The 2001-2002 Official PFA

FOOTBALLERS FACTFILE

The Football Bible

Edited by

Barry J Hugman

Assistant Editor

Ian Nannestad

Photographs by

Colorsport

AFS Publication

The Official PFA Footballers Factfile
is produced in association with
The Association of Football Statisticians
email: enquiries@the-afs.com
Telephone: 0207 498 8906

First Published in Great Britain in 2001 by AFS
a division of Exxus Limited
18 St Philip Square
London
SW8 3RS

www.exxus.co.uk

The CIP catalogue record for this book
Is available from the British Library

Photographs copyright Colorsport

ISBN: 0-946531-34X

Typeset and Designed by
Typecast (Artwork and Design)
8 Mudford Road
Yeovil, Somerset BA21 4AA

Distributed by Book Representation and Distribution Ltd
Hadleigh Hall, London Road, Hadleigh, SS7 2DE
Tel: 01702 552912
Fax 01702 556065
E-mail: mail@bookreps.com
www.bookreps.com

Printed and Bound in Great Britain by
Butler & Tanner, London and Frome

Acknowledgements

Now into its seventh year, the *Factfile* continues to expand and reach out, not only as a media tool and invaluable to those in the game, but as a part-work which, in due course, will cover the season-by-season record of every player's complete career and should be of interest to all who follow this great game of ours. As a book with a heavy workload, I would once again like to express my thanks to **Gordon Taylor**, the chief executive, and all those at the PFA, including **Brendon Batson** and **Garry Nelson**, who are genuinely supporting and helping to establish the *Factfile*. Their help is much appreciated.

I am grateful to all those at EXXUS, who are the new publishers of the *Factfile*, including **Mark Baber**, managing director, and a major influence in the Association of Football Statisticians' involvement with the *Factfile*; senior soccer analysts and researchers, **Kevin Glumart**, **Graham Cull**, **Trevor Bugg**, **Terry O'Neill** and **Mike Murphy**, for their collation, checking and auditing of the statistics; web/graphic designer, **James Kilbane**, for designing the new look to the *Factfile* cover. Many thanks also to **Nick Taylor** and **Ben Smith** for their work on the IT side and to **Ron Hockings**, author of several books on international football and keeper of the world's most comprehensive database of internationals, for his help on this edition. I am also grateful to **Graham Hortop** and **Jamil Hussein** for their help and diligence in keeping up to date with the latest transfers, and to **Ray Kidd** and **Andy Young** for their efforts on the sales and marketing side.

The massive task of editing the text this year was carried out by the assistant editor, **Ian Nannestad**, who has been a long-standing contributor to the *Factfile* for his own club Lincoln City and who also provided a substantial input on the text for the 2000-01 *Factfile*. Co-author of two books on the history of the Imps, he has been a member of the AFS since 1980 and joined the staff of Exxus earlier in the year. He also has a strong interest in the early history of the game and in the future he is likely to have a major role in the AFS quarterly report.

The *Factfile* team were also lucky to be able to call upon **David Barber** (English FA), **Sandy Bryson** (Scottish FA), **Zoe Ward** (FA Premier League), **Ceri Stennett** (FA of Wales), and **Marshall Gillespie** (editor of the Northern Ireland Football Yearbook). Others who gave their time were **Roy Grant**, **Alan Platt**, **Jenny Hugman**, and many Premier and Football League members up and down the country.

For the seventh year, **Jonathan Ticehurst**, managing director of Windsor Insurance Brokers' Sports Division, has thrown his weight behind the *Factfile*, both financially and vocally. His and Windsor's support, as with the *British Boxing Board of Control Yearbook*, is greatly appreciated.

For details provided on players, I have listed below, in alphabetical order, the names of the "team", without whose help this book would not have been possible to produce. Once again, I thank every one of them for all the hard work they put in.

Audrey Adams *(Watford):* Producer and statistician for BBC Radio Sport and a Watford supporter since the days of Cliff Holton, Audrey was the club statistician for the *Ultimate Football Guide*.

Geoff Allman *(Walsall):* A university lecturer by trade, he saw his first ever game in February 1944, Walsall versus Wolves. Has written for Walsall's programme for over 30 seasons and, at one time or another, has provided articles for more than half of the clubs currently in the Premiership and Football League. Geoff is also a Methodist local preacher and press officer.

Mark Barrowclough *(Manchester City):* Mark has been a City supporter since 1965, getting his first season ticket in the 1973-74 season and having one ever since. He met his wife, Dawn, who was working for City in the commercial department at the time. Mark has done matchball sponsorship and sponsored reserve team football matches, and has also produced some match reports for the City programme.

Stuart Basson *(Chesterfield):* Stuart is the AFS club statistician for Chesterfield FC. His latest book *Chesterfield FC – The Official History* was published by Yore Publications in December and, like *Lucky Whites & Spireites*, sold out in record time. Stuart was also involved with the birth of a new trust, the Chesterfield Football Supporters Society, which aims to secure the long-term future of the Spireites and restore their reputation in the football world.

Ian Bates *(Bradford):* Will be celebrating his 50th year watching Bradford City on 25 December 2001. His main hobby is City, but he also enjoys cricket as well, and has been umpiring for 17 years and loves it. Ian had to stop refereeing, which he did at local level for 19 years, after injuring his back.

David Batters *(York City):* A supporter since 1948, David is the club historian and a contributor to the matchday programme. Is the author of *York City, the Complete Record 1922-1990*, and the compiler of *Images of Sport - York City FC*. Also commentates on matches for York Hospital Radio.

Harry Berry *(Blackburn Rovers):* Early next year, Harry will complete 50 years of following Blackburn Rovers, having been born only three miles from Ewood Park, living within 15 miles all his life, and a season ticket holder ever since starting work. Has been for many years a road runner and completed a few marathons. By profession he is a financial director and works for the largest manufacturer in Blackburn.

Eddie Brennan *(Sunderland):* A season ticket holder at the Stadium of Light, and a former contributor to the *Carling Ultimate Football Guide*, Eddie has been a regular supporter since 1976.

Jim Brown *(Coventry City):* The club's official statistician and contributor to the programme, he also pens a column for the *Coventry Evening Telegraph* answering readers' queries. He is the author of *Coventry City – The Elite era (1998)* and *The Illustrated History (2000)* in addition to being co-author of the *Breedon Complete Record (1991)*. A life member of the AFS, he has been a Coventry fan since 1962 and has almost a complete collection of Coventry programmes since the war.

Mark Brown *(Plymouth Argyle):* Helped on the *PFA Factfile* profiles by his wife Nicola, Mark has been supporting the club for over 25 years, having been introduced to them at the tender age of five by his Argyle-mad family. Follows most of their games, whether home or away, and is a member of the travel club.

Trevor Bugg *(Hull City):* A supporter of the Tigers for over 30 years, he is now employed as a football statistician with Exxus and also contributes to Hull City's official web site, as well as the matchday programme.

Wallace Chadwick *(Burnley):* A Burnley fan for over 40 years, during which time the Clarets have topped all four divisions and come within 90 minutes of relegation from the Football League. A regular contributor to the club programme, he now lives in hope that the club can recapture the glory days which he unfortunately took for granted before becoming old enough to know better!

Gary Chalk *(Southampton):* A member of the hagiology group of Saints' historians committed to the collection and dissemination of accurate information on the history of Southampton FC. Currently the club's official co-historian and statistician, Gary co-authored *Saints: A Complete History 1885-1987* and *The Alphabet of the Saints 1992* with Duncan Holley, and more recently contributed to the successful *Match of the Millenium* project published by Hagiology Publishing.

Paul Clayton *(Charlton Athletic):* Paul wrote a regular feature in the club programme between 1993 and 1998, having previously written other articles for the now defunct Charlton Athletic magazine and Valiants' Viewpoint (Supporters' Club newsletter/fanzine). Has also provided the Charlton statistics for a number of publications, including the *Ultimate Football Guide*, since 1987 to its final publication in 1999, along with the Charlton player information for the *Factfile* since its inception in 1995. A member of the AFS, he is a long-standing season ticket holder at The Valley and rarely misses a game, home or away, despite living in Wiltshire.

Grant Coleby *(Exeter City):* A member of both the Exeter City Supporters' Club and the Association of Football Statisticians, Grant has been the official contributor to the *Factfile* since its inception.

Eddie Collins *(Nottingham Forest):* A Forest supporter since 1956, and a member of the Associated Football Statisticians, this is the first publication he has been involved in.

David Copping *(Barnsley):* Life-long Barnsley fan who commentated on hospital radio for many years and then moved on to the club's videos. He has also written regularly in their matchday programme for the last 13 seasons and on player profiles for a new internet site.

Frank Coumbe *(Brentford):* Has not missed a competitive Brentford home game since December 1977, a club record. He has also been the Bees' statistician for this publication since it began, and acted in a similar capacity for the *Ultimate Football Guide* until its demise. Frank also writes in club programmes. The highlight of 2000-01 was Brentford reaching the final of the LDV Vans Trophy, while the lowlight is the probability of a groundshare with Woking for the 2002-03 season.

Peter Cullen *(Bury):* Peter is Bury FC's official historian, and author of three publications to date – *Bury FC 1885-1985*, *Bury FC - A Pictorial History* and more recently, *Bury FC - The Official History*. He has also been involved with the club's match programme as editor or contributor for the past 21 years.

John Curtis *(Scunthorpe United):* A life-long Scunthorpe fan, John reports on the club in his role as deputy sports editor at the *Scunthorpe Evening Telegraph* and is a former editor of the award-winning club matchday programme.

Carol Dalziel *(Tranmere Rovers):* Has been watching Tranmere for over 30 years, is a regular contributor to the matchday programme, and operates the club's electronic scoreboard.

Denise Dann *(Aston Villa):* In her own words, Denise is a mad, crazy Villa supporter, who follows them up and down the country without fail. Her only previous football work was to help with the club's profiles required for the *Premier League: The Players* publication. She was assisted by her husband, Paul.

Gareth Davies and **Geraint Parry** *(Wrexham):* Peter and Gareth are co-authors on the Tempus *Wrexham FC 1872-1950* compilation in the popular series and intend to complete *1950-To Date* in the near future. Gareth continues to write articles for the Wrexham programme, as well as contributing to the Welsh Football Magazine and Holyhead Hotspur (Cymru Alliance League) and Swansea City programmes – topical pieces on football in Wales.

David Downs *(Reading):* David is a former schoolteacher who took early retirement to become the Reading Football Club's welfare and child protection officer. He is a regular contributor to the club programme, and has published his latest book, *One Hundred Greats of Reading FC* during the past season. David, his family, and friends starred in the Pizza Hut television advertisement shown during Nationwide Sky Soccer last season.

Ray Driscoll *(Chelsea):* A life-long Blues' fan, born and bred two miles away from Stamford Bridge, whose 40 years spectating encompasses the era from Jimmy Greaves to Jimmy Floyd Hasselbaink. An all-round sports 'nut', he has contributed to many football books as well as other sports books, such as cricket, golf, rugby and tennis. He has also contributed to more 'cerebral' literature such as reference books.

Mark Evans *(Leeds United):* Has supported United for over 30 years and describes his association with the club as one of the loves of his life. The Leeds' statistician for the *Ultimate Football Guide* for nearly nine years, he was also involved in my two editions of the *FA Carling Premiership: The Players.*

Keith Evemy *(Fulham):* A regular supporter, both home and away, since 1943, Keith missed Fulham's only previous (to 1998-99 and 2000-01) post-war honour, the Second Division championship in 1948-49, being away on military service. Has contributed to the club programme for more than 20 years. The *Factfile* wishes Keith all the very best for the future as he has decided to step down from next year's edition. He will be decidedly missed.

Colin Faiers *(Cambridge United):* A Cambridge United fan for over 30 years, Colin has witnessed their rise from non-league football. A chartered accountant in the day, he is the club statistician and occasional contributor to the club programme and web site.

Harold Finch *(Crewe Alexandra):* Club historian for Alexandra, Harold has now completed 67 years of supporting them. Although no longer programme editor he is still a regular contributor to the programme and provides all club statistics. His publication, *Crewe Alexandra FC – A Pictorial History of the Club* has proved to be extremely popular with collectors.

Mick Ford and **Richard Lindsey** *(Millwall):* A life-long Millwall fan, Mick will see MFC in the First Division, which will be his 50th season as a Millwall supporter. Despite living in Worcester, he only misses a handful of games a season and without the understanding of his wife, Sue, would find it difficult to continue his passion. Has an extensive memorabilia collection which he adds to when the right items come up. Meanwhile, his *Factfile* partner, Richard, the author of *Millwall: The Complete Record*, continues to help establish the Millwall FC Museum at the New Den.

Andrew Frazier *(Kidderminster Harriers):* Has been following the Harriers since 1978, and hasn't missed a game, home or away, for over eight years. Is a contributor to the club programme, the club statistician, and a member of the Association of Football Statisticians.

Jon Gibbes *(Torquay United):* Saw his first game on Boxing Day 1970 aged seven, the beginning of an unhealthy obsession with Torquay United which at times leads to the woeful neglect of wife, Julie, and children, Rosie and Tommy. After having disproved the long-held belief that the club was formed in 1898, Jon co-wrote the club's *Official Centenary History 1899-1999* with Leigh Edwards and John Lovis.

Paul Godfrey *(Cheltenham Town):* Paul first watched football as a toddler when his father was on the committee of the local Cheltenham club, St Marks CA, prior to graduating to Town in the late 1970s and continuing to watch them both during and after his studies at Oxford University. Has so far spent ten seasons as the club's programme editor, and between October 1990 and February 2000 has seen every home and away first-team match. Is currently writing for the *Gloucester Citizen* newspaper, while working on the *Official History of Cheltenham Town FC.*

Dave Goody *(Southend United):* A season ticket holder and life-long Shrimpers fan, Dave is now putting his large collection of Southend United programmes and memorabilia to good use, co-authoring a series of books in Tempus Publishing's *Archive Photograph Series* with noted football author and fellow fan, Peter Miles, bringing the total of Southend United books authored by him to four.

Frank Grande *(Northampton Town):* Author of *The Cobblers, A History of Northampton Town FC* and a *Who's Who*, Frank also compiled the *Definitive History* of the club and the *Centenary History*. Now working on a biography of Tommy Fowler, the club's longest serving player. Has been a contributor to the club programme for over 20 years.

Roy Grant *(Oxford United):* A life-long Oxford United fan, Roy previously produced the Oxford United matchday programme and had a spell as club statistician. A contributor in the *Footballer's Factfile* since its first issue, Roy has also written for several football club programmes as well as contributing to football websites and productions such as the *Official Football League Yearbook* and the *Ultimate Football Guide*.

Michael Green *(Bolton Wanderers):* Despite being a fanatical Newcastle United supporter, Michael covers Bolton for the *Factfile* and his excellent efforts are much appreciated. Having a yearning to get involved in the area of freelance journalism, preferably concerning football or popular entertainment (music, films etc), he has enrolled on a substantial writing course to further himself in this field. Has also formed a band called Pub Monkey with some friends, playing lead guitar.

Alan Harding *(Swindon Town):* Alan has been supporting Swindon Town since 1968, is a season ticket holder, travels home and away, and has been researching match stats and line-up details, plus details of players since 1981. Is also a member of the AFS and this is the first time he has assisted with anything like this.

Roger Harrison *(Blackpool):* A life-long supporter who has seen the Pool play every other league side both home and away, and joint programme editor and club statistician, Roger has contributed to other publications, including *Rothmans* and the *Ultimate Football Guide*.

Richard and **Janey Hayhoe** *(Tottenham Hotspur):* Janey and Richard long for the day that their team can fill them with the same pride and show the same progress as their daughter Holly, now three-years old. Richard hopes that another new arrival will bring them similar fulfilment … that arrival being Glenn Hoddle of course!

Des Hinks *(Stockport County):* Des, who has been following his beloved Hatters for 37 years, independently covers every game, at home and abroad, for the club's website and information telephone line. He also edits and produces their award-winning reserve-team match programme.

Ray Hugman *(Luton Town):* Looking to build himself a career in writing, Ray, who lives in Hatfield and has supported Queens Park Rangers since a lad, enjoys watching his football at Luton these days. He is especially interested in assessing and analysing player skills throughout a match.

Mike Jay *(Bristol Rovers):* Mike, the club's official historian and programme contributor, has had three books published on Bristol Rovers, namely *The Complete Record (1883-1987)*, *Pirates in Profile, a Who's Who of Players (1920-1994)*, and *Bristol Rovers FC Images of England Photographic History 1999.* He is currently working in conjunction with Stephen Byrne on a detailed history of the club which is due to be published in the near future.

Darran and **Chris Jennison** *(Wimbledon):* Darran and Chris are family stand season ticket holders, where they sit with their sons, Daniel and Elliott. Chris has supported Wimbledon for over 25 years.

Colin Jones *(Swansea City):* A fan since the early 1960s, and a contributor to the club programme during the last six years (was the editor last season), Colin played non-league football before being involved in training and coaching.

Andrew Kirkham *(Sheffield United):* A Blades' supporter since 1953, and a regular contributor to the club programme and handbook since 1984, Andrew is a member of the AFS and 92 club. He was a contributor to *Sheffield United: The First 100 Years*, and co-author of *A Complete Record of Sheffield United Football Club, 1889-1999.*

Geoff Knights *(Macclesfield Town):* Following a career move to Cheshire, Geoff started following Macclesfield Town in the late '80s and rarely misses a match these days, whether it be home or away. Describing himself as an ordinary supporter who stands on the terraces, and one who enjoys the friendly atmosphere of a small club, he keeps detailed statistics and records on the club, which are used in response to media and other enquiries.

Geoffrey Lea *(Wigan Athletic):* A life-long supporter who first started watching the club back in their non-league days. As editor of the matchday programme for the last six seasons, Geoff performs a number of jobs for the club as a labour of love, being matchday press liaison officer and Clubcall reporter. Has also worked for a number of local radio stations following the club's progress.

Philip Lonkhurst *(Arsenal):* A life-long Arsenal fan, Philip has held a season ticket since he was ten-years old, and has played for Herts County as a schoolboy, before moving up to the mid-Herts Premier League, as a central defender. Has a good library of Arsenal memorabilia.

Gordon Macey *(Queens Park Rangers):* Has supported Queens Park Rangers since the early 1960s and has been collecting and compiling statistics on the club, at all levels, for many seasons. He is a life member of the Association of Football Statisticians and is recognised by many areas of the media as the 'expert' on QPR. In 1993, Gordon was appointed as the club's official historian, following the publication of his successful *Complete Record of Queens Park Rangers* book, and to mark the Millennium he published an update of the club history in August 1999. His three children are all regular attendees at the Rangers' games and help with some of the research at newspaper and local archives. Gordon's work, as an implementer of Financial and Logistic Business Systems involves travel throughout Europe and other parts of the world. This gives him the opportunity of watching football (and his other interest of ice hockey) in a number of different countries.

Steve McGhee *(Derby County):* A supporter since 1969, Steve used to produce a magazine on the club's programmes/history. As a programme collector since 1975, he has a complete collection of Derby home games back to the war and 98 per-cent of the aways.

John Maguire *(Manchester United):* John has been busy writing several new booklets during the past 12 months (and updating existing titles), all of which are now available in the London branch of Sportspages (look at their internet site) as well as in Manchester. A member of the AFS for many years, he has been a one-club man for the *Factfile* since its inception in 1995, and is proud to be part of the team.

Carl Marsden *(Oldham Athletic):* Carl is chairman of SAFE (Secure Athletic's Future Existence – *http://www.safe-oafc.org.uk*), maintains *The Oldham Athletic E-Zine* at *http://www.oafc.co.uk* and, naturally, is a Latics fanatic. **Ross Coyne**, who helps Carl on the *Factfile*, is a life-long Oldham Athletic fan and prominent member of SAFE, who regularly travels nationwide to watch his beloved Blues in action.

Carl Marston *(Colchester City):* Has been reporting on the fortunes of Colchester United since they regained their Football League status in 1992, both for the *East Anglian Daily Times* and the *Green 'Un* newspapers. Carl has only missed a handful of games during the last nine years, usually when away, running for Suffolk in cross country races.

Wade Martin *(Stoke City):* A Stoke supporter since birth, he has written numerous books on the club, including the Definitive History – *A Potter's Tale* – and a Who's Who series – *The Master Potters*. Wade acts as the club's historian and was a contributor to the club's programme for many years.

Tony Matthews *(West Bromwich Albion):* Official statistician, historian and curator at *The Hawthorns*, his 50 publications include the complete records of *Aston Villa, Birmingham City, Stoke City, Walsall, West Bromwich Albion and Wolverhampton Wanderers*; the *Essential History of Wolves*; full *A-Z Encyclopaedias of Villa* (published in 2001), *Blues, Stoke City, Tottenham Hotspur* (published in 2001), *WBA & Wolves; Who's Who* on *Villa, Blues, Manchester United (1945-85), WBA* and Wolves; wartime and photographic books and also contributes to eight matchday programmes in the Premiership and Nationwide Leagues. He is currently working on the *A-Z of Manchester United* (175,000 words, plus stats) and the essential *History of Leicester City*.

Paul Morant *(Leyton Orient):* Is 31-years old, and works for an insurance company in London. Has not missed a game, home and away, for over three years, and, where possible, also attends youth and reserve-team games.

Ian Nannestad *(Lincoln City):* Ian has followed the Imps for around 35 years and is the co-author with his brother Donald of *A Who's Who of Lincoln City, 1892-1994* and *Lincoln City FC: The Official History*.

Adrian and **Caroline Newnham** and **Tim Carder** *(Brighton & Hove Albion):* Caroline and Adrian are life-long supporters who met through watching the Albion and are actively involved in the campaign to secure the Seagulls a permanent stadium at Falmer. Adrian is a former editor of the Albion fanzine, *Scars and Stripes,* and undertakes matchday tours of Brighton's temporary ground at Withdean. Both are proud to say they saw every first team game of this championship winning season. Tim is chairman of both the Supporters' Club and the Albion's Collectors and Historians Society. Along with Roger Harris, he co-authored *Seagulls: The Story of Brighton and Hove Albion FC* and *Albion A-Z: A Who's Who of Brighton and Hove Albion FC*. He too attended all first team games this season – and managed to see his first championship winning side after 36 years of loyal support! Tim is also a respected local historian on matters ranging far beyond the Albion.

John Northcutt *(West Ham United):* Has supported the Hammers since 1959 and is the co-author of West Ham books, *The Complete Record* and the *Illustrated History*. A regular contributor to the club programme, John was the club adviser to the *Ultimate Football Guide*.

Richard Owen *(Portsmouth):* A life-long supporter and official club historian for Portsmouth, Richard performs a number of jobs for the club as a labour of love. Is a regular contributor to the club programme for the past 23 years and has missed only a handful of away matches in the last 25 years, watching Pompey on 104 league grounds. An avid programme collector, with almost a complete set of post-war Portsmouth home and away issues, he co-published the *Centenary Pictorial History of Portsmouth FC* and *A Team Collection*, which featured every team picture of Pompey since 1898, in 1998. He is now working on his third book, entitled *100 Pompey Legends,* and has built up an almost full library of club histories of all British Football League clubs.

Steve Peart and **Dave Finch** *(Wycombe Wanderers):* A former programme editor of the club and a supporter for over 20 years, Steve put together the player profiles, while the club statistics were supplied by Dave, the official Wycombe statistician. Both were authors of *Wycombe Wanderers 1887-1996 - The Official History*, published in 1996. Dave has supported Wycombe regularly since 1964 and is the club's statistician, having been part of their programme editorial team since 1990.

Steve Phillipps *(Rochdale):* A Rochdale supporter for over 35 years and the club's official historian, Steve is the author of *The Survivors, The Story of Rochdale AFC (1990)* and *The Definitive Rochdale (1995)*. Is currently working on the *Official History of Rochdale AFC*, due out later this year. A founder member of the Association of Football Statisticians, away from football he is a university lecturer.

Terry Phillips *(Cardiff City):* Chief soccer writer for the *South Wales Echo* since 1994, and a sports journalist for over 30 years – *Kent Evening Post* (1970-1977), *Derby Evening Telegraph* (1977-1986), *Gloucester Citizen* (1986-1994) – Terry has previously covered clubs at all levels, including Brian Clough's Nottingham Forest, Derby County, Gillingham, and Gloucester City. His specialist subjects are Cardiff City FC and Cardiff Devils (Ice Hockey).

Andrew Pinfield *(Halifax Town):* As the Halifax Town commercial manager, and a life-long supporter of the club, Andrew is also the club's programme editor. Collects Halifax Town memorabilia.

Alan Platt *(Liverpool):* Is a dedicated football statistician and a follower of Liverpool FC since 1960, and whilst resident in London, a member and official of the London branch of the LFC Supporters Club. He has assisted Barry Hugman in an editorial capacity on all his football publications since 1980, namely the four updates of the *Football League Players Records*, the two editions of *Premier League Players* and, for the last six years, the *PFA Factfile*, when not working overseas in his profession of transport planner. Now resident in Manchester, his main interest today is in non-league football and he keeps detailed records on all the senior semi-professional leagues, having compiled a database of over 6,000 players participating in that level of football.

Kevan Platt *(Norwich City):* Kevan has been club secretary at Carrow Road for approaching three years and has over 21 years full-time service, in total, to the Canaries behind him. His support of City began in 1968 when his 'Carrow Road debut' coincided with that of Canary legend to be, Duncan Forbes, with whom he would share an office some 15 or so years later. Having watched his favourite team on over 65 different league grounds, Kevan classes himself as a fan first and foremost, but his current position gives him a real insight into every aspect of the club's administration.

Dave Prentice *(Everton):* Everton correspondent for the *Liverpool Echo* since 1993 and author of a club history five years earlier, when he was reporting on both Everton and Liverpool for the *Daily Post*, Dave completed his Mersey set when reporting on Tranmere Rovers for three years from 1990.

Mike Purkiss *(Crystal Palace):* Having supported Palace since 1950 and produced stats on them since 1960, Mike is the author of the *Complete History of Crystal Palace, 1905-1989*. Was the club statistician for the *Ultimate Football Guide* and also contributed to *Premier League: The Players*.

Mick Renshaw *(Sheffield Wednesday):* Has followed Wednesday for over 40 years and is a great supporter of European soccer. Mick also produced the club section for the *Ultimate Football Guide*.

Mick Robinson *(Peterborough United):* Another life-long fan, for a number of years Mick has contributed to the club programme and was the joint editor of the *Official Peterborough History*. Was also club statistician for the *Ultimate Football Guide*.

Jeff Searle *(Barnet):* Jeff has been supporting the Bees for nearly 20 years and is a committee member of the *Keep Barnet Alive* campaign. He follows the Bees home and away without fail and hopes they can return to the league at the first attempt.

Phil Sherwin *(Port Vale):* Phil is the Port Vale club statistician and has been a fan since 1968, when they had to seek re-election to the old Fourth Division. Travelling to away games since 1973, he has only missed a handful of games since then and has contributed to the club programme, various books on the club, the now defunct *League Directory*, and the local newspaper, radio and television.

Derrick Slasor *(Middlesbrough):* First saw the Boro play in December 1946 and, as the managing director of Trapezium Transport Services, was well known in the area for sponsoring various club activities.

Mike Slater *(Wolverhampton Wanderers):* The Wolves' contributor to the *Factfile* since its inception, Mike wrote a book on the club's history called *Molineux Memories*, which he published in 1988. Well-known as the eight-time compiler of the *Brain of Wolves' Quiz*, he also produced a booklet in 1996 containing all of Wolves' competitive results and records against every other club.

Gordon Small *(Hartlepool United):* Having supported United since October 1965, experiencing two promotions, two relegations, and several close calls, 2000-01 was another good season, with the club reaching the Play-Offs for the second year running.

Dave Smith *(Leicester City):* Dave has been the club historian and statistician for Leicester City for several years. Has written a regular column in the club programme since the 1980s, and also contributes a regular feature to the local weekly sports newspaper. Is also the co-author of a number of club publications, including the official club history *Of Fossils & Foxes*.

Jim Smith *(Bournemouth):* Jim is a committed Bournemouth fan about to clock up a quarter of a century of watching the Cherries. Born in London in 1964, he moved to Wimborne in Dorset, aged eight, and started going to watch Bournemouth after the club offered his school free tickets in return for allowing them to train on its grounds!

Gerry Somerton *(Rotherham United):* Having provided the information for the *Factfile* on Rotherham United since its inception, Gerry is deputy sports editor of the *Rotherham Advertiser* as well as acting as co-editor of the club's matchday programme for many years and is the club's historian. Has written two best selling books on the club's history and his third – *The Ronnie Moore Story* – is due out in October. Works on a part-time basis for BBC Radio Sheffield.

Paul Stead *(Huddersfield Town):* A life-long supporter of his hometown football club, and proud parent of Gracie (a future Terrier fan), Paul is now in his fourth year with the *Factfile*. Also contributes to the Huddersfield TV web site, covering an array of topics on the club.

David Steele *(Carlisle United):* A programme contributor since 1989, as well as producing more general historical articles, David has now profiled many ex-Carlisle players.

Richard Stocken *(Shrewsbury Town):* Following Shrewsbury Town for almost 45 years through thick and mostly thin, Richard is a collector of club programmes and memorabilia and has contributed to a number of publications over the years. Due to write a best seller on Shrewsbury come retirement, he is a senior manager with one of the big four banks in his spare time.

Bill Swann *(Newcastle United):* A supporter since the Jackie Milburn days of the early 1950s, and a long-term shareholder in the club along with his wife and three children, all season ticket holders, he is a keen collector of memorabilia connected with the club, and a member of the AFS. Bill has now consolidated his information on club matches, teams, scorers, and players into a database for easy access and analysis. He assisted in the production of the club's volume in the *Complete Record* series, and this is his sixth year as a contributor to the *Factfile*. His 15-year-old son Richard, also a Newcastle fanatic, supplied much of the 'anorak' information for the player biographies.

Colin Tattum *(Birmingham City):* Colin is the senior sportswriter on the *Birmingham Evening Mail*, with special responsibility for football and Birmingham City.

Paul Taylor *(Mansfield Town):* A Mansfield Town supporter of more than 30 years standing, Paul has contributed to many publications over the last few years, including the club's *Centenary History* published in 1997. He is President of the Stags Supporters' Club, the club's official historian, and this season became the official Mansfield Town statistician for the AFS.

Richard and **Sarah Taylor** and **Ian Mills** *(Notts County):* Richard Taylor – a life-long Notts County fan from a Notts County family, he has travelled the length and breadth of the land in following the Magpies and has seen them on all but a few current league grounds and many non-current grounds too. In the summer, he umpires cricket matches to while away the close season. Sarah Taylor – like her father and two brothers, Sarah became a dedicated fan at an early age and has made regular excursions home from university to support the Magpies. Having missed only a handful of games during her three years as an undergraduate, she was due to sit her finals for a degree in law in the summer. Ian Mills – Ian supplies the County stats, Richard the words, and Sarah the typing. Having seen his first game at Gay Meadow in 1959-60, Ian, who ran the matchday programme sales, has been hooked ever since, missing just one match since 1970.

Les Triggs *(Grimsby Town):* A retired librarian, Les first saw the Mariners in a wartime league match whilst the club was in exile at Scunthorpe's Old Show Ground, and has been a regular supporter since their days as a then First Division club. Became involved in the historical side of the club when asked to assist in the staging of the Centenary Exhibition in 1978. The co-author of the Grimsby Town volume in the *Complete Record* series, and the Grimsby statistician for the former *Ultimate Football Guide*, he is also an occasional contributor to the club fanzine.

Roger Triggs *(Gillingham):* Roger has been a Gillingham supporter for over 40 years and has been collecting statistics and records on the club since he was a schoolboy. Co-author of the highly acclaimed centenary book *Home of the Shouting Men,* produced in 1993, Roger has since produced his images collection in conjunction with Tempus Publishing Company, and in August 2001 will be bringing out a complete *Who's Who of Gillingham's Football League Players 1920-1938 & 1950-2001*.

Frank Tweddle *(Darlington):* The club's official historian and statistician, Frank has contributed articles to the Darlington programme for the last 26 seasons and has supported the Quakers for well over 40 years. As well as being a member of the 92 Club and the AFS, he is the author of *Darlington's Centenary History* published in 1983, and *The Definitive Darlington 1883-2000,* published in late 2000, as well as producing work for various other football publications.

Paul Voller *(Ipswich Town):* Has been a life-long Ipswich Town fan and started attending matches at Portman Road in 1963. A member of the Ipswich Town Supporters Management Committee with responsibilities for media and publishing, he edits the supporters' page in the matchday magazine and also edits the supporters' fortnightly pages in the local evening paper (We are allocated two tabloid size pages on alternate Saturdays throughout the season). Was the Ipswich statistician for the *Rothmans Yearbooks* and provided the Ipswich statistics for the *Football Club Directories* in the 1990s.

Tony Woodburn and **Martin Atherton** *(Preston North End):* Both being North End fans for over 30 years, Tony and Martin provide statistical and historical information on the club for the National Football Museum's permanent Preston North End collection, as well as writing for the club programme and, of course, the *Factfile*. Tony is a member of the Association of Football Statisticians, the 92 club, and the Scottish 38 club, whilst Martin works for the Institute for Football Studies, a joint education and research venture between the National Football Museum and the University of Central Lancashire in Preston.

David Woods *(Bristol City):* A regular at Ashton Gate since March 1958, and a shareholder since 1972, David has written four books on Bristol City, the most recent being *Bristol City – The Modern Era 1967-2000*, published by Desert Island. A life member of the Association of Football Statisticians, as well as belonging to the 92 Club after visiting all the Football League grounds, completing his experience at Lincoln on 18 April 1970. Official club historian from 1981-1986, he has had two spells (1982-86 and 1995-97) of writing regularly in the Bristol City programme, as well as featuring in the Bristol Rovers' programme from 1987-1993. The statistician to *Rothmans Football Yearbook* for 1983-84 and the *Football Club Directory* from 1985 to 1998, David has also written articles for the *Footballer* Magazine, and has just had published a history on *Bristol Bulldogs Speedway*. An old boy of Bristol Technical School of Engineering, he is currently researching with his brother Tony, a history of technical and commercial school education in Bristol.

Finally, on the production side of the book, my thanks go to Jean Bastin, of Typecast (Artwork & Design), for her patience and diligent work on the typesetting and design, which again went far beyond the call of normal duty and was much appreciated.

Forewords

I am extremely pleased to give the PFA's full endorsement and recommendation to *Footballers' Factfile*. In this modern age of such tremendous interest in the professional football game it is good to have at hand the definitive book on statistics and profiles for every one of our members playing in first team football throughout the Premier League and Football League in England and Wales.

This book gives the background to what the game is all about - the players. Having to deal with 4,000 PFA members, the *Factfile* gives me a valuable source of information in an easily accessible, attractive and enjoyable format. It is a must for anybody involved in the game as an administrator, spectator, commentator and is especially invaluable for any football "Brain of Britain" or football quiz aspirant!

I hope that with the financial investment in academies and coaching, and an appreciation of the necessary skills for success on the international stage emphasising technique, possession football and flair, that we can copy our past with qualification for the World Cup in 2002.

The publication has again been sponsored by Windsor Insurance Brokers, the key figures in our industry with regard to the protection of players against injury, and compiled by Barry Hugman, whose record in this field is unsurpassed. Barry has a team of over 90 people who provide him with the invaluable aspects of local information which gives this book such credibility.

Gordon Taylor,
Chief Executive, The Professional Footballers' Association,

There is no doubt in my mind that the *Footballers' Factfile* goes from strength to strength as the years go by. Barry Hugman and his research team are to be congratulated, yet again, on this season's publication, which I see on the desk or in the bookcase of almost everybody connected with the game today.

The Windsor Insurance Group continues its close association with professional football that was first established over 25 years ago. Together, with the Professional Footballers' Association, we manage the Players Permanent Disablement Fund, whereby every registered player in the English leagues receives an insurance benefit if his career is ended through injury or sickness. The level of benefit is continually reviewed and was increased significantly in recent times.

Our close links with the Professional Footballers' Association, and the clubs, leagues, and national associations, give us a unique position from which we can offer advice on insurance related matters to all in football. And, we are more than happy to continue to support and again lend our name as sponsors to this excellent publication.

Jonathan Ticehurst,
Managing Director of the Sports Division, Windsor Insurance Brokers Limited.

Editorial Introduction

Following on from last year's edition, the *Factfile* portrays the statistical career record of every FA Carling Premiership and Nationwide League player who made an appearance in 2000-01, whether it be in league football, the Football League Cup (Worthington Cup), FA Cup (Sponsored by AXA), Charity Shield, European Cup, UEFA Cup, Inter-Toto Cup, or in the Play Offs. Not included are Welsh Cup matches. It goes beyond mere statistics, however, with a write up on all of the 2,300 plus players involved, and also records faithfully last season's playing records separately by club.

The work falls into three sections, all inter-relating. Firstly, the main core, PFA Footballers' Factfile: A-Z (pages 9 to 338); secondly, Where Did They Go? (pages 339 to 342); lists all players shown in the previous edition of the *Factfile* who either moved on or did not play in 2000-01; and thirdly, FA Carling Premiership and Nationwide League Clubs: Summary of Appearances and Goals for 2000-01 (pages 345 to 367). Below is an explanation on how to follow the *PFA Footballers' Factfile.*

As the title suggests, all players are listed in alphabetical order and are shown by Surnames first, followed by full Christian names, with the one the player is commonly known by shown in **bold.** Any abbreviation or pseudonym is bracketed.

Birthplace/date: You will note that several players who would be predominately classified as British, were born in places like Germany and India, for example. My book, *Premier and Football League Players' Records*, which covers every man who has played league football since the war, has, in the past, used the family domicile as a more realistic "birthplace". But, for our purposes here, I have reverted to that which has been officially recorded.

Height and Weight: Listed in feet and inches, and stones and pounds, respectively. It must be remembered that a player's weight can frequently change and, on that basis, the recorded data should be used as a guide only, especially as they would have been weighed several times during the season.

Club Honours: Those shown, cover careers from the Conference and FA Trophy upwards. For abbreviations, read:- European Honours: EC (European Cup), ESC (European Super Cup), ECWC (European Cup Winners' Cup) and UEFAC. English Honours: FAC (FA Cup), FLC (Football League Cup), CS (Charity Shield), FMC (Full Members Cup, which takes in the Simod and Zenith Data sponsorships), AMC (Associated Members Cup - Freight Rover, Sherpa Van, Leyland DAF, Autoglass, Auto Windscreens and LDV Vans), AIC (Anglo-Italian Cup), GMVC (GM Vauxhall Conference), FC (Football Conference), NC (Nationwide Conference), FAT (FA Trophy), FAYC (FA Youth Cup). Scottish Honours: SPD (Scottish Premier Division), S Div 1/2 (Scottish Leagues), SC (Scottish Cup), SLC (Scottish League Cup). Welsh Honours: WC (Welsh Cup). Please note that medals awarded to P/FL, FLC, and AMC winners relate to players who have appeared in 25%, or over, of matches, while FAC, EC, and UEFAC winners medals are for all-named finalists, including unused subs. For our purposes, however, Charity Shield winners' medals refer to men who either played or came on as a sub. Honours applicable to players coming in from abroad are not shown at present, but the position will be reviewed in future editions.

International Honours: For abbreviations, read:- E (England), NI (Northern Ireland), S (Scotland), W (Wales) and Ei (Republic of Ireland). Under 21 through to full internationals give total appearances (inclusive of subs), while schoolboy (U16s and U18s) and youth representatives are just listed. The cut-off date used for appearances was up to and including 30 June.

Player Descriptions: Gives position and playing strengths and, in keeping the work topical, a few words on how their season went in 2000-01. This takes into account, in a positive fashion, key performances, along with value to the team, injuries, honours, and other points of interest, etc.

Career Records: Full appearances, plus substitutes and goals, are given for all Carling Premiership and Nationwide League games and, if a player who is in the book has played in any of the senior Scottish Leagues, his appearances with the club in question will also be recorded at the point of signing. Other information given, includes the origination of players (clubs in the non-leagues, junior football, or from abroad), registered signing dates (if a player signs permanently following a loan spell, for our purposes, we have shown the initial date as being the point of temporary transfer. Also, loan transfers are only recorded if an appearance is made), transfer fees (these are the figures that have been reported in newspapers and magazines and should only be used as a guide to a player's valuation), and a breakdown of matches by P/FL (Premiership and Football League), PL (Premier League), FL (Football League), FLC (Football League Cup), FAC (FA Cup), and Others. Other matches will take in the Play Offs, Anglo-Italian Cup, Auto Windscreens Shield, Charity Shield, and any major European competition. All of these matches are lumped together for reasons of saving space. Scottish appearances for players on loan to P/FL clubs in 1999-2000 are shown at the point of transfer and do not include games following their return to Scotland. That also applies to players transferred from England to Scotland.

Career statistics are depicted as
Appearances + Substitutes/Goals

Whether you wish to analyse someone for your fantasy football team selection or would like to know more about a little-known player appearing in the lower reaches of the game, the *PFA Footballers' Factfile* should provide you with the answer.

Barry J. Hugman, Editor, PFA Footballers' Factfile

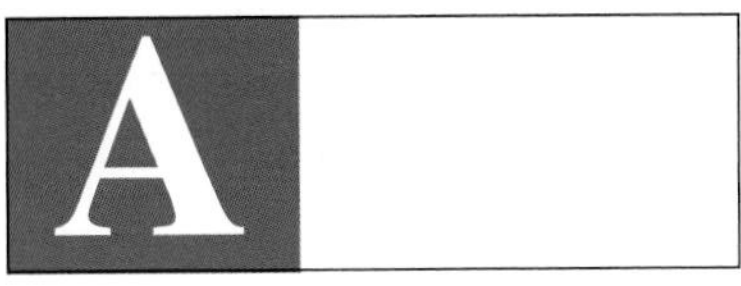

ABBEY Benjamin (Ben) Charles
Born: London, 13 May 1978
Height: 5'7" Weight: 11.0
Out of favour at Oxford, Ben spent the first month of last season on loan at Ryman League club Aldershot Town before signing for Third Division Southend United. He became an instant favourite with the Roots Hall fans after scoring two goals on his debut against Macclesfield. A small and lively striker with great pace and agility, he was released in the summer.
Oxford U (£30,000 from Crawley T on 29/9/1999) FL 0+10 FAC 0+1/1 Others 0+1
Southend U (Free on 27/10/2000) FL 15+9/8 FAC 4/1 Others 3+1/1

ABBEY George Peterson
Born: Port Harcourt, Nigeria, 20 October 1978
Height: 5'10" Weight: 10.10
George was affected by a string of minor injuries: knee, shoulder, groin strain, hamstring and also a bout of 'flu, nevertheless his overall performance at right back for Macclesfield showed steady improvement. He is now much more of a team player, although he still retains his natural individual flair and enthusiasm.
Macclesfield T (Signed from Sharks FC, Port Harcourt, Nigeria on 20/8/1999) FL 25+11 FLC 4+1 FAC 1+2

ABBEY Nathanael (Nathan)
Born: Islington, 11 July 1978
Height: 6'1" Weight: 12.0
Nathan began the 2000-01 campaign as second-choice 'keeper to newcomer Mark Ovendale at Luton. He came back to enjoy two lengthy runs in the side and the pair effectively shared duties during the campaign. A talented young goalkeeper he produced some commanding performances and arguably the save of the season at Kenilworth Road in the game against Wrexham in October. He was one of five players released by the Hatters in the summer.
Luton T (From trainee on 2/5/1996) FL 54+1 FLC 3 FAC 8 Others 2

ABBEY Zema
Born: Luton, 17 April 1977
Height: 6'1" Weight: 12.11
Zema started the 2000-01 season at Cambridge with a flourish and scored five league goals before suffering a dip in form. In December he moved on to Norwich City for a substantial fee and made an immediate impact for the Canaries. Although regularly in the squad he was often used as a substitute, netting his first goal for his new club in the home game against Queens Park Rangers. A pacy centre forward who can also operate in a wide role, his excellent close control enables him to go past defenders with ease. He also possesses an excellent spring in his jump that allows him to beat much taller players in the air.
Cambridge U (Signed from Hitchin T on 11/2/2000) FL 16+6/5 FLC 1+1 FAC 1 Others 1
Norwich C (£350,000 on 15/12/2000) FL 11+9/1

ABIDALLAH Nabil
Born: Amsterdam, Holland, 5 August 1982
Height: 5'7" Weight: 9.6
International Honours: Morocco: Yth
Nabil joined Ipswich Town from Ajax's youth programme and made steady progress in the reserves last term. He stepped up for his first-team debut when he came on for the final eleven minutes at home to Everton in February and also featured in the closing stages of the home game with Bradford City the following month. He is a predominantly right-footed creative midfield player with a similar style to that of Keiron Dyer.
Ipswich T (Free from Ajax, Holland on 19/7/2000) PL 0+2

ACHTERBERG John
Born: Utrecht, Holland, 8 July 1971
Height: 6'1" Weight: 13.8
Having signed a new three-year contract towards the end of the 1999-2000 season, John started last term as first-choice 'keeper for Tranmere and remained so until sidelined by an ankle injury. Although out of action for several weeks, he returned to the team in the new year continuing to see off the challenge of his younger rival Joe Murphy. Calm and efficient, he has good handling skills and produced many sterling performances to save Rovers from some heavy defeats as they eventually dropped down to the Second Division.
Tranmere Rov (Free from PSV Eindhoven, Holland, ex NAC Breda, on 22/9/1998) FL 72+3 FLC 11+1 FAC 7

ACUNA Donoso **Clarence** Williams
Born: Coya Rancagua, Chile, 8 February 1975
Height: 5'8" Weight: 11.6
International Honours: Chile: 52; Yth
Three times a championship winner in Chile with Universidad, Clarence signed for Newcastle in the close season but had to wait until October to make his Premiership debut. His first goal came in the home win over Leeds and he netted again when the Magpies completed the double over their Yorkshire rivals. One of his best performances came at Bradford when he notched a point-saving goal, but he missed the last few games of the campaign with a bout of tendonitis. A short stocky box-to-box midfielder he frequently makes telling runs into the opposition penalty area. Having had a season to acclimatise himself on Tyneside it seems likely he will become increasingly influential in Newcastle's midfield in 2001-02.
Newcastle U (£900,000 from Universidad de Chile, ex O'Higgins, on 25/10/2000) PL 23+3/3 FLC 1 FAC 2

ADAMS Daniel (Danny) Benjamin
Born: Manchester, 3 January 1976
Height: 5'8" Weight: 13.8
This former Bury trainee joined Macclesfield Town on a two-year contract last August, making his debut from the subs' bench in the Worthington Cup home tie against Bolton Wanderers and proceeding to make the left-back position his own. A gritty and determined player, Danny feeds the ball well to the midfield and enjoys pushing forward on the overlap.
Macclesfield T (£25,000 from Altrincham on 31/8/2000) FL 36+1 FLC 1+1 FAC 1 Others 1

ADAMS Neil James
Born: Stoke, 23 November 1965
Height: 5'8" Weight: 10.12
Club Honours: Div 1 '87, Div 2 '91
International Honours: E: U21-1
Although he scored Oldham's opening goal of the 2000-01 campaign in the 4-1 win over Port Vale, Neil had a somewhat troubled time last season. He suffered a cruciate knee ligament injury after falling awkwardly in the game at Stoke in October, and although he battled back to fitness and managed a couple of appearances towards the end of the season he was released when his contract expired in the summer. A very experienced right wing back he can still deliver a fine cross from the flank.
Stoke C (Signed from QM Rangers on 1/7/1985) FL 31+1/4 FLC 3 FAC 1 Others 3
Everton (£150,000 on 7/7/1986) FL 17+3 FLC 4+1/1 Others 5+1
Oldham Ath (Loaned on 11/1/1989) FL 9
Oldham Ath (£100,000 on 21/6/1989) F/PL 93+36/23 FLC 13+2/1 FAC 10+2/2 Others 1+1
Norwich C (£250,000 on 17/2/1994) P/FL 164+18/25 FLC 16+1/4 FAC 7/1
Oldham Ath (Free on 6/7/1999) FL 47/4 FLC 4 FAC 2/1 Others 1

ADAMS Stephen (Steve) Marc
Born: Plymouth, 25 September 1980
Height: 6'0" Weight: 11.10
Steve is one of several promising youngsters at Plymouth but had a frustrating time with injuries in the 2000-01 season. A versatile player who can play either in midfield or defence, his main attributes are his pace and the accuracy of his passing.
Plymouth Arg (From trainee on 6/7/1999) FL 13+5 FAC 1 Others 1+1

ADAMS Tony Alexander
Born: Romford, 10 October 1966
Height: 6'3" Weight: 13.11
Club Honours: Div 1 '89, '91; PL '98; FLC '87, '93; FAC '93, '98; ECWC '94; CS '98
International Honours: E: 66; B-4; U21-5; Yth
An exceptional central defender who commands respect at every level of the game, Tony started the 2000-01 season very much in the same vein as the previous two campaigns: absent for almost every other

game up to the Christmas period due to back problems, minor knocks, and general wear and tear. However when he did play his superb leadership qualities were very much in evidence. As ever, he showed total commitment while his ferocious tackling and excellent positional sense added stability to the Arsenal defence. The most successful Arsenal captain, he is closing in on David O'Leary's appearance record and in January he announced his retirement from the international scene in order to let his body recover from the demands of the modern game. Despite being in the twilight of his career, his loyalty to the Gunners has been rewarded with an extended contract and he remains a vital figure in the continued success of the Highbury team.
Arsenal (From apprentice on 30/1/1984) F/PL 490+4/32 FLC 58+1/5 FAC 50+1/7 Others 55/4

ADAMSON Christopher (Chris)
Born: Ashington, 4 November 1978
Height: 5'1" Weight: 11.0
Chris began last season as second-choice 'keeper to Brian Jensen at West Bromwich Albion and made a single first-team appearance in the FA Cup third round tie at Blackburn when Jensen was injured. The Baggies then signed Russell Hoult, pushing Chris further down the pecking order and although he played regularly for the reserves he finished the campaign on the transfer list.
West Bromwich A (From trainee on 2/7/1997) FL 12 FAC 2
Mansfield T (Loaned on 30/4/1999) FL 2
Halifax T (Loaned on 1/7/1999) FL 7

ADEBOLA Bamberdele (Dele)
Born: Lagos, Nigeria, 23 June 1975
Height: 6'3" Weight: 12.8
Dele seemed to be set for a move to Las Palmas during the close season but the deal broke down and he remained at Birmingham City throughout the 2000-01 campaign. He responded by working hard in training and won his place back in the squad, although he was often used as a substitute. He was particularly effective in the Worthington Cup run, scoring five goals for Blues on the way to the final when he made the starting line-up against Liverpool. His strong dribbling caused tremendous problems in the earlier rounds both for Spurs, against whom he scored twice in a 3-1 win at White Hart Lane, and Newcastle. However he had the misfortune to suffer a bad knee injury when he collided with a post in the penultimate game of the regular season and is not expected to return until the turn of the year. A powerful striker he showed a good turn of pace when in full flow and also improved his heading.
Crewe Alex (From trainee on 21/6/1993) FL 98+26/39 FLC 4+3/2 FAC 8+2/3 Others 10+1/2
Birmingham C (£1,000,000 on 6/2/1998) FL 86+43/31 FLC 13+4/8 FAC 2+1/2 Others 1+2/1

AGGREY James (Jimmy) Emmanuel
Born: Hammersmith, 26 October 1978
Height: 6'3" Weight: 13.6
Surprisingly good on the ground for one so tall, Jimmy has always possessed the ability to succeed but his progress at Torquay has sometimes been hampered by a suspect temperament. However he emerged with a more mature, focused attitude last season and this resulted in a series of commanding performances in the second half of the season. He developed a fine understanding in the centre of defence with the experienced Lee Russell and it came as no surprise when Jimmy picked up the Gulls' 'Player of the Season' award.
Fulham (From trainee at Chelsea on 2/7/1997)
Airdrieonians (Free on 30/6/1998)
Torquay U (Free on 22/10/1998) FL 85+8/2 FLC 4 FAC 5+1 Others 5

Jimmy Aggrey

AGNEW Stephen (Steve) Mark
Born: Shipley, 9 November 1965
Height: 5'10" Weight: 11.9
Club Honours: Div 1 '96
This experienced midfielder captained York City last season, his leadership and commitment proving significant in the closing weeks of the campaign as the Minstermen pulled themselves clear of the Third Division relegation zone. He scored three goals including a vital 20-yard strike to equalise in the FA Cup replay at Reading, that proved to be the springboard for a shock 3-1 victory for the Third Division club. He was released in May.
Barnsley (From apprentice on 10/11/1983) FL 186+8/29 FLC 13/3 FAC 20/4 Others 6+1
Blackburn Rov (£700,000 on 25/6/1991) FL 2 FLC 2
Portsmouth (Loaned on 21/11/1992) FL 3+2 Others 2
Leicester C (£250,000 on 9/2/1993) F/PL 52+4/4 FLC 4+1 FAC 2 Others 2
Sunderland (£250,000 on 11/1/1995) P/FL 56+7/9 FLC 4 FAC 2+1/1
York C (Free on 10/7/1998) FL 76+5/4 FLC 2 FAC 6/1 Others 1

AGYEMANG Patrick
Born: Walthamstow, 29 September 1980
Height: 6'1" Weight: 12.0
Patrick broke through to win a regular place in the Wimbledon first-team squad in 2000-01 and after a long wait he netted his first senior goal for the Dons in the FA Cup fifth round tie against Wycombe Wanderers. However once he had scored he went on to register several more goals and quickly became something of a cult hero with the Dons' faithful. He capped a fine year by being voted the club's 'Most Improved Player' and the coming season should see him go from strength to strength.
Wimbledon (From trainee on 11/5/1999) FL 16+13/4 FLC 1+1 FAC 6/1
Brentford (Loaned on 18/10/1999) FL 3+9 FAC 1

AINSWORTH Gareth
Born: Blackburn, 10 May 1973
Height: 5'9" Weight: 12.5
Gareth's season didn't kick off until January last term due to injury but once he was back, Wimbledon showed a significant upturn in form. A speedy right winger who laid on many goals for his colleagues, he is a true character and entertainer and regularly worth the entrance fee alone. Unfortunately he broke a wrist during the Stockport away match and so missed another short spell but was soon back in the team. The Dons' faithful were left with the feeling that had he been fit all season an automatic promotion place would have been there for the taking.
Preston NE (Signed from Northwich Vic, ex Blackburn Rov YTS, on 21/1/1992) FL 2+3 Others 1/1
Cambridge U (Free on 17/8/1992) FL 1+3/1 FLC 0+1
Preston NE (Free on 23/12/1992) FL 76+6/12 FLC 3+2 FAC 3+1 Others 8+1/1
Lincoln C (£25,000 on 31/10/1995) FL 83/37 FLC 8/3 FAC 2 Others 4/1
Port Vale (£500,000 on 12/9/1997) FL 53+2/10 FLC 2/1 FAC 2
Wimbledon (£2,000,000 on 3/11/1998) P/FL 13+9/4 FAC 5+1/1

AISTON Samuel (Sam) James
Born: Newcastle, 21 November 1976
Height: 6'1" Weight: 12.10
Club Honours: Div 1 '96
International Honours: E: Sch
This skilful left winger joined Shrewsbury Town in July 2000 and was a near ever-present last season. He is a very talented player capable of rounding opponents with ease, but still needs to develop greater composure when delivering his final ball. He netted two goals during the campaign including a brilliant individual effort in the 2-2 draw at Lincoln when he ran half the length of the pitch before finishing with a fine shot.
Sunderland (Free from Newcastle U juniors on 14/7/1995) P/FL 5+15 FLC 0+2 FAC 0+2
Chester C (Loaned on 21/2/1997) FL 14 FLC 1 Others 2
Chester C (Loaned on 27/11/1998) FL 11 Others 1
Stoke C (Loaned on 6/8/1999) FL 2+4 FLC 1
Shrewsbury T (Loaned on 24/12/1999) FL 10
Shrewsbury T (Free on 21/7/2000) FL 40+2/2 FLC 2 FAC 1

AKINBIYI Adeola (Ade) Peter
Born: Hackney, 10 October 1974
Height: 6'1" Weight: 12.9
International Honours: Nigeria: 1
Signed by Leicester City in the close season for a club record fee it was originally thought that Ade would play alongside an experienced striker in his early days in the Premiership but he soon found that he was

thrust into the deep end after the two potential partners, Stan Collymore and Tony Cottee, quickly departed from Filbert Street. Things were tough for Ade throughout his inaugural campaign with the Foxes, as he suffered both from the lack of a reliable service and the need to adapt to a series of different front-line partners. The signing of Dean Sturridge was a turning point for him and he eventually went on to finish as the club's leading scorer with a double-figure tally. A strong and speedy striker he has the attributes to become a handful for any defence. Ade is a cousin of Bristol City's Kay Odejayi.

Norwich C (From trainee on 5/2/1993) P/FL 22+27/3 FLC 2+4/2 FAC 1+2 Others 0+1
Hereford U (Loaned on 21/1/1994) FL 3+1/2
Brighton & Hove A (Loaned on 24/11/1994) FL 7/4
Gillingham (£250,000 on 13/1/1997) FL 63/28 FLC 2 FAC 2/1 Others 0+1
Bristol C (£1,200,000 on 28/5/1998) FL 47/21 FLC 5/4 FAC 1
Wolverhampton W (£3,500,000 on 7/9/1999) FL 36+1/16
Leicester C (£5,000,000 on 28/7/2000) PL 33+4/9 FAC 4/1 Others 2

Ade Akinbiyi

ALCIDE Colin James
Born: Huddersfield, 14 April 1972
Height: 6'2" Weight: 13.10

The powerfully built player had a mixed time for York City in 2000-01. Although not a regular in the line-up in the first half of the campaign he came off the subs' bench to score an important goal in the Minstermen's 3-1 FA Cup win at Reading. He then had a successful spell mid-term in the centre of defence where he impressed with his composure, before returning to his more familiar position as a striker. He was particularly effective in the win at Mansfield last March, and struck up a useful partnership with Lee Nogan up front in the closing weeks of the season. Colin has a good touch on the ball and is very effective in the air whether playing in defence or attack. He was reported to have moved to Cambridge United in the summer.

Lincoln C (£15,000 from Emley on 5/12/1995) FL 105+16/27 FLC 7+2/2 FAC 3+3/2 Others 3+1
Hull C (Loaned on 4/2/1999) FL 5/1
Hull C (£50,000 on 10/3/1999) FL 22+2/3 FLC 3+1/2 FAC 0+2
York C (£80,000 on 23/11/1999) FL 33+20/7 FLC 1 FAC 2+1/1 Others 2

ALDRIDGE Paul John
Born: Liverpool, 2 December 1981
Height: 5'11" Weight: 11.7

Paul continued to make steady progress at Tranmere in 2000-01, and made the subs' bench on the opening day of the season for the game at Wimbledon. It was a very disappointing campaign for Rovers who struggled unsuccessfully to avoid relegation, and Paul managed just one more appearance, also as a substitute, during the season. A regular in the club's successful reserve team he is a young midfield player with an uncompromising approach who is full of enthusiasm for the game. Paul is the son of former Tranmere boss John Aldridge.

Tranmere Rov (From trainee on 24/3/2000) FL 0+6

ALEKSIDZE Rati
Born: Georgia, 6 August 1978
Height: 6'0" Weight: 12.4
International Honours: Georgia: 9

This dynamic young striker almost rescued Chelsea's season in his initial first-team outing as a substitute. The Blues were trailing at Swiss club St Gallen in the UEFA Cup when his late drive hit the crossbar and rebounded to safety - so close to scoring the away goal which would have secured victory. Rati is a left-sided attacker with an impressive pedigree in his homeland - he was Georgian Player of the Year in 2000 and captained both Dinamo Tbilisi and the national U21 side. Indeed Chelsea have been long-time admirers of his talents and he spent a trial period at Stamford Bridge back in the 1996-97 season when he played for the club's youth and reserve sides. The Blues had closely monitored his progress in the interim and fought a protracted battle to secure a work permit. He was limited to a handful of substitute appearances last term but will expect to feature more regularly in 2001-02.

Chelsea (£120,000 + from Dinamo Tbilisi, Georgia on 17/2/2000) PL 0+2 Others 0+1

ALEXANDER Gary George
Born: Lambeth, 15 August 1979
Height: 5'11" Weight: 13.0

Gary became Swindon Town's major signing during the 2000 close season when he arrived from West Ham for a substantial fee. He took time to settle in, not least because of the weight of expectation placed on him, and was dropped for a short period but finished the campaign strongly. A tall striker who works tirelessly he has great awareness about him in the penalty box. He was reported to have signed for Hull City in the summer.

West Ham U (From trainee on 6/7/1998)
Exeter C (Loaned on 19/8/1999) FL 37/16 FLC 1 FAC 3/1 Others 4/2
Swindon T (£300,000 on 11/8/2000) FL 30+7/7 FLC 3 FAC 2+1 Others 2+1/2

ALEXANDER Graham
Born: Coventry, 10 October 1971
Height: 5'10" Weight: 12.7
Club Honours: Div 2 '00

An injury at Bolton last August saw Graham miss his first league game since signing for Preston, but he went on to feature regularly for the club last season, his only other absences coming with a brief suspension and when he suffered a broken rib on Boxing Day that led to a punctured lung and two-months on the sidelines. He scored a penalty against his home-town club Coventry in the Worthington Cup tie, the winner against local rivals Burnley and in all added seven goals during the campaign. A popular right back his positive overlapping, powerful free kicks and sound defensive play were a feature of the run-in to the play-offs.

Scunthorpe U (From trainee on 20/3/1990) FL 149+10/18 FLC 11+1/2 FAC 12/1 Others 13+3/3
Luton T (£100,000 on 8/7/1995) FL 146+4/15 FLC 17/2 FAC 6+1 Others 6+2
Preston NE (£50,000 on 25/3/1999) FL 90/11 FLC 9/3 FAC 6/3 Others 6

ALEXANDERSSON Niclas
Born: Halmstad, Sweden, 29 December 1971
Height: 6'2" Weight: 11.8
International Honours: Sweden: 51

Having ended his final season at Sheffield Wednesday as fans' player of the year, Niclas found himself blighted by injury at Goodison last term. A goal-scoring right winger, he whetted the Everton fans' appetites with a series of strikes in the club's pre-season fixtures but an injury in the last of those games against Manchester City, however, was just the first of a series of problems. He returned for a short run in the line-up before another injury sustained on international duty with Sweden cut two more months out of his season. An ankle problem and a dose of 'flu meant that it was March before he finally returned regularly to first-team action. He scored his first goal with a decisive strike at West Ham and also netted in the crucial home game with Bradford City when Everton secured a Premiership place once more.

Sheffield Wed (£750,000 from Gothenburg, Sweden, ex Halmstad, on 9/12/1997) PL 73+2/8 FLC 4+1/2 FAC 8/2
Everton (£2,500,000 on 20/7/2000) PL 17+3/2 FLC 2 FAC 1

AL JABER Sami Abdullah
Born: Riyadh, Suadi Arabia, 11 December 1972
Height: 5'8" Weight: 12.1
International Honours: Saudi Arabia:

A prolific scorer in Saudi Arabia where he was nicknamed the 'Blue Wolf' Sami appropriately joined the First Division Wolves last season on an extended five-month trial. He impressed in pre-season games and after eventually gaining a work permit made his debut from the subs' bench

at Wimbledon. He featured in a handful of early season games before returning home to take part in the Asian Cup in which he captained his country's team that was narrowly beaten in the final by Japan. However he returned to Molineux with an injury and made just one more appearance as a substitute before going back home in the new year. A vastly experienced international, he is a striker who although not tall, looked very sharp and possessed a neat touch on the ball.
Wolverhampton W (Loaned from Al Hilal, Saudi Arabia on 13/9/2000) FL 0+4 FLC 1

ALLAN Jonathan (Jon) Michael
Born: Carlisle, 24 May 1983
Height: 5'10" Weight: 11.12
Jon stepped up from the youth ranks to sign a professional contract with Carlisle at the end of the 1999-2000 campaign and went on to make his senior debut in the LDV Vans Trophy tie at Kidderminster, when he came off the subs' bench for the final 35 minutes. A powerful young striker with good pace he will be hoping to gain more first-team experience in 2001-02.
Carlisle U (From trainee on 24/5/2000) Others 0+1

ALLEN Bradley James
Born: Romford, 13 September 1971
Height: 5'8" Weight: 11.0
International Honours: E: U21-8; Yth
Bradley took advantage of Lee Ashcroft's departure from Grimsby to establish himself as a regular in the line-up in the early part of the 2000-01 campaign. Unfortunately he then suffered an injury in the match at Watford in November that developed into tendonitis, leading to a long spell on the sidelines. He eventually returned to the team in March but his hopes of playing a role in the Mariners' struggle to remain in the First Division were then dashed by an achilles heel injury in only his second full game back. He is a lively striker whose speed in the box, and accuracy in front of goal were sorely missed last season.
Queens Park R (From juniors on 30/9/1988) F/PL 56+25/27 FLC 5+2/5 FAC 3+2 Others 1
Charlton Ath (£400,000 on 28/3/1996) FL 30+10/9 FLC 3+1/2 FAC 0+2 Others 1+1
Colchester U (Loaned on 24/2/1999) FL 4/1
Grimsby T (Free on 12/7/1999) FL 27+25/11 FLC 4+4/3 FAC 0+2/1

ALLEN Graham
Born: Bolton, 8 April 1977
Height: 6'1" Weight: 12.8
International Honours: E: Yth
Graham was out of favour at Tranmere at the beginning of the 2000-01 season and it was only when Dave Challinor was sidelined with a broken leg in November that he returned to a regular place in the line-up. He went on to produce some solid displays in what was a very disappointing campaign for the Birkenhead club and finished the season as club captain. An uncompromising defender who can play either at right back or centre half, he relishes the chance to go forward and join the attack when the opportunity presents itself. He was due to be out of contract in the summer and at the time of writing his future was unclear.
Everton (From trainee on 10/12/1994) PL 2+4
Tranmere Rov (Free on 28/8/1998) FL 83+4/5 FLC 8+2 FAC 6

ALLISON Wayne Anthony
Born: Huddersfield, 16 October 1968
Height: 6'1" Weight: 12.6
Club Honours: Div 2 '96
Very much a favourite of the Tranmere faithful for his all-action displays, Wayne found it difficult to hit his best form in a struggling side last term and when the goals dried up he spent some time in the reserve team before resuming his place in the attack later on. Nevertheless he still finished as the club's joint-second-top scorer with six goals. A traditional, old-fashioned centre forward he dominates in the air, leads the line well and creates chances with his bustling, awkward style.
Halifax T (From trainee on 6/7/1987) FL 74+10/23 FLC 3/2 FAC 4+1/2 Others 8+1/3
Watford (£250,000 on 26/7/1989) FL 6+1
Bristol C (£300,000 on 9/8/1990) FL 149+46/48 FLC 4+5/2 FAC 12+1/5 Others 6+2/2
Swindon T (£475,000 on 22/7/1995) FL 98+3/31 FLC 9/3 FAC 7/2 Others 3
Huddersfield T (£800,000 on 11/11/1997) FL 71+3/15 FLC 3+1/2 FAC 6/2
Tranmere Rov (£300,000 on 3/9/1999) FL 72+4/22 FLC 4+2/1 FAC 4+1/4

ALLOTT Mark Stephen
Born: Manchester, 3 October 1977
Height: 5'11" Weight: 12.6
Mark started the 2000-01 campaign on a high, signing a deal which committed him to Oldham Athletic for three more years and producing an impressive showing and a goal in the 4-1 opening day rout of Port Vale. However he then endured another stop-start season as competition for front-line slots became fierce and the subs' bench beckoned on a regular basis. A striker who holds the ball well, he has good movement but has still yet to consistently fulfil his goal-scoring potential.
Oldham Ath (From trainee on 14/10/1995) FL 96+43/27 FLC 6+3/2 FAC 7+6 Others 1+1

ALLSOP Daniel (Danny)
Born: Australia, 10 August 1978
Height: 6'1" Weight: 12.0
International Honours: Australia: U23-7; Yth
Danny found himself unable to break into Manchester City's first-team squad at the start of the 2000-01 campaign and joined Bristol Rovers on loan in October. He made a handful of appearances for the Pirates before returning to Maine Road, but soon afterwards he was on his way again, this time to Notts County. He quickly established a successful partnership up front with Mark Stallard and signed permanently for the Magpies for a substantial fee in December. A big strong target man who can play either in the centre of attack or on the right flank, his confidence improved as the season progressed and he registered a respectable double-figure goal tally.
Manchester C (£10,000 from Port Melbourne, Australia on 7/8/1998) P/FL 3+26/4 FLC 0+7/1 Others 1+1/1
Notts Co (Loaned on 5/11/1999) FL 3/1
Wrexham (Loaned on 25/2/2000) FL 3/4
Bristol Rov (Loaned on 12/10/2000) FL 4+2
Notts Co (£300,000 on 22/11/2000) FL 26+3/13 FAC 4

ALOISI John
Born: Adelaide, Australia, 5 February 1976
Height: 6'0" Weight: 12.13
International Honours: Australia: 21; Yth
Having missed much of the previous campaign through injury, great things were expected from John at Coventry last term, but the reality was that it proved to be another frustrating season for him. Out of the team at the start of the season, he got his first start in the Worthington Cup tie at home to Preston. He grasped the opportunity with both hands netting an impressive hat-trick and followed this up with goals in successive Premiership matches against Charlton and Spurs, the latter a stunning effort. However after two more starts he was sidelined by hamstring trouble, and although he scored an excellent goal on his return at Bradford he was then dropped and rarely featured in the first team thereafter. In April he returned to Australia to play for his country in the World Cup qualifiers and netted six goals in a 22-0 win over Tonga, only to suffer further hamstring problems against Fiji that cut short his involvement at Highfield Road, although he recovered in time to feature again for his country during the summer.
Portsmouth (£300,000 from Cremonese, Italy, ex Adelaide City, Standard Liege, Royal Antwerp, on 8/8/1997) FL 55+5/25 FLC 6/3 FAC 1
Coventry C (£650,000 on 18/12/1998) PL 18+24/10 FLC 2+1/3 FAC 0+2

[ALPAY] OZALAN Fehmi
Born: Karisyaled, Turkey, 29 May 1973
Height: 6'2" Weight: 13.7
International Honours: Turkey: 52
Alpay arrived at Aston Villa in the summer after impressing with Turkey in the Euro 2000 finals. Seen as a replacement for Ugo Ehiogu he quickly established himself in the team and proved to be an excellent buy for Villa boss John Gregory. He went on to be a near ever-present, missing a handful of games due to a hamstring injury and suspensions. A tough-tackling central defender who is good in the air and can also play the ball out from the defence, he is strong, composed and a good reader of the game. He remained a regular for Turkey winning his 50th cap last October.
Aston Villa (£5,600,000 from Fenerbahce, Turkey, ex Altay, Besiktas, on 31/7/2000) PL 33 FLC 1 FAC 2

ALSOP Julian Mark
Born: Nuneaton, 28 May 1973
Height: 6'4" Weight: 14.0
Club Honours: Div 3 '00
Although not a prolific goal-scorer Julian proved a valuable signing for Cheltenham last season. He suffered from the lack of a regular partner and occasionally played as a lone forward but always caused problems for defenders with his height and strength on the ball. He is a hard working striker who is

a very effective target man, adept at holding the ball up and laying it off for his colleagues.
Bristol Rov (£15,000 from Halesowen on 14/2/1997) FL 20+13/4 FLC 2/1 FAC 1/1 Others 2
Swansea C (Loaned on 20/1/1998) FL 5/2
Swansea C (£30,000 on 12/3/1998) FL 73+12/14 FLC 4+2 FAC 6+1/1 Others 5
Cheltenham T (Free on 3/7/2000) FL 29+10/5 FLC 2 FAC 1+1/1

AMANKWAAH Kevin
Born: Harrow, 19 May 1982
Height: 6'1" Weight: 12.0
International Honours: E: Yth
Kevin looked a star in the making during an impressive run in the Bristol City first team shortly after the start of last season but then suffered a knee ligament injury in the game at Millwall. Although he recovered fitness, he was unable to displace Matt Hill in the starting line-up and featured on only a handful of occasions in the second half of the campaign. A pacy young defender he can play at right back, right wing back or at centre half if required.
Bristol C (From trainee on 16/6/2000) FL 12+7 FAC 0+1 Others 1+1

AMEOBI Foluwashola (Shola)
Born: Zaria, Nigeria, 12 October 1981
Height: 6'2" Weight: 12.0
International Honours: E: U21-5
Shola had a tremendous season at Newcastle in 2000-01 for he started off in the Academy side and finished as a regular for both the first team and England U21s. Injuries to the club's more senior strikers presented him with a first-team opportunity from the subs' bench against Chelsea in September and he came on to torment the Blues' defence, at the same time endearing himself to the Toon Army with his display. His first start came in the Boxing Day win over Leeds and after that he became a near regular in the team, netting his first Premiership goal against Coventry in January. A tall lanky striker with an awkward looking style he has a good touch and he leads the line adroitly, holding the ball up when necessary to bring colleagues into play, but not afraid to go it alone if the opportunity presents itself. While clearly there are still some raw edges to his game he is a very promising youngster and he signed a four-year contract for the Magpies last September. His performances earned him a call up to the England U21 squad and after making his debut in the friendly with Spain he netted twice in the 4-0 win over Finland.
Newcastle U (From trainee on 19/10/1998) PL 12+8/2 FAC 2

AMPADU Patrick **Kwame**
Born: Bradford, 20 December 1970
Height: 5'10" Weight: 11.10
Club Honours: AMC '94
International Honours: RoI: U21-4; Yth
Kwame joined Exeter City in the 2000 close season and earned himself a regular place in the Grecians' midfield in 2000-01. Essentially a ball-winning player in the centre of the park he showed precise judgement in the tackle and excellent distribution. He scored his only goal of the campaign in the Worthington Cup tie at Swindon last August. He was placed on the open to offers list in the summer.
Arsenal (From trainee on 19/11/1988) FL 0+2
Plymouth Arg (Loaned on 31/10/1990) FL 6/1 Others 1
West Bromwich A (£50,000 on 24/6/1991) FL 27+22/4 FLC 6+1 FAC 1 Others 5/1
Swansea C (£15,000 on 16/2/1994) FL 128+19/12 FLC 8+1/1 FAC 5+1/1 Others 16/1
Leyton Orient (Free on 30/7/1998) FL 69+3/1 FLC 8 FAC 4+1/1 Others 1
Exeter C (Free on 18/7/2000) FL 29+7 FLC 1/1 FAC 0+1

ANDERSEN Trond
Born: Kristiansand, Norway, 6 January 1975
Height: 6'2" Weight: 12.8
International Honours: Norway: 12; B-1; U21; Yth
Trond enjoyed another hugely successful season for Wimbledon in 2000-01 turning in some crucial performances and finding time to contribute some valuable goals. A versatile player who can take any defensive or midfield position, he has the ability to run all day and often seems to do so. A member of the Norway national team during the campaign he could provide a solid backbone for the Dons in years to come.
Wimbledon (£2,500,000 from Molde, Norway on 9/8/1999) P/FL 75+3/5 FLC 6 FAC 8/1

ANDERSON Iain
Born: Glasgow, 23 July 1977
Height: 5'8" Weight: 9.10
Club Honours: Div 2 '00
International Honours: S: U21-14
Signed permanently by Preston on the first day of pre-season training following a successful loan spell in 1999-2000, Iain's story last season was one of injuries and comeback goals. A long-range volley at Sheffield Wednesday, the winner at Wolves and the last of five against Queens Park Rangers all marked his return from yet another spell in the treatment room. Typical of his bad luck was when he received both head and hamstring injuries in the same incident against Fulham. A fast and tricky ball-playing winger who can operate on both flanks, he is most dangerous on the left from where he can cut inside and unleash powerful shots.
Dundee (From juniors on 10/8/1994) SL 90+37/16 SLC 3+5 SC 6+3/2 Others 6+1/2 (Signed by Toulouse, France on 28/7/1999)
Preston NE (Loaned from Toulouse, France on 18/2/2000) FL 30+13/8 FLC 2 Others 1+2

ANDERSON Ijah Massai
Born: Hackney, 30 December 1975
Height: 5'8" Weight: 10.6
Club Honours: Div 3 '99
Brentford's longest-serving player lined up in an unfamiliar centre back role for the opening game of 2000-01 at Northampton. Unfortunately that was to be the extent of his senior experience for the season as he ruptured a knee ligament in training shortly afterwards and was out of action for the remainder of the campaign. Ijah usually appears at left back for the Bees and it is hoped he will make a full recovery by the start of the coming season.
Southend U (From trainee at Tottenham H on 2/8/1994)
Brentford (Free on 31/7/1995) FL 154+4/4 FLC 15/1 FAC 4+3 Others 8+1

ANDERTON Darren Robert
Born: Southampton, 3 March 1972
Height: 6'1" Weight: 12.5
Club Honours: FLC '99
International Honours: E: 29; B-1; U21-12; Yth
Darren featured regularly for Tottenham in the first half of last season only missing a brief spell early on with a groin problem. He did well in the period up to Christmas, netting in the 3-1 win over Ipswich in the opening game and going on to score a total of four goals, although three of these came from the penalty spot. However he was then sidelined by an achilles injury early in the new year and did not appear in the first team at all after mid-February. At his best Darren is an international class midfield player with great vision and accuracy both when crossing the ball and shooting for goal.
Portsmouth (From trainee on 5/2/1990) FL 53+9/7 FLC 3+2/1 FAC 7+1/5 Others 2
Tottenham H (£1,750,000 on 3/6/1992) PL 206+18/30 FLC 21/5 FAC 22+1/5

ANDREASSON Marcus
Born: Liberia, 13 July 1978
Height: 6'4" Weight: 12.2
Marcus suffered some back problems during the 2000-01 pre-season which prevented him being selected for Bristol Rovers in the early part of the campaign, but he soon earned a short run in the team netting his first league goal in the 3-1 victory at Swindon. He subsequently fell out of favour and did not feature at all after October. He is a central defender whose height and pace are his best assets.
Bristol Rov (Free from Osters IF, Sweden on 28/7/1998) FL 5+1 FLC 2 (Free to Kalmar, Sweden on 31/8/1999)
Bristol Rov (Free on 24/3/2000) FL 9/1 FLC 2

ANDREWS John Henry
Born: Cork, 27 September 1978
Height: 6'1" Weight: 12.8
John had a disappointing campaign for Mansfield in 2000-01 when he was unable to produce consistent form and spent a lengthy period out injured. His best performance of the campaign came in the 3-0 Worthington Cup victory at Wrexham when the Stags turned a first leg deficit around to record a 3-1 aggregate win. A right-sided or central defender he was made available on a free transfer in the summer.
Coventry C (From trainee on 15/5/1997. Free to Shepshed Dynamo during 1998 close season)
Mansfield T (Free from Grantham T on 21/10/1999) FL 34+4/1 FLC 4 FAC 2 Others 2

ANDREWS Keith Joseph
Born: Dublin, 13 September 1980
Height: 5'11" Weight: 11.5
Keith's previous experience of senior football amounted to around five minutes before the start of the 2000-01 campaign but he made such tremendous progress that he

was regarded as a regular in the Wolves' first team by the summer. His fortunes began to change after joining Oxford United on loan in November where he scored a fine goal on his debut. On his return caretaker-manager John Ward gave him a surprise chance for the Wanderers just before Christmas and he showed great promise in a short spell in the line-up. Absent for a run of three games he came back with an outstanding performance against West Bromwich Albion, tackling well and spraying the ball around confidently. A young midfield battler who seems to have all the attributes needed for his position, he will be aiming to consolidate his place in the team in 2001-02.

Wolverhampton W (From trainee on 26/9/1997) FL 20+4 FAC 2
Oxford U (Loaned on 10/11/2000) FL 4/1 Others 1

ANGEL Juan Pablo Aranzo
Born: Medellin, Colombia, 24 October 1975
Height: 6'0" Weight: 11.6
International Honours: Colombia: 15; Yth

A prolific goal-scorer in Argentina with River Plate, Juan Pablo joined Aston Villa in January for a new club record fee. However he took some time to settle into English football and domestic problems also hindered his progress. He rarely featured for the first team but there were signs by the end of the campaign that he had begun to get used to life at Villa Park. He netted his all-important first goal in the 3-2 win over Coventry, chesting down Gareth Southgate's cross before volleying the ball home. A member of the Colombian squad for their World Cup qualifying campaign he will be hoping to score many more goals for Villa in the coming season.

Aston Villa (£9,500,000 + from River Plate, Argentina, ex Atletico Nacional, on 19/1/2001) PL 7+2/1 FAC 1

ANGEL Mark
Born: Newcastle, 23 August 1975
Height: 5'10" Weight: 11.10

This pacy winger returned to the North-east last August but never really established himself in the Darlington first team despite some capable displays when coming on as substitute. He scored one goal for the Quakers in his brief time at the club, netting in the Worthington Cup second round defeat at Bradford City. Mark was subsequently released at the end of November and later moved north of the border to sign for Queen of the South.

Sunderland (Free from Walker Central on 31/12/1993)
Oxford U (Free on 9/8/1995) FL 40+33/4 FLC 4+4 FAC 4+2 Others 2+1/1
West Bromwich A (Free on 2/7/1998) FL 4+21/1 FLC 0+1 FAC 1+1
Darlington (Free on 8/8/2000) FL 1+4 FLC 2+1/1

ANGELL Brett Ashley Mark
Born: Marlborough, 20 August 1968
Height: 6'2" Weight: 13.11
Club Honours: Div 2 '00

This much-travelled striker celebrated his arrival at Walsall by scoring twice on his debut as he helped the Saddlers fight back from a two-goal deficit to win 3-2 at Rotherham. His bustling style was effective whether starting a game or coming on as substitute (something he did over twenty times during the season), and he ended his first campaign at Bescot Stadium on a high note with a hat-trick in the final Second Division game at Northampton. A big and powerful target man, he holds the ball up well and has an instinct for finding scoring positions.

Portsmouth (From trainee on 1/8/1986)
Derby Co (£40,000 from Cheltenham T on 19/2/1988)
Stockport Co (£33,000 on 20/10/1988) FL 60+10/28 FLC 3 FAC 3/1 Others 8/4
Southend U (£100,000 on 2/8/1990) FL 109+6/47 FLC 7+1/4 FAC 3/2 Others 9+1/10
Everton (£500,000 on 17/1/1994) PL 16+4/1 FLC 0+1
Sunderland (£600,000 on 23/3/1995) FL 10 FLC 1/1
Sheffield U (Loaned on 30/1/1996) FL 6/2
West Bromwich A (Loaned on 28/3/1996) FL 0+3
Stockport Co (£120,000 on 19/8/1996) FL 122+4/50 FLC 16+3/7 FAC 7/4 Others 4+1/1
Notts Co (Loaned on 9/12/1999) FL 6/5
Preston NE (Loaned on 24/2/2000) FL 9+6/8
Walsall (Free on 27/7/2000) FL 23+18/13 FLC 2+1 FAC 1+2/1 Others 0+1

ANGUS Stevland Dennis
Born: Westminster, 16 September 1980
Height: 6'0" Weight: 12.0
Club Honours: FAYC '99

Stevland was a member of West Ham's successful U19 squad in 1999-2000 and joined Bournemouth on loan at the start of last season to cover for the injured Eddie Howe. He gave some promising performances for the Cherries in the early weeks of the campaign but then went down with glandular fever and returned early to Upton Park. A talented young central defender he will be hoping to gain more senior experience in 2001-02.

West Ham U (From trainee on 2/7/1999)
Bournemouth (Loaned on 11/8/2000) FL 7+2

ANTHROBUS Stephen (Steve) Anthony
Born: Lewisham, 10 November 1968
Height: 6'2" Weight: 13.0

Steve featured regularly for Oxford United at the beginning of last season but then fell out of favour following a managerial change and he was eventually released at the end of the campaign. He is an experienced hard-working target man who is effective in the air and adept at holding the ball up to bring his colleagues in to play.

Millwall (From juniors on 4/8/1986) FL 19+2/4 FLC 3 Others 1
Wimbledon (£150,000 on 16/2/1990) F/PL 27+1 FLC 1 FAC 2
Peterborough U (Loaned on 21/1/1994) FL 2
Chester C (Loaned on 26/8/1994) FL 7
Shrewsbury T (£25,000 on 8/8/1995) FL 60+12/16 FLC 4+1 FAC 5+3/1 Others 7+2/1
Crewe Alex (£75,000 on 24/3/1997) FL 53+8/9 FLC 2+1
Oxford U (Free on 1/7/1999) FL 38+18/3 FLC 6 FAC 4+1 Others 2+2/1

ANTONY Paul Mark
Born: Barnet, 4 March 1982
Height: 5'11" Weight: 12.0

Having developed through the youth system at Carlisle, Paul stepped up to the professional ranks in June 2000 and continued to make steady progress in the reserves. He made his debut in senior football in the LDV Vans Trophy tie at Kidderminster last December when he produced a battling performance on a saturated pitch. He is a promising midfield player who will be looking to gain more first-team experience in the 2001-02 campaign.

Carlisle U (From trainee on 6/6/2000) Others 1

APPLEBY Matthew (Matty) Wilfred
Born: Middlesbrough, 16 April 1972
Height: 5'8" Weight: 11.12

This highly efficient midfield player was again a regular in the Barnsley line-up at the start of the 2000-01 season. However he suffered a calf injury in the FA Cup third round tie against Leeds and was then diagnosed as having a double hernia. He eventually came back into contention very late in the campaign and played in the final game at right back. A natural ball winner whose usual role is to provide a link between defence and attack he always gives 100 per cent effort for the cause.

Newcastle U (From trainee on 4/5/1990) F/PL 18+2 FLC 2+1 FAC 2 Others 2+2
Darlington (Loaned on 25/11/1993) FL 10/1 Others 1
Darlington (Free on 15/6/1994) FL 77+2/7 FLC 2 FAC 4 Others 8/3
Barnsley (£200,000 on 19/7/1996) F/PL 131+8/7 FLC 10+3 FAC 6+2 Others 3

APPLEBY Richard (Richie) Dean
Born: Middlesbrough, 18 September 1975
Height: 5'9" Weight: 11.4
Club Honours: Div 3 '00
International Honours: E: Yth

Richie had a frustrating time with injuries at Swansea last term and a heel problem restricted him to just two outings from the subs' bench in the first half of the season. He spent a further period when he was sidelined with his foot in plaster, but returned to make a handful more appearances as a substitute in the closing matches. A very skilful wide midfield player, he has the ability to open up opposition defences and provides many chances for his colleagues.

Newcastle U (From trainee on 12/8/1993) Others 2
Ipswich T (Free on 12/12/1995) FL 0+3 Others 1
Swansea C (Free on 16/8/1996) FL 87+23/11 FLC 4+3 FAC 5+1/2 Others 3+3/1

APPLETON Michael Antony
Born: Salford, 4 December 1975
Height: 5'9" Weight: 12.4
Club Honours: Div 2 '00

Michael scored Preston North End's first goal of the 2000-01 season at Grimsby, and followed this up with early strikes in the first two home games against Sheffield United and Wimbledon. He showed consistent form and scored the goal that inflicted Fulham's first defeat of the season, when he netted directly from a corner. A 30-yard rocket followed against Crewe in November and it came as a shock when he was transferred to fellow play-off hopefuls West Bromwich Albion in mid-January. Replacing the injured Derek McInnes he added a degree of

steel to the Baggies' centre line but in the end although both North End and Albion reached the play-offs neither was successful in their hopes of a Premiership spot. Michael is a hard-tackling tenacious midfield player with good passing skills.
Manchester U (From trainee on 1/7/1994) FLC 1+1
Wimbledon (Loaned on 22/6/1995) Others 4
Lincoln C (Loaned on 15/9/1995) FL 4 Others 1
Grimsby T (Loaned on 17/1/1997) FL 10/3
Preston NE (£500,000 on 8/8/1997) FL 90+25/12 FLC 7+1/1 FAC 9+1/1 Others 6+1/1
West Bromwich A (£750,000 on 19/1/2001) FL 15 Others 2

ARANALDE Zigor
Born: Guipuzcoa, Spain, 28 February 1973
Height: 6'1" Weight: 13.5
A former team-mate of Pedro Matias, Zigor joined Walsall from Spanish Second Division club CD Logrones shortly before the start of last season. He made an immediate impact at Bescot Stadium, impressing with his raids down the left flank and seemed to have a telepathic understanding with Matias. A regular all season in midfield for the Saddlers he always played with great enthusiasm and 100 per cent commitment.
Walsall (Free from CD Logrones, Spain, ex Albacete, Marbella, Seville, on 11/8/2000) FL 45 FLC 4 FAC 3 Others 3

ARBER Mark Andrew
Born: Johannesburg, South Africa, 9 October 1977
Height: 6'1" Weight: 12.11
Mark was a near ever-present for Barnet last season producing some assured performances at centre back for the Bees. A no-nonsense defender who is nevertheless comfortable on the ball, he was a constant threat to opposition defences at set pieces and scored a number of important goals during the campaign. Perhaps his most outstanding contribution was at Hull City when he stopped a certain goal with an absolutely astonishing header after Lee Harrison had been beaten. Mark has developed into a favourite of the Underhill fans largely due to his passion and commitment to the cause. He was placed on the open to offer list in the summer.
Tottenham H (From trainee on 27/3/1996)
Barnet (£75,000 on 18/9/1998) FL 123+2/15 FLC 4 FAC 3 Others 8/1

ARCA Julio Andres
Born: Quilmes Bernal, Argentine, 31 January 1981
Height: 5'10" Weight: 11.6
International Honours: Argentina: Yth (World Youth '01)
Peter Reid raised a few eyebrows when he paid out a substantial fee for this relatively unknown Argentinian youngster, but Julio soon showed the Sunderland faithful why he was valued so highly and he quickly became a crowd favourite. Just 25 minutes into his debut against West Ham he headed home Kevin Kilbane's cross and became the new hero on Wearside. Although he was absent early in the new year due to international commitments he returned to score superb goals against Manchester United and Ipswich. A left-sided midfielder or winger, he combines outstanding ball skills with some aggressive tackling and was a real thorn in the side of many a Premiership right back last term. An unmistakable sight with socks around his ankles and golden boots, the youngster looks to have an outstanding career ahead of him with both club and country. He was a member of the Argentina U20 team that won the World Youth Championships in the summer, and was voted 'Young Player of the Year' by members of the Supporters' Association.
Sunderland (£3,500,000 from Argentinos Juniors, Argentine on 31/8/2000) PL 26+1/2 FLC 2/1 FAC 1

ARDLEY Neal Christopher
Born: Epsom, 1 September 1972
Height: 5'11" Weight: 11.9
International Honours: E: U21-10
Neal continued to feature regularly for Wimbledon in the 2000-01 campaign when he was mostly used in a right-sided midfield role, although he played some matches in a more central position where he proved very effective. A set-piece specialist he delivers powerful free kicks and accurate corners to set up chances for his colleagues. At the time of writing there appeared to be some doubt as to whether he would be starting the coming season with the Dons, but should he depart he will be sorely missed.
Wimbledon (From trainee on 29/7/1991) F/PL 185+31/15 FLC 21+3/5 FAC 25+4/3

ARMSTRONG Alun
Born: Gateshead, 22 February 1975
Height: 6'1" Weight: 11.13
Club Honours: Div 1 '98
Out of favour at the Riverside Alun featured briefly in Worthington Cup action for Middlesbrough before grabbing the chance of regular first-team football with a move to Ipswich in December. He made his debut from the subs' bench in the tremendous win at Anfield and his first goal followed a week later when he sealed another win against Southampton with a crucial third goal. His partnership up front with Marcus Stewart blossomed to such an extent that boss George Burley was soon convinced that he could allow David Johnson to go to Nottingham Forest. As a striker he is an unselfish runner who shields the ball well and is good in the air, with a goal-poacher's instinct for being in the right place at the right time. He scored eight goals for Ipswich but there were none sweeter than the two he scored on his return to the Riverside Stadium which enabled Town to beat his old team. Both came within five minutes of the restart, the first a 25-yard volley and the second a deft flick from Stewart's cross. The home fans gave him a standing ovation when he left the field.
Newcastle U (From trainee on 1/10/1993)
Stockport Co (£50,000 on 23/6/1994) FL 151+8/48 FLC 22/8 FAC 10+1/5 Others 7
Middlesbrough (£1,500,000 on 16/2/1998) P/FL 10+19/9 FLC 4
Huddersfield T (Loaned on 23/3/2000) FL 4+2
Ipswich T (£500,000 + on 8/12/2000) PL 15+6/7 FAC 2/1

ARMSTRONG Christopher (Chris)
Born: Newcastle, 5 August 1982
Height: 5'10" Weight: 10.8
Chris made tremendous progress for Bury in 2000-01 for having begun the season as an untried trainee he stepped up to the professional ranks and featured regularly for the Shakers in the second half of the campaign. He looked very confident in a left-back role showing good skills on the ball, accurate distribution and strength in the air. Chris is the younger brother of Burnley's Gordon Armstrong.
Bury (From trainee on 2/3/2001) FL 22/1 Others 3

ARMSTRONG Christopher (Chris) Peter
Born: Newcastle, 19 June 1971
Height: 6'0" Weight: 13.3
Club Honours: Div 1 '94; FLC '99
International Honours: E: B-1
Chris had a very frustrating time with injuries at Tottenham last term and had few opportunities to impress. He missed the first few months of the campaign due to a groin problem before returning with a bang when he came off the subs' bench to net a dramatic winner against Sunderland in November. He then enjoyed a brief run in the team, also scoring in the 3-3 draw at Bradford before he was sidelined again by injury and remained out of action until the end of the season. An athletic striker with great ability in the air he will be hoping to have made a full recovery in time for the start of the 2001-02 campaign.
Wrexham (Free from Llay Welfare on 3/3/1989) FL 40+20/13 FLC 2+1 FAC 0+1 Others 5+1/3
Millwall (£50,000 on 16/8/1991) FL 11+17/5 FLC 3+1/2 FAC 0+1 Others 0+1
Crystal Palace (£1,000,000 on 1/9/1992) F/PL 118/45 FLC 8/6 FAC 8/5 Others 2/1
Tottenham H (£4,500,000 on 30/6/1995) PL 117+24/48 FLC 15/10 FAC 9+5/4 Others 3

ARMSTRONG Steven **Craig**
Born: South Shields, 23 May 1975
Height: 5'11" Weight: 12.10
Craig started the 2000-01 season alternating between the left- and right-back positions and seemed to struggle to find his best form at a time when Huddersfield were slipping down the First Division table. However a switch to a midfield role proved a positive move and he established himself as a regular in the Terriers' line-up. A predominantly left-footed player he went on to produce some excellent performances, scoring several fine goals and occasionally deputising as team captain. He is likely to be a key figure for the club again in 2001-02 as they attempt to return to Division One at the first attempt.
Nottingham F (From trainee on 2/6/1992) P/FL 24+16 FLC 6+2/2 FAC 1
Burnley (Loaned on 29/12/1994) FL 4
Bristol Rov (Loaned on 8/1/1996) FL 4
Bristol Rov (Loaned on 28/3/1996) FL 9+1
Gillingham (Loaned on 18/10/1996) FL 10 FLC 2 Others 1
Watford (Loaned on 24/1/1997) FL 3
Watford (Loaned on 14/3/1997) FL 12
Huddersfield T (£750,000 on 26/2/1999) FL 94+2/4 FLC 6+1 FAC 2

ARMSTRONG Gordon Ian
Born: Newcastle, 15 July 1967
Height: 6'0" Weight: 12.11
Club Honours: Div 3 '88

Although no longer a first-team regular at Turf Moor Gordon remained an important member of the Burnley squad in 2000-01. His appearances were mostly to cover for injury and suspension to one of the regular back three, but he was also occasionally used in a sweeper role. Whatever was asked of him his experience and professionalism shone through and he never let the side down. Possibly his finest performance of the season came in the 2-1 win against champions Fulham on a night when his gritty qualities were transmitted throughout the side. He is the older brother of Bury's Chris Armstrong.

Sunderland (From apprentice on 10/7/1985) FL 331+18/50 FLC 25+4/3 FAC 19/4 Others 18+1/4
Bristol C (Loaned on 24/8/1995) FL 6
Northampton T (Loaned on 5/1/1996) FL 4/1 Others 1
Bury (Free on 16/7/1996) FL 49+22/4 FLC 5+2/2 FAC 2+1 Others 1+1
Burnley (Free on 27/8/1998) FL 76+5/3 FLC 2 FAC 3+2

ARMSTRONG Joel
Born: Chesterfield, 25 September 1981
Height: 5'11" Weight: 12.7

Although denied first-team action by the fine form of regular 'keeper Mike Pollitt, Joel was actually the only Chesterfield player to appear on every team-sheet in 2000-01. He played in the Worthington Cup first round first leg tie at Port Vale when he showed considerable bravery and also came on as a substitute for the last few minutes of the final game of the season against Halifax. Agile and quick to come off his line he is a fine goalkeeping prospect.

Chesterfield (Trainee) FL 3+1 FLC 1 Others 1

ARMSTRONG Stephen Mark
Born: Birkenhead, 23 July 1976
Height: 5'10" Weight: 10.10

Although born in England Stephen arrived at Watford last October via a rather circuitous route. Having been brought up in South Africa, he then studied in the United States where he was a star of college soccer with Butler University and also featured for the Premier Development League club Mid-Michigan Bucks. Although he then had the opportunity of signing for DC United he chose to go to Europe where he spent the summer in Sweden before joining the Hornets on a 12-month contract. A talented left winger with a good scoring record for his college team, he struggled to break into the squad at Vicarage Road and made only a handful of appearances from the subs' bench. He was released in the summer.

Watford (Free from Vastra Frolunda IF, Sweden, ex Butler University in USA, on 27/10/2000) FL 0+3

ARNISON Paul Simon
Born: Hartlepool, 18 September 1977
Height: 5'10" Weight: 10.12

Paul had a mixed first full season with his home-town club. He started the campaign out injured with a torn calf muscle but soon returned to establish himself at right back in preference to the more experienced Darren Knowles. He was again sidelined by injury in February and was only able to make a brief re-appearance in the first team before the end of the campaign. Paul is a versatile player who can also turn out in midfield or in the centre of defence.

Newcastle U (From trainee on 1/3/1996)
Hartlepool U (Free on 10/3/2000) FL 31+4/2 FLC 1 FAC 1 Others 5/1

ARNOTT Andrew (Andy) John
Born: Chatham, 18 October 1973
Height: 6'1" Weight: 13.2

Andy again had a wretched time with injuries at Colchester in the 2000-01 campaign and never seemed to be able to shake off his long-standing groin problem. He featured in a handful of games for the U's but his only start in a Second Division game came in the home match with Northampton in November when he appeared as a makeshift target man. A versatile player who was more at home in midfield and defence he was unable to recover full fitness and eventually announced his retirement from the game in February.

Gillingham (From trainee on 13/5/1991) FL 50+23/12 FLC 2+3 FAC 10+2/1 Others 3+2
Leyton Orient (£15,000 on 25/1/1996) FL 47+3/6 FLC 2 FAC 2 Others 1
Fulham (£23,000 on 17/6/1997) FL 0+1 Others 0+2
Brighton & Hove A (£20,000 on 23/10/1998) FL 27+1/2 FLC 1 FAC 1 Others 1
Colchester U (Free on 24/9/1999) FL 5+10 FLC 0+1 Others 1

ARPHEXAD Pegguy Michel
Born: Abymes, Guadeloupe, 18 May 1973
Height: 6'2" Weight: 13.5
Club Honours: FLC '00, '01; FAC '01; UEFAC '01

Pegguy was signed by Liverpool manager Gerard Houllier in the summer on a 'Bosman' free transfer to provide cover for first-choice goalkeeper Sander Westerveld following the departure of Brad Friedel. However he saw even less first-team action last season than he had at Filbert Street, being selected only for two Worthington Cup ties against Chelsea in the third round and at Stoke City in the fourth round when the Reds slaughtered potentially difficult opponents by a margin of 8-0. A spectacular shot stopper, he may be considered unfortunate not to have received an extended run in the team in view of Westerveld's uncertain form in the first half of the campaign. It remains to be seen whether he suffers the same anonymous fate of most reserve 'keepers at Anfield in the last forty years.

Leicester C (Free from Lens, France on 20/8/1997) PL 17+4 FLC 4 FAC 3+1
Liverpool (Free on 13/7/2000) FLC 2

ARTELL David John
Born: Rotherham, 22 November 1980
Height: 6'2" Weight: 13.9

This young Rotherham defender stepped up to make his first appearance in the starting line-up last season and grabbed the opportunity with both hands as he went on to become a regular in the Millers' first team. Big and strong, he is also very effective in the opposing penalty area as he demonstrated by scoring some useful goals. He was rewarded for his progress by being offered an extended contract towards the end of the campaign.

Rotherham U (From trainee on 1/7/1999) FL 35+2/4 FAC 3 Others 1

ASABA Carl Edward
Born: London, 28 January 1973
Height: 6'2" Weight: 13.4

Carl was again a key figure up front for Gillingham last term and once he had got used to First Division football he scored regularly, including a fine hat-trick in the 4-1 win over Crystal Palace on Boxing Day. Moving on to Sheffield United in early March he quickly made an impression at Bramall Lane scoring several goals in the run-in to the end of the season including one in the Sheffield 'derby' against Wednesday. A big powerful striker he creates chances with his effective runs and fine ball control and has an excellent scoring record himself.

Brentford (Free from Dulwich Hamlet on 9/8/1994) FL 49+5/25 FLC 5 FAC 4 Others 7/2
Colchester U (Loaned on 16/2/1995) FL 9+3/2
Reading (£800,000 on 7/8/1997) FL 31+2/8 FLC 7+2/4 FAC 3/1
Gillingham (£600,000 on 28/8/1998) FL 65+12/36 FLC 3/2 FAC 1+1 Others 9/2
Sheffield U (£92,500 + on 8/3/2001) FL 10/5

ASHBEE Ian
Born: Birmingham, 6 September 1976
Height: 6'1" Weight: 13.7
International Honours: E: Yth

Ian had another fine season for Cambridge United in 2000-01 and once again missed only a handful of games. A versatile player who can feature in midfield or anywhere in the back four he scored two goals in the 6-1 win over Rotherham in September and also netted with a great 25-yard free kick in the crucial 2-0 win at Northampton towards the end of the campaign.

Derby Co (From trainee on 9/11/1994) FL 1
Cambridge U (Free on 13/12/1996) FL 154+11/9 FLC 6 FAC 13 Others 4+1

ASHBY Barry John
Born: Park Royal, 2 November 1970
Height: 6'2" Weight: 13.8
Club Honours: FAYC '89

A near ever-present for Gillingham last season, Barry was once again a dominant force at the heart of the defence. Although troubled by a calf injury towards the end of the campaign he was an automatic choice in the club's first season in Division One. A reliable central defender, he is always dangerous at set pieces and is very effective pushing down the right wing from where he can deliver an accurate cross into the box.

Watford (From trainee on 1/12/1988) FL 101+13/3 FLC 6 FAC 4 Others 2+1
Brentford (Signed on 22/3/1994) FL 119+2/4 FLC 11 FAC 9/1 Others 11+1
Gillingham (£140,000 on 8/8/1997) FL 160+2/5 FLC 10 FAC 12/1 Others 9/1

ASHCROFT Lee
Born: Preston, 7 September 1972
Height: 5'10" Weight: 11.10
International Honours: E: U21-1
Lee joined Wigan Athletic at the start of the 2000-01 campaign as a replacement for Stuart Barlow but he had a frustrating time with injuries and found it difficult to establish a regular place in the line-up. A quick forward who likes to run at defenders, he is able to play on either flank, as an out-and-out striker or in a position just behind the front two. He netted his first goals for the Latics with a double in the 2-2 draw at Brentford in December.
Preston NE (From trainee on 16/7/1991) FL 78+13/13 FLC 3 FAC 5 Others 6+2/1
West Bromwich A (£250,000 on 1/8/1993) FL 66+24/17 FLC 2+3 FAC 3+1/1 Others 8+3
Notts Co (Loaned on 28/3/1996) FL 4+2
Preston NE (£150,000 on 5/9/1996) FL 63+1/22 FLC 4 FAC 5/5 Others 2+1
Grimsby T (£500,000 on 12/8/1998) FL 52+9/15 FLC 7/2 FAC 1
Wigan Ath (£250,000 on 9/8/2000) FL 23+7/5 FLC 1 FAC 2+1/1 Others 0+2

ASHDOWN Jamie Lawrence
Born: Wokingham, 30 November 1980
Height: 6'3" Weight: 14.10
Jamie began the 2000-01 campaign as third-choice 'keeper for Reading but stepped up to make his Football League debut when he replaced Phil Whitehead for the final 25 minutes of the home game against Oldham in September. The following month he went out on loan to Bishops Stortford to gain more experience of first-team football but then broke a finger. On recovering fitness he had another loan spell at Gravesend & Northfleet. Tall and commanding, he is likely to step up to a regular place on the subs' bench in 2001-02 now that Scott Howie has been released.
Reading (From trainee on 26/11/1999) FL 0+1

ASHER Alistair Andrew
Born: Leicester, 14 October 1980
Height: 6'0" Weight: 11.6
Alistair began the 2000-01 campaign as a regular in the Mansfield Town side but then suffered a loss of form and dropped back to the reserves. He gradually regained his confidence going on to captain the Stags' second string and eventually earned a recall to the senior team in the new year. A versatile defender who can play at right back or centre half, he is cool under pressure and has good distribution.
Mansfield T (From trainee on 23/6/1999) FL 52+11 FLC 2+2 FAC 1+1 Others 2+1

ASHFORD Ryan Marc
Born: Honiton, 13 October 1981
Height: 5'11" Weight: 11.13
A highly-rated third-year scholar in the Southampton Academy, Ryan was given his senior debut at Mansfield Town in the Worthington Cup second round second leg tie last September. Unfortunately his contribution to the match was brief and he was stretchered off with an ankle injury after just 20 minutes. A left-sided defender Ryan signed a full professional contract for the Saints in January.
Southampton (From trainee on 15/1/2001) FLC 1

ASHINGTON Ryan David
Born: Torbay, 28 March 1983
Height: 5'10" Weight: 11.10
This forceful young midfielder made an impressive debut for Torquay United early on last season, rattling Southend's crossbar in the process and retained his place in the squad until the beginning of November. He only featured a couple of times from the subs' bench in the second half of the campaign but made sufficient progress to ensure a professional contract for the coming season. Ryan picked up the Gulls' 'Young Player of the Year' award.
Torquay U (Trainee) FL 9+5 FLC 1+1 FAC 0+1

ASHTON Dean
Born: Crewe, 24 November 1983
Height: 6'1" Weight: 13.11
International Honours: E: Yth
Dean began 2000-01 one of many promising youngsters at Crewe's Academy but made such tremendous progress that by the end of the campaign he was a regular in the first team and one of the hottest properties in the First Division. He made his debut from the subs' bench at Gillingham in October and after winning a place in the line-up in the new year he scored his first gaol against Burnley in February. An exciting striker who only signed professional forms mid-way through the season he finished the campaign with eight goals. He made his debut for England U17s in the summer, scoring against Italy.
Crewe Alex (From trainee on 6/2/2001) FL 12+9/8 FAC 1+1

ASHTON Jonathan (Jon) Frank
Born: Plymouth, 4 August 1979
Height: 5'11" Weight: 12.0
This young defender joined Exeter City from Devon rivals Plymouth in the summer of 2000 and appeared regularly in the early part of last season, but injuries and loss of form meant that he struggled to find a place in the team after September. He rarely featured in the second half of the campaign and was released in May. Jon is a quick right back with great determination in the tackle.
Plymouth Arg (From trainee on 29/7/1997) FL 27+7 FLC 1+2 FAC 5 Others 2
Exeter C (Free on 18/7/2000) FL 7+6 FLC 0+2 Others 1

ASKEY John Colin
Born: Stoke, 4 November 1964
Height: 6'0" Weight: 12.2
Club Honours: GMVC '95, '97; FAT '96
International Honours: E: SP-1
Macclesfield Town's longest-serving and most respected player, John initially played on the right wing last season which restricted his goalscoring opportunities, but then mid-way through the campaign he moved up to the forward line often appearing as the sole striker. While his pace may not be what it was, he is still a very skilful player who holds the ball up well and makes intelligent use of possession. He was appointed reserve-team manager in January 2001 and having completed the UEFA "B" coaching certificate will move up to a full-time coaching role with Macclesfield in the 2001-2002 season as well as remaining a member of the first team squad on non-contract forms.
Macclesfield T (Free from Milton U during 1985-86) FL 134+20/28 FLC 9+3/2 FAC 7/1 Others 2+1

ASPIN Neil
Born: Gateshead, 12 April 1965
Height: 6'0" Weight: 13.10
Club Honours: AMC '93
This vastly experienced defender was a regular in the centre of defence for Darlington in the first half of last season but after a couple of injuries he lost his regular first team place around Christmas and could not regain it. His contract was surprisingly terminated in January and he signed for local rivals Hartlepool where he strengthened a squad already pushing for a promotion place. He made his first appearances as substitute and later gave some fine performances as a stand-in right back before dropping out of the reckoning in the closing weeks of the season. Dominant in the air and strong in the tackle he regularly joined the attack at corners and set pieces but failed to register a goal. He was released by Pool in the summer and was reported to have signed for Harrogate Town.
Leeds U (From apprentice on 6/10/1982) FL 203+4/5 FLC 9/1 FAC 17 Others 11
Port Vale (£200,000 on 28/7/1989) FL 343+5/3 FLC 20 FAC 24 Others 18
Darlington (Free on 13/7/1999) FL 50 FLC 3 FAC 5 Others 2
Hartlepool U (Free on 23/1/2001) FL 5+5 Others 0+1

ASPINALL Warren
Born: Wigan, 13 September 1967
Height: 5'9" Weight: 12.8
Club Honours: AMC '85, '97; Div 3 '99
International Honours: E: Yth
This veteran midfielder began the 2000-01 campaign on a month-to-month contract at Brighton and came on from the subs' bench for the final 15 minutes of the home game with Rochdale last August. Sadly that was to be his last appearance in senior football for he suffered an ankle injury playing for the reserves shortly afterwards that required an operation. Complications set in and he contracted a flesh-eating infection that attacked his ankle ligaments, a lengthy stay in hospital followed and Warren finally announced his retirement on doctor's advice in November. He has since assisted with the Albion reserve team and is aiming to become involved in coaching in the future.
Wigan Ath (From apprentice on 31/8/1985) FL 21+12/10 FLC 1 FAC 2+3/2 Others 1+5/2
Everton (£150,000 on 4/2/1986) FL 0+7 FLC 0+1 Others 0+2
Wigan Ath (Loaned on 6/2/1986) FL 18/12 Others 2/2
Aston Villa (£300,000 on 19/2/1987) FL 40+4/14 FLC 4/2 FAC 1+1
Portsmouth (£315,000 on 26/8/1988) FL 97+35/21 FLC 8+3/3 FAC 4+5/2 Others 6+1/2
Bournemouth (Loaned on 27/8/1993) FL 4+2/1

Swansea C (Loaned on 14/10/1993) FL 5 Others 1
Bournemouth (£20,000 on 31/12/1993) FL 26+1/8 FLC 4 FAC 1 Others 1
Carlisle U (Free on 8/3/1995) FL 99+8/12 FLC 8/3 FAC 6 Others 10+1/1
Brentford (£50,000 on 21/11/1997) FL 41+2/5 FLC 4 FAC 1+1 Others 2
Colchester U (Free on 9/2/1999) FL 22/5 FLC 2
Brighton & Hove A (Free on 24/9/1999) FL 19+13/3 FAC 3 Others 2

ASTAFJEVS Vitalijs
Born: Riga, Latvia, 3 April 1971
Height: 5'11" Weight: 12.5
International Honours: Latvia: 75

Vitalijs enjoyed an excellent season for Bristol Rovers and produced superb performances in the Worthington Cup ties against Everton and Sunderland. An experienced midfielder he chipped in with a number of fine goals including a brace in the remarkable 6-2 victory at Brentford at the end of August. He was again a regular for Latvia and now holds the Pirates' record for most-capped player.

Bristol Rov (£150,000 from Skonto Riga, Latvia on 28/1/2000) FL 47+10/7 FLC 5 FAC 1 Others 3/2

ATHERTON Peter
Born: Orrell, 6 April 1970
Height: 5'11" Weight: 13.12
International Honours: E: U21-1; Sch

Signed on a free transfer during the close season Peter started the 2000-01 campaign at right back for Bradford City before switching to the centre of defence following an injury to Andy O'Brien. He was an ever-present in the line-up until he dropped back to the subs' bench for the game against Southampton in February, then two days later was transferred to Birmingham on loan until the end of the season. He made an impressive debut for the Blues in a 2-1 win over local rivals West Bromwich Albion and apart from a short spell out with hamstring trouble he featured regularly until the end of the campaign. He is a solid defender whose strengths are his tackling and positional sense.

Wigan Ath (From trainee on 12/2/1988) FL 145+4/1 FLC 8 FAC 7 Others 12+1
Coventry C (£300,000 on 23/8/1991) F/PL 113+1 FLC 4 FAC 2
Sheffield Wed (£800,000 on 1/6/1994) PL 214/9 FLC 16 FAC 18 Others 3
Bradford C (Free on 6/7/2000) PL 25 FLC 3 FAC 1 Others 4
Birmingham C (Loaned on 15/2/2001) FL 10 Others 2

ATKINS Mark Nigel
Born: Doncaster, 14 August 1968
Height: 6'0" Weight: 13.2
Club Honours: PL '95
International Honours: E: Sch

This vastly experienced midfielder made a surprise return to the Football League last March when he left Conference club Doncaster Rovers to join Hull City's charge towards the Third Division play-offs. He partnered Gary Brabin in the Tigers' engine room and soon showed that he was another successful capture by Brian Little, impressing with his calm authority in the centre of the park. Mark is a versatile player who can also play at full back if required. He was released in May.

Scunthorpe U (From juniors on 9/7/1986) FL 45+5/2 FLC 3+1 FAC 5 Others 6+1
Blackburn Rov (£45,000 on 16/6/1988) F/PL 224+33/35 FLC 20+2/4 FAC 11+3 Others 17+2/1
Wolverhampton W (£1,000,000 on 21/9/1995) FL 115+11/8 FLC 12+1/2 FAC 11+1 Others 2/1
York C (Free on 5/8/1999) FL 10/2 FLC 2 (Free to Doncaster Rov on 4/11/1999)
Hull C (Free on 21/3/2001) FL 8 Others 1+1

ATKINSON Brian
Born: Darlington, 19 January 1971
Height: 5'10" Weight: 12.5
International Honours: E: U21-6

Brian's fifth season with Darlington was again unfortunately dogged by injury problems and he did not make a first team start until October. Alas, further injury problems limited his involvement after the turn of the year and he only returned for the last half dozen games of the campaign, when his ability to hold the ball in midfield and prompt the attack was again appreciated. He was entrusted with penalties and slotted home four during his spells in the side.

Sunderland (From trainee on 21/7/1989) FL 119+22/4 FLC 8+2 FAC 13/2 Others 2+3
Carlisle U (Loaned on 19/1/1996) FL 2 Others 1
Darlington (Free on 10/8/1996) FL 139+19/10 FLC 9 FAC 11+1/2 Others 5+1/1

AUSTIN Dean Barry
Born: Hemel Hempstead, 26 April 1970
Height: 5'11" Weight: 12.4

Although released by Crystal Palace on a free transfer at the end of the 1999-2000 campaign, Dean found himself back at Selhurst Park with a new two-year contract at the start of last season. His rehabilitation was complete when he was appointed club captain in succession to Neil Ruddock and he went on to become a regular in the Eagles' starting line-up. He appeared both at right back and as a right-sided central defender and netted three important goals in the springtime when the Palace forwards were struggling to find the net.

Southend U (£12,000 from St Albans C on 22/3/1990) FL 96/2 FLC 4/1 FAC 2 Others 7
Tottenham H (£375,000 on 4/6/1992) PL 117+7 FLC 7+2 FAC 16+1
Crystal Palace (Free on 8/7/1998) FL 100+4/6 FLC 15+1 FAC 3 Others 2

AUSTIN Kevin Levi
Born: Hackney, 12 February 1973
Height: 6'0" Weight: 14.0

Having recovered from a ruptured achilles tendon suffered at the start of the 1999-2000 campaign, Kevin made an appearance from the subs' bench in the Worthington Cup tie against Rotherham but otherwise found opportunities at Barnsley very limited last term. He subsequently joined Second Division Brentford on loan in October where he produced some commanding performances but no permanent deal was pursued. After returning to Oakwell he went on to make his full international debut for Trinidad & Tobago against Panama in a World Cup qualifying tie but then ruptured his other achilles tendon while training on international duty in February and was again sidelined for a lengthy period. A powerful central defender who has good pace he can also play at left back.

Leyton Orient (Free from Saffron Walden on 19/8/1993) FL 101+8/3 FLC 4/1 FAC 6 Others 7
Lincoln C (£30,000 on 31/7/1996) FL 128+1/2 FLC 9 FAC 6 Others 4
Barnsley (Free on 5/7/1999) FL 3 FLC 2+1
Brentford (Loaned on 27/10/2000) FL 3

AWFORD Andrew (Andy) Terence
Born: Worcester, 14 July 1972
Height: 5'10" Weight: 12.0
International Honours: E: U21-9; Yth; Sch

Andy had the misfortune to suffer a serious neck injury playing for Portsmouth against Sheffield United in the opening game of last season and although he bravely fought back to appear against Queens Park Rangers he announced his retirement from playing at the beginning of December. An experienced defender he fell just short of 300 league games for Pompey who were his only professional club. Still under 30 Andy is keen to remain in football and was appointed chief scout at Fratton Park at the turn of the year.

Portsmouth (From trainee on 24/7/1989) FL 293+20/3 FLC 29+1 FAC 17 Others 12

AXELDAHL Jonas Michael
Born: Holm, Sweden, 2 September 1970
Height: 5'11" Weight: 11.7

Having topped the scoring charts in the Avon Insurance Combination in the 1999-2000 campaign, Jonas moved on to Second Division Cambridge United in the close season. He soon formed a useful partnership up front for the U's with Zema Abbey and featured regularly until being sidelined by knee ligament trouble in the new year. The injury required corrective surgery and he had yet to recover full fitness by the end of the campaign when he was released. He is an experienced right-footed striker with good mobility.

Ipswich T (Free from Foggia, Italy, ex Halmstad, Malmo FF, Osters IF, on 31/7/1999) FL 1+15 FLC 0+3 FAC 0+1
Cambridge U (Free on 21/8/2000) FL 12+6/2 FLC 2 FAC 1/1 Others 2/1

AYRES James Martin
Born: Luton, 18 September 1980
Height: 6'3" Weight: 13.0

One of several youngsters to graduate from Luton Town's youth scheme in recent seasons James was loaned to Stevenage Borough last September to gain some valuable experience of first-team football. On his return he featured for the Hatters in the LDV Vans Trophy tie at Peterborough but this was his only senior appearance of the campaign and he was released shortly afterwards. A strong and forceful central defender he later had a brief spell with Dagenham & Redbridge before joining Kettering Town.

Luton T (From trainee on 9/2/1999) Others 2

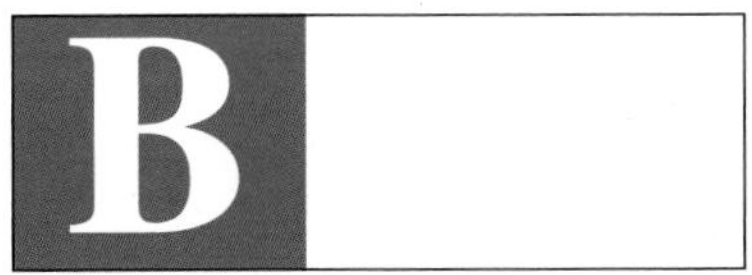

BAARDSEN Per **Espen**
Born: San Rafael, USA, 7 December 1977
Height: 6'5" Weight: 13.13
Club Honours: FLC '99
International Honours: Norway: 4; U21; USA: Yth

Having failed to make a senior appearance for Tottenham in 1999-2000, Espen moved on to Watford in the close season and went straight in the Hornets' first team. Still relatively inexperienced for a goalkeeper, he took a while to develop an understanding with his fellow-defenders. However, once he had settled in he had a frustrating time with injuries which caused him to be substituted three times during the campaign. Tall and strongly built, he impressed with his shot-stopping capabilities but then lost his place around the turn of the year when he seemed to suffer a dip in confidence. However he returned to the side in February with renewed assurance, only to be carried off at Grimsby in April with a groin injury that brought a premature end to his season.

Tottenham H (Free from San Francisco All Blacks, USA, on 16/7/1996) PL 22+1 FLC 3 FAC 2+1
Watford (£1,250,000 on 3/8/2000) FL 27 FLC 2

BABAYARO Celestine
Born: Kaduna, Nigeria, 29 August 1978
Height: 5'8" Weight: 11.0
Club Honours: FLC '98; ESC '98; FAC '00; CS '00
International Honours: Nigeria: 24; U23 (OLYM '96); Yth (World-U17 '93)

The popular 'Baba' endured something of a stop-go season at Chelsea in 2000-01. In September he jetted off to Sydney to represent his country in the Olympic Games, but his hopes of a second successive gold medal were dashed when he received a red card against Australia and then watched from the sidelines as Nigeria fell at the hands of Chile in the quarter-final. Returning to Stamford Bridge he found a new coach, Claudio Ranieri, in place and then had to readjust to the new formation implemented by the incoming regime. Whichever system Chelsea adopt Baba is vital to their attacking options, as his buccaneering forays down the left flank and accurate crosses are major elements in their attacking armoury. With Graeme Le Saux missing for the majority of the season and Jon Harley loaned to Wimbledon, Baba was the only recognised left wing back that Chelsea could call on for much of the campaign and he responded in his own inimitable enthusiastic fashion.

Chelsea (£2,250,000 from Anderlecht, Belgium on 20/6/1997) PL 76+9/3 FLC 5+1 FAC 7+1 Others 24+3/3

BABBEL Markus
Born: Munich, Germany, 8 September 1972
Height: 6'3" Weight: 12.10
Club Honours: UEFAC '01; FLC '01; FAC '01
International Honours: Germany: 51

Markus took a big risk when he chose to exercise his option to leave Munich last summer on a 'Bosman' free transfer to join a former European heavyweight club fallen on relatively hard times in the shape of Liverpool. However he can feel well satisfied with the move after finishing the 2000-01 season with two domestic cup winners medals, a UEFA Cup winners medal and the prospect of another season of Champions' League football. Primarily a central defender, it was not immediately clear where he would fit into the Liverpool formation. However, Vegard Heggem's long-term injury left a gap at right back and this is where he spent the majority of the campaign. To his credit he filled the position with distinction and although not a natural attacking player he was always willing to push down the flank. He was also adept at creeping forward on the blind side of defenders at corners and free kicks and scoring with headers, most notably the opening goal of the UEFA Cup final against Deportivo Alaves. Ever-present in the Premiership he missed just three cup games all season. Cool and composed on the ball, if there was an award for consistency at Anfield he would surely have won.

Liverpool (Free from Bayern Munich, Germany, ex SV Hamburg, on 10/7/2000) PL 38/3 FLC 4/1 FAC 5/1 Others 13/1

BACON Daniel (Danny) Stephen
Born: Mansfield, 20 September 1980
Height: 5'10" Weight: 10.12

Danny managed to stay clear of serious injuries last season and featured regularly in the Mansfield Town squad, although mainly used from the subs' bench. He is a fast and skilful striker who always causes defenders problems and if he continues to progress at a similar rate he should have an excellent future in the game. He was leading scorer for the Stags' successful reserve side in 2000-01.

Mansfield T (From trainee on 5/1/2000) FL 13+17/3 FLC 1+2 FAC 0+2 Others 1/1

BAGHERI Karim
Born: Abassi, Iran, 20 February 1974
Height: 6'1" Weight: 12.5
International Honours: Iran:

Karim joined Charlton Athletic from Pirouzi in the close season with a reputation as a goal-scoring midfield player. His time at the Valley was unfortunately beset by injury and personal problems and he made just one appearance in the Premiership, coming on for the final 18 minutes at Portman Road against Ipswich Town when he was employed in a defensive midfield role. A veteran of his country's 1998 World Cup finals team, Karim won a further six caps for Iran last season scoring eight goals, including six in the 19-0 victory over Guam last November.

Charlton Ath (£400,000 from Pirouzi, Iran, ex Tractorsazi, Pirouzi, Armenia Bielefeld, on 17/8/2000) PL 0+1

BAILEY Alan
Born: Macclesfield, 1 November 1978
Height: 5'9" Weight: 11.12

A series of niggling injuries restricted Alan to just one league start for Stockport County last term and apart from a couple of outings from the subs' bench he failed to make the first-team squad. A striker who can play down the middle or wide on the right-hand side he was pushed down the pecking order at Edgeley Park following the arrival of Finnish international Shefki Kuqi and then former Ayr United marksman Glynn Hurst. A pacy striker who holds the ball up well he was released in the summer.

Manchester C (From trainee on 2/7/1997) Others 0+1
Macclesfield T (Loaned on 29/1/1999) FL 5+5/1
Stockport Co (Free on 4/8/1999) FL 6+12/1 FLC 0+2 FAC 1/1

BAIRD Andrew (Andy) Crawford
Born: East Kilbride, 18 January 1979
Height: 5'10" Weight: 12.6

Andy was plagued by injuries at Wycombe last term although he featured regularly in the first half of the campaign. However he then damaged his cruciate ligament in the FA Cup fifth round replay against Wimbledon and this brought his season to a premature close. A fearless and hard-working striker who is capable of scoring spectacular goals he is expected to be fit again by Christmas.

Wycombe W (From trainee on 18/3/1998) FL 54+19/13 FLC 2+7/2 FAC 8+2/2 Others 3+1

BAKALLI Adrian
Born: Brussels, Belgium, 22 November 1976
Height: 6'3" Weight: 13.6

Unable to break through to the first team at Watford last term, Adrian had an unsuccessful trial with Belgian club Lierse SK in October before his contract at Vicarage Road was cancelled by mutual consent the following month. He subsequently had trials with several more clubs including Reading and Luton before signing a short-term contract for Swindon Town on the transfer deadline day. However he received few opportunities at the County Ground and made his only appearance in the final game of the season at Stoke when he played in a support role just behind the front two before being substituted at half-time. A tall and powerful attacking midfield player he was released by the Robins in the summer.

Watford (£100,000 from RWD Molenbeek, Belgium on 19/1/1999) PL 0+2 (Freed on 2/12/2000)
Swindon T (Free, via trials at Lierse SK, Reading, Luton, on 23/3/2001) FL 1

BAKER Steven (Steve) Richard
Born: Pontefract, 8 September 1978
Height: 5'10" Weight: 11.11
International Honours: RoI: U21-4

This stylish Middlesbrough defender joined Hartlepool on loan last October to strengthen a team badly hit by injuries. He acquitted himself well in a two-month stay at the Victoria Ground and there was talk of a permanent move but no deal could be reached and he returned to the Riverside Stadium to continue his development in the reserves.

Middlesbrough (From trainee on 24/7/1997) P/FL 6+2 FLC 2+2 FAC 0+1
Huddersfield T (Loaned on 6/8/1999) FL 3
Darlington (Loaned on 23/3/2000) FL 4+1
Hartlepool U (Loaned on 28/9/2000) FL 9

BAKKE Eirik
Born: Sogndal, Norway, 13 September 1977
Height: 6'2" Weight: 12.9
International Honours: Norway: 14; U21; Yth

Very much the find of the 1999-2000 season for Leeds United, Eirik began last term in the starting line-up only to be stretchered off against Everton with an injury that kept him out for six games. He returned to put in a superb performance in the 1-0 Champions' League victory over AC Milan. Two games later he scored his first of the season, and hit a post in the 6-0 hammering of Besiktas, but surprisingly had to wait until January to score his first Premiership goal, netting in the 4-0 victory at Manchester City. Eirik then remained in the first-team picture for the rest of the campaign. A strong and powerful midfielder, he possesses a great deal of skill and looks to have a fine future both at Elland Road and at international level with Norway.

Leeds U (£1,000,000 + from Sogndal, Norway on 13/7/1999) PL 48+10/4 FLC 3 FAC 5/4 Others 19+3/3

Eirik Bakke

BALDRY Simon Jonathan
Born: Huddersfield, 12 February 1976
Height: 5'10" Weight: 11.6

Simon was in and out of the Huddersfield Town line-up last season and never really established himself as a first-team regular. A right winger with good close control he is always willing to run at defenders and gained a number of 'Man of the Match' awards during the campaign. Having now featured in over 100 league games for the Terriers he will be aiming to finally win a regular place in the team in 2001-02.

Huddersfield T (From trainee on 14/7/1994) FL 70+50/6 FLC 3+5 FAC 2+1 Others 1+2/1
Bury (Loaned on 8/9/1998) FL 0+5

BALIS Igor
Born: Czechoslavakia, 5 January 1970
Height: 5'11" Weight: 11.4
International Honours: Slovakia: 38

Igor was recruited by West Bromwich Albion manager Gary Megson to bolster his squad at a time when injuries and suspensions were causing some concern. However he took time to settle down and only started one game all season, although he came off the subs' bench on a number of occasions. A very quick right wing back with plenty of international experience he will be looking to establish himself in the line-up in 2001-02.

West Bromwich A (£150,000 from Slovan Bratislava, Slovakia, ex Spartak Trnava, on 14/12/2000) FL 1+6 FAC 0+1

BALL Kevin Anthony
Born: Hastings, 12 November 1964
Height: 5'10" Weight: 12.6
Club Honours: Div 1 '96, '99

Kevin joined Burnley from Fulham in the 2000 close season and quickly established himself as a never-say-die competitor and ball winner in the Clarets' midfield. Playing usually in a central role with a licence to block any opposition threats he remained as effective as ever. Disciplinary problems are of course a by-product of his style of play and his dismissal in the local derby against Blackburn led to a suspension that coincided with the team's worst run of the campaign. He contributed two goals, the first of which came in a 3-0 win over Preston last April.

Portsmouth (From apprentice at Coventry C on 6/10/1982) FL 96+9/4 FLC 8+1 FAC 8 Others 6
Sunderland (£350,000 on 16/7/1990) P/FL 329+10/21 FLC 23+3/4 FAC 16 Others 7/2
Fulham (£200,000 on 9/12/1999) FL 15+3 FAC 2
Burnley (Free on 24/7/2000) FL 40/2 FLC 4 FAC 1

BALL Michael John
Born: Liverpool, 2 October 1979
Height: 5'10" Weight: 11.2
International Honours: E: 1; U21-7; Yth; Sch

After a period when it seemed that Michael's undoubted potential as a young defender of the highest class was not to be realised with Everton, he bounced back with the most consistently influential displays of his career. The turning point came almost by accident, when he was forced by an injury crisis from his usual left-back berth to play in central defence against Arsenal. Such was the quality and poise of his performance against strikers of the class of Denis Bergkamp and Nwankwo Kanu that he remained in that role for the next 25 games! His development was acknowledged by England coach Sven Goran Eriksson, who handed him a first full cap against Spain in February. Michael ended the season with a flourish, coolly converting a penalty kick in the Blues' last match against Sunderland. He later admitted that the 2000-01 campaign had been the most important in his brief career. He came through it with flying colours and is already eagerly looking forward to the new season.

Everton (From trainee on 17/10/1996) PL 102+19/8 FLC 7+3 FAC 7+1

BALMER Stuart Murray
Born: Falkirk, 20 September 1969
Height: 6'0" Weight: 12.11
Club Honours: AMC '99
International Honours: S: Yth; Sch

Stuart found first-team opportunities at Wigan somewhat limited in 2000-01 due to injury and the consistent form of Pat McGibbon and Arjan De Zeeuw, however he always performed well when called into the side. A strong right-footed central defender he scored his only goal of the campaign in the 1-0 win at Bury that coincided with his 100th Football League appearance for the Latics. Stuart was released in the summer.

Glasgow Celtic (From juniors in 1987)
Charlton Ath (£120,000 on 24/8/1990) FL 201+26/8 FLC 15 FAC 9+1 Others 11+1
Wigan Ath (£200,000 on 18/9/1998) FL 99+2/4 FLC 7 FAC 8 Others 12/1

BAMBER Michael (Mike) John
Born: Preston, 1 October 1980
Height: 5'7" Weight: 10.2

Opportunities for this pacy Macclesfield right back were limited in the 2000-01 season but when called upon he put in some excellent performances and was a regular and reliable member of the reserve side. His day will surely come as he looks to be a good prospect for the future.

Macclesfield T (From trainee at Blackpool on 16/12/1999) FL 2+4 FLC 0+1 Others 0+1

BANCE Daniel (Danny) Robert
Born: Plymouth, 27 September 1982
Height: 5'10" Weight: 11.7

Danny is a promising youngster who made his Football League debut for Plymouth in the 3-0 defeat against Kidderminster Harriers on Easter Monday. A local-born full back he will be looking to gain more first-team experience in the 2001-02 campaign.

Plymouth Arg (Trainee) FL 1

BANGER Nicholas (Nicky) Lee
Born: Southampton, 25 February 1971
Height: 5'9" Weight: 11.6

Out of favour at Dundee Nicky joined Scunthorpe on loan in early November. Unfortunately his Iron career lasted just two minutes as he tore his groin shortly after coming on as a substitute against Hartlepool. The injury required surgery and he was out of action for some time. Nicky is a wide midfield player or striker who has good pace and an eye for goal.

Southampton (From trainee on 25/4/1989) F/PL 18+37/8 FLC 2+2/3 FAC 0+2 Others 1
Oldham Ath (£250,000 on 4/10/1994) FL 44+20/10 FLC 6/1 FAC 2+1 Others 0+1
Oxford U (Free on 24/7/1997) FL 41+22/8 FLC 6+2/1 FAC 3
Dundee (Free on 9/11/1999) SL 2+4 SLC 0+1 SC 1+1
Scunthorpe U (Loaned on 3/11/2000) FL 0+1

BANKOLE Ademola (Ade)
Born: Abeokuta, Nigeria, 9 September 1969
Height: 6'3" Weight: 12.10

'George' rejoined Crewe Alexandra in July 2000 and began last season as second choice in goal to Jason Kearton, but his patience was eventually rewarded when he stepped up to take over the 'keeper's jersey at Nottingham Forest on Boxing Day and went on to retain his place until almost the very end of the campaign. A big strong goalkeeper he will be hoping to remain first choice again in 2001-02.

Doncaster Rov (Free from Shooting Stars, Ibadan, Nigeria on 30/11/1995)
Leyton Orient (Free on 27/12/1995)
Crewe Alex (Free on 25/9/1996) FL 6 FLC 1
Queens Park R (£50,000 on 2/7/1998) FL 0+1
Crewe Alex (£50,000 on 19/7/2000) FL 21 FLC 0+1 FAC 3

BANKS Christopher (Chris) Noel
Born: Stone, 12 November 1965
Height: 5'11" Weight: 12.2
Club Honours: NC '99
International Honours: E: SP-2

Chris missed only a handful of matches for Cheltenham Town in the 2000-01 season and also scored his first league goal for many years in the 1-1 draw with local rivals Kidderminster in November. Although no longer as quick as he once was, he has a sharp football brain and reads the game well from the centre of defence. He is at his best alongside a big defender who attacks the ball while Chris drops deeper to cover space and pick up runners. His value to the team was recognised by his colleagues who voted him 'Players' Player of the Season'.

Port Vale (From juniors on 3/12/1982) FL 50+15/1 FLC 3+3 FAC 4 Others 8+4
Exeter C (Free on 24/6/1988) FL 43+2/1 FLC 2 FAC 1 Others 2 (Free to Bath C during 1989 close season)
Cheltenham T (Free on 11/8/1994) FL 81+1/1 FLC 4 FAC 4 Others 3

BANKS Steven (Steve)
Born: Hillingdon, 9 February 1972
Height: 6'0" Weight: 13.2

Having spent the majority of the 1999-2000 season as Jussi Jaaskelainen's deputy, Steve was looking to get a sustained run in goal for Bolton last term. When his rival damaged a cruciate ligament early in the new year he was given his chance, but although generally confident boss Sam Allardyce eventually opted to bring in Matt Clarke on loan and Steve returned to his place on the subs' bench. An experienced 'keeper he is now entering the stage of his career when he needs regular first-team football to reach his full potential.

West Ham U (From trainee on 24/3/1990) Others 1
Gillingham (Free on 25/3/1993) FL 67 FAC 7 Others 2
Blackpool (£60,000 on 18/8/1995) FL 150 FLC 13 FAC 8 Others 10
Bolton W (£50,000 on 25/3/1999) FL 19+1 FLC 6 FAC 5 Others 3

BAPTISTE Jairzinho **Rocky** Alon
Born: Clapham, 7 August 1972
Height: 6'2" Weight: 11.10

Ade Bankole

Having developed with Willesden Constantine, a club that has produced several Football League players in recent seasons, Rocky only stepped up to Conference football last September but was an immediate hit with Hayes, scoring a hat-trick within four minutes in the 4-3 win at Northwich. His goal-scoring exploits attracted the attention of then Luton manager Ricky Hill and he signed for the Hatters in mid-October. He made his debut from the subs' bench at Bury but when Hill was replaced as boss he fell out of favour and was subsequently loaned back to Hayes. A tall intelligent striker with good technique he was released at the end of April and signed for Farnborough Town during the summer.

Luton T (Free from Hayes on 23/10/2000) FL 0+3

BARACLOUGH Ian Robert
Born: Leicester, 4 December 1970
Height: 6'1" Weight: 12.2
Club Honours: Div 3 '98
International Honours: E: Yth

Ian is a left-sided defender who normally operates as a wing back but can also play in a left-sided central role in a 5-3-2 formation. He had the misfortune to suffer a cracked fibula playing for Queens Park Rangers against Crewe at the end of last August and it was not until November that he returned to first-team duties. Despite Rangers poor results during the campaign he maintained consistent form and always made a positive contribution to the side. Ian was one of 15 players released by the Loftus Road club in the summer and he was reported to have signed for Notts County during the break.

Leicester C (From trainee on 15/12/1988) FAC 1 Others 0+1
Wigan Ath (Loaned on 22/3/1990) FL 8+1/2
Grimsby T (Loaned on 21/12/1990) FL 1+3
Grimsby T (Free on 13/8/1991) FL 1
Lincoln C (Free on 21/8/1992) FL 68+5/10 FLC 7/1 FAC 4 Others 7
Mansfield T (Free on 6/6/1994) FL 47/5 FLC 7 FAC 4 Others 4
Notts Co (Signed on 13/10/1995) FL 107+4/10 FLC 5+1/1 FAC 8 Others 2
Queens Park R (£50,000 on 19/3/1998) FL 120+5/1 FLC 7 FAC 6

BARKER Christopher (Chris) Andrew
Born: Sheffield, 2 March 1980
Height: 6'0" Weight: 11.8

It was felt that Chris would not be a regular in the Barnsley team last season when boss Dave Bassett brought in left back Matteo Corbo, but he saw off the challenge with ease. Solid rather than spectacular he has a good left foot, tackles hard and distributes the ball accurately. He was an ever-present after Nigel Spackman took over as manager in January and signed a new contract that should see him remaining at Oakwell until the summer of 2004. Chris became the first player to win the Barnsley 'Young Player of the Year' award on two occasions.

Barnsley (Signed from Alfreton on 24/8/1998) FL 67+2 FLC 8+1 FAC 2 Others 0+1

Chris Barker

BARKER Richard (Richie) Ian
Born: Sheffield, 30 May 1975
Height: 6'0" Weight: 13.5
International Honours: E: Yth; Sch

A successful ankle ligament operation in the summer of 2000 ensured that Richie was fit for the start of last season. He struggled to make an impact for Macclesfield in the first half of the campaign when he was mostly employed as the solo forward, and after failing to agree new terms he moved on to Rotherham early in the new year. Although not an automatic choice at Millmoor he demonstrated a great attitude by giving his best whenever he was called upon and always worked hard. Richie netted his first Rotherham goal in style on the way to a comprehensive win against Bristol Rovers and will be looking to win a regular place in the starting line-up in 2001-02.

Sheffield Wed (From trainee on 27/7/1993) Others 1+1 (Free to Linfield on 22/8/1996)
Doncaster Rov (Loaned on 29/9/1995) FL 5+1 Others 0+1
Brighton & Hove A (Free on 19/12/1997) FL 48+12/12 FLC 1+1/1 FAC 1/1 Others 1
Macclesfield T (Free on 5/7/1999) FL 58/23 FLC 6/2 FAC 3 Others 1/1
Rotherham U (£60,000 on 3/1/2001) FL 7+12/1

BARLOW Martin David
Born: Barnstaple, 25 June 1971
Height: 5'7" Weight: 10.3

Martin returned to the Plymouth Argyle line-up at the start of last season after recovering from long-term injury problems but subsequently fell out of favour following a change in management and in March he went on loan to Yeovil Town. However he made just one appearance from the subs' bench for the Conference high flyers before he suffered a serious knee injury and returned to Home Park. When fully fit he is a talented play maker in the centre of midfield. Martin was released by the Pilgrims in the summer.

Plymouth Arg (From trainee on 1/7/1989) FL 294+35/24 FLC 11+1/2 FAC 19 Others 17+1

BARLOW Stuart
Born: Liverpool, 16 July 1968
Height: 5'10" Weight: 11.0
Club Honours: AMC '99

Having joined Tranmere Rovers on a 'Bosman' free transfer in the close season Stuart took some time to settle in at Prenton Park and made little impact in the first half of the campaign. Surprisingly recalled to the team on New Year's Day he responded with a gutsy performance to stake his case for a regular spot and subsequently began to show some much-improved form. An experienced striker he creates problems for defenders with his acceleration and neat ball control. A high point of the season was the FA Cup fifth round replay against Southampton when he hit the winner for Rovers as they turned a three-goal deficit into a famous 4-3 victory.

Everton (Free from Sherwood Park on 6/6/1990) F/PL 24+47/10 FLC 3+5/1 FAC 4+3/2 Others 0+2
Rotherham U (Loaned on 10/1/1992) Others 0+1
Oldham Ath (£450,000 on 20/11/1995) FL 78+15/31 FLC 5+1 FAC 6+1/1 Others 1
Wigan Ath (£45,000 on 26/3/1998) FL 72+11/40 FLC 6/3 FAC 5/3 Others 9+3/6
Tranmere Rov (Free on 5/7/2000) FL 12+15/2 FLC 1+3/1 FAC 2+2/1

BARMBY Nicholas (Nick) Jonathan
Born: Hull, 11 February 1974
Height: 5'7" Weight: 11.3
Club Honours: FLC '01; UEFAC '01
International Honours: E: 19; B-2; U21-4; Yth; Sch

Following his controversial transfer from city neighbours Everton to Liverpool in the summer and his return to the England squad, Nick must have been disappointed to miss out on most of Liverpool's triumphs at the end of the 2000-01 season due mainly to an ill-timed ankle injury that troubled him intermittently in the latter months of the campaign and flared up again in the FA Cup semi-final against Wycombe Wanderers. Although primarily considered to be a right-sided midfielder he was often employed on the opposite flank following the long-term injury to Patrik Berger and featured in every game up to the turn of the year, but only intermittently thereafter. A paltry return of two Premiership goals included one in the Anfield 'derby' game against his former club but he made a significant contribution to the Reds early progress in the UEFA Cup with four goals, one apiece in the away legs with Rapid Bucharest and Slovan Liberec, and one in each leg of the third round tie with Olympiakos. In addition he scored the vital breakthrough goal in the closing stages of the FA Cup fourth round game at Leeds. On the international front he played in the dismal England defeat by Germany at Wembley last October without distinction and although included in new manager Sven Goran Eriksson's first team selection and scoring an excellent opening goal in the 3-0 victory over Spain in March injuries then kept him out of the reckoning.

Tottenham H (From trainee on 9/4/1991) PL 81+6/20 FLC 7+1/2 FAC 12+1/5
Middlesbrough (£5,250,000 on 8/8/1995) PL 42/8 FLC 4/1 FAC 3/1
Everton (£5,750,000 on 2/11/1996) PL 105+11/18 FLC 2+3/3 FAC 12/3
Liverpool (£6,000,000 on 19/7/2000) PL 21+5/2 FLC 2+4/1 FAC 2+3/1 Others 6+3/4

BARNARD Darren Sean
Born: Rintein, Germany, 30 November 1971
Height: 5'9" Weight: 12.3
International Honours: E: Sch. W: 15

Darren sometimes struggled to find his best form for Barnlsey in 2000-01 although his season was badly disrupted by a knee injury that kept him out of action from the end of December until late February. Asked to play on the left side of a midfield four, he nevertheless often showed that he had one of the best left feet in the First Division and his passing and crossing remained of a high standard. Once he had returned to fitness he also won a recall to the Wales international team.

Chelsea (£50,000 from Wokingham T on 25/7/1990) F/PL 18+11/2 FLC 1+1 FAC 1+1
Reading (Loaned on 18/11/1994) FL 3+1
Bristol C (£175,000 on 6/10/1995) FL 77+1/15 FLC 4/1 FAC 6 Others 6/1
Barnsley (£750,000 on 8/8/1997) P/FL 117+15/21 FLC 14+2/5 FAC 7/2 Others 3

BARNES Paul Lance
Born: Leicester, 16 November 1967
Height: 5'11" Weight: 13.6

Now approaching the veteran stage of his career Paul was never able to hold down a regular place in the Bury line-up during the 2000-01 campaign. A hamstring injury in early October caused a brief lay-off and although he returned to the side he found himself largely relegated to the subs' bench in the second half of the season. He subsequently moved on loan to Conference outfit Nuneaton Borough in March where he enjoyed some success scoring 10 goals in just nine games. Paul is a hard working striker with a proven record as a goal-scorer throughout his career. He was reported to have signed for Doncaster Rovers shortly after the end of the season.

Notts Co (From apprentice on 16/11/1985) FL 36+17/14 FAC 0+1 Others 4+6/5

Stoke C (£30,000 on 23/3/1990) FL 10+14/3 FLC 0+2 Others 3+1/2
Chesterfield (Loaned on 8/11/1990) FL 1 FAC 1/1
York C (£50,000 on 15/7/1992) FL 147+1/76 FLC 10/5 FAC 5 Others 16/4
Birmingham C (£350,000 on 4/3/1996) FL 15/7
Burnley (£350,000 + on 6/9/1996) FL 63+2/30 FLC 5 FAC 5/1
Huddersfield T (Signed on 16/1/1998) FL 13+17/2 FLC 0+3 FAC 1+1
Bury (£40,000 on 15/3/1999) FL 31+23/8 FLC 0+1 FAC 4 Others 2

BARNES Philip (Phil) Kenneth
Born: Sheffield, 2 March 1979
Height: 6'1" Weight: 11.1
Phil started last season as deputy to Tony Caig in the Blackpool goal but eventually made the position his own after seeing off a challenge from on-loan 'keeper John Kennedy. A good shot stopper with a safe pair of hands he grew in confidence and contributed a number of clean sheets to the Bloomfield Road club's promotion campaign.
Rotherham U (From trainee on 25/6/1997) FL 2
Blackpool (£100,000 on 22/7/1997) FL 48 FLC 4 FAC 1 Others 6

BARNESS Anthony
Born: Lewisham, 25 March 1973
Height: 5'10" Weight: 13.1
Club Honours: Div 1 '00
Having joined Bolton on a free transfer in the close season, Anthony went on to become an invaluable member of the Wanderers' squad last term. Although able to play anywhere in defence or midfield he was used mainly at right back where his experience was put to good effect. He was given a run of games in the opening months of the campaign and was later drafted in and out of the team as required by boss Sam Allardyce. A solid no-frills type of player, he is likely to continue to be a vital part of the Wanderers' set up in 2001-02.
Charlton Ath (From trainee on 6/3/1991) FL 21+6/1 FLC 2 FAC 3 Others 1+1/1
Chelsea (£350,000 on 8/9/1992) PL 12+2 FLC 2 Others 2+1
Middlesbrough (Loaned on 12/8/1993) Others 1
Southend U (Loaned on 2/2/1996) FL 5
Charlton Ath (£165,000 on 8/8/1996) P/FL 83+13/3 FLC 5 FAC 3+1 Others 1+1
Bolton W (Free on 6/7/2000) FL 17+3 FLC 2 FAC 2 Others 3

BARNETT Gary Lloyd
Born: Stratford on Avon, 11 March 1963
Height: 5'9" Weight: 10.8
Club Honours: Div 3 '84
This experienced player featured twice for Kidderminster in a wide-left midfield role last September as the Harriers began their first-ever Football League campaign. Gary then stepped back to focus on his role as assistant-manager at Aggborough working with boss Jan Molby to ensure the team reached a respectable mid-table placing by the end of the season.
Coventry C (From apprentice on 22/1/1981)
Oxford U (Free on 7/7/1982) FL 37+8/9 FLC 6+2/1 FAC 5 Others 1
Wimbledon (Loaned on 24/2/1983) FL 5/1
Fulham (Loaned on 19/12/1984) FL 0+2/1
Fulham (£20,000 on 12/9/1985) FL 167+13/30 FLC 17/3 FAC 8+1/1 Others 8+2/1
Huddersfield T (Signed on 20/7/1990) FL 92+8/11 FLC 11/3 FAC 10/2 Others 7+2/1
Leyton Orient (Signed on 20/8/1993) FL 47+16/7 FLC 3 FAC 4 Others 5+2/1 (Free to Barry T during 1995 close season)
Kidderminster Hrs (Free on 11/8/1999) FL 2

BARNETT Jason Vincent
Born: Shrewsbury, 21 April 1976
Height: 5'9" Weight: 11.6
Jason was out of favour at Lincoln City at the start of last season but soon forced his way into the team appearing at right back and as a third centre back on occasions when a five man defence was used. His long throws and ability to push forward gave the Imps extra attacking options. He missed a number of games in the second half of the campaign after suffering a bout of pneumonia but recovered to win his place back.
Wolverhampton W (From trainee on 4/7/1994)
Lincoln C (£5,000 on 26/10/1995) FL 166+15/4 FLC 7 FAC 8+1 Others 13

BARRAS Anthony (Tony)
Born: Billingham, 29 March 1971
Height: 6'0" Weight: 13.0
Tony enjoyed another successful season for Walsall in 2000-01 forming an effective partnership in the centre of defence with Andy Tillson. Always ready to push forward he snatched a vital equaliser at Reading in April and then in the play-off final against the same opponents he stirred the hearts of all Saddlers' supporters by trying to get back onto the pitch after being concussed during extra time. He is a brave and hard-working central defender who combines aerial power with a useful touch on the floor.
Hartlepool U (From trainee on 6/7/1989) FL 9+3 FLC 2 FAC 1 Others 1
Stockport Co (Free on 23/7/1990) FL 94+5/5 FLC 2 FAC 7 Others 19+1
Rotherham U (Loaned on 25/2/1994) FL 5/1
York C (£25,000 on 18/7/1994) FL 167+4/11 FLC 16/2 FAC 10/1 Others 8+1/1
Reading (£20,000 on 19/3/1999) FL 4+2/1
Walsall (£20,000 on 16/7/1999) FL 52+8/5 FLC 7/1 FAC 4/1 Others 4

BARRASS Matthew (Matt) Robert
Born: Bury, 28 February 1980
Height: 5'11" Weight: 12.0
Matt had an unfortunate time with injuries during 2000-01 when he was absent for all but a few weeks of the campaign. He contracted glandular fever during the pre-season and although he made a brief return to action in September he then suffered cartilage damage during training and required corrective surgery. He eventually returned to fitness in the closing weeks of the season to make a late appearance from the subs' bench in the final game at Brentford. Matt is a promising young right back who is strong in the tackle and effective in the air.
Bury (From trainee on 19/5/1999) FL 28+2/1 FLC 1+1 Others 1

BARRETT Adam Nicholas
Born: Dagenham, 29 November 1979
Height: 5'10" Weight: 12.0
Adam began the 2000-01 campaign as a regular in the heart of Plymouth's defence but subsequently fell out of favour following a change of management and was rather surprisingly sold to Third Division rivals Mansfield Town for a bargain fee. At Field Mill he was sidelined with an ankle problem for a lengthy spell in the new year and when he returned to the first team he aggravated the injury which then required surgery, thus bringing his disrupted season to an end. A commanding left-footed central defender he is effective in the air and very comfortable on the ball.
Plymouth Arg (Free from USA football scholarship on 13/1/1999) FL 47+5/3 FLC 4 FAC 6+1 Others 1
Mansfield T (£10,000 on 1/12/2000) FL 8/1 Others 1

BARRETT Daniel (Danny) Thomas
Born: Bradford, 25 September 1980
Height: 6'0" Weight: 11.12
Danny made just one senior appearance for Chesterfield last season coming off the bench for the closing minutes of the 1-0 defeat at Brighton in May. He had been kept out of action by injuries earlier in the campaign and was loaned to Stafford Rangers in February to aid his return to fitness. A young striker who can also play in defence he is learning to make effective use of his height and pace.
Chesterfield (From trainee on 2/7/1999) FL 0+3

BARRETT Graham
Born: Dublin, 6 October 1981
Height: 5'10" Weight: 11.7
Club Honours: FAYC '00
International Honours: RoI: U21-10; Yth (UEFA-U16 '98); Sch
Having captained Arsenal's FA Youth Cup winning team in 1999-2000 Graham became a regular for the reserves last term and started his first game at senior level in the Worthington Cup third round tie against Ipswich. He joined Bristol Rovers on a three-month loan towards the end of the year to gain more first-team experience but made just one appearance from the subs' bench before picking up a severe throat infection and the problem was diagnosed as glandular fever. He eventually resumed playing for the U19s in March and worked his way back up to the second string by the end of the campaign. An exciting young striker he holds the ball up well and has superb finishing skills. Graham continued to represent the Republic of Ireland at U21 level winning a further five caps during the season.
Arsenal (From trainee on 14/10/1998) PL 0+2 FLC 1
Bristol Rov (Loaned on 15/12/2000) FL 0+1

BARRETT Paul David
Born: Newcastle, 13 April 1978
Height: 5'11" Weight: 11.5
International Honours: E: Yth
Paul appeared regularly for Wrexham in the early part of the 2000-01 campaign before losing his place last November and he only featured briefly after that. He is a hard-working midfield player who can play on either flank bringing aggression and enthusiasm to the Robins' team. His only

goal last season came in the 4-0 win over Bangor in the FA Wales Premier Cup.
Newcastle U (From trainee on 20/6/1996)
Wrexham (Free on 24/3/1999) FL 47+5/2 FLC 0+1 FAC 2+1 Others 1

BARRETT Scott
Born: Ilkeston, 2 April 1963
Height: 6'0" Weight: 14.4
Club Honours: GMVC '92; FAT '92

Scott spent last season as second-choice 'keeper to Ashley Bayes at Leyton Orient. Although he made a brief return to the first team in March when Bayes was rested he soon found himself back on the subs' bench. He was offered a further 12-month contract at Brisbane Road and will also be the club's goalkeeping coach next term.
Wolverhampton W (Signed from Ilkeston T on 27/9/1984) FL 30 FLC 1 FAC 1 Others 3
Stoke C (£10,000 on 24/7/1987) FL 51 FLC 2 FAC 3 Others 4
Colchester U (Loaned on 10/1/1990) FL 13
Stockport Co (Loaned on 22/3/1990) FL 10 Others 2
Gillingham (Free on 14/8/1992) FL 51 FLC 7 FAC 4 Others 4
Cambridge U (Free on 2/8/1995) FL 119 FLC 6 FAC 7 Others 3
Leyton Orient (Free on 25/1/1999) FL 56 FLC 2 FAC 1 Others 3

BARRICK Dean
Born: Hemsworth, 30 September 1969
Height: 5'9" Weight: 12.0
Club Honours: Div 3 '96

Dean was never able to hold down a place in the Bury line-up last season and played much of his football with the club's reserve team. He eventually moved to Doncaster Rovers on loan at the end of March and featured regularly for the Conference club in the closing weeks of the campaign. An experienced and consistent left back, he signed permanent forms for Rovers in May.
Sheffield Wed (From trainee on 7/5/1988) FL 11/2
Rotherham U (£50,000 on 14/2/1991) FL 96+3/7 FLC 6 FAC 8 Others 5/1
Cambridge U (£50,000 on 11/8/1993) FL 90+1/3 FLC 7/1 FAC 7/1 Others 6
Preston NE (Signed on 11/9/1995) FL 98+11/1 FLC 7+1/1 FAC 5 Others 6
Bury (Free on 3/7/1998) FL 37+10/1 FLC 5+2 FAC 2+1
Ayr U (Loaned on 19/2/1999) SL 11 SC 2

BARRON Michael James
Born: Chester le Street, 22 December 1974
Height: 5'11" Weight: 11.9

Michael was badly missed by Hartlepool during the early part of last season when he was sidelined with a knee injury. He made his long-awaited return to the team in November and shortly afterwards, Pool commenced a run of 21 league games without defeat. He was soon playing as if he had never been away and went on to captain the club to their second consecutive appearance in the end-of-season play-offs. He is a reliable central defender who reads the game well and is excellent at organising the back line.
Middlesbrough (From trainee on 2/2/1993) P/FL 2+1 FLC 1 Others 3+3
Hartlepool U (Loaned on 6/9/1996) FL 16
Hartlepool U (Free on 8/7/1997) FL 137+2/1 FLC 5 FAC 5 Others 15

BARROWCLOUGH Carl
Born: Barnsley, 25 September 1981
Height: 5'10" Weight: 11.2

One of several promising youngsters to emerge from Barnsley's youth scheme in recent seasons Carl made his senior debut for the Tykes against Gillingham and made his mark by winning the penalty that put the Tykes on the road to victory. He went on to make a handful more appearances and will be hoping to gain further experience in the 2001-02 season. A tricky winger with the ability to beat defenders and deliver a telling cross, he is the son of the former Barnsley and Newcastle player Stewart Barrowclough.
Barnsley (From trainee on 15/3/2001) FL 2+5

BARRY Gareth
Born: Hastings, 23 February 1981
Height: 6'0" Weight: 12.6
International Honours: E: 6; U21-7; Yth

Having burst on the Premiership scene with Aston Villa in the 1999-2000 campaign Gareth had a settling-in period last season. A regular in the first team for most of the time he produced some consistent performances although he was more solid than spectacular. Now an established figure in the defence he impressed with his composure and a maturity beyond his years. Very comfortable on the ball he is not afraid to take players on and occasionally featured in midfield where he looked equally at home. A regular member of the full international squad in the first half of the campaign he added four more caps before dropping back into the U21s. Gareth remains a cornerstone of John Gregory's long-term plans at Villa Park and signed a new contract during the season to keep him at the club for the next four years.
Aston Villa (From trainee on 27/2/1998) PL 87+7/3 FLC 9 FAC 10+1 Others 7/1

Gareth Barry

BARRY-MURPHY Brian
Born: Cork, Ireland, 27 July 1978
Height: 6'0" Weight: 12.4
International Honours: RoI: U21-6; Yth

Preston's young Irish midfielder made his first start in the team in the Worthington Cup tie at Shrewsbury last season, but it was not until the Boxing Day game against Wolves that he featured in league action. He appeared regularly from the subs' bench in the second half of the campaign and great things are expected of him at Deepdale providing he continues to develop in similar fashion. Mainly a wide left-sided midfield player he has a powerful shot, and looks very classy on the ball, distributing with confidence and accuracy.

Preston NE (Free from Cork C on 3/8/1999) FL 2+13 FLC 1+3 FAC 1 Others 1

Chris Bart-Williams

BART-WILLIAMS Christopher (Chris) Gerald
Born: Freetown, Sierra Leone, 16 June 1974
Height: 5'11" Weight: 11.6
Club Honours: Div 1 '98
International Honours: E: B-1; U21-16; Yth

Nottingham Forest boss David Platt appointed Chris as the club captain at the start of last season and soon afterwards he was switched to play in defence as a sweeper. He adapted to the move without any problems and indeed he showed some inspirational form in his new position. A very cultured player, his vision and passing were unmatched and he proved to be a deadly marksman from set pieces. Chris finished as Forest's leading scorer with 15 goals, but with one year remaining on his contract he went on the transfer list and his future at the City Ground seemed in doubt at the time of writing.

Leyton Orient (From trainee on 18/7/1991) FL 34+2/2 FLC 4 Others 2
Sheffield Wed (£275,000 on 21/11/1991) F/PL 95+29/16 FLC 14+2/4 FAC 9+3/2 Others 1+3/2
Nottingham F (£2,500,000 on 1/7/1995) F/PL 183+7/27 FLC 14/2 FAC 14/2 Others 7+1

BARTHEZ Fabien Alain
Born: Lavelanet, France, 28 June 1971
Height: 5'11" Weight: 12.8
Club Honours: PL '01
International Honours: France: 41

Forget the fact that Fabien Barthez turned up for his first day's training at Manchester United 35 miles down the wrong end of the East Lancs Road. And no, he wasn't given directions by his French compatriot Gerard Houllier, contrary to popular belief. Certainly, in terms of direction, he didn't need an A-Z to keep United's goal under guard last term, and he proved himself a worthy successor to the legendary Peter Schmeichel in his first full season of Premiership action. Of course, there's so much more to him than meets the eye, and Sir Alex Ferguson knew he wasn't only getting a world-class goalkeeper when he signed him from Monaco in the close season, but also a 'showman' into the bargain. While some of his antics made Schmeichel's sorties on opposing goals tame by comparison, the facts don't lie - he kept 15 clean sheets in the Premiership up to the beginning of February, and was highly influential in the Champions' League with

Fabien Barthez

some masterful performances. So what of his season? Well, after a baptism of fire in the Charity Shield opener against Chelsea at Wembley, he put together a run of eight games before sustaining a hamstring injury at Everton that kept him out of the important Champions' League openers against Dynamo Kiev and PSV. Fortunately, or unfortunately in his case, he returned for the Premiership match against Arsenal at Highbury, where fellow compatriot, Thierry Henry, scored one of the goals of the season against him. Against Leeds in March, he emerged as both hero and villain, narrowly avoiding a red card and then saving a vital penalty to earn United a share of the points. He remained first-choice 'keeper for France and was also voted into the PFA's Premiership team. Fabien is the son of Alain Barthez a former rugby union scrum half with Narbonne and France.

Manchester U (£7,800,000 from AS Monaco, France, ex Toulouse, Olympique Marseille, on 7/6/2000) PL 30 FAC 1 Others 13

BARTLETT Thurston **Shaun**
Born: Cape Town, South Africa, 31 October 1972
Height: 6'1" Weight: 12.4
International Honours: South Africa:

An experienced international striker, Shaun joined Charlton Athletic on loan from Swiss club FC Zurich last November and made his debut later that week when he came on a s a 67th minute substitute against Liverpool. He made the starting line-up for the home game against Manchester United and scored twice in a thrilling encounter that saw the Addicks come back from two goals down to earn a 3-3 draw. He continued to score on a fairly regular basis at The Valley but did not find the net away from home until he blasted in the only goal of the game in an excellent win at Stamford Bridge against Chelsea. Shaun is quick, has good close control and is excellent in the air. He has a tremendous shot and scored with a thunderous volley against Leicester City at The Valley that was later voted 'Goal of the Season' by 'Match of the Day' viewers. Shaun remained a regular for South Africa during the season.

Charlton Ath (Loaned from FC Zurich, Switzerland, ex Cape Town Spurs, Colorado Rapids, NY/NJ Metro Stars, Cape Town Spurs, on 1/12/2000) PL 16+2/7 FAC 2

BARTON Warren Dean
Born: Stoke Newington, 19 March 1969
Height: 6'0" Weight: 12.0
International Honours: E: 3; B-3

Having completed six seasons at Newcastle Warren is one of the club's longest serving players and he remains a cornerstone of the Geordies' defence. He got off to an unfortunate start in 2000-01 receiving a red card at Derby and then tearing a groin muscle in training, however he returned after a lengthy lay off to keep his place in the team until the end of the season. A versatile player he is primarily a right back, but also featured at left back, in the centre of defence and in a 'holding' midfield role. Sound in the tackle, he has a sharp positional awareness, and is very effective when pushing down the wing to deliver crosses into the box.

Maidstone U (£10,000 from Leytonstone on 28/7/1989) FL 41+1 FLC 0+2 FAC 3/1 Others 7
Wimbledon (£300,000 on 7/6/1990) F/PL 178+2/10 FLC 16/1 FAC 11 Others 2
Newcastle U (£4,500,000 on 5/6/1995) PL 138+21/4 FLC 11/1 FAC 19+3 Others 14+2

Shaun Bartlett

BARTRAM Vincent (Vince) Lee
Born: Birmingham, 7 August 1968
Height: 6'2" Weight: 13.4

Although he took a little time to find his best form, Vince appeared in every first-team game for Gillingham last season. He became the first goalkeeper to win the Nationwide 'Save of the Month' award twice in the same season when he was selected in both August and September and went on to make his 150th first-team appearance for the Gills. He was outstanding in the latter stages of the campaign when his agility and reflex saves made a significant contribution in helping the club retain their First Division status.

Wolverhampton W (From juniors on 17/8/1985) FL 5 FLC 2 FAC 3
Blackpool (Loaned on 27/10/1989) FL 9 Others 2
Bournemouth (£65,000 on 24/7/1991) FL 132 FLC 10 FAC 14 Others 6
Arsenal (£400,000 on 10/8/1994) PL 11 FLC 0+1
Huddersfield T (Loaned on 17/10/1997) FL 12
Gillingham (Free on 20/3/1998) FL 142 FLC 8 FAC 10 Others 10

BASHAM Michael (Mike)
Born: Barking, 27 September 1973
Height: 6'2" Weight: 13.9
Club Honours: AMC '94
International Honours: E: Yth; Sch

After producing the best performances of any centre back at Barnet in the 2000-01 pre-season games, injuries limited Mike to just a handful of appearances during the course of the season. A cultured defender with fine distribution he eventually moved to York City shortly before the transfer deadline where he impressed in the centre of defence in the closing weeks of the campaign. He scored with a close-range header in the Minstermen's vital relegation battle at Torquay.

West Ham U (From trainee on 3/7/1992)
Colchester U (Loaned on 18/11/1993) FL 1
Swansea C (Free on 24/3/1994) FL 27+2/1 FAC 6 Others 8+2
Peterborough U (Free on 18/12/1995) FL 17+2/1 FLC 1 FAC 0+1
Barnet (Free on 5/8/1997) FL 74+1/2 FLC 2 FAC 0+1 Others 7+1
York C (Free on 14/3/2001) FL 6+1/1

BASHAM Steven (Steve) Brian
Born: Southampton, 2 December 1977
Height: 5'11" Weight: 12.0
Club Honours: Div 2 '00

After waiting exactly a year for a goal, Steve marked his 50th appearance for Preston with the winner against Portsmouth in September but then suffered a double fracture of the right leg against Tranmere towards the end of October after netting what once again proved to be the deciding goal. At his best he is a sharp and incisive goal-scorer with excellent ball control and powerful shooting from a short backlift. It is hoped he will be fully fit in time for the start of the 2001-02 campaign.

Southampton (From trainee on 24/5/1996) PL 1+18/1 FLC 0+1
Wrexham (Loaned on 6/2/1998) FL 4+1
Preston NE (£200,000 on 5/2/1999) FL 37+15/14 FLC 5+1/1 FAC 0+1

BASS Jonathan (Jon) David
Born: Weston super Mare, 1 January 1976
Height: 6'0" Weight: 12.2
International Honours: E: Sch

Jon missed the first part of last season at Birmingham after suffering a blood clot in his shoulder but received few first-team opportunities on his return to fitness and was placed on the transfer list. A very disciplined right back who reads the game well, his only senior game came when he came on from the subs' bench for the final five minutes of the game at Sheffield Wednesday in March. Jon was released by the Blues in the summer.

Birmingham C (From juniors on 27/6/1994) FL 60+8 FLC 7+1 FAC 5
Carlisle U (Loaned on 11/10/1996) FL 3
Gillingham (Loaned on 23/3/2000) FL 4+3

BASSEDAS Christian Gustavo
Born: Buenos Aires, Argentine, 16 February 1973
Height: 5'9" Weight: 11.7
International Honours: Argentina: 22

Four times a championship winner in Argentina with Velez Sarsfield, Christian signed for Newcastle United in July 2000 but his Premiership debut was delayed until November after he broke a bone in his foot during the club's pre-season tour of the USA. He eventually began to settle into the midfield, scoring his first goal against Chelsea at the end of January, but is not expected to hit his best form until the 2001-02 campaign. A neat and undemonstrative midfield player with a sure touch and good technique he is able to play anywhere across the line, but is probably more comfortable on the left-hand side.

Newcastle U (£4,100,000 from Velez Sarsfield, Argentine on 6/7/2000) PL 17+5/1 FLC 1+1 FAC 2

BASSILA Christian
Born: Paris, France, 5 October 1977
Height: 6'4" Weight: 13.6
International Honours: France: U21

A former French U21 international, Christian joined West Ham on loan from Rennes last August and made his debut from the substitutes' bench against Manchester United soon afterwards. Unfortunately he suffered a bad knee injury during the game and it was not until January that he returned to the first team again when he featured in the FA Cup third round tie at Walsall. In all he made four appearances as a substitute for the Hammers, amounting to just 78 minutes of first-team football during the season. He is a hard-working ball winner in the centre of the park.

West Ham U (Loaned from Stade Rennais, France, ex Lyon, on 28/8/2000) PL 0+3 FAC 0+1

BATES James (Jamie) Alan
Born: Croydon, 24 February 1968
Height: 6'2" Weight: 14.0
Club Honours: Div 3 '92, '99

Jamie had another fine season in the Wycombe Wanderers defence in 2000-01 when he was an automatic selection in the side apart from a brief spell out with a hamstring injury at the turn of the year. He twice scored a brace of goals, against Harrow Borough in the FA Cup and Bury in the Second Division, and produced a superb performance in the FA Cup semi-final against Liverpool. A rock solid defender with a reputation for blasting free kicks through defensive walls he surprisingly announced his retirement from the game at the end of the campaign. After fifteen years and over 600 games for Brentford and Wycombe he will be greatly missed by all at Adams Park.

Brentford (From trainee on 1/6/1987) FL 399+20/18 FLC 37+3/3 FAC 20+1/2 Others 44/1
Wycombe W (Free on 25/3/1999) FL 76+4/4 FLC 8/1 FAC 9+2/2 Others 1

BATTERSBY Anthony (Tony)
Born: Doncaster, 30 August 1975
Height: 6'0" Weight: 12.7

This skilful striker was one of a number of Lincoln City players who experienced an upturn in fortunes following the arrival of new manager Alan Buckley at the start of March. After struggling to cope with the style of the previous management Tony showed a dramatic change fitting in well with the system adopted by Buckley. He began to find the net again and started to create chances for colleagues with his ability to hold up the ball and turn his man. Having at one point appeared certain to be released he ended the campaign by signing a new contract.

Sheffield U (From trainee on 5/7/1993) FL 3+7/1 FLC 1+1 Others 2+1/1
Southend U (Loaned on 23/3/1995) FL 6+2/1
Notts Co (£200,000 on 8/1/1996) FL 20+19/8 FLC 1 FAC 0+3 Others 4
Bury (£125,000 on 3/3/1997) FL 37+11/8 FLC 3+1/1 FAC 2
Lincoln C (£75,000 on 8/8/1998) FL 66+24/16 FLC 4/1 FAC 2+2/1 Others 8+1/2
Northampton T (Loaned on 24/9/1999) FL 0+3/1

BATTY David
Born: Leeds, 2 December 1968
Height: 5'8" Weight: 12.0
Club Honours: Div 2 '90, Div 1 '92; CS '92
International Honours: E: 42; B-5; U21-7

December 16, was a special day at Elland Road last season, for after 78 minutes and Leeds 2-0 to the good against Sunderland, 40,000 fans voiced their acclaim as David Batty stepped on to the pitch as a replacement for Olivier Dacourt to confirm that he had finally recovered from his injury problems. He became a regular fixture in the side from the turn of the year, and coincidentally his presence in the team saw an upturn in form and fortune for United and he started to establish a formidable partnership with Dacourt, looking as if he had never been away. His calm approach, tactical awareness and ability to read the game shone through and he produced some exceptional performances, particularly in the home games with Manchester United and Deportivo La Coruna (if only that volley had gone in against Deportivo the roof at Elland Road would have come off!). Having passed through his injury nightmare all at the club hope for better times, and as a model professional he deserves them.

Leeds U (From trainee on 3/8/1987) F/PL 201+10/4 FLC 17 FAC 12 Others 17
Blackburn Rov (£2,750,000 on 26/10/1993) PL 53+1/1 FLC 6 FAC 5 Others 6
Newcastle U (£3,750,000 on 2/3/1996) PL 81+2/3 FLC 6 FAC 9/1 Others 16
Leeds U (£4,400,000 on 9/12/1998) PL 39+3 FLC 2 FAC 2 Others 11+1

BAYES Ashley John
Born: Lincoln, 19 April 1972
Height: 6'1" Weight: 13.5
International Honours: E: Yth

Ashley finally made the 'keeper's jersey his own at Leyton Orient last season. Full of confidence and an excellent shot stopper, he is a huge favourite of the Brisbane Road faithful. Some of the highlights of his campaign came in the cup ties against Newcastle and Tottenham when he performed creditably well and prevented both Alan Shearer and Sergei Rebrov from scoring against the O's.

Brentford (From trainee on 5/7/1990) FL 4 FLC 5 FAC 2 Others 1
Torquay U (Free on 13/8/1993) FL 97 FLC 7 FAC 9 Others 6
Exeter C (Free on 31/7/1996) FL 127 FLC 6 FAC 8 Others 4
Leyton Orient (Free on 5/7/1999) FL 56 FLC 6 FAC 5 Others 5

BAYLISS David (Dave) Anthony
Born: Liverpool, 8 June 1976
Height: 5'11" Weight: 12.4

Rochdale's longest-serving player, Dave was again in great form at the centre of defence in the 2000-01 campaign, rarely having an off-day, and missing just a handful of games during the season through suspension. He played his 200th game for the club in the 3-0 win against Exeter last April and celebrated by scoring with a header.

Rochdale (From trainee on 10/6/1995) FL 160+17/9 FLC 10 FAC 4+3 Others 11+1

BAZELEY Darren Shaun
Born: Northampton, 5 October 1972
Height: 5'10" Weight: 11.7
Club Honours: Div 2 '98
International Honours: E: U21-1

Darren was omitted from the Wolves' team at the start of last season but soon won a regular place back featuring either at right back or in a more advanced role. Although his form was a little patchy he was still able to deliver some telling crosses but then suffered a torn cartilage in the game at Sheffield Wednesday shortly before Christmas. Corrective surgery was required and he failed to return to match fitness before the end of the campaign.

Watford (From trainee on 6/5/1991) FL 187+53/21 FLC 13+5/2 FAC 12+1/3 Others 9+1/1
Wolverhampton W (Free on 13/7/1999) FL 69+1/4 FLC 7 FAC 3

BEADLE Peter Clifford William James
Born: Lambeth, 13 May 1972
Height: 6'1" Weight: 13.7

While never being assured of a permanent place in Bristol City's line-up last season, Peter featured regularly in the first-team squad and was often used from the subs' bench, coming on to try and change the course of a game. He finally won over his critics, who had resented his previous

affiliation with the blue side of Bristol, with a fine performance in the 'derby' match against Bristol Rovers when he made one goal and scored another with a diving header in City's 3-2 victory. A big strong target man who leads the line well, he also possesses deft control and considerable skill on the ball.
Gillingham (From trainee on 5/5/1990) FL 42+25/14 FLC 2+4/2 FAC 1+1 Others 1
Tottenham H (£300,000 on 4/6/1992)
Bournemouth (Loaned on 25/3/1993) FL 9/2
Southend U (Loaned on 4/3/1994) FL 8/1
Watford (Signed on 12/9/1994) FL 12+11/1 FLC 1
Bristol Rov (£50,000 on 17/11/1995) FL 98+11/39 FLC 2+1 FAC 5/2 Others 7+1/1
Port Vale (£300,000 on 6/8/1998) FL 18+5/6 FLC 2 FAC 1
Notts Co (£250,000 on 18/2/1999) FL 14+8/3 FLC 1+3
Bristol C (£200,000 on 19/10/1999) FL 40+18/10 FLC 1 FAC 6+2/1 Others 5+2/4

Peter Beagrie

BEAGRIE Peter Sydney
Born: Middlesbrough, 28 November 1965
Height: 5'8" Weight: 12.0
International Honours: E: B-2; U21-2
Peter underwent a summer operation to resolve an achilles tendon problem and missed the pre-season friendlies and Inter Toto Cup matches for Bradford City. He was in and out of the team during the 2000-01 campaign and missed a number of games due to a torn calf muscle. Rather surprisingly he joined Second Division Wigan Athletic on a short-term contract in March to assist with their push for promotion. Peter proved a talented addition to the Latics' squad and scored a crucial last-minute winner at Wycombe but was subsequently released in the summer. He is a tricky winger, superb at delivering crosses and always willing to track back and help out in defence. His great enthusiasm for the game rubs off on his team-mates, and he is always willing to help the youngsters out.
Middlesbrough (From juniors on 10/9/1983) FL 24+9/2 FLC 1 Others 1+1
Sheffield U (£35,000 on 16/8/1986) FL 81+3/11 FLC 5 FAC 5 Others 4
Stoke C (£210,000 on 29/6/1988) FL 54/7 FLC 4 FAC 3/1
Everton (£750,000 on 2/11/1989) F/PL 88+26/11 FLC 7+2/3 FAC 7+2 Others 5+1/1
Sunderland (Loaned on 26/9/1991) FL 5/1
Manchester C (£1,100,000 on 24/3/1994) F/PL 46+6/3 FLC 8/1 FAC 4+1/1
Bradford C (£50,000 on 2/7/1997) P/FL 113+18/20 FLC 9/3 FAC 5+1 Others 0+1
Everton (Loaned on 26/3/1998) PL 4+2
Wigan Ath (Free on 16/2/2001) FL 7+3/1 Others 2

BEALL Matthew John
Born: Enfield, 4 December 1977
Height: 5'7" Weight: 10.12
'Billy', as he is known, started the season on the treatment table but was soon back in action for Leyton Orient and featured in a handful of games in the first half of the campaign. He subsequently joined Conference outfit Dover on loan in February before returning to play his part in midfield and help the team to the play-off final. An excellent tackler who uses the ball well he was reported to have signed a new 12-month contract for the O's at the end of the season.
Cambridge U (From trainee on 28/3/1996) FL 73+8/7 FLC 2 FAC 6/2 Others 1+1
Leyton Orient (Signed on 26/10/1998) FL 55+18/3 FLC 2 FAC 6+2 Others 4

BEASANT David (Dave) John
Born: Willesden, 20 March 1959
Height: 6'4" Weight: 14.3
Club Honours: Div 4 '83, Div 2 '89; Div 1 '98; FAC '88; FMC '90
International Honours: E: 2; B-7
This veteran goalkeeper seems to get better as he gets older. Big Dave had another excellent season as Nottingham Forest's first choice 'keeper, missing just one First Division game and saving the day on numerous occasions with some world-class saves. Confident coming out for corners and a reassuring presence between the sticks he continued to extend his record as the oldest player to have appeared for Forest in Football League action. He was released at the end of the season.
Wimbledon (£1,000 from Edgware T on 7/8/1979) FL 340 FLC 21 FAC 27 Others 3
Newcastle U (£800,000 on 13/6/1988) FL 20 FLC 2 FAC 2 Others 1
Chelsea (£725,000 on 14/1/1989) F/PL 133 FLC 11 FAC 5 Others 8
Grimsby T (Loaned on 24/10/1992) FL 6
Wolverhampton W (Loaned on 12/1/1993) FL 4 FAC 1
Southampton (£300,000 on 4/11/1993) PL 86+2 FLC 8 FAC 9
Nottingham F (Free on 22/8/1997) P/FL 139 FLC 8+1 FAC 6

BEATTIE James Scott
Born: Lancaster, 27 February 1978
Height: 6'1" Weight: 12.0
International Honours: E: U21-5
Having endured a nightmare time with injuries and loss of form in the 1999-2000 season, James bounced back last term in fine style. He hit a rich vein of form especially in the autumn when he netted ten goals in a run of ten games to win the 'Carling Player of the Month' for December. His exploits included a dramatic 25-yard free-kick in the 3-2 win over Chelsea and a stunning 40-yard effort at Sunderland. A powerfully built striker he is very effective in the air, packs a powerful shot and links well with his partner up front Marian Pahars.
Blackburn Rov (From trainee on 7/3/1995) PL 1+3 FLC 2 FAC 0+1
Southampton (£1,000,000 on 17/7/1998) PL 59+31/16 FLC 4+3/1 FAC 6+1/1

BEAUCHAMP Joseph (Joey) Daniel
Born: Oxford, 13 March 1971
Height: 5'10" Weight: 12.11
Although now approaching the veteran stage of his career, Joey was a regular member of the Oxford United first-team squad last season and continued to show that he is a potential match winner. He sometimes struggled to find his best form but also produced some excellent displays and netted two brilliant goals - a long-range cracker at Walsall and a 30-yarder in the 2-1 win at Swansea in November. Still very much a tricky winger, he netted a total of seven goals and the United fans will be hoping for a few more seasons from one of their most loyal players.
Oxford U (From trainee on 16/5/1989) FL 117+7/20 FLC 6+1/2 FAC 8/3 Others 5+1
Swansea C (Loaned on 30/10/1991) FL 5/2 Others 1
West Ham U (£1,000,000 on 22/6/1994)
Swindon T (£850,000 on 18/8/1994) FL 39+6/3 FLC 7+2/1 FAC 2 Others 4
Oxford U (£75,000 on 4/10/1995) FL 201+34/42 FLC 22+1/8 FAC 12+3/1 Others 2+4

BEAUMONT Christopher (Chris) Paul
Born: Sheffield, 5 December 1965
Height: 5'11" Weight: 11.12
Chris spent most of last season on the subs' bench for Chesterfield and only made the starting line-up on four occasions. He usually came on if an experienced hand was needed to cover for the withdrawal of a defender or midfielder and although no player can be happy being a permanent substitute, he put the team before himself and proved to be a valued squad member. For a player who arrived at Saltergate as a right winger, Chris performed as a stand-in centre-half with great aplomb! He was released in the summer.
Rochdale (Free from Denaby U on 21/7/1988) FL 31+3/7 FLC 0+1/1 FAC 2/1 Others 2
Stockport Co (£8,000 on 21/7/1989) FL 238+20/39 FLC 14+3/3 FAC 15/2 Others 34+2/7
Chesterfield (£30,000 on 22/7/1996) FL 132+26/6 FLC 11+3 FAC 7+2/1 Others 6+4

BEAVERS Paul Mark
Born: Blackpool, 2 October 1978
Height: 6'3" Weight: 13.5
This strong, bustling centre forward initially joined Darlington on loan shortly after the start of last season and made his debut in the Worthington Cup second round tie against Bradford City. He then scored the winner on his home debut against Carlisle United after coming off the subs' bench, but after just three more appearances he went on loan to Irish League club Coleraine for three months and played in the Nationwide Gold Cup final. He made two more starts on his return but failed to win a regular first team place. He was released in the summer.

Sunderland (From trainee on 14/4/1997)
Shrewsbury T (Loaned on 7/12/1998) FL 2 Others 1
Oldham Ath (Signed on 25/3/1999) FL 10+1/2 FLC 0+1 Others 0+1
Hartlepool U (Loaned on 23/3/2000) FL 2+5 Others 1
Darlington (Free on 8/9/2000) FL 3+4/1 FLC 1

BECKETT Luke John
Born: Sheffield, 25 November 1976
Height: 5'11" Weight: 11.6

Luke signed for Chesterfield during the 2000 close season in a deal that later attracted controversy. He took a while to find full fitness and was sidelined with a thigh injury in October but on his return he showed why he was such a sought-after player scoring seven goals in as many games as the Spireites consolidated their position at the top of the table. A striker with a proven scoring record he holds the ball up well, links intelligently with team-mates and is never afraid to go in where it hurts.

Barnsley (From trainee on 20/6/1995)
Chester C (Free on 11/6/1998) FL 70+4/25 FLC 5/5 FAC 4/2 Others 1
Chesterfield (£75,000 on 19/7/2000) FL 38+3/16 FLC 4/2 FAC 1 Others 3

BECKHAM David Robert Joseph
Born: Leytonstone, 2 May 1975
Height: 6'0" Weight: 11.12
Club Honours: FAYC '92; PL '96, '97, '99, '00, '01; FAC '96, '99; CS '96, '97; EC '99
International Honours: E: 42; U21-9; Yth

In another outstanding season for Manchester United and England, David continued to juggle his showbiz lifestyle, with that of a professional footballer with amazing dexterity. While his stint on the 'Parkinson Show' dispelled some media myths about his private life, what emerged was his dedication and gratitude towards a sport that has made him into a legend. On the playing front, his season opened in spectacular fashion with three goals in successive games against Ipswich, West Ham, and Bradford. Having netted a goal in every other game throughout October, he drew a blank during the early stages of the Champions' League. Back on the Premiership trail, he netted the all-important winner against Manchester City in the first 'derby' for four years, and in December negotiated a lucrative pay rise plus a package of shares, and a valuable boot deal with Adidas. Voted sixth in the annual FIFA 'World Player of the Year' award, an ITV documentary revealed that he was just a normal, quiet sensitive lad with an exceptional football talent, rather than the figure the media circus would have us believe. His performance level dipped a little in March but there was nothing any of the opposition could do to stop United winning their seventh Premiership title in nine years. On the international front, he played in England's disappointing World Cup loss to Germany and was then given the captaincy for the friendly against Italy in November. New coach Sven-Goran Eriksson clearly saw qualities in him that the media had missed and his decision to keep David as skipper proved a masterstroke when he netted a superb strike against Finland and followed this up with two classic free-kicks against Mexico and Greece in the summer, thus at least achieving the effect of taking attention away from his new Mohican hairstyle!

Manchester U (From trainee on 29/1/1993) PL 187+19/44 FLC 5+2 FAC 18+2/5 Others 63+3/9
Preston NE (Loaned on 28/2/1995) FL 4+1/2

BEDEAU Anthony (Tony) Charles Osmond
Born: Hammersmith, 24 March 1979
Height: 5'10" Weight: 11.0

After missing the start of the 2000-2001 campaign through injury Tony stormed back in style netting twice in the Worthington Cup tie against Gillingham and following this up with the Gulls' equaliser in the 1-1 draw with Lincoln. Such form attracted the attentions of scouts from higher clubs but he then seemed to lose his confidence and the goals dried up and after netting at Hull in mid-December he managed just one more in the remainder of the campaign. A striker who is strong on the ball and has good pace, he will be hoping that the goals return in the coming season.

Torquay U (From trainee on 28/7/1997) FL 116+38/36 FLC 6+1/3 FAC 8+3/1 Others 1+8

BEECH Christopher (Chris)
Born: Congleton, 5 November 1975
Height: 5'10" Weight: 11.12
International Honours: E: Yth; Sch

Chris once again had to be content with a bit part at Rotherham last season although he can consider himself rather unlucky not to have played more often. He started the season in the team before picking up an injury and he was unable to command a regular spot thereafter. A dogged left-sided defender, distribution is one of his strong points as he rarely wastes the ball. He never let the side down whenever called upon.

Manchester C (From trainee on 12/11/1992)
Cardiff C (Free on 7/8/1997) FL 46/1 FLC 2 FAC 6
Rotherham U (Free on 30/6/1998) FL 37+8 FLC 5 FAC 0+1

BEECH Christopher (Chris) Stephen
Born: Blackpool, 16 September 1974
Height: 5'11" Weight: 11.12

Chris missed the start of the 2000-01 season at Huddersfield with a groin injury and eventually made his return in a goalless draw at Stockport County. However he was then sidelined by an achilles problem in October and this brought his campaign to a premature close. A skilful attacking midfield player he had been a driving force in the centre of the park in what turned out to be a very disappointing season for the Terriers. Chris was sorely missed in his absence not least for the valuable goals he scores.

Blackpool (From trainee on 9/7/1993) FL 53+29/4 FLC 4+4 FAC 1 Others 3+3/2
Hartlepool U (Free on 18/7/1996) FL 92+2/23 FLC 5/1 FAC 3/1 Others 3/1
Huddersfield T (£65,000 on 27/11/1998) FL 57+5/11 FLC 5/1 FAC 2/2

BEETON Alan Matthew
Born: Watford, 4 October 1978
Height: 5'11" Weight: 11.12

Alan found it difficult to break into the Wycombe team last term and had to wait until November until he came into the side for the injured Chris Vinnicombe. However he only played a handful of games before moving on to Ryman League outfit Chesham United early in the new year. He is a left-sided defender with great stamina and fine attacking skills.

Wycombe W (From trainee on 1/7/1997) FL 39+16 FLC 4+1 FAC 5+2

BELL Leon Earl
Born: Hitchin, 19 December 1980
Height: 5'7" Weight: 9.7

Having developed in Barnet's youth team Leon continued to make progress at Underhill in the 2000-01 campaign. A talented right-sided midfield player with good close control and thoughtful distribution, the highlight of his season was a fine performance when coming off the subs' bench for the final half hour against Carlisle in March. He was placed on the open to offers list in the summer.

Barnet (From trainee on 2/7/1999) FL 7+5 FLC 0+1 Others 3

Mickey Bell

BELL Michael (Mickey)
Born: Newcastle, 15 November 1971
Height: 5'9" Weight: 11.4

Although not as effective going forward for Bristol City as in previous years Mickey still had a fine season at Ashton Gate in 2000-01 and was honoured by being selected for the PFA Division Two team for the second successive year. A regular for most of the campaign he missed a handful of games in the spring after suffering a broken toe. He is a stylish left-sided defender who can play either at full back or in a wing-back role.

Northampton T (From trainee on 1/7/1990) FL 133+20/10 FLC 7+1 FAC 5/1 Others 9+2/1
Wycombe W (£45,000 on 21/10/1994) FL 117+1/5 FLC 5 FAC 9/2 Others 3+1
Bristol C (£150,000 on 2/7/1997) FL 152+2/24 FLC 10 FAC 12 Others 6

BELLAMY Craig Douglas
Born: Cardiff, 13 July 1979
Height: 5'9" Weight: 10.12
International Honours: W: 12; U21-8; Yth; Sch

Having missed most of the 1999-2000 campaign through injury Craig enjoyed a good pre-season for Norwich but after appearing in the opening league game at Barnsley he was then sold to Coventry City for a substantial fee, arriving as a replacement for Robbie Keane. A fast and instinctive striker with good close ball skills he netted twice in his first three games including a brilliant solo effort at Maine Road but subsequently goals were hard to come by. His form improved after he was switched to a role on the left of midfield where he had more time and less exposure to the physical challenges from central defenders and he was particularly outstanding in this role in the game at Leicester. Despite the club's relegation worries his spirit never diminished and he always gave 100% for the cause. Craig again featured regularly for Wales and was reported to have joined Newcastle for a substantial fee during the close season.
Norwich C (From trainee on 20/1/1997) FL 71+13/32 FLC 6/2 FAC 1
Coventry C (£6,500,000 on 17/8/2000) PL 33+1/6 FLC 3/1 FAC 2/1

Craig Bellamy

BENALI Francis Vincent
Born: Southampton, 30 December 1968
Height: 5'10" Weight: 11.0
International Honours: E: Sch

Francis found himself on the fringes of the first-team squad at Southampton in the 2000-01 campaign following the emergence of Wayne Bridge and he made just one early season appearance, coming on from the subs' bench in the closing stages of the 5-0 defeat at Old Trafford. With no further opportunities on the horizon he moved on loan to Nottingham Forest where he soon won a regular place in the team. He made 15 appearances during a three-month loan period at the City Ground and impressed with some solid defensive displays. He returned to the Dell and featured from the bench again on a further three occasions in the closing matches. A left-sided central defender who can feature either at full back or in a more central role he has been a loyal servant to the Saints and a model professional for the club.
Southampton (From apprentice on 5/1/1987) F/PL 269+37/1 FLC 24+7 FAC 21 Others 3+1
Nottingham F (Loaned on 12/1/2001) FL 15

BENEFIELD James (Jimmy) Patrick
Born: Torbay, 6 May 1983
Height: 5'10" Weight: 11.2

This midfielder made steady progress in the Torquay United youth team last season and made his bow in senior football when he came on from the subs' bench to replace Kevin Hill for the final 30 minutes of the Gulls game at Brighton in September. Still a trainee at Plainmoor he will be hoping for more first-team experience in the 2001-02 campaign.
Torquay U (Trainee) FL 0+1

BENJAMIN Trevor Junior
Born: Kettering, 8 February 1979
Height: 6'2" Weight: 13.2
International Honours: E: U21-1

Trevor joined Leicester City during the close season and was considered to be an investment for the future by new boss Peter Taylor. He spent much of the 2000-01 campaign on the subs' bench but always looked prepared to put himself about whenever he was given the chance. He scored his first Premiership goal in the 3-0 win at Middlesbrough in November, and after missing out for England U21s in Italy when he was in the squad for the abandoned fixture, he won his first cap in the end-of-season friendly against Mexico. A promising young striker he will have benefited from his limited taste of Premiership football and will be looking to challenge for a regular place next term.
Cambridge U (From trainee on 21/2/1997) FL 96+27/35 FLC 7+3/4 FAC 9+1/5 Others 3/2
Leicester C (£1,000,000 + on 14/7/2000) PL 7+14/1 FLC 0+1 FAC 1+2

BENNETT Dean Alan
Born: Wolverhampton, 13 December 1977
Height: 5'10" Weight: 11.0
Club Honours: NC '00
International Honours: E: SP-1

Dean featured regularly in the centre of the park for Football League newcomers Kidderminster. He took time to settle in to the higher level required and was one of several players transfer listed in January but responded positively by raising his game. A lively midfielder, his strength lies in his ability to pick up the ball from deep and run at opposition defenders.
West Bromwich A (Free from Aston Villa juniors on 19/12/1996) FL 0+1 (Free to Bromsgrove Rov on 14/9/98)
Kidderminster Hrs (£30,000 on 29/1/1999) FL 35+7/4 FLC 2 FAC 1+2 Others 1

BENNETT Ian Michael
Born: Worksop, 10 October 1971
Height: 6'0" Weight: 12.10
Club Honours: Div 2 '95; AMC '95

Ian was first-choice 'keeper for Birmingham City throughout the 2000-01 campaign when he missed just one senior game. He made his 300th appearance for the club in the Worthington Cup final against Liverpool and although he saved Dietmar Hamann's penalty in the decisive shoot-out he was unable to prevent the Blues' going down to defeat. A fine shot stopper with good reflexes and quick foot movement, he also showed he is no slouch on the ground.
Newcastle U (From trainee at Queens Park R on 20/3/1989)
Peterborough U (Free on 22/3/1991) FL 72 FLC 10 FAC 3 Others 4
Birmingham C (£325,000 on 17/12/1993) FL 253 FLC 36 FAC 15 Others 13

Tom Bennett

BENNETT Thomas (Tom) McNeill
Born: Falkirk, 12 December 1969
Height: 5'11" Weight: 11.8

Having enjoyed two successful loan spells at Walsall in the 1999-2000 season Tom joined the Saddlers on a permanent basis in the summer and immediately took over as club captain. Despite being held back by a persistent groin strain he was inspirational in driving his side forward and he contributed six goals including a great drive in the win against Brentford. A classy midfield player who tackles hard and passes the ball intelligently he played a major role for the club in the play-offs and it was his in-swinging corner that led to the goal which set the Saddlers on their way to victory in the semi-final against Stoke.

Aston Villa (From apprentice on 16/12/1987)
Wolverhampton W (Free on 5/7/1988) FL 103+12/2 FLC 7 FAC 5+2 Others 3+1
Stockport Co (£75,000 on 23/6/1995) FL 105+5/5 FLC 20/2 FAC 10 Others 6+1
Walsall (Loaned on 30/12/1999) FL 4/1
Walsall (Free on 23/3/2000) FL 41+4/7 FLC 1+1 FAC 2 Others 3

BENNION Christopher (Chris)
Born: Edinburgh, 30 August 1980
Height: 6'2" Weight: 12.2

Having coming up through the ranks at Middlesbrough this aspiring young 'keeper was loaned out to Shelbourne at the beginning of the 2000-01 campaign before being recalled to the Riverside to receive his first taste of senior action in a Worthington Cup tie against Macclesfield Town. With several more senior players ahead of him in the pecking order at the Riverside he was released in the summer.

Middlesbrough (From trainee on 5/7/1999) FLC 1

BENT Marcus Nathan
Born: Hammersmith, 19 May 1978
Height: 6'2" Weight: 12.4
International Honours: E: U21-2

Marcus began the 2000-01 season on top form for Sheffield United, scoring a Worthington Cup hat-trick against Lincoln and netting twice in the First Division game against Tranmere. However the goals then dried up and despite some effective approach play he struggled to find the net. In November he was sold to Blackburn Rovers where he featured regularly, netting a stunning equaliser at Norwich on New Year's Day. A deceptively fast striker he is very good in the air, adept at finding space in the box and able to create opportunities for others with his running.

Brentford (From trainee on 21/7/1995) FL 56+14/8 FLC 7/1 FAC 8/3 Others 5+1/1
Crystal Palace (£150,000 + on 8/1/1998) P/FL 13+15/5 FLC 0+2 FAC 0+1
Port Vale (£375,000 on 15/1/1999) FL 17+6/1 FLC 1
Sheffield U (£300,000 on 28/10/1999) FL 48/20 FLC 5/3 FAC 3/1
Blackburn Rov (£1,300,000 + on 24/11/2000) FL 21+7/8 FAC 5+1/3

BERESFORD David
Born: Middleton, 11 November 1976
Height: 5'5" Weight: 11.4
International Honours: E: Yth; Sch

David started the 2000-01 campaign on the fringes of the Huddersfield Town squad and in September he joined Port Vale on loan making his debut in the local 'derby' at home to Stoke City. He subsequently kept his place for the next three matches but all were lost by Vale without a goal being scored and he returned to the McAlpine Stadium. He made just one further appearance as a substitute on his return and did not feature at all in the first team after October. A speedy little right winger, he is full of tricks and crosses the ball accurately.

Oldham Ath (From trainee on 22/7/1994) P/FL 32+32/2 FLC 3+3 FAC 0+1 Others 3
Swansea C (Loaned on 11/8/1995) FL 4+2
Huddersfield T (£350,000 on 27/3/1997) FL 24+11/3 FLC 2+3 FAC 1+1
Preston NE (Loaned on 17/12/1999) FL 1+3 FAC 0+1 Others 1
Port Vale (Loaned on 15/9/2000) FL 4

BERESFORD Marlon
Born: Lincoln, 2 September 1969
Height: 6'1" Weight: 13.6

Marlon again failed to make a significant breakthrough at Middlesbrough last season and received his only senior action when he came on from the subs' bench in the home game against Arsenal in November after Mark Crossley had been sent off. Later in the season he returned to his first professional club Sheffield Wednesday to cover for an injury crisis, but the Owls lost all four games that he appeared in and there was no attempt to pursue a permanent move. Marlon is a competent shot stopper with excellent distribution but will be hoping for more regular first-team action in the coming season.

Sheffield Wed (From trainee on 23/9/1987)
Bury (Loaned on 25/8/1989) FL 1
Northampton T (Loaned on 27/9/1990) FL 13 Others 2
Crewe Alex (Loaned on 28/2/1991) FL 3
Northampton T (Loaned on 15/8/1991) FL 15
Burnley (£95,000 on 28/8/1992) FL 240 FLC 18 FAC 20 Others 16
Middlesbrough (£500,000 on 10/3/1998) P/FL 8+1 FLC 3
Sheffield Wed (Loaned on 12/1/2000) FL 4

BERG Henning
Born: Eidsvell, Norway, 1 September 1969
Height: 6'0" Weight: 12.7
Club Honours: PL '95, '99, '00
International Honours: Norway: 82; U21

Facing something of a make-or-break season in his career at Manchester United, Henning made just a single appearance for the Reds when he came on from the subs' bench in the Premiership game against West Ham in August before rejoining his former club Blackburn Rovers in a three-month loan deal at the beginning of the following month. Quickly establishing himself at Ewood Park, he was very much the man that made it all happen for Rovers. A near ever-present he dominated at the back, and after signing permanently in December he guided the team to promotion back to the top flight. A competitive centre half he rarely lost out in physical encounters and was always involved in the action supporting his colleagues and imposing his will on opposition strikers. He was selected for the PFA's First Division representative team in April.

Blackburn Rov (£400,000 from Lillestrom, Norway, ex VIF, on 26/1/1993) PL 154+5/4 FLC 16 FAC 10 Others 9
Manchester U (£5,000,000 on 12/8/1997) PL 49+17/2 FLC 3 FAC 7 Others 22+5/1
Blackburn Rov (£1,750,000 on 8/9/2000) FL 41/1 FLC 1 FAC 3

BERGER Patrik
Born: Prague, Czechoslovakia, 10 November 1973
Height: 6'1" Weight: 12.6
Club Honours: FAC '01; UEFAC '01
International Honours: Czech Republic: 41; Czechoslovakia: 2; Yth (UEFA-U16 '90)

After enjoying his best season to date for Liverpool in 1999-2000 Patrik spent much of last term on the sidelines with an ankle injury. On his return to the team in September he played in seven games scoring in the 4-0 victory at Derby and the Anfield 'derby' game against Everton, but just as he was getting back to his best the injury flared up again at Leeds and he flew out to the United States for corrective surgery. His second comeback coincided with Liverpool's finest display of the season, the 2-0 victory over deadly rivals Manchester United at the end of March. He remained a regular in the squad until the end of the season featuring from the subs' bench in both the FA and UEFA Cup Finals and it was his delightfully weighted through ball that set Michael Owen free for his winning goal in the game at Cardiff.

Liverpool (£3,250,000 from Borussia Dortmund, Germany, ex Slavia Prague, on 15/8/1996) PL 94+31/27 FLC 8+2/2 FAC 4+3 Others 16+3/4

BERGERSEN Kent
Born: Oslo, Norway, 8 February 1967
Height: 5'10" Weight: 10.8

Kent spent the 2000 close summer playing on loan in Norway for Moss FK but on his return to Stockport County he failed to establish himself in the first-team line-up. A fractured bone in his foot sidelined him in December but after returning for a single appearance from the subs' bench at Nottingham Forest he left Edgeley Park in April and signed again for Moss. He is a popular midfield player who despite a certain lack of pace causes problems for defenders down either flank thanks to his close control and sharp brain.

Raith Rov (Signed from Valerengen, Norway on 29/11/1996) SL 6/1 (Free to Panionios, Greece on 16/1/1997)
Stockport Co (Free from Stromsgodset, Norway on 10/9/1999) FL 18+8/1 FAC 1

BERGKAMP Dennis
Born: Amsterdam, Holland, 18 May 1969
Height: 6'0" Weight: 12.5
Club Honours: PL '98; CS '98
International Honours: Holland: 79; U21

Dennis started the 2000-01 campaign on the bench at Arsenal but when fully fit he was invariably included in the starting line-up, however his campaign was again hampered by a string of minor injuries and he flitted in and out of the team. Despite his fear of flying and his non-appearance in the Champions League away games, Dennis's best moments occurred in this competition. He put in a sublime performance against Lazio at Highbury setting up both goals for Freddie Ljungberg in an impressive victory and also scored a memorable effort against Lyon to earn the Gunners a valuable point. A very talented striker with the ability to score and create goals from nothing, Dennis called time on an impressive international career after Euro 2000, finishing with 36 goals in 79 appearances. He pledged to see his career out at Highbury midway through

Dennis Bergkamp (right) and Danny Higginbotham

the season, thus ending a long-running contract saga.

Arsenal (£7,500,000 from Inter Milan, Italy, ex Ajax, on 3/7/1995) PL 159+13/60 FLC 14/8 FAC 20+1/8 Others 20+2/7

BERGSSON Gudni
Born: Reykjavik, Iceland, 21 July 1965
Height: 6'1" Weight: 12.3
Club Honours: Div 1 '97
International Honours: Iceland: 77; U21-4; Yth

'The Iceman' continued to defy his advancing years at Bolton last term and was again a rock at the heart of the defence. Although at times he held the right-back position, he mostly stood tall as a central defender, marshalling the defence superbly. He really came into his own when Colin Hendry arrived, and while this pairing may have been the oldest in the First Division by some distance, they were surely also one of the best. Gudni also had a marvellous goal-scoring record, notching eight goals in the regular season and another two in the play-offs. His importance to the team was recognised when he was deservedly voted as the Wanderers' 'Player of the Year'.

Tottenham H (£100,000 from Valur, Iceland on 15/12/1988) F/PL 51+20/2 FLC 4+2 FAC 2+2 Others 5+1
Bolton W (£115,000 on 21/3/1995) P/FL 202+7/21 FLC 23+2/1 FAC 10 Others 8+2/2

Gudni Bergsson

BERHALTER Gregg
Born: Tenafly, New Jersey, USA, 1 August 1973
Height: 6'1" Weight: 12.7
International Honours: United States: 21

This experienced USA international defender had a number of trials with English clubs following his release by Cambuur in the 2000 close season but it was not until well into the new year that he linked up with Crystal Palace. He made a couple of appearances in the starting line-up but spent most of his time on the subs' bench. A regular for the USA international squad he assisted with their campaign to qualify for the 2002 World Cup finals.

Crystal Palace (Free from Cambuur, Holland, ex University of North Carolina, FC Zwolle, Sparta Rotterdam, on 16/2/2001) FL 4+1

BERKLEY Austin James
Born: Dartford, 28 January 1973
Height: 5'10" Weight: 11.6

Austin joined Barnet in the summer of 2000 and impressed for the Bees in pre-season matches. However persistent ankle problems then kept him out of the side and he was restricted to just two outings in the LDV Vans Trophy ties against Rushden and Peterborough. An exciting winger with some neat touches he will be looking to find first-team football on a regular basis in 2001-02. He was placed on the open to offers list in the summer.

Gillingham (From trainee on 13/5/1991) FL 0+3 Others 0+3
Swindon T (Free on 16/5/1992) FL 0+1 FLC 0+1 Others 3+1/1
Shrewsbury T (Free on 29/7/1995) FL 152+20/12 FLC 5+2 FAC 6+1 Others 12+1/1
Barnet (Free on 4/7/2000) Others 1+1

BERKOVIC Eyal
Born: Haifa, Israel, 2 April 1972
Height: 5'7" Weight: 10.6
Club Honours: SLC '00
International Honours: Israel: 71; U21

Although he netted an early hat-trick for Celtic in the UEFA qualifying match against Jeunesse Esch, Eyal rarely featured under new boss Martin O'Neill and early in the new year Blackburn manager Graham Souness brought him on loan to Ewood Park. He remained on the bench for a time as Souness had no wish to upset the balance of a successful team but he produced a masterly display at Grimsby, when he took the opportunity of a rare start to dominate the game and headed the second goal for Rovers. An experienced midfield play maker his quick feet, perpetual seeking of the ball and ability to flick the telling pass without effort more than compensate for deficiencies in winning the ball.

Southampton (Loaned from Maccabi Tel Aviv, Israel on 11/10/1996) PL 26+2/4 FLC 5+1/2 FAC 1
West Ham U (£1,700,000 on 30/7/1997) PL 62+3/10 FLC 6 FAC 7+1/2
Glasgow Celtic (£5,500,000 on 20/7/1999) SL 29+3/9 SLC 0+2 SC 1 Others 3+3
Blackburn Rov (Loaned on 9/2/2001) FL 4+7/2 FAC 3

Eyal Berkovic

BERNARD Narada Michael
Born: Bristol, 30 January 1981
Height: 5'2" Weight: 10.5
Narada featured regularly in the Arsenal U19 Academy team in 1999-2000 before moving on to Second Division Bournemouth in the close season. He went on to make his senior debut for the Cherries in the FA Cup tie against Swansea and enjoyed a short run in the first-team squad in the new year. A promising youngster he can play either at left back or on the left-hand side of midfield. Narada is the son of a former Bristol rugby union player and was named after 1970s soul star Narada Michael Walden.
Arsenal (From trainee at Tottenham H on 9/7/1999)
Bournemouth (Free on 31/7/2000) FL 6+8 FAC 1 Others 2

BERNARD Olivier
Born: Paris, France, 14 October 1979
Height: 5'9" Weight: 12.6
Olivier joined Newcastle United last October and after playing a handful of games for the reserves he moved on loan to Darlington to gain some first-team experience. He was unfortunately injured on his debut at York City but when he returned to action his class shone through. His clever footwork and penetrating runs down the left flank were a joy to watch and his keenness to push forward was rewarded with a goal against Shrewsbury Town at Feethams when he slotted home inside the six-yard box: not a position normally associated with a left back!
Newcastle U (Signed from Lyon, France, on 26/10/2000)
Darlington (Loaned on 13/3/2001) FL 9+1/2

BERRY Trevor John
Born: Haslemere, 1 August 1974
Height: 5'7" Weight: 11.2
Club Honours: AMC '96
International Honours: E: Yth
An old-fashioned right-winger, Trevor was unable to carve out a regular first-team place at Rotherham last season mainly because the club employed a formation that used three strikers. The majority of his appearances were as a substitute but he showed a willingness to fill in anywhere by playing as a striker when required. He subsequently joined Scunthorpe on loan in February where he featured on either flank or just behind the front two. He scored a great equaliser against Southend but with the club set to extend his loan into a second month he tore a hamstring at Torquay at the beginning of March and this ruled him out for the rest of the season. His talent on the ball and pace and directness make him a difficult opponent for lower division defenders.
Aston Villa (£50,000 from trainee at Bournemouth on 3/4/1992)
Rotherham U (£20,000 on 8/9/1995) FL 126+47/20 FLC 3+3 FAC 9+4/3 Others 9+3/1
Scunthorpe U (Loaned on 9/2/2001) FL 6/1

BERTOS Leonida (Leo) Christos
Born: Wellington, New Zealand, 20 December 1981
Height: 6'0" Weight: 12.6
International Honours: New Zealand: Sch
A former New Zealand Secondary Schools international, Leo played senior football for Wellington Olympic before turning up at Barnsley last season and asking for a trial. He signed professional forms for the Tykes at the beginning of September and after doing well in the U19 and reserve teams he stepped up to make his Football League debut against Preston towards the end of the campaign. An attacking midfield player he performed extremely well in a variety of roles in the club's junior teams and thoroughly deserved his chance of senior football. The club feel he has a big future and he signed a contract that tied him to Oakwell until the summer of 2003.
Barnsley (Signed from Wellington Olympic, New Zealand on 1/9/2000) FL 0+2

BESWETHERICK Jonathan (Jon) Barry
Born: Liverpool, 15 January 1978
Height: 5'11" Weight: 11.4
Jon was first choice at left back for Plymouth Argyle last season when he made more first team appearances than any other player at the club. He is tenacious in the tackle and is effective pushing forward down the left flank from where he delivers dangerous crosses that often lead to goal-scoring opportunities. Jon has now played over 100 games for the Pilgrims but although he came close on a number of occasions he is still looking to score his first senior goal.
Plymouth Arg (From trainee on 27/7/1996) FL 106+8 FLC 3 FAC 13 Others 3

BETSY Kevin Eddie Lewis
Born: Seychelles, 20 March 1978
Height: 6'1" Weight: 11.12
International Honours: E: SP-1
Another season on the fringe of the Fulham side saw this talented youngster make five appearances in league matches and a further two in the Worthington Cup. Kevin played most of his football in the club's successful reserve team for whom he netted seven goals in 16 games. At first-team level he was tried as both a right-sided and central midfielder and certainly did not let anyone down when he appeared in the team.
Fulham (£80,000 + from Woking on 16/9/1998) FL 3+11/1 FLC 2+1 FAC 0+1 Others 1
Bournemouth (Loaned on 3/9/1999) FL 1+4
Hull C (Loaned on 26/11/1999) FL 1+1 Others 1

BETTNEY Christopher (Chris) John
Born: Chesterfield, 27 October 1977
Height: 5'10" Weight: 11.4
After signing non-contract forms for Macclesfield during the 2000 close season Chris made only two short appearances from the subs' bench. However, after failing to impress sufficiently to earn a full-time contract he was released by Macc at the start of last October. He subsequently linked up with former England star Chris Waddle at Unibond League club Worksop Town.
Sheffield U (From trainee on 15/5/1996) FL 0+1
Hull C (Loaned on 26/9/1997) FL 28+2/1 FLC 2 Others 1
Chesterfield (Free on 3/7/1999) FL 7+6 FLC 3
Rochdale (Free on 5/11/1999) FL 12+12 FAC 0+1 Others 3+2
Macclesfield T (Free on 24/7/2000) FL 0+2

BETTS Robert
Born: Doncaster, 21 December 1981
Height: 5'10" Weight: 11.0
A former captain of the Coventry City youth team Robert spent much of last term in the reserves, before moving on loan to Plymouth Argyle to gain further experience of first-team football. He played in three senior games and one from the subs' bench for the Third Division club producing some impressive displays before returning to Highfield Road where he made a further senior appearance when he came off the subs' bench for the last 10 minutes of the final game against Bradford City. A tenacious young midfield player he is the grandson of former Manchester United wing half Maurice Setters.
Doncaster Rov (Trainee) FL 2+1
Coventry C (From trainee on 23/12/1998) PL 0+3
Plymouth Arg (Loaned on 16/2/2001) FL 3+1

BHUTIA Bhaichung
Born: Gangtok, Sikkim, India, 15 December 1976
Height: 5'8" Weight: 10.2
International Honours: India: 46
Bhaichung had a very mixed time at Bury in 2000-01. He began the season as a regular in the line-up and netted a superb goal in the 2-1 win at Rotherham in August but then seemed to lose his form and dropped out the side. In January he returned in a free midfield role operating just behind the front two strikers and produced some excellent performances, but he received few opportunities after the arrival of Jon Newby and Colin Cramb and he eventually returned to India on international duty at the end of March. He won a further six caps for his

country during the season, netting goals in the World Cup qualifiers against Yemen and Brunei.
Bury (Signed from East Bengal, India on 29/9/1999) FL 17+17/3 FLC 2 FAC 2+3 Others 2

BIDSTRUP Stefan
Born: Helsingoer, Denmark, 24 February 1975
Height: 6'2 Weight: 13.6
Stefan joined Wigan Athletic last November in the Danish mid-season break, making his debut from the subs' bench against Cambridge shortly afterwards and then scoring on his first start in the FA Cup tie against non-league Dorchester. However he failed to win a regular place after manager Bruce Rioch departed and at the end of the campaign his contract was cancelled by mutual agreement. He subsequently returned to Denmark where he signed for AaB Aalborg. Stefan is a left-sided midfielder with an excellent work rate who likes to push forward to assist the attack.
Wigan Ath (£450,000 from Lyngby, Denmark on 10/11/2000) FL 10+5/2 FAC 2/1

BIGNOT Marcus
Born: Birmingham, 22 August 1974
Height: 5'10" Weight: 11.2
International Honours: E: SP-1
Marcus joined Bristol Rovers in August 2000 and scored his first-ever senior goal in only his second match for his new club in the 2-1 Worthington Cup victory at Plymouth. He followed this up with a goal for the Pirates after just 27 seconds against Bristol City at Ashton Gate, setting a new record for the quickest strike in a Bristol 'derby'. One of the most consistent players for Rovers during the season he subsequently followed his old manager Ian Holloway to Queens Park Rangers. Having initially appeared as a right wing back for the Loftus Road club he later switched to a central midfield role where his ball-winning talents were much in evidence.
Crewe Alex (£150,000 + from Kidderminster Hrs on 1/9/1997) FL 93+2 FLC 8 FAC 3
Bristol Rov (Free on 7/8/2000) FL 26/1 FLC 5/2 FAC 1 Others 3
Queens Park R (Signed on 16/3/2001) FL 8+1/1

BILLY Christopher (Chris) Anthony
Born: Huddersfield, 2 January 1973
Height: 5'11" Weight: 11.8
Chris had a fine season for Bury in 2000-01, when he was an ever-present in Second Division matches and showed some excellent form. Once again used in a variety of positions he featured at right back, in midfield and occasionally as a central defender during the campaign. A hard working player who always gave 100 per cent effort he was voted 'Player of the Season' by the Shakers' supporters, but was out of contract in the summer and his future was uncertain at the time of writing.
Huddersfield T (From trainee on 1/7/1991) FL 76+18/4 FLC 8+2 FAC 5 Others 15+2/2
Plymouth Arg (Signed on 10/8/1995) FL 107+11/9 FLC 5 FAC 8/1 Others 5+1
Notts Co (Free on 2/7/1998) FL 3+3 FLC 2
Bury (Free on 17/9/1998) FL 113+6/4 FLC 3 FAC 6/1 Others 1+1

BIMSON Stuart James
Born: Liverpool, 29 September 1969
Height: 5'11" Weight: 11.12
A calf injury caused Stuart to miss out after starting the season as Lincoln's left back. He then suffered a stress fracture of the foot and was only restored to the first team at the beginning of March. The change of management at Sincil Bank saw him become a first choice with his ball playing skills fitting the new style adopted by the team.
Bury (£12,500 from Macclesfield T on 6/2/1995) FL 36 FLC 5 Others 3
Lincoln C (Free on 29/11/1996) FL 82+16/3 FAC 5+1 Others 8+1/1

BIRCH Gary Stephen
Born: Birmingham, 8 October 1981
Height: 5'10" Weight: 11.6
This promising young Walsall striker netted a fine 25-yarder on his debut in senior football for the Saddlers against Wigan in an LDV Vans Trophy tie last January. He subsequently moved on loan to Exeter City in March and did well in his spell with the Devon club, scoring two goals and quickly becoming a favourite with the club's fans. Enthusiastic, quick and skilful, Gary has a good eye for goal and is always looking to punish defenders.
Walsall (From trainee on 31/10/1998) Others 2/1
Exeter C (Loaned on 22/3/2001) FL 6+3/2

BIRCH Mark
Born: Stoke, 5 January 1977
Height: 5'10" Weight: 12.5
This former Stoke trainee joined Carlisle United in August 2000 and went on to become a near ever-present in his first season of Third Division football. Although he understandably looked a little raw early in the campaign, he grew in confidence as the season progressed and gave a particularly outstanding display in March against Leyton Orient when he was moved into a midfield role. Mark is a promising young wing back who will be looking to build on this impressive foundation in 2001-02.
Stoke C (From trainee on 8/7/1995. Free to Northwich Vic on 22/7/98)
Carlisle U (£10,000 on 10/8/2000) FL 44 FLC 2 FAC 3 Others 1

BIRCHAM Marc Stephen John
Born: Wembley, 11 May 1978
Height: 5'10" Weight: 12.4
Club Honours: Div 2 '01
International Honours: Canada: 13; U23-1
Marc took some time to recover from an injury suffered back in February 2000 and was only used sparingly by Millwall at the start of the 2000-01 campaign. He then went down with a bout of tonsillitis before injuries and suspensions to others allowed him back in the team. When fit he produced some excellent performances and captained the team on a number of occasions. He is a hard-working central midfield player with some creative touches who can also play at full back. Marc again featured for Canada at international level, winning a further three caps.
Millwall (From trainee on 22/5/1996) FL 64+16/3 FLC 3+1 FAC 5+1/1 Others 5+1

Marc Bircham

BIRD Anthony (Tony)
Born: Cardiff, 1 September 1974
Height: 5'10" Weight: 12.8
Club Honours: Div 3 '00
International Honours: W: U21-8; Yth
Tony linked up with his old boss Jan Molby when he signed for Kidderminster in July 2000 and impressed in the pre-season scoring seven times in eight games. However when the campaign kicked-off in earnest the goals dried up and it took until April before he registered a league goal. One of several players transfer-listed in January, he eventually forced his way back into the team in a new role in midfield where he added a physical presence to the side.
Cardiff C (From trainee on 4/8/1993) FL 44+31/13 FLC 8/2 FAC 4+1/1 Others 12+4/3 (Free to Barry T in January 1996)
Swansea C (£40,000 on 8/8/1997) FL 51+35/18 FLC 5+2/1 FAC 2+1 Others 3+3/3
Kidderminster Hrs (Free on 14/7/2000) FL 16+9/1 FLC 2 FAC 1+1/1 Others 1+1/1

BIRMINGHAM David Paul
Born: Portsmouth, 16 April 1981
Height: 5'6" Weight: 10.0
After recovering from long-term injury problems, David did well with Portsmouth reserves in the early part of the 2000-01 campaign and made a further senior appearance from the subs' bench in the Worthington Cup tie at Blackburn. He was subsequently loaned to Ryman League club Bognor Regis Town in December before his contract was cancelled by mutual consent and he then joined Bournemouth on non-contract forms for the closing weeks of the season, although he made no first-team appearances for the Cherries. A young defender with some potential he is quick, hard working and courageous in the tackle.
Portsmouth (From trainee at Bournemouth on 4/8/1999) FL 1+1 FLC 0+1

BISCAN Igor
Born: Yugoslavia, 4 May 1978
Height: 6'3" Weight: 12.8
Club Honours: FLC '01
International Honours: Croatia: 12
Liverpool manager Gerard Houllier signed Igor in December following injuries to both Patrik Berger and Dieter Hamann that left the Reds a bit thin on resources in midfield. After debuting as substitute at home to Ipswich he made the starting line-up for the Worthington Cup tie at home to Fulham and then played a part in the stunning victories over Manchester United and Arsenal operating in central midfield alongside Steve Gerrard. After enjoying a run in the team he lost his regular place as other players came back to fitness and was selected only intermittently after February, missing out in the climactic closing weeks of the season. It is far too early to pass judgement on Igor but he will have a tough job to win a regular place for the Reds in the coming season.
Liverpool (£3,500,000 from Dynamo Zagreb, Croatia, ex Samobar, on 7/12/2000) PL 8+5 FLC 4/1 FAC 3+1

BISHOP Ian William
Born: Liverpool, 29 May 1965
Height: 5'9" Weight: 10.12
International Honours: E: B-1
Ian rarely featured for Manchester City last term and it was not until September that he made his first senior appearance of the season coming off the subs' bench in the 1-1 draw with Middlesbrough. He scored his only goal in the Worthington Cup tie against Wimbledon and made his final appearance for City from the bench in the FA Cup victory over Birmingham before crossing the Atlantic to join MLS club Miami Fusion. An influential midfield player, he always seems to be able to calm things down in the centre of the park and has the ability to pick out his colleagues with some thoughtful passing.
Everton (From apprentice on 24/5/1983) FL 0+1
Crewe Alex (Loaned on 22/3/1984) FL 4
Carlisle U (£15,000 on 11/10/1984) FL 131+1/14 FLC 8/1 FAC 5/1 Others 4
Bournemouth (£35,000 on 14/7/1988) FL 44/2 FLC 4 FAC 5 Others 1
Manchester C (£465,000 on 2/8/1989) FL 18+1/2 FLC 4/1 Others 1
West Ham U (£500,000 on 28/12/1989) F/PL 240+14/12 FLC 21+1/1 FAC 22+1/3 Others 4+1/1
Manchester C (Free on 26/3/1998) P/FL 53+25/2 FLC 4+5 FAC 3+2/2 Others 0+1

BJORNEBYE Stig Inge
Born: Elverum, Norway, 11 December 1969
Height: 5'10" Weight: 11.9
Club Honours: FLC '95
International Honours: Norway: 76; B-1; U21; Yth
Despite his vast experience in the game Stig Inge took time to find his feet in the First Division with Blackburn last term and it was a while before he settled down in the left-back position. A solid defender who is a great positional player, he tackles strongly and is a calming influence on the back line. His attacking strengths were less in evidence but he used the ball with care and produced some exceptional crosses with his left foot.
Liverpool (£600,000 from Rosenborg, Norway, ex Strommen, Kongsvinger, on 18/12/1992) PL 132+7/2 FLC 16 FAC 11+2 Others 16/2
Blackburn Rov (£300,000 on 28/6/2000) FL 30+3/1 FLC 2 FAC 2+1

BLACK Kingsley Terence
Born: Luton, 22 June 1968
Height: 5'9" Weight: 11.2
Club Honours: FLC '88; FMC '92; AMC '98
International Honours: E: Sch. NI: 30; B-3; U21-1
Kingsley had a disappointing time at Grimsby in the 2000-01 campaign, for after featuring several times early on he fell out of favour following a change of management. He moved on loan to Lincoln City in October where he linked up once again with his old boss Alan Buckley and proved an asset to the Imps on the left flank with his accurate crosses and set-piece balls giving a good service to the front men. He subsequently returned to Blundell Park when his four-week loan expired but spent the remainder of the campaign in the reserves. He was reported to have signed a two-year contract for the Imps in May following his release by the Mariners.
Luton T (From juniors on 7/7/1986) FL 123+4/26 FLC 16+2/1 FAC 5+1/2 Others 3+2/1
Nottingham F (£1,500,000 on 2/9/1991) F/PL 80+18/14 FLC 19+1/5 FAC 4 Others 4+2/1
Sheffield U (Loaned on 2/3/1995) FL 8+3/2
Millwall (Loaned on 29/9/1995) FL 1+2/1 FLC 0+1
Grimsby T (£25,000 on 16/7/1996) FL 91+50/8 FLC 14+2 FAC 5+2 Others 2+5/1
Lincoln C (Loaned on 13/10/2000) FL 5

BLACK Michael James
Born: Chigwell, 6 October 1976
Height: 5'8" Weight: 11.8
Club Honours: FAYC '94
International Honours: E: Sch
Unable to get a game at Tranmere, Michael joined Southend United on loan last December and the move was made permanent shortly afterwards. A quick and skilful winger he scored his first goal for the Blues in the 2-1 defeat at Kidderminster last February. Michael was released on a free transfer in the summer. He is the elder brother of Tommy Black.
Arsenal (From trainee on 1/7/1995) Others 0+1
Millwall (Loaned on 3/10/1997) FL 13/2 Others 1
Tranmere Rov (Free on 14/7/1999) FL 7+15 FLC 1+4/1
Southend U (Free on 29/12/2000) FL 10+5/1 Others 1

BLACK Thomas (Tommy) Robert
Born: Chigwell, 26 November 1979
Height: 5'7" Weight: 11.4
Tommy joined Crystal Palace from Arsenal in the summer of 2000 along with another young player Julian Gray shortly before Steve Coppell departed as manager. He was mostly used on the wide right-side of midfield where his pace and ability to deliver accurate crosses proved most effective. His performances soon made him a crowd favourite and he was rarely absent from the first-team squad throughout last season. Tommy is the brother of Southend's Michael Black.
Arsenal (From trainee on 3/7/1998) PL 0+1 FLC 1
Carlisle U (Loaned on 25/8/1999) FL 5/1
Bristol C (Loaned on 17/12/1999) FL 4
Crystal Palace (£250,000 + on 21/7/2000) FL 30+10/4 FLC 8/1 FAC 0+1

BLACKWELL Dean Robert
Born: Camden, 5 December 1969
Height: 6'1" Weight: 12.7
International Honours: E: U21-6
Dean scored the goal that nobody saw and in the end never counted when he netted in the fog-bound FA Cup tie for Wimbledon against Notts County before the match was abandoned. This seemed to sum up a frustrating season for him as he was sidelined for long periods with groin and achilles injuries and was only fit to take his place in the side for a short time. A strong towering central defender whose positional play is second to none he will be hoping for a return to fitness in 2001-02 so that he can resume his formidable partnership with Mark Williams at the heart of the Dons' defence.
Wimbledon (From trainee on 7/7/1988) F/PL 180+25/1 FLC 20 FAC 23+1 Others 1
Plymouth Arg (Loaned on 15/3/1990) FL 5+2

BLACKWOOD Michael Andrew
Born: Birmingham, 30 September 1979
Height: 5'10" Weight: 11.10
Michael joined Wrexham during the 2000 summer break and appeared in the line up for the opening match of the season against Bristol City but picked up a cartilage injury which required surgery. It was not until March that he returned to full fitness and he then featured mostly from the subs' bench. He is a very promising wide left-sided midfield player but was nevertheless released on a free transfer in the summer.
Aston Villa (From trainee on 14/4/1998)
Chester C (Loaned on 3/9/1999) FL 9/2
Wrexham (Free on 18/7/2000) FL 3+12 FAC 0+1

BLAKE Mark Antony
Born: Nottingham, 16 December 1970
Height: 5'11" Weight: 13.0
International Honours: E: U21-9; Yth; Sch
This experienced player proved to be a mainstay in the centre of the park for the Stags' last season, although his form was a little inconsistent at times. He chipped in with some very useful goals throughout the campaign including an amazing 40-yard lob over the Barnet 'keepers' head in the 3-3 draw at Underhill last August. A hard-tackling midfielder he was released on a free transfer in May.
Aston Villa (From trainee on 1/7/1989) FL 26+5/2 FLC 1+1 FAC 2 Others 2
Wolverhampton W (Loaned on 17/1/1991) FL 2
Portsmouth (£400,000 on 5/8/1993) FL 15 Others 4+1
Leicester C (£360,000 on 24/3/1994) P/FL 42+7/4 FLC 4 Others 3
Walsall (Free on 23/8/1996) FL 51+10/5 FLC 2 FAC 0+4 Others 2+2/1
Mansfield T (Free on 13/8/1999) FL 78+6/9 FLC 4 FAC 3/1 Others 3

BLAKE Nathan Alexander
Born: Cardiff, 27 January 1972
Height: 5'11" Weight: 13.2
Club Honours: WC '92, '93; Div 3 '93, Div 1 '97
International Honours: W: 20; B-1; U21-5; Yth

With his future at Ewood Park apparently in some doubt Nathan arrived for pre-season training in great shape and in fine form, to such an extent that he became a first-choice striker for Blackburn last term. He scored regularly but now added a degree of bite up front, a feature that had often been missing from his play in previous seasons. He established a useful partnership with Matt Jansen but was then sidelined by an achilles injury that required surgery. He returned briefly in the new year only to be out of action again with a thigh problem and it was only towards the very end of the campaign that he returned, scoring on his comeback at Gillingham.

Cardiff C (From trainee at Chelsea on 20/8/1990) FL 113+18/35 FLC 6+2 FAC 10/4 Others 13+2/1
Sheffield U (£300,000 on 17/2/1994) P/FL 55+14/34 FLC 3+1/1 FAC 1 Others 1
Bolton W (£1,500,000 on 23/12/1995) F/PL 102+5/38 FLC 10+1/8 FAC 6/2
Blackburn Rov (£4,250,000 on 30/10/1998) P/FL 37+14/12 FLC 3/1 FAC 5+3/2

BLAKE Noel Lloyd George
Born: Jamaica, 12 January 1962
Height: 6'1" Weight: 14.2

Exeter City's manager, Noel only assumed defensive duties for a handful of games last season at a time when the Grecians were on a depressing run of games without a victory. A strong and powerful central defender his brief comeback was ended when he tore a thigh muscle in the 'derby' match against Torquay in January. Noel ultimately saw the Devon club to safety and was reported to have been offered a further 12-months contract at St James Park.

Aston Villa (Signed from Sutton Coldfield T on 1/8/1979) FL 4
Shrewsbury T (Loaned on 1/3/1982) FL 6
Birmingham C (£55,000 on 15/9/1982) FL 76/5 FLC 12 FAC 8
Portsmouth (£150,000 on 24/4/1984) FL 144/10 FLC 14/1 FAC 10/2 Others 5/1
Leeds U (Free on 4/7/1988) FL 51/4 FLC 4+1 FAC 2 Others 4
Stoke C (£175,000 on 9/2/1990) FL 74+1/3 FLC 6 FAC 3+1 Others 4+1
Bradford C (Loaned on 27/2/1992) FL 6
Bradford C (Free on 20/7/1992) FL 38+1/3 FLC 2+1 FAC 5/1 Others 4
Dundee (Free on 10/12/1993) SL 52+2/2 SLC 2 SC 5 Others 3
Exeter C (Free on 18/8/1995) FL 135+12/10 FLC 6 FAC 6 Others 3+2

BLAKE Robert (Robbie) James
Born: Middlesbrough, 4 March 1976
Height: 5'9" Weight: 12.6

Having scored twice for Bradford City in four pre-season Inter Toto outings, Robbie was loaned to Nottingham Forest for three months at the start of the 2000-01 campaign. He impressed early on at the City Ground scoring in the 4-3 win at Barnsley and there was talk of a permanent move but this fizzled out and he went back to Valley Parade at the end of November. He looked very sharp in reserve games on his return and was eventually called up for Premiership action, featuring either out wide on the right of midfield or up front as a striker which is his favoured position. A tricky player who loves taking on opponents, he is willing to shoot from any distance and netted four more goals for City during the season.

Darlington (From trainee on 1/7/1994) FL 54+14/21 FLC 4+2/1 FAC 3+1 Others 3+1/1
Bradford C (£300,000 on 27/3/1997) P/FL 90+37/30 FLC 5+3/2 FAC 6/1 Others 3+1/2
Nottingham F (Loaned on 22/8/2000) FL 9+2/1 FLC 1

BLATHERWICK Steven (Steve) Scott
Born: Hucknall, 20 September 1973
Height: 6'1" Weight: 14.6

Steve has grown in stature as a central defender under the tutelage of Chesterfield manager Nicky Law. Previously an effective and commanding defender he has added more steel, reads the game far better than before and is more able to supervise his fellow defenders. His trademark is a single buccaneering run every game towards the opponents' box that invariably causes panic and delights the Spireites fans. Steve was elected to the PFA's Division Three team.

Nottingham F (From trainee at Notts Co on 2/8/1992) FL 10 FLC 2 FAC 1 Others 2
Wycombe W (Loaned on 18/2/1994) FL 2 Others 1
Hereford U (Loaned on 11/9/1995) FL 10/1 Others 2
Reading (Loaned on 27/3/1997) FL 6+1
Burnley (£150,000 on 18/7/1997) FL 16+8 FLC 5 FAC 1+1 Others 3
Chesterfield (Loaned on 18/9/1998) FL 2
Chesterfield (£50,000 on 1/12/1998) FL 81+5/2 FLC 6 FAC 2 Others 7/2

BLATSIS Con
Born: Melbourne, Australia, 6 July 1977
Height: 6'3" Weight: 13.7
International Honours: Australia: 2; U23; Yth

This young Australian defender signed a three-year contract for Derby County last August having earlier taken part in the World Club Championships in Brazil for South Melbourne. He played on the right side of defence in the Rams' opening two games of 2000-01 before joining up with the Australian Olympic squad. His first-team opportunities at Pride Park were then restricted by injury and transfers-in, and in January he went on loan to Sheffield Wednesday. He looked solid in the centre of defence in his first few games at Hillsborough but failed to maintain his form and returned to Derby where he featured in the reserves' title winning squad. Con made his full international debut when coming on from the subs' bench for Australia against South Korea last October and then made the starting line-up for the trip to Colombia in February.

Derby Co (£150,000 from South Melbourne, Australia on 15/8/2000) PL 2
Sheffield Wed (Loaned on 29/12/2000) FL 6 FAC 2

BLEIDELIS Imants
Born: Latvia, 16 August 1975
Height: 5'10" Weight: 11.11
International Honours: Latvia: 50

Signed by former Southampton boss David Jones shortly before he left The Dell, Imants had to wait over a month for his work permit and immediately after his arrival there was a change in management at the club. He did well in the Saints' reserve team before stepping up to make his senior debut in the Worthington Cup tie at Mansfield last September. However his first-team opportunities under boss Glenn Hoddle were few and far between and it was not until February that he made his bow in the Premiership when he came on from the subs' bench against Bradford City. A full Latvian international he is a quick and dangerous right winger.

Southampton (£600,000 from Skonto Riga, Latvia on 10/2/2000) PL 0+1 FLC 1+1 FAC 0+1

BLOOMER Matthew (Matt) Brian
Born: Grimsby, 3 November 1978
Height: 6'0" Weight: 13.0

Matt was again kept on the fringe of the Grimsby Town squad last season as new boss Lennie Lawrence opted for experience in the fight against relegation. Generally restricted to reserve-team outings he always performed creditably when called up for first-team action. He had a lengthy spell on the sidelines with a foot injury in the second half of the campaign and was released in the summer reportedly joining Hull City soon afterwards. Matt is a young central defender who is from a well-known football family.

Grimsby T (From juniors on 3/7/1997) FL 3+9 FLC 0+2 Others 0+1

BLOOMER Robert (Bob) Stephen
Born: Sheffield, 21 June 1966
Height: 5'10" Weight: 12.7
Club Honours:FAT '98; NC '99

This experienced player made a handful of appearances for Cheltenham Town last season either at right back or in midfield before announcing his retirement at the end of the campaign. He played a key role for the Robins in the 0-0 draw at Watford in the Worthington Cup first round first leg and also scored a spectacular goal against Brighton. Having already passed his UEFA 'B' coaching badge he is to take charge of Cheltenham's youth team in the 2001-02 season. Earlier in the campaign he was rewarded with a benefit match against his old club Bristol Rovers.

Chesterfield (From juniors on 21/8/1985) FL 120+21/15 FLC 2+2 FAC 5+1 Others 9+1/1
Bristol Rov (£20,000 on 22/3/1990) FL 11+11
Cheltenham T (Free on 15/8/1992) FL 6+17/1 FLC 2+2 Others 1+1

BOA MORTE Luis Pereira
Born: Lisbon, Portugal, 4 August 1977
Height: 5'10" Weight: 11.5
Club Honours: PL '98; Div 1 '01; CS '98, '99
International Honours: Portugal: 2; U21; Yth

Luis joined Fulham on a full season's loan from Southampton last term and exceeded all expectations by scoring 21 goals for the first team. An exciting young striker, his

pace and ball control proved too much for most Division One defences. His performances won him a call up to the full Portugal international squad and he made his debut in the friendly with France in April. Luis was reported to have joined Fulham on a permanent basis in the summer.
Arsenal (£1,750,000 + from Sporting Lisbon, Portugal on 25/6/1997) PL 6+19 FLC 3/2 FAC 2+3/1 Others 2+4/1
Southampton (£500,000 + on 27/8/1999) PL 6+8/1 FLC 0+2 FAC 1
Fulham (Loaned on 31/7/2000) FL 21+18/18 FLC 5+1/3 FAC 1

BOATENG George
Born: Nkawkaw, Ghana, 5 September 1975
Height: 5'9" Weight: 11.7
International Honours: Holland: U21-18
George had an excellent season for Aston Villa in 2000-01 and apart from a brief spell out with an ankle injury he was an ever-present in the first team. He looked very comfortable in a central midfield role tackling fiercely and battling away in the centre of the park. However there is much more to his game than this, and he not only has a superb engine and a fine shot but he also has the ability to spray passes around the field to his colleagues. More inclined to lay the ball off rather than shoot himself he scored just once, netting in the 2-1 win at Leeds shortly before Christmas.
Coventry C (£250,000 from Feyenoord, Holland, ex Excelsior, on 19/12/1997) PL 43+4/5 FLC 3/1 FAC 8/1
Aston Villa (£4,500,000 on 22/7/1999) PL 59+7/3 FLC 8/1 FAC 8 Others 4

BOERTIEN Paul
Born: Haltwhistle, 21 January 1979
Height: 5'10" Weight: 11.2
This young left back did well in Derby County's reserves last season and earned a call-up for his Premiership debut against Sunderland in March as a replacement for the injured Seth Johnson. He gave an impressive performance that day and suspensions later on in the campaign meant he played a key role in the closing matches. He was particularly outstanding in the home game with Leicester when he scored a goal and was voted 'Man of the Match', and also in the vital game at Old Trafford.
Carlisle U (From trainee on 13/5/1997) FL 16+1/1 FLC 0+2 FAC 1 Others 1
Derby Co (£250,000 on 25/3/1999) PL 7+4/1 FLC 0+1 FAC 1+2
Crewe Alex (Loaned on 11/2/2000) FL 2

BOGARDE Winston
Born: Rotterdam, Holland, 22 October 1970
Height: 6'2" Weight: 13.6
International Honours: Holland: 20
The end of August was a time of comings and goings within Chelsea's central defensive complement: out went popular Brazilian Emerson Thome to Sunderland and in came Dutch superstar Winston Bogarde from Barcelona on a 'Bosman' free transfer. His arrival had an element of farce with press reports claiming that Chelsea boss Luca Vialli was unaware of his transfer but a few days later Vialli was on his way and Winston began his career at Stamford Bridge under new coach Claudio Ranieri. The classy defender took time to settle and then suffered a knee injury at Ipswich on Boxing Day and this brought a premature end to his first-team involvement.
Chelsea (Free from Barcelona, Spain, ex Excelsior, Sparta Rotterdam, Ajax, AC Milan, on 1/9/2000) PL 2+7 FLC 1 Others 1

BOGIE Ian
Born: Newcastle, 6 December 1967
Height: 5'7" Weight: 12.0
International Honours: E: Sch
An immensely talented midfielder, Ian joined Kidderminster on the eve of the 2000-01 campaign but it took a while for him to settle in as he struggled to pick up fitness. As the season progressed he was then hampered by a back injury and found himself in and out of the side. He was then transfer-listed in January and eventually released from his contract in March when he returned to the North-East.
Newcastle U (From apprentice on 18/12/1985) FL 7+7 FLC 0+1 FAC 1+2 Others 3/1
Preston NE (Signed on 9/2/1989) FL 67+12/12 FLC 3+1 FAC 3 Others 4+1
Millwall (£145,000 on 16/8/1991) FL 44+7/1 FLC 1 FAC 2 Others 3
Leyton Orient (Signed on 14/10/1993) FL 62+3/5 FLC 2 FAC 2 Others 8+1
Port Vale (£50,000 on 23/3/1995) FL 133+21/9 FLC 9/1 FAC 8+2/2 Others 8
Kidderminster Hrs (Free on 17/8/2000) FL 14+7/1 FLC 2 FAC 2+1/1 Others 1+1

BOHINEN Lars
Born: Vadso, Norway, 8 September 1969
Height: 6'0" Weight: 12.10
International Honours: Norway: 49; U21; Yth
After a disappointing time in 1999-2000 the Norwegian international midfielder returned to Scandinavia in the summer to train with his local side in order to prepare properly for the upcoming season with Derby County. A skilful player with good passing abilities he still tended to struggle with the more physical side of the game. Unable to get into the first team he was restricted to reserve appearances only, returning for one game at Chelsea before his contract was cancelled in January and he moved on to Danish club Lyngby.
Nottingham F (£450,000 from Young Boys of Berne, Switzerland, ex Valergengen, Viking, on 5/11/1993) F/PL 59+5/7 FLC 7+1/2 FAC 2/1 Others 1
Blackburn Rov (£700,000 on 14/10/1995) PL 40+18/7 FLC 3+2/1 FAC 2+1/1
Derby Co (£1,450,000 on 27/3/1998) PL 47+9/1 FLC 2 FAC 3

BOKSIC Alen
Born: Makarska, Yugoslavia, 31 January 1970
Height: 6'1" Weight: 12.8
International Honours: Croatia: 32
A fast strong-running forward with a powerful shot in either foot Alen scored two goals on his debut for Middlesbrough against Coventry City last term. Although a little injury prone he fearlessly entered every goalmouth melee and sprayed passes around for his colleagues to fasten on to. One of the bright spots in an otherwise dour season for Boro', he was one of the manager's most inspired buys. A proven goal scorer he is a lethal finisher and finished the campaign as the club's leading scorer.
Middlesbrough (£2,500,000 from Lazio, Italy, ex Hajduk Split, AS Cannes, Olympique Marseille, Lazio, Juventus, on 11/8/2000) PL 26+2/12 FLC 0+1 FAC 2+1

BOLAND William (Willie) John
Born: Ennis, Ireland, 6 August 1975
Height: 5'9" Weight: 11.2
International Honours: RoI: B-1; U21-11; Yth; Sch
Willie had the misfortune to suffer a fractured fibula playing for Cardiff City at Barnet at the end of last August and it was not until early December that he returned to first-team action. Once fully fit he showed his true value with some outstanding displays and played an important role for the Bluebirds' successful promotion campaign. He is a quality midfield player who works hard and shows good movement and passing ability.
Coventry C (From juniors on 4/11/1992) PL 43+20 FLC 6+1 FAC 0+1
Cardiff C (Free on 24/6/1999) FL 45+8/2 FLC 4 FAC 2+4 Others 1

BOLDER Adam Peter
Born: Hull, 25 October 1980
Height: 5'8" Weight: 11.0
This promising Derby County youngster spent most of the 2000-01 campaign developing in the club's reserve team assisting them to their league title. He was a non-playing substitute on a number of occasions for the senior team and came on for the final few minutes of the key end-of-season game at Old Trafford. A tenacious midfield player of great potential he can play on either flank.
Hull C (From trainee on 9/7/1999) FL 18+2 Others 2+1
Derby Co (Signed on 3/4/2000) PL 0+2

BOLIMA Cedric
Born: Kinshasa, Zaire, 26 September 1979
Height: 5'11" Weight: 12.7
Having spent the 1999-2000 campaign in the Lens second string, Cedric crossed the Channel to try his luck in the Nationwide League last season. He had trials at Swansea and Rotherham where he made a single appearance from the subs' bench, replacing Alan Lee for the final five minutes at Bournemouth. A young striker he eventually returned to France and linked up with the CFA (Fourth Division) team US St Malo in January.
Rotherham U (Free from RC Lens, France on 12/10/2000) FL 0+1

BOLLAND Paul Graham
Born: Bradford, 23 December 1979
Height: 5'11" Weight: 11.0
Paul had a rough time with injuries at Notts County last season and was only able to make intermittent appearances for the first team. A hard-working and competitive midfield player who often seems to cover every blade of grass for the Magpies' cause,

he will be hoping to avoid the treatment room and establish himself in the team during the 2001-02 campaign.
Bradford C (From trainee on 20/3/1998) FL 4+8 FLC 2
Notts Co (£75,000 on 14/1/1999) FL 37+8/1 FLC 1+3 FAC 1+1 Others 1+1

BONNER Mark
Born: Ormskirk, 7 June 1974
Height: 5'10" Weight: 11.0
Mark missed a significant portion of Cardiff City's 2000-01 campaign through injury but when present he exerted considerable influence in the centre of the park. He scored his first goal in two seasons when he netted a last-minute equaliser against Hartlepool in November paving the way for a remarkable 3-2 for the Bluebirds. He is a gutsy and tenacious central midfield player with a thoughtful approach to the game.
Blackpool (From trainee on 18/6/1992) FL 156+22/14 FLC 15+3 FAC 11 Others 10+3/1
Cardiff C (Free on 17/7/1998) FL 67+13/2 FLC 6 FAC 4 Others 2
Hull C (Loaned on 8/1/1999) FL 1/1

BOOK Steven (Steve) Kim
Born: Bournemouth, 7 July 1969
Height: 5'11" Weight: 11.1
Club Honours: FAT '98; NC '99
International Honours: E: SP-3
Steve was again an ever-present in goal for Cheltenham Town in Third Division matches in 2000-01 and to date he has appeared in every single Football League match that the Whaddon Road club has played. He began the campaign in fine form producing a particularly breathtaking stop in the 2-0 win at Hull in September. While his agility and reflexes were never in doubt his form showed a slight dip towards the end of the season but nevertheless he was offered a new three-year contract by the Robins. Steve is the son of the former Northampton and Doncaster 'keeper Kim Book.
Cheltenham T (Signed from Forest Green Rov on 23/7/1997) FL 92 FLC 4 FAC 4 Others 2

BOOTH Andrew (Andy) David
Born: Huddersfield, 6 December 1973
Height: 6'0" Weight: 13.0
International Honours: E: U21-3
This big hard-working striker scored Sheffield Wednesday's first goal of the 2000-01 campaign to earn the club a 1-1 draw at Wolves and featured regularly for the Owls until a surprise loan move to Tottenham in the new year. Desperate for a big man up front with Les Ferdinand, Steffen Iversen and Chris Armstrong all out injured, boss David Pleat turned to Andy as a short-term solution. He did well in his stay at White Hart Lane but with his contract at Hillsborough due to run out in the summer he was then sold to his former club Huddersfield on transfer deadline day. A classic target man and a hard worker, he made an instant impact with a 'Man of the Match' performance on his return, scoring in the 4-1 defeat of Portsmouth at the McAlpine Stadium. Clearly showing all the benefits of a player that has gained experience from playing at the highest level, Andy will be hoping to stay clear of injuries and lead the Terriers' attack in 2000-01.
Huddersfield T (From trainee on 1/7/1992) FL 109+14/54 FLC 6+1/3 FAC 8/3 Others 12+1/4
Sheffield Wed (£2,700,000 on 8/7/1996) P/FL 124+9/28 FLC 10+1/1 FAC 9+1/5
Tottenham H (Loaned on 30/1/2001) PL 3+1
Huddersfield T (£200,000 on 22/3/2001) FL 8/3

BOOTY Martyn James
Born: Kirby Muxloe, 30 May 1971
Height: 5'8" Weight: 11.2
This experienced full-back appeared regularly for Southend United in the 2000-01 campaign, doing well in a back four that was considerably more water-tight than in recent seasons. Although not really suited to the forward-running style favoured by new manager David Webb, Martyn's strong tackling and defensive astuteness meant he never let the Blues down. He was placed on the open to offers list in the summer.
Coventry C (From trainee on 30/5/1989) FL 4+1 FLC 2 FAC 2
Crewe Alex (Free on 7/10/1993) FL 95+1/5 FLC 6 FAC 8/1 Others 13
Reading (£75,000 on 18/1/1996) FL 62+2/1 FLC 10+1 FAC 7/1
Southend U (Free on 7/1/1999) FL 78+2 FLC 4 FAC 5 Others 2

BOSHELL Daniel (Danny) Kevin
Born: Bradford, 30 May 1981
Height: 5'11" Weight: 11.10
The 2000-01 campaign was only Danny's second as a professional but after making a promising impact he rather disappointingly spent much of the season on the subs' bench. He was often the unfortunate player to depart from midfield when Oldham switched to playing five at the back or needed to introduce pace and goals into the game. A promising young midfield play maker he is still highly rated at Boundary Park and was awarded a new long-term deal in January.
Oldham Ath (From trainee on 10/7/1998) FL 15+11/1 FLC 3/1 FAC 2 Others 1

BOTHROYD Jay
Born: London, 7 May 1982
Height: 6'3" Weight: 13.6
Club Honours: FAYC '00
International Honours: E: U21-1; Yth; Sch
A member of the Arsenal team that won the FA Youth Cup in 1999-2000 Jay joined Coventry City in the close season as a long-term prospect for the Sky Blues. After making his senior debut in a Worthington Cup tie against Preston he was given a tough baptism in the Premiership when he was chosen to lead the attack against Manchester United in November. Although slightly overawed by the occasion he was later recalled for the FA Cup tie at Maine Road when he performed well and subsequently made a number of short appearances as a substitute. His efforts for England U18s were rewarded in May with an appearance for the U21s from the subs' bench in the friendly against Mexico when he scored with a spectacular overhead kick.
Arsenal (From trainee on 8/7/1999)
Coventry C (£1,000,000 on 13/7/2000) PL 3+5 FLC 0+1 FAC 1

BOUANANE Emad
Born: Paris, France, 22 November 1976
Height: 6'1" Weight: 12.4
Emad joined Wrexham on a one-year contract and featured regularly for the Robins through until last February before falling out of favour. A capable left back he became a cult figure with the Racecourse Ground fans famous for his foraging runs upfield, taking on all-comers and generally finishing with a cracking shot.
Wrexham (Free from Avranches, France, ex Beauvais, Boissy, Brive, on 30/8/2000) FL 13+4 FAC 1 Others 1

BOULD Stephen (Steve) Andrew
Born: Stoke, 16 November 1962
Height: 6'4" Weight: 14.2
Club Honours: Div 1 '89, '91; PL '98; ECWC '94; FAC '98; CS '98
International Honours: E: 2; B-1
One of the saddest events of the 2000-01 season for many Sunderland fans was the retirement of team captain Steve Bould. Although the ex-England centre back had only been at the club for just over a year his contribution at the Stadium of Light was immense, helping the Black Cats find their feet in the Premiership following promotion. He made only one substitute appearance last term, replacing the injured Stan Varga in the 4-2 loss at Maine Road in August before conceding defeat to a persistent toe injury. Having left with the best wishes of all, Steve is reportedly looking to gain coaching qualifications to enable him to stay in the game.
Stoke C (From apprentice on 15/11/1980) FL 179+4/6 FLC 13/1 FAC 10 Others 5
Torquay U (Loaned on 19/10/1982) FL 9 FAC 2
Arsenal (£390,000 on 13/6/1988) F/PL 271+16/5 FLC 33/1 FAC 27+2 Others 18+6/2
Sunderland (£500,000 on 9/7/1999) PL 19+2 FAC 2

BOULDING Michael Thomas
Born: Sheffield, 8 February 1975
Height: 5'10" Weight: 11.4
Michael was again mainly used as a substitute by Mansfield last season, much to the frustration of the club's supporters A left-sided striker with electric pace he is capable of causing all kind of problems for defenders. This was best demonstrated in the home game with Hartlepool in September when he came off the subs' bench for the last ten minutes and helped turn a 3-1 deficit into a 4-3 victory. A former professional tennis player, Michael was out of contract in the summer.
Mansfield T (Signed from Hallam FC on 2/8/1999) FL 28+38/12 FLC 2+2 FAC 2+1 Others 1+1

BOUND Matthew Terence
Born: Melksham, 9 November 1972
Height: 6'2" Weight: 14.6
Club Honours: Div 3 '00
Matthew was again a regular in the Swansea City defence last season and was a near ever-present apart from suspension and a brief period in the new year when he was dropped. A big strong left-sided central defender his talents won him a place on the

standby list for Wales for their World Cup qualifying ties although he has yet to make his international debut.

Southampton (From trainee on 3/5/1991) F/PL 2+3
Hull C (Loaned on 27/8/1993) FL 7/1
Stockport Co (£100,000 on 27/10/1994) FL 44/5 FLC 1 FAC 3/1 Others 3/1
Lincoln C (Loaned on 11/9/1995) FL 3+1 Others 1
Swansea C (£55,000 on 21/11/1997) FL 155+1/7 FLC 8/2 FAC 8 Others 7+1/2

BOWEN Jason Peter
Born: Merthyr Tydfil, 24 August 1972
Height: 5'7" Weight: 11.0
Club Honours: AMC '94
International Honours: W: 2; B-1; U21-5; Yth; Sch

Jason was used in a role just behind the front two for Cardiff City in 2000-01 and became one of five Bluebirds' players to hit a double-figure tally of Third Division goals. He looked more comfortable in this position than playing as an out-and-out striker and it was the case that when Jason played well, the team played well. He is a very talented player with pace, movement and good ball control.

Swansea C (From trainee on 1/7/1990) FL 93+31/26 FLC 6+1/2 FAC 9+2/1 Others 15+3/8
Birmingham C (£350,000 on 24/7/1995) FL 35+13/7 FLC 4+6/2 FAC 1+4 Others 2/2
Southampton (Loaned on 2/9/1997) PL 1+2
Reading (£200,000 on 24/12/1997) FL 12+3/1 FLC 1+1 FAC 5
Cardiff C (Free on 12/1/1999) FL 77+19/26 FLC 4/2 FAC 9+1 Others 1

BOWER Mark James
Born: Bradford, 23 January 1980
Height: 5'10" Weight: 11.0

Although he featured for Bradford in an Inter Toto Cup tie against FK Atlantas and also in a Worthington Cup game against Darlington, Mark failed to make a real breakthrough at Valley Parade in the early part of last season and joined York City in a long-term loan deal in November. He featured regularly for the Minstermen, producing some impressive displays in the centre of defence and contributed a goal in the 2-1 home defeat by Plymouth as he helped them to safety from relegation once more.

Bradford C (From trainee on 28/3/1998) FL 1+2 FLC 1 Others 1
York C (Loaned on 16/2/2000) FL 15/1
York C (Loaned on 30/11/2000) FL 21/1 FAC 3 Others 0+1

BOWLING Ian
Born: Sheffield, 27 July 1965
Height: 6'3" Weight: 14.8

Ian began the 2000-01 campaign as first choice 'keeper for Mansfield but lost his place early on to Bobby Mimms. He then suffered a broken toe in a domestic accident and after being released by the Stags he moved on to Conference club Kettering Town. A fine shot stopper who commands his area he had been Mansfield's regular goalkeeper for the previous six years.

Lincoln C (£2,000 from Gainsborough Trinity on 23/10/1988) FL 59 FLC 3 FAC 2 Others 4
Hartlepool U (Loaned on 17/8/1989) FL 1
Bradford C (Loaned on 25/3/1993) FL 7
Bradford C (£27,500 on 28/7/1993) FL 29 FLC 2 FAC 2+1 Others 1
Mansfield T (Free on 11/8/1995) FL 174 FLC 9 FAC 9 Others 8

BOWRY Robert (Bobby) John
Born: Hampstead, 19 May 1971
Height: 5'9" Weight: 10.8
Club Honours: Div 1 '94
International Honours: St Kitts & Nevis

Bobby was very much a fringe player at Millwall last season but was a regular with the club's reserve team where he acted as a mentor for the many promising youngsters coming through at The New Den. He is a neat and skilful midfield player who is quick to push forward to help the attack and tracks back to help out in defence when needed. He was released in the summer.

Crystal Palace (Free from Carshalton on 4/4/1992) F/PL 36+14/1 FLC 10 FAC 1
Millwall (£220,000 on 5/7/1995) FL 125+15/5 FLC 9+1 FAC 6 Others 4

BOWYER Lee David
Born: London, 3 January 1977
Height: 5'9" Weight: 10.6
International Honours: E: U21-13; Yth

Despite a season overshadowed by a much publicised and at the time of writing unresolved problem, Lee continued to produce the goods on the football pitch last term. A dynamic and tireless performer in the centre of the park for Leeds he showed he was one of the best all-round midfield players in the country. His goal-scoring ability makes him of great value to the team and he again weighed in with some telling contributions, none more so than in the Champions' League, where he was the tournament's joint-top scorer at the quarter-final stage. His speculative 25-yard effort that slipped through the AC Milan goalkeeper's fingers in the last minute of their tie at Elland Road set the club on their way to European success and indeed his performances were a model of consistency throughout the season.

Charlton Ath (From trainee on 13/4/1994) FL 46/8 FLC 6+1/5 FAC 3/1 Others 2
Leeds U (£2,600,000 on 5/7/1996) PL 157+6/30 FLC 5+1/1 FAC 15/3 Others 30/11

BOYCE Emmerson Orlando
Born: Aylesbury, 24 September 1979
Height: 5'11" Weight: 11.10

Emmerson had a good season for Luton Town in 2000-01 despite playing in a struggling team and was a near ever-present missing just four matches. A calm and cultured defender who is equally at home either as a full back or central defender, he provided some invaluable experience to help the youngsters around him. He is quick, strong in the tackle and makes effective surging runs deep into the opposition territory. He won the young supporters' 'Player of the Season' award as a reward for his efforts.

Luton T (From trainee on 2/4/1998) FL 66+7/4 FLC 6 FAC 2+3 Others 2

BOYD Adam Mark
Born: Hartlepool, 25 May 1982
Height: 5'9" Weight: 10.12

The 2000-01 campaign was a season of learning for Hartlepool's promising young forward. Having enjoyed some success in the previous season he received few senior opportunities and he failed to make much of an impact. Adam is still only 19 and he will be aiming to make the breakthrough in the coming season as Pool boss Chris Turner plans to work with a trimmed down first-team squad.

Hartlepool U (From trainee on 20/9/1999) FL 3+6/1 FAC 0+1 Others 0+2

BOYD Walter
Born: Jamaica, 1 January 1972
Height: 5'11" Weight: 11.10
Club Honours: Div 3 '00
International Honours: Jamaica

Walter featured in a number of early-season games for Swansea last term but after returning from a spell of international duty later in the autumn he struggled with some niggling injuries and it was not until mid-April that he returned to the first team. He scored two late goals on his first start for the Swans against Wycombe but was out of contract in the summer and at the time of writing his future was uncertain. An enigmatic striker he can show tremendous ability on the ball and is willing to take on the opposition from anywhere in the park. He was recalled to the Jamaica squad during the 2000 close season and made intermittent appearances during the campaign, winning a further seven caps.

Swansea C (Free from Arnett Gardens, Jamaica on 11/10/1999) FL 35+9/10 FLC 2 FAC 1+1 Others 2

BRABIN Gary
Born: Liverpool, 9 December 1970
Height: 5'11" Weight: 14.8
International Honours: E: SP-3

Previously a regular under Warren Joyce, Gary wasn't a first choice in the early weeks of Brian Little's reign at Hull City last season, but recovered to become a leading figure as the Tigers reached the Third Division play-offs. A powerful midfield player who also showed he could perform in the centre of defence if required, he further enhanced his reputation with the Boothferry Park fans by refusing to consider a transfer at the time of the club's financial crisis in the spring. He was made available to offers in the summer.

Stockport Co (From trainee on 14/12/1989) FL 1+1 Others 1+1
Doncaster Rov (£45,000 from Runcorn on 26/7/1994) FL 58+1/11 FLC 2 FAC 2 Others 4
Bury (£125,000 on 29/3/1996) FL 5
Blackpool (£200,000 on 30/7/1996) FL 50+13/5 FLC 7+1 FAC 2 Others 2+2
Lincoln C (Loaned on 11/12/1998) FL 3+1 Others 1
Hull C (Free on 8/1/1999) FL 89+6/9 FLC 5+1 FAC 5 Others 3

BRACEY Lee Michael Ian
Born: Barking, 11 September 1968
Height: 6'2" Weight: 13.6

After the trials and tribulations of his first season at Hull, Lee regained his place in the Tigers' goal at the start of 2000-01. However new manager Brian Little decided to draft in Paul Musselwhite from Sheffield Wednesday and Lee was relegated to the subs' bench from the middle of September. He featured only twice more during the campaign, replacing the injured Musselwhite at Brighton in March and then standing-in for him in the following match at Plymouth. He was placed on the open to offers list in the summer.

West Ham U (From trainee on 6/7/1987)
Swansea C (Free on 27/8/1988) FL 99 FLC 8 FAC 11 Others 10
Halifax T (£47,500 on 17/10/1991) FL 73 FLC 2 FAC 1 Others 2
Bury (£20,000 on 23/8/1993) FL 65+2 FLC 4 FAC 2 Others 1
Ipswich T (£40,000 on 5/8/1997)
Hull C (Free on 5/7/1999) FL 19+1 FLC 6 FAC 3 Others 1

BRADBURY Lee Michael
Born: Isle of Wight, 3 July 1975
Height: 6'2" Weight: 13.10
International Honours: E: U21-3

One of the few players to remain a regular for Portsmouth in 2000-01 following a series of managerial changes Lee netted 10 valuable goals to finish as second-top scorer. A tireless and hard-working striker who can kick with either foot he holds the ball up well and upsets defenders with his bustling style.

Portsmouth (Free from Cowes on 14/8/1995) FL 41+13/15 FLC 1+2 FAC 4/2
Exeter C (Loaned on 1/12/1995) FL 14/5
Manchester C (£3,000,000 + on 1/8/1997) FL 34+6/10 FLC 6/1
Crystal Palace (£1,500,000 on 29/10/1998) FL 28+4/6 FLC 3+1/1 FAC 1/1
Birmingham C (Loaned on 25/3/1999) FL 6+1 Others 1+1
Portsmouth (£380,000 on 14/10/1999) FL 70+4/20 FLC 3+1 FAC 2/1

BRADLEY Shayne
Born: Gloucester, 8 December 1979
Height: 5'11" Weight: 13.2
International Honours: E: Sch

Shayne joined Mansfield Town for a club record fee as a replacement for Tony Lormor and made his debut as substitute in the 'home' Worthington Cup tie against Wrexham at Meadow Lane. He seemed to be settling in well when he picked up an ankle injury after just a handful of appearances. He then suffered a succession of injuries and afterwards seemed to struggle for fitness although he did score some useful goals. He is a traditional bustling centre forward who leads his line well and possesses a powerful shot.

Southampton (From trainee on 16/1/1998) PL 0+4
Swindon T (Loaned on 25/3/1999) FL 6+1
Exeter C (Loaned on 17/9/1999) FL 6+2/1 FAC 1
Mansfield T (£50,000 + on 22/8/2000) FL 21+5/7 FLC 0+1 FAC 0+2 Others 1

BRADSHAW Carl
Born: Sheffield, 2 October 1968
Height: 5'11" Weight: 11.11
Club Honours: AMC '99
International Honours: E: Yth

Carl was again hampered by injuries at Wigan in the 2000-01 campaign but when he was in the side he proved both consistent and reliable. He netted with two penalties, giving him a 100 per cent record from spot kicks, and added a stunning 30-yarder in the 1-1 draw with Reading in October. A hard tackling right back he passed the landmark of 300 Football League appearances during the season. Carl was one of a number of players released by the Latics in the summer.

Sheffield Wed (From apprentice on 23/8/1986) FL 16+16/4 FLC 2+2 FAC 6+1/3 Others 1
Barnsley (Loaned on 23/8/1986) FL 6/1
Manchester C (£50,000 on 30/9/1988) FL 1+4 FAC 0+1 Others 0+1
Sheffield U (£50,000 on 7/9/1989) F/PL 122+25/8 FLC 10+1/2 FAC 12+1/3 Others 4
Norwich C (£500,000 on 28/7/1994) P/FL 55+10/2 FLC 6+1/1 FAC 2
Wigan Ath (Free on 6/10/1997) FL 109+11/11 FLC 6/1 FAC 5 Others 9+1/1

BRADSHAW Gary
Born: Hull, 30 December 1982
Height: 5'6" Weight: 10.6

After bursting into senior football with Hull City towards the end of 1999-2000, Gary returned to the youth ranks last term as he continued to learn his trade. He made two appearances from the subs' bench shortly before Christmas as Tigers' manager Brian Little decided to ease him gently into first-team football. He is a nippy striker with good ball skills who will be looking to make further progress in the 2001-02 campaign.

Hull C (From trainee on 14/7/2000) FL 5+9

BRADSHAW Mark
Born: Ashton under Lyne, 7 September 1969
Height: 5'10" Weight: 12.0
Club Honours: GMVC '95, '97, FC '98
International Honours: E: SP-1

Mark started last season in fine style for Halifax Town netting on the opening day in the 2-2 draw at Carlisle United and following this up with a spectacular volley at home to local rivals Rochdale. However he was dropped following the home defeat by York, and in November he went on loan to Conference outfit Southport. He rarely featured for the Shaymen in the second half of the campaign and was released in May. He is a left back who is always willing to push forward down the flank to help the attack.

Blackpool (From trainee on 9/12/1987) FL 34+8/1 FLC 3/1 FAC 5+1 Others 1+2 (Free to Stafford R during 1991 close season)
York C (Loaned on 16/4/1991) FL 0+1
Halifax T (Free from Macclesfield T on 18/5/1995) FL 73+10/7 FLC 5 FAC 2+1 Others 1/1

BRADY Garry
Born: Glasgow, 7 September 1976
Height: 5'10" Weight: 11.0
International Honours: S: Yth; Sch

Unable to get in the team at Newcastle Garry joined Norwich City on loan last September where he impressed with his awareness and passing skills before returning north. In February he went to Portsmouth in another loan deal making a promising debut against Burnley at Fratton Park under the new management of Graham Rix. His footwork and accurate distribution were a pleasure to watch over his first few games but as the threat of relegation loomed he was left out of the side. A hard-working midfield player he eventually joined Pompey on a permanent basis in March and will be hoping to gain regular first-team football in 2001-02.

Tottenham H (From trainee on 9/9/1993) PL 0+9 FAC 1+1
Newcastle U (£650,000 on 15/7/1998) PL 3+6 FAC 2+1
Norwich C (Loaned on 22/3/2000) FL 6
Norwich C (Loaned on 4/9/2000) FL 2 FLC 2
Portsmouth (Free on 1/3/2001) FL 8

BRADY Matthew (Matt) John
Born: Marylebone, 27 October 1977
Height: 5'11" Weight: 11.10

Matt found it hard to win a regular place at Wycombe last season with Steve Brown and Martyn Lee in such fine form and only featured in a handful of first-team games. He produced a superb performance in the LDV Vans Trophy tie at Leyton Orient crowned by his only goal of the campaign but he was released by boss Lawrie Sanchez in the summer. He is a wide-left midfield player who can deliver a useful cross into the box.

Barnet (From trainee on 3/7/1996) FL 2+8 (Free to Boreham Wood on 6/11/1998)
Wycombe W (Signed on 11/11/1999) FL 6+6/2 FAC 2+1 Others 2+1/1

BRAGSTAD Bjorn Otto
Born: Trondheim, Norway, 15 January 1971
Height: 6'4" Weight: 13.5
International Honours: Norway: 14

This Norwegian international centre back arrived at Derby County in the summer of 2000 with an outstanding reputation however he found it difficult to settle at first which didn't help his introduction into a less than steady defence. Originally part of a back four, he struggled once Jim Smith moved to playing three centre backs and with the team hovering near the foot of the table he lost his place. The introduction of Chris Riggott and the signing of Taribo West meant an extended spell in the reserves, however he assisted the second string to a successful defence of their title, captaining the team on occasions. The Rams' supporters have still to see the best of the hard-tackling defender and he will be hoping for a higher profile at Pride Park in 2000-01.

Derby Co (£1,500,000 from Rosenborg, Norway on 4/8/2000) PL 10+2 FLC 3/2 FAC 1

BRAMBLE Tesfaye (Tes)
Born: Ipswich, 20 July 1980
Height: 6'1" Weight: 13.10

Tes is a skilful striker with the build of an old-fashioned centre forward. He joined Southend United from Dr Martens League club Cambridge City last January after previously having trials with a number of clubs including Tottenham Hotspur, and is clearly a great prospect. Although often used in a wide-left role he quickly settled down and by the end of the season was scoring regularly. With the advantage of a

full pre-season training behind him his speed and sharpness should cause problems for many Third Division defences in the coming season. Tes is the brother of Ipswich Town's Titus Bramble.
Southend U (Signed from Cambridge C on 19/1/2001) FL 12+4/6 Others 2+1

BRAMBLE Titus Malachi
Born: Ipswich, 21 July 1981
Height: 6'1" Weight: 13.10
International Honours: E: U21-5
After a tremendous pre-season Titus found himself in the Ipswich Town team on merit when the 2000-01 campaign began at White Hart Lane. He retained his place for the visit of Manchester United and went on to score his first goal in the following game with Sunderland when he surged up the field, exchanged passes with Marcus Stewart and fired the ball into the net. He has a very strong physique and the Portman Road fans really enjoy it when he goes on a 'surge' leaving defenders in his wake. His strength and power are awesome and some of the best strikers in the Premiership found him to be a difficult opponent. Titus also made a vital contribution to Town's excellent Worthington Cup run, scoring a late equaliser against Millwall and netting with a low shot following a corner in the home tie with Coventry. His fine performances earned him a place in the England U21 team against Georgia back in August and he went on to win four more caps during the campaign. He is the brother of Southend's Tes Bramble.
Ipswich T (From trainee on 24/8/1998) FL 25+5/1 FLC 4+1/2 FAC 2+1
Colchester U (Loaned on 29/12/1999) FL 2

Titus Bramble

BRAMMER David (Dave)
Born: Bromborough, 28 February 1975
Height: 5'10" Weight: 12.0
Club Honours: AMC '01
Dave had a remarkable change of fortunes in the 2000-01 campaign, for having begun the season on the transfer list at Port Vale he finished it by winning the supporters' 'Player of the Year' award. He netted four goals including a great individual effort in the local 'derby' at Stoke and a blistering 30-yard drive to give Vale a 1-0 win at Colchester. A busy midfield man he was at the hub of many of the team's best moves and won numerous 'Man of the Match' awards. Dave crowned a fine season by appearing for Vale in their LDV Vans Trophy final victory over Brentford at Cardiff's Millenium Stadium.
Wrexham (From trainee on 2/7/1993) FL 118+19/12 FLC 6+2 FAC 8+2/1 Others 13+2/1
Port Vale (£350,000 + on 24/3/1999) FL 71+2/3 FLC 2 FAC 2/1 Others 7

BRANAGAN Keith Graham
Born: Fulham, 10 July 1966
Height: 6'0" Weight: 13.2
Club Honours: Div 1 '97
International Honours: RoI: 1; B-1
Having joined Ipswich as cover for Richard Wright at the end of the 1999-2000 campaign Keith made his debut for the club in the Worthington Cup tie with Coventry. He kept his place for the home defeat by Derby and made a single further appearance in the Premiership game with Coventry towards the end of the season after Wright was injured in the pre-match warm up. On that occasion he made a fantastic goal-line save to prevent John Eustace from equalising and from his resulting clearance Ipswich scored their second goal to clinch victory.
Cambridge U (From juniors on 4/8/1983) FL 110 FLC 12 FAC 6 Others 6
Millwall (£100,000 on 25/3/1988) FL 46 FLC 1 FAC 5 Others 1
Brentford (Loaned on 24/11/1989) FL 2 Others 1
Gillingham (Loaned on 1/10/1991) FL 1
Bolton W (Free on 3/7/1992) P/FL 214 FLC 33 FAC 10 Others 6
Ipswich T (Free on 7/4/2000) PL 2 FLC 1

BRANCH Graham
Born: Liverpool, 12 February 1972
Height: 6'2" Weight: 12.2
Graham began the 2000-01 on the subs' bench at Burnley and it was not until mid-September that he won a place in the Clarets' starting line-up. He was mainly used in a wide-left midfield role where his tricky runs down the wing were always exciting to watch. His performances continued to improve as the campaign wore on and he seldom looked out of place at First Division level. Graham's season finished prematurely after he suffered a knee injury in the heavy defeat at Blackburn last April.
Tranmere Rov (Free from Heswall on 2/7/1991) FL 55+47/10 FLC 4+8/1 FAC 1+2 Others 2+1
Bury (Loaned on 20/11/1992) FL 3+1/1 Others 1
Wigan Ath (Loaned on 24/12/1997) FL 2+1
Stockport Co (Free on 31/7/1998) FL 10+4/3 FLC 1
Burnley (Free on 31/12/1998) FL 71+28/9 FLC 4+2 FAC 2+3 Others 1

BRANCH Paul **Michael**
Born: Liverpool, 18 October 1978
Height: 5'10" Weight: 11.7
International Honours: E: U21-1; Yth; Sch
Michael played well for Wolves in the opening game of the 2000-01 campaign against Sheffield Wednesday but was then sidelined by a torn hamstring and was unable to return to the starting line-up for several weeks. Often used as a lone striker he found goals hard to come by and was mostly used on the right wing in the second half of the campaign covering for the injured Darren Bazeley. A pacy and versatile forward he needs to try and increase his goal output.
Everton (From trainee on 24/10/1995) PL 16+25/3 FLC 0+1 FAC 1+2
Manchester C (Loaned on 29/10/1998) FL 4
Wolverhampton W (£500,000 + on 25/11/1999) FL 56+9/10 FLC 2+1 FAC 4

BRANDON Christopher (Chris) William
Born: Bradford, 7 April 1976
Height: 5'7" Weight: 10.3
Chris appeared for Torquay in the opening game of the 2000-01 campaign at Kidderminster but then had the misfortune to go down with a pelvic injury. He made an abortive return against Halifax at the end of September but was forced to sit out the rest of the season. He is as an attacking right-sided midfielder who is not afraid to run at defenders and head for a goal.
Torquay U (Free from Bradford PA on 5/8/1999) FL 42+2/5 FLC 2 FAC 4/1 Others 2

BRANIFF Kevin Robert
Born: Belfast, 4 March 1983
Height: 5'11" Weight: 12.0
International Honours: NI: Yth; Sch
Kevin is another of the talented youngsters on Millwall's books. He made his senior debut against Brighton in the Worthington Cup first round first leg tie, scoring a wonderful goal when he curled the ball in from the edge of the box to give the Lions a 2-1 victory. A quick and skilful striker he was unable to win a regular place in the line-up due to the form of the club's front men but will be looking to extend his first-team experience in 2001-02. Kevin was capped by Northern Ireland at U18 level during the season, appearing in the UEFA tournament qualifying ties against Portugal and Norway.
Millwall (From trainee on 12/4/2000) FL 2+3 FLC 3+1/1 FAC 0+1

BRANNAN Gerard (Ged) Daniel
Born: Prescot, 15 January 1972
Height: 6'0" Weight: 12.3
Having begun the 2000-01 campaign as a regular with Scottish Premier League club Motherwell Ged was transferred to Wigan Athletic in March. He gave some solid performances for the Second Division club but missed out on the play-off semi-finals due to a hamstring injury. A strong and determined midfielder he is perhaps best used on the right-hand side from where he is particularly adept at making late surging runs in to the penalty box.
Tranmere Rov (From trainee on 3/7/1990) FL 227+11/20 FLC 26+1/4 FAC 10+1 Others 26+1/1
Manchester C (£750,000 on 12/3/1997) FL 38+5/4 FLC 2 FAC 1
Norwich C (Loaned on 21/8/1998) FL 10+1/1 FLC 1
Motherwell (£378,000 on 28/10/1998) SL 81/16 SLC 3+1 SC 7/2
Wigan Ath (£175,000 on 16/2/2001) FL 12+1

BRANSTON Guy Peter Bromley
Born: Leicester, 9 January 1979
Height: 6'0" Weight: 13.12

Guy was a tower of strength on the left side of the back three for Rotherham last season, playing a major role in the club's battle for a second successive promotion. Very strong in the tackle and excellent in the air, he is never perturbed by opponents and in addition to defending superbly he came up with some vital goals. However he accumulated a number of bookings leading to several spells out through suspension and this is an area of his game where he needs to show improvement.

Leicester C (From trainee on 3/7/1997)
Colchester U (Loaned on 9/2/1998) FL 12/1 Others 1
Colchester U (Loaned on 7/8/1998) FL 0+1
Plymouth Arg (Loaned on 20/11/1998) FL 7/1 Others 1
Lincoln C (Loaned on 10/8/1999) FL 4 FLC 2
Rotherham U (£50,000 on 15/10/1999) FL 71/10 FLC 2 FAC 3 Others 2

BRASS Christopher (Chris) Paul
Born: Easington, 24 July 1975
Height: 5'10" Weight: 12.6

Chris proved unable to displace any of the talented Burnley defenders at the start of last season and went out on loan to Halifax Town in September. Employed in a midfield role by the Shaymen he added extra bite in the centre of the park before returning to Turf Moor. In March he made a permanent move to York City and captained the Minstermen on his full debut for the club at Leyton Orient. He produced some very impressive performances in the closing weeks of the campaign and he is expected to play an important role at Bootham Crescent in the 2001-02 campaign. Chris is a commanding central defender who is strong in the tackle and has good distribution.

Burnley (From trainee on 8/7/1993) FL 120+14/1 FLC 8+1 FAC 6+1 Others 8+2
Torquay U (Loaned on 14/10/1994) FL 7 FAC 2 Others 1
Halifax T (Loaned on 22/9/2000) FL 6
York C (Free on 15/3/2001) FL 8+2/1

BRAYSON Paul
Born: Newcastle, 16 September 1977
Height: 5'4" Weight: 10.10
International Honours: E: Yth

Having failed to score a senior goal in his previous two seasons at Reading, Paul proved to be something of a revelation at Cardiff last season, netting 15 goals from just 25 starts. He earned his place in the Bluebirds' line-up despite facing stiff competition and he showed himself to be a clever striker with an excellent eye for goal. Having received such a boost to his career he will be looking forward to the challenge of Second Division football in 2001-02.

Newcastle U (From trainee on 1/8/1995) FLC 1+1
Swansea C (Loaned on 30/1/1997) FL 11/5
Reading (£100,000 on 26/3/1998) FL 15+26/1 FLC 0+2 FAC 1+1 Others 2
Cardiff C (Free on 16/3/2000) FL 32+17/16 FLC 1 FAC 0+3 Others 1

BRAZIER Matthew (Matt) Ronald
Born: Leytonstone, 2 July 1976
Height: 5'8" Weight: 11.6

Matt had a fair season operating down the left hand side for Cardiff City in 2000-01. He experienced his ups and downs, notably producing some quality play and experiencing a lengthy absence through illness. A versatile player who can play at wing back, as a winger or in midfield he scored two goals last season.

Queens Park R (From trainee on 1/7/1994) P/FL 36+13/2 FLC 3+2/1 FAC 3
Fulham (£65,000 on 20/3/1998) FL 4+5/1 FAC 2+1 Others 1
Cardiff C (Loaned on 28/8/1998) FL 11/2
Cardiff C (£100,000 on 9/7/1999) FL 43+13/3 FLC 2+3/1 FAC 5+1/1 Others 1

BREACKER Timothy (Tim) Sean
Born: Bicester, 2 July 1965
Height: 6'0" Weight: 13.0
Club Honours: FLC '88
International Honours: E: U21-2

This experienced right wing back started just nine matches for Queens Park Rangers in the first half of last season before succumbing to a persistent ankle injury. He eventually announced his retirement from the game in April and was appointed as reserve team coach at Loftus Road following the departure of Iain Dowie and Des Bulphin.

Luton T (From apprentice on 15/5/1983) FL 204+6/3 FLC 22+2 FAC 21 Others 7
West Ham U (£600,000 on 12/10/1990) F/PL 229+11/8 FLC 20+1 FAC 27+1 Others 7
Queens Park R (Loaned on 2/10/1998) FL 2
Queens Park R (Free on 10/2/1999) FL 39+3/2 FLC 3 FAC 2

BREBNER Grant Iain
Born: Edinburgh, 6 December 1977
Height: 5'10" Weight: 12.0
Club Honours: FAYC '95
International Honours: S: U21-17; Sch

Unable to win a regular place in the Hibernian team Grant joined Stockport County for a three-month loan period only to suffer a knee injury in only his fourth game for the Hatters. A cartilage operation followed and although he forced his way back into the first-team picture he returned to Easter Road where he featured regularly in the closing stages of the campaign. A talented playmaker in the centre of the park he is skilful on the ball and has a good eye for goal.

Manchester U (Free from Hutchinson Vale BC on 17/3/1995)
Cambridge U (Loaned on 9/1/1998) FL 6/1
Hibernian (Loaned on 26/2/1998) SL 9/1
Reading (£300,000 on 15/6/1998) FL 38+3/10 FLC 4/1 FAC 1
Hibernian (£400,000 on 19/8/1999) SL 27+2 SLC 3 SC 3+1/1
Stockport Co (Loaned on 13/10/2000) FL 3+3

BRECKIN Ian
Born: Rotherham, 24 February 1975
Height: 6'0" Weight: 12.9
Club Honours: AMC '96

Ian signed a new three-year contract for Chesterfield at the start of last season and celebrated with a goal in the opening day win over York when he ran through from his own half, exchanged passes with David Reeves and shot home. He is the perfect foil for the more physical Steve Blatherwick in the middle of defence, always looking composed, in the right place and ready with a perfectly-timed tackle should the need arise. Ian made his 300th League appearance at Hull in April and in recognition of his growing maturity he skippered the side for much of the campaign.

Rotherham U (From trainee on 1/11/1993) FL 130+2/6 FLC 6 FAC 5 Others 11
Chesterfield (£100,000 on 25/7/1997) FL 166+4/7 FLC 15/1 FAC 6/1 Others 9/1

BREEN Gary Patrick
Born: Hendon, 12 December 1973
Height: 6'2" Weight: 12.0
International Honours: RoI: 38; U21-9

With Coventry's embarrassment of riches in the central defensive positions, Gary found it hard to win a regular place in his favoured role. He got his chance in September when Paul Williams was suspended but after three successive defeats he was switched to right back again where he won much praise for his speed and skill on the ball. An injury to Mo Konjic at Christmas meant he was back in the centre of defence, a position he maintained until the end of the season with some outstanding performances. He proved unquestionably that he has matured into one of the top defenders in the Premiership and became something of a cult hero with the Sky Blues' fans. A regular for the Republic of Ireland he equalled the club record for most caps in the spring and was deservedly voted 'Player of the Year' by both the supporters and his team-mates.

Maidstone U (From Charlton Ath juniors on 6/3/1991) FL 19
Gillingham (Free on 2/7/1992) FL 45+6 FLC 4 FAC 5 Others 1
Peterborough U (£70,000 on 5/8/1994) FL 68+1/1 FLC 6 FAC 6 Others 6/1
Birmingham C (£400,000 on 9/2/1996) FL 37+3/2 FLC 4 FAC 1
Coventry C (£2,400,000 on 1/2/1997) PL 108+8/2 FLC 8+3 FAC 11

BREITENFELDER Friedrich Johann
Born: Vienna, Austria, 16 June 1980
Height: 6'2" Weight: 12.13

Friedrich signed for Luton Town in August 2000 after impressing during pre-season trials but struggled to win a regular place in the first team squad after being hampered by a series of injuries. A tall and rangy right-sided midfield player he showed good positional sense, some accurate passing and was comfortable on the ball. He was one of five players released by the Hatters at the end of April.

Luton T (Free from NCN St Polten, Austria, ex Rapid Vienna, Casino Bregenz, on 11/8/2000) FL 2+3

BRENNAN Dean James Gary
Born: Dublin, 17 June 1980
Height: 5'9" Weight: 11.8

Dean joined Luton Town in the 2000 close season from Sheffield Wednesday along with Peter Holmes but struggled to make an impact at first-team level for the Hatters. A hard running left-sided midfield player who is also comfortable in a role as striker he provided a threat with his forward runs but only made a handful of appearances early in

the campaign. He was one of several players placed on the transfer list by new boss Joe Kinnear in the summer.
Sheffield Wed (Signed from Stella Maris YC on 21/11/1997)
Luton T (Free on 11/8/2000) FL 2+7 FLC 1+2

BRENNAN James (Jim) Gerald
Born: Toronto, Canada, 8 May 1977
Height: 5'9" Weight: 12.5
International Honours: Canada: 25 (Gold Cup 2000); U23-1
Although he featured a number of times early on last season Jim struggled to hold down a regular first-team place with Nottingham Forest and found himself out of the squad in September. Although he returned towards the end of the year he never seemed particularly comfortable in the role he was asked to play and he eventually joined Huddersfield Town on the transfer deadline day as cover for injuries. However he only made two brief appearances from the subs' bench for the Terriers and then received a red card in a reserve game that led to him being suspended. An attacking wing back with good pace he continued to appear for Canada during the season and was a member of their squad for the Confederations Cup tournament over the summer.
Bristol C (Free from Sora Lazio, Canada on 25/10/1994) FL 51+4/3 FLC 6 FAC 1
Nottingham F (£1,500,000 on 29/10/1999) FL 31+6 FLC 2 FAC 4
Huddersfield T (Loaned on 21/3/2001) FL 0+2

BRESLAN Geoffrey (Geoff) Francis
Born: Torquay, 4 June 1980
Height: 5'8" Weight: 11.0
This wide left-sided midfield player struggled to break into the Exeter City first team in 2000-01 and made just two appearances from the subs' bench during the campaign. He has a good touch on the ball and can deliver an accurate cross but has yet to fulfil the promise he showed as a trainee at St James Park. Geoff had a spell on loan at Dr Martens League club Tamworth in the autumn and was placed on the open to offers list in the summer.
Exeter C (From trainee on 7/1/1999) FL 40+26/4 FLC 4 FAC 3+3 Others 6/1

BREVETT Rupis (Rufus) Emanuel
Born: Derby, 24 September 1969
Height: 5'8" Weight: 11.6
Club Honours: Div 2 '99; Div 1 '01
Last season was undoubtedly Rufus's best in a Fulham shirt and he saw off strong challenges from Paul Trollope and Terry Phelan to retain the left-back spot on a regular basis. A strong and determined defender he impressed with his overlapping runs down the wing while both his passing and tackling improved under Jean Tigana's tuition.
Doncaster Rov (From trainee on 8/7/1988) FL 106+3/3 FLC 5 FAC 4 Others 10+1
Queens Park R (£250,000 on 15/2/1991) F/PL 141+11/1 FLC 9+1 FAC 8
Fulham (£375,000 on 28/1/1998) FL 117+1/1 FLC 13+1 FAC 8 Others 2

BRIDGE Wayne Michael
Born: Southampton, 5 August 1980
Height: 5'10" Weight: 11.11
International Honours: E: U21-2; Yth
Wayne was without doubt the most improved player on Southampton's books last season. An ever-present for the Saints in Premiership matches it looks as if he will be a fixture in the line-up for the foreseeable future. A left-sided wing back who can also play in midfield he was on the subs' bench for England in the U21 game in Italy that fell victim to the fog but added a further cap when he appeared in the friendly against Spain in February.
Southampton (From trainee on 16/1/1998) PL 68+12/1 FLC 5+1 FAC 6

BRIDGE-WILKINSON Marc
Born: Nuneaton, 16 March 1979
Height: 5'6 Weight: 11.8
Club Honours: AMC '01
Marc had an excellent campaign with Port Vale in 2000-1. He netted with two great strikes in the first home game of the season against Oxford and went on to finish with a double-figure tally in all competitions. A near ever-present for Vale he also developed a reputation as a successful penalty taker, ending with a 100 per cent record from five attempts including a crucial spot kick in the LDV Vans Trophy final victory over Brentford. Marc is a left-sided midfield player with a calm approach to the game and a powerful and effective long-range shot. He was the joint-winner of Vale's 'Young Player of the Year' award.
Derby Co (From trainee on 26/3/1997) PL 0+1
Carlisle U (Loaned on 5/3/1999) FL 4+3
Port Vale (Free on 4/7/2000) FL 40+2/9 FLC 1/1 FAC 2/1 Others 7/3

BRIDGES Michael
Born: North Shields, 5 August 1978
Height: 6'1" Weight: 10.11
Club Honours: Div 1 '96, '99
International Honours: E: U21-3; Yth; Sch
A striker of undoubted skill and talent and Leeds United's leading scorer in 1999-2000, Michael began last term in a three-man attack at Elland Road. Surprisingly he failed to find the net in the opening games and was subsequently rested. He returned to the fore at Besiktas in October only to be stretchered off after 28 minutes. He was then diagnosed with an ankle injury and this kept him out of action for the remainder of the season. His qualities were sorely missed up front by United.
Sunderland (From trainee on 9/11/1995) P/FL 31+48/16 FLC 8+3/5 FAC 2
Leeds U (£4,500,000 + on 29/7/1999) PL 38+3/19 FLC 2 FAC 1+1 Others 16/2

BRIGGS Keith
Born: Ashton under Lyne, 11 December 1981
Height: 5'10" Weight: 11.6
Having broken into the Stockport County line-up in 1999-2000 Keith found first-team opportunities hard to come by at Edgeley Park last term and made just one senior appearance, coming off the subs' bench in the FA Cup third round tie at Preston. A product of the Hatters' successful youth system, he is a pacy defender who is comfortable either at right back or in a wing-back role.
Stockport Co (From trainee on 27/8/1999) FL 4+3/1 FLC 2/1 FAC 0+1

BRIGHTWELL David John
Born: Lutterworth, 7 January 1971
Height: 6'2" Weight: 13.5
David became manager Brian Little's first signing for Hull in June 2000 and he quickly became a commanding figure on the left of a three-man defence. The highlight of his time at Boothferry Park came when he netted a late free kick that proved to be the winner in the Humber 'derby' at Scunthorpe in December. With the Tigers hitting financial problems in the new year, David elected to move on to Darlington where he immediately established himself in the heart of the defence alongside Craig Liddle. Strong in the air and uncompromising in the tackle he gave the defence a more solid look, producing a series of resolute displays. He is the younger brother of Ian Brightwell.
Manchester C (From juniors on 11/4/1988) F/PL 35+8/1 FLC 2+1 FAC 5+2/1
Chester C (Loaned on 22/3/1991) FL 6
Lincoln C (Loaned on 11/8/1995) FL 5 FLC 2
Stoke C (Loaned on 11/9/1995) FL 0+1 Others 1
Bradford C (£30,000 on 22/12/1995) FL 23+1 FAC 1 Others 2
Blackpool (Loaned on 12/12/1996) FL 1+1
Northampton T (Free on 29/7/1997) FL 34+1/1 FLC 2 FAC 5 Others 2+1
Carlisle U (Free on 10/7/1998) FL 78/4 FLC 4 FAC 2 Others 3
Hull C (Free on 27/6/2000) FL 24+3/2 FLC 2 FAC 2 Others 1
Darlington (Free on 15/2/2001) FL 12+2

BRIGHTWELL Ian Robert
Born: Lutterworth, 9 April 1968
Height: 5'10" Weight: 12.5
International Honours: E: U21-4; Yth
Ian enjoyed a splendidly consistent season at Walsall in 2000-01, missing only two games all season. Playing on the right-hand side of the defence he was strong in the air, solid on the ground and impressive in the tackle. He is the brother of David Brightwell and the son of Olympic athletes Ann Packham and Robbie Brightwell.
Manchester C (From juniors on 7/5/1986) F/PL 285+36/18 FLC 29+2 FAC 19+4/1 Others 4+3
Coventry C (Free on 2/7/1998) FLC 1
Walsall (Free on 11/2/2000) FL 52+2 FLC 4 FAC 3 Others 3

BRISCO Neil Anthony
Born: Wigan, 26 January 1978
Height: 6'0" Weight: 11.5
Club Honours: AMC '01
Neil didn't have much of a look-in at Port Vale in the first half of last season and it wasn't until February that he made the starting line-up as a replacement for the suspended Tommy Widdrington. He seized his chance to hold down a regular place as the club embarked on a 16-game unbeaten run and he also appeared in the LDV Vans Trophy final victory over Brentford. A powerful midfield player he scored his first goal in senior football when he netted a

superb last-minute effort in the 2-1 win over Bournemouth.
Manchester C (From trainee on 4/3/1997)
Port Vale (Free on 7/8/1998) FL 28+2/1 FAC 2 Others 4+1

BRISCOE Lee Stephen
Born: Pontefract, 30 September 1975
Height: 5'11" Weight: 11.12
International Honours: E: U21-5
Lee soon settled into an attacking left-back role in the Burnley side in 2000-01, filling a position that had been a problem for some time. Although he likes to go forward, his qualities were nevertheless best seen at the back and his experience of higher-grade football proved invaluable for the Clarets. Unfortunately he suffered a knee injury in the home win against Norwich which kept him out of action for three months and then had another spell out after straining a hamstring at Hillsborough towards the end of the campaign. Lee is one of the younger members of the Burnley squad and should be a regular choice in the first team once again in the coming season.
Sheffield Wed (From trainee on 22/5/1994) PL 48+30/1 FLC 5+2 FAC 0+2 Others 2+1
Manchester C (Loaned on 20/2/1998) FL 5/1
Burnley (Free on 14/7/2000) FL 25+4 FLC 3

Lee Briscoe

BRISSETT Jason Curtis
Born: Wanstead, 7 September 1974
Height: 5'10" Weight: 12.7
Having signed for Leyton Orient on a free transfer during the close season Jason featured in a number of early-season games but seemed unable to settle in at Brisbane Road and moved on to Stevenage Borough towards the end of the year. He featured in a couple of games for the Conference club but was hampered by an ankle injury and was released in the summer. He is a wide left-sided midfield player with a good turn of pace and a useful cross.
Peterborough U (From trainee at Arsenal on 14/6/1993) FL 27+8 FLC 5+1/1 FAC 2+1/1 Others 3+1/1
Bournemouth (Free on 23/12/1994) 96+28/8 FLC 5+2 FAC 4 Others 6+2/2
Walsall (Free on 31/7/1998) FL 32+10/2 FLC 4/1 FAC 1 Others 3+2
Cheltenham T (Loaned on 11/11/1999) FL 5+3 Others 1+1
Leyton Orient (Free on 10/7/2000) FL 2+2 FLC 1+1

BRKOVIC Ahmet
Born: Dubrovnik, Croatia, 23 September 1974
Height: 5'7" Weight: 10.8
Ahmet was again an influential part of Leyton Orient's midfield last season when he was a regular member of the first-team squad. A skilful player who always seems to have time on the ball, he has excellent distribution and is capable of creating chances out of nothing. Out of contract at the end of the season he was reported to have been released on a free transfer.
Leyton Orient (Free from HNK Dubrovnik, Croatia on 14/10/1999) FL 59+10/8 FLC 3/2 FAC 4+2 Others 2+2

BROAD Stephen
Born: Epsom, 10 June 1980
Height: 6'0" Weight: 11.5
Stephen joined Southend United on loan just before the transfer deadline last season and made his debut in the 1-1 draw at Third Division champions Chesterfield. A composed character, he immediately formed a strong central defensive partnership with Phil Whelan and was a key figure in the Blues victory over Hartlepool which ended the Pool's 21-match unbeaten run. He produced some impressive displays being strong in the air and confident on the ground. A former youth-team captain at Stamford Bridge, he was released in the summer and reportedly joined Southend on a permanent basis soon afterwards.
Chelsea (From trainee on 9/2/1998)
Southend U (Loaned on 31/3/2001) FL 10

BROADHURST Karl Matthew
Born: Portsmouth, 18 March 1980
Height: 6'1" Weight: 11.7
Karl missed several weeks in the early part of last season with an ankle problem, but then injuries to Neil Young and Steve Purches allowed him into the Bournemouth first team and after an uncertain start he held down a regular place in the second half of the campaign. A promising central defender who is comfortable on the ball he featured mainly in a right-back role in 2000-01. Karl has signed a new three-year contract that will keep him at Dean Court until 2004.
Bournemouth (From trainee on 3/7/1998) FL 41+5 FLC 3 FAC 3 Others 2

BROCK Stuart Alan
Born: West Bromwich, 26 September 1976
Height: 6'1" Weight: 13.8
Club Honours: NC '00
Stuart started the 2000-01 season as Kidderminster's second-choice goalkeeper behind Tim Clarke, but soon displaced him in the side and gave a series of performances as good as any since he joined the club. He eventually lost his place following the defeat at Carlisle in February and made no further senior appearances during the campaign.
Aston Villa (From trainee on 10/5/1995)
Northampton T (Free on 27/3/1997. Free to Solihull Borough during 1997 close season)
Kidderminster Hrs (Free on 17/9/1997) FL 21 FLC 1 FAC 3

BROMBY Leigh
Born: Dewsbury, 2 June 1980
Height: 6'0" Weight: 11.8
International Honours: E: Sch
This young Sheffield Wednesday defender eventually broke into the first team last December and went on to produce a series of assured performances in the left-back position. Although essentially a central defender he never let the team down and retained his place in the Owls' line-up even when more experienced players were available.
Sheffield Wed (Free from Liversedge on 9/7/1998) FL 17+1 FAC 1+1
Mansfield T (Loaned on 10/12/1999) FL 10/1 Others 1

BROOKER Paul
Born: Hammersmith, 25 November 1976
Height: 5'8" Weight: 10.0
Club Honours: Div 3 '01
This exciting winger made a permanent move to Brighton in the summer of 2000 but after starting the first few games his form dropped off and he was relegated to the subs' bench for much of the autumn. He came back into the side in December as his confidence increased he returned to his best form. Paul has good pace and excellent ball control and can play on either flank if required.
Fulham (From trainee on 1/7/1995) FL 13+43/4 FLC 1+2/1 FAC 1+3/1 Others 3+3
Brighton & Hove A (£25,000 on 18/2/2000) FL 40+16/5 FLC 1+1 FAC 0+2 Others 2/1

BROOKER Stephen Michael Lord
Born: Newport Pagnel, 21 May 1981
Height: 5'10" Weight: 12.4
Club Honours: AMC '01
Unable to break into the first team at Vicarage Road, Stephen joined Port Vale on loan last January and proved an instant success. He scored in his second game for Vale in the LDV Vans Trophy tie against Notts County and very soon afterwards was signed in a permanent deal. He went on to net a number of vital goals, notably the winner just six minutes from time in the LDV Vans final against Brentford at Cardiff's Millenium Stadium. Full of enthusiasm he is a burly young striker with an excellent shot and a great eye for goal.
Watford (From trainee on 9/7/1999) PL 0+1 FAC 0+1
Port Vale (£15,000 on 5/1/2001) FL 20+3/8 Others 5/2

BROOKS Jamie Paul
Born: Oxford, 12 August 1983
Height: 5'9" Weight: 10.9
One of several promising youngsters on Oxford's books Jamie made his Football League debut from the subs' bench at Swindon in October before stepping up to sign a professional contract shortly before

Christmas. He then burst on the scene towards the end of the campaign with a 'Man of the Match' performance against Swansea when he set up one goal and scored another. A talented winger who can play on either flank he has already attracted attention from bigger clubs.
Oxford U (From trainee on 13/12/2000) FL 3+1/1

BROOMES Marlon Charles
Born: Birmingham, 28 November 1977
Height: 6'0" Weight: 12.12
International Honours: E: U21-2; Yth; Sch
Despite his obvious athleticism Marlon failed to make much of an impact with Blackburn last term and in fact slipped down the pecking order of defenders during the campaign. He made a handful of early season appearances for Rovers and then joined Queens Park Rangers on loan towards the end of October. He quickly became popular with the Loftus Road faithful with some fine performances and Rangers' boss Gerry Francis tried to make the deal permanent, but was unable to agree terms and so Marlon returned to Ewood Park where he played no further part in the club's successful season. He remains a central defender of considerable potential but really needs to gain regular first-team football to enable him to fulfil this.
Blackburn Rov (From trainee on 28/11/1994) P/FL 24+7/1 FLC 3 FAC 4
Swindon T (Loaned on 22/1/1997) FL 12/1
Queens Park R (Loaned on 25/10/2000) FL 5

BROUGH John Robert
Born: Ilkeston, 8 January 1973
Height: 6'0" Weight: 13.0
Club Honours: NC '99
John began last season in Cheltenham Town's line-up but was hampered by hamstring trouble early on, and shortly after he had recovered he had the misfortune to suffer a serious knee ligament injury playing against Macclesfield in October. It was not until towards the end of the campaign that his rehabilitation was complete and he made no further senior appearances. He is a versatile player who is essentially a central defender but has occasionally appeared as a makeshift striker.
Notts Co (From trainee on 9/7/1991)
Shrewsbury T (Free on 6/7/1992) FL 7+9/1 FLC 1+1 FAC 1 Others 1 (Free to Telford during 1994 close season)
Hereford U (Free on 4/11/1994) FL 70+9/3 FLC 5 FAC 4/1 Others 4+3
Cheltenham T (Signed on 16/7/1998) FL 19+28/2 FLC 1+1 FAC 2/1 Others 0+1

BROUGH Michael
Born: Nottingham, 1 August 1981
Height: 6'0" Weight: 11.7
A graduate of Notts County's youth system, Michael gained further senior experience when he was called up for a run in the first team in the new year and he again made a solid impact, scoring his first-ever Football League goal with a superb left-foot shot to clinch a 1-0 win at Swansea in February. A promising central midfield ball-winner with a never-say-die attitude he will be hoping to win a regular place in the squad in 2001-02.
Notts Co (From trainee on 1/7/1999) FL 22+5/1 FAC 1+2

BROUGH Scott
Born: Scunthorpe, 10 February 1983
Height: 5'6" Weight: 9.10
Formerly on Leeds United's books as an associate schoolboy Scott progressed from the Scunthorpe juniors into the first-team squad last November while still doing his 'A'-Levels at college. He made a handful of appearances as a substitute and will be hoping for a better look-in at first team level next season. He is a skilful winger who can operate on either flank and has good pace and a directness about his play.
Scunthorpe U (From juniors on 9/11/2000) FL 0+4 FAC 0+1 Others 0+1

BROUGHTON Drewe Oliver
Born: Hitchin, 25 October 1978
Height: 6'3" Weight: 12.10
Out of favour at Peterborough Drewe spent time on loan at Dagenham & Redbridge and Stevenage in the first half of last season before joining Third Division new boys Kidderminster, again on loan, at the turn of the year. He scored on his debut at Mansfield and did well enough at Aggborough to earn a permanent transfer, going on to find the net regularly in the closing weeks of the campaign. Drewe is a big and bustling target man who has a good first touch.
Norwich C (From trainee on 6/5/1997) FL 3+6/1
Wigan Ath (Loaned on 15/8/1997) FL 1+3
Brentford (£100,000 on 30/10/1998) FL 1
Peterborough U (£100,000 on 17/11/1998) FL 19+16/8 FLC 2 Others 1+1/1
Kidderminster Hrs (£50,000 on 22/1/2001) FL 19/7

BROWN Aaron Wesley
Born: Bristol, 14 March 1980
Height: 5'10" Weight: 11.12
International Honours: E: Sch
Aaron came on in leaps and bounds at Bristol City last season and was particularly impressive in the FA Cup fourth round replay win at Kingstonian. He opened his goal-scoring account with a brace in the 3-1 victory over Luton Town towards the end of the campaign and if he can add a bit of steel to his tackling he may soon attract attention from higher-grade clubs. Aaron is the older brother of Marvin Brown who also plays for City.
Bristol C (From trainee on 7/11/1997) FL 51+11/4 FLC 0+2 FAC 6 Others 4+1
Exeter C (Loaned on 6/1/2000) FL 4+1/1

BROWN Daniel (Danny)
Born: Bethnal Green, 12 September 1980
Height: 6'0" Weight: 12.0
Danny established himself as the first choice on the left side of midfield for Barnet last season and managed to rediscover some of the form that he had shown during the previous campaign. Danny has great vision and when pushing forward he can deliver an excellent cross, as was demonstrated in the 2-1 defeat at Hull City. He was placed on the open to offers list in the summer.
Leyton Orient (From trainee on 5/5/1998) Others 1
Barnet (Free on 25/5/1999) FL 42+11/3 FLC 0+1 FAC 1+1 Others 5

BROWN David Alistair
Born: Bolton, 2 October 1978
Height: 5'10" Weight: 12.6
David struggled to hold down a regular starting place for Hull City in the first half of the 2000-01 campaign and his future began to look bleak when the club recruited a new attacking duo of Kevin Francis and Rodney Rowe but then he switched to a midfield role with considerable success. Still essentially a striker his future at Boothferry Park seemed in doubt at the time of writing as he was placed on the open to offers list in the summer.
Manchester U (From trainee on 27/10/1995)
Hull C (Free on 26/3/1998) FL 108+23/23 FLC 9+1/5 FAC 10/3 Others 5+1

BROWN Grant Ashley
Born: Sunderland, 19 November 1969
Height: 6'0" Weight: 11.12
Lincoln's longest-serving player experienced both the high and low points of his career during his 11th season at Sincil Bank. Although normally a right-sided player he filled in as a left-sided central defender during the first half of the campaign. Grant broke a club record when he made his 425th senior appearance against Morecambe in the LDV Vans Trophy in November but two months later his season came to an end when he suffered a double fracture of the left leg in a local 'derby' clash with Hull City. By the start of May he was back in light training and hoping to be match fit for the start of the 2001-2002 campaign.
Leicester C (From trainee on 1/7/1988) FL 14 FLC 2
Lincoln C (Loaned on 20/8/1989) FL 14/1 FLC 2 Others 1
Lincoln C (£60,000 on 4/1/1990) FL 355+2/14 FLC 20/1 FAC 15 Others 19+1/2

BROWN John **Keith**
Born: Edinburgh, 24 December 1979
Height: 6'0" Weight: 11.0
International Honours: S: Yth
Keith found his first-team opportunities at Barnsley very limited at the start of the 2000-01 season, and after making just a single appearance against Birmingham at the end of August he joined Oxford United for a two-month loan period. He performed consistently well at left back during his stay at the Manor Ground, helping the U's to back-to-back wins in his first two games. On his return to Oakwell he was made reserve team captain and did a good job bringing on the youngsters coming up from the academy. A versatile defender who can play either in central defence or at left back he reads the game well and is strong in the tackle.
Blackburn Rov (From trainee on 16/1/1997)
Barnsley (Loaned on 10/9/1999) FL 4
Barnsley (£100,000 on 20/12/1999) FL 4+3 Others 3
Oxford U (Loaned on 10/11/2000) FL 3 FAC 2 Others 1

BROWN Marvin Robert
Born: Bristol, 6 July 1983
Height: 5'9" Weight: 11.1
International Honours: E: Yth
Marvin has been very much a star-in-waiting for almost two seasons at Bristol

City, but still has to follow his elder brother Aaron and cement a regular first-team place. He continued to make steady progress in the 2000-01 campaign but his first-team appearances were limited to outings from the subs' bench. A very promising young striker he needs to gain more senior experience to begin to fulfil his obvious promise. He made two appearances for England U17s during the season.
Bristol C (From trainee on 18/7/2000) FL 0+7 FLC 0+1 FAC 0+1 Others 0+1

BROWN Michael (Mickey) Antony
Born: Birmingham, 8 February 1968
Height: 5'9" Weight: 11.12
Club Honours: Div 3 '94
Mickey had a stop-start season at Shrewsbury in 2000-01 and although he featured regularly in the squad he was often on the subs' bench. A versatile player who is essentially a wide right midfielder he can also play up front or at full back. Wherever he featured Mickey always gave 100 per cent and looked capable of creating danger with his speed. Forever a hero at Gay Meadow following the goal he scored at Exeter in May 2000 to secure Football League status, he created a new club record of league appearances when he overtook Colin Griffin's tally of 406 before being released at the end of the campaign.
Shrewsbury T (From apprentice on 11/2/1986) FL 174+16/9 FLC 17/2 FAC 10/1 Others 11
Bolton W (£100,000 on 15/8/1991) FL 27+6/3 FLC 0+1 FAC 3 Others 2
Shrewsbury T (£25,000 on 23/12/1992) FL 66+1/11 FLC 8/1 FAC 3 Others 2
Preston NE (£75,000 on 30/11/1994) FL 11+5/1 FLC 0+1 Others 1
Rochdale (Loaned on 13/9/1996) FL 5
Shrewsbury T (£20,000 on 12/12/1996) FL 111+50/16 FLC 3+2 FAC 4+1 Others 6+1

BROWN Michael Robert
Born: Hartlepool, 25 January 1977
Height: 5'9" Weight: 11.8
International Honours: E: U21-4
Michael had an excellent season with Sheffield United in 2000-01, playing a key role in the centre of the park. A hard-working left-sided midfield player with the ability to win the ball he was able to create many openings for others with his perceptive passing. Absent for only a handful of occasions until March he then injured ankle ligaments in training causing him to miss the remainder of the season.
Manchester C (From trainee on 13/9/1994) F/PL 67+22/2 FLC 2+4 FAC 10+1/2 Others 4
Hartlepool U (Loaned on 27/3/1997) FL 6/1
Portsmouth (Loaned on 19/11/1999) FL 4
Sheffield U (Signed on 17/12/1999) FL 57+3/4 FLC 4/1

BROWN Simon James
Born: Chelmsford, 3 December 1976
Height: 6'2" Weight: 15.0
Simon began the 2000-01 campaign as first choice 'keeper for Colchester United and retained his place until Andy Woodman arrived from Brentford in November. He also played in the humiliating FA Cup defeat by Yeovil, when Woodman was ineligible, but appeared only once in the second half of the season. Simon remains a promising young goalkeeper who is an excellent shot stopper but he needs to try and develop a more commanding presence in the penalty area.
Tottenham H (From trainee on 1/7/1995)
Lincoln C (Loaned on 19/12/1997) FL 1
Colchester U (Free on 20/7/1999) FL 56 FLC 5 FAC 2 Others 1

BROWN Steven (Steve) Byron
Born: Brighton, 13 May 1972
Height: 6'1" Weight: 13.10
Club Honours: Div 1 '00
Steve was a regular in central defence for Charlton Athletic in the early part of last season but lost his place when Mark Fish arrived from Bolton in November and from then on was used mainly as a substitute. He is a reliable centre half who is strong and commanding in the air, has good distribution under pressure and rarely makes a bad pass. He also has a very powerful right-foot shot which is often employed usefully at set pieces. An extremely versatile player, Steve can also play in midfield or at right back, and in the past has even been used as an emergency goalkeeper.
Charlton Ath (From trainee on 3/7/1990) P/FL 183+42/7 FLC 10+2 FAC 18/1 Others 3+2

BROWN Steven (Steve) Ferold
Born: Northampton, 6 July 1966
Height: 6'0" Weight: 11.8
Steve had a memorable season for Wycombe Wanderers in 2000-01 and performed to his usual high standards throughout the campaign. He scored three goals in the first six league games and also netted a late and controversial equaliser against Wimbledon in the FA Cup fifth round to keep the Chairboys remarkable run going. He subsequently achieved national headlines and great sympathy when he received a second booking while celebrating the winning goal in the FA Cup sixth round tie at Leicester City. A very popular left-sided midfield player who is effective in the tackle he accumulated several yellow cards in the closing stages of the campaign and this is an area of his game where he needs to show improvement.
Northampton T (From juniors on 11/8/1983) FL 14+1/3 (Free to Irthlingborough T in December 1985)
Northampton T (Free on 21/7/1989) FL 145+13/19 FLC 10/1 FAC 12/2 Others 10+1/1
Wycombe W (£60,000 on 9/2/1994) FL 250+20/21 FLC 20+2/3 FAC 20+5/2 Others 10+2/1

BROWN Wayne Lawrence
Born: Barking, 20 August 1977
Height: 6'0" Weight: 12.6
Wayne was the player who made way for Hermann Hreidarsson at Ipswich last term and he found himself on the substitutes bench for the opening game at Tottenham. A promising central defender he was then troubled by injury for much of the season and was only able to make a total of four first-team appearances, all from the subs' bench. There was talk of a transfer to Wimbledon during the early stages of the campaign but nothing materialised and he eventually joined First Division Queens Park Rangers in a loan deal on the transfer deadline day. Unfortunately he then suffered further injury problems in only his second game for the West London club and he returned to Portman Road early.
Ipswich T (From trainee on 16/5/1996) P/FL 21+10 FLC 2 FAC 1 Others 1+1
Colchester U (Loaned on 16/10/1997) FL 0+2
Queens Park R (Loaned on 22/3/2001) FL 2

BROWN Wesley (Wes) Michael
Born: Manchester, 13 October 1979
Height: 6'1" Weight: 12.4
Club Honours: EC '99; PL '99; '01
International Honours: E: 3; U21-8; Yth; Sch
If there were an award for 'Comeback Player of the Year' in the 2000-01 season Wes would surely have won it hands down. For after a 15-month absence with a ruptured cruciate ligament that nearly wrecked his career, his re-emergence was one of Manchester United's most glittering success stories. Not only did he help to solve Sir Alex Ferguson's central defensive problems caused by the long-term absence of Jaap Stam but he also earned rave reviews for his cameo role for England as a substitute in their vital World Cup qualifier against Finland in Helsinki in October. His performances won praise from both Ferguson and stand-in England boss Howard Wilkinson. Once Stam returned from injury, Wes combined well with the big Dutchman and in February there was serious speculation that he might become a future England captain. Ironically he then missed the friendly against Spain in February, which just goes to show that football can be a funny old game. Now firmly established as a first-team regular, the Brown-Stam partnership looks set to become a feature of United's back line for many years to come. He was selected for the PFA's Premiership team in April.
Manchester U (From trainee on 13/11/1996) PL 37+7 FLC 1+1 FAC 3 Others 12+3

BROWNING Marcus Trevor
Born: Bristol, 22 April 1971
Height: 6'0" Weight: 12.10
International Honours: W: 5
Marcus was in and out of the Gillingham team in the first half of last season and it was only in January that he gained a regular first-team place following injuries to Andy Hessenthaler and Ty Gooden. An effective ball winner in central midfield, he began to show his best form towards the end of the season, working hard and producing some excellent passes.
Bristol Rov (From trainee on 1/7/1989) FL 152+22/13 FLC 7+3 FAC 8/1 Others 13+5/3
Hereford U (Loaned on 18/9/1992) FL 7/5
Huddersfield T (£500,000 on 17/2/1997) FL 25+8 FLC 2+2
Gillingham (Loaned on 20/11/1998) FL 1
Gillingham (£150,000 on 25/3/1999) FL 22+13 FLC 4 FAC 1+2 Others 0+1

BRUCE Paul Mark
Born: Lambeth, 18 February 1978
Height: 5'11" Weight: 12.0
After a successful 1999-2000 campaign for

Queens Park Rangers Paul found himself limited to a handful of appearances from the subs' bench in the first half of last season. He was a regular in the reserves and had a brief run in the starting line-up in the new year before being sidelined by injury. A left-sided midfield player he was one of 15 players released by Rangers in the summer.
Queens Park R (From trainee on 15/7/1996) FL 17+7/2 FLC 0+1 FAC 3+1
Cambridge U (Loaned on 25/3/1999) FL 2+2

BRUMWELL Phillip (Phil)
Born: Darlington, 8 August 1975
Height: 5'8" Weight: 11.0
Phil ended a five-year spell at Darlington in the 2000 close season when he joined Third Division rivals Hull City. His versatility seemed to make him an excellent addition to the Tigers' small squad but he was unable to establish himself in the starting line-up and readily agreed a return to Darlington at the end of November. Phil covered for various positions in defence and midfield and was a near-ever present for the remainder of the campaign. A local boy he really relished playing for his home-town club and was extremely glad to be back. Phil always produces committed displays whenever he is called upon and has now completed almost two hundred games for the Quakers.
Sunderland (From trainee on 30/6/1994)
Darlington (Free on 11/8/1995) FL 106+50/1 FLC 5+2 FAC 7+5/2 Others 8+3
Hull C (Free on 10/8/2000) FL 1+3 FLC 1+1
Darlington (Free on 30/11/2000) FL 19+2 FAC 0+2 Others 3

BRYAN Marvin Lee
Born: Paddington, 2 August 1975
Height: 6'0" Weight: 12.2
Marvin started off as a regular on the right side of the back three for Rotherham United in 2001-02 before suffering an injury that kept him out of the side. He was initially used mainly as a substitute on his return and it was not until March that he managed to regain his place in the line-up on the right-hand side of midfield.
Queens Park R (From trainee on 17/8/1992)
Doncaster Rov (Loaned on 8/12/1994) FL 5/1
Blackpool (£20,000 on 10/8/1995) FL 172+10/4 FLC 10+3 FAC 8 Others 12
Bury (Free on 23/3/2000) FL 6+3
Rotherham U (Free on 10/7/2000) FL 23+5 FLC 2 FAC 1 Others 1

BRYANT Simon Christopher
Born: Bristol, 22 November 1982
Height: 5'9" Weight: 10.7
Simon made excellent progress for Bristol Rovers last season in what was generally a disappointing campaign for the club. He featured regularly in the first team and netted his first senior goal with a spectacular 25-yard strike at Cambridge in September. He then went on to become the Pirates youngest-ever captain when he skippered the side in the final game of the season against Wrexham. A combative midfield player his efforts were rewarded by a call-up to the England U18 squad and he made his debut against the Faroe Islands.
Bristol Rov (From trainee on 17/1/2000) FL 36+9/1 FLC 5+3 FAC 1 Others 3

BRYNGELSSON Fredrik
Born: Sweden, 10 April 1975
Height: 6'3" Weight: 13.0
Having signed from Swedish club BK Hacken during the summer, Fredrik played in six of the first seven fixtures for Stockport County last term but then lost his place following the surprise Worthington Cup defeat by Blackpool. A knee injury then hindered his progress and he made just one more first-team appearance before the end of the campaign. Tall, quick and comfortable on the ball he possesses all the attributes to be a successful defender but sometimes seems to find it difficult to come to terms with the physical side of the game.
Stockport Co (£80,000 from BK Hacken, Sweden, ex IFK Goteborg, Norrby IF, on 25/7/2000) FL 4+1 FLC 2

BUBB Alvin Ryan
Born: Paddington, 11 October 1980
Height: 5'6" Weight: 10.7
This young Queens Park Rangers prospect received limited opportunities for the reserve team last season due to injuries. However, he stepped up to make his Football League debut on the final day of the campaign when he came on from the subs' bench in the closing minutes of Rangers game at Wolves. A striker who prefers playing on the right-hand side he was one of 15 players released by the Loftus Road club in the summer.
Queens Park R (From trainee on 16/11/1998) FL 0+1

BUBB Byron James
Born: Harrow, 17 December 1981
Height: 5'7" Weight: 10.5
Byron found it difficult to break into a strong Millwall line-up last season and only made a handful of senior appearances. He continued his development in the reserves where he proved to be a fast and tricky winger who can deliver a good cross. He was released by the Lions in the summer.
Millwall (From trainee on 30/12/1998) FL 3+5

BUCKLE Paul John
Born: Hatfield, 16 December 1970
Height: 5'8" Weight: 11.10
Club Honours: Div 3 '92
After being left out for the first handful of games at the start of the 2000-01 campaign Paul came back into the Exeter City team in September and grabbed his chance with both hands. His consistent performances in central midfield made him a key figure for the Grecians and his distribution was superb. His stunning 25-yard effort in the 3-1 home win against York was one of the highlights of the season at St James Park.
Brentford (From trainee on 1/7/1989) FL 42+15/1 FLC 5+1 FAC 3+1 Others 6+5
Torquay U (Free on 3/2/1994) FL 57+2/9 FLC 8 FAC 3 Others 1
Exeter C (Free on 13/10/1995) FL 22/2 FAC 1 Others 2
Northampton T (Free on 30/8/1996)
Wycombe W (Free on 18/10/1996)
Colchester U (Free on 28/11/1996) FL 96+9/7 FLC 4 FAC 2 Others 10/3
Exeter C (Free on 2/7/1999) FL 66+2/4 FAC 4+1 Others 6/1

BUGGIE Lee David
Born: Bury, 11 February 1981
Height: 5'9" Weight: 11.0
This promising Bury youngster joined Rochdale on loan last September to gain experience of first-team football. He went on to make two appearances from the subs' bench before returning to Gigg Lane and soon afterwards he went to Unibond League club Whitby Town, also on loan. He subsequently continued to develop in the Shakers' reserves and made one senior appearance from the subs' bench in the LDV Vans tie against Kidderminster in January. A stocky striker he was released by Bury in the summer.
Bolton W (From trainee on 18/2/1998)
Bury (Free on 27/5/1999) FL 0+1 Others 0+1
Rochdale (Loaned on 15/9/2000) FL 0+2

BUKRAN Gabor
Born: Hungary, 16 November 1975
Height: 5'11" Weight: 12.2
International Honours: Hungary: 1; U21; Yth
Gabor impressed for Walsall in the Worthington Cup games against West Ham last season when his use of the ball was seen to best effect and seemed to be reaching top form again in mid-season when he netted twice in a game against Cambridge. However he then received an uncharacteristic red card at Bury that seemed to affect his performances although he returned to feature again towards the end of the campaign. He is a stylish midfield player who finishes well, however, he was released in the summer.
Walsall (Free from Xerez CD, Spain on 5/8/1999) FL 63+10/4 FLC 8/3 FAC 3+1 Others 1+1

BULL Ronald (Ronnie) Rodney
Born: Hackney, 26 December 1980
Height: 5'8" Weight: 10.12
Ronnie found it difficult to replace regular left back Robbie Ryan in the Millwall line-up last season and was restricted to just a handful of first-team outings as cover when Ryan was suspended. He continued his development in the club's reserves where he showed himself to be a tenacious defender who loves to push down the flank. Ronnie will be hoping to gain more first-team opportunities in the 2001-02 campaign.
Millwall (From trainee on 12/5/1999) FL 8+4 Others 1

BULLOCK Anthony (Tony) Brian
Born: Warrington, 18 February 1972
Height: 6'1" Weight: 12.13
Tony joined Macclesfield Town on a one-year contract following some impressive performances in the 2000-01 pre-season games. His fine form continued into the new campaign but after suspension he lost his place to Lee Martin and moved to Lincoln on transfer deadline day as an experienced back-up for regular 'keeper Alan Marriott. However he made just two first-team appearances for the Imps before he was injured in a reserve game. An excellent shot stopper with a huge kick and a long throw he was released in May.
Barnsley (£20,000 from Leek T on 27/3/1997) FL 37+1 FLC 4 FAC 5

Macclesfield T (Free on 26/7/2000) FL 24 FLC 4 Others 1
Lincoln C (Free on 21/3/2001) FL 2

BULLOCK Darren John
Born: Worcester, 12 February 1969
Height: 5'9" Weight: 12.10
Darren started the 2000-01 season in scintillating form as the Shakers spent the opening two months riding high near the top of the Second Division table. That success was due in no small way to his own contribution as he hit top form, scoring four goals in the opening seven games. He then suffered a thigh injury at the end of September that kept him sidelined for two months and shortly after returning he fell foul of disciplinary problems. Never able to win his place back, he moved on loan to Sheffield United on the transfer deadline day, linking up once again with his old boss Neil Warnock. He went on to make his debut in the Sheffield 'derby' at Hillsborough but after some promising displays a hernia injury ended his hopes of a permanent deal. He is a combative midfield player with excellent ball-winning skills.
Huddersfield T (£55,000 from Nuneaton Borough on 19/11/1993) FL 127+1/16 FLC 11/1 FAC 8/2 Others 9/1
Swindon T (£400,000 on 24/2/1997) FL 55+11/2 FLC 2 FAC 1
Bury (£150,000 + on 15/2/1999) FL 43+6/5 FLC 4/2 FAC 5/1 Others 1/1
Sheffield U (Loaned on 22/3/2001) FL 6

BULLOCK Lee
Born: Stockton, 22 May 1981
Height: 5'9" Weight: 11.7
Lee had a very good season for York City in 2000-01 especially in the closing weeks of the campaign when he played a full part in the Minstermen's revival. A good all-round player who is strong both in the air and on the ground, he gave plenty support to the front men with some strong running from midfield and netted vital goals in the victories over Halifax Town and Radcliffe Borough. A talented young midfield player he will be looking to win a regular place in the starting line-up in 2001-02.
York C (From trainee on 29/6/1999) FL 45+12/3 FLC 2+1 FAC 2+1/1

BULLOCK Martin John
Born: Derby, 5 March 1975
Height: 5'5" Weight: 10.7
International Honours: E: U21-1
Martin missed the start of the 2000-01 season with a groin injury that required corrective surgery and it was not until January that he made his first appearance in the starting line-up for Barnsley. He was rarely absent after that, performing either wide on the right-hand side of midfield or in a more central role. At his best when attacking defenders in open play he can also deliver a telling cross. Out of contract in the summer, he was released on a free transfer.
Barnsley (£15,000 from Eastwood T on 4/9/1993) F/PL 108+77/4 FLC 14+3 FAC 4+11/3 Others 1
Port Vale (Loaned on 14/1/2000) FL 6/1

BULMAN Dannie
Born: Ashford, Surrey, 24 January 1979
Height: 5'10" Weight: 12.3
Dannie had a fine season at Wycombe in 2000-01 when he firmly established himself in the team and produced some excellent displays in the centre of the park. He is a tigerish midfield player who is strong in the tackle and has the knack of successfully threading diagonal passes through defences to set up chances for his colleagues. Probably the most improved player for the Chairboys last term he fails to recognise any cause as a lost one.
Wycombe W (£5,000 + from Ashford T on 17/6/1998) FL 51+25/6 FLC 5+1 FAC 8+4 Others 4

BURCHILL Mark James
Born: Broxburn, 18 August 1980
Height: 5'8" Weight: 10.2
Club Honours: SLC '00
International Honours: S: 6; U21-15; Sch
Mark got off to an explosive start at Celtic last term netting a hat-trick within four minutes in the 7-0 thrashing of Luxembourg's Jeunesse Esch in a UEFA Cup qualifying round tie. However he failed to win a regular place in Martin O'Neill's team and was soon on his way to Birmingham City in a loan deal. He did well at St Andrews netting five goals from seven starts and becoming a huge crowd favourite to the extent that the fans raised a petition to pressure the club into signing him permanently. However the transfer eventually fell through and in February he joined Ipswich Town on loan for the remainder of the season, primarily as cover for Marcus Stewart. He made his debut in the home game with Everton and created a tremendous impression being denied a penalty as early as the seventh minute. He also had a shot blocked and a flying header saved before he turned provider with his crosses from the left wing creating goals for Matt Holland and Alun Armstrong. He scored in the following game against Bradford, when he got the slightest touch on Hermann Hreidarsson's goal-bound header, but although he made further substitute appearances he never featured again in the starting line-up and returned to Celtic Park once the season had ended. He is an effective striker blessed with blinding pace, the ability to kick with either foot, the knack of being in the right place at the right time and great movement off the ball.
Glasgow Celtic (From Celtic BC on 3/6/1997) SL 17+34/21 SLC 3+2 SC 1+2/1 Others 3+1
Birmingham C (Loaned on 22/9/2000) FL 4+9/4 FLC 3+1/1
Ipswich T (Loaned on 22/1/2001) PL 2+5/1

BURGESS Benjamin (Ben)
Born: Buxton, 9 November 1981
Height: 6'3" Weight: 14.4
International Honours: RoI: Yth
This promising Blackburn Rovers striker made an early season appearance in the Worthington Cup second round second leg tie against Portsmouth before jetting off to Australia where he joined NSL club Northern Spirit on loan for the remainder of the 2000-01 campaign. The move was a success and despite being hampered by niggling injuries he scored a creditable 16 goals in 26 appearances. Having tasted regular first-team action, Ben will be aiming to gain more senior experience at Ewood Park in the coming season.
Blackburn Rov (From trainee on 25/11/1998) FL 1+1 FLC 1

BURGESS Daryl
Born: Birmingham, 24 January 1971
Height: 5'11" Weight: 12.4
Daryl was rarely used by West Bromwich Albion boss Gary Megson last term and apart from a handful of senior outings he played most of his football in the reserves. An experienced defender whose versatility makes him a useful squad member, he received a testimonial match against Newcastle United in May but soon afterwards he was released by the Baggies. He was reported to have signed for Northampton Town in the summer.
West Bromwich A (From trainee on 1/7/1989) FL 317+15/10 FLC 19+3/3 FAC 9 Others 14

BURGESS Oliver David
Born: Bracknell, 12 October 1981
Height: 5'10" Weight: 11.7
Oliver was yet another of Queens Park Rangers' successful U19 team who received an introduction to first-team football last season. A promising central midfield player he came on from the subs' bench for the final 30 minutes of the home match with Blackburn at the beginning of April. He later featured in both legs of the FA Academy League final when Rangers were narrowly defeated by Nottingham Forest.
Queens Park R (Trainee) FL 0+1

BURGESS Richard Daniel
Born: Bromsgrove, 18 August 1978
Height: 5'8" Weight: 11.4
Richard began the 2000-01 campaign with Dr Martens Premier Division outfit Worcester City but received few early season opportunities and moved on to neighbours Bromsgrove Rovers at the end of August. His performances soon attracted the attention of Football League scouts and after a proposed move to Northampton fell through he signed for Port Vale in March. A small and nippy striker he showed plenty of promise in the reserves, scoring a hat-trick in the game at Oldham, and made his Football League debut when coming off the subs' bench in the closing stages of the game at Millwall. He was reported to have signed a 12-month contract for Vale in the summer.
Aston Villa (From trainee on 5/7/1996)
Stoke C (Free on 17/5/1997. Free to Worcester C on 31/3/2000)
Port Vale (Loaned from Bromsgrove Rov on 22/3/2001) FL 0+1

BURLEY Adam Gareth
Born: Sheffield, 27 November 1980
Height: 5'10" Weight: 12.6
Having broken into the Sheffield United team in 1999-2000 Adam continued his football education with the reserves last season apart from a couple of early outings from the subs' bench. He spent time on loan with Nigel Clough's Burton Albion in the new year and was a member of the Blades'

successful reserve team that won the Avon Insurance league and cup double.
Sheffield U (From trainee on 5/7/1999) FL 0+3/1 FLC 0+3

BURLEY Craig William
Born: Irvine, 24 September 1971
Height: 6'1" Weight: 13.0
Club Honours: SLC '97; SPD '98
International Honours: S: 42; U21-7; Yth; Sch
Craig was sidelined by a calf injury in the opening weeks of the 2000-01 campaign and it was not until the end of September that he returned to full fitness. A midfield schemer he prefers a role on the right-hand side from where he can link up between defence and attack and deliver some telling crosses into the opposition penalty area. After the success of the previous season he played a more muted role as the Rams struggled to avoid relegation. Although possessing a venomous shot he only scored four goals, the most notable being that which earned three vital points against Sunderland in March. A regular for Scotland at international level, he is the nephew of Ipswich boss George Burley.
Chelsea (From trainee on 1/9/1989) P/FL 85+28/7 FLC 8 FAC 12+5/4 Others 3
Glasgow Celtic (£2,500,000 on 24/7/1997) SL 61+3/20 SLC 7 SC 6/1 Others 12/1
Derby Co (£3,000,000 on 2/12/1999) PL 42/7 FLC 3/2 FAC 2

Craig Burley

BURNELL Joseph (Joe) Michael
Born: Bristol, 10 October 1980
Height: 5'10" Weight: 11.1
Having generally played in a midfield role for Bristol City in 1999-2000, a spate of injuries enabled Joe to feature in defence last season. A tough-tackling player who is comfortable at either right back or in the centre of the defence, he produced some stirring displays and was deservedly rewarded with a long-term contract at Ashton Gate.
Bristol C (From trainee on 24/7/1999) FL 34+6 FAC 0+3 Others 4/1

BURNETT Wayne
Born: Lambeth, 4 September 1971
Height: 5'11" Weight: 12.6
Club Honours: AMC '98
International Honours: E: Yth
Having finally shaken off the groin problem that had dogged him for so long, Wayne eventually won his place back in Grimsby Town's line-up last November. He gradually returned to his old form but was then sidelined by a knee injury in the new year and it was not until the final day of the season that he made a return to the squad. When fully fit he is a creative midfield player able to deliver a telling pass. He was released in the summer.
Leyton Orient (From trainee on 13/11/1989) FL 34+6 FLC 3+1/1 FAC 3+1 Others 4
Blackburn Rov (£90,000 on 19/8/1992)
Plymouth Arg (Signed on 9/8/1993) FL 61+9/3 FLC 3 FAC 8 Others 4+1
Bolton W (£100,000 on 12/10/1995) F/PL 0+2
Huddersfield T (Signed on 6/9/1996) FL 44+6 FLC 6+1/1 FAC 1+1
Grimsby T (£100,000 on 9/1/1998) FL 62+12/4 FLC 3+2 FAC 0+2 Others 8/3

BURNS Jacob Geoffrey
Born: Sydney, Australia, 1 April 1978
Height: 5'9" Weight: 11.12
International Honours: Australia: 2; U23-19
Jacob joined Leeds United last August after a successful pre-season trial and won an early appearance in the first-team squad due to the club's injury problems. He found himself on the bench at Barcelona in the Champions' League, and because of the worsening situation he made his Premiership debut in central midfield in the 3-1 win against Charlton in October. He remained in the first-team picture, making another eight appearances including some in the European matches against Real Madrid and Lazio. Self-assured and very focused he looks to have a promising future at Elland Road.
Leeds U (£250,000 from Parramatta Power, Australia, ex Sydney U, on 31/8/2000) PL 3+1 FLC 1 Others 3+1

BURNS Liam
Born: Belfast, 30 October 1978
Height: 6'0" Weight: 12.12
International Honours: NI: U21-13; Yth
Liam had few first-team opportunities at Port Vale in 2000-01 and it is for an appearance in an unaccustomed role that his season will be remembered. When 'keeper Mark Goodlad was carried off just 30 minutes into the home game with Wigan in March Liam came off the bench, took over in goal and produced a very capable performance to earn Vale a point in a 0-0 draw. He is a dependable central defender who always tries his best whatever the circumstances.
Port Vale (From trainee on 2/7/1997) FL 31+11 FAC 2 Others 0+1

BURROWS David
Born: Dudley, 25 October 1968
Height: 5'9" Weight: 11.8
Club Honours: CS '89; Div 1 '90; FAC '92
International Honours: E: B-3; U21-7
David had a disappointing campaign at Birmingham City in 2000-01. He was sidelined early on after pulling a hamstring in the final pre-season game then aggravated the problem in the opening minutes of his debut against Sheffield United in September. Although he looked accomplished and capable on the ball at left back when he was chosen he remained a reserve to Martin Grainger, only getting the occasional opportunity due to injuries or suspensions. After being left out of the Worthington Cup final team he asked for a transfer and his request was granted by the Blues' management.
West Bromwich A (From apprentice on 8/11/1986) FL 37+9/1 FLC 3+1 FAC 2 Others 1
Liverpool (£550,000 on 20/10/1988) F/PL 135+11/3 FLC 16 FAC 16+1 Others 14
West Ham U (Signed on 17/9/1993) PL 29/1 FLC 3/1 FAC 3
Everton (Signed on 6/9/1994) PL 19 FLC 2 FAC 2
Coventry C (£1,100,000 on 2/3/1995) PL 106+5 FLC 9 FAC 9
Birmingham C (Free on 4/7/2000) FL 8+5 FLC 0+2

BURROWS Mark
Born: Kettering, 14 August 1980
Height: 6'3" Weight: 12.8
Mark joined Exeter City in July 2000 and made his Football League debut for the Grecians against Darlington. Apart from a period around the turn of the year he appeared regularly and he will be looking to firmly establish a place in the line-up in the coming season. A tall central defender he is effective in the air and his physical presence was useful when both defending and attacking at set pieces.
Coventry C (From trainee on 19/1/1998)
Exeter C (Free on 18/7/2000) FL 21+8 FLC 2 FAC 1

BURTON Deon John
Born: Ashford, 25 October 1976
Height: 5'9" Weight: 11.9
International Honours: Jamaica: 36
2000-01 was a season of contrasting fortunes for Deon. He started well, netting in the opening game with Southampton, but by November his form and confidence had dipped and he spent a short time on the transfer list. Injuries led to a recall at the turn of the year, however, and he responded enthusiastically. His most important goal of the season was a fine header that earned the Rams a point at Anfield over Easter. Blessed with a great deal of pace, he is at his best when running directly at defenders while his off-the-ball movement can cause trouble for opposing defences. Deon continued to lead the attack for Jamaica throughout the campaign winning a further 12 caps.
Portsmouth (From trainee on 15/2/1994) FL 42+20/10 FLC 3+2/2 FAC 0+2/1
Cardiff C (Loaned on 24/12/1996) FL 5/2 Others 1
Derby Co (£1,000,000 + on 9/8/1997) PL 66+35/21 FLC 5+2/1 FAC 9+1/3
Barnsley (Loaned on 14/12/1998) FL 3

BURTON-GODWIN Osagyefo (Sagi) Lenin Ernesto
Born: Birmingham, 25 November 1977
Height: 6'2" Weight: 13.6
Club Honours: AMC '01

Sagi had a roller coaster of a season at Port Vale in 2000-01. He suffered a loss of form in the autumn and also had some disciplinary problems resulting in a lengthy lay off. However he returned to the first team in February and looked a completely different player, proving a colossus in defence as Vale kept six successive clean sheets and went on a run of only one defeat in 21 games. He featured in the LDV Vans Trophy final victory over Brentford in April and finished the campaign strongly. Sagi is a powerful central defender who is good in the air and uses his physical strength to good effect.

Crystal Palace (From trainee on 26/1/1996) P/FL 19+6/1 FLC 1 FAC 0+1 Others 0+1
Colchester U (Free on 26/5/1999) FL 9 FLC 2
Sheffield U (Free on 19/11/1999)
Port Vale (Free on 14/1/2000) FL 43+6/2 FLC 2/1 FAC 1 Others 4+1

Sagi Burton-Godwin

BUSBY Hubert George Albert
Born: Kingston, Ontario, Canada, 18 June 1969
Height: 6'4" Weight: 13.10

Hubert joined Oxford United at the beginning of the 2000-01 campaign following a spell in Portugal. He was on the subs' bench for several early-season games and stepped up to make his debut at Wycombe when he replaced the injured Richard Knight at the break. He was not offered a permanent contract at the Manor Ground and after a brief period with Crystal Palace he signed for US-A League club Vancouver Whitecaps in March. However his stay with the Canadian club was also to be brief, for after three appearances in pre-season matches he was released. A very experienced 'keeper he was called up to the Jamaican national squad in the new year and featured as an unused substitute in a World Cup qualifying game.

Oxford U (Free from SC Caldas, Portugal, ex Detroit Wheels, Telstar, Montreal Impact, Toronto Lynx, on 21/8/2000) FL 0+1

BUSHELL Stephen (Steve) Paul
Born: Manchester, 28 December 1972
Height: 5'9" Weight: 11.6

This Blackpool midfielder was again affected by niggling injuries in the 2000-01 season. He was an ever-present in the Tangerines' line-up until injury put him out of action in October and after that he struggled to regain a regular place in the side. A hard-working player he often made a significant contribution when coming off the subs' bench in the second half of the campaign. He was released on a free transfer in the summer.

York C (From trainee on 25/2/1991) FL 156+18/10 FLC 8+1/2 FAC 5 Others 11+2/1
Blackpool (Free on 2/7/1998) FL 64+15/6 FLC 8 FAC 5+1 Others 3+1

BUTLER Philip **Anthony (Tony)**
Born: Stockport, 28 September 1972
Height: 6'2" Weight: 12.0

Tony was one of the most consistent performers for West Bromwich Albion last season when he was a near ever-present. A determined, hard-working and resilient central defender he always tried his hardest whether at home or away and never shirked a challenge. He netted his first goal for the Baggies with a header in the local 'derby' defeat away to Birmingham City.

Gillingham (From trainee on 13/5/1991) FL 142+6/5 FLC 12 FAC 12+1 Others 5+1/1
Blackpool (£225,000 on 30/7/1996) FL 98+1 FLC 7 FAC 4 Others 4/1
Port Vale (£115,000 on 25/3/1999) FL 19
West Bromwich A (£140,000 on 23/3/2000) FL 51/1 FLC 4 FAC 1 Others 2

BUTLER Lee Simon
Born: Sheffield, 30 May 1966
Height: 6'2" Weight: 13.6
Club Honours: Div 3 '97

Halifax Town's popular 'keeper broke a finger on the opening day of last season and had to be replaced at half time. On his return the Shaymen suffered an embarrassing 5-1 defeat at Mansfield which was to prove the downfall of manager Mark Lillis, but Lee then returned to his best form before going down with a knee injury in February that put him out of action for several weeks. He came back for the last few games of the campaign and will be looking to be first choice once again in 2001-02. He is an agile goalkeeper who once again produced many crucial saves.

Lincoln C (Free from Haworth Colliery on 16/6/1986) FL 30 FLC 1 FAC 1
Aston Villa (£100,000 on 21/8/1987) FL 8 Others 2
Hull C (Loaned on 18/3/1991) FL 4
Barnsley (£165,000 on 22/7/1991) FL 118+2 FLC 5 FAC 9 Others 4
Scunthorpe U (Loaned on 5/2/1996) FL 2
Wigan Ath (Free on 5/7/1996) FL 63 FLC 3 FAC 2 Others 2
Dunfermline Ath (Signed on 3/7/1998) SL 35 SLC 1 SC 2
Halifax T (Signed on 24/9/1999) FL 71 FAC 4 Others 3

BUTLER Martin Neil
Born: Wordsley, 15 September 1974
Height: 5'11" Weight: 11.9

Martin formed a lethal spearhead with Jamie Cureton for Reading last season, the pair scoring almost 60 goals between them and making a massive contribution to the Royals' promotion campaign. Strong and incisive he is a very hard-working striker who owes much of his improved sharpness to work done with Niall Clark, the club's sports scientist. Martin's efforts were recognised when he was selected for the PFA's Second Division team and also won the club's 'Player of the Year' award.

Walsall (From trainee on 24/5/1993) FL 43+31/8 FLC 2+1 FAC 2+5/2 Others 2+2/2
Cambridge U (£22,500 on 8/8/1997) FL 100+3/41 FLC 9/5 FAC 9+2/5 Others 3+1/1
Reading (£750,000 + on 1/2/2000) FL 59+3/28 FLC 1+1 FAC 3/2 Others 4+1/2

Martin Butler

BUTLER Paul John
Born: Manchester, 2 November 1972
Height: 6'2" Weight: 13.0
Club Honours: Div 2 '97; Div 1 '99
International Honours: RoI: 1; B-1

With the arrival of Stan Varga and Emmerson Thome at Sunderland last term, Paul found the task of holding down a regular first-team slot somewhat difficult. Although he started as first choice alongside Varga, he soon lost out to Jody Craddock and was restricted to appearances in the Worthington Cup. In November he joined Wolves on loan and made an immediate impact, striking the bar on his debut against Blackburn and giving the defence a more assured look. The Wanderers were anxious to recruit him but a permanent deal was delayed due to a change in management. However, once Dave Jones was installed as boss he was duly signed up and carried on where he had left off. Unfortunately he was sidelined shortly afterwards by a torn muscle in his groin and the injury required corrective surgery. A big strong-tackling central defender he is decisive in the tackle and more than useful in the air.

Rochdale (From trainee on 5/7/1991) FL 151+7/10 FLC 8+1 FAC 6+2 Others 12+1
Bury (£100,000 on 22/7/1996) FL 83+1/4 FLC 8 FAC 2 Others 3/1

Sunderland (£600,000 + on 15/7/1998) P/FL 78+1/3 FLC 11+1/1 FAC 4
Wolverhampton W (Loaned on 17/11/2000) FL 5
Wolverhampton W (£1,000,000 on 31/1/2001) FL 7

BUTLER Thomas Anthony
Born: Dublin, Ireland, 25 April 1981
Height: 5'8" Weight: 10.8
International Honours: RoI: U21-2; Yth
Thomas continued to make steady progress at Sunderland last term and following an early-season outing from the subs' bench in the Worthington Cup tie at Luton he spent two months on loan at Darlington in the autumn where he thrilled the Feethams crowds with his darting runs. After returning to the Stadium of Light he went on to gain some valuable Premiership experience towards the end of the campaign with several appearances as a substitute. He is equally at home in midfield, where he possesses a good short-passing game, or wide on the left, where his ability to beat a man can be used to good effect. Thomas made his debut for the Republic of Ireland U21s against Portugal at the beginning of June featuring as a substitute, and was then promoted to the starting line-up for the game in Estonia when he put on a superb display, providing the crosses for each of his side's three goals.
Sunderland (From trainee on 25/6/1998) PL 0+5 FLC 0+2
Darlington (Loaned on 13/10/2000) FL 8 FAC 2

BUTT Nicholas (Nicky)
Born: Manchester, 21 January 1975
Height: 5'10" Weight: 11.3
Club Honours: FAYC '92; CS '96, '97; PL '96, '97, '99, '00, 01; FAC '96; EC '99
International Honours: E: 14; U21-7; Yth; Sch
Despite some stories in the national press suggesting that Nicky might be the one Red most likely to be surplus to requirements, Sir Alex Ferguson quickly rubbished such claims and gave due praise to a player who continues to be just as effective as any of the big name stars at Old Trafford. He started the season in excellent fashion against Bradford City at Old Trafford in September and then notched his first goal against Everton in his next Premiership game at Goodison Park. His reputation was further enhanced with a courageous display against PSV in the Champions' League and a call-up to the England squad for the friendly against Italy in November. The following month was also productive as Nicky netted two further goals against Middlesbrough and Derby and he went on to feature in almost three-quarters of the champions' Premiership games during the campaign.
Manchester U (From trainee on 29/1/1993) PL 164+42/19 FLC 5 FAC 18+2/1 Others 45+11/3

BUTTERFIELD Daniel (Danny) Paul
Born: Boston, 21 November 1979
Height: 5'10" Weight: 11.10
Club Honours: AMC '98
International Honours: E: Yth
This talented youngster established himself as a regular member of the Grimsby Town squad last season, playing either in defence or midfield depending on the formation employed. He showed outstanding form in the vital end-of-season games as he helped the club to escape relegation. Fast and tenacious wherever he is played, it seems only a matter of time before he is sold to a bigger club. Danny has been voted 'Young Player of the Year' by the Mariners' fans for the past two seasons.
Grimsby T (From trainee on 7/8/1997) FL 57+21/1 FLC 9+1 FAC 3+2 Others 1+1/1

BUTTERS Guy
Born: Hillingdon, 30 October 1969
Height: 6'3" Weight: 14.2
International Honours: E: U21-3
Guy had the satisfaction of scoring Gillingham's first-ever goal in Division One when he netted from the edge of the box on the opening day of last season against Stockport in just 64 seconds! He appeared regularly until being sidelined by hamstring trouble following the pulsating 4-4 draw at Wimbledon in October, and it was not until the new year that he returned to first team action. Unfortunately he then suffered a bad knee injury in the FA Cup third round tie at Bournemouth and failed to make a full recovery before the summer. An effective central defender he is useful in the air and possesses a deadly left-foot shot from long range.
Tottenham H (From trainee on 5/8/1988) FL 34+1/1 FLC 2+1 FAC 1
Southend U (Loaned on 13/1/1990) FL 16/3 Others 2
Portsmouth (£375,000 on 28/9/1990) FL 148+6/6 FLC 15+1/1 FAC 7 Others 7+2
Oxford U (Loaned on 4/11/1994) FL 3/1 Others 1
Gillingham (£225,000 on 18/10/1996) FL 134+2/15 FLC 8 FAC 14/1 Others 11

BUTTERWORTH Adam Lawrence
Born: Paignton, 9 August 1982
Height: 6'2" Weight: 13.0
A former Exeter trainee, Adam later played for the Torquay United youth team before following his colleague Luke Guttridge to Cambridge United at the start of the 2000-01 campaign. He featured regularly in the centre of defence for the U's reserves and stepped up to make his Football League debut from the subs' bench in the final game of the season at Swansea. A promising defender with a good first touch and sound passing ability he was rewarded with a contract at the end of the campaign.
Cambridge U (From Torquay U juniors, ex Exeter C trainee, on 1/7/2000) FL 0+1

BYFIELD Darren
Born: Sutton Coldfield, 29 September 1976
Height: 5'11" Weight: 11.11
Darren received regular first-team football at Walsall last season as manager Ray Graydon used him either to give the team a flying start or from the subs' bench to provide fresh legs later in the game. He netted some vital goals, scoring with his first touch after coming on as a substitute against Notts County and heading the late equaliser at Bournemouth, but his finest hour came in the second half of extra time in the play-off final against Reading when he hit the unforgettable 20-yard match-winner that took Walsall back to Division One. He is a pacy striker with quick reactions in the box and a great eye for goal.
Aston Villa (From trainee on 14/2/1994) PL 1+6 FLC 1 FAC 0+1 Others 1
Preston NE (Loaned on 6/11/1998) FL 3+2/1 Others 1
Northampton T (Loaned on 13/8/1999) FL 6/1 FLC 1/1
Cambridge U (Loaned on 17/9/1999) FL 3+1
Blackpool (Loaned on 6/3/2000) FL 3
Walsall (Free on 21/6/2000) FL 21+19/9 FLC 2+2/1 FAC 2+1 Others 2+2/1

BYRNE Christopher (Chris) Thomas
Born: Manchester, 9 February 1975
Height: 5'9" Weight: 10.4
Club Honours: GMVC '97
International Honours: E: SP-1
Chris spent much of the 2000-01 campaign recovering from a serious knee injury, eventually returning to the Stockport County first-team as a late substitute in the game at Nottingham Forest in April to be greeted by a huge cheer from the travelling fans. Unfortunately that was to be his only senior game for the Hatters and he was given a free transfer by boss Andy Kilner in the summer. A pacy skilful midfield player he was reported to have signed for Macclesfield Town in the summer.
Crewe Alex (From trainee on 21/6/1993. Free to Flixton on 1/8/1994)
Sunderland (Signed from Macclesfield T on 11/6/1997) FL 4+4 FLC 1+1
Stockport Co (£200,000 on 21/11/1997) FL 43+13/11 FLC 3/1 FAC 1+1
Macclesfield T (Loaned on 27/8/1999) FL 5

BYRNE Paul
Born: Newcastle, Natal, South Africa, 26 November 1982
Height: 5'9" Weight: 11.0
This Port Vale trainee featured regularly for the youth team last season and after a few outings for the reserves he was promoted to the first team, making his Football League debut in the 3-0 win at Bristol Rovers in April. He gave a fine performance but although he occasionally appeared on the subs' bench afterwards he made no further first-team appearances. A promising left-sided midfield player Paul will be aiming to gain further senior experience in 2001-02.
Port Vale (Trainee) FL 1

BYWATER Stephen (Steve) Michael
Born: Manchester, 7 June 1981
Height: 6'3" Weight: 13.2
Club Honours: FAYC '99
International Honours: E: U21-2; Yth
This young West Ham 'keeper featured regularly for the reserve team last term and sat on the subs' bench for Premiership matches on several occasions. He appeared just once in the first team for the visit to Bradford in February when he put on a solid display. Steve was called up to the England U21 squad during the season and won his first cap in the friendly against Mexico in the summer.
Rochdale (Trainee) Others 1
West Ham U (£300,000 + on 7/8/1998) PL 4+1
Wycombe W (Loaned on 23/9/1999) FL 2
Hull C (Loaned on 23/11/1999) FL 4

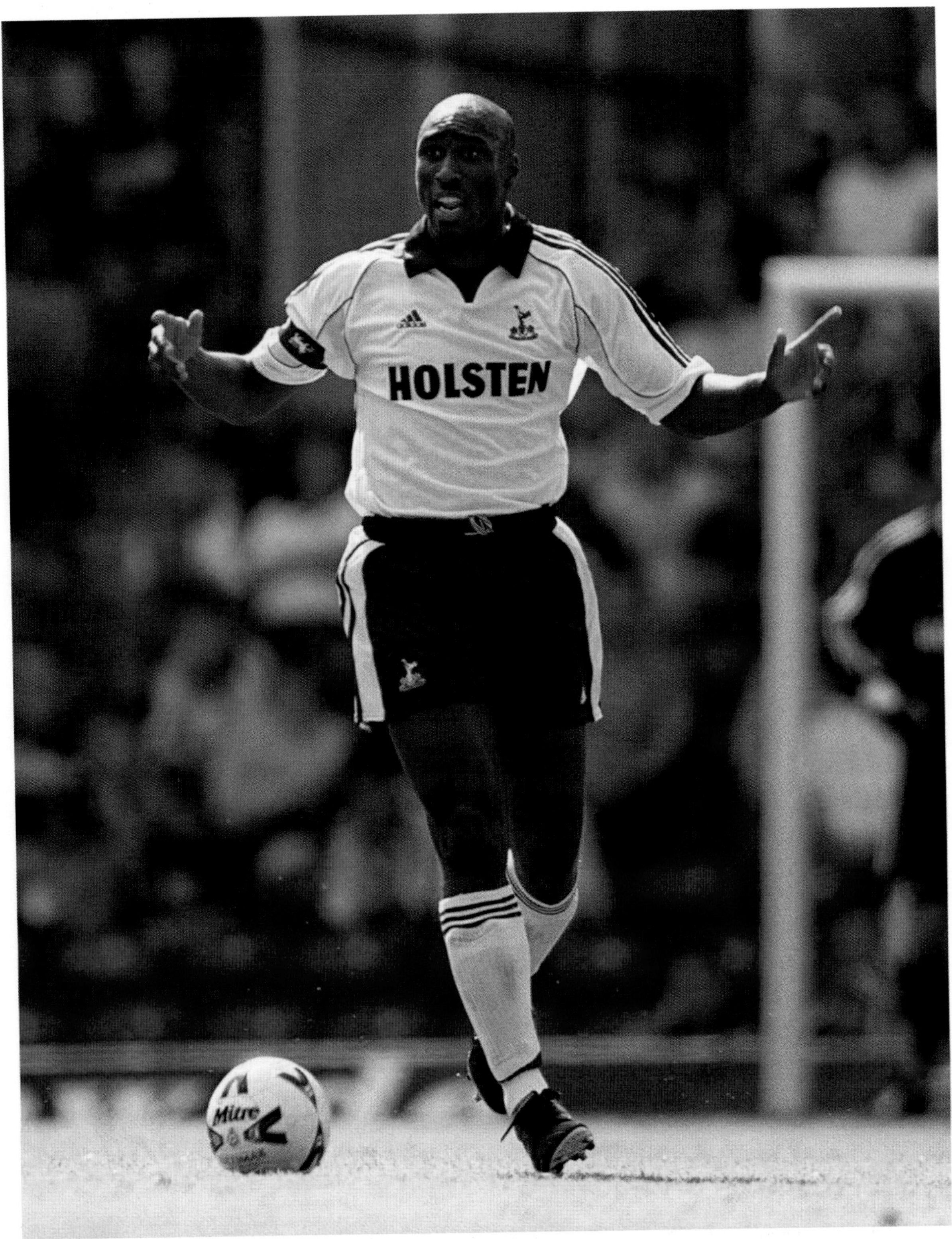

Sol Campbell

CADAMARTERI Daniel (Danny) Leon
Born: Bradford, 12 October 1979
Height: 5'7" Weight: 11.12
Club Honours: FAYC '98
International Honours: E: U21-3; Yth

Danny possesses all the qualities bar one required to become a lethal Premiership striker. Powerful in possession, a direct and pacy runner and capable of fierce shooting, the one quality he craves more than most is consistency. During a three-goal-in-four-game burst for Everton in November he looked a top class forward against defences of the quality of Arsenal and Chelsea, but he couldn't maintain that form consistently and dropped down to the substitutes' bench again. Equally at home as a right winger or a central striker, Danny will hope that 2001-02 is the season when everything clicks for him.

Everton (From trainee on 15/10/1996) PL 36+54/13 FLC 6+3/2 FAC 6+3
Fulham (Loaned on 4/11/1999) FL 3+2/1

CADIOU Frederic
Born: Paris, France, 20 April 1969
Height: 6'0" Weight: 12.5

Having been released by French Division Two club Wasquehal at the end of the 1999-2000 campaign Frederic joined Leyton Orient on a non-contract basis in October. An experienced striker he featured in a handful of games as a substitute but was unable to settle at Brisbane Road and soon returned across the Channel.

Leyton Orient (Free from Wasquehal, France on 6/10/2000) FL 0+3

CAHILL Timothy (Tim)
Born: Sydney, Australia, 6 December 1979
Height: 5'10" Weight: 10.11
Club Honours: Div 2 '01

Tim turned in some excellent performances for Second Division champions Millwall last season and also contributed a number of crucial goals. A box-to-box midfield player he is strong in the tackle and good in the air despite having a rather slight build. Tim's importance to the Lions was recognised when he was selected for the PFA's Second Division team at the end of the campaign.

Millwall (Signed from Sydney U, Australia on 31/7/1997) FL 120+3/27 FLC 6+1/1 FAC 1+2 Others 8+1/1

CAIG Antony (Tony)
Born: Whitehaven, 11 April 1974
Height: 6'1" Weight: 13.4
Club Honours: Div 3 '95; AMC '97

Tony began the 2000-01 season as first-choice Blackpool 'keeper before losing his place to Phil Barnes last September. He later moved to Premiership club Charlton Athletic where he linked up once again with Mervyn Day his former manager at Carlisle. Although third-choice at The Valley he made his Premiership debut as a half-time replacement for the injured Dean Kiely against Derby County at The Valley when he made several fine saves and kept a clean sheet. He appeared to have done enough to retain his place in the team, but the following week he was replaced by Sasa Ilic and did not feature again for the Addicks. He was released on a free transfer in the summer.

Carlisle U (From trainee on 10/7/1992) FL 223 FLC 16 FAC 13 Others 29
Blackpool (£40,000 on 25/3/1999) FL 49 FLC 2 FAC 3 Others 2
Charlton Ath (Free on 3/11/2000) PL 0+1

CALDERWOOD Colin
Born: Glasgow, 20 January 1965
Height: 6'0" Weight: 12.12
Club Honours: Div 4 '86; FLC '99
International Honours: S: 36

Having recovered from a broken leg suffered towards the end of the 1999-2000 campaign Colin found it difficult to win his place back in the Nottingham Forest line-up last term and only featured in a couple of first-team games. Shortly before the transfer deadline he crossed the Trent to join neighbours Notts County in a loan deal, with the Magpies in need of cover when several senior defenders were out with injuries. However although he made several appearances at Meadow Lane he never seemed to find his best form and returned to the City Ground when the period was completed, subsequently announcing his retirement at the end of the season.

Mansfield T (Signed from Inverness Caledonian on 19/3/1982) FL 97+3/1 FLC 4 FAC 6/1 Others 7
Swindon T (£30,000 on 1/7/1985) FL 328+2/20 FLC 35 FAC 17/1 Others 32
Tottenham H (£1,250,000 on 22/7/1993) PL 152+11/6 FLC 19+1 FAC 15+1/1
Aston Villa (£225,000 on 24/3/1999) PL 23+3 FLC 3+1
Nottingham F (£70,000 on 15/3/2000) FL 7+1
Notts Co (Loaned on 13/3/2001) FL 5

CALDWELL Stephen (Steve)
Born: Stirling, 12 September 1980
Height: 6'0" Weight: 11.5
International Honours: S: 1; U21-7; Yth

A product of the Newcastle United youth system, Steve broke into the first-team squad last season making his senior debut when he came off the subs' bench at Manchester City in September. He received his first start in the Worthington Cup tie against Bradford City when he scored what proved to be the winner and went on to make a handful more appearances during the campaign. A promising young central defender he is sound in the air, strong in the tackle and is able to cover ground quickly. He has been a regular for Scotland U21s in the last couple of seasons and last term he was joined in the team by his younger brother Gary who is also on Newcastle's books but has yet to appear in the first team. Steve also made his senior debut for his country in the friendly against Poland in April.

Newcastle U (From trainee on 30/10/1997) PL 5+4 FLC 1/1

CALVO-GARCIA Alexander (Alex)
Born: Ordizia, Spain, 1 January 1972
Height: 5'10" Weight: 11.12

Alex took a while to recover from the broken leg he sustained in November 1999 but by last October he had established himself as a regular again in the Scunthorpe United midfield. Rarely absent from then on he contributed four goals, all coming towards the end of the campaign, but he was unable to guide the Iron into the play-offs. He is a skilful, hard-working midfield player who is at his best when getting forward into the box.

Scunthorpe U (Free from Eibar, Spain on 4/10/1996) FL 136+16/21 FLC 9/3 FAC 15/2 Others 7/2

CAMARA Aboubacar (Titi) Sidiki
Born: Guinea, 17 November 1972
Height: 6'1" Weight: 12.8
International Honours: Guinea

Pushed out of contention at Anfield by the summer signing of Emile Heskey, Titi failed to make the first-team squad at all and in December he was sold to West Ham United. He went on to make his debut in the Premiership fixture at Leicester but only featured in half-a-dozen games for the Hammers before being sidelined by a knee injury. A fast and direct forward his best performance came in the FA Cup third round tie at Walsall when he combined well with Frank Lampard in the 3-2 victory.

Liverpool (£2,600,000 from Olympique Marseille, France, ex St Etienne, RC Lens, on 14/6/1999) PL 22+11/9 FLC 0+2 FAC 2/1
West Ham U (£1,500,000 on 21/12/2000) PL 5+1 FAC 1

CAMARA Mohamed
Born: Conakry, Guinea, 25 June 1975
Height: 5'11" Weight: 11.6

Initially signed on loan from French Second Division club Le Havre where he had rarely featured in the first team in 1999-2000, Mohamed made his debut for Wolves from the subs' bench against Burnley and looked very lively attacking down the left flank. Although his opportunities were to some extent restricted by Lee Naylor's fine form he joined Wanderers permanently in November and featured regularly as a substitute for the remainder of the campaign, although his only subsequent start came at Watford in April. An enthusiastic left-sided defender he will be aiming to feature more regularly in 2001-02.

Wolverhampton W (Loaned from Le Havre, France, ex AS Beauvais, on 11/8/2000) FL 4+14 FLC 1+1 FAC 0+1

CAME Shaun Raymond
Born: Crewe, 15 June 1983
Height: 6'3" Weight: 11.12

Shaun was awarded his first professional contract by Macclesfield Town last September and made his senior debut in the difficult LDV Vans Trophy match at Chesterfield. He appeared regularly for the reserve and youth sides and produced some useful performances when re-introduced to the first team as cover towards the end of the season. A promising central defender who is

good in the air, he is the son of the former Bolton Wanderers player Mark Came.
Macclesfield T (From trainee on 5/7/2000) FL 3+4 Others 0+1

CAMERON David (Dave) Anthony
Born: Bangor, Wales, 24 August 1975
Height: 6'1" Weight: 13.8
This target man was signed by Lincoln City in the summer of 2000 and started last season partnering Tony Battersby in the Imps front line. Dave scored a memorable goal against his former club Brighton in August but soon afterwards lost his place due to suspension. He was then mainly used from the subs' bench. He found goals hard to come by in first-team football but netted regularly for City's reserves for whom he finished as top scorer with 12.
Falkirk (Signed from Dunipace Juniors on 17/8/1994)
East Stirling (Free on 31/8/1995) SL 0+8 (Free to Pencaitland & Ormiston during 1997 close season)
St Mirren (Signed from Whitehall Welfare on 2/2/1999) SL 3+8
Brighton & Hove A (Free from British Army on 8/7/1999) FL 6+11 FLC 0+1 Others 0+1 (Free to Worthing on 31/3/2000)
Lincoln C (Free on 5/7/2000) FL 10+6/2 FLC 2 FAC 0+1 Others 0+5

CAMERON Martin George William
Born: Dunfermline, 16 August 1978
Height: 6'1" Weight: 12.11
Club Honours: SCC '00
Martin adapted quickly to full-time soccer after signing for Bristol Rovers during the 2000-01 close season and made his mark by scoring with a brave header on his first start in the Worthington Cup tie at Plymouth. Unfortunately he then sustained a broken ankle shortly afterwards and was sidelined for two months. He returned to the Pirates' line-up only to suffer a further ankle injury against Reading on Boxing Day, but after corrective surgery he was back by the end of the season. A big striker with a good goals-per-game record he will be aiming to win a regular place for Rovers in 2001-02.
Alloa Ath (Signed from Craigmillar Thistle on 11/10/1997) SL 60+27/39 SLC 3+3/3 SC 7+2/3 Others 5/3
Bristol Rov (£100,000 on 11/7/2000) FL 6+8/2 FLC 1/1

CAMM Mark Liam
Born: Mansfield, 1 October 1981
Height: 5'8" Weight: 10.12
This busy right-sided defender began the 2000-01 season on monthly contracts with Lincoln before eventually earning a more permanent deal. He made his Football League debut in December against Rochdale and showed promise both in his defensive qualities and his ability to push forward. Mark was offered a one-year contract by the Imps in the summer.
Sheffield U (From trainee on 5/7/1999)
Lincoln C (Free on 14/8/2000) FL 3 Others 0+2

CAMPBELL Andrew (Andy) Paul
Born: Stockton, 18 April 1979
Height: 5'11" Weight: 11.7
International Honours: E: U21-4; Yth
Having burst on the scene at Middlesbrough the previous season Andy found it difficult to win a regular place in what was a struggling side for most of last term. He eventually joined Bolton on a three-month loan spell in March to provide extra options up front for boss Sam Allardyce in the vital closing stages of the season. However after three starts and a handful of appearances from the subs' bench he was recalled to the Riverside to cover for injuries. A skilful young striker with good pace he will be hoping for better fortune in 2001-02.
Middlesbrough (From trainee on 4/7/1996) F/PL 28+24/4 FLC 5+5/1 FAC 2+2/1
Sheffield U (Loaned on 10/12/1998) FL 5/1
Sheffield U (Loaned on 25/3/1999) FL 6/2
Bolton W (Loaned on 9/3/2001) FL 3+3

CAMPBELL Jamie
Born: Birmingham, 21 October 1972
Height: 6'1" Weight: 12.11
Jamie signed for Exeter from Brighton in 2000 close season and was a virtual ever-present in the left back position in 2000-01. Dangerous going forward and at set plays he scored against local rivals Torquay in the 1-1 draw on Boxing Day and also netted in the home game against Southend. He performed consistently well throughout the campaign and took over as captain when Chris Curran was injured. He was deservedly voted as City's 'Player of the Year' at the end of the campaign.
Luton T (From trainee on 1/7/1991) FL 10+26/1 FLC 1+1 FAC 1+3 Others 1+2
Mansfield T (Loaned on 25/11/1994) FL 3/1 FAC 2
Cambridge U (Loaned on 10/3/1995) FL 12
Barnet (Free on 11/7/1995) FL 50+17/5 FLC 3+3/1 FAC 4+2/1 Others 1
Cambridge U (Free on 8/8/1997) FL 91/6 FLC 7 FAC 6/1 Others 4
Brighton & Hove A (Free on 7/7/1999) FL 22+1/1 FLC 2 FAC 3 Others 2
Exeter C (Free on 11/7/2000) FL 42/2 FLC 1 FAC 1 Others 1

CAMPBELL Kevin Joseph
Born: Lambeth, 4 February 1970
Height: 6'1" Weight: 13.8
Club Honours: FAYC '88; FLC '93; FAC '93; ECWC '94; Div 1 '98
International Honours: E: B-1; U21-4
Evertonians had already taken Super Kevin to their hearts when his goals helped save the club from relegation in 1998 - and he went on to pass some notable milestones in 2000-01. He finished club top scorer for the third successive season, a feat not managed for almost a decade at Goodison, and was also named as captain of the club - an achievement he was justifiably proud of. Kevin did not show quite the same dash and drive he had managed in previous campaigns but he was asked to lead the line on his own on numerous occasions due to injuries sustained by strike partners Duncan Ferguson and Francis Jeffers. He also had injury problems of his own to overcome and did not start a Premiership match for the club until mid-September, but after that he remained pretty much an ever-present. Having signed a lucrative new contract during the season Kevin seems happy to see out his playing years at a club whose fans have taken him to their hearts.
Arsenal (From trainee on 11/2/1988) F/PL 124+42/46 FLC 14+10/6 FAC 13+6/2 Others 15+4/5
Leyton Orient (Loaned on 16/1/1989) FL 16/9
Leicester C (Loaned on 8/11/1989) FL 11/5 Others 1/1
Nottingham F (£3,000,000 on 1/7/1995) F/PL 79+1/32 FLC 2 FAC 11/3 Others 3 (£2,500,000 to Trabzonspor, Turkey on 7/8/1998)
Everton (£3,000,000 on 25/3/1999) PL 61+2/30 FLC 1+3/1 FAC 6

CAMPBELL Paul Andrew
Born: Middlesbrough, 29 January 1980
Height: 6'1" Weight: 11.0
This promising youngster made a number of appearances from the subs' bench for Darlington at the start of last season including a memorable outing in the Worthington Cup tie against Nottingham Forest when he headed a superb equaliser in Darlington's shock first-round victory at the City Ground. Alas, just as his displays had earned him a starting place in the team he sustained a serious groin injury that at first threatened to keep him out for the remainder of the campaign. However he surprisingly returned in mid-January and had another brief run in the side before injury ruled him out again.
Darlington (From trainee on 8/7/1998) FL 24+16/5 FLC 1+4/1 FAC 1 Others 3+1

CAMPBELL Stuart Pearson
Born: Corby, 9 December 1977
Height: 5'10" Weight: 10.8
Club Honours: FLC '97, '00
International Honours: S: U21-14
Stuart initially joined Grimsby Town on a month's loan last September but created such a favourable impression that he stayed until the end of the season, establishing himself as a regular in the Mariners' first team. A versatile midfield player he mostly appeared on the right-hand side from where he made some penetrating runs into the box. He was reported to have signed a three-year contract for the Blundell Park club during the summer.
Leicester C (From trainee on 4/7/1996) PL 12+25 FLC 2+5 FAC 3+3
Birmingham C (Loaned on 23/3/2000) FL 0+2
Grimsby T (Loaned on 15/9/2000) FL 38/2 FAC 2

CAMPBELL Sulzeer (Sol) Jeremiah
Born: Newham, 18 September 1974
Height: 6'2" Weight: 14.1
Club Honours: FLC '99
International Honours: E: 40; B-1; U21-11; Yth (UEFA-U18 '93)
Sol had a somewhat frustrating time at White Hart Lane last season when he missed long spells through injury and the media seemed to focus on his contractual position rather than his football skills. He was absent for two months in the autumn with a dislocated shoulder and after returning to his customary place in the centre of defence he helped the team reach the FA Cup semi-final only to meet with disappointment not just at the defeat by bitter North London rivals Arsenal but also because of the ankle injury he suffered that was to keep him out of action until the summer break. A rock solid defender, club captain and a regular for his country he was as always a key figure at the

back for Spurs. Due to be out of contract in the close season he had yet to reach a decision on his future at the time of writing but it seemed likely that he might be playing his football elsewhere in the 2001-02 campaign. He was reported to have signed for North London rivals Arsenal during the summer.

Tottenham H (From trainee on 23/9/1992) PL 246+9/10 FLC 28/4 FAC 28+2/1 Others 2

CANOVILLE Lee
Born: Ealing, 14 March 1981
Height: 6'1" Weight: 11.3
International Honours: E: Yth; Sch

A former England U16 international Lee attended the FA School of Excellence at Lilleshall before signing for Arsenal. Having developed in the Gunners' U19 and reserve teams he stepped up to make his senior debut in the Worthington Cup third round defeat by Ipswich Town. Early in the new year he joined Northampton Town on loan where he made a handful of first-team appearances at right back before returning to Highbury where he featured again in the second string. A versatile player he is most comfortable playing either in the heart of the defence or in a central midfield role. Out of contract in the summer his future was unclear at the time of writing.

Arsenal (From trainee on 3/7/1998, having earlier been transferred from Millwall juniors for an undisclosed fee on 9/7/1997) FLC 0+1
Northampton T (Loaned on 26/1/2001) FL 2

CAPLETON Melvyn (Mel) David
Born: Hackney, 24 October 1973
Height: 5'11" Weight: 12.0

Mel started last season as second-choice 'keeper at Southend United but managed just one appearance from the subs' bench when he came on for the injured Andy Woodman against Halifax, before he suffered a badly broken leg playing in a reserve match against Brentford. The injury put him out of action for a lengthy period and it was not until the final weeks of the campaign that he resumed full training once more.

Southend U (From trainee on 1/7/1992)
Blackpool (Free on 1/8/1993) FL 9+2 FLC 1 (Free to Grays Ath on 18/10/1995)
Leyton Orient (Free on 14/9/1998) FLC 1
Southend U (Free on 23/10/1998) FL 54+3 FLC 2 FAC 1 Others 1

CARBON Matthew (Matt) Phillip
Born: Nottingham, 8 June 1975
Height: 6'2" Weight: 13.6
International Honours: E: U21-4

Matt had a rather disappointing campaign for West Bromwich Albion in 2000-01 when he was in and out of the first team, often being sidelined by niggling injuries. He played his best football alongside Tony Butler at the heart of the Baggies' defence between November and late January but thereafter struggled to hold down a first team slot and lost his place altogether when Phil Gilchrist arrived towards the end of March. An effective central defender who is strong in the air he was out of contract in the summer and his future was uncertain at the time of writing.

Lincoln C (From trainee on 13/4/1993) FL 66+3/10 FLC 4/1 FAC 3 Others 4+3
Derby Co (£385,000 on 8/3/1996) P/FL 11+9 FLC 1 FAC 0+1
West Bromwich A (£800,000 on 26/1/1998) FL 106+7/5 FLC 7+2 FAC 4

CARBONARI Horacio Angel
Born: Argentina, 2 May 1973
Height: 6'3" Weight: 13.4

Enjoying his third season at Derby last term, Horacio was one of the more consistent players in the Rams' defence. Preferring to play in the pivotal role within a three-man back line he found it harder when asked to play in a back four formation. He possesses a thundering shot often seen at dead-ball situations and this has led to him receiving the nickname 'Bazooka'. Not the quickest of players, he compensates for this with an excellent ability to read the game. Although he suffered two successive red cards early in the season he was a model of consistency upon his return, the arrival of Colin Todd as coach making a notable difference.

Derby Co (£2,700,000 from Athletico Rosario Central, Argentina on 1/7/1998) PL 84+1/8 FLC 2 FAC 8

CARBONE Benito (Beni)
Born: Begnara, Italy, 14 August 1971
Height: 5'6" Weight: 10.8
International Honours: Italy: U21 (UEFA-U21 '94)

Beni joined Bradford City on a four-year contract in the close season and was an ever-present in the Bantams' team until he was dropped by boss Jim Jeffries in mid-January and placed on the transfer list. To his credit he turned down a proposed move to Middlesbrough and announced his intention of fighting to win back his place in the line-up. He eventually returned after missing just five games but proved unable to prevent the club slipping out of the Premiership. An immense talent, he is one of the most exciting players to appear at Valley Parade in City's recent history and his skills were much appreciated by the club's supporters. On his day he can produce some brilliant play running at opposition defences with great pace and tight control. He was deservedly voted 'Player of the Year' by the Bantams' supporters.

Sheffield Wed (£3,000,000 from Inter Milan, Italy, ex Torino, Reggina, Casert, Ascoli, Napoli, on 18/10/1996) PL 86+10/25 FLC 3+1 FAC 7/1
Aston Villa (Signed on 21/10/1999) PL 22+2/3 FAC 6/5
Bradford C (Free on 10/8/2000) PL 29+2/5 FLC 2/2 FAC 0+1

CAREY Brian Patrick
Born: Cork, 31 May 1968
Height: 6'3" Weight: 14.4
International Honours: RoI: 3; U21-1

Wrexham's club captain once again proved an inspirational figure at the heart of the defence in the 2000-01 campaign. He missed two months in the autumn with a knee problem but otherwise was rarely absent from the Robins' line-up. Brian remains a powerful and effective central defender who contributes his fair share of goals - he netted another three last season.

Manchester U (£100,000 from Cork C on 2/9/1989)
Wrexham (Loaned on 17/1/1991) FL 3
Wrexham (Loaned on 24/12/1991) FL 13/1 FAC 3 Others 3
Leicester C (£250,000 on 16/7/1993) F/PL 51+7/1 FLC 3 FAC 0+1 Others 4
Wrexham (£100,000 on 19/7/1996) FL 193/7 FLC 9 FAC 20 Others 8

CAREY Louis Anthony
Born: Bristol, 20 January 1977
Height: 5'10" Weight: 11.10
International Honours: S: U21-1

This cool and cultured defender had a fine season with Bristol City in 2000-01 when he was an ever-present in Second Division games and confidently took on the role of captain when Keith Millen was absent through injury. He impressed with his mazy runs to the by-line and was one of the club's best players during the campaign. Although only in his early 20s he has now made more than 200 first-team appearances for City and looks likely to become a fixture in the line-up over the next few seasons.

Bristol C (From trainee on 3/7/1995) FL 205+7/3 FLC 11+1 FAC 15 Others 8+2

CARLISLE Clarke James
Born: Preston, 14 October 1979
Height: 6'1" Weight: 12.7
International Honours: E: U21-3

Clarke joined Queens Park Rangers for a substantial fee shortly after the end of the 1999-2000 campaign and quickly became a favourite of the Loftus Road faithful after producing some fine performances. He was one of the very few players to feature regularly for Rangers in the first half of last season but then suffered a cruciate ligament injury in the home game with Fulham at the end of January that sidelined him until the summer. He is a strong central defender with good pace who is able to read the game in front of him. He was rewarded with a debut for England U21s against Georgia at the end of August and he went on to win further caps against Germany and Finland.

Blackpool (From trainee on 13/8/1997) FL 85+8/7 FLC 4+1 FAC 3/1 Others 5
Queens Park R (£250,000 on 25/5/2000) FL 27/3 FLC 2 FAC 3

CARLISLE Wayne Thomas
Born: Lisburn, 9 September 1979
Height: 6'0" Weight: 11.6
International Honours: NI: U21-6; Yth; Sch

This pacy wide right-sided midfield player failed to make the breakthrough to regular first-team football at Crystal Palace in 2000-01 but he was a member of the squad throughout the campaign. He will be aiming to displace Tommy Black in the Eagles starting line-up in the coming season.

Crystal Palace (From trainee on 18/9/1996) FL 29+17/3 FLC 3+3 FAC 1

CARPENTER Richard
Born: Sheerness, 30 September 1972
Height: 6'0" Weight: 13.0
Club Honours: Div 3 '01

Although playing for most of the season with an injury, Richard made a tremendous impression at Brighton in 2000-01. An

effective midfield player he is strong in the tackle, has a terrific right-foot shot and distributes the ball accurately. One free kick in particular stands out - the 25-yard bullet drive which opened the scoring in the FA Cup first round victory at Aldershot and was featured on 'Match of the Day'.
Gillingham (From trainee on 13/5/1991) FL 107+15/4 FLC 2+1 FAC 9+1 Others 7/1
Fulham (£15,000 on 26/9/1996) FL 49+9/7 FLC 4/1 FAC 2/1 Others 2
Cardiff C (£35,000 on 29/7/1998) FL 69+6/2 FLC 3+1 FAC 8+1 Others 1
Brighton & Hove A (Free on 4/7/2000) FL 42/6 FLC 2 FAC 2/1 Others 1

CARR Darren John
Born: Bristol, 4 September 1968
Height: 6'2" Weight: 13.7
This experienced Brighton centre half featured in the first two games of last season replacing the suspended Danny Cullip, but then lost his place in the squad and eventually moved out on loan to Rotherham as cover for the suspended Guy Branston. He gave a fine performance for the Millers in the vital clash with promotion rivals Millwall and also appeared in an LDV Vans Trophy tie before departing. He subsequently went on loan to Lincoln in January to cover for injuries and suspensions. He made a steady debut in the local 'derby' win over Hull City but made just two further appearances before his return to the South Coast. Darren then had a third spell on loan at relegation threatened Carlisle where he stayed for the final three months of the campaign slotting in well with the Cumbrians defence and ably assisting their escape from relegation to the Conference. He is a big strong central defender with a no-nonsense style who is particularly effective in the air. He remains on the open to offers list at Brighton.
Bristol Rov (From trainee on 20/8/1986) FL 26+4 FLC 2+2 FAC 3 Others 2
Newport Co (Loaned on 30/10/1987) FL 4
Newport Co (£3,000 on 28/1/1988) FL 5
Sheffield U (£8,000 on 10/3/1988) FL 12+1/1 FLC 1 FAC 3+1 Others 1
Crewe Alex (£35,000 on 18/9/1990) FL 96+8/5 FLC 8 FAC 12/2 Others 10
Chesterfield (£30,000 on 21/7/1993) FL 84+2/4 FLC 9 FAC 6+3 Others 8
Gillingham (£75,000 on 7/8/1998) FL 22+8/2 FLC 2 FAC 1 Others 3+1
Brighton & Hove A (£25,000 on 14/7/1999) FL 18+3 FAC 3 Others 2
Rotherham U (Loaned on 30/11/2000) FL 1 Others 1
Lincoln C (Loaned on 19/1/2001) FL 3
Carlisle U (Loaned on 9/2/2001) FL 10

CARR Stephen
Born: Dublin, 29 August 1976
Height: 5'9" Weight: 12.2
Club Honours: FLC '99
International Honours: RoI: 18; U21-12; Yth; Sch
Stephen had another fantastic season at Tottenham last term only interrupted by a groin injury that kept him out of action from December through until March. Confident in his wing-back position, he loved to get forward down the flank and his initiative earned him three goals: one in the 3-1 opening day win at home to Ipswich, another in the home defeat by Derby in October and a third in the penultimate game of the season at Leicester. Solid in his defending role, his strength in the tackle and pace make him a hard player to beat. Spurs are likely to rely heavily on his organisational skills at the back in the coming season, particularly if Sol Campbell opts to leave. He was again a regular for the Republic of Ireland and has now assumed the defensive role previously taken by Dennis Irwin. He also won recognition from his fellow professionals when he was selected for the PFA's Premiership team in April.
Tottenham H (From trainee on 1/9/1993) PL 160+4/6 FLC 18/1 FAC 12+1 Others 6

Stephen Carr

CARRAGHER James (Jamie) Lee Duncan
Born: Bootle, 28 January 1978
Height: 6'1" Weight: 13.0
Club Honours: FAYC '96; FLC '01; FAC '01; UEFAC '01
International Honours: E: 3; B-2; U21-27; Yth
Jamie enjoyed another exceptional season at Liverpool last term playing in all but four of the Reds gruelling 63-match programme and winning Worthington Cup, FA Cup and UEFA Cup winners medals. The most versatile player in Liverpool's squad he can play anywhere along the back four and as a defensive midfield player in the centre or on the flanks. Last season he switched positions frequently in the opening weeks before establishing himself at left back. Although right-footed he performed excellently in his new role and never better than in the titanic clashes with Roma and Barcelona in the UEFA Cup when Liverpool were constantly under pressure and living on a knife edge. He remained on the fringe of the England squad, featuring from the subs' bench against Italy in November and in the summer friendly with Mexico. With Sol Campbell and Rio Ferdinand looking like a settled pairing in central defence for the foreseeable future his best hope of future international honours would appear to be at right back.
Liverpool (From trainee on 9/10/1996) PL 115+11/2 FLC 12+1 FAC 10 Others 19

CARRAGHER Matthew (Matt)
Born: Liverpool, 14 January 1976
Height: 5'9" Weight: 11.4
Club Honours: Div 3 '97; AMC '01
Matt had a fine season for Port Vale in 2000-01 when he was a near ever-present and captained the team that defeated Brentford to win the LDV Vans Trophy final at Cardiff's Millenium Stadium. Having previously mostly appeared at right back he spent much of the campaign as a sweeper, a role he adapted to with ease. He helped make the Vale defence one of the tightest in the division, often flying in with last-ditch tackles to save the situation.
Wigan Ath (From trainee on 25/11/1993) FL 102+17 FLC 6+1/1 FAC 10+1/2 Others 7+1
Port Vale (Free on 3/7/1997) FL 115+3/1 FLC 6 FAC 2 Others 7

CARRATT Philip (Phil)
Born: Stockport, 22 October 1981
Height: 5'10" Weight: 12.7
This local-born youngster made his Football League debut from the subs' bench for Stockport against Watford just 24 hours after signing his first professional contract for the club. A product of the Hatters' highly successful youth set-up he made just one more substitute appearance during the campaign but is highly regarded at Edgeley Park and will be hoping for more senior action in 2001-02. Phil is a promising striker who creates opportunities with his pace and unpredictability.
Stockport Co (From trainee on 28/9/2000) FL 0+2

CARRICK Michael
Born: Wallsend, 28 July 1981
Height: 6'0" Weight: 11.10
Club Honours: FAYC '99
International Honours: E: 1 U21-4; Yth
Having been used sparingly by West Ham boss Harry Redknapp in 1999-2000, Michael found himself thrust into regular first-team action at the beginning of last season due to an injury crisis. He went on to establish himself as a regular in the first team and indeed rarely missed a match. An elegant left-sided midfielder who is effective with his passes, both long and short, he seems to have all the time in the world on the ball. Awarded 'Man of the Match' in the Premiership games at Sunderland and Charlton he deservedly won the title of 'Young Hammer of the Year' and clearly follows in the long-standing tradition of cultured midfield players at Upton Park. Michael featured regularly for England U21s during the campaign and made his full international debut when he came on as a half-time substitute in the friendly game against Mexico at the end of May.
West Ham U (From trainee on 25/8/1998) PL 36+5/2 FLC 4 FAC 4 Others 0+1
Swindon T (Loaned on 12/11/1999) FL 6/2
Birmingham C (Loaned on 23/2/2000) FL 1+1

Michael Carrick

CARRIGAN Brian
Born: Glasgow, 26 September 1979
Height: 5'8" Weight: 10.10
Club Honours: S Div 2 '00
International Honours: S: U21-1
A summer capture from Clyde, Brian got off to the worst possible start at Stockport County when he injured a hamstring on the first day of pre-season training. Once he had recovered however he struggled to break into the first-team squad and only occasionally showed flashes of the skill that had produced so many goals north of the border. He netted five goals in a Cheshire Senior Cup game against Macclesfield and also grabbed the vital winner against Sheffield Wednesday during County's great end-of-season battle to avoid the drop. At the time of writing his future at Edgeley Park seemed to be in some doubt following an off-the-field incident.
Clyde (Signed from Kilsyth Rangers on 21/12/1996) SL 80+31/25 SLC 2+2/2 SC 4+6/7 Others 2
Stockport Co (£250,000 on 18/8/2000) FL 3+10/1 FLC 1 FAC 1+1

CARROLL David (Dave) Francis
Born: Paisley, 20 September 1966
Height: 6'0" Weight: 12.0
Club Honours: FAT '91, '93; GMVC '93
International Honours: E: Sch
A pelvic injury sustained during the first half of last season meant that Dave's first-team appearances were severely restricted at Wycombe last term. His goal at Bury in March was his 100th for the club in all competitions although arguably much more important was his coolly taken equaliser at Wimbledon in the FA Cup fifth round replay. A right-sided midfield player who is comfortable on the ball he has been rewarded with another year's contract by the Chairboys.
Wycombe W (£6,000 from Ruislip Manor in 1988 close season) FL 276+14/41 FLC 21+2/1 FAC 29+2/6 Others 14/3

CARROLL Roy Eric
Born: Enniskillen, 30 September 1977
Height: 6'2" Weight: 12.9
Club Honours: AMC '99
International Honours: NI: 9; U21-11; Yth
Roy had another very successful season for Wigan Athletic in 2000-01 and once again there was speculation about a transfer deal with a Premiership club. A broken toe saw him miss three months of the campaign but he returned in February to help the Latics in their push towards the play-offs. Roy is now a highly accomplished goalkeeper with more than 200 Football League appearances to his name and this was demonstrated in the greater maturity of his performances. He is now firmly established as first choice 'keeper for Northern Ireland and added a further five caps during the season.
Hull C (From trainee on 7/9/1995) FL 46 FLC 2 FAC 1 Others 1
Wigan Ath (£350,000 on 16/4/1997) FL 135 FLC 11 FAC 8 Others 15

CARRUTHERS Christopher (Chris) Paul
Born: Kettering, 19 August 1983
Height: 5'10" Weight: 12.3
A local youngster, Chris made his debut for Northampton Town shortly before the end of the 2000-01 season against Port Vale. A promising central defender or midfielder he created an immediate impression by 'nutmegging' a Vale player with almost his first touch of the ball. He went on to feature twice more for the Cobblers and will be looking to gain more senior experience in 2001-02.
Northampton T (Trainee) FL 1+2

CARRUTHERS Martin George
Born: Nottingham, 7 August 1972
Height: 5'11" Weight: 11.9
After the fireworks of the previous season, Martin never found the same goal-scoring form for Southend in the 2000-01 campaign and finally departed to Scunthorpe for a cut-price fee on transfer deadline day. Iron manager Brian Laws hoped that his presence would help the team towards the play-offs but he only netted once for the Glanford Park club and will be hoping to improve on this in the coming season. Martin is a talented striker who works hard and has an excellent goal-scoring record.
Aston Villa (From trainee on 4/7/1990) F/PL 2+2 FAC 0+1 Others 0+1
Hull C (Loaned on 31/10/1992) FL 13/6 Others 3
Stoke C (£100,000 on 5/7/1993) FL 60+31/13 FLC 7+3/1 FAC 3+1 Others 10+4/6
Peterborough U (Signed on 18/11/1996) FL 63+4/21 FLC 5+1/2 FAC 6/4 Others 6
York C (Loaned on 29/1/1999) FL 3+3
Darlington (Signed on 25/3/1999) FL 11+6/2
Southend U (£50,000 on 17/9/1999) FL 69+1/26 FLC 2 FAC 5 Others 5+1/3
Scunthorpe U (£20,000 on 22/3/2001) FL 8/1

CARSLEY Lee Kevin
Born: Birmingham, 28 February 1974
Height: 5'10" Weight: 11.11
International Honours: RoI: 16; U21-1
Lee found himself out of favour at Blackburn at the beginning of last season and rarely featured for the first team. It was therefore no surprise when he moved on to Coventry City at the beginning of December and he went on to make his debut in the 1-0 home win over Leicester. An all-action midfield player he took some time to settle back in the Premier League, a situation not helped by the fact that the Sky Blues were struggling. He took over the anchor role in midfield from Carlton Palmer and provided good protection for the back four in a low-key fashion. He took on the penalty duties and scored his first in the Everton home defeat while he also acted as stand-in captain in the absence of Moustapha Hadji and Paul Williams. Despite hitting a rich vein of personal form in the closing matches - his performances against Derby and Leicester were excellent - he proved unable to prevent the club from dropping down to the First Division.
Derby Co (From trainee on 6/7/1992) P/FL 122+16/5 FLC 10+3 FAC 12 Others 3
Blackburn Rov (£3,375,000 on 23/3/1999) P/FL 40+6/10 FLC 4/1 FAC 4/1
Coventry C (£2,500,000 on 1/12/2000) PL 21/2 FAC 2

CARSS Anthony (Tony) John
Born: Alnwick, 31 March 1976
Height: 5'10" Weight: 12.0
Tony made a handful of appearances for Carlisle United in the early part of last season but although he produced a particularly effective performance at Darlington he was quickly on his way to Oldham in October. He went on to have a spectacular season at Boundary Park scoring the 'Goal of the Season' to clinch a 1-0 victory over Bristol Rovers on Easter Monday. Operating mainly in a central midfield role he worked tirelessly and deservedly received the Latics' 'Player of the Season' award following some excellent performances.
Blackburn Rov (From trainee at Bradford C on 29/8/1994)
Darlington (Free on 11/8/1995) FL 33+24/2 FLC 5/1 FAC 2+1 Others 4
Cardiff C (Free on 28/7/1997) FL 36+6/1 FLC 2 FAC 5+1 Others 1
Chesterfield (Free on 7/9/1998) FL 26+9/1 FLC 2 FAC 1 Others 1+1
Carlisle U (Free on 11/8/2000) FL 6+1 FLC 2
Oldham Ath (Free on 13/10/2000) FL 35/2 FAC 3

CARTER Alfonso (Alfie) Jermaine
Born: Birmingham, 23 August 1980
Height: 5'10" Weight: 10.6
Alfie made just a brief appearance in Walsall's first team last season, replacing Paul Hall for the final 10 minutes of the away win at Wrexham before being released by the Saddlers. He subsequently joined Dr Martens League club Bromsgrove Rovers and later had an extended trial at Gillingham featuring for the reserve team on several occasions. He is a young hard-running midfield player.
Walsall (From trainee on 30/4/1999) FL 1+2 FLC 0+1

CARTERON Patrice
Born: Saint-Brieuc, France, 30 July 1970
Height: 6'0" Weight: 12.3
This experienced right back joined Sunderland on loan last March as a

replacement for Chris Makin who had just been sold to Ipswich. Thrust immediately into action, Patrice set about winning himself a contract for the 2000-01 season with a series of dazzling displays down the right-hand side, regularly linking up with the midfield and attack, and popping up in goal-scoring positions on a number of occasions. Indeed, he scored his first Premiership goal in such circumstances, rounding off a typical run against Newcastle with a superb finish. With his loan spell over at the end of the season it was unclear at the time of writing whether boss Peter Reid would be pursuing a permanent deal.

Sunderland (Loaned from St Etienne, France, ex Laval, Rennes, Lyon, on 16/3/2001) PL 8/1

CARTWRIGHT Lee
Born: Rawtenstall, 19 September 1972
Height: 5'8" Weight: 11.0
Club Honours: Div 3 '96; Div 2 '00

A knee operation during the summer meant Preston's longest serving player missed the start of last season, and it was not until mid-September that Lee made his first league appearance for North End. Having regained his regular place on the right-hand side of midfield, Lee celebrated 300 league games for the club with a win at Fulham. He moved briefly back to his original position in central midfield in February, and showed that he had not forgotten how to make best use of his pace and acceleration, reminding all that his slight frame hides a determined and effective tackler.

Preston NE (From trainee on 30/7/1991) FL 263+64/21 FLC 17+2/2 FAC 17+4/1 Others 20+5/1

CARTWRIGHT Mark Neville
Born: Chester, 13 January 1973
Height: 6'2" Weight: 13.6
Club Honours: Div 3 '01

Mark joined Brighton on trial during the summer of 2000 and completed a permanent move at the end of August. He made his debut on the opening day of the season when he replaced Michel Kuipers for the second half of the 2-0 defeat at Southend and retained his place in the Seagulls line-up until early October when Kuipers returned to the team. He had to wait until February before he had another brief run in the side and when he returned he went on to create a club record of six consecutive clean sheets, albeit separated by a period of several months. Mark is a reliable 'keeper who is not afraid to put himself in painful situations when defending his goal. He was released in May and was reported to have signed for Shrewsbury Town.

Stockport Co (From trainee at York C on 17/8/1991. Freed during 1992 close season)
Wrexham (Signed following a USA soccer scholarship on 5/3/1994) FL 37 FLC 2 FAC 6 Others 6
Brighton & Hove A (Free on 10/8/2000) FL 12+1 FLC 2

CASEY Ryan Peter
Born: Coventry, 3 January 1979
Height: 6'1" Weight: 11.2
International Honours: RoI: Yth

Although it took some time to get going Ryan's 2000-01 season appeared to be taking off at the turn of the year when he scored the equaliser for Swansea against Peterborough and seemed to be on the verge of winning a regular place in the first-team squad. However he then had the misfortune to suffer a ruptured medial ligament and a depressed fracture of the tibia in the LDV Vans Trophy match against Reading and the injury put him out of action for the remainder of the campaign. A promising wide left midfield player he signed a new one-year contract for the Swans in April.

Swansea C (From trainee on 7/5/1997) FL 13+33/2 FLC 1+1 FAC 0+2 Others 2+1

CASKEY Darren Mark
Born: Basildon, 21 August 1974
Height: 5'8" Weight: 11.9
International Honours: E: Yth (UEFA-U18 '93); Sch

Although still very much a creative force in midfield for Reading last season, Darren was unable to repeat his success or goal-scoring feats of the previous campaign. He eventually lost the captain's armband to Phil Parkinson and was increasingly confined to the substitutes bench for the final two months. Still an expert at dead-ball situations, he nevertheless managed a respectable double-figure tally of goals for the Royals. He was granted a free transfer in May as Reading boss Alan Pardew sought to restructure his squad following the disappointing defeat by Walsall in the play-off final. He was reported to have signed for Notts County in the summer.

Tottenham H (From trainee on 6/3/1992) PL 20+12/4 FLC 3+1/1 FAC 6+1
Watford (Loaned on 27/10/1995) FL 6/1
Reading (£700,000 on 28/2/1996) FL 180+22/35 FLC 10+2/4 FAC 9+1/5 Others 8+1/1

CASTLE Stephen (Steve) Charles
Born: Barkingside, 17 May 1966
Height: 5'11" Weight: 12.10

Having returned to Leyton Orient on a free transfer in the close season Steve missed the majority of the 2000-01 campaign with a knee injury. He eventually returned to regular first-team action in the closing weeks of the campaign when he played an influential role in guiding the O's into the play-off final. He is an inspirational figure in the centre of midfield where he works tirelessly for the cause.

Leyton Orient (From apprentice on 18/5/1984) FL 232+11/55 FLC 15+1/5 FAC 23+1/6 Others 18+2
Plymouth Arg (£195,000 on 30/6/1992) FL 98+3/35 FLC 5/1 FAC 8/2 Others 6/1
Birmingham C (£225,000 on 21/7/1995) FL 16+7/1 FLC 11 FAC 1 Others 3/1
Gillingham (Loaned on 15/2/1996) FL 5+1/1
Leyton Orient (Loaned on 3/2/1997) FL 4/1
Peterborough U (Free on 14/5/1997) FL 96+6/17 FLC 7+1 FAC 4+1/2 Others 6+1/1
Leyton Orient (Free on 10/7/2000) FL 2+7 FAC 0+1 Others 2+1

CASTLEDINE Stewart Mark
Born: Wandsworth, 22 January 1973
Height: 6'1" Weight: 12.13

After making just one first-team appearance for Wimbledon in the previous two seasons it was not surprising that Stewart looked a little rusty in his early games at Wycombe last term. However he never managed to establish himself in a very strong Wanderers line-up and he made most of his appearances from the subs' bench. A hard-working midfield player with an eye for goal he will be hoping to win a regular place in the coming season.

Wimbledon (From trainee on 2/7/1991) F/PL 18+10/4 FLC 4/3 FAC 2+3
Wycombe W (Loaned on 25/8/1995) FL 7/3
Wycombe W (Free on 7/7/2000) FL 6+11 FLC 0+3/1 FAC 0+2 Others 0+1

CAU Jean-Michel
Born: Ajaccio, France, 27 October 1980
Height: 6'3" Weight: 13.4

Jean-Michel was one of three players signed by Darlington from French National Division club GFCO Ajaccio on the transfer deadline. He made his debut the following week when he came on from the subs' bench against Leyton Orient but the proliferation of strikers at Feethams in the latter part of the season limited any further opportunities. He is a tall and skilful forward who likes to take on opponents. He was released on a free transfer in the summer.

Darlington (Free from GFCO Ajaccio, France, ex Istres, on 22/3/2001) FL 0+1

CHADWICK Luke Harry
Born: Cambridge, 18 November 1980
Height: 5'11" Weight: 11.0
Club Honours: PL '01
International Honours: E: U21-9; Yth

With the exception of Wes Brown, Luke was the one Manchester United player who made the biggest impact on the Old Trafford stage last term. After spending two spells on loan in Belgium with Royal Antwerp he shone in United's short-lived Worthington Cup campaign before making his first full Premiership appearance of the season against Derby in November. A regular substitute in Sir Alex Ferguson's well-oiled machine he netted his first goal of the campaign against Bradford City in January before adding another with an important strike in the 1-1 draw against Leeds at Elland Road.

Manchester U (From trainee on 8/2/1999) PL 6+10/2 FLC 3 FAC 0+1 Others 1+2

CHALK Martyn Peter Glyn
Born: Swindon, 30 August 1969
Height: 5'6" Weight: 10.0

This hard-working central midfield player enjoyed a much better season at Wrexham in 2000-01 and featured more regularly in the first-team squad. He performed consistently well in the first half of the campaign although he dropped out of the squad for a couple of months in the new year. Martyn can also play wide on the right of midfield if required.

Derby Co (£10,000 from Louth U on 23/1/1990) FL 4+3/1 FAC 3/1 Others 0+1
Stockport Co (£40,000 on 30/6/1994) FL 29+14/6 FLC 7+1/2 FAC 2+3 Others 2+2
Wrexham (£25,000 on 19/2/1996) FL 119+41/10 FLC 3+3 FAC 12+3 Others 7

CHALLINOR David (Dave) Paul
Born: Chester, 2 October 1975
Height: 6'1" Weight: 12.6
International Honours: E: Yth; Sch

Having featured regularly for Tranmere in the early part of the 2000-01 campaign Dave had the misfortune to suffer a broken leg in the game at Nottingham Forest last November. He eventually returned to first-team action in the spring but failed to fully establish himself in the side before the end of the season. Although famed for his phenomenally long throws that still create chaos in opposition defences there is much more to his game. He is a good all-round midfield player who distributes the ball intelligently.

Tranmere Rov (Signed from Bromborough Pool on 18/7/1994) FL 118+16/6 FLC 16+1 FAC 9+2

CHALLIS Trevor Michael
Born: Paddington, 23 October 1975
Height: 5'9" Weight: 11.4
International Honours: E: U21-2; Yth

After undergoing a groin operation in the 2000-01 close season Trevor had wait patiently to regain a regular place in the Bristol Rovers side. However once he had recovered fitness he then ran in to disciplinary problems that caused him to miss a number of games in the second half of the campaign. An attacking wing back who also featured in midfield and at left back, Trevor has a high work rate and neat distribution.

Queens Park R (From trainee on 1/7/1994) F/PL 12+1 FAC 2
Bristol Rov (Free on 15/7/1998) FL 93+7/1 FLC 6 FAC 7 Others 3

CHALQI Khalid
Born: Oujda, Morocco, 28 April 1971
Height: 6'2" Weight: 13.1

This experienced midfielder joined Torquay last November after languishing in Creteil's reserves and although he initially displayed a tendency to hold the ball too long he soon adapted to the pace of Third Division football. Good in the air and strong in the tackle he still needs to work to improve his disciplinary record. However he showed a willingness to support the attack from a central midfield position and scored with a header on his debut for the Gulls at York.

Torquay U (Free from Creteil, France, ex Vincennes, Creteil, Aubervilliers, Noisy-le-Sac, Uniao Madeira, Creteil, Naval, on 2/11/2000) FL 20+1/1 FAC 2/1 Others 1

CHAMBERLAIN Alec Francis Roy
Born: March, 20 June 1964
Height: 6'2" Weight: 13.9
Club Honours: Div 1 '96; Div 2 '98

Watford's senior professional with more than 650 first appearances as a goalkeeper for five different clubs, Alec started the 2000-01 season on the bench following the summer signing of Espen Baardsen. However he regained his first-team place when Baardsen was injured and proved as reliable as ever when called upon. He had the unusual experience for a 'keeper of coming on three times as a substitute during the season - replacing Baardsen against Cheltenham, Crewe and Grimsby.

Ipswich T (Free from Ramsey T on 27/7/1981)
Colchester U (Free on 3/8/1982) FL 188 FLC 11 FAC 10 Others 12
Everton (£80,000 on 28/7/1987)
Tranmere Rov (Loaned on 1/11/1987) FL 15
Luton T (£150,000 on 27/7/1988) FL 138 FLC 7 FAC 7 Others 7
Sunderland (Free on 8/7/1993) FL 89+1 FLC 9 FAC 8 Others 1
Watford (£40,000 on 10/7/1996) P/FL 142+2 FLC 11+1 FAC 8 Others 3

CHAMBERS Adam Craig
Born: West Bromwich, 20 November 1980
Height: 5'10" Weight: 11.8
International Honours: E: Yth

Adam spent most of the 2000-01 season in West Bromwich Albion's reserve team or sitting on the subs' bench for the first team but stepped up to make his Football League debut at Stockport last September. A versatile player who can occupy several positions he prefers a defensive role in the main. The twin brother of Albion's James Chambers he scored his first goal in senior football when he netted in the 2-0 win over Portsmouth in February.

West Bromwich A (From trainee on 8/1/1999) FL 4+7/1 FLC 1+1 Others 0+1

Adam Chambers

CHAMBERS James Ashley
Born: West Bromwich, 20 November 1980
Height: 5'10" Weight: 11.8
International Honours: E: Yth

Having been introduced to the West Bromwich Albion first team in the 1999-2000 campaign James had an excellent season last term when he was as a regular in the line-up from August until sidelined by an injury in February. Although he occasionally filled in at right back, he produced his best displays playing as a central defender alongside Tony Butler. Cool under pressure and with a confident approach, he showed excellent distribution and will be looking to make further progress in 2001-02. James is the twin brother of Albion's Adam Chambers.

West Bromwich A (From trainee on 8/1/1999) FL 37+6 FLC 4 FAC 1

CHAPMAN Benjamin (Ben)
Born: Scunthorpe, 2 March 1979
Height: 5'7" Weight: 11.0

Ben had a disappointing time at Grimsby Town in 2000-01. He managed just two senior appearances from the subs' bench as new boss Lennie Lawrence opted for experience in the back line and missed the last few weeks of the season after being sent off in a reserve game and then suffering a shoulder injury. A hard-tackling left back he was made available on a free transfer at the end of the season.

Grimsby T (From trainee on 11/7/1997) FL 1+3 FAC 1 Others 0+1

CHARLERY Kenneth (Kenny) Leroy
Born: Stepney, 28 November 1964
Height: 6'1" Weight: 13.12
International Honours: St Lucia: 4

This veteran striker scored three times for Barnet in the early part of last season including the winner in the 2-1 victory over Chesterfield at Saltergate. He was then sold to Conference outfit Boston United in September where he continued to find the net regularly, finishing the campaign as the York Street club's leading scorer with 13 goals. Although now past his prime he is a useful target man and still has a good eye for goal.

Maidstone U (£35,000 from Fisher on 1/3/1989) FL 41+18/11 FLC 1+3/1 FAC 0+3 Others 5+4
Peterborough U (£20,000 on 28/3/1991) FL 45+6/19 FLC 10/5 FAC 3/1 Others 11/7
Watford (£350,000 on 16/10/1992) FL 45+3/13 FLC 3 FAC 1 Others 0+1
Peterborough U (£150,000 on 16/12/1993) FL 70/24 FLC 2 FAC 2+1/3 Others 2/1
Birmingham C (£350,000 on 4/7/1995) FL 8+9/4 FLC 3+1/2 Others 2+1
Southend U (Loaned on 12/1/1996) FL 2+1
Peterborough U (Signed on 9/2/1996) FL 55+1/12 FLC 4/1 FAC 6/6 Others 6/1
Stockport Co (£85,000 on 25/3/1997) FL 8+2
Barnet (£80,000 on 7/8/1997) FL 106+18/37 FLC 7+1 FAC 3 Others 5+2/1

CHARLES Gary Andrew
Born: Newham, 13 April 1970
Height: 5'9" Weight: 11.8
Club Honours: FMC '92; FLC '96
International Honours: E: 2; U21-4

Gary replaced Davor Suker at half time in the first home Premiership game of the season against Leicester but that was the extent of his first-team football for West Ham in 2000-01. In September he joined Birmingham City on loan but after making his debut in a 1-1 draw against rivals West Bromwich Albion he was affected by hamstring problems and was in and out of the side. He subsequently featured regularly for the Hammers' reserves but was hampered by a number of niggling injuries. An experienced right back or wing back his strengths are his speed and crossing.

Nottingham F (From trainee on 7/11/1987) F/PL 54+2/1 FLC 9 FAC 8+2/1 Others 4+2

Leicester C (Loaned on 16/3/1989) FL 5+3
Derby Co (£750,000 on 29/7/1993) FL 61/3 FLC 5+1 FAC 1 Others 9
Aston Villa (Signed on 6/1/1995) PL 72+7/3 FLC 9+1 FAC 5+2 Others 6+3/1 (£1,500,000 to Benfica, Portugal on 14/1/1999)
West Ham U (£1,200,000 on 6/10/1999) PL 2+3 FLC 1
Birmingham C (Loaned on 15/9/2000) FL 3

CHARLES Julian
Born: Plaistow, 5 February 1977
Height: 5'9" Weight: 11.0
International Honours: St Vincent & Grenadines: 2

Julian had to wait until last March before he finally broke into the Brentford first-team squad and he featured regularly in the closing matches of the season. He is a pacy young striker and was mostly used by the Bees as a second-half substitute to run at opposition defences. Julian made his debut in international football in 2000-01 appearing for St Vincent against Honduras and Jamaica in World Cup qualifying matches.

Brentford (£25,000 from Hampton & Richmond Borough on 23/12/1999) FL 4+8

CHARLTON Simon Thomas
Born: Huddersfield, 25 October 1971
Height: 5'8" Weight: 11.10
International Honours: E: Yth

Signed by Bolton during the close season Simon proved another excellent recruit for Wanderers' boss Sam Allardyce. He won a regular first-team place from October but a hamstring problem then put him out of action for some time, and although he featured occasionally it was not until March that he returned to the starting line-up as a first choice. He then grabbed the opportunity with both hands and was a revelation for the remainder of the campaign, holding down the left-back spot with some fine performances. A strong and composed defender, he impressed with his accurate distribution, crossing ability and skill on the ball.

Huddersfield T (From trainee on 1/7/1989) FL 121+3/1 FLC 9/1 FAC 10 Others 14
Southampton (£250,000 on 8/6/1993) PL 104+10/2 FLC 9+4/1 FAC 8+1
Birmingham C (£250,000 on 5/12/1997) FL 69+3 FLC 3 FAC 3
Bolton W (Free on 12/7/2000) FL 18+4 FAC 3+1 Others 3

CHARNOCK Philip (Phil) Anthony
Born: Southport, 14 February 1975
Height: 5'11" Weight: 11.2

Phil eventually recovered from his long-term pelvic and groin injury problems after more than 12 months on the sidelines but it was not until April that he returned to the Crewe Alexandra starting line-up. He is a hard-working midfield player who uses possession intelligently and strikes the ball well.

Liverpool (From trainee on 16/3/1993) FLC 1 Others 0+1
Blackpool (Loaned on 9/2/1996) FL 0+4
Crewe Alex (Signed on 30/9/1996) FL 115+19/7 FLC 12+1 FAC 4 Others 6

CHARVET Laurent Jean
Born: Beziers, France, 8 May 1973
Height: 5'10" Weight: 12.3
Club Honours: ECWC '98

Laurent started the 2000-01 season on the Newcastle bench, but stepped in to the side following Warren Barton's suspension and after producing a 'Man of the Match' performance against Coventry he retained his place until he was sold to Manchester City at the end of October. Brought in to fill the right-back position he had a baptism of fire at Highbury when the Blues lost 5-0 but went on to enjoy a short run in the team before being sidelined by an achilles injury. He eventually returned to action at the end of February when he looked much more settled in the team. An experienced and versatile defender he is quick, sound in the air and very effective when pushing down the wing. He was placed on the open to offers list in the summer.

Chelsea (Loaned from Cannes, France on 22/1/1998) PL 7+4/2 FLC 0+1 Others 0+1
Newcastle U (£750,000 on 23/7/1998) PL 37+3/1 FLC 3 FAC 6 Others 4
Manchester C (£1,000,000 + on 26/10/2000) PL 16+4 FAC 0+1

Steve Chettle

CHETTLE Stephen (Steve)
Born: Nottingham, 27 September 1968
Height: 6'1" Weight: 13.3
Club Honours: FMC '89, '92; FLC '89, '90; Div 1 '98
International Honours: E: U21-12

Steve was appointed club captain by Barnsley boss Dave Bassett at the start of the 2000-01 season and he remained a regular in the squad throughout the campaign despite being troubled by a niggling back problem. A cultured defender, he increasingly took on the role of mentor to the many youngsters introduced to the first-team squad and was always solid and reliable. A popular figure with the club's fans he was awarded a one-year extension to his contract during the campaign.

Nottingham F (From apprentice on 28/8/1986) F/PL 398+17/11 FLC 49+3/1 FAC 36+1 Others 21+2/2
Barnsley (Free on 26/11/1999) FL 60/2 FLC 3 FAC 1 Others 3

CHILLINGWORTH Daniel Thomas
Born: Cambridge, 13 September 1981
Height: 6'0" Weight: 12.6

Daniel missed several weeks in the early part of last season with an ankle injury but once fit he struggled to break into the Cambridge United first-team squad. He made just one appearance during the campaign, coming on from the subs' bench in the closing stages of the Second Division game against Oldham in March and later the same month he was loaned to Dr Martens League club Cambridge City to gain more first-team experience. He is a promising young striker who is big and strong.

Cambridge U (From trainee on 14/2/2000) FL 0+4 Others 0+1

CHILVERS Liam Christopher
Born: Chelmsford, 6 November 1981
Height: 6'1" Weight: 13.5
Club Honours: FAYC '00

This Arsenal youngster was a member of the Gunners team that won the FA Youth Cup and finished runners-up to West Ham in the U19 Academy final in 1999-2000. He continued to develop with the Gunners' reserves in 2000-01 and spent a month loan at Northampton Town at the turn of the year where he made his Football League debut in the local 'derby' match against Peterborough last December. A big, strong and mobile defender Liam produced a series of competent performances for the Cobblers and will be aiming to make a breakthrough into the senior team at Highbury in the coming season.

Arsenal (From trainee on 18/7/2000)
Northampton T (Loaned on 22/12/2000) FL 7

CHIPPO Youssef
Born: Boujaad, Morocco, 10 June 1973
Height: 5'10" Weight: 10.10
International Honours: Morocco

Youssef had a disappointing season at Coventry last term and eventually lost his place in central midfield following the Worthington Cup defeat by Ipswich in November. Although he featured regularly from the subs' bench he made only one more start and at the time of writing a summer move away from Highfield Road seemed to be on the cards. At his best he has great pace and skill on the ball and is capable of scoring some outstanding goals.

Coventry C (£1,200,000 from FC Porto, Portugal, ex Al Arabi, on 16/7/1999) PL 51+14/2 FLC 5/2 FAC 3/2

CHRISTIE Iyseden
Born: Coventry, 14 November 1976
Height: 6'0" Weight: 12.6

Iyseden missed the start of last season due to suspension but quickly regained his place in the Leyton Orient squad and made several useful contributions from the subs' bench. He was just beginning to make a case for a place in the starting line-up when he suffered a ruptured knee ligament in the Worthington Cup second round second leg tie against Newcastle and was sidelined for the remainder of the campaign. A very quick striker with a good left foot and an eye for goal he will be hoping to return for the O's in the coming season.

Coventry C (From trainee on 22/5/1995) PL 0+1 FLC 0+1
Bournemouth (Loaned on 18/11/1996) FL 3+1
Mansfield T (Loaned on 7/2/1997) FL 8
Mansfield T (Free on 16/6/1997) FL 44+37/18 FLC 4/5 FAC 0+4 Others 2+1
Leyton Orient (£40,000 on 2/7/1999) FL 23+20/9 FLC 4+1/1 FAC 1+1 Others 1

CHRISTIE Malcolm Neil
Born: Stamford, 11 April 1979
Height: 5'6" Weight: 11.4
International Honours: E: U21-6

Having spent the close season battling meningitis, Malcolm missed the opening games of the 2000-01 season for Derby but made up for it by scoring twice on his first appearance against Middlesbrough in September. Fast and direct, he had little time to play his way back in as injuries to others often meant he was employed as a lone forward. Despite this he never gave less than 100 per cent for the team, though the pressures involved resulted in fewer goals as the season wore on. It is not to be forgotten that this was only his second season as a regular member of the side. A great favourite with the home fans, he rewarded them with a superb winning goal at Old Trafford in May to finally secure County's Premiership status. It is to be hoped that the return from injury of Branko Strupar will allow Malcolm to maintain his rate of progress. He made his debut for England U21s against Finland in October and added a further five caps during the season.

Derby Co (£50,000 + from Nuneaton Borough on 2/11/1998) PL 39+18/13 FLC 4+1/2 FAC 3/2

Malcolm Christie

CLAPHAM James (Jamie) Richard
Born: Lincoln, 7 December 1975
Height: 5'9" Weight: 10.11

Jamie made an excellent start to the 2000-01 season at Ipswich playing either at left wing back or on the left side of midfield depending on the team tactics. He retained his place in the starting line-up until dropping back to the bench for the home game against Tottenham at the end of the year. His place in the side came under increasing threat in the second half of the season, firstly from Martijn Reuser who was preferred in midfield, then from Chris Makin for the wing-back slot and he spent much of the final two months of the campaign on the bench. He was not despondent however, and made some telling contributions when he was given the opportunity. Jamie is particularly dangerous going forward and is an excellent crosser of the ball, creating numerous scoring opportunities for his forwards. He is also a bit of a dead-ball specialist, taking corners and free kicks around the box, as typified by his goal at Bradford when he curled a free kick over the wall and into the net. He is the son of the former Shrewsbury Town and Chester player Graham Clapham.

Tottenham H (From trainee on 1/7/1994) PL 0+1 Others 4
Leyton Orient (Loaned on 29/1/1997) FL 6
Bristol Rov (Loaned on 27/3/1997) FL 4+1
Ipswich T (£300,000 on 9/1/1998) P/FL 139+10/7 FLC 14+1/3 FAC 3+2 Others 6/1

CLARE Daryl Adam
Born: Jersey, 1 August 1978
Height: 5'9" Weight: 11.12
Club Honours: AMC '98
International Honours: RoI: B-1; U21-6

Despite a change in management at Grimsby in the early part of last season Daryl was mainly restricted to appearances from the subs' bench in the opening matches. He subsequently moved on loan to Northampton but was unable to recapture the goal-scoring form he had shown in an earlier loan period at Sixfields and returned to Blundell Park after four games. He then had another loan spell at Cheltenham in the new year but although he gave some committed performances for the Robins he returned early with a hamstring injury. Daryl than made a brief come back in the Mariners' squad following the departure of David Neilsen, but he was released at the end of the season. He is a pacy striker able to harry opposition defenders into errors and with a good eye for goal.

Grimsby T (From trainee on 9/12/1995) FL 34+45/9 FLC 1+8/1 FAC 1+4 Others 4+2
Northampton T (Loaned on 12/11/1999) FL 9+1/3
Northampton T (Loaned on 24/11/2000) FL 3+1 Others 0+1
Cheltenham T (Loaned on 30/12/2000) FL 4

CLARE Robert
Born: Belper, 28 February 1983
Height: 6'1" Weight: 11.7

The emergence of Robert was undoubtedly one of the high spots of a difficult season for Stockport County in 2000-01. Initially introduced at full back he was subsequently switched to sweeper to shore up a defence that was leaking too many goals. A classy defender with great composure and an excellent ability to read the game in one so young, his influence on the team was such that the Hatters lost just four times in his 19 starts. With several bigger clubs apparently monitoring his progress he signed a new long-term contract for County towards the end of the season.

Stockport Co (From trainee on 10/3/2000) FL 19+3 FAC 2

CLARIDGE Stephen (Steve) Edward
Born: Portsmouth, 10 April 1966
Height: 5'11" Weight: 12.10
Club Honours: Div 3 '91, Div 2 '95; AMC '95; FLC '97

Pompey's well-travelled marksman had another eventful season in 2000-01. He got off to a great start netting a hat-trick against Wolves at the end of August and was then the surprise choice to succeed Tony Pulis as boss in October. He netted on his managerial debut, and indeed finished the campaign as Pompey's leading scorer, but when Graham Rix took over as manager at the end of February he went on the transfer list. He subsequently joined Millwall on loan on the deadline day and proved an inspirational signing for Lions' manager Mark McGhee. He was a great help to Neil Harris and Richard Sadlier and scored twice in the vital 4-0 win over promotion rivals Rotherham, the second of which was a brilliant chip from 25 yards out. An experienced striker who is full of tricks, he has an excellent first touch and holds the ball up well.

Bournemouth (Signed from Fareham on 30/11/1984) FL 3+4/1 Others 1 (£10,000 to Weymouth in October 1985)
Crystal Palace (Signed on 11/10/1988)
Aldershot (£14,000 on 13/10/1988) FL 58+4/19 FLC 2+1 FAC 6/1 Others 5/2
Cambridge U (£75,000 on 8/2/1990) FL 56+23/28 FLC 2+4/2 FAC 1 Others 6+3/1
Luton T (£160,000 on 17/7/1992) FL 15+1/2 FLC 2/3 Others 2/1
Cambridge U (£195,000 on 20/11/1992) FL 53/18 FLC 4/3 FAC 4 Others 3
Birmingham C (£350,000 on 7/1/1994) FL 86+2/35 FLC 14+1/2 FAC 7 Others 9+1/5
Leicester C (£1,200,000 on 1/3/1996) P/FL 53+10/17 FLC 8/2 FAC 4/1 Others 3+1/1
Portsmouth (Loaned on 23/1/1998) FL 10/2
Wolverhampton W (£400,000 on 26/3/1998) FL 4+1 FAC 1
Portsmouth (£200,000 on 10/8/1998) FL 94+10/34 FLC 4+2 FAC 2+2/1
Millwall (Loaned on 21/3/2001) FL 6/3

CLARK Benjamin (Ben)
Born: Consett, 24 January 1983
Height: 6'1" Weight: 13.6
International Honours: E: Yth; Sch

A member of the England U18 set-up Ben made his senior debut for Sunderland in the 2-1 Worthington Cup win at Luton last September and certainly did not look out of his depth. A solid defender who is confident on the ball he will be hoping to gain further experience in the first-team in 2001-02.

Sunderland (From trainee on 5/7/2000) FLC 1

CLARK Ian David
Born: Stockton, 23 October 1974
Height: 5'11" Weight: 11.7

An injury meant that Ian was out of the first-team picture at Hartlepool for the first three months of last season. He then resumed his friendly battle with Sam Shilton for the left-back position but there was rarely anything to choose between them. Ian finished the season as first choice and was offered a new contract by manager Chris Turner. He is a left-sided utility man who can also play in midfield and attack and likes to push forward and take defenders on.

Doncaster Rov (Free from Stockton on 11/8/1995) FL 23+22/3 FLC 1+2 FAC 1+1 Others 4/1
Hartlepool U (Free on 24/10/1997) FL 104+27/15 FLC 3 FAC 4+2 Others 11+2/1

CLARK Lee Robert
Born: Wallsend, 27 October 1972
Height: 5'8" Weight: 11.7
Club Honours: Div 1 '93, '99, '01
International Honours: E: U21-11; Yth; Sch

Lee had a tremendous season for First Division champions Fulham last term when he was a near ever-present and scored seven valuable goals. An attacking central midfield player his forward runs often left space for others to come through and he set up many chances for his colleagues while still finding time to help out in defence. He was one of six team-mates named in the PFA's Division One team.

Newcastle U (From trainee on 9/12/1989) F/PL 153+42/23 FLC 17 FAC 14+2/3 Others 7+5/1
Sunderland (£2,750,000 on 25/6/1997) FL 72+1/16 FLC 4+1 FAC 4 Others 3
Fulham (£3,000,000 on 13/7/1999) FL 87/15 FLC 10/1 FAC 5

Lee Clark

CLARK Peter James
Born: Romford, 10 December 1979
Height: 6'1" Weight: 12.7

Peter enjoyed an excellent first season at Stockport County last term following his summer move from Carlisle and his performances made him a firm favourite with the Edgeley Park faithful. A pacy defender who appeared at left back and centre half he looked particularly impressive in the first half of the campaign and scored a brilliant solo goal in the Hatters' 2-0 win over Fulham on New Year's Day.

Carlisle U (From trainee at Arsenal on 6/8/1998) FL 77+2/1 FLC 2 FAC 2 Others 3
Stockport Co (£75,000 on 7/7/2000) FL 33+4/2 FLC 2 FAC 3

CLARK Simon
Born: Boston, 12 March 1967
Height: 6'1" Weight: 12.12

Simon joined Colchester United in July 2000 and was appointed club captain for last season. He performed consistently well for the U's, shaking off the effects of a mid-season car accident to lead the team by example. A defender who is dominant both in the air and on the ground, he was usually employed on the left-hand side of a three-man back line.

Peterborough U (Free from Stevenage Borough on 25/3/1994) FL 102+5/4 FLC 5 FAC 12 Others 7+1/1
Leyton Orient (£20,000 on 16/6/1997) FL 98/9 FLC 6 FAC 9 Others 5
Colchester U (Free on 5/7/2000) FL 33+1 FLC 4 FAC 0+1

CLARKE Andrew (Andy) Weston
Born: Islington, 22 July 1967
Height: 5'10" Weight: 11.7
Club Honours: GMVC '91
International Honours: E: SP-2

Although now approaching the twilight of his career, Andy appeared in all but four of Peterborough's Second Division games last term. Featuring either as an out-and-out striker or wide on the left-hand side of midfield he netted eleven goals in all competitions to finish as second-top scorer for Posh. Still quick and able to mesmerise defenders with his neat footwork, he looks to have several more seasons football left in him.

Wimbledon (£250,000 from Barnet on 21/2/1991) F/PL 74+96/17 FLC 13+12/4 FAC 9+8/2
Port Vale (Loaned on 28/8/1998) FL 2+4
Northampton T (Loaned on 15/1/1999) FL 2+2
Peterborough U (Free on 4/5/1999) FL 69+10/24 FLC 1/1 FAC 6/2 Others 5/2

CLARKE Christopher (Chris) Edward
Born: Leeds, 18 December 1980
Height: 6'3" Weight: 12.10

Chris only featured intermittently for Halifax Town in the first half of last season before winning a regular place in the new year. He went on to produce a series of outstanding displays and opened his goal-scoring account for the Shaymen with a close-range goal in 3-0 victory over Barnet in March. A tall and powerful defender he is the twin brother of Matthew who also plays for Halifax.

Halifax T (From trainee at Wolverhampton W on 5/7/1999) FL 26+1/1 FLC 1 Others 1

CLARKE Clive Richard
Born: Dublin, 14 January 1980
Height: 6'1" Weight: 12.3
Club Honours: AMC '00
International Honours: RoI: U21-9; Yth

Having featured regularly in the Stoke City line-up in the 1999-2000 campaign, Clive was somewhat disconcerted by the arrival of Tony Dorigo at the Britannia Stadium in the close season and found that he was second choice to the former England star for much of last term. A talented young left-sided player with excellent distribution he mostly appeared at full back but can also play in midfield if required. Clive again featured regularly for the Republic of Ireland U21 squad and will be aiming to win his place back in the City line-up in 2001-02.

Stoke C (From trainee on 25/1/1997) FL 53+12/1 FLC 8+2 FAC 2+1 Others 13/1

CLARKE Darrell James
Born: Mansfield, 16 December 1977
Height: 5'10" Weight: 11.6

Darrell had another very useful season for Mansfield Town in 2000-01, confirming that he is one of the Stags' up-and-coming stars. He is a left-sided midfield player who likes to get forward and scored a useful number of goals for the Stags during the campaign. He was a regular in the team apart from suspension and the odd minor injury.

Mansfield T (From trainee on 3/7/1996) FL 137+24/24 FLC 7/2 FAC 4+1/1 Others 2+2

CLARKE Matthew (Matt) John
Born: Sheffield, 3 November 1973
Height: 6'4" Weight: 13.10

Matt played in every game for Bradford City until he was dropped by manager Jim Jeffries shortly before Christmas. A transfer request followed and in March he joined Bolton in a loan deal until the end of the season. At the time Wanderers had something of a goalkeeping crisis and Matt quickly took advantage of the situation. He started the away game at Wimbledon and then held his position for the remainder of the campaign producing some fine displays in the play-offs to help the club through to the Premiership. A big, strong, imposing 'keeper he is very confident and commands his area well.

Rotherham U (From trainee on 28/7/1992) FL 123+1 FLC 4 FAC 3 Others 11
Sheffield Wed (£325,000 + on 10/7/1996) PL 2+2
Bradford C (Free on 5/7/1999) PL 38 FLC 2 FAC 2 Others 3
Bolton W (Loaned on 20/3/2001) FL 8 Others 3

CLARKE Matthew Paul
Born: Leeds, 18 December 1980
Height: 6'3" Weight: 12.7

This tall Halifax Town striker spent time on loan with Unibond League clubs Gainsborough Trinity and Frickley Athletic last autumn but on his return to The Shay he switched to a role in the centre of defence for the club's reserves. He performed impressively in his new position and featured regularly in the senior squad in the second half of the campaign. Matthew scored his first-ever Football League goal when he headed home from a corner in the 3-0 win at Southend last February. He is the twin brother of Halifax colleague Chris Clarke.

Halifax T (From trainee at Wolverhampton W on 5/7/1999) FL 20+18/1 FAC 2+1 Others 1+2

CLARKE Peter Michael
Born: Southport, 3 January 1982
Height: 6'0" Weight: 12.0
International Honours: E: Yth; Sch

The captain of England U18s and a regular schoolboy international throughout his formative footballing years, Peter finally made his first team breakthrough at Everton in 2001. Introduced as a substitute after half an hour of the crucial away match at Coventry, he performed creditably in an unaccustomed right-back role. A powerful defender, good in the air and strong in the tackle, he sat on the substitutes' bench on four further occasions without adding to his first-team experience. However having made the decisive breakthrough he will now be keen to add to his senior opportunities at Goodison.

Everton (From juniors on 19/1/1999) PL 0+1

CLARKE Timothy (Tim) Joseph
Born: Stourbridge, 16 May 1965
Height: 6'3" Weight: 15.2
Club Honours: AMC '96; NC '00

This big commanding goalkeeper began last season as first choice for Kidderminster but went down with an injury at the end of August and was replaced by Stuart Brock. He eventually re-established himself in the team in February although he then suffered a dip in form in the closing matches. Tim was released by the Harriers in May and was reported to have signed for Halesowen Town. During the summer break he was loaned to Barry Town for whom he appeared in the European Champions' League qualifying matches for 2001-02.

Coventry C (£25,000 from Halesowen T on 22/10/1990)
Huddersfield T (£15,000 on 22/7/1991) FL 70 FLC 7 FAC 6 Others 8 (Free to Altrincham on 19/8/93)
Rochdale (Loaned on 12/2/1993) FL 2
Shrewsbury T (Free on 21/10/1993) FL 30+1 FLC 3 Others 1 (Free to Witton A during 1996 close season)
York C (Free on 7/9/1996) FL 17 FLC 1 FAC 4 Others 1
Scunthorpe U (Signed on 21/2/1997) FL 78 FLC 5 FAC 6 Others 5
Kidderminster Hrs (Free on 6/10/1999) FL 25 FLC 1 Others 2

CLARKSON Ian Stewart
Born: Solihull, 4 December 1970
Height: 5'10" Weight: 12.12
Club Honours: AMC '91; NC '00

Ian was appointed captain of new boys Kidderminster at the start of last season and featured regularly before losing his place in the closing weeks of the campaign. An experienced right back he had previously retired from the game through injury but a loophole in the regulations allowed him to resume his professional career.

Birmingham C (From trainee on 15/12/1988) FL 125+11 FLC 12 FAC 5+1 Others 17+1
Stoke C (£40,000 on 13/9/1993) FL 72+3 FLC 6 FAC 5 Others 8+2
Northampton T (Free on 2/8/1996) FL 91+3/1 FLC 7+2 FAC 6 Others 10/1
Kidderminster Hrs (Free on 5/11/2000) FL 37+1 FLC 2 FAC 3 Others 1

CLARKSON Philip (Phil) Ian
Born: Garstang, 13 November 1968
Height: 5'10" Weight: 12.5

Phil was in the Blackpool first-team squad for most of the 2000-01 campaign but was in and out of the starting line-up, spending long periods on the subs' bench. He is an attacking midfield player with a good turn of speed and an eye for goal. He will be aiming to feature more regularly in the coming season.

Crewe Alex (£22,500 from Fleetwood T on 15/10/1991) FL 76+22/27 FLC 6+2/1 FAC 3+2/2 Others 7+4/1
Scunthorpe U (Loaned on 30/10/1995) FL 4/1
Scunthorpe U (Free on 13/2/1996) FL 45+3/18 FLC 2/1 FAC 3/2 Others 1
Blackpool (£80,000 on 6/2/1997) FL 153+16/35 FLC 10+1/2 FAC 6+2/4 Others 10/2

CLEGG George Gerald
Born: Manchester, 16 November 1980
Height: 5'10" Weight: 11.12

After scoring regularly for Manchester United reserves George was loaned to Second Division Wycombe Wanderers to cover for injuries and suspensions. He made his senior debut against Port Vale in March and the following week made the starting line-up for the historic FA Cup sixth round tie at Leicester. Although mostly used as a substitute, he showed many neat touches and good ball control before returning to Old Trafford at the end of the season. He was released on a free transfer in the summer.

Manchester U (From trainee on 5/7/1999)
Wycombe W (Loaned on 2/3/2001) FL 2+8 FAC 1

CLEGG Michael Jaime
Born: Ashton under Lyne, 3 July 1977
Height: 5'8" Weight: 11.8
Club Honours: FAYC '95
International Honours: E: U21-2

A very capable defender, Michael had a frustrating time at Manchester United last term when his career seemed to make little progress. He mostly featured in the club's reserve team and his senior appearances were limited to the Worthington Cup ties at Watford and Sunderland. Facing the rather unenviable task of trying to displace one of the Neville brothers or Dennis Irwin in the Reds' line-up, he may well have quite a wait before he wins a regular place in the squad. Primarily a full back he is a solid tackler and excellent on the overlap.

Manchester U (From trainee on 1/7/1995) PL 4+5 FLC 7 FAC 3+1 Others 1+2
Ipswich T (Loaned on 16/2/2000) FL 3
Wigan Ath (Loaned on 23/3/2000) FL 6

CLELAND Alexander (Alex)
Born: Glasgow, 10 December 1970
Height: 5'8" Weight: 11.6
Club Honours: SPL '95, '96, '97; SC '94, '96
International Honours: S: B-2; U21-11; Sch

A neat and tidy right back, Alex was plagued by injury problems for Everton throughout the 2000-01 season. He had made just two first-team starts in arguably his most effective position of right wing back, when a hamstring injury cut his season short. He returned in January for a vital away trip to Coventry but played only 31 minutes of the Blues' victory before succumbing to an unrelated calf injury. That was his final act of the campaign although he proved his fitness with a series of reserve team run-outs before the season's close. A popular member of the first-team squad, Alex will be hoping for better luck next season.

Dundee U (From juniors on 18/6/1987) SL 131+20/8 SLC 10+1 SC 7+2 Others 8+1/1
Glasgow R (Signed on 26/1/1995) SL 90+6/4 SLC 8+2 SC 13+1 Others 13+1
Everton (Free on 3/7/1998) PL 21+11 FLC 5+2 FAC 2

CLEMENCE Stephen Neal
Born: Liverpool, 31 March 1978
Height: 5'11" Weight: 11.7
Club Honours: FLC '99
International Honours: E: U21-1; Yth; Sch

Stephen continued to make steady progress at Tottenham last season when he became a regular in the first team, holding his place as a result of some good solid performances. A skilful central midfield player he grew in confidence as the campaign wore on and added a much-needed degree of continuity in the centre of the park. A player who likes to get forward into the opponents' box and is prepared to go out wide to get possession, he managed just a single goal, netting at the near post in the 3-2 win at Sunderland. Stephen is the son of the former England goalkeeper Ray Clemence.

Tottenham H (From trainee on 3/4/1995) PL 64+20/2 FLC 6+1 FAC 7+1/1 Others 2+1

CLEMENT Neil
Born: Reading, 3 October 1978
Height: 6'0" Weight: 12.3
International Honours: E: Yth; Sch

Having enjoyed a successful loan spell at The Hawthorns towards the end of the 1999-2000 campaign Neil returned to sign permanently for West Bromwich Albion in the summer. A stylish left wing back he had an exceptional season with the Baggies, producing a string of consistent performances and scoring some fine goals. Confident on the ball and firm in the tackle he created several chances for his colleagues with his powerful runs down the flank and also developed into something of a specialist with free kicks. He was deservedly voted 'Player of the Year' by the club's supporters. Neil is the son of the former Queens Park Rangers and England full back Dave Clement.

Chelsea (From trainee on 8/10/1995) PL 1 FLC 0+2 FAC 0+1
Reading (Loaned on 19/11/1998) FL 11/1 Others 1
Preston NE (Loaned on 25/3/1999) FL 4
Brentford (Loaned on 23/11/1999) FL 7+1
West Bromwich A (£100,000 + on 23/3/2000) FL 52+1/5 FLC 4/2 FAC 1 Others 2

CLIST Simon James
Born: Shaftesbury, 13 June 1981
Height: 5'9" Weight: 11.0

Simon was a regular in the Bristol City line-up last season and at times showed some excellent form. A central midfield player, his deft touches and intelligent runs off the

ball provided City with some creative inspiration in the centre of the park. He was voted 'Young Player of the Season' by members of the supporters' club.
Bristol C (From trainee at Tottenham H on 24/7/1999) FL 44+3/4 FAC 6/2 Others 1+3

COATES Jonathan Simon
Born: Swansea, 27 June 1975
Height: 5'8" Weight: 10.4
Club Honours: Div 3 '00
International Honours: W: B-1; U21-5; Yth
After appearing regularly in the Swansea City squad at the start of last season, Jonathan had the misfortune to suffer a knee ligament injury in the match at Rotherham at the end of October. It was not until March that he returned to first-team action, but he was again sidelined by hamstring trouble and it was only in the last few games that he came back into the side. When fully fit he is an exciting left winger with excellent skills on the ball.
Swansea C (From trainee on 8/7/1993) FL 174+31/18 FLC 10+2/1 FAC 8 Others 10+3

COBIAN Juan Manuel
Born: Buenos Aires, Argentine, 11 September 1975
Height: 5'9" Weight: 12.0
Having featured in just a handful of games for Aberdeen in the 1999-2000 campaign Juan joined Swindon Town in the close season. However he featured on only a handful of occasions, and following his appearance at Walsall on New Year's Day he was restricted to reserve-team football and a couple of outings from the subs' bench in the LDV Vans Trophy. He is a right wing back who is comfortable and composed on the ball when pushing forward.
Sheffield Wed (Signed from Boca Juniors, Argentine on 13/8/1998) PL 7+2 FLC 1
Charlton Ath (Free on 5/8/1999)
Aberdeen (Free on 1/11/1999) SL 2+1 SLC 1
Swindon T (Free on 27/7/2000) FL 3 FLC 2 FAC 1 Others 0+2

COCHRANE Justin Vincent
Born: Hackney, 26 January 1982
Height: 6'0" Weight: 11.8
Justin was a member of the successful Queens Park Rangers U19 team last season and played in both legs of the Academy League final when Rangers narrowly lost out to Nottingham Forest. A promising midfield player, he made his Football League debut when he came on from the subs' bench for the home game against Stockport at the end of April but had the misfortune to receive a rather harsh red card just 17 minutes after coming on the field.
Queens Park R (From trainee on 16/7/1999) FL 0+1

COID Daniel (Danny) John
Born: Liverpool, 3 October 1981
Height: 5'11" Weight: 11.7
Danny had an excellent season for Blackpool in 2000-01 when he firmly established himself as a regular in the first team line-up. He began the season playing as a right wing back but moved forward into midfield after the arrival of Gary Parkinson in March. A versatile player who can also play on the left side, he netted the winner against Macclesfield last October with an unstoppable shot from the edge of the box.
Blackpool (From trainee on 24/7/2000) FL 58+10/2 FLC 4 FAC 4 Others 5

COLDICOTT Stacy
Born: Redditch, 29 April 1974
Height: 5'8" Weight: 11.8
Stacy was a regular for Grimsby Town last season, rarely absent apart from minor injuries, and he once again played a vital part in yet another battle by the Mariners to avoid relegation. A competitive and hard-tackling midfield player he scored the winner in the vital end-of-season game against Watford.
West Bromwich A (From trainee on 4/3/1992) FL 64+40/3 FLC 8+1 FAC 2+2/1 Others 7+3
Cardiff C (Loaned on 30/8/1996) FL 6
Grimsby T (£125,000 on 6/8/1998) FL 111+7/3 FLC 11/2 FAC 4+1

COLE Andrew (Andy) Alexander
Born: Nottingham, 15 October 1971
Height: 5'11" Weight: 11.12
Club Honours: Div 1 '93; PL '96, '97, '99, '00, '01; FAC '96, '99; CS '97; EC '99
International Honours: E: 13; B-1; U21-8; Yth, Sch
Andy started the 2000-01 season like a man on a mission, clearly determined to rewrite the Manchester United records books almost on his own. Having started the campaign with goals against Newcastle (his 10th in 11

Andy Cole

games against his former club), West Ham and Bradford in the Premiership, his superb hat-trick against Anderlecht at Old Trafford in the Champions' League in September earned him the title of United's all-time European Cup goal scorer. His first effort that night was United's 300th in all European games, while his second was the Reds 200th in the European Cup. Deservedly recalled to the England side for the friendly against France in Paris in September, he then played in the dismal defeat by Germany in October. Despite requiring surgery to an achilles heel in December, he started the new year with a vengeance, netting in successive games against Sunderland, Everton and Chelsea. After signing a new four-year contract in February his Champions' League effort against Valencia helped United through to the quarter-final stages. With a vital first goal for England against Albania in March, his club and international future looked to be on a secure footing.

Arsenal (From trainee on 18/10/1989) FL 0+1 Others 0+1
Fulham (Loaned on 5/9/1991) FL 13/3 Others 2/1
Bristol C (£500,000 on 12/3/1992) FL 41/20 FLC 3/4 FAC 1 Others 4/1
Newcastle U (£1,750,000 on 12/3/1993) F/PL 69+1/55 FLC 7/8 FAC 4/1 Others 3/4
Manchester U (£6,000,000 on 12/1/1995) PL 154+30/89 FLC 2 FAC 19+2/9 Others 48+5/18

Ashley Cole

COLE Ashley
Born: Stepney, 20 December 1980
Height: 5'8" Weight: 10.8
International Honours: E: 3; U21-3; Yth

Ashley had a fantastic first full season for Arsenal in 2000-01. Capitalising on the chance brought about by an early injury to regular left back Silvinho, he seized his opportunity and proved to be a revelation for the Gunners. His surging runs, timely tackles and stinging crosses won praise from all quarters and he won a regular place in the England U21 team from the beginning of the campaign. An extended run in the side then brought him to the attention of new national team coach Sven Goran Eriksson and he was awarded his first full England cap in the World Cup qualifier against Albania in March. Ashley showed a maturity beyond his years, putting in accomplished performances against the cream of Europe in the Champions League and looks to have a long, successful and exciting career ahead of him at both club and international level.

Arsenal (From trainee on 23/11/1998) PL 16+2/3 FLC 1+1 FAC 5+1 Others 8+1
Crystal Palace (Loaned on 25/2/2000) FL 14/1

COLE Joseph (Joe) John
Born: Islington, 8 November 1981
Height: 5'9" Weight: 11.0
Club Honours: FAYC '99
International Honours: E: 1; U21-3; Yth; Sch

Having recovered from the broken leg that brought his 1999-2000 campaign to a premature close, Joe was thrust straight into first-team action for West Ham at the start of last term due to the club's long injury list. He remained in the team until suffering an injury in the clash with Newcastle in November that put him out for two months. But once back he retained his place through to the summer break. He had outstanding games against Manchester United and Liverpool at Upton Park and his only apparent weakness was a limited goal tally. An extremely talented midfield player he has unbelievable skill and pace for one so young while he also has great stamina and tackles well. Joe was a regular for England at U21 level before making his long-awaited full international debut when he replaced Steven Gerrard for the second half of the friendly against Mexico at the end of May.

West Ham U (From trainee on 11/12/1998) PL 43+17/6 FLC 5+1/1 FAC 5+1 Others 2+3

COLEMAN Christopher (Chris)
Born: Swansea, 10 June 1970
Height: 6'2" Weight: 14.6
Club Honours: WC '89, '91; Div 1 '94, '01; Div 2 '99
International Honours: W: 31; U21-3; Yth; Sch

The one blot on Fulham's fantastic season was the horrific car accident last January that left their popular skipper's future career in doubt. He required a series of operations on his badly damaged leg and was still on crutches when receiving the championship trophy at the final home game of the season, however Chris is absolutely determined to be back in action during the club's first season in the top flight for over 30 years. He had played so well in the period prior to the accident that he was named in the PFA Divisional awards for the fourth successive season. 'Cookie', as he is affectionately known, played a huge part in the 11 successive victories at the start of the campaign when the defence conceded just six goals, and it was this spell that set up the title.

Swansea C (From Manchester C juniors on 1/9/1987) FL 159+1/2 FLC 8 FAC 13/1 Others 15
Crystal Palace (£275,000 on 19/7/1991) F/PL 143+11/13 FLC 24+2/2 FAC 8/1 Others 2
Blackburn Rov (£2,800,000 on 16/12/1995) PL 27+1 FLC 2 FAC 2
Fulham (£2,100,000 on 1/12/1997) FL 136/8 FLC 13/2 FAC 11/1 Others 3

COLEMAN Simon
Born: Worksop, 13 March 1968
Height: 6'0" Weight: 11.8

This experienced centre back was signed by Rochdale in the summer of 2000 to bring some much-needed organisational skills to the defence, but was injured during the pre-season and managed only one game before Christmas. He was then recalled to face Shrewsbury in February, but unfortunately for Simon, Dale slumped to their worst-ever home defeat. At his best he is a commanding defender who is also very useful when coming up to join the attack for set pieces.

Mansfield T (From juniors on 29/7/1985) FL 96/7 FLC 9 FAC 7 Others 7/1
Middlesbrough (£600,000 on 26/9/1989) FL 51+4/2 FAC 5 Others 10/1
Derby Co (£300,000 on 15/8/1991) FL 62+8/2 FLC 5+1 FAC 5 Others 12
Sheffield Wed (£250,000 on 20/1/1994) PL 11+5/1 FLC 3 FAC 2
Bolton W (£350,000 on 5/10/1994) P/FL 34/5 FLC 4 FAC 2
Wolverhampton W (Loaned on 2/9/1997) FL 3+1
Southend U (Free on 20/2/1998) FL 98+1/9 FLC 6 FAC 2 Others 2
Rochdale (Free on 10/7/2000) FL 5

COLES Daniel (Danny) Richard
Born: Bristol, 31 October 1981
Height: 6'1" Weight: 11.5

Danny is one of many exciting products of Bristol City's Academy set-up and continued to make steady progress in the reserves last season. A promising young central defender he made a handful of first-team appearances and will be hoping for more senior experience in the 2001-02 campaign.

Bristol C (From trainee on 7/6/2000) FL 1+2 Others 1

COLLETT Andrew (Andy) Alfred
Born: Stockton, 28 October 1973
Height: 6'0" Weight: 12.10

Andy made the Darlington goalkeeping spot his own last season despite stiff competition from Dutch understudy Frank Van Der Geest. He made some brilliant saves including a penalty stop from Benito Carbone in the Worthington Cup tie against Bradford City, while he almost single-handedly denied Hartlepool a win in the local 'derby' at Feethams. However he broke a thumb during his heroics in the latter game and was forced onto the sidelines for the next seven games before returning to the side for the last few games of the campaign.

Middlesbrough (From trainee on 6/3/1992) PL 2 Others 3
Bristol Rov (Loaned on 18/10/1994) FL 4
Bristol Rov (£10,000 on 23/3/1995) FL 103 FLC 4 FAC 7 Others 8
Darlington (Free on 6/8/1999) FL 50 FLC 4 FAC 4 Others 3

COLLINS James Ian
Born: Liverpool, 28 May 1978
Height: 5'8" Weight: 10.0

Another young player to come up through

the ranks at Crewe, James featured in a handful of first-team games in the early part of last season but found it difficult to claim a regular place in the squad. He eventually moved on loan to Dr Martens League club Halesowen Town in March and was released at the end of the campaign. He is a young midfield player who is skilful on the ball and works hard.

Crewe Alex (From trainee on 4/7/1996) FL 15+9/1 FLC 1+3 FAC 0+1

COLLINS James Michael
Born: Newport, 23 August 1983
Height: 6'2" Weight: 13.0
International Honours: W: Yth

James emerged as one of several promising youngsters at Cardiff City last season making his senior debut when he came off the subs' bench to replace Robbie Earnshaw in the closing minutes of the FA cup first round tie against Bristol Rovers. He made a handful more appearances, mostly as a substitute, and will be looking to see more first-team action in the 2001-02 campaign. James started out as a central defender, but has since switched to playing as a striker. He was capped for Wales at U17 and U18 levels during the season.

Cardiff C (From trainee on 5/4/2001) FL 0+3 FAC 0+2 Others 1

COLLINS John Angus Paul
Born: Galashiels, 31 January 1968
Height: 5'7" Weight: 10.10
Club Honours: SC '95; Div 1 '01
International Honours: S: 58; U21-8; Yth

John became Jean Tigana's first signing for Fulham - and what an inspired choice that proved to be. A regular in the first half of the season he was then affected by a series of niggling injuries but remained an influential figure for the First Division champions. While his vast experience in midfield helped the club's younger players adapt to the new 'pass, pass, pass' regime of the manager he rarely lost possession himself and when he did he was quick to win it back again.

Hibernian (Free from Hutchison Vale BC on 9/8/1984) SL 155+8/16 SLC 7+3/1 SC 17/3 Others 4/1
Glasgow Celtic (Signed on 13/7/1990) SL 211+6/47 SLC 22/3 SC 21/3 Others 13/1 (Free to AS Monaco, France on 2/7/1996)
Everton (£2,500,000 on 7/8/1998) PL 52+3/3 FLC 3+2/1 FAC 4
Fulham (£2,000,000 on 21/7/2000) FL 25+2/3

COLLINS Lee
Born: Bellshill, 3 February 1974
Height: 5'8" Weight: 11.6

Lee linked up once again with his old boss Steve McMahon and apart from an early-season injury he was a regular in the Blackpool line-up last season. He is a hard-working battling player who performed both in a central and wide right-sided midfield role for the Tangerines during the 2000-01 campaign.

Albion Rov (Signed from Pollock on 25/11/1993) SL 43+2/1 SLC 2 SC 2 Others 2
Swindon T (£15,000 on 15/11/1995) FL 52+11/2 FAC 4 Others 1
Blackpool (Free on 24/7/2000) FL 23+5 FLC 2 FAC 2 Others 1

COLLINS Lee David
Born: Birmingham, 10 September 1977
Height: 6'1" Weight: 12.6

Lee was loaned to Cambridge United at the beginning of last season but failed to make it beyond the subs' bench at the Abbey Stadium. However he produced some fine performances for Stoke reserves on his return to the Potteries and was called up to the first team for the FA Cup first round replay against Nuneaton Borough. He subsequently continued his development in the second string before going out on loan to Dr Martens League club Moor Green in the closing stages of the campaign. A tall and commanding central defender he was reported to have joined Halesowen Town in the summer.

Aston Villa (From trainee on 5/7/1996)
Stoke C (Free on 19/2/1999) FL 4 FAC 0+1

COLLINS Samuel (Sam) Jason
Born: Pontefract, 5 June 1977
Height: 6'3" Weight: 14.0

Sam was regarded as an automatic choice for Bury throughout much of last season, despite struggling to find his best form at times. However he limped out of the action with an achilles injury in the Shakers' home game against Notts County in March and missed the remainder of the campaign as a result. Sam is a powerful central defender who is effective in the air and capable of some crunching tackles. He is the younger brother of Macclesfield's Simon Collins.

Huddersfield T (From trainee on 6/7/1994) FL 34+3 FLC 6+1 FAC 3
Bury (£75,000 on 2/7/1999) FL 52+1/2 FLC 4 FAC 0+2

COLLINS Simon Jonathan
Born: Pontefract, 16 December 1973
Height: 5'11" Weight: 13.0

Simon started the 2000-2001 season with some strong performances in the centre of the Macclesfield Town defence. Unfortunately he was then sidelined following a cartilage operation and later with knee ligament damage and did not regain his position on a regular basis. He moved on loan to Shrewsbury Town in the new year where he began to establish a useful partnership with new signing Matt Redmile. However he was recalled early due to an injury crisis and subsequently featured for Macc in the closing weeks of the campaign. He is a powerful central defender who tackles effectively and is good in the air. Simon is the elder brother of Bury's Sam Collins. He was out of contract in the summer.

Huddersfield T (From trainee on 1/7/1992) FL 31+21/3 FLC 6+3/2 FAC 1+4 Others 1+3
Plymouth Arg (£60,000 on 6/3/1997) FL 81+3/5 FLC 2 FAC 1 Others 1
Macclesfield T (Free on 5/7/1999) FL 52+4/3 FLC 3 FAC 2 Others 1
Shrewsbury T (Loaned on 16/2/2001) FL 12

COLLINS Wayne Anthony
Born: Manchester, 4 March 1969
Height: 6'0" Weight: 12.0
Club Honours: Div 2 '97

Wayne had another frustrating season at Fulham last term as he was unable to break into the first team on a regular basis. He was named as a substitute on no less than a dozen occasions but he only came off the bench twice to add to a handful of starts in league games, although he was still a very valued member of the first team squad. A versatile player he can appear in either full-back position or in a variety of midfield roles. He was released in the summer.

Crewe Alex (£10,000 from Winsford U on 29/7/1993) FL 102+15/14 FLC 5/1 FAC 8+1 Others 14+1/2
Sheffield Wed (£600,000 on 1/8/1996) PL 16+15/6 FLC 2 FAC 1
Fulham (£400,000 + on 23/1/1998) FL 37+21/4 FLC 10+1/2 FAC 6+2/2 Others 4

COLLIS David (Dave) John
Born: London, 8 November 1981
Height: 5'11" Weight: 12.2

This versatile Charlton youngster featured regularly for the Addicks' reserve team last season playing either at right back or in midfield. In March he was loaned to Third Division Barnet to gain experience of first team football and made two appearances for the Bees in a central midfield role before returning to the Valley. Strong in the tackle, Dave will be aiming to gain further senior experience in the 2001-02 campaign.

Charlton Ath (From trainee on 17/5/2000)
Barnet (Loaned on 11/3/2001) FL 1+1

COLLYMORE Stanley (Stan) Victor
Born: Cannock, 22 January 1971
Height: 6'3" Weight: 13.10
International Honours: E: 3

Having made such an impact under Martin O'Neill, Stan's career at Leicester under Peter Taylor was extremely brief amounting to a handful of appearances, mostly from the subs' bench, and a single goal in the 2-0 victory at Chelsea. His relationship with the new boss never seemed to get on a steady footing and in October he moved on to Bradford City. He made the perfect start at Valley Parade netting with a superb overhead kick in the 1-1 draw against Leeds but after half-a-dozen games he went on the transfer list and was eventually allowed to move to Spanish club Real Oviedo on a free transfer. That too failed to work out and before the end of the season he had announce his retirement from the game. Stan is a very talented footballer and on his day can be more than a match for even the best defenders but until he can resolve his much-publicised problems he is unlikely to reach his full potential.

Wolverhampton W (From trainee on 13/7/1989)
Crystal Palace (£100,000 from Stafford R on 4/1/1991) FL 4+16/1 FLC 2+3/1
Southend U (£100,000 on 20/11/1992) FL 30/15 FAC 3/3
Nottingham F (£2,000,000 on 5/7/1993) F/PL 64+1/41 FLC 9/2 FAC 2/1 Others 2/1
Liverpool (£8,500,000 on 3/7/1995) PL 55+6/26 FLC 2+2 FAC 9/7 Others 5+2/2
Aston Villa (£7,000,000 on 16/5/1997) PL 34+11/7 FLC 1 FAC 5/3 Others 9+1/5
Fulham (Loaned on 19/7/1999) FL 3+3 FLC 1+2/1
Leicester C (£250,000 + on 11/2/2000) PL 7+4/5 Others 0+1
Bradford C (Free on 27/10/2000) PL 5+2/2 FLC 1

CONLON Barry John
Born: Drogheda, 1 October 1978
Height: 6'3" Weight: 13.7
International Honours: RoI: U21-7

Having finished leading scorer for York City in 1999-2000 Barry found himself relegated to the subs' bench after just two games last term and in November he moved to Colchester United on a long-term loan. He immediately impressed the Layer Road faithful with his physical presence up front and scored eight goals in his stay with the U's. The club were keen to buy him at the end of the season but at the time of writing no deal had been agreed. Barry is an effective striker who is able to undo opposition defences with his passing ability and close control and has a good eye for goal.

Manchester C (From trainee at Queens Park R on 14/8/1997) FL 1+6 FLC 0+1
Plymouth Arg (Loaned on 26/2/1998) FL 13/2
Southend U (£95,000 on 4/9/1998) FL 28+6/7 FAC 1 Others 1
York C (£100,000 on 20/7/1999) FL 33+15/11 FLC 2+2 FAC 1 Others 0+1
Colchester U (Loaned on 9/11/2000) FL 23+3/8 FAC 1 Others 1

CONNELL Darren Stephen
Born: Liverpool, 3 February 1982
Height: 5'8" Weight: 10.8

After being released by Blackpool, Darren had trials with Bolton during the 2000 close season before signing a 12-month contract for Macclesfield Town. He appeared regularly for Macc's reserve and youth teams but made just a single first team appearance when he came on as a last minute substitute in the away win at Lincoln last February. A promising striker he was released on a free transfer in the summer.

Blackpool (Trainee) FL 1+2
Macclesfield T (Free on 1/9/2000) FL 0+1

CONNELL Lee Anthony
Born: Bury, 24 June 1981
Height: 6'0" Weight: 12.0

One of several promising youngsters on the books at Bury, Lee continued his development in the club's reserve team in 2000-01, stepping up to make two senior appearances. He featured in an unaccustomed right-back role in the LDV Vans Trophy tie against Chesterfield in January, and then appeared as a second half substitute in the Shakers' 3-0 home win over Swansea in March when he played in the centre of defence and scored Bury's third goal.

Bury (From trainee on 9/7/1999) FL 1+2/1 Others 1

CONNELLY Gordon Paul John
Born: Glasgow, 1 November 1976
Height: 5'11" Weight: 12.4
International Honours: S: Yth; Sch

Gordon began last season at Southend United, but although he featured regularly in the first-team squad under Brian Little he moved on to Carlisle soon after David Webb became manager. He quickly found a regular berth on the right side of midfield at Brunton Park and produced some determined displays for the Cumbrian club. He only scored a couple of goals himself but had great satisfaction in setting up United's goal in a 1-1 draw against his former colleagues at Roots Hall in April. He is a busy, hard-working player who operates wide on the right-hand side of midfield and is always willing to push forward to help the attack. He was released on a free transfer.

Airdrieonians (Signed from Milngarvie W on 11/8/1995) SL 16+17/1 SC 0+1 Others 3+2/1
York C (Free on 10/8/1998) FL 28/4 FLC 2 FAC 3 Others 1
Southend U (£50,000 on 1/7/1999) FL 37+5/2 FLC 2 FAC 1 Others 1
Carlisle U (Free on 6/11/2000) FL 21+7/1 FAC 3/1

CONNELLY Sean Patrick
Born: Sheffield, 26 June 1970
Height: 5'10" Weight: 11.10

This long-serving Stockport County defender had a disappointing time last season and never established himself as a first-team regular at Edgeley Park. He subsequently joined Wolves linking up with his old boss Dave Jones in a loan deal shortly before the transfer deadline. Used as cover when Kevin Muscat was absent through suspension and international commitments he made a steady start and proved a calming influence on the Wanderers' defence. An experienced right back he was out of contract in the summer and at the time of writing it was unclear where he would be at the start of the 2001-02 campaign.

Stockport Co (Free from Hallam on 12/8/1991) FL 292+10/6 FLC 29/1 FAC 15+2 Others 15+1
Wolverhampton W (Loaned on 21/3/2001) FL 6

CONNOLLY Karl Andrew
Born: Prescot, 9 February 1970
Height: 5'10" Weight: 11.2
Club Honours: WC '95

Karl joined Queens Park Rangers on a free transfer under the Bosman ruling at the end of May 2000. He made a couple of appearances from the subs' bench in the early part of last season but it was not until mid-October that he won a regular place in the starting line-up. He continued to feature until March when a change in management brought a new formation and he dropped out of the team. He is an attacking left-sided midfield player who created numerous goal opportunities for the front line through his ability to hold the ball and beat defenders.

Wrexham (Free from Napoli, in local Sunday League, on 8/5/1991) FL 337+21/88 FLC 22/4 FAC 37+1/16 Others 32+1/6
Queens Park R (Free on 31/5/2000) FL 17+6/4 FLC 1 FAC 2+1

CONNOLLY Paul
Born: Liverpool, 29 September 1983
Height: 6'0" Weight: 11.9

Paul made his Football League debut for Plymouth Argyle in the final game of the 2000-01 season when he came off the subs' bench to replace David Friio for the last 20 minutes of the game against Rochdale. He then proceeded to give an accomplished performance at right back helping the Argyle defence to secure a clean sheet. Paul will be looking to receive more first team opportunities in the coming season.

Plymouth Arg (Trainee) FL 0+1

CONNOR Daniel (Dan) Brian
Born: Dublin, 31 January 1981
Height: 6'2" Weight: 12.9
International Honours: RoI: Yth

Dan was again understudy to Mark Tyler at Peterborough last term and made just two first-team appearances both coming in the LDV Vans Trophy ties. An imposing young 'keeper he set a new club record for appearances as an unused substitute during the season.

Peterborough U (From trainee on 29/4/1998) FL 2+1 Others 2

CONNOR Paul
Born: Bishop Auckland, 12 January 1979
Height: 6'1" Weight: 11.5
Club Honours: AMC '00

With the wealth of strikers at Stoke manager Gudjon Thordarson's disposal, Paul's chances at the Britannia Stadium were limited to a handful of outings, mostly from the subs' bench. In December he went out on loan to Second Division rivals Cambridge United where his arrival lifted the team. He showed an excellent eye for goal, netting five times for the U's before returning to the Potteries. Rochdale manager Steve Parkin then signed him for a club record fee in a bid to boost his attack and came up trumps. Paul was an immediate hit at Spotland, scoring ten times in 14 games including a hat-trick in the 6-0 win over Halifax Town. He is a promising young striker who makes intelligent runs and is a strong finisher.

Middlesbrough (From trainee on 4/7/1996)
Hartlepool U (Loaned on 6/2/1998) FL 4+1
Stoke C (Free on 25/3/1999) FL 18+18/7 FLC 3+3/3 FAC 0+1 Others 2+3
Cambridge U (Loaned on 9/11/2000) FL 12+1/5 FAC 1
Rochdale (£100,000 on 9/3/2001) FL 14/10

CONSTANTINE Leon
Born: Hackney, 24 February 1978
Height: 6'2" Weight: 11.10

Leon attracted the attention of Football League scouts after scoring freely for Ryman League club Edgware Town in the 1999-2000 campaign and joined Millwall last August following a short trial. He subsequently spent most of the 2000-01 season developing in the reserves where he acquitted himself well: a hat-trick against Wycombe being the highlight of his campaign. He made his Football League debut when he came on from the subs' bench for the closing stages of the match at Peterborough in September. Leon is a lanky striker who has a good eye for goal and uses his height and strength to put defences under pressure.

Millwall (Signed from Edgware T on 31/8/2000) FL 0+1 Others 1

CONVERY Mark Peter
Born: Newcastle, 29 May 1981
Height: 5'6" Weight: 10.5

Mark spent the early part of last season on loan in Denmark with Hvidovre and on his

return he had a short trial at Reading before signing for Darlington. He made his debut for the Quakers in the LDV Vans Trophy tie at Port Vale, however he was limited to appearances from the subs' bench until an injury to Mark Ford allowed him to make his first league start on Easter Saturday and he then held his place for the next few games. Mark is a busy midfield player who covers every blade of grass in his efforts to gain possession for his colleagues and to support the attack.
Sunderland (From trainee on 24/3/1999)
Darlington (Free on 30/1/2001) FL 5+6 Others 1

COOK James (Jamie) Steven
Born: Oxford, 2 August 1979
Height: 5'10" Weight: 11.6
Jamie featured in a handful of early season games for Oxford United and scored the winner at Bury to give the U's their first win of the campaign. However he then fell out of favour following a change in management and was released by new boss David Kemp. He subsequently had a brief trial at Darlington before joining Boston United along with the Weatherstone brothers. He featured regularly for the Conference club in the closing matches and netted two goals in the 5-3 victory over Hereford on the last day of the season.
Oxford U (From trainee on 1/7/1997) FL 33+44/7 FLC 1+4 FAC 3+4 Others 3

COOK Lee
Born: Hammersmith, 3 August 1982
Height: 5'9" Weight: 11.7
Lee stepped up to make his Football League debut for Watford when he came off the subs' bench during the second half of the 2-1 defeat at Grimsby last April. He did well enough to justify his inclusion on a handful more occasions and will be hoping to gain further senior experience in 2001-02. He is a promising left-sided striker who has good technical skill on the ball and is very effective when running at opposing defenders.
Watford (Signed from Aylesbury U on 19/11/1999) FL 2+2

COOK Paul Anthony
Born: Liverpool, 22 June 1967
Height: 5'11" Weight: 11.0
Paul had mixed fortunes in the 2000-01 season, seeming to suffer a loss of form in the early part of the campaign before once again becoming the creative element in the Clarets' midfield. He was seldom out of the team apart from injuries and suspension mostly performing in a role as the link man between defence and attack. He is a talented midfield player with good vision and passing ability who is never afraid to go for goal when the opportunity arises.
Wigan Ath (Signed from Marine on 20/7/1984) FL 77+6/14 FLC 4 FAC 6+1 Others 5+1/1
Norwich C (£73,000 on 23/5/1988) FL 3+3 Others 1+1
Wolverhampton W (£250,000 on 1/11/1989) FL 191+2/19 FLC 7/1 FAC 5+2 Others 6+1/1
Coventry C (£600,000 on 18/8/1994) PL 35+2/3 FLC 3 FAC 3
Tranmere Rov (£250,000 on 29/2/1996) FL 54+6/4 FLC 8 FAC 1
Stockport Co (£250,000 on 24/10/1997) FL 48+1/3 FLC 1+1 FAC 2
Burnley (Free on 12/3/1999) FL 94+2/7 FLC 4+1 FAC 6/2

COOKE Andrew (Andy) Roy
Born: Shrewsbury, 20 January 1974
Height: 6'0" Weight: 12.8
A regular in the Burnley team for the last five years, Andy started the 2000-01 season well enough as the Clarets surprised the First Division with their early results. However manager Stan Ternent then restructured the strike force using Glen Little or Graham Branch as the supply line to the sometimes-isolated Andy Payton, and when Ian Moore arrived from Stockport Andy moved on to Stoke City. A City supporter in his younger days he quickly won over the fans with an honest, hard-working style and established a promising partnership with Peter Thorne. He was hampered by some niggling injuries but remained a first-choice at the Britannia Stadium when fit.
Burnley (Signed from Newtown on 1/5/1995) FL 134+37/52 FLC 8+2/6 FAC 7+3/2 Others 9+2/2
Stoke C (£350,000 on 1/12/2000) FL 21+1/6 Others 3+2/1

COOKE Stephen Lee
Born: Walsall, 15 February 1983
Height: 5'8" Weight: 9.8
International Honours: E: Yth
Having developed through the ranks at Aston Villa Stephen stepped up to make his bow in senior football when he came off the subs' bench to replace Julian Joachim for the final 15 minutes of the Inter Toto semi-final second leg against Celta Vigo. A talented midfield player he spent the remainder of the campaign developing in the club's junior teams. He was a regular for England U17s, winning six caps during the season.
Aston Villa (From trainee on 22/2/2000) Others 0+1

COOKE Terence (Terry) John
Born: Birmingham, 5 August 1976
Height: 5'7" Weight: 11.4
Club Honours: FAYC '95
International Honours: E: U21-4; Yth
Manchester City's skilful right winger was unable to break into the first team at Maine Road last season and spent two months on loan at Sheffield Wednesday in the autumn. He impressed with his fast and direct wing play and manager Paul Jewell tried to sign him on a permanent basis but the two clubs failed to agree on a fee. Terry went back to Hillsborough in mid-December for a second loan spell but failed to make a significant impact and returned to City after the four weeks were over.
Manchester U (From trainee on 1/7/1994) PL 1+3 FLC 1+2/1 Others 0+1
Sunderland (Loaned on 29/1/1996) FL 6
Birmingham C (Loaned on 29/11/1996) FL 1+3
Wrexham (Loaned on 30/10/1998) FL 10 Others 1
Manchester C (£1,000,000 on 13/1/1999) FL 27+7/7 FLC 3+1/1 Others 3
Wigan Ath (Loaned on 7/3/2000) FL 10/1
Sheffield Wed (Loaned on 21/9/2000) FL 12+1/1
Sheffield Wed (Loaned on 15/12/2000) FL 4

Terry Cooke

COOPER Colin Terence
Born: Sedgefield, 28 February 1967
Height: 5'10" Weight: 11.9
Club Honours: Div 1 '98
International Honours: E: 2; U21-8
A professional with the highest standards, able to combine football skills with great determination, Colin possessed the ideal qualities to help in Middlesbrough's ultimately successful struggle against relegation last season. A versatile defender with immaculate ball distribution his tackling is solidly reliable and he added to his many 'Man of the Match' awards winning much acclaim from the Boro' supporters. He also showed again that he is still able to tuck away a couple of goals each season in spite of a certain reluctance to go forward too often.
Middlesbrough (From juniors on 17/7/1984) FL 183+5/6 FLC 18 FAC 13 Others 19+1/2
Millwall (£300,000 on 25/7/1991) FL 77/6 FLC 6 FAC 2 Others 2
Nottingham F (£1,700,000 on 21/6/1993) F/PL 179+1/20 FLC 14/2 FAC 12/1 Others 7
Middlesbrough (£2,500,000 on 22/8/1998) PL 83+2/3 FLC 7 FAC 3

COOPER Kevin Lee
Born: Derby, 8 February 1975
Height: 5'7" Weight: 10.7
In a season that saw Stockport County sell four key players it was perhaps Kevin's departure to First Division rivals Wimbledon that hit the Edgeley Park faithful hardest. Five goals and many more assists from 34 appearances represented a decent return from the midfield man who was equally as happy rolling up his sleeves

and defending at the other end of the field. County's loss was definitely the Dons' gain when Kevin moved on for a substantial fee shortly before the transfer deadline. He became an instant hit with the club's fans and scored in consecutive home matches towards the end of the season against Nottingham Forest and Crewe. A hard-working tricky winger who can operate down both flanks he also occasionally featured in a more central role.

Derby Co (From trainee on 2/7/1993) FL 0+2 FLC 0+2 Others 0+1
Stockport Co (£150,000 on 24/3/1997) FL 146+22/21 FLC 7+5/2 FAC 6 Others 1
Wimbledon (£800,000 + on 15/3/2001) FL 11/3

COOPER Richard Anthony
Born: Nottingham, 27 September 1977
Height: 5'9" Weight: 10.12
International Honours: E: Yth; Sch

Richard broke into the first-team squad at Nottingham Forest towards the end of the year and made appearances from the subs' bench against Sheffield United and Burnley before dropping back to the reserves. In March he joined Third Division York City on loan where he produced some fine performances and became a firm favourite with the club's supporters. A tough-tackling defender or midfield player he featured in a wide-right role for the Minstermen and was reported to have signed permanently for them in the summer.

Nottingham F (From trainee on 2/10/1996) FL 0+3
York C (Loaned on 2/3/2001) FL 14

COOTE Adrian
Born: Great Yarmouth, 30 September 1978
Height: 6'2" Weight: 12.0
International Honours: NI: 6; B-1; U21-14

This locally-born centre forward enjoyed a fantastic season of reserve-team football for Norwich City in 2000-01 averaging a goal per game, but he was unfortunately unable to match that success when called upon at senior level. A brave, whole-hearted performer with a useful left foot he is very strong in the air. Adrian earned a call-up to the full Northern Ireland squad for their World Cup qualifiers against the Czech Republic and Bulgaria in March, only to miss out through injury. A couple of goals at senior level would probably set him off on an excellent league career as he certainly knows where the goal is.

Norwich C (From trainee on 3/7/1997) FL 20+34/3 FLC 1+5 FAC 0+1

COPPINGER James
Born: Middlesbrough, 10 January 1981
Height: 5'7" Weight: 10.6
International Honours: E: Yth

James is a young striker brought to Newcastle as a player of potential, who has been learning his trade in the club's junior and reserve sides. Although small of stature he is lively, nimble and very alert in and around the penalty area. A loan spell at Hartlepool in the 1999-2000 campaign clearly helped him mature and he stepped up to make his senior debut for Newcastle when he came off the subs' bench for the final 15 minutes of the home game with Tottenham last August. Having signed a new three-year contract with the Magpies during the season he will be aiming to feature more regularly in the senior squad in 2001-02.

Newcastle U (£250,000 + from trainee at Darlington on 27/3/1998) PL 0+1
Hartlepool U (Loaned on 10/3/2000) FL 6+4/3 Others 1

CORAZZIN Giancarlo (Carlo) Michele
Born: Canada, 25 December 1971
Height: 5'10" Weight: 12.7
International Honours: Canada: 53 (Gold Cup 2000)

After joining Oldham Athletic during the 2000 summer break this experienced striker had a solid but unspectacular season in 2000-01. He struggled to score goals and although he managed to hit a respectable double-figure tally, four of these came in the 5-1 thrashing of Wrexham in February. A combination of several factors including niggling injuries and a loss of confidence were to blame and Carlo will be determined to set the record straight next term. He continued to be a regular for Canada, winning a further eight caps during the season and featuring in the prestigious end-of-season Confederations Cup tournament.

Cambridge U (£20,000 from Vancouver 86ers, Canada on 10/12/1993) FL 104+1/39 FLC 4/2 FAC 5 Others 3/2
Plymouth Arg (£150,000 on 28/3/1996) FL 61+13/22 FLC 1+1 FAC 0+2/1 Others 2+1
Northampton T (Free on 2/7/1998) FL 63+15/30 FLC 5+2/1 FAC 3 Others 1/1
Oldham Ath (Free on 31/7/2000) FL 37+1/7 FLC 3/1 FAC 3/1

CORBETT Andrew (Andy) John
Born: Worcester, 20 February 1982
Height: 6'0" Weight: 11.4

This local-born player progressed through the Kidderminster youth and reserve teams before being handed his first professional contract in the summer of 2000. He made his Football League debut when coming off the subs' bench in the home game against Leyton Orient in September but generally found his first-team opportunities limited and in March he went out on loan to Redditch United. However Andy clearly did enough to impress the management at Aggborough and was given a two-year extension to his contract at the end of the campaign. A traditional-style centre forward, he will be hoping to feature more regularly in the coming season.

Kidderminster Hrs (From juniors on 4/7/2000) FL 3+3

CORBO Mateo Andres
Born: Montevideo, Uruguay, 21 April 1976
Height: 5'11" Weight: 12.7

Having recovered from a serious knee injury suffered in the 1999-200 season, Mateo joined Barnsley last September and had a baptism of fire on his debut against Fulham. He recovered from that mauling to become a favourite of the fans at Oakwell and his defence-splitting pass that allowed Bruce Dyer to net the only goal against Sheffield Wednesday will be long remembered. An experienced left back who also featured on the left side of midfield he showed some neat touches with his passing but fell out of favour following a change in management and spent most of the second half of the campaign in the reserves.

Barnsley (£250,000 from Real Oviedo, Spain, ex Racing Club, on 29/8/2000) FL 10+7 FLC 2/1 FAC 0+1

CORDEN Simon **Wayne**
Born: Leek, 1 November 1975
Height: 5'9" Weight: 11.3

This skilful midfield player joined Mansfield in the summer of 2000 having been acquainted with Stags' manager Billy Dearden from their time together at Port Vale. Apart from occasional losses of form he appeared regularly for the Field Mill club last season, contributing some spectacular goals, notably in the Worthington Cup tie at Wrexham and the home game with Exeter in February. On the latter occasion he cut in from the touchline, beat three defenders and scored with a great shot from 20 yards out. Wayne is a speedy left winger who crosses the ball well and was a great asset to the Stags in 2000-01.

Port Vale (From trainee on 20/9/1994) FL 30+36/1 FLC 4 FAC 2+1/1
Mansfield T (Free on 3/7/2000) FL 31+3/3 FLC 4/2 FAC 1 Others 1

CORDONE Carlos **Daniel**
Born: Buenos Aires, Argentine, 6 January 1974
Height: 5'9" Weight: 11.10

A regular scorer in his homeland of Argentina, Daniel was out of contract in the summer of 2000 and joined Newcastle on a one-year deal. He is a strong-running striker with a good turn of pace, able to play anywhere across the attack or in a more supporting role just behind the front line. Signed primarily as cover for the main strike force of Alan Shearer and Carl Cort he was given an early opportunity in the side and scored in each of the first two home games last term, but he was unable to maintain this scoring rate and he lost his place in November after which he mainly appeared as a substitute.

Newcastle U (Loaned from Racing Club, Argentine, ex Velez Sarsfield, on 16/8/2000) PL 12+9/2 FLC 1+3/1 FAC 0+2

CORNFORTH John Michael
Born: Whitley Bay, 7 October 1967
Height: 6'1" Weight: 13.12
Club Honours: Div 3 '88; AMC '94
International Honours: W: 2

John is arguably one of the best play makers on the books of Exeter City but his appearances were severely restricted last season by a persistent calf injury. His experience and excellent distribution were invaluable for the Grecians when he was able to play, although he failed to find the net during the campaign. He was appointed player-coach at St James Park in October.

Sunderland (From apprentice on 11/10/1985) FL 21+11/2 FLC 0+1 Others 1+3
Doncaster Rov (Loaned on 6/11/1986) FL 6+1/3 Others 2

Shrewsbury T (Loaned on 23/11/1989) FL 3 Others 2
Lincoln C (Loaned on 11/1/1990) FL 9/1
Swansea C (£50,000 on 2/8/1991) FL 147+2/16 FLC 14 FAC 11/1 Others 19/1
Birmingham C (£350,000 on 26/3/1996) FL 8
Wycombe W (£50,000 on 5/12/1996) FL 35+12/6 FLC 6 FAC 2/2 Others 0+2
Peterborough U (Loaned on 13/2/1998) FL 3+1
Cardiff C (Free on 6/8/1999) FL 6+4/1 FLC 1+2
Scunthorpe U (Free on 4/11/1999) FL 2+2/1 Others 1
Exeter C (Free on 18/2/2000) FL 23+1/2

CORNWALL Lucas (Luke) Clarence
Born: Lambeth, 23 July 1980
Height: 5'11" Weight: 11.6
Luke made his senior debut for Fulham in the Worthington Cup ties at the beginning of last season before returning to the club's reserve team for whom he finished the campaign as leading scorer. With too many experienced strikers ahead of him to have any realistic chance of a First Division appearance at Craven Cottage he joined Grimsby Town on loan as Mariners' boss Lennie Lawrence sought to add some firepower up front. After taking a short time to settle in he began to fulfil his obvious potential, scoring two goals in the 3-1 win over fellow strugglers Tranmere and a vital winner against West Bromwich Albion at The Hawthorns. A pacy striker with considerable goal-scoring potential, he will be hoping to gain more first-team experience in 2001-02.
Fulham (From trainee on 6/7/1998) FL 1+3/1 FLC 2+1
Grimsby T (Loaned on 13/3/2001) FL 9+1/4

CORT Carl Edward Richard
Born: Southwark, 1 November 1977
Height: 6'4" Weight: 12.7
International Honours: E: U21-12
Carl joined Newcastle in the close season and quickly endeared himself to the club's fans by scoring four minutes into his home debut, unfortunately he also injured a hamstring in the same match and corrective surgery was required. Returning to the team again he suffered further hamstring problems unconnected with the first injury and was sidelined for six months. He eventually re-emerged in the home game against Middlesbrough in March, when he was again on target with a terrific drive from the edge of the penalty area, and he went on to finish as the club's joint-top scorer, albeit with just six goals. Tall and strong with a good turn of speed, he is an awkward opponent to deal with in the box, but he also works hard in all areas of the pitch for the sake of his team.
Wimbledon (From trainee on 7/6/1996) PL 54+19/16 FLC 8+2/7 FAC 6+4/2
Lincoln C (Loaned on 3/2/1997) FL 5+1/1
Newcastle U (£7,000,000 on 6/7/2000) PL 13/6 FLC 2/1

COTTEE Anthony (Tony) Richard
Born: West Ham, 11 July 1965
Height: 5'9" Weight: 12.6
Club Honours: FLC '00
International Honours: E: 7; U21-8; Yth
Although not the first player to appear in all four senior divisions in England in a single season, Tony is certainly the only one to do so since the formation of the Premiership. He began his journey at Leicester where he struggled to establish himself under new boss Peter Taylor and appeared just twice from the subs' bench, before enjoying a short spell at Norwich where he linked up well with Iwan Roberts. He netted two goals for the Canaries but was then drawn back to London by the offer of a position as player-manager of Barnet, who at the time were seen as candidates for promotion from the Third Division. His first game in charge produced a 7-0 demolition of Blackpool but although he scored regularly himself, including a hat-trick against Scunthorpe in December, the Bees hit a poor run of form, dropping towards the lower reaches of the table and he was replaced by former boss John Still in March. Tony moved on to Second Division promotion candidates Millwall to complete his trip around the divisions, providing some invaluable experience in the closing weeks of the campaign. However he made just two senior appearances from the subs' bench for the Lions before being released in the summer. Tony is still a quality striker who is full of tricks and able to deliver a rasping shot.
West Ham U (From apprentice on 1/9/1982) FL 203+9/92 FLC 19/14 FAC 24/11 Others 1/1
Everton (£2,300,000 on 2/8/1988) F/PL 161+23/72 FLC 19+4/11 FAC 15+6/4 Others 11+2/12
West Ham U (Signed on 7/9/1994) PL 63+4/23 FLC 8/4 FAC 5/1 (Signed by Selangor, Malaysia on 3/3/1997)
Leicester C (£500,000 on 14/8/1997) PL 66+19/27 FLC 9/5 FAC 3+2/2 Others 0+1
Birmingham C (Loaned on 14/11/1997) FL 4+1/1
Norwich C (Free on 11/9/2000) FL 5+2/1 FLC 1+1/1
Barnet (Free on 31/10/2000) FL 16/9 FAC 2/1
Millwall (Free on 22/3/2001) FL 0+2

COTTERILL James Michael
Born: Barnsley, 3 August 1982
Height: 6'0" Weight: 12.4
This young Scunthorpe United trainee broke into the first team in the midst of an injury crisis in March and had an excellent debut against high-fliers Brighton. Given a run of four matches he certainly didn't look out of his depth and was rather unlucky to be left out when more experienced players became available. A solidly built central defender who can also play at full back, James was reported to have been offered terms for next season.
Scunthorpe U (Trainee) FL 4

COUSINS Jason Michael
Born: Hayes, 14 October 1970
Height: 5'11" Weight: 12.4
Club Honours: GMVC '93; FAT '93
Jason began last season on the subs' bench at Wycombe until injuries allowed him to break into the starting line-up. Once in the team he produced some of the best football of his career turning in many impressive displays, especially when used in a five-man defence. A central defender with immaculate timing both in the air and when tackling, he always gives 100 per cent commitment for the cause.
Brentford (From trainee on 13/7/1989) FL 20+1 Others 2+2
Wycombe W (Free on 1/7/1991) FL 257+20/6 FLC 18+2/1 FAC 33+1 Others 18

COWAN Thomas (Tom)
Born: Bellshill, 28 August 1969
Height: 5'9" Weight: 11.10
Tom joined Cambridge United in the 2000 close season as a replacement for Clive Wilson and earned a regular place in the U's line-up last term. A tough-tackling left-sided defender he worked tirelessly in the back line all season. Strong in the air and with a powerful long throw he also found time to get forward to score a couple of valuable goals.
Clyde (Free from Netherdale BC on 11/7/1988) SL 16/2 SC 2
Glasgow R (Signed on 9/2/1989) SL 8+4 SC 0+1 Others 2
Sheffield U (£350,000 on 1/8/1991) F/PL 45 FLC 5 FAC 2 Others 1
Stoke C (Loaned on 1/10/1993) FL 14 FLC 1 Others 3
Huddersfield T (£150,000 on 24/3/1994) FL 137/8 FLC 13/1 FAC 9/1 Others 6
Burnley (£20,000 on 12/3/1999) FL 17+3 FLC 2 Others 0+1
Cambridge U (Loaned on 22/2/2000) FL 4
Cambridge U (Free on 20/7/2000) FL 41/2 FLC 1 FAC 1

COWE Steven (Steve) Mark
Born: Gloucester, 29 September 1974
Height: 5'7" Weight: 10.10
Steve started the 2000-01 season on the fringes of the Swindon Town first team but won a mid-season recall to the starting line-up in an unfamiliar midfield role. He netted twice in the FA Cup demolition of Gateshead but was then sidelined with an achilles injury early in the new year and he spent the remainder of the campaign out of action. A small nippy striker with some neat touches he was released in the summer.
Aston Villa (From trainee on 7/7/1993)
Swindon T (£100,000 on 22/3/1996) FL 59+38/11 FLC 3+3 FAC 2+3/2

COX Ian Gary
Born: Croydon, 25 March 1971
Height: 6'0" Weight: 12.2
International Honours: Trinidad & Tobago: 5
Burnley's success last season on their return to the First Division was based around a solid three-man defence and Ian was a key member of that trio along with Steve Davis and Mitchell Thomas. Good in the air and on the ground, fast, strong in the tackle and cool at all times Ian looked a class act and worth every penny of the fee that brought him to Turf Moor from Bournemouth. A member of Ian Porterfield's Trinidad & Tobago squad, he contributed to their campaign to reach the World Cup finals in 2002 winning four more caps.
Crystal Palace (£35,000 from Carshalton on 8/3/1994) F/PL 2+13 FAC 1+2/1
Bournemouth (Free on 28/3/1996) FL 172/16 FLC 14 FAC 10 Others 11/1
Burnley (£500,000 on 4/2/2000) FL 52+3/2 FLC 4 FAC 2

COX Neil James
Born: Scunthorpe, 8 October 1971
Height: 6'0" Weight: 13.7
Club Honours: FLC '94; Div 1 '95
International Honours: E: U21-6
Neil became increasingly influential at right back for Watford last term as he became accustomed to the club's style of play during his second season at Vicarage Road. Strong going forward and a dead-ball specialist, he had the distinction of scoring the Hornets' first goal of the season with an astute free kick at Huddersfield and netted several more times including a brace in the 3-1 win over Queens Park Rangers in October. Like the rest of the defence he wobbled a bit in mid-season, but came back strongly towards the end of the campaign. He was placed on the transfer list by new boss Gianluca Vialli in the summer.
Scunthorpe U (From trainee on 20/3/1990) FL 17/1 FAC 4 Others 4+1
Aston Villa (£400,000 on 12/2/1991) F/PL 26+16/3 FLC 5+2 FAC 4+2/1 Others 2
Middlesbrough (£1,000,000 on 19/7/1994) P/FL 103+3/3 FLC 14+1 FAC 5/1 Others 2
Bolton W (£1,200,000 on 27/5/1997) P/FL 77+3/7 FLC 9/1 FAC 1+1 Others 3
Watford (£500,000 on 5/11/1999) P/FL 63+2/5 FLC 5 FAC 2

Neil Cox

COYNE Daniel (Danny)
Born: Prestatyn, 27 August 1973
Height: 5'11" Weight: 13.0
International Honours: W: 1; B-1; U21-9; Yth; Sch
Danny was in great form in goal for First Division Grimsby Town throughout the 2000-01 campaign, earning the Mariners points on many occasions with some stunning saves. He gave an exceptional performance in the relegation battle at Queens Park Rangers when he defied the home strikers almost single-handedly to ensure a vital 1-0 victory. A fine shot stopper with excellent positioning and lightning reactions, he will be aiming for a recall to the Wales international squad in the coming season. He was deservedly voted as the supporters' 'Player of the Year'.
Tranmere Rov (From trainee on 8/5/1992) FL 110+1 FLC 13 FAC 2 Others 2
Grimsby T (Free on 12/7/1999) FL 90 FLC 5 FAC 3

CRADDOCK Jody Darryl
Born: Redditch, 25 July 1975
Height: 6'1" Weight: 12.4
Jody enjoyed an impressive season at Sunderland in 2000-01 when he finally established himself as a first-choice central defender at the Stadium Of Light. Powerful in the air, a crisp tackler, a dependable man-marker and as quick as any defender in the Premiership, Jody is an excellent prospect. A near ever-present last term he has seen off stiff competition to get this far and will be aiming to consolidate his position in the team in 2001-02.
Cambridge U (Free from Christchurch on 13/8/1993) FL 142+3/4 FLC 3/1 FAC 6 Others 5
Sunderland (£300,000 + on 4/8/1997) P/FL 85+6 FLC 7+2 FAC 3+1 Others 3
Sheffield U (Loaned on 27/8/1999) FL 10

CRAMB Colin
Born: Lanark, 23 June 1974
Height: 6'0" Weight: 12.6
Club Honours: B&Q '93
Unable to get a regular game at Crewe at the beginning of last season, Colin joined Notts County on loan in September and featured in a handful of games for the Magpies. On his return to Gresty Road he enjoyed a brief run in the first team, netting a double in the 2-0 win over Wolves, but then fell out of favour again in the new year and moved to Bury on loan in what proved an inspirational deal by Shakers' boss Andy Preece. Colin forged a fine partnership with youngster Jon Newby and became a highly popular figure with the Gigg Lane faithful. He scored five times in fifteen outings for the Second Division club and impressed with his superb touch, vision and skill. Colin is a strong-running striker with a preference for ground play rather than aerial combat.
Hamilton Ac (From juniors on 1/6/1993) SL 29+19/10 SC 0+1 Others 1+3
Southampton (£75,000 on 8/6/1993) PL 0+1
Falkirk (Signed on 30/8/1994) SL 6+2/1 SLC 0+1
Hearts (Signed on 1/3/1995) SL 3+3/1
Doncaster Rov (£25,000 on 15/12/1995) FL 60+2/25 FLC 2/1 FAC 1/1 Others 1/1
Bristol C (£250,000 on 10/7/1997) FL 38+15/9 FLC 3+1 FAC 1/1 Others 1+1
Walsall (Loaned on 27/2/1999) FL 4/4 Others 2
Crewe Alex (£200,000 on 6/8/1999) FL 43+7/10 FLC 5+1/1 FAC 2
Notts Co (Loaned on 11/9/2000) FL 2+1
Bury (Loaned on 16/2/2001) FL 15/5

CRANE Anthony (Tony) Steven
Born: Liverpool, 8 September 1982
Height: 6'1" Weight: 12.6
This young Sheffield Wednesday midfielder made his debut in senior football against Nottingham Forest last September and went on to feature regularly for the Owls in the first half of the 2000-01 campaign. Tall and skilful his strength in the air proved to be useful both in defence and attack. Tony scored with headers in consecutive games against Watford and Norwich last November and looks to have an excellent future in the game.
Sheffield Wed (From trainee on 15/9/1999) FL 7+8/2 FLC 3+2 FAC 0+2

CRESSWELL Richard Paul Wesley
Born: Bridlington, 20 September 1977
Height: 6'0" Weight: 11.8
International Honours: E: U21-4
Richard played for Sheffield Wednesday in the first four games of last season before moving back to the Premiership when he signed for Leicester City. Although he showed some lively form, he never quite grasped the opportunity of a place partnering Ade Akinbiyi up front for the Foxes. He netted with a bullet header in the FA Cup third round tie against his old club York City but having failed to establish himself in the first team at Filbert Street he moved out on loan to Preston in March. He found life easier in the First Division scoring on his debut just four minutes after coming on as a substitute against Wolves. Alternating between the starting line-up and the subs' bench, he also netted at Barnsley, and generally combined well with Jon Macken and David Healy. A lively and hard-working striker who is useful in the air, he will have to fight hard to win a regular first-team place at Leicester in 2001-02.
York C (From trainee on 15/11/1995) FL 72+23/21 FLC 3+3 FAC 4+2/3 Others 4
Mansfield T (Loaned on 27/3/1997) FL 5/1
Sheffield Wed (£950,000 + on 25/3/1999) PL 7+24/2 FLC 1+1/1 FAC 0+3
Leicester C (£750,000 on 5/9/2000) PL 3+5 FLC 1 FAC 0+2/1 Others 0+2
Preston NE (Loaned on 12/3/2001) FL 5+6/2 Others 1+2

CRICHTON Paul Andrew
Born: Pontefract, 3 October 1968
Height: 6'1" Weight: 12.2
Starting 2000-01 as Burnley's only goalkeeper with first-team experience, Paul performed solidly enough in the opening matches of the season but although selected for the visit to Huddersfield he was delayed in traffic on the way to the ground and the recently arrived Nik Michopolous stepped into the breach. Michopolous played a blinder and from that point on remained first choice. Paul became a fixture on the subs' bench and his only subsequent first-team action came at the Hawthorns against his former club West Bromwich when he performed capably well. He was reported to have signed for Norwich City in the summer.
Nottingham F (From juniors on 23/5/1986)
Notts Co (Loaned on 19/9/1986) FL 5
Darlington (Loaned on 30/1/1987) FL 5
Peterborough U (Loaned on 27/3/1987) FL 4
Darlington (Loaned on 28/9/1987) FL 3 FLC 1 Others 1
Swindon T (Loaned on 24/12/1987) FL 4
Rotherham U (Loaned on 9/3/1988) FL 6
Torquay U (Loaned on 25/8/1988) FL 13 FLC 2
Peterborough U (Signed on 3/11/1988) FL 47 FAC 5 Others 3
Doncaster Rov (Free on 25/8/1990) FL 77 FLC 5 FAC 3 Others 5
Grimsby T (Free on 9/7/1993) FL 133 FLC 7 FAC 8 Others 2
West Bromwich A (£250,000 on 9/9/1996) FL 32 FLC 1 FAC 1

Burnley (Loaned on 7/8/1998) FL 1
Burnley (£100,000 on 19/11/1998) FL 81+1 FLC 4 FAC 4 Others 2

CROFT Gary
Born: Burton on Trent, 17 February 1974
Height: 5'9" Weight: 11.8
International Honours: E: U21-4
Injuries and the competition for places in defence made the 2000-01 campaign another indifferent season for Gary at Ipswich Town. He was in the starting line-up for the season's opener at Tottenham but Fabian Wilnis then took over from him in the next game and Gary was unable to win his place back, apart from a couple of brief spells when Wilnis was injured. However he did enough in these games to show that when fully fit he can still do a useful job for the team. A talented defender he will be hoping for a return to first-team football in 2001-02.
Grimsby T (From trainee on 7/7/1992) FL 139+10/3 FLC 7 FAC 8+2/1 Others 3
Blackburn Rov (£1,700,000 on 29/3/1996) PL 33+7/1 FLC 6 FAC 4+2
Ipswich T (£800,000 on 21/9/1999) P/FL 20+9/1 FLC 3+1 FAC 1 Others 2+1

CROFTS Andrew Lawrence
Born: Chatham, 29 May 1984
Height: 5'9" Weight: 10.2
This Gillingham youngster did well enough with the reserve and U19 teams last term to earn a call-up to the first-team squad towards the end of the season. He made his senior debut when he came off the subs' bench for the final 15 minutes of the penultimate home game against Watford. A promising striker he became the third-youngest player to appear for the Gills in a Football League match.
Gillingham (Trainee) FL 0+1

CROOKS Lee Robert
Born: Wakefield, 14 January 1978
Height: 6'0" Weight: 12.1
International Honours: E: Yth
Lee was very much on the fringes of the Manchester City first-team squad last season and although he made the starting line-up for both legs of the Worthington Cup tie against Gillingham he made just two appearances from the subs' bench in Premiership matches. In December he joined Second Division Northampton Town on loan where he looked very useful in a defensive midfield role. Unfortunately he injured an ankle in his second game for the Sixfields club and was injured again on his return. He was subsequently sold to Barnsley in March but had a knee injury when he joined the club and this was aggravated as he tried to start to regain fitness. He subsequently underwent surgery in mid-April and is expected to be fit for the start of the 2001-02 season. A versatile defender who is best used either as a centre half or right back he makes effective forward runs and has a powerful long-range shot.
Manchester C (From trainee on 14/1/1995) P/FL 52+24/2 FLC 5+2 FAC 5 Others 3
Northampton T (Loaned on 26/12/2000) FL 3
Barnsley (£190,000 on 2/3/2001)

CROSBY Andrew (Andy) Keith
Born: Rotherham, 3 March 1973
Height: 6'2" Weight: 13.7
Club Honours: Div 3 '01
This ever-reliable central defender was controversially sent off in Brighton's first home game of the 2000-01 campaign and then had to bide his time before he could get back in the side, but injuries and suspensions for Cullip and Wicks led to a recall. Andy is a steady player who goes about his business in a quiet but effective manner, he is excellent in the air and comfortable when playing the ball on the ground.
Doncaster Rov (From trainee at Leeds U on 4/7/1991) FL 41+10 FLC 1+1 FAC 2 Others 4+1/1
Darlington (Free on 10/12/1993) FL 179+2/3 FLC 10 FAC 11/1 Others 9
Chester C (Free on 8/7/1998) FL 41/4 FLC 3 FAC 1 Others 1
Brighton & Hove A (£10,000 on 28/7/1999) FL 64+6/5 FLC 3 FAC 1+1 Others 4

CROSS Garry Robert
Born: Chelmsford, 7 October 1980
Height: 5'9" Weight: 12.0
Garry was always on the fringe of the Southend United squad last season but was unable to establish himself in the first team and in January he moved on to Ryman League outfit Slough Town. A stocky and tough-tackling right back he remains a promising youngster and there is still time for him to return to the professional game.
Southend U (From trainee on 2/7/1999) FL 11+5 FLC 1+1 Others 1

CROSSLEY Mark Geoffrey
Born: Barnsley, 16 June 1969
Height: 6'0" Weight: 16.0
International Honours: E: U21-3. W: 3; B-1
The powerfully built 'keeper is a proven shot stopper who covers his area fearlessly and with confidence, but he received few chances at Middlesbrough in 2000-01 due to the excellent form shown by Mark Scwarzer. Although firmly settled on Teesside he will not be satisfied with his position as a second choice in the line-up and will be hoping to change this state of affairs in the coming season.
Nottingham F (From trainee on 2/7/1987) F/PL 301+2 FLC 39+1 FAC 32 Others 18
Millwall (Loaned on 20/2/1998) FL 13
Middlesbrough (Free on 25/7/2000) PL 4+1 FLC 2

CROUCH Peter James
Born: Macclesfield, 30 January 1981
Height: 6'7" Weight: 11.12
International Honours: E: Yth
Peter joined Queens Park Rangers in July 2000 thus linking up again with Rangers' boss Gerry Francis who had coached him as a junior at Tottenham. He made his Football League debut on the opening day of the season against Birmingham City and very quickly became a regular first-team player. Despite featuring in a struggling team he made great progress during the campaign, finishing up as leading scorer and sweeping the board at the end-of-season 'Player of the Year' awards. He is a very tall striker who uses his height to good effect, yet also has good ball control and the ability to beat defenders on the ground. He was reported to have signed for Portsmouth in the summer.
Tottenham H (From trainee on 2/7/1998)
Queens Park R (£60,000 on 28/7/2000) FL 38+4/10 FLC 1+1 FAC 3/2

CROWE Dean Anthony
Born: Stockport, 6 June 1979
Height: 5'5" Weight: 11.3
Dean joined Bury on loan during July 2000, commencing his second loan spell at Gigg Lane within a period of a few months. He began well, netting a goal in the Shakers' pre-season games in the Isle of Man Festival, but when the campaign started in earnest he found himself mostly on the subs' bench. He made just one start and returned to Stoke at the beginning of October to continue his development in the club's reserve team. Dean is a quick and lively striker with a committed approach to the game. He was placed on the open to offers list in the summer.
Stoke C (From trainee on 5/9/1996) FL 29+31/12 FLC 2+3 Others 2/1
Northampton T (Loaned on 11/2/2000) FL 3+2
Bury (Loaned on 23/3/2000) FL 4/1
Bury (Loaned on 11/8/2000) FL 1+6/1

CROWE Jason William
Born: Sidcup, 30 September 1978
Height: 5'9" Weight: 10.9
International Honours: E: Yth
Left out of the Portsmouth team by manager Tony Pulis early last season, Jason was loaned out to Third Division Brentford for two months in the autumn. Fast and with good positional sense he looked well above Second Division standard and on his return to Fratton Park he was given an extended run in the Pompey first team. A talented young right wing back he has good man-to-man marking skills and is also effective as a sweeper. A dead-ball specialist he will be aiming for regular first-team football in 2001-02.
Arsenal (From trainee on 13/5/1996) FLC 0+2 FAC 0+1
Crystal Palace (Loaned on 10/11/1998) FL 8
Portsmouth (£750,000 + on 7/7/1999) FL 42+6 FLC 3 FAC 1+1
Brentford (Loaned on 12/9/2000) FL 9 FLC 2

CRYAN Colin
Born: Dublin, 23 March 1981
Height: 5'10" Weight: 13.4
Colin made his senior debut for Sheffield United when he came on as a late substitute in the Worthington Cup tie against Colchester United and went on to receive a couple more outings from the bench last term. A powerfully built midfielder who has come up through the ranks he works hard to support both attack and defence. He was a regular in the Blades' successful reserve team featuring in the Avon Insurance League Cup final victory over Stoke.
Sheffield U (From trainee on 6/8/1999) FL 0+1 FLC 0+2

CUDICINI Carlo
Born: Milan, Italy, 6 September 1973
Height: 6'1" Weight: 12.3
Club Honours: FAC '00; CS '00

Although he had made only three first-team appearances during his initial year-long loan period at Chelsea, the club were impressed sufficiently by Carlo's ability to exercise their option of a permanent transfer from Serie C club Castel di Sangro. He made an early appearance in the third Premiership match of the 2000-01 campaign at Villa Park when Ed de Goey sustained a hamstring injury in the pre-match warm-up, stepping in with a heroic performance to defy the home forwards and earn a valuable away point for Chelsea. This was the first of seven consecutive appearances and it turned out to be a baptism of fire for Carlo as the Blues began a dismal autumn with the departure of Luca Vialli and UEFA Cup elimination. De Goey returned for a short spell, but was surprisingly dropped for the New Year's Day return match against Villa and Carlo stepped in to great effect for the remainder of the season as the revitalised Blues put together a strong run which lifted them to sixth place in the Premiership and a UEFA Cup qualification. He is a good shot stopper and extremely agile for such a big man but having succeeded De Goey he now has an uncertain future himself following the arrival of Mark Bosnich.

Chelsea (£160,000 from Castel di Sangro, Italy, ex AC Milan, Prato, Lazio, on 6/8/1999) PL 24+1 FLC 1 FAC 3 Others 2+1

CULKIN Nicholas (Nick) James
Born: York, 6 July 1978
Height: 6'2" Weight: 13.7

Nick joined Bristol Rovers for a 12-month loan spell after impressing in a testimonial match for former Manchester United and Pirates' defender Lee Martin in the 1999-2000 campaign. Full of confidence and a brave shot stopper, he quickly won over the Rovers' supporters showing some fine positional sense and the ability to organise his defence. He was a near ever-present for the Second Division club, missing just one game in a 55-match season and returned to Old Trafford having benefited from the experience of regular first-team football.

Manchester U (£250,000 from trainee at York C on 27/9/1995) PL 0+1
Hull C (Loaned on 24/12/1999) FL 4
Bristol Rov (Loaned on 14/7/2000) FL 45 FLC 5 FAC 1 Others 3

CULLEN David **Jonathan (Jon)**
Born: Durham City, 10 January 1973
Height: 6'0" Weight: 12.0

Jon was a regular in the Peterborough United squad until last October when he lost his place following a change of formation by manager Barry Fry. He rarely featured in the following months and after undergoing a cartilage operation at the beginning of the year he joined Third Division Carlisle United shortly before the transfer deadline. He played regularly for the Cumbrians in the closing stages of the season and was unlucky not to get on the score sheet on his home debut against Torquay. An elegant and cultivated midfield player, he is comfortable either in a central role or a position on the left-hand side.

Doncaster Rov (From trainee on 16/9/1991) FL 8+1 FLC 2+1/1 FAC 0+1 Others 1 (Free to Spennymoor in September 1993)
Hartlepool U (Free from Morpeth on 27/3/1997) FL 33+1/12 FLC 2 FAC 1 Others 2
Sheffield U (£250,000 on 26/1/1998) FL 0+4
Shrewsbury T (Loaned on 10/9/1999) FL 10/1
Halifax T (Loaned on 17/12/1999) FL 11/5
Peterborough U (£35,000 on 3/3/2000) FL 24+7/4 FLC 0+1 FAC 1 Others 3/1
Carlisle U (Loaned on 16/3/2001) FL 10+1

CULLIP Daniel (Danny)
Born: Bracknell, 17 September 1976
Height: 6'1" Weight: 12.7
Club Honours: Div 3 '01

Danny missed the first few games of the 2000-01 campaign due to suspension but went on to become one of the key figures in Brighton's Third Division title-winning team. A no-nonsense centre half who commands the penalty area and is not afraid to put himself where it hurts he has tremendous heading ability and excellent distribution. He will be aiming to produce a similar level of performance in the coming season as the Seagulls face the challenge of higher-grade football. He was selected by his fellow professionals for the PFA Third Division team.

Oxford U (From trainee on 6/7/1995)
Fulham (Free on 5/7/1996) FL 41+9/2 FLC 8 FAC 2 Others 1
Brentford (£75,000 on 17/2/1998) FL 15 FLC 2
Brighton & Hove A (£50,000 on 17/9/1999) FL 70+1/4 FLC 2 FAC 6/1 Others 3/1

CUMMINGS Warren
Born: Aberdeen, 15 October 1980
Height: 5'9" Weight: 11.8
International Honours: S: U21-7

A product of the Chelsea youth system, Warren joined Second Division Bournemouth on loan last October and made his Football League debut in the 5-2 win at Bury. He made an excellent contribution in his three-month stay at Dean Court and helped the Cherries turn their season around to become challengers for a place in the play-offs. He returned to Stamford Bridge for a while before joining West Bromwich Albion on loan in March as Baggies' boss Gary Megson sought extra options on the left-hand side. A strong left back with good pace he appeared regularly for Scotland at U21 level winning three more caps during the season.

Chelsea (From trainee on 5/7/1999)
Bournemouth (Loaned on 20/10/2000) FL 10/1 Others 1
West Bromwich A (Loaned on 21/3/2001) FL 1+2

CUMMINS Michael Thomas
Born: Dublin, 1 June 1978
Height: 6'0" Weight: 11.11
Club Honours: AMC '01
International Honours: RoI: U21-2; Yth

Michael had a fine season at Port Vale in 2000-01 the high point of which was his appearance in the LDV Vans Trophy final victory over Brentford in April. Like many of his colleagues he seemed to struggle to find his form early on and it was only after Christmas that he began to perform at his best. He is a hard-tackling wing back who is comfortable on the ball and particularly adept at sneaking up on the blind side when coming up to help the attack, a skill that enabled him to score twice in Second Division matches during the campaign.

Middlesbrough (From trainee on 1/7/1995) PL 1+1
Port Vale (Free on 17/3/2000) FL 55+2/3 FLC 2 FAC 2 Others 7/1

CUNNINGHAM Craig John
Born: Knowsley, 9 September 1982
Height: 5'8" Weight: 10.4

A second-year trainee at Wigan Athletic, Craig stepped up to make his senior debut from the subs' bench in the LDV Vans Trophy defeat at Walsall. Quick, good in the air and possessing neat ball control, his appearances were restricted mainly to youth level. A right-sided midfield player he can play out wide or in a more central role. He was one of several youngsters not to be offered a professional contract by the Latics and was released in the summer.

Wigan Ath (Trainee) Others 0+1

CUNNINGHAM Kenneth (Kenny) Edward
Born: Dublin, 28 June 1971
Height: 6'0" Weight: 11.8
International Honours: RoI: 33; B-2; U21-4; Yth

The hugely popular Wimbledon defender was absent with a groin injury for much of the 2000-01 campaign and it was not until the end of January that he returned to action with the first team. A true captain, Kenny led by example and forged an effective partnership with Mark Williams in the centre of defence, winning much acclaim for his performances. With his right-back role reallocated the Dons' missed his over lapping runs and pinpoint crosses but were just glad to have him back. He also made a return to the Republic of Ireland international squad and added to his already impressive tally of caps.

Millwall (Signed from Tolka Rov on 18/9/1989) FL 132+4/1 FLC 10 FAC 1 Others 5+1/1
Wimbledon (Signed on 9/11/1994) P/FL 215+1 FLC 22+1 FAC 30+1

CURETON Jamie
Born: Bristol, 28 August 1975
Height: 5'8" Weight: 10.7
International Honours: E: Yth

Jamie netted from a penalty kick for Bristol Rovers in the opening game of the 2000-01 season against Bournemouth but was then sold to Reading for a substantial fee as the Royals acted quickly to replace the injured Nicky Forster. The move proved a great success as he went on to forge a very productive partnership up front with Martin Butler and finished the campaign as joint-top scorer in the Second Division with Millwall's Neil Harris. His tally included hat-tricks against Brentford and Luton Town, and a spell when he scored in six consecutive games, while he also netted the Royals' first goal in the play-off final against Walsall. Hard working, quick and elusive in the box his deadly finishing makes him almost the complete striker.

Norwich C (From trainee on 5/2/1993) P/FL 13+16/6 FLC 0+1 FAC 0+2

Bournemouth (Loaned on 8/9/1995) FL 0+5 Others 0+1
Bristol Rov (£250,000 on 20/9/1996) FL 165+9/72 FLC 7+1/2 FAC 10/2 Others 6/2
Reading (£250,000 on 21/8/2000) FL 37+6/26 FLC 2/1 FAC 2+1/1 Others 5/2

CURLE Keith
Born: Bristol, 14 November 1963
Height: 6'1" Weight: 12.12
Club Honours: AMC '86; FMC '88
International Honours: E: 3; B-4

Having joined Sheffield United as a player-coach in the close season it was not until late October that Keith won a regular place in the starting line-up when he replaced Lee Sandford in the centre of defence. Although his initial performances were not particularly convincing he returned later in the campaign and gave some fine displays. An experienced central defender he has great anticipation and the confidence to bring the ball forward out of defence.

Bristol Rov (From apprentice on 20/11/1981) FL 21+11/4 FLC 3 FAC 1
Torquay U (£5,000 on 4/11/1983) FL 16/5 FAC 1/1 Others 1
Bristol C (£10,000 on 3/3/1984) FL 113+8/1 FLC 7+1 FAC 5 Others 14+1
Reading (£150,000 on 23/10/1987) FL 40 FLC 8 Others 5
Wimbledon (£500,000 on 21/10/1988) FL 91+2/3 FLC 7 FAC 5 Others 6/1
Manchester C (£2,500,000 on 14/8/1991) F/PL 171/11 FLC 18/2 FAC 14 Others 1
Wolverhampton W (£650,000 on 2/8/1996) FL 148+2/9 FLC 7/1 FAC 11/1 Others 2
Sheffield U (Free on 10/7/2000) FL 23+2 FLC 2

Curle Keith

CURRAN Christopher (Chris)
Born: Birmingham, 17 September 1971
Height: 5'11" Weight: 12.4

Exeter City's club captain was a virtual ever-present last season until suffering a knee injury against Carlisle in February that sidelined him for several weeks. Chris is a hard-working and committed central defender whose ability to read the game was once again an asset for the Grecians. His long service in football was rewarded with a benefit match against Everton in August 2000.

Torquay U (From trainee on 13/7/1990) FL 144+8/4 FLC 15 FAC 8 Others 10/1
Plymouth Arg (£40,000 on 22/12/1995) FL 26+4 FLC 1+1 FAC 1 Others 4
Exeter C (£20,000 on 31/7/1997) FL 101+6/5 FLC 6 FAC 8 Others 6

CURRIE Darren Paul
Born: Hampstead, 29 November 1974
Height: 5'11" Weight: 12.7

Darren was once again a key figure for Barnet last season, finishing as the club's joint-top goalscorer and injecting a high level of skill to the Bees' midfield. Although not blessed with great pace, he has the ability to pass the best of defenders with his intricate foot work while he delivers crosses accurately and has a good eye for goal. A high point of the campaign was his hat-trick in the 7-0 thrashing of Blackpool last November when he scored with two cracking free-kicks and an exquisite individual effort. Despite Barnet's relegation from the Football League Darren was once again named in the PFA Third Division team of the year. He is the nephew of the former Sheffield United and QPR star Tony Currie.

West Ham U (From trainee on 2/7/1993)
Shrewsbury T (Loaned on 5/9/1994) FL 10+2/2
Shrewsbury T (Loaned on 3/2/1995) FL 5
Leyton Orient (Loaned on 16/11/1995) FL 9+1
Shrewsbury T (£70,000 on 7/2/1996) FL 46+20/8 FLC 2+1/1 FAC 3
Plymouth Arg (Free on 26/3/1998) FL 5+2
Barnet (Free on 13/7/1998) FL 120+7/19 FLC 5/1 FAC 3/2 Others 6

CURTIS John Charles
Born: Nuneaton, 3 September 1978
Height: 5'10" Weight: 11.9
Club Honours: FAYC '95
International Honours: E: B-1; U21-16; Yth; Sch

Having joined Blackburn during the close season, John settled in quickly at Ewood Park and went on to be an ever-present for Rovers in First Division games last term. Although happy to play right back he also settled easily into the role of right-sided player in a back three and showed an astonishing degree of consistency throughout the campaign. Dependable, quick in the tackle and constructive with his use of the ball he was a manager's dream, producing quality displays week-in, week-out. A talented youngster he will look forward to meeting the challenge of Premiership football in 2001-02.

Manchester U (From trainee on 3/10/1995) PL 4+9 FLC 5 Others 0+1
Barnsley (Loaned on 19/11/1999) FL 28/2 Others 1+1
Blackburn Rov (£2,250,000 on 1/6/2000) FL 46 FLC 4 FAC 5

CURTIS Thomas (Tom) David
Born: Exeter, 1 March 1973
Height: 5'8" Weight: 11.7

After signing for Portsmouth during the close season Tom appeared regularly in the opening matches of 2000-01 but then had the misfortune to suffer a broken ankle when he fell awkwardly during the Worthington Cup first round second leg tie against Cambridge United. The injury kept him out of action until the end of the campaign and he will be hoping to return to the Pompey first team in 2001-02. He is a busy midfield player who forces opponents into errors with his tenacity.

Derby Co (From juniors on 1/7/1991)
Chesterfield (Free on 12/8/1993) FL 235+5/12 FLC 20+1 FAC 14/1 Others 11+1
Portsmouth (£150,000 on 4/8/2000) FL 4 FLC 1+1

CUSACK Nicholas (Nicky) John
Born: Maltby, 24 December 1965
Height: 6'0" Weight: 12.8
Club Honours: Div 3 '00

Nicky began the 2000-01 season playing in the unaccustomed role of striker for Swansea alongside Steve Watkin before reverting to a more familiar midfield 'holding' role midway through the campaign. He was rarely absent from the squad apart from a period in April when he picked up a hamstring injury at Bristol Rovers and by the time he had returned to action the Swans had been relegated. A hard-working player who links well between attack and defence when playing in the centre of the park, he signed an extension to his contract that is likely to see him remain with the Swans for the rest of his playing career.

Leicester C (Signed from Alvechurch on 18/6/1987) FL 5+11/1 FAC 0+1 Others 1+1
Peterborough U (£40,000 on 29/7/1988) FL 44/10 FLC 4/1 FAC 4/1 Others 2
Motherwell (£100,000 on 2/8/1989) SL 68+9/17 SLC 5/4 SC 3+1/2 Others 1+1/1
Darlington (£95,000 on 24/1/1992) FL 21/6
Oxford U (£95,000 on 16/7/1992) FL 48+13/10 FLC 3/2 FAC 4+2/1 Others 2+1
Wycombe W (Loaned on 24/3/1994) FL 2+2/1
Fulham (Free on 4/11/1994) FL 109+7/14 FLC 6+4/1 FAC 7+1/1 Others 5+2/3
Swansea C (£50,000 on 30/10/1997) FL 147+11/10 FLC 5/1 FAC 9/1 Others 4+1

CUTLER Neil Anthony
Born: Birmingham, 3 September 1976
Height: 6'1" Weight: 12.0
International Honours: E: Yth; Sch

Third-choice 'keeper at Aston Villa behind David James and Peter Enckelman, Neil spent two months at Second Division Oxford United last autumn to gain some valuable experience of first-team football. He had the difficult task of replacing fans' favourite Richard Knight at a time when the team were enduring a poor patch of results but he stuck to his task well producing some good performances before returning to Villa Park. An excellent shot stopper Neil is entering a period in his career when he needs to experience regular first-team football to enable him to fulfil his full potential. He was released on a free transfer during the summer.

West Bromwich A (From trainee on 7/9/1993)
Chester C (Loaned on 27/3/1996) FL 1
Crewe Alex (Signed on 30/7/1996)
Chester C (Loaned on 30/8/1996) FL 5
Chester C (Free on 8/7/1998) FL 23 FLC 1 FAC 1 Others 1
Aston Villa (Signed on 30/11/1999) PL 0+1
Oxford U (Loaned on 15/12/2000) FL 11

DABIZAS Nikolaos (Nicos)
Born: Amyndaeo, Greece, 3 August 1973
Height: 6'1" Weight: 12.7
International Honours: Greece: 44; U21; Yth

Nicos had a frustrating time with injuries at Newcastle last term. He unfortunately damaged a cruciate knee ligament in only the second game of the season. After returning to Greece for surgery he underwent a long period of rehabilitation and it was not until April that he returned to match fitness. After a single reserve game he was back in the first team for the home game with West Ham and immediately added an assurance and solidity that had been missing from the Magpies' defence all season. An experienced centre back who is strong in the tackle and effective in the air, he ended the season in fine style and will be hoping for better fortune in 2001-02.

Newcastle U (£1,300,000 from Olympiakos, Greece on 13/3/1998) PL 73+6/7 FLC 3 FAC 14/2 Others 8/1

Nicos Dabizas

DACOURT Olivier
Born: Montreuil-sous-Bois, France, 25 September 1974
Height: 5'9" Weight: 11.12
International Honours: France: 3; U21

This classy midfield player cost Leeds United a then club record fee when he signed from Lens during the summer. After being sent off in his first competitive game against Munich 1860 in the Champions League preliminary round, he went on to become one of the finds of the season, producing numerous 'Man of the Match' displays. A tireless worker he sometimes seems to run without stopping throughout the whole 90 minutes while he closes opponents down consistently and makes valuable tackles and interceptions. Olivier is equally adept going forward, playing incisive passes and getting in long-range efforts, indeed his first United goal came from a long-range free kick in the victory over Arsenal in November. Probably more than any other player he benefited from the return of David Batty to the side and the pair soon established a formidable partnership in the centre of the park. His contributions at club level were recognised by the French selectors and he made his full international debut in the Confederations Cup match against South Korea during the close season.

Everton (£4,000,000 from Strasbourg, France, ex Thovars, on 7/8/1998) PL 28+2/2 FLC 4/1 FAC 2 (£6,500,000 to RC Lens, France on 29/6/99)
Leeds U (£7,200,000 on 18/7/2000) PL 33/3 FAC 1 Others 14

DADASON Rikhardur (Rikki)
Born: Reykjavik, Iceland, 26 April 1972
Height: 6'4" Weight: 12.0
International Honours: Iceland: 40; U21-10; Yth

Rikki joined Stoke City at the end of the Scandinavian 2000 season and made a dream start to his career at the Britannia Stadium when he came on as a substitute in the closing stages of the Worthington Cup tie against Barnsley and scored a dramatic winner to earn City a home tie with Liverpool in the next round. He subsequently took some time to adjust to his new surroundings and often featured from the subs' bench although he still managed to score eight goals in all competitions. He is a tall striker with a powerful left-foot shot. An experienced international he featured regularly for Iceland during the campaign and scored a number of goals, including strikes in successive games against Malta and Bulgaria in the summer.

Stoke C (Free from Viking, Norway, ex Fram Reykjavik, Kalamata, KR Reykjavik, on 31/10/2000) FL 13+15/6 FLC 0+1/1 FAC 0+1 Others 3+2/1

DAGNOGO Moussa Moustapha
Born: Paris, France, 30 January 1972
Height: 6'0" Weight: 12.11

Having been released by Portuguese outfit Uniao Madeira at the end of the 1999-2000 campaign, this experienced striker returned home and took advantage of the French players' union's pre-season training facilities, scoring regularly for their select team in the friendly matches arranged. He subsequently crossed the Channel and after trials with Aberdeen he joined Bristol Rovers on a three-month contract towards the end of September. Moussa made his debut for the Pirates as a substitute in the 3-3 draw with Luton when he had a powerful header cleared off the line but although he scored regularly for the reserves he made just one further appearance from the subs' bench before moving on. He then re-emerged at St Mirren in the new year, scoring the winner against Dundee on his debut, but although he featured in a handful of games for the Buddies he failed to win a long-term contract and departed before the end of the season.

Bristol Rov (Free from Unaio de Madeira, Portugal, ex Pau, Les Lilas, Moissy-Cramayel, Angouleme, Racing Paris, on 29/9/2000) FL 0+2

DAILLY Christian Eduard
Born: Dundee, 23 October 1973
Height: 6'0" Weight: 12.10
Club Honours: SC '94
International Honours: S: 27; B-1; U21-34; Yth; Sch

Early-season attempts to pair Christian with Craig Short in the centre of defence for Blackburn were not without merit but his style did not seem to fit in with manager Graham Souness's requirements. Although he won a recall for Scotland against Australia in November he failed to make any real impact at Ewood Park and it was no real surprise when he moved on to West Ham early in the new year. He went straight into the Hammers' side at Charlton and then played brilliantly in the cup victories at Manchester United and Sunderland. However the FA Cup was not always a happy hunting ground for him as he suffered a broken foot in the quarter-final tie against Tottenham and the injury kept him on the sidelines for a month. Strong in the air and a decisive tackler he is a versatile player although he has mostly featured as a central defender in recent seasons.

Dundee U (From juniors on 2/8/1990) SL 110+33/18 SLC 9/1 SC 10+2 Others 8+1/1
Derby Co (£1,000,000 on 12/8/1996) PL 62+5/4 FLC 6 FAC 4+1
Blackburn Rov (£5,300,000 on 22/8/1998) P/FL 60+10/4 FLC 5+1 FAC 4 Others 2
West Ham U (£1,750,000 on 18/1/2001) PL 11+1 FAC 3

DALGLISH Paul
Born: Glasgow, 18 February 1977
Height: 5'10" Weight: 10.0
International Honours: S: U21-7

Paul struggled to make an impact at Norwich last season and although he made a number of appearances as a substitute his only start came in the Worthington Cup tie at Derby. He was allowed to join Wigan Athletic on loan in March but after a handful of games he had the misfortune to receive two red cards in successive games and was subsequently ruled out through suspension. A direct, mobile striker with pace to burn, he is at his best when played wide down the right where his strong running causes defenders real problems. Paul is the son of former Liverpool star Kenny Dalglish.

Glasgow Celtic (From juniors on 20/7/1995)
Liverpool (Free on 14/8/1996)
Newcastle U (Free on 21/11/1997) PL 6+5/1 FLC 2/1
Bury (Loaned on 21/11/1997) FL 1+11 FAC 1
Norwich C (£300,000 on 25/3/1999) FL 25+18/2 FLC 3+1 FAC 1
Wigan Ath (Loaned on 22/3/2001) FL 5+1

DALLA BONA Samuelle (Sam)
Born: Venice, Italy, 6 February 1981
Height: 6'1" Weight: 12.0
International Honours: Italy: Yth

Chelsea boss Luca Vialli gave Sam his first start in the UEFA Cup first round home leg

against St Gallen last September - a match that proved to be his last in charge of the Blues before Claudio Ranieri took over the reins. Subsequently given his chance when Roberto Di Matteo broke his leg, he responded superbly. He opened his goal-scoring account with a rasping 20-yarder at Everton and followed this with a glorious solo effort against Bradford City after a mazy dribble. A rangy, long-striding midfield player who can deliver inch-perfect long-distance passes, Sam is a confirmed devotee of the English Premiership and admits that its pace, aggression and physical contact have been crucial elements in developing his game. Conversely, his meteoric ascent can only be good news for the Italian national side for whom he seems bound to figure at some point in the future.
Chelsea (Signed from Atalanta, Italy on 16/10/1998) PL 26+5/2 FAC 1 Others 1+2

Sam Dalla Bona

DALY Jonathan (Jon) Marvin
Born: Dublin, Ireland, 8 January 1983
Height: 6'1" Weight: 12.4
International Honours: RoI: Yth
Jon added just one senior appearance for Stockport County last season, making the starting line-up for the Worthington Cup first round second leg tie against Blackpool. A couple of minor knee operations subsequently hindered his progress but he remains a promising young striker and there is plenty time ahead of him to break into the County first team.
Stockport Co (From trainee on 18/1/2000) FL 0+4 FLC 1

DANIELSSON Helgi Valur
Born: Rejkjavic, Iceland, 13 July 1981
Height: 6'0" Weight: 12.0
International Honours: Iceland: 1; U21;Yth
One of the many talented youngsters on Peterborough's books Helgi spent the summer months on loan in Iceland before returning to London Road where he made his Football League debut when coming on as a late substitute at Bristol City in October. He subsequently featured in several games towards the end of the campaign and will be looking to gain further senior experience in 2001-02. A very talented midfield prospect he has excellent distribution and always seems to have time on the ball. Helgi made his bow at U21 level for Iceland in the friendly with Sweden last August and was a regular in the line-up all season, also making the experimental national squad for the Millenium Cup tournament in January when he made his full international debut from the subs' bench against India.
Peterborough U (Free from Fylkir, Iceland on 16/10/1998) FL 3+3

DANILEVICIUS Tomas
Born: Lithuania, 18 July 1978
Height: 6'3" Weight: 12.7
International Honours: Lithuania: 8
Tomas impressed while on trial with Arsenal back in the summer, scoring in a friendly against Barcelona in Amsterdam before manager Arsene Wenger returned to sign him last December. A tall striker who can be used as a target man or to hold up play he made his debut from the subs' bench against Sunderland at the end of December and added a couple more appearances as a substitute before joining Dunfermline Athletic on loan. Capped by Lithuania at every level he will be hoping to see more regular first-team action at Highbury in the coming season.
Arsenal (Signed from FC Lausanne, Switzerland, ex FK Baltai, FK Atlantas, Beveren, Brugge, on 21/12/2000) PL 0+2 FAC 0+1
Dunfermline Ath (Loaned on 16/3/2001) SL 3

DARBY Julian Timothy
Born: Bolton, 3 October 1967
Height: 6'0" Weight: 11.4
Club Honours: AMC '89
International Honours: E: Sch
Julian joined Carlisle United as a player-coach under boss Ian Atkins shortly before the start of the 2000-01 campaign and featured regularly in the first half of the season either in defence or in a midfield role. A vastly experienced player he concentrated on his coaching duties after Christmas as the Cumbrian side successfully fought to avoid dropping down to the Conference. He scored just one goal during the campaign, when he joined the attack in the closing stages of the home game with Scunthorpe in October. He was out of contract in the summer.
Bolton W (From trainee on 22/7/1986) FL 258+12/36 FLC 25/8 FAC 19/3 Others 31+1/5
Coventry C (£150,000 on 28/10/1993) PL 52+3/5 FLC 3/1 FAC 2+2
West Bromwich A (£200,000 on 24/11/1995) FL 32+7/1 FAC 1 Others 4
Preston NE (£150,000 on 13/6/1997) FL 20+15/1 FLC 1+1 FAC 4+2/1 Others 4+2/1
Rotherham U (Loaned on 26/3/1998) FL 3
Carlisle U (Free on 10/8/2000) FL 15+3/1 FLC 2 FAC 1 Others 1

D'ARCY Ross
Born: Balbriggan, 21 March 1978
Height: 6'0" Weight: 12.2
International Honours: RoI: U21-6
Ross did well in the 2000-01 pre-season games for Barnet, but faced with considerable competition for a place in the centre of the Bees' defence he made just a handful of appearances from the subs' bench in the early part of the campaign. He subsequently had a spell on loan at Conference outfit Dover but spent most of the remainder of the season languishing in the reserve team. He is a solid centre back who is strong in the tackle and has good distribution.
Tottenham H (From trainee on 1/7/1995)
Barnet (Free on 22/12/1999) FL 1+5 Others 0+1

DARLINGTON Jermaine Christopher
Born: Hackney, 11 April 1974
Height: 5'7" Weight: 10.10
Jermaine continued to show excellent form for Queens Park rangers last season despite playing in a struggling team. He was mostly used as the right wing back in a 5-3-2 formation, but was equally successful when switched to a left-wing role in a 4-4-2 line-up. He suffered a slight dip in form towards the end of the first half of the season, but reclaimed his place around Christmas and held on to it until the end of the campaign.
Charlton Ath (From trainee on 30/6/1992) FL 1+1 (Free to Dover Ath on 23/9/1993)
Queens Park R (£25,000 from Aylesbury U on 25/3/1999) FL 70+1/2 FLC 2 FAC 6

DARLOW Kieran Brian
Born: Bedford, 9 November 1982
Height: 6'0" Weight: 13.12
Kieran continued to make good progress in the York City reserves and juniors last season and made just one senior appearance, coming on from the subs' bench for the final 30 minutes of the home defeat at the hands of Exeter City in February. He is a promising young left winger with good pace who will be hoping to feature more regularly in the first team in the 2001-02 campaign.
York C (Trainee) FL 0+3

D'AURIA David Alan
Born: Swansea, 26 March 1970
Height: 5'10" Weight: 12.6
Club Honours: WC '94
International Honours: W: Yth
David suffered another injury-wrecked season at Chesterfield in 2000-01. Having recovered from long-term back problems he started four straight league games in December constituting his best run for the Spireites since joining the club in November 1999. He then made the odd senior appearance before a foot injury brought his season to an early conclusion. When fully fit he is a talented and hard-working central midfield player.
Swansea C (From trainee on 2/8/1988) FL 27+18/6 FLC 2+2 FAC 1 Others 4 (Free transfer to Merthyr Tydfil during 1991 close season)
Scarborough (Signed from Barry T on 22/8/1994) FL 49+3/8 FLC 3+2/1 FAC 4+1 Others 2
Scunthorpe U (£40,000 on 6/12/1995) FL 103+4/18 FLC 6 FAC 7/1 Others 4+1
Hull C (Free on 16/7/1998) FL 52+2/4 FLC 5+2 FAC 5 Others 2/1
Chesterfield (£50,000 on 25/11/1999) FL 8+3 FAC 0+1 Others 1

DAVENPORT Calum Raymond Paul
Born: Bedford, 1 January 1983
Height: 6'4" Weight: 14.4
International Honours: E: Yth

A product of Coventry's youth scheme, Calum played for the Sky Blues in two consecutive FA Youth Cup finals and was a regular member of the reserve team that finished runners-up in the Premier Reserve League last term. He stepped up to make his senior debut in the final game of the season against Bradford City when he came on as a half-time substitute. Strong in the air and comfortable on the ball the young central defender won praise for his cool and assured performance and looks to have a bright future in the game.

Coventry C (From trainee on 6/1/2000) PL 0+1

DAVIDSON Callum Iain
Born: Stirling, 25 June 1976
Height: 5'10" Weight: 11.8
Club Honours: S Div 1 '97
International Honours: S: 14; U21-2

Signed by Leicester City in the close season, Callum replaced Steve Guppy at left wing back last term. His presence provided the Foxes' defence with a more solid look but he was injured in the opening game against Aston Villa and then just as he was beginning to recapture his best form in mid-season he was affected by back problems. Nevertheless he eventually opened his Leicester goal account in the return game at Villa Park in April. His intermittent injury problems, which also affected his ankle, kept him out of contention for more international honours for much of the campaign although he did win further caps against Latvia and Poland.

St Johnstone (From juniors on 8/6/1994) SL 39+5/4 SLC 1 Others 3
Blackburn Rov (£1,750,000 on 12/2/1998) P/FL 63+2/1 FLC 3+1 FAC 6 Others 1+1
Leicester C (£1,700,000 on 12/7/2000) PL 25+3/1 FLC 1 FAC 2 Others 0+1

DAVIDSON Ross James
Born: Chertsey, 13 November 1973
Height: 5'9" Weight: 12.4

Despite missing part of last season through injury Ross appeared regularly for Shrewsbury last season. A solid dependable right back he likes to push forward down the flank and has an excellent delivery into the box. He was also the preferred choice for taking free kicks and corners. He was released by the Third Division club at the end of the season.

Sheffield U (Signed from Walton & Hersham on 5/6/1993) FL 2 Others 2
Chester C (Free on 26/1/1996) FL 132/5 FLC 11 FAC 3+1 Others 4
Barnet (Free on 5/11/1999) FL 8+1 Others 1
Shrewsbury T (Free on 9/3/2000) FL 40+3 FLC 2/1 FAC 1 Others 1

DAVIES Alexander (Alex) John
Born: Swansea, 2 November 1982
Height: 6'1" Weight: 13.0

Still in his second year as a trainee at Swansea, Alex was called up to the first-team squad to sit on the subs' bench at Bury when regular 'keeper Roger Freestone was suspended and received a surprise call to action when Jason Jones received a red card. His first task was to face a penalty kick and although he saved the first effort a retake was ordered and the ball duly dispatched into the net. Nevertheless he made a good impression during the remainder of the match and pulled off some fine saves. He subsequently continued his development in the Swans' U19s but will be aiming for more senior experience next term.

Swansea C (Trainee) FL 0+1

DAVIES Benjamin (Ben) James
Born: Birmingham, 27 May 1981
Height: 5'6" Weight: 10.7

Ben found his opportunities at Kidderminster limited last season and after making his senior debut in the LDV Vans Trophy tie against Carlisle he only featured a couple more times. A hard-working midfield player with excellent passing ability he was rewarded with a contract extension at the end of the campaign. He will be hoping to become more involved in the first team in 2001-02 when the Harriers are expected to put a greater emphasis on youth.

Walsall (From trainee at Stoke C on 11/8/1999)
Kidderminster Hrs (Free on 1/3/2000) FL 2+1 Others 1

Davies Kevin

DAVIES Kevin Cyril
Born: Sheffield, 26 March 1977
Height: 6'0" Weight: 13.6
International Honours: E: U21-3; Yth

Injuries limited Kevin's involvement at Southampton last season but he still managed to feature in over half the Premiership games, scoring just a single goal against Tottenham over the Christmas period. A cracked toe suffered at the end of August kept him out of action for a while and later in the season he was sidelined with an ankle problem. Having previously operated as a target man, new boss Glenn Hoddle used him in a deeper right-sided midfield role where his speed was put to good effect. A talented player who is strong in the air he will be hoping to avoid the treatment room next term.

Chesterfield (From trainee on 18/4/1994) FL 113+16/22 FLC 7+2/1 FAC 10/6 Others 9+2/1
Southampton (£750,000 on 14/5/1997) PL 20+5/9 FLC 3+1/3 FAC 1
Blackburn Rov (£7,250,000 on 2/6/1998) P/FL 11+12/1 FLC 3 FAC 2/1 Others 1
Southampton (Signed on 18/8/1999) PL 40+10/7 FLC 1+1 FAC 3/1

DAVIES Simon
Born: Haverfordwest, 23 October 1979
Height: 5'10" Weight: 11.4
International Honours: W: 2; B-1; U21-10; Yth

Simon broke into the Tottenham first-team squad in the second half of last season and impressed with two smashing goals in the 4-0 win over Stockport County in the FA Cup fifth round. He went on to score in the 2-1 win over Bradford City in April and with a stunning right-foot shot in the defeat at Leicester the following month. Brimming with confidence and favouring a role as an out-and-out striker role he is now close to winning a regular place in the team. He continued to represent Wales winning four more U21 caps before stepping up to win his first full cap as a substitute in the World Cup qualifier against Ukraine in March and then replacing the injured Robbie Savage in the starting line-up for the return game in Kiev.

Peterborough U (From trainee on 21/7/1997) FL 63+2/6 FLC 4 FAC 3 Others 3
Tottenham H (£700,000 on 10/1/2000) PL 10+6/2 FLC 0+1 FAC 0+1/2

DAVIES Simon Ithel
Born: Winsford, 23 April 1974
Height: 6'0" Weight: 11.11
Club Honours: FAYC '92
International Honours: W: 1

A close season signing from Macclesfield, Simon scored Rochdale's first goal of the 2000-01 campaign when he netted from the penalty spot in the 1-1 draw with Darlington. However although he appeared regularly in the early matches he lost his place at the end of September and rarely featured after that. He is a wide left midfield player who is capable of producing flashes of trickery on the wing. He was out of contract in the summer.

Manchester U (From trainee on 6/7/1992) PL 4+7 FLC 4+2 Others 2+1/1
Exeter C (Loaned on 17/12/1993) FL 5+1/1 FAC 1
Huddersfield T (Loaned on 29/10/1996) FL 3
Luton T (£150,000 on 5/8/1997) FL 10+12/1 FLC 3+1 FAC 0+1 Others 3
Macclesfield T (Signed on 17/12/1998) FL 39+9/3 FLC 2 FAC 3 Others 1/1
Rochdale (Free on 4/8/2000) FL 7+5/1 FLC 1+1 FAC 0+1 Others 0+1

DAVIS Kelvin Geoffrey
Born: Bedford, 29 September 1976
Height: 6'1" Weight: 14.0
International Honours: E: U21-3; Yth

Last season was Kelvin's first as number one 'keeper for Wimbledon following the departure of Neil Sullivan to Spurs. He grabbed the opportunity enthusiastically and went on to produce a string of fine performances throughout the campaign. A fine shot stopper who possesses a powerful kick he still needs to work on handling crosses, but with age on his side he certainly looks to have a bright future ahead of him. Kelvin's progress was recognised when he came runner-up in the supporters' poll for 'Player of the Season'.

Luton T (From trainee on 1/7/1994) FL 92 FLC 7 FAC 2 Others 6
Torquay U (Loaned on 16/9/1994) FL 2 FLC 1 Others 1
Hartlepool U (Loaned on 8/8/1997) FL 2 FLC 1
Wimbledon (£600,000 + on 14/7/1999) FL 45 FLC 4 FAC 6

DAVIS Sean
Born: Clapham, 20 September 1979
Height: 5'10" Weight: 12.0
Club Honours: Div 1 '01
International Honours: E: U21-4

Sean was undoubtedly one of the success stories for Fulham in 2000-01 when he finally established himself as a regular in the first team. Given the responsibility of being the 'holding' midfield player he responded brilliantly. Not only did he prove to be an effective link between defence and attack he also got forward to score some of the most important goals of the season. His injury time winner at Blackburn made promotion a near certainty, while his superb strike that earned a 1-1 draw against Sheffield Wednesday made certain of the First Division championship. His excellent progress was recognised when he stepped up to make his debut for England U21s against Finland in March. He was also honoured by his fellow professionals with a place in the PFA First Division team.

Fulham (From trainee on 2/7/1998) FL 53+20/6 FLC 6+4/3 FAC 2+1/1

DAVIS Solomon (Sol) Sebastian
Born: Cheltenham, 4 September 1979
Height: 5'8" Weight: 11.0

Now firmly established in the Swindon Town defence, Sol again did well in the 2000-01 campaign although he accumulated a number of yellow cards and this is an area of his game where he still needs to show improvement. A solid tough-tackling left back he never shirks a challenge and always gives 100 per cent commitment to the team. He was rarely seen as an attacking force last term, but combined well with Andy Williams to provide the cross from which Giuliano Grazioli netted the winner at home to Oxford in October.

Swindon T (From trainee on 29/5/1998) FL 84+11 FLC 5 FAC 4 Others 1

DAVIS Stephen (Steve) Mark
Born: Hexham, 30 October 1968
Height: 6'2" Weight: 14.7
Club Honours: Div 4 '92

Burnley's captain and defensive colossus had another fine season in 2000-01. A commanding figure in the back three, Steve proved a match for most of the best strikers the First Division had to offer and it was significant that one of the Clarets heaviest defeats, 5-0 at Nottingham Forest, came on one of his very rare off-days. A fine sight bringing the ball out of defence, he kept up his fine record as a goalscorer adding another six in league and cup games. He is solid both in the air and on the ground and leads the team by example.

Southampton (From trainee on 6/7/1987) FL 5+1
Burnley (Loaned on 21/11/1989) FL 7+2
Notts Co (Loaned on 28/3/1991) FL 0+2
Burnley (£60,000 on 17/8/1991) FL 162/22 FLC 10/2 FAC 18/1 Others 13
Luton T (£750,000 on 13/7/1995) FL 137+1/21 FLC 19/3 FAC 5/2 Others 10/1
Burnley (£800,000 on 21/12/1998) FL 105/16 FLC 5/1 FAC 6 Others 1

DAVISON Aidan John
Born: Sedgefield, 11 May 1968
Height: 6'1" Weight: 13.12
Club Honours: AMC '98
International Honours: NI: 3; B-1

Aidan spent most of the 2000-01 campaign as third-choice 'keeper at Bradford City behind Gary Walsh and Matt Clarke. He played in two early season Worthington Cup ties and also appeared a couple of times in the Premiership at the very end of the campaign. An excellent shot stopper with quick reflexes he showed some superb form for the Bantams' reserve team and will be hoping to get back in the first team in 2001-02.

Notts Co (Signed from Billingham Synthonia on 25/3/1988) FL 1
Bury (£6,000 on 7/10/1989)
Millwall (Free on 14/8/1991) FL 34 FLC 3 FAC 3 Others 2
Bolton W (£25,000 on 26/7/1993) P/FL 35+2 FAC 8 Others 4
Hull C (Loaned on 29/11/1996) FL 9 Others 1
Bradford C (Free on 14/3/1997) FL 10
Grimsby T (Free on 16/7/1997) FL 77 FLC 10 FAC 7 Others 10
Sheffield U (Free on 6/8/1999) FL 1+1
Bradford C (Loaned on 4/1/2000) PL 7+1 FLC 2 Others 2+1

DAWS Nicholas (Nick) John
Born: Manchester, 15 March 1970
Height: 5'11" Weight: 13.2
Club Honours: Div 2 '97

Bury's captain and longest-serving player was once again a virtual ever-present in the Shakers' team in the 2000-01 campaign. After a somewhat disappointing time the previous season, Nick seemed to have rediscovered his appetite for the game with a number of fine battling performances in central midfield. He also played the occasional game at full back when required and pitched in with six goals in all - his best total for some time.

Bury (£10,000 from Altrincham on 13/8/1992) FL 356+13/16 FLC 25+3/3 FAC 19/1 Others 15+4/3

DAWSON Andrew (Andy)
Born: Northallerton, 20 October 1978
Height: 5'9" Weight: 10.2

Scunthorpe's left-back continued to look one of the best in Division Three during 2000-01 with his strong defensive tackling plus his ability to get forward at every opportunity. He also became something of a free-kick expert during the campaign with four goals from just outside the box, including a crucial strike in the FA Cup victory over First Division Burnley. Apart from injuries and suspensions he was an ever-present for the Iron last season. Andy was voted 'Player of the Year' by the club's supporters.

Nottingham F (From trainee on 31/10/1995) FLC 1
Scunthorpe U (£70,000 on 18/12/1998) FL 105+3/6 FLC 4 FAC 6/1 Others 6/1

DAWSON Andrew (Andy) Stephen
Born: York, 8 December 1979
Height: 6'0" Weight: 11.7

Andy joined Carlisle United on a non-contract basis last December but his only senior appearance came from the subs' bench in the LDV Vans Trophy tie at Kidderminster and in February he moved on to join Conference club Scarborough. Andy is a versatile youngster who can play both in midfield and defence.

York C (From trainee on 2/7/1998) FL 18+10/1 FLC 2 FAC 1 Others 1
Carlisle U (Free on 5/12/2000) Others 0+1

DAWSON Kevin Edward
Born: Northallerton, 18 June 1981
Height: 6'0" Weight: 10.10

Kevin struggled to make an impact at Nottingham Forest last season and made just one first-team appearance in the 3-0 defeat by Blackburn in September. In March he went on loan to struggling Third Division outfit Barnet where he produced some fine performances notably in the 2-1 win over Southend but was unable to lead them away from the relegation zone. A small and stocky central defender he nevertheless has a commanding presence and reads the game well. Kevin was placed on the open to offers list in the summer.

Nottingham F (From trainee on 25/6/1998) FL 5+3 FAC 1
Barnet (Loaned on 9/3/2001) FL 5

DAY Christopher (Chris) Nicholas
Born: Walthamstow, 28 July 1975
Height: 6'3" Weight: 13.6
International Honours: E: U21-6; Yth (UEFA-U18 '93)

Unable to break into the first team at Watford Chris moved on loan to Lincoln City last December to fill in for the injured Alan Marriott. His experience served the Imps well at a time when the team was struggling to find its form. He proved an excellent shot stopper as well as proving a commanding figure in the box. He returned to Vicarage Road after three months at Sincil Bank. Released by the Hornets in the summer he was reported to have signed for Queens Park Rangers.

Tottenham H (From trainee on 16/4/1993) Others 4
Crystal Palace (£225,000 + on 9/8/1996) FL 24 FLC 2 FAC 2
Watford (£225,000 on 18/7/1997) PL 11 FLC 1 Others 1
Lincoln C (Loaned on 4/12/2000) FL 14 Others 4

DAY James (Jamie) Russell
Born: Bexley, 13 September 1979
Height: 5'7" Weight: 10.12
International Honours: E: Sch

Jamie began the 2000-1 season with high hopes of establishing himself in the Bournemouth side. He made the starting line-up for the opening game at Bristol Rovers but then found his first-team opportunities somewhat limited and started on only a handful more occasions. He is a promising left-sided midfield player with some neat touches and good passing skills. He was reported to have signed for Dover Athletic in the summer.

Arsenal (From trainee on 3/7/1997)
Bournemouth (£20,000 on 3/3/1999) FL 15+5/1 FLC 1+1 FAC 4+1 Others 2

DEANE Brian Christopher
Born: Leeds, 7 February 1968
Height: 6'3" Weight: 12.7
International Honours: E: 3; B-3

Brian struggled again with illness and injuries at Middlesbrough in 2000-01 and a tally of two goals from 13 starts was never likely to set the Tees alight although the fans could be forgiven for demanding more. The inspirational striker would move heaven and earth to regain his scoring rate when he gets back in the groove, but it was a long hard slog for him last term. An experienced striker who is particularly effective in the air he possesses a powerful shot and will be hoping for a better run of fortune in 2001-02.

Doncaster Rov (From juniors on 14/12/1985) FL 59+7/12 FLC 3 FAC 2+1/1 Others 2+2
Sheffield U (£30,000 on 19/7/1988) F/PL 197/82 FLC 16/11 FAC 23+1/11 Others 2/2
Leeds U (£2,900,000 on 14/7/1993) PL 131+7/32 FLC 8+3/2 FAC 13+3/4 Others 3
Sheffield U (£1,500,000 on 29/7/1997) FL 24/11 FLC 4/2 FAC 1 (£1,000,000 to Benfica, Portugal on 15/1/1998)
Middlesbrough (£3,000,000 on 16/10/1998) PL 66+14/17 FLC 4+1 FAC 3/1

DEARDEN Kevin Charles
Born: Luton, 8 March 1970
Height: 5'11" Weight: 13.4

Kevin began last season on the bench for Wrexham and it was not until mid-September that he replaced Kristian Rogers in the Robins' goal. He then retained his position for the remainder of the campaign producing an excellent performance in the Boxing Day game against Port Vale at the Racecourse Ground. Although not particularly tall he is a fine shot stopper who is able to dominate his penalty area. He was released on a free transfer in the summer.

Tottenham H (From trainee on 5/8/1988) PL 0+1 FLC 1
Cambridge U (Loaned on 9/3/1989) FL 15
Hartlepool U (Loaned on 31/8/1989) FL 10
Swindon T (Loaned on 23/3/1990) FL 1
Peterborough U (Loaned on 24/8/1990) FL 7
Hull C (Loaned on 10/1/1991) FL 3
Rochdale (Loaned on 16/8/1991) FL 2
Birmingham C (Loaned on 19/3/1992) FL 12
Brentford (Free on 30/9/1993) FL 205 FLC 17 FAC 13 Others 19
Barnet (Loaned on 5/2/1999) FL 1
Wrexham (Free on 4/6/1999) FL 81 FLC 3 FAC 6

DE BILDE Gilles Roger Gerard
Born: Zellik, Belgium, 9 June 1971
Height: 5'11" Weight: 11.6
International Honours: Belgium: 25

This experienced Belgian striker had rather a disappointing season with Sheffield Wednesday in 2000-01 and in October he moved on a three-month loan to Premiership club Aston Villa. Boss John Gregory was seeking a replacement for the injured Luc Nilis, but Gilles failed to impress in a handful of appearances and no permanent deal was pursued. On his return to Hillsborough caretaker-manager Peter Shreeves restored him to the line-up and he scored a vital winner for the Owls at Birmingham. Gilles added to his total of caps when he appeared for Belgium against Bulgaria last August.

Sheffield Wed (£3,000,000 from PSV Eindhoven, Holland, ex Aalst, Anderlecht, on 19/7/1999) PL 50+9/13 FLC 5/2 FAC 4
Aston Villa (Loaned on 12/10/2000) PL 4

DE BLASIIS Jean Yves
Born: Bordeaux, France, 25 September 1973
Height: 5'9" Weight: 11.5
International Honours: France: Yth

Having eventually recovered following a cruciate ligament injury sustained towards the end of the 1999-2000 campaign Jean Yves returned to the Norwich City first-team squad last December but failed to hold down a regular place in the starting line-up. A versatile player he is by preference a midfielder but he can also play in either full back position where his tenacity comes to good use. He was released on a free transfer in the summer.

Norwich C (Free from Paris Red Star, France on 31/7/1999) FL 28+7 FLC 1+1 FAC 1

DEFOE Jermaine Colin
Born: Beckton, 7 October 1982
Height: 5'7" Weight: 10.4
International Honours: E: U21-2; Yth; Sch

Jermaine was one of the stars of West Ham's U19 team that won the FA Academy play-offs in 1999-2000 and he made a quick step up to the Hammers' first team last term when he made his senior debut in the Worthington Cup second round tie at Walsall, snatching the winner just minutes after coming off the subs' bench. However this was just a taste of what was to follow. At the end of October he was loaned to Second Division Bournemouth and made a sensational start by scoring in each of his first ten league games to establish a new club record. The Cherries' fortunes quickly changed for the better as they moved up the table to challenge for a play-off place with Jermaine scoring freely all season. His tally of 19 goals in all competitions included several fine efforts, notably a brilliant individual strike at Oxford on Boxing Day when he collected the ball in his own half and ran through the opposition defence before chipping the 'keeper. He eventually returned to Upton Park at the end of the Nationwide season and went on to make his Premiership debut for the Hammers when he came on from the subs' bench in the final game at Middlesbrough. He is a quick and lively striker with an eye for goal and the knack of finding space in the penalty box. A regular for England at U18 level he was promoted to the U21s in the summer, scoring on his debut against Mexico and also featuring in the UEFA qualifying game in Greece.

West Ham U (£400,000 + from trainee at Charlton Ath on 15/10/1999) PL 0+1 FLC 0+1/1
Bournemouth (Loaned on 26/10/2000) FL 27+2/18 FAC 1/1 Others 1

DE GOEY Eduard (Ed) Franciscus
Born: Gouda, Holland, 20 December 1966
Height: 6'6" Weight: 15.0
Club Honours: FLC '98; ECWC '98; ESC '98; FAC '00; CS '00
International Honours: Holland: 31; U21-17

Rarely can a player have suffered such a contrast in fortunes as Chelsea goalkeeper Ed De Goey. After breaking two long-standing club records and gaining an FA Cup winner's medal in 1999-2000 he had a distinctly disappointing campaign last term and found his automatic status as first-choice 'keeper under threat. His season began brightly enough with a Charity Shield medal in August against Manchester United but it began to unravel just two matches later when his judgement was called into question following a 2-0 defeat at struggling Bradford City. Worse was to follow five days later at Villa Park when he injured a hamstring in the pre-match warm-up and was forced onto the sidelines as Carlo Cudicini deputised. Normal service seemed to have been resumed as he regained his place for the 3-0 home win over Liverpool and stayed in for the next 14 matches but Cudicini was then recalled for the New Year's Day fixture against Aston Villa and another bombshell dropped shortly after with the club's shock acquisition of Manchester United's outcast goalkeeper Mark Bosnich. Effectively relegated to third-choice at Stamford Bridge his future at the club must now be under question.

Chelsea (£2,250,000 from Feyenoord, Holland, ex Sparta Rotterdam, on 10/7/1997) PL 115 FLC 5 FAC 13 Others 35

DELANEY Damien
Born: Cork, 20 July 1981
Height: 6'3" Weight: 13.10
International Honours: RoI: U21-1; Yth

Capped by the Republic of Ireland at U18 level Damien made the big step up from Cork City to Premiership club Leicester last October and impressed new manager Peter Taylor sufficiently to gain his senior debut in the FA Cup third round tie against York. He made the starting line-up for the fourth round tie against Aston Villa where he performed with a maturity beyond his years and had his first taste of league action against Manchester United. A left-sided midfield player or defender of immense promise and undoubted class he will be hoping for further senior action in 2001-02.

Leicester C (£50,000 from Cork C on 9/11/2000) PL 3+2 FAC 1+1

DELANEY Dean
Born: Dublin, 15 September 1980
Height: 6'1" Weight: 13.2
Club Honours: FAYC '98
International Honours: RoI: U21-6

Dean was second-choice 'keeper to Mark Goodlad at Port Vale last season and received few opportunities due to the fine form of his rival. He made his senior debut at Wrexham on Boxing Day when he came on from the subs' bench in the final minute after Goodlad had received a red card and also featured on a number of occasions

towards the end of the campaign. Dean continued to represent the Republic of Ireland at U21 level winning further caps against Netherlands and Portugal.
Everton (From trainee on 23/9/1997)
Port Vale (Free on 16/6/2000) FL 7+1 Others 1

DELANEY Mark Anthony
Born: Fishguard, 13 May 1976
Height: 6'1" Weight: 11.7
International Honours: W: 9
Mark began the 2000-01 season with some disciplinary problems having received a red card for his country during the summer and another in an early Inter Toto Cup game but although he quickly put these troubles behind him he had a frustrating time with injuries and never really established himself in the Aston Villa first team last season. He spent time out with two separate knee injuries and was also sidelined in the spring with a badly bruised ankle. When fit he originally found himself competing with Steve Stone for the right-wing-back position, however a change of formation during the second half of the campaign saw them both appear in the same line-up overlapping down the right flank. He continued to appear for Wales winning five more caps during the season.
Cardiff C (Free from Carmarthen on 3/7/1998) FL 28 FLC 2 FAC 5/1
Aston Villa (£250,000 + on 10/3/1999) PL 37+12/1 FLC 1+3 FAC 4+1 Others 1

DELAP Rory John
Born: Sutton Coldfield, 6 July 1976
Height: 6'0" Weight: 12.10
Club Honours: AMC '97
International Honours: RoI: 6; B-1; U21-4
Rory had a mixed season at Pride Park last term. A regular in the Derby County first team where he played in a variety of positions according to the tactics used, his preference was for either a role on the right side of midfield or as a right wing back. Injuries even forced Jim Smith to use him as an emergency striker on occasions. Very fast going forward, but less so when tracking back, he scored what was arguably the Rams' 'Goal of the Season' with a long-range strike in the away game at Leicester.
Carlisle U (From trainee on 18/7/1994) FL 40+25/7 FLC 4+1 FAC 0+3 Others 12+2
Derby Co (£500,000 + on 6/2/1998) PL 97+6/11 FLC 7/2 FAC 2+1

DEMPSEY Paul
Born: Birkenhead, 3 December 1981
Height: 5'11" Weight: 12.0
This skilful right-sided wing back featured for Sheffield United reserves for much of last season before moving to Northampton Town on the transfer deadline day. Paul went on to make his debut for the Cobblers in the 2-1 defeat at Oldham and played regularly in the closing matches of the campaign.
Sheffield U (From trainee on 7/7/2000)
Northampton T (Free on 12/3/2001) FL 5+1

DERRY Shaun Peter
Born: Nottingham, 6 December 1977
Height: 5'10" Weight: 10.13
Club Honours: Div 3 '98
Shaun switched from a central midfield role to right back for Portsmouth at the beginning of last season and alternated roles during the campaign depending on the formation employed. He was a regular in the team until sidelined by a back injury that kept him out of action from the end of February. A powerful composed defender he has a great first touch, a good turn of pace and is very strong pushing forward.
Notts Co (From trainee on 13/4/1996) FL 76+3/4 FLC 4+1 FAC 6+1/1 Others 3
Sheffield U (£700,000 on 26/1/1998) FL 62+10 FLC 4 FAC 7/1
Portsmouth (£300,000 + on 16/3/2000) FL 36+1/1 FLC 4 FAC 1

DERVELD Fernando
Born: Vlissingen, Holland, 22 October 1976
Height: 6'2" Weight: 12.8
Fernando started the 2000-01 season in fine style for Norwich, using his excellent turn of pace and great strength to impose himself upon his opponents. A loss of form in the autumn left him out of the side and when new manager Nigel Worthington took over it became clear that his future opportunities would become limited. West Bromwich Albion boss Gary Megson then signed him on loan in February, perhaps recalling the fine display he had put on against the Baggies earlier in the season. Signed as cover for the left side of defence and midfield he featured only a couple of times before returning to Carrow Road. He later had a trial in Denmark with Odense and his contract was eventually cancelled by mutual consent during the summer break.
Norwich C (£150,000 + from Haarlem, Holland on 23/3/2000) FL 20+2/1 FLC 3
West Bromwich A (Loaned on 6/2/2001) FL 1+1

DESAILLY Marcel
Born: Accra, Ghana, 7 September 1968
Height: 6'1" Weight: 13.5
Club Honours: ESC '98; FAC '00; CS '00
International Honours: France: 85 (WC '98, UEFA '00); B-1; U21
The Rock. Never was a nickname so appropriate as this great defender maintained his reputation as one of the world's best while, seemingly at times, things fell apart around him. Before the season began he added a European Championship winner's medal to his collection of honours and soon afterwards he replaced his close friend and ex-Chelsea colleague Didier Deschamps as captain of France. However his tried and trusted central defensive partnership with Frank Leboeuf looked to be under strain at Stamford Bridge as Leboeuf began the season out of favour, and Marcel was partnered by a number of players until new

Marcel Desailly

manager Claudio Ranieri decided to give impressive youngster John Terry an extended run in the first team. Marcel had acted as a mentor in Terry's rise to prominence and the pairing became established throughout the second half of the campaign as the Blues improved to claim a UEFA Cup berth. Given the upheavals in a traumatic season at Stamford Bridge, Marcel has remained one of the few constants around which Ranieri is determined to rebuild a new team that will be serious contenders on all fronts.
Chelsea (£4,600,000 from AC Milan, Italy, ex Nantes, Marseilles, on 14/7/1998) PL 87+1/3 FLC 1 FAC 12 Others 26/1

DEVANEY Martin Thomas
Born: Cheltenham, 1 June 1980
Height: 5'10" Weight: 11.12
This exciting youngster continued to make progress at Cheltenham last season and netted the club's first-ever Football League hat-trick in the 5-2 victory over Plymouth in September. He featured regularly until manager Steve Cotterill preferred more experienced players towards the end of the campaign. A talented youngster with good skills on the ball he is still learning the game but if he continues to work hard he should develop into a more than useful striker.
Coventry C (From trainee on 4/6/1997)
Cheltenham T (Free on 5/8/1999) FL 42+18/16 FLC 3 FAC 1+1 Others 1

DEVLIN Paul John
Born: Birmingham, 14 April 1972
Height: 5'9" Weight: 11.5
Club Honours: AIC '95
Having committed himself to a further four years with Sheffield United Paul continued to be a key player in the 2000-01 campaign. Despite being regularly marked by two opposition defenders he still managed to create many chances with his foraging down the right-hand side but his goal tally was somewhat reduced. He is a speedy right winger with tenacity and excellent ball control.
Notts Co (£40,000 from Stafford R on 22/2/1992) FL 132+9/25 FLC 11+1/1 FAC 8/1 Others 17+2/4
Birmingham C (Signed on 29/2/1996) FL 61+15/28 FLC 8+1/4 FAC 3+1/2
Sheffield U (£200,000 + on 13/3/1998) FL 108+20/22 FLC 7+3/3 FAC 7/1 Others 2
Notts Co (Loaned on 23/10/1998) FL 5

DE-VULGT Leigh Stewart
Born: Swansea, 17 March 1981
Height: 5'9" Weight: 11.2
International Honours: W: Yth
Swansea's injury problems gave Leigh the chance of an appearance from the subs' bench at Rotherham last October and he went on to receive occasional first-team opportunities during the remainder of the campaign. He mostly featured at right back, producing some solid defensive work and pushing forward to deliver accurate crosses from the flank. He was reported to have signed a new two-year deal for the club during the summer.
Swansea C (From trainee on 5/7/1999) FL 6+3 Others 3

DE WAARD Raymond
Born: Rotterdam, Holland, 27 March 1973
Height: 6'1" Weight: 13.6
Although he made several appearances from the subs' bench for Norwich City last season this leggy winger made only one start and in the new year his contract was cancelled. He subsequently joined Dutch side AZ Alkmaar where he featured in a handful of games towards the end of the campaign. Very much a winger in the traditional sense he can outwit opposition defenders with his pace and close control.
Norwich C (£150,000 + from Cambuur Leeuwarden, Holland, ex Excelsior, on 23/3/2000) FL 4+6 FLC 1+2

DEWHURST Robert (Rob) Matthew
Born: Keighley, 10 September 1971
Height: 6'3" Weight: 14.0
Rob joined Scunthorpe on a monthly contract in the summer of 2000 and showed his experience and strength at centre-half in pre-season friendlies. His only first team opportunity came in the Worthington Cup tie at Wigan when he was sent off for a professional foul after just 20 minutes. Rob was released by the Iron in September and after a brief spell at Unibond League outfit Gainsborough Trinity he signed for North Ferriby United.
Blackburn Rov (From trainee on 15/10/1990) FL 13 FLC 2 Others 1
Darlington (Loaned on 20/12/1991) FL 11/1 Others 1
Huddersfield T (Loaned on 2/10/1992) FL 7
Hull C (Free on 5/11/1993) FL 132+6/13 FLC 8 FAC 8/1 Others 7
Exeter C (Free on 9/8/1999) FL 21+2/2 FLC 2 FAC 2+1 Others 0+1
Scunthorpe U (Free on 25/7/2000) FLC 1

DE ZEEUW Adrianus (Arjan) Johannes
Born: Castricum, Holland, 16 April 1970
Height: 6'1" Weight: 13.11
This classy defender was among the best in the Second Division last season and his excellent performances for Wigan Athletic were rewarded when he was named in the PFA's divisional team in April. A composed central defender who is powerful in the air and strong in the tackle he skippered the Latics to a place in the play-offs. He completed a century of games for Wigan and he swept the board at the club's end-of-season awards, winning both 'Players' Player of the Year' and the supporters' 'Player of the Year'.
Barnsley (£250,000 from Telstar, Holland, ex Vitesse 22, on 3/11/1995) F/PL 138/7 FLC 12 FAC 14
Wigan Ath (Free on 2/7/1999) FL 84/4 FLC 7 FAC 5 Others 5

DIAWARA Kaba
Born: Toulon, France, 16 December 1975
Height: 5'11" Weight: 11.12
International Honours: France: U21
Having made little impact at Paris St Germain in 1999-2000 Kaba joined Blackburn Rovers last August in a long-term loan deal. He featured mostly from the subs' bench at Ewood Park, netting his only goal in the Worthington Cup first round tie against Rochdale. In September Premiership club West Ham stepped in to take over his contract but he failed to establish himself in the Hammers' first team despite fine performances in the victories over Southampton and Middlesbrough. A powerful burly striker he is quick for a big man and well suited to the physical nature of the English game.
Arsenal (£2,500,000 from Bordeaux, France on 29/1/1999) PL 2+10 FAC 1+2 (£2,000,000 to Marseille, France on 8/7/99)
Blackburn Rov (Loaned from Paris St Germain, France on 22/8/2000) FL 1+4 FLC 1/1
West Ham U (Loaned from Paris St Germain, France on 22/9/2000) PL 6+5

DIBBLE Andrew (Andy) Gerald
Born: Cwmbran, 8 May 1965
Height: 6'3" Weight: 16.8
International Honours: W: 3; U21-3; Yth; Sch
With first choice goalkeepers Carlo Nash and Lee Jones unavailable veteran Andy Dibble answered Stockport's emergency call for the daunting trip to Blackburn last November. Unfazed, he went on to produce a 'Man of the Match' performance keeping the Rovers' forwards at bay with a series of magnificent saves until he was eventually beaten by Craig Hignett's injury-time free kick. He went on to enjoy two brief runs in the side before stepping back to the sidelines.
Cardiff C (From apprentice on 27/8/1982) FL 62 FLC 4 FAC 4
Luton T (£125,000 on 16/7/1984) FL 30 FLC 4 FAC 1 Others 1
Sunderland (Loaned on 21/2/1986) FL 12
Huddersfield T (Loaned on 26/3/1987) FL 5
Manchester C (£240,000 on 1/7/1988) P/FL 113+3 FLC 14 FAC 8+1 Others 2
Aberdeen (Loaned on 20/10/1990) SL 5
Middlesbrough (Loaned on 20/2/1991) FL 19 Others 2
Bolton W (Loaned on 6/9/1991) FL 13 Others 1
West Bromwich A (Loaned on 27/2/1992) FL 9
Glasgow R (Signed on 11/3/1997) SL 7
Luton T (Free on 15/9/1997) FL 1 FLC 2
Middlesbrough (Free on 30/1/1998) FL 2 (Free to Altrincham during 1998 close season)
Hartlepool U (Free on 25/3/1999) FL 6 FLC 2 Others 2+1
Carlisle U (Loaned on 8/10/1999) FL 2
Stockport Co (Free on 10/8/2000) FL 9+1

DI CANIO Paolo
Born: Rome, Italy, 9 July 1968
Height: 5'9" Weight: 11.9
A veritable genius for West Ham, Paolo is the one man who excites the Upton Park faithful and makes the side tick. He was again in breathtaking form last season, showing off a fine array of skills and creating numerous scoring opportunities for his colleagues. Among his many fine goals there were three amazing efforts: at Charlton where he rode one tackle and crashed an unstoppable 18-yarder into the roof of the net; at Old Trafford in the FA Cup tie when he ignored offside claims and coolly slotted the ball home to earn the Hammers a surprise victory; and in the final home game against Southampton when he picked up on the ball on the edge of the area, ghosted past two defenders before tucking it in the corner of the net. As ever Paolo always came up

with the unexpected and when Everton goalkeeper Paul Gerrard lay injured on the ground he opted to catch the ball rather than take the easy option of tapping into an empty net. His decision won plaudits from FIFA president Sepp Blatter, but Hammers' boss Harry Redknapp was probably not so gushing in praise of his maverick striker.

Glasgow Celtic (Signed from AC Milan, Italy, ex AC Milan, Lazio, Ternana, Juventus, Napoli, on 3/7/1996) SL 25+1/12 SLC 2 SC 6/3 Others 2+1
Sheffield Wed (£3,000,000 on 8/8/1997) PL 39+2/15 FLC 4/2 FAC 3
West Ham U (£1,700,000 on 28/1/1999) PL 72+2/29 FLC 7/2 FAC 4/1 Others 10/1

DICHIO Daniele (Danny) Salvatore Ernest
Born: Hammersmith, 19 October 1974
Height: 6'3" Weight: 12.3
Club Honours: Div 1 '99
International Honours: E: U21-1; Sch

Danny continued to wait patiently in the wings as Niall Quinn's understudy at Sunderland last season and has now performed this role for over three seasons. Strong in the air and not afraid to compete where it hurts, his contributions are always wholehearted however intermittently he is called up for duty. His early season games were restricted to outings in the Worthington Cup before he got his chance in the Premiership against Ipswich on New Year's Day. He scored in a 4-1 win and followed this up with the winner against the same opposition three weeks later when he netted with a trademark diving header to put the Wearsiders through to the fifth round of the FA Cup. Generally however he was restricted to cameo appearances from the substitutes' bench.

Queens Park R (From trainee on 17/5/1993) P/FL 56+19/20 FLC 6/2 FAC 3+3 (Free to Sampdoria, Italy during 1997 close season)
Barnet (Loaned on 24/3/1994) FL 9/2
Sunderland (£750,000, via loan spell at Lecce, Italy on 28/1/1998) P/FL 20+56/11 FLC 11+1/6 FAC 3+3/1 Others 1+2

DICKOV Paul
Born: Livingston, 1 November 1972
Height: 5'6" Weight: 11.9
Club Honours: ECWC '94
International Honours: S: 3; U21-4; Yth; Sch

Paul had an early-season run for Manchester City last term but was sidelined for two months at the turn of the year after damaging knee ligaments in the game against Leeds United. Back in the first-team reckoning by March he was unlucky to receive a red card at Goodison and escaped further punishment when the decision was later rescinded. A firm favourite with the Maine Road faithful his goal tally included one in the abandoned Worthington Cup fifth round tie against Ipswich Town. A tireless forager up front he will be hoping to feature more regularly at first-team level in 2001-02. He stepped up to make his full debut for Scotland against San Marino last October.

Arsenal (From trainee on 28/12/1990) PL 6+15/3 FLC 2+2/3
Luton T (Loaned on 8/10/1993) FL 8+7/1
Brighton & Hove A (Loaned on 23/3/1994) FL 8/5
Manchester C (£1,000,000 on 23/8/1996) P/FL 105+44/33 FLC 9+3/4 FAC 5+4/1 Others 3/2

DICKSON Hugh Robinson
Born: Downpatrick, 28 August 1981
Height: 6'2" Weight: 11.2

This young defender joined Wigan Athletic from Irish league club Glentoran at the start of last season. He went on to make his senior debut in the FA Cup second round replay against Notts County and featured in a handful more games later in the campaign. A versatile defender who can play either at centre half or right back, Hugh has good pace and is strong in the challenge. He was placed on stand-by for the Northern Ireland U21 squad in March and will be looking to win a regular place in the Latics' first-team squad in the coming season. Hugh is a cousin of Preston's David Healy.

Wigan Ath (Free from Glentoran on 25/8/2000) FL 0+1 FAC 0+1 Others 2

DI MATTEO Roberto (Robbie)
Born: Berne, Switzerland, 29 May 1970
Height: 5'10" Weight: 12.5
Club Honours: FAC '97. '00; FLC '98; ECWC '98; ESC '98; CS '00
International Honours: Italy: 34

This dynamic midfield player endured a roller-coaster time in the year 2000 - battling his way back into first-team contention following a serious ankle injury and a fractured arm, scoring the winning goal in the FA Cup Final and dominating the midfield in Chelsea's exciting Charity Shield triumph. With the sale of Didier Deschamps and Dan Petrescu he seemed poised to reclaim his favoured central midfield position but shortly after Gianluca Vialli's shock departure as Chelsea manager the fates dealt Robbie a terrible blow. During the catastrophic UEFA Cup defeat at the hands of Swiss club St Gallen in September he suffered a badly broken left leg and this brought his season to a premature close. He was sorely missed for his steadying influence and drive in midfield and in his absence the team plunged from being Premiership contenders to a position of mid-table obscurity. The fact that Chelsea have won six major trophies since Robbie's arrival in July 1996 after years of under-achievement speaks volumes for his contribution to the club's transformation into one of the modern-day giants.

Chelsea (£4,900,000 from Lazio, Italy, ex FC Aarau, FC Zurich, Schaffhausen, on 17/7/1996) PL 108+11/15 FLC 9+1/3 FAC 15+2/5 Others 23+6/3

DINNING Tony
Born: Wallsend, 12 April 1975
Height: 6'0" Weight: 12.11

After making a bright start at Stockport last season Tony was surprisingly sold to First Division rivals Wolves for something of a bargain fee at the end of September. Although he made his debut for Wanderers in the heart of the defence his more usual role was in the centre of the park where he produced some intelligent play. He also scored a number of important goals including a cheeky penalty at Bolton and a fine volley against Watford. An attacking central midfield player he is capable of scoring spectacular goals.

Newcastle U (From trainee on 1/10/1993)
Stockport Co (Free on 23/6/1994) FL 159+32/25 FLC 12+5/3 FAC 5+7 Others 6+1/2
Wolverhampton W (£600,000 + on 22/9/2000) FL 31/6 FAC 1

DIOMEDE Bernard
Born: St Doulchard, France, 23 January 1974
Height: 5'7" Weight: 11.4
International Honours: France: 8

Bernard made his Liverpool debut in the away leg of the UEFA Cup tie against Rapid Bucharest in September and his Premiership debut against Sunderland nine days later. However following a rather unconvincing display in the return match with Rapid he played virtually no part in the rest of the campaign save for a brief substitute appearance at Manchester City in February. In fairness it should be stated that he was sidelined with knee and cartilage injuries for two months but even when available he was not called upon. With so much midfield talent available at Anfield it seems unlikely that he will remain with the club for much longer.

Liverpool (£3,000,000 from Auxerre, France on 5/7/2000) PL 1+1 Others 2

Michele Di Piedi

DI PIEDI Michele
Born: Italy, 4 December 1980
Height: 6'6" Weight: 13.7

This young striker was mostly used as a substitute by Sheffield Wednesday last season but proved a useful acquisition and netted some spectacular goals. Michele scored his first goal for the Owls with a 25-yard drive at Grimsby last August to earn the club their first victory back in the First Division and his arrival on the pitch invariably excited the Wednesday fans. Full of flair, enthusiasm and passion he will be looking to feature more regularly in the starting line-up in 2001-02.

Sheffield Wed (Free from Perugia, Italy on 15/8/2000) FL 6+19/4 FLC 0+3/1

DISLEY Craig Edward
Born: Worksop, 24 August 1981
Height: 5'10" Weight: 11.0
Craig produced some fine performances for Mansfield Town reserves in 2000-01 but although he made the odd appearance as cover for injury and suspension it was not until last February that he was given an extended run in the first team. He is a promising young midfield player whose pace and persistence going forward make him a thorn in the side of opposition defenders.
Mansfield T (From trainee on 23/6/1999) FL 18+11 FAC 2 Others 1

DIXON Lee Michael
Born: Manchester, 17 March 1964
Height: 5'9" Weight: 11.8
Club Honours: Div 1 '89, '91; PL '98; FAC '93, '98; ECWC '94; CS '98, '99
International Honours: E: 22; B-4
Lee had another fine season for Arsenal last term and now stands fourth in the list of appearances made for the Gunners behind George Armstrong, Tony Adams and David O'Leary. That he has reached this marvellous goal is a testament to a player who has been constantly written off as being 'over the hill' during the last few seasons. He draws on his vast experience, fantastic stamina and excellent attitude to remain Arsenal's first-choice right back. He reads the game superbly, times his tackles to perfection and is equally comfortable going forward and creating attacking moves. As ever he was a key figure at Highbury as the club reached a high position in the Premiership and enjoyed lengthy runs in the FA Cup and Champions League.
Burnley (From juniors on 21/7/1982) FL 4 FLC 1
Chester C (Free on 16/2/1984) FL 56+1/1 FLC 2 FAC 1 Others 3
Bury (Free on 15/7/1985) FL 45/5 FLC 4 FAC 8/1 Others 1
Stoke C (£40,000 on 18/7/1986) FL 71/5 FLC 6 FAC 7 Others 4
Arsenal (£400,000 on 29/1/1988) F/PL 436+9/25 FLC 45 FAC 50/1 Others 62/2

D'JAFFO Laurent
Born: Aquitane, France, 5 November 1970
Height: 6'0" Weight: 13.5
A calf injury delayed Laurent's start to his first full season with Sheffield United until October but thereafter he featured in most games, although rarely completing the full 90 minutes. Always giving 100 per cent effort he worked hard for the team as a target man and scored some valuable goals including one in the Sheffield 'derby' at Hillsborough before injury brought his campaign to a premature close.
Ayr U (Signed from Red Star Paris, France on 13/10/1997) SL 21+3/10 SC 2+1
Bury (Free on 28/7/1998) FL 35+2/8 FLC 4+1/1 FAC 1
Stockport Co (£100,000 on 13/8/1999) FL 20+1/7 FLC 2/1
Sheffield U (£100,000 + on 4/2/2000) FL 22+15/6 FAC 0+1

DJORDJIC Bojan
Born: Belgrade, Yugoslavia, 6 February 1982
Height: 5'10" Weight: 11.5
A promising young midfield player with an eye for goal Bojan made his Premiership debut for Manchester United in the final game of the 2000-01 season when he replaced Dennis Irwin with 15 minutes to go. He scored his first senior goal for the Reds in Tommy Boyd's testimonial game at Parkhead and will be looking forward to more first-team games in 2001-02. Bojan is the son of the former Red Star Belgrade and Yugoslavia player Branko Djordjic.
Manchester U (£1,000,000 from Bromma Pojkarna, Sweden on 18/2/1999) PL 0+1

DOANE Benjamin (Ben) Nigel David
Born: Sheffield, 22 December 1979
Height: 5'10" Weight: 12.0
Although a regular in Sheffield United's successful reserve side last season Ben had to wait until the last few matches of the season before he appeared in the first team. He impressed at right back in the game at Grimsby in April when his searching cross provided the opening for the winning goal and went on to play twice more. An adaptable defender with good positional sense he will be hoping to gain further senior experience in 2001-02.
Sheffield U (From trainee on 15/7/1998) FL 3+1 FLC 0+1

DOBIE Robert **Scott**
Born: Workington, 10 October 1978
Height: 6'1" Weight: 12.8
Scott had his best season to date for Carlisle United and his excellent form attracted interest from higher-level clubs on a number of occasions. He featured both on the right flank and in a more central role as a second striker alongside Ian Stevens during the campaign. A big powerful front man he uses his pace and height to good effect and notched several vital goals for the Cumbrians including the winners against Leyton Orient and Macclesfield in March.
Carlisle U (From trainee on 10/5/1997) FL 101+35/24 FLC 2+6 FAC 4+1/2 Others 6+1
Clydebank (Loaned on 3/11/1998) SL 6

DOBSON Michael William
Born: Isleworth, 9 April 1981
Height: 5'11" Weight: 12.4
Michael enjoyed a tremendous first season in senior football for Brentford in 2000-01. He made his debut from the subs' bench against Swansea last August but suffered a torn cartilage in the Worthington Cup tie at Tottenham the following month. He went on to become a first-team regular from December under Ray Lewington and appeared in the side that narrowly lost out to Port Vale in the LDV Vans Trophy final when he scored the Bees only goal of the match. Michael is a right wing back who can also play on the left side or in the centre of defence and possesses a fine long throw. He is the son of 1960s Brentford winger George Dobson.
Brentford (From trainee on 30/6/1999) FL 23+3 FLC 0+1 Others 7/3

DODD Ashley Michael
Born: Stafford, 7 January 1982
Height: 5'10" Weight: 10.2
International Honours: E: Sch
Ashley joined Port Vale on loan last March as cover for the log-jam of fixtures in the closing weeks of the season. He impressed at reserve level before stepping up to the first team for the final three games of the campaign. A clever midfield player he showed a cool head and looked comfortable on the ball. Released by United in the summer he was reported to have signed a 12-month contract for Vale.
Manchester U (From trainee on 9/9/1999)
Port Vale (Loaned on 22/3/2001) FL 3

DODD Jason Robert
Born: Bath, 2 November 1970
Height: 5'10" Weight: 12.3
International Honours: E: U21-8
Southampton's 'Mr Reliable' and an automatic choice for the right-back position, Jason captained the Saints in 2000-01 when he was once again a key figure in the defence. Not the fastest of defenders he more than makes up for this with his excellent reading of the game. He took over penalty-taking duties from the injured Matt LeTissier during the season with a certain amount of success. He received a well-deserved benefit match at the end of the campaign.
Southampton (£50,000 from Bath C on 15/3/1989) F/PL 301+20/9 FLC 36+2/1 FAC 29/3 Others 5

Gary Doherty

DOHERTY Gary Michael Thomas
Born: Carndonagh, 31 January 1980
Height: 6'2" Weight: 13.1
International Honours: RoI: 8; U21-7; Yth
This talented youngster broke through to earn a regular first-team place at Tottenham in the second half of last season. He quickly showed his goal-scoring potential, netting with a great header in the 4-2 win over Newcastle and following that with a late winner in the FA Cup third round tie at Leyton Orient. He seemed to favour the rough and tumble of the cup, because he also scored in the sixth round game against West Ham and in the semi-final defeat by

Arsenal. Gary is very versatile and is equally at home in defence or playing as a striker using his height to good effect at both ends of the pitch. He continued to represent the Republic of Ireland during the campaign winning a further three caps at U21 level and also featuring five times for the full squad.
Luton T (From trainee on 2/7/1997) FL 46+24/12 FLC 0+3/1 FAC 6+2/2 Others 1+1
Tottenham H (£1,000,000 on 22/4/2000) PL 18+6/3 FAC 5/3

DOHERTY Thomas (Tommy) Edward
Born: Bristol, 17 March 1979
Height: 5'8" Weight: 9.13
Tommy missed the first two months of last season with a knee injury but although he recovered fitness he only managed one first-team game for Bristol City during the campaign when he appeared in the LDV Vans Trophy tie at Plymouth. A combative midfield player he will be looking to put his injury problems behind him in 2001-02 and make a return to a regular place in the first team.
Bristol C (From trainee on 8/7/1997) FL 37+17/3 FLC 3+1/1 FAC 1+1 Others 1

DOIG Christopher (Chris) Ross
Born: Dumfries, 13 February 1981
Height: 6'2" Weight: 12.6
International Honours: S: U21-6; Yth; Sch
Chris featured regularly for Nottingham Forest at the beginning of last season before being sidelined by an ankle ligament injury in October. It was not until April that he returned to action with the first team but he began to establish a useful partnership with Jon Olav Hjelde in the heart of the defence in the closing stages of the campaign. A tall and commanding central defender he continued to appear for Scotland at U21 level winning three more caps during the season.
Queen of the South (Associated Schoolboy) SL 2+2
Nottingham F (From trainee on 7/3/1998) P/FL 23+5 FLC 3+1 FAC 1

DOLAN Joseph (Joe)
Born: Harrow, 27 May 1980
Height: 6'3" Weight: 12.12
Club Honours: Div 2 '01
International Honours: NI: U21-6; Yth
Joe was an ever-present for Millwall last season until suffering a broken leg against Bristol Rovers in February that put him out of action until the end of the campaign. He is a powerful central defender who has a great turn of speed and is very difficult to knock off the ball. Joe was a regular for Northern Ireland at U21 level before his injury, winning a further three caps.
Millwall (Free from Chelsea juniors on 15/4/1998) FL 45+1/3 FLC 5 FAC 3/1 Others 5

DOMI Didier
Born: Paris, France, 2 May 1978
Height: 5'10" Weight: 11.4
International Honours: France: U21; Yth
Although a broken rib, somehow incurred on an air flight, disrupted his pre-season training Didier appeared regularly for Newcastle in the first half of last season but in December he fell out of favour and soon afterwards he was sold to his former club Paris St Germain. A classy defender who can play either at left back or in a wing-back role he is composed on the ball with a good touch and the ability to deliver a telling cross.
Newcastle U (£3,250,000 + from Paris St Germain, France on 5/1/1999) PL 44+11/3 FLC 2+1 FAC 5+3/1 Others 4

DOMINGUEZ Jose Manuel Martins
Born: Lisbon, Portugal, 16 February 1974
Height: 5'3" Weight: 10.0
Club Honours: Div 2 '95; FLC '99
International Honours: Portugal: 3; U21; Yth
Jose was only on the fringes of the Tottenham first team last season and was restricted to just a handful of early season outings from the subs' bench. It was therefore no surprise when he was transferred to the Bundesliga club Kaiserslautern in November where he went on to feature in the team that reached the UEFA Cup semi-finals before going down to Deportivo Alaves. He is a quick and skilful winger who can also play up front.
Birmingham C (£180,000 from Benfica, Portugal on 9/3/1994) FL 15+20/3 FLC 1+2 FAC 2+1 Others 2+2/1 (£1,800,000 to Sporting Lisbon, Portugal on 1/8/1995)
Tottenham H (£1,600,000 on 12/8/1997) PL 12+33/4 FLC 2+6/1 FAC 2+1 Others 0+2

DONNELLY Paul Michael
Born: Stoke, 16 February 1981
Height: 5'7" Weight: 11.10
Paul appeared regularly for Port Vale reserves last season before stepping up to make the briefest of first-team appearances when he came on as a last minute substitute for Liam Burns in the penultimate away game at Oxford. A promising right-sided defender he will be hoping for more senior experience in the 2001-02 campaign.
Port Vale (From trainee on 1/7/1999) FL 4+1

DONNELLY Simon Thomas
Born: Glasgow, 1 December 1974
Height: 5'9" Weight: 11.0
Club Honours: SC '95; SPD '98
International Honours: S: 10; U21-11
Simon missed almost the whole of the 2000-01 campaign with persistent hamstring trouble but eventually returned to first-team action last April when he came off the subs' bench to score a cracking winner against Barnsley. He also appeared as a substitute in the last two games of the season and he will be hoping he has finally put his long-standing injury problems behind him. Simon can play as an attacking midfield player or as a striker and in the past has shown a good goals-per-game record.
Glasgow Celtic (From juniors on 27/5/1993) SL 113+33/30 SLC 11+6/4 SC 8+5/2 Others 13+7/6
Sheffield Wed (Free on 9/7/1999) P/FL 3+12/2 FLC 1+2 FAC 0+3

DONOVAN Kevin
Born: Halifax, 17 December 1971
Height: 5'8" Weight: 11.2
Club Honours: AMC '98
Kevin missed the early part of last season through injury, but returned to the squad at the end of September and quickly showed that he had returned to his best form. Whether playing in his favoured position wide on the right of midfield or in the hole behind a lone striker he produced some fine performances. He created numerous chances for his colleagues with his pace and ability to run at and beat opposition defenders and netted five valuable goals himself. He was reported to have signed for Barnsley during the summer.
Huddersfield T (From trainee on 11/10/1989) FL 11+9/1 FLC 1+1 FAC 1/2 Others 4
Halifax T (Loaned on 13/2/1992) FL 6
West Bromwich A (£70,000 on 1/10/1992) FL 139+29/19 FLC 9+2/6 FAC 7+1/3 Others 15+1/4
Grimsby T (£300,000 on 29/7/1997) FL 150+6/24 FLC 13+1/2 FAC 11/1 Others 9/3

DOOLAN John
Born: Liverpool, 7 May 1974
Height: 6'1" Weight: 13.0
John was once again a hugely influential figure for Barnet in the 2000-01 season. A tough-tackling central midfield player who also distributes the ball well, his value to the Bees was shown at the turn of the year when the team had a disastrous run of results while he was sidelined with an ankle injury. Any chances of the Underhill club reaching the play-offs rapidly disappeared and they never fully recovered resulting in their relegation from the Football League in May. He was placed on the open to offers list in the summer.
Everton (From trainee on 1/6/1992)
Mansfield T (Free on 2/9/1994) FL 128+3/10 FLC 8/1 FAC 7/2 Others 4+1/1
Barnet (£60,000 on 13/1/1998) FL 132+2/7 FLC 5+1/1 FAC 4 Others 5

Tony Dorigo

DORIGO Anthony (Tony) Robert
Born: Australia, 31 December 1965
Height: 5'9" Weight: 10.10
Club Honours: Div 2 '89, Div 1 '92; FMC '90; CS '92
International Honours: E: 15; B-7; U21-11
Stoke managed to secure Tony's services from under the noses of Wolves during the 2000 close season and although he some-

times struggled with the volume of matches he had a fine season at the Britannia Stadium and was appointed team captain in the autumn. An experienced left back his quality was an asset to City and he impressed with his excellent vision. Tony announced his retirement from football in the summer after playing in more then 500 Football League and Premiership games during the previous 18 years.
Aston Villa (From apprentice on 19/7/1983) FL 106+5/1 FLC 14+1 FAC 7 Others 2
Chelsea (£475,000 on 3/7/1987) FL 146/11 FLC 14 FAC 4 Others 16/1
Leeds U (£1,300,000 on 6/6/1991) F/PL 168+3/5 FLC 12+1 FAC 16 Others 9/1 (Free to Torino, Italy during 1997 close season)
Derby Co (Free on 23/10/1998) PL 37+4/1 FLC 4 FAC 4/2
Stoke C (Free on 14/7/2000) FL 34+2 FLC 3 FAC 1 Others 1

DORRIAN Christopher (Chris) Stewart
Born: Harlow, 3 April 1982
Height: 5'9" Weight: 10.0
A member of the Leyton Orient U19 team that was successful in the Youth Alliance Cup final against Bradford City, Chris made a promising Football League debut at Plymouth on the opening day of last season. He went on to feature in a handful of early-season games for the O's deputising when Matthew Joseph was injured or on international duty before stepping down. A talented young right back he will be hoping to gain further senior experience in 2001-02.
Leyton Orient (From trainee on 10/7/2000) FL 2 FLC 1

DOUGLAS Jonathan
Born: Monaghan, 22 November 1981
Height: 5'10" Weight: 12.12
International Honours: RoI: Yth
Previously capped by the Republic of Ireland at U16 and U18 levels, this slender lad made his senior debut for Blackburn Rovers in the Worthington Cup tie against West Ham at the end of October and also later featured in the FA Cup third round tie against Chester City. A promising young midfield player he appeared surprisingly at ease with his ability to spot the breaking striker and deliver a measured pass to him.
Blackburn Rov (From trainee on 10/2/2000) FLC 0+1 FAC 0+1

DOUGLAS Stuart Anthony
Born: Enfield, 9 April 1978
Height: 5'9" Weight: 11.5
Stuart was plagued by hamstring problems during the first half of the 2000-01 season and it was not until the new year that he featured regularly for Luton Town. A hard-working forward who is always willing to chase lost causes he was badly missed during his absence and made an immediate difference to the strike force on his return.
Luton T (From trainee on 2/5/1996) FL 102+35/18 FLC 11+2/3 FAC 8+2/2 Others 1+1

DOUGLIN Troy Alexander
Born: Coventry, 7 May 1982
Height: 6'0" Weight: 11.8
After breaking into the Torquay United first team early last season and playing five consecutive matches, this strong young centre back was invited up to Celtic for a trial which developed into a six month loan. He featured in the U18s and U21s and the Bhoys were sufficiently impressed to wish to keep him but were not prepared to pay the asking price. As a result Troy returned to Plainmoor to find his route to the first team blocked by Jimmy Aggrey and Lee Russell.
Torquay U (From trainee on 4/7/2000) FL 3 FLC 2

DOWIE Iain
Born: Hatfield, 9 January 1965
Height: 6'1" Weight: 13.11
International Honours: NI: 59; U23-1; U21-1
Iain was mainly employed as an assistant coach at Queens Park Rangers last season. He played on several occasions as a central defender in the reserves and made a single first-team appearance from the subs' bench against Bolton in February when injuries decimated the side of front line strikers. Iain, who holds a UEFA 'A' coaching badge, subsequently left the Loftus Road club shortly after the departure of manager Gerry Francis.
Luton T (£30,000 from Hendon on 14/12/1988) FL 53+13/16 FLC 3+1 FAC 1+2 Others 5/4
Fulham (Loaned on 13/9/1989) FL 5/1
West Ham U (£480,000 on 22/3/1991) FL 12/4
Southampton (£500,000 on 3/9/1991) F/PL 115+7/30 FLC 8+3/1 FAC 6/1 Others 4
Crystal Palace (£400,000 on 13/1/1995) P/FL 19/6 FAC 6/4
West Ham U (£500,000 on 8/9/1995) PL 58+10/8 FLC 10+1/2 FAC 3+1/1
Queens Park R (Signed on 30/1/1998) FL 16+15/2 FLC 0+1 FAC 0+2

DOWNER Simon
Born: Romford, 19 October 1981
Height: 5'11" Weight: 12.0
On the fringes of the Leyton Orient first team at the start of 2000-01, Simon went on to win a regular place in the starting line-up by the end of the season partnering Dean Smith in the centre of defence. A promising centre half he has an excellent turn of speed, a crisp tackle and never knows when he is beaten. His progress has already been tracked by a number of bigger clubs and he spent a week on trial at Newcastle during the campaign.
Leyton Orient (From trainee on 4/10/1999) FL 44+12 FLC 2+2 FAC 3+1 Others 5

DOWNEY Christopher (Chris) Anthony
Born: Warrington, 19 April 1983
Height: 5'10" Weight: 9.11
Chris made great progress at Bolton last term. Starting off as a second-year trainee with the U19s he moved up to the reserves and then made his senior debut when he came off the subs' bench for the last 25 minutes of the final game of the regular season against Sheffield United. Selected as the Academy team's 'Player of the Year' he is a pacy centre forward with bags of enthusiasm.
Bolton W (Trainee) FL 0+1

DOYLE Daire Michael
Born: Dublin, 18 October 1980
Height: 5'11" Weight: 11.12
After developing in Coventry's U19s Daire first arrived on trial at Kidderminster last September and impressed the Harriers management by scoring a hat-trick for the reserves. However it was not until January that a permanent move was agreed and he went on to make his Football League debut at Mansfield towards the end of the same month. He featured fairly regularly on the left side of midfield for the Aggborough club and was particularly effective in the local 'derby' match at Cheltenham in April.
Coventry C (Signed from Cherry Orchard on 15/9/1998)
Kidderminster Hrs (Free on 12/1/2001) FL 13+2

DOZZELL Jason Alvin Winans
Born: Ipswich, 9 December 1967
Height: 6'1" Weight: 13.8
Club Honours: Div 2 '92
International Honours: E: U21-9; Yth
Jason appeared regularly for Colchester United in the first half of last season but he suffered a toe injury towards the end of the year and following surgery he was sidelined until the summer break. A vastly experienced central midfield player he has excellent distribution and at his best can dictate the pace and flow of games. Jason was released on a free transfer in the summer.
Ipswich T (From apprentice on 20/12/1984) F/PL 312+20/52 FLC 29+1/3 FAC 22/12 Others 22/4
Tottenham H (£1,900,000 on 1/8/1993) PL 68+16/13 FLC 8+2 FAC 4+1/1
Ipswich T (Free on 2/10/1997) FL 8/1 FLC 2/1
Northampton T (Free on 19/12/1997) FL 18+3/4 FAC 1 Others 3
Colchester U (Free on 14/10/1998) FL 83+7/9 FLC 6/1 FAC 3 Others 2+1

DRAPER Mark Andrew
Born: Long Eaton, 11 November 1970
Height: 5'10" Weight: 12.4
Club Honours: FLC '96
International Honours: E: U21-3
Southampton's only cash signing during the close season, Mark came to The Dell in search of a new challenge having spent a large part of the 1999-2000 campaign exiled from the Premiership in Spain. An experienced campaigner, he took some time to settle on the south coast and his progress was hampered by a series of niggling injuries and some indifferent form. He made the starting line-up for the opening games but then found himself relegated to the subs' bench. Perhaps his best performance of the season came at Middlesbrough in February when he scored the winner with a cracking drive from the edge of the penalty area. An experienced midfield player who doesn't give the ball away easily, he links well between defence and attack.
Notts Co (From trainee on 12/12/1988) FL 206+16/40 FLC 14+1/2 FAC 10/2 Others 21+2/5
Leicester C (£1,250,000 on 22/7/1994) PL 39/5 FLC 2 FAC 2
Aston Villa (£3,250,000 on 5/7/1995) PL 108+12/7 FLC 11+1/2 FAC 10/2 Others 12+1
Southampton (£1,500,000 on 21/7/2000) PL 16+6/1 FLC 1 FAC 3+1

DREYER John Brian
Born: Alnwick, 11 June 1963
Height: 6'1" Weight: 13.2

This vastly experienced defender joined Cambridge United during the 2000 close season to help bolster a young defence. He proved a tower of strength in the early part of the campaign forming an excellent partnership with Andy Duncan and retaining a regular place in the line-up until the last couple of months of the season. John is a versatile and hard-working player who can appear in the centre of defence, at full back and in midfield. He was placed on the transfer list in May.
Oxford U (Signed from Wallingford on 8/1/1985) FL 57+3/2 FLC 10+1 FAC 2 Others 3
Torquay U (Loaned on 13/12/1985) FL 5
Fulham (Loaned on 27/3/1988) FL 12/2
Luton T (£140,000 on 27/6/1988) FL 212+2/13 FLC 13+1/1 FAC 14 Others 8/1
Stoke C (Free on 15/7/1994) FL32+17/3 FLC 5 FAC 1 Others 4+1/1
Bolton W (Loaned on 23/3/1995) FL 1+1 Others 1+1
Bradford C (£25,000 on 6/11/1996) P/FL 72+8/2 FLC 8+2 FAC 3/3
Cambridge U (Free on 18/7/2000) FL 40 FLC 2 FAC 1 Others 1/1

DRURY Adam James
Born: Cambridge, 29 August 1978
Height: 5'10" Weight: 11.8
Adam featured regularly for Peterborough United last term until being sold to Norwich City for a substantial fee shortly before the transfer deadline. A promising defender he had once been on the Canaries' books as a schoolboy but this time he went straight in the first team, making his debut against Grimsby Town. For one so young, he has already gained a wealth of experience playing mainly at left back, but also in the centre of defence for Posh. A good tackler, he is very quick and enjoys getting forward when the opportunity arises. Next season will be the true test of Adam's capabilities as he settles in to football at a higher level.
Peterborough U (From trainee on 3/7/1996) FL 138+10/2 FLC 8 FAC 9 Others 10+1
Norwich C (£275,000 on 21/3/2001) FL 6

Dion Dublin

DRYDEN Richard Andrew
Born: Stroud, 14 June 1969
Height: 6'0" Weight: 13.12
Club Honours: Div 4 '90
This experienced Southampton central defender spent two months on loan at Second Division Northampton last autumn. The Cobblers kept a clean sheet in his first three games but he then missed several matches through injury and eventually returned to The Dell before going out on loan again, this time to Swindon. Although he got off to an unfortunate start by heading an own goal in the opening minutes of his debut, he was effective in shoring up a leaky defence before moving on to assist relegation-threatened Luton on a short-term contract in February. Brought in to replace Adrian Whitbread when he returned to Portsmouth, Richard added some much needed stability to the back line but was unable to prevent the club dropping into the Third Division. A commanding left-sided central defender he is effective in the tackle and has good distribution.
Bristol Rov (From trainee on 14/7/1987) FL 12+1 FLC 2+1 FAC 0+2 Others 2
Exeter C (Loaned on 22/9/1988) FL 6
Exeter C (£10,000 on 8/3/1989) FL 86/13 FLC 7/2 FAC 2 Others 4
Notts Co (£250,000 on 9/8/1991) FL 30+1/1 FLC 1+1 FAC 2+1 Others 2
Plymouth Arg (Loaned on 18/11/1992) FL 5 Others 1
Birmingham C (£165,000 on 19/3/1993) FL 48 FLC 5 FAC 1
Bristol C (£140,000 on 16/12/1994) FL 32+5/2 FLC 4 FAC 1+1 Others 2
Southampton (£150,000 on 6/8/1996) PL 44+3/1 FLC 7/3
Stoke C (Loaned on 3/11/1999) FL 3
Stoke C (Loaned on 23/3/2000) FL 8+2 Others 1+1
Northampton T (Loaned on 8/9/2000) FL 9+1
Swindon T (Loaned on 24/11/2000) FL 7 FAC 1
Luton T (Free on 2/2/2001) FL 20

DRYSDALE Leon Anthony
Born: Walsall, 3 February 1981
Height: 5'9" Weight: 11.6
Leon is one of several youngsters developing in the wings at Shrewsbury. Introduced to the first team in short spells he gave some committed performances and looks to have a good future in the game. He is a strong tackling right-sided defender who likes to push forward although he is still seeking his first goal in Third Division football.
Shrewsbury T (From trainee on 2/7/1999) FL 18+2 FLC 0+1

DUBERRY Michael Wayne
Born: Enfield, 14 October 1975
Height: 6'1" Weight: 13.6
Club Honours: FLC '98; ECWC '98; ESC '98
International Honours: E: U21-5
After limited appearances for Leeds United in the 1999-2000 campaign Michael began last season in the first-team picture, and with all the team's injury problems he found himself playing right from the off. His height and strength made him a formidable opponent and he began to show his real form, especially in the 1-0 home defeat of AC Milan. Unfortunately in the very next game at Derby he fell awkwardly on the stroke of half-time injuring his achilles

tendon, which caused him to miss the remainder of the campaign. Michael also had to contend with some much publicised off the field problems but hopefully with these now behind him he will return to a regular place in the first-team squad in 2001-02.

Chelsea (From trainee on 7/6/1993) PL 77+9/1 FLC 8 FAC 12/2 Others 9
Bournemouth (Loaned on 29/9/1995) FL 7 Others 1
Leeds U (£4,000,000 + on 29/7/1999) PL 17+1/1 FLC 0+1 FAC 1 Others 5

DUBLIN Dion
Born: Leicester, 22 April 1969
Height: 6'1" Weight: 12.4
Club Honours: Div 3 '91
International Honours: E: 4

Dion struggled to recapture his best form for Aston Villa in the 2000-01 campaign and by his own high standards suffered something of a barren time. Nevertheless he remained a regular in the first team and actually finished the season as the club's leading scorer with nine goals in all competitions. He is a strong and determined centre forward who is very effective in the air and is able to play in a central defensive role if required.

Norwich C (Free from Oakham U on 24/3/1988)
Cambridge U (Free on 2/8/1988) FL 133+23/52 FLC 8+2/5 FAC 21/11 Others 14+1/5
Manchester U (£1,000,000 on 7/8/1992) PL 4+8/2 FLC 1+1/1 FAC 1+1 Others 0+1
Coventry C (£2,000,000 on 9/9/1994) PL 144+1/61 FLC 11+2/4 FAC 13/7
Aston Villa (£5,750,000 on 6/11/1998) PL 76+7/31 FLC 5/3 FAC 4+2/1 Others 3/1

DUCROS Andrew (Andy) John
Born: Evesham, 16 September 1977
Height: 5'4" Weight: 10.6
International Honours: E: Sch

Andy joined Kidderminster for a club record fee in July 2000 and did well in the early part of last season, using his tricky ball skills to baffle opposition defences. However he struggled with injuries in the second half of the campaign and was often restricted to appearances from the subs' bench. He is essentially an attacking midfield player who is best used in a free role behind the main strikers. He is due to undergo a knee operation over the summer break and should return to full fitness for the start of the 2001-02 season.

Coventry C (From trainee on 16/9/1994) PL 2+6 FLC 0+1(Free to Nuneaton Borough on 6/8/99)
Kidderminster Hrs (£100,000 on 24/7/2000) FL 29+5/2 FLC 1 FAC 3

DUDFIELD Lawrence (Lawrie) George
Born: Southwark, 7 May 1980
Height: 6'1" Weight: 13.9

This young Leicester City prospect was loaned to Lincoln last September where he showed much promise. His pace and direct running at defenders caused problems for opposing teams but he was given only two first-team starts and returned early to Filbert Street. Lawrie then joined Chesterfield on loan in December where he made a fine impact creating several goals for others and scoring three himself, including the winner against Blackpool in February just two minutes after coming on as a substitute. He is a tall left-sided striker who brings pace and width to the attack. He was reported to have signed for Hull City in the summer.

Leicester C (Signed from Kettering T on 6/6/1997) PL 0+2
Lincoln C (Loaned on 15/9/2000) FL 2+1
Chesterfield (Loaned on 14/12/2000) FL 4+10/3 Others 3+1/1

DUDGEON James Fleming
Born: Newcastle, 19 March 1981
Height: 6'2" Weight: 12.4
International Honours: S: Yth

James gained his first experience of senior football during a long-term loan spell at Lincoln City last season. Apart from a period of suspension after receiving two red cards he was a first-team regular for the Imps playing as a right-sided central defender. Strong in the air and effective as a man-marker, he also provided a number of goals, with his late winner against Plymouth Argyle in April giving Lincoln the three points they needed to ensure survival in the Football League.

Barnsley (From trainee on 19/7/1999)
Lincoln C (Loaned on 22/11/2000) FL 20+2/3 Others 3

DUDLEY Craig Bryan
Born: Ollerton, 12 September 1979
Height: 5'10" Weight: 11.2
Club Honours: Div 3 '98
International Honours: E: Yth

Craig had a frustrating time at Oldham in the 2000-01 campaign after starting off with realistic claims to a regular place in the starting line-up. However, faced with increased competition, he found opportunities limited and although he hit a purple patch in October with three goals in two games he was dogged by injuries and illness. A skilful and pacy right-sided striker he signed a new long-term deal in January.

Notts Co (From trainee on 2/4/1997) FL 11+20/3 FLC 1+2/1 FAC 1+2
Shrewsbury T (Loaned on 8/1/1998) FL 3+1
Hull C (Loaned on 10/11/1998) FL 4+3/2
Oldham Ath (Free on 25/3/1999) FL 28+23/9 FLC 2 FAC 5+1/3
Chesterfield (Loaned on 20/8/1999) FL 0+2

DUFF Damien Anthony
Born: Dublin, Ireland, 2 March 1979
Height: 5'10" Weight: 9.7
International Honours: RoI: 20; B-1; Yth; Sch

Damien was a regular in the starting line-up for Blackburn Rovers last term although he was hampered by two spells of hamstring trouble. The team always seemed to have a better balance when he was taking men on down the left wing, while his defensive qualities improved during the season to such an extent that he was able to play at wing back when required. He netted just once during the campaign but it was worth waiting for - a brilliant solo effort at Birmingham that clinched victory in a vital game. He was honoured by his fellow professionals with a place in the PFA's First Division team.

Blackburn Rov (Signed from Lourdes Celtic on 5/3/1996) P/FL 100+26/11 FLC 9+1/3 FAC 12+4/2 Others 1

DUFF Michael James
Born: Belfast, 11 January 1978
Height: 6'1" Weight: 11.8
Club Honours: FAT '98; NC '99

Michael was used by Cheltenham at right back or on the right-hand side of midfield last season. Tall, strong and with excellent crossing ability his height proved an asset in both attack and defence. He netted a number of important goals when coming up for set pieces including a brace of headers in the 2-1 win over Lincoln in April.

Cheltenham T (From trainee on 17/8/1996) FL 70/7 FLC 2 FAC 4 Others 2

DUFFIELD Peter
Born: Middlesbrough, 4 February 1969
Height: 5'6" Weight: 10.4

Peter began the 2000-01 campaign in great form for York City scoring three goals in the opening seven games but then had the great misfortune to suffer a double fracture of his right leg in the home game against Scunthorpe in September. After a long convalescence he battled back to fitness and will be looking to return to the Minstermen's line-up in the 2001-02 season. He is a busy striker who can hold the play up and link well with his colleagues.

Middlesbrough (From apprentice on 4/11/1986)
Sheffield U (Free on 20/8/1987) FL 34+24/14 FLC 3+5/2 FAC 6+2/1 Others 3+2/3
Halifax T (Loaned on 7/3/1988) FL 12/6 Others 1
Rotherham U (Loaned on 7/3/1991) FL 17/4
Blackpool (Loaned on 23/7/1992) FL 3+2/1 FLC 0+1
Crewe Alex (Loaned on 15/1/1993) FL 0+2 FAC 0+1
Stockport Co (Loaned on 19/3/1993) FL 6+1/4 Others 2+1
Hamilton Ac (Signed on 24/9/1993) SL 69+3/39 SLC 2/1 SC 2 Others 3/3
Airdrie (Signed on 21/7/1995) SL 19+5/6 SLC 2+2/2 SC 3/3 Others 1
Raith Rov (Signed on 2/3/1996) SL 37+14/11 SLC 2+1/3 SC 2 Others 1+1
Morton (Signed on 8/11/1997) SL 25/9 SLC 1 SC 1
Falkirk (Signed on 27/8/1998) SL 10+7/3
Darlington (Signed on 15/1/1999) FL 31+16/14 FLC 0+2 FAC 2/1 Others 3
York C (Free on 3/7/2000) FL 6/3 FLC 1

DUGUID Karl Anthony
Born: Letchworth, 21 March 1978
Height: 5'11" Weight: 11.7

Karl never quite managed to repeat his excellent form of the previous season in 2000-01 although he continued to feature regularly in the Colchester United first team. He again showed his versatility by appearing as both a right wing back and a striker, although when played up front he found goals hard to come by and endured a long lean spell before returning to form in the closing matches. One of the few players to have successfully emerged from the U's youth team in recent years his lightning pace makes him ideal for a number of positions.

Colchester U (From trainee on 16/7/1996) FL 120+52/28 FLC 5+3 FAC 5+3/1 Others 2+5

DUKE David
Born: Inverness, 7 November 1978
Height: 5'10" Weight: 11.3

After joining Swindon Town during the 2000 close season David made his Football League debut in the opening game against Colchester and went on to become a regular member of the first-team squad until he suffered an injury to his left knee at the beginning of March. He is a neat left-sided player with a useful long throw who featured both at full back and in a wide midfield role.

Sunderland (Free from Redby CA on 3/7/1997)
Swindon T (Free on 10/8/2000) FL 24+8/1 FLC 4 FAC 1+2 Others 3

DUNBAVIN Ian Stuart
Born: Huyton, 27 May 1980
Height: 6'2" Weight: 13.0

In only his second season of senior football Ian showed much more confidence for Shrewsbury Town in 2000-01 and shared goalkeeping duties with the veteran Paul Edwards. Very quick off his line and with a powerful kick he will be looking to take over as first choice in the coming season now that Edwards has been released.

Liverpool (From trainee on 26/11/1998)
Shrewsbury T (Free on 17/1/2000) FL 26+3 FLC 2 FAC 1

DUNCAN Andrew (Andy)
Born: Hexham, 20 October 1977
Height: 5'11" Weight: 13.0
International Honours: E: Sch

Having missed most of the 1999-2000 campaign with a broken leg Andy returned to first-team action with Cambridge United last term and forged an excellent partnership with new signing John Dreyer in the back line during the first half of the season. He went on to become a near ever-present for the U's scoring his only goal with a last-minute header to earn a point at Brentford. Andy is a cultured defender whose confidence and strength are assets to the United defence.

Manchester U (From trainee on 10/7/1996)
Cambridge U (£20,000 on 9/1/1998) FL 115+1/3 FLC 9 FAC 4 Others 5

DUNFIELD Terence (Terry)
Born: Canada, 20 February 1982
Height: 5'7" Weight: 10.6
International Honours: E: Yth; Canada: Yth

Having made just a handful of appearances for the reserve team in 1999-2000, Terry made considerable progress and stepped up to make his Premiership debut for Manchester City in the final game of the 2000-01 season against Chelsea. He came off the subs' bench to replace the injured Jeff Whitley after just 32 minutes and gave a solid no-frills, performance, not looking at all out of his depth. Terry also played in the Manchester Senior Cup final at Old Trafford against neighbours United, scoring the fourth and best goal of the night. A talented young defender he was capped by England at U16 level when he appeared in a friendly against Turkey back in 1999 but has since opted to play for Canada and captained the team in the World U20 Youth Championship finals in Argentina during the summer.

Manchester C (From trainee on 5/5/1999) PL 0+1

DUNN David John Ian
Born: Blackburn, 27 December 1979
Height: 5'10" Weight: 12.3
International Honours: E: U21-10; Yth

David came of age for Blackburn Rovers last term and firmly established himself as a regular in the first-team line-up. He netted a remarkable hat-trick of penalties in the 6-1 Worthington Cup victory over Rochdale and impressed with a willingness to take on opponents and some fine dribbling skills in the last third of the field. Never reluctant to shoot from long-range he showed a capacity to battle away in midfield as well as sparkle in the opposition penalty area. David was also a regular for England at U21 level, often captaining the side. He was honoured by his fellow professionals when he was voted in to the PFA's First Division team.

Blackburn Rov (From trainee on 30/9/1997) P/FL 68+11/15 FLC 7+3/5 FAC 7+2/2

David Dunn

DUNN Mark Anthony
Born: Newport, Gwent, 18 September 1982
Height: 5'8" Weight: 11.3

Mark is another of the promising youngsters to develop through Notts County's youth system and although still on a scholars' contract he stepped up to make his senior debut in the LDV Vans Trophy tie at Port Vale last January. A talented young defender he will be hoping to gain further first-team experience in 2001-02.

Notts Co (Trainee) Others 1

DUNNE Joseph (Joe) John
Born: Dublin, 25 May 1973
Height: 5'9" Weight: 11.6
International Honours: RoI: U21-1; Yth; Sch

Joe was Colchester United's 'Mr Reliable' in 2000-01 once again producing a series of gutsy displays throughout the campaign. He suffered a serious gash to his face at Luton in November, but although the wound required more than 30 stitches he was back in action in a matter of weeks. A committed right wing back he scored just one goal during the season, netting with a great header to earn the U's a vital 1-0 win at Oxford in January.

Gillingham (From trainee on 9/8/1990) FL 108+7/1 FLC 7 FAC 5+1 Others 4+2
Colchester U (Free on 27/3/1996) FL 79+22/3 FLC 3+1/1 FAC 5+1 Others 7+1 (Free to Dover Ath during 1999 close season)
Colchester U (Free on 14/12/1999) FL 50+4/1 FLC 3 FAC 0+1 Others 1

DUNNE Richard Patrick
Born: Dublin, 21 September 1979
Height: 6'1" Weight: 14.0
Club Honours: FAYC '98
International Honours: RoI: 10; B-1; U21-4; Yth; (UEFA-U18 '98); Sch

Richard made only four first-team appearances for Everton last term before making the short trip down the East Lancs Road to sign for his old boss Joe Royle at Manchester City in October. He made his debut at full back in the away game at Southampton before going on to establish himself in the centre of the defence. He formed a solid partnership with Steve Howey in middle of the back line and with a little more protection from City's midfield, might have given the team a better chance of survival at the top level. Very quick for a big man and particularly effective in the air, he was a regular member of the Republic of Ireland squad winning seven more caps.

Everton (From trainee on 8/10/1996) PL 53+7 FLC 4 FAC 8
Manchester C (£3,000,000 on 20/10/2000) PL 24+1 FAC 3

DUNNING Darren
Born: Scarborough, 8 January 1981
Height: 5'6" Weight: 11.12

Darren joined Bristol City on loan in the early part of last season to gain some experience of first-team football and proved an immediate hit with the club's supporters. He added much-needed steel in the centre of the park in his brief spell at Ashton Gate before returning to Lancashire to continue his development in the reserves. He went on to make his debut for Blackburn in the Worthington Cup tie against West Ham and later also featured in the FA Cup game against Chester and an end-of-season match with Gillingham. The captain of Rovers' reserve team he is a versatile midfield player who is more comfortable in a central role rather than in a position wide on the left.

Blackburn Rov (From trainee on 25/2/1999) FL 1 FLC 1 FAC 1
Bristol C (Loaned on 12/8/2000) FL 9

DURKAN Keiron John
Born: Chester, 1 December 1973
Height: 5'11" Weight: 12.10
Club Honours: WC '95
International Honours: RoI: U21-3

Having concluded the 1999-2000 season in fine form it was rather surprising that the Macclesfield right winger got off to a slow start in the 2000-2001 campaign and spent the month of October on loan at York where he impressed with his direct style of play before returning to the Moss Rose club. However his season changed dramatically at the beginning of January when he was reinstated on the right wing. He provided Macc with some much-needed width on the flank, tackling well and beating defenders to deliver quality pin-point crosses. He also began scoring again, notably two goals from superbly taken free kicks in the home win against Barnet.

Wrexham (From trainee on 16/7/1992) FL 43+7/3 FLC 3+1 FAC 4+2/2 Others 15/1
Stockport Co (£95,000 on 16/2/1996) FL 52+12/4 FLC 10+1 FAC 4/3 Others 4+2
Macclesfield T (£15,000 on 25/3/1998) FL 92+11/13 FLC 4+3 FAC 2+3 Others 1+1
York C (Loaned on 5/10/2000) FL 7

DURNIN John Paul
Born: Bootle, 18 August 1965
Height: 5'10" Weight: 12.3

Out of contract in the summer of 2000, John spent time training with Tranmere Rovers to keep in shape before linking up with Football League new boys Kidderminster in October. He added much-needed experience to the squad and quickly settled in, scoring from close range on his debut at Lincoln and then adding two more the following Tuesday in the 2-1 win at Darlington. He went on to score in three consecutive games over the new year and finished the season as the Harriers' joint-leading scorer. A vastly experienced striker who has scored regularly throughout his career he was released in May.

Liverpool (Free from Waterloo Dock on 29/3/1986) FLC 1+1
West Bromwich A (Loaned on 20/10/1988) FL 5/2
Oxford U (£225,000 on 10/2/1989) FL 140+21/44 FLC 7/1 FAC 7/1 Others 4+1/1
Portsmouth (£200,000 on 15/7/1993) FL 118+63/31 FLC 14+3/2 FAC 5+2 Others 4+2
Blackpool (Loaned on 1/11/1999) FL 4+1/1 FAC 1/1
Carlisle U (Free on 3/12/1999) FL 20+2/2 Others 1
Kidderminster Hrs (Free on 13/10/2000) FL 28+3/9 FAC 1

DUXBURY Lee Edward
Born: Keighley, 7 October 1969
Height: 5'10" Weight: 11.13

The Oldham skipper had another honourable campaign at Boundary Park in 2000-01. A workaholic in the centre of midfield he had his best season yet for the club in front of goal, managing to get into double figures despite operating in a relatively withdrawn role. A virtual ever-present in the side apart from a short absence with a hamstring injury in December Lee continued to add steel, tenacity and guile to the Latics' midfield, working in tandem with veteran John Sheridan.

Bradford C (From trainee on 4/7/1988) FL 204+5/25 FLC 18+1/3 FAC 11 Others 13
Rochdale (Loaned on 18/1/1990) FL 9+1 FAC 1
Huddersfield T (£250,000 on 23/12/1994) FL 29/2 FLC 1 Others 3
Bradford C (£135,000 on 15/11/1995) FL 63/7 FLC 2 FAC 5 Others 3
Oldham Ath (£350,000 on 7/3/1997) FL 172+2/24 FLC 9/1 FAC 12/3 Others 3

DYCHE Sean Mark
Born: Kettering, 28 June 1971
Height: 6'0" Weight: 13.10
Club Honours: Div 2 '01

Having been plagued by injuries in the previous season Sean was again sidelined at the start of the 2000-01 campaign but recovered to feature regularly for Second Division champions Millwall, sharing responsibilities in the centre of defence with Stuart Nethercott and Joe Dolan. He is an effective defender who is good in the air, strong in the tackle and reads the game well.

Nottingham F (From trainee on 20/5/1989)
Chesterfield (Free on 1/2/1990) FL 219+12/8 FLC 9 FAC 13/1 Others 16
Bristol C (£350,000 on 11/7/1997) FL 14+3 FLC 2+1
Luton T (Loaned on 4/1/1999) FL 14/1 Others 1
Millwall (£150,000 on 5/7/1999) FL 34 FLC 0+1 FAC 2

DYER Alexander (Alex) Constantine
Born: Forest Gate, 14 November 1965
Height: 6'0" Weight: 12.0

This experienced left-footed player made a number of appearances for Notts County early on last season but found himself surplus to requirements and moved on to Kingstonian at the end of November. He stayed there only briefly however and at the beginning of the new year he signed for another Conference club Hayes. A loyal servant of the Magpies in recent seasons he can perform either in defence or midfield.

Blackpool (From apprentice at Watford on 20/10/1983) FL 101+7/19 FLC 8+1/1 FAC 4+1 Others 7/1
Hull C (£37,000 on 13/2/1987) FL 59+1/14 FLC 2 FAC 4/1
Crystal Palace (£250,000 on 11/11/1988) FL 16+1/2 FLC 3+1 FAC 1+1 Others 3+1/3
Charlton Ath (£100,000 on 30/11/1990) FL 60+18/13 FLC 2+1 FAC 1/1 Others 3+1
Oxford U (Free on 26/7/1993) FL 62+14/6 FLC 4/1 FAC 5/1 Others 5
Lincoln C (Free on 21/8/1995) FL 1 FLC 1
Barnet (Free on 1/9/1995) FL 30+5/2 Others 1 (Freed on 9/5/1996)
Huddersfield T (Signed from FC Maia, Portugal on 13/8/1997) FL 8+4/1 FLC 3/1
Notts Co (Free on 2/3/1998) FL 58+20/6 FLC 3+2 FAC 5+1 Others 0+1

DYER Bruce Antonio
Born: Ilford, 13 April 1975
Height: 6'0" Weight: 11.3
International Honours: E: U21-11

Bruce found his opportunities somewhat limited at Barnsley early last season and went on the transfer list at the beginning of September. However he maintained that he didn't want to leave Oakwell and was soon back in the team. He subsequently hit a purple patch of scoring following a change in management to finish as the Tykes' leading scorer with 16 goals in all competitions. At best he is a powerful striker who has the physique to put any defender under pressure. He showed that he still has an eye for goal and is extemely dangerous when attacking down the right-hand side. Bruce eventually agreed a new two-year deal that will keep him at Oakwell until the summer of 2003.

Watford (From trainee on 19/4/1993) FL 29+2/6 FLC 4/2 FAC 1 Others 2/1
Crystal Palace (£1,100,000 on 10/3/1994) F/PL 95+40/37 FLC 9+5/1 FAC 7+3/6 Others 3+2
Barnsley (£700,000 on 23/10/1998) FL 68+30/28 FLC 7+1/1 FAC 2+2/1 Others 2+1/3

DYER Keiron Courtney
Born: Ipswich, 29 December 1978
Height: 5'7" Weight: 9.7
International Honours: E: 8; B-2; U21-11; Yth

Kieron was again a key figure in the Newcastle United team in 2000-01 and although primarily a midfield player his talents and versatility enable him to play almost anywhere. He spent much of the season covering for injuries as a makeshift striker but wherever he appeared he always tried his best. Early in the new year he began to suffer with pains in his shin and the problem was eventually diagnosed as being a stress fracture, corrective surgery was required and he was sidelined for the remainder of the campaign. Quick and lively, he has good ball control and is seen at his most exciting when running at opposition defences at pace, driving into the box to threaten the goal.

Ipswich T (From trainee on 3/1/1997) FL 79+12/9 FLC 11/1 FAC 5 Others 5+1/2
Newcastle U (£6,000,000 on 16/7/1999) PL 52+8/8 FLC 4/1 FAC 6+1/1 Others 3

Keiron Dyer

DYSON Jonathan (Jon) Paul
Born: Mirfield, 18 December 1971
Height: 6'1" Weight: 12.12

Jon completed his 200th league appearance for Huddersfield Town last term and was awarded a testimonial year in recognition of his long service with the Terriers. A versatile defender he enjoyed a regular partnership alongside Chris Lucketti in the heart of the defence at a time when the team looked to be pulling away from the relegation zone. An assured approach to the game, some strong tackling and good distribution skills made him an important member of the squad. Always capable of scoring at set pieces, he netted twice during the season.

Huddersfield T (From juniors on 29/12/1990) FL 182+31/9 FLC 17+4 FAC 10 Others 7+4

The Royal Bank
of Scotland

EADEN Nicholas (Nicky) Jeremy
Born: Sheffield, 12 December 1972
Height: 5'9" Weight: 12.8

Nicky was a near ever-present for Birmingham City last season featuring mainly on the right wing in place of the injured Jon McCarthy. Dependable and consistent throughout the campaign he was very much an unsung hero for the Blues. He impressed with some clever use of the ball and determined tackling and made the starting line-up for the Worthington Cup final against Liverpool when City lost out so narrowly in a penalty shoot-out.

Barnsley (From juniors on 4/6/1991) F/PL 281+12/10 FLC 18+3/3 FAC 20 Others 4+1
Birmingham C (Free on 6/7/2000) FL 44+1/2 FLC 10/1 FAC 1 Others 1+1/1

Nicky Eaden

EADIE Darren Malcolm
Born: Chippenham, 10 June 1975
Height: 5'8" Weight: 11.6
International Honours: E: U21-7; Yth

Darren featured regularly for Leicester City in the early part of last season but his run in the team was halted by a back injury in October. On his return to fitness he struggled to establish a regular place in the squad, although he was not helped by a knee problem that required surgery in mid-season. He scored for the Foxes at West Ham to clinch City's first victory at Upton Park for over 30 years. A striker or left-sided midfield player, his electrifying pace and direct style can unsettle even the best defenders.

Norwich C (From trainee on 5/2/1993) P/FL 153+15/35 FLC 25+1/2 FAC 7+1/1 Others 1+1
Leicester C (£3,000,000 on 10/12/1999) PL 31+9/2 FLC 1 FAC 3+1 Others 2

EARNSHAW Robert
Born: Zambia, 6 April 1981
Height: 5'8" Weight: 10.10
International Honours: W: U21-10; Yth

Having previously been something of a fringe player for Cardiff City, Robert firmly established himself in the team last season and finished as the club's leading scorer with a total of 25 goals. He netted a hat-trick in the FA Cup tie against Bristol Rovers and another in the Third Division game with Torquay during a particularly hot phase when he scored ten goals in a run of seven games. A quick and exciting striker he celebrates every goal with an elaborate routine featuring a somersault. Robert won three more caps for Wales at U21 level, was voted the Bluebirds' 'Young Player of the Year' for the third time in a row and was also selected for the PFA's Third Division team.

Cardiff C (From trainee on 4/8/1998) FL 26+26/21 FLC 0+2 FAC 4+1/6 Others 0+1
Greenock Morton (Loaned on 20/1/2000) SL 3/2 SC 1

EASTER Jermaine Maurice
Born: Cardiff, 15 January 1982
Height: 5'8" Weight: 12.4
International Honours: W: Yth

This promising youngster was unable to make a breakthrough at Wolves and after being released in March he joined Third Division Hartlepool whose manager Chris Turner had previously been youth coach at Molineux. A striker who has a good goal-scoring record in junior football, he was given an early promotion to the first-team squad by being named as a substitute in the end-of-season games but got little chance to prove himself. Earlier in the campaign Jermaine won two further caps for Wales at U18 level when he captained the side in their UEFA tournament qualifying games.

Wolverhampton W (From trainee on 6/7/2000)
Hartlepool U (Free on 17/3/2001) FL 0+4 Others 0+2

EASTON Clint Jude
Born: Barking, 1 October 1977
Height: 5'11' Weight: 10.8
Club Honours: Div 2 '98
International Honours: E: Yth

Having shown considerable promise during the 1999-2000 campaign Clint must have been a little disappointed at his inability to pin down a regular first-team place for Watford last term. When selected he caught the eye with his assertive play and willingness to take responsibility and manager Graham Taylor was supportive, commending his patience and commitment. A left-sided midfield player, he turned down the opportunity of a transfer to Luton to stay and press his claims for the Hornets but was reported to have signed for Norwich City during the close season.

Watford (From trainee on 5/7/1996) P/FL 50+14/1 FLC 4+4/1 FAC 3+1 Others 3

EATON Adam Paul
Born: Wigan, 2 May 1980
Height: 5'11" Weight: 11.2
Club Honours: FAYC '98

Adam continued to develop at Preston last term and made an impressive full debut at left back in the FA Cup third round tie against Stockport. The consistent form of Rob Edwards restricted his further involvement, although he also made the line-up in the final game of the regular season against West Bromwich Albion. A young left-sided player his pace, strong tackling and positional play in both defence and wide midfield indicate he has considerable potential.

Everton (From trainee on 2/6/1997)
Preston NE (Free on 29/6/1999) FL 1 FAC 1 Others 0+1

EBDON Marcus
Born: Pontypool, 17 October 1970
Height: 5'10" Weight: 12.4
International Honours: W: U21-2; Yth

Marcus was the safecracker in Chesterfield's midfield last season. Whereas some try to blow opposing defences open with a big boot, he prefers the locksmith's art, picking teams apart with precision passes. With others around him to do the fetching and carrying, Marcus concentrated on creativity last term, and the Spireites' few off games mostly occurred in his absence. Marcus is a free-kick specialist and scored a 40-yarder in the 2-0 win over Exeter in December.

Everton (From trainee on 16/8/1989)
Peterborough U (Free on 15/7/1991) FL 136+11/15 FLC 14+2 FAC 12+3/1 Others 11+1
Chesterfield (£100,000 on 21/3/1997) FL 130+7/7 FLC 10+1/1 FAC 6 Others 5/3

ECKHARDT Jeffrey (Jeff) Edward
Born: Sheffield, 7 October 1965
Height: 6'0" Weight: 11.7

This strong and whole-hearted defender did not figure regularly for Cardiff City in 2000-01 but still did an effective job when required. A consistent and versatile defender who never gives less than 100 per cent in any game that he plays, he is a qualified chiropodist and plans to follow that career when he retires from the game.

Sheffield U (From juniors on 23/8/1984) FL 73+1/2 FLC 7 FAC 2 Others 5
Fulham (£50,000 on 20/11/1987) FL 245+4/25 FLC 13 FAC 5+1 Others 15/3
Stockport Co (£50,000 on 21/7/1994) FL 56+6/7 FLC 6+2/1 FAC 5/4 Others 2
Cardiff C (£30,000 on 22/8/1996) FL 129+11/14 FLC 5+2/1 FAC 11+1/1 Others 5/1

EDDS Gareth James
Born: Sydney, Australia, 3 February 1981
Height: 5'11" Weight: 10.12
International Honours: Australia: Yth

This young full back broke through to feature a number of times for Nottingham Forest in the second half of last season, scoring his first-ever senior goal in the 3-1 win over Grimsby. Gareth is a promising youngster who is strong in the tackle, shows great awareness with his passing and possesses a fierce shot. He will be looking to win a regular first-team slot at the City Ground in the coming season. He was called up for the Australia U20 team in the summer and appeared for them in both the East Asian Games and World Youth Championship tournaments.

Nottingham F (From trainee on 19/2/1998) FL 11+4/1 FAC 1

EDGE Roland
Born: Gillingham, 25 November 1978
Height: 5'9" Weight: 11.6

A talented defender, who gained rave reviews in the 1999-2000 campaign, Roland was troubled by a series of niggling injuries during the course of last season and never really got a decent run in the Gillingham line-up. Although linked with a big-money move to Premiership Leicester City in the summer his injuries very much restricted his appearances and nothing materialised. A promising left back he has good ball control and neat distribution. Out of contract in the summer, his future was unclear at the time of writing.

Gillingham (From trainee on 10/7/1997) FL 45+9/1 FLC 3 FAC 10+1 Others 5

EDGHILL Richard Arlon
Born: Oldham, 23 September 1974
Height: 5'9" Weight: 11.5
International Honours: E: B-1; U21-3

Richard started the 2000-01 season as club captain of Manchester City and in his usual position in the team. However he was dropped after the early season home defeat by Coventry and in November he joined Birmingham City on loan, making an encouraging debut in the 3-2 win over Burnley. Signed to play at right back he was troubled by a niggling injury and returned to Maine Road after just three appearances. He was eventually recalled for the away game on New Year's Day, ironically for the game at Coventry, when he produced a sound display but only featured for the first team on a handful more occasions. An experienced full back who can play on either flank, his work rate is never in question as he covers plenty of ground both in his defensive duties and when pushing forward to help the attack.

Manchester C (From trainee on 15/7/1992) P/FL 169+1/1 FLC 17 FAC 7 Others 3
Birmingham C (Loaned on 14/11/2000) FL 3

EDINBURGH Justin Charles
Born: Basildon, 18 December 1969
Height: 5'10" Weight: 12.0
Club Honours: FAC '91; FLC '99

Justin featured regularly at left back for Portsmouth until last December when he was sidelined by an achilles problem. He then tore a calf muscle in training and as a result was laid off until the end of the season. He is a tenacious no-frills defender who is strong in the tackle and has an educated left foot. He was sorely missed by Pompey in the second half of the campaign and will be competing with young Jamie Vincent for the left-back role in 2001-02.

Southend U (From trainee on 5/8/1988) FL 36+1 FLC 2+1 FAC 2 Others 4+1/1
Tottenham H (£150,000 on 30/7/1990) F/PL 190+23/1 FLC 25+4 FAC 27+1 Others 4+2
Portsmouth (£175,000 on 6/3/2000) FL 27+1 FLC 3

EDMONDSON Darren Stephen
Born: Coniston, 4 November 1971
Height: 6'0" Weight: 12.11
Club Honours: Div 3 '95; AMC '97

Darren featured regularly for York City at the start of last season but then suffered damaged knee ligaments and spent four months out of action. He returned to first team duty in April and once again showed consistent form in a right-wing-back role. He is a hard tackling defender who always gives 100 per cent commitment to the cause.

Carlisle U (From trainee on 17/7/1990) FL 205+9/9 FLC 15/1 FAC 15/3 Others 22/3
Huddersfield T (£200,000 + on 3/3/1997) FL 28+9 FLC 2 FAC 2+2
Plymouth Arg (Loaned on 11/9/1998) FL 4
York C (Free on 23/3/2000) FL 29+1 FLC 2 FAC 2

[EDU] EDUARDO Cesar Gaspar
Born: Sao Paulo, Brazil, 15 May 1978
Height: 6'1" Weight: 11.4

Edu was close to joining Arsenal in the summer of 2000 but the deal was delayed to allow him time to sort out his documentation and it was not until January that he finally arrived at Highbury. He made his debut as substitute at Leicester but lasted only fifteen minutes before a pulled hamstring caused him to be withdrawn. This kept him out for over a month and he next appeared off the subs' bench in the home game against West Ham. A skilful, versatile midfielder with a huge amount of talent, he will be hoping to reach peak fitness and challenge for a regular place in the new season. Edu links up with his former Corinthians' team-mate Silvinho at Highbury.

Arsenal (£6,000,000 from Corinthians, Brazil on 18/1/2001) PL 2+3

EDWARDS Andrew (Andy) David
Born: Epping, 17 September 1971
Height: 6'3" Weight: 12.10

Andy was yet again a rock-like figure in the heart of defence for Peterborough last season. A virtual ever-present he captained the side with great authority and provided one of the highlights of the campaign when he sold a dummy to Chelsea's Frank Leboeuf in the FA Cup tie at Stamford Bridge. He is a commanding central defender who is good in the air, quick to recover and tackle back, and a constant danger when coming up to support the attack at set pieces.

Southend U (From trainee on 14/12/1989) FL 141+6/5 FLC 5 FAC 4 Others 9/2
Birmingham C (£400,000 on 6/7/1995) FL 37+3/1 FLC 12/1 FAC 2 Others 5/1
Peterborough U (Signed on 29/11/1996) FL 199/7 FLC 10 FAC 15/1 Others 15/1

EDWARDS Akenhaton **Carlos**
Born: Port of Spain, Trinidad, 24 October 1978
Height: 5'11" Weight: 11.9
International Honours: Trinidad & Tobago: 15

Carlos joined Wrexham on a three-year contract last August along with Hector Sam after finally securing a work permit. He proved to be an exciting wide right midfield player, capable of causing problems for any defence and he was particularly outstanding in the early season encounter at Bury when he ran the home defenders ragged with an excellent display of wing play. An established international for Trinidad & Tobago he appeared regularly in the squad during their qualifying campaign for the 2002 World Cup finals, winning a further ten caps after arriving at the Racecourse Ground.

Wrexham (£125,000 from Defence Force, Trinidad on 8/8/2000) FL 31+5/4 FLC 1+1 FAC 1

EDWARDS Christian (Chris) Nicholas Howells
Born: Caerphilly, 23 November 1975
Height: 6'2" Weight: 12.8
International Honours: W: 1; B-2; U21-7

Something of a forgotten man at Nottingham Forest, Chris made a comeback last season and after returning to the first team in September he went on to emerge as one of the best players on the books at the City Ground. A big centre back who has a no-nonsense approach to defending, he is effective in the air and brave in the tackle. A useful man to have up front for corners, he scored three goals and was also recalled to the full Welsh squad during the campaign.

Swansea C (From trainee on 20/7/1994) FL 113+2/4 FLC 5 FAC 4 Others 9+1
Nottingham F (£175,000 + on 26/3/1998) P/FL 42+6/3 FAC 1
Bristol C (Loaned on 11/12/1998) FL 3
Oxford U (Loaned on 24/2/2000) FL 5/1

EDWARDS Craig Alfred
Born: London, 8 July 1982
Height: 5'10" Weight: 11.4

Craig made his debut in senior football for Southend United in the LDV Vans Trophy tie with Cheltenham and also came on from the subs' bench in the final game of last season against Mansfield. A young midfield player he faces a difficult task to win a regular place in the Blues first team in 2001-02 but he will be hoping to feature more regularly in the squad.

Southend U (Trainee) FL 0+1 Others 1

EDWARDS Michael
Born: Hessle, 25 April 1980
Height: 6'1" Weight: 12.0

Michael scored Hull City's first goal of 2000-01 at Blackpool and capped a fine season when he netted the final goal of their regular campaign to clinch a draw at Southend and the Tigers' first play-off qualification. Initially played out of position at right wing back, he looked much more comfortable when employed as a right back after Tigers reverted to a back four. His consistent performances were rewarded with a new three-year contract in March.

Hull C (From trainee on 16/7/1998) FL 124+9/5 FLC 6+1 FAC 9/2 Others 7+1

EDWARDS Neil Ryan
Born: Aberdare, 5 December 1970
Height: 5'9" Weight: 11.10

International Honours: W: U21-1; Yth; Sch
Neil was again the undisputed number one 'keeper at Rochdale in 2000-01 and also captained the side. He demonstrated his shot stopping skills on many occasions, helping Dale to maintain one of the best defensive records away from home of any club in the Football League. He missed just a couple of games last season and is now approaching 400 appearances in senior football.
Leeds U (From trainee on 10/3/1989) Others 1
Stockport Co (£5,000 on 3/9/1991) FL 163+1 FLC 11 FAC 11 Others 31
Rochdale (£25,000 on 3/11/1997) FL 156 FLC 6 FAC 8+1 Others 9

EDWARDS Paul
Born: Liverpool, 22 February 1965
Height: 5'11" Weight: 11.5
Club Honours: Div 3 '94
Paul shared goalkeeping duties for Shrewsbury with Ian Dunbavin last season and when selected he produced some very sound performances, never letting the team down. His consistency was recognised when he was voted as the supporters' 'Player of the Year', but after nine years and more than 300 appearances for the Gay Meadow club he was released at the end of the campaign. He is an experienced 'keeper who handles the ball well and is strong when defending against close-range shots.
Crewe Alex (Free from Leek T on 24/2/1989) FL 29 FLC 4 FAC 3 Others 4
Shrewsbury T (Free on 6/8/1992) FL 312 FLC 16 FAC 19+1 Others 18

EDWARDS Robert (Rob)
Born: Manchester, 23 February 1970
Height: 5'9" Weight: 12.4
Rob joined Chesterfield last September and his arrival galvanised the Spireites charge to the top of the Third Division table. A wide left-sided player who is at home in the defence or midfield, he tackles clinically, has a good turn of pace and the ability to pick out forwards with seductive crosses. Rob got forward to score important goals, but his enjoyment was most evident when tormenting opposition defenders to set up chances for others.
Crewe Alex (From trainee on 11/7/1988) FL 110+45/44 FLC 8/5 FAC 13+5/5 Others 9+8/4
Huddersfield T (£150,000 on 8/3/1996) FL 109+29/14 FLC 12+1/1 FAC 7+1/1
Chesterfield (£20,000 on 8/9/2000) FL 34/4 FLC 2 FAC 1 Others 4

EDWARDS Robert (Rob) William
Born: Kendal, 1 July 1973
Height: 6'0" Weight: 12.2
Club Honours: Div 2 '00
International Honours: W: 4; B-2; U21-17; Yth
Rob was a consistently strong performer in defence for Preston last season and his experience proved vital in enabling the side to adapt to Division One football. His 400th senior club appearance came at Wolverhampton on Boxing Day before a deadleg at Sheffield United put him out for four games. An efficient left back he is also excellent on the overlap and his accurate crosses led to several goals for his team-mates.
Carlisle U (From trainee on 10/4/1990) FL 48/5 FLC 4 FAC 1 Others 2+1
Bristol C (£135,000 on 27/3/1991) FL 188+28/5 FLC 16+3/1 FAC 13+2 Others 12+1/2
Preston NE (Free on 5/8/1999) FL 78+5/2 FLC 9 FAC 6 Others 5/1

EDWORTHY Marc
Born: Barnstaple, 24 December 1972
Height: 5'8" Weight: 11.10
After overcoming a serious ankle injury sustained in the previous season, Marc had high hopes at Coventry at the start of the 2000-01 campaign. He played consistently well at right back in the early matches with his overlapping runs being a key feature of his play. However he was then switched to the troublesome left-back position to cover for injuries and looked much less comfortable there, before picking up a groin strain that kept him out for several weeks. He was back in action on New Year's Day when he scored his first goal for the Sky Blues with a speculative shot that foxed Nicky Weaver of Manchester City, but was then sidelined by a calf problem. On his return he soon lost his place to Barry Quinn and spent the remainder of the season on the subs' bench and in the reserves.
Plymouth Arg (From trainee on 30/3/1991) FL 52+17/1 FLC 5+2 FAC 5+2 Others 2+2
Crystal Palace (£350,000 on 9/6/1995) F/PL 120+6 FLC 8+1/1 FAC 8 Others 8
Coventry C (£850,000 + on 28/8/1998) PL 44+12/1 FLC 4 FAC 3

Ugo Ehiogu

EHIOGU Ugochuku (Ugo)
Born: Hackney, 3 November 1972
Height: 6'2" Weight: 14.10
Club Honours: FLC '96
International Honours: E: 2; B-1; U21-15
Following a much-publicised transfer request and the arrival of Alpay during the close season, Ugo's first-team opportunities at Aston Villa suddenly became very limited at the beginning of the 2000-01 season. He featured in just a couple of Premiership games and it came as no real surprise when he moved on to Middlesbrough for a new club record fee in October. He readily joined in Boro's backs-to-the-wall fight to save their Premiership place and showed some fine spirit at all times. Well received by the Riverside faithful, his aerial power and control allied to some tough and relentless tackling enabled him to dominate the centre of defence and won a deserved recall for England against Spain in February when he scored in the 3-0 victory.
West Bromwich A (From trainee on 13/7/1989) FL 0+2
Aston Villa (£40,000 on 12/7/1991) F/PL 223+14/12 FLC 23+1/1 FAC 22+2/1 Others 18/1
Middlesbrough (£8,000,000 on 20/10/2000) PL 21/3 FAC 3

EKELUND Ronald (Ronnie) Michael
Born: Angreb, Denmark, 21 August 1972
Height: 5'11" Weight: 12.8
International Honours: Denmark: U21; Yth
Having spent the 1999-2000 campaign with Toulouse, Ronnie was released in the close season and linked up with Second Division Walsall last December after he had recovered from an elbow injury. He quickly impressed with some neat and tidy passing but left before the end of the campaign, crossing the Atlantic to sign for MLS club San Jose Earthquakes. An experienced midfield player with plenty of skill, he had previously been at Southampton when Saddlers' boss Ray Graydon was on the coaching staff there.
Southampton (Loaned from Barcelona, Spain, ex Brondby IF, on 15/9/1994) PL 15+2/5 FLC 2+1
Manchester C (Loaned from Barcelona, Spain on 23/12/1995) PL 2+2 FAC 1+1
Walsall (Free from Toulouse, France, ex OB, on 1/12/2000) FL 2+7/1 FAC 0+1 Others 1+1

EKOKU Efangwu (Efan) Goziem
Born: Manchester, 8 June 1967
Height: 6'2" Weight: 12.0
International Honours: Nigeria: 5
Efan joined Sheffield Wednesday in a long-term loan deal last October as manager Paul Jewell sought to boost a flagging attack. His bustle and pace proved effective and he earned a place in the hearts of the Owls' fans by scoring both goals in the Worthington Cup victory over Sheffield United in November. He produced a series of steady performances and scored a number of goals as the club's fortunes improved in the second half of the season.
Bournemouth (£100,000 from Sutton U on 11/5/1990) FL 43+19/21 FLC 0+2 FAC 5+2/2 Others 3+1/2
Norwich C (£500,000 on 26/3/1993) PL 26+11/15 FLC 3/1 FAC 1+1 Others 3/1
Wimbledon (£900,000 on 14/10/1994) PL 102+21/37 FLC 11+2/4 FAC 16+1/3 (£500,000 to Grasshopper Zurich, Switzerland on 27/8/99)
Sheffield Wed (Loaned on 20/10/2000) FL 31+1/7 FLC 3/2 FAC 1+1

EL KHALEJ Tahar
Born: Morocco, 16 June 1968
Height: 6'3" Weight: 13.8
International Honours: Morocco

A versatile player who is comfortable at centre back, wing back or in a midfield anchor role, Tahar showed great enthusiasm and grit in his performances for Southampton last season. A regular in the line-up for most of the season he also continued to be a member of the Moroccan national squad and is now approaching 100 caps for his country. He has adapted well to the English game and has become a popular character at The Dell easily recognisable in his silver boots.
Southampton (£300,000 from Benfica, Portugal, ex KAC Marrakesh, Uniao Leiria, on 10/3/2000) PL 36+7/2 FLC 1+2 FAC 1+1

Tahar El Khalej

ELLINGTON Nathan Levi Fontaine
Born: Bradford, 2 July 1981
Height: 5'10" Weight: 12.10
Nathan established himself as Bristol Rovers' main striker last season following the departure of Jason Roberts. He scored a remarkable individual goal in the second match of the campaign and went on to find the net regularly, despite playing alongside a constant flow of different partners. His mature performances won him respect from opponents and supporters alike and he finished as the club's leading scorer with 18 goals in all competitions. A talented young striker he has good pace and excellent close control.
Bristol Rov (£150,000 from Walton & Hersham on 18/2/1999) FL 49+40/20 FLC 5/2 FAC 1+1 Others 4+1/1

ELLIOTT Matthew (Matt) Stephen
Born: Wandsworth, 1 November 1968
Height: 6'3" Weight: 14.10
Club Honours: FLC '00
International Honours: S: 15
After his heroics of the previous season, Matt had a quiet campaign for Leicester City last term by his own high standards. He was again a regular for the Foxes, providing a solid presence in the centre of defence but the goals seemed to dry up and he netted only twice. Oddly, this was the year in which Matt actually notched his first international goal against San Marino in October, and he also managed to hit the woodwork against the same opposition in the return fixture at Hampden Park in March. A groin problem picked up in that game rather affected his form during the closing weeks before a knee ligament injury suffered at Pride Park on Easter Monday brought his season to a premature close. A summer operation loomed.
Charlton Ath (£5,000 from Epsom & Ewell on 9/5/1988) FLC 1
Torquay U (£10,000 on 23/3/1989) FL 123+1/15 FLC 9/2 FAC 9/2 Others 16/1
Scunthorpe U (£50,000 on 26/3/1992) FL 61/8 FLC 6 FAC 2 Others 8
Oxford U (£150,000 on 5/11/1993) FL 148/21 FLC 16/1 FAC 11/2 Others 6
Leicester C (£1,600,000 on 18/1/1997) PL 161/22 FLC 15+1/3 FAC 15/2 Others 4

ELLIOTT Robert (Robbie) James
Born: Newcastle, 25 December 1973
Height: 5'10" Weight: 11.6
International Honours: E: U21-2; Yth
Sidelined with an injury at the start of last season it was not until October that Robbie returned to action for Bolton Wanderers in 2000-01. Initially employed at left back, as the season wore on he was switched to a midfield role and adapted well to the change of position. A tough-tackling player who is also very useful on the ball, he performed consistently throughout the campaign and even grabbed a couple of vital goals for the Wanderers.
Newcastle U (From trainee on 3/4/1991) F/PL 71+8/9 FLC 5 FAC 7+3 Others 5+1
Bolton W (£2,500,000 + on 2/7/1997) P/FL 71+15/5 FLC 4+2/2 FAC 5 Others 5+2

ELLIOTT Steven (Steve) William
Born: Swadlincote, 29 October 1978
Height: 6'1" Weight: 14.0
International Honours: E: U21-2
The locally-born centre back had a disappointing season at Pride Park. Having commenced the campaign in the first team he seemed set for an extended run, but the club's early season defensive frailties meant a change in both formation and personnel. He was then sidelined by injury and once fit he had to be content with a return to the Rams' successful reserve side. Strong in the tackle and with good distribution skills, he will be looking to feature more often at first-team level in 2001-02.
Derby Co (From trainee on 26/3/1997) PL 33+7 FLC 7+1 FAC 2+2

ELLIOTT Stuart Thomas
Born: Willesden, 27 August 1977
Height: 5'9" Weight: 12.0
After a series of loan spells at various clubs Stuart finally made the break from Newcastle United and signed for Darlington in the summer of 2000. He immediately made an impact with some tenacious midfield displays and his ability to pick out runners with pinpoint passes. He scored an amazing goal which proved to be the winner in the Worthington Cup first round tie against Nottingham Forest at the City Ground, picking up a loose clearance from Dave Beasant in the centre circle and firing it straight back into the net. However he was surprisingly transferred to Plymouth Argyle in March following an influx of new signings at Feethams. He proved a useful acquisition for the Pilgrims covering for the injured David Worrell on the right side of defence but was released at the end of the season.
Newcastle U (From trainee on 28/8/1995)
Hull C (Loaned on 28/2/1997) FL 3
Swindon T (Loaned on 20/2/1998) FL 1+1
Gillingham (Loaned on 23/10/1998) FL 4+1
Hartlepool U (Loaned on 29/1/1999) FL 5
Wrexham (Loaned on 22/3/1999) FL 8+1 Others 1
Bournemouth (Loaned on 3/12/1999) FL 6+2
Stockport Co (Loaned on 25/2/2000) FL 4+1
Darlington (Free on 21/7/2000) FL 20+4 FLC 3+1/3 FAC 1+1 Others 3/1
Plymouth Arg (Free on 7/3/2001) FL 11+1

ELLIOTT Wade Patrick
Born: Eastleigh, 14 December 1978
Height: 5'9" Weight: 11.1
International Honours: E: Sch
Wade made excellent progress at Bournemouth last season and after taking a while to establish himself in the first team he became an automatic choice by the end of the campaign. A pacy right winger with the ability to run at players with the ball, he hit a double-figure tally of goals and his achievements were recognised when he received the Dean Court Supporters Club 'Player of the Season' award and a new three-year contract for the Cherries.
Bournemouth (£5,000 from Bashley on 4/2/2000) FL 33+15/12 FLC 0+1 FAC 3/2 Others 0+1

ELLIS Anthony (Tony) Joseph
Born: Salford, 20 October 1964
Height: 5'11" Weight: 11.0
Tony started the 2000-01 season where he had left off at the end of the previous campaign, namely scoring goals. He netted four times from eight starts including a last gasp equaliser against First Division Blackburn in the Worthington Cup but then hit something of a lean patch. He featured regularly for Dale until March when he lost his place to new signing Paul Connor and made just one more appearance in the closing weeks of the campaign. Now reaching the veteran stage of his career he is a hard working striker who holds the ball up well and has an excellent scoring record. He was out of contract in the summer.
Oldham Ath (Free from Horwich RMI on 22/8/1986) FL 5+3 FLC 1 Others 1
Preston NE (£23,000 on 16/10/1987) FL 80+6/26 FLC 3 FAC 5 Others 11+1/5
Stoke C (£250,000 on 20/12/1989) FL 66+11/19 FLC 5+1/1 FAC 1+4 Others 3+2
Preston NE (£140,000 on 14/8/1992) FL 70+2/48 FLC 4/2 FAC 6/3 Others 6/3
Blackpool (£165,000 on 25/7/1994) FL 140+6/54 FLC 10+1/6 FAC 7/1 Others 8/3
Bury (£75,000 on 12/12/1997) FL 24+14/8 FLC 2+2

Stockport Co (£25,000 on 3/2/1999) FL 17+3/6 FLC 1+1
Rochdale (Free on 1/11/1999) FL 55+4/17 FLC 1/1 FAC 1+1 Others 5+1

ELLIS Clinton (Clint)
Born: Ealing, 7 July 1977
Height: 5'7" Weight: 12.0
International Honours: E: Yth; Sch
This former Chelsea trainee spent several years out of the professional game before being encouraged to prove his fitness and resume his full time football career with Bristol Rovers. A quick and skilful striker, he showed some neat touches but struggled to break into the Pirates first team although he featured regularly from the subs' bench. Clint scored his only goal of the campaign in the 2-1 defeat by Colchester in October but was released by Rovers in the summer.
Bristol Rov (Free from Willesden Constantine on 23/3/2000) FL 2+13/1 FLC 2+2 FAC 0+1 Others 0+1

ELLISON Kevin
Born: Liverpool, 23 February 1979
Height: 6'1" Weight: 12.8
Signed from non-league Altrincham last February this attacking midfielder had previously had trials with Everton, Wigan Athletic and Manchester City before Peter Taylor decided to invest in his potential for the future. Kevin was thrust into the squad for the fixture at Old Trafford in March after Arnie Gunnlaugsson was taken ill, and came on for the last five minutes to make his debut in senior football. He will need to develop at his own pace next term but will be aiming for more first-team experience during the season.
Leicester C (£50,000 + from Altrincham on 13/2/2001) PL 0+1

EMBERSON Carl Wayne
Born: Epsom, 13 July 1973
Height: 6'2" Weight: 14.7
Club Honours: FAYC '91
This experienced goalkeeper was again second choice to James Walker at Walsall in the 2000-01 campaign. When called up for action in the 3-0 win over Stoke last October he seemed to be on the edge of an extended run in the team, but he lost his place soon afterwards and then only appeared in the two LDV Vans Trophy games. A useful back-up 'keeper he was released by the Saddlers in the summer.
Millwall (From trainee on 4/5/1991) Others 1
Colchester U (Loaned on 17/12/1992) FL 13
Colchester U (£25,000 on 6/7/1994) FL 178+1 FLC 9 FAC 8 Others 16
Walsall (Free on 28/6/1999) FL 6+2 FLC 1 Others 2

EMBLEN Neil Robert
Born: Bromley, 19 June 1971
Height: 6'1" Weight: 13.11
Neil featured regularly for Wolves in the early part of last season, mostly being used in midfield or defence, although on one occasion he appeared as a makeshift striker. However after signing a new three-year contract he found it hard going and lost his place in the team before eventually returning to the line-up in April. A very versatile player he is effective in the air and makes determined runs with the ball. He is the brother of Wycombe's Paul Emblen.
Millwall (£175,000 from Sittingbourne on 8/11/1993) FL 12 Others 1
Wolverhampton W (£600,000 on 14/7/1994) FL 80+8/9 FLC 2+2/1 FAC 7+2 Others 2+1
Crystal Palace (£2,000,000 on 21/8/1997) PL 8+5 FAC 1+1/2
Wolverhampton W (£900,000 on 26/3/1998) FL 102+12/7 FLC 8+1/1 FAC 6+1

EMMERSON Scott
Born: Durham, 10 October 1982
Height: 5'9" Weight: 12.7
York City's highly-rated youngster did well in reserve team football and was thrust into senior action early in the new year. Given his first start at Rochdale in February he responded by scoring the only goal of the game with a close-range effort. The result victory lifted the Minstermen off the bottom of the Third Division and on their way to a nine-match unbeaten run which took them clear of danger. Scott is a lively striker who will be aiming to extend his first-team experience at Bootham Crescent in the 2001-02 campaign.
York C (Trainee) FL 3+5/1

ENHUA Zhang
Born: China, 28 April 1973
Height: 6'0" Weight: 13.12
International Honours: China
Zhang joined Grimsby Town on loan from Chinese League champions Dalian Shide in December and proved to be a great success in his stay at Blundell Park. A class act in the centre of defence he is good in the air, has fine positional sense and reads the game well. He established a solid partnership with Paul Groves at the back for the Mariners and also found time to net the winner against Burnley when he headed home a corner. An experienced international, he returned to China at the beginning of April and joined up with his country's squad for the World Cup qualifiers.
Grimsby T (Loaned from Dalian Shide, China on 15/12/2000) FL 16+1/3

EPESSE-TITI Steeve
Born: Bordeaux, France, 5 September 1979
Height: 6'1" Weight: 13.3
This young French defender joined Wolves from Bordeaux in the 2000 close season but failed to make an impression at Molineux and moved to Third Division Exeter City last March. He did well on his debut against Blackpool and featured regularly for the Grecians in the closing matches of the campaign. Cool under pressure, Steeve has good pace and technical ability but was out of contract in the summer.
Wolverhampton W (Free from Bordeaux, France on 7/8/2000)
Exeter C (Free on 22/3/2001) FL 5+1

ERANIO Stefano
Born: Genoa, Italy, 29 December 1966
Height: 5'11" Weight: 12.2
International Honours: Italy: 20
Stefano had a mixed season at Derby in 2001-02 being in and out of the side until the closing matches when he came in and gave some eye-catching performances, scoring goals against Leicester and Arsenal. A right-sided midfielder who can also play at right back, his ball control and intelligent passing make him one of the team's most creative players as well as one of the hardest working. He made his hundredth senior appearance for the Rams in the FA Cup replay with Blackburn Rovers but as the season concluded he made the decision to return to Italy in the summer to concentrate on a career in coaching.
Derby Co (Free from AC Milan, Italy, ex Genoa, on 15/7/1997) PL 83+12/7 FLC 5 FAC 8/3

ERIBENNE Chukwunyeaka (Chukki) Osondu
Born: Westminster, 2 November 1980
Height: 5'10" Weight: 11.12
Chukki got off to a great start at Bournemouth last season, scoring a fine goal in the opening game at Bristol Rovers to earn the Cherries a 1-1 draw. He featured regularly in the early weeks of the campaign but failed to add to his goal tally and later dropped back to the fringe of the first-team squad. He is a powerful young striker who will be looking to gain further senior experience in 2001-02.
Coventry C (From trainee on 19/1/1998)
Bournemouth (Free on 4/7/2000) FL 6+11/1 FLC 2 FAC 0+3 Others 2

ESSANDOH Roy
Born: Belfast, 17 February 1976
Height: 6'0" Weight: 12.3
International Honours: NI: Yth
Roy's big break at Wycombe was one of the fairy tale stories of English football last season. Having returned from a spell in Finland, he had trials with a number of clubs including Conference outfit Rushden & Diamonds before his agent came across an appeal for a striker on the internet by Wycombe manager Lawrie Sanchez. He was signed up and after a couple of run-outs made the subs' bench for the FA Cup sixth round tie at Leicester. Introduced into the game in the second half he scored a dramatic last-minute header to send the Chairboys into the semi-final for the first time ever. A tall and athletic striker who is very effective in the air, he won a contract at Adams Park until the end of the season but was then released in the summer.
Motherwell (From Cumbernauld Juniors on 9/12/1994) SL 0+5 Others 0+1 (Free to St Polten, Austria on 30/6/1997)
East Fife (Free on 23/2/1998) SL 5 (Free to VPS Vassa, Finland on 8/5/1998)
Wycombe W (Free from Rushden & Diamonds on 28/2/2001) FL 8+5 FAC 0+2/1

ETHERINGTON Matthew
Born: Truro, 14 August 1981
Height: 5'10" Weight: 11.2
International Honours: E: Yth
This promising Tottenham youngster featured in the Worthington Cup second round first leg tie at Brentford at the beginning of last season, but it was not until the second half of the campaign that he

made much of an impact at senior level. He appeared several times from the subs' bench in the closing matches and made the starting line-up for the final game against Manchester United at White Hart Lane. A left-sided midfield player, Matthew exudes confidence on the ball and uses his excellent vision to bring his colleagues into play.
Peterborough U (From trainee on 15/8/1998) FL 43+8/6 FLC 1+1 FAC 2+1 Others 2
Tottenham H (£500,000 on 10/1/2000) PL 2+9 FLC 1

EUELL Jason Joseph
Born: Lambeth, 6 February 1977
Height: 6'0" Weight: 12.7
International Honours: E: U21-6
Jason switched from an attacking midfield role to playing as an out-and-out striker last term with great success and at times he appeared to keep Wimbledon's play-off hopes alive almost single-handedly with his goals. He found the net regularly all season despite having a number of different partners up front and produced a quality of play that would grace any Premiership squad. His pace and control were too much for many First Division defences to handle as his goals-per-game ratio showed, and Dons' fans look forward to another bagful of goals in 2001-02.
Wimbledon (From trainee on 1/6/1995) P/FL 118+23/41 FLC 15+2/4 FAC 14+5/2 Others 2+2

EUSTACE John Mark
Born: Solihull, 3 November 1979
Height: 5'11" Weight: 11.12
This young midfielder made further progress at Coventry last term and was a regular starter in central midfield until the Chelsea debacle in October. He then dropped back to the bench and was restricted to substitute appearances over the winter months as boss Gordon Strachan chose to rest him, but returned again to the line-up in January. His all-action style endeared him to the Sky Blues' fans and he seemed to relish the physical aspect of his game, but although he regularly got up to help the attack his goals were few and far between.
Coventry C (From trainee on 5/11/1996) PL 34+14/3 FLC 5+1/2 FAC 2+2/1
Dundee U (Loaned on 17/2/1999) SL 8+3/1 SC 2

EUSTACE Scott Douglas
Born: Leicester, 13 June 1975
Height: 6'0" Weight: 14.2
This left-sided central defender arrived at Lincoln in the summer of 2000 on a two-year contract but injured his left knee in pre-season. He returned to the reserves in September and was given a 12-minute run-out as a substitute for the first team at Leyton Orient later that month. However his injury persisted and he was still not fully fit when his contract was cancelled in October due to off the field matters.
Leicester C (From trainee on 9/7/1993) FL 0+1
Mansfield T (Free on 9/6/1995) FL 90+8/6 FLC 3 FAC 5/1 Others 3+1
Chesterfield (Free on 7/8/1998) FLC 0+1
Cambridge U (Free on 8/1/1999) FL 49+3/1 FLC 2 FAC 3
Lincoln C (Free on 12/7/2000) FL 0+1

Jason Euell

EVANS Gareth Joseph
Born: Leeds, 15 February 1981
Height: 6'0" Weight: 11.12
International Honours: E: Yth
Gareth stepped up to make his senior debut for Leeds United during the club's early-season injury crisis when he came off the substitutes' bench for the final 15 minutes of the Champions' League qualifier at Munich 1860. He followed this up two weeks later when coming on after 58 minutes to make his Premiership debut against Manchester City and later featured on the bench in the Champions' League games, but his domestic appearances were otherwise restricted to the club's reserve team. This local-born left back played in the same school side as his Leeds United colleague Alan Smith.
Leeds U (From trainee on 26/3/1998) PL 0+1 Others 0+1

EVANS Kevin
Born: Carmarthen, 16 December 1980
Height: 6'2" Weight: 12.10
International Honours: W: U21-4; Yth
Having been a central defender in his Leeds United days, Cardiff City manager Bobby Gould switched Kevin to a midfield role in a pre-season game and the move was so effective that he stayed in that position. Although he spent much of last season on a learning curve he featured regularly for the Bluebirds without really finding consistent form. He netted his first senior goal with a 20-yarder in the 2-0 home victory over Darlington and scored a total of five times during the campaign. Kevin continued to represent Wales at U21 level winning further caps against Norway and Poland in the autumn.
Leeds U (From trainee on 13/1/1998)
Swansea C (Loaned on 17/1/2000) FL 1+1
Cardiff C (Free on 31/8/2000) FL 24+6/3 FLC 1 FAC 3/2 Others 0+1

EVANS Michael (Micky) James
Born: Plymouth, 1 January 1973
Height: 6'1" Weight: 13.4
International Honours: RoI: 1
Having joined Bristol Rovers on loan at the start of the 2000-01 campaign, Micky scored with a fine left-foot shot on his debut at Peterborough but after signing permanently he found his progress hampered by a viral infection. His goal tally was a little disappointing and it was no real surprise that he was allowed to return to Plymouth Argyle on transfer deadline day for a nominal fee. He showed he had lost none of his confidence in front of goal by scoring four times in ten appearances in the remaining weeks of the season for the Third Division club. Micky

is an experienced striker who works hard and has the ability to hold the ball up.
Plymouth Arg (From trainee on 30/3/1991) FL 130+33/38 FLC 8+1 FAC 10+2/3 Others 10/2
Southampton (£500,000 on 4/3/1997) PL 14+8/4 FLC 2+1/1
West Bromwich A (£750,000 on 27/10/1997) FL 35+28/6 FLC 3+3/2 FAC 2+2/1
Bristol Rov (£250,000 on 18/8/2000) FL 19+2/4 FLC 2 Others 3/2
Plymouth Arg (£30,000 on 22/3/2001) FL 10/4

EVANS Paul Simon
Born: Oswestry, 1 September 1974
Height: 5'8" Weight: 11.6
Club Honours: Div 3 '94, '99
International Honours: W: U21-4; Yth
Paul had another excellent season for Brentford in 2000-01 when he was a near ever-present. He provided inspirational leadership, organising the team on the field and netting his usual share of long-range goals including a cracking 30-yarder in the 2-1 win over Walsall last October. He won a runners-up medal in the LDV Vans Trophy as a member of the Bees side that were defeated 2-1 by Port Vale at the Millenium Stadium. A powerful ball-winning midfield player he is also the team's penalty taker.
Shrewsbury T (From trainee on 2/7/1993) FL 178+20/26 FLC 12+2/4 FAC 12+1/2 Others 12/4
Brentford (£110,000 on 3/3/1999) FL 90/17 FLC 6 FAC 2 Others 9/3

EVANS Stephen (Steve) James
Born: Caerphilly, 25 September 1980
Height: 6'1" Weight: 11.6
International Honours: W: U21-2; Yth
Having recovered from the knee injuries that troubled him in 1999-2000 Steve found it difficult to break into the Crystal Palace first-team squad last season and made just a single appearance, coming off the subs' bench in the last minute of the end-of-season game at Portsmouth. A promising left-sided midfield player he won two caps for Wales at U21 level.
Crystal Palace (From trainee on 31/10/1998) FL 0+6 FLC 0+1

EVANS Thomas (Tommy) Raymond
Born: Doncaster, 31 December 1976
Height: 6'0" Weight: 13.2
International Honours: NI: Yth
Tommy was once again first-choice goalkeeper for Scunthorpe United last season and he was the club's only ever-present during the campaign. He is a good shot-stopper, has worked hard on improving his distribution and handling of crosses and is particularly effective in one-on-one situations. He was due to be out of contract in the summer and at the time of writing it was unclear whether he would start the 2001-02 campaign at Glanford Park.
Sheffield U (From trainee on 3/7/1995)
Crystal Palace (Free on 14/6/1996)
Scunthorpe U (Free on 22/8/1997) FL 102+1 FLC 5 FAC 7 Others 3

EVANS Duncan **Wayne**
Born: Abermule, 25 August 1971
Height: 5'10" Weight: 12.5
This ever-consistent Rochdale defender was mostly employed at right back last season, although he occasionally played as a third centre back. His partnership with Lee Todd became arguably the best full-back pairing in the Third Division and his influence on the team was immense. It was no coincidence that Dale's worst two defeats of the season came after he was carried off in the home game with Shrewsbury and then missed the next match through injury. He even managed two goals, though Wayne himself would probably be the only one prepared to claim that he meant them!
Walsall (Free from Welshpool on 13/8/1993) FL 173+10/1 FLC 14+1/1 FAC 15+1 Others 12+3
Rochdale (Free on 2/7/1999) FL 91/3 FLC 4/1 FAC 4 Others 6

EVATT Ian Ross
Born: Coventry, 19 November 1981
Height: 6'3" Weight: 13.11
Captain of Derby County's U19 team in the 1999-2000 campaign, Ian spent most of last term developing in the Rams' reserves before making his Premiership debut in the final game against Ipswich when he came off the subs' bench to replace Thordur Gudjonsson for the last 15 minutes. An inspirational defender he signed a three-year contract in July 2000 and will be hoping for more senior experience in 2001-02.
Derby Co (From trainee on 3/12/1998) PL 0+1

EVERS Sean Anthony
Born: Hitchin, 10 October 1977
Height: 5'9" Weight: 9.11
Sean began the 2000-01 campaign at Reading where he was confined to reserve-team football apart from a single first-team appearance in the Worthington Cup first round first leg tie against Leyton Orient. He was loaned to St Johnstone in October and featured in a handful of games for the Scottish Premier League club before returning to the Madejski Stadium. Still unable to break into the Royals' line-up, he moved on to Plymouth in March where he featured mostly from the subs' bench in the closing weeks of the season. A busy bustling midfielder with some neat touches he will be aiming for a return to the form he previously displayed in his spell at Luton Town next term.
Luton T (From trainee on 16/5/1996) FL 43+9/6 FLC 9/1 FAC 2 Others 6
Reading (£500,000 on 25/3/1999) FL 8+10 FLC 1+1 FAC 4 Others 2+1
St Johnstone (Loaned on 13/10/2000) SL 5+1
Plymouth Arg (Free on 8/3/2001) FL 2+5

EYJOLFSSON Sigurdur (Sigi)
Born: Iceland, 1 December 1973
Height: 6'2" Weight: 12.0
International Honours: Iceland: Yth
Sigi made just a single appearance for Walsall last term, coming off the subs' bench to replace Jorge Leitao in the Worthington Cup tie against Kidderminster, before moving to Belgian club RC Harelbeke. Once a star of US College soccer and capped by Iceland at U18 level, he is a tall striker who holds the ball up well and is very mobile.
Walsall (Free from IF Akranes, Iceland, ex North Carolina University, on 27/1/1999) FL 1+22/2 FLC 1+4/3 FAC 0+1 Others 0+1/1
Chester C (Loaned on 7/1/2000) FL 9/3 Others 1

EYRE John Robert
Born: Hull, 9 October 1974
Height: 6'0" Weight: 12.7
John was badly affected by injuries last season but recovered to play an influential role in Hull City's campaign to reach the play-offs. He suffered a recurrence of a back problem in September and didn't fully recover until February, however he came back with two goals in the 2-1 win over Barnet and ended up competing with Rodney Rowe for a place as Kevin Francis's strike partner. John finished the term by netting the Tigers' winner in the play-off semi-final first leg against Leyton Orient to make him the club's leading scorer for the season. He is a striker with good skills on the ball who is capable of upsetting defences with his direct style. He was placed on the open to offers list in the summer.
Oldham Ath (From trainee on 16/7/1993) P/FL 4+6/1 FLC 0+2
Scunthorpe U (Loaned on 15/12/1994) FL 9/8
Scunthorpe U (£40,000 on 4/7/1995) FL 151+13/43 FLC 9/2 FAC 12/3 Others 8+1/3
Hull C (Free on 5/7/1999) FL 43+9/13 FLC 5/3 FAC 4+1/2 Others 3+2/1

EYRE Richard Paul
Born: Poynton, 15 September 1976
Height: 5'11" Weight: 11.6
Richard found it difficult to break into the Port Vale first team last season, being restricted to reserve-team football with the exception of two appearances in the first-team line-up and a handful of outings from the subs' bench. An enthusiastic right-winger he was released by Vale in the summer.
Port Vale (From trainee on 29/6/1995) FL 26+22/1 FLC 1+2 FAC 1 Others 0+1

EYRES David
Born: Liverpool, 26 February 1964
Height: 5'11" Weight: 11.8
Club Honours: Div 2 '00
A veteran left winger and consummate professional, David was rewarded with a new one-year contract at Preston during the summer of 2000, and had a permanent place on the bench in the early season. However, frustrated by a lack of first-team football, he left for Oldham in October where his arrival marked a turning point in the club's campaign, as a desperate run of six points from 11 games suddenly became one of just four defeats in 19 Second Division matches. Employed either as a left wing back or out-and-out winger, he provided some much-needed width and the occasional goal. It was no surprise when he agreed a new contract that will keep him at Boundary Park until at least the end of the 2001-02 season.
Blackpool (£10,000 from Rhyl on 15/8/1989) FL 147+11/38 FLC 11+1/1 FAC 11/2 Others 13+2/4
Burnley (£90,000 on 29/7/1993) FL 171+4/37 FLC 17/7 FAC 14/8 Others 9/3
Preston NE (£80,000 on 29/10/1997) FL 85+23/19 FLC 3+4 FAC 10/3 Others 5/3
Oldham Ath (Free on 13/10/2000) FL 30/3 FAC 3 Others 1

FABIANO Nicolas
Born: Paris, France, 8 February 1981
Height: 5'11" Weight: 11.10
International Honours: France: Yth

This talented youngster joined Swansea City for an extended loan period last February as the club sought to stave off the threat of relegation from the Second Division. He featured regularly during his spell at Vetch Field scoring on his first appearance in the starting line-up at Northampton, but was unable to save the Swans from the drop. He is a pacy wide-right midfield player with excellent skills on the ball. A member of the France U18 squad that won the 2000 UEFA championship, he stepped up to the U20s last term and made the squads for both the Toulon tournament and the FIFA World Youth championships in Argentina.

Swansea C (Loaned from Paris St Germain, France on 6/2/2001) FL 12+4/1

FACEY Delroy Michael
Born: Huddersfield, 22 April 1980
Height: 5'11' Weight: 13.10

Although he featured several times early on for Huddersfield Town last season, Delroy failed to win a regular place in the line-up although he continued to impress in the reserves. He received more opportunities when Lou Macari took over as manager although he was still often used from the subs' bench. A quick strong forward he had the McAlpine Stadium buzzing with his whole-hearted approach and netted ten goals to finish joint-top scorer with Kevin Gallen. Delroy will be looking to forge a striking partnership with Andy Booth in the 2001-02 campaign.

Huddersfield T (From trainee on 13/5/1997) FL 29+33/13 FLC 1+1 FAC 1+2

FALLON Rory Michael
Born: Gisbourne, New Zealand, 20 March 1982
Height: 6'2" Weight: 11.10
International Honours: E: Yth

A regular in the England U18 squad last season Rory was the leading scorer for Barnsley's reserve team and fully justified his promotion to the first-team squad towards the end of the campaign when he made his senior debut in the home game against Preston. A lanky striker who is well thought of at Oakwell, he not only has an eye for goal but has a good touch on the ball and can bring others into the game.

Barnsley (From trainee on 23/3/1999) FL 1

FARRELL David (Dave) William
Born: Birmingham, 11 November 1971
Height: 5'10" Weight: 11.9

Dave had another fine season for Peterborough in 2000-01 when he was a near ever-present and netted nine goals. The best of these was probably Posh's 'Goal of the Season' at Notts County when he turned the Magpies' defence inside out with a run down the left flank before cutting in to deliver a great shot into the roof of the net. A wide left-sided midfield player he causes defenders all sorts of problems with his blistering pace and mazy runs down the wing.

Aston Villa (£45,000 from Redditch U on 6/1/1992) F/PL 5+1 FLC 2
Scunthorpe U (Loaned on 25/1/1993) FL 4+1/1 Others 2
Wycombe W (£100,000 on 14/9/1995) FL 44+16/6 FLC 6 FAC 3+2 Others 2
Peterborough U (Free on 21/7/1997) FL 140+18/20 FLC 7+2/2 FAC 9/1 Others 8/4

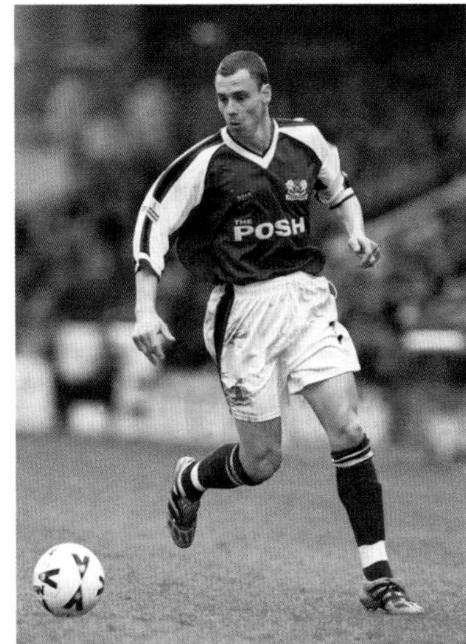

Dave Farrell

FARRELL Sean Paul
Born: Watford, 28 February 1969
Height: 6'0" Weight: 13.7
Club Honours: Div 3 '98

Sean struggled with injuries at Notts County in 2000-01 and was restricted to just a handful of appearances in the starting line-up and several outings from the subs' bench. A big and strong traditional-style centre forward with a heart to match, he always battled back but managed only three goals during the season. Sean was released by the Magpies in the summer.

Luton T (From apprentice on 5/3/1987) FL 14+11/1 FAC 2+1/1 Others 1+2/2
Colchester U (Loaned on 1/3/1988) FL 4+5/1
Northampton T (Loaned on 13/9/1991) FL 4/1
Fulham (£100,000 on 19/12/1991) FL 93+1/31 FLC 5+1/3 FAC 2/3 Others 8/1
Peterborough U (£120,000 on 5/8/1994) FL 49+17/21 FLC 4+2/1 FAC 4+1/3 Others 3+1/1
Notts Co (£80,000 on 14/10/1996) FL 58+30/22 FLC 2+1 FAC 6+1/1 Others 1

FARRELLY Gareth
Born: Dublin, 28 August 1975
Height: 6'0" Weight: 13.0
International Honours: RoI: 6; B-1; U21-11; Yth; Sch

Surely Bolton's most improved player last season, Gareth was a touch of class at the heart of a successful team. Consistently outstanding throughout the campaign he was at his most dangerous when on the ball. With the ability and the vision to pick out the right pass almost every time and also in possession of a mean shot when he chose to let fly, he represented a constant threat to opposing defences even though his final tally of goals was a little disappointing. However he capped a fine season by netting the vital first goal in the play-off final against Preston.

Aston Villa (From trainee on 21/1/1992) PL 2+6 FLC 0+1
Rotherham U (Loaned on 21/3/1995) FL 9+1/2
Everton (£700,000 + on 9/7/1997) PL 18+9/1 FLC 2/1 FAC 1
Bolton W (Free on 12/11/1999) FL 44+8/4 FLC 1 FAC 2+2 Others 3/1

Gareth Farrelly

FAULCONBRIDGE Craig Michael
Born: Nuneaton, 20 April 1978
Height: 6'1" Weight: 13.0

Craig is a hard-working Wrexham striker who always provides a threat to opposition defences in the air and holds the ball up well on the ground. He scored some vital goals last season including the winners at home to both Bristol Rovers and Port Vale, and forged a useful partnership with the evergreen Kevin Russell when the veteran midfielder was pressed into service up front. Craig lost his automatic place in the line-up to newcomer Lee Trundle in the new year.

Coventry C (From trainee on 5/7/1996)
Dunfermline Ath (Loaned on 27/3/1998) SL 1+12/1 SLC 0+1
Hull C (Loaned on 18/12/1998) FL 4+6 FAC 1 Others 1+1
Wrexham (Free on 6/8/1999) FL 56+18/18 FLC 3+1 FAC 3+2/1 Others 2/1

FEAR Peter Stanley
Born: Sutton, 10 September 1973
Height: 5'10" Weight: 11.7
International Honours: E: U21-3

Peter had a disappointing time at Oxford in 2000-01 and struggled to make his mark although managerial changes and the club's relegation problems did not aid his cause. His best spell came when he was reunited with his former Wimbledon boss, Joe Kinnear when he scored two goals and gave some effective displays. However when Kinnear left for Luton he found himself relegated to the subs' bench losing out to the many talented youngsters on the U's books. He is a hard-working midfield player who closes down opponents quickly and sets up chances for his colleagues. He was released in the summer.

Wimbledon (From trainee on 2/7/1992) PL 51+22/4 FLC 9+2/1 FAC 4
Oxford U (Free on 13/7/1999) FL 27+11/3 FLC 3 FAC 3+1 Others 2

FEENEY Warren
Born: Belfast, 17 January 1981
Height: 5'10" Weight: 11.6
International Honours: NI: Yth; Sch

This former Northern Ireland U18 international joined Bournemouth in a loan deal shortly before the transfer deadline last term and scored in his second appearance, coming off the subs' bench to net from close range in the 3-0 win at Swansea. A young and pacy striker he quickly endeared himself to the Cherries' fans with his high work rate and scored some vital goals in the closing weeks of the season. He was reported to have signed a permanent deal for Bournemouth during the summer.

Leeds U (Signed from St Andrew's BC on 26/1/1998)
Bournemouth (Loaned on 22/3/2001) FL 3+7/4

FENTON Graham Anthony
Born: Wallsend, 22 May 1974
Height: 5'10" Weight: 12.10
Club Honours: FLC '94, '96, '00
International Honours: E: U21-1

Graham joined Stoke City on a short-term contract in the 2000 close season but although he made a few first-team appearances he failed to win a longer deal at the Britannia Stadium and eventually moved on to St Mirren at the end of September. He was a regular in the line-up at Love Street but proved unable to prevent the team finishing the campaign at the bottom of the Scottish Premier League. He is a skilful right-sided striker who can hold the ball up and lay it off well.

Aston Villa (From trainee on 13/2/1992) PL 16+16/3 FLC 2+5
West Bromwich A (Loaned on 10/1/1994) FL 7/3
Blackburn Rov (£1,500,000 on 7/11/1995) PL 9+18/7 FLC 0+2 FAC 0+1
Leicester C (£1,100,000 on 8/8/1997) PL 13+21/3 FLC 3+2/1 FAC 0+4 Others 0+2
Walsall (Free on 20/3/2000) FL 8+1/1
Stoke C (Free on 11/8/2000) FL 2+3/1 FLC 2

FENTON Nicholas (Nicky) Leonard
Born: Preston, 23 November 1979
Height: 5'10" Weight: 10.4
International Honours: E: Yth

Unable to break in to the Manchester City side Nicky returned to Bournemouth for a month-long loan spell at the start of the 2000-01 campaign and appeared in a handful of games before returning to Maine Road. Shortly afterwards he went on loan again to Notts County having impressed assistant manager Gary Brazil during a previous spell at Meadow Lane and the deal became permanent in November. He featured regularly in the Magpies defence either as a centre half or at right back where he gave some composed performances.

Manchester C (From trainee on 26/11/1996) FL 15 FLC 3+1 Others 1
Notts Co (Loaned on 7/10/1999) FL 13/1 Others 1
Bournemouth (Loaned on 23/3/2000) FL 8
Bournemouth (Loaned on 11/8/2000) FL 4+1
Notts Co (£150,000 on 18/9/2000) FL 30/2 FLC 1 FAC 5

FERDINAND Leslie (Les)
Born: Acton, 8 December 1966
Height: 5'11" Weight: 13.5
Club Honours: FLC '99
International Honours: E: 17; B-1

Les began the 2000-01 season partnering new signing Sergei Rebrov up front for Tottenham and got off to a good start, scoring with a header in the 3-1 defeat of Premiership newcomers Ipswich Town in the opening game. Looking lean and focused he returned to the exciting form that he had displayed in his younger days and netted regularly throughout the campaign to finish as the club's leading scorer. Probably his finest performance in a Spurs shirt came in the home game with Leicester when he almost single-handedly destroyed the opposition defence with three superbly taken goals. Ironically, Les did not get to take the ball home with him that day after a disappointed City defender kicked it into the crowd in frustration, and it was only after a public appeal that he received his prize several weeks later! Strong, pacy and good in the air he received his reward with a new two-year contract that should see him as a major part of new boss Glenn Hoddle's plans for the future.

Queens Park R (£15,000 from Hayes on 12/3/1987) F/PL 152+11/80 FLC 11+2/7 FAC 6+1/3 Others 1
Brentford (Loaned on 24/3/1988) FL 3
Newcastle U (£6,000,000 on 7/6/1995) PL 67+1/41 FLC 6/3 FAC 4+1/2 Others 5/4
Tottenham H (£6,000,000 on 5/8/1997) PL 71+11/22 FLC 5+3 FAC 12+1

Les Ferdinand

FERDINAND Rio Gavin
Born: Peckham, 8 November 1978
Height: 6'2" Weight: 12.1
International Honours: E: 15; U21-5; Yth

Although speculation of a big money transfer began to mount from the beginning of last season, Rio remained a steady figure in the heart of the West Ham defence in the opening months before he was eventually sold to Leeds United for a new club record fee in November. His first two appearances for United ended in defeats at Leicester City and Southampton, but he soon began to settle and got better and better. He established a great partnership with Lucas Radebe in the heart of the defence and this coincided with an upturn in the club's fortunes. His performances were indeed of the highest order, and when Radebe was sidelined by injury Rio took over the captain's armband. He also weighed in with his first goals for the club with headers against Deportivo La Coruna in the Champions' League and in the 2-1 win at Liverpool. An immensely talented, thoughtful and stylish defender, he is very comfortable on the ball and displays excellent distribution. A regular for England under Sven Goran Eriksson he looks to have a great future in the game.

West Ham U (From trainee on 27/11/1995) PL 122+5/2 FLC 12+1 FAC 9 Others 9
Bournemouth (Loaned on 8/11/1996) FL 10 Others 1
Leeds U (£18,000,000 on 27/11/2000) PL 23/2 FAC 2 Others 7/1

FERGUSON Barry
Born: Dublin, 7 September 1979
Height: 6'3" Weight: 12.10
International Honours: RoI: U21-6

This young Coventry City centre back began 2000-01 on loan at Hartlepool where he featured regularly in the early season games. He then returned to Highfield Road before going out on loan again, this time to Second Division Northampton Town last December for an extended period. Primarily at Sixfields to gain experience Barry made a handful of appearances in the first team covering for injuries.

Coventry C (Signed from Home Farm on 4/9/1998)
Colchester U (Loaned on 23/3/2000) FL 5+1
Hartlepool U (Loaned on 28/7/2000) FL 4 FLC 1
Northampton T (Loaned on 29/12/2000) FL 1+2

FERGUSON Darren
Born: Glasgow, 9 February 1972
Height: 5'10" Weight: 11.10
Club Honours: PL '93
International Honours: S: U21-5; Yth

Darren provided some quality play in the centre of midfield for Wrexham last season, his silky midfield skills more than compensating for a slight lack of pace. He rejected a proposed move to Wigan last February and instead committed himself to the Robins for the near future with a three-year deal. Always dangerous at set pieces with his curling free kicks Darren also contributed ten goals in league and cup games during 2000-01.

Manchester U (From trainee on 11/7/1990) F/PL 20+7 FLC 2+1
Wolverhampton W (£250,000 on 13/1/1994) FL 94+23/4 FLC 13+2/3 FAC 9+2/3 Others 6
Wrexham (Free on 17/9/1999) FL 80/13 FLC 2/1 FAC 6/1 Others 1

Darren Ferguson

FERGUSON Duncan
Born: Stirling, 27 December 1971
Height: 6'4" Weight: 14.6
Club Honours: SL '94; SLC '94; FAC '95
International Honours: S: 7; B; U21-7; Yth; Sch

It was with a huge sense of frustration that Evertonians watched their cult hero produce some of the most consistent goal scoring of his Goodison career only to fall victim to the injury curse that has plagued his whole career. When fully fit and focussed Duncan is a difficult centre forward to halt. His aerial strength is formidable and he is more adept on the floor than many give him credit for. Everton fans were thrilled when he returned from Newcastle United in a cut-price deal - and confirmed the Everton tattoo was still prominently displayed on his shoulder. Two goals after stepping off the substitutes' bench on his home debut against Charlton helped add to his legendary status. A dreadful tackle in that match sparked the start of many injury problems, however, including one bizarre incident when he broke his hand detaining an alleged intruder at his family home! The six goals he scored still proved invaluable in Everton's bid to avoid relegation and he will hope to produce a more sustained contribution next season.

Dundee U (Signed from Carse Thistle on 1/2/1990) SL 75+2/28 SLC 2+1/2 SC 6/4
Glasgow R (£4,000,000 on 20/7/1993) SL 8+6/2 SLC 2+2/3 SC 0+3 Others 1
Everton (£4,400,000 on 4/10/1994) PL 110+6/37 FLC 8/1 FAC 8+1/4
Newcastle U (£7,000,000 + on 25/11/1998) PL 24+6/8 FAC 6+2/3 Others 2+1/1
Everton (£3,750,000 on 19/8/2000) PL 9+3/6 FAC 1

FERNANDES Fabrice
Born: Paris, France, 29 October 1979
Height: 5'9" Weight: 11.7
Club Honours: Div 1 '01
International Honours: France: U21

Signed on a long-term loan from Rennes, Fabrice looked a terrific prospect on the left of a midfield for Fulham early on last season. He seemed to have all the attributes of a quality midfield player: brilliant ball control, pace and a superb shot, and few of the club's fans will forget his wonderful equalising goal against Manchester United in the FA Cup. However he struggled to fit into the team structure at Craven Cottage and was subsequently was allowed to join Glasgow Rangers in the new year where he scored a great goal on his debut but was restricted to outings from the subs' bench.

Fulham (Loaned from Rennes, France on 3/8/2000) FL 23+6/2 FLC 4+2/1 FAC 1

FERRER Albert Llopes
Born: Barcelona, Spain, 6 June 1970
Height: 5'7" Weight: 10.6
Club Honours: ESC '98
International Honours: Spain: 36; U23 (OLYM '92)

This superb Spanish international right back was still recovering from an ankle injury at the start of the 2000-01 season and the arrival of Christian Panucci on a long-term loan seemed to put his future at Stamford Bridge in doubt. However his luck changed when Claudio Ranieri took over as boss and he returned for the Blues in the 3-0 victory over Liverpool in October, retaining his place in the side while Panucci was released to join Monaco. A feature of Signor Ranieri's stewardship has been his willingness to vary his formations and Albert showed himself to be equally adept playing in a flat back four or pushed further forward into a right wing-back role within a five-man midfield. He broke the 100-appearance barrier for the club last season and has certainly been one of the most popular of the so-called 'Foreign Legion'.

Chelsea (£2,200,000 from Barcelona, Spain on 15/8/1998) PL 66+3 FLC 0+1 FAC 7 Others 22/1

FESTA Gianluca
Born: Cagliari, Italy, 15 March 1969
Height: 6'0" Weight: 13.6

This experienced central defender has a tough no-nonsense tackling style with an almost mischievous sense of adventure going forward, often leaving a mountain to climb when he needs to get back into position quickly. The big Italian has now completed five seasons with Middlesbrough where the fans adore him, while from the club viewpoint he remains one of the best buys Bryan Robson ever made. It was good news for all at the club when he declared himself to be settled on Teesside thus ruling out a bid from his old boss Claudio Ranieri at Chelsea.

Middlesbrough (£2,700,000 from Inter Milan, Italy, ex Cagliari, on 18/1/1997) F/PL 124+6/9 FLC 18/1 FAC 11/1

FETTIS Alan William
Born: Belfast, 1 February 1971
Height: 6'1" Weight: 12.10
International Honours: NI: 25; B-3; Yth; Sch

Alan had an outstanding season with York City in 2000-01 and his consistent displays were a huge factor in the Minstermen's successful battle in avoiding the dreaded drop into the Conference. He is an excellent goalkeeper who is both brave and agile. It was no surprise when he made a clean sweep of the end-of-season awards, winning the 'Clubman of the Year', Junior Reds and Supporters Club titles for best player.

Hull C (£50,000 from Ards on 14/8/1991) FL 131+4/2 FLC 7+1 FAC 5 Others 7
West Bromwich A (Loaned on 20/11/1995) FL 3
Nottingham F (£250,000 on 13/1/1996) PL 4 FLC 1 FAC 0+1
Blackburn Rov (£300,000 on 12/9/1997) P/FL 9+2 FAC 1
York C (Free on 1/3/2000) FL 59 FLC 1 FAC 4

FICKLING Ashley Spencer
Born: Sheffield, 15 November 1972
Height: 5'10" Weight: 11.6
International Honours: E: Sch

Ashley endured a disappointing season in 2000-01 when he only managed three league starts and was placed on the transfer-list early on. A trial at Mansfield failed to bring a permanent move and he then picked up a back injury in February that ruled him out for the remainder of the campaign. He is a solid and versatile defender who can play anywhere across the back four. He was released in the summer.

Sheffield U (From juniors on 26/7/1991) FLC 2+1 Others 3
Darlington (Loaned on 26/11/1992) FL 14 Others 1
Darlington (Loaned on 12/8/1993) FL 1 FLC 1
Grimsby T (Free on 23/3/1995) FL 26+13/2 FLC 2+1 FAC 2+1
Darlington (Loaned on 26/3/1998) FL 8
Scunthorpe U (Free on 24/7/1998) FL 55+13/1 FLC 4 FAC 3+1 Others 3

FILAN John Richard
Born: Sydney, Australia, 8 February 1970
Height: 5'11" Weight: 13.2
International Honours: Australia: 1; U23

Having recovered from the shoulder injury that kept him out of action for the second half of the 1999-2000 campaign, John had to wait until September before he was able to displace Alan Kelly as Blackburn's regular 'keeper. Generally cool under pressure and performing competently he retained his place in the line-up until boss Graham Souness brought in Brad Friedel in November and subsequently only featured as cover for injuries.

Cambridge U (£40,000 from Budapest St George, Australia on 12/3/1993) FL 68 FLC 6 FAC 3 Others 3
Coventry C (£300,000 on 2/3/1995) PL 15+1 FLC 2
Blackburn Rov (£700,000 on 10/7/1997) P/FL 61+1 FLC 5 FAC 5

FINNAN Stephen (Steve) John
Born: Limerick, 20 April 1976
Height: 5'10" Weight: 11.6
Club Honours: Div 3 '98; Div 2 '99; Div 1 '01
International Honours: RoI: 7; B-1; U21-8

2000-01 was the season that Steve had always promised since signing for Fulham. He missed only one First Division match in his favoured right-back position and his combination play with Bjarne Goldbaek down the flank was the catalyst for several of the club's best performances. His passing and crossing were much improved and on the

occasions when he had to defend, his timing in the tackle and speed of recovery invariably kept the opposition at bay. He added further caps for the Republic of Ireland side and was also selected for the PFA's Division One side.
Birmingham C (£100,000 from Welling U on 12/6/1995) FL 9+6/1 FLC 2+2 Others 2+1
Notts Co (Loaned on 5/3/1996) FL 14+3/2 Others 3/1
Notts Co (£300,000 on 31/10/1996) FL 71+9/5 FLC 4 FAC 7/1 Others 1
Fulham (£600,000 on 13/11/1998) FL 101+1/6 FLC 7+1 FAC 9/1 Others 1

Steve Finnan

FINNIGAN John Francis
Born: Wakefield, 29 March 1976
Height: 5'8" Weight: 10.11
John was given the captain's armband for Lincoln City at the start of the 2000-01 campaign and formed an effective centre midfield partnership with his former Nottingham Forest colleague Justin Walker. His passing ability and battling qualities were very much in evidence with the only disappointment being his failure to find the net during the season.
Nottingham F (From trainee on 10/5/1993)
Lincoln C (£50,000 on 26/3/1998) FL 118+2/3 FLC 6 FAC 8/1 Others 7

FISH Mark Anthony
Born: Capetown, South Africa, 14 March 1974
Height: 6'3" Weight: 13.2
International Honours: South Africa (ANC '96)
Mark began last season in fine style at Bolton partnering Gudni Bergsson in the heart of the defence, but in November he elected for a move back into the Premiership when he signed for Charlton Athletic. He was immediately thrust into the side making his debut against Ipswich Town at Portman Road. Although primarily a central defender Mark played several games for the Addicks at right back but wherever he was employed he looked a class act. He is strong in the air, very comfortable on the ground and loves to run with the ball into the opposition half. He built a solid relationship with Richard Rufus at the heart of the Charlton defence and linked up well with his former Bolton colleague Andy Todd when the latter broke into the side at the end of December. Mark made a number of appearances for South Africa early last term to become Bolton's most-capped player but has since announced his retirement from international football.
Bolton W (£2,500,000 from Lazio, Italy, ex Orlando Pirates, on 16/9/1997) P/FL 102+1 FLC 12+1/1 FAC 6 Others 5
Charlton Ath (£700,000 on 10/11/2000) PL 24/1 FAC 3

FITZGERALD Scott Brian
Born: Westminster, 13 August 1969
Height: 6'0" Weight: 12.12
International Honours: RoI: B-1; U21-4
Scott found it difficult to break into the Millwall first team at the start of the 2000-01 campaign and after making just a single appearance from the subs' bench he was transferred to Colchester United in October. He was an ever-present at Layer Road until the final week of the season and did an effective job in shoring up a leaky defence. He was mostly employed by the U's as a sweeper in a three-man back line but also featured occasionally at left back.
Wimbledon (From trainee on 13/7/1989) F/PL 95+11/1 FLC 13 FAC 5 Others 1
Sheffield U (Loaned on 23/11/1995) FL 6
Millwall (Loaned on 11/10/1996) FL 7
Millwall (£50,000 + on 28/7/1997) FL 79+3/1 FLC 4 FAC 2 Others 5
Colchester U (Free on 17/10/2000) FL 30 FAC 1 Others 1

FITZPATRICK Ian Matthew
Born: Manchester, 22 September 1980
Height: 5'9" Weight: 10.6
International Honours: E: Yth; Sch
Having started 2000-01 on the subs' bench for Halifax, Ian netted his first goal of the season at Mansfield Town and followed this up with a stunning goal in the 2-1 win at Torquay. Shortly afterwards he picked up a calf injury but although he returned to fitness he struggled to win his place back and was mainly restricted to outings in the reserves. He is essentially a striker but can also play wide on the left or just behind the front two.
Manchester U (From trainee on 8/7/1998)
Halifax T (Free on 2/3/2000) FL 11+9/2 FLC 1+1

FITZPATRICK Lee Gareth
Born: Manchester, 31 October 1978
Height: 5'10" Weight: 11.7
Lee had a mixed time for Hartlepool in the 2000-01 campaign. He began the season in fine style, scoring both goals in a great 2-0 win at Lincoln on the opening day, but his form was subsequently a little patchy, and when Pool signed Mark Tinkler he was relegated to the subs' bench. He is a promising young midfield player who makes darting runs at opposition defences. Lee was surprisingly released in the summer.
Blackburn Rov (From trainee on 2/7/1996)
Hartlepool U (Loaned on 17/9/1999) FL 6+4/1
Hartlepool U (Free on 27/1/2000) FL 22+15/5 FLC 2/1 Others 1+4

FITZPATRICK Trevor Joseph James
Born: Frimley, 19 February 1980
Height: 6'1" Weight: 12.10
International Honours: RoI: Yth
Trevor had a disappointing campaign at Southend last season and never really established himself in the first team. Although he scored a number of goals when coming off the subs' bench he was made available to transfer in December and ultimately released from his contract in March. He headed for Ireland and after a brief trial was reported to have signed a contract for Shelbourne in May. Very skilful on the ball and with a good eye for goal, Trevor will be aiming to prove Blues' manager Dave Webb wrong in the 2001-02 campaign.
Southend U (From trainee on 6/7/1998) FL 17+36/8 FLC 1+2 FAC 0+2 Others 0+2

FLACK Steven (Steve) Richard
Born: Cambridge, 29 May 1971
Height: 6'2" Weight: 13.2
Last season saw the Steve Flack of old as he re-established himself as the first-choice target man for Exeter City. Although he sustained medial ligament damage against Scunthorpe in November Steve came firing back on all cylinders just six weeks later. He finished the season as the Grecians' leading scorer and among the highlights of a great campaign were a superb individual effort in the home game with Southend and a spell in March when he scored in five consecutive matches to equal a club record.
Cardiff C (£10,000 from Cambridge C on 13/11/1995) FL 6+5/1
Exeter C (£10,000 on 13/9/1996) FL 147+45/44 FLC 7+1 FAC 9+2/5 Others 6+2/2

FLAHAVAN Aaron Adam
Born: Southampton, 15 December 1975
Height: 6'1" Weight: 11.12
After some time as second-choice 'keeper at Portsmouth Aaron finally took over the jersey after Russell Hoult was sold to West Bromwich Albion early in the new year. He performed soundly in the closing weeks of the campaign, keeping several clean sheets and producing his fair share of spectacular saves. An accomplished shot stopper who commands his area well, he faces an important season in 2001-02 as he bids to establish himself as the number one 'keeper at Fratton Park. He is the brother of the Southend goalkeeper Darryl Flahaven. Fratton Park.
Portsmouth (From trainee on 15/2/1994) FL 93 FLC 11 FAC 1

FLAHAVAN Darryl James
Born: Southampton, 28 November 1978
Height: 5'10" Weight: 12.1
Darryl signed for Southend from Conference club Woking last October and took over between the posts when Andy Woodman's loan spell came to an end the following month. He proved to be a goalkeeper of exceptional talent, and immediately won over the Blues' fans with his performances, remaining first choice for the remainder of the season. He is very agile, shows good command of his area and has a powerful kick. Darryl is the younger brother of Portsmouth 'keeper Aaron Flahaven

Southampton (From trainee on 14/5/1996. Free to Woking on 13/8/1998)
Southend U (Free on 16/10/2000) FL 29 FAC 4 Others 6

FLEMING Craig
Born: Halifax, 6 October 1971
Height: 6'0" Weight: 12.10

Craig was again a consistent performer in the heart of the Norwich City defence in the 2000-01 campaign. Solid and dependable, he is a fierce competitor who is always prepared to throw his body in the way of a goal-bound shot. He signed a new contract midway through the season and played his 150th game for the Canaries in March.

Halifax T (From trainee on 21/3/1990) FL 56+1 FLC 4 FAC 3 Others 3+2
Oldham Ath (£80,000 on 15/8/1991) F/PL 158+6/1 FLC 12+1 FAC 11 Others 4
Norwich C (£600,000 on 30/6/1997) FL 132+5/7 FLC 15 FAC 3+1

FLEMING Curtis
Born: Manchester, 8 October 1968
Height: 5'11" Weight: 12.8
Club Honours: Div 1 '95
International Honours: RoI: 10; U23-2; U21-5; Yth

The Republic of Ireland defender, currently enjoying the tenth year of his Middlesbrough career, is still a firm favourite with most of the Riverside fans. His role has changed many times over the years and probably peaked during the early days of Bryan Robson's reign at the club when he adapted quite naturally to the art of the overlapping wing back. A regular in the Boro' line-up again last term his ability to soak up the pressure and recover lost balls from attackers was in evidence, added to a gritty and resolute attitude. Going forward he showed he could deliver some very telling crosses and he fitted in well in an ever-changing line-up.

Middlesbrough (£50,000 from St Patricks on 16/8/1991) F/PL 240+18/3 FLC 24+2/1 FAC 16+1 Others 7+1

FLEMING Terence (Terry) Maurice
Born: Marston Green, 5 January 1973
Height: 5'9" Weight: 10.9

Terry joined Plymouth on a three-year contract in the 2000 close season and made the starting line-up for the first few weeks of the campaign. However he struggled to win a regular place following a change in management at Home Park and in March he rejoined his old boss John Beck at Cambridge United. He scored a goal for the U's on his debut against Wrexham and provided a welcome boost for the team in the centre of the park. Terry is a combative midfield ball winner who possesses an effective long throw.

Coventry C (From trainee on 2/7/1991) F/PL 8+5 FLC 0+1
Northampton T (Free on 3/8/1993) FL 26+5/1 FLC 2 FAC 0+1 Others 0+1
Preston NE (Free on 18/7/1994) FL 25+7/2 FLC 4 FAC 0+1 Others 3+2
Lincoln C (Signed on 7/12/1995) FL 175+8/8 FLC 11+1/2 FAC 11/2 Others 4
Plymouth Arg (Free on 4/7/2000) FL 15+2 FLC 2 FAC 2 Others 0+2
Cambridge U (Free on 8/3/2001) FL 9+1/1

FLETCHER Carl Neil
Born: Camberley, 7 April 1980
Height: 5'10" Weight: 11.7

Having broken through at Bournemouth in the 1999-2000 campaign, Carl firmly established himself in the first team last season and rarely missed a game. A midfield player who is strong in the tackle and capable of scoring spectacular goals, he formed a strong partnership in the centre of the park with Richard Hughes. His performances earned him a new three-year contract with the Cherries.

Bournemouth (From trainee on 3/7/1998) FL 63+7/9 FLC 2 FAC 5/1 Others 1+1

FLETCHER Gary
Born: Widnes, 4 June 1981
Height: 5'10" Weight: 11.7

After developing through the Northwich Victoria youth set-up Gary became one of the hottest properties in non-league football last season with his scoring exploits against Bury and Leyton Orient in the FA Cup. He attracted the attention of a number of clubs before joining Hull City in a loan deal last March. A promising young striker he was mostly used from the subs' bench by the Tigers who have to decide on a permanent deal over the summer.

Hull C (Loaned from Northwich Vic on 16/3/2001) FL 1+4

Steve Fletcher

FLETCHER Steven (Steve) Mark
Born: Hartlepool, 26 June 1972
Height: 6'2" Weight: 14.9

Steve had another good season for Bournemouth in 2000-01 when he missed just one Second Division match and provided many of the chances for the free-scoring Jermain Defoe. A tall striker, he uses his height to good effect and holds the ball up well to bring his colleagues into play. Steve is the Cherries' longest-serving player and will start his tenth season with the club in 2001-02 having now passed 300 Football League games for them.

Hartlepool U (From trainee on 23/8/1990) FL 19+13/4 FLC 0+2/1 FAC 1+2 Others 2+2/1
Bournemouth (£30,000 on 28/7/1992) FL 293+18/60 FLC 26/3 FAC 17/3 Others 13/2

FLITCROFT David (Dave) John
Born: Bolton, 14 January 1974
Height: 5'11" Weight: 13.5

Dave was again a key figure in the centre of the park for Rochdale last season. In partnership with Gary Jones he never gave opponents any respite and his will to win was clear in every game. Apart from a brief spell out while undergoing a hernia operation in the autumn he rarely missed a game and even took over in goal after Neil Edwards was sent off at Southend. Dave is a battling midfield player with a good long-range shot. He is the younger brother of Blackburn's Garry Flitcroft.

Preston NE (From trainee on 2/5/1992) FL 4+4/2 FLC 0+1 Others 0+1
Lincoln C (Loaned on 17/9/1993) FL 2 FLC 0+1
Chester C (Free on 9/12/1993) FL 146+21/18 FLC 10+1 FAC 7 Others 8/1
Rochdale (Free on 5/7/1999) FL 80+4/2 FLC 3+1 FAC 1+2 Others 5+1

FLITCROFT Garry William
Born: Bolton, 6 November 1972
Height: 6'0" Weight: 12.2
International Honours: E: U21-10; Yth; Sch

A near-ever present for Blackburn last season, Garry was something of an unsung hero and his value as a defensive organiser only became apparent in his absence. Captain of the team he provided bite and a physical presence in midfield where he generally performed in a role just in front of the central defenders. He became more adventurous in the second half of the campaign and pushed forward to score vital goals in the FA Cup win over Bolton and the 2-0 victory over Huddersfield. He is the brother of Preston's Dave Flitcroft.

Manchester C (From trainee on 2/7/1991) PL 109+6/13 FLC 11+1 FAC 14/2
Bury (Loaned on 5/3/1992) FL 12
Blackburn Rov (£3,200,000 on 26/3/1996) P/FL 125+7/8 FLC 5+2/1 FAC 8+1/2 Others 2/1

Garry Flitcroft

FLO Tore Andre
Born: Stryn, Norway, 15 June 1973
Height: 6'4" Weight: 13.8
Club Honours: FLC '98; ECWC '98; ESC '98; FAC '00; CS '00
International Honours: Norway: 56; U21

One of the outcomes of Gianluca Vialli's departure as manager of Chelsea was an end to the controversial rotation policy he had operated. Unfortunately this meant that Tore Andre could not be guaranteed a regular starting place and after requesting a transfer he was sold for a substantial fee to Glasgow Rangers at the end of November. Sadly missed by the Stamford Bridge faithful, Tore Andre scored a memorable double at Old Trafford before leaving, to turn a 3-1 deficit into a thoroughly deserved 3-3 draw: a diving header through the 'keeper's legs and a clinical 'pass' into the net from a diagonal angle. In a world away from Chelsea's fluent passing game he had spent Euro 2000 gazing mournfully skywards as Norway lumped high balls from one end of the pitch to the other and sadly under-used one of their star players.

Chelsea (£300,000 from Brann Bergen, Norway, ex Sogndal, Tromso, on 4/8/1997) PL 59+53/34 FLC 7+2/3 FAC 5+5/1 Others 23+9/12

FLOWERS Timothy (Tim) David
Born: Kenilworth, 3 February 1967
Height: 6'2" Weight: 14.0
Club Honours: PL '95; FLC '00
International Honours: E: 11; U21-3; Yth

Tim was in outstanding form in the early part of last season winning the Carling Premiership 'Player of the Month' award for September after conceding just one goal from open play in the first eight league fixtures. He was being widely touted for an England recall and his prospects seemed bright when club manager Peter Taylor took temporary charge of the national team. However a series of back and hip injuries rather wrecked his season thereafter. Indeed, the hip trouble proved so severe that he was out of first-team contention from the turn of the year until Easter and his inspirational presence was clearly missed by the rest of City's rearguard. Tim is now resigned to living with the hip problems until he eventually retires when he will require a major operation.

Wolverhampton W (From apprentice on 28/8/1984) FL 63 FLC 5 FAC 2 Others 2
Southampton (£70,000 on 13/6/1986) F/PL 192 FLC 26 FAC 16 Others 8
Swindon T (Loaned on 23/3/1987) FL 2
Swindon T (Loaned on 13/11/1987) FL 5
Blackburn Rov (£2,400,000 on 4/11/1993) PL 175+2 FLC 14 FAC 13+1 Others 12
Leicester C (£1,100,000 + on 30/7/1999) PL 51 FLC 5+1 FAC 2 Others 2

FLYNN Lee David
Born: Hampstead, 4 September 1973
Height: 5'9" Weight: 12.0

Lee joined Barnet from Conference club Hayes last January and immediately went into the Bees' first team. He took a while to adapt to Third Division football but once he had settled in he produced some consistent displays at left back or left wing back depending on the formation employed. He was placed on the open to offers list in the summer.

Barnet (£13,500 from Hayes on 10/1/2001) FL 17 Others 1

FLYNN Michael (Mike) Anthony
Born: Oldham, 23 February 1969
Height: 6'0" Weight: 11.0

Stockport County's inspirational skipper rarely missed a game last season and was one of the cornerstones in a defence that conceded just four goals in the final nine games to provide the foundation on which the Hatters' built their successful First Division survival campaign. An uncompromising central defender he led the team by example and now stands in fifth place in the club's all-time appearance list. Mike is likely to remain an important figure for County in the near future as he signed a new long-term contract during the season.

Oldham Ath (From apprentice on 7/2/1987) FL 37+3/1 FLC 1+1/1 FAC 1 Others 2
Norwich C (£100,000 on 22/12/1988)
Preston NE (£125,000 on 4/12/1989) FL 134+2/7 FLC 6 FAC 6+1/1 Others 13
Stockport Co (£125,000 on 25/3/1993) FL 360+1/14 FLC 32/2 FAC 20/1 Others 19

Mike Flynn

FLYNN Sean Michael
Born: Birmingham, 13 March 1968
Height: 5'8" Weight: 11.8

Tranmere secured Sean's services during the close season and he went on to feature regularly for Rovers last term. A determined and diligent right-sided or central midfielder he provided inspirational leadership from the centre of the park, constantly encouraging his team-mates with his never-say-die approach. He will be an important figure for Rovers in 2001-02 as they attempt to win back their place in Division One at the first time of asking.

Coventry C (£20,000 from Halesowen T on 3/12/1991) F/PL 90+7/9 FLC 5/1 FAC 3
Derby Co (£250,000 on 11/8/1995) F/PL 39+20/3 FLC 3 FAC 3
Stoke C (Loaned on 27/3/1997) FL 5
West Bromwich A (£260,000 on 8/8/1997) FL 99+10/8 FLC 11/1 FAC 0+2
Tranmere Rov (Free on 18/7/2000) FL 35/1 FLC 5 FAC 4

FOLAN Anthony (Tony) Stephen
Born: Lewisham, 18 September 1978
Height: 5'11" Weight: 11.8
Club Honours: Div 3 '99
International Honours: RoI: U21-6

This very talented left-sided midfield player began the 2000-01 season as a regular in the Brentford first-team squad and netted the winner at Oxford last August. He then fell out of favour before suffering an injury that required a cartilage operation in December. Once he had recovered fitness Tony appeared regularly in the squad towards the end of the campaign but was unable to recover his best form during this period.

Crystal Palace (From trainee on 22/9/1995) PL 0+1 Others 1
Brentford (£100,000 on 22/9/1998) FL 31+28/7 FLC 2+3 FAC 3+1/2 Others 2

FOLEY Dominic Joseph
Born: Cork, 7 July 1976
Height: 6'1" Weight: 12.8
International Honours: RoI: 6; U21-8

Having done well with the Republic of Ireland in their Nike Cup tournament matches during the close season, Dominic got off to a great start in the 2000-01 campaign when he came off the subs' bench against Barnsley to score a spectacular last-minute winner. However despite a declaration of support from Hornets' boss Graham Taylor he was unable to claim a regular first-team place and then had the misfortune to suffer a stress fracture of the fibula in December that kept him on the sidelines for some time. A tall striker he will be hoping to make a breakthrough at Vicarage Road in the coming season.

Wolverhampton W (£35,000 from St James' Gate on 31/8/1995) FL 4+16/3 FLC 0+3 FAC 0+1 Others 0+2
Watford (Loaned on 24/2/1998) FL 2+6/1
Notts Co (Loaned on 7/12/1998) FL 2 Others 1
Watford (Free on 11/6/1999) P/FL 5+12/2 FLC 2+3

FOLLAND Robert (Rob) William
Born: Swansea, 16 September 1979
Height: 5'9" Weight: 11.0
International Honours: W: U21-1; Yth

Rob was very much a forgotten figure at Oxford United for much of last season. He played a number of early season games under Dennis Smith but was then overlooked by his successor David Kemp and it was only in the final two games that he returned to the first team. However despite the disappointment of relegation the season ended on something of a personal high for him as he scored United's only goal at Notts County and was then offered a 12-month extension to his contract by the club. Rob is a promising young striker who can also play at wing back if required.

Oxford U (From trainee on 3/7/1998) FL 18+12/2 FLC 4+2 FAC 4+1/1 Others 1

FORAN Mark James
Born: Aldershot, 30 October 1973
Height: 6'4" Weight: 14.3
Mark joined Bristol Rovers shortly before the start of the 2000-01 campaign and made an excellent debut in the opening game against Bournemouth. However he subsequently struggled to retain his place and was one of 13 players transfer-listed by the Pirates in January. He turned down the opportunity of a loan spell at Carlisle United and to his credit forced his way back into the side for the final two matches. He is a central defender who uses his height to great advantage and is always a threat at set pieces.
Millwall (From trainee on 3/11/1990)
Sheffield U (£25,000 on 28/8/1993) FL 10+1/1 FLC 1 Others 0+1
Rotherham U (Loaned on 26/8/1994) FL 3
Wycombe W (Loaned on 11/8/1995) FL 5 FLC 2
Peterborough U (£40,000 on 8/2/1996) FL 22+3/1 FAC 1 Others 2
Lincoln C (Loaned on 22/1/1997) FL 1+1
Oldham Ath (Loaned on 3/3/1997) FL 0+1
Crewe Alex (£25,000 + on 12/12/1997) FL 25+6/1 FLC 2 FAC 1
Bristol Rov (Free on 11/8/2000) FL 9+3 FLC 1+1 Others 1

FORBES Adrian Emmanuel
Born: Ealing, 23 January 1979
Height: 5'8" Weight: 11.10
International Honours: E: Yth
Although a regular in the Norwich City squad Adrian often found himself on the subs' bench last term. He never seemed to be able to establish himself in any one particular position, but his versatility proved an asset as he performed in a number of different roles during the campaign. Predominantly recognised as a wing man, where his speed and direct style made him a difficult opponent for full backs, he was also often used as a central striker where again his pace and ability to turn defenders unsettled many a back line. He also contributed some terrific goals, notably a spectacular winner at home to Birmingham and a great solo effort in the home draw with Blackburn. Adrian signed a new one-year deal in March and he will hope for a regular place in the starting line-up in 2001-02.
Norwich C (From trainee on 21/1/1997) FL 66+46/8 FLC 1+4 FAC 2+2

FORBES Scott Hugh
Born: Canewdon, 3 December 1976
Height: 5'8" Weight: 11.2
Another of Southend's non-league bargains, Scott joined from Essex Senior League outfit Saffron Walden Town in the 2000 close season and made his Football League debut on the opening day of the campaign when he came on from the subs' bench against Brighton. He soon earned a regular place in the starting line-up and remained in the Blues' team throughout the season. A left-sided midfielder with a huge amount of stamina, Scott makes up for his small frame with an all-action style, often winning tackles and headers against opponents much larger than himself.
Southend U (Free from Braintree on 10/8/2000) FL 27+7/3 FLC 0+1 FAC 4/1 Others 4

FORD James Anthony
Born: Portsmouth, 23 October 1981
Height: 5'8" Weight: 11.0
Another of the many promising youngsters to develop through Bournemouth's successful youth system, James was very much on the fringe of the first-team squad last season. He featured from the subs' bench on a handful of occasions in the early part of the campaign and spent time on loan with Dorchester Town in the new year to gain experience of senior football. A promising midfield player, he will be looking to gain more first-team action in the coming season.
Bournemouth (From trainee on 12/4/2000) FL 0+5

FORD Mark Stuart
Born: Pontefract, 10 October 1975
Height: 5'8" Weight: 10.10
Club Honours: FAYC '93
International Honours: E: U21-2; Yth
Mark joined Torquay United in the 2000 close season after a spell in Belgium and inherited the captaincy from the injured Brian Healy. He coolly dispatched four penalties during his stay including one in the local 'derby' with Exeter. In the midst of a fierce relegation scrap, it was surprising to say the least when the Gulls agreed to let their skipper move to rivals Darlington. He immediately became an integral part of the Quakers' team, his vision and experience in the centre of the park being major factors in the club's improved performances towards the end of the campaign. A combative central midfield player he passes the ball accurately and is also capable of moving forward to score spectacular goals from the edge of the box.
Leeds U (From trainee on 5/3/1993) PL 27+2/1 FLC 7 FAC 5 Others 0+1
Burnley (£250,000 on 18/7/1997) FL 43+5/1 FLC 2 FAC 1+1 Others 5+1 (Free to KFC Lommelse, Belgium during 1999 close season)
Torquay U (Free on 17/7/2000) FL 28/3 FLC 2 FAC 2/1 Others 1
Darlington (£15,000 on 19/2/2001) FL 11/2

FORD Michael (Mike) Paul
Born: Bristol, 9 February 1966
Height: 6'0" Weight: 12.6
Club Honours: WC '88
Having effectively retired from playing at the end of the 1999-2000 campaign Mike was appointed youth-team manager at Oxford United in the close season but was forced back into action by an injury crisis at the Manor Ground. He made a single first-team appearance at full back against Bristol City in September, putting on a competent display before returning to the back room. Soon afterwards he was appointed caretaker-manager following Dennis Smith's departure and he had a second brief spell in charge of team affairs at the very end of the season when he was responsible for introducing several youngsters into senior football.
Leicester C (From apprentice on 11/2/1984)
Cardiff C (Free from Devizes T on 19/9/1984) FL 144+1/13 FLC 6 FAC 9 Others 7
Oxford U (£150,000 on 10/6/1988) FL 273+16/18 FLC 27+1/2 FAC 12+1/1 Others 8/1
Cardiff C (Free on 29/7/1998) FL 48+3 FLC 4 FAC 10/1
Oxford U (Free on 28/9/2000) FL 1

FORD Robert (Bobby) John
Born: Bristol, 22 September 1974
Height: 5'9" Weight: 11.0
Bobby continued to play a key role for Sheffield United last season and apart from a suspension and a short spell out with a foot injury in the autumn he rarely missed a match for the Blades. He worked hard in midfield helping out in both defence and attack, and every now and again producing a telling pass. Although his goal tally from open play was disappointing he was nominated as the club's regular penalty taker for a while, but after netting from his first three spot kicks he met with failure against Nottingham Forest.
Oxford U (From trainee on 6/10/1992) FL 104+12/7 FLC 14+2/1 FAC 10/2 Others 7/1
Sheffield U (£400,000 on 28/11/1997) FL 118+11/6 FLC 8+2/1 FAC 12+4 Others 2

FORD Ryan
Born: Worksop, 3 September 1980
Height: 5'9" Weight: 10.4
Ryan continued to make steady progress with the Notts County reserve team last season and stepped up to make a single first-team appearance in the LDV Vans Trophy tie at Port Vale. A promising young midfield player with good passing skills, he will be aiming to break into the senior squad more often in the 2001-02 campaign.
Manchester U (From trainee on 11/7/1997)
Notts Co (Free on 1/2/2000) FL 0+1 Others 1

FORD Tony
Born: Grimsby, 14 May 1959
Height: 5'10" Weight: 13.0
Club Honours: Div 3 '80; FLGC '82
International Honours: E: B-2
Rochdale's 41-year-old assistant manager continued to defy his years and was again a regular in the midfield in the 2000-01 campaign. Although perhaps now lacking some pace, his pinpoint crosses nevertheless set up numerous goals for colleagues. Already holder of the record number of senior appearances for an outfield player he established two new landmarks last season. He became Rochdale's oldest-ever Football League player, succeeding 1950's player Jack Warner, and played his 900th Football League game against Scunthorpe in February, a milestone only previously reached by Peter Shilton.
Grimsby T (From apprentice on 1/5/1977) FL 321+34/55 FLC 31+3/4 FAC 15+4/2 Others 2
Sunderland (Loaned on 27/3/1986) FL 8+1/1
Stoke C (£35,000 on 8/7/1986) FL 112/13 FLC 8 FAC 9 Others 6/1
West Bromwich A (£145,000 on 24/3/1989) FL 114/14 FLC 7 FAC 4/1 Others 2+1
Grimsby T (£50,000 on 21/11/1991) FL 59+9/3 FLC 1 FAC 3
Bradford C (Loaned on 16/9/1993) FL 5 FLC 2
Scunthorpe U (Free on 2/8/1994) FL 73+3/9 FLC 4/1 FAC 7/1 Others 4 (Free to Barrow on 22/8/1996)
Mansfield T (Free on 25/10/1996) FL 97+6/7 FLC 4/1 FAC 4/1 Others 5
Rochdale (Free on 6/7/1999) FL 64+8/4 FLC 4 FAC 4 Others 3+1

FORDE Fabian Wesley
Born: Harrow, 26 October 1981
Height: 5'11" Weight: 13.7
Fabian did well with the reserve and youth

teams at Watford last term and stepped up to join the professional ranks in March. A promising striker with a good scoring record at junior level he made his Football League debut in the last game of the season at Burnley when he came off the subs' bench in the closing minutes.
Watford (From trainee on 7/3/2001) FL 0+1

FORGE Nicolas
Born: Roanne, France, 13 May 1971
Height: 6'0" Weight: 12.8
Having been released by Valence at the end of the 1999-2000 season following their relegation from the French Second Division Nicolas spent the early part of last term recovering from injury. He then failed to find a new club during the transfer window at the turn of the year and subsequently joined Leyton Orient on a non-contract basis in March and went on to make a single first team appearance at Cardiff as cover for the suspended Dave McGhee. An experienced central midfield player he was allowed to return home soon afterwards.
Leyton Orient (Free from ASOA Valence, France, following an injury and trials at Darlington and Notts Co, ex Troyes, Martigues, on 2/3/2001) FL 1

FORINTON Howard Lee
Born: Boston, 18 September 1975
Height: 5'11" Weight: 11.4
Howard had a frustrating time at Peterborough in 2000-01 when injuries and loss of form meant that he rarely featured in the first team. An early-season hernia operation kept him out until December and in the new year he was loaned out to Conference title-hopefuls Yeovil Town. However in his second game for them he suffered a broken nose and injured ankle and knee ligaments when falling awkwardly and he failed to recover match fitness before the summer break. A bustling all-action striker with a good eye for goal he will be hoping for a change in fortune in the coming season.
Birmingham C (Signed from Yeovil T on 14/7/1997) FL 0+4/1 FLC 1+1
Plymouth Arg (Loaned on 18/12/1998) FL 8+2/3 FLC 1+2
Peterborough U (£250,000 on 17/9/1999) FL 21+12/8 FLC 1 FAC 2+2 Others 2

FORREST Craig Lorne
Born: Vancouver, Canada, 20 September 1967
Height: 6'5" Weight: 14.4
Club Honours: Div 2 '92
International Honours: Canada: 56 (Gold Cup 2000)
A good safe all-round goalkeeper, Craig began the 2000-01 campaign as second choice to Shaka Hislop at West Ham and then missed several weeks in the autumn due to a hernia problem. However he was back in action in the new year and took over for a brief run in the team when his rival was sidelined by injury. He subsequently dropped out of the first-team picture and suffered further injury problems with a broken finger. Craig continued to represent Canada and featured for them in both World Cup qualifiers and the Confederations Cup tournament during the season.
Ipswich T (From apprentice on 31/8/1985) F/PL 263 FLC 16 FAC 11 Others 14
Colchester U (Loaned on 1/3/1988) FL 11
Chelsea (Loaned on 26/3/1997) PL 2+1
West Ham U (£500,000 on 23/7/1997) PL 26+4 FLC 3 FAC 4 Others 1

FORREST Martyn William
Born: Bury, 2 January 1979
Height: 5'10" Weight: 12.2
Martyn made steady progress at Bury last season when he was much more involved at first-team level than he had been in 1999-2000. He enjoyed a sustained run in the team during the second half of the campaign and impressed with his commitment and undoubted skill on the ball. He also showed his leadership skills when captaining the Shakers' reserve team and skippering the first team when Nick Daws was unavailable. Martyn is a highly-rated midfield player who will be looking to establish himself as a regular in the line-up in 2001-02.
Bury (From trainee on 16/7/1997) FL 29+14 FLC 0+2 FAC 0+1 Others 1

FORRESTER Jamie Mark
Born: Bradford, 1 November 1974
Height: 5'6" Weight: 11.0
Club Honours: FAYC '93
International Honours: E: Yth (UEFA-U18 '93); Sch
Jamie signed for Northampton on a permanent basis during the 2000 close season and justified the large fee paid by Cobblers' manager Kevin Wilson by finishing the campaign as the club's leading scorer with 19 league and cup goals. He is a lively striker with an eye for goal, equally effective with either foot and capable of holding the ball up well.
Leeds U (£60,000 from Auxerre, France on 20/10/1992) PL 7+2 FAC 1+1/2
Southend U (Loaned on 1/9/1994) FL 3+2
Grimsby T (Loaned on 10/3/1995) FL 7+2/1
Grimsby T (Signed on 17/10/1995) FL 27+14/6 FLC 0+2 FAC 3+1/3
Scunthorpe U (Signed on 21/3/1997) FL 99+2/37 FLC 6/2 FAC 7/4 Others 7 (Free to FC Utrecht, Holland on 1/6/1999)
Walsall (Free on 30/12/1999) FL 2+3
Northampton T (£150,000 on 21/3/2000) FL 51+2/23 FLC 2 FAC 2/2

FORSSELL Mikael
Born: Steinfurt, Germany, 15 March 1981
Height: 6'1" Weight: 12.8
International Honours: Finland: 13; U21; Yth
This classy young Chelsea striker spent the whole of last season on loan at Crystal Palace as he continued with his football education. Although in and out of the Eagles starting line-up in the first few months of the campaign he made himself an automatic choice by scoring 11 goals in a run of 13 matches and made a significant contribution to Palace's run to the Worthington Cup semi-final. He showed excellent ball control and looked particularly impressive when receiving through balls to feet. Mikael also broke through to become a regular member of the Finland international squad.
Chelsea (Free from HJK Helsinki, Finland on 18/12/1998) PL 4+6/1FLC 1 FAC 1+2/2 Others 1
Crystal Palace (Loaned on 23/2/2000) FL 44+8/16 FLC 8/2 FAC 1+1

FORSTER Nicholas (Nicky) Michael
Born: Caterham, 8 September 1973
Height: 5'10" Weight: 11.5
International Honours: E: U21-4
Nicky had the misfortune to suffer torn knee ligaments playing in a pre-season friendly for Reading against Charlton Athletic and it was only towards the very end of last term that he recovered sufficiently to take his place on the subs' bench. He was particularly effective in the home leg of the play-off semi-final against Wigan when he turned the game, setting up Martin Butler for the equaliser and winning the penalty which he put in from the rebound after Jamie Cureton's kick was saved. Now fully fit, he will vie with Butler and Cureton for a place in the Royals' strike force in the coming season.
Gillingham (Signed from Horley T on 22/5/1992) FL 54+13/24 FLC 3+2 FAC 6/2
Brentford (£100,000 on 17/6/1994) FL 108+1/39 FLC 11/3 FAC 8/1 Others 7+1/4
Birmingham C (£700,000 on 31/1/1997) FL 24+44/11 FLC 2+2/1 FAC 3+1
Reading (£650,000 on 23/6/1999) FL 31+14/11 FLC 3 FAC 2 Others 1+4/1

FORSYTH Richard Michael
Born: Dudley, 3 October 1970
Height: 5'11" Weight: 13.0
Club Honours: GMVC '94
International Honours: E: SP-3
Having joined Peterborough in July 2000 Richard took time to settle in at London Road but quickly showed that he was an excellent acquisition for boss Barry Fry. He controlled the centre of midfield and made the team click in the first half of the season, but was badly hampered by injuries after Christmas and rarely featured afterwards. He was sorely missed by Posh and the team appeared much less fluid in his absence.
Birmingham C (£50,000 from Kidderminster Hrs on 13/7/1995) FL 12+14/2 FLC 7+2 FAC 2 Others 3+1
Stoke C (£200,000 on 25/7/1996) FL 90+5/17 FLC 7/1 FAC 4 Others 1+1
Blackpool (Free on 5/7/1999) FL 10+3 FAC 0+2 Others 0+1
Peterborough U (Free on 14/7/2000) FL 25+5/2 FLC 2 FAC 5/1 Others 0+1

FORTUNE Jonathan (Jon) Jay
Born: Islington, 23 August 1980
Height: 6'2" Weight: 11.4
Having spent time on loan with Mansfield in 1999-2000 Jon returned to Field Mill for a second loan spell last September as Stags' manager Billy Dearden attempted to plug a leaky defence. His influence was immediately felt on his debut at Exeter when the team recorded their first clean sheet of the season and he went on to produce a series of fine performances in his three months with the club. Jon then returned to the Valley to continue his development with Charlton reserves. He is a commanding central defender with good pace and excellent distribution. He is the nephew of the Cardiff striker Leo Fortune-West.
Charlton Ath (From trainee on 2/7/1998)
Mansfield T (Loaned on 18/2/2000) FL 4
Mansfield T (Loaned on 31/8/2000) FL 14

FORTUNE Quinton
Born: Cape Town, South Africa, 21 May 1977
Height: 5'11" Weight: 11.11
International Honours: South Africa

Quinton got off to a flyer in the 2000-01 campaign when he scored twice in Manchester United's six-goal thrashing of Bradford City in September, and despite only making fleeting appearances in the side up to December he managed an appearance as a substitute in the Champions' League encounter against Dynamo Kiev. Still very much on the fringe of United's first-team, a knee injury kept him out for two months in the new year but the big test of establishing himself full-time will start in earnest come August. He continued to appear for South Africa in their campaign to qualify for the 2002 world Cup finals. He was placed on the open to offers list in the summer.

Manchester U (£1,500,000 from Atletico Madrid, Spain on 27/8/1999) PL 10+3/4 FLC 2 Others 2+6/2

FORTUNE-WEST Leopold (Leo) Paul Osborne
Born: Stratford, 9 April 1971
Height: 6'3" Weight: 13.10

This big and powerful striker began last season at Rotherham where he netted just one goal in seven outings. However just days after pledging his future to the Millers he was on his way to Cardiff City, where he once again proved how useful he is at disrupting lower division defences. He was particularly effective when Andy Legg delivered his long throws into the box, as Leo would draw defenders to him allowing others such as Scott Young to move in to score. He was one of five Bluebirds to reach a double-figure goal tally as he featured in a promotion-winning team for the second year in a row. He is the uncle of the young Charlton prospect Jay Fortune.

Gillingham (£5,000 from Stevenage Borough on 12/7/1995) FL 48+19/18 FLC 3+1/2 FAC 3+1/2
Leyton Orient (Loaned on 27/3/1997) FL 1+4
Lincoln C (Free on 6/7/1998) FL 7+2/1 FLC 2
Rotherham U (Loaned on 8/10/1998) FL 5/4
Brentford (£60,000 on 17/11/1998) FL 2+9 FAC 0+1 Others 2+1/1
Rotherham U (£35,000 on 26/2/1999) FL 59/26 FLC 4 FAC 2 Others 2
Cardiff C (£300,000 on 11/9/2000) FL 28+9/12 FAC 4/1

FOSTER James **Ian**
Born: Liverpool, 11 November 1976
Height: 5'7" Weight: 11.0
Club Honours: NC '00
International Honours: E: SP-1; Sch

The leading scorer in Kidderminster's promotion-winning season, Ian began 2000-01 as a regular in the starting line-up but went down with a hamstring injury only to return to the team in October. However the problem refused to go away and a further breakdown in January put him out for the remainder of the campaign. He is a small speedy striker with a good eye for goal.

Hereford U (Free from Liverpool juniors on 15/7/1996) FL 4+15 FLC 2+1 Others 0+1 (Free to Barrow during 1998 close season)
Kidderminster Hrs (Free on 13/8/1999) FL 9+1/2 FLC 1 FAC 2 Others 1

FOSTER Stephen (Steve)
Born: Mansfield, 3 December 1974
Height: 6'1" Weight: 12.0
Club Honours: FAT '97

Steve once again proved to be one of the most consistent and reliable players for Bristol Rovers last season. A near ever-present for the Pirates he also found time to score the winning goals at Wycombe and Oxford. He is a powerful central defender who is very effective as a man-to-man marker. Steve was deservedly voted as the supporters' club 'Player of the Season'.

Mansfield T (From trainee on 15/7/1993) FL 2+3 FLC 2 (Free to Telford on 22/1/1994)
Bristol Rov (£150,000 from Woking on 23/5/1997) FL 160+4/6 FLC 12 FAC 11 Others 10

FOSTER Stephen (Steve) John
Born: Warrington, 10 September 1980
Height: 5'11" Weight: 11.8
International Honours: E: Sch

Another product of Crewe Alexandra's successful youth system Steve returned to first-team action last term after missing the whole of the 1999-2000 campaign with a cruciate ligament injury. He scored his first goal for the club in the Worthington Cup tie against Bury and went on to feature regularly during the season. A powerful central defender who is effective in the air he will be hoping to continue to progress at Gresty Road in the coming season.

Crewe Alex (From trainee on 19/9/1998) FL 21+10 FLC 2+1/1 FAC 3

FOSTERVOLD Knut Anders
Born: Norway, 4 October 1971
Height: 6'2" Weight: 13.10

Having appeared for Molde in their UEFA Cup ties against Rayo Vallecano last September, Knut Anders joined Grimsby Town in November for a three-month loan period that coincided with the Norwegian close season. A vastly experienced player he became an instant favourite of the Blundell Park faithful after some fine performances but he returned home in February. He is a powerful left-sided defender who is very strong in the challenge.

Grimsby T (Loaned from Molde FK, Norway, ex Eik Tonsberg, on 20/11/2000) FL 9+1

FOTIADIS Panos **Andrew**
Born: Hitchin, 6 September 1977
Height: 5'11" Weight: 11.7
International Honours: E: Sch

Andrew was dogged throughout the 2000-01 campaign by hamstring and groin problems and these not only prevented him from getting a decent run in the Luton Town team but also cost him the chance of a call-up to the Cyprus national team. A lively striker with good skills on the ball and a useful scoring record, he will be hoping to steer clear of injuries in the coming season.

Luton T (From juniors on 26/7/1996) FL 42+56/11 FLC 2+6/1 FAC 4/1 Others 3+2

FOWLER Jason Kenneth
Born: Bristol, 20 August 1974
Height: 6'3" Weight: 11.12

Ian Foster

Jason had a frustrating time in 2000-01 when he seemed to be lacking in energy. It took the medical staff some time to find the cause of this but he was eventually diagnosed as suffering from an over-active thyroid. He featured in a handful of first team games for Cardiff City and by the end of the season had been given the all-clear. At his best Jason is one of the Bluebirds most creative forces in midfield with a great touch, good passing skills and the ability to produce the unexpected.

Bristol C (From trainee on 8/7/1993) FL 16+9 FLC 1+2 Others 1+1
Cardiff C (Signed on 19/6/1996) FL 138+7/14 FLC 8/1 FAC 12+2/4 Others 3/1

FOWLER Robert (Robbie) Bernard
Born: Liverpool, 9 April 1975
Height: 5'11" Weight: 11.10
Club Honours: FLC '95, '01; FAC '01; UEFAC '01
International Honours: E: 18; B-1; U21-8; Yth (UEFA-U18 '93)

Another frustrating season for the mercurial Liverpool striker ended happily in a blaze of glory as Robbie played his part in the Reds' triple strike for cup glory and returned in style to the England national team. Plagued by injury in recent seasons he began the 2000-01 campaign on the sidelines with an ankle problem. Once fit he spent much of the remainder of the season as the odd man out, for although manager Gerard Houllier rotated his strikers around he seemed to prefer Emile Heskey and Michael Owen as his first-choice pairing. In truth he was a shadow of his former self when he returned in September but once off the mark he began to score regularly, particularly in the Worthington Cup ties. A hat-trick in the 8-0 slaughter of Stoke City was followed by one of his best performances in recent seasons in the semi-final second leg victory over Crystal Palace, while his 30-yard dipping volley in the final against Birmingham City was a contender for 'Goal of the Season' and deserved to be the winner. However as Liverpool's season approached its frenetic conclusion he became more marginalised and must have been hugely disappointed to be on the bench for both the FA and UEFA Cup Finals, although he came on in both matches, scoring an outstanding goal against Deportivo Alaves. He was again in top form for the final Premiership match of the season at Charlton when he scored twice and linked up well with his striking partner Michael Owen, before being recalled to the England team in May, scoring in the 4-0 victory over Mexico and also playing in the World Cup qualifier in Greece.

Liverpool (From trainee on 23/4/1992) P/FL 202+24/117 FLC 32/27 FAC 21+3/12 Others 24+7/11

FOX Christian
Born: Stonehaven, 11 April 1981
Height: 5'10" Weight: 11.5

This promising York City youngster was bedevilled by injuries last season, suffering from hamstring trouble early on and then damaging a knee cartilage. An initial operation appeared to have resolved the problem and he returned to the first team at the end of December before it flared up again. Further surgery was required and it is hoped that he will be fully fit by the start of the 2001-02 campaign. Christian is a midfield player with good control and the ability to run at opposition defenders.

York C (From trainee on 29/6/1999) FL 31+11/1 FLC 1 FAC 2 Others 2

FOX Ruel Adrian
Born: Ipswich, 14 January 1968
Height: 5'6" Weight: 10.10
Club Honours: FLC '99
International Honours: E: B-2

Ruel had a superb season at West Bromwich Albion in 2000-01 when his vast experience was a major factor in the club reaching the play-offs. Operating mostly in a free role just behind the front two, he was the instigator of numerous attacking moves, his intelligent passing and thoughtful promptings standing out time and time again. He also delivered many teasing corners and free-kicks to set up chances for the Baggies' prolific strike force. Awarded the captain's armband when Derek McInnes was sidelined by injury he soldiered on towards the end of the campaign despite a nagging groin strain.

Norwich C (From apprentice on 20/1/1986) F/PL 148+24/22 FLC 13+3/3 FAC 11+4 Others 12+4
Newcastle U (£2,250,000 on 2/2/1994) PL 56+2/12 FLC 3/1 FAC 5 Others 4/1
Tottenham H (£4,200,000 on 6/10/1995) PL 95+11/13 FLC 7+3/1 FAC 11+1/1 Others 1
West Bromwich A (£200,000 on 26/8/2000) FL 36+2/1 FLC 3 FAC 1 Others 2

FOXE Hayden
Born: Australia, 23 June 1977
Height: 6'4" Weight: 13.5
International Honours: Australia: 10; U23; Yth

Although he signed forms for West Ham United last August, Hayden was not actually registered until March after the club's application for a work permit was rejected on several occasions. The problem was eventually resolved when he married his French girlfriend and thus became qualified to take up paid employment in England. A tall central defender who is good in the air and comfortable on the ball he featured in a handful of Premiership games for the Hammers before joining up with the Australian squad for their World Cup qualifying campaign. Earlier in the season he had featured in all three of the 'Olyroos' matches in the Sydney Olympics.

West Ham U (Free from Sanfrecce Hiroshima, Japan, ex Ajax, Arminia Bielefeld, on 14/3/2001) PL 3+2

FOY Keith Patrick
Born: Dublin, 30 December 1981
Height: 5'11" Weight: 12.3
International Honours: U21-1; Yth (UEFA-U16 '98)

When Alan Rogers was injured last November, Keith stepped in to fill the vacant left-wing-back position for Nottingham Forest and went on to retain his place until early in the new year. A promising youngster who is very comfortable defending he has plenty skill on the ball and likes to push forward down the flank to send crosses into the penalty box. Previously capped by the Republic of Ireland at U18 level he made his debut for the U21s in the 3-0 victory over Estonia at the beginning of June.

Nottingham F (From trainee on 8/1/1999) FL 17+3/1

FRADIN Karim
Born: St Martin d'Hyeres, France, 2 February 1972
Height: 5'10" Weight: 13.0

Karim continued to make a major contribution at Stockport County in 2000-01, working tirelessly in midfield and scoring six vital goals, including back-to-back strikes against Crewe and QPR at the end of the season. An athletic box-to-box player he is comfortable on the ball, rarely gives away possession and seems to have the knack of being in the right place at the right time. He signed an extension to his contract during the campaign that will keep him at Edgeley Park until 2004.

Stockport Co (Free from OGC Nice, France on 19/11/1999) FL 46+6/7 FAC 2+1/1

FRAIN John William
Born: Birmingham, 8 October 1968
Height: 5'9" Weight: 11.9
Club Honours: AMC '91

This hard-working player featured in a wide-left midfield role and also as a left wing back for Northampton last season but missed a lengthy part of the campaign with hamstring problems. John contributed two goals for the Cobblers, netting in the FA Cup victory over Frickley Athletic and the 2-1 defeat by Oldham last April.

Birmingham C (From apprentice on 10/10/1986) FL 265+9/23 FLC 28/1 FAC 12 Others 22/2
Northampton T (Free on 24/1/1997) FL 165+1/4 FLC 9 FAC 8/1 Others 13/2

FRAMPTON Andrew (Andy) James Kerr
Born: Wimbledon, 3 September 1979
Height: 5'11" Weight: 10.10

Andy spent most of last season in Crystal Palace's reserve team unable to break Craig Harrison's hold on the left-back position. His first-team outings mostly came as cover for injuries and suspensions in the second half of the campaign. Tall and pacy he is strong in the air and a good reader of the game. He will be hoping to feature more regularly in the Eagles' senior team in the coming season.

Crystal Palace (From trainee on 8/5/1998) FL 18+7 FLC 3 FAC 2

FRANCIS Damien Jerome
Born: Wandsworth, 27 February 1979
Height: 6'1" Weight: 11.2

Damien was a revelation in his first season as a regular for Wimbledon last term and succeeded Robbie Earle as the box-to-box player in midfield in almost seamless fashion. He played with poise, skill and commitment until suffering a knee ligament injury in the FA Cup tie with Middlesbrough that unfortunately put him out of action until the end of the campaign.

Wimbledon (From trainee on 6/3/1997) P/FL 30+10/8 FLC 5+3 FAC 5

FRANCIS Kevin Michael Derek
Born: Birmingham, 6 December 1967
Height: 6'7" Weight: 16.10
Club Honours: Div 2 '95; AMC '95

Having recovered from a serious achilles tendon injury, Kevin began last season without a club. He spent time training with his old boss Barry Fry at Peterborough and occasionally turned out for North West Counties League outfit Castleton Gabriels before joining Exeter City on non-contract forms last November. He scored once for the Grecians in seven league appearances before joining Hull City at the end of the year and quickly became a huge favourite of the Tigers' fans after netting four times in a spell of five games. A giant striker who upsets opposition defences with his physical presence, he was a key figure in the Boothferry Park club's rise up the table to the play-offs. He was released at the end of the season.

Derby Co (Free from Mile Oak Rov on 2/2/1989) FL 0+10 FLC 1+2 FAC 1+2/1 Others 0+1
Stockport Co (£45,000 on 21/2/1991) FL 147+5/88 FLC 12/5 FAC 9/6 Others 25/18
Birmingham C (£800,000 on 20/1/1995) FL 32+41/13 FLC 6+5/5 FAC 3+3/2 Others 4/1
Oxford U (£100,000 + on 17/2/1998) FL 27+9/8 FAC 0+3 Others 0+1
Stockport Co (Free on 10/3/2000) FL 4 (Freed during 2000 close season)
Exeter C (Free from Castleton Gabriels on 10/11/2000) FL 3+4/1 FAC 1 Others 1
Hull C (Free on 22/12/2000) FL 22/5 Others 2

FRANDSEN Per
Born: Copenhagen, Denmark, 6 February 1970
Height: 6'1" Weight: 12.6
Club Honours: Div 1 '97
International Honours: Denmark: 20; U21; Yth

It was a case of the prodigal son returns when Per rejoined Bolton in June 2000. His time at Blackburn had not been particularly successful and he now had the perfect opportunity to re-establish himself as one of the best midfield players outside the Premiership. However, restored in a central midfield role for Wanderers, he sometimes struggled to find his best form and it was only in the play-offs that he really showed what he was capable of. Nevertheless he was still an important member of the team and was particularly effective taking set-piece kicks.

Bolton W (£1,250,000 from FC Copenhagen, Denmark, ex Lille, on 7/8/1996) F/PL 129+1/17 FLC 15+1/4 FAC 4+1 Others 3/1
Blackburn Rov (£1,750,000 + on 22/9/1999) FL 26+5/5 FAC 4/1
Bolton W (£1,600,000 on 24/7/2000) FL 35+4/7 FLC 1+1 FAC 2+2 Others 2+1/1

FRASER Stuart James
Born: Cheltenham, 1 August 1978
Height: 6'0" Weight: 12.6

Stuart joined Exeter from Stoke City during the 2000 summer break and was second-choice goalkeeper for the Grecians last season. Despite having to undergo a hernia operation last October he still managed a handful of appearances in the first team at St James Park. He will be aiming to feature more regularly in the coming campaign.

Stoke C (Signed from Cheltenham T on 8/7/1996) FL 0+1
Exeter C (Free on 18/7/2000) FL 5+1 FLC 1 Others 1

FRASER Stuart Thomas
Born: Edinburgh, 9 January 1980
Height: 5'9" Weight: 11.4
International Honours: S: U21-5

Stuart continued to impress the Luton Town supporters last season. Equally at home on either flank as a wing back, his strong and decisive tackling made life uncomfortable for opposing players. After coming through a slight dip in form over the Christmas period he had the misfortune to suffer a broken fibula in the FA Cup third round replay at Queens Park Rangers and failed to return to action before the summer. He was reported to have signed a new one-year contract in the close season.

Luton T (From trainee on 2/4/1998) FL 36+8/1 FLC 6 FAC 9 Others 3

FREDGAARD Carsten
Born: Denmark, 20 May 1976
Height: 6'0" Weight: 12.6
International Honours: Denmark: 1; U21-9; Yth

Carsten again struggled to break into the first team at Sunderland last term and the only senior action he saw came in a Worthington Cup tie at Luton. In November he joined First Division promotion hopefuls Bolton Wanderers on loan as manager Sam Allardyce sought to boost his midfield, but although he featured in a handful of games he made little impact and returned to the Stadium of Light. A tall and pacy left winger he eventually moved back to Denmark in the summer signing a long-term contract with FC Copenhagen.

Sunderland (£1,800,000 from Lyngby, Denmark on 5/7/1999) PL 0+1 FLC 3+1/2
West Bromwich A (Loaned on 9/2/2000) FL 5
Bolton W (Loaned on 17/11/2000) FL 1+4

FREEDMAN Douglas (Dougie) Alan
Born: Glasgow, 21 January 1974
Height: 5'9" Weight: 11.2
International Honours: S: B-1; U21-8; Sch

Dougie began the 2000-01 campaign at Nottingham Forest where he featured in several of the early matches without making much of an impact and subsequently returned to one of his former clubs, Crystal Palace. His goal-scoring touch seemed to come back at Selhurst Park as he netted four times in his first four games but he then spent some time on the subs' bench and the goal supply began to dry up. He is an intelligent striker who can turn defenders and displays some neat touches. He scored three goals in the final two games of the season including the vital winner in the final game of the season at Stockport that saved Palace's Division One status for another year.

Queens Park R (From trainee on 15/5/1992)
Barnet (Free on 26/7/1994) FL 47/27 FLC 6/5 FAC 2 Others 2
Crystal Palace (£800,000 on 8/9/1995) F/PL 72+18/31 FLC 3+2/1 FAC 2+1 Others 3+2/2
Wolverhampton W (£800,000 on 17/10/1997) FL 25+4/10 FAC 5+1/2
Nottingham F (£950,000 on 12/8/1998) P/FL 50+20/18 FLC 8+1/4 FAC 3+1/1
Crystal Palace (£600,000 on 23/10/2000) FL 16+10/11 FAC 1+1

FREEMAN Darren Barry Andduet
Born: Brighton, 22 August 1973
Height: 5'11" Weight: 13.0
Club Honours: Div 3 '99, '01

This versatile Brighton player appeared for the first month of last season while suffering from a hernia problem before succumbing to surgery which kept him out of the reckoning until mid December. When Darren returned to the Seagulls' line-up he never quite seemed to regain the form he had shown in 1999-200 and although he produced a solid performance in the away victory at Torquay he was subsequently relegated to the subs' bench. The hernia problem flared up again in April and a further operation was required which effectively ended his campaign. Essentially a wide midfield player, although he can also play at centre forward, he was released in the summer.

Gillingham (Free from Horsham on 31/1/1995) FL 4+8 FAC 0+1 Others 2/1
Fulham (£15,000 + on 4/7/1996) FL 32+14/9 FLC 2 Others 3/1
Brentford (Free on 7/7/1998) FL 16+6/6 FLC 4/1 FAC 3/2 Others 1
Brighton & Hove A (Free on 8/7/1999) FL 41+13/12 FLC 2+1 FAC 3/1 Others 1+1

FREEMAN David
Born: Dublin, 25 November 1979
Height: 5'10" Weight: 11.10
International Honours: RoI: U21-1; Yth

David joined Port Vale on loan last September and impressed on his debut at Bournemouth, but only featured twice more for the Second Division club before returning to the City Ground. He subsequently enjoyed a brief run in the Nottingham Forest first-team squad after Christmas and will be looking to feature more regularly in 2001-02. He is a busy little striker with a good touch, plenty of pace and a useful shot.

Nottingham F (From trainee on 9/12/1996) FL 2+6 FAC 0+1
Port Vale (Loaned on 8/9/2000) FL 2+1

FREEMAN Mark Wayne
Born: Walsall, 27 January 1970
Height: 6'2" Weight: 13.8
Club Honours: FAT '98; NC '99

Mark was again a regular in the centre of defence for Cheltenham Town last season before his season was cut short by a back injury. Tall and strong, he is at his best when defending crosses or close-marking opponents. Although sometimes beaten for pace by nippy strikers, he relishes a physical battle against a big target man and rarely comes off second best. A big-hearted character he is one of several long-serving players who have been with the Robins since their days in the Dr Martens League. Released in the summer he was reported to have signed for Boston United.

Wolverhampton W (Signed from Bilston T on 27/10/1987. Free to Bilston T during 1988 close season)
Cheltenham T (Signed from Gloucester C on 4/3/1996) FL 61+4/2 FLC 3 FAC 4 Others 2

FREESTONE Christopher (Chris) Mark
Born: Nottingham, 4 September 1971
Height: 5'11" Weight: 11.7
Club Honours: AMC '97

Chris had a disappointing time for Shrewsbury in 2000-01. Manager Kevin Ratcliffe persevered with him in the early weeks of the campaign but his only goals came in the Worthington Cup tie against Preston and against Cheltenham in the FA Cup. He eventually lost his place and started just one game in the second half of the season. He was on the open to offers list in the summer.

Middlesbrough (£10,000 from Arnold T on 2/12/1994) P/FL 2+7/1 FLC 1+1/1 FAC 0+2
Carlisle U (Loaned on 3/3/1997) FL 3+2/2 Others 2
Northampton T (£75,000 on 8/12/1997) FL 40+17/13 FLC 4/3 FAC 1+2 Others 6+1/3
Hartlepool U (£75,000 on 25/3/1999) FL 24+13/7 FLC 2 FAC 2 Others 3
Cheltenham T (Loaned on 11/2/2000) FL 5/2
Shrewsbury T (Free on 21/7/2000) FL 16+4 FLC 2/1 FAC 1/1 Others 0+1

FREESTONE Roger
Born: Newport, 19 August 1968
Height: 6'3" Weight: 14.6
Club Honours: Div 2 '89; Div 3 '00; AMC '94
International Honours: W: 1; U21-1; Yth; Sch

Roger was once again first-choice 'keeper for Swansea last season and his only absences came as a result of injury or suspension. Despite playing in a side struggling towards the foot of the Second Division he was regularly included in the Welsh international squad, although he failed to add to his single cap. A reliable shot stopper with a safe pair of hands he has now made more than 500 senior appearances for the Swans.

Newport Co (From trainee on 2/4/1986) FL 13 Others 1
Chelsea (£95,000 on 10/3/1987) FL 42 FLC 2 FAC 3 Others 6
Swansea C (Loaned on 29/9/1989) FL 14 Others 1
Hereford U (Loaned on 9/3/1990) FL 8
Swansea C (£45,000 on 5/9/1991) FL 438+1/3 FLC 26 FAC 27 Others 42

FRENCH Daniel John
Born: Peterborough, 25 November 1979
Height: 5'11" Weight: 11.4

One of the many talented youngsters at Peterborough, Daniel spent two months on loan at Conference club Boston United to give him the chance of an extended run of first-team football. On his return to London Road he made two appearances in the LDV Vans Trophy ties before another loan spell at Bedford. He subsequently returned and featured again for Posh towards the end of the season. A very quick right winger who delivers an excellent cross he will be hoping to gain more senior experience in the 2001-02 campaign.

Peterborough U (From trainee on 6/7/1998) FL 1+7 FAC 0+1 Others 1+1

FREUND Steffen
Born: Brandenburg, Germany, 19 January 1970
Height: 5'11" Weight: 11.6
Club Honours: FLC '99
International Honours: Germany: 21; U21; Yth

A regular for Tottenham in the early part of the 2000-01 campaign Steffen was sidelined in November with a hamstring problem and although he made a quick return to fitness he then suffered knee ligament damage that brought his season to an early conclusion in April. A strong midfield anchorman he was often forced to play below full match fitness but always gave 100 per cent in every game. He performed a key role holding the midfield together, often forming the first line of defence. He shows tremendous determination when keeping possession and uses the ball intelligently to create opportunities from the centre of the park.

Tottenham H (£750,000 from Borussia Dortmund, Germany, ex Motor Sud, Stahl Brandenburg, Schalke 04, on 29/12/1998) PL 60+5 FLC 8 FAC 10 Others 4

FRIEDEL Bradley (Brad) Howard
Born: Lakewood, USA, 18 May 1971
Height: 6'3" Weight: 14.7
International Honours: USA: 68

Conjecture had arisen pre-season that Brad would team up again with Graham Souness at Blackburn last term, but it was not until November that a work permit was obtained for him. He was quickly installed as first-team goalkeeper and after a slow start he soon began to exude confidence. Although Rovers' dominance of opponents meant he had few chances to really shine he convinced the final few doubters with a point-saving display against Wimbledon. His fine form also won him preference over Kasey Keller for the USA national team in their World Cup qualifying campaign.

Liverpool (£1,000,000 from Columbus Crew, USA on 23/12/1997) PL 25 FLC 4 Others 1+1
Blackburn Rov (Free on 7/11/2000) FL 27 FAC 6

FRIIO David
Born: Thionville, France, 17 February 1973
Height: 6'0" Weight: 11.7

Having been released by French club Valence at the end of the 1999-2000 season David joined Plymouth Argyle on non-contract forms last November. He became an instant hero with the Pilgrims' fans after producing a fine performance on his debut in the 2-0 success at arch-rivals Exeter City. A gifted midfielder who is very comfortable on the ball he added a touch of class to the Plymouth side. He also showed that he has a good eye for goal netting five times during the campaign. He subsequently signed a two-year contract with the club and is likely to play an important role in the 2001-02 season.

Plymouth Arg (Free from ASOA Valence, France, ex Epinal, Nimes, on 30/11/2000) FL 26/5 Others 1

FULLARTON James (Jamie)
Born: Glasgow, 20 July 1974
Height: 5'10" Weight: 10.6
International Honours: S: U21-17

This hard-tackling midfield player eventually signed a new one-year contract with Crystal Palace in the summer of 2000 and featured in the first three games of last season before being dropped. Jamie was later one of a number of players placed on the transfer list at Selhurst Park and in November he signed for Scottish Premier League club Dundee United. His career at Tannadice Park had hardly begun when he suffered a serious ankle injury at Kilmarnock that put him out of action for several months.

St Mirren (Free from Motherwell BC on 13/6/1991) SL 93+9/3 SLC 2 SC 4 Others 4+1 (Transferred to Bastia, France during 1996 close season)
Crystal Palace (Free on 7/8/1997) P/FL 40+7/1 FLC 2+1 FAC 3 Others 1
Bolton W (Loaned on 25/3/1999) FL 1

FULLER Ricardo Dwayne
Born: Kingston, Jamaica, 31 October 1979
Height: 6'2" Weight: 12.4
International Honours: Jamaica

This exciting young striker originally arrived in England for a trial with Charlton Athletic in December 1999. He was on the verge of signing for the Addicks when a medical revealed a back problem that required corrective surgery. Once fully fit again he was released to join South London neighbours Crystal Palace shortly before the transfer deadline last season. He featured regularly for the Eagles in the closing matches without managing to score. Ricardo is an experienced international for Jamaica and he returned to the national squad in the new year contributing to their campaign to qualify for the 2002 World Cup finals.

Crystal Palace (Free from Tivoli Gardens, Jamaica on 19/2/2001) FL 2+6

FURLONG Paul Anthony
Born: Wood Green, 1 October 1968
Height: 6'0" Weight: 13.8
Club Honours: FAT '88
International Honours: E: SP-5

Placed on the transfer list in the summer by Birmingham City Paul joined Queens Park Rangers on a three-month loan at the beginning of the 2000-01 season, but after scoring the winner against Crewe he fractured his patella tendon and returned to St Andrews prematurely. He subsequently made a brief return to the Blues' squad in March before being sidelined by hamstring trouble but was back in action by the end of the campaign. He is a big strong striker who holds the ball up well and shoots with power and accuracy.

Coventry C (£130,000 from Enfield on 31/7/1991) FL 27+10/4 FLC 4/1 FAC 1+1 Others 1
Watford (£250,000 on 24/7/1992) FL 79/37 FLC 7/4 FAC 2 Others 4
Chelsea (£2,300,000 on 26/5/1994) PL 44+20/13 FLC 3+1 FAC 5+4/1 Others 7/3
Birmingham C (£1,500,000 on 17/7/1996) FL 102+18/49 FLC 11/3 FAC 5/3 Others 4
Queens Park R (Loaned on 18/8/2000) FL 3/1

FUTCHER Benjamin (Ben) Paul
Born: Manchester, 20 February 1981
Height: 6'4" Weight: 12.4

Oldham's abundance of central defenders restricted opportunities for Ben last season and he was almost exclusively limited to reserve-team action. However he remains a promising youngster who uses his height to good effect and clearly is still part of the club's long-term plans as he signed a further 12-month contract during the campaign. Ben is the son of the former Oldham and Barnsley defender Paul Futcher.

Oldham Ath (From trainee on 5/7/1999) FL 2+8 FAC 0+1

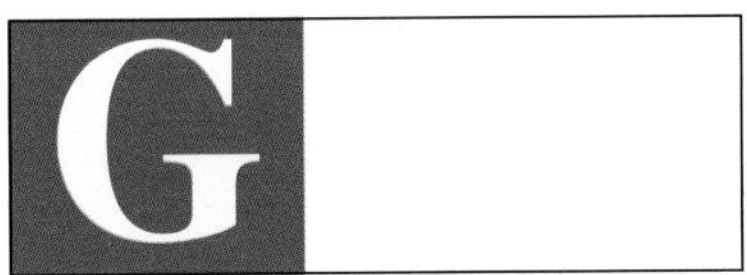

GABBIADINI Marco
Born: Nottingham, 20 January 1968
Height: 5'10" Weight: 13.4
Club Honours: Div 3 '88
International Honours: E: B-1; U21-2
This experienced striker produced some sterling performances for Northampton Town last season although it took him a while to find his goal-scoring touch. Strong and determined on the ball his talents make him an ideal choice to play behind the forwards but the Cobblers' injury problems meant that he was often used as an out-and-out striker.
York C (From apprentice on 5/9/1985) FL 42+18/14 FLC 4+3/1 Others 4/3
Sunderland (£80,000 on 23/9/1987) FL 155+2/74 FLC 14/9 FAC 5 Others 9/4
Crystal Palace (£1,800,000 on 1/10/1991) FL 15/5 FLC 6/1 FAC 1 Others 3/1
Derby Co (£1,000,000 on 31/1/1992) F/PL 163+25/50 FLC 13/7 FAC 8+1/3 Others 16+1/8 (Free to Panionios, Greece during 1997 close season)
Birmingham C (Loaned on 14/10/1996) FL 0+2
Oxford U (Loaned on 31/1/1997) FL 5/1
Stoke C (Free on 24/12/1997) FL 2+6 FAC 1/1
York C (Free on 20/2/1998) FL 5+2/1
Darlington (Free on 8/7/1998) FL 81+1/47 FLC 4/1 FAC 4/1 Others 5+1/3
Northampton T (Free on 28/6/2000) FL 34+10/6 FLC 2/1 FAC 1+1 Others 1

GABBIDON Daniel (Danny) Leon
Born: Cwmbran, 8 August 1979
Height: 5'10" Weight: 11.2
International Honours: W: U21-14; Yth
Danny joined Cardiff City for a substantial fee last August and immediately established himself in the first team, going on to become a near ever-present in the Bluebirds' promotion season. Although previously mainly used as a right back he played in every position across the back division. A quality defender he continued to represent Wales at U21 level winning a further six caps during the campaign.
West Bromwich A (From trainee on 3/7/1998) FL 20 FLC 4+1 FAC 2
Cardiff C (£175,000 + on 10/8/2000) FL 42+1/3 FLC 2 FAC 4

GADSBY Matthew John
Born: Sutton Coldfield, 6 September 1979
Height: 6'1" Weight: 11.12
Matthew received limited opportunities at Walsall in 2000-01 but on each of his first-team appearances he gave an outstanding performance. Despite being used sparingly he featured from the subs' bench in all three of the play-off matches when he battled hard for every ball. A versatile young defender or midfield player he will be hoping for more chances in the coming campaign.
Walsall (From trainee on 12/2/1998) FL 6+9 FAC 0+1 Others 2+5

GAIN Peter Thomas
Born: Hammersmith, 11 November 1976
Height: 6'1" Weight: 11.0
International Honours: RoI: U21-1; Yth
This left-sided midfield man again found his appearances for Lincoln City restricted by injury during the 2000-2001 campaign. After recovering from a lengthy spell out with a medial knee ligament problem, Peter won his place back in the squad and finished the season as a first-team regular. He is a skilful player who passes accurately and is at his best when taking on defenders. He also contributed six goals for the Imps.
Tottenham H (From trainee on 1/7/1995)
Lincoln C (Loaned on 31/12/1998) FL 0+1 Others 1
Lincoln C (Signed on 26/3/1999) FL 39+20/7 FLC 3+1 FAC 4/1 Others 3+1

GALL Kevin Alexander
Born: Merthyr Tydfil, 4 February 1982
Height: 5'9" Weight: 11.1
International Honours: W: Yth; Sch
Kevin joined Second Division Bristol Rovers on transfer deadline day after being released by Newcastle United. A promising striker, he scored his first senior goal within minutes of coming off the subs' bench on his debut at Stoke and also netted in the penultimate game of the season against Wycombe. Earlier in the campaign he had appeared for Wales U18s in their UEFA tournament qualifying matches.
Newcastle U (From trainee on 29/4/1999)
Bristol Rov (Free on 22/3/2001) FL 3+7/2

GALLACHER Kevin William
Born: Clydebank, 23 November 1966
Height: 5'8" Weight: 11.6
International Honours: S: 53; B-2; U21-7; Yth
Kevin had a delayed start last season due to a thigh injury and it was not until September that he made his first appearance for Newcastle, coming off the subs' bench to score against his old club Coventry. However after a handful more appearances he succumbed to a series of injuries which disrupted his campaign: a torn right hamstring was followed in turn by injuries to each of his calves leading to three months on the sidelines. He eventually returned to the Magpies' squad in January but it was not until the last few games that he reappeared in the starting line-up. Although now in the latter stages of his career he remains as lively and hard-working as ever, and can always be relied upon to give his all for the team, whether he is played as an out-and-out striker or playing just behind the front line. His 50th cap for Scotland came in the World Cup qualifier against San Marino in October and he was honoured with the captaincy of the side to mark the occasion, while a few days later he scored the goal that earned a vital point for his country in Croatia. Kevin comes from a footballing family as his grandfather, father and brother all played the game professionally in Scotland. He was released on a free transfer in the summer.
Dundee U (Signed from Duntocher BC on 2/9/1983) SL 118+13/27 SLC 13/5 SC 20+3/5 Others 15+6/3
Coventry C (£900,000 on 29/1/1990) F/PL 99+1/28 FLC 11/7 FAC 4 Others 2
Blackburn Rov (£1,500,000 on 22/3/1993) P/FL 132+12/46 FLC 8+2/3 FAC 13/4 Others 1+1
Newcastle U (£700,000 on 1/10/1999) PL 27+12/4 FLC 2/1 FAC 5+1/1

GALLEN Kevin Andrew
Born: Chiswick, 21 September 1975
Height: 5'11" Weight: 12.10
International Honours: E: U21-4; Yth (UEFA-U18 '93); Sch
Huddersfield Town's only summer purchase, Kevin joined on a one-year contract and quickly found himself as the Terriers' first-choice striker. He was soon on the goal-scoring trail with a wonderful strike in the away victory at Sheffield Wednesday but then suffered a hamstring injury that hampered him in the early part of the season. He scored regularly in the first half of the campaign but less often after Christmas, even so he finished as the club's joint-top scorer with Delroy Facey. A hard-working striker he holds the ball well and is a good passer, linking well with others around him. Kevin was released in the summer.
Queens Park R (From trainee on 22/9/1992) P/FL 126+45/36 FLC 9+3/2 FAC 6+2/2
Huddersfield T (Free on 10/8/2000) FL 30+8/10 FAC 1

Kevin Gallen

GALLIMORE Anthony (Tony) Mark
Born: Crewe, 21 February 1972
Height: 5'11" Weight: 12.6
Club Honours: Div 3 '95; AMC '98
Tony was once again the first-choice left back for Grimsby Town last season but was dogged by injuries that caused him to miss several matches. However he recovered fitness in time to feature for the Mariners in the vital run-in to the end of the campaign and played an important role as the club staved off the threat of relegation from the First Division. He is a solid defender with a powerful left foot who is capable of making useful runs down the flank.
Stoke C (From trainee on 11/7/1990) FL 6+5
Carlisle U (Loaned on 3/10/1991) FL 8
Carlisle U (Loaned on 26/2/1992) FL 8

Carlisle U (£15,000 on 25/3/1993) FL 124/9 FLC 8/1 FAC 8 Others 24/1
Grimsby T (£125,000 on 28/3/1996) FL 187+10/4 FLC 16/2 FAC 11 Others 10

GALLOWAY Michael (Mick) Anthony
Born: Nottingham, 13 October 1974
Height: 5'11" Weight: 12.4

Mick found opportunities at Chesterfield restricted last season and moved on loan to Carlisle in November, the deal becoming permanent two months later. A hard-working midfielder, his arrival helped spark a revival in the Cumbrians' fortunes and he set up some vital goals with his wickedly accurate corner kicks including both strikes in the 2-1 win over Mansfield in January. He is a midfield grafter who passes the ball neatly and is a fine striker of a dead ball with either foot. He was made available on a free transfer in the summer.

Notts Co (From trainee on 15/6/1993) FL 17+4 FLC 2 FAC 0+1 Others 4
Gillingham (£10,000 + on 27/3/1997) FL 58+17/5 FLC 3+1 FAC 1+2 Others 5
Lincoln C (Loaned on 29/9/1999) FL 5
Chesterfield (£15,000 on 5/11/1999) FL 18+2/1 FLC 2+1 Others 3
Carlisle U (Free on 9/11/2000) FL 26/1 FAC 2

GAMBLE Joseph (Joe) Finbar
Born: Cork, 14 January 1982
Height: 5'7" Weight: 11.2
International Honours: RoI: Yth

Joe joined Reading from League of Ireland club Cork City in August 2000 and gave some impressive performances in the reserve and youth teams. He made his senior debut when coming off the subs' bench for the final 15 minutes of the Worthington Cup first round first leg tie against Leyton Orient and made a couple more appearances later in the season, before being loaned out to Crawley Town in March to gain some regular first-team football. A tenacious midfield player with plenty of skill on the ball he featured regularly for the Republic of Ireland at U18 level during the campaign.

Reading (Free from Cork C on 8/8/2000) FL 0+1 FLC 0+1 FAC 0+1

GANNON James (Jim) Paul
Born: Southwark, 7 September 1968
Height: 6'2" Weight: 13.0

Jim was still recovering from a cruciate ligament injury at the beginning of last term although he enjoyed a testimonial match against Manchester City shortly before the start of the season. He eventually recovered fitness towards the end of the year, but then left Edgeley Park in rather acrimonious circumstances and signed a short-term contract for Crewe Alexandra. Used as cover by boss Dario Gradi his vast experience proved of value in a young team and whenever he was called upon he performed well. An effective central defender who is strong in the air he was released by the Railwaymen in the summer.

Sheffield U (Signed from Dundalk on 27/4/1989)
Halifax T (Loaned on 22/2/1990) FL 2
Stockport Co (£40,000 on 7/3/1990) FL 350+33/52 FLC 34+4/3 FAC 19+1/1 Others 37+2/8
Notts Co (Loaned on 14/1/1994) FL 2
Crewe Alex (Free on 21/12/2000) FL 5+2 FAC 3

GARCIA Richard
Born: Perth, Australia, 4 September 1981
Height: 6'1" Weight: 11.2
Club Honours: FAYC '99
International Honours: Australia: Yth

A key member of West Ham's 1998-99 FA Youth Cup winning side when he had scored in every round of the tournament, Richard joined Leyton Orient on a three-month loan deal at the start of last term to gain experience of first-team football. He was a regular in the O's line-up and had just agreed to stay at Brisbane Road for the remainder of the season when he had the misfortune to injure a cruciate knee ligament in the game at Cheltenham and this kept him out of action until the summer. A promising young striker who has represented Australia at U17 level he was a prolific scorer for the Hammers' junior teams.

West Ham U (From trainee on 16/9/1998)
Leyton Orient (Loaned on 11/8/2000) FL 18/4 FLC 3

GARDNER Anthony
Born: Stone, 19 September 1980
Height: 6'5" Weight: 13.8

Having joined Spurs midway through the 1999-2000 campaign, Anthony spent some 15 months in the reserves before finally making his senior debut when he came on from the subs' bench in the 2-1 defeat at Derby in March. He was then included in the starting line-up at Highbury when an injury-ravaged side kept the Gunners at bay for 70 minutes before finally going down 2-0 and featured regularly in the closing weeks of the campaign. A tall central defender with lightning pace, he will be hoping for more opportunities in the coming season.

Port Vale (From trainee on 31/7/1998) FL 40+1/4 FLC 2 FAC 1
Tottenham H (£1,000,000 on 28/1/2000) PL 5+3

GARDNER Ricardo Wayne
Born: Jamaica, 25 September 1978
Height: 5'9" Weight: 11.0
International Honours: Jamaica: 37

Ricardo spent the first two months of the 2000-01 season recovering from a knee ligament injury sustained in the previous campaign, but once he had recovered fitness he returned to his old form. A real box of tricks on the left wing and a firm crowd favourite at the Reebok Stadium, he is one of Bolton's brightest and most consistent players. Always difficult to predict what he will do when he receives the ball he proved to be one of the most naturally-gifted players in the First Division last term. He seemed to thrive in big games, netting vital goals in both rounds of the play-offs to help Wanderers back into the Premiership. He also featured regularly for Jamaica when fit, assisting in their campaign to qualify for the 2002 World Cup finals.

Bolton W (£1,000,000 from Harbour View, Jamaica on 17/8/1998) FL 72+19/10 FLC 11+1/2 FAC 4+3 Others 6/2

Ricardo Gardner

GARNER Darren John
Born: Plymouth, 10 December 1971
Height: 5'9" Weight: 12.7
Club Honours: AMC '96

Previously an attacking midfielder, Darren was asked to adopt a more defensive role on the right-hand side for Rotherham in 2000-01. He responded magnificently with some outstanding performances and had missed only a handful of games before suffering a broken leg in the vital promotion clash at Reading at the beginning of March. He was sorely missed in the last two months of the Millers' push for promotion to the First Division.

Plymouth Arg (From trainee on 15/3/1989) FL 22+5/1 FLC 2+1 FAC 1 (Free to Dorchester T on 19/8/1994)
Rotherham U (£20,000 on 26/6/1995) FL 201+6/20 FLC 10+2 FAC 15/6 Others 9/1

GARNETT Shaun Maurice
Born: Wallasey, 22 November 1969
Height: 6'2" Weight: 13.4
Club Honours: AMC '90

This imperious defender has long been a mainstay of Oldham Athletic's back line and it was no surprise therefore that he continued to be a virtual ever-present in 2000-01, regardless of what defensive system was adopted. His strength in the air remains unquestioned and he is very much a no-nonsense player who is fierce in the tackle and rarely outfought.

Tranmere Rov (From trainee on 15/6/1988) FL 110+2/5 FLC 13/1 FAC 4 Others 15+2
Chester C (Loaned on 1/10/1992) FL 9
Preston NE (Loaned on 11/12/1992) FL 10/2 Others 1
Wigan Ath (Loaned on 26/2/1993) FL 13/1
Swansea C (£200,000 on 11/3/1996) FL 15 FLC 2
Oldham Ath (£150,000 on 19/9/1996) FL 161+4/9 FLC 6 FAC 12 Others 4

GARRATT Martin Blake George
Born: York, 22 February 1980
Height: 5'8" Weight: 10.7

This left-sided midfield player signed for Lincoln City on a non-contract basis after a spell with St Patrick's in the League of Ireland. He showed promise on his debut against Blackpool in the LDV Vans Trophy but was only given a couple of chances in league games at a time when the Imps were struggling at the foot of the Third Division. Martin was released at the beginning of March and signed for Conference club Hednesford Town.

York C (From trainee on 2/7/1998) FL 35+10/1 FLC 2+1 FAC 3 Others 0+1
Mansfield T (Free on 23/3/2000) FL 4+2 (Freed during 2000 close season)
Lincoln C (Free from St Patricks on 29/12/2000) FL 2 Others 1

GASCOIGNE Paul John
Born: Gateshead, 27 May 1967
Height: 5'10" Weight: 11.12
Club Honours: FAYC '85; FAC '91. SPL '96, '97; SLC '97; SC '96
International Honours: E: 57; B-4; U21-13; Yth

Many believed Everton boss Walter Smith to be taking an unnecessary gamble when he signed English football's fading Enfant Terrible from Middlesbrough on a free transfer. But Paul repaid his old Glasgow Rangers' manager's faith by getting himself into the best shape he had been in for years - and showed a consistency and quality of performance to match. The old drawing power was still there - 15,000 for a pre-season friendly at Tranmere and 13,000 at Plymouth - and while the legs weren't quite as quick, the speed of thought was still evident. Initially employed as a 'supersub', capable of coming on and influencing the final quarter of matches, 'Gazza' forced his way into the Everton starting line-up and stayed there for nine successive matches. Such was the quality and energy he displayed in a televised draw at Leicester in September that some analysts were suggesting that Kevin Keegan should include him in his England squad for the World Cup qualifier against Germany. The fairy tale comeback ended with a torn thigh muscle against Aston Villa in November, but Paul had proved his fitness again by the end of the season and was intent on starting the 2001-02 season - the 15th of his professional career - with the same zest he had shown for the last one.

Newcastle U (From apprentice on 13/5/1985) FL 83+9/21 FLC 8/1 FAC 4/3 Others 2+1
Tottenham H (£2,000,000 on 18/7/1988) FL 91+1/19 FLC 14+1/8 FAC 6/6 (£5,500,000 to Lazio, Italy on 1/5/1992)
Glasgow R (£4,300,000 on 10/7/1995) SL 64+10/30 SLC 7/4 SC 7+1/3 Others 16/2
Middlesbrough (£3,450,000 on 27/3/1998) P/FL 39+2/4 FLC 3+2 FAC 2
Everton (Free on 20/7/2000) PL 10+4 FLC 0+1

GAUGHAN Steven (Steve) Edward
Born: Doncaster, 14 April 1970
Height: 6'0" Weight: 12.6

Steve started last season as a regular in the Halifax Town line-up and scored in the 2-1 defeat at Kidderminster Harriers in August. However he then spent three months on loan at Cork City returning to the The Shay in February when he made a couple of appearances before being sidelined by an injury. He is an experienced central midfield player with a high work rate and good distribution. He was released in the summer.

Doncaster Rov (Free from Hatfield Main Colliery on 21/1/1988) FL 42+25/3 FLC 2+2 FAC 4+1 Others 5+1
Sunderland (Free on 1/7/1990)
Darlington (£10,000 on 21/1/1992) FL 159+12/15 FLC 8 FAC 6/1 Others 10+1
Chesterfield (£30,000 on 16/8/1996) FL 16+4 FLC 1+1/1 FAC 0+1 Others 1
Darlington (Signed on 21/11/1997) FL 35+12/3 FLC 2 FAC 5 Others 2
Halifax T (Free on 14/7/1999) FL 35+12/1 FLC 2+1/1 FAC 2 Others 1

GAUNT Ian Thomas Francis
Born: Bromsgrove, 28 September 1981
Height: 6'1" Weight: 12.4

This powerfully-built Walsall trainee had very mixed experiences in his two senior games last term. Making his debut in the LDV Vans Trophy tie against Wigan he snatched a last-minute winner but in the next round against Stoke he received a red card as he battled to stem the tide for a weakened Saddler's line-up in danger of being over-run. A promising young defender he had a brief loan spell at Moor Green towards the end of the season.

Walsall (Trainee) Others 2/1

GAVILAN Zarate **Diego** Antonio
Born: Paraguay, 1 March 1980
Height: 5'8" Weight: 10.7
International Honours: Paraguay: 12

Diego was on the subs' bench for most of the early matches for Newcastle last season coming on the field on a couple of occasions, but he was sidelined for a lengthy spell after straining the medial ligaments in his knee and was unable to break back into the squad on his return to fitness. A rather slight figure, he is a quick and neat midfield player who has good control with both feet and an eye for goal.

Newcastle U (£2,000,000 from Cerro Porteno, Paraguay on 4/2/2000) PL 2+5/1 FLC 0+1

GAVIN Jason Joseph
Born: Dublin, 14 March 1980
Height: 6'1" Weight: 12.7
International Honours: RoI: U21-6; Yth (UEFA-U18 '98)

A talented youngster Jason made steady progress with Middlesbrough last season. Now established as a first-team squad member he is a tough and uncompromising defender of whom great things are predicted for in the future. His aerial power is quite brilliant and he never shirks a tackle, coming away with the ball to initiate intelligent attacking moves and surge up field when the situation demands. Jason is a product of the Boro' youth system, joining the club straight from school, and won five more caps for the Republic of Ireland at U21 level last term.

Middlesbrough (From trainee on 26/3/1997) PL 14+8 FLC 3 FAC 0+1

GAYLE John
Born: Bromsgrove, 30 July 1964
Height: 6'2" Weight: 15.4
Club Honours: AMC '91

John clearly did not figure in Shrewsbury Town manager Kevin Ratcliffe's plans last season and was restricted to just one brief substitute appearance before being released. He moved on to Torquay United in December where he was used mainly as a substitute to add weight to the attack in the final twenty minutes. His high point for the Gulls came with a scrambled late winner in the vital game against Darlington that helped the Devon club retain their Football League status. Although clearly past his prime John is a striker who still possesses the ability to hold the ball up and his mere physical presence unsettled opposition defenders. He was released in the summer.

Wimbledon (£30,000 from Burton A on 1/3/1989) FL 17+3/2 FLC 3
Birmingham C (£175,000 on 21/11/1990) FL 39+5/10 FAC 2 Others 8+1/4
Walsall (Loaned on 20/8/1993) FL 4/1
Coventry C (£100,000 on 13/9/1993) PL 3 FLC 1+2
Burnley (£70,000 on 17/8/1994) FL 7+7/3 FLC 1+1/1 FAC 1+1/1
Stoke C (£70,000 on 23/1/1995) FL 14+12/4 FLC 2 FAC 0+1 Others 3+1
Gillingham (Loaned on 14/3/1996) FL 9/3
Northampton T (£25,000 on 10/2/1997) FL 35+13/7 FLC 1+1/2 FAC 4 Others 9+1/4
Scunthorpe U (Free on 27/7/1998) FL 38+11/4 FLC 3 FAC 1 Others 4
Shrewsbury T (Free on 25/11/1999) FL 17+2/2 Others 1
Torquay U (Free on 14/12/2000) FL 5+8/1

GAYLE Marcus Anthony
Born: Hammersmith, 27 September 1970
Height: 6'1" Weight: 12.9
Club Honours: Div 3 '92
International Honours: E: Yth. Jamaica: 14

Marcus continued to remain popular with the Wimbledon faithful last term and was a regular in the line-up before completing the surprise move of the year to Glasgow Rangers in March. A versatile player who can either take a left-midfield role or play up front, he is particular effective in the air and his skills are equally useful when helping the defence or leading the attack. Having been a key figure for the Dons over several years he will be missed by all at the club.

Brentford (From trainee on 6/7/1989) FL 118+38/22 FLC 6+3 FAC 6+2/2 Others 14+6/2
Wimbledon (£250,000 on 24/3/1994) P/FL 198+38/37 FLC 23+1/7 FAC 18+7/3

GEARY Derek Peter
Born: Dublin, 19 June 1980
Height: 5'6" Weight: 10.8

This Sheffield Wednesday youngster made his senior debut in the Worthington Cup tie at Oldham last September and went on to produce an excellent performance in the 'derby' match against Sheffield United in the same competition, coming off the subs' bench to mark the Blades' danger man Paul Devlin out of the game. Derek then featured in a number of games towards the end of the season, starting his first league game on the final day of the campaign against Crewe. He

is a hard-working right back who times his tackles well and has a good positional sense.
Sheffield Wed (Signed from Cherry Orchard on 17/11/1997) FL 1+4 FLC 4+1

GELLERT Brian
Born: Kolding, Denmark, 10 May 1977
Height: 5'11" Weight: 12.7
Having been released by Italian club Brescia, Brian joined Notts County at the end of October but found it difficult to break into the first team and made just one appearance for the Magpies in the LDV Vans Trophy tie at Port Vale. A promising young midfield player who is comfortable on the ball and has good distribution, he was released in the summer.
Notts Co (Signed from Xanthi, Greece, ex IF Kolding, Brescia, on 27/10/2000) Others 1

GEMMILL Scot
Born: Paisley, 2 January 1971
Height: 5'11" Weight: 11.6
Club Honours: FMC '92; Div 1 '98
International Honours: S: 17; B-2; U21-4
A precise and intelligent passer of the ball, coupled with a good midfield engine, Scot enjoyed his most consistent season to date in Everton's colours. It took him some time to force his way into the starting line-up last season, but when he did step in for the injured Paul Gascoigne he stayed there for the rest of the campaign. A clinically incisive pass against Chelsea which created a goal out of nothing for team-mate Danny Cadamarteri showed the vision and the quality he possesses, and he also weighed in with a couple of well-struck goals - ironically home and away to Coventry City. It spoke volumes for his re-emergence at Goodison that he missed only two of Everton's last 23 games of the season. Scot will be hoping to build on a solid season at Goodison Park during 2001-02.
Nottingham F (From trainee on 5/1/1990) F/PL 228+17/21 FLC 29+2/3 FAC 19+2/1 Others 13+1/4
Everton (£250,000 on 25/3/1999) PL 38+11/4 FLC 2 FAC 1+2

GEORGE Liam Brendan
Born: Luton, 2 February 1979
Height: 5'9" Weight: 11.3
International Honours: RoI: U21-4; Yth (UEFA-U18 '98)
Liam had another good campaign for Luton Town in 2000-01 despite the club's relegation problems and finished as leading scorer for the second season in a row. He was mostly used in a role behind the front two where he was able to find the freedom to run at opposing defenders. A promising striker with excellent control and nimble footwork it remains to be seen how long the Hatters will be able to hold on to him. He continued to represent the Republic of Ireland at U21 level winning a further cap against Cyprus in February.
Luton T (From trainee on 20/1/1997) FL 79+19/20 FLC 3+6 FAC 9/4 Others 1+1

GERRARD Paul William
Born: Heywood, 22 January 1973
Height: 6'2" Weight: 14.4
International Honours: E: U21-18
After years spent in the shadows at Goodison Park, Paul was unquestionably first-choice goalkeeper for Everton last term. Involved in one of the more bizarre incidents of the season - when West Ham striker Paolo Di Canio chose to catch the ball rather than strike it at an unguarded net after Paul had collapsed with a knee injury - as soon as he was fit again he was restored instantly to the starting line-up. An outstanding shot stopper, he made a crucial penalty save in the home match with Bradford City which ultimately preserved Everton's Premiership place for another season. But he attracted some criticism for occasional lapses of concentration, a flaw he has worked relentlessly at ironing out of his game.
Oldham Ath (From trainee on 2/11/1991) P/FL 118+1 FLC 7 FAC 7 Others 2+1
Everton (£1,000,000 + on 1/7/1996) PL 74+1 FLC 5 FAC 3
Oxford U (Loaned on 18/12/1998) FL 16

GERRARD Steven George
Born: Huyton, 30 May 1980
Height: 6'2" Weight: 12.4
Club Honours: FLC '01; FAC '01; UEFAC '01
International Honours: E: 5; U21-4; Yth
Having coped admirably with all the pressures of being a star at such a young age Steven found himself having to be nursed along for much of last season by Liverpool boss Gerard Houllier to enable him to continue playing despite being troubled by a persistent back problem. Already he is close to being the complete midfielder: balanced and composed on the ball, committed and tigerish in the tackle with excellent ball control and superb passing skills. To cap it all he is a player of excellent character and temperament who is modest in his public persona and less carried away by his achievements than his many admirers. He scored ten goals last season, all impressive strikes, but none could match his 35-yard bullet in the 2-0 win over Manchester at the end of March. Although he understandably began to tire in the closing weeks of the campaign he rallied again at the very end, scoring the second goal in the unforgettable UEFA Cup final against Deportivo Alaves and driving the team on to victory in the final league match at Charlton to earn a place in the Champions' League for 2001-02. He again featured for England appearing against Finland at Anfield in March and following this up with two outstanding displays against Mexico and in the World Cup qualifier in Greece. He was honoured by his fellow professionals when he was selected for the PFA's Premiership team in April and was voted as PFA 'Young Player of the Year'.
Liverpool (From trainee on 26/2/1998) PL 59+15/8 FLC 4 FAC 4+2/1 Others 10/2

GHENT Matthew Ian
Born: Burton, 5 October 1980
Height: 6'3" Weight: 14.1
International Honours: E: Yth; Sch
This young 'keeper joined Lincoln on a non-contract basis last November as cover for Alan Marriott. An injury to Marriott gave him his chance to make his Football League debut as a substitute at Carlisle and he retained his place for the FA Cup second round clash with Dagenham & Redbridge when he produced some outstanding saves to keep the Imps in the game only to let in a last minute winner. He left Lincoln in January and later joined Forest Green Rovers.
Aston Villa (From trainee on 13/10/1997)
Lincoln C (Free on 1/12/2000) FL 0+1 FAC 1

GIALLANZA Gaetano
Born: Dornach, Switzerland, 6 June 1974
Height: 6'0" Weight: 11.12
Having enjoyed a successful loan spell at Carrow Road towards the end of the 1999-2000 campaign Gaetano joined Norwich City on a permanent basis in the close season. A rangy frontrunner, with a cool head in front of goal, 'Tano' was just settling into the rigours of English football when he was cruelly cut down by a cruciate ligament injury sustained in the home game against Sheffield United in October. Prior to this he had already scored five goals and was showing signs of establishing an excellent partnership with Iwan Roberts. He is unlikely to return to action before the end of 2001 following a complication in the surgery process.
Bolton W (Loaned from Nantes, France on 25/3/1998) PL 0+3
Norwich C (Free from Nantes, France on 23/3/2000) FL 7+7/2 FLC 3+1/3

GIBB Alistair (Ally) Stuart
Born: Salisbury, 17 February 1976
Height: 5'9" Weight: 11.7
Ally continued where he had left off at the end of the 1999-2000 campaign for Stockport last season, firmly establishing himself as a first choice on the right-hand side of the defence. Comfortable in a flat back four, his blistering pace and ability to cross the ball accurately on the run is also perfect for the modern day wing-back role. A tireless worker down the flank Ally can push forward to deliver accurate crosses and also showed himself to be something of a dead-ball specialist for County, taking most of the corners on the right.
Norwich C (From trainee on 1/7/1994)
Northampton T (Loaned on 22/9/1995) FL 9/1
Northampton T (£30,000 on 5/2/1996) FL 51+71/3 FLC 8+4 FAC 5+3 Others 6+3
Stockport Co (£50,000 on 18/2/2000) FL 51+2 FLC 2 FAC 2

GIBBENS Kevin
Born: Southampton, 4 November 1979
Height: 5'10" Weight: 12.13
Having missed a large part of the 1999-2000 season through injury Kevin fought his way back to the fringes of the Southampton first team last term. He made his first senior appearance of the season as a late substitute against Arsenal in November but never managed to establish himself in the squad and received just a handful of first-team outings afterwards. He is a box-to-box midfield player who is tigerish in the tackle and has excellent distribution.
Southampton (From trainee on 16/1/1998) PL 5+3 FLC 2 FAC 1
Stockport Co (Loaned on 9/9/1999) FL 1+1 FLC 2

GIBBS Nigel James
Born: St Albans, 20 November 1965
Height: 5'7" Weight: 11.11
Club Honours: FAYC '82; Div 2 '98
International Honours: E: U21-5; Yth

Nigel came on as a substitute at Huddersfield on the first day of the season, thus clocking up his 18th campaign as a senior player with Watford. However ill-timed knee and groin injuries restricted his first-team opportunities and all seven of his appearances came in away games. As ever he remained the ideal squad man, capable of playing in any defensive position, although right back continued to be his forte. Now approaching 500 games for the Hornets he was rewarded for his enthusiasm and loyalty with an extension to his contract, thus giving him the chance to overhaul Luther Blissett's club record of appearances.

Watford (From apprentice on 23/11/1983) P/FL 385+22/5 FLC 25/2 FAC 39+2 Others 17

GIBBS Paul Derek
Born: Gorleston, 26 October 1972
Height: 5'10" Weight: 11.10

Paul was a surprise signing by Brentford in the 2000 close season but having got into the Bees' first team he suffered an injury in the Worthington Cup tie at Bristol City. He returned to action two months later and went on to take full advantage of Ijah Anderson's long-term injury to establish himself as a regular in the team. A skilful attacking left wing back with good positional sense, he scored his first goal for the Bees with a curling free kick in the 3-1 win at Wigan last April. Paul won a runners-up medal in the LDV Vans Trophy when he appeared in the final against Port Vale at Cardiff's Millenium Stadium.

Colchester U (Signed from Diss T on 6/3/1995) FL 39+14/3 FAC 1+1 Others 8+1
Torquay U (Free on 26/7/1997) FL 40+1/7 FLC 4/1 FAC 3/1 Others 3/1
Plymouth Arg (Free on 7/7/1998) FL 30+4/3 FLC 2
Brentford (Free on 10/7/2000) FL 26+1/1 FLC 1 FAC 1 Others 6

GIBSON Paul Richard
Born: Sheffield, 1 November 1976
Height: 6'3" Weight: 13.0
Club Honours: FAYC '95

Paul spent the 2000-01 campaign as second-choice 'keeper to Darren Ward at Notts County and was limited to occasional outings in the senior team when Ward was unavailable. A promising youngster he did little wrong when called into service but was released by the Magpies in the summer.

Manchester U (From trainee on 1/7/1995)
Mansfield T (Loaned on 20/10/1997) FL 13
Hull C (Loaned on 6/11/1998) FL 4
Notts Co (Free on 25/3/1999) FL 11 FLC 2 Others 1
Rochdale (Loaned on 4/2/2000) FL 5

GIBSON Robin John
Born: Crewe, 15 November 1979
Height: 5'6" Weight: 10.7

Robin began the 2000-01 campaign on the subs' bench for Wrexham following the arrival of Carlos Edwards and it was not until February that he regained a regular place in the Robins' line-up. Generally playing in a wide-right-midfield role he has good pace and the ability to take on and beat defenders, while he is also willing to help out the defence when required. His only goal of the season came in the 1-1 draw at Port Vale at the beginning of April.

Wrexham (From trainee on 3/7/1998) FL 38+21/3 FLC 1+1 FAC 1+2/1 Others 2+4

GIER Robert (Rob) James
Born: Bracknell, 6 January 1980
Height: 5'9" Weight: 11.7

Having developed through the ranks at Wimbledon, Rob made his Football League debut from the subs' bench in the 4-0 win at Crewe last October and went on to enjoy a short run in the first team before dropping back into the reserves. He returned again at the very end of the season and will be hoping to gain more senior experience in 2001-02. Once he had settled down he produced some fine performances in the heart of the defence and although he still has a lot to learn he can be pleased with his progress last term. A promising young central defender he is an assured performer and has the confidence to run the ball out of defence.

Wimbledon (From trainee on 11/5/1999) FL 13+1 FLC 1+1

GIGGS Ryan Joseph
Born: Cardiff, 29 November 1973
Height: 5'11" Weight: 10.9
Club Honours: ESC '91; FAYC '92; FLC '92; PL '93, '94, '96, '97, '99, '00, '01; CS '93, '94, '96, '97; FAC '94, '96, '99; EC '99
International Honours: W: 32; U21-1; Yth. E: Sch

One sometimes wonders whether there's a clause in Ryan's contract demanding

Ryan Giggs

excellence on the really big European nights for while his consistency in the Premiership remained of the highest order, his form in the Champions' League earned him rave notices both at home and abroad. Despite not recording a goal in Europe during the early stages of the tournament, his unofficial title of 'provider supreme' was never in doubt. In the Premiership he was an ever-present throughout August and September, and opened his account with one of Manchester United's three goals against Everton in September. Netting against Charlton in November, and Bradford in January, he missed three Premiership games on the trot with hamstring problems, but soon returned to spearhead the vital run-in to both the Premiership and European campaigns. With a new five-year contract in the bag in April, Ryan goes into his eleventh year at the Old Trafford hopeful of even more honours. He continued to feature regularly for Wales when fit during the campaign. He was honoured by his fellow professionals with a place in the PFA's Premiership team in April.

Manchester U (From trainee on 1/12/1990) F/PL 291+30/64 FLC 17+4/6 FAC 36+3/7 Others 60+4/13

GILCHRIST Philip (Phil) Alexander
Born: Stockton on Tees, 25 August 1973
Height: 5'11" Weight: 13.12
Club Honours: FLC '00

Phil proved a steady deputy in a number of positions for Leicester last term but he was unable was unable to establish a regular place in the starting line-up. Several clubs tried to prise him from Filbert Street on loan, but he was eventually sold to West Bromwich Albion on the transfer deadline day. Ironically, the deal was initially secured as a loan so that the paperwork could be finalised the following day. He immediately established himself in the centre of defence at The Hawthorns and gave the back line a much more secure look in the closing stages of the campaign. However unfortunately for Baggies' fans he was unable to guide the team past Bolton Wanderers in the play-offs and a place in the promised land of the Premiership.

Nottingham F (From trainee on 5/12/1990)
Middlesbrough (Free on 10/1/1992)
Hartlepool U (Free on 27/11/1992) FL 77+5 FLC 4+1 FAC 4 Others 5
Oxford U (£100,000 on 17/2/1995) FL 173+4/10 FLC 16 FAC 9/1 Others 3
Leicester C (£500,000 on 10/8/1999) PL 23+16/1 FLC 6+1 FAC 4+1
West Bromwich A (£500,000 on 22/3/2001) FL 8 Others 2

GILES Martyn
Born: Cardiff, 10 April 1983
Height: 6'0" Weight: 12.0
International Honours: W: Yth

Martyn is one of several talented youngsters on Cardiff City's books and was given his Football League debut last March when he came on as a substitute in the home game against Hull City. He later stepped in on a handful of occasions for Matt Brazier making the starting line-up at Darlington where he gave a creditable performance. A promising left wing back he was a member of the Bluebirds team that won the Welsh Youth Cup and also featured for Wales U17s against Italy in December.

Cardiff C (From trainee on 23/3/2001) FL 1+4

GILKES Michael Earl Glenis McDonald
Born: Hackney, 20 July 1965
Height: 5'8" Weight: 10.10
Club Honours: FMC '88; Div 3 '86, Div 2 '94
International Honours: Barbados: 6

Michael made only a handful of appearances for Millwall last season when he found it difficult to break into a very strong first-team squad. He played regularly for the reserves where his experience proved invaluable in bringing the youngsters on. He is a talented winger who still has the ability to take on and beat defenders and tracks back well to help his own back line. Michael made his international debut for Barbados in a World Cup tie against Costa Rica in July 2000 and went on to feature regularly for the Bajan Rockets in their remaining qualifying round games. He was released by Millwall in the summer.

Reading (From Leicester C juniors on 10/7/1984) FL 348+45/43 FLC 25+7/6 FAC 31+2/1 Others 26+2/2
Chelsea (Loaned on 28/1/1992) FL 0+1 Others 0+1
Southampton (Loaned on 4/3/1992) FL 4+2
Wolverhampton W (£155,000 on 27/3/1997) FL 33+5/1 FLC 0+1 FAC 2
Millwall (Free on 7/7/1999) FL 28+4/2 FLC 0+2

GILKS Matthew (Matty)
Born: Oldham, 4 June 1982
Height: 6'1" Weight: 12.7

Matty progressed from Rochdale's youth team to the reserves last season and his fine displays won him a regular place on the subs' bench for the first team. He was thrown in at the deep end when regular 'keeper Neil Edwards missed the match away to runaway leaders Chesterfield in March, and performed competently, making a tremendous save late on to keep the score at 1-1. He played twice more when Edwards was injured and looks to be an excellent prospect.

Rochdale (Trainee) FL 2+1

GILL Jeremy (Jerry) Morley
Born: Clevedon, 8 September 1970
Height: 5'7" Weight: 11.0
International Honours: E: SP-1

Jerry had his best season to date for Birmingham City in 2000-01, seeing off the challenge of a string of on-loan right backs to retain his place. He acted with dignity after being left out of the Worthington Cup final team and this helped cement his reputation as a huge crowd favourite. Always dogged in the tackle and wholly committed to the cause, Jerry formed an effective partnership with Nicky Eaden down the right-hand side and went on to play some of the best football of his career.

Leyton Orient (Free from Trowbridge T on 16/12/1988. Free to Weston super Mare on 1/7/1990)
Birmingham C (£30,000 from Yeovil T on 14/7/1997) FL 29+17 FLC 9+1 FAC 2 Others 1

GILL Matthew James
Born: Cambridge, 8 November 1980
Height: 5'11" Weight: 12.10

Matthew missed the start of the 2000-01 campaign while recovering from a close-season hernia operation and it was not until October that he returned to action with Peterborough United. He was switched from a midfield role to full back on his return but then suffered a bad knee injury against Brentford at the beginning of March and was sidelined until the summer break. A product of Posh's successful youth system, his capacity for hard work rather belies his somewhat frail stature.

Peterborough U (From trainee on 2/3/1998) FL 42+23/2 FLC 2 FAC 4 Others 2+3

GILL Wayne John
Born: Chorley, 28 November 1975
Height: 5'9" Weight: 11.0

Wayne joined Tranmere during the close season and was seen as a natural replacement for Alan Mahon, but after a bright start that brought him three goals he suffered a dip in form and lost his place in November. Although he rarely featured in the second half of the campaign, he worked hard in the reserves to try and win his place back. A skilful and hard-working midfield play maker, he has an excellent turn of speed and is good at creating space in the opposition penalty box.

Blackburn Rov (From trainee on 12/7/1994) FLC 3
Blackpool (Signed on 6/3/2000) FL 12/7
Tranmere Rov (Free on 5/7/2000) FL 7+9/2 FLC 3+2/1 FAC 0+1

GILLESPIE Keith Robert
Born: Bangor, 18 February 1975
Height: 5'10" Weight: 11.3
Club Honours: FAYC '92
International Honours: NI: 36; U21-1; Yth; Sch

Unable to establish himself in the Blackburn team at the beginning of last season, Keith joined Wigan Athletic for a loan spell in December but proved unable to reproduce the penetrating runs that had characterised his game in the Premiership and he was back at Ewood Park at the end of the month. However he was recalled to the Rovers' first-team soon after his return and although he struggled to find consistent form he impressed with his ability to track back and cover the break. A talented right winger who on his day is fast and tricky on the ball, he will be aiming for a regular first-team place in 2001-02.

Manchester U (From trainee on 3/2/1993) PL 3+6/1 FLC 3 FAC 1+1/1
Wigan Ath (Loaned on 3/9/1993) FL 8/4 Others 2
Newcastle U (£1,000,000 on 12/1/1995) PL 94+19/11 FLC 7+1/1 FAC 9+1/2 Others 11+5
Blackburn Rov (£2,250,000 on 18/12/1998) P/FL 36+20/3 FLC 3 FAC 4+1/1
Wigan Ath (Loaned on 1/12/2000) FL 4+1 FAC 2

GINOLA David Desire Marc
Born: Gassin, France, 25 January 1967
Height: 6'0" Weight: 11.10
Club Honours: FLC '99
International Honours: France: 17; B-2; U21

Aston Villa's big name signing during the close season, there were high expectations of what David might do for the club in 2000-01, but in the end his campaign was something of a disappointment. He was in and out of the side all season, often hampered by niggling injuries and rarely completed a full 90 minutes. Despite this he regularly showed that he is an extremely talented footballer: strong, quick and skilful, with a powerful shot and plenty of flair. Very often operating in a free role that enabled him to play down either flank he impressed with some two-footed trickery and the delivery of pinpoint crosses. However he seemed to save the best until last, turning on some eye-catching displays in the closing matches. He scored with a cracking right-foot free-kick in the 2-2 draw with West Ham and followed this up with an inspirational performance and a fine goal at Charlton.

Newcastle U (£2,500,000 from Paris St Germain, France, ex Toulon, Racing Paris, Brest, on 6/7/1995) PL 54+4/6 FLC 6 FAC 4 Others 7+1/1
Tottenham H (£2,000,000 on 18/7/1997) PL 100/12 FLC 13/4 FAC 11/5 Others 2+1
Aston Villa (£3,000,000 on 1/8/2000) PL 14+13/3 FAC 1

Shay Given

GIVEN Seamus (Shay) John
Born: Lifford, 20 April 1976
Height: 6'0" Weight: 13.4
Club Honours: Div 1 '96
International Honours: RoI: 31; U21-5; Yth

Despite the well-publicised dearth of clean sheets at Newcastle last term, Shay had one of his best-ever seasons in goal for the Magpies. Agile and quick on his feet with a safe pair of hands, he is often described as small for his position, but he was rarely exposed in the air and comfortably handled the pressure created by high balls being delivered into the box. After signing a new contract in September he was named 'Man of the Match' in the home game with Liverpool when he defied the Reds' attack time after time to earn a surprise victory. Injured and substituted at Derby just before Christmas he missed the home win over Leeds and was then kept on the bench by Steve Harper's fine form. A transfer request followed but this was soon withdrawn and shortly afterwards he was back in the line-up. He continued to play well for the remainder of the season, and was in particularly good form in the away 'derby' at Sunderland. He capped a fine season by being recalled to the Republic of Ireland team after losing his place through injury the previous summer.

Blackburn Rov (From Glasgow Celtic juniors on 8/8/1994) PL 2 FLC 0+1
Swindon T (Loaned on 4/8/1995) FL 5
Sunderland (Loaned on 19/1/1996) FL 17
Newcastle U (£1,500,000 on 14/7/1997) PL 103 FLC 3+1 FAC 12 Others 8

GLASS James (Jimmy) Robert
Born: Epsom, 1 August 1973
Height: 6'1" Weight: 13.4

Having been released by Brentford at the end of the 1999-2000 campaign, Jimmy joined Oxford United during the summer on a monthly contract. A regular on the subs' bench in the first half of the season he made just a couple of starts in the first team before being released early in the new year. He subsequently had a brief spell with Dr Martens League outfit Crawley Town before moving on to Kingstonian in March. He is an agile 'keeper who is reliable on crosses and an excellent shot stopper.

Crystal Palace (From trainee on 4/7/1991)
Portsmouth (Loaned on 10/2/1995) FL 3
Bournemouth (Free on 8/3/1996) FL 94 FLC 4 FAC 4 Others 7
Swindon T (Free on 24/6/1998) FL 11 FLC 1
Carlisle U (Loaned on 22/4/1999) FL 3/1
Cambridge U (Free on 20/1/2000)
Brentford (Free on 23/3/2000) FL 1+1
Oxford U (Free on 8/8/2000) FL 1 Others 1

GLASS Stephen
Born: Dundee, 23 May 1976
Height: 5'9" Weight: 11.0
Club Honours: SLC '96
International Honours: S: 1; B-2; U21-11; Sch

Stephen came off the transfer list at Newcastle during the close season and resolved to fight for his place in the Magpies' first team in 2000-01. He came off the subs' bench in the second game of the season against Derby to score with a stunning 25-yard volley into the roof of the net, but after starting the next two games he was mostly used as a squad player, featuring as a substitute with only occasional appearances in the line-up. He is a pacy winger with good crossing ability and a keen eye for goal.

Aberdeen (Free from Crombie Sports on 25/10/1994) SL 93+13/7 SLC 10/2 SC 7+2 Others 3/2
Newcastle U (£650,000 on 22/7/1998) PL 24+19/7 FLC 3 FAC 3+4 Others 2+3

GLEDHILL Lee
Born: Bury, 7 November 1980
Height: 5'10" Weight: 11.2

Lee once again found opportunities at Barnet rather limited last season due to the outstanding form of Sam Stockley and he made the starting line-up just once, for the game against Plymouth in March. He produced some fine performances in the Bees' reserve team, captaining the side on occasions and will be hoping to get a decent run of first-team football in the 2000-01 campaign. He is an effective right wing back who makes useful forays down the flank to support the attack. He was placed on the open to offers list in the summer.

Barnet (From trainee on 2/7/1999) FL 9+7 FAC 1+1 Others 2

GLENNON Matthew (Matty) William
Born: Stockport, 8 October 1978
Height: 6'2" Weight: 14.9

This young Bolton Wanderers goalkeeper had a short loan spell at Bristol Rovers early in the 2000-01 campaign where he made a single appearance deputising for the injured Nick Culkin. Matty produced a superb 'Man of the Match' display against Wigan Athletic keeping a clean sheet in a goalless draw. In November he moved on to Carlisle, also on loan and quickly became a favourite of the Brunton Park faithful with some confident displays, his ability to command the area proving an inspiration to the defenders in front of him. He produced an excellent penalty save at York but he saved his best performance for the FA Cup tie against Arsenal when he made some magnificent saves to restrict the Gunners to a single goal. Matty deservedly received the Cumbrians' 'Player of the Year' award at the end of the campaign. He was reported to have signed for Hull City in the summer.

Bolton W (From trainee on 3/7/1997)
Bristol Rov (Loaned on 15/9/2000) FL 1
Carlisle U (Loaned on 10/11/2000) FL 29 FAC 3 Others 1

GLOVER Edward **Lee**
Born: Kettering, 24 April 1970
Height: 5'11" Weight: 12.1
Club Honours: FLC '89; FMC '92
International Honours: S: U21-3; Yth

Lee signed for Macclesfield after a successful pre-season trial but took time to settle in at the start of the 2000-01 campaign. Although not always the first-choice striker, he eventually began to show his value and finished up as the club's leading scorer, his tally including some crucial strikes, notably a last-gasp penalty at Hartlepool to level the scores and two splendid goals in the win at Barnet. He is a skilful forward who holds the ball up well on the edge of the box, turns defenders quickly and can certainly move up a gear when going for goal. Away from football Lee is in his third year of a four-year part-time course studying for a BSc (Hons) degree in Sports Science.

Nottingham F (From apprentice on 2/5/1987) F/PL 61+15/9 FLC 6+5/2 FAC 8+2/1 Others 4+1/1
Leicester C (Loaned on 14/9/1989) FL 3+2/1
Barnsley (Loaned on 18/1/1990) FL 8 FAC 4
Luton T (Loaned on 2/9/1991) FL 1
Port Vale (£200,000 on 2/8/1994) FL 38+14/7 FLC 5+1/4 FAC 0+2 Others 3+2/2

Rotherham U (£150,000 on 15/8/1996) FL 70+15/29 FLC 5 FAC 9+1/3 Others 1+1
Huddersfield T (Loaned on 3/3/1997) FL 11
Macclesfield T (Free on 5/7/2000) FL 29+8/8 FLC 0+1 FAC 1 Others 1/2

GOATER Leonard **Shaun**
Born: Hamilton, Bermuda, 25 February 1970
Height: 6'1" Weight: 12.0
Club Honours: AMC '96
International Honours: Bermuda: 19; Yth

The Bermudian international had a disappointing start to his first season in the Premiership. He was sidelined with a knee injury during the pre-season and it was not until the game at Southampton in October that he appeared for the first time, coming on as a substitute for Paulo Wanchope in a 2-0 win for the Blues. He broke his Premiership duck in December with a goal in the 5-0 win over Everton at Maine Road and began to find the net more regularly in the second half of the campaign, netting an injury-time winner in the FA Cup fourth round tie against Coventry and the only goal of the game at Newcastle to earn some vital points for City. An effective target man who works hard for the cause he will be hoping to score more regularly in the 2001-02 campaign.

Manchester U (Free from North Village, Bermuda on 8/5/1989)
Rotherham U (Free on 25/10/1989) FL 169+40/70 FLC 13+4/4 FAC 12+3/7 Others 15+5/5
Notts Co (Loaned on 12/11/1993) FL 1
Bristol C (£175,000 on 17/7/1996) FL 67+8/40 FLC 7/2 FAC 5 Others 5+1/1
Manchester C (£400,000 on 26/3/1998) P/FL 108+8/49 FLC 9/7 FAC 8+1/7 Others 3/1

Shaun Goater

GOLDBAEK Bjarne
Born: Nykobing Falster, Denmark, 6 October 1968
Height: 5'10" Weight: 12.4
Club Honours: Div 1 '01
International Honours: Denmark: 28; B-1; U21; Yth

Bjarne was one of the most consistent players in the Fulham squad in 2000-01 and missed only two First Division matches, making a significant contribution to the club's championship season. His exciting runs down the right flank made him a great favourite with the club's fans, the only disappointment being that despite his ferocious shot he only scored twice. A dependable right-sided midfield player he can also feature at wing back.

Chelsea (£350,000 from FC Copenhagen, Denmark, ex Naestved, FC Schalke, Kaiserslautern, Tennis Borussia, FC Koln, on 10/11/1998) PL 15+14/5 FLC 3 FAC 2+4 Others 1+1
Fulham (£500,000 + on 18/1/2000) FL 57+5/5 FLC 3 FAC 2

GOMA Alain
Born: Sault, France, 5 October 1972
Height: 6'0" Weight: 13.0
International Honours: France: 2; B-1; U21; Yth

After missing a large part of the 1999-2000 season through injury Alain came back into the Newcastle United team last term and began to forge a solid partnership with Aaron Hughes in the centre of the defence. However he continued to attract injuries, suffering a broken nose against Charlton and a broken hand against Chelsea. It was something of a surprise when he put in a transfer request and in March he moved on to Fulham for a substantial fee. He eventually made his debut at the end of April but featured in only a handful of games before the end of the campaign. A big strong centre half who likes bringing the ball out of defence he is particularly effective as a man-to-man marker.

Newcastle U (£4,750,000 from Paris St Germain, France, ex Auxerre, on 9/7/1999) PL 32+1/1 FLC 4 FAC 2 Others 2
Fulham (£4,000,000 on 16/3/2001) FL 3

GOODEN Ty Michael
Born: Canvey Island, 23 October 1972
Height: 5'8" Weight: 12.6
Club Honours: Div 2 '96

Although he appeared in Gillingham's first-ever Division One game against Stockport last August, Ty was plagued by injuries to his knee, hamstring and ankle last term and was absent for large parts of the season. A hard-working left-sided midfield player he likes to get forward at every opportunity and can create as well as score goals.

Swindon T (Free from Wycombe W on 17/9/1993) P/FL 118+28/9 FLC 6+1/1 FAC 7+1/1 Others 3+1
Gillingham (£75,000 on 4/1/2000) FL 32+2/4 FLC 2 Others 3/1

GOODFELLOW Marc David
Born: Burton, 20 September 1981
Height: 5'8" Weight: 10.6

Marc won rave reviews after scoring freely for the Stoke City reserve and youth teams last season and broke into the first team in style - scoring an outstanding late winner in the Worthington Cup tie against Charlton. He went on to make a handful of senior appearances and will be looking to feature more regularly in the squad in the coming season. He is a talented young striker with electric pace, an excellent shot in both feet and an eye for a goal-scoring opportunity.

Stoke C (From juniors on 29/1/1999) FL 0+7 FLC 0+2/1 FAC 0+1 Others 2/1

GOODHIND Warren Ernest
Born: Johannesburg, South Africa, 16 August 1977
Height: 5'11" Weight: 11.6

Warren showed that he had made a full recovery from the broken leg he suffered back in November 1998, turning in a string of impressive performances for Barnet last season. His commitment to the cause made him a favourite of the Underhill club's fans in what was a very disappointing campaign overall. An effective central defender he is now the Bees longest serving player following the departure of Paul Wilson. He was placed on the open to offers list in the summer.

Barnet (From trainee on 3/7/1996) FL 73+20/3 FLC 5+1 FAC 2 Others 4/1

GOODISON Ian
Born: Jamaica, 21 November 1972
Height: 6'3" Weight: 12.10
International Honours: Jamaica

This cultured defender displayed class throughout the 2000-01 campaign and played a crucial role in helping Hull City to the play-offs. After struggling to establish himself in his first season in England he showed he had adapted well to the Third Division, forming a formidable central defensive partnership with Tigers' skipper Justin Whittle. Ian now holds the Tigers record for international appearances, having won 26 caps since arriving at Boothferry Park.

Hull C (Free from Olympic Gardens, Jamaica on 22/10/1999) FL 53+1/1 FLC 1 FAC 4+1 Others 3

GOODLAD Mark
Born: Barnsley, 9 September 1979
Height: 6'0" Weight: 13.2
Club Honours: AMC '01

Mark had an excellent first season as Port Vale's regular goalkeeper, rarely being absent and finishing the campaign as a joint-winner of the club's 'Young Player of the Year' award. A fine shot stopper and excellent at handling crosses, a high point of his campaign was appearing in the Vale team that defeated Brentford to win the LDV Vans Trophy at Cardiff's Millenium Stadium.

Nottingham F (From trainee on 2/10/1996)
Scarborough (Loaned on 5/2/1999) FL 3
Port Vale (Signed on 23/3/2000) FL 40+1 FLC 2 FAC 2 Others 6

GOODMAN Donald (Don) Ralph
Born: Leeds, 9 May 1966
Height: 5'10" Weight: 13.2
Club Honours: Div 3 '85

This vastly experienced striker began the 2000-01 campaign with Scottish Premier League club Motherwell where he was mostly used from the subs' bench. Don returned to the Midlands on the transfer deadline day to boost Walsall's promotion campaign and despite his advancing years he proved very effective, netting three goals including the first equaliser against Reading in the play-off final. He is an experienced striker with an outstanding work rate, powerful running and great aerial ability. He was reported to have signed a new 12-month contract with the Saddlers in the summer.

Bradford C (Free from Collingham on 10/7/1984) FL 65+5/14 FLC 5+1/2 FAC 2+3/4 Others 4+1/2
West Bromwich A (£50,000 on 27/3/1987) FL 140+18/60 FLC 11/1 FAC 7/1 Others 5/1
Sunderland (£900,000 on 6/12/1991) FL 112+4/40 FLC 9/1 FAC 3/1 Others 4/2
Wolverhampton W (£1,100,000 on 6/12/1994) FL 115+10/33 FLC 8+1/4 FAC 16+1/2 Others 3 (Free to Hiroshima Antlers, Japan during 1998 close season)
Barnsley (Loaned on 25/12/1998) FL 5+3 FAC 2
Motherwell (Signed on 30/3/1999) SL 39+16/9 SLC 4+1 SC 4/3
Walsall (Free on 22/3/2001) FL 8/2 Others 3/1

Don Goodman

GOODRIDGE Gregory (Greg) Ronald St Clair
Born: Barbados, 10 July 1971
Height: 5'6" Weight: 10.0
International Honours: Barbados

Greg had a rather frustrating time at Bristol City in 2000-01 and although he featured a number of times from the subs' bench he made the starting line-up on only one occasion. He rather surprisingly went on loan to Cheltenham in February and made a big impression in his first month at Whaddon Road. He became a key figure for the Robins helping the team stage a late bid for a place in the play-offs, but proved a little less effective following a spell on international duty and returned to Ashton Gate at the end of the campaign. Greg is a skilful and exciting winger with a tremendous long throw. He continued to captain the Barbados national team, leading them to their best-ever World Cup qualifying performance and a place in the finals of the Copa Caribe tournament in May and winning a further 11 caps during the season.

Torquay U (Free from Lambada, St Vincent on 24/3/1994) FL 32+6/4 FLC 4/1 FAC 2+1 Others 3+1/1
Queens Park R (£350,000 on 9/8/1995) PL 0+7/1 FLC 0+1 FAC 0+1
Bristol C (£50,000 on 19/8/1996) FL 76+41/14 FLC 10+2/1 FAC 5+3/1 Others 2+4/1
Cheltenham T (Loaned on 24/2/2001) FL 10+1/1

GOPE-FENEPEJ John
Born: Noumea, New Caledonia, 16 November 1978
Height: 5'11" Weight: 12.7

Signed on a three-month loan deal from Nantes, John never really established himself in the Bolton Wanderers' first team and he made just two appearances from the subs' bench before returning across the Channel. A promising central defender he has yet to break into the French club's first team.

Bolton W (Loaned from Nantes, France on 22/9/2000) FL 0+2

GORAM Andrew (Andy) Lewis
Born: Bury, 13 April 1964
Height: 5'11" Weight: 12.6
Club Honours: SPD '92, '93, '95, '96, '97; SLC '93, '97; SC '92, '93, '96
International Honours: S: 43; U21-1

They say that everything comes to those who wait, but even Andy probably couldn't believe his dream move at the end of the 2000-01 campaign. Twenty years after Tommy Docherty tried to sign him for Manchester United when he was manager, a goalkeeping crisis prompted Sir Alex Ferguson to sign Andy from Motherwell in March. At 36, the former Scottish international goalkeeper was considered a stop-gap signing and he appeared just twice for United, making his debut in the 4-2 win over Coventry in April and also featuring in the defeat at Southampton the following month. Andy is that rarity in the modern game a double international, having played both football and cricket for Scotland.

Oldham Ath (Free from West Bromwich A juniors on 22/8/1981) FL 195 FLC 10 FAC 7 Others 3
Hibernian (£325,000 on 9/10/1987) SL 138/1 SLC 7 SC 13 Others 4
Glasgow R (£1,000,000 on 27/6/1991) SL 184 SLC 19 SC 26 Others 31
Notts Co (Free on 3/9/1998) FL 1
Sheffield U (Free on 7/9/1998) FL 7 FLC 2
Motherwell (Free on 12/1/1999) SL 57 SLC 4 SC 8
Manchester U (£100,000 on 22/3/2001) PL 2

GORDON Dean Dwight
Born: Croydon, 10 February 1973
Height: 6'0" Weight: 13.4
Club Honours: Div 1 '94
International Honours: E: U21-13

For the second consecutive season Dean was blighted by injuries that kept him out of action for much of the campaign. When fully fit he is an exciting winger who races down the flank to deliver some telling crosses, while he is almost legendary for his powerful shots and his tenacious tackling. His absences coincided with the worst of Boro's performances but when he appeared he always gave his all for the cause.

Crystal Palace (From trainee on 4/7/1991) F/PL 181+20/20 FLC 16+3/2 FAC 14+1/1 Others 5+1
Middlesbrough (£900,000 on 17/7/1998) PL 53+9/4 FLC 5 FAC 3

GORDON Kenyatta Gavin
Born: Manchester, 24 June 1979
Height: 6'1" Weight: 12.0

Gavin began last season in fine form at Lincoln causing plenty of problems for opposing defenders and netting ten goals including two against Cardiff at Ninian Park. After the Imps were knocked out of the FA Cup he was sold to Cardiff City for a club record fee and following a couple of appearances from the subs' bench he made the starting line-up for the home game with Exeter City on New Year's Day. The Bluebirds won 6-1 and Gavin netted with a header, but he then spent much of the remainder of the campaign in the treatment room. The problem was eventually diagnosed as a displaced joint and has now been rectified. At his best Gavin is a bustling striker who works hard to harass defenders and is good in the air.

Hull C (From trainee on 3/7/1996) FL 22+16/9 FLC 1+4/1 Others 1+1
Lincoln C (£30,000 on 7/11/1997) FL 87+12/28 FLC 2/1 FAC 9/2 Others 4+1
Cardiff C (£275,000 + on 18/12/2000) FL 4+6/1

GORRE Dean
Born: Surinam, 10 September 1970
Height: 5'8" Weight: 11.7
International Honours: Holland: U21

Dean was hampered by a hamstring injury in the early part of last season and this restricted his efforts to win a regular place in the Huddersfield Town starting line-up. Once fully fit however he became unhappy with a place on the subs' bench and targeted a move away from the club. However he eventually returned to his best form but was unable to prevent the Terriers from being relegated to the Second Division. A skilful midfield playmaker who can create an opening out of nothing, he will be hoping for better fortune in the 2001-02 campaign.

Huddersfield T (£330,000 from Ajax, Holland on 16/9/1999) FL 49+13/6 FLC 4/1 FAC 1+1

GOTTSKALKSSON Olafur
Born: Keflavik, Iceland, 12 March 1968
Height: 6'3" Weight: 13.12
Club Honours: S Div 1 '99
International Honours: Iceland: 9; U21-7; Yth

Olafur immediately established himself as first-choice goalkeeper for Brentford last season after signing from Hibernian during the 2000 summer break. An excellent shot stopper his assured performances inspired confidence in the Bees' defence and he made early-season penalty saves against Wycombe and Notts County. He has also been known to join the attack for late corners when the situation requires and almost scored against Swindon last April when he headed narrowly over the bar. He won a runners-up medal in the LDV Vans Trophy after appearing for Brentford in the final against Port Vale last April.

Hibernian (Signed from Keflavik, Iceland, ex IA Akranes, KR Reykjavik, on 29/7/1997) SL 64 SLC 4 SC 2
Brentford (Free on 11/7/2000) FL 45 FLC 4 FAC 1 Others 7

GOUGH Richard Charles
Born: Stockholm, Sweden, 5 April 1962
Height: 6'0" Weight: 12.0
Club Honours: SPD '83, '89, '90, '91, '92, '93, '94, '95, '96, '97; SLC '89, '91, '93, '94, '97; SC '92, '93, '96
International Honours: S: 61; U21-5

After an outstanding first full season with Everton, the final year of Richard's glittering career was blighted by injuries. He remained club captain throughout the campaign, but was prevented from showing his inspirational leadership qualities on the pitch by a succession of injury problems. Stretchered off with knee ligament damage in only his second appearance of the season, he did not return until January. Even then niggling problems meant he made just seven further appearances before he called time for good on his playing career. Taking time out to consider his career options with his family in California, the chances are that Richard's talents will not be lost to the game for good.

Dundee U (From Wits University, South Africa on 21/3/1980) SL 160+8/24 SLC 33+3/9 SC 19/2 Others 30+1/3
Tottenham H (£750,000 on 17/8/1986) FL 49/2 FLC 10 FAC 6
Glasgow R (£1,500,000 on 2/10/1987) SL 318/26 SLC 35/3 SC 37/2 Others 34/4 (Free to San Jose, USA on 21/5/1998)
Nottingham F (Free on 5/3/1999) PL 7
Everton (Free on 11/6/1999) PL 38/1 FAC 3+1

GOULD James Robert
Born: Kettering, 15 January 1982
Height: 5'9" Weight: 11.8

This Northampton Town youngster was a regular in the club's reserve team last season and featured several times on the subs' bench. He made his first appearance in the starting line-up for the LDV Vans Trophy game at Millwall scoring the Cobblers' goal in a 4-1 defeat, but when further opportunities arose he was struck down with appendicitis. James is a wing back who can play on either flank if required.

Northampton T (From trainee on 13/7/2000) FL 0+1 Others 1+1/1

GOWER Mark
Born: Edmonton, 5 October 1978
Height: 5'11" Weight: 11.12
Club Honours: FLC '99
International Honours: E: Yth; Sch

Tony Cottee's major signing in his reign as Barnet manager, Mark joined the Bees from Spurs last January. Although he is a very skilful midfield player, he took time to adjust to the physical demands of the Third Division and he found himself relegated to the subs' bench for the last month of the season. Mark scored his first goal for the Bees when he netted with a header in the 2-1 defeat at Hull in March. He was placed on the open to offers list in the summer.

Tottenham H (From trainee on 1/4/1997) FLC 0+2
Motherwell (Loaned on 12/3/1999) SL 8+1/1
Barnet (£32,500 on 19/1/2001) FL 10+4/1 Others 1/1

GRAHAM David
Born: Edinburgh, 6 October 1978
Height: 5'10" Weight: 11.5
International Honours: S: U21-8

After failing to establish himself at Dunfermline, David had a spell on loan with Inverness Caledonian Thistle before joining Torquay United on a short-term contract on transfer deadline day. A quick and busy striker he played an important role in ensuring the Gulls survival netting two goals in five games including one in the final-day decider at Barnet.

Glasgow R (From juniors on 1/7/1995) SL 0+3 Others 1+1
Dunfermline Ath (Signed on 15/11/1998) SL 17+23/4 SLC 1 SC 3/1 Others 0+1
Inverness Caledonian Thistle (Loaned on 5/1/2001) SL 0+2 SC 0+2
Torquay U (Free on 22/3/2001) FL 5/2

GRAHAM Gareth Lee
Born: Belfast, 6 December 1978
Height: 5'7" Weight: 10.2
International Honours: NI: U21-5

Gareth was again unable to establish himself in the Brentford first-team squad last season and it was not until the closing stages of the campaign that he finally appeared, coming off the subs' bench for the final two minutes of the 2-2 draw at home to Luton. A combative and hard-working midfield player he was out of contract in the summer.

Crystal Palace (From trainee on 19/3/1997) FL 0+1
Brentford (Free on 28/9/1999) FL 5+9

GRAINGER Martin Robert
Born: Enfield, 23 August 1972
Height: 5'11" Weight: 12.0

One of the vital members of the Birmingham City team, Martin had a solid campaign in 2000-01 and could always be relied on to provide 100 per cent effort for the cause. An experienced midfield player he strikes the ball sweetly with his left foot and is always a danger from set pieces, his tally of eight last season putting him among the Blues' leading scorers. The high point of his campaign was appearing in the team that was so narrowly defeated by Liverpool in the Worthington Cup final at Cardiff's Millenium Stadium. He was honoured by his fellow professionals when he was selected for the PFA's First Division team in April.

Colchester U (From trainee on 28/7/1992) FL 37+9/7 FLC 3 FAC 3+2 Others 3/1
Brentford (£60,000 on 21/10/1993) FL 100+1/12 FLC 6/1 FAC 9/1 Others 8/2
Birmingham C (£400,000 on 25/3/1996) FL 155+18/20 FLC 18+2/2 FAC 8+1/1 Others 4

GRANT Anthony (Tony) James
Born: Liverpool, 14 November 1974
Height: 5'10" Weight: 10.2
Club Honours: CS '95
International Honours: E: U21-1

Tony had to wait patiently for his first chance of regular Premiership football last season. After a single appearance as a substitute when he replaced Richard Edgehill in the home defeat by Coventry City in August he was sidelined for six weeks with a stress fracture of the foot, before joining West Bromwich Albion on loan as cover for the injured Derek McInnes. He made a handful of appearances for the Baggies and although boss Gary Megson was keen on a permanent deal he subsequently returned to Maine Road. He was back in the first-team squad in the new year, featuring from the subs' bench in the home game against Leeds and appearing more regularly towards the end of the campaign as Joe Royle's team fought unsuccessfully against relegation. He is a hard-tackling midfield player with excellent vision and the ability to deliver a measured pass.

Everton (From trainee on 8/7/1993) PL 43+18/2 FLC 5+1 FAC 4+4 Others 2+2/1
Swindon T (Loaned on 18/1/1996) FL 3/1
Tranmere Rov (Loaned on 2/9/1999) FL 8+1 FLC 1/1
Manchester C (£450,000 on 24/12/1999) P/FL 9+9 FAC 2+1
West Bromwich A (Loaned on 1/12/2000) FL 3+2

GRANT Gareth Michael
Born: Leeds, 6 September 1980
Height: 5'9" Weight: 10.4

Gareth featured a couple of times for Bradford City in the Inter Toto Cup matches in pre-season scoring his first senior goal in the 4-1 home victory over Lithuanian outfit FK Atlantas and netting another in the 7-2 Worthington Cup win over Darlington. A pacy and skilful striker he spent February on loan at Lincoln where he made a bright start creating a goal on his debut and scoring in his second match. However, the Imps were struggling in the Third Division at the time and Gareth returned to Valley Parade after a change of manager at Sincil Bank. He made a handful of appearances from the subs' bench in Premiership matches and will be hoping for more senior experience in 2001-02.

Bradford C (From trainee on 28/4/1998) P/FL 2+12 FLC 3+4/1 Others 0+2/1
Halifax T (Loaned on 12/2/1999) FL 0+3 Others 0+1
Lincoln C (Loaned on 9/2/2001) FL 3 Others 1/1

GRANT John Anthony Carlton
Born: Manchester, 9 August 1981
Height: 5'11" Weight: 11.0

A graduate of the successful Crewe Alexandra Academy scheme, John featured in a handful of games at the beginning of last season but was then sidelined by injuries. He eventually recovered in the new year and in March he went on loan to Unibond League outfit Hyde United. A promising young striker with an eye for goal he will hoping to make a breakthrough into the first team at Gresty Road in the coming season.

Crewe Alex (From trainee on 7/7/1999) FL 1+5 FLC 1+3

GRANT Peter
Born: Glasgow, 30 August 1965
Height: 5'9" Weight: 11.9
Club Honours: SPL '86, '88; SC '89
International Honours: S: 2; B-2; U21-10; Yth; Sch

Although he joined Bournemouth as a player-coach, Peter featured regularly in the first three months of the 2000-01 season before stepping back to make way for younger players in the squad. A hard-working, thoughtful midfield player his experience proved an asset in the centre of the park for the Cherries.

Glasgow Celtic (From juniors on 27/7/1982) SL 338+27/15 SLC 40+3/3 SC 34+4/1 Others 27/1
Norwich C (£200,000 on 22/8/1997) FL 64+4/3 FLC 4+1 FAC 2
Reading (Free on 20/8/1999) FL 27+2/1 FLC 3 FAC 0+4 Others 2
Bournemouth (Free on 18/8/2000) FL 14+1 FLC 2 Others 1

GRANVILLE Daniel (Danny) Patrick
Born: Islington, 19 January 1975
Height: 5'11" Weight: 12.5
Club Honours: FLC '98, ECWC '98
International Honours: E: U21-3

Danny featured in a couple of early matches for Manchester City last term before joining Norwich City on loan in October. He did well in his short stay at Carrow Road where he featured both at left back and in a more attacking left-sided role. He subsequently returned to Maine Road but it was not until the away game at Coventry on New Year's Day that he made the starting line-up. From then on he featured in almost every game as City battled unsuccessfully for Premiership survival. A speedy defender with a high work rate he likes to get forward to support the attack and can deliver a useful cross.

Cambridge U (From trainee on 19/5/1993) FL 89+10/7 FLC 3+2 FAC 2+2 Others 4+2
Chelsea (£300,000 + on 21/3/1997) PL 12+6 FLC 3 Others 4+1/1
Leeds U (£1,600,000 on 8/7/1998) PL 7+2 FLC 1 FAC 3 Others 0+1
Manchester C (£1,000,000 on 7/8/1999) P/FL 44+10/2 FLC 0+3 FAC 5
Norwich C (Loaned on 27/10/2000) FL 6

GRAVES Wayne Alan
Born: Scunthorpe, 18 September 1980
Height: 5'8" Weight: 12.10

After scoring as a substitute in the opening home game, Wayne became a regular for Scunthorpe United during the opening two months of the 2000-01 campaign. A tigerish midfielder with great pace and work-rate it was not until March that he received another run in the team and he then featured regularly for the Iron in the remaining matches. He will be in his third full season as a professional in 2001-02 and will looking to establish a regular place in the starting line-up at Glanford Park.

Scunthorpe U (From trainee on 24/3/1999) FL 34+22/2 FLC 3+1 FAC 0+4 Others 2

GRAVESEN Thomas
Born: Vejle, Denmark, 11 March 1976
Height: 5'10" Weight: 12.4
International Honours: Denmark: 16

A summer signing from SV Hamburg, Thomas suffered the indignity of being red-carded in a pre-season friendly for his new club. It was a harsh decision, but meant he was suspended for the opening day of the Premiership season at Leeds. Whether the decision had an impact on his game or not is uncertain, but he rarely lived up to the reputation he brought with him from the Bundesliga. Instead Everton got an energetic, strong-running midfielder with a good range of passing and a solid shot from distance. Strangely he failed to build on two goals in his opening five Premiership matches, but wasn't helped by being asked to play in a variety of positions during an Everton injury crisis - including the sweeper role he fills for the Danish national team. Despite the difficulties, Thomas made a consistent and solid start to his first full season in the English Premiership.

Everton (£2,500,000 from SV Hamburg, Germany, ex Vejle BK, on 9/8/2000) PL 30+2/2 FLC 1 FAC 2

Thomas Gravesen

Andy Gray

GRAY Andrew (Andy) David
Born: Harrogate, 15 November 1977
Height: 6'1" Weight: 13.0
International Honours: S: Yth

Andy again struggled to make some impact on the Nottingham Forest first-team squad last season and rarely featured at all before breaking through in December. He subsequently appeared fairly regularly, mostly being employed as an orthodox right back. However he looked far more comfortable playing on the right-hand side of midfield and seemed to struggle to settle down in his new role.

Leeds U (From trainee on 1/7/1995) PL 13+9 FLC 3+1 FAC 0+2
Bury (Loaned on 11/12/1997) FL 4+2/1
Nottingham F (£175,000 on 2/9/1998) P/FL 26+22 FLC 2+3 FAC 4+1
Preston NE (Loaned on 23/2/1999) FL 5
Oldham Ath (Loaned on 25/3/1999) FL 4

GRAY Ian James
Born: Manchester, 25 February 1975
Height: 6'2" Weight: 13.0

An excellent shot stopper, Ian had missed just one game for Rotherham last season before picking up an injury in February and from then on he had a battle on his hands with Paul Pettinger for the number one spot. He made a superb penalty-kick save to earn a point at Bristol Rovers but suffered a slight dip in form as the campaign reached its climax. He kept three successive clean sheets on two occasions during the season.

Oldham Ath (From trainee on 16/7/1993)
Rochdale (Loaned on 18/11/1994) FL 12 Others 3
Rochdale (£20,000 on 17/7/1995) FL 66 FLC 4 FAC 5 Others 4
Stockport Co (£200,000 + on 30/7/1997) FL 14+2 FLC 3
Rotherham U (Free on 10/7/2000) FL 33 FLC 2 FAC 3 Others 1

GRAY Julian Raymond
Born: Lewisham, 21 September 1979
Height: Weight:

This tall wide-left midfield player joined Crystal Palace from Arsenal in the summer of 2000 and featured regularly for the Eagles in the first half of last season before dropping out of the squad. He has plenty of speed, is a good crosser of the ball and is strong in the air. Julian scored his first league goal with a header in the 2-1 win at Huddersfield last August.

Arsenal (From trainee on 13/7/1998) PL 0+1
Crystal Palace (£250,000 + on 21/7/2000) FL 12+11/1 FLC 1+4

GRAY Kevin John
Born: Sheffield, 7 January 1972
Height: 6'0" Weight: 14.0

Huddersfield defender Kevin joined Stockport in a loan deal on the eve of the 2000-01 season and was a surprise inclusion in the line-up for the opening game at Gillingham. However he was on his way back to the McAlpine Stadium within a matter of days after suffering injury and illness during his first game for County. Once back he had to settle for a place on the substitutes' bench, and it was not until late October that he regained a regular place in the first team. A committed defender with a

no-nonsense approach he was always in the thick of the action and looked most comfortable when playing alongside Jon Dyson in the heart of the back line.
Mansfield T (From trainee on 1/7/1990) FL 129+12/3 FLC 8/1 FAC 6+1 Others 12+2/2
Huddersfield T (Signed on 18/7/1994) FL 170+16/5 FLC 11+1 FAC 13 Others 3
Stockport Co (Loaned on 11/8/2000) FL 1

GRAY Martin David
Born: Stockton on Tees, 17 August 1971
Height: 5'9" Weight: 11.4
Martin was appointed Darlington club captain at the start of last season after his commitment and passion had shown through in the 1999-2000 campaign. He continued where he had left off and impressed again with both effort and consistency in midfield. After missing only one game up to the end of January he suffered a back injury and was ruled out for the remainder of the season. Although he has come close on a number of occasions Martin is still looking for his first goal for the Quakers after over 80 outings.
Sunderland (From trainee on 1/2/1990) FL 46+18/1 FLC 6+2 FAC 0+3 Others 3+1
Aldershot (Loaned on 9/1/1991) FL 3+2 Others 1
Fulham (Loaned on 20/10/1995) FL 6 Others 1
Oxford U (£100,000 on 28/3/1996) FL 115+6/4 FLC 9 FAC 4
Darlington (Free on 7/6/1999) FL 65+1 FLC 5+1 FAC 5 Others 6

GRAY Michael
Born: Sunderland, 3 August 1974
Height: 5'7" Weight: 10.10
Club Honours: Div 1 '96, '99
International Honours: E: 3
Michael enjoyed an excellent season with Sunderland in 2000-01 when he was one of the club's most consistent players and rarely missed a match. Officially appointed team captain following the retirement of Steve Bould, he wasted no time in announcing how proud he was to be leading his home-town club and his displays certainly reflected this. A pacy left back who was always willing to fly down the wing, he produced some particularly fine performances during the season's 'derby' matches, supplying a brilliant pinpoint cross for Niall Quinn to head home the winner at St James Park against Newcastle and then firing home the only goal of the game against Middlesbrough at the Stadium of Light - his only success of the campaign.
Sunderland (From trainee on 1/7/1992) P/FL 274+21/15 FLC 21+4 FAC 13+1/1 Others 2

GRAY Philip (Phil)
Born: Belfast, 2 October 1968
Height: 5'10" Weight: 12.5
International Honours: NI: 26; U23-1; Yth; Sch
Phil impressed in the 2000-01 pre-season matches for Burnley, netting with a spectacular strike in the friendly with Manchester City and going on to hit the equaliser at Bolton on the opening day of the season. He partnered Andy Cooke up front for the Clarets in the first few games but then lost his place once Andy Payton returned from injury and was soon on his way to Oxford where he did well in a struggling side. He scored one of the U's quickest-ever goals when he netted after just six seconds at Bournemouth and went on to finish the campaign as leading scorer with nine goals. A combative and inventive striker he is an excellent leader of the front line. Phil remained a member of the Northern Ireland international squad and won five more caps during the season.
Tottenham H (From apprentice on 21/8/1986) FL 4+5 FAC 0+1
Barnsley (Loaned on 17/1/1990) FL 3 FAC 1
Fulham (Loaned on 8/11/1990) FL 3 Others 2/1
Luton T (£275,000 on 16/8/1991) FL 54+5/22 FLC 4/3 FAC 2/1 Others 2
Sunderland (£800,000 on 19/7/1993) FL 108+7/34 FLC 9/4 FAC 8/3 Others 2 (Free to Nancy, France during 1996 close season)
Luton T (£400,000 from Fortuna Sittard, Holland on 19/9/1997) FL 74+7/21 FLC 9/3 FAC 3/3 Others 0+1
Burnley (Free on 20/7/2000) FL 5/1 FLC 2+1
Oxford U (Free on 10/11/2000) FL 21+2/7 FAC 2/2 Others 1

GRAY Stuart Edward
Born: Harrogate, 18 December 1973
Height: 5'11" Weight: 11.2
International Honours: S: U21-7
Stuart was mostly restricted to reserve-team football at Reading last season apart from a brief run in the first team in the new year when he filled in at left back for the injured Matthew Robinson. He was subsequently allowed to join Conference outfit Rushden & Diamonds in March and he assisted in the closing weeks of their championship-winning team, thus ensuring the possibility of a quick return to the Football League in the coming season. He is a steady but unspectacular defender with a powerful shot.
Glasgow Celtic (Signed from Giffnock North AFC on 7/7/1992) SL 19+9/1 SC 1 Others 2+1
Reading (£100,000 on 27/3/1998) FL 46+6/2 FLC 8 FAC 1+1 Others 2

GRAY Wayne William
Born: Camberwell, 7 November 1980
Height: 5'10" Weight: 12.10
Wayne joined Port Vale on loan last October to gain some valuable first-team experience and made his debut in the 2-0 defeat at Peterborough. He went on to make a further appearance from the subs' bench before returning to Selhurst Park where he featured regularly as a substitute in the second half of the campaign, although he managed just one goal, netting in the FA Cup fifth round replay against Wycombe. A promising striker who has pace in abundance, 2001-02 will be a big season for him as he seeks to win a regular first-team place with the Dons.
Wimbledon (From trainee on 10/2/1999) P/FL 1+11 FAC 0+4/1
Swindon T (Loaned on 3/3/2000) FL 8+4/2
Port Vale (Loaned on 6/10/2000) FL 2+1

GRAYSON Neil
Born: York, 1 November 1964
Height: 5'10" Weight: 12.10
Club Honours: NC '99
International Honours: E: SP-4
Neil suffered a broken ankle playing for Cheltenham against York in only the second match of last season but recovered quickly to win his place back and finished the campaign as the Robins' leading scorer. One of the highlights of his campaign was scoring a hat-trick in the 3-1 win over Cardiff City in April. Although not the tallest of players, Neil is strong on the ball and an effective target man.
Doncaster Rov (Free from Rowntree Mackintosh on 22/3/1990) FL 21+8/6 FAC 1+1 Others 2+1/1
York C (Free on 28/3/1991) FL 0+1
Chesterfield (Free on 16/8/1991) FL 9+6 FLC 2 FAC 1 Others 1 (Free to Gateshead during 1992 close season)
Northampton T (Free from Boston U on 19/6/1994) FL 103+17/31 FLC 7+1 FAC 3 Others 10/3 (Transferred to Hereford U on 4/8/1997)
Cheltenham T (Signed on 5/3/1998) FL 62+12/23 FLC 2/1 FAC 2+1/2 Others 2

GRAYSON Simon Nicholas
Born: Ripon, 16 December 1969
Height: 6'0" Weight: 13.7
Club Honours: FLC '97
Simon joined Sheffield Wednesday on loan from Blackburn at the start of last season and performed competently at right back for the Owls without tempting manager Paul Jewell to pursue a permanent deal. He returned to Ewood Park making his only first-team appearance of the campaign in the Worthington Cup tie with Portsmouth, but soon found himself out of favour to such an extent that he was not even considered for the reserves. In January he moved on to First Division rivals Stockport County in a long-term loan deal that proved a huge success. He appeared regularly for the Hatters in a central midfield role where his committed approach to every game endeared him to players and fans alike. Tenacious and enthusiastic he is a versatile player who can feature either in defence or midfield.
Leeds U (From trainee on 13/6/1988) FL 2 Others 1+1
Leicester C (£50,000 on 13/3/1992) F/PL 175+13/4 FLC 16+2/2 FAC 9 Others 13+1
Aston Villa (£1,350,000 on 1/7/1997) PL 32+16 FLC 1+1 FAC 4+1/2 Others 6+3
Blackburn Rov (£750,000 + on 29/7/1999) FL 31+3 FLC 1+1 FAC 2+1
Sheffield Wed (Loaned on 11/8/2000) FL 5
Stockport Co (Loaned on 12/1/2001) FL 13 FAC 1

GRAZIOLI Giuliano Stefano Luigi
Born: Marylebone, 23 March 1975
Height: 5'11" Weight: 12.11
Giuliano had a somewhat frustrating campaign at Swindon last term and after being placed on the transfer list in November he was then sidelined for several weeks after tearing a stomach muscle. He started just ten games, although he featured in many more from the subs' bench and scored just twice, although one of these was a late winner against local rivals Oxford in October, thus ensuring that he remained a favourite of the club's supporters. A pacy enthusiastic striker who is always looking for the ball, he will be hoping for a change of fortune in the coming season.
Peterborough U (Free from Wembley on 19/10/1995) FL 23+18/16 FLC 1+2 FAC 0+3/1 Others 0+2
Swindon T (Free on 15/7/1999) FL 21+26/10 FLC 3+2

GREAVES Mark Andrew
Born: Hull, 22 January 1975
Height: 6'1" Weight: 13.0

Having previously been established at centre back, Mark switched to a midfield role for Hull City last season. A tough tackling box-to-box player he proved to be a great competitor for the Tigers in the centre of the park before receiving an untimely set back in February when he suffered medial ligament damage during the win at Shrewsbury. He returned in time to appear in the play-offs and also signed a new three-year contract for the Boothferry Park club.

Hull C (Free from Brigg T on 17/6/1996) FL 124+24/9 FLC 7 FAC 11/1 Others 6+1

GREEN Francis James
Born: Nottingham, 25 April 1980
Height: 5'9" Weight: 11.6

Francis continued to progress at a steady rate with Peterborough last term and featured regularly in the first-team squad although he was often used from the subs' bench. A quick and powerful young striker he scored seven goals, a figure that represents his best tally to date. He will be looking to firmly establish himself in the line-up in 2001-02.

Peterborough U (£25,000 + from Ilkeston T on 2/3/1998) FL 31+32/9 FLC 2+1 FAC 3 Others 3+2/1

GREEN Richard Edward
Born: Wolverhampton, 22 November 1967
Height: 6'1" Weight: 13.7

Richard signed a new contract for Northampton in the 2000 close season and produced some sterling performances in the Cobblers' defence during the 2000-01 campaign, generally featuring in a back three alongside Ian Sampson and Richard Hope. A reliable central defender his performances never wavered even after it was announced that he would be released in the summer.

Shrewsbury T (From trainee on 19/7/1986) FL 120+5/5 FLC 11/1 FAC 5 Others 5/1
Swindon T (Free on 25/10/1990)
Gillingham (Free on 6/3/1992) FL 206+10/16 FLC 12+1 FAC 16+1/1 Others 6+1
Walsall (Signed on 10/8/1998) FL 22+8/1 FLC 2 FAC 2 Others 1
Rochdale (Loaned on 24/9/1999) FL 6
Northampton T (Free on 7/1/2000) FL 55+4/2 FLC 2 FAC 2 Others 2

GREEN Robert Paul
Born: Chertsey, 18 January 1980
Height: 6'2" Weight: 12.2
International Honours: E: Yth

Although second-choice 'keeper to Andy Marshall at Norwich last term, Robert stepped up to make a handful of appearances in the closing weeks of the season. He has established an excellent reputation for himself with his sound handling of the ball and positive distribution. He has a tremendous temperament and a real physical presence and both should stand him in good stead for the regular exertions of senior football that lie ahead. Having signed a new long-term deal with the Canaries the 2001-02 campaign promises to be a very important one in his career if, as seems likely at the time of writing, the man blocking his way to regular first-team football eventually leaves Carrow Road.

Norwich C (From juniors on 3/7/1997) FL 9+1

GREEN Ryan Michael
Born: Cardiff, 20 October 1980
Height: 5'8" Weight: 11.0
International Honours: W: 2; U21-16; Yth

Having previously only made a single first-team appearance for Wolves, Ryan stepped in to cover for injuries last term and enjoyed a short run of games in the early part of the season. However he then lost his place and after requesting a transfer linked up with former Wanderers' boss Colin Lee at Torquay in March. He made his debut for the Gulls as a sweeper but then moved to right back and made the position his own with a series of assured defensive displays. He remained a regular for Wales at U21 level winning six more caps during the campaign.

Wolverhampton W (From trainee on 25/10/1997) FL 6+2 FLC 2 FAC 0+2
Torquay U (Loaned on 2/3/2001) FL 10

GREEN Scott Paul
Born: Walsall, 15 January 1970
Height: 5'10" Weight: 12.5
Club Honours: Div 1 '97; AMC '99

Scott signed a new two-year contract for Wigan Athletic at the start of the 2000-01 season and featured regularly during the campaign. An attacking right back, he showed plenty of confidence on the ball and contributed two goals including a vital late equaliser at Swindon in September. Scott is a tireless worker with a good engine who is a popular figure with the Latics' supporters.

Derby Co (From trainee on 20/7/1988)
Bolton W (£50,000 on 17/3/1990) P/FL 166+54/25 FLC 19+4/1 FAC 20+3/4 Others 16+4/1
Wigan Ath (£300,000 on 30/6/1997) FL 128+15/5 FLC 13 FAC 13 Others 12+1

GREENACRE Christopher (Chris) Mark
Born: Halifax, 23 December 1977
Height: 5'11" Weight: 12.8

Chris started the 2000-01 season in spectacular style for Mansfield with an amazing goal in the opening game at Cheltenham when he chipped the ball over the home 'keeper's head from inside the centre circle. This was just the start as he scored goals almost at will throughout the campaign including a hat-trick in the 5-1 home win over Halifax in September, finishing up as the Stags' leading scorer. He is a pacy hard-working striker who finds space in the box and has a good eye for goal.

Manchester C (From trainee on 1/7/1995) FL 3+5/1 FAC 0+1
Cardiff C (Loaned on 22/8/1997) FL 11/2
Blackpool (Loaned on 5/3/1998) FL 2+2
Scarborough (Loaned on 10/12/1998) FL 10+2/2 Others 1
Mansfield T (Free on 5/11/1999) FL 77/28 FLC 4/1 FAC 2/1 Others 2+1

GREENE David Michael
Born: Luton, 26 October 1973
Height: 6'3" Weight: 14.4
International Honours: RoI: U21-14

David joined Cardiff City on a three-year deal in July 2000, but although he featured regularly in the early-season games he had few opportunities to make an impact after new owner Sam Hammam arrived and began to bring in new faces. He eventually moved on to Cambridge United in March where he made his club debut in the local 'derby' at Peterborough, which proved to be his only appearance for the U's in the closing weeks of the campaign. David is a big strong right-sided central defender who is good in the air.

Luton T (From juniors on 3/9/1991) FL 18+1 FLC 2 FAC 1 Others 0+1
Colchester U (Loaned on 23/11/1995) FL 14/1 Others 2
Brentford (Loaned on 1/3/1996) FL 11
Colchester U (£30,000 on 21/6/1996) FL 153/15 FLC 10 FAC 7 Others 10/2
Cardiff C (Free on 21/7/2000) FL 10 FLC 2 Others 1
Cambridge U (Free on 22/3/2001) FL 1

GREENING Jonathan
Born: Scarborough, 2 January 1979
Height: 5'11" Weight: 11.7
Club Honours: EC '99
International Honours: E: U21-10; Yth

For a player who was seemingly on his way out of Old Trafford in the summer Jonathan certainly made his presence felt when the 2000-01 season began. Having impressed in United's early-season defeat of Bradford City in the Premiership he also appeared twice in Worthington Cup matches, deputised for Ryan Giggs in the 3-1 Champions' League reverse against PSV and featured in the Premiership against Aston Villa and Leicester. Despite becoming a regular member of the England U21 side, the lack of first-team opportunities became too much of a burden for him, and he asked for a transfer again in March. He is a talented young attacking midfield player with great pace and an eye for goal.

York C (From trainee on 23/12/1996) FL 5+20/2 FLC 0+1 Others 1
Manchester U (£500,000 + on 25/3/1998) PL 4+10 FLC 6 FAC 0+1 Others 3+3

GREGAN Sean Matthew
Born: Guisborough, 29 March 1974
Height: 6'2" Weight: 14.7
Club Honours: Div 2'00

Club captain Sean started the 2000-01 season at centre half for Preston although he later alternated between that role and a position in central midfield. Wherever he played his aggressive ball winning, both on the ground and in the air, upset opponents and delighted the Preston fans in equal measure, and he remained an iconic figure at the club. Personal milestones of 150 games for North End and 350 career games were followed by six weeks out after a cartilage operation in January, and on his return he scored the winner against Norwich at Carrow Road with an amazing 50-yard lob.

Darlington (From trainee on 20/1/1991) FL 129+7/4 FLC 8 FAC 7 Others 10+1/1
Preston NE (£350,000 on 29/11/1996) FL 166+5/11 FLC 12 FAC 13/1 Others 10

Sean Gregan

GREGG Matthew (Matt) Stephen
Born: Cheltenham, 30 November 1978
Height: 5'11" Weight: 12.0

Despite some promising performances in the final matches of the 1999-2000 campaign Matt once again found himself reserve 'keeper at Crystal Palace last season. His first-team opportunities were restricted to early season Worthington Cup ties when Stuart Taylor was unavailable and later as stand-in for the suspended Alex Kolinko. An alert and agile shot stopper he will be hoping to see more regular senior action in 2001-02.

Torquay U (From trainee on 4/7/1997) FL 32 FLC 5 FAC 1 Others 1
Crystal Palace (£400,000 on 24/10/1998) FL 7 FLC 2+1
Swansea C (Loaned on 12/2/1999) FL 5

GREGORY David Spencer
Born: Hadleigh, 23 January 1970
Height: 5'10" Weight: 12.8

David again gave excellent service to Colchester United in 2000-01 although he found goals hard to come by. He featured regularly in the first team until he cracked a bone in his foot playing against Port Vale in March and he failed to recover fitness by the summer break. A hard-working central midfield player he has reportedly been offered a month-to-month contract for the coming season.

Ipswich T (From trainee on 31/3/1987) F/PL 16+16/2 FLC 3+2 FAC 1 Others 3+2/4
Hereford U (Loaned on 9/1/1995) FL 2 Others 1
Peterborough U (Free on 4/7/1995) FL 0+3 FLC 1 FAC 1 Others 2
Colchester U (Free on 8/12/1995) FL 196+13/20 FLC 8+1/2 FAC 8/2 Others 14/2

GRIEMINK Bart
Born: Holland, 29 March 1972
Height: 6'4" Weight: 15.4

Bart joined Swindon Town in July 2000 following a successful loan period the previous season and was immediately installed as the Robins' first-choice 'keeper. He retained his place until the new year when he dropped out through suspension, and when his understudy Steve Mildenhall came in his form was such that Bart failed to win his place back. Despite his height he is very agile and gets down well to cover ground shots.

Birmingham C (Free from WK Emmen, Holland on 9/11/1995) FL 20 FLC 3 FAC 1 Others 1+1
Peterborough U (£25,000 on 11/10/1996) FL 58 FLC 1 FAC 4 Others 4
Swindon T (Loaned on 5/2/2000) FL 4
Swindon T (Free on 27/7/2000) FL 24+1 FLC 4 FAC 2 Others 2

GRIFFIN Andrew (Andy)
Born: Billinge, 7 March 1979
Height: 5'9" Weight: 10.10
International Honours: E: U21-2; Yth

Andy is a talented young full back whose versatility and technical ability make him an important member of the Newcastle United defence. Powerful in the tackle and with good positional sense he is rarely exposed defensively, while his pace and stamina allow him to push down the wing in support of the attack. Having played through the pre-season period, he was disappointed when a groin strain kept him out of the side during the opening games last term but he returned with a 'Man of the Match' performance in the Worthington Cup tie against Leyton Orient and went on to become a near-regular in the Magpies squad. Unfortunately he was then sidelined by a hernia operation in early May and his campaign came to a premature close. A regular in the England U21 squad he added a further cap in the friendly against Spain in February.

Stoke C (From trainee on 5/9/1996) FL 52+5/2 FLC 4+1 FAC 2
Newcastle U (£1,500,000 + on 30/1/1998) PL 33+7/1 FLC 5 FAC 5 Others 1

GRIFFIN Antony Richard
Born: Bournemouth, 22 March 1979
Height: 5'11" Weight: 11.2

Antony had to wait until the end of September for a chance in Cheltenham's first team last season but when the opportunity arose he grabbed it with both hands, scoring a spectacular goal in the 5-2 win over Plymouth Argyle. A speedy right-sided player who made most of his appearances at right-back Antony suffered a succession of injuries including hamstring pulls and groin strains that prevented him from establishing himself as a regular for the Robins. A hard-working and versatile player he can also play as a wing back or in midfield.

Bournemouth (From trainee on 7/7/1997) FL 1+5
Cheltenham T (Signed on 27/7/1999) FL 28+18/1 FLC 2 FAC 1 Others 0+1

GRIFFIN Charles (Charlie) John
Born: Bath, 25 June 1979
Height: 6'0" Weight: 12.7

Charlie scored regularly for Swindon Town reserves at the beginning of the 2000-01 campaign netting two hat-tricks but he received few senior opportunities and in October he went on loan to Woking. He subsequently joined the Conference club permanently the following month and finished the season as the club's leading scorer. He is a promising young striker who has the ability to be in the right place at the right time and is a proven goal-scorer in non-league football.

Swindon T (£10,000 from Chippenham T on 29/1/1999) FL 8+20/2 FLC 0+1 FAC 0+1

GRIFFITHS Carl Brian
Born: Welshpool, 15 July 1971
Height: 5'11" Weight: 11.10
International Honours: W: B-1; U21-2; Yth

Carl had another excellent season at Leyton Orient last term and again finished as the club's leading scorer. Now established as one of the most dangerous finishers in the lower divisions he was sorely missed in the play-offs when he missed out due to suspension. A quality striker with a proven scoring record he will be hoping to continue in similar vein next term.

Shrewsbury T (From trainee on 26/9/1988) FL 110+33/54 FLC 7+4/3 FAC 6/2 Others 7+3/3
Manchester C (£500,000 on 29/10/1993) PL 11+7/4 FLC 0+1 FAC 2
Portsmouth (£200,000 on 17/8/1995) FL 2+12/2 FLC 0+1
Peterborough U (£225,000 on 28/3/1996) FL 6+10/2 FLC 0+2/1 FAC 1+1/1 Others 0+1
Leyton Orient (Loaned on 31/10/1996) FL 5/3
Leyton Orient (£100,000 on 7/3/1997) FL 60+5/29 FLC 7+1/3 FAC 5/2 Others 2
Wrexham (Loaned on 13/1/1999) FL 4/3 Others 1/1
Port Vale (£100,000 on 25/3/1999) FL 3+5/1 FLC 0+2/1
Leyton Orient (£80,000 on 16/12/1999) FL 46+2/18 FLC 2+1 FAC 3/4

GRIFFITHS Gareth John
Born: Winsford, 10 April 1970
Height: 6'4" Weight: 14.0

This tall and imposing central defender again found first-team opportunities at a premium for Wigan Athletic in the 2000-01 season. Tremendously strong in the air, he proved an invaluable squad member despite being affected by niggling injuries. He scored his only goal of the campaign with a header in the 1-1 draw at Rotherham in November. Gareth was released in the summer when his contract expired.

Port Vale (£1,000 from Rhyl on 8/2/1993) FL 90+4/4 FLC 8 FAC 7/1 Others 7
Shrewsbury T (Loaned on 31/10/1997) FL 6
Wigan Ath (Free on 2/7/1998) FL 44+9/2 FLC 4/1 FAC 5 Others 5+1

GRIMANDI Gilles
Born: Gap, France, 11 November 1970
Height: 6'0" Weight: 12.7
Club Honours: PL '98; FAC '98; CS '98, '99

A valuable utility player for Arsenal, Gilles breaks up attacks and uses the ball intelligently, hitting long, accurate passes

around the pitch and can slot in equally comfortably in midfield or defence. He is particularly effective when playing alongside Patrick Viera in the centre of midfield, providing the perfect foil for his colleague's driving forward runs. Gilles featured in the majority of Arsenal's Premiership games last season, scoring just once in the home game against Everton at Highbury in April.
Arsenal (£1,500,000 from Monaco, France, ex FC Gap, on 25/6/1997) PL 74+14/4 FLC 7 FAC 9+4/1 Others 19+3/1

GRITTON Martin
Born: Glasgow, 1 June 1978
Height: 6'1" Weight: 12.7
Martin got off to a good start last season, coming off the subs' bench to score a last minute equaliser against Hull in Plymouth's first home game. However, he struggled to hold down a regular first-team place and was mostly restricted to appearances as a substitute. He was loaned to Conference high flyers Yeovil at the end of February where he made four appearances before returning to Home Park for the closing weeks of the campaign.
Plymouth Arg (Free from Porthleven on 7/8/1998) FL 15+27/7 FLC 2+1/1 FAC 0+4 Others 3/1

GRONKJAER Jesper
Born: Nuuk, Denmark, 12 August 1977
Height: 6'1" Weight: 12.8
International Honours: Denmark: 19
A tall, right-footed left winger, who can also operate as a central striker, Jesper impressed the Chelsea hierarchy with some fine performances in an otherwise dismal Denmark side in Euro 2000 but it was not until December that he signed up for the Blues. After two fleeting substitute appearances he made his full debut in a tricky FA Cup fourth round tie at Gillingham when his sensational intervention eased the Blues through after a mighty scare - he scored a goal with either foot and hit the same post twice after mazy dribbles. Three days later he opened his Premiership account against Newcastle, smashing home a fierce left-footed half volley to secure another Chelsea home victory. He gradually became acclimatised to Premiership football and the Stamford Bridge faithful will be looking forward to seeing him in full flow in 2001-02. Two interesting facts about Jesper: he made his Champions' League debut for Aalborg against Porto while still at school and he is the only Greenland-born player to appear in the Premiership!
Chelsea (£7,800,000 from Ajax, Holland, ex Aalborg BK, on 21/12/2000) PL 6+8/1 FAC 1+1/2

GROVES Paul
Born: Derby, 28 February 1966
Height: 5'11" Weight: 11.5
Club Honours: AMC '98
Having spent part of the 1999-2000 campaign covering for injuries in the centre of defence, Paul remained in his new role for Grimsby Town for virtually all of last season, forming an effective partnership with Chinese international Zhang Enhua. The Mariners' club captain and a model professional he performed with his customary coolness, always appearing in command of the situation. Fittingly it was Paul who scored the goal that gave Grimsby a 1-0 victory over champions Fulham on the final day of the season, thus ensuring beyond doubt that the club would retain First Division status.
Leicester C (£12,000 from Burton A on 18/4/1988) FL 7+9/1 FLC 1/1 FAC 0+1 Others 0+1
Lincoln C (Loaned on 20/8/1989) FL 8/1 FLC 2
Blackpool (£60,000 on 25/1/1990) FL 106+1/21 FLC 6/1 FAC 9/4 Others 13/3
Grimsby T (£150,000 on 12/8/1992) FL 183+1/38 FLC 10+1/2 FAC 12/2 Others 4/1
West Bromwich A (£600,000 on 8/7/1996) FL 27+2/4 FLC 2/1 FAC 1
Grimsby T (£250,000 on 21/7/1997) FL 180/28 FLC 20/5 FAC 9/1 Others 10/2

GUDJOHNSEN Eidur Smari
Born: Reykjavik, Iceland, 15 September 1978
Height: 6'1" Weight: 13.0
Club Honours: CS '00
International Honours: Iceland: 13; U21-11; Yth
Chelsea won the race for Eidur's signature last summer - the negotiations being helped along by his father who had played against then-boss Luca Vialli in the 1990 European Cup Winners Cup Final! Initially he made sporadic substitute appearances within Vialli's rotation system but after the Italian's departure and the subsequent sale of Tore Andre Flo he came into his own. He marked his first Chelsea start with his first goal for the club against Liverpool and hit a purple patch in December with a brace against Derby County, a fierce drive against Bradford City and a classic Boxing Day double at Portman Road. He went on to become Jimmy Floyd Hasselbaink's regular strike partner for the second half of the season and their productive combination was crucial to Chelsea's much-improved form that resulted in a UEFA Cup spot. An alert, intelligent front-runner with excellent ball control and dribbling skills, Eidur had a superb first season in the Premiership and became a firm crowd favourite in the process.
Bolton W (Free from KR Reykjavik, Iceland, ex Valur, PSV Eindhoven, on 6/8/1998) FL 48+7/18 FLC 8+1/4 FAC 4+1/4 Others 4/1
Chelsea (£4,000,000 on 12/7/2000) PL 17+13/10 FLC 0+1 FAC 1+2/3 Others 0+3

GUDJONSSON Bjarni
Born: Iceland, 26 February 1979
Height: 5'9" Weight: 11.9
Club Honours: AMC '00
International Honours: Iceland: 8; U21-15; Yth
Bjarni featured regularly for Stoke City last season contributing several important goals including two crackers in the 3-2 defeat of Barnsley in the Worthington Cup third round. A very skilful player he was mostly employed in the 'hole' between the strikers and the midfield line where it was thought he would have more influence on the game, although he is equally capable of playing wide on the right-hand side of a midfield four. Bjarni is the son of Stoke boss Gudjon Thordarson. He was placed on the open to offers list in the summer.
Newcastle U (£500,000 from Akranes, Iceland on 14/7/1997. £125,000 to KRC Genk on 12/11/1998)
Stoke C (£250,000 on 10/3/2000) FL 48+2/7 FLC 5/2 FAC 2 Others 6+4/2

GUDJONSSON Thordur
Born: Akranes, Iceland, 14 October 1973
Height: 5'9" Weight: 12.5
International Honours: Iceland: 42; U21-10; Yth
With Derby struggling against relegation, it was felt that more attacking options were required to add some variety to an injury-hit side and Jim Smith looked to the Las Palmas and Iceland attacking midfielder to provide these. Signed initially on loan with an option available on a permanent deal, he had previously been with Belgian club Genk where he had enjoyed a productive spell playing alongside current Rams' striker Branko Strupar. A versatile player who is equally at home playing just behind the front two or in a left-sided midfield role, he made his debut as a substitute in the home game against Spurs in March, but rarely made the starting line-up. After due consideration the club decided not to pursue a permanent signing.
Derby Co (Loaned from Las Palmas, Spain, ex IA Akranes, KA Akureyrar, VFL Bochum, RC Genk, on 2/3/2001) PL 2+8/1

GUDMUNDSSON Johann Birnir
Born: Reykjavik, Iceland, 5 December 1977
Height: 5'9" Weight: 13.0
International Honours: Iceland: 3; U21-11; Yth
Johann made just two senior appearances for Watford last season, both in Worthington Cup ties, and in November he went on loan to Cambridge United where he played a handful of games before returning. Increasingly homesick he was eventually released by the Hornets and after briefly going back to Iceland he signed for Lyn Oslo in time for the start of the new Scandinavian 2001 season. He is a neat right winger with good skills on the ball.
Watford (Signed from IBK Keflavik, Iceland on 26/3/1998) P/FL 7+15/2 FLC 1+2 FAC 0+1
Cambridge U (Loaned on 9/11/2000) FL 3

GUERET Willy July
Born: Guadeloupe, 3 August 1973
Height: 6'1" Weight: 13.5
Having been second-choice 'keeper with French Division Two club Le Mans in the 1999-2000 campaign, Willy joined Millwall in July 2000 as cover for Tony Warner. He produced some impressive displays in the reserves and eventually made his Football League debut against Bristol Rovers in February. He is a fine shot stopper who commands his box and did exceptionally well to keep a total of nine clean sheets in 13 senior appearances. He will be looking to receive more regular first-team action in the coming season.
Millwall (Free from Le Mans, France on 31/7/2000) FL 11 Others 2

GUERRERO Mario **Ivan**
Born: Honduras, 30 November 1977
Height: 5'7" Weight: 10.3
International Honours: Honduras

A regular in the Honduras national team, Ivan arrived at Coventry with his friend and compatriot Jairo Martinez after captaining his country's team in the Sydney Olympics. A left back who likes to attack, he made his debut at Sunderland in October and impressed with his touch and control. He subsequently played three more games but began to look a little out of his depth and spent the remainder of the campaign in the Sky Blues' reserve team with the occasional trip back to Central America for internationals.

Coventry C (Signed from Motagua, Honduras on 24/10/2000) PL 3 FLC 1

GUINAN Stephen (Steve) Anthony
Born: Birmingham, 24 December 1975
Height: 6'1" Weight: 13.7

Steve started last season by signing a new two-year contract for Plymouth but although he played regularly in the early games it was not until the end of September that he scored his first goal. He then found it difficult to hold down a place in the starting line-up and the majority of his subsequent appearances came from the subs' bench. A tall and powerful striker he failed to add to his single strike and will be looking for a change in fortune in front of goal in the 2001-02 campaign. He was placed on the open to offers list in the summer.

Nottingham F (From trainee on 7/1/1993) F/PL 2+5 FLC 2/1
Darlington (Loaned on 14/12/1995) FL 3/1
Burnley (Loaned on 27/3/1997) FL 0+6
Crewe Alex (Loaned on 19/3/1998) FL 3
Halifax T (Loaned on 16/10/1998) FL 12/2
Plymouth Arg (Loaned on 24/3/1999) FL 11/7
Scunthorpe U (Loaned on 10/9/1999) FL 2+1/1
Cambridge U (Free on 24/12/1999) FL 4+2 FAC 0+2 Others 1
Plymouth Arg (Free on 23/3/2000) FL 15+15/3 FLC 2 FAC 2 Others 0+1

GUNNARSSON Brynjar Bjorn
Born: Iceland, 16 October 1975
Height: 6'1" Weight: 11.12
International Honours: Iceland: 29; U21-8; Yth

An ever-present for Stoke City in their Second Division games last term Brynjar performed consistently well throughout the campaign. Equally adept in the centre of defence or in a midfield role he is very effective at winning the ball and bringing it forward. He featured regularly for the Iceland national team and was also City's 'Player of the Season'.

Stoke C (£600,000 from Orgryte IS, Sweden on 4/1/2000) FL 67+1/6 FLC 6/1 FAC 1 Others 11+1/1

GUNNLAUGSSON Arnar (Arnie) Bergmann
Born: Akranes, Iceland, 6 March 1973
Height: 6'0" Weight: 11.10
Club Honours: FLC '00
International Honours: Iceland: 30; U21-6; Yth

Although immensely popular with the fans, Arnie has generally proved more effective for Leicester when appearing from the bench than he has when in the starting line-up. Indeed he netted four valuable goals last term after appearing from the dug out, and most were memorable contributions to the Foxes' campaign - a curled shot from the edge of the box against Derby, a sweetly struck free kick against Newcastle and a controlled volley at Aston Villa to clinch victory in the FA Cup tie. Blessed with good technique, excellent close control and an eye for a strike on goal, it is not hard to see why he is so popular on the terraces, yet he often gives the impression of being slightly too much of an individualist to fit neatly into the team pattern, which perhaps explains his relatively few starting berths. Arnie also suffered his share of injury and illness during the season, including a bout of appendicitis in December. He is the twin brother of Preston's Bjarke Gunnlaugsson.

Bolton W (£100,000 from IA Akranes, Iceland, ex Feyenoord, IFC Nuremberg, Sochaux, on 7/8/1997) P/FL 24+18/13 FLC 6+3/2 FAC 1+1
Leicester C (£2,000,000 on 5/2/1999) PL 10+18/3 FLC 1+2 FAC 2+4/1 Others 0+1
Stoke C (Loaned on 3/3/2000) FL 10+3/2 Others 5/1

Arnie Gunnlaugsson

GUNNLAUGSSON Bjarke Bergman
Born: Akranes, Iceland, 6 March 1973
Height: 5'9" Weight: 11.7
Club Honours: Div 2 '00
International Honours: Iceland: 27; U21-4; Yth

Bjarke began the 2000-01 campaign with a niggling groin strain sustained the day before the season started and this kept him out of action for a month. His recovery was only brief, but on his second comeback, he scored an injury-time winner against Norwich that proved to be his only goal of the season. Very quick on the ball and with fast feet he struggled through to the end of the campaign, making short substitute appearances thus delaying an operation on his injured hip until the summer. A good link player, he will be hoping for an injury free 2001-02. Bjarke is the twin brother of Leicester's Arnar Gunnlaugsson.

Preston NE (Free from KR Reykjavik, Iceland, ex IA Akranes, Feyenoord, I FC Nuremberg, Waldhof Mannheim, Molde FK, on 30/9/1999) FL 17+28/2 FLC 0+1 FAC 3+3/1 Others 2/4

GUPPY Stephen (Steve) Andrew
Born: Winchester, 29 March 1969
Height: 5'11" Weight: 11.12
Club Honours: FAT '91, '93; GMVC '93; FLC '00
International Honours: E: 1; B-1; U21-1; SP-1

After being a regular choice under Martin O'Neill, Steve found himself in competition with Callum Davidson for the left-wing-back berth under Peter Taylor and mostly lost out to his rival. He tried hard to impress when coming on from the subs' bench and continued to look the most deadly crosser of a ball in the Foxes' squad but was still unable to win a regular place in the starting line-up. His situation seemed to unsettle him somewhat and it remains to be seen what will happen in the coming season.

Wycombe W (Signed from Colden Common on 1/9/1989) FL 41/8 FLC 4 FAC 8/2 Others 10
Newcastle U (£150,000 on 2/8/1994) FLC 0+1
Port Vale (£225,000 on 25/11/1994) FL 102+3/12 FLC 7 FAC 8 Others 7+1/1
Leicester C (£950,000 on 28/2/1997) PL 133+13/9 FLC 15 FAC 9/1 Others 4

GURNEY Andrew (Andy) Robert
Born: Bristol, 25 January 1974
Height: 5'10" Weight: 11.6

Andy was a regular in the Reading squad in the first half of the 2000-01 campaign and scored a cracking goal from 20 yards in the 3-0 win over Cambridge United before being edged out of the side in the new year. He rarely featured thereafter but was recalled for the two play-off semi-finals against Wigan when he performed well. An experienced right wing back he is very effective pushing down the flank and always gives 100 per cent for the cause. He was given a free transfer by the Royals at the end of the season.

Bristol Rov (From trainee on 10/7/1992) FL 100+8/9 FLC 7/1 FAC 5 Others 15
Torquay U (Free on 10/7/1997) FL 64/10 FLC 6 FAC 5/1 Others 3
Reading (£100,000 on 15/1/1999) FL 55+12/3 FLC 5 FAC 5+1 Others 5+1

GUTTRIDGE Luke
Born: Barnstaple, 27 March 1982
Height: 5'5" Weight: 9.7

This former Torquay trainee joined Cambridge United in the 2000 close season and after a couple of brief appearances from the subs' bench in LDV Vans Trophy ties he was drafted in for his first start in the home game against Oldham. He made a dramatic entrance, scoring a fine goal within the first two minutes and was deservedly voted 'Man of the Match', but he suffered an ankle injury that kept him out of action for a while afterwards. Luke is a busy combative midfield player with excellent distribution.

Torquay U (Trainee) FL 0+1
Cambridge U (Free on 15/8/2000) FL 1/1 Others 0+2

HAALAND Alf-Inge (Alfie) Rasdal
Born: Stavanger, Norway, 23 November 1972
Height: 5'10" Weight: 12.12
International Honours: Norway: 34

After showing an interest in signing Alfie during his spell in charge at Everton, Manchester City boss Joe Royle brought him to Maine Road on a five-year contract in the summer. He started in the centre of defence in pre-season but then moved into midfield and scored in City's first home game of the 2000-01 campaign against Sunderland. Soon afterwards he took on the role of club captain and also switched to the right-back position, going on to appear in almost every match for the Blues apart from the occasional absence through injury or suspension. A versatile player his need to focus on defensive duties meant that he scored just three goals during the campaign.

Nottingham F (Signed from Bryne, Norway on 25/1/1994) F/PL 66+9/7 FLC 2+5 FAC 5+1 Others 2+3
Leeds U (£1,600,000 on 17/7/1997) PL 57+17/8 FLC 3 FAC 5+1 Others 7+2
Manchester C (£2,500,000 on 16/6/2000) PL 35/3 FLC 5 FAC 3

Alfie Haaland

HACKETT Christopher (Chris) James
Born: Oxford, 1 March 1983
Height: 6'0" Weight: 11.6

After making a few substitute appearances at the start of last season Chris broke into the Oxford United side following his first start in the FA Cup tie at Chester. He scored his first senior goal against Northampton the following week and also netted a second goal against Wycombe as he enjoyed an extended run in the team. However he was then sidelined by a hernia injury and failed to return before the end of the campaign. A speedy winger or striker he will be hoping to gain more senior experience in 2001-02.

Oxford U (From trainee on 20/4/2000) FL 10+8/2 FAC 1 Others 0+1

HACKWORTH Anthony (Tony)
Born: Durham, 19 May 1980
Height: 6'1" Weight: 13.
International Honours: E: Yth

One of several talented youngsters to emerge at Leeds in recent years, Tony's entry into first-team football had been delayed by a string of injuries over recent seasons but he finally stepped up to make his senior debut in the Champions' League game against Barcelona at the Nou Camp Stadium. The tall striker then went on to feature in a couple more early-season games from the substitutes' bench. Having put some much publicised off the field problems behind him, he will be aiming to win a regular place in the first-team squad in 2001-02.

Leeds U (From trainee on 23/5/1997) FLC 0+1 Others 0+2

HADDOW Alexander (Alex)
Born: Aldershot, 8 January 1982
Height: 5'8" Weight: 11.2

A graduate of Reading's Academy, Alex found himself mainly restricted to reserve-team football in 2000-01 and his only senior opportunity came when he replaced Andy Gurney at left wing back for the final 10 minutes of the home game against Brentford. A left-sided player who can also feature in a wide-midfield role he has a devastating turn of pace and is a neat passer of the ball. He appeared for the Royals' second-string in the Avon Insurance Combination Cup final against Norwich but was given a free transfer by boss Alan Pardew in his end-of-season clearout.

Reading (From trainee on 18/3/2000) FL 1+2 FLC 1

HADJI Moustapha
Born: Ifrane, Morocco, 16 November 1971
Height: 6'0" Weight: 11.10
International Honours: Morocco

After such a scintillating first season in the Premiership Moustapha failed to maintain the same high level of performance for Coventry City in 2000-01. Absent for the opening matches, he was appointed team captain but he struggled to find his best form early on. He netted with an exquisite chip in the defeat at Highbury and after switching from midfield to an attacking role in November he scored good goals against Aston Villa and Everton, but rarely looked the world-class player he can be. His best performance was probably at Leicester when he bamboozled defenders with his silky skills and cheeky footwork. He netted twice in the vital game at Villa Park including a stunning second, but sadly it proved in vain and he was unable to prevent the Sky Blues from being relegated to the First Division. At the time of writing his future was unclear, but it appeared he might be playing elsewhere in the 2001-02 campaign.

Coventry C (£4,000,000 from Deportivo La Coruna, Spain, ex Nancy, Sporting Lisbon, on 3/8/1999) PL 61+1/12 FLC 4+1 FAC 3/1

Moustapha Hadji

HADLAND Phillip (Phil) Jonathan
Born: Warrington, 20 October 1980
Height: 5'11" Weight: 11.8

Phil joined Rochdale in the 2000 close season and featured regularly for the Third Division club in 2000-01 although he was often used from the subs' bench. He came on for the final quarter of an hour of the opening game against Darlington and scored his first goal in senior football in only his third appearance when he netted the equaliser against Cardiff. A speedy winger, capable of mazy runs, Phil will be looking to feature regularly in the starting line-up for Dale in 2001-02.

Reading (From trainee on 22/6/1999) FLC 1
Rochdale (Free on 8/8/2000) FL 12+20/2 FLC 0+1 FAC 1 Others 1

HADLEY Stewart
Born: Dudley, 30 December 1973
Height: 6'0" Weight: 13.2
Club Honours: NC '00

Stewart got off to a great start with Kidderminster last season, scoring four times in the first four games including the club's historic first-ever goal in the Football League when he netted after 14 minutes of the opening day encounter with Torquay United. However the goal supply dried up and he found himself in and out of the side for the remainder of the campaign, often featuring from the subs' bench. A hard-working striker he still finished up as the Harriers' joint-leading scorer with nine goals in all competitions.

Derby Co (Free from Halesowen T on 6/7/1992)
Mansfield T (Signed on 9/2/1994) FL 100+24/31 FLC 6+2 FAC 7/1 Others 5+1/3
Kidderminster Hrs (Free on 24/6/1998) FL 18+15/6 FLC 2/1 FAC 2+1/2 Others 1

HAHNEMANN Marcus Stephen
Born: Seattle, USA, 15 June 1972
Height: 6'3" Weight: 16.2
International Honours: United States: 4
With Maik Taylor in superb form in the Fulham goal last season, Marcus had little chance to impress. The regular 'keeper for the club's championship-winning reserve team he stepped up to gain some senior experience in the two legs of the Worthington Cup first round tie against Northampton Town at the beginning of the season and then featured a couple of times in the closing matches.
Fulham (£80,000 from Colorado Rapids, USA on 9/7/1999) FL 2 FLC 2

HALFORD Stephen (Steve) Paul
Born: Bury, 21 September 1980
Height: 5'10" Weight: 12.10
Another youngster to graduate through the ranks at Bury, this promising central defender had a handful of first-team outings last season as cover for Steve Redmond. He performed well enough to suggest that he has a good future in the game, but with his contract due to expire it was uncertain at the time of writing whether he would remain at Gigg Lane.
Bury (From trainee on 9/7/1999) FL 3+2

HALL Gareth David
Born: Croydon, 12 March 1969
Height: 5'8" Weight: 12.0
Club Honours: Div 2 '89; Div 1 '96; FMC '90
International Honours: E: Sch. W: 9; U21-1
Gareth found himself out of favour at Swindon in the first half of last season under boss Colin Todd but was recalled to the team on Boxing Day following a change of management. However although he subsequently made a handful of appearances for the Robins he failed to establish himself as a regular in the line-up and was released in the summer. A versatile player who has featured both in defence and midfield at his best he has an excellent first touch and displays good passing skills.
Chelsea (From apprentice on 25/4/1986) F/PL 120+18/4 FLC 12+1 FAC 6 Others 10+4/1
Sunderland (£300,000 on 20/12/1995) P/FL 41+7 FLC 3 FAC 2
Brentford (Loaned on 3/10/1997) FL 6
Swindon T (Free on 22/5/1998) FL 80+7/3 FLC 4 FAC 4 Others 1+1

HALL Marcus Thomas
Born: Coventry, 24 March 1976
Height: 6'1" Weight: 12.2
International Honours: E: B-1; U21-8
After suffering a frustrating time with injury problems in 1999-2000 Marcus was pleased to start last season as first-choice left back for Coventry City. His knee appeared to have healed but it gave way after the game at Charlton in September and further surgery was required. After convalescence it was January before he returned to the team and he had a storming game in the FA Cup tie at Maine Road. In April he reached the milestone of 100 Premiership appearances but his performances towards the end of the campaign were a little inconsistent as the Sky Blues struggled unsuccessfully to avoid relegation.
Coventry C (From trainee on 1/7/1994) PL 86+17/1 FLC 13+1/2 FAC 8+2

HALL Paul Anthony
Born: Manchester, 3 July 1972
Height: 5'9" Weight: 11.0
International Honours: Jamaica: 33
Having enjoyed a successful spell on loan with Walsall in 1999-2000 Paul made a permanent move to the Bescot Stadium in the close season. He featured regularly for the Saddlers all season and netted a number of useful goals including two in the space of 15 minutes in the 5-1 hammering of Swansea in January. A lively right-sided midfield player he provided plenty of thrust and served up some delicious crosses for the club's powerful strike force.
Torquay U (From trainee on 9/7/1990) FL 77+16/1 FLC 7 FAC 4+1/2 Others 5+1/1
Portsmouth (£70,000 on 25/3/1993) FL 148+40/37 FLC 10+3/1 FAC 7+1/2 Others 6+2/2
Coventry C (£300,000 on 10/8/1998) PL 2+8 FLC 2+1/1
Bury (Loaned on 18/2/1999) FL 7
Sheffield U (Loaned on 17/12/1999) FL 1+3/1
West Bromwich A (Loaned on 10/2/2000) FL 4
Walsall (Free on 17/3/2000) FL 46+6/10 FLC 4 FAC 3/1 Others 3

Wayne Hall

HALL Wayne
Born: Rotherham, 25 October 1968
Height: 5'9" Weight: 10.6
This ever-popular left back York City left back received a testimonial match against Middlesbrough in August 2000 but his 13th season at Bootham Crescent proved somewhat unlucky as he suffered from a string of niggling injuries that severely restricted his first-team opportunities. However he played sufficient games to reach fourth place in the Minstermen's all-time appearance list before being released in May. Wayne is a reliable defender known for his consistency.
York C (Free from Hatfield Main on 15/3/1989) FL 353+20/9 FLC 27+1 FAC 13+2/1 Others 21+1/1

HALLE Gunnar
Born: Larvik, Norway, 11 August 1965
Height: 5'11" Weight: 11.2
Club Honours: Div 2 '91
International Honours: Norway: 64; U21
This hard-working defender missed four months of the 2000-01 campaign for Bradford City after suffering a broken foot playing against West Ham in September and was out for four months. Once fit again Gunnar found it difficult to get back in the first team, although he regularly appeared for the reserves either at full back or as a central defender. He eventually returned to the side at the beginning of April but despite performing as well as ever he was unable to prevent the Bantams from being relegated back to the First Division.
Oldham Ath (£280,000 from Lillestrom, Norway on 15/2/1991) F/PL 185+3/17 FLC 16/2 FAC 8/2 Others 4
Leeds U (£400,000 on 13/12/1996) PL 65+5/4 FLC 3+1 FAC 8+1 Others 2
Bradford C (£200,000 on 11/6/1999) PL 47+4 FLC 3/1 FAC 2 Others 2

HALLIDAY Kevin Joseph
Born: Swindon, 8 July 1983
Height: 5'11" Weight: 12.0
A scholar on Swindon Town's books, Kevin spent most of last season learning his trade with the club's reserve and youth teams. He made his debut in senior football when he came off the subs' bench in the LDV Vans Trophy game at Millwall and had his moment of glory in the penalty shoot-out that decided the tie. Nominated as the Robins' fifth penalty taker he confidently hammered the ball past the 'keeper to score what proved to be the decisive goal. He is a promising left back who will be hoping to gain more first-team experience in the coming season.
Swindon T (Trainee) Others 0+1

HALLIDAY Stephen (Steve) William
Born: Sunderland, 3 May 1976
Height: 5'10" Weight: 12.12
After being released by Carlisle United at the end of the 1999-2000 campaign Steve began last season at Conference outfit Doncaster Rovers. He then made a surprise return to Brunton Park in October and although he seldom made the same impact as he had in his previous spell he still proved to be a quality performer with the ability to hold the ball and link well with his colleagues. Almost exclusively used from the subs' bench his form improved as the campaign progressed. Steve is a clever striker who is comfortable on the ball.
Hartlepool U (From trainee on 5/7/1994) FL 111+29/25 FLC 8+3 FAC 4+1/1 Others 5+1

Motherwell (Free on 7/7/1998) SL 3+6 SLC 3+2/2 (Free to Doncaster Rov on 26/7/2000)
Carlisle U (Loaned on 14/2/2000) FL 16/7 Others 2/1
Carlisle U (Free on 20/10/2000) FL 3+21/1 FAC 0+2 Others 1

HAMANN Dietmar
Born: Waldsasson, Germany, 27 August 1973
Height: 6'3" Weight: 12.2
Club Honours: FLC '01; FAC '01; UEFAC '01
International Honours: Germany: 32; U21; Yth

Dietmar was a key figure for Liverpool last term as the defensive anchor in midfield and went on to win three cup winners' medals for the Reds' treble-winning side. He played consistently well throughout the season and his only absence from the first team came in December when he was sidelined for five games with a knee injury. An early personal highlight was scoring two goals, including the late winner, in a somewhat fortuitous 3-2 home victory over Manchester City back in September. However in general he was rarely seen as an attacking force as manager Gerard Houllier adopted a more cautious style of play especially in their UEFA Cup campaign. On the international stage he survived the fall out following Germany's ignominious exit from Euro 2000 and was the architect of his team's early revenge against England in the World Cup qualifying game at Wembley when he scored the only goal with a quickly taken free kick that caught David Seaman off guard. There is little doubt that this efficient and unspectacular player will remain a linchpin of Liverpool's search for more honours in the coming season.

Newcastle U (£4,500,000 from Bayern Munich, Germany, ex Wacker Munchen, on 5/8/1998) PL 22+1/4 FLC 1 FAC 7/1
Liverpool (£8,000,000 on 23/7/1999) PL 53+5/3 FLC 2+3 FAC 7/1 Others 13

HAMILTON Derrick (Des) Vivian
Born: Bradford, 15 August 1976
Height: 5'11" Weight: 13.0
International Honours: E: U21-1

Mostly restricted to outings in Newcastle reserves last season, Des spent two loan spells with Second Division Tranmere Rovers where he impressed with his mature and reliable style of play. Injury cut short the first period, but he returned in the new year when he again made a significant contribution to Rovers' struggle against relegation. He is a powerfully built midfield player who tackles forcefully and is always willing to launch an attack.

Bradford C (From trainee on 1/6/1994) FL 67+21/5 FLC 6/1 FAC 6 Others 4+1/2
Newcastle U (£1,500,000 + on 27/3/1997) PL 7+5 FLC 1+1/1 FAC 1 Others 2+1
Sheffield U (Loaned on 16/10/1998) FL 6
Huddersfield T (Loaned on 15/2/1999) FL 10/1
Norwich C (Loaned on 22/3/2000) FL 7
Tranmere Rov (Loaned on 25/10/2000) FL 2 FLC 1
Tranmere Rov (Loaned on 10/1/2001) FL 3+1 FAC 3

HAMILTON Gary Ian
Born: Banbridge, 6 October 1980
Height: 5'9" Weight: 11.10
International Honours: NI: U21-10; Yth; Sch

This young Blackburn prospect joined Rochdale on loan as cover last August and made a handful of appearances from the subs' bench before returning to Ewood Park where he made his senior debut for Rovers in the Worthington Cup tie against Portsmouth. He subsequently went down with a back injury, then fell out of favour with the management at Ewood Park and after being informed he would be released at the end of the campaign he had a two-match trial at Wigan in the new year. Gary is a promising striker with the knack of being in the right place at the right time but still needs to work on his finishing. He continued to represent Northern Ireland at U21 level winning seven further caps during the season.

Blackburn Rov (From trainee on 17/10/1997) FLC 0+1
Rochdale (Loaned on 11/8/2000) FL 0+3

HAMILTON Ian Richard
Born: Stevenage, 14 December 1967
Height: 5'9" Weight: 11.3

Having fallen out of favour at Bramall Lane Ian moved on to Notts County at the start of 2000-01 where he saw regular first-team action up until the closing stages of the season. A hard-working player with shrewd distribution he was generally deployed in a central midfield role by the Magpies.

Southampton (From apprentice on 24/12/1985)
Cambridge U (Signed on 29/3/1988) FL 23+1/1 FLC 1 FAC 2 Others 2
Scunthorpe U (Signed on 23/12/1988) FL 139+6/18 FLC 6 FAC 6+1 Others 14+1/3
West Bromwich A (£160,000 on 19/6/1992) FL 229+11/23 FLC 13+2/1 FAC 10+1/1 Others 14+2/3
Sheffield U (Signed on 26/3/1998) FL 38+7/3 FLC 6/1 FAC 2+3 Others 2
Grimsby T (Loaned on 4/11/1999) FL 6/1
Notts Co (Free on 18/8/2000) FL 23+2 FLC 3+1 FAC 3+1 Others 1

HAMMOND Dean John
Born: Hastings, 7 March 1983
Height: 6'0" Weight: 11.10

This young Brighton trainee made his debut in senior football when he came off the subs' bench to replace Paul Watson for the final 30 minutes of the LDV Vans tie against Cardiff last December. Dean is a promising midfield player who will be looking to gain further first-team experience in the 2001-02 campaign.

Brighton & Hove A (Trainee) Others 0+1

HAMMOND Elvis Zark
Born: Accra, Ghana, 6 October 1980
Height: 5'10" Weight: 10.10

Elvis featured mostly for the U19 and reserve teams at Fulham last season, making his senior debut in the Worthington Cup second round tie at Chesterfield when he replaced Luke Cornwall at half-time. A very quick striker he reads the game well and stands every chance of a successful career in football providing he continues to work at his game.

Fulham (From trainee on 1/7/1999) FLC 0+1

HAMSHAW Matthew Thomas
Born: Rotherham, 1 January 1982
Height: 5'9" Weight: 11.9
International Honours: E: Yth; Sch

This speedy direct right winger stepped up to first-team action with Sheffield Wednesday last season, featuring regularly in the early matches of the campaign. He scored his first senior goal with a back post header in the Worthington Cup tie against Oldham in September and also netted in the FA Cup game against Norwich. Previously capped by England at U16 and U17 levels he won six caps for the U18s last term.

Sheffield Wed (From trainee on 5/1/1999) FL 9+9 FLC 3/1 FAC 1/1

HANCOCK Glynn Roy
Born: Biddulph, 24 May 1982
Height: 6'0" Weight: 12.2

After gaining senior experience during the summer of 2000 in Sweden with Second Division club Trollhattans FK, Glynn returned to Stockport and quickly made an impressive Football League debut against West Bromwich Albion in September. He added a further appearance from the subs' bench against Preston before stepping back to captain the reserve team in the Avon Insurance League. A strong and powerful central defender he will be hoping to feature in the first-team squad again in the coming season.

Stockport Co (From trainee on 27/8/1999) FL 1+1

HANDYSIDE Peter David
Born: Dumfries, 31 July 1974
Height: 6'1" Weight: 13.8
Club Honours: AMC '98
International Honours: S: U21-7

After missing all of the 1999-2000 campaign with a serious ankle injury Peter made a successful return to action with Grimsby Town last September. He showed he had lost none of his class but struggled to retain his place following the arrival of Zhang Enhua and it was only when the Chinese international departed that he was able to resume as a first choice in the Mariners' line-up. Peter is a formidable central defender who brings the ball out of defence with confidence and shows excellent distribution.

Grimsby T (From trainee on 21/11/1992) FL 181+9/4 FLC 18+1 FAC 12+1 Others 13+1

HANLON Richard (Richie) Kenneth
Born: Wembley, 26 May 1978
Height: 6'1" Weight: 13.7

Richie continued to make steady progress at Peterborough last term but never seemed to be able to establish himself in the first team and only played in fits and starts. He is a forceful midfield player with a fine left-foot shot and a ferocious striker of a dead ball. However despite making over 20 appearances for Posh he failed to register a goal.

Southend U (From trainee at Chelsea on 10/7/1996) FL 1+1 (Free to Welling U during 1997 close season)

Peterborough U (Signed from Rushden & Diamonds on 9/12/1998) FL 0+4/1 Others 1 (Free to Welling U on 12/8/1999)
Peterborough U (Free on 17/12/1999) FL 30+12/2 FLC 1+1 FAC 0+1 Others 3+2

HANMER Gareth Craig
Born: Shrewsbury, 12 October 1973
Height: 5'6" Weight: 10.3

Gareth was in and out of the Shrewsbury team last season partly as a result of being affected by injuries and partly through being out of favour. He is a left-sided defender who is very effective pushing forward and can deliver quality crosses into the box. He was released by manager Kevin Ratcliffe in the summer.

West Bromwich A (£20,000 from Newtown on 18/6/1996)
Shrewsbury T (£10,000 on 25/7/1997) FL 134+6/1 FLC 7 FAC 6 Others 4

HANSEN Bo
Born: Denmark, 16 June 1972
Height: 5'11" Weight: 11.10
International Honours: Denmark: 1

Bo had a fantastic season for Bolton Wanderers in 2000-01. Although he had previously played as a centre forward, boss Sam Allardyce saw his potential in other areas and the hunch proved to be a masterstroke. Featuring mainly on the wings or just behind one or two other front-line strikers he was a revelation. Quick and skilful, with bags of pace and willing to chase every ball he swiftly become a real crowd favourite and will be aiming to retain his place as a regular in the line-up in 2001-02.

Bolton W (£1,000,000 from Brondby, Denmark on 12/2/1999) FL 54+25/14 FLC 5+2/1 FAC 2+2/1 Others 3+5

HANSEN John Schnabel
Born: Mannheim, Germany, 14 September 1973
Height: 5'11" Weight: 13.1

After making a big impression in his first season at Cambridge United, John struggled to find his best form last term and after failing to establish himself as a regular in the team he was placed on the transfer list. An attacking left-sided midfield player his only goal of the campaign provided the U's with the winner in their FA Cup first round tie against Rochdale.

Cambridge U (£5,000 from Esbjerg, Denmark on 16/2/2000) FL 19+9/3 FLC 1 FAC 0+2/1 Others 1

HANSON Christian
Born: Middlesbrough, 3 August 1981
Height: 6'1" Weight: 11.5
International Honours: E: Yth; Sch

Capped by England at U16 and U18 levels, Christian developed through the ranks at Middlesbrough before joining Second Division Cambridge United on loan last March to gain some experience of first-team football. A talented left-sided defender, he appeared for the U's in the final eight matches of the campaign when he performed with great composure on the ball.

Middlesbrough (From trainee on 5/8/1998)
Cambridge U (Loaned on 22/3/2001) FL 8

HANSSON Mikael
Born: Norrkoping, Sweden, 15 March 1968
Height: 5'10" Weight: 11.2
Club Honours: AMC '00
International Honours: Sweden: 1

Mikael was a regular in the Stoke City line-up last season, his appearances being only slightly limited by a recurring leg injury. An experienced right wing back whose main attribute is undoubtedly his electric pace, he is particularly effective when pushing up the flank. His influence on the team was such that when he was on song they rarely lost.

Stoke C (Free from IFK Norrkoping, Sweden, ex Soderkopings, on 3/12/1999) FL 60+5/2 FLC 4 FAC 2 Others 11+1/1

Marlon Harewood

HARDY Adam Neil
Born: Uitenhage, South Africa, 22 February 1983
Height: 5'10" Weight: 13.0

One of several promising youngsters at Bradford City Adam spent most of last season learning his football in the club's reserve and youth teams where he generally featured in midfield. He stepped up to make his senior debut when he came on from the subs' bench in the Worthington Cup match at home to Darlington in September.

Bradford C (Trainee) FLC 0+1

HARDY Philip (Phil)
Born: Ellesmere Port, 9 April 1973
Height: 5'8" Weight: 11.8
Club Honours: WC '95
International Honours: RoI: U21-9

This experienced Wrexham left back endured a frustrating 2000-01 season missing long spells with a series of injuries. After knee surgery in the summer he did not return to fitness until last November, but soon afterwards further knee problems put him out of action until February, and then after just one game he tore a calf muscle. It was not until the final weeks of the campaign that he saw regular first-team action. At his best Phil is a consistent defender who is quick in the tackle and rarely gives his opponent much room. He was reported to have signed for Port Vale in the summer.

Wrexham (From trainee on 24/11/1990) FL 346+3/1 FLC 19 FAC 36 Others 38

HAREWOOD Marlon Anderson
Born: Hampstead, 25 August 1979
Height: 6'1" Weight: 11.0

Marlon again featured regularly in the Nottingham Forest first-team squad last term although he was still unable to establish himself as a regular in the starting line-up. A very persistent player who is good at holding the ball up, he possesses most of the key attributes required of a striker: height, pace and strength on the ball. However, despite showing considerable determination he has yet to develop a composure in front of goal. A favourite of the City Ground fans he finished the season on a high with two goals in the final game at Tranmere.

Nottingham F (From trainee on 9/9/1996) P/FL 43+48/8 FLC 7+3/3 FAC 2+2
Ipswich T (Loaned on 28/1/1999) FL 5+1/1

HARGREAVES Christian (Chris)
Born: Cleethorpes, 12 May 1972
Height: 5'11" Weight: 12.2

Chris spent much of last season playing in a left-wing-back role for Northampton due to the club's injury problems. Previously known as a quality left-sided midfield player his speed and skill on the ball enabled him to

make the switch with ease. He suffered a knee injury against Millwall last February that required a cartilage operation and brought his campaign to a premature close.
Grimsby T (From trainee on 6/12/1989) FL 15+36/5 FLC 2+2/1 FAC 1+2/1 Others 2+4
Scarborough (Loaned on 4/3/1993) FL 2+1
Hull C (Signed on 26/7/1993) FL 34+15 FLC 1 FAC 2+1/1 Others 3+1
West Bromwich A (Free on 13/7/1995) FL 0+1 Others 0+1
Hereford U (Free on 19/2/1996) FL 57+4/6 FLC 3+1 FAC 1 Others 2
Plymouth Arg (Free on 20/7/1998) FL 74+2/5 FLC 4 FAC 11/2 Others 1
Northampton T (Free on 7/7/2000) FL 29+2 FLC 1 FAC 2 Others 1

HARKIN Maurice (Mo) Presley
Born: Londonderry, 16 August 1979
Height: 5'9" Weight: 11.11
International Honours: NI: U21-9; Yth

While he featured regularly for Northern Ireland U21s last season Mo found it difficult to establish himself in the Wycombe Wanderers line-up and he rarely featured in the second half of the campaign. A talented midfield playmaker he impressed with his close control and always threatened from the edge of the box but was released at the end of the season.
Wycombe W (From trainee on 14/2/1997) FL 26+47/2 FLC 5+2/1 FAC 4+4 Others 4/1

Steve Harkness

HARKNESS Steven (Steve)
Born: Carlisle, 27 August 1971
Height: 5'10" Weight: 11.2
International Honours: E: Yth

Steve made just one appearance for Blackburn at the start of last season before being sold to Sheffield Wednesday in September and went straight into the team at left back, rarely missing a game apart from injury or suspension. Quick in the tackle and enthusiastic his experience proved invaluable for the Hillsborough club. He scored just once during the campaign, hitting the winner in the home match against Birmingham City with a crisp low drive.
Carlisle U (From trainee on 23/3/1989) FL 12+1
Liverpool (£75,000 on 17/7/1989) F/PL 90+12/2 FLC 11+4/1 FAC 5+1 Others 13+3 (£750,000 to Benfica on 9/3/1999)
Huddersfield T (Loaned on 24/9/1993) FL 5 Others 1
Southend U (Loaned on 3/2/1995) FL 6
Blackburn Rov (£400,000 on 8/9/1999) FL 17 FLC 2+1 FAC 1
Sheffield Wed (£200,000 on 29/9/2000) FL 28+2/1 FAC 2

HARLEY Jonathan (Jon)
Born: Maidstone, 26 September 1979
Height: 5'9" Weight: 10.3
Club Honours: FAC '00
International Honours: E: U21-3; Yth

After making such a startling impact at Chelsea in the 1999-2000 campaign Jon was loaned out to Wimbledon soon after new boss Claudio Ranieri arrived at Stamford Bridge. He made a cracking start with the Dons, grabbing two goals in the 4-0 win at Crewe but his subsequent performances didn't quite match those high standards. He was then recalled at short notice in November to take his place on the subs' bench at Goodison Park. The schedule was so tight that he flew from Stansted still wearing a Wimbledon tracksuit! In all he made a handful of appearances for the Blues last term but with Ranieri having expressed his desire to give the team a young, English backbone this promising left-sided midfield player may still yet work his way through to a regular place in the first team.
Chelsea (From trainee on 20/3/1997) PL 19+11/2 FLC 0+1 FAC 7 Others 1+3
Wimbledon (Loaned on 20/10/2000) FL 6/2

HARPER James (Jamie) Alan John
Born: Chelmsford, 9 November 1980
Height: 5'10" Weight: 11.7

Unable to break into the senior team at Highbury this talented youngster joined Cardiff City on loan with a view to a permanent transfer. No deal could be reached and he returned to Arsenal before moving on to Reading shortly afterwards. Jamie went straight into the Royals' first team and quickly justified his substantial transfer fee by scoring a superb goal on his debut against Rotherham United. A talented midfielder who plays with an assured arrogance and determination, he is likely to become a key figure at the Madejski Stadium in the coming season.
Arsenal (From trainee on 8/7/1999)
Cardiff C (Loaned on 29/12/2000) FL 3
Reading (£400,000 on 28/2/2001) FL 9+3/1 Others 1+1

HARPER Kevin Patrick
Born: Oldham, 15 January 1976
Height: 5'6" Weight: 10.10
International Honours: S: B-1; U21-7; Sch

After some impressive performances for Portsmouth towards the end of the 1999-2000 campaign there were high expectations of this pacy winger at Fratton Park last term, but unfortunately he was dogged by a persistent hamstring problem that restricted him to little more than a dozen starts. A right-footed player who is able to operate either on the wing or in a midfield role he is adept at knocking on through balls for the front men to put away.
Hibernian (Signed from Hutchison Vale BC on 3/8/1992) SL 73+23/15 SLC 4+5 SC 9+1/3
Derby Co (£300,000 + on 11/9/1998) PL 6+26/1 FLC 1+5 FAC 0+3/1
Walsall (Loaned on 17/12/1999) FL 8+1/1
Portsmouth (£300,000 on 6/3/2000) FL 27+9/4 FAC 1

HARPER Lee Charles Phillip
Born: Chelsea, 30 October 1971
Height: 6'1" Weight: 13.11

Lee began last season as the first-choice 'keeper for Queens Park Rangers. He showed consistent form despite the club's poor results and although he was dropped in favour of Ludo Miklosko in November he returned to the line-up in the new year and kept his place for the remainder of the campaign. Although he was one of the most consistent Rangers players in a very disappointing season he was released in the summer.
Arsenal (£150,000 from Sittingbourne on 16/6/1994) PL 1
Queens Park R (£125,000 + on 11/7/1997) FL 117+1 FLC 8+1 FAC 4

HARPER Stephen (Steve) Alan
Born: Easington, 14 March 1975
Height: 6'2" Weight: 13.0

One of the few local-born players in the Newcastle first-team pool Steve is now second only to Rob Lee in terms of length of service on Tyneside, but he again made relatively few appearances last term. Lively and alert, he is a good shot stopper and is comfortable when fielding high balls into the box. A cartilage operation during the summer slowed his pre-season preparation but he started the new campaign on the bench. However his only early-season action came in the Worthington Cup ties and it was not until Shay Given was injured at Derby shortly before Christmas that he came into the reckoning. He had a fine game in the Boxing Day win over Leeds and indeed kept Given out of the team for a short while until he himself went down with a foot injury, and on his recovery he returned to a place on the bench. A qualified referee, Steve is also studying for a Social Sciences degree with the Open University.
Newcastle U (Free from Seaham Red Star on 5/7/1993) PL 29+2 FLC 4 FAC 7+1 Others 6
Bradford C (Loaned on 18/9/1995) FL 1
Hartlepool U (Loaned on 29/8/1997) FL 15
Huddersfield T (Loaned on 18/12/1997) FL 24 FAC 2

HARPER Steven (Steve) James
Born: Newcastle under Lyme, 3 February 1969
Height: 5'10" Weight: 11.12
Club Honours: Div 4 '92

This experienced defender suffered an early setback in the 2000-01 campaign after suffering a leg injury when playing for Hull City against Plymouth. He soon returned to his familiar left-wing-back role, and settled down to the consistent performances that have been the hallmark of his time at Boothferry Park. Steve was a regular in the Tiger's line-up until the club's financial problems led to him joining Third Division rivals Darlington in February. He slotted in straight away for the Quakers playing on the left hand side either at full back or in midfield where his guile and experience were invaluable. He likes to overlap and link with the forwards and his tricky footwork down the flank contributed a number of goals for the side, but none for himself.

Port Vale (From trainee on 29/6/1987) FL 16+12/2 FLC 1+2 Others 1+1
Preston NE (Signed on 23/3/1989) FL 57+20/10 FLC 1+1 FAC 1+2 Others 6+1/1
Burnley (Free on 23/7/1991) FL 64+5/8 FLC 1+2 FAC 10/3 Others 8
Doncaster Rov (Free on 7/8/1993) FL 56+9/11 FLC 2+1/1 FAC 3 Others 4
Mansfield T (£20,000 on 8/9/1995) FL 157+3/18 FLC 6 FAC 8/1 Others 7
Hull C (Free on 13/7/1999) FL 63+2/4 FLC 5 FAC 7 Others 3
Darlington (Free on 15/2/2001) FL 17

HARRIS Andrew (Andy) David Douglas
Born: Springs, South Africa, 26 February 1977
Height: 5'10" Weight: 11.11

Having been badly affected by injuries in 1999-2000 Andy returned to the Leyton Orient line-up at the start of last season in the new position of central midfield. The switch proved a great success and he went on be a near ever-present for the O's. An effective box-to-box player he is an excellent tackler and capable of both breaking up and creating attacks. He was rewarded with a new two-year contract in the summer.

Liverpool (From trainee on 23/3/1994)
Southend U (Free on 10/7/1996) FL 70+2 FLC 5 FAC 3
Leyton Orient (Free on 5/7/1999) FL 55+4 FLC 8 FAC 4 Others 1+1

HARRIS Jason Andre Sebastian
Born: Sutton, 24 November 1976
Height: 6'1" Weight: 11.7

Largely out of favour since Brian Little's arrival at Hull, Jason's remained an attraction for other clubs and he had several trials before moving on loan to Shrewsbury Town in March. However he made just one start at Gay Meadow and had little chance to make any real impact before returning to Boothferry Park. He is a young striker with sufficient pace to upset most Third Division defenders. He was placed on the open to offers list in the summer. Jason is the older brother of Crystal Palace's Richard Harris.

Crystal Palace (From trainee on 3/7/1995) FL 0+2 FLC 0+2
Bristol Rov (Loaned on 22/11/1996) FL 5+1/2 Others 1/1
Lincoln C (Loaned on 11/8/1997) FL 0+1
Leyton Orient (£20,000 on 23/9/1997) FL 22+15/7 FLC 1 FAC 2 Others 1+1
Preston NE (Signed on 28/8/1998) FL 9+25/6 FAC 2+1/1 Others 2+2
Hull C (£30,000 + on 12/7/1999) FL 19+19/4 FLC 0+3 FAC 0+1 Others 1+2
Shrewsbury T (Loaned on 16/3/2001) FL 1+3

HARRIS Neil
Born: Orsett, 12 July 1977
Height: 5'11" Weight: 12.9
Club Honours: Div 2 '01

Neil had another fine campaign for Second Division champions Millwall in 2000-01, finishing leading scorer for the third successive season and registering an amazing tally of three hat-tricks. A talented striker with excellent close control he can shoot with either foot and is a constant threat both in the air and on the ground. His goals provided one of the foundation stones on which the Lions' success was built and he is likely to be a key figure in their First Division campaign in 2001-02. Neil was one of three Millwall players selected for the PFA's Second Division team at the end of the season.

Millwall (£30,000 from Cambridge C on 26/3/1998) FL 112+10/67 FLC 4+1 FAC 3+2/1 Others 10+1/3

HARRIS Richard
Born: Croydon, 23 October 1980
Height: 5'11" Weight: 10.9

This versatile young Crystal Palace player had another season disrupted by injury in 2000-01. He featured in the first-team squad for a short period last autumn making the starting line-up on two occasions. Richard possesses a prodigious throw that can cause havoc in opposition defences. He is the brother of Jason Harris.

Crystal Palace (From trainee on 22/12/1997) FL 2+7 FLC 2+2

HARRISON Craig
Born: Gateshead, 10 November 1977
Height: 6'0" Weight: 11.13

Craig missed the whole of the 1999-2000 campaign through illness and injury but became a regular in the Crystal Palace line-up last term after signing permanently following a successful loan period. A pacy left back he is powerful in the tackle and possesses good distribution skills. Apart from a short absence due to a dislocated shoulder he rarely missed a game for the Eagles and his performances improved as the season wore on.

Middlesbrough (From trainee on 4/7/1996) F/PL 19+5 FLC 4+2 FAC 2
Preston NE (Loaned on 15/1/1999) FL 6 Others 1
Crystal Palace (£200,000 on 11/8/2000) FL 30+2 FLC 8 FAC 2

HARRISON Gerald (Gerry) Randall
Born: Lambeth, 15 April 1972
Height: 5'10" Weight: 12.12
International Honours: E: Sch

Having been released by Sunderland, Gerry signed for Halifax Town on a one-month contract last August and scored a cracking goal in the 2-2 draw against Leyton Orient but was released by the Shaymen the following month. A powerful midfielder known for his penetrating runs he can also play as a central defender.

Watford (From trainee on 18/12/1989) FL 6+3 Others 1
Bristol C (Free on 23/7/1991) FL 25+13/1 FLC 2+2 FAC 1 Others 4+1
Cardiff C (Loaned on 24/1/1992) FL 10/1
Hereford U (Loaned on 19/11/1993) FL 6 FAC 1 Others 1
Huddersfield T (Free on 24/3/1994)
Burnley (Free on 5/8/1994) FL 116+8/3 FLC 5+1 FAC 6+2 Others 7+1
Sunderland (Free on 29/7/1998) FLC 1
Luton T (Loaned on 24/12/1998) FL 14 Others 1
Hull C (Loaned on 25/3/1999) FL 8
Hull C (Loaned on 1/10/1999) FL 3
Halifax T (Free on 18/8/2000) FL 7+2/1 FLC 2

HARRISON Lee David
Born: Billericay, 12 September 1971
Height: 6'2" Weight: 12.7

Lee was once again first-choice goalkeeper for Barnet for most of last season and demonstrated his value to the team on many occasions. He suffered a groin injury in the home game with Hull City in September and although he made a quick recovery it was not until December that he regained his place in the starting line-up. Sadly he was stretchered off with damaged knee ligaments in the opening minutes of Barnet's crucial final league game against Torquay. A fine shot stopper he will be aiming to make a recovery by the early part of the 2001-02 campaign. He was placed on the open to offers list in the summer.

Charlton Ath (From trainee on 3/7/1990)
Fulham (Loaned on 18/11/1991) Others 1
Gillingham (Loaned on 24/3/1992) FL 2
Fulham (Free on 18/12/1992) FL 11+1 FAC 1 Others 6
Barnet (Free on 15/7/1996) FL 183 FLC 9 FAC 3 Others 12

HARSLEY Paul
Born: Scunthorpe, 29 May 1978
Height: 5'9" Weight: 11.5

After being an ever-present for virtually two seasons, Paul was out of favour at Scunthorpe for much of the 2000-01 campaign, making only three league starts in a five-month spell. He returned to the team in the new year at right-back and adapted well to the role, playing a big part in Scunthorpe's surge back up towards the play-offs. Paul opened his goal-scoring account for the season in the 4-3 win at Halifax last March when he netted straight from a corner. Released in the summer he was reported to have signed for the Shaymen.

Grimsby T (From trainee on 16/7/1996)
Scunthorpe U (Free on 7/7/1997) FL 110+18/5 FLC 6 FAC 4+2/1 Others 5+1

HART Gary John
Born: Harlow, 21 September 1976
Height: 5'9" Weight: 12.8
Club Honours: Div 3 '01

Despite starting the 2000-01 season as centre forward, Brighton manager Micky Adams soon switched Gary to a wider role where it was felt his pace would be more beneficial. He worked hard to adapt to his new position and the results were clearly visible as he become more involved in the games, showing an increased work rate and more effective tackling. He was a near ever-

present for the Seagulls as they went on to win the Third Division championship in style.
Brighton & Hove A (£1,000 from Stansted on 18/6/1998) FL 127+5/28 FLC 4+2 FAC 5 Others 4+1/1

HARTE Ian Patrick
Born: Drogheda, 31 August 1977
Height: 5'10" Weight: 11.8
International Honours: RoI: 31; U21-3
Ian is now recognised as not only one of the best left backs in the country, but also one of the deadliest exponents of the dead-ball situation, indeed he scored a hat-trick of free kicks at Blackburn during the pre-season period. Although having little competition for his place in recent campaigns the signing of Dominic Matteo meant this was no longer the case, and in December he was dropped for nine games, and was subsequently linked to other clubs by the media. He returned at Villa Park in January, scoring in United's victory and never looked back, keeping his place until the end of the season. He remains the club's penalty taker, but is equally effective with his explosive free kicks, as Deportivo La Coruna found out to their cost when his superb effort opened the scoring in the Champions' League quarter-final. A typical modern full back, he is much admired across Europe, and remains an integral part of the future plans for club and country.
Leeds U (From trainee on 15/12/1995) PL 120+7/19 FLC 5+2/1 FAC 11+2/3 Others 32/5

HARTSON John
Born: Neath, 5 April 1975
Height: 6'1" Weight: 14.6
International Honours: W: 24; U21-9; Yth
John worked very hard at Wimbledon at the start of last season and was appointed club captain. He scored regularly for the Dons throughout the campaign but it came as no real surprise when he finally agreed a move to struggling Coventry City in the new year. He had a goal controversially disallowed on his debut for the Sky Blues against West Ham and a penalty decision turned down late in the game but did enough to show that he had lost none of his aggression and power. His attitude and commitment provided an immediate boost to the whole team and they lost only one of his first six games as he contributed some wonderful headed goals and brought the best out of his colleague Craig Bellamy. He had a storming game at Old Trafford where he scored two goals and generally gave Wes Brown the run around, but none of this was enough to keep Coventry in the Premiership. A big bustling centre forward capable of upsetting any defence, he has a fine shot in either foot and is also very effective in the air. He continued to represent Wales scoring twice to earn a draw in Armenia in March and also netting in the 1-1 draw with the Ukraine.
Luton T (From trainee on 19/12/1992) FL 32+22/11 FLC 0+1 FAC 3+3/2 Others 2
Arsenal (£2,500,000 on 13/1/1995) PL 43+10/14 FLC 2+4/1 FAC 2+1/1 Others 8+1/1
West Ham U (£3,200,000 + on 14/2/1997) PL 59+1/24 FLC 6/6 FAC 7/3
Wimbledon (£7,000,000 on 15/1/1999) P/FL 46+3/19 FLC 7/2 FAC 1
Coventry C (Signed on 8/2/2001) PL 12/6

HASLAM Steven Robert
Born: Sheffield, 6 September 1979
Height: 5'11" Weight: 10.10
International Honours: E: Yth; Sch
Steven had another solid if unspectacular campaign for Sheffield Wednesday in 2000-01. He established himself in a midfield 'holding' role until a change of formation in the new year saw him lose his place. He has excellent distribution while his tenacity and calmness under pressure are an asset to the side. Steven is tied to a long-term contract at Hillsborough and looks to have a great future in the game.
Sheffield Wed (From trainee on 12/9/1996) P/FL 42+10/1 FLC 3+1 FAC 5

HASSELBAINK Jerrel (Jimmy Floyd)
Born: Surinam, 27 March 1972
Height: 6'2" Weight: 13.4
Club Honours: CS '00
International Honours: Holland: 13
Despite a solid defence and some beautiful flowing football in midfield, one of Chelsea's failings in recent seasons has been the absence of a prolific goal-scorer. Having recognised the problem the Blues then paid out a club record fee to secure the services of this former Leeds United cult hero. Jimmy immediately paid back a large slice of that fee on his debut at Wembley when he ran the Manchester United defence ragged in the Charity Shield and netted the opener in Chelsea's 2-0 victory. After scoring against London rivals West Ham and Arsenal, Jimmy Floyd returned to haunt

Jimmy Floyd Hasselbaink

Manchester United in September when he blasted the Blues ahead at Old Trafford with a sensational pile driver. The goals continued to flow as Jimmy Floyd vied with Marcus Stewart for the honour of Premiership top-scorer. A classic four-timer against Coventry was followed by two the next week against Tottenham before his fortunes took a turn for the worse. Recalled by Holland for the November friendly in Spain he equalised with a typical drive from the edge of the box but then received a red card and a second followed just 10 days later in the Premiership game at Goodison Park. He started 2001 with a bang, scoring consistently until the end of the season, his haul including another high-velocity screamer in the FA Cup fifth round tie at Highbury and consecutive doubles against both Everton and Liverpool. His 23rd Premiership goal of the season in the final match at Maine Road clinched the 'Golden Boot' and, perhaps more importantly, Chelsea's UEFA Cup qualification. In the process he became the first Chelsea striker since Kerry Dixon to score 20 league goals in a season. The Blues now have a potent strike force and Jimmy Floyd's vibrant partnerships with Eidur Gudjohnsen and Gianfranco Zola resulted in 68 Premiership goals last term - the third-highest total. An abrasive character who is totally single-minded in his pursuit of goals Jimmy Floyd is now approaching cult status at Stamford Bridge.

Leeds U (£2,000,000 from Boavista, Portugal, ex Campomaiorense, on 18/7/1997) PL 66+3/34 FLC 5/2 FAC 9/5 Others 4/1 (£12,000,000 to Atletico Madrid, Spain on 20/8/1999)
Chelsea (£15,000,000 on 12/7/2000) PL 35/23 FLC 1 FAC 2/2 Others 3/1

HASSELL Robert (Bobby) John Francis
Born: Derby, 4 June 1980
Height: 5'9" Weight: 12.6

Bobby stayed relatively free of injuries last term and enjoyed an extended run in the Mansfield Town first team. Playing mostly in a midfield role he tackled as strong as ever and passed the ball well. He scored his first goal in senior football with a fierce right-foot drive to help the Stags to a 3-2 victory over Darlington in the closing stages of the season.

Mansfield T (From trainee on 3/7/1998) FL 56+7/2 FLC 4+1 FAC 2

HATCHER Daniel (Danny) Ian
Born: Newport, IoW, 24 December 1983
Height: 5'10" Weight: 11.8

A regular for Leyton Orient's successful U19 team Danny first came to attention when he was included in the senior squad for the FA Cup game against Tottenham. Although he didn't make his debut that day he went on to appear as a substitute in the LDV Vans Trophy game against Wycombe shortly afterwards and featured from the bench in a couple of Third Division games. He also appeared in the Football League Youth Alliance Cup final at Cardiff's Millenium Stadium when he came on and almost scored as the O's went on to win the trophy. Danny is a very quick and direct striker who will be looking to gain further senior experience in 2001-02.

Leyton Orient (Trainee) FL 0+2 Others 0+1

HATSWELL Wayne Mervin
Born: Swindon, 8 February 1975
Height: 6'0" Weight: 13.10

Wayne joined Oxford United from Conference club Forest Green Rovers last December and after making his Football League debut from the subs' bench at Oldham he quickly established himself as a regular in the U's first-team. Introduced at left back he took some time to adjust to his new surroundings and looked more comfortable when he played in a central defensive role. A big strong left-footed defender he will be aiming to make further progress in the coming season.

Oxford U (£35,000 from Forest Green Rov on 1/12/2000) FL 26+1 Others 1

HAWE Steven (Steve) John
Born: Magherafelt, 23 December 1980
Height: 5'11" Weight: 11.7
International Honours: NI: U21-2; Yth; Sch

This young Blackburn Rovers defender began the 2000-01 campaign on loan at Blackpool and played in the opening two games of the season for the Tangerines. He later joined Third Division rivals Halifax Town for an extended loan period making his debut for the Shaymen from the subs' bench at Darlington. He featured in a number of games around the turn of the year but then fell out of favour. Nevertheless he stepped up to represent Northern Ireland at U21 level, making his debut against the Czech Republic in March. He was out of contract in the summer.

Blackburn Rov (From trainee on 31/12/1997)
Blackpool (Loaned on 11/8/2000) FL 2
Halifax T (Loaned on 10/11/2000) FL 6+2 FAC 1 Others 1

Peter Hawkins

HAWKINS Peter Steven
Born: Maidstone, 19 September 1978
Height: 6'0" Weight: 11.6

Peter received his big break at Wimbledon last term and fitted admirably into the left-back role. Despite suffering an ankle injury towards the end of the year he came back to regain his place and can be satisfied with the progress he made over the 12 months. Quick in the tackle and always willing to push forward down the wing he showed his versatility by occasionally standing in at right back.

Wimbledon (From trainee on 6/3/1997) FL 29+1 FLC 3 FAC 5
York C (Loaned on 22/2/2000) FL 14

HAWLEY Karl Leon
Born: Walsall, 6 December 1981
Height: 5'7" Weight: 12.0

After having done well at reserve level for Walsall Karl stepped up to make his senior debut when he came off the subs' bench for the final 20 minutes of the LDV Vans Trophy second round tie against Wigan and also featured in the next round against Stoke. A very promising lively front-runner he joined the professional ranks in January and will be aiming to gain more first-team experience in the coming season.

Walsall (From trainee on 26/1/2001) Others 0+2

HAWORTH Simon Owen
Born: Cardiff, 30 March 1977
Height: 6'2" Weight: 13.8
Club Honours: AMC '99
International Honours: W: 5; B-1; U21-12; Yth

Simon had a great start to the 2000-01 campaign, scoring regularly for Wigan Athletic before being sidelined by a hamstring injury. He returned to finish the season as top scorer for the Latics and also had the distinction of becoming the first player to score a hat trick at the JJB Stadium when he did so in the 3-1 win over Colchester in September. Quick, skilful and with an ability to score spectacular goals he looks capable of playing at a higher level.

Cardiff C (From trainee on 7/8/1995) FL 27+10/9 FLC 4 FAC 0+1 Others 4/1
Coventry C (£500,000 on 4/6/1997) PL 5+6 FLC 2/1 FAC 0+1
Wigan Ath (£600,000 on 2/10/1998) FL 80+10/34 FLC 7/5 FAC 4/4 Others 11+1/4

HAY Christopher (Chris) Drummond
Born: Glasgow, 28 August 1974
Height: 5'11" Weight: 12.5

Chris made a number of appearances from the subs' bench for Huddersfield Town in the early part of last season and started in the two Worthington Cup ties but otherwise spent his time developing in the reserves where he was a regular goal-scorer. Injury kept him out of action for some of the time but will be looking to push for a regular place in the first team in 2001-02. A striker who can kick with either foot he has plenty of skill and shows a good eye for goal.

Glasgow Celtic (Free from Giffnock North AFC on 27/5/1993) SL 9+16/4 SC 0+3 Others 0+2/1
Swindon T (£330,000 on 6/8/1997) FL 73+21/30 FLC 2+2 FAC 2+1
Huddersfield T (£70,000 on 23/3/2000) FL 2+9 FLC 2

HAY Daniel (Danny) John
Born: Auckland, New Zealand, 15 May 1975
Height: 6'4" Weight: 14.11
International Honours: New Zealand: 11

Danny was pushed forward ahead of schedule due to the injury crisis at Elland Road and made his senior debut for Leeds United when he came off the substitutes' bench in the final minute to replace Lucas Radebe in the Champions' League game in Barcelona. He remained in the first-team picture, and again substituted for the injured Radebe, at half-time in the 4-2 home win over Tottenham when he had an inspired 45 minutes, looking solid and adept at bringing the ball out of defence. He made three more appearances for the first team before returning to the reserves where he played regularly for the remainder of the campaign. A New Zealand international central defender he missed out on their World Cup qualifying matches due to a nagging groin injury.

Leeds U (£200,000 from Perth Glory, Australia on 25/8/1999) PL 2+2 FLC 1 Others 0+1

Barry Hayles

HAYLES Barrington (Barry) Edward
Born: Lambeth, 17 May 1972
Height: 5'9" Weight: 13.0
Club Honours: GMVC '96; Div 2 '99; Div 1 '01
International Honours: E: SP-2. Jamaica: 6

One of three strikers to appear regularly for Fulham last term Barry linked well with both Louis Saha and Luis Boa Morte as boss Jean Tigana rotated his attacking force. A thorn in the side of opposition defences he netted 18 goals in 35 league appearances a much-improved figure on his 1999-2000 tally. A busy striker he impressed again with his pace, strength on the ball and eye for goal. Barry made his international debut for Jamaica against Trinidad & Tobago in February and subsequently featured regularly for the Reggae Boyz in their campaign to qualify for the 2002 World Cup finals.

Bristol Rov (£250,000 from Stevenage Borough on 4/6/1997) FL 62/32 FLC 4/1 FAC 5/2 Others 3+2/2
Fulham (£2,100,000 on 17/11/1998) FL 75+25/31 FLC 6+2/3 FAC 7+1/3

HAYTER James (Jamie) Edward
Born: Sandown, IoW, 9 April 1979
Height: 5'9" Weight: 11.2

One of several promising youngsters at Bournemouth, Jamie hit the headlines last October when he scored four goals in the 5-2 win at Bury, including a hat-trick in a six-minute spell. With Jermain Defoe firmly established up front however, he often found himself playing in a midfield role last season where his high work rate and an ability to create chances for others proved particularly useful.

Bournemouth (From trainee on 7/7/1997) FL 66+32/15 FLC 1+2/1 FAC 4/1 Others 2+2/1

HAYWARD Steven (Steve) Lee
Born: Pelsall, 8 September 1971
Height: 5'11" Weight: 12.5
Club Honours: AMC '97; Div 2 '99
International Honours: E: Yth

This hard-working midfield player saw his first-team opportunities disappear at Fulham with the signing of John Collins and apart from a brief outing from the subs' bench against Barnsley he was restricted to appearing in the early rounds of the Worthington Cup and regular reserve-team football. Barnsley's new manager Nigel Spackman then swooped to bring him to Oakwell early in the new year. He settled in well, scoring on his debut with a tremendous 30-yard shot. He was a regular in the side before suffering a serious knee injury against Tranmere in March that is likely to keep him out of action for most of the 2001-02 campaign. Hard working, strong in the tackle and the possessor of a vicious shot he mostly featured in the centre of midfield for the Tykes.

Derby Co (From juniors on 17/9/1988) FL 15+11/1 FLC 0+2 FAC 1 Others 3+4
Carlisle U (£100,000 on 13/3/1995) FL 88+2/14 FLC 6/1 FAC 4 Others 15/1
Fulham (£175,000 on 23/6/1997) FL 108+7/7 FLC 16+3/1 FAC 9+2/3 Others 3
Barnsley (£25,000 on 19/1/2001) FL 10/1

HAZELL Reuben
Born: Birmingham, 24 April 1979
Height: 5'11" Weight: 12.0

This promising Tranmere youngster was a cornerstone of the club's successful reserve team last season but it was only towards the end of the campaign that he broke through to feature regularly in the first-team squad. A pacy and cultured defender he enjoys getting forward and supporting his front-line colleagues whenever he can. Reuben is the nephew of the former Queens Park rangers star Bob Hazell.

Aston Villa (From trainee on 20/3/1997)
Tranmere Rov (Free on 5/8/1999) FL 32+4/1 FLC 7 FAC 3

HEALD Gregory (Greg) James
Born: Enfield, 26 September 1971
Height: 6'1" Weight: 12.8
International Honours: E: Sch

Greg was a regular in the Barnet line-up last season although he never quite managed to show the outstanding form he had displayed in 1999-2000. A powerful central defender he still provided an effective presence when moving up to assist the attack and netted a useful number of goals during the campaign. He was placed on the open to offers list in the summer.

Peterborough U (£35,000 from Enfield on 8/7/1994) FL 101+4/6 FLC 8 FAC 8+1 Others 11/2
Barnet (Signed on 8/8/1997) FL 141/13 FLC 8/1 FAC 4 Others 7/1

HEALD Paul Andrew
Born: Wath on Dearne, 20 September 1968
Height: 6'2" Weight: 14.0

A little unlucky not to have taken over the 'keeper's jersey at Wimbledon following the departure of Neil Sullivan, Paul was second choice to Kelvin Davis last term, being restricted to just a couple of appearances from the subs' bench and a place in the starting line-up for the final game of the season against Norwich. A firm favourite of the Dons' supporters he has good command over his box and possesses an extremely powerful kick.

Sheffield U (From trainee on 30/6/1987)
Leyton Orient (Signed on 2/12/1988) FL 176 FLC 13 FAC 9 Others 21
Coventry C (Loaned on 10/3/1992) PL 2
Swindon T (Loaned on 24/3/1994) PL 1+1
Wimbledon (£125,000 on 25/7/1995) P/FL 22+2 FLC 7

David Healy

HEALY David Jonathan
Born: Downpatrick, 5 August 1979
Height: 5'8" Weight: 11.0
International Honours: NI: 12; B-1; U21-8; Yth; Sch

David began the 2000-01 campaign at Old Trafford but despite his successes on the international front with Northern Ireland he made little headway in the first-team squad. He appeared as a substitute in the Worthington Cup game against Sunderland in November and also in the Premiership against Ipswich the following month before joining Preston North End for a new club record fee shortly afterwards. He provided an immediate return on the investment by scoring in the fourth minute of his debut at Sheffield United and five goals in his first seven starts. A quick and mobile striker, David is surprisingly adept in the air, as his great spring and powerful header at Norwich demonstrated. His partnership up front with Jon Macken bodes well for the future and he finished his first half-season at Deepdale with a tally of 10 goals. A nippy striker with an excellent eye for goal he continued to be a regular for his country for whom he scored three times during the campaign. David is a cousin of Wigan Athletic's Hugh Dickson.

Manchester U (From trainee on 28/11/1997) PL 0+1 FLC 0+2
Port Vale (Loaned on 25/2/2000) FL 15+1/3
Preston NE (£1,500,000 on 29/12/2000) FL 19+3/9 FAC 1 Others 3/1

HEARY Thomas Mark
Born: Dublin, 14 February 1978
Height: 5'10" Weight: 11.12
International Honours: RoI: U21-4; Yth; (UEFA-U18 '98); Sch

Having signed a new contract for Huddersfield Town during the summer Thomas featured in a number of games in the early part of the 2000-01 campaign before establishing himself as a regular in the first team under new manager Lou Macari. A quiet but confident defender he briefly appeared at left back and in midfield but looked much more assured in his customary right-back position. Strong in the tackle and an excellent passer of the ball, he was rewarded with a further extension to his contract at the McAlpine Stadium.

Huddersfield T (From trainee on 17/2/1996) FL 33+7 FLC 2+1 FAC 2

HEATH Robert
Born: Newcastle under Lyme, 31 August 1978
Height: 5'8" Weight: 10.0

Robert was on the fringes of the Stoke City first-team squad at the start of the 2000-01 campaign and made his only senior appearance of the campaign in Worthington Cup first round first leg tie at York when he scored in a 5-1 victory. However his progress was subsequently blighted by injury and he was only offered monthly terms in the summer. When fully fit he is a hard-working midfield player who can also play at full back.

Stoke C (From trainee on 15/7/1996) FL 11+8 FLC 1+1/1 FAC 0+1 Others 2

HEATHCOTE Michael (Mick)
Born: Kelloe, 10 September 1965
Height: 6'2" Weight: 12.5

Mick fought back from injury to win a new one-year contract for Plymouth at the start of last season. Unfortunately he suffered a further injury during the pre-season and it was not until October that he appeared in the first team. He bolstered the centre of Argyle's defence on his return but was again sidelined in December and failed to make a recovery before the end of the campaign. His commanding influence over the Pilgrims' team was sorely missed. A popular figure at Home Park he has been rewarded a testimonial match due to take place against Sunderland at the end of July.

Sunderland (£15,000 from Spennymoor on 19/8/1987) FL 6+3 Others 0+1
Halifax T (Loaned on 17/12/1987) FL 7/1 FAC 1
York C (Loaned on 4/1/1990) FL 3 Others 1
Shrewsbury T (£55,000 on 12/7/1990) FL 43+1/6 FLC 6 FAC 5 Others 4
Cambridge U (£150,000 on 12/9/1991) FL123+5/13 FLC 7/1 FAC 5+2/2 Others 7/2
Plymouth Arg (£70,000 on 27/7/1995) FL 195+4/13 FLC 9/1 FAC 18/3 Others 9

HECKINGBOTTOM Paul
Born: Barnsley, 17 July 1977
Height: 5'11" Weight: 12.0

Paul appeared in the first dozen games of last season in his customary left-back spot for Darlington, but went down with a strained groin in the first leg of the Worthington Cup tie with Bradford City and was forced to rest. He returned two months later, perhaps too soon, and although he had occasional outings through to February he was forced into another period of inactivity that lasted until the end of the season. He remains a strong-tackling defender capable of penetrating runs down the flank.

Sunderland (From trainee at Manchester U on 14/7/1995)
Scarborough (Loaned on 17/10/1997) FL 28+1 Others 1
Hartlepool U (Loaned on 25/9/1998) FL 5/1
Darlington (Free on 25/3/1999) FL 71+2/2 FLC 4 FAC 4/1 Others 6

HEDMAN Magnus Carl
Born: Stockholm, Sweden, 19 March 1973
Height: 6'4" Weight: 13.10
International Honours: Sweden: 36; B-1; U21; Yth

Magnus had a frustrating time at Coventry in 2000-01, for having been first-choice 'keeper at the start of the campaign he was affected by a series of injuries, then lost his place to his young rival Chris Kirkland and to cap it all the Sky Blues were relegated to the First Division. He injured a knee playing for Sweden in the autumn and was then sidelined by ankle trouble just before Christmas, then featured only briefly on his return before losing his place. His shot-stopping skills were as brilliant as ever but while he was less reluctant than previous to stay on his line at corners this remained an area where he needed to show improvement. Having rarely featured during the second half of the campaign he is unlikely to be happy with a prolonged spell on the subs' bench in 2001-02.

Coventry C (£500,000 from AIK Solna, Sweden on 24/7/1997) PL 100 FLC 5 FAC 10

HEFFERNAN Paul
Born: Dublin, Ireland, 29 December 1981
Height: 5'10" Weight: 10.7

This promising young striker continued to develop at reserve level with Notts County in 2000-01, stepping up to make appearances from the subs' bench for the first team on two occasions. Very quick and with a great eye for goal he will be aiming to break through into the senior squad more often in the coming season.

Notts Co (Signed from Newtown, Co Wicklow on 22/10/1999) FL 0+3 Others 0+1

HEGGEM Vegard
Born: Trondheim, Norway, 13 July 1975
Height: 5'10" Weight: 11.12
International Honours: Norway: 21; U21

Two years ago the Norwegian international looked set to be Liverpool's right back for a generation but a recurring hamstring injury curtailed his 1999-2000 campaign and again hampered him last term. He made a comeback in September as substitute at West Ham and started the games at home to Rapid Bucharest in the UEFA Cup and at Derby. However he was stretchered off after only five minutes of the game at Pride Park with the same hamstring problem and the date of his return to full fitness was continually put back until the season ran out. However even when he regains fitness he will find it difficult to force his way back into a Liverpool back four that now seems firmly established.

Liverpool (£3,500,000 from Rosenborg, Norway, ex Orkdal, on 27/7/1998) PL 38+16/3 FLC 2+2 FAC 1 Others 5+1

HEGGS Carl Sydney
Born: Leicester, 11 October 1970
Height: 6'1" Weight: 12.10

Carl became Ian Atkins' first signing for Carlisle in August 2000 and although his appearances were restricted by injury he came back bravely to feature in the final games of the season. A hard-working striker who never lets his opponents relax he netted some vital goals for the Cumbrians including a 25-yard strike against Chesterfield, which was one of the best goals seen at Brunton Park all season, and a top-quality volley to clinch a point at Lincoln in the vital end-of-season clash.

West Bromwich A (£25,000 from Leicester U on 22/8/1991) FL 13+27/3 FLC 2 FAC 0+1 Others 6+3/1
Bristol Rov (Loaned on 27/1/1995) FL 2+3/1
Swansea C (£60,000 on 27/7/1995) FL 33+13/7 FLC 2 FAC 2 Others 4+1/1
Northampton T (£40,000 on 31/7/1997) FL 29+17/5 FLC 3+2/2 FAC 4+1/1 Others 3+1/4 (£65,000 to Rushden & Diamonds on 23/10/1998)
Chester C (Loaned on 10/3/2000) FL 11/2
Carlisle U (Free on 1/8/2000) FL 16+14/5 FLC 1 FAC 0+3 Others 1

HEINOLA Antti Juhani
Born: Helsinki, Finland, 20 March 1973
Height: 5'10" Weight: 12.3
International Honours: Finland: 8; U21

Having finally recovered from a cruciate ligament injury suffered in the summer of 1999, Antti struggled to win his place back

in the Queens Park Rangers' team last season. He was a regular member of the reserve side but only made a couple of appearances from the subs' bench for the first team. In March he announced his retirement from football and returned to Finland to study for an Economics degree at Helsinki University.
Queens Park R (£150,000 from Heracles, Holland, ex HJK Helsinki, Emmen, on 15/1/1998) FL 23+11 FLC 3+1 FAC 1

HEISELBERG Kim
Born: Tarm, Denmark, 21 September 1977
Height: 5'11" Weight: 11.7
International Honours: Denmark: U21; Yth
Kim joined Swindon Town in August 2000 but although he made the starting line-up for two early-season matches he never really seemed to settle at the County Ground and after being placed on the transfer list in November he left the club shortly afterwards. Capped by Denmark at U21 level he is an attacking left back.
Sunderland (£125,000 from Esbjerg, Denmark on 20/3/1997. Released on 12/3/1998)
Swindon T (Free from FC Midtjyllan, Denmark on 11/8/2000) FL 1 FLC 1

HELGUSON Heidar
Born: Iceland, 22 August 1977
Height: 6'0" Weight: 12.2
International Honours: Iceland: 17; U21-6; Yth
After enjoying a promising start with Watford in the Premiership Heidar had a rather disappointing time last term. He missed the opening of the season with a shin injury, but was soon off the mark at home to Sheffield United and went on to find the net in four consecutive matches. However as the campaign progressed he hit a frustrating goal drought which gradually eroded his confidence and eventually saw him relegated to the subs' bench. An all-action centre forward he finished the campaign with eight goals but will be hoping for a better haul in 2001-02.
Watford (£1,500,000 from SK Lillestrom, Norway, ex Throttur, on 13/1/2000) P/FL 37+12/14 FLC 2+2/1 FAC 0+1

HELIN Petri Juhani
Born: Helsinki, Finland, 13 December 1969
Height: 5'11" Weight: 13.2
International Honours: Finland: 21
Petri joined Second Division Luton Town during the Scandinavian close season and made a fine debut for the Hatters, scoring a late equaliser to save a point at Bury. He added stability in the centre of the park and featured regularly apart from a short absence in the new year with a foot problem. An experienced right-sided midfield player he distributes the ball accurately and can deliver a fine defence-splitting pass. Petri added to his tally of caps during his stay at Kenilworth Road when he came on for his country from the subs' bench in the closing stages of the World Cup qualifier against England at Anfield.
Luton T (Free from FC Jokerit, Finland, ex Ikast, PPT Pon, HJK Helsinki, on 2/11/2000) FL 23/1 FAC 3 Others 1

HEMMINGS Anthony (Tony) George
Born: Burton, 21 September 1967
Height: 5'10" Weight: 12.10
Club Honours: FAT '96; GMVC '97
International Honours: E: SP-1
Tony linked up with his old boss Ian Atkins at Carlisle shortly before the start of the 2000-01 campaign and initially featured in a left-wing-back role. He appeared regularly in the first two months of the campaign but always looked more comfortable going forward and it was no surprise when he later switched to playing on the left side of midfield. He failed to register a goal but provided the cross from the left flank that enabled Scott Dobie to equalise in the 1-1 draw against Plymouth in February. He was out of contract in the summer.
Wycombe W (£25,000 from Northwich Vic on 8/9/1993) FL 28+21/12 FLC 1+5 FAC 2+2/1 Others 3+3/1 (Free to Macclesfield T on 31/10/1995)
Chester C (£30,000 from Ilkeston T on 21/1/2000) FL 19/2
Carlisle U (Free on 8/8/2000) FL 16+6 FLC 1 FAC 2

HENCHOZ Stephane
Born: Billens, Switzerland, 7 September 1974
Height: 6'1" Weight: 12.10
Club Honours: FLC '01; FAC '01; UEFAC '01
International Honours: Switzerland: 50; U21; Yth
After such an effective season in the Liverpool defence in 1999-2000 Stephane looked a little unsure at the start of last term and briefly lost his place in the team as manager Gerard Houllier experimented with different defensive formations. A return to his original defensive formation in late November saw Stephane's partnership with Sami Hyppia blossom again and he went on to play in all but three of the remaining games of the campaign, gaining winners' medals in the FA Cup, Worthington Cup and UEFA Cup as the Reds strode to a remarkable treble. A trojan in defence he occasionally showed a lack of composure under pressure but nevertheless the Henchoz-Hyppia partnership is probably Liverpool's strongest central defensive pairing since the days of Alan Hansen and Mark Lawrenson. At the end of the season he was voted as the top Swiss player playing outside the country and there is no doubt this honour was well deserved.
Blackburn Rov (£3,000,000 from Hamburg, Germany, ex FC Bulle, Neuchatel Xamax, on 14/7/1997) PL 70 FLC 3+1 FAC 6 Others 2
Liverpool (£3,750,000 on 20/7/1999) PL 61 FLC 8 FAC 7 Others 10

HENDERSON Darius Alexis
Born: Sutton, 7 September 1981
Height: 6'0" Weight: 12.8
Having broken into the Reading first team at the end of 1999-2000 Darius continued to develop at a steady rate last term. His first-team opportunities were very much limited by the consistent form of Martin Butler and Jamie Cureton but he made a handful of appearances, mostly from the subs' bench. A powerfully built bustling striker he was a regular in the Royals' reserve team that did so well in the Avon Combination last term.
Reading (From trainee on 15/12/1999) FL 2+8 FLC 1 Others 0+1

HENDERSON Kevin Malcolm
Born: Ashington, 8 June 1974
Height: 6'3" Weight: 13.2
Hartlepool's hard-working front-runner was finally rewarded with a regular first-team place in 2000-01. He steadily grew in confidence and scored regularly throughout the campaign, finishing with a tally of 17 league goals, thus making him the club's most successful striker for 10 years. Crucially for Pool he appeared in the disappointing end of season play-offs against Blackpool when not fully fit. He is a big strong striker who works hard and has good pace.
Burnley (Signed from Morpeth T on 17/12/1997) FL 0+14/1 FLC 0+2 Others 0+4/1
Hartlepool U (Free on 2/7/1999) FL 63+12/25 FLC 2+1 FAC 1+1 Others 5+1/3

HENDON Ian Michael
Born: Ilford, 5 December 1971
Height: 6'0" Weight: 12.10
Club Honours: FAYC '90; CS '91; Div 3 '98
International Honours: E: U21-7; Yth
This skilful right wing back began last season at Northampton Town but was quickly snapped up by First Division Sheffield Wednesday where he quickly made the right back position his own. His influence was such that he was clearly missed when absent through injury and he contributed two goals including a 25-yard deflected free kick that earned the Owls a point against local rivals Sheffield United last December. Ian reads the game well and is very composed on the ball, using his dribbling talents to play his way out of defence.
Tottenham H (From trainee on 20/12/1989) FL 0+4 FLC 1 Others 0+2
Portsmouth (Loaned on 16/1/1992) FL 1+3
Leyton Orient (Loaned on 26/3/1992) FL 5+1
Barnsley (Loaned on 17/3/1993) FL 6
Leyton Orient (£50,000 on 9/8/1993) FL 130+1/5 FLC 8 FAC 7 Others 12/1
Birmingham C (Loaned on 23/3/1995) FL 4
Notts Co (£50,000 on 24/2/1997) FL 82/6 FLC 5/1 FAC 8+1
Northampton T (£30,000 on 25/3/1999) FL 60/3 FLC 4 FAC 1/1 Others 1
Sheffield Wed (£40,000 + on 12/10/2000) FL 31/2 FAC 2

HENDRIE Lee Andrew
Born: Birmingham, 18 May 1977
Height: 5'10" Weight: 10.3
International Honours: E: 1; B-1; U21-13; Yth
Lee featured regularly in the Aston Villa side last season and produced a string of consistent displays. Although remaining relatively free from injuries in comparison to recent years, he suffered some disciplinary problems receiving red cards on two occasions. However his performances appeared to get progressively better as the season wore on and he returned to his best form in the final weeks. A spell of three

goals in three games confirmed this - the final one in the sequence being a superb strike smashed into the roof of the net in the 2-2 draw with West Ham. He is a creative midfield player with good pace and the skill to unlock the tightest of defences.
Aston Villa (From trainee on 18/5/1994) PL 91+26/13 FLC 4+2/3 FAC 6+8 Others 6+3

HENDRY Edward **Colin** James
Born: Keith, 7 December 1965
Height: 6'1" Weight: 12.7
Club Honours: FMC '87; PL '95; SLC '98; SPD '99; SC '99
International Honours: S: 51; B-1
Colin appeared for Coventry in the opening day defeat by Middlesbrough last term but then fell out of favour and made only one further appearance from the subs' bench. In December he joined Bolton Wanderers on loan where he proved to be the signing of the season. Initially coming for three months he quickly slotted into the team and established a formidable partnership at the heart of the defence with Gudni Bergsson. He was particularly outstanding in his early games for the Wanderers and the deal was eventually made permanent in March. Despite his advancing years he was a commanding, never-say-die figure at the back and also chipped in with some important goals. A regular for Scotland he netted two goals in the World Cup qualifier against San Marino.
Dundee (Signed from Islavale on 1/7/1983) SL 17+24/2 SC 2+3/1
Blackburn Rov (£30,000 on 11/3/1987) FL 99+3/22 FLC 4 FAC 3 Others 13/1
Manchester C (£700,000 on 16/11/1989) FL 57+6/5 FLC 4+1/1 FAC 5/2 Others 4/2
Blackburn Rov (£700,000 on 8/11/1991) P/FL 229+5/12 FLC 23 FAC 17+1 Others 11
Glasgow R (£4,000,000 on 5/8/1998) SL 18+3 SLC 3+1 SC 3 Others 4+1
Coventry C (£750,000 on 3/3/2000) PL 10+1
Bolton W (£250,000 on 15/12/2000) FL 22/3 FAC 1 Others 3

HENRY Anthony Francis
Born: Stepney, 13 September 1979
Height: 6'1" Weight: 13.8
This young central defender was still recovering from a fractured foot when the 2000-2001 season started. He made his come back for Lincoln in the reserves last September only to find himself out of favour at Sincil Bank. He had two loan spells at Conference club Northwich Victoria before eventually making his first and only Third Division appearance of the campaign against Leyton Orient in February. His lack of regular first-team football showed and he was substituted after only 45 minutes of what proved to be manager Phil Stant's final match before he left the club. Anthony was released at the end of the campaign.
West Ham U (From trainee on 6/6/1997)
Lincoln C (Free on 5/8/1999) FL 15+3/1 FAC 2 Others 1/1

HENRY Karl Levi Daniel
Born: Wolverhampton, 26 November 1982
Height: 6'1" Weight: 10.13
International Honours: E: Yth
Captain of Stoke City's U19 Academy team, Karl stepped up to make his debut in senior football when he came off the subs' bench for the final 20 minutes of the LDV Vans Trophy tie against Walsall. A talented young midfield player he is comfortable on the ball and has the vision to open up defences. Having signed an extension to his contract during the season he went on to make his debut for England U18s against Switzerland at the end of May.
Stoke C (From trainee on 30/11/1999) Others 0+1

HENRY Nicholas (Nick) Ian
Born: Liverpool, 21 February 1969
Height: 5'6" Weight: 10.12
Club Honours: Div 2 '91
Nick had a somewhat difficult time at Tranmere last season, for after featuring regularly in the opening matches he was diagnosed as suffering from a blood disorder that affected his energy levels. The problem was eventually treated but he then found it hard to win his place back in the team when he was fully fit. A hard-working midfield player he is sharp in the tackle and passes the ball intelligently. He was released on a free transfer in the summer.
Oldham Ath (From trainee on 6/7/1987) F/PL 264+9/19 FLC 30+4/3 FAC 21 Others 5
Sheffield U (£500,000 on 28/2/1997) FL 13+3 FAC 2+1 Others 2
Walsall (Free on 25/3/1999) FL 8
Tranmere Rov (Free on 5/7/1999) FL 45+5/1 FLC 9+1/1 FAC 5+3/1

Thierry Henry

HENRY Thierry
Born: Paris, France, 17 August 1977
Height: 6'1" Weight: 12.2
International Honours: France: 29 (UEFA '00); Yth; (UEFA-U18 '96)
Now established as one of the world's top strikers Thierry enjoyed another excellent season with Arsenal. He notched up 22 goals during the campaign, including a spectacular 30-yard strike against Manchester United at Highbury in October and the vital headed winner in the Champions League clash in Lyon. A striker with lightning pace he also possesses fantastic skill, a wide shooting range and the ability to conjure chances from nothing. Despite playing mostly in a central role he often pulls out onto the flanks where his speed enables him to pass opposition full backs with ease. A regular for his country he finished fourth in the 'European Footballer of the Year' poll and collected the French 'Player of the Year' award. He was also honoured by his fellow professionals who voted him into the PFA's Premiership team.
Arsenal (£8,000,000 from Juventus, Italy, ex Monaco, on 6/8/1999) PL 53+13/34 FLC 2/1 FAC 6+1/1 Others 21+5/12

HERBERT Robert
Born: Durham, 29 August 1983
Height: 5'8" Weight: 11.0
This young Halifax Town prospect came on from the subs' bench in the opening game of last season at Carlisle but only featured occasionally in the first team thereafter. An energetic midfield player with good distribution he was affected by a series of niggling injuries but continued to look useful in his appearances in the club's reserves. He will be aiming to extend his senior experience in the 2001-02 campaign.
Halifax T (From trainee on 28/10/2000) FL 4+9/1 FLC 0+1 FAC 0+1 Others 0+1

HERNANDEZ Ferdino (Dino) Francio
Born: Amersfoort, Holland, 25 July 1971
Height: 5'11" Weight: 11.6
Having been released by AZ Alkmaar, Dino had trials with a number of clubs including Barnsley, Clydebank (where he made a single Scottish League appearance) and Dunfermline before signing a three-month contract for Wigan Athletic at the beginning of November. He featured in the FA Cup first round tie against Dorchester but otherwise failed to break into the Latics' first team and returned to Holland shortly before Christmas. A left-footed midfield player or striker he is comfortable on the ball, has good pace and can deliver an effective cross from the wing.
Clydebank (Free from AZ Alkmaar, Holland, via trial at Barnsley, ex Quick, FC Utrecht, on 15/8/2000) SL 1 (Freed on 31/8/2000)
Wigan Ath Free, via trial at Dunfermline Ath, on 2/11/2000) FAC 1

HERRERA Roberto (Robbie)
Born: Torquay, 12 June 1970
Height: 5'7" Weight: 10.6
Never the world's most adventurous when overlapping, Robbie had always compensated for this with a solid defensive game and tidy if cautious distribution. When Torquay switched from a wing back system to a 4-4-2 formation last season this appeared to suit his style as a left back perfectly, but he seemed to suffer a loss of

form not helped by a series of niggling injuries and did not feature for the Gulls after the end of March. He was released at the end of the season.
Queens Park R (From trainee on 1/3/1988) FL 4+2 FLC 1+2 Others 1+1
Torquay U (Loaned on 17/3/1992) FL 11
Torquay U (Loaned on 24/10/1992) FL 5
Fulham (Signed on 29/10/1993) FL 143+2/1 FLC 15 FAC 13 Others 7+1
Torquay U (£30,000 on 4/8/1998) FL 102+2/1 FLC 5 FAC 5 Others 3

HESKEY Emile William Ivanhoe
Born: Leicester, 11 January 1978
Height: 6'2" Weight: 13.12
Club Honours: FLC '97, '00, '01; FAC '01; UEFAC '01
International Honours: E: 16; B-1; U21-16; Yth
Although one or two observers questioned Liverpool manager Gerard Houllier's wisdom when he signed Emile towards the end of the 1999-2000 campaign those doubts were laid to rest when he netted a hat-trick in the 4-0 win at Derby in October. A run of 12 goals in 12 games confirmed that he was one of the top strikers in the country and at times he outshone both Robbie Fowler and Michael Owen in the Reds' attack as he provided a physical presence and aerial threat lacking from the more lightweight forwards. He continued to score consistently throughout the season and even when rested due to the manager's rotation policy he came off the bench to net some vital late goals, most notably the winner with a bullet header in the FA Cup semi-final against Wycombe Wanderers when the team had seemingly run out of ideas against a stubborn defence. He ran himself into the ground in the epic UEFA Cup struggles with Roma and Barcelona often playing as a lone striker. Understandably he tired towards the end of the season but Houllier kept faith with him and selected him for the starting line-ups for both the FA Cup and UEFA Cup finals. Much more than a 'target' striker, he can shield and hold the ball well, is difficult to dispossess and has surprising pace for such a big man. His England career continued with an appearance in the World Cup qualifier in Finland in October and he then became a regular in the squad under new coach Sven Goran Eriksson who selected him for all five international matches during his reign.
Leicester C (From trainee on 3/10/1995) PL 143+11/40 FLC 25+2/6 FAC 11 Others 5
Liverpool (£11,000,000 on 10/3/2000) PL 45+3/17 FLC 3+1 FAC 3+2/5 Others 9+2/3

HESSENTHALER Andrew (Andy)
Born: Dartford, 17 June 1965
Height: 5'7" Weight: 11.5
International Honours: E: SP-1
Andy was appointed player-manager of Gillingham when Peter Taylor departed for Leicester and led the club through an excellent campaign in which they established themselves in the First Division. Voted the Nationwide 'Player of the Month' for September - the first ever player-manager to receive the award - his season came to an abrupt end in the FA Cup third round tie at Bournemouth in January when he sustained a horrific gash to his left leg that kept him out of action until the summer. A very competitive central midfield player who provides inspirational leadership in the centre of the park he also contributed two goals during the season.
Watford (£65,000 from Redbridge Forest on 12/9/1991) FL 195/12 FLC 13/1 FAC 5/2 Others 4
Gillingham (£235,000 on 7/8/1996) FL 176+8/16 FLC 18/2 FAC 13+1/2 Others 9+1/3

Andy Hessenthaler

HEWLETT Matthew (Matt) Paul
Born: Bristol, 25 February 1976
Height: 6'2" Weight: 11.3
International Honours: E: Yth
Matt joined Swindon Town in the 2000 close season following a disappointing campaign with Bristol City and went on to provide one of the few success stories at the County Ground last term. He put in some sterling displays in the opening matches before being sidelined by a cruciate ligament injury in October but fought his way back into the line-up in February and was a key figure in the Robins' successful struggle against relegation. He is an attacking midfielder who tackles well and has good skill on the ball.
Bristol C (From trainee on 12/8/1993) FL 111+16/9 FLC 10+2 FAC 4+1/2 Others 7+2/1
Burnley (Loaned on 27/11/1998) FL 2 Others 1
Swindon T (Free on 27/7/2000) FL 25+1 FLC 4 Others 1

HEYWOOD Matthew (Matty) Stephen
Born: Chatham, 26 August 1979
Height: 6'2" Weight: 14.0
Although he was unable to break into a strong Burnley squad last term Matty captained the reserve team before moving on to Swindon Town in January where he helped to shore up a defence that had leaked goals during the first half of the season. He went on to produce some inspired performances and also weighed in with a couple of goals including an important winner at Brentford which helped to ease the club's relegation fears. He is a powerful no-nonsense central defender who tackles well and distributes the ball sensibly.
Burnley (From trainee on 6/7/1998) FL 11+2 FAC 1 Others 1
Swindon T (Free on 22/1/2001) FL 21/2 Others 2

HIBBERT Anthony (Tony) James
Born: Liverpool, 20 February 1981
Height: 5'8" Weight: 11.3
Club Honours: FAYC '98
A regular at the heart of midfield in Everton's championship winning reserve side, Tony showed he could successfully make the step up to Premiership level with a handful of appearances in the run-in to the season. His courage was highlighted on his first-team debut at West Ham when a fully committed challenge with the imposing figure of Stuart Pearce earned a vital penalty for his side, and saw the Hammers' hard-man red-carded! Tony made two more substitute appearances after that and will be anxious to build on his first-team flirtation next season.
Everton (From trainee on 1/7/1998) PL 1+2

HICKS Stuart Jason
Born: Peterborough, 30 May 1967
Height: 6'1" Weight: 13.0
Stuart quickly settled into a central defensive role at Mansfield last season and his experience proved invaluable to the youngsters around him. His tenacity and never-say-die attitude made him an instant hit with the fans before he went down with a series of injuries after the turn of the year. He eventually needed an operation to reconstruct cruciate knee ligaments and he is expected to be out of action for some time.
Peterborough U (From apprentice on 10/8/1984)
Colchester U (Free from Wisbech on 24/3/1988) FL 57+7 FLC 2 FAC 5/1 Others 5
Scunthorpe U (Free on 19/8/1990) FL 67/1 FLC 4 FAC 4/1 Others 8
Doncaster Rov (Free on 10/8/1992) FL 36 FLC 2 FAC 1 Others 2
Huddersfield T (Signed on 27/8/1993) FL 20+2/1 FLC 3 FAC 3 Others 1
Preston NE (Signed on 24/3/1994) FL 11+1 FLC 2 Others 1/1
Scarborough (Signed on 22/2/1995) FL 81+4/2 FLC 5 FAC 4 Others 3
Leyton Orient (Free on 5/8/1997) FL 77+1 FLC 9 FAC 6 Others 2+1
Chester C (Free on 25/2/2000) FL 13
Mansfield T (Free on 13/7/2000) FL 25 FLC 4 FAC 1

HIGGINBOTHAM Daniel (Danny) John
Born: Manchester, 29 December 1978
Height: 6'1" Weight: 12.6
Having signed during the close season Danny immediately slotted into the left-wing back role at Derby last term. He took time to settle and often found himself on the substitutes' bench early on, but as the season progressed he displayed a fine touch on the ball and an aggressive tackling technique. However some of his best performances came when he played as a left-sided centre

back later in the campaign and it may well be that this turns out to be his best position.
Manchester U (From trainee on 10/7/1997) PL 2+2 FLC 1 Others 1+1
Derby Co (£2,000,000 on 12/7/2000) PL 23+3 FLC 3+1 FAC 2+1

HIGGINS Alexander (Alex) John
Born: Sheffield, 22 July 1981
Height: 5'9" Weight: 11.6
International Honours: E: Yth; Sch
After developing through the ranks at Hillsborough Alex joined Queens Park Rangers on the transfer deadline day last March but featured mainly in the reserve side at Loftus Road. He was called up for his Football League debut when he came on from the subs' bench for the final ten minutes of the last game of the season at Wolves. A promising midfield player he will be aiming to gain further senior experience in the 2001-02 campaign. Out of contract in the summer, he was released by Rangers.
Sheffield Wed (From trainee on 16/11/1998)
Queens Park R (Free on 22/3/2001) FL 0+1

HIGGS Shane Peter
Born: Oxford, 13 May 1977
Height: 6'2" Weight: 12.12
Shane was again Cheltenham Town's second-choice goalkeeper last season. He was an ever-present for the reserves and made his senior debut for the Robins when he appeared in the LDV Vans Trophy tie against Southend. Later in the season he made a single appearance from the subs' bench when he replaced the injured Steve Book for the last hour of the Third Division game at Barnet when he gave a competent performance. Shane is a useful shot stopper but needs to gain further first team experience.
Bristol Rov (From trainee on 17/7/1995) FL 10 Others 2 (Free to Worcester C on 11/7/1998)
Cheltenham T (£10,000 on 21/6/1999) FL 0+1 Others 1

HIGNETT Craig John
Born: Prescot, 12 January 1970
Height: 5'9" Weight: 11.10
Club Honours: Div 1 '95
Craig had a disappointing time at Blackburn last season after his big money transfer from Barnsley in the summer. He suffered an achilles injury before the start of the campaign and it was not until October that he eventually appeared for the first team. He then struggled to establish himself in the side, often featuring as a substitute rather than making the starting line-up. When given his chance he produced some solid rather than spectacular performances although he netted stunning goals from free kicks against Stockport and Bolton.
Crewe Alex (From trainee at Liverpool on 11/5/1988) FL 108+13/42 FLC 9+1/4 FAC 11+1/8 Others 6+1/3
Middlesbrough (£500,000 on 27/11/1992) F/PL 126+30/33 FLC 19+3/12 FAC 9+2/3 Others 5+1
Aberdeen (Free on 1/7/1998) SL 13/2 SLC 2
Barnsley (£800,000 on 26/11/1998) FL 62+4/28 FLC 2 FAC 6/5 Others 3/2
Blackburn Rov (£2,250,000 on 14/7/2000) FL 15+15/3 FAC 2+3/2

HILEY Scott Patrick
Born: Plymouth, 27 September 1968
Height: 5'9" Weight: 11.5
Club Honours: Div 4 '90
Having been out of favour with Portsmouth boss Tony Pulis at the start of last season, Scott's career at Fratton Park was resurrected by Steve Claridge and he went on to hit some of his best-ever form. Playing either at right back or in the centre of defence he performed consistently well, even when the team was struggling, and impressed the Pompey faithful with his excellent first touch, ability to read the game and composure in difficult situations. His fine performances won him the supporters' 'Player of the Year' award.
Exeter C (From trainee on 4/8/1986) FL 205+5/12 FLC 17 FAC 14 Others 16+2
Birmingham C (£100,000 on 12/3/1994) FL 49 FLC 7 FAC 1 Others 2
Manchester C (£250,000 on 23/2/1996) P/FL 4+5
Southampton (Free on 4/8/1998) PL 30+2 FAC 1
Portsmouth (£200,000 on 3/12/1999) FL 38+4 FLC 1 FAC 2

HILL Clinton (Clint) Scott
Born: Huyton, 19 October 1978
Height: 6'0" Weight: 11.6
A rugged and powerful defender, Clint again produced some committed displays for Tranmere last season while managing a considerable improvement in his disciplinary record, for although he accumulated a number of yellow cards he received no red ones during the campaign. Solid at the back he continued to provide a threat when moving up to join the attack and netted six valuable goals. He is likely to be a key figure for Rovers next term as they seek to win promotion back to the First Division.
Tranmere Rov (From trainee on 9/7/1997) FL 108+2/14 FLC 17/3 FAC 6+1/1

HILL Daniel (Danny) Ronald
Born: Enfield, 1 October 1974
Height: 5'9" Weight: 11.10
International Honours: E: U21-4; Yth
Danny had a disappointing time at Cardiff in 2000-01 for although he enjoyed an early season run in the team he soon lost his place and his only senior appearance after mid-October came in the LDV Vans Trophy tie against Brighton. Earlier in the campaign he scored a goal of rare quality when he netted with a delicate chip in the 1-1 draw, also against Brighton. He is a creative midfield player who is capable of opening up opposing defences. With no recognised reserve team at Ninian Park he had few opportunities at any level and was released in May.
Tottenham H (From trainee on 9/9/1992) PL 4+6 FLC 0+2 Others 1
Birmingham C (Loaned on 24/11/1995) FL 5 FLC 2
Watford (Loaned on 15/2/1996) FL 1
Cardiff C (Loaned on 19/2/1998) FL 7
Oxford U (Free on 30/7/1998) FL 1+8 FLC 0+1
Cardiff C (Free on 12/11/1998) FL 33+25/4 FLC 2 FAC 3+3 Others 3

HILL Keith John
Born: Bolton, 17 May 1969
Height: 6'0" Weight: 12.6
Keith started the 2000-01 season in excellent form in central defence for Rochdale, but lost his place through injury. He then had to bide his time as the partnership between Dave Bayliss and Mark Monington proved equally successful. Dale manager Steve Parkin elected to change his centre half partnership only if one became unavailable through injury or suspension. Keith regained his place for two short spells only to have to drop out again through injury or suspension. He is a commanding centre half known for his consistent performances. He was reported to have signed for Cheltenham in the summer.
Blackburn Rov (From juniors on 9/5/1987) F/PL 89+7/3 FLC 6/1 FAC 5+1 Others 3+2
Plymouth Arg (Signed on 23/9/1992) FL 117+6/2 FLC 9 FAC 10 Others 9
Rochdale (Free on 3/7/1996) FL 171+5/6 FLC 10 FAC 8 Others 6/1

HILL Kevin
Born: Exeter, 6 March 1976
Height: 5'8" Weight: 10.3
This all-action midfield dynamo gave his best performances for Torquay last season when left free to roam in the centre of midfield although he was also used in a wide left role at times. Kevin has the stamina to get from box to box, the knack of arriving unmarked in scoring positions and surprisingly good heading ability for his height but it was still a surprise that he should finish the 2000-01 campaign as the Gulls leading scorer. He contributed to the club's late dash to safety with headed goals in the vital end-of-season games against York and Barnet.
Torquay U (Free from Torrington on 8/8/1997) FL 135+24/23 FLC 8+1/1 FAC 11/1 Others 6+1/1

HILL Matthew (Matt) Clayton
Born: Bristol, 26 March 1981
Height: 5'7" Weight: 12.6
After making his debut in 1999-2000, Matt became a regular in Bristol City's back four last season. A versatile defender who can play either at left back or centre half he impressed with his tigerish tackling and speedy recovery. One of several promising graduates from City's youth set-up he was voted 'Young Player of the Year' by the club's Junior Strikers section.
Bristol C (From trainee on 22/2/1999) FL 40+11 FLC 1 FAC 6 Others 3+2

HILL Nicholas (Nicky) Damien
Born: Accrington, 26 February 1981
Height: 6'0" Weight: 12.3
Nicky was finally given an extended run in the Bury first team last March when Sam Collins was sidelined by injury and he grabbed his opportunity with both hands. He performed with the confidence and ability of a seasoned professional in the closing weeks of the campaign only to miss the final two games after breaking his nose in a training ground accident. One of several promising

youngsters on the books at Gigg Lane, Nicky is a big strong central defender.
Bury (From trainee on 9/7/1999) FL 12+3 Others 2+1

HILLIER David
Born: Blackheath, 19 December 1969
Height: 5'10" Weight: 12.5
Club Honours: FAYC '88; Div 1 '91
International Honours: E: U21-1
After undergoing a knee operation in the summer of 2000 to resolve problems he had encountered in the final months of the 1999-2000 campaign, David then had the misfortune to suffer a broken toe in the treatment room. He eventually returned to the Bristol Rovers first team at Swindon in October but managed just three starts during the season. He is an experienced central midfield player who is comfortable on the ball and is an expert with dead-ball kicks.
Arsenal (From trainee on 11/2/1988) F/PL 82+22/2 FLC 13+2 FAC 13+2 Others 5+4
Portsmouth (£250,000 on 2/11/1996) FL 62+5/4 FLC 3/2 FAC 4/1
Bristol Rov (£15,000 on 24/2/1999) FL 55+1 FLC 4 FAC 1 Others 1+1

HILLS John David
Born: Blackpool, 21 April 1978
Height: 5'9" Weight: 11.2
This left-sided Blackpool defender missed the first ten weeks of the 2000-01 campaign after pulling a hamstring in a pre-season friendly. He returned to the Tangerines' first team at Mansfield in October but suffered a recurrence of the injury at the turn of the year and was absent for much of the second half of the season. John likes to get forward and delivers a good cross from the flank. His enthusiasm and commitment to the cause make him a crowd favourite. He was back in the team for the play-offs and scored a valuable goal in the second leg of the semi-final against Hartlepool.
Blackpool (From trainee on 27/10/1995)
Everton (£90,000 on 4/11/1995) PL 1+2
Swansea C (Loaned on 30/1/1997) FL 11/1
Swansea C (Loaned on 22/8/1997) FL 7
Blackpool (£75,000 on 16/1/1998) FL 96+2/6 FLC 3 FAC 6 Others 6+1/1

HIMSWORTH Gary Paul
Born: Pickering, 19 December 1969
Height: 5'8" Weight: 10.6
Now in his second spell at Darlington this busy utility player featured in the majority of games in the first four months of last season before suffering a knee injury in the FA Cup tie at Luton in December. He spent some time out of action and failed to make a further appearance during the campaign. Although at his best on the left this skilful and adroit player can fulfil any number of roles in defence and midfield.
York C (From trainee on 27/1/1988) FL 74+14/8 FLC 5 Others 5+2
Scarborough (Free on 5/12/1990) FL 83+9/6 FLC 7+2/1 FAC 1+1 Others 6+1
Darlington (Free on 16/7/1993) FL 86+8/8 FLC 5+1 FAC 6 Others 7/4
York C (£25,000 on 16/2/1996) FL 60+9/3 FLC 4 FAC 6+2/1 Others 3/1
Darlington (Signed on 5/3/1999) FL 41+7/1 FLC 4+1 FAC 4+1

HINCHCLIFFE Andrew (Andy) George
Born: Manchester, 5 February 1969
Height: 5'10" Weight: 13.7
Club Honours: FAC '95; CS '95
International Honours: E: 7; U21-1; Yth
This experienced Sheffield Wednesday defender had a frustrating time in the 2000-01 season when he was dogged by an ongoing achilles problem. After appearing in the early fixtures he spent a couple of months out, returning in November for three matches before aggravating the injury and he was then out until April when he made just one further first-team appearance. When fully fit he is a hard-working left back with a good cross who adds a touch of class to the team.
Manchester C (From apprentice on 13/2/1986) FL 107+5/8 FLC 11/1 FAC 12/1 Others 4/1
Everton (£800,000 on 17/7/1990) F/PL 170+12/7 FLC 21+2/1 FAC 12+2/1 Others 8
Sheffield Wed (£2,850,000 on 30/1/1998) P/FL 85/7 FLC 4 FAC 6

HINDS Richard Paul
Born: Sheffield, 22 August 1980
Height: 6'2" Weight: 11.0
Richard began to establish himself in the Tranmere first team in the early stages of last season producing a number of calm and mature displays in defence. A key player in the club's reserves his campaign came to a premature end in March when he suffered a leg injury. A centre back who passes the ball accurately he can also play in a midfield role if required.
Tranmere Rov (From juniors on 20/7/1998) FL 30+7 FLC 3+3 FAC 5

HINTON Craig
Born: Wolverhampton, 26 November 1977
Height: 6'0" Weight: 12.0
Club Honours: NC '00
This solid and reliable central defender was the only player to be ever-present for Kidderminster in their inaugural season in the Football League. He also proved useful when moving up to assist the attack at set pieces and he contributed goals against Leyton Orient and Shrewsbury. Craig was rewarded for some fine displays when he took over as captain in the closing matches and was deservedly voted 'Player of the Year' by the Harriers' supporters.
Birmingham C (From trainee on 5/7/1996)
Kidderminster Hrs (Free on 12/8/1998) FL 46/2 FLC 2 FAC 3 Others 2

HISLOP Neil **Shaka**
Born: Hackney, 22 February 1969
Height: 6'4" Weight: 14.4
Club Honours: Div 2 '94
International Honours: E: U21-1. Trinidad & Tobago: 7
Shaka had a somewhat disappointing season at West Ham last term although he played in all but four of the club's Premiership games. Despite knee problems, a virus and a shoulder injury he mostly played on, while the constant changes in the Hammers back line didn't make things any easier for him. A fine shot stopper he was particularly impressive in the 1-1 draw at Ipswich in October. On the international front he continued to feature occasionally for Trinidad & Tobago but for much of the campaign he was second choice in goal behind Crewe's Clayton Ince.
Reading (Signed from Howard University, USA on 9/9/1992) FL 104 FLC 10 FAC 3 Others 9
Newcastle U (£1,575,000 on 10/8/1995) PL 53 FLC 8 FAC 6 Others 4
West Ham U (Free on 8/7/1998) PL 93 FLC 10 FAC 7 Others 9

HITCHEN Steven (Steve) James
Born: Salford, 28 November 1976
Height: 5'8" Weight: 11.8
Although he is a right-footed player Steve started the 2000-2001 season at Macclesfield in the left-back position but was then sidelined for over six weeks with a knee injury. He returned in November to play at right back, a role to which he is more accustomed and kept his place in the Macc line-up for the remainder of the season. Steve is a defender who is effective in the tackle, distributes the ball well and likes to push forward down the flanks.
Blackburn Rov (From trainee on 4/7/1995)
Macclesfield T (Free on 14/7/1997) FL 75+4 FLC 4+1 FAC 5 Others 1

HITZLSPERGER Thomas
Born: Munich, Germany, 5 April 1982
Height: 6'0" Weight: 12.5
International Honours: Germany: Yth
Having developed with Bayern Munich from a very early age Thomas opted for a change of scene last summer and was snapped up by Aston Villa. A technically gifted midfield play maker with a cultured left foot he mostly featured in the reserve and youth teams at Villa Park last term but stepped up for his senior debut when coming on as a substitute for the final six minutes of the home game with Liverpool in January. Capped by Germany at youth level he first came to prominence playing for his country in the 1999 World U17 Youth Championships in New Zealand.
Aston Villa (Free from Bayern Munich, Germany on 8/8/2000) PL 0+1

HJELDE Jon Olav
Born: Levanger, Norway, 30 April 1972
Height: 6'1" Weight: 13.7
Club Honours: Div 1 '98
The big Norwegian had a mixed start to the 2000-01 campaign with Nottingham Forest, heading home the winner in the opening game of the season against West Bromwich Albion and then falling victim to a hip injury that kept him out of action until February. He returned for the home win against Grimsby and proceeded to put on some of his best defensive performances since joining the club. A tall central defender he is strong in the air and solid on the ground.
Nottingham F (£600,000 from Rosenborg, Norway on 8/8/1997) P/FL 75+14/4 FLC 7/2 FAC 4

HJORTH Jesper
Born: Denmark, 3 April 1975
Height: 6'0" Weight: 12.4
This popular Dane was again a great favourite of the Darlington fans last season.

Although he seldom featured for the whole game and was often used from the subs' bench he impressed with his strong running, close control and powerful shooting. He netted just one goal during the campaign, scoring from just inside the box in the 2-1 defeat at Blackpool last November. He was released by the Quakers in the summer.

Darlington (Signed from OB Odense, Denmark on 11/11/1999) FL 16+29/7 FLC 4 FAC 0+4 Others 4+2

HOBSON Gary
Born: Hull, 12 November 1972
Height: 6'1" Weight: 13.3

Gary joined York City from Chester in July 2000 but had a frustrating time in his first season at Bootham Crescent. He impressed at the heart of the defence in the early games but was then sidelined by a knee injury that required surgery and it was not until the closing weeks of the campaign that he returned to take a place on the subs' bench. He is a left-footed defender who can play either as a centre half or left back.

Hull C (From trainee on 17/7/1991) FL 135+7 FLC 13+1 FAC 2+2/1 Others 6
Brighton & Hove A (£60,000 on 27/3/1996) FL 92+6/1 FLC 7 FAC 4+1 Others 3
Chester C (Signed on 7/1/2000) FL 20
York C (Free on 17/7/2000) FL 8+3 FLC 1

HOCKING Matthew (Matt) James
Born: Boston, 30 January 1978
Height: 5'11" Weight: 11.12

Matt enjoyed two extended spells in the centre of defence for York City last season and acquitted himself very well on both occasions. A versatile player who has previously played at right back and on the right side of midfield he has good pace and reads the game well.

Sheffield U (From trainee on 16/5/1996)
Hull C (£25,000 on 19/9/1997) FL 55+2/2 FLC 6 FAC 4 Others 4
York C (£30,000 on 25/3/1999) FL 54+10/2 FLC 2+1 FAC 1+2 Others 1

HOCKLEY Matthew (Matt)
Born: Paignton, 5 June 1982
Height: 5'10" Weight: 11.7

This first-year professional made his debut senior football for Torquay against Southend United in an FA Cup tie last November and confirmed his reputation as an effective man-marker the following Saturday when he blotted out Barnet star Darren Currie to pave the way for a vital win for the Gulls. He is a calm and efficient defender who can play either in the centre of defence or at right back. He is the brother of Wayne Hockley a former trainee at Plainmoor who made a couple of appearances for the Gulls in the 1996-97 season.

Torquay U (From trainee on 4/7/2000) FL 4+2/1 FAC 2 Others 1

HODGE John
Born: Skelmersdale, 1 April 1969
Height: 5'7" Weight: 11.12
Club Honours: AMC '94

John is a talented wide right-sided midfield player with the ability to run at opposition defenders and cross the ball accurately. He opened his goal account for Northampton in the 2-1 win against Bury last January with a cracking effort which saw him dance his way through the opposition defence before shooting home from the edge of the box. John also had a spell at wing back for the Cobblers last season when the club was beset by injury problems.

Exeter C (Signed from Falmouth T on 12/9/1991) FL 57+8/10 FLC 3/1 FAC 2 Others 8+2/1
Swansea C (Signed on 14/7/1993) FL 87+25/10 FLC 6+2/3 FAC 6 Others 13+4
Walsall (Free on 23/9/1996) FL 67+9/12 FLC 5 FAC 7+1/2 Others 5+2
Gillingham (Free on 10/7/1998) FL 8+41/1 FLC 4+1 FAC 3+2/1 Others 2+4
Northampton T (£25,000 on 7/3/2000) FL 29+12/1 FLC 0+2 FAC 0+1

HODGES John Kenneth
Born: Leicester, 22 January 1980
Height: 6'0" Weight: 11.13

John was signed by Plymouth Argyle during the 2000 close season with the aim of providing regular 'keeper Jon Sheffield with some competition. He made his debut for the Pilgrims at Brighton in October and enjoyed a brief run in the team before losing his place following the FA Cup defeat by Conference outfit Chester City. Shortly afterwards Romain Larrieu arrived at Home Park and John was released.

Leicester C (From trainee on 3/7/1998)
Plymouth Arg (Free on 4/7/2000) FL 2 FAC 2

HODGES Lee Leslie
Born: Plaistow, 2 March 1978
Height: 5'5" Weight: 10.2
International Honours: E: Sch

Without doubt Scunthorpe's most talented player, Lee continued to shine on the left side of attack last season when he was too good for many division three defences. Quick, direct and very skilful, he was a regular in the Scunthorpe side and got himself on the score sheet regularly with a mixture of spectacular long-range strikes and penalties. Due to be out of contract in the summer he was transfer-listed in February and at the time of writing it seems unlikely that he will still be at Glanford Park at the start of the 2001-02 campaign. He missed the last few games due to a cartilage operation but was honoured by winning a place in the PFA's Third Division team in April.

West Ham U (From trainee on 2/3/1995) PL 0+3 FAC 0+3
Exeter C (Loaned on 13/9/1996) FL 16+1
Leyton Orient (Loaned on 28/2/1997) FL 3
Plymouth Arg (Loaned on 6/11/1997) FL 9 Others 1
Ipswich T (Loaned on 20/11/1998) FL 0+4
Southend U (Loaned on 25/3/1999) FL 10/1
Scunthorpe U (£50,000 on 8/7/1999) FL 71+7/14 FLC 4 FAC 6/1 Others 1/1

HODGES Lee Leslie
Born: Epping, 4 September 1973
Height: 6'0" Weight: 12.1
International Honours: E: Yth

Lee enjoyed an excellent time for Reading in the first half of last season when he was a regular in the first team but he lost his place following a dip in form at the turn of the year and rarely featured afterwards. A creative midfield player he sets up openings for others and contributes the occasional goal himself. He was out of contract at the end of the campaign and was released by the Royals.

Tottenham H (From trainee on 29/2/1992) PL 0+4
Plymouth Arg (Loaned on 26/2/1993) FL 6+1/2
Wycombe W (Loaned on 31/12/1993) FL 2+2 FAC 1 Others 1
Barnet (Free on 31/5/1994) FL 94+11/26 FLC 6+1 FAC 6+1/4 Others 3+1
Reading (£100,000 on 29/7/1997) FL 58+21/10 FLC 7+3 FAC 7+1/1 Others 0+2

HODGSON Richard James
Born: Sunderland, 1 October 1979
Height: 5'10" Weight: 11.8

After arriving from Nottingham Forest in the summer, Richard appropriately made his Darlington debut against his former club at the City Ground in the shock Worthington Cup victory in early September. He subsequently featured in the majority of games although many of his appearances came from the subs' bench. He is a tricky direct left winger who is dangerous when cutting in from the flank and able to deliver accurate crosses for his team-mates.

Nottingham F (From trainee on 8/10/1996)
Scunthorpe U (Free on 9/3/2000) FL 1
Darlington (Free on 7/8/2000) FL 20+15/2 FLC 2+1 FAC 2+1/2 Others 2+1/1

HOGG Lewis James
Born: Bristol, 13 September 1982
Height: 5'8" Weight: 10.8

Lewis stepped up to make his Football League debut from the subs' bench for Bristol Rovers on the opening day of the 2000-01 season and shortly afterwards netted two goals in the Pirates' remarkable 6-2 win at Brentford. He went on to produce a series of solid performances throughout the campaign, scoring an important equaliser in the Worthington Cup tie at Everton and finishing on a high when he won the 'Young Player of the Season' award. Lewis is a promising ball-winning midfield player who will be looking to make further progress for the Pirates in the coming season.

Bristol Rov (From trainee on 14/9/1999) FL 31+3/3 FLC 5/1 FAC 1 Others 1

HOLDEN Dean Thomas John
Born: Salford, 15 September 1979
Height: 6'0" Weight: 11.0
International Honours: E: Yth

Dean spent most of the 2000-01 campaign recovering from a broken leg sustained the previous March and it was not until the final game of the season that he returned to first-team action for Bolton. It was something of a fairy tale comeback for, playing against Sheffield United, the team against whom he had suffered his injury, he netted a last-minute goal to earn the Wanderers a point in a 1-1 draw. A promising young defender he will be looking to reclaim his place in the starting line-up in 2001-02.

Bolton W (From trainee on 23/12/1997) FL 7+6/1 FLC 2 FAC 3+1

HOLDER Jordan Andrew
Born: Oxford, 22 October 1982
Height: 5'10" Weight: 11.5

One of many promising youngsters on Oxford United's books Jordan stepped up to make two appearances from the subs' bench at the end of last season. A talented striker with the club's youth team he signed a professional contract for the U's and will be looking to gain more senior experience in 2001-02.
Oxford U (Trainee) FL 0+2

HOLDSWORTH David Gary
Born: Walthamstow, 8 November 1968
Height: 6'1" Weight: 12.10
International Honours: E: U21-1; Yth
David was in fine form for Birmingham City in the early part of last season, marshalling the defence with a calm assurance and reading the play very well. However he had his tonsils removed in November and ended up back in a hospital trauma ward after suffering severe haemorrhaging, he then had trouble eating and drinking and lost a stone in weight before finally setting out on the road to recovery. He made a surprise return to the subs' bench for the Worthington Cup final and subsequently returned to first-team action for the Blues. David is the twin brother of Bolton's Dean Holdsworth.
Watford (From apprentice on 8/11/1986) FL 249+9/11 FLC 20/2 FAC 14+1/1 Others 8+2
Sheffield U (£450,00 on 8/10/1996) FL 93/4 FLC 7 FAC 13/3 Others 5
Birmingham C (£1,200,000 on 22/3/1999) FL 75+6/7 FLC 9/1 FAC 1 Others 4+1

HOLDSWORTH Dean Christopher
Born: Walthamstow, 8 November 1968
Height: 5'11" Weight: 11.13
Club Honours: Div 3 '92
International Honours: E: B-1
Dean had a fine season with Bolton Wanderers in 2000-01 when he finally won over his critics at the Reebok Stadium. Finishing as the club's second-top scorer he showed that there is much more to his game as a striker than hitting the back of the net. His approach play took on a new dimension, his skill at holding up the ball and his willingness to help the team defend proving invaluable throughout the campaign. He also netted some fine goals, one particular effort against Wolves in October being particularly memorable, and in March he registered the 200th senior goal of his career against Nottingham Forest. Out of contract in the summer it was unclear at the time of writing whether he would remain with the Wanderers. He is the twin brother of David Holdsworth.
Watford (From apprentice on 12/11/1986) FL 2+14/3 Others 0+4
Carlisle U (Loaned on 11/2/1988) FL 4/1
Port Vale (Loaned on 18/3/1988) FL 6/2
Swansea C (Loaned on 25/8/1988) FL 4+1/1
Brentford (Loaned on 13/10/1988) FL 2+5/1
Brentford (£125,000 on 29/9/1989) FL 106+4/53 FLC 7+1/6 FAC 6/7 Others 12+2/9
Wimbledon (£720,000 on 20/7/1992) PL 148+21/58 FLC 16+3/11 FAC 13+7/7
Bolton W (£3,500,000 on 3/10/1997) P/FL 83+35/37 FLC 8+3/2 FAC 5+1/3 Others 5/3

HOLLAND Christopher (Chris) James
Born: Clitheroe, 11 September 1975
Height: 5'9" Weight: 11.5
International Honours: E: U21-10; Yth
Chris was sidelined by a knee injury and then achilles trouble during the early part of last season before returning to the Huddersfield Town squad in November. However he continued to be plagued by injury problems, later suffering a broken toe and these prevented him having a decent run in the team. An energetic midfield player who sometimes seems to cover every blade of grass, he is strong in the tackle and has a good partnership with Craig Armstrong in the centre of the park.
Preston NE (Trainee) FL 0+1 Others 1
Newcastle U (£100,000 on 20/1/1994) PL 2+1 FLC 0+1
Birmingham C (£600,000 on 5/9/1996) FL 39+31 FLC 7+5 FAC 4 Others 1+1
Huddersfield T (£150,000 on 3/2/2000) FL 45+1/1 FLC 1 FAC 1

HOLLAND Matthew (Matt) Rhys
Born: Bury, 11 April 1974
Height: 5'9" Weight: 11.12
International Honours: RoI: 11; B-1
A club captain who leads by example, Matt continued his incredible record of not missing a game since he joined Ipswich in 1997, although he did sit out the first half of the Worthington Cup tie at Millwall. He epitomises all that is good about the club - he gives maximum effort in every game, seems to cover every blade of grass on the pitch and plays in the right spirit, hard but fair - he did not pick up a single yellow card during the 2000-01 season. His goal tally was reduced, but not for want of trying as he could often be found in the opponents' penalty box in support of his attack. All three of the league goals he scored came in the last quarter of the game and helped set Town on their way to victory. The goals themselves were also similar in their execution, right-foot shots from the edge of the penalty area after good football had created the opportunity, and all were scored at Portman Road. Matt continued his international career with the Republic of Ireland and netted his first international goals against Andorra and Portugal.
West Ham U (From trainee on 3/7/1992)
Bournemouth (Signed on 27/1/1995) FL 97+7/18 FLC 6 FAC 3 Others 3
Ipswich T (£800,000 on 31/7/1997) P/FL 176/28 FLC 21+1/6 FAC 9 Others 7/2

HOLLAND Paul
Born: Lincoln, 8 July 1973
Height: 5'11" Weight: 12.10
International Honours: E: U21-4; Yth; Sch
Paul began the 2000-01 campaign in impressive form for Bristol City and scored with a header in the 2-0 victory at Wrexham in the opening game. However after just half-a-dozen first-team outings he suffered a serious knee injury that brought his season to a very early conclusion. An experienced midfield player he combines creative touches with a degree of bite in the centre of the park.
Mansfield T (From juniors on 4/7/1991) FL 149/25 FLC 11 FAC 7/3 Others 9/1
Sheffield U (£250,000 on 20/6/1995) FL 11+7/1 FLC 2/1
Chesterfield (Signed on 5/1/1996) FL 108+6/11 FLC 11+1/2 FAC 11 Others 1
Bristol C (£200,000 on 23/9/1999) FL 27+5/1 FLC 2/1 FAC 3 Others 4/1

HOLLIGAN Gavin Victor
Born: Lambeth, 13 June 1980
Height: 5'10" Weight: 12.0
This promising young striker joined Exeter City on a month's loan last October but failed to find the net in three outings for the Grecians and returned to Upton Park. Later in the season he spent a loan period at his former club Kingstonian where he scored twice in seven games. He was released on a free transfer in the summer.
West Ham U (£100,000 from Kingstonian on 5/3/1999) PL 0+1
Leyton Orient (Loaned on 17/9/1999) FL 1 FLC 1
Exeter C (Loaned on 17/10/2000) FL 3

HOLLOWAY Christopher (Chris) David
Born: Swansea, 5 February 1980
Height: 5'10" Weight: 11.7
International Honours: W: U21-2
Chris failed to start a game for Exeter City last season and was restricted to just a handful of outings from the subs' bench. His absence was partly a result of niggling injuries, including a freak training ground accident that required over 30 stitches to a leg wound. When fully fit Chris is a promising midfield player with a neat touch and good distribution. He was released by the Grecians in the summer.
Exeter C (From trainee on 9/7/1998) FL 51+17/2 FLC 2+1 FAC 1+1 Others 3

HOLLOWAY Darren
Born: Crook, 3 October 1977
Height: 5'10" Weight: 12.2
International Honours: E: U21-1
Primarily a defender, Darren started the 2000-01 season at Sunderland in midfield to cover for injuries and suspensions. However although he was very effective in the opening day win over Arsenal he lost his place to Darren Williams after just a handful of appearances and was soon on his way to Wimbledon. After taking some time to settle in he began to prove his worth to the Dons, forging a very effective partnership with Gareth Ainsworth down the right-hand side. A hard-working player he is very versatile and can play in both midfield and defence down the centre or on the right flank, although he mostly featured at right back for Wimbledon.
Sunderland (From trainee on 12/10/1995) P/FL 46+12 FLC 3 FAC 2 Others 3
Carlisle U (Loaned on 29/8/1997) FL 5
Bolton W (Loaned on 14/12/1999) FL 3+1
Wimbledon (£1,250,000 on 2/10/2000) FL 30+1 FAC 4

HOLLUND Martin
Born: Stord, Norway, 11 August 1974
Height: 6'0" Weight: 12.9
International Honours: Norway: U21
Martin had a disappointing time at Hartlepool in 2000-01 after having made great progress the previous season. He began as the club's first-choice goalkeeper but lost his place to newcomer Anthony Williams following the 3-1 home defeat by Shrewsbury and never managed to get back in the team. However he is still part of

manager Chris Turner's plans and was offered a new contract at the end of the campaign.
Hartlepool U (Free from SK Brann Bergen, Norway on 21/11/1997) FL 114 FLC 3 FAC 4 Others 8

HOLMES Paul
Born: Stocksbridge, 18 February 1968
Height: 5'10" Weight: 11.3

Paul began the 2000-01 campaign at right back for Torquay but eventually lost his place to Steve Tully before returning to the line-up later in the season when he took over at left back from the injured Robbie Herrera. He struggled at times to find his best form and will be hoping for a more successful time in 2001-02. An experienced performer who has good pace and kicks well with either foot, Paul can play in either full back position, as a sweeper or in a wide midfield role.
Doncaster Rov (From apprentice on 24/2/1986) FL 42+5/1 FAC 3+1/1 Others 1
Torquay U (£6,000 on 12/8/1988) FL 127+12/4 FLC 9 FAC 9+2 Others 13+3
Birmingham C (£40,000 on 5/6/1992) FL 12 FAC 1
Everton (£100,000 on 19/3/1993) PL 21 FLC 4 FAC 1 Others 0+2
West Bromwich A (£80,000 on 12/1/1996) FL 102+1/1 FLC 5 FAC 4 Others 3
Torquay U (Free on 11/11/1999) FL 58+4/2 FLC 2 FAC 3 Others 1+1

HOLMES Peter James
Born: Bishop Auckland, 18 November 1980
Height: 5'10" Weight: 10.6
International Honours: E: Yth; Sch

A product of the FA School of Excellence and previously capped by England at U16 level Peter joined Luton Town in the 2000 close season after three years as a professional at Hillsborough. He made his Football League debut from the subs' bench in the opening day defeat by Notts County but although he featured regularly in the first half of the campaign he never managed to establish himself in the team in what was a very difficult season for the Hatters. He is a young midfield player who has good ball control and can hit the ball with either foot. Peter was placed on the transfer list at Kenilworth Road in the summer.
Sheffield Wed (From trainee on 2/12/1997)
Luton T (Free on 1/8/2000) FL 12+6/1 FLC 2+1 FAC 1

HOLMES Richard
Born: Grantham, 7 November 1980
Height: 5'10" Weight: 10.7

Richard had a disappointing campaign for Notts County in 2000-01 when he rarely featured at first-team level following an early-season switch of formation. A quick right back who is sharp in the tackle he will be hoping to return to the Magpies line-up in the coming season.
Notts Co (From trainee on 23/3/1999) FL 44+10 FLC 3+1 FAC 2+1 Others 1

HOLMES Steven (Steve) Peter
Born: Middlesbrough, 13 January 1971
Height: 6'2" Weight: 13.0

Steve proved to be one of Lincoln City's most consistent players in a season that saw the Imps fighting against relegation. He was a very effective central defender but also provided a steady supply of goals both from set-piece moves and from the penalty spot. He finished the campaign as City's leading scorer in Third Division games with the remarkable tally for a defender of 11 goals.
Lincoln C (From trainee on 17/7/1989)
Preston NE (£10,000 from Guisborough T, ex Gainsborough Trinity, on 14/3/1994) FL 13/1 FAC 3 Others 1
Hartlepool U (Loaned on 10/3/1995) FL 5/2
Lincoln C (Loaned on 20/10/1995) FL 12/1 Others 2
Lincoln C (£30,000 on 15/3/1996) FL 167+2/28 FLC 8/2 FAC 8/1 Others 7/1

HOLT Andrew (Andy)
Born: Stockport, 21 May 1978
Height: 6'1" Weight: 12.7

Andy rather surprisingly lost his place at left back in Oldham Athletic's line-up following some useful early-season displays and in March he moved on loan to Hull City where he mostly featured on the left-hand side of midfield. He played an important role in guiding the Tigers into the play-offs scoring crucial goals in the draw at Torquay and in the local 'derby' with Scunthorpe, the latter coming with a spectacular free-kick from the edge of the box. A versatile player with a terrific long throw his direct style makes him a threat when pushing forward from the back. Andy was reported to have joined Hull for a substantial fee during the summer break.
Oldham Ath (From trainee on 23/7/1996) FL 104+20/10 FLC 8 FAC 6+4 Others 3
Hull C (Loaned on 15/3/2001) FL 10/2 Others 2

HOLT Gary James
Born: Irvine, 9 March 1973
Height: 6'0" Weight: 12.11
Club Honours: SC '98
International Honours: S: 3

Having featured regularly for Kilmarnock last term Gary was the subject of a pre-deadline day swoop by Norwich City who beat off several rivals for his signature. He is a hard-working combative player in the middle of the park - winning the ball and distributing it simply to keep his side moving forward. Strong in the air he also enjoys getting forward into the opposition penalty area to help out in attack.
Stoke C (Free from Glasgow Celtic N/C on 20/10/1994)
Kilmarnock (Free on 18/8/1995) SL 138+13/9 SLC 10+1 SC 13 Others 8
Norwich C (£100,000 on 22/3/2001) FL 3+1

HOLT Grant
Born: Carlisle, 12 April 1981
Height: 6'1" Weight: 12.7

This promising young striker featured in a handful of games for Halifax in the early part of last season and scored with a header in the Worthington Cup tie against Tranmere in what proved to be the only occasion that he made the starting line-up. Grant subsequently spent most of the remainder of the campaign out on loan, firstly with Workington and later with Barrow before being released in May.
Halifax T (Signed from Workington on 16/9/1999) FL 0+6 FLC 1/1 Others 1

HOOPER Dean Raymond
Born: Harefield, 13 April 1971
Height: 5'11" Weight: 11.6
International Honours: E: SP-1

Dean had an in-and-out season at Peterborough in 2000-01 with injuries and loss of form limiting his appearances. A fiery hard-tackling right back who is comfortable on the ball he occasionally deputised as skipper. He will be hoping for better fortune in the coming season.
Swindon T (£15,000 from Hayes on 3/3/1995) FL 0+4 FLC 0+2 Others 2 (Free to Hayes on 4/10/1996)
Peterborough U (Loaned on 15/12/1995) FL 4
Peterborough U (Signed from Kingstonian on 6/8/1998) FL 92+8/2 FLC 6 FAC 5+2 Others 4+1

HOPE Christopher (Chris) Jonathan
Born: Sheffield, 14 November 1972
Height: 6'1" Weight: 12.7

After signing for First Division newcomers Gillingham during the close season, Chris settled in well at the Priestfield Stadium last term and went on to become an ever-present for his new club. A very solid central defender he was excellent in the air and a constant danger at set pieces, indeed he was rather unfortunate to finish with a tally of just three goals for the season.
Nottingham F (From Darlington juniors on 23/8/1990)
Scunthorpe U (£50,000 on 5/7/1993) FL 278+9/19 FLC 13+1 FAC 18/1 Others 18/2
Gillingham (£250,000 on 12/7/2000) FL 46/2 FLC 4 FAC 2/1

Richard Hope

HOPE Richard Paul
Born: Stockton, 22 June 1978
Height: 6'2" Weight: 12.6

Richard was once again a rock-like figure playing alongside Ian Sampson in the Northampton Town defence during 2000-01. Although absent with a thigh injury in the early part of the campaign he soon returned and was rarely absent for the remainder of the season. He is a central defender with a commanding presence in the air who is also an effective tackler on the ground. Richard is the son of the former Sheffield United and Hartlepool goalkeeper John Hope.

Blackburn Rov (From trainee on 9/8/1995)
Darlington (Free on 17/1/1997) FL 62+1/1 FLC 3 FAC 1 Others 0+1
Northampton T (Signed on 18/12/1998) FL 61+8 FLC 1 FAC 2+1 Others 4

HOPKIN David
Born: Greenock, 21 August 1970
Height: 5'9" Weight: 11.0
International Honours: S: 7; B-1

David became Bradford City's record signing when he arrived from Leeds United in July 2000. He played in the opening games of last season but then suffered damage to his ankle ligaments in the Worthington Cup match at Darlington and was out of action for four months. His hard tackling and forceful play in midfield were sorely missed by City during his absence but he returned for just five games before he was sold to Crystal Palace, one of his former clubs. Welcomed back at Selhurst Park he added his class and battling qualities to the Eagles' successful fight against relegation.

Greenock Morton (Signed from Port Glasgow BC on 7/7/1989) SL 33+15/4 SLC 2/2 SC 2/1
Chelsea (£300,000 on 25/9/1992) PL 21+19/1 FLC 0+1 FAC 3+2
Crystal Palace (£850,000 on 29/7/1995) FL 79+4/21 FLC 6/6 FAC 3 Others 4/2
Leeds U (£3,250,000 on 23/7/1997) PL 64+9/6 FLC 7 FAC 6 Others 6+1
Bradford C (£2,500,000 on 12/7/2000) PL 8+3 FLC 1 Others 3+1
Crystal Palace (£1,500,000 on 15/3/2001) FL 8+1/1

HOPKINS Gareth
Born: Cheltenham, 14 June 1980
Height: 6'2" Weight: 13.8

Having previously only appeared as a substitute, Gareth made his first start for Cheltenham against Chesterfield last September but was mostly restricted to reserve-team football last season. In March he went out on loan to Dr Martens League club Cinderford Town to gain further experience and he was rewarded with a one-year extension to his contract in the summer. He is a tall and powerful striker with good pace but needs to try and win a regular place in the Robins first-team squad in the coming season.

Cheltenham T (From trainee on 27/7/1998) FL 1+4 FLC 0+1 FAC 0+1 Others 1

HOPPER Tony
Born: Carlisle, 31 May 1976
Height: 5'11" Weight: 12.8
Club Honours: AMC '97

After being released by Carlisle United at the end of the 1999-2000 campaign, Tony joined League of Ireland outfit Bohemians and featured for them in UEFA Cup action in the early part of last season. He came back to the North West in the new year, firstly joining non-league Workington and then returning to Brunton Park in February. A hard-working defensive midfielder, he can always be depended upon to give 100 per cent commitment to his home-town club. He was released in the summer.

Carlisle U (From trainee on 18/7/1994) FL 75+25/1 FLC 2+1 FAC 3+1/1 Others 7+4 (Free to Bohemians during 2000 close season)
Carlisle U (Free from Workington on 14/2/2001) FL 4+5

HORE John
Born: Liverpool, 18 August 1982
Height: 5'11" Weight: 11.12

Another product of the Carlisle youth team, John made two senior appearances last December, featuring in the league game against Macclesfield and the LDV Vans tie at Kidderminster. A strong left-footed striker he will be aiming to gain further senior experience for the Cumbrians in 2001-02.

Carlisle U (From trainee on 12/6/2000) FL 2 Others 1

HORLOCK Kevin
Born: Erith, 1 November 1972
Height: 6'0" Weight: 12.0
Club Honours: Div 2 '96
International Honours: NI: 25; B-2

Kevin had a rather disappointing season at Manchester City in 2000-01. He started off as a regular in the first team but seemed to find it hard to adapt to the pace of Premiership football and then fractured an ankle playing against Charlton at the turn of the year. He took some time to recover match fitness but towards the end of the campaign he returned to the reserve team and scored one of the goals as City beat United's second string at Old Trafford to take the Manchester Senior Cup. An attacking midfield player he continued to feature for Northern Ireland in their World Cup qualifying campaign matches.

West Ham U (From trainee on 1/7/1991)
Swindon T (Free on 27/8/1992) F/PL 151+12/22 FLC 15+2/1 FAC 12/3 Others 5+2
Manchester C (£1,250,000 on 31/1/1997) P/FL 129+3/30 FLC 12/3 FAC 5 Others 3/1

HORNE Barry
Born: Rhyl, 18 May 1962
Height: 5'9" Weight: 12.2
Club Honours: WC '86; FAC '95; CS '95
International Honours: W: 59

Barry's arrival at Kidderminster in August 2000 brought much needed experience to the newly-promoted team. Operating in a central midfield role he scored with a cracking 25-yard drive to clinch victory over Torquay in the Harriers' first-ever Football League game but generally took some time to settle in at Aggborough. Although he featured regularly in the squad he was one of several players transfer-listed in January and after being released in March he linked up with Second Division Walsall to assist with their promotion campaign. After two brief appearances from the subs' bench he went on to give an assured display to help the Saddlers beat Northampton in the final Second Division game of the season. A vastly experienced midfield anchor man he has a combative approach to the game that inspires his team-mates. He was released in the summer.

Wrexham (Free from Rhyl on 26/6/1984) FL 136/17 FLC 10/1 FAC 7/2 Others 15/3
Portsmouth (£60,000 on 17/7/1987) FL 66+4/7 FLC 3 FAC 6
Southampton (£700,000 on 22/3/1989) FL 111+1/6 FLC 15+2/3 FAC 15/3 Others 7/1
Everton (£675,000 on 1/7/1992) PL 118+5/3 FLC 12+1 FAC 11+1 Others 3
Birmingham C (£250,000 on 10/6/1996) FL 33 FLC 3 FAC 3
Huddersfield T (Free on 13/10/1997) FL 55+9/1 FLC 7 FAC 2
Sheffield Wed (Free on 23/3/2000) PL 7
Kidderminster Hrs (Free on 11/8/2000) FL 21+6/1 FLC 2 FAC 3 Others 2
Walsall (Free on 23/3/2001) FL 1+2

HORSFIELD Geoffrey (Geoff) Malcolm
Born: Barnsley, 1 November 1973
Height: 5'10" Weight: 11.0
Club Honours: FC '98; Div 2 '99

Signed by Birmingham City for a new club record fee in the close season, Geoff had an up and down campaign for the Blues in 2000-01. Hampered by a series of niggling injuries he rarely operated at full capacity but nevertheless finished leading scorer for the club in all competitions. He seemed to save some of his best performances for the Worthington Cup ties, terrorising the Newcastle defence in the fourth round tie and then scoring twice in the semi-final second leg win over Ipswich. The final against Liverpool, when the team came so close to victory, was another high point. He scored fairly regularly throughout the campaign, netting his last goal in the play-off semi-final second leg at Preston when Blues again lost out on penalties. A big bustling centre forward his aggressive style, determination and close control made life hard for opposition defences.

Scarborough (From juniors on 10/7/1992) FL 12/1 FAC 1 Others 0+2 (Free to Halifax T on 31/3/1994)
Halifax T (Free from Witton A on 8/5/1997) FL 10/7 FLC 4/1
Fulham (£325,000 on 12/10/1998) FL 54+5/22 FLC 6/6 FAC 8+1/3
Birmingham C (£2,000,000 + on 12/7/2000) FL 25+9/7 FLC 5+1/3 FAC 0+1 Others 2/1

HOTTE Mark Stephen
Born: Bradford, 27 September 1978
Height: 5'11" Weight: 11.1

A product of the Oldham Athletic youth set-up, Mark made steady progress towards establishing himself in the first team last season. Comfortable on the ball, this imaginative player is now regarded as an ideal foil for the club's stoppers and what he lacks in height he more than makes up for in terms of pace and quick thinking. Such attributes make him ideal for the role of sweeper in which he was generally employed during the campaign.

Oldham Ath (From trainee on 1/7/1997) FL 59+6 FLC 2 FAC 2+1 Others 2

HOUGHTON Scott Aaron
Born: Hitchin, 22 October 1971
Height: 5'7" Weight: 12.4
Club Honours: FAYC '90
International Honours: E: Yth; Sch

Scott featured regularly for Southend under Brian Little in the opening games of the 2000-01 campaign but was sold to Leyton Orient shortly after new manager David Webb arrived at Roots Hall. Although injured on his debut at Torquay he soon returned and claimed the winning goal in the FA Cup replay against Norwich Victoria when the ball entered the net off his backside! He subsequently shared the left-wing slot with John Martin but appeared in the heartbreaking play-off final against Blackpool when he scored the O's second goal. A wide-left midfield player, on his day he is one of the finest crossers of the ball in the lower divisions.

Tottenham H (From trainee on 24/8/1990) FL 0+10/2 FLC 0+2 Others 0+2
Ipswich T (Loaned on 26/3/1991) FL 7+1/1
Gillingham (Loaned on 17/12/1992) FL 3
Charlton Ath (Loaned on 26/2/1993) FL 6
Luton T (Free on 10/8/1993) FL 7+9/1 FLC 2+1 FAC 0+1 Others 2
Walsall (£20,000 on 2/9/1994) FL 76+2/14 FLC 0+1/1 FAC 10/3 Others 4
Peterborough U (£60,000 + on 12/7/1996) FL 57+13/13 FLC 6+2 FAC 7/1 Others 1+1/1
Southend U (Signed on 20/11/1998) FL 75+4/9 FLC 3+1 FAC 1 Others 1
Leyton Orient (Free on 6/10/2000) FL 17+4/1 FAC 3/1 Others 4/1

HOULT Russell
Born: Ashby de la Zouch, 22 November 1972
Height: 6'3" Weight: 14.9

Russell was an ever-present for Portsmouth in the first half of the 2000-01 season until acting-manager Steve Claridge was tempted by West Bromwich Albion's offer and he returned to the Midlands where he had spent most of his career. He soon replaced Brian Jensen as the Baggies' first-choice 'keeper and immediately inspired confidence in the defence, producing some outstanding performances to help the club to a place in the end-of-season play-offs. A goalkeeper who shows good command of his area he is particularly adept at handling awkward crosses.

Leicester C (From trainee on 28/3/1991) FL 10 FLC 3 Others 1
Lincoln C (Loaned on 27/8/1991) FL 2 FLC 1
Bolton W (Loaned on 3/11/1993) FL 3+1 Others 1
Lincoln C (Loaned on 12/8/1994) FL 15 Others 1
Derby Co (£300,000 on 17/2/1995) F/PL 121+2 FLC 8 FAC 7
Portsmouth (£300,000 + on 21/1/2000) FL 40 FLC 4
West Bromwich A (£500,000 on 5/1/2001) FL 13 Others 2

HOWARD Jonathan (Jon)
Born: Sheffield, 7 October 1971
Height: 5'11" Weight: 12.6

Jon thrived for Chesterfield in a more successful team last season, looking lively, quick-witted and completely at home in a team that played passing football. His contribution was heavily restricted by knee ligament damage sustained at Southend in December shortly after he scored two goals in the 4-1 defeat of Leyton Orient. Fortunately he had recovered by March and hit a late equaliser against Rochdale in his comeback game. He was released in the summer.

Rotherham U (From trainee on 10/7/1990) FL 25+11/5 FLC 0+1 FAC 4/2 Others 3+1 (Free to Buxton on 11/11/94)
Chesterfield (Free on 9/12/1994) FL 139+68/34 FLC 10+3/1 FAC 12+1/2 Others 9+3/2

HOWARD Michael (Mike) Anthony
Born: Birkenhead, 2 December 1978
Height: 5'9" Weight: 11.13
Club Honours: Div 3 '00

A regular for Swansea last season apart from the occasional absence due to suspension, Mike remained a very much under-rated defender. Versatile enough to play either as a left back or on the left-hand side of midfield when a three-man back-line was employed, he is sound defensively and effective when pushing up the flank.

Tranmere Rov (From trainee on 9/7/1997)
Swansea C (Free on 6/2/1998) FL 118+5/1 FLC 7 FAC 8 Others 5

HOWARD Steven (Steve) John
Born: Durham, 10 May 1976
Height: 6'2" Weight: 14.6

Steve played regularly up front for Northampton in the 2000-01 season alongside Marco Gabbiadini and Jamie Forrester until he surprisingly moved to neighbours Luton Town on the transfer deadline day. He scored from the penalty spot in his second game for the Hatters at Wycombe and also added two more in the final two games of the campaign. He is a strong and powerful centre forward who holds the ball up well to bring his colleagues into play.

Hartlepool U (Free from Tow Law on 8/8/1995) FL 117+25/27 FLC 7+1/1 FAC 5/2 Others 7/3
Northampton T (£120,000 on 22/2/1999) FL 67+19/18 FLC 4 FAC 2+1 Others 2
Luton T (£50,000 on 22/3/2001) FL 12/3

HOWARTH Neil
Born: Farnworth, 15 November 1971
Height: 6'2" Weight: 13.6
Club Honours: GMVC '95, '97; FAT '96
International Honours: E: SP-1

Neil began last season as first choice at right back for Cheltenham Town and scored a late equaliser in the opening day draw with Mansfield but was then affected by hamstring problems. He subsequently found it difficult to regain his place and was restricted to sporadic appearances on the right or in the centre of defence. When fully fit he is a good all-round defender who is comfortable on the ball, useful in the air and possesses good positional play.

Burnley (From trainee on 2/7/1990) FL 0+1
Macclesfield T (Free on 3/9/1993) FL 49+11/3 FLC 3 FAC 2+2 Others 2
Cheltenham T (£7,000 on 24/2/1999) FL 62+5/5 FLC 4 FAC 3+1/1 Others 2

HOWARTH Russell Michael
Born: York, 27 March 1982
Height: 6'1" Weight: 13.10
International Honours: E: Yth

Russell only made a couple of senior appearances in the Worthington Cup and LDV Vans Trophy for York City last season due to the outstanding form of Alan Fettis. However he continued to remain an integral part of the England youth set-up regularly featuring in the U18 squad and winning three more caps.

York C (From trainee on 26/8/1999) FL 5+1 FLC 3 Others 1

HOWE Edward (Eddie) John Frank
Born: Amersham, 29 November 1977
Height: 5'10" Weight: 11.10
International Honours: E: U21-2

Eddie had the misfortune to suffer a knee injury shortly before the start of the 2000-01 campaign and it was not until the end of October that he returned to first-team duties for Bournemouth. Once fit however he re-established himself in the team and formed an effective partnership in the centre of defence with Jason Tindall. Eddie is a commanding centre half who is calm on the ball and likes to get forward for set pieces.

Bournemouth (From trainee on 4/7/1996) FL 145+17/6 FLC 11+1/1 FAC 10/2 Others 7+2

HOWE Stephen **Robert (Bobby)**
Born: Cramlington, 6 November 1973
Height: 5'7" Weight: 10.4
International Honours: E: Yth

Bobby had a somewhat mixed season for Swindon Town in 2000-01 starting off with some lively intelligent displays and scoring with an excellent free kick against Exeter City in the Worthington Cup tie. He continued to work hard, remaining a member of the first-team squad until suffering an achilles injury early in the new year that kept him out of action until the summer break. At his best he is a strong-running attacking midfield player who is a good passer of the ball.

Nottingham F (From trainee on 5/12/1990) P/FL 6+8/2 FLC 2 Others 1+1
Ipswich T (Loaned on 17/1/1997) FL 2+1 FLC 1
Swindon T (£30,000 on 16/1/1998) FL 70+13/5 FLC 3+1/1 FAC 4/2

HOWELL Dean George
Born: Burton, 29 November 1980
Height: 6'1" Weight: 12.5

Dean signed a one-year contract for Crewe in the 2000 close season but managed only one appearance from the subs' bench for the Railwaymen. He joined Third Division Rochdale on loan in March to provide extra options on the left hand side and played a prominent role in Dale's excellent draw at Hartlepool. However, with other players coming back from injury and further new signings, Dean managed only one more start before returning to Gresty Road. He is a left-sided defender with good pace who enjoys moving down the flank to support the attack. Out of contract in the summer it was unclear at the time of writing where he would be playing at the start of the 2001-02 campaign.

Notts Co (From trainee on 1/7/1999) FL 0+1
Crewe Alex (Free on 26/7/2000) FL 0+1
Rochdale (Loaned on 1/3/2001) FL 2+1

HOWELLS Lee David
Born: Perth, Australia, 14 October 1968
Height: 5'11" Weight: 11.12
Club Honours: FAT '98; NC '99
International Honours: SP-2

Lee was a regular choice with Mark Yates in the centre of midfield for Cheltenham Town last season. Having played for the club since their Dr Martens League days he is one of the more experienced heads at Whaddon Road but his form seemed to dip at times and he had some disciplinary problems which he needs to avoid in the future. He is a hard-running and effective midfield player who is strong in the tackle.

Bristol Rov (From apprentice on 17/10/1986. Freed on 1/7/1988)
Cheltenham T (Signed from Brisbane Lions, Australia on 1/12/1991) FL 81/4 FLC 2 FAC 4/1 Others 2

HOWEY Lee Matthew
Born: Sunderland, 1 April 1969
Height: 6'3" Weight: 14.6
Club Honours: Div 1 '96

Lee returned to action for Northampton reserves last February after being out of action with a knee injury since Boxing Day 1999. He went on to appear twice for the Cobblers in the closing stages of the season and will be hoping he has finally put his injury problems behind him. A strong and committed central defender he began studying for his UEFA 'B' coaching certificate during his long lay-off. Lee is the brother of Steve Howey. He was released on a free transfer in the summer.

Ipswich T (From trainee on 2/10/1986. Free to Blyth Spartans in March 1988)
Sunderland (Free from Bishop Auckland on 25/3/1993) P/FL 39+30/8 FLC 1+4/2 FAC 2+4/1 Others 0+1
Burnley (£200,000 on 11/8/1997) FL 24+2 FLC 5/1 FAC 2 Others 0+1
Northampton T (£50,000 on 6/11/1998) FL 47+1/6 FLC 2 FAC 1 Others 2

HOWEY Stephen (Steve) Norman
Born: Sunderland, 26 October 1971
Height: 6'2" Weight: 11.12
Club Honours: Div 1 '93
International Honours: E: 4

Having finally departed from St James Park after a decade with Newcastle, Steve linked up with Premiership new boys Manchester City in the summer. He soon established himself as a commanding figure in the centre of the Blues' defence at the beginning of last season and when Richard Dunne arrived from Everton the two forged a solid defensive partnership. Rarely absent all season he contributed six vital goals including a late equaliser in the game at Old Trafford. Steve is the younger brother of Northampton's Lee Howey.

Newcastle U (From trainee on 11/12/1989) F/PL 167+24/6 FLC 14+2/1 FAC 21+2 Others 10+2
Manchester C (£2,000,000 + on 14/8/2000) PL 36/6 FLC 2 FAC 1

HOWIE Scott
Born: Motherwell, 4 January 1972
Height: 6'2" Weight: 13.7
Club Honours: S Div 2 '93
International Honours: S: U21-5

Scott was again second-choice 'keeper at Reading in 2000-01 and was unable to displace Phil Whitehead, being limited to a couple of first-team outings in the LDV Vans Trophy games at Hereford and Swansea. He appeared regularly in the Royals' successful reserve team and made an appearance in the Avon Insurance Combination Cup final against Norwich. A tall and well-built goalkeeper he has excellent reflexes and is a fine shot stopper. Scott was released on a free transfer in the summer.

Clyde (Signed from Ferguslie U on 7/1/1992) SL 55 SLC 3 SC 4 Others 1
Norwich C (£300,000 on 12/8/1993) PL 1+1
Motherwell (£300,000 on 13/10/1994) SL 69 SLC 4 SC 5 Others 1
Reading (£30,000 on 26/3/1998) FL 84+1 FLC 6 FAC 4 Others 7

HREIDARSSON Hermann
Born: Iceland, 11 July 1974
Height: 6'1" Weight: 13.1
Club Honours: Div 3 '99
International Honours: Iceland: 37; U21-6

Hermann played for Wimbledon against Tranmere in the opening game of last season before he moved back into the Premiership to join Ipswich for a club record fee and went straight into the team for the game at Tottenham. He went on to miss just two games through an injury caused by overstretching in an attempt to clear his lines in the home game with Leeds but took part in every other Premiership match for Town, scoring a goal against Manchester City at Maine Road when he headed home a corner. Earlier he thought he had netted in the game with Bradford at Portman Road and made a

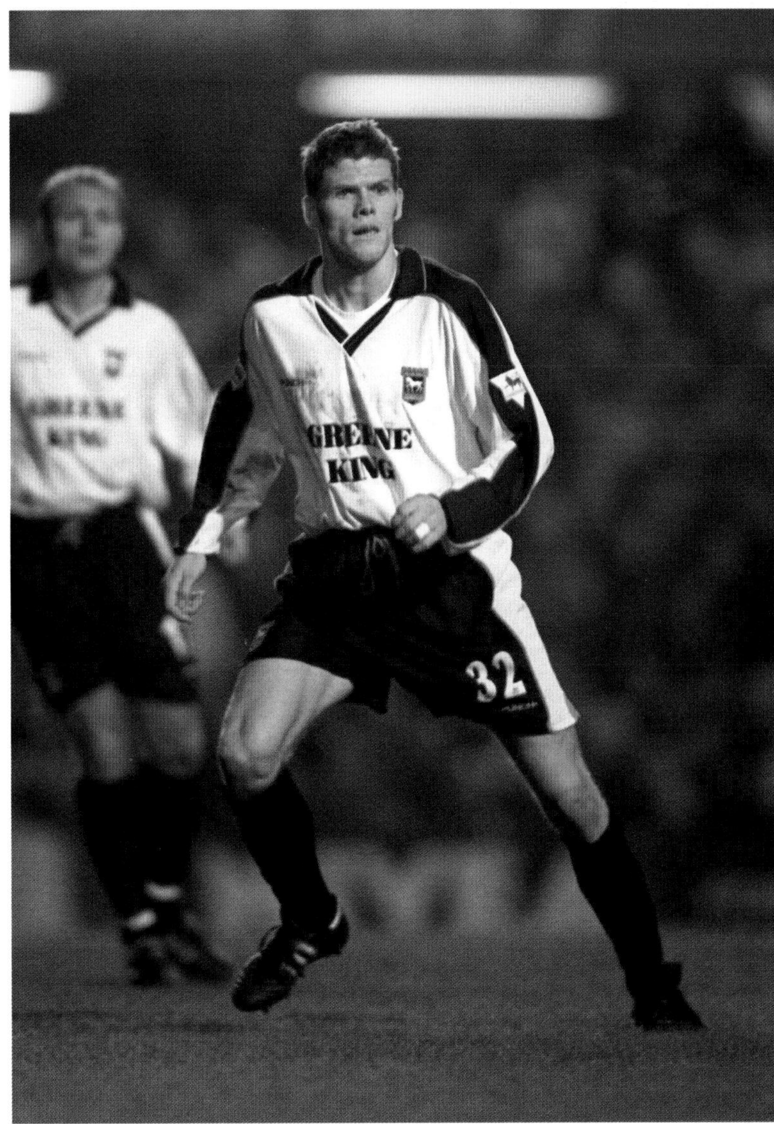

Hermann Hreidarsson

celebratory dive into the crowd but, unbeknown to him, Mark Burchill had got a touch to his goal-bound header and claimed the goal. Hermann played in central defence or as the left-sided wing back and his performances in the latter position allowed him the freedom to go marauding deep into the opponents half - an aspect of his game that endeared him to the Town fans. He was runner-up in the supporters' 'Player of the Year' vote and he continued his international career with Iceland, captaining them on occasions.

Crystal Palace (Signed from IBV, Iceland on 9/8/1997) P/FL 32+5/2 FLC 5/1 FAC 4 Others 2
Brentford (£850,000 on 24/9/1998) FL 41/6 FLC 2 FAC 2/1 Others 3/1
Wimbledon (£2,500,000 on 14/10/1999) P/FL 25/1 FAC 2
Ipswich T (£4,000,000 + on 19/8/2000) PL 35+1/1 FLC 7 FAC 2

HUCK William Roger Fernend
Born: Paris, France, 17 March 1979
Height: 5'10" Weight: 11.13

William again failed to break through to win a regular place in the Bournemouth first team last season and was very much on the fringe of the squad, starting just one Second Division game and making a number of appearances from the subs' bench. He is a very quick left-sided midfielder who is able to run at opposition defenders and put in a good cross.

Arsenal (Signed from Monaco, France on 6/11/1998)
Bournemouth (£50,000 on 25/3/1999) FL 11+22 FLC 0+5/1 Others 2

HUCKERBY Darren Carl
Born: Nottingham, 23 April 1976
Height: 5'10" Weight: 11.12
International Honours: E: B-1; U21-4

Darren again found it difficult to win a place in the starting line-up at Leeds in 2000-01 and mostly found himself on the substitutes' bench. He scored one of United's goals in the 6-0 Champions' League win over Besiktas and netted a double in the 3-2 Worthington Cup defeat by Tranmere but was increasingly marginalised towards the end of the year. Shortly after Christmas he moved across the Pennines to join Manchester City and made an immediate impact on his debut from the subs' bench winning and then converting a consolation penalty as the Blues went down 4-1. However after a run of eight games in the starting line-up he was relegated to the bench again and added just one more goal, a fine individual effort in the FA Cup victory over Birmingham City. A tricky striker with lightning pace he will be aiming to win a regular place in the line-up at Maine Road in 2001-02.

Lincoln C (From trainee on 14/7/1993) FL 20+8/5 FLC 2 Others 1/2
Newcastle U (£400,000 on 10/11/1995) PL 0+1 FAC 0+1
Millwall (Loaned on 6/9/1996) FL 6/3
Coventry C (£1,000,000 on 23/11/1996) PL 85+9/28 FLC 2+1 FAC 12/6
Leeds U (£4,000,000 on 12/8/1999) PL 11+29/2 FLC 1+1/2 FAC 1+2 Others 1+11/2
Manchester C (£2,250,000 + on 29/12/2000) PL 8+5/1 FAC 3/1

HUDSON Daniel (Danny) Robert
Born: Doncaster, 25 June 1979
Height: 5'9" Weight: 10.3

Danny was restricted to just one start and a handful of appearances from the subs' bench for Rotherham in 2000-01 but he never let the side down. A young midfielder he likes to get forward and has the ability to deliver excellent free kicks. His only appearance in the starting line-up came in the home win against Bournemouth in March.

Rotherham U (From trainee on 25/6/1997) FL 29+19/5 FLC 0+2 FAC 3+2/2 Others 3+1

HUDSON Mark
Born: Bishop Auckland, 24 October 1980
Height: 5'10" Weight: 11.3

Another product of Middlesbrough's youth system, Mark did well with the reserve team last season and went on to make his Premiership debut when he came off the subs' bench in the 1-0 win against Liverpool on Boxing Day. He featured sparingly in the second half of the campaign making a total of four appearances, all as a substitute. A talented youngster who has played in midfield and as a striker he was due to be out of contract in the summer and at the time of writing his future was unclear.

Middlesbrough (From trainee on 5/7/1999) PL 0+3 FAC 0+1

HUDSON Mark Alexander
Born: Guildford, 30 March 1982
Height: 6'1" Weight: 12.1

A promising central defender in the Fulham U19 and reserve teams Mark received his first taste of senior action in the two legs of the Worthington Cup second round tie against Chesterfield last season. Very strong in the air, his distribution has improved greatly under the new regime at Craven Cottage and he looks to be a bright prospect.

Fulham (From trainee on 6/4/1999) FLC 2

HUGHES Aaron William
Born: Magherafelt, 8 November 1979
Height: 6'0" Weight: 11.2
International Honours: NI: 20; B-2; Yth

Aaron finally established himself as a regular in the Newcastle United team in 2000-01 when he produced some fine displays. A versatile defender he played in the opening game at left back but was then moved to the centre of the defence where he became a fixture until he was rested in April. The return from injury of Nicos Dabizas and the arrival of Andy O'Brien saw him finish the campaign back in a left-back role. He is an excellent reader of the game, comfortable on the ball and adept at using his distribution skills to turn defence into attack. A regular again for Northern Ireland he signed a new five-year contract for the Magpies last September.

Newcastle U (From trainee on 11/3/1997) PL 72+8/2 FLC 5 FAC 3+2 Others 0+2

HUGHES Andrew (Andy) John
Born: Manchester, 2 January 1978
Height: 5'11" Weight: 12.1
Club Honours: Div 3 '98

Andy featured regularly in the Notts County squad last season although he spent some time on the subs' bench. A talented right-sided midfielder his lightning bursts down the flank enthused the Meadow Lane faithful and he contributed a number of valuable goals. The Magpies' penalty expert he was out of contract in the summer and at the time of writing it was not clear where he would be playing in 2001-02.

Oldham Ath (From trainee on 20/1/1996) FL 18+15/1 FLC 1+1 FAC 3+1 Others 1+2
Notts Co (£150,000 on 29/1/1998) FL 85+25/17 FLC 6+1/1 FAC 10/2 Others 2

HUGHES Bryan
Born: Liverpool, 19 June 1976
Height: 5'10" Weight: 11.2
Club Honours: WC '95

One of the most talented players in the Birmingham City squad, Bryan produced occasional moments of brilliance last term, notably when he netted a superb goal on the turn in the 2-0 win over Watford in March. Often used on the left of midfield from where he could cut inside and float the ball in to good effect, he did well when coming off the subs' bench in the Worthington Cup final against Liverpool, nearly scoring with a superb 30-yard chip.

Wrexham (From trainee on 7/7/1994) FL 71+23/12 FLC 2 FAC 13+3/7 Others 14+1/3
Birmingham C (£750,000 + on 12/3/1997) FL 143+26/22 FLC 14+5/2 FAC 5+2/2 Others 3+2

HUGHES Ceri Morgan
Born: Pontypridd, 26 February 1971
Height: 5'10" Weight: 12.7
International Honours: W: 8; B-2; Yth

In and out the Portsmouth team all last season due to niggling injuries, Ceri's vast experience in the game was an important factor for the club until he was finally sidelined at the beginning of February. A versatile midfield player he particularly impressed with his ability to read the game, a willingness to track back and some great crosses.

Luton T (From trainee on 1/7/1989) FL 157+18/17 FLC 13/1 FAC 11/2 Others 6
Wimbledon (£400,000 + on 4/7/1997) PL 21+10/1 FLC 2+1 FAC 2+3
Portsmouth (£150,000 on 21/1/2000) FL 31+3/2 FLC 3 FAC 0+1

HUGHES Robert **David**
Born: Wrexham, 1 February 1978
Height: 6'4" Weight: 14.0
International Honours: W: B-2 ; U21-13; Yth

David started the 2000-01 campaign a little uncertainly in the centre of the Shrewsbury Town defence but quickly found his feet and went on to produce some excellent form in the first half of the season. He moved on to Cardiff in February for a substantial fee as the Bluebirds sought to firm up their defence in the run-in to their promotion challenge. He took time to settle in at Ninian Park but by the end of the season had begun to do an effective job in sealing up the back line. David is a tall commanding central defender with a powerful long throw.

Aston Villa (From trainee on 5/7/1996) PL 4+3
Carlisle U (Loaned on 26/3/1998) FL 1

Shrewsbury T (Free on 22/9/1999) FL 42+4/3 FLC 1 FAC 4 Others 2
Cardiff C (£450,000 on 9/2/2001) FL 11+1

HUGHES Garry
Born: Birmingham, 19 November 1979
Height: 6'0" Weight: 12.2
Garry produced some excellent displays at right back for Northampton in the first half of last season before dropping back into the club's reserve team where he was mostly played as a central defender. He scored his first-ever senior goal with a shot from the edge of the box in the 2-1 against Oldham last October after rising from his sick bed to play in the game. Gary appeared regularly on the bench as an unused substitute in the second half of the campaign but was released in the summer.
Northampton T (From trainee on 7/7/1998) FL 13+5/1 FLC 2 FAC 1+2 Others 2

HUGHES Ian
Born: Bangor, 2 August 1974
Height: 5'10" Weight: 12.8
Club Honours: Div 2 '97
International Honours: W: U21-12; Yth
Ian once again captained Blackpool in 2000-01 and rarely missed a match during the campaign. A hard-tackling central defender he is strong in the air and very popular with the Tangerines' supporters. He performed consistently well all season, netting with a late header in the 2-0 victory at York and adding a vital goal in the play-off final against Leyton Orient.
Bury (From trainee on 19/11/1991) FL 137+24/1 FLC 13+3 FAC 6+2 Others 14+4/1
Blackpool (£200,000 on 12/12/1997) FL 113+9/2 FLC 10/1 FAC 5 Others 7+1/1

HUGHES Lee
Born: Smethwick, 22 May 1976
Height: 5'10" Weight: 11.6
International Honours: E: SP-4
West Bromwich Albion's leading scorer yet again, Lee was as sharp as ever during the 2000-01 season, scoring his usual mix of stunning goals and gifts handed to him on a plate. He hit a purple patch in November, netting successive hat-tricks against Gillingham and Preston and his partnerships with Jason Roberts and Bob Taylor certainly caused a lot of problems for opposing sides. A fast and direct striker who is a real workaholic and has a superb eye for goal, he scored in the first leg of the play-off semi-final against Bolton but was unable to lead the Baggies to a place in the Premiership.
West Bromwich A (£250,000 + from Kidderminster Hrs on 19/5/1997) FL 137+19/78 FLC 10+3/4 FAC 6/2 Others 2/1

HUGHES Leslie **Mark**
Born: Wrexham, 1 November 1963
Height: 5'11" Weight: 13.0
Club Honours: FAC '85, '90, '94, '97; ECWC '91, '98; ESC '91; FLC '92, '98; PL '93, '94; CS '93, '94
International Honours: W: 72; U21-5; Yth; Sch
Mark started the 2000-01 campaign in the Premiership with Everton but failed to register a goal in nine appearances. In October he moved on to join Graham Souness at Blackburn and made a huge initial impact with some stunning goals including two on his debut against Tranmere. However as the season wore on he seemed to lose much of his sharpness although he retained a strong physical presence that proved effective in breaking down stubborn defences. A vastly experienced striker he is coming to the end of his playing career and is also employed as the manager for the full Wales international team.
Manchester U (From apprentice on 5/11/1980) FL 85+4/37 FLC 5+1/4 FAC 10/4 Others 14+2/2 (£2,500,000 to Barcelona on 1/7/86)
Manchester U (£1,500,000 on 20/7/1988) F/PL 251+5/82 FLC 32/12 FAC 34+1/13 Others 27+1/8
Chelsea (£1,500,000 on 6/7/1995) PL 88+7/25 FLC 7+3/3 FAC 13+1/9 Others 1+3/2
Southampton (£650,000 on 15/7/1998) PL 50+2/2 FLC 5 FAC 2+2
Everton (Free on 14/3/2000) PL 15+3/1 FLC 1
Blackburn Rov (Free on 2/10/2000) FL 21+8/5 FAC 3+2

HUGHES Michael Eamonn
Born: Larne, 2 August 1971
Height: 5'7" Weight: 10.13
International Honours: NI: 58; U23-2; U21-1; Yth; Sch
Having suffered a broken leg in the penultimate game of the 1999-2000 campaign, Michael spent much of last season recuperating and it was not until March that he returned to the Wimbledon first team. Once back he showed that he could still be a handful to any defence as Birmingham found out to their cost when he came off the subs' bench and changed the course of the game. A wide left-sided midfield player who can also play as a striker he returned to the Northern Ireland squad in the spring.
Manchester C (From trainee on 17/8/1988) FL 25+1/1 FLC 5 FAC 1 Others 1 (£450,000 to RS Strasbourg, France in 1992 close season)
West Ham U (Loaned on 29/11/1994) PL 15+2/2 FAC 2
West Ham U (Loaned on 2/10/1995) PL 28 FLC 2 FAC 3/1
West Ham U (Free on 12/8/1996) PL 33+5/3 FLC 5 FAC 2
Wimbledon (£1,600,000 on 25/9/1997) P/FL 75+14/9 FLC 5+1/2 FAC 6+1/2

HUGHES Richard
Born: Glasgow, 25 June 1979
Height: 5'9" Weight: 9.12
International Honours: S: U21-8; Yth
Richard was one of Bournemouth's key players in the 2000-01 campaign when he was a near ever-present and formed a strong partnership in the centre of midfield with Carl Fletcher. A talented youngster with a useful left-foot shot he chipped in with some crucial goals during the campaign as the Cherries narrowly missed out on a place in the end-of-season play-offs. He featured regularly for Scotland at U21 level winning a further three caps.
Arsenal (Free from Atalanta, Italy on 11/8/1997)
Bournemouth (£20,000 on 5/8/1998) FL 107+2/12 FLC 9+1 FAC 6/1 Others 5

HUGHES Stephen John
Born: Reading, 18 September 1976
Height: 6'0" Weight: 12.12
Club Honours: FAYC '94; PL '98; CS '98
International Honours: E: U21-8; Yth; Sch
A left-sided midfielder capable of striking a football ever so sweetly - as witnessed by a stunning FA Cup free-kick at Watford - Stephen appeared only fitfully in the Everton midfield last season. He was selected in Walter Smith's first starting line-up of the season and stayed there for six games without ever showing the authority or style he was clearly capable of. Another seven-match run in the first team ended with a debilitating dose of 'flu and he struggled to force his way back into the reckoning. He was reported to have signed for Watford in the summer.
Arsenal (From trainee on 15/7/1995) PL 22+27/4 FLC 5+3/1 FAC 7+7/1 Others 2+4/1
Fulham (Loaned on 26/7/1999) FL 3 FLC 1
Everton (£500,000 + on 10/3/2000) PL 27+2/1 FLC 1+1 FAC 2/1

HULBERT Robin James
Born: Plymouth, 14 March 1980
Height: 5'9" Weight: 10.5
International Honours: E: Yth; Sch
Robin featured regularly in the Bristol City squad in the early part of last season but then went down with a groin problem that kept him out of action for three months and it was not until towards the end of the campaign that he returned to the side. A hard-tackling player who usually operates on the right-hand side of midfield he will be aiming to establish himself firmly in the starting line-up in 2001-02.
Swindon T (From trainee on 25/9/1997) FL 12+17 FLC 1+1 FAC 2
Bristol C (£25,000 on 23/3/2000) FL 15+6 FLC 0+2

HULME Kevin
Born: Farnworth, 2 December 1967
Height: 5'10" Weight: 13.2
Club Honours: FAT '96; FC '98
This combative midfield player struggled to win a regular first-team place for York City last season before he tore a medial knee ligament at Barnet in January. The injury put him on the long-term sick list and his career effectively came to a close in March when he was released on medical grounds. Kevin scored three crucial goals for the Minstermen netting two in the 3-2 victory over Shrewsbury and also in the 2-1 success over Torquay.
Bury (£5,000 from Radcliffe Borough on 16/3/1989) FL 82+28/21 FLC 4+3/2 FAC 4+1/1 Others 4+8/2
Chester C (Loaned on 26/10/1989) FL 4
Doncaster Rov (£42,500 on 14/7/1993) FL 33+1/8 FLC 2/1 FAC 1 Others 2
Bury (£42,500 on 11/8/1994) FL 24+5 FLC 2 FAC 2 Others 2
Lincoln C (Signed on 28/9/1995) FL 4+1 FAC 1 Others 1+1 (Free to Macclesfield T on 15/12/1995)
Halifax T (Free on 22/11/1996) FL 32+1/4 FLC 4+1 Others 2
York C (Free on 10/9/1999) FL 34+4/7 FLC 2 FAC 4 Others 2

HULSE Robert (Rob) William
Born: Crewe, 25 October 1979
Height: 6'1" Weight: 11.4

Having previously made just a handful of appearances from the subs' bench Rob made excellent progress at Crewe last season and featured in most of the club's First Division games. His first goal of the season came against Barnsley towards the end of September and he followed this up with doubles at Tranmere and Grimsby, eventually going on to finish as the Railwaymen's leading scorer with 11 goals. A very promising young striker he uses his height to good effect and has established an excellent partnership up front with Dean Ashton.

Crewe Alex (From trainee on 25/6/1998) FL 22+15/12 FLC 2+1 FAC 1+1

HUME Iain
Born: Brampton, Ontario, Canada, 31 October 1983
Height: 5'7" Weight: 11.2
International Honours: Canada: Yth

Iain continued to make excellent progress at Tranmere last season when he was a regular in the successful reserve team and made a number of appearances as a substitute for the first team. An assured and unflappable striker who can kick with either foot he will be aiming to win a regular place in Rovers' first-team squad in 2001-02. He was a regular for the Canada U20 team and featured in their squad for the World Youth Championships in Argentina during the summer.

Tranmere Rov (From juniors on 6/11/2000) FL 0+13 FAC 0+1

HUMPHREYS Richard (Richie) John
Born: Sheffield, 30 November 1977
Height: 5'11" Weight: 14.6
International Honours: E: U21-3; Yth

Although he had a short run in the Sheffield Wednesday line-up last September Richie was again on the fringes of the first-team squad at Hillsborough in 2000-01 and in the new year he opted for a transfer to Second Division Cambridge United. He made an instant impact at the Abbey Stadium scoring three goals in seven matches but then suffered a broken bone in his foot at Luton that put him out for of the season. He is a stocky young striker with good skills on the ball. Out of contract in the summer his future was uncertain at the time of writing.

Sheffield Wed (From trainee on 8/2/1996) P/FL 34+33/4 FLC 4+2 FAC 5+4/4
Scunthorpe U (Loaned on 13/8/1999) FL 6/2
Cardiff C (Loaned on 22/11/1999) FL 8+1/2 FAC 1 Others 1
Cambridge U (Free on 2/2/2001) FL 7/3

HUNT Andrew (Andy)
Born: Grays, 9 June 1970
Height: 6'0" Weight: 12.0
Club Honours: Div 1 '00

Andy started the 200-01 campaign as a first choice in the Charlton line-up, scoring once in the opening day thrashing of Manchester City and a further two at Highbury the following week. However he managed only a handful more appearances before being struck down by post-viral fatigue syndrome and this eventually brought about his retirement from the game on medical grounds. When fit Andy is a hard working striker who holds the ball up well to bring others into the game. He is also good in the air and scores a fair proportion of his goals with his head.

Newcastle U (£150,000 from Kettering T on 29/1/1991) FL 34+9/11 FLC 3/1 FAC 2/2 Others 3
West Bromwich A (£100,000 on 25/3/1993) FL 201+11/76 FLC 12/4 FAC 7/2 Others 8+1/3
Charlton Ath (Free on 2/7/1998) P/FL 83+3/35 FLC 3 FAC 5/1

HUNT James Malcolm
Born: Derby, 17 December 1976
Height: 5'8" Weight: 10.3

This enthusiastic midfield dynamo was a fixture in the Northampton Town line-up last season until suffering medial knee ligament damage at Rotherham on Easter Monday which put him out of action for the final few games. Operating as a box-to-box player he appeared to cover every blade of grass in matches and still had time to contribute the occasional goal for the Cobblers.

Notts Co (From trainee on 15/7/1994) FL 15+4/1 FAC 0+1 Others 2+2/1
Northampton T (Free on 7/8/1997) FL 112+22/4 FLC 6+2 FAC 5+3/1 Others 8+1

HUNT Jonathan (Jon) Richard
Born: Camden, 2 November 1971
Height: 5'10" Weight: 11.12
Club Honours: Div 2 '95; AMC '95

Jon joined Wimbledon last September on a contract to the end of the season but after playing regularly in his first few weeks with the club he soon lost his place as established players returned from injury and he then found it difficult to get back in the side. A wide midfield player who can play on either flank he is also something of a dead-ball specialist. He was released by the Dons in the summer.

Barnet (From juniors in 1989-90) FL 12+21 FLC 1 FAC 0+1 Others 6+2
Southend U (Free on 20/7/1993) FL 41+8/6 FLC 1+3 FAC 1 Others 6+1
Birmingham C (£50,000 on 16/9/1994) FL 67+10/18 FLC 10+5/2 FAC 3+1/1 Others 8/4
Derby Co (£500,000 on 23/5/1997) PL 7+18/2 FLC 2+2 FAC 0+3
Sheffield U (Loaned on 20/8/1998) FL 4+1/1
Ipswich T (Loaned on 20/10/1998) FL 2+4
Sheffield U (Signed on 12/3/1999) FL 16+6/1 FLC 2+2 FAC 3
Cambridge U (Loaned on 23/3/2000) FL 3+4/1
Wimbledon (Free on 18/9/2000) FL 8+4 FLC 1+1 FAC 0+2/1

HUNT Nicholas (Nicky) Brett
Born: Bolton, 3 September 1983
Height: 6'1" Weight: 10.6

Nicky began the 2000-01 campaign as a first-year academy boy at Bolton but made such fine progress that he moved up to the reserve team in the new year and went on to make his Football League debut against Sheffield United in the final game of the regular season, coming off the subs' bench for the final seven minutes to replace Colin Hendry. A quick centre back, he will be hoping to gain further senior experience in the coming season.

Bolton W (Trainee) FL 0+1

HUNTER Barry Victor
Born: Coleraine, 18 November 1968
Height: 6'3" Weight: 13.2
International Honours: NI: 15; B-2; Yth

Barry began last term as a first-choice at centre back for Reading alongside Adrian Viveash, but lost his place following a hamstring injury and then found it difficult to get back in the side. A stylish defender he has a good touch on the ball and is very effective in the air. He created a small piece of history by becoming the first professional footballer to be selected to appear on the BBC television programme 'The Weakest Link'.

Newcastle U (Signed from Coleraine on 2/11/1987. Freed during 1988 close season)
Wrexham (£50,000 from Crusaders on 20/8/1993) FL 88+3/4 FLC 6 FAC 7+1/1 Others 15/1
Reading (£400,000 on 12/7/1996) FL 76+8/4 FLC 5/1 FAC 3+1/1 Others 6+1
Southend U (Loaned on 12/2/1999) FL 5/2

HUNTER Leon David
Born: Walthamstow, 27 August 1981
Height: 5'10" Weight: 10.10

Another product of the Southend United youth set-up, Leon made his debut in senior football when he came off the subs' bench for the final 15 minutes of the Worthington Cup tie at Birmingham City. He was unable to force himself into the first team on a regular basis and had a spell on loan with Dr Martens League club Chelmsford City in January. Leon is a wide midfield player who will be hoping to break into the squad at Roots Hall in the coming season.

Southend U (Trainee) FLC 0+1

HUNTER Roy Ian
Born: Saltburn, 29 October 1973
Height: 5'10" Weight: 12.8

Roy was again badly affected by injury problems last season. He lasted just two minutes when making a return to the Northampton reserve team last September and it was not until March that he finally appeared to have recovered from his long-standing knee injury. After a few outings from the subs' bench he made the starting line-up for the final game of the campaign at home to Walsall. When fully fit he is a dynamic midfield player for the Cobblers and he will be hoping that his injury problems are now behind him.

West Bromwich A (From trainee on 4/3/1992) FL 3+6/1 Others 4+1
Northampton T (Free on 2/8/1995) FL 111+26/13 FLC 9 FAC 9/2 Others 12/1

HURST Glynn
Born: Barnsley, 17 January 1976
Height: 5'10" Weight: 11.10

Glynn was in fine goal-scoring form for Ayr United last season netting 17 times in 19 appearances including a hat-trick against Falkirk and five in a 6-0 win at Morton. Such prolific exploits persuaded Stockport County manager Andy Kilner to bring him to Edgeley Park where he proved a perfect foil for Shefki Kuqi and Aaron Wilbraham in a three-pronged strike force. Surprisingly he didn't register a goal for the Hatters himself but still impressed with his blistering pace and unselfish running off the ball.

Barnsley (From trainee at Tottenham H on 13/7/1994) FL 0+8 FLC 1 (Freed on 27/3/1997)
Swansea C (Loaned on 15/12/1995) FL 2/1
Mansfield T (Loaned on 18/11/1996) FL 5+1 Others 0+1
Ayr U (£30,000 from Emley on 23/3/1998) SL 78/49 SLC 6/2 SC 10 Others 1+2
Stockport Co (£150,000 on 16/2/2001) FL 10+1

HURST Paul Michael
Born: Sheffield, 25 September 1974
Height: 5'4" Weight: 9.4
Club Honours: AMC '96

After being on the substitutes' bench for Rotherham during the opening month of the 2000-01 campaign Paul was promoted to the starting line-up at the beginning of September and seized his opportunity to retain his place for the rest of the season. He mainly featured on the left side of midfield although he is equally at home at left back, and surprised everyone when he out-jumped much taller opponents to head a vital winner against Colchester United in February.

Rotherham U (From trainee on 12/8/1993) FL 185+38/11 FLC 5+1 FAC 15+2/2 Others 14+1

HUTCHINGS Carl Emil
Born: Hammersmith, 24 September 1974
Height: 5'11" Weight: 11.0

Carl found himself out of favour at Bristol City last autumn and in December he moved to Exeter for a loan period. Unfortunately the Grecians lost all three games in which he appeared but he then made a permanent move to Southend where he linked up with his old boss David Webb. After a few games in midfield he dropped back to form an effective central defensive partnership with Phil Whelan. His experience proved invaluable as he helped to guide the younger members of the team through some difficult matches towards the end of the campaign, but nevertheless he was released at the end of the season.

Brentford (From trainee on 12/7/1993) FL 144+18/7 FLC 9+1 FAC 11+1 Others 11+3
Bristol C (£130,000 on 6/7/1998) FL 33+9/3 FLC 4+1/2 FAC 2+2 Others 1
Brentford (Loaned on 11/2/2000) FL 7+1
Exeter C (Loaned on 30/11/2000) FL 2 Others 1
Southend U (Free on 29/12/2000) FL 14 FAC 1

HUTCHINSON Edward (Eddie) Stephen
Born: Kingston, 23 February 1982
Height: 6'1" Weight: 12.7

Eddie joined Brentford from non-league football during the 2000 summer break but missed a substantial part of last season with a shin injury. It was not until April that he finally made his debut in senior football when he came on as a substitute against Swindon. A neat central midfield player he will be looking to establish a regular presence in the Bees' first-team squad in the 2001-02 campaign.

Brentford (£75,000 from Sutton U on 21/7/2000) FL 5+2

HUTCHISON Donald (Don)
Born: Gateshead, 9 May 1971
Height: 6'1" Weight: 11.8
International Honours: S: 10; B-1

A summer capture from Everton, Don was without doubt one of the 'steals' of the 2000-01 season and his acquisition represents another outstanding piece of business by Sunderland boss Peter Reid. Although he took a little time to settle in with his new team-mates his season took off after netting two goals in a Worthington Cup tie at Bristol Rovers and he never looked back. He can play in midfield or attack although the former is probably his best position as his superb reading of the game and passing ability can be used to maximum effect. His season was littered with high points, notably an equalising goal in the North-East 'derby' against Newcastle in November and two further strikes from quickly-taken free-kicks against Manchester City and West Ham. He continued to feature regularly for Scotland and his superb contribution to Sunderland's campaign was recognised when he was voted the Supporters Association's 'Player of the Year'.

Hartlepool U (From trainee on 20/3/1990) FL 19+5/2 FLC 1+1 FAC 2 Others 1
Liverpool (£175,000 on 27/11/1990) F/PL 33+12/7 FLC 7+1/2 FAC 1+2 Others 3+1/1
West Ham U (£1,500,000 on 30/8/1994) PL 30+5/11 FLC 3/2 FAC 0+1
Sheffield U (£1,200,000 on 11/1/1996) FL 70+8/5 FLC 3+2 FAC 5/1 Others 2+1
Everton (£1,000,000 + on 27/2/1998) PL 68+7/10 FLC 4+1/1 FAC 9
Sunderland (£2,500,000 on 19/7/2000) PL 30+2/8 FLC 2/2 FAC 3

HYDE Graham
Born: Doncaster, 10 November 1970
Height: 5'8" Weight: 11.11

Graham had a frustrating time at Birmingham last season and made little impact at first-team level featuring in just a handful of games. An experienced central midfield player who is always on the move and available for a pass, he performed professionally when called upon and was neat and tidy on the ball.

Sheffield Wed (From trainee on 17/5/1988) F/PL 126+46/11 FLC 17+3/2 FAC 13+5/2 Others 8/1
Birmingham C (Free on 5/2/1999) FL 34+13/1 FLC 2+2/1 FAC 2

HYDE Micah Anthony
Born: Newham, 10 November 1974
Height: 5'9" Weight: 11.5
Club Honours: Div 2 '98
International Honours: Jamaica: 5

Micah missed the opening games of last season through suspension, but made a scoring return against Sheffield United and seemed set to carry on the impressive form he had shown in 1999-2000. His shooting in particular seemed improved and he was briefly leading scorer after netting doubles against Blackburn and Nottingham Forest and a memorable goal at home to Crewe. However, he then suffered a recurrence of a knee injury that caused a dip in his form at the turn of the year, and an attack of chicken pox was a source of further frustration. Micah received an end-of-season boost when he was called up for Jamaica, making his debut from the subs' bench in the World Cup qualifier against Honduras in April and retaining his place in the squad for the next few games. A combative central midfield player he has now made over 250 league appearances for the Hornets.

Cambridge U (From trainee on 19/5/1993) FL 89+18/13 FLC 3 FAC 7+2 Others 4+1
Watford (£225,000 on 21/7/1997) P/FL 133+11/15 FLC 10/2 FAC 7 Others 3

HYYPIA Sami
Born: Porvoo, Finland, 7 October 1973
Height: 6'4" Weight: 13.5
Club Honours: FLC '01; FAC '01; UEFAC '01
International Honours: Finland: 39; U21; Yth

After a slow start to the 2000-01 campaign, Sami settled down in the Liverpool back line alongside Stephane Henchoz and he was soon back to his best form helping the Reds to win three major trophies and clinch a place in the Champions' League for 2001-02. His performances in the UEFA Cup clashes with Roma and Barcelona were Herculean as he exuded coolness and authority to ensure that while the Reds might be outplayed in midfield their opponents were denied the space and opportunity to exploit their domination. His power in the air was also in evidence in the opposition penalty area and he scored four goals, none more vital than his late winner at Coventry in April in a match Liverpool might easily have lost. A 'stopper' centre half in the grand tradition of Ron Yeats, Larry Lloyd and Mark Wright he is arguably a more complete player than any of his predecessors. He was joined at Anfield by his compatriot Jari Litmanen in January and both remained mainstays of the Finland national team last term.

Liverpool (£2,600,000 from Willem II, Holland, ex MyPa, on 7/7/1999) PL 73/5 FLC 8/1 FAC 8 Others 11

Sami Hyypia

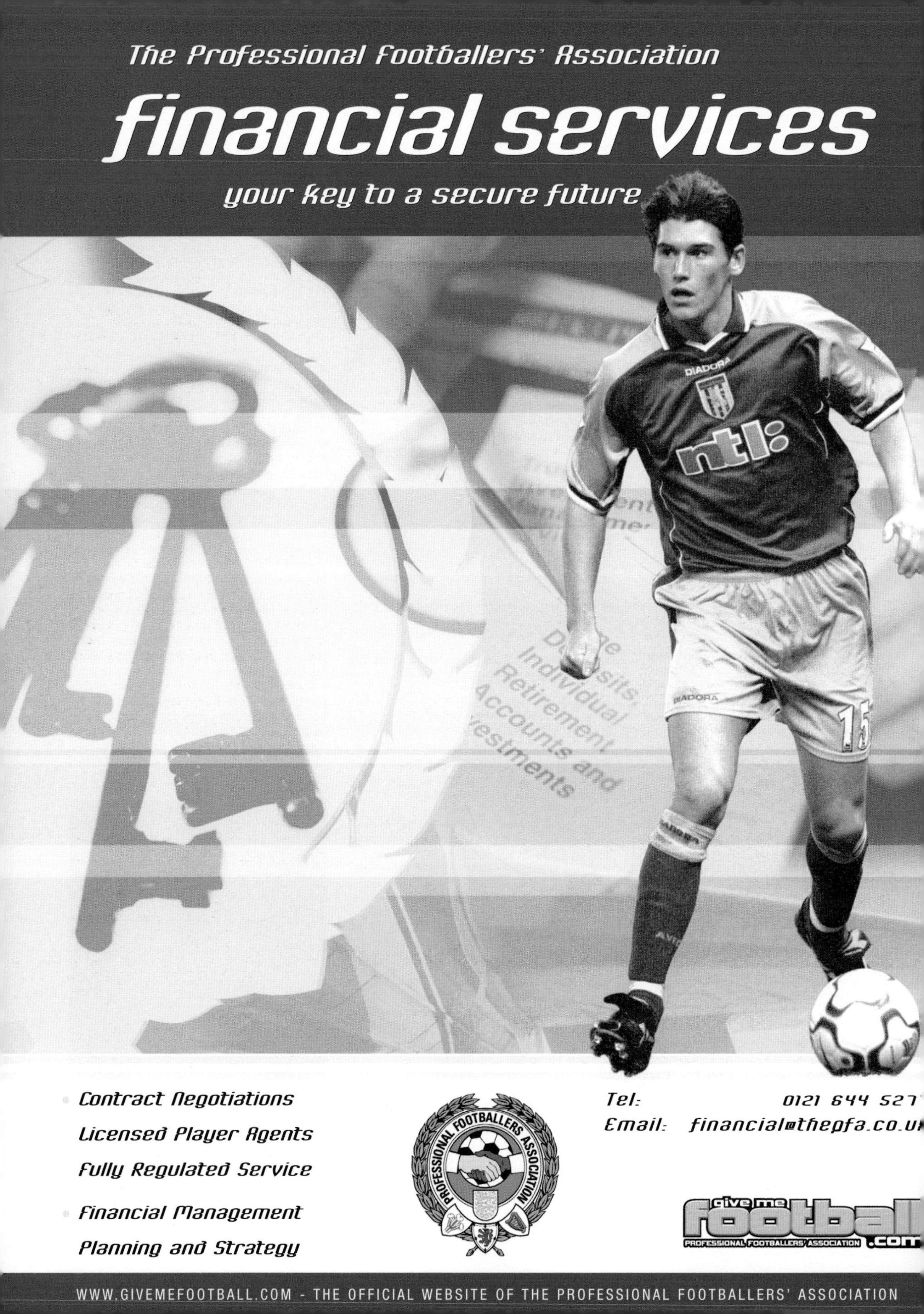
The Professional Footballers' Association
financial services
your key to a secure future
DIADORA
ntl:
Contract Negotiations
Licensed Player Agents
Fully Regulated Service
Financial Management
Planning and Strategy
PROFESSIONAL FOOTBALLERS ASSOCIATION
Tel: 0121 644 527
Email: financial@thepfa.co.u
give me football .com
PROFESSIONAL FOOTBALLERS' ASSOCIATION
WWW.GIVEMEFOOTBALL.COM - THE OFFICIAL WEBSITE OF THE PROFESSIONAL FOOTBALLERS' ASSOCIATION

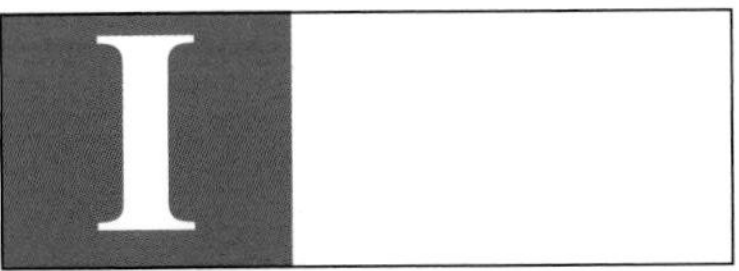

IBEHRE Jabo Oshevire
Born: Islington, 28 January 1983
Height: 6'2" Weight: 12.10

Jabo continued to make steady progress at Leyton Orient last term and after a couple of brief appearances early on in the season he dropped out of the first-team picture for a while. He played for the U19s in the Football League Youth Alliance Cup final before being thrust into the senior team at the end of the campaign due to injuries and suspensions. He made an immediate impact by scoring twice on his first start at Macclesfield and retained his place for the play-offs. A quick, strong centre forward he will be looking to feature more regularly for the O's in 2001-02.

Leyton Orient (Trainee) FL 1+7/2 FLC 0+1 Others 3

IFILL Paul
Born: Brighton, 20 October 1979
Height: 6'0" Weight: 12.10
Club Honours: Div 2 '01

Having come up through the ranks at Millwall, Paul is still learning the game but came on in leaps and bounds last season. He is a very fast, tricky winger who has the ability to turn defences inside out and can also deliver a telling cross. As well as being an excellent provider he is something of a goal-scorer too and one of the highlights of a great campaign was his hat-trick in the 5-1 win at Cambridge in April.

Millwall (From trainee on 2/6/1998) FL 78+16/18 FLC 2/1 FAC 4 Others 6+1

IGOE Samuel (Sammy) Gary
Born: Staines, 30 September 1975
Height: 5'6" Weight: 10.0

Sammy played an important role in Reading's quest for promotion last season, although he was often used from the subs' bench and it was only in the later stages of the campaign that he featured regularly in the starting line-up. Looking more effective when played out wide on the right rather than in a central role he chipped in with some valuable goals including two fine efforts in the 5-0 home win against Oldham Athletic. He is an attacking midfield player who crosses the ball accurately and is comfortable on the ball.

Portsmouth (From trainee on 15/2/1994) FL 100+60/11 FLC 8+5 FAC 2+3
Reading (£100,000 on 23/3/2000) FL 18+19/6 FLC 2 FAC 2 Others 5

Jabo Ibehre

ILIC Sasa
Born: Melbourne, Australia, 18 July 1972
Height: 6'4" Weight: 14.0
International Honours: Yugoslavia: 1

Sasa found himself mainly on the subs' bench for Charlton at the start of last season making only one start - in the Worthington Cup tie against Stoke at The Valley. He then picked up a rib injury at the end of October that sidelined him for two months before finally claiming his place in the Addicks line-up last January after Dean Kiely was injured. Given a decent run in the side Sasa had a shaky start but quickly found his form and a series of steady performances earned him a recall to the Yugoslavian international squad towards the end of the season.

Charlton Ath (Free from St Leonards Stamcroft on 5/10/1997) P/FL 51 FLC 3 FAC 2 Others 3
West Ham U (Loaned on 24/2/2000) PL 1

IMPEY Andrew (Andy) Rodney
Born: Hammersmith, 13 September 1971
Height: 5'8" Weight: 11.2
Club Honours: FLC '00
International Honours: E: U21-1

Andy was the first-choice right wing back for Leicester City for much of the 2000-01 season and was particularly impressive during City's excellent early run when he seemed to adapt very quickly to the requirements of the new Peter Taylor regime. He seemed less effective after returning from injury in the spring when the whole team was suffering from a more general malaise, but turned in a useful performance at left back in the Easter defeat by Manchester City.

Queens Park R (£35,000 from Yeading on 14/6/1990) F/PL 177+10/13 FLC 15+1/3 FAC 7+3/1 Others 0+2/1
West Ham U (£1,300,000 on 26/9/1997) PL 25+2 FLC 4 FAC 3
Leicester C (£1,600,000 on 25/11/1998) PL 74+6/1 FLC 5+2 FAC 6+1 Others 2

INCE Clayton
Born: Trinidad, 13 July 1972
Height: 6'3" Weight: 14.2
International Honours: Trinidad & Tobago

Clayton again rarely featured for Crewe Alexandra last season and in October he moved to Scottish club Dundee for a loan period, although he failed to make a senior appearance there either. His only first-team game for the Railwaymen came when he replaced Ade Bankole in the closing stages of the game at Birmingham in March. However he continued to appear regularly for Trinidad & Tobago, being the first-choice 'keeper for their World Cup qualifying campaign. Despite his lack of experience at Gresty Road he is actually the club's most capped player, having appeared in 29 international matches since joining the Railwaymen.

Crewe Alex (£50,000 from Defence Force, Trinidad on 21/9/1999) FL 0+2

INCE Paul Emerson Carlyle
Born: Ilford, 21 October 1967
Height: 5'11" Weight: 12.2
Club Honours: CS '93, '94; FAC '90, '94; ECW '91; ESC '91; FLC '92; PL '93, '94

International Honours: E: 53; B-1; U21-2; Yth

Middlesbrough's skipper in 2000-01 Paul led the team by sheer determination and example and his battling displays in the centre of the park ensured that no one was ever left in any doubt as to who controlled the midfield. He tackled with frightening zeal and showed a gritty tenaciousness and ferocity in the application of his football skills. If only Boro' could find another ten with the same spirit that he shows they would never find themselves in relegation trouble again!

West Ham U (From apprentice on 18/7/1985) FL 66+6/7 FLC 9/3 FAC 8+2/1 Others 4/1
Manchester U (£1,000,000 on 14/9/1989) F/PL 203+3/24 FLC 23+1/2 FAC 26+1/1 Others 24/1 (£8,000,000 to Inter Milan, Italy on 13/7/1995)
Liverpool (£4,200,000 on 22/7/1997) PL 65/14 FLC 6/1 FAC 3/1 Others 7/1
Middlesbrough (£1,000,000 on 3/8/1999) PL 62/5 FLC 5/1 FAC 3

INGIMARSSON Ivar
Born: Iceland, 20 August 1978
Height: 6'0" Weight: 12.7
International Honours: Iceland: 2; U21-14; Yth

Ivar began the 2000-01 campaign as an attacking central midfield player for Brentford but made an early-season switch to centre back where he proved to be a revelation, performing very much in the style of fellow countryman Hermann Hreidarsson, another former player for the Griffin Park club. He performed equally well in both positions putting his passing skills and excellent positional sense to good use. Ivar won a runners-up medal in the LDV Vans Trophy when he appeared for the Bees in the 2-1 defeat by Port Vale last April and added a further cap for Iceland when he appeared in the friendly fixture with Poland last November.

Torquay U (Loaned from IBV Vestmannaeyjar, Iceland on 21/10/1999) FL 4/1
Brentford (£150,000 on 18/11/1999) FL 63+4/4 FLC 4 FAC 1 Others 9/1

INGLEDOW Jamie Graeme
Born: Barnsley, 23 August 1980
Height: 5'6" Weight: 9.7

Jamie joined Chesterfield in July 2000 and his patient work on fitness paid off when he established himself as a regular in the line-up in the new year. He brought sound defensive qualities to the centre of midfield and also contributed in attack, being particularly adept at making and receiving passes on the edge of opponents' penalty boxes. Jamie netted three goals for the Spireites, the first being an injury-time winner in the tense battle with promotion rivals Brighton last October.

Rotherham U (From trainee on 1/7/1998) FL 17+8/2 FLC 3 FAC 5 Others 2+1
Chesterfield (Free on 19/7/2000) FL 14+10/3 FLC 0+1 Others 3

INGLETHORPE Alexander (Alex) Matthew
Born: Epsom, 14 November 1971
Height: 5'11" Weight: 11.6

An attacking midfielder who can play up front, Alex appeared regularly for Exeter City in the early part of the 2000-01 campaign before falling out of favour and moving on loan to Canvey Island last December. He featured for the Ryman League club in their FA Cup tie against Southend United and once back at St James Park he eventually won a recall to the Grecians team in February. He was released in May.

Watford (From juniors on 1/7/1990) FL 2+10/2 FLC 1+2 Others 1+1/1
Barnet (Loaned on 23/3/1995) FL 5+1/3
Leyton Orient (Signed on 19/5/1995) FL 105+18/32 FLC 6/4 FAC 3+5 Others 3+3/1
Exeter C (Loaned on 24/2/2000) FL 0+1 Others 1
Exeter C (Free on 18/7/2000) FL 11+7/2 FLC 2

INGLIS John
Born: Edinburgh, 16 October 1966
Height: 6'0" Weight: 13.0
Club Honours: SLC '96

Having spent some time in Bulgaria John returned to link up with Third Division outfit Carlisle United at the end of September. He featured on several occasions in defence for the Cumbrians, often looking impressive, but it was not enough to earn a permanent deal and in January he signed for Raith Rovers on a short-term contract to the end of the season.

East Fife (Signed from Hutcheson Vale on 15/7/1983) SL 38+18/1 SC 1
Brechin C (Free on 17/12/1986) SL 51+2/4 SLC 2 SC 4
Meadowbank Thistle (Signed on 14/12/1988) SL 47+3/4 SLC 0+1 SC 1
St Johnstone (Signed on 23/6/1990) SL 139+1/2 SLC 9 SC 16 Others 2
Aberdeen (Signed on 28/10/1994) SL 96+2/4 SLC 12/1 SC 6+1 Others 4 (Free to Levski Sofia, Bulgaria on 28/10/1999)
Aberdeen (Free on 2/8/2000)
Carlisle U (Free on 29/9/2000) FL 8

INGRAM Rae
Born: Manchester, 6 December 1974
Height: 5'11" Weight: 12.8

Rae featured at centre back for Macclesfield Town for most of the 2000-2001 season and apart from a two-month absence with a knee injury at the turn of the year he was a near ever-present for the Moss Rose club. A skilful defender who can also play at right back, he controls the ball well, passes accurately and moves round opponents with ease. He scored his first-ever league goal in the home win against Cheltenham last October 2000, volleying home after he had moved up to receive a flick-on from Lee Glover. He was reported to have signed for Port Vale in the summer.

Manchester C (From trainee on 9/7/1993) P/FL 18+5 FLC 1 FAC 4
Macclesfield T (Free on 19/3/1998) FL 95+8/1 FLC 6 FAC 4+1 Others 1+1

INNES Mark
Born: Glasgow, 27 September 1978
Height: 5'10" Weight: 12.1

After starting the 2000-01 season on the transfer list, Mark finally cemented a first-team place at Oldham Athletic when a switch from midfield to left back saw him unexpectedly oust Andy Holt from the side. Such was the transformation in his fortunes that he finally came off the list in April and now looks to have a much brighter future at Boundary Park.

Oldham Ath (From trainee on 10/10/1995) FL 52+16/1 FLC 4+2 FAC 4 Others 1+1

INVINCIBLE Daniel (Danny)
Born: Australia, 31 March 1979
Height: 6'4" Weight: 12.2
International Honours: Australia: Sch

Danny was very much the find of the season for Swindon Town last term. Spotted by then-boss Colin Todd while on a trial at West Ham he was quickly signed up and became a great favourite with the club's fans. He netted regularly during the campaign, finishing as leading scorer, while his spectacular injury-time winner against Peterborough United in the final home game of the season ensured that the Robins avoided the ignominy of being relegated for a second year in a row. An attacking right-sided midfield player he possesses great pace and delights at running at defenders.

Swindon T (Free from Marconi Stallions, Australia on 10/8/2000) FL 32+10/9 FLC 1+1/1 FAC 3 Others 2

IPOUA Gui (Guy)
Born: Douala, Cameroon, 14 January 1976
Height: 6'1" Weight: 12.0

Guy was still recovering from an ankle operation at the start of the 2000-01 campaign and his season didn't start until the end of September, but by early January he was already Scunthorpe's leading scorer having had an amazing spell in November when he hit a hat-trick against Hartlepool and followed this with four goals in a 6-0 thrashing of Mansfield. Due to be out of contract in the summer he reportedly refused a new deal with the Iron and was sold to Gillingham for a bargain fee just before transfer deadline day. Although he only featured from the subs' bench for the Gills in the closing weeks of the season he did enough to suggest he may be able to take the place vacated by Carl Asaba when he moved on to Sheffield United. He is a strong powerful striker with a very direct style. Guy is the brother of the Cameroon international Samuel Ipoua.

Bristol Rov (Free from Seville, Spain on 7/8/1998) FL 15+9/3 FLC 1+1 FAC 3+1 Others 1
Scunthorpe U (Free on 27/8/1999) FL 50+15/23 FAC 5/4 Others 2
Gillingham (£25,000 on 19/3/2001) FL 0+9

IRELAND Craig
Born: Dundee, 29 November 1975
Height: 6'3" Weight: 13.9

Craig began the 2000-01 campaign on an extended loan at Airdrie and scored on his debut in a 5-1 win at Morton. He moved south of the border in the new year to link up with his old boss Jocky Scott at Notts County in another long-term loan deal and impressed with some assured performances in the back line. He is an accomplished central defender who can also play at left back if required.

Aberdeen (From juniors on 5/10/1994) SLC 1
Dunfermline Ath (Free on 12/2/1996) SL 61+6/2 SLC 0+2 SC 0+1
Dundee (Free on 27/10/1999) SL 14/1 SC 1

Airdrieonians (Loaned on 12/10/2000) SL 12/2 Others 1
Notts Co (Loaned on 2/2/2001) FL 16

IRONS Kenneth (Kenny)
Born: Liverpool, 4 November 1970
Height: 5'10" Weight: 12.2
Huddersfield Town's midfield maestro suffered from some niggling injuries last season and found it difficult to hit his best form for much of the campaign. A skilful play maker he was always at the hub of play and impressed with his high quality passing and close control. Often used from the subs' bench he also seemed to be unsettled by news of a transfer bid by his old club Tranmere but hopefully he will recover full fitness and return to a regular place in the Terriers' line-up in 2000-01.
Tranmere Rov (From trainee on 9/11/1989) FL 313+39/54 FLC 24+7/7 FAC 14+2/3 Others 28+3/3
Huddersfield T (£450,000 on 18/6/1999) FL 57+16/3 FLC 7/2 FAC 1

IRWIN Joseph **Denis**
Born: Cork, 31 October 1965
Height: 5'8" Weight: 11.0
Club Honours: CS '93, '96, '97; ECWC '91; ESC '91; FLC '92; PL '93, '94, '96, '97, '99, '00, '01; FAC '94, '96; EC '99
International Honours: RoI: 56; B-1; U23-1; U21-3; Yth; Sch
Denis started his tenth season at Manchester United vying for his customary left-back slot with the likes of the Neville brothers and Mickael Silvestre. Proving that he's not quite ready for the footballer's 'zimmer frame' just yet, he certainly gave the youngsters a run for their money with ten full appearances before the end of the year. In the Champions' League too he showed he could still take a mean penalty, netting from the spot in both ties against Anderlecht in the autumn. He celebrated his 500th senior game at Old Trafford appropriately on St. Patrick's Day and continued to appear for the Republic of Ireland at international level.
Leeds U (From apprentice on 3/11/1983) FL 72/1 FLC 5 FAC 3 Others 2
Oldham Ath (Free on 22/5/1986) FL 166+1/4 FLC 19/3 FAC 13 Others 5
Manchester U (£625,000 on 20/6/1990) F/PL 346+10/22 FLC 28+3 FAC 42+1/7 Others 76/4

IVERSEN Steffen
Born: Oslo, Norway, 10 November 1976
Height: 6'1" Weight: 11.10
Club Honours: FLC '99
International Honours: Norway: 24; U21; Yth
After appearing for Norway in the Euro 2000 finals Steffen found himself playing in a wide-right role as Les Ferdinand and Sergei Rebrov took the main strikers positions for Spurs last season. He featured regularly early on but was then sidelined by a knee injury that required corrective surgery and it was not until the end of February that he returned to first-team action. He netted with a glancing header in the 3-0 win over Coventry and also scored a neat goal against Bradford City in April. Having signed a new four-year contract back in September he will be hoping for a better degree of fortune next term.
Tottenham H (£2,700,000 from Rosenborg, Norway, ex Nationalkam, on 7/12/1996) PL 92+14/31 FLC 9+1/4 FAC 9+2/3 Others 4/1

Kenny Irons

IWELUMO Christopher (Chris) Robert
Born: Coatbridge, 1 August 1978
Height: 6'3" Weight: 13.8
Chris made a handful of early-season appearances for Stoke City last term, scoring within two minutes of coming off the subs' bench in the 5-1 Worthington Cup win at York and heading an excellent winner in the home game with Millwall. He then went on loan to Third Division York City where he scored three goals including one in the 3-1 FA Cup second round replay victory over Reading. He returned to the Britannia Stadium in February and soon afterwards moved out on loan again this time to Cheltenham where he scored a well-taken goal on his debut against Mansfield. However he subsequently suffered a groin injury and failed to recapture the form of his early games. He is a tall, powerfully built target man with a good touch for such a big man.
St Mirren (From juniors on 5/8/1996) SL 7+19 SLC 0+3/1 SC 1+1/1 Others 0+2 (Free to Aarhus Fremad, Denmark during 1998 close season)
Stoke C (£25,000 from AGF Aarhus, Denmark on 1/3/2000) FL 0+5/1 FLC 0+2/1 Others 0+1
York C (Loaned on 10/11/2000) FL 11+1/2 FAC 4/1
Cheltenham T (Loaned on 13/2/2001) FL 2+2/1

IZZET Kemal (Kem)
Born: Whitechapel, 29 September 1980
Height: 5'8" Weight: 10.5
After developing through the ranks at Charlton, Kem joined Colchester United in a loan deal on the transfer deadline day. He proved an inspirational signing for U's boss Steve Whitton and within a matter of weeks a permanent move was arranged. Kem gave the Colchester midfield a new competitive edge with his sharp tackling and boundless energy and he scored his first senior goal to earn a vital point in the 2-2 draw with Peterborough in April. Kem is the younger brother of Leicester City's Muzzy Izzet.
Charlton Ath (From trainee on 11/1/1999)
Colchester U (Signed on 22/3/2001) FL 5+1/1

IZZET Mustafa (Muzzy) Kemal
Born: Mile End, 31 October 1974
Height: 5'10" Weight: 10.12
Club Honours: FLC '97, '00
International Honours: Turkey: 2
Muzzy showed excellent form for Leicester City throughout the 2000-01 season, taking on extra responsibility when his partner Neil Lennon departed for Celtic, and thriving in a role as the forward-breaking midfielder. He managed to score goals on a regular basis but injuries took a greater toll than in previous years and seemed to stifle his international ambitions at times. He was sidelined by injury after the disastrous FA Cup defeat by Wycombe and the same problem flared up again on his return against Coventry ruling him out for the rest of the season. He was sorely missed in his absence when his true value to the team became apparent. Muzzy is the older brother of Colchester's Kem Izzet.
Chelsea (From trainee on 19/5/1993)
Leicester C (£650,000 + on 28/3/1996) P/FL 168+2/28 FLC 19+1/3 FAC 12/4 Others 7/1

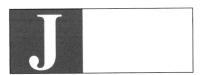

JAASKELAINEN Jussi
Born: Vaasa, Finland, 19 April 1975
Height: 6'3" Weight: 12.10
International Honours: Finland: 7; U21; Yth

Jussi started last season just as successfully as he had ended the 1999-2000 campaign. Having firmly established himself as Bolton's first-choice 'keeper, he showed some excellent form, improving his game to the extent that he has few visible weaknesses. A phenomenal shot stopper, he commanded his box with some authority and he played with much greater confidence than previously. Unfortunately he suffered a cruciate ligament injury playing against Tranmere in January and this ruled him out of action for the remainder of the season.

Bolton W (£100,000 + from VPS Vassa, Finland, ex MPS, on 14/11/1997) FL 94+1 FLC 7 FAC 4 Others 2

JACK Rodney Alphonso
Born: Kingstown, St Vincent, 28 September 1972
Height: 5'7" Weight: 10.9
International Honours: St Vincent & Grenadines

Rodney was again a key figure for Crewe Alexandra in 2000-01 although he missed several weeks in the middle part of the campaign with injuries. On his day a potential match winner he is an exciting player with a fine turn of speed and an explosive shot. A skilful striker he featured in both wide-right and wide-left positions during the campaign. He added two further caps for St Vincent in their unsuccessful campaign to qualify for the 2002 World Cup finals.

Torquay U (Free from Lambada, St Vincent on 10/10/1995) FL 82+5/24 FLC 6/1 FAC 6 Others 6/3
Crewe Alex (£650,000 on 14/8/1998) FL 81+11/17 FLC 7/2 FAC 4

JACKSON Kirk Stewart
Born: Doncaster, 16 October 1976
Height: 5'11" Weight: 12.0

This free-scoring striker was in great form for Worksop Town in the early part of last season, netting six times in the 12-0 thrashing of Frickley Athletic and by the time he signed for Darlington in March he had amassed a total of 40 goals. He made an immediate impact for the Quakers scoring with a well-placed shot on his debut at Carlisle and adapting well to the higher level of football, although he failed to add to his goal tally.

Sheffield Wed (From trainee on 15/5/1995)
Scunthorpe U (Free on 23/7/1996) FL 0+4/1 Others 0+1
Chesterfield (Free on 6/8/1997) FL 0+3 FLC 0+1 FAC 0+1 Others 1 (Free to Grantham T on 7/8/1998)
Darlington (£30,000 from Worksop T on 1/3/2001) FL 5+5/1

JACKSON Mark Graham
Born: Barnsley, 30 September 1977
Height: 6'0" Weight: 11.12
International Honours: E: Yth

Mark suffered a disastrous start to last season when he cracked an ankle in the opening game and was ruled out for two months. However he returned to become a regular in the Scunthorpe United side, playing mainly at right back before being switched to centre defence which looks to be his best position. Mark scored his first league goal in the 4-3 win at Halifax in March when he netted with a close-range header.

Leeds U (From trainee on 1/7/1995) PL 11+8 FAC 4
Huddersfield T (Loaned on 29/10/1998) FL 5
Barnsley (Loaned on 14/1/2000) FL 1
Scunthorpe U (Free on 9/3/2000) FL 34+4/1 FAC 5 Others 1

JACKSON Matthew (Matt) Alan
Born: Leeds, 19 October 1971
Height: 6'1" Weight: 12.12
Club Honours: FAC '95
International Honours: E: U21-10; Sch

Despite being sidelined by injuries for a lengthy spell in the autumn Matt produced another season full of composed and authorative displays at the heart of the Norwich City defence in 2000-01. An assured central defender who combines a resolute approach to defending with a desire to retain possession he remains club captain at Carrow Road.

Luton T (From juniors on 4/7/1990) FL 7+2 FLC 2 Others 0+1
Preston NE (Loaned on 27/3/1991) FL 3+1 Others 1
Everton (£600,000 on 18/10/1991) F/PL 132+6/4 FLC 9 FAC 14/2 Others 4
Charlton Ath (Loaned on 26/3/1996) FL 8 Others 2
Queens Park R (Loaned on 20/8/1996) FL 7
Birmingham C (Loaned on 31/10/1996) FL 10
Norwich C (£450,000 on 24/12/1996) FL 158+3/6 FLC 6 FAC 5

JACKSON Michael Douglas
Born: Cheltenham, 26 June 1980
Height: 5'7" Weight: 10.10

Having come up through the ranks at Cheltenham Michael continued to make steady progress last season. He started a Football League game for the first time when he played in the local 'derby' at Kidderminster in November, producing a fine performance and also appearing in a handful more senior games. His opportunities were to some extent limited by the form of the regular midfield pairing of Lee Howells and Mark Yates but he will be hoping to gain further first-team experience in the 2001-02 campaign.

Cheltenham T (From trainee on 1/8/1997) FL 2+6 FLC 0+2 FAC 0+1 Others 1

JACKSON Michael James
Born: Runcorn, 4 December 1973
Height: 6'0" Weight: 13.8
Club Honours: Div 2 '97, '00
International Honours: E: Yth

Suspended for the first three games of the 2000-01 season, this central defensive kingpin was unable to reclaim a regular starting place for Preston until November when Colin Murdock was suspended. However once back he retained his place, scoring his first goal of the campaign in the home draw with Fulham going on to make his 150th league appearance for North End. Having returned to his best form and adapted to First Division football, a back injury then led to his season ending prematurely. A consistent central defender his timing of vital tackles and decisive heading are his key attributes.

Crewe Alex (From trainee on 29/7/1992) FL 5 FLC 1 FAC 1 Others 2
Bury (Free on 13/8/1993) FL 123+2/9 FLC 9/1 FAC 3 Others 12
Preston NE (£125,000 on 26/3/1997) FL 163+4/16 FLC 13 FAC 13 Others 8

JACKSON Richard
Born: Whitby, 18 April 1980
Height: 5'8" Weight: 10.12

A regular in the Derby County reserve side on the right-hand side of defence last season, Richard received his first start in the Premiership at Everton in August. His opportunities were limited after that as manager Jim Smith preferred to opt for more experienced players, and a broken cheekbone sustained in a training ground accident in early January then ruled him out of action for the reserves until early April. He returned to the senior squad for the final game of the season against Ipswich when he came on for Chris Riggott at half-time.

Scarborough (From trainee on 27/3/1998) FL 21+1 FLC 2
Derby Co (£30,000 + on 25/3/1999) PL 1+3 FLC 1

JACOBS Wayne Graham
Born: Sheffield, 3 February 1969
Height: 5'9" Weight: 11.2

Wayne had a difficult time with injuries at Bradford City last term spending three months of the campaign on the sidelines, firstly with an ankle ligament injury suffered in an Inter Toto Cup match and then undergoing an operation for a double hernia. As befits the club's longest-serving player he bounced back each time and fought his way into the team again. A left-sided player who is equally at home at full back or in a midfield role, he is strong in the tackle and has good distribution. Wayne is a great servant of the Valley Parade club and readily offers his services as a speaker at supporters' meetings.

Sheffield Wed (From apprentice on 3/1/1987) FL 5+1 FLC 3 Others 1
Hull C (£27,000 on 25/3/1988) FL 127+2/4 FLC 7 FAC 8 Others 6
Rotherham U (Free on 5/8/1993) FL 40+2/2 FLC 4 FAC 1 Others 2
Bradford C (Free on 5/8/1994) P/FL 222+8/11 FLC 16+2 FAC 11/2 Others 7

JACOBSEN Anders
Born: Norway, 18 April 1968
Height: 6'3" Weight: 13.7
Club Honours: AMC '00

Anders joined Notts County last September and after a slow start he established himself as a regular in the first team. A cultured and

thoughtful central defender he became the linchpin of the Magpies' back line and was a major influence in their rise up the Second Division table in the second half of the season. He was released by the Magpies at the end of the season.
Sheffield U (Signed from IK Start, Norway on 24/12/1998) FL 8+4 FAC 0+1
Stoke C (Free on 11/8/1999) FL 29+4/2 FLC 3 FAC 1 Others 6+1
Notts Co (Free on 6/9/2000) FL 27+2/2 FAC 5

JAGIELKA Philip (Phil) Nikodem
Born: Manchester, 17 August 1982
Height: 5'11" Weight: 12.8
International Honours: E: Yth
Phil continued to be introduced slowly to senior football at Sheffield United last season and apart from some early outings in the Worthington Cup he was restricted to appearances from the subs' bench until he made the starting line-up for the final three games. A promising midfield player who is comfortable on the ball he was capped by England U18s against Switzerland. He is the brother of Steve Jagielka.
Sheffield U (From trainee on 8/5/2000) FL 3+13 FLC 3

JAGIELKA Stephen (Steve)
Born: Manchester, 10 March 1978
Height: 5'8" Weight: 11.5
Steve had his best season yet at Shrewsbury in 2000-01 even though he spent part of the campaign on the subs' bench. He was used in a midfield role, where his speed going forward troubled opposition defenders and he scored a respectable total of six goals. He is the older brother of Sheffield United's Phil Jagielka.
Stoke C (From trainee on 15/7/1996)
Shrewsbury T (Free on 30/7/1997) FL 52+59/9 FLC 3+3 FAC 3+1/1 Others 1+1/1

JAMES David Benjamin
Born: Welwyn Garden City, 1 August 1970
Height: 6'5" Weight: 14.5
Club Honours: FAYC '89; FLC '95
International Honours: E: 4; B-1; U21-10; Yth
David had an excellent season in 2000-01 when he was an ever-present for Aston Villa in domestic matches despite breaking a nose at Everton early on. He is a big powerful 'keeper who has a commanding presence in the penalty box. Quick to release the ball he also possesses a prodigious throw while his kicking and reading of the game are of a high standard. His consistent form was recognised by the England selectors and he featured regularly in the squad all season winning further caps in the friendly matches against Italy, Spain and Mexico.
Watford (From trainee on 1/7/1988) FL 89 FLC 6 FAC 2 Others 1
Liverpool (£1,000,000 on 6/7/1992) PL 213+1 FLC 22 FAC 19 Others 22
Aston Villa (£1,800,000 on 23/6/1999) PL 67 FLC 6 FAC 8 Others 4

JAMES Kevin Ernest
Born: Southwark, 3 January 1980
Height: 5'9" Weight: 10.7
Kevin spent four years at Charlton without making their first team and after being released in the 1999-2000 close season he linked up with Canvey Island for whom he impressed in a pre-season friendly against Gillingham. A successful trial period followed and he then signed a 12-month contract for the Gills. A tricky right winger he made just a handful of appearances for the first team, mostly from the subs' bench but was a regular in the club's reserve team throughout the season.
Charlton Ath (From trainee on 2/7/1998)
Gillingham (Free on 21/8/2000) FL 1+6 FLC 0+1

JAMES Lutel Malik
Born: Manchester, 2 June 1972
Height: 5'9" Weight: 11.0
International Honours: St Kitts & Nevis
Lutel found his opportunities severely limited at Bury in 2000-2001 and was mostly used from the subs' bench. His best performance of the season came in the 1-1 draw with Wycombe at the end of April when he used his skill and pace to good effect when running at opposition defenders. An experienced wing-man he was out of contract in the summer.
Scarborough (Free from Yorkshire Amateurs on 22/2/1993) FL 0+6 (Free to Guiseley during 1993 close season)
Bury (Free from Hyde U on 26/10/1998) FL 34+34/4 FLC 2+2 FAC 1+2/1 Others 2+1

JANSEN Matthew (Matt) Brooke
Born: Carlisle, 20 October 1977
Height: 5'11" Weight: 10.13
Club Honours: AMC '97
International Honours: E: U21-6; Yth
Matt had a great season with Blackburn Rovers in 2000-01 after a rather disappointing time the previous term. He bagged a hatful of goals and became the idol of the Ewood Park faithful with some fine performances. Full of tricks he showed good balance, quick feet and a desire to keep on going through challenges rather than fall to the ground. Composed in front of goal with the ability to think and place his shot he is also a constant aerial threat despite his lack of height. He will be hoping to continue to display such form for Rovers in the Premiership in the coming season. He was honoured by his fellow professionals with a place in the PFA's First Division team.
Carlisle U (From trainee on 18/1/1996) FL 26+16/10 FLC 4+1/3 FAC 1+3 Others 3+3
Crystal Palace (£1,000,000 + on 12/2/1998) P/FL 23+3/10 FLC 4 FAC 0+1 Others 2
Blackburn Rov (£4,100,000 on 19/1/1999) P/FL 57+24/30 FLC 3+1/2 FAC 4+3/2

JARMAN Lee
Born: Cardiff, 16 December 1977
Height: 6'3" Weight: 13.3
International Honours: W: U21-9; Yth
Having been released by Exeter City at the end of the 1999-2000 campaign Lee joined Oxford United on a monthly contract in the close season and did well enough to earn himself a one-year deal. He was a regular for the U's before Christmas but then fell out of favour and was eventually released in the summer. A tall central defender with an excellent right foot he can also play at right back if required.
Cardiff C (From trainee on 23/8/1995) FL 78+16/1 FLC 3+2 FAC 3+3/1 Others 5+2 (Free to Merthyr Tydfil 1/11/1999)
Exeter C (Free on 10/3/2000) FL 7 Others 0+1
Oxford U (Free on 26/7/2000) FL 15+6/1 FLC 2 FAC 2

JARRETT Jason Lee Mee
Born: Bury, 14 September 1979
Height: 6'0" Weight: 12.4
Having had a trial at Bury towards the end of the 1999-2000 campaign, Jason was taken on by his home-town club on a short-term contract in the close season and made such great progress that boss Andy Preece eventually rewarded him with an 18-month contract in March. He featured in the first team on a number of occasions in the opening half of the campaign but struggled to win a place after Christmas. Jason is an attacking midfield player who excels at linking defence and attack.
Blackpool (From trainee on 3/7/1998) FL 2 FAC 0+1 Others 1
Wrexham (Free on 8/10/1999) FL 1
Bury (Free on 13/7/2000) FL 13+12/2 FAC 0+2 Others 2/1

JASZCZUN Antony (Tommy) John
Born: Kettering, 16 September 1977
Height: 5'10" Weight: 10.10
Tommy is a left-sided defender who performed equally well in the full-back and wing-back roles for Blackpool during the 2000-01 season. He played consistently well and showed an eagerness to attack opposing defences down the flank and an ability to cross the ball with accuracy. He took advantage of John Hills' injury problems to feature regularly in the first team throughout the season but failed to add to his goals tally for the Tangerines.
Aston Villa (From trainee on 5/7/1996) FLC 0+1
Blackpool (£30,000 on 20/1/2000) FL 51+3 FLC 4 Others 4/1

JAVARY Jean-Phillipe
Born: Montpellier, France, 10 January 1978
Height: 6'0" Weight: 12.6
International Honours: France: Yth (UEFA-U18 '96)
This combative midfield player began the 2000-01 campaign at Raith, but after a single appearance he was on his way to Brentford. At Griffin Park he appeared alongside Paul Evans in the centre of the park but then dropped out of contention and was restricted to the occasional first-team appearance. He joined Third Division Plymouth Argyle in March on non-contract forms and went on to make four league appearances for the Pilgrims but was released at the end of the season by manager Paul Sturrock. Jean-Phillipe is a former youth international for France and played in the U18 team that won the European Championship in 1996 featuring players such as Mikael Silvestre and Thierry Henry.
Raith Rov (Signed from Montpellier, France, ex ASOA Valence, RCD Espanyol, on 20/1/2000) SL 11+1
Brentford (Free on 18/8/2000) FL 4+2 FLC 2 Others 1
Plymouth Arg (Free on 28/2/2001) FL 4

JEANNIN Alexandre (Alex)
Born: France, 30 December 1970
Height: 6'1" Weight: 11.12

Alex was one of a trio of French players signed by Darlington on transfer deadline day. A commanding left-sided central defender he went straight into the side two days later and immediately slotted into the back line, providing the accurate through ball that led to the Quakers' second goal. He remained in the side until the end of the season and was rewarded with a two-year contract.

Darlington (Free from Troyes, France on 22/3/2001) FL 11

JEFFERS Francis
Born: Liverpool, 25 January 1981
Height: 5'10" Weight: 10.7
Club Honours: FAYC '98
International Honours: E: U21-6; Yth; Sch

After forging a fruitful partnership with Kevin Campbell the previous season - statistically one of the most effective in the Premiership - Francis was forced to go it alone in 2000-01 because of injury to his partner. It made little difference, with the young striker enjoying a devastating scoring burst to start the season. The intelligence and timing of his runs made him elusive for defenders to pick up, and his finishing was invariably excellent. With five goals in his first five Premiership outings he was rubbing shoulders with the leading scorers in the country, until a sixth goal in a Worthington Cup tie at Bristol Rovers was followed by an ankle ligament injury and five months on the sidelines. Typically he scored in his comeback game before succumbing again to injury, then a dislocated shoulder in a home game against Manchester City ended his season for good. After turning down offers of a new contract at Everton he was reported to have signed for Arsenal in the summer.

Everton (From trainee on 20/2/1998) PL 37+12/18 FLC 2+2/1 FAC 6+1/1

JEFFREY Michael (Mike) Richard
Born: Liverpool, 11 August 1971
Height: 5'11" Weight: 11.6
Club Honours: AMC '96

Mike joined Grimsby Town in August 2000 making him Alan Buckley's last signing before his surprise departure at the end of the month. He initially partnered Bradley Allen up front but then found himself relegated behind Steve Livingstone and newcomer David Nielsen in the pecking order of strikers at Blundell Park. He won a recall to the side in the new year and produced an excellent performance in the 2-1 win over Portsmouth at the end of January. Although a little lightweight, Mike has the ability to run at defenders and creates many chances for his colleagues.

Bolton W (From trainee on 9/2/1989) FL 9+6 FLC 1+2 FAC 1 Others 2+1
Doncaster Rov (£20,000 on 5/3/1992) FL 48+1/19 FLC 4 Others 2/1
Newcastle U (£60,000 on 4/10/1993) PL 2 FLC 1/1 Others 0+2
Rotherham U (£80,000 on 22/6/1995) FL 22/5 FLC 3/1 FAC 1 Others 3 (£205,000 to Fortuna Sittard, Holland on 16/1/1996)
Kilmarnock (Signed on 14/7/1999) SL 10+8/2 SLC 3+2/1 SC 1 Others 1+3
Grimsby T (Free on 10/8/2000) FL 15+14/1 FLC 3+1 FAC 1/1

JELLEYMAN Gareth Anthony
Born: Holywell, 14 November 1980
Height: 5'10" Weight: 10.6
International Honours: W: U21-1; Yth

Gareth had a wretched time with injuries at Peterborough last season and received few first-team opportunities. He missed the opening weeks of the campaign following a close-season hernia operation and was sidelined again at the turn of the year with tendonitis in his knee, before finally suffering a serious knee injury in March that was expected to keep him out of action for some time. He is a talented young left back who is quick and very strong in the tackle.

Peterborough U (From trainee on 5/8/1998) FL 20+8 FAC 1+2 Others 5+1

JEMSON Nigel Bradley
Born: Hutton, 10 October 1969
Height: 5'11" Weight: 12.10
Club Honours: FLC '90; AMC '96
International Honours: E: U21-1

Nigel proved an excellent signing for Shrewsbury Town manager Kevin Ratcliffe last season. He was a near ever-present and finished the campaign as leading scorer with a tally of 15 goals in Third Division games. An experienced striker he holds the ball up well, produces some lovely flick-ons and always gives 100 per cent for the cause.

Preston NE (From trainee on 6/7/1987) FL 28+4/8 FAC 2/1 Others 5+1/5
Nottingham F (£150,000 on 24/3/1988) FL 45+2/13 FLC 9/4 FAC 3+1/3 Others 1
Bolton W (Loaned on 23/12/1988) FL 4+1
Preston NE (Loaned on 15/3/1989) FL 6+3/2 Others 2/1
Sheffield Wed (£800,000 on 17/9/1991) F/PL 26+25/9 FLC 3+4 FAC 3+3/1 Others 2+2/1
Grimsby T (Loaned on 10/9/1993) FL 6/2 Others 1
Notts Co (£300,000 on 8/9/1994) FL 7+7/1 FLC 2+2/1 Others 1
Watford (Loaned on 12/1/1995) FL 3+1
Rotherham U (Loaned on 15/2/1996) FL 16/5 Others 3/4
Oxford U (£60,000 on 23/7/1996) FL 68/27 FLC 12/6 FAC 2
Bury (£100,000 on 5/2/1998) FL 17+12/1 FLC 0+2 FAC 0+1
Ayr U (Free on 21/7/1999) SL 9+3/5 SLC 1
Oxford U (Free on 27/1/2000) FL 13+5
Shrewsbury T (Free on 21/7/2000) FL 41/15 FLC 2 FAC 1 Others 1

JENAS Jermaine Anthony
Born: Nottingham, 18 February 1983
Height: 5'11" Weight: 11.2
International Honours: E: Yth

This promising Nottingham Forest youngster made an assured senior debut in the FA Cup third round game with Wolves last season and also appeared in the First Division game against Crystal Palace before dropping back to the reserves. A hard-tackling midfield player who distributes the ball accurately he won representative honours with the England U17 and U18 teams during the season.

Nottingham F (From trainee on 19/2/2000) FL 1 FAC 1

JENKINS Iain
Born: Prescot, 24 November 1972
Height: 5'9" Weight: 11.12
International Honours: NI: 5; B-1

Iain joined his old boss Kevin Ratcliffe at Shrewsbury Town in July 2000 but a series of niggling injuries restricted his appearances and he was eventually sidelined in January by a long-term groin problem. A left-sided defender he will be hoping to make a full recovery in time for the start of the 2001-02 campaign.

Everton (From trainee on 4/6/1991) PL 3+2 FLC 0+1
Bradford C (Loaned on 31/12/1992) FL 6 Others 1
Chester C (Free on 13/8/1993) FL 155+5/1 FLC 7+2 FAC 11+1 Others 12
Dundee U (Signed on 27/3/1998) SL 13+1 SLC 1 SC 2
Shrewsbury T (Free on 11/7/2000) FL 16 FLC 2 FAC 1 Others 1

JENKINS Lee David
Born: Pontypool, 28 June 1979
Height: 5'9" Weight: 11.0
Club Honours: Div 3 '00
International Honours: W: U21-9; Yth; Sch

Lee had his most productive season to date at Swansea in 2000-01 and was a regular in the first-team squad for most of the campaign before picking up a hip injury in mid-April. A competitive midfield player with tremendous stamina and a high work rate he showed his versatility by occasionally taking on the left back role. Lee again featured regularly for Wales at U21 level winning a further four caps.

Swansea C (From trainee on 20/12/1996) FL 77+33/2 FLC 1+1 FAC 2+1 Others 8

JENKINS Stephen (Steve) Robert
Born: Merthyr Tydfil, 16 July 1972
Height: 5'11" Weight: 12.3
Club Honours: AMC '94
International Honours: W: 14; U21-2; Yth

Steve was sidelined with a knee injury shortly after the start of the 2000-01 season and it was not until October that he returned to the Huddersfield Town line-up. A hard-working defender he came back in commanding form before he was loaned out to Birmingham City as part of a proposed exchange deal involving Peter Ndlovu. He did well at St Andrews but was hampered by a calf injury and a permanent deal failed to materialise. He subsequently returned to the McAlpine Stadium but was unable to prevent the Terriers from being relegated to the Second Division. Strong in the tackle and very influential at the back, he was recalled to the Wales international team for their World Cup qualifying matches against Poland and Ukraine in the summer.

Swansea C (From trainee on 1/7/1990) FL 155+10/1 FLC 12+1 FAC 10+1 Others 26
Huddersfield T (£275,000 on 3/11/1995) FL 191+1/3 FLC 15 FAC 12
Birmingham C (Loaned on 15/12/2000) FL 3 FLC 1

JENSEN Brian
Born: Copenhagen, Denmark, 8 June 1975
Height: 6'1" Weight: 12.4

Brian had an excellent first half to the

2000-01 season for West Bromwich Albion but then seemed to suffer losses of concentration and he was replaced in the team by new signing Russell Hoult early in the new year. An excellent shot stopper with a powerful kick he will be hoping to regain his position as number one 'keeper at The Hawthorns in the 2001-02 campaign.

West Bromwich A (£100,000 from AZ Alkmaar, Holland, ex B93, Hvidovre, on 3/3/2000) FL 45 FLC 4

JENSEN Claus William
Born: Nykobing, Denmark, 29 April 1977
Height: 5'11" Weight: 12.6
International Honours: Denmark: 11; U21

Claus became Charlton Athletic's record signing in the 2000 close season and immediately made an impact on the club's supporters with some excellent displays in midfield. Extremely comfortable on the ball, he can deliver a 40-yard pass with accuracy and is a constant danger with his set-piece kicks. He found the net on four occasions last season and three of his goals proved to be memorable for different reasons. The first came after a wonderful one-two with Jonatan Johansson at Derby, the second was a blaster from the edge of the box at Leeds and the third was a freak goal at Manchester City when an attempted clearance by Nicky Weaver cannoned off Claus's leg and looped over the hapless 'keeper into an empty net. Claus also established himself as a regular member of the Denmark international squad, winning a further eight caps last season and scoring his first goal in the 5-0 victory over Malta last March.

Bolton W (£1,600,000 from Lyngby, Denmark, ex Naestved, on 14/7/1998) FL 85+1/8 FLC 12/2 FAC 6 Others 5
Charlton Ath (£4,000,000 on 21/7/2000) PL 37+1/5 FLC 2 FAC 2

JEPSON Ronald (Ronnie) Francis
Born: Stoke, 12 May 1963
Height: 6'1" Weight: 13.7
Club Honours: Div 2 '97

The oldest member of a Burnley squad not renowned for its youth, Ronnie began last season in his familiar place on the subs' bench. He was a popular replacement when he came on, geeing up the team in the later stages of games, never afraid to get stuck in and always willing to have a pot at goal. Unfortunately he missed most of the second half of the campaign with an achilles tendon injury that required an operation and at the time of writing it remained to be seen whether he would return to action at Turf Moor in 2001-02.

Port Vale (Free from Nantwich T on 23/3/1989) FL 12+10 FLC 1+1 FAC 1+1
Peterborough U (Loaned on 25/1/1990) FL 18/5
Preston NE (£80,000 on 12/2/1991) FL 36+2/8 FLC 2 Others 3/4
Exeter C (£60,000 on 29/7/1992) FL 51+3/21 FLC 6/2 FAC 3/1 Others 4/1
Huddersfield T (£80,000 on 7/12/1993) FL 95+12/36 FLC 6+1/2 FAC 4/3 Others 6/1
Bury (£40,000 on 27/7/1996) FL 31+16/9 FLC 7/1 FAC 0+3 Others 1+1/2
Oldham Ath (£30,000 on 16/1/1998) FL 9/4
Burnley (Free on 29/7/1998) FL 4+55/3 FLC 2+4 FAC 0+3

JERVIS David John
Born: Retford, 18 January 1982
Height: 5'9" Weight: 11.3

A first-year professional at Mansfield, David made his Football League debut last September when he came off the subs' bench in the 5-1 drubbing of Halifax and he made the starting line-up for the first time at Cardiff the following month. Playing wide on the left hand side of the defence he likes to push forward and passes the ball accurately. He was reported to have signed a new contract for the Stags in the summer.

Mansfield T (From trainee on 3/7/2000) FL 17+5 FAC 2

JESS Eoin
Born: Aberdeen, 13 December 1970
Height: 5'9" Weight: 11.10
Club Honours: SLC '89
International Honours: S: 18; B-2; U21-14

Having fallen out of favour at Aberdeen Eoin joined Bradford City on loan at the end of December initially for three months and then until the end of the season. He scored on his debut at Leicester in City's first away win and went on to form a useful central midfield partnership with Stuart McCall. A hard-tackling player he impressed with his enthusiasm and whole-hearted performances although it remains to be seen whether he will come to Valley Parade on a permanent basis in the close season.

Aberdeen (Free from Glasgow R juniors on 13/11/1987) SL 167+34/50 SLC 19+2/4 SC 14+2/3 Others 8+2/6
Coventry C (£1,750,000 on 24/2/1996) PL 28+11/1 FLC 1 FAC 4/2
Aberdeen (£700,000 on 3/7/1997) SL 108+3/29 SLC 8+1/1 SC 6/1
Bradford C (Loaned on 29/12/2000) PL 17/3 FAC 1

JEVONS Philip (Phil)
Born: Liverpool, 1 August 1979
Height: 5'11" Weight: 11.10
Club Honours: FAYC '98

A willing and strong-running striker, Phil finished top scorer for Everton's title-winning reserve team without ever quite forcing himself into the first-team picture. He made four substitute appearances, including one after only 25 minutes in a crucial match at Coventry City when his intelligent running helped create a goal for Kevin Campbell. An enthusiastic and popular player at Goodison, he is anxious for the opportunity to prove himself.

Everton (From trainee on 10/11/1997) PL 2+6 FLC 1

JOACHIM Julian Kevin
Born: Boston, 20 September 1974
Height: 5'6" Weight: 12.2
International Honours: E: U21-9; Yth; (UEFA-U18 '93)

Julian was not expected to feature much for Aston Villa last term after a public falling out with manager John Gregory during the summer. However, although he was the subject of much transfer speculation throughout the campaign, he featured on a fairly regular basis and showed his value as a goal-scorer by netting eight times from 13 starts. An able striker with lightning pace and a willingness to run at defenders he seems likely to be on the move from Villa Park during the close season.

Leicester C (From trainee on 15/9/1992) F/PL 77+22/25 FLC 7+2/3 FAC 4+1/1 Others 4+2/2
Aston Villa (£1,500,000 on 24/2/1996) PL 90+51/40 FLC 10+1/3 FAC 8+4/2 Others 6+3/1

JOB Josephe-Desire
Born: Lyon, France, 1 December 1977
Height: 5'10" Weight: 11.3
International Honours: Cameroon: (ANC '00)

Signed up by Middlesbrough during the close season this exciting young striker was used sparingly in the 2000-01 campaign. With greased lightening in each boot and the ability to run at defenders he can play equally well on either wing and also through the middle. The pieces are slowly being moved into place for Boro's projected onslaught on the Premiership and Josephe-Desire is very much a part of those plans.

Middlesbrough (£3,000,000 from RC Lens, France, ex Lyon, on 7/8/2000) PL 8+4/3 FLC 1+1

Josephe-Desire Job

JOBSON Richard Ian
Born: Holderness, 9 May 1963
Height: 6'1" Weight: 13.5
Club Honours: Div 2 '91
International Honours: E: B-2

After successfully helping Manchester City gain promotion to the Premiership, Richard found few senior opportunities at Maine Road last term and his only appearances in the first team came in the early-season Worthington Cup games against Gillingham. In November he returned to Watford where had begun his professional career. Signed as cover for the injured Darren Ward he became the Hornets' oldest first-team player in almost 50 years, but looked a little rusty and after two games he returned north. He subsequently joined First Division strugglers Tranmere on loan at the end of December where he was brought in to shore up a leaky defence. He later signed for Rovers on a permanent basis but although he produced some consistent displays he was unable to prevent the club from being relegated at the end of the campaign. A vastly experienced centre half whose fitness belies his years he has a no-nonsense approach to his defensive work.

Watford (£22,000 from Burton A on 5/11/1982) FL 26+2/4 FLC 2 FAC 0+1 Others 5+1
Hull C (£40,000 on 7/2/1985) FL 219+2/17 FLC 12 FAC 13/1 Others 9
Oldham Ath (£460,000 on 30/8/1990) P/FL 188+1/10 FLC 19/1 FAC 13 Others 4
Leeds U (£1,000,000 on 26/10/1995) PL 22/1 FLC 3 FAC 1
Southend U (Loaned on 23/1/1998) FL 8/1
Manchester C (Free on 12/3/1998) FL 49+1/4 FLC 4+1 FAC 2
Watford (Loaned on 7/11/2000) FL 2
Tranmere Rov (Free on 28/12/2000) FL 16 FAC 5

JOHANSEN Rune Buer
Born: Oslo, Norway, 4 September 1973
Height: 5'10" Weight: 11.10

Rune netted regularly for Tromso in the Norwegian 2000 season and at the end of the campaign he joined Second Division Bristol Rovers on loan. He made his debut for the Pirates as a substitute against Walsall and made the starting line-up for the FA Cup tie at Cardiff. However soon afterwards he returned to Scandinavia and later featured from the subs' bench again for Tromso at the start of their 2001 domestic season. Rune is a slightly built striker who sometimes found it difficult to adapt to the hurly burly of lower division football.

Bristol Rov (Loaned from Tromso, Norway, ex Askim, Fredrikstad, Moss, Sogndal, Kongsvinger, on 10/11/2000) FL 0+2 FAC 1

JOHANSSON Jonatan (JJ) Lillebror
Born: Stockholm, Sweden, 16 August 1975
Height: 6'1" Weight: 12.8
Club Honours: SPL '99, '00; SLC '99
International Honours: Finland: 30

JJ as he became known at The Valley missed the first few games of last season through injury but once fit became a favourite of the Charlton supporters after scoring against Southampton in his second match for the club. The goals came fairly regularly in the first half of the campaign and he scored in four consecutive games in September, but the supply began to dry up after Christmas. Nevertheless he still finished up as the Addicks' leading scorer. He linked up well with both Matt Svensson and Shaun Bartlett in a central striking role and used his pace and ability to turn defenders and set up goals for his colleagues. A regular choice for his country he won a further five caps last season, appearing in both World Cup qualifying ties against England.

Glasgow R (From FC Flora Tallinn, Estonia, ex TPS Turku, on 13/8/1997) SL 22+25/14 SLC 4/1 SC 2+4/3 Others 9+8/7
Charlton Ath (£3,250,000 + on 1/8/2000) PL 27+4/11 FLC 2/3

JOHN Stern
Born: Trinidad, 30 October 1976
Height: 6'1" Weight: 12.12
International Honours: Trinidad & Tobago

Although Stern featured for Nottingham Forest in the opening matches of the 2000-01 campaign he was sidelined by a knee injury in September and this kept him out of action for two months. He returned to the squad in November and went on to finish the season looking very sharp, netting two goals and being rather unlucky not to score more. While his striking partnership with David Johnson is still in its early stages of development there were definite signs that the two might come good in 2001-02. When fit Stern was a regular for Trinidad & Tobago scoring eight goals in 16 international appearances.

Nottingham F (£1,500,000 + from Columbus Crew, USA on 22/11/1999) FL 29+17/5 FLC 2/1 FAC 3+1

JOHNROSE Leonard (Lenny)
Born: Preston, 29 November 1969
Height: 5'10" Weight: 12.6
Club Honours: Div 2 '97

After having been a key man in Burnley's surge to promotion in 1999-2000, Lenny missed the start of last season's First Division campaign with a knee injury. Once fit he struggled to make the starting line-up following the arrival of Kevin Ball at Turf Moor, although for a while he vied for a place with Paul Cook. Lenny's best spell in a season he will want to forget came in January when he scored a last-minute equaliser in the FA Cup tie at Scunthorpe and followed this with a fine performance and a goal against Barnsley. He was later sidelined again with an achilles tendon injury that required surgery.

Blackburn Rov (From trainee on 16/6/1988) FL 20+22/11 FLC 2+1/1 FAC 0+3 Others 2
Preston NE (Loaned on 21/1/1992) FL 1+2/1
Hartlepool U (£50,000 on 28/2/1992) FL 59+7/11 FLC 5+1/4 FAC 5/1 Others 5
Bury (Signed on 7/12/1993) FL 181+7/19 FLC 16+2/2 FAC 9/1 Others 9/1
Burnley (£225,000 on 12/2/1999) FL 46+20/4 FLC 2 FAC 1+2/1 Others 1

JOHNSEN Jean **Ronny**
Born: Norway, 10 June 1969
Height: 6'2" Weight: 13.2
Club Honours: PL '97, '99, '01; CS '97; FAC '99; EC '99
International Honours: Norway: 42

Although everyone at Manchester United

JJ Johansson

was delighted to see Ronny returning to first-team action after a dreadful spate of injuries that had once threatened to curtail his career, it was a season of great contrasts for him. Not content with making a low-key comeback he scored United's opening goal of the Premiership campaign against Newcastle at Old Trafford and looked to be back at his best. However after completing only seven Premiership games the injury jinx struck again and more surgery was required in January on his 'good' knee, keeping him out for another six weeks. He was back in the first team again in April and was due to spend the summer training with Norwegian club Eik Tonsberg in a bid to speed up his return to match fitness.
Manchester U (£1,200,000 from Besiktas, Turkey, ex Lyn, Lillestrom, on 26/7/1996) PL 76+13/6 FLC 3 FAC 8+2/1 Others 27+2/1

JOHNSON Andrew (Andy)
Born: Bedford, 10 February 1981
Height: 5'9" Weight: 9.7
International Honours: E: Yth
A regular for Birmingham City for much of 2000-01 although he was often on the subs' bench, Andy had a season of high and low points. His wonder goal in the 2-0 win at Preston in February was certainly one of the former while he will forever be remembered for missing the decisive penalty in the Worthington Cup final shoot-out against Liverpool later the same month. However he responded with great maturity and the incident didn't seem to affect his play in the remaining matches, indeed soon afterwards he scored another cracking solo effort against Crewe. He is a tough-tackling midfield player who always gives 100 per cent effort for the cause. Andy was deservedly voted 'Young Player of the Season' by the Blues' fans.
Birmingham C (From juniors on 11/3/1998) FL 35+25/5 FLC 4+9/4 Others 1+1

JOHNSON Andrew (Andy) James
Born: Bristol, 2 May 1974
Height: 6'0" Weight: 13.0
Club Honours: Div 1 '98
International Honours: E: Yth. W: 7
Andy had a bit of a stop-start season in 2000-01 for Nottingham Forest. A regular in the early weeks of the season he missed the important turn-of-the year period through injury before returning again to the line-up. A key figure in the midfield engine room for Forest he sometimes seems to run without stopping for the full 90 minutes of a match. A box-to-box player in the centre of the park his inspirational play regularly lifted his team-mates.
Norwich C (From trainee on 4/3/1992) F/PL 56+10/13 FLC 6+1/2 FAC 2
Nottingham F (£2,200,000 on 4/7/1997) P/FL 102+16/9 FLC 5+1/1 FAC 2

JOHNSON Damien Michael
Born: Lisburn, 18 November 1978
Height: 5'9" Weight: 11.2
International Honours: NI: 12; U21-11; Yth
Damien was converted by Blackburn boss Graham Souness to a central midfield role last term and the switch looked like being a success in the opening months of the campaign. However he was then sidelined by a back problem for several weeks and it was not until April that he returned to the Rovers' team. He produced a fine display in the win at Grimsby when he was full of running and trickery. A talented midfield player who previously featured wide on the right he has good pace and a liking for the hard work and decisive tackling required for a more central position. He continued to appear for Northern Ireland during the campaign winning several more caps.
Blackburn Rov (From trainee on 2/2/1996) P/FL 37+16/2 FLC 9+3 FAC 1+4 Others 0+1
Nottingham F (Loaned on 29/1/1998) FL 5+1

JOHNSON David Anthony
Born: Kingston, Jamaica, 15 August 1976
Height: 5'6" Weight: 12.3
Club Honours: FAYC '95; Div 2 '97
International Honours: E: B-1; Sch. Jamaica: 4
David started the 2000-01 season at Ipswich more like his old self and seemed to relish playing on the Premiership stage at last. However, despite all his efforts he was unable to notch that elusive first Premiership goal. It was not for want of trying though and luck was not with him either. Fabien Barthez brought off an excellent save to deny his goal-bound header against Manchester United, while in the next home game against Sunderland he had what appeared to be a perfectly good goal disallowed. Bradford's Clarke also pulled off a magnificent save to deny him yet again. If one of those opportunities had gone in, who knows what might have happened but Town manager George Burley finally seemed to decide that his style was not compatible with that of his striking partner Marcus Stewart and early in the new year he was sold to Nottingham Forest. Bought to solve David Platt's goal-scoring problems he managed to hit the back of the net just twice in 19 games at the City Ground. However he impressed as a quality player and given better service and a regular strike partner the goals will surely come next term.
Manchester U (From trainee on 1/7/1994)
Bury (Free on 5/7/1995) FL 72+25/18 FLC 8+3/4 FAC 1+1 Others 3+2/1
Ipswich T (£800,000 on 14/11/1997) P/FL 121+10/55 FLC 13/5 FAC 7/2 Others 7
Nottingham F (£3,000,000 + on 12/1/2001) FL 19/2

JOHNSON Gavin
Born: Stowmarket, 10 October 1970
Height: 5'11" Weight: 12.0
Club Honours: Div 2 '92; Div 3 '97
After beginning the 2000-01 season on the subs' bench for Colchester United Gavin won a recall to the side and went on to play a key role in the campaign to secure another year of Second Division football for the U's. He scored just one goal during the season, netting a real cracker with a 30-yard free kick to secure a 1-0 win over Reading in November. He mostly featured in a left-wing-back role although he can also operate in central midfield if required.
Ipswich T (From trainee on 1/3/1989) P/FL 114+18/11 FLC 10+1/2 FAC 12/2 Others 3+1/1
Luton T (Free on 4/7/1995) FL 4+1
Wigan Ath (£15,000 on 15/12/1995) FL 82+2/8 FLC 4 FAC 3 Others 1
Dunfermline Ath (Free on 1/7/1998) SL 18 SC 0+1
Colchester U (Free on 12/11/1999) FL 57+7/2 FLC 3+1 FAC 1

Gavin Johnson

JOHNSON Ian Robert
Born: Liverpool, 7 March 1983
Height: 6'1" Weight: 12.5
A trainee at Wigan, Ian appeared mostly in the youth and reserve teams during the 2000-01 campaign but stepped up to make a promising debut from the subs' bench in the LDV Vans Trophy tie at Oldham Athletic. He also appeared in the second round tie at Walsall in the same competition and will be looking to gain further senior experience in the 2001-02 season. A right-sided midfield player, he is the grandson of former Liverpool manager Ronnie Moran.
Wigan Ath (Trainee) Others 0+2

JOHNSON Joel
Born: Manchester, 28 April 1983
Height: 5'8" Weight: 12.8
This Wigan trainee spent most of last season developing in the youth and reserve teams but he experienced his first taste of senior action in the LDV Vans Trophy second round tie at Walsall in January. Joel is a pacy striker but was released by the Latics at the end of his apprenticeship.
Wigan Ath (Trainee) Others 1

JOHNSON Lee David
Born: Newmarket, 7 June 1981
Height: 5'6" Weight: 10.7
Lee joined Brighton after being released by Watford and featured regularly for the Seagulls' reserves last season, making his only senior appearance in the LDV Vans tie against Cardiff when he scored the first goal in a 2-0 victory. A tigerish midfield player he was eventually released in March and then spent a trial period with Brentford where he featured in the reserves. Lee is the son of the Latvia national team manager Gary Johnson.

Watford (From trainee on 3/10/1998)
Brighton & Hove A (Free on 4/9/2000) Others 1/1

JOHNSON Leon Dean
Born: Shoreditch, 10 May 1981
Height: 6'0" Weight: 12.4

Leon seized his chance to establish himself as a regular in the Southend United first team last January and established an excellent pairing with Kevin Maher in the centre of the park. A tall and elegant central midfield player he is adept at making important tackles and blocks to frustrate opponents. He scored his first goal in senior football at Chesterfield in March and will be looking to gain more experience in the coming season.

Southend U (From trainee on 17/11/1999) FL 19+1/1 FAC 0+1 Others 6

JOHNSON Marvin Anthony
Born: Wembley, 29 October 1968
Height: 6'0" Weight: 13.6

Marvin had the misfortune to suffer a neck injury in only the second game of the 2000-01 campaign and he spent most of the remainder of the season trying to recover full fitness. The problem was eventually diagnosed as a slipped disc but although he made a brief come-back in December it was not until the closing stages of the season that he seemed to finally shake it off. Currently the longest-serving player at Kenilworth Road, Marvin has been a rock in the centre of defence in recent seasons and a shining example to the younger players. Quick, strong in the tackle and difficult to pass he was sorely missed by the Hatters and they struggled all season in his absence.

Luton T (From apprentice on 12/11/1986) FL 341+14/6 FLC 26+2/2 FAC 19+1/1 Others 13

JOHNSON Michael Owen
Born: Nottingham, 4 July 1973
Height: 5'11" Weight: 11.12
Club Honours: AIC '95
International Honours: Jamaica: 7

This popular Birmingham City defender was a model of consistency last season and formed an excellent partnership with Darren Purse in the heart of the back line. Very quick and with a good leap Michael enhanced his reputation as one of the best centre halves outside the Premier League. A great recovery tackler, he decided to turn down overtures by Jamaica after they left him out of their early-season games.

Notts Co (From trainee on 9/7/1991) FL 102+5 FLC 9 FAC 4 Others 15+1
Birmingham C (£225,000 on 1/9/1995) FL 192+32/12 FLC 22+6/4 FAC 6+3 Others 10

JOHNSON Richard Mark
Born: Newcastle, Australia, 27 April 1974
Height: 5'11" Weight: 12.0
Club Honours: Div 2 '98
International Honours: Australia: 1

Richard spent virtually the whole of the 2000-01 campaign recovering from a cruciate ligament injury suffered in the closing stages of the previous season. He made his long-awaited return to the Watford first-team at the end of April when he came off the subs' bench against Tranmere and returned to the starting line-up for the final game at Burnley. An experienced central midfield player he possesses a powerful long-range shot and when fully fit is capable of dominating the centre of the park.

Watford (From trainee on 11/5/1992) P/FL 205+25/20 FLC 13+1/1 FAC 13+1/1 Others 5+1

JOHNSON Roger
Born: Ashford, 28 April 1983
Height: 6'3" Weight: 11.0

After making his senior debut for Wycombe at the end of the 1999-2000 campaign, Roger found it difficult to break into the first-team squad last season and his only opportunity came from the subs' bench at Reading in March when he gave an assured performance. A talented young central defender he is still on a scholar's contract and has plenty of time to establish himself in the game.

Wycombe W (Trainee) FL 0+2

JOHNSON Ross Yorke
Born: Brighton, 2 January 1976
Height: 6'0" Weight: 12.12

Ross missed the first half of the 2000-01 season for Colchester with a long-term knee injury but returned to action in December and had a lengthy run of first-team action in the new year. He is a right-sided central midfield player with a classy style of play and a powerful long throw.

Brighton & Hove A (From trainee on 22/7/1994) FL 113+19/2 FLC 3+3 FAC 4 Others 4+1
Colchester U (Free on 12/1/2000) FL 34+2

JOHNSON Seth Art Maurice
Born: Birmingham, 12 March 1979
Height: 5'10" Weight: 11.0
International Honours: E: 1; U21-12; Yth

All in all 2000-01 was quite a season for this combative Derby midfielder. Generally operating on the left-hand side of midfield, his no-nonsense style earned him numerous yellow cards but there was a marked maturity in his play during the campaign. An automatic first-team choice for Jim Smith, he also showed himself as an able deputy for Darryl Powell as team captain when called upon. Injury forced him to miss six weeks of the action at the turn of the year. He can also play as a left-sided wing back when required but it is in midfield where his passing abilities are put to best use. A regular in the England U21 set-up he became the first County player to represent his country at full international level for nine years when he came on as a second half substitute in November's friendly in Italy. It was almost a dream debut as his first touch of the ball forced a great save from the opposing 'keeper.

Crewe Alex (From trainee on 12/7/1996) FL 89+4/6 FLC 5 FAC 2/1 Others 0+3
Derby Co (£3,000,000 on 21/5/1999) PL 66/2 FLC 5+1 FAC 0+1

JOKANOVIC Slavisa
Born: Novi Sad, Yugoslavia, 16 August 1968
Height: 6'3" Weight: 13.10
International Honours: Yugoslavia: 58

Chelsea were in desperate need of an experienced central midfield player following Roberto Di Matteo's injury and manager Claudio Ranieri made his first signing to bring this much-travelled player to Stamford Bridge. A league winner with three different clubs: Vojvodina, Partizan Belgrade and Deportivo La Coruna he struggled at first to cope with the pace of the Premiership and made the majority of his appearances as a second-half substitute. A hard-working, aggressive midfielder player he uses his height to good advantage in dead-ball situations.

Chelsea (£1,700,000 from Deportivo la Coruna, Spain, ex Novi Sad, Vojvodina, Partizan Belgrade, Real Oviedo, Tenerife, on 16/10/2000) PL 7+12 FLC 1 FAC 2

JONES Barry
Born: Prescot, 30 June 1970
Height: 5'11" Weight: 11.12
Club Honours: WC '95

Barry again performed consistently in defence for York City last season but fell out of favour after Mike Basham and Chris Brass arrived at Bootham Crescent in the new year and was released in May. Steady and reliable he can play either at right back or in the centre of the defence.

Liverpool (Free from Prescot Cables on 19/1/1989) Others 0+1
Wrexham (Free on 10/7/1992) FL 184+11/5 FLC 14+1/1 FAC 11+2 Others 21+1
York C (£40,000 on 17/12/1997) FL 130+4/5 FLC 6/1 FAC 4 Others 1

JONES Darren Lee
Born: Newport, 26 August 1983
Height: 6'0" Weight: 12.6
International Honours: W: Yth; Sch

Darren is yet another of the promising youngsters to develop through Bristol City's Academy set-up. A former Wales schools international he signed a long-term contract for City last September and stepped up to make his senior debut from the subs' bench in the LDV Vans Trophy tie at Plymouth. He is a versatile player who has featured both at centre half and in a midfield role.

Bristol C (From trainee on 22/9/2000) Others 0+1

JONES Eifion Pritchard
Born: Caernarfon, 28 September 1980
Height: 6'3" Weight: 13.0
International Honours: W: Yth

This young Blackpool central defender made several senior appearances in the early part of last season but later dropped back into the reserves as manager Steve McMahon opted for more experience at the back. The 2001-02 season will be Eifion's second full campaign at Bloomfield Road and he will be looking to win a regular place in the first-team squad.

Liverpool (From trainee on 6/10/1997)
Blackpool (Signed on 23/3/2000) FL 5+3 FLC 4

JONES Gary
Born: Huddersfield, 6 April 1969
Height: 6'1" Weight: 12.9
Club Honours: Div 3 '98

Gary found it hard to establish himself in the Halifax Town line-up at the start of last season but after being relegated to the subs' bench in September he scored his first goal of the campaign at Cardiff. He found the net fairly regularly after that but missed several matches after suffering a knee injury at Shrewsbury and only returned to action in the final week of the season. He is a hard-working striker who formed an excellent partnership with Steve Kerrigan up front for the Shaymen.

Doncaster Rov (Free from Rossington Main on 26/1/1989) FL 10+10/2 FLC 1 (Free to Grantham on 1/11/1989)
Southend U (£25,000 from Boston U, ex Kettering T, on 3/6/1993) FL 47+23/16 FLC 3/1 FAC 2 Others 6+1/2
Lincoln C (Loaned on 17/9/1993) FL 0+4/2 Others 0+1
Notts Co (£140,000 on 1/3/1996) FL 103+14/38 FLC 5+1/1 FAC 9+1/7 Others 2+1
Scunthorpe U (Loaned on 21/2/1997) FL 9+2/5
Hartlepool U (Signed on 10/3/1999) FL 42+3/7 FLC 2 FAC 2/1 Others 2+2
Halifax T (Free on 23/3/2000) FL 38+3/6 FLC 2 FAC 1 Others 2/2

JONES Gary Roy
Born: Birkenhead, 3 June 1977
Height: 5'10" Weight: 12.0

Gary missed the first two games of the 2000-01 campaign through suspension, but thereafter was a fixture in Rochdale's midfield. Undoubtedly the side's most improved player, and a huge favourite with the fans, he was at the hub of everything covering every blade of grass and contesting every tackle week-in, week-out. He also contributed a major share of goals, especially when the strikers were going through a lean spell.

Swansea C (Signed from Caernarfon T on 11/7/1997) FL 3+5 FLC 0+1
Rochdale (Free on 15/1/1998) FL 103+17/17 FLC 2+1 FAC 4+3 Others 6+2/2

JONES Gary Steven
Born: Chester, 10 May 1975
Height: 6'3" Weight: 14.0

Having joined Nottingham Forest on a free transfer during the close season Gary went on to feature regularly for the First Division club in 2000-01 without ever really establishing himself in any one role. He was initially used as a striker but failed to make much impact and went on to appear in almost every outfield position during the season, although he seemed most comfortable either in midfield or at the back where his strength in the tackle could be used to good effect.

Tranmere Rov (From trainee on 5/7/1993) FL 117+61/28 FLC 17+2/2 FAC 9+2/3 Others 1+1
Nottingham F (Free on 3/7/2000) FL 22+9/1 FLC 1+1 FAC 1

JONES Thomas **Gethin**
Born: Llanbyther, 8 August 1981
Height: 5'11" Weight: 12.4

Gethin followed in the footsteps of Wales international Mark Delaney when he joined Cardiff City from League of Wales club Carmarthen Town last August. He made an immediate impact at Ninian Park and was called up for his senior debut in the Worthington Cup tie against Crystal Palace soon after signing. He also made a couple of Third Division appearances from the subs' bench but then had the misfortune to suffer a broken leg in a reserve game against Plymouth in September. A promising central defender he remains very much part of the Bluebirds plans for the future and was offered a further year's extension to his 12-month contract by owner Sam Hammam.

Cardiff C (Free from Carmarthen on 11/8/2000) FL 0+2 FLC 1

JONES Jason Andrew
Born: Wrexham, 10 May 1979
Height: 6'2" Weight: 12.7
International Honours: W: U21-2; Yth

In his third full season as understudy to the consistent Roger Freestone, Jason once again saw little first-team action at Swansea. For much of the campaign he was confined to outings in the FA Wales Premier Cup matches and when he got his chance at Bury when Freestone was suspended he promptly received a red card himself. He later made two further Second Division appearances and received a reward for his efforts in the close season when he made his debut for Wales at U21 level against Poland. A promising young goalkeeper he will be hoping for more senior experience next term.

Swansea C (From trainee at Liverpool on 29/12/1997) FL 7

JONES Keith Aubrey
Born: Dulwich, 14 October 1965
Height: 5'8" Weight: 11.2
Club Honours: Div 1 '00
International Honours: E: Yth; Sch

Keith missed the start of last term for Reading after suffering a hamstring injury in a pre-season friendly at Kingstonian and it was not until the end of September that he returned to first-team action. Used very much as a squad player, his vast experience proved invaluable in the centre of the park for the Royals and he contributed a single goal, netting in the 4-0 FA Cup victory over Grays Athletic. A hard-working competitive midfield player he can be very effective when used in a man-to-man marking role.

Chelsea (From apprentice on 16/8/1983) FL 43+9/7 FLC 9+2/3 FAC 1 Others 4+1
Brentford (£40,000 on 3/9/1987) FL 167+2/13 FLC 15/2 FAC 13/4 Others 16/1
Southend U (£175,000 on 21/10/1991) FL 88+2/11 FLC 4 FAC 5 Others 9/1
Charlton Ath (£150,000 on 16/9/1994) P/FL 142+16/6 FLC 6+1 FAC 4+3/1 Others 3
Reading (Free on 7/7/2000) FL 18+5 FAC 3/1 Others 2

JONES Lee
Born: Pontypridd, 9 August 1970
Height: 6'3" Weight: 14.4
Club Honours: AMC '94

A close season signing from Bristol Rovers, Lee began the 2000-01 campaign as first choice in goal for Stockport County and apart from occasional absences he did well to hold off challenges from Carlo Nash and Andy Dibble and emerge as the Hatters' regular 'keeper. Tall, strong, brave and agile he showed an impeccable temperament during the pressure-cooker final weeks of the season when the club's First Division status was on the line. A goals-against tally of just four in a run of eight vital games provided County with a platform to beat the drop.

Swansea C (£7,500 from AFC Porth on 24/3/1994) FL 6 Others 1
Bristol Rov (Signed on 7/3/1998) FL 76 FLC 6 FAC 7 Others 4
Stockport Co (£50,000 on 19/7/2000) FL 27 FLC 2 FAC 2

JONES Philip **Lee**
Born: Wrexham, 29 May 1973
Height: 5'9" Weight: 10.8
International Honours: W: 2; B-1; U21-14; Yth

Signed from Tranmere during the close season, Lee made a bright start to the 2000-01 campaign at Barnsley, scoring the winner against Norwich on the opening day and following this up with a double in the next home game against West Bromwich Albion. Managerial changes at Oakwell meant that he appeared in a variety of positions during the season but he looked more comfortable when used as a striker where his speed off the mark always made him a handful for opposition defenders. He missed several matches due to injuries and his longest run in the team came when Nigel Spackman took over as manager and played him on the left-hand side of midfield. However a bout tendonitis caused his season to end prematurely in the new year.

Wrexham (From trainee on 5/7/1991) FL 24+15/10 FLC 2 FAC 1+2/1 Others 4+1/2
Liverpool (£300,000 on 12/3/1992) PL 0+3 FLC 0+1
Crewe Alex (Loaned on 3/9/1993) FL 4+4/1
Wrexham (Loaned on 26/1/1996) FL 20/9
Wrexham (Loaned on 31/1/1997) FL 2+4
Tranmere Rov (£100,000 on 27/3/1997) FL 58+28/16 FLC 7+3/2 FAC 0+1
Barnsley (Free on 3/7/2000) FL 15+12/5 FLC 2+3/1

JONES Marcus Lee
Born: Stone, 24 June 1974
Height: 6'2" Weight: 13.2

After beginning the 2000-01 campaign with non-league Scarborough, Marcus joined Cheltenham Town last November as cover for an injury crisis. He mostly featured in the reserves at centre half but also played in a central midfield role on occasions. He found first-team opportunities limited at Whaddon Road and in February he moved on to join Yeovil to assist in their fight for the Conference title.

Cheltenham T (Signed from Scarborough on 17/11/2000) FL 1+1 Others 1

JONES Mark Andrew
Born: Walsall, 7 September 1979
Height: 5'9" Weight: 11.7
International Honours: E: Yth; Sch

Following his release by Wolves Mark joined Chesterfield in the 2000 close season but took a long time to reach full match fitness, due in part to a lack of reserve games to bring him on. A quick-witted and pacy striker, he scored on his only start for the Spireites in the LDV Vans Trophy game at Rotherham, but moved on to Raith Rovers

in the new year. He netted on his debut for the Scottish First Division outfit and settled in well, hitting four goals in eight appearances.
Wolverhampton W (From trainee on 25/9/1996) FL 0+3 FLC 0+2
Cheltenham T (Loaned on 4/10/1999) FL 3
Chesterfield (Free on 9/8/2000) FL 0+3 FAC 0+1 Others 1/1

JONES Matthew Graham
Born: Llanelli, 1 September 1980
Height: 5'11" Weight: 11.5
Club Honours: FAYC '97
International Honours: W: 8; B-1; U21-7; Yth
Matthew was very much on the fringes of the Leeds United first-team squad at the beginning of the 2000-01 campaign but after playing in the Premiership game at Leicester in December he moved on to the Filbert Street club shortly afterwards. Seen by boss Peter Taylor as a potential long-term replacement for Neil Lennon in the central midfield anchor role, he looked particularly impressive on his debut against Charlton. Although his form dipped at times he was inspirational in the FA Cup victory over Bristol City and clearly has plenty of natural ability. Matthew continued to appear for Wales and suffered a foot injury in the World Cup qualifier against Ukraine in March, but he returned to action for the last couple of games of the season.
Leeds U (From trainee on 3/9/1997) PL 11+12 FLC 1+1 FAC 0+2 Others 4+2
Leicester C (£3,250,000 on 13/12/2000) PL 10+1 FAC 3

JONES Matthew Neil
Born: Shrewsbury, 11 October 1980
Height: 6'0" Weight: 12.0
Matthew was one of several youngsters on the verge of the Shrewsbury Town first team last season. He recovered from a hernia operation to make a handful of senior appearances before spending a month on loan at Conference club Southport at the turn of the year. He is a right-sided defender who is composed on the ball and always looks to push forward. Matthew was released in the summer.
Shrewsbury T (From trainee on 2/7/1999) FL 5+2

JONES Nathan Jason
Born: Rhondda, 28 May 1973
Height: 5'7" Weight: 10.12
Club Honours: Div 3 '01
Out of contract at Southend, Nathan joined Brighton in the 2000 close season and appeared mostly in a wide left-midfield role for the Seagulls in 2000-01. He quickly became a crowd favourite with his entertaining style and elaborate shimmies and shuffles, which in turn earned him his own 'soccer skills' feature on the Sky Sports programme 'Soccer AM'. A high point was scoring twice in the 6-2 home victory over Torquay, a result that heralded a transformation of the Seagulls' fortunes after a shaky start and which paved the way for their ultimately successful Third Division championship campaign.
Luton T (£10,000 from Merthyr Tydfil on 30/6/1995. Freed on 20/12/1995)
Southend U (Free from Numancia, Spain on 5/8/1997) FL 82+17/2 FLC 6+2 FAC 3+1/1 Others 0+3
Scarborough (Loaned on 25/3/1999) FL 8+1
Brighton & Hove A (Free on 7/7/2000) FL 27+13/4 FLC 1+1/1 FAC 2 Others 1

JONES Paul Neil
Born: Liverpool, 3 June 1978
Height: 6'1" Weight: 13.2
After bursting on the scene at Oldham in the second half of the 1999-2000 campaign Paul had a very frustrating time last term. His progress was impeded when a fractured cheekbone ruled him out for several weeks, and then a 70-minute appearance at Oxford in early December proved to be his final contribution as he was struck by problems with shin splints soon afterwards. He underwent corrective surgery in May and is expected to be fit for the start of the 2001-02 season. A powerful 'stopper' centre half he will be hoping to regain his place in the Latics' team.
Tranmere Rov (From trainee on 27/12/1995. Free to Barrow during 1997 close season)
Oldham Ath (Free from Leigh RMI on 15/11/1999) FL 26+2/3 FLC 3 Others 0+1

JONES Paul Steven
Born: Chirk, 18 April 1967
Height: 6'3" Weight: 14.8
International Honours: W: 21
After recovering from a serious back injury that at one point seemed to threaten to end his career, Paul reclaimed his place as Southampton's number one goalkeeper at the start of the 2000-01 campaign. Apart from a brief spell early in the season when his form dipped he went from strength to strength, establishing a new post-war club record early in the new year with a run of seven straight Premiership clean sheets and 667 minutes without conceding a goal. His agility and shot stopping capabilities will stand him in good stead for a few more seasons to come and he signed an extension to his contract that will bind him to the Saints until 2005.
Wolverhampton W (£40,000 from Kidderminster Hrs on 23/7/1991) FL 33 FLC 2 FAC 5 Others 4
Stockport Co (£60,000 on 25/7/1996) FL 46 FLC 11 FAC 4 Others 4
Southampton (£900,000 on 28/7/1997) PL 135 FLC 13 FAC 9

JONES Scott
Born: Sheffield, 1 May 1975
Height: 5'10" Weight: 12.8
Scott joined Bristol Rovers on loan shortly before the start of the 2000-01 campaign and made an impressive debut in the opening game against Bournemouth. He signed permanently shortly afterwards and settled in well with the Pirates, featuring regularly during the season and contributing some vital goals. A versatile left-sided defender he has good distribution and is a constant danger when joining the attack at set pieces.
Barnsley (From trainee on 1/2/1994) F/PL 76+7/4 FLC 7/1 FAC 4+3/2
Mansfield T (Loaned on 7/8/1997) FL 6 FLC 2
Bristol Rov (£200,000 on 10/8/2000) FL 37+2/3 FLC 3 FAC 1 Others 1+1

JONES Stephen (Steve) Gary
Born: Cambridge, 17 March 1970
Height: 6'1" Weight: 12.12
Still out of favour at Bristol City Steve joined Wycombe in July 2000 on a three-month loan deal to replace the injured Sean Devine. He made a highly impressive debut at Stoke on the opening day of the season but after a handful of appearances he suffered a broken bone in his left foot in the match at Brentford and returned to Ashton Gate where he played no further senior games. An experienced striker who is quick for his size, his abrasive style of play means defenders find him difficult to handle.
West Ham U (£22,000 from Billericay T on 16/11/1992) PL 8+8/4 FAC 2+2/1 Others 1+1
Bournemouth (£150,000 on 21/10/1994) FL 71+3/26 FLC 4/3 FAC 3/1 Others 3
West Ham U (Signed on 16/5/1996) PL 5+3 FLC 0+1 FAC 2 Others 1
Charlton Ath (£400,000 on 14/2/1997) P/FL 28+24/8 FLC 3+1 FAC 1 Others 1+2
Bournemouth (Loaned on 24/12/1997) FL 5/4 Others 1/1
Bristol C (£425,000 + on 10/9/1999) FL 12+2/2 FLC 2 FAC 2+1
Brentford (Loaned on 21/1/2000) FL 6+2 Others 2
Southend U (Loaned on 17/3/2000) FL 9/2
Wycombe W (Loaned on 17/7/2000) FL 5 FLC 1

JONES Stephen (Steve) Robert
Born: Bristol, 25 December 1970
Height: 5'10" Weight: 12.2
Club Honours: Div 3 '00
Steve had a wretched time with injuries at Swansea last term after making a promising start to the campaign. He underwent a groin and stomach operation in mid-October and shortly after returning to first-team action he injured a thigh at Walsall on Boxing Day. He eventually came back in March only to suffer an ankle injury in the FA Wales Premier Cup tie against TNS Llansantffraid. When fully fit he is a gutsy right back who defends solidly and always gives 100 per cent effort in every game. He was released by the Swans in the summer.
Swansea C (£25,000 from Cheltenham T on 14/11/1995) FL 140+6/4 FLC 2+1 FAC 9 Others 8

JONES Stuart Clive
Born: Bristol, 24 October 1977
Height: 6'1" Weight: 14.0
Stuart started the 2000-01 season as first-choice 'keeper for Torquay United but lost his place through injury and had to be content with sharing duties with Ryan Northmore. He had been out of the team for some time when Andy Petterson's loan spell ended but he came back for the vital last game at Barnet and ended the campaign as a hero after saving a penalty. Stuart is an excellent shot stopper but still needs to develop greater consistency when handling crosses.
Sheffield Wed (£20,000 + from Weston super Mare on 26/3/1998)
Torquay U (£30,000 on 3/2/2000) FL 32 FLC 2 FAC 2 Others 1

JONES William (Billy) Kenneth
Born: Chatham, 26 March 1983
Height: 6'0" Weight: 11.7

A regular in Leyton Orient's successful U19 team last term, Billy scored the winning goal from the penalty spot in the Football League Youth Alliance Cup final against Bradford at the Millennium Stadium. He stepped up to make his senior debut when he replaced the injured Matt Lockwood against Kidderminster in February. A promising left back with good vision and accurate distribution he will be hoping for more senior action in the coming season.

Leyton Orient (Trainee) FL 1

JONK Wim
Born: Volendam, Holland, 12 October 1966
Height: 6'0" Weight: 12.2
International Honours: Holland: 48

Sheffield Wednesday badly missed this midfield play maker after he was sidelined with a groin injury in only the second match of the 2000-01 season and was absent for the remainder of the campaign. An influential figure in the centre of the park his calm approach and defence-splitting passes would have been of great value to the Owls as they struggled to cope with the rigours of the First Division. He was released in the summer.

Sheffield Wed (£2,500,000 from PSV Eindhoven, Holland, ex FC Volendam, Ajax, Inter Milan, on 12/8/1998) P/FL 69+1/5 FLC 4 FAC 7

JORDAN Andrew (Andy) Joseph
Born: Manchester, 14 December 1979
Height: 6'1" Weight: 13.1
International Honours: S: U21-4

Having signed a new contract for Bristol City in the Summer of 2000 Andy found it difficult to break into the first team at Ashton Gate in the early part of last season and at the end of October he moved on to Third Division high flyers Cardiff City. However after a brief run in the first team at Ninian Park he lost his place and with few reserve matches his opportunities were severely limited. Andy is a strong-tackling and committed central defender. He is the son of the former Scotland centre forward Joe Jordan.

Bristol C (From trainee on 5/12/1997) FL 10+1 FLC 1+1 FAC 1 Others 1
Cardiff C (£30,000 on 26/10/2000) FL 3+2 FAC 1

JORDAN Scott Douglas
Born: Newcastle, 19 July 1975
Height: 5'10" Weight: 11.8

Scott was on the fringe of York City's first team in 2000-01 and after nine seasons at Bootham Crescent he moved on to Conference club Scarborough in March. He managed just one goal for the Minstermen, netting with a cracking effort from 18 yards in the 4-1 FA Cup win over non-league Radcliffe Borough. He is a composed midfield player with fine distribution.

York C (From trainee on 21/10/1992) FL 123+44/12 FLC 5+1/1 FAC 7+3/3 Others 7+4

[JORDAO] BATISTA Adelion Jose Martins
Born: Malange, Angola, 30 August 1971
Height: 6'3" Weight: 12.10

Having joined West Bromwich Albion towards the end of last August Jordao made his first-team debut at Barnsley just 24 hours after signing. A strong, athletic player who is comfortable on the ball, it was hoped he would link up with Richard Sneekes and Derek McInnes in the engine-room but he never really settled into Albion's style of play. His best spell came in the six-week period leading up to early December but he was continuously in and out of the side during the second half of the season. He scored his first goal in English football in the 4-2 home defeat by Derby County in the Worthington Cup.

West Bromwich A (£350,000 from Sporting Braga, Portugal, ex Estrela Amadora, Campomaiorense, Lece, on 25/8/2000) FL 28+7/1 FLC 3/1 FAC 1 Others 0+2

JORGENSEN Claus Beck
Born: Denmark, 24 April 1979
Height: 5'11" Weight: 11.0

Claus missed just three Second Division games for Bournemouth last season and contributed a useful tally of goals, mostly in the first half of the campaign. He is a hard working midfield player with the ability to take on and beat opposing defenders. Out of contract at the end in the summer it was not clear at the time of writing whether he would remain with the Cherries for the 2001-02 season.

Bournemouth (Free from AC Horsens, Denmark on 12/7/1999) FL 77+10/14 FLC 6/1 FAC 6 Others 1+1

JORGENSEN Henrik
Born: Denmark, 12 January 1979
Height: 6'2" Weight: 14.0

Henrik joined Notts County at the end of the Scandinavian 2000 season and produced some highly-accomplished displays for the reserve team. A talented young central defender he made a handful of appearances for the Magpies' first team and was reported to have signed a new one-year contract in the summer.

Notts Co (Signed from B1909, Denmark, ex Odense BK, on 27/10/2000) FL 3+2 Others 1

JOSEPH David
Born: Guadeloupe, 22 November 1976
Height: 5'10" Weight: 12.7

David joined Notts County shortly before the start of last season in a 12-month loan deal from Montpellier where he had featured in the reserve team during 1999-2000. He adapted quickly to the English game and featured regularly in the squad although he was often on the subs' bench. He is an exciting young striker who is very quick and has the ability to turn and beat defenders in one move.

Notts Co (Loaned from Montpellier, France on 7/8/2000) FL 13+14/4 FLC 3+1 FAC 0+1 Others 1

JOSEPH Marc Ellis
Born: Leicester, 10 November 1976
Height: 6'0" Weight: 12.10

Marc missed the first couple of months of last season for Cambridge United while recovering from injury but on his return he gave some solid performances featuring regularly through to the end of the campaign. He is a classy central defender who is comfortable on the ball when pushing forward. Marc was out of contract in the summer and at the time of writing it was unclear whether he would remain at the Abbey Stadium or seek new pastures.

Cambridge U (From trainee on 23/5/1995) FL 136+17 FLC 7 FAC 5+2 Others 7+1

JOSEPH Matthew (Matt) Nathan Adolphus
Born: Bethnal Green, 30 September 1972
Height: 5'8" Weight: 10.7
International Honours: E: Yth. Barbabos: 2

A near ever-present for Leyton Orient last term Matt was a key figure in helping the team into the play-off final. An accomplished right back and an excellent man-marker he is difficult to knock off the ball and sets up many attacks with his fine surging runs. Matt made his international debut in the autumn for Barbados, featuring in World Cup qualifiers against Guatemala and the USA, and was deservedly voted 'Player of the Year' by the O's supporters for the second season in a row.

Arsenal (From trainee on 17/11/1990)
Gillingham (Free on 7/12/1992. Free to Ilves, Finland during 1993 close season)
Cambridge U (Signed on 19/11/1993) FL 157+2/6 FLC 6+1 FAC 7 Others 5
Leyton Orient (£10,000 on 22/1/1998) FL 130+3/1 FLC 7+1 FAC 10+1 Others 5+1

JULES Mark Anthony
Born: Bradford, 5 September 1971
Height: 5'8" Weight: 11.1

Mark was an ever-present in the Halifax Town squad under Mark Lillis in the early part of last season but when Paul Bracewell took over as manager he fell out of favour. He subsequently buckled down to some hard work and after a series of impressive performances in the reserves he forced his way back into the team in March, going on to play a vital role in the Shaymen's successful campaign to avoid relegation down to the Conference.

Bradford C (From trainee on 3/7/1990) FLC 0+1
Scarborough (Free on 14/8/1991) FL 57+20/16 FLC 6+2/2 FAC 1+1 Others 6/4
Chesterfield (£40,000 on 21/5/1993) FL 155+31/4 FLC 12+3/2 FAC 13+2 Others 10+1
Halifax T (Free on 5/7/1999) FL 54+8/1 FLC 3 FAC 2 Others 1

JUPP Duncan Alan
Born: Guildford, 25 January 1975
Height: 6'0" Weight: 12.12
International Honours: S: U21-9

With Kenny Cunningham sidelined for an extended period at the beginning of last term Duncan looked set for a decent run in the Wimbledon side, but after just a few games he was sidelined by an ankle injury and rarely featured afterwards. A dependable right back known for his charging runs down the flank he will be hoping to win a regular place in the Dons' team in the coming season.

Fulham (From trainee on 12/7/1993) FL 101+4/2 FLC 10+2 FAC 9+1/1 Others 9+1/1
Wimbledon (£125,000 + on 27/6/1996) P/FL 22+6 FLC 8+1 FAC 3+2

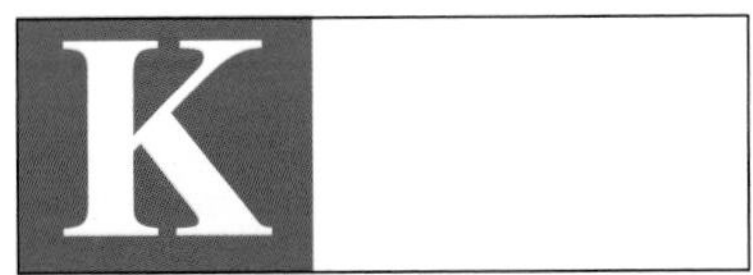

KAAK Anton (Tom) Christian
Born: Winterswijk, Holland, 31 March 1978
Height: 5'10" Weight: 12.7

Tom joined Darlington in the 2000 close season and immediately impressed with his strong running and neat link up play. He made his debut in the opening league game at Rochdale and when he scored in successive home games against Plymouth and York his position looked secure for some time. However after only a handful of appearances he was deemed surplus to requirements and was allowed to leave. He had a trial period with Scottish Division Two outfit Clydebank where he scored once in two games before returning to Holland where he linked up with Ijsselmeervogels.

Darlington (Free from Heracles, Holland, ex De Graafschap, on 21/7/2000) FL 7+1/2 FLC 0+2

KABBA Stephen (Steve)
Born: Lambeth, 7 March 1981
Height: 5'10" Weight: 11.12

This young Crystal Palace striker continued his progress in the club's reserve side in the 2000-01 season, his achievements including a four-goal tally in a 5-4 win over Norwich reserves last April. He made a brief appearance for the first team when he came on as a substitute for the second period of extra time in the Worthington Cup Fourth Round tie against Tranmere. The game went to a penalty shoot-out and Steve achieved his moment of glory when he scored from the deciding spot kick. He also came on as a late substitute against Norwich in February.

Crystal Palace (From trainee on 29/6/1999) FL 1+1 FLC 0+1

KACHLOUL Hassan
Born: Agadir, Morocco, 19 February 1973
Height: 6'1" Weight: 11.12
International Honours: Morocco

Hassan got off to a great start last season with two fine goals in the opening game at Derby to earn Southampton a 2-2 draw but then netted only two more goals all season. A talented attacking midfielder, he is at his best when cutting in from the left flank. Due to be out of contract in the summer there was considerable speculation about his future towards the end of the campaign and this seemed to have an unsettling effect on him. At the time of writing there has been no firm news as to whether he would stay with the Saints or be on his way, although the latter seemed much more likely.

Southampton (£250,000 from St Etienne, France, ex Nimes, Dunkerque, Metz, on 20/10/1998) PL 73+13/14 FLC 5 FAC 4+2/1

KANCHELSKIS Andrei
Born: Kirovograd, USSR, 23 January 1969
Height: 5'10" Weight: 13.4
Club Honours: ESC '91; FLC '92; PL '93, '94; FAC '94; CS '93, '94; SPD '99, '00; SC '99, '00; SLC '99
International Honours: Russia: 36; CIS 6; USSR: 17 (UEFA-U21 '90)

Andrei was a regular for Glasgow Rangers last season until October but after that he fell out of favour at Ibrox. Having previously played for Joe Royle at Everton he linked up with him for the second time in his career when he joined Manchester City in a three-month loan deal at the end of January. Making his debut as a second-half substitute in the 1-1 draw against Liverpool at Maine Road he caused many problems for the Reds with his pace on the right wing. He then featured regularly in the starting line-up scoring his only goal for the Blues in the FA Cup defeat at Anfield before returning north of the border.

Manchester U (£650,000 from Shakhtar Donetsk, Ukraine, ex Dinamo Kiev, on 26/3/1991) F/PL 96+27/28 FLC 15+1/3 FAC 11+1/4 Others 10/1
Everton (£5,000,000 on 25/8/1995) PL 52/20 FLC 2/1 FAC 6/1 (£8,000,000 to Fiorentina, Italy on 29/1/1997)
Glasgow R (£5,500,000 on 15/7/1998) SL 57+8/12 SLC 4/1 SC 10+2/2 Others 13+10/3
Manchester C (Loaned on 30/1/2001) PL 7+3 FAC 1/1

KANDOL Tresor Osmar
Born: Zaire, 30 August 1981
Height: 6'2" Weight: 11.7

A promising youngster who graduated from Luton Town's youth set-up Tresor made steady progress last season but failed to establish himself as a regular in the Hatters' first team. He scored with a header in his first appearance of the campaign at Wycombe and then netted a brace in the 3-3 draw at Bristol Rovers in September. However some well-publicised off-the-field problems seemed to affect his form and he rarely featured in the first team after Christmas. A tall and skilful striker he was released in the summer.

Luton T (From trainee on 26/9/1998) FL 9+12/3 FLC 3+1/2 Others 0+1

KANOUTE Frederic
Born: Sainte Foy Les Lyon, France, 2 September 1977
Height: 6'4" Weight: 12.10
International Honours: France: B-1; U21

Frederic is a centre forward who appears to have all the attributes required to be a top player in his position: pace, quick feet, strength and skill. However although he did well for the Hammers last term, finishing up as the leading scorer, he was hampered by a niggling hamstring problem that prevented him from performing at full capacity for much of the campaign. He was unstoppable in November and ran the Leeds and Southampton defences ragged in away wins for the Hammers. While he was on fire at Christmas and the New Year netting seven goals in a run of five games including doubles in the 5-0 win over Charlton and in the FA Cup victory over Walsall. Media stories of an impending transfer began to circulate towards the end of the season and at the time of writing it was unclear whether he would remain at Upton Park for the start of the 2001-02 campaign.

West Ham U (£4,000,000 from Lyon, France on 23/3/2000) PL 40/13 FLC 3 FAC 4/3

Frederic Kanoute

KANU Nwankwo
Born: Owerri, Nigeria, 1 August 1976
Height: 6'4" Weight: 13.3
Club Honours: CS '99
International Honours: Nigeria: 25; U23 (OLYM '96); Yth (World-U17 '93)

By his own high standards the 2000-01 campaign was not one of Kanu's best. In and out of the Arsenal team he still had his moments, notably when he came off the subs' bench in the league clash against Tottenham at Highbury and produced a marvellous back-heel to set up Thierry Henry for a goal in the 2-0 victory. At times he can appear awkward, but his ability to hold up the ball and take pressure off the defence can be vital and there is no doubt that he is an extraordinary talent. Kanu finished fifth in this year's 'African Footballer of the Year' voting and again featured for Nigeria although this was a cause of occasional friction between club and country.

Arsenal (£4,500,000 from Inter Milan, Italy, ex Fed Works, Iwuanyanwu National, Ajax, on 4/2/1999) PL 42+28/21 FLC 1/1 FAC 0+8/1 Others 21+9/6

KAREMBEU Christian Lali
Born: Lifou, New Caledonia, 3 December 1970
Height: 5'11" Weight: 11.7
International Honours: France: 51

Christian brought an abundance of talent to the Riverside when he signed for Middlesbrough during the summer and it soon became clear that his transfer fee was a real bargain. A midfielder-cum-striker with a lot to offer he soon proved his worth, winning over the fans with his exciting brand of soccer. Mostly used in an attacking midfield role, he will be hoping that the Boro' team he plays for next term is a more successful one.

Middlesbrough (£2,100,000 from Real Madrid, Spain, ex Nantes, Sampdoria, on 7/8/2000) PL 31+2/4 FLC 1 FAC 1+1

KARIC Amir
Born: Oramovica Ponja, Yugoslavia, 31 December 1973
Height: 5'11" Weight: 12.8
International Honours: Slovenia: 10
Amir appeared in the UEFA Champions' League qualifying matches for the 1999-2000 Slovenian champions NK Maribor before joining Ipswich Town last autumn. He made his first-team debut in the home leg of the Worthington Cup tie with Millwall and gave some glimpses of his potential with some excellent crosses but found it hard to break into the side at Portman Road. He later had a short loan spell at Crystal Palace where he made three appearances at left back as cover for the suspended Craig Harrison. An experienced left-sided defender he is particularly effective when delivering free kicks. A member of the Slovenian international team he featured in their squad for the Euro 2000 finals.
Ipswich T (£700,000 from NK Maribor, Slovenia, ex NK Maribor, Gamba Osaka, on 18/9/2000) FLC 0+3
Crystal Palace (Loaned on 2/3/2001) FL 3

KARLSEN Kent
Born: Oslo, Norway, 17 February 1973
Height: 6'2" Weight: 13.3
International Honours: Norway: U21
Kent joined Luton Town from Valerenga during the Norwegian close season to add competition for places, but after a handful of appearances he was sidelined by a knee injury and did not return until the final game against Port Vale. A big powerful central defender he possesses good passing skills and is very strong in the tackle.
Luton T (Free from FC Valerenga, Norway, ex Hamarkameratene, Lillestrom, on 3/11/2000) FL 4+2 FAC 2 Others 1

KARLSSON Par
Born: Sweden, 29 May 1978
Height: 5'8" Weight: 10.10
International Honours: Sweden: U21
Wimbledon beat off the attempts of several more fashionable clubs at home and abroad to land this Swedish U21 international for a bargain fee last September. A left-sided midfield player who enjoys going forward but also does his fair share of tracking back into defence, he netted his first goal for the Dons at home to Preston in January. Par took some time to settle in at his new club but is likely to show his full potential in the coming season.
Wimbledon (£40,000 from IFK Gothenburg, Sweden, ex Karlskoya, on 7/9/2000) FL 7+9 FLC 1 FAC 5/1

KAVANAGH Graham Anthony
Born: Dublin, 2 December 1973
Height: 5'10" Weight: 12.11
Club Honours: AMC '00
International Honours: RoI: 3; B-1; U21-9; Yth; Sch
Graham was once again a key figure for Stoke City last season and his performances made a great contribution towards the club's campaign to reach the play-offs. He continued to be employed in a central-midfield role although he played in a more defensive capacity hence his reduced goal output. A very talented midfielder he was reported to have gone on the transfer list during the summer as he sought higher-grade football in a bid to boost his international ambitions. He was selected for the PFA's Second Division team in April.
Middlesbrough (Signed from Home Farm on 16/8/1991) F/PL 22+13/3 FLC 1 FAC 3+1/1 Others 7
Darlington (Loaned on 25/2/1994) FL 5
Stoke C (£250,000 + on 13/9/1996) FL 198+8/35 FLC 16+2/7 FAC 6 Others 15/4

KAY Antony Roland
Born: Barnsley, 21 October 1982
Height: 5'11" Weight: 11.8
International Honours: E: Yth
Having developed through the ranks at Barnsley, Antony made his Football League debut against Norwich on the opening day of last season but was rather unfortunately substituted early on after a sending off led to a reorganisation of the line-up. He was then hit by a number of minor injuries and didn't force himself back into the first-team picture on a regular basis until late in the season. A stylish midfielder who is comfortable on the ball and hard-working when not in possession he impressed in the handful of appearances he made. He made his debut for England U18s against Switzerland at the end of the season.
Barnsley (From trainee on 25/10/1999) FL 3+4

KAY Stephen **Benjamin (Ben)**
Born: Wigan, 22 September 1982
Height: 5'10" Weight: 11.6
Ben was one of several promising youngsters to make his senior debut for Wigan in the LDV Vans Trophy second round tie at Walsall in January. A promising central defender he spent the remainder of the season developing in the club's reserve and youth teams. He was voted 'Young Player of the Year' and his performances also earned him a 12-month professional contract in the summer.
Wigan Ath (Trainee) Others 1

KEANE Michael Thomas Joseph
Born: Dublin, 29 December 1982
Height: 5'7" Weight: 10.10
International Honours: RoI: Yth
A tough-tackling all-action midfield player Michael graduated from the Preston youth team to win a regular place in the reserves last season before stepping up to make his Football League debut against Blackburn in the penultimate match of the regular campaign. Predominantly left-footed he is nippy around the pitch and is one of many fine prospects coming through the ranks at Deepdale.
Preston NE (From trainee on 7/8/2000) FL 0+2

KEANE Robert (Robbie) David
Born: Dublin, 8 July 1980
Height: 5'9" Weight: 11.10
International Honours: RoI: 25; B-1; Yth; (UEFA-U18 '98)
A young striker of immense talent, Robbie joined Leeds United on loan from Inter Milan last December only a matter of months after his move to Italy. He arrived at Elland Road like a breath of fresh air and had an immediate effect on a side that seemed to be temporarily struggling. He scored against Middlesbrough in his first full game and followed this with five in his next seven games including a superb overhead kick to defeat his old Coventry City team-mates. Unfortunately for Robbie he was cup-tied for the Champions League' and then had to battle with Alan Smith to partner Mark Viduka in domestic matches. With his great awareness, unselfish running, and a dazzling array of skills he is a superb young talent. Although on loan he may well sign permanently in the close season and would certainly add to the glittering array of young players at Elland Road.
Wolverhampton W (From trainee on 26/7/1997) FL 66+7/24 FLC 7+2/3 FAC 3+2/2
Coventry C (£6,000,000 on 20/8/1999) PL 30+1/12 FAC 3 (£13,000,000 to Inter Milan, Italy on 31/7/1999)
Leeds U (£12,000,000 on 22/12/2000) PL 12+6/9 FAC 2

KEANE Roy Maurice
Born: Cork, 10 August 1971
Height: 5'10" Weight: 12.10
Club Honours: FMC '92; CS '93, '96, '97; PL '94, '96, '97, '99, '00, '01; FAC '94, '96, '99
International Honours: RoI: 52; U21-4; Yth; Sch
Roy started his seventh season at Old Trafford in his customary sublime manner, and despite missing three consecutive Premiership games in September, was clearly determined to lead the Reds to further glories on both the domestic and European stage. While his on-field activities were beyond reproach, he did manage to cause a minor controversy in November with some remarks about prawn sandwiches and more specifically those who indulge in them. One area where Roy's own appetite was a bit subdued was in the goal-scoring stakes. Having netted eight goals by the turn of the year during the previous campaign, his first effort of 2000-01 came against Charlton in December. Not that it particularly bothered him. The main reason for the drought was that he was playing a more disciplined role, thus allowing David Beckham to get forward more. Netting one of United's six goals in the Premiership match against Arsenal in February, Roy was highly influential during the Champions' League run and was in the thick of things as the competition reached its exciting and ultimately disappointing finale. He remained of course a cornerstone of the Republic of Ireland national team and was a key figure in their highly promising start to their qualifying campaign for the 2002 World Cup finals. He was also honoured by his fellow professionals by being voted into the PFA's Premier Division team once again.
Nottingham F (£10,000 from Cobh Ramblers on 12/6/1990) F/PL 114/22 FLC 17/6 FAC 18/3 Others 5/2
Manchester U (£3,750,000 on 22/7/1993) PL 205+8/26 FLC 9+2 FAC 31+1/1 Others 62/15

KEARTON Jason Brett
Born: Ipswich, Australia, 9 July 1969
Height: 6'1" Weight: 11.10
Club Honours: FAC '95

Jason was again first-choice 'keeper for Crewe Alexandra at the beginning of last season but lost his place at the turn of the year to Ade Bankole and only returned to the side at the very end of the campaign. A very popular 'keeper with the Gresty Road faithful he has now made over 200 appearances for the Railwaymen and will be hoping to become the club's regular goalie once more in 2001-02.

Everton (Free from Brisbane Lions, Australia on 31/10/1988) PL 3+3 FLC 1 FAC 1
Stoke C (Loaned on 13/8/1991) FL 16 Others 1
Blackpool (Loaned on 9/1/1992) FL 14
Notts Co (Loaned on 19/1/1995) FL 10 Others 2
Crewe Alex (Free on 16/10/1996) FL 190+1 FLC 15 FAC 7 Others 6

KEATES Dean Scott
Born: Walsall, 30 June 1978
Height: 5'6" Weight: 10.10

Although not always a first choice for Walsall last term, Dean came back again and again to lift the side when they were in danger of slipping out of the promotion race. His tackling and use of the ball were inspirational and he also came up with some vital goals, including a penalty against Port Vale, and an in-swinging corner in the play-off semi-final against Stoke. He follows in the Saddlers' tradition of battling all-action midfielders and remains a key member of the squad.

Walsall (From trainee on 14/8/1996) FL 119+27/8 FLC 14+1/1 FAC 9+2 Others 14+1/3

KEEBLE Christopher (Chris) Mark
Born: Colchester, 17 September 1978
Height: 5'9" Weight: 11.5

Chris had a frustrating time for Colchester United last season, spending much of the campaign in the reserves. He made the starting line-up on a handful of occasions but had the misfortune to rupture an achilles tendon in the final match against Wycombe and the injury is expected to keep him out of action until the end of the year. A promising central midfield player he is the son of Vic Keeble who played for Colchester, Newcastle and West Ham in the 1950s.

Ipswich T (From trainee on 2/6/1997) FL 0+1
Colchester U (Free on 23/3/2000) FL 12+9/2 FLC 1+1 Others 1

KEEGAN Michael Jerard
Born: Wallasey, 12 May 1981
Height: 5'10" Weight: 11.0

Michael enjoyed a brief run in the Swansea City team at the start of the 2000-01 campaign before losing his place. A very promising young wide-right midfield player, he has neat ball control and can deliver accurate crosses from the flanks. Unfortunately as the Swans have no regular reserve team he was forced to spend long spells of the season with no competitive action.

Swansea C (From trainee on 5/7/1999) FL 7+1 FLC 1+1 FAC 1+1 Others 4

KEELER Justin Jack
Born: Hillingdon, 17 April 1978
Height: 5'11" Weight: 11.6

Justin spent three months on loan with Dr Martens League club Dorchester Town at the beginning of last season and although he did well with Bournemouth reserves on his return he only managed a handful of appearances from the subs' bench at first-team level. An attacking midfield player he was eventually allowed to join Dorchester on a permanent basis towards the end of the campaign.

Bournemouth (Free from Christchurch on 10/1/2000) FL 0+4 Others 0+3

KEEN Kevin Ian
Born: Amersham, 25 February 1967
Height: 5'8" Weight: 10.10
International Honours: E: Yth; Sch

This experienced player joined Macclesfield Town on a one-year contract at the start of last season and after taking time to settle in he teamed up with Chris Priest to form an effective partnership in the centre of the park. Kevin is a hard-working attacking midfielder who is adept at scoring long-distance goals when picking up stray balls on the edge of the box. Kevin made his 450th League appearance during the 2000-2001 season and is working towards his UEFA 'A' coaching certificate. He was appointed assistant manager of the Macc reserve team in January and later signed an extension to his contract at Moss Rose.

West Ham U (From apprentice on 8/3/1984) FL 187+32/21 FLC 21+1/5 FAC 15+7/1 Others 14+2/3
Wolverhampton W (£600,000 on 7/7/1993) FL 37+5/7 FLC 2+1 FAC 5/1 Others 4/1
Stoke C (£300,000 on 19/10/1994) FL 147+30/10 FLC 13+3/2 FAC 6 Others 3+1
Macclesfield T (Free on 11/9/2000) FL 30+2/2 FLC 1+1 FAC 0+1

KEEN Peter Alan
Born: Middlesbrough, 16 November 1976
Height: 6'0" Weight: 12.0

Despite an encouraging end to the 1999-2000 campaign, Peter had to wait until late October for a first-team appearance in goal for Carlisle. He returned in style, scoring the Cumbrians' second goal in the 3-2 defeat at Blackpool with a huge wind-assisted kick, making him the second Carlisle 'keeper to register a goal in little more than 12 months! Despite this he lost his place soon afterwards and later moved on loan to Darlington as cover for the injured Andy Collett. Peter made his debut for the Quakers in the defeat at Barnet but then rapidly grew in confidence and was only on the losing side once in seven games before Collett returned to the line-up. He was released in the summer.

Newcastle U (From trainee on 25/3/1996)
Carlisle U (Free on 4/8/1999) FL 9/1
Darlington (Loaned on 13/3/2001) FL 7

KEISTER John Edward Samuel
Born: Manchester, 11 November 1970
Height: 5'8" Weight: 11.0
International Honours: Sierra Leone: 3

John linked up with his old boss Kevin Ratcliffe at Shrewsbury last October as the Town manager sought to add some bite in the centre of the park. He produced some characteristically determined performances as a ball-winning midfield player but departed for a brief spell at Stevenage in the new year. He later moved on to Margate where he assisted in their Dr Martens League championship-winning team in the closing stages of the season.

Walsall (Free from Faweh FC on 18/9/1993) FL 78+28/2 FLC 4+1 FAC 10+2 Others 2+2
Chester C (Free on 7/1/2000) FL 8+2 Others 1
Shrewsbury T (Free on 13/10/2000) FL 8 FAC 1

KEITH Joseph (Joe) Richard
Born: Plaistow, 1 October 1978
Height: 5'7" Weight: 10.6

Joe started the first five games of last season for Colchester United but then lost his place in the team to Gavin Johnson. He subsequently asked to go on the transfer list but then regained his first team slot in February and withdrew his request, finishing the campaign in fine form. He is an attacking left-sided defender who can play either at full back or in a wing-back role.

West Ham U (From trainee on 9/7/1997)
Colchester U (Free on 5/7/1999) FL 66+6/4 FLC 3+2/1 FAC 1 Others 1

KELL Richard
Born: Bishop Auckland, 15 September 1979
Height: 6'1" Weight: 10.13
International Honours: E: Sch

After failing to break into the first team at Middlesbrough, Richard joined Torquay United on loan before signing a short-term contract. He quickly adapted to life in the Third Division, seeming to possess that rare ability to find time and space in the centre of the park. He created a fine partnership with Khalid Chalqi and played an important role in ensuring that the Gulls avoided the drop to the Conference. He netted a fine goal on his debut at Lincoln and went on to impress with some telling passing and a willingness to push forward. He was out of contract in the summer and at the time of writing his future was uncertain.

Middlesbrough (From trainee on 2/7/1998)
Torquay U (Free on 8/2/2001) FL 15/3

KELLER Marc
Born: Colmar, France, 14 January 1968
Height: 5'11" Weight: 12.4
International Honours: France: 5

Marc featured just once for West Ham in the 2000-01 campaign when he made the starting line-up for the Worthington Cup second round second leg tie against Walsall. In October he was loaned to Portsmouth and produced some effective midfield displays before going back to Upton Park following a change of management at the First Division club. He subsequently joined Blackburn Rovers in something of a surprise move early in the new year. However he found it difficult to break into an in-form side although he featured several times from the subs' bench, coming on to play out wide where he showed patience on the ball and a disciplined approach. An experienced wide midfield player or wing back Marc was due to leave Ewood Park in the summer to take up a post as director of football at Strasbourg.

West Ham U (Free from Karlsruhe, Germany, ex Colmer, Mulhouse, Strasbourg, on 27/7/1998) PL 36+8/5 FLC 5+1/1 Others 6+1
Portsmouth (Loaned on 22/9/2000) FL 3
Blackburn Rov (Free on 12/1/2001) FL 0+2 FAC 0+3

KELLY Alan Thomas
Born: Preston, 11 August 1968
Height: 6'2" Weight: 14.3
International Honours: RoI: 33; U23-1; Yth

Alan started the 2000-01 season as first-choice goalkeeper for Blackburn but lost his place to John Filan early on following a 2-0 defeat by Sheffield United and soon dropped even further down the line after Brad Friedel arrived. Then, with all Stockport's five goalkeepers out injured, he answered boss Andy Kilner's emergency call and showed his class with top-class performances against Bolton and Sheffield Wednesday before returning once more to Ewood Park. He is the younger brother of Oldham's Gary Kelly.

Preston NE (From apprentice on 25/9/1985) FL 142 FLC 1 FAC 8 Others 13
Sheffield U (£200,000 on 24/7/1992) P/FL 213+3 FLC 15 FAC 22 Others 2
Blackburn Rov (£675,000 on 30/7/1999) FL 36+1 FLC 4 FAC 3
Stockport Co (Loaned on 3/4/2001) FL 2

KELLY David Thomas
Born: Birmingham, 25 November 1965
Height: 5'11" Weight: 12.1
Club Honours: Div 1 '93
International Honours: RoI: 26; B-3; U23-1; U21-3

Having joined Sheffield United on a 12-month contract in the close season, David went on to be a regular in the starting line-up for much of last season, only dropping back to the subs' bench in February. Despite his advancing years he showed he could still take a half-chance and his goal at Blackburn when he charged down a kick from the visiting 'keeper typified his attitude. A hard-working striker who never seemed to stop chasing he was joint second-top scorer for the Blades.

Walsall (Signed from Alvechurch on 21/12/1983) FL 115+32/63 FLC 11+1/4 FAC 12+2/3 Others 14+3/10
West Ham U (£600,000 on 1/8/1988) FL 29+12/7 FLC 11+3/5 FAC 6 Others 2+1/2
Leicester C (£300,000 on 22/3/1990) FL 63+3/22 FLC 6/2 FAC 1 Others 2/1
Newcastle U (£250,000 on 4/12/1991) FL 70/35 FLC 4/2 FAC 5/1 Others 4/1
Wolverhampton W (£750,000 on 23/6/1993) FL 76+7/26 FLC 5/2 FAC 11/6 Others 4/2
Sunderland (£1,000,000 on 19/9/1995) P/FL 32+2/2 FLC 2+1 FAC 3
Tranmere Rov (£350,000 on 5/8/1997) FL 69+19/21 FLC 16+1/13 FAC 11+1/3
Sheffield U (Free on 21/7/2000) FL 21+14/6 FLC 4/2 FAC 1

KELLY Garry
Born: Drogheda, 9 July 1974
Height: 5'8" Weight: 11.8
International Honours: RoI: 38; U21-5; Yth; Sch

Leeds United's longest-serving player Garry began the 2000-01 season in his customary right-back slot and remained there until the turn of the year, producing some consistent performances particularly in the Champions' League. However he then suffered some niggling injuries that caused him to miss a number of matches, and as this coincided with the return to form of Danny Mills, he found it difficult to win his place back. An excellent defender and reader of the game, he is never slow to get forward and has the ability to work the flanks at great pace. Garry also has a tremendous will to win, and captains the side in the absence of Lucas Radebe.

Leeds U (Signed from Home Farm on 24/9/1991) PL 236+9/2 FLC 21+1 FAC 23+1 Others 26+1

KELLY Gary Alexander
Born: Preston, 3 August 1966
Height: 5'11" Weight: 13.6
Club Honours: FAYC '85
International Honours: RoI: B-1; U23-1; U21-8

This veteran 'keeper has now made over 200 appearances for Oldham Athletic and still shows few signs of surrendering his first-team place to long-suffering deputy David Miskelly. He was again a near ever-present last season and continued to perform capably for the Latics as a spell of seven clean sheets in 14 Second Division games at the turn of the year clearly showed. He is the older brother of Blackburn 'keeper Alan Kelly.

Newcastle U (From apprentice on 20/6/1984) FL 53 FLC 4 FAC 3 Others 2
Blackpool (Loaned on 7/10/1988) FL 5
Bury (£60,000 on 5/10/1989) FL 236 FLC 14 FAC 13 Others 29
Oldham Ath (£10,000 on 27/8/1996) FL 202 FLC 11 FAC 15 Others 4

KENNA Jeffrey (Jeff) Jude
Born: Dublin, 27 August 1970
Height: 5'11" Weight: 12.2
International Honours: RoI: 27; B-1; U21-8; Yth; Sch

After bravely fighting back from two achilles operations, Jeff found his path to the Blackburn Rovers first team blocked by John Curtis and he was restricted to a handful of appearances in his less-favoured left back position. He subsequently requested a transfer and then moved on loan to Tranmere Rovers where his experience proved invaluable in what was ultimately an unsuccessful struggle against relegation. An experienced right back, he is capable of covering in any position in the defence.

Southampton (From trainee on 25/4/1989) F/PL 110+4/4 FLC 4 FAC 10+1 Others 3
Blackburn Rov (£1,500,000 on 15/3/1995) P/FL 153+2/1 FLC 16+2 FAC 13 Others 7
Tranmere Rov (Loaned on 20/3/2001) FL 11

KENNEDY Jonathan (Jon)
Born: Rotherham, 30 November 1980
Height: 6'1" Weight: 14.10

This powerfully built goalkeeper joined Blackpool for an extended loan period last October and was given a run of seven consecutive games in the Tangerines' starting line-up. He later dropped back to the subs' bench before eventually returning to the Stadium of Light.

Sunderland (£80,000 from Worksop T on 19/5/2000)
Blackpool (Loaned on 17/10/2000) FL 6 FAC 1

KENNEDY Mark
Born: Dublin, 15 May 1976
Height: 5'11" Weight: 11.9
International Honours: RoI: 31; U21-7; Yth; Sch

After a fine season for Manchester City in the First Division in 1999-2000, Mark found the step up to the Premiership a difficult one. He made a quiet start to the new season and seemed to lack the confidence and pace he had previously shown. He often found himself on the subs' bench but then tore medial ligaments in his knee in the game at Sunderland just before Christmas. He returned to fitness early in the new year only to pick up an achilles injury playing for the reserves and it was not until mid-March that he was back on the bench for the first team. A traditional-style left winger he featured again for the Republic of Ireland last term and during the summer he was reported to have signed for Wolves.

Millwall (From trainee on 6/5/1992) FL 37+6/9 FLC 6+1/2 FAC 3+1/1
Liverpool (£1,500,000 on 21/3/1995) PL 5+11 FLC 0+2 FAC 0+1 Others 0+2
Queens Park R (Loaned on 27/1/1998) FL 8/2
Wimbledon (£1,750,000 on 27/3/1998) PL 11+10 FLC 4+1/1 FAC 2
Manchester C (£1,000,000 + on 15/7/1999) P/FL 56+10/8 FLC 5+4/3 FAC 2

KENNEDY Peter Henry James
Born: Lurgan, 10 September 1973
Height: 5'9" Weight: 11.11
Club Honours: Div 2 '98
International Honours: NI: 9; B-1

Peter missed the start of the 2000-01 season due to an achilles tendon problem and then suffered a heel injury that required corrective surgery. He returned to first-team action for Watford in December, and immediately gave the team a more balanced look with his cultured left foot prompting from the centre of the park. A left-sided midfield player who is an expert at delivering free kicks and corners his return to fitness also led to a recall to the Northern Ireland squad. He was placed on the open to offers list in the summer.

Notts Co (£100,000 from Portadown on 28/8/1996) FL 20+2 FLC 1 FAC 2+1/1 Others 0+1
Watford (£130,000 on 10/7/1997) P/FL 108+7/18 FLC 9/2 FAC 7/2 Others 3

KENNEDY Richard Joseph
Born: Waterford, 28 August 1978
Height: 5'10" Weight: 10.12

Richard struggled to break into the Brentford first-team squad in 2000-01 and was eventually released last March when he signed for League of Wales club Barry Town. His only start for the Bees came at Notts County last August when he replaced Simon March in the pre-match warm-up, and the only other senior action he saw was when he came on as a last-minute substitute in the LDV Vans Trophy tie against Oxford last December.

Crystal Palace (From trainee on 29/3/1997)
Wycombe W (Free on 15/10/1998)
Brentford (Free on 14/7/1999) FL 5+5 Others 1+1

KENNY Patrick (Paddy) Joseph
Born: Halifax, 17 May 1978
Height: 6'1" Weight: 14.6

Paddy had another excellent campaign in goal for Bury in 2000-01 and for the second season in a row he was an ever-present in the first team. He produced some fine performances in the early part of the season, saving a penalty in the game at Oxford in September and enjoying a spell when he conceded just one goal in 568 minutes of football. An excellent shot stopper and in possession of an enormous kick, Paddy remains an outstanding prospect for the Shakers.

Bury (£10,000 + from Bradford PA on 28/8/1998) FL 92 FLC 4 FAC 6 Others 4

KENTON Darren Edward
Born: Wandsworth, 13 September 1978
Height: 5'10" Weight: 11.11

Darren enhanced his reputation as one of the best youngsters outside the Premiership with a string of impressive displays for Norwich City last season. His laid back approach to the game sometimes belies his determination and tenacity but he is an excellent tackler and can match most opponents in the air. A versatile defender who can play in any position across the back line he prefers a central role but is more often seen at right back.

Norwich C (From trainee on 3/7/1997) FL 76+12/4 FLC 8+1 FAC 0+2

Darren Kenton

KEOWN Martin Raymond
Born: Oxford, 24 July 1966
Height: 6'1" Weight: 12.4
Club Honours: PL '98; FAC '98; CS '98, '99
International Honours: E: 38; B-1; U21-8; Yth

A fiercely competitive centre back of the highest order, Martin is strong, quick and aggressive in the tackle. A regular in the Arsenal side over the past eight seasons, his formidable partnership with Tony Adams has been the bedrock of the Gunners' success during this period. His strength in the air makes him a threat when joining the attack for set pieces although he scored only twice last term, both goals coming in a vital Champions' League match against Shakhtjor Donetsk at Highbury. A regular again in the full England squad he missed a lengthy spell last term due to injury.

Arsenal (From apprentice on 2/2/1984) FL 22 FAC 5
Brighton & Hove A (Loaned on 15/2/1985) FL 21+2/1 FLC 2/1 Others 2/1
Aston Villa (£200,000 on 9/6/1986) FL 109+3/3 FLC 12+1 FAC 6 Others 2
Everton (£750,000 on 7/8/1989) F/PL 92+4 FLC 11 FAC 12+1 Others 6
Arsenal (£2,000,000 on 4/2/1993) PL 236+18/4 FLC 16+2/1 FAC 23+2 Others 36+5/3

KERR Brian
Born: Motherwell, 12 October 1981
Height: 5'8" Weight: 11.2
International Honours: S: Yth; Sch

A product of Newcastle's Academy scheme, Brian started the 2000-01 campaign playing in the youth and reserve teams and did well enough to earn a call up to the senior squad, making his debut as a late substitute at Coventry at the beginning of September. He then dislocated a shoulder in training shortly afterwards and after returning to action suffered a repeat of the same injury towards the end of the campaign. A tidy midfield player with a deft touch on the ball he is always keen to push forward and will be looking to gain more senior experience in 2001-02. He was rewarded for his progress with a new four-year contract last September.

Newcastle U (From trainee on 4/12/1998) PL 0+1

KERR Dylan
Born: Valetta, Malta, 14 January 1967
Height: 5'9" Weight: 11.4
Club Honours: Div 2 '94

This experienced left back had the briefest of careers with Football League new boys Kidderminster last season, his sole first-team experience comprising the final three minutes of the home game against Leyton Orient after he had came on from the subs' bench. His contract at Aggborough was cancelled shortly afterwards and he then had brief spells in non-league football with Harrogate Town and Slough before joining Scottish Division Three outfit Hamilton Academicals in January. He featured regularly for them until the end of the campaign, scoring three goals in 17 appearances.

Sheffield Wed (From juniors on 1/9/1984. Freed during 1985 close season)
Leeds U (Free from Arcadia Shepherds, South Africa on 8/2/1989) F/PL 6+7 FLC 2 FAC 1 Others 0+4
Doncaster Rov (Loaned on 22/8/1991) FL 7/1
Blackpool (Loaned on 31/12/1991) FL 12/1 Others 1
Reading (£75,000 on 15/7/1993) FL 84+5/5 FLC 8+1 FAC 2 Others 3+1
Carlisle U (Free on 16/9/1996) FL 0+1
Kilmarnock (Free on 11/10/1996) SL 63 SLC 2 SC 6+1 Others 2
Kidderminster Hrs (Free on 7/9/2000) FL 0+1

KERR Scott
Born: Leeds, 11 December 1981
Height: 5'8" Weight: 10.8

One of Bradford City's highly-rated youngsters Scott joined the professional ranks last summer and went on to make his senior debut in the Inter Toto Cup second round first leg tie in Lithuania against FK Atlantas. He later featured as a substitute in a Worthington Cup tie against Darlington and also came on in the final Premiership match of the season at Coventry. A promising young midfield player he has a great engine and never stops running throughout the 90 minutes. He was reported to have signed for Hull City in the summer.

Bradford C (From trainee on 4/7/2000) PL 0+1 FLC 0+1 Others 1

KERRIGAN Steven (Steve) John
Born: Baillieston, 9 October 1972
Height: 6'1" Weight: 12.4
Club Honours: S Div 2 '97

Steve got off to a great start in 2000-01, scoring for Halifax Town in the first two games of the campaign. Despite appearing in a struggling team he netted regularly throughout the season and finished as the club's leading scorer with 20 goals in all competitions. He is a pacy striker who is strong in the air and capable of some excellent link up play.

Albion Rov (Free from Newmains Juveniles on 22/7/1992) SL 46+7/14 SLC 2/1 SC 1 Others 1
Clydebank (Signed on 11/2/1994) SL 17+13 SLC 1+1 Others 2+1/2
Stranraer (Signed on 4/11/1995) SL 19+2/5 SC 1
Ayr U (Signed on 25/6/1996) SL 26+7/17 SLC 2/2 SC 1 Others 2/2
Shrewsbury T (£25,000 on 21/1/1998) FL 63+13/15 FLC 2+1 FAC 3/3
Halifax T (Signed on 23/3/2000) FL 47+1/22 FLC 1+1 FAC 1 Others 2/1

KETSBAIA Temuri
Born: Georgia, 18 March 1968
Height: 6'0" Weight: 13.0
International Honours: Georgia: 48

A surprise summer signing for Wolves, Temuri made a stunning debut against Sheffield Wednesday and almost scored in the first minute when he was brought down by the 'keeper to earn a penalty. He subsequently scored a cracking goal from 20 yards and had another first-half effort ruled out in an explosive display. However he became quieter as the season progressed and it seemed that the club was unsure of which position he could be best employed in. He was then in and out of the side and was sidelined for a while in the new year by a knee operation. An exciting and unpredictable striker he can always be relied upon to give whole-hearted commitment to the cause. He continued to feature regularly for Georgia for whom he holds the record for total goals scored.

Newcastle U (Free from AEK Athens, Greece, ex Dynamo Sukhumi, Dynamo Tbilisi, Anorthosis Famagusta, on 10/7/1997) PL 41+37/8 FLC 1+1 FAC 8+8/4 Others 7+6/2
Wolverhampton W (£900,000 on 10/8/2000) FL 14+8/3 FLC 3+1/1

KEWELL Harold (Harry)
Born: Sydney, Australia, 22 September 1978
Height: 6'0" Weight: 11.10
Club Honours: FAYC '97
International Honours: Australia: 9; Yth

One of the best youngsters in the Premiership and named 'PFA Young Player of the Year', the previous season, Harry looked set to take the Champions' League by storm in 2000-01. Unfortunately he picked up a bad achilles injury during the pre-season which ruled him out until December, and also caused him the heartbreak of missing the Olympic Games tournament in his homeland. Harry took a while to get going on his return but soon showed glimpses of his old self, he terrorised the Manchester United defence after coming on as a half-time substitute and scored his first of the season with a typical left-foot strike against Southampton in April. His return to form coincided with Leeds' march up the table and into Europe once more. Harry is a marvellous talent who has the ability to become a major world star, and he should take further steps along that road in the coming season.

Leeds U (Signed from the Australian Academy of Sport on 23/12/1995) PL 112+11/23 FLC 6/3 FAC 12/5 Others 22+3/5

KIDD Ryan Andrew
Born: Radcliffe, 6 October 1971
Height: 6'0" Weight: 12.10
Club Honours: Div 3 '96, Div 2 '00

Diagnosed with a serious neck injury at the end of the 1999-2000 season, Ryan underwent surgery during the summer and was out of the Preston North End squad until returning as a substitute in the Worthington Cup tie at Coventry. Although a regular on the bench he only made six starts until April when he replaced the injured Michael Jackson in the line-up. Due a testimonial in 2001-02, Ryan has matured into a reliable left-sided defender able to play centrally or on the flank, with excellent tackling and heading skills.

Port Vale (From trainee on 12/7/1990) FL 1 FLC 0+2 Others 0+1
Preston NE (Free on 15/7/1992) FL 236+17/9 FLC 16+3/1 FAC 18 Others 19+1/1

KIELY Dean Laurence
Born: Salford, 10 October 1970
Height: 6'1" Weight: 13.5
Club Honours: Div 2 '97; Div 1 '00
International Honours: E: Yth; Sch. RoI: 4; B-1

Dean began last season as first-choice goalkeeper for Premiership new boys Charlton Athletic and never looked like losing his place. He made several excellent saves including one from a Nelson Vivas spot kick against Arsenal at The Valley. It was while making another penalty save from Derby's Craig Burley that he injured his groin and he took no further part in the campaign after this. Dean is an excellent shot stopper who commands his area well and will be looking to reclaim his place at the start of the 2001-02 campaign.

Coventry C (From trainee on 30/10/1987)
York C (Signed on 9/3/1990) FL 210 FLC 9 FAC 4 Others 16
Bury (£125,000 on 15/8/1996) FL 137 FLC 13 FAC 4 Others 3
Charlton Ath (£1,000,000 on 26/5/1999) P/FL 70 FLC 3 FAC 6

KILBANE Kevin Daniel
Born: Preston, 1 February 1977
Height: 6'0" Weight: 12.10
International Honours: RoI: 25; U21-11

The 2000-01 campaign was one of highs and lows for Kevin at Sunderland. He started off in promising fashion, scoring a superb goal against Derby at the Stadium of Light when he cut in from an unfamiliar right-wing position and curled a magnificent 20-yard strike past Mart Poom. However, a dip in form saw him relegated to the bench before he was restored to the starting line-up and finished on another high with a trio of great goals against Tottenham, Southampton and Charlton. An exciting left winger with pace, strength on the ball and good heading ability he will be hoping to start the 2001-02 season in a similar vein of form. Kevin remained a regular for the Republic of Ireland and was particularly impressive against Holland in September.

Preston NE (From trainee on 6/7/1995) FL 39+8/3 FLC 4 FAC 1 Others 1+1
West Bromwich A (£1,000,000 on 13/6/1997) FL 105+1/15 FLC 12/2 FAC 4/1
Sunderland (£2,500,000 on 16/12/1999) PL 43+7/5 FLC 1 FAC 0+3/1

KILFORD Ian Anthony
Born: Bristol, 6 October 1973
Height: 5'10" Weight: 11.0
Club Honours: Div 3 '97; AMC '99

Ian once again showed his versatility for Wigan Athletic last season, appearing in a variety of roles during the campaign. Essentially a right-sided midfielder, he was effective when pushing forward into the opposition penalty box and scored four vital goals. He had the misfortune to suffer a broken wrist early into the new year and the injury kept him on the sidelines for the remainder of the season.

Nottingham F (From trainee on 3/4/1991) FL 0+1
Wigan Ath (Loaned on 23/12/1993) FL 2+1/2 FAC 0+1
Wigan Ath (Free on 13/7/1994) FL 168+30/30 FLC 14+2/1 FAC 14+2/2 Others 13+2/2

KILLEN Christopher (Chris) John
Born: Wellington, New Zealand, 8 October 1981
Height: 5'11" Weight: 11.3
International Honours: New Zealand: 4; Yth

This young Manchester City striker spent three months on loan at Wrexham last autumn to gain experience of first-team football and slotted in well for the Robins. Chris was initially signed as a replacement for the suspended Craig Faulconbridge and went on to produce some impressive performances up front for the Racecourse Ground club before returning to Maine Road. Already a full international for New Zealand Chris won further caps last August in the Merdeka Cup Tournament in Malaysia and also captained his country's U20 team which narrowly failed to qualify for the World Finals in Argentina.

Manchester C (Free from Miramar Rangers, New Zealand on 8/3/1999)
Wrexham (Loaned on 8/9/2000) FL 11+1/3

KILTY Mark Thomas
Born: Sunderland, 24 June 1981
Height: 5'11" Weight: 12.5

After making only a handful of appearances for Darlington in the first half of last season, Mark established himself as a regular member of the Quakers team in December and retained his place until suffering a knee injury against Hull City in April that ruled him out for the remainder of the campaign. He filled various defensive roles with great determination and enthusiasm and slammed in his first goal for the club against Shrewsbury Town, when he blasted a cross into the roof of the net following a surging run from midfield. A tenacious tackler who is equally strong in the air, Mark looks an exciting prospect for the years to come.

Darlington (From trainee on 17/7/1999) FL 19+3/1 FLC 1 FAC 0+1 Others 3

KIMBLE Alan Frank
Born: Dagenham, 6 August 1966
Height: 5'9" Weight: 12.4
Club Honours: Div 3 '91

This ever-dependable left back again produced many a fine performance for Wimbledon last term. Unfortunately he was hampered by a string of injuries (tendons and hamstring) and these somewhat restricted his opportunities. He continued to retain his role as a set-piece specialist and his experience proved invaluable in bringing on the youngsters in the team.

Charlton Ath (From juniors on 8/8/1984) FL 6
Exeter C (Loaned on 23/8/1985) FL 1 FLC 1
Cambridge U (Free on 22/8/1986) FL 295+4/24 FLC 23+1 FAC 29/1 Others 22
Wimbledon (£175,000 on 27/7/1993) P/FL 189+17 FLC 21+3/1 FAC 26

KINET Christophe
Born: Huy, Belgium, 31 December 1972
Height: 5'8" Weight: 10.12
Club Honours: Div 2 '01

Although not always featuring regularly for Second Division champions Millwall last season Christophe again proved to be a clever and tricky winger. He has a good shot with either foot and is very effective when cutting in from the flank to take on defenders. He also developed something of an eye for goal, netting a hat-trick in the LDV Vans Trophy tie against Northampton Town in December.

Millwall (£75,000 from Racing Strasbourg, France, ex Germinal, on 9/2/2000) FL 18+12/2 FLC 3/1 FAC 1+2 Others 2+2/3

KING Ledley Brenton
Born: Stepney, 12 October 1980
Height: 6'2" Weight: 13.6
International Honours: E: U21-7; Yth

Ledley came of age at Tottenham in the 2000-01 season and after being given an opportunity from the subs' bench in the 2-1 win over Liverpool in November he seized his chance with both hands to establish himself in the team. A talented defender who is extremely strong in the challenge he has a good turn of speed. He showed a willingness to get forward and was rewarded with two senior goals, the first away at Bradford in December coming after just ten seconds, thus setting a new official record as the Premiership's fastest goal. Experience will bring greater maturity to his raw talents and Ledley is likely to feature as a significant force as Glenn Hoddle rebuilds the Spurs line up for the 2001-02 campaign. He continued to represent England U21 during the campaign winning three more caps.

Tottenham H (From trainee on 22/7/1998) PL 20+2/1 FAC 4+1/1

KING Marlon Francis
Born: Dulwich, 26 April 1980
Height: 6'1" Weight: 11.12

Signed from Third Division Barnet for a substantial fee during the close season Marlon took some time to settle in at Gillingham and it was not until November that he netted for the first team. However after this he went from strength to strength and the goals began to flow to the extent that he finished the campaign as the club's leading scorer with 15 goals from 26 starts. A promising young striker he is very quick over ten yards, is cool in front of goal and works tirelessly for the cause.

Barnet (From trainee on 9/9/1998) FL 36+17/14 FLC 0+2 FAC 0+1 Others 2+2
Gillingham (£255,000 on 28/6/2000) FL 26+12/15 FLC 3 FAC 1+1

KING Simon Daniel Roy
Born: Oxford, 11 April 1983
Height: 5'11" Weight: 12.4

Another of the promising youngsters at Oxford United, Simon made his Football League debut against Port Vale in the penultimate game of the 2000-01 season and retained his place for the final match at Notts County. A talented left back he stepped up to the professional ranks last December and will be aiming to gain more first-team experience in the coming campaign.

Oxford U (From trainee on 13/12/2000) FL 2

KINKLADZE Georgiou (Georgi)
Born: Tbilisi, Georgia, 6 November 1973
Height: 5'8" Weight: 11.2
International Honours: Georgia: 42

2000-01 was very much a stop-start season for Derby's Georgian international play maker. Never fully match-fit having undergone a hernia operation during the close season and then suffered various injuries during the campaign, his appearances were mostly from the substitute's bench - a frustrating situation both for the player and the fans who regard him as the most creative player at the club. Blessed with a vision for the killer pass he can also conjure up goals and goal-scoring situations from virtually nothing. A season-long fight against relegation was not necessarily the best of stages for his individual talents and it was not until the very last few matches that he played a regular role in his preferred position just behind the front two strikers.

Manchester C (£2,000,000 from Mretebi Tbilisi, Georgia, ex Mretebi, on 17/8/1995) P/FL 105+1/20 FLC 6 FAC 9/2 (£5,000,000 to Ajax, Holland on 15/5/1998)
Derby Co (Signed on 26/11/1999) PL 25+16/2 FLC 2 FAC 2

KINSELLA Mark Anthony
Born: Dublin, 12 August 1972
Height: 5'9" Weight: 11.8
Club Honours: GMVC '92; FAT '92; Div 1 '00
International Honours: RoI: 24; B-1; U21-8; Yth

This immensely influential right-sided midfield player once again had a terrific season as captain of Charlton Athletic in 2000-01. Controlling the centre of the park Mark linked up well with Graham Stuart to generate most of the Addicks' attacking movements. He reads the game well and is an excellent passer of the ball, not afraid to hit a 40-yard pass to change the direction of play. Mark did not get forward as much as in previous seasons and only found the net on a couple of occasions scoring in the opening day victory over Manchester City and netting a beautifully worked goal against Aston Villa at The Valley late in the season. Mark remained a regular for the Republic of Ireland winning a further eight caps.

Colchester U (Free from Home Farm on 18/8/1989) FL 174+6/27 FLC 11/3 FAC 11/1 Others 9+1/5
Charlton Ath (£150,000 on 23/9/1996) P/FL 186+5/19 FLC 3+2 FAC 8+1/3 Others 3

KIPPE Frode
Born: Oslo, Norway, 17 January 1978
Height: 6'4" Weight: 13.10
Club Honours: AMC '00
International Honours: Norway: B-1; U21

Having enjoyed a very successful time on loan at Stoke in the 1999-2000 campaign, Frode joined City again last October in a deal that allowed him to stay until the end of the season. However although he showed he has the stature and strength to make a good centre back he was hampered by a series of knee injuries that restricted appearances. He returned to Liverpool in the summer and will be hoping to make a breakthrough at Anfield in the near future.

Liverpool (£700,000 from Lillestrom, Norway, ex Kilbotn, on 7/1/1999) FLC 0+1
Stoke C (Loaned on 24/12/1999) FL 15/1 Others 5
Stoke C (Loaned on 13/10/2000) FL 15+4 Others 5

KIRKLAND Christopher (Chris)
Born: Leicester, 2 May 1981
Height: 6'3" Weight: 11.7
International Honours: E: U21-1; Yth

Having previously played only one senior game for Coventry City before the start of last season Chris made tremendous progress during 2000-01 and by the summer he could rightly claim that he was the club's number one goalkeeper. He got an unexpected call up to first team duty against Tottenham in October due to Magnus Hedman's injury and although he was controversially sent off the following week at Stamford Bridge (a decision later rescinded) he went on to enjoy a short run in the line-up. He created a great impression with some fine performances and after another short spell in the team over Christmas he took over from the out-of-form Hedman in March. Growing in confidence all the time he was particularly inspiring in the home game with Chelsea when he pulled off half a dozen outstanding saves. Despite the disappointment of relegation for the Sky Blues he capped a fine personal season when he made his debut for England U21s against Mexico during the summer.

Coventry C (From trainee on 6/5/1998) PL 23 FLC 3+1 FAC 1

KISHISHEV Radostin Prodanov
Born: Bulgaria, 30 July 1974
Height: 5'10" Weight: 12.4
International Honours: Bulgaria: 44

Radostin made his Premiership debut for Charlton in the opening game of last season at right back and performed well but shortly afterwards lost his place in the team and it was not until November that he won a recall. He looked much more comfortable playing as a wing back in a 5-3-2 formation but it was only when he was switched to a wide midfield role that he found his best form. He is a good tackler, comfortable on the ball and not afraid to attempt the unexpected. Radostin was a regular for the Bulgaria international team during 2000-01.

Charlton Ath (£300,000 + from Liteks Lovech, Bulgaria, ex Neftokhimik Burgas, Bursapor, on 14/8/2000) PL 25+2 FLC 1 FAC 2

KITSON David (Dave)
Born: Hitchin, 21 January 1980
Height: 6'3" Weight: 12.11

Dave switched from playing on the left wing to a role as an out-and-out striker for Ryman League club Arlesey Town at the start of the 2000-01 campaign and proved a revelation, scoring almost a goal a game. His form soon attracted the attention of Football League clubs and he joined Second Division Cambridge United in March. He went on to make his debut against Stoke and featured in a handful of games towards the end of the season, netting his first senior goal with a header at Swansea in the final game. Dave is a lanky striker with a great eye for goal and he will be looking to gain a regular first-team place at the Abbey Stadium in 2001-02.

Cambridge U (Signed from Arlesey T on 16/3/2001) FL 6+2/1

KITSON Paul
Born: Murton, 9 January 1971
Height: 5'11" Weight: 10.12
International Honours: E: U21-7

Although he featured as a substitute for West Ham in the early season games against Leicester and Manchester United, Paul once again spent much of the 2000-01 season in the reserve team. He had a month on loan at Crystal Palace last autumn, but failed to score in four games before returning to the Hammers second string where he netted three times in ten outings. Still a useful striker, he is capable of holding the ball up well and creating chances with his pace and persistence.

Leicester C (From trainee on 15/12/1988) FL 39+11/6 FLC 5/3 FAC 1+1/1 Others 5/1
Derby Co (£1,300,000 on 11/3/1992) FL 105/36 FLC 7/3 FAC 5/1 Others 13+1/9
Newcastle U (£2,250,000 on 24/9/1994) PL 26+10/10 FLC 3+2/1 FAC 6+1/3 Others 0+1
West Ham U (£2,300,000 on 10/2/1997) PL 43+13/15 FLC 2+3/1 FAC 2+1/1 Others 3+5/2
Charlton Ath (Loaned on 21/3/2000) FL 2+4/1
Crystal Palace (Loaned on 14/9/2000) FL 4

KIWOMYA Christopher (Chris) Mark
Born: Huddersfield, 2 December 1969
Height: 5'9" Weight: 11.2
Club Honours: Div 2 '92

Chris made a promising start to the 2000-01 season with Queens Park Rangers, scoring a number of goals before suffering an injury at the end of September. He came back just three games later but this proved to be too soon as he aggravated the problem and was sidelined until the turn of the year. He subsequently returned to first-team action but failed to capture his early-season form in a struggling side. A pacy striker he can either play on the left-hand side or in a central role. Chris was one of 15 players released by Rangers in the summer.

Ipswich T (From trainee on 31/3/1987) F/PL 197+28/51 FLC 14+1/8 FAC 14/2 Others 5+1/3
Arsenal (£1,500,000 on 13/1/1995) PL 5+9/3 Others 1+2 (Free to Selangor, Malaysia on 21/8/1997)
Queens Park R (Free on 28/8/1998) FL 74+12/25 FLC 4+1/2 FAC 3+2/3

Chris Kiwomya

KNIGHT Leon Leroy
Born: Hackney, 16 September 1982
Height: 5'4" Weight: 9.10
International Honours: E: Yth

This promising Chelsea youngster joined Queens Park Rangers on loan at the beginning of March and featured regularly for the First Division club in the closing weeks of the campaign. Previously capped by England at U16 and U17 levels he stepped up to the U18s last season. Although a striker at youth level, Leon was often used in a wide midfield role at Loftus Road where he showed good pace and ball control and became popular with the fans in his short stay. He remained until the end of the season before returning to Stamford Bridge.

Chelsea (From trainee on 17/9/1999)
Queens Park R (Loaned on 9/3/2001) FL 10+1

KNIGHT Richard
Born: Burton, 3 August 1979
Height: 6'1" Weight: 14.0
International Honours: E: Yth

Having been released by Derby County at the end of the 1999-2000 campaign Richard signed for Second Division Oxford United where he had previously enjoyed two successful loan spells. Installed as the U's first-choice 'keeper he produced a string of accomplished displays and apart from a period when he was replaced by the on-loan Neil Cutler he was rarely absent all season. A promising goalkeeper who showed a level of maturity beyond his years he deservedly won the club's 'Player of the Year' award.

Derby Co (Signed from Burton A on 25/6/1997)
Carlisle U (Loaned on 26/3/1999) FL 6
Birmingham C (Loaned on 4/8/1999) FLC 0+1
Hull C (Loaned on 7/10/1999) FL 1
Macclesfield T (Loaned on 3/12/1999) FL 3
Oxford U (Loaned on 19/1/2000) FL 1+1
Oxford U (Free on 13/3/2000) FL 44 FLC 2 FAC 2

KNIGHT Zatyiah (Zat)
Born: Solihull, 2 May 1980
Height: 6'6" Weight: 13.8

Zat made his first-team debut for Fulham in the Worthington Cup first round second leg tie against Northampton and then featured in both legs of the second round against Chesterfield. Signed as a central defender he also played in a central midfield role for the reserve team last term. Skilful on the ball his passing skills improved considerably during the season while his height caused problems for the opposition at corners and free kicks.

Fulham (Signed from Rushall Olympic on 19/2/1999) FLC 3
Peterborough U (Loaned on 25/2/2000) FL 8

KNOWLES Darren Thomas
Born: Sheffield, 8 October 1970
Height: 5'6" Weight: 11.6

Having been an automatic choice at right back for Hartlepool over the previous three years, Darren spent much of the 2000-01 season as reserve to the younger Paul Arnison. However he returned to the first team in the new year resuming with his usual commitment. He is a great clubman, and a player who always gives 100 per cent yet is rarely in trouble with referees. He was released in the summer.

Sheffield U (From trainee on 1/7/1989)
Stockport Co (£3,000 on 14/9/1989) FL 51+12 FLC 2+4 Others 14+1
Scarborough (Free on 4/8/1993) FL 139+5/2 FLC 11+1 FAC 9 Others 7
Hartlepool U (Free on 27/3/1997) FL 164+4/2 FLC 7+1 FAC 5 Others 10

KOEJOE Samuel (Sammy)
Born: Paramaribo, Surinam, 17 August 1974
Height: 6'1" Weight: 12.2

Sammy was mostly restricted to outings from the subs' bench for Queens Park Rangers last season and only made the starting line-up on a handful of occasions as cover for injuries. He was a regular in the first-team squad until mid-January but was then sidelined by injury and featured only once more as a substitute in the remainder of the campaign. He is a big bustling striker with good pace.

Queens Park R (£250,000 from Salzburg, Austria, ex DWV Amsterdam, Lustenau, on 29/11/1999) FL 13+19/3 FLC 1+1 FAC 3+2

KOLINKO Aleksandrs (Alex)
Born: Latvia, 18 June 1975
Height: 6'3" Weight: 13.7
International Honours: Latvia: 21

Alex joined Crystal Palace from Latvian club Skonto Riga for whom he had appeared in the UEFA Champions' League qualifying competition in the early part of the season. His career at Selhurst Park got off to a shaky start, but as his English improved so did his performances on the pitch. He developed into a good all-round 'keeper and became a favourite of the Eagles' fans. He produced a particularly inspirational performance to keep a clean sheet in the FA Cup third round tie against Premiership Sunderland. Alex is the first-choice 'keeper for Latvia and featured regularly in their World Cup qualifying matches during the season.

Crystal Palace (£600,000 from Skonto Riga, Latvia, ex Metals Riga, on 15/9/2000) FL 35 FLC 7 FAC 2

Alex Kolinko

KONCHESKY Paul Martyn
Born: Barking, 15 May 1981
Height: 5'10" Weight: 10.12
International Honours: E: Yth

This promising youngster was unlucky not to have played more games for Charlton last season and was only kept out of the team by the consistent form of England international Chris Powell at left back. Paul has the distinction of being the Addicks' youngest-ever debutant and has the potential to be a top-class player. A skilful left-sided defender who can also play in midfield he appeared at right back in the early part of the campaign and then briefly displaced Powell at the turn of the year. Already capped by

England U16s and U18s he was called up to the U21 squad last season and will be aiming to making his debut at this level in the near future.
Charlton Ath (From trainee on 25/5/1998) P/FL 20+16 FLC 4+1 FAC 2+1

KONJIC Muhamed (Mo)
Born: Bosnia, 14 May 1970
Height: 6'4" Weight: 13.7
International Honours: Bosnia-Herzegovina: 21
Mo had another frustrating season at Coventry in 2000-01. After working hard to get fit in the summer he got his chance in the Ipswich home game and did well enough to earn a brief run in the team. However he then picked up a groin injury at Everton on Boxing Day and when he returned for the home game against the same opponents the following month he found himself substituted early on. He subsequently spent the remainder of the campaign either injured or in the reserves. An experienced centre half his defensive play was solid and he showed a good amount of skill on the ground.
Coventry C (£2,000,000 from AS Monaco, France, ex Slobada Tuzla, Croatia Belisce, Croatia Zagreb, FC Zurich, on 5/2/1999) PL 14+2 FLC 2+1

KORSTEN Willem
Born: Boxtell, Holland, 21 January 1975
Height: 6'3" Weight: 12.10
International Honours: Holland: U21
Despite another injury-dogged season at Tottenham last term Willem did well when called upon and bagged three goals late on. He had a particularly good game in the final match against champions Manchester United, scoring with two fine 20-yard efforts as Spurs went on to win 3-1. An attacking left-sided midfield player who can also feature as a striker, his towering frame makes him a little cumbersome in the air but his power and strength on the ground are his greatest assets. Having finished on a high he will be hoping to resume in similar vein at the start of the 2001-02 campaign.
Leeds U (Loaned from Vitesse Arnhem, Holland, ex NEC Nijmegen, on 11/1/1999) PL 4+3/2 FAC 2+1
Tottenham H (£1,500,000 on 9/7/1999) PL 12+11/3 FLC 1 FAC 0+3

KOUMAS Jason
Born: Wrexham, 25 September 1979
Height: 5'10" Weight: 11.0
International Honours: W: 1
A near-automatic selection for Tranmere from October Jason showed some fine form last season despite appearing in a struggling side. A creative and stylish midfield player he grew in maturity as the campaign progressed and also developed into the main focus for the Rovers' attack, finishing up as leading scorer with ten goals. His performances attracted the attention of bigger clubs and at the beginning of June he made his debut in international football for Wales when he came off the subs' bench in the closing stages of the World Cup qualifier against Ukraine. Blessed with stamina, vision and pace, it looks increasingly likely as though his future lies away from Prenton Park.
Tranmere Rov (From trainee on 27/11/1997) FL 54+31/15 FLC 8+5/1 FAC 5/1

KOZLUK Robert (Rob)
Born: Mansfield, 5 August 1977
Height: 5'8" Weight: 11.7
International Honours: E: U21-2
Seemingly out of favour at Bramall Lane following the arrival of Gus Uhlenbeek, Rob made one substitute appearance before moving on loan to Huddersfield where he made a tremendous impact in a two-month spell at the McAlpine Stadium. He returned to Bramall Lane a much more confident player while his concentration was improved and his speed, timing and anticipation in defence were of a higher quality. A hard-working full back he quickly went on to become a fixture in the Blades' line-up although his first goal is still awaited despite several long-range efforts.
Derby Co (From trainee on 10/2/1996) PL 9+7 FLC 3 FAC 2+1
Sheffield U (Signed on 12/3/1999) FL 69+7 FLC 2 FAC 3
Huddersfield T (Loaned on 7/9/2000) FL 14

KRISTINSSON Birkir
Born: Vestmannaeyjar, Iceland, 15 March 1964
Height: 6'1" Weight: 11.12
International Honours: Iceland: 70
Birkir linked up with Stoke City last October to help out with a goal-keeping crisis at the club and when Carl Muggleton suffered a dip in form he stepped in and held his place in the team until Gavin Ward recovered fitness. A vastly experienced international 'keeper who had previously enjoyed brief spells with Birmingham City and Bolton he was hugely popular with the fans and gave some fine performances. He also established something of a record by being the first shareholder to play for the City first team.
Stoke C (Free from IB Vestmannaeyjar, Iceland, ex Fram Reykjavik, SK Brann Bergen, IFK Norrkoping, IB Vestmannaeyjar, Lustenau, on 3/11/2000) FL 18 Others 4

KUIPERS Michel
Born: Amsterdam, Holland, 26 June 1974
Height: 6'2" Weight: 14.10
Club Honours: Div 3 '01
Michel suffered the ignominy of being substituted at half time in the opening game of last season at Southend but by September he was back in the Brighton line-up and he remained the club's first-choice 'keeper for all but a short spell for the remainder of the campaign. An excellent shot stopper he was formerly in the Dutch marines and bought himself out to pursue a career in professional football.
Bristol Rov (Free from SDW Amsterdam, Holland on 20/1/1999) FL 1
Brighton & Hove A (Free on 4/7/2000) FL 34 FAC 2 Others 2

KULCSAR George
Born: Budapest, Hungary, 12 August 1967
Height: 6'2" Weight: 13.4
International Honours: Australia: 3
George was mostly limited to reserve team football at Queens Park Rangers at the beginning of the 2000-01 campaign and it was not until the team adopted a 4-4-2 formation in the new year that he received a run in the side. A change of management saw another switch in tactics and he lost his place again towards the end of the season. An effective central midfield player George was released from his contract by mutual consent in mid-May.
Bradford C (£100,000 from Royal Antwerp, Belgium on 7/3/1997) FL 23+3/1
Queens Park R (£250,000 on 17/12/1997) FL 42+14/1 FLC 0+2 FAC 2

KUQI Shefki
Born: Albania, 10 November 1976
Height: 6'2" Weight: 13.10
International Honours: Finland: 17
Signed up by Stockport County boss Andy Kilner at the end of January, Shefki's arrival at Edgeley Park gave the whole club a boost both on and off the field. A striker in the old-fashioned English centre forward mould, he was a revelation as his powerful play reaped an early dividend with six goals from 17 appearances. Perhaps more important was his role in taking the weight off his striking partner Aaron Wilbraham, thus helping the youngster to top the club's scoring charts. Shefki also featured for Finland during the campaign winning two further caps after joining County.
Stockport Co (£300,000 from FC Jokerit, Finland, ex HJK Helsinki, on 31/1/2001) FL 17/6 FAC 1

KYLE Kevin Alistair
Born: Stranraer, 7 June 1981
Height: 6'3" Weight: 13.7
International Honours: S: U21-3
Some impressive form in Sunderland's reserve and youth teams earned Kevin his first U21 cap for Scotland against Latvia last September and he subsequently spent much of the remainder of the campaign out on loan as he gained valuable first-team experience to prepare him for Premiership football. He firstly joined Huddersfield Town where he made his Football League debut as a substitute against Bolton. Then it was on to Darlington at the beginning of November where he scored twice and showed neat footwork as well as tremendous aerial strength. He returned to Wearside after suffering an injury in the FA Cup replay at Luton but then went out again to Rochdale in January where he made his debut in the televised game against Leyton Orient. He made a big impression on his first start against Cardiff, but returned to the Stadium of Light after a month and went on make a handful of appearances from the subs' bench in the closing weeks of the season. A tall and skilful striker his physical style and aerial power suggest he is a potential long-term successor to Niall Quinn. He won a total of two caps for Scotland at U21 level last term.
Sunderland (Free from Ayr Boswell on 25/9/1998) PL 0+3
Huddersfield T (Loaned on 8/9/2000) FL 0+4
Darlington (Loaned on 1/11/2000) FL 5/1 FAC 3/1
Rochdale (Loaned on 26/1/2001) FL 3+3

Frank Lampard

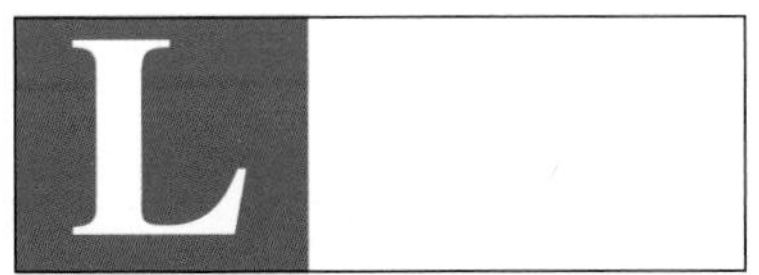

LACEY Damian James
Born: Bridgend, 3 August 1977
Height: 5'9" Weight: 11.3
Club Honours: Div 3 '00

Damian missed the opening weeks of the 2000-01 campaign after sustaining stress fractures to his right heel bone and it was not until late November that he returned to first-team action for Swansea City. He scored a rare goal in the LDV Vans Trophy tie against Brentford, but then went down with an ankle injury in mid-March that put him on the sidelines for the remainder of the campaign. A hard-working competitive midfield player he signed a two-and-a-half-year extension to his contract in January.
Swansea C (From trainee on 1/7/1996) FL 63+15/1 FLC 3 FAC 2+1 Others 5/1

LAMBERT Rickie Lee
Born: Liverpool, 16 February 1982
Height: 5'10" Weight: 11.2

A former Blackpool trainee, Rickie initially joined Macclesfield on youth forms last December and then signed on a non-contract basis the following month. He played most of his football for the youth and reserve teams during the 2000-2001 season making a very positive contribution in the centre of the park and scoring some well-taken goals. He made his senior debut for Macc in the home defeat by Chesterfield in March and appeared fairly regularly towards the end of the campaign, putting in some fine performances. A promising midfield player he signed a 12-month contract in May.
Blackpool (From trainee on 17/7/2000) FL 0+3
Macclesfield T (Free on 2/3/2001) FL 4+5

LAMBOURDE Bernard
Born: Guadaloupe, 11 May 1971
Height: 6'1" Weight: 12.4
Club Honours: FLC '98; CS '00

Faced with fierce competition for a place at Chelsea, Bernard failed to make the first team at the beginning of the 2000-01 campaign and in September he joined Portsmouth on loan. Deputising for Shaun Derry in defence he showed some neat touches for Pompey but was sent back when Steve Claridge took over as manager in mid-October. On his return to Stamford Bridge he eventually received the briefest of opportunities at senior level, making a two-minute appearance as a substitute against Manchester United in February. A valued utility member of Chelsea's squad since his signing, he is a good all-round footballer who is equally at home in central defence, at full back or in the midfield 'holding' role.
Chelsea (£1,600,000 from Bordeaux, France, ex Cannes, on 10/7/1997) PL 29+11/2 FLC 6+1 FAC 5 Others 3+5/1
Portsmouth (Loaned on 8/9/2000) FL 6

LAMEY Nathan James
Born: Leeds, 14 October 1980
Height: 5'8" Weight: 13.0

Nathan struggled to break in to the Cambridge United squad last season and was restricted to just a handful of appearances from the subs' bench. He was released in January and subsequently moved on to Ryman League club Hitchin Town. He is a promising young striker with good pace.
Wolverhampton W (From trainee on 25/10/1997)
Cambridge U (Free on 10/8/1999) FL 2+4

LAMPARD Frank James
Born: Romford, 20 June 1978
Height: 6'0" Weight: 12.6
International Honours: E: 2; B-1; U21-19; Yth

Frank had an excellent season for West Ham last term when he was a key figure in the club's successful fight to avoid relegation. Always in the action he scored nine valuable goals including two in the vital 3-1 win over Derby and a cracking effort in the FA Cup tie at Walsall, while his surging run set up the winner at Sunderland to earn a place in the FA Cup quarter-final. He also won a further England cap in the friendly against Spain when he made two goals, but then missed the last few games of the season after having a groin operation. Placed in a difficult situation at Upton Park after his father and uncle were replaced as the Hammers' management team, he was reported to have joined Premiership rivals Chelsea in the summer.
West Ham U (From trainee on 1/7/1995) PL 132+16/23 FLC 15+1/9 FAC 13/2 Others 10/4
Swansea C (Loaned on 6/10/1995) FL 8+1/1 Others 1+1

LANCASHIRE Graham
Born: Blackpool, 19 October 1972
Height: 5'10" Weight: 11.12
Club Honours: Div 4 '92, Div 3 '97

Graham was again beset by injuries last season. He had managed just one outing from the subs' bench before a long spell out of action and returned for just three more brief appearances before being injured again. He was badly missed when Dale's goal supply dried up and finally scored on his first full appearance of the season which came in the record 7-1 home defeat at the hands of Shrewsbury, featuring regularly in the squad thereafter. When fully fit he is a quick striker with a good goals-per-game record. Out of contract in the summer, his future was uncertain at the time of writing.
Burnley (From trainee on 1/7/1991) FL 11+20/8 FLC 1+1 FAC 2+2/1 Others 2+4
Halifax T (Loaned on 20/11/1992) FL 2 Others 1+1
Chester C (Loaned on 21/1/1994) FL 10+1/7
Preston NE (£55,000 on 23/12/1994) FL 11+12/2 Others 1+1
Wigan Ath (£35,000 on 12/1/1996) FL 20+10/12 FLC 2+1/4
Rochdale (£40,000 on 2/10/1997) FL 54+29/23 FLC 3+1/1 FAC 0+1 Others 3+3/1

LANGLEY Richard Barrington Michael
Born: Harlesden, 27 December 1979
Height: 5'10" Weight: 11.4
International Honours: E: Yth

Richard's excellent progress provided one of the highlights in a disappointing season for Queens Park Rangers in 2000-01. He was one of the very few players to hold down a regular place in the first team but had the misfortune to suffer a cruciate ligament injury against Fulham at the end of January and this put him out of action for the remainder of the campaign. An attacking central midfield player he will be hoping to make a full recovery for the 2001-02 season.
Queens Park R (From trainee on 31/12/1996) FL 69+6/5 FLC 4/1 FAC 6

Richard Langley

LARKIN Colin
Born: Dundalk, Ireland, 27 April 1982
Height: 5'9" Weight: 10.4
International Honours: RoI: Yth

Colin continued to develop steadily for Wolves last term, mostly featuring in the club's reserve team where he was a regular scorer. He had two outings for the first team as a substitute, the first at Gillingham in August and the second on the final day of the season. A pacy young striker he also featured for the Republic of Ireland U18s during the campaign.
Wolverhampton W (From trainee on 19/5/1999) FL 1+2 FLC 0+1/1

LARRIEU Romain
Born: Mont-de-Marsan, France, 31 August 1975
Height: 6'4" Weight: 13.11

Like his colleague David Friio, Romain was released by French National Division outfit Valence at the end of the 1999-2000 campaign and joined Third Division Plymouth Argyle on non-contract forms last November. A tall and agile goalkeeper he made his debut at home to Bristol City in the LDV Vans Trophy tie, keeping a clean sheet in the 3-0 victory before going on to take over as first-choice 'keeper in the second half of the season. He was reported to have signed a two-year deal with the Pilgrims during the summer break.

Plymouth Arg (Free from ASOA Valence, France, ex Montpellier, on 30/11/2000) FL 14+1 Others 2

LARUSSON Bjarnolfur (Bjarne)
Born: Iceland, 11 March 1976
Height: 5'11" Weight: 12.8
International Honours: Iceland: U21-10; Yth

Bjarne signed for Scunthorpe after a trial last September and quickly established himself as a first choice in the United midfield. Hard-working and skilful, he passes the ball accurately and has a powerful shot which brought him a number of long-range goals. He netted with a brilliant 25-yard free-kick in the 4-0 victory over York in February and is very capable of getting more from a midfield position. Out of contract in the summer he was released on a free transfer.

Hibernian (Signed from IB Vestmannaeyar, Iceland on 17/10/1997) SL 3+4/1
Walsall (Free on 25/9/1998) FL 45+14/3 FLC 0+1 FAC 4/1 Others 6/1
Scunthorpe U (Free on 8/9/2000) FL 33/4 FAC 5 Others 1

[LAUREN] LAUREANO Bisan-Etame Mayer
Born: Lodhji Krib, Cameroon, 19 January 1977
Height: 5'11" Weight: 11.4
International Honours: Cameroon: (ANC '00, OLYM '00)

Lauren has experienced phenomenal success since the beginning of the year 2000. After helping Cameroon to victory in the African Nations Cup he was named 'Player of the Tournament', and subsequently joined Arsenal in May of that year. He then went on to star for his country in the Sydney Olympics, scoring one of the goals in the penalty shoot-out that saw the team win their country's first-ever gold medals by defeating Spain in the final. Finally he was named as runner-up in the 'African Footballer of the Year' award. He also scored on his first start for Arsenal in the Premiership victory over Liverpool at Highbury and went on to feature regularly for the Gunners. Lauren is a skilful, resilient player equally comfortable in the centre or on the right of midfield. He is a tough tackler with the creative ability to start attacking moves.

Arsenal (£7,200,000 from Real Mallorca, Spain, ex Cant Sevilla, Utrera, Seville, Levante, on 16/6/2000) PL 15+3/2 FAC 4 Others 6+5/1

[LAURENCO] DA SILVA Luis Carlos
Born: Luanda, Angola, 5 June 1983
Height: 5'6" Weight: 10.7
International Honours: Portugal: Yth

This talented young striker was a member of the Sporting Lisbon team who were national champions at U16 level in 1998-99 and after progressing to the club's B team in the Portuguese Second Division he joined Bristol City on loan last March. He scored twice for the reserves at Barnet and was promoted to the subs' bench for the first team, making a sensational debut at Bury when he came on to score the winner. Having been capped earlier in the season for the U18s, he stepped up to represent Portugal at U20 level in the prestigious Toulon Tournament during the summer.

Bristol C (Loaned from Sporting Lisbon, Portugal on 22/3/2001) FL 1+2/1

LAVIN Gerard
Born: Corby, 5 February 1974
Height: 5'10" Weight: 11.0
International Honours: S: U21-7

Gerard remained out of favour at Bristol City last season although whenever called up to the first team he did all that was asked of him. He went on loan to Wycombe Wanderers in January where he damaged his knee on his debut and after struggling on for two more games he returned to Ashton Gate. He subsequently had a trial with Northampton Town towards the end of the campaign and was reported to have made a permanent move to Sixfields during the summer. Gerard is an experienced right back with good positional sense and the ability to push down the flank and beat defenders.

Watford (From trainee on 11/5/1992) FL 121+5/2 FLC 11/1 FAC 6 Others 2+1
Millwall (£500,000 on 23/11/1995) FL 67+7 FLC 2 FAC 3+1 Others 8/1
Bristol C (Free on 6/8/1999) FL 21+1 FLC 3 FAC 2 Others 1
Wycombe W (Loaned on 19/1/2001) FL 2 Others 1

LAW Gareth Martin
Born: Torquay, 20 August 1982
Height: 6'0" Weight: 12.8

This nippy young striker developed a reputation for being in the right place at the right time at youth level for Torquay United and was rewarded with a professional contract last November. He made his first-team debut from the subs' bench in the LDV Vans Trophy tie against Bristol Rovers shortly afterwards and featured on a number of occasions later in the campaign. Gareth scored his first goal in senior football when he netted in the 2-1 win over Darlington in April.

Torquay U (From trainee on 21/11/2000) FL 2+8/1 Others 0+1

LAWRENCE Denis William
Born: Trinidad, 1 August 1974
Height: 6'7" Weight: 12.7
International Honours: Trinidad & Tobago: 30

This extremely tall central defender joined Wrexham shortly before the transfer deadline last March after undergoing trials at a number of clubs including Newcastle United and Bolton. Denis made his senior debut for the Robins when he came on from the subs' bench for the final minutes of the game at Reading in April and featured occasionally in the run-in to the end of the campaign. He is an impressive figure who is very composed on the ball and has excellent distribution. Denis is an established Trinidad & Tobago international who has appeared regularly in their qualifying campaign for the 2002 World Cup finals. Since his arrival in Wales he has won ten more caps and scored his first international goal in the Copa Caribe game against Martinique.

Wrexham (£100,000 from Defence Force, Trinidad on 10/3/2001) FL 1+2

LAWRENCE James (Jamie) Hubert
Born: Balham, 8 March 1970
Height: 5'11" Weight: 12.11
Club Honours: FLC '97
International Honours: Jamaica: 9

Jamie was hampered by a series of injuries for Bradford City last term - hip, toe and wrist - and these severely restricted his appearances. Used both on the right-hand side of midfield and at right back he showed tremendous defensive ability and a real bite in the tackle. However he was even better in an attacking role, taking the ball down the wing, beating defenders and delivering some fine crosses. He made his debut in international football for Jamaica against Trinidad & Tobago at the end of February and subsequently featured regularly for the Reggaeboyz in their World Cup qualifying campaign.

Sunderland (Signed from Cowes on 15/10/1993) FL 2+2 FLC 0+1
Doncaster Rov (£20,000 on 17/3/1994) FL 16+9/3 FLC 2 FAC 1 Others 3
Leicester C (£125,000 on 6/1/1995) P/FL 21+26/1 FLC 3+4/2 FAC 1+1
Bradford C (£50,000 on 17/6/1997) P/FL 105+13/9 FLC 6+1 FAC 4+1/1 Others 0+2

LAWRENCE Liam
Born: Retford, 14 December 1981
Height: 5'10" Weight: 11.3

This right-sided midfielder received further senior experience at Mansfield in the second half of the 2000-01 campaign although he was again mainly used from the subs' bench. An enthusiastic youngster who reads the game well Liam will be looking to establish himself in the starting line-up at Field Mill in the coming season.

Mansfield T (From trainee on 3/7/2000) FL 7+13/4 Others 0+1

LAWRENCE Matthew (Matty) James
Born: Northampton, 19 June 1974
Height: 6'1" Weight: 12.12
Club Honours: Div 2 '01
International Honours: E: Sch

Matty had a fine season for Second Division champions Millwall in 2000-01 missing only one game and being one of the most consistent players in the side. He is a very thoughtful central defender with the ability to make even complicated tasks appear simple. An excellent all-round defender he is strong in the tackle, possesses a good turn of speed and delivers an accurate cross. His value to the team was recognised when he was selected for the PFA's Second Division team and was voted as the supporters' club 'Player of the Year'.

Wycombe W (£20,000 from Grays Ath on 19/1/1996) FL 13+3/1 FLC 4 FAC 1 Others 0+1
Fulham (Free on 7/2/1997) FL 57+2 FLC 4+1 FAC 2 Others 5
Wycombe W (£86,000 + on 2/10/1998) FL 63/4 FLC 4 FAC 6 Others 3
Millwall (£200,000 on 21/3/2000) FL 54 FLC 4 FAC 3 Others 4

LAWSON Ian James
Born: Huddersfield, 4 November 1977
Height: 5'11" Weight: 11.5

Ian had a season to forget at Stockport County last term as a catalogue of niggling injuries forced him down the pecking order of strikers at Edgeley Park. He started just one game, against Portsmouth in October, and although he came off the bench another nine times he failed to add to his tally of goals for County. At his best his timing in the air makes him a formidable opponent while he has good pace and an eye for goal.

Huddersfield T (From trainee on 26/1/1995) FL 13+29/5 FLC 1+4 FAC 1+1
Blackpool (Loaned on 6/11/1998) FL 5/3
Blackpool (Loaned on 8/1/1999) FL 4
Bury (£75,000 on 16/7/1999) FL 20+5/11 FLC 2 FAC 3+1 Others 1
Stockport Co (£150,000 on 17/2/2000) FL 14+11/4

LAZARIDIS Stanley (Stan)
Born: Perth, Australia, 16 August 1972
Height: 5'9" Weight: 11.12
International Honours: Australia: 41; U23; Yth

Stan was a constant menace on the left wing for Birmingham City last term, supplying a constant stream of crosses for his colleagues. He missed several weeks in the early part of the campaign when he returned to Australia to play for his country in the Sydney Olympics, but his form held up throughout the season. Whenever he was out of the team, the Blues missed his ability to keep hold of the ball or dribble it deep into opposition territory. He remained a regular for Australia, featuring in the Confederations Cup tournament in the summer and in their campaign to qualify for the 2002 World Cup finals.

West Ham U (£300,000 from West Adelaide, Australia on 8/9/1995) PL 53+16/3 FLC 6+1 FAC 9+1 Others 0+1
Birmingham C (£1,600,000 on 29/7/1999) FL 52+10/4 FLC 8+2 FAC 1+1 Others 2+2

LEABURN Carl Winston
Born: Lewisham, 30 March 1969
Height: 6'3" Weight: 13.0

Carl started the first two games of 2000-01 for Wimbledon but then lost his place and featured only once more from the subs' bench during the campaign. A tall, strong and powerful centre forward he is an awkward player for defenders to handle as he showed in several reserve appearances towards the end of the season. He was released by the Dons in the summer.

Charlton Ath (From apprentice on 22/4/1987) FL 276+46/53 FLC 19/5 FAC 19+2/4 Others 9+5/4
Northampton T (Loaned on 22/3/1990) FL 9
Wimbledon (£300,000 on 9/1/1998) P/FL 36+23/4 FLC 5+6/1 FAC 4

LEADBITTER Christopher (Chris) Jonathan
Born: Middlesbrough, 17 October 1967
Height: 5'9" Weight: 10.6
Club Honours: Div 3 '91

Chris had a frustrating time at Plymouth last season. Injury kept him out of action until September and after a brief run in the team he was sidelined again in January with a serious knee injury. An all-action central midfield player he was released by the Pilgrims in the summer.

Grimsby T (From apprentice on 4/9/1985)
Hereford U (Free on 21/8/1986) FL 32+4/1 FLC 2 FAC 2 Others 3
Cambridge U (Free on 2/8/1988) FL 144+32/18 FLC 12/3 FAC 16+2/3 Others 11+2/1
Bournemouth (£25,000 on 16/8/1993) FL 45+9/3 FLC 6+1 FAC 5 Others 2
Plymouth Arg (Free on 27/7/1995) FL 46+6/1 FLC 2 FAC 6/1 Others 5+1/1 (Free to Dorchester T during 1997 close season)
Torquay U (Free on 27/11/1997) FL 58+5/2 FLC 1 FAC 1+2 Others 5+1
Plymouth Arg (Free on 6/7/1999) FL 37+3/2 FLC 1 FAC 8 Others 2

LEBOEUF Frank
Born: Marseille, France, 22 January 1968
Height: 6'0" Weight: 12.6
Club Honours: FAC '97, '00; FLC '98; ECWC '98; ESC '98; CS '00
International Honours: France: 40 (WC '98, UEFA '00)

A permanent fixture at Chelsea since his arrival in July 1996, Frank featured in the FA Charity Shield victory over Manchester United, but then received a two-week internal club ban that led to him missing the opening Premiership matches of the season. At the turn of the year he seemed destined to leave Stamford Bridge; he had lost his first-team place to the impressive John Terry and was poised to sign for Monaco, but the protracted deal broke down as the French transfer 'window' of 31 January passed. A groin injury suffered while on international duty with France in February seemed to prematurely curtail his season but he came on as a substitute in the final match of the season at Maine Road in what could prove to be a valedictory appearance. That same weekend Chelsea increased the competition for central defensive places by signing compatriot William Gallas from Marseille and it increasingly looked as if Frank would return to France to complete his career. Although not always popular with opposing supporters, Frank has cult-like status with the Chelsea faithful who have taken his buccaneering style to their hearts.

Chelsea (£2,500,000 from Strasbourg, France, ex Hyeres, Meaux, Laval, on 12/7/1996) PL 142+2/17 FLC 8/1 FAC 17+1/3 Others 33+1/3

LEE Alan Desmond
Born: Galway, 21 August 1978
Height: 6'2" Weight: 13.9
International Honours: RoI: U21-5

Alan was plucked from Burnley's reserve team by Rotherham following the departure of Leo Fortune-West and although he took a while to net his first goal he never looked back once he had made the breakthrough. A strong and very quick striker, he grabbed his first-ever Football League hat-trick in the 3-1 home win against Cambridge United in February and went on to reach double figures. With age on his side he should have a bright future at Millmoor.

Aston Villa (From trainee on 21/8/1995)
Torquay U (Loaned on 27/11/1998) FL 6+1/2 Others 2/1
Port Vale (Loaned on 2/3/1999) FL 7+4/2
Burnley (£150,000 on 8/7/1999) FL 2+13 FLC 1+1 FAC 0+2 Others 1/1
Rotherham U (£150,000 on 21/9/2000) FL 29+2/13 FAC 3/1 Others 1/1

LEE Christian Earl
Born: Aylesbury, 8 October 1976
Height: 6'2" Weight: 11.7

After a lengthy spell out of action with a serious knee injury Christian joined Third Division Rochdale on loan last autumn as cover for Clive Platt and Tony Ellis. The high spot of his stay at Spotland was coming off the bench against Macclesfield and scoring a goal that inspired Dale to come back from 2-0 down. Still unable to get into the Gills' line-up he moved to Leyton Orient on loan at the beginning of March, again covering for injuries, but after just three senior appearances he returned to the Priestfield Stadium. Once back he was immediately on his way to Bristol Rovers in yet another loan deal, rejoining caretaker manager Garry Thompson who he had known from their Northampton days. He scored two goals for Rovers, the first a glancing header in the Bristol 'derby', and produced some promising displays in his spell at the Memorial Stadium.

Northampton T (From trainee at Doncaster Rov on 13/7/1995) FL 25+34/8 FLC 2/2 FAC 3+3 Others 6+2
Gillingham (£35,000 + on 3/8/1999) FL 1+2 FLC 1+1
Rochdale (Loaned on 20/10/2000) FL 2+3/1
Leyton Orient (Loaned on 6/3/2001) FL 2+1
Bristol Rov (Free on 22/3/2001) FL 8+1/2

LEE David John Francis
Born: Basildon, 28 March 1980
Height: 5'11" Weight: 11.8

Signed from Tottenham during the 2000 summer break, David made his Football League debut for Southend in the opening game of last season against Brighton when he scored a cracking goal to clinch a 2-0 victory. He quickly established himself as a regular in the Blues' first team and contributed a number of useful goals. He is a classy midfield player who also made a fair number of appearances as a makeshift striker. He was reported to have joined Hull City in the summer.

Tottenham H (From trainee on 17/7/1998)
Southend U (Free on 2/8/2000) FL 37+5/8 FLC 2 FAC 3 Others 5/2

LEE David Mark
Born: Whitefield, 5 November 1967
Height: 5'7" Weight: 11.0
Club Honours: Div 1 '97; AMC '99

Having joined Carlisle United shortly before the start of last season, David came off the bench in the opening match against Halifax to inspire the Cumbrians' recovery from a two-goal deficit to take a point. However although he featured regularly as a substitute he only started one Third Division match and left Brunton Park in November. He subsequently spent several weeks training with Halifax Town before joining Conference outfit Morecambe in January.

Bury (From juniors on 8/8/1986) FL 203+5/35 FLC 15/1 FAC 6 Others 19+1/4
Southampton (£350,000 on 27/8/1991) F/PL 11+9 FAC 0+1 Others 1+1
Bolton W (£300,000 on 2/11/1992) P/FL 124+31/17 FLC 19+1/2 FAC 13+2 Others 8+1/1

Wigan Ath (£250,000 on 16/7/1997) FL 61+22/11 FLC 6+3/2 FAC 4+2/2 Others 5+4/1
Blackpool (Loaned on 18/10/1999) FL 9/1 FAC 1 Others 1
Carlisle U (Free on 11/8/2000) FL 1+12 FLC 1+1

LEE Graeme Barry
Born: Middlesbrough, 31 May 1978
Height: 6'2" Weight: 13.7

2000-01 was almost a lost season for Hartlepool's highly rated young central defender. In the early weeks of the campaign he was kept out of the first team by a knee injury, then after the briefest of returns in September further complications set in and he required surgery. Determined not to give up, he recovered sufficiently to return to the first team in April and he played in the last seven games of the season.

Hartlepool U (From trainee on 2/7/1996) FL 125+10/13 FLC 5+2/1 FAC 6 Others 10+2/2

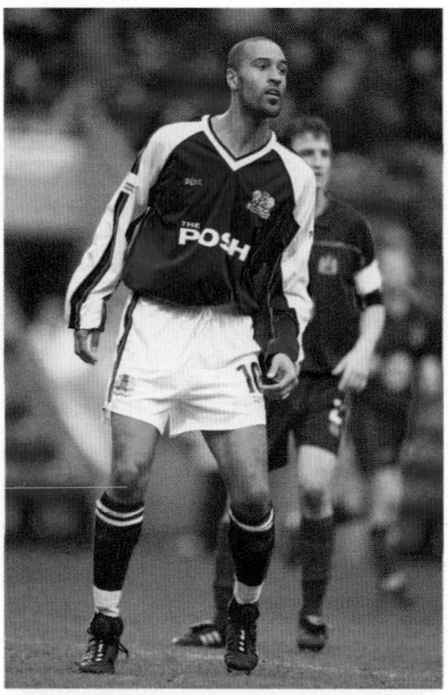

Jason Lee

LEE Jason Benedict
Born: Forest Gate, 9 May 1971
Height: 6'3" Weight: 13.8
Club Honours: Div 2 '98

It was not until mid-September that Jason was able to resume first-team action for Peterborough following the knee injury he had picked up during the 1999-2000 end-of-season play-offs. After a brief run in the team he was again sidelined by injury at the turn of the year, but after a cartilage operation he returned to action before the summer break. A big and awkward striker he showed his goal-scoring potential for Posh by netting seven times from 18 starts.

Charlton Ath (From trainee on 2/6/1989) FL 0+1 Others 0+2
Stockport Co (Loaned on 6/2/1991) FL 2
Lincoln C (£35,000 on 1/3/1991) FL 86+7/21 FLC 6 FAC 2+1/1 Others 4
Southend U (Signed on 6/8/1993) FL 18+6/3 FLC 1 FAC 1 Others 5+3/3
Nottingham F (£200,000 on 4/3/1994) F/PL 41+35/14 FLC 4+3/1 FAC 0+5 Others 4+2
Charlton Ath (Loaned on 5/2/1997) FL 7+1/3
Grimsby T (Loaned on 27/3/1997) FL 2+5/1 FAC 1
Watford (£200,000 on 16/6/1997) FL 36+1/11 FLC 4 FAC 4 Others 1
Chesterfield (£250,000 on 28/8/1998) FL 17+11/1 FAC 0+2 Others 0+2
Peterborough U (£50,000 on 3/1/2000) FL 37+16/14 FAC 4/1 Others 2+1/1

LEE Martyn James
Born: Guildford, 10 September 1980
Height: 5'6" Weight: 9.0

Martyn made excellent progress at Wycombe in 2000-01 and established himself as a regular in the first-team squad in the second half of the season. He set up several goals for his colleagues and scored three himself including a cracking 25-yarder against Reading. He is a skilful all-action midfield player who has quick feet and possesses a lightning-quick turn that regularly bamboozles opposition defenders.

Wycombe W (From trainee on 30/1/1999) FL 18+10/3 FAC 4+1 Others 1+1

LEE Robert (Rob) Martin
Born: West Ham, 1 February 1966
Height: 5'11" Weight: 11.13
Club Honours: Div 1 '93
International Honours: E: 21; B-1; U21-2

Newcastle United's longest-serving player signed a new two-year contract in the summer of 2000 and had another fine season at St James Park. Calm on the ball and with good vision, he tended to sit deeper in midfield than earlier in his career, delivering sweeping passes to change the angle of attack, or alternatively probing opposition defences with long balls into the heart of the box. Because of injuries he was pressed into service as an emergency sweeper at West Ham where he turned in an excellent performance, and this option was occasionally used in subsequent games. He made the 700th senior appearance of his career at Bradford City in March, but the second half of the season was disrupted by a series of injuries, beginning with a hamstring strain at the end of the year and ending with an injury to his left knee that required surgery to shave the cartilage and remove floating bone debris, thus bringing his season to a premature end in April.

Charlton Ath (Free from Hornchurch on 12/7/1983) FL 274+24/59 FLC 16+3/1 FAC 14/2 Others 10+2/3
Newcastle U (£700,00 on 22/9/1992) F/PL 277+10/43 FLC 19+1/3 FAC 27/5 Others 25/4

LEGG Andrew (Andy)
Born: Neath, 28 July 1966
Height: 5'8" Weight: 10.7
Club Honours: WC '89, '91; AIC '95
International Honours: W: 6

Andy was a hugely influential figure for Cardiff City in their promotion campaign last season during which he made a successful switch to playing as a sweeper. A hard-working and committed player his long throw once again proved to be a powerful weapon for the Bluebirds. He was rewarded for his efforts with a recall to the Wales team for the World Cup qualifier in Armenia and was also voted the club's 'Player of the Year' for the second year in succession.

Swansea C (Signed from Britton Ferry on 12/8/1988) FL 155+8/29 FLC 9+1 FAC 16/4 Others 15+3/5
Notts Co (£275,000 on 23/7/1993) FL 85+4/9 FLC 11 FAC 7+1 Others 13+2/6
Birmingham C (Signed on 29/2/1996) FL 31+14/5 FLC 3+1 FAC 2+1
Ipswich T (Loaned on 3/11/1997) FL 6/1 FLC 1
Reading (£75,000 on 20/2/1998) FL 12 FLC 1
Peterborough U (Loaned on 15/10/1998) FL 5
Cardiff C (Free on 16/12/1998) FL 99+6/7 FLC 6 FAC 9+3

LEITAO Jorge Manuel Vasconcelos
Born: Oporto, Portugal, 14 January 1974
Height: 5'11" Weight: 13.4

Having impressed during a pre-season tour of Scotland, Jorge joined Walsall for a substantial fee last August and went on to prove himself to be worth many times that sum. A very talented striker with great pace, ability in the air and above all finishing power, he had a fine season with the Saddlers finishing up as leading scorer with 21 goals. After having given up his studies for a Sports Science degree course in order to come to the Bescot Stadium he was voted 'Player of the Season' by the club's supporters.

Walsall (£150,000 from SC Farense, Portugal, ex Avintes, on 10/8/2000) FL 40+4/18 FLC 4/2 FAC 3/1 Others 3

LEMARCHAND Stephane
Born: Saint-Lo, France, 6 August 1971
Height: 5'10" Weight: 11.7

Having been released by Louhans-Cuiseaux at the end of the 1999-2000 campaign Stephane took advantage of the French players' union's pre-season training facilities and featured regularly for their select team in friendly games. He subsequently crossed the Channel to join Carlisle United and after impressing in a number of reserve games he was promoted to the first team. He went on to feature on a handful of occasions, netting a fine individual goal in the 2-2 draw at home to Cardiff, but with no permanent contract on offer he moved on for a trial at Rotherham. He made a brief appearance for the Millers as a substitute in the FA Cup win over Northampton Town but was again unable to win a long-term contract and he departed shortly afterwards.

Carlisle U (Free from Caen, France, ex Caen, Mulhouse, on 29/9/2000) FL 4+1/1
Rotherham U (Free on 3/11/2000) FAC 0+1

LENNON Neil Francis
Born: Lurgan, 25 June 1971
Height: 5'9" Weight: 13.2
Club Honours: FLC '97, '00
International Honours: NI: 39; B-1; U23-1; U21-2; Yth

Leicester City's fiery right-footed midfield dynamo struggled to find his best form during the early weeks of the 2000-01 season while playing under the shadow of mounting speculation about an impending transfer to Celtic. He eventually linked up with his former mentor, Martin O'Neill, in December where he collected an array of medals as the Bhoys walked off with the

Scottish League Cup, FA Cup and Premiership title. A regular for Northern Ireland he was treated disgracefully by some sections of his own supporters during a subsequent World Cup tie in Belfast because of his Catholic background and his new club allegiance, but showed great character to put those incidents behind him as the sporting world rallied to his support.

Manchester C (From trainee on 26/8/1989) FL 1
Crewe Alex (Free on 9/8/1990) FL 142+5/15 FLC 8+1/1 FAC 16/1 Others 15+1
Leicester C (£750,000 on 23/2/1996) P/FL 169+1/6 FLC 23/3 FAC 8 Others 7

LEONHARDSEN Oyvind
Born: Kristiansund, Norway, 17 August 1970
Height: 5'10" Weight: 11.2
International Honours: Norway: 73; U21; Yth

Oyvind had a mixed season at Tottenham last term. Perhaps his best performance came in the 3-1 win over Derby County in October when he netted two goals before limping off with a hamstring injury. It was not until Christmas that he returned to the line-up and although he retained his place in the squad he missed a further six weeks in the spring. A very talented midfield player he provided width to the attack with some accurate long balls to the flanks and displayed a sure touch in front of goal. Oyvind featured regularly for Norway during the campaign scoring both goals in the 2-1 win over Bulgaria in April.

Wimbledon (£660,000 from Rosenborg, Norway, ex Clausenengen, Molde, on 8/11/1994) PL 73+3/13 FLC 7+2/1 FAC 17/2
Liverpool (£3,500,000 on 3/6/1997) PL 34+3/7 FLC 4+2 FAC 1 Others 3+2
Tottenham H (£3,000,000 on 6/8/1999) PL 44+3/7 FLC 4/2 FAC 3+1/1 Others 4/1

LE SAUX Graeme Pierre
Born: Jersey, 17 October 1968
Height: 5'10" Weight: 12.2
Club Honours: PL '95; FLC '98; ESC '98; CS '00
International Honours: E: 36; B-2; U21-4

Following England's ignominious exit from Euro 2000 there was one piece of short-term good news for the national side with the return to full fitness of Graeme Le Saux who filled the problem position at left back. In just his fourth start of the last season he was appointed stand-in skipper for Chelsea under new boss Claudio Ranieri for the vital game at Old Trafford and he produced an inspirational performance, creating all three of the Blues' goals against the reigning champions and securing the draw with a sensational goal-line clearance to deny Andy Cole. Unfortunately, just three matches later his campaign was interrupted with a red card at Sunderland and he then joined an appallingly long injury list at Stamford Bridge with an achilles tendon problem that sidelined him until the first week of January. His absence left Chelsea unbalanced in defence, while his surging runs down the left flank were sorely missed - one of several factors contributing to a relatively under-achieving season for the Blues.

Chelsea (Free from St Paul's, Jersey on 9/12/1987) F/PL 77+13/8 FLC 7+6/1 FAC 7+1 Others 8+1
Blackburn Rov (£750,000 on 25/3/1993) PL 127+2/7 FLC 10 FAC 8 Others 6+1
Chelsea (£5,000,000 on 8/8/1997) PL 80+5/1 FLC 5/1 FAC 7+2/1 Others 17+2

LESCOTT Aaron Anthony
Born: Birmingham, 2 December 1978
Height: 5'8" Weight: 10.9

Unable to get a game at Aston Villa, Aaron moved down a division to join Sheffield Wednesday last October and proved a useful acquisition for Owls' boss Paul Jewell. He made his debut in midfield against West Bromwich Albion but showed his versatility when covering at full back when required. Young, quick and full of enthusiasm he put in some effective challenges wherever he played and looks to have a bright future at Hillsborough. He is the older brother of Joleon Lescott.

Aston Villa (From trainee on 5/7/1996) FAC 0+1
Lincoln C (Loaned on 14/3/2000) FL 3+2
Sheffield Wed (£100,000 on 3/10/2000) FL 17+13 FLC 3 FAC 2

LESCOTT Joleon Patrick
Born: Birmingham, 16 August 1982
Height: 6'2" Weight: 13.0
International Honours: E: Yth

Joleon had a superb season for Wolves in 2000-01, and after making his first-team debut back in August he went on to feature regularly throughout the campaign only losing his place when Paul Butler arrived at Molineux in the new year. A powerful central defender, he produced some superb displays for one so young and even scored two goals himself including a header to earn Wanderers a point at Wimbledon. Previously capped for England at U17 level he stepped up to appear for the U18s last term. Joleon is the younger brother of Sheffield Wednesday's Aaron Lescott.

Wolverhampton W (From trainee on 18/8/1999) FL 31+6/2 FLC 5 FAC 2

LESTER Jack William
Born: Sheffield, 8 October 1975
Height: 5'10" Weight: 11.8
Club Honours: AMC '98
International Honours: E: Sch

Signed as a provider of goals rather than a scorer, Jack produced a pleasant surprise by netting seven times for Nottingham Forest in the early part of last season, all his efforts coming away from the City Ground. Amongst these was a fine hat-trick in the 3-1 win at Gillingham in November, however shortly afterwards he suffered a bad groin injury against Portsmouth that was to keep him out of action for the remainder of the campaign. He is a small but effective striker with pace, skill and an excellent work rate.

Grimsby T (From juniors on 8/7/1994) FL 93+40/17 FLC 13+4/6 FAC 7+2/2 Others 4+4
Doncaster Rov (Loaned on 20/9/1996) FL 5+6/1
Nottingham F (£300,000 on 28/1/2000) FL 30+4/9

LE TISSIER Matthew (Matt) Paul
Born: Guernsey, 14 October 1968
Height: 6'1" Weight: 13.8
International Honours: E: 8; B-6; Yth

Matt had yet another nightmare time with injuries at Southampton last term. After enjoying a brief run in the line-up at the beginning of the season he was sidelined by a series of calf and knee problems and it was not until shortly before the end of the campaign that he recovered anything like match fitness. However he made the starting line-up for the last game of the season against Arsenal, which was the final Premiership match to be played on The Dell, and with a sense of the grand occasion he netted a spectacular late winner with a left-foot shot on the turn from the edge of the penalty area. An immensely creative talent in midfield and a great goal-scorer - he needs 14 more to overhaul Mike Channon's club record of 185 league goals - he was reported to have signed a new two-year deal for the Saints at the end of the season.

Southampton (From apprentice on 17/10/1986) F/PL 377+62/162 FLC 44+8/27 FAC 30+2/12 Others 11+1/9

LEVER Mark
Born: Beverley, 29 March 1970
Height: 6'3" Weight: 13.5
Club Honours: AMC '98

A close-season free-transfer signing for Bristol City Mark looked impressive in the opening games of the 2000-01 campaign but then had the misfortune to suffer a serious knee injury in the Worthington Cup first round first leg against Brentford. He failed to recover match fitness by the end and it is hoped that he will return in time for the start of the coming season. Mark is a commanding central defender who is powerful in the air and a forceful tackler.

Grimsby T (From trainee on 9/8/1988) FL 343+18/8 FLC 22+2 FAC 17+3 Others 18
Bristol C (Free on 24/7/2000) FL 2 FLC 1

LEWIS Edward (Eddie) James
Born: Cerritos, California, USA, 17 May 1974
Height: 5'9" Weight: 11.12
International Honours: USA: 28

When Eddie played the full 90 minutes in Fulham's opening 2-0 win against Crewe, he could hardly have imagined that this would be his only league start of the season. It was his misfortune that Jean Tigana brought in Sean Davis as the 'holding' midfielder with such success and moved John Collins into Eddie's position on the left side of midfield. He played his part in Fulham's Worthington Cup runs and scored his first goal for the club in the fourth round win against Derby County. His form in the reserve side was excellent and he found the net nine times in nine games including successive hat-tricks against Swindon and Oxford. His pace and accurate crossing could well unlock some Premiership defences in 2001-02 if he is given the chance. He featured regularly for the USA in the early part of the campaign but struggled to retain his place in the new year.

Fulham (£1,300,000 from San Jose Clash, USA on 17/3/2000) FL 7+8 FLC 6/1

LEWIS Graham
Born: Reading, 15 February 1982
Height: 5'10" Weight: 11.12

This hard-working striker signed a three-month contract for Lincoln City after completing his time as a trainee with the club. He showed promise in three brief appearances from the subs' bench but failed to make the starting line-up and was released in October. Graham later signed for Conference club Northwich Victoria.

Lincoln C (From trainee on 19/7/2000) FL 3+4 FLC 0+1

LEWIS Karl **Junior**
Born: Wembley, 9 October 1973
Height: 6'5" Weight: 12.4

Junior produced some excellent performances for First Division new boys Gillingham in the first half of last season when he was rarely absent from first-team duties. Such form drew the attention of his old boss Peter Taylor and in January he moved to Leicester on loan, the deal becoming permanent in March. He took over the anchor role in midfield, sitting just in front of the back line, and performed his duties steadily and effectively. He settled in well, keeping his passes deliberate and simple, but usually finding a blue shirt. When the team was playing on form, Junior even found the confidence to supply the odd defence-splitting ball, but found himself a little overwhelmed in the aftermath of the Wycombe FA Cup debacle, when he was asked to shoulder the main midfield responsibilities while Muzzy Izzet and Robbie Savage were injured. However in the summer he could look back on a season of tremendous progress and look forward to the prospect of a regular first-team place for the Foxes in 2001-02.

Fulham (From trainee on 3/7/1992) FL 4+1 FAC 1 (Free to Dover Ath during 1993 close season)
Gillingham (Free from Hendon on 3/8/1999) FL 47+12/8 FLC 4+2 FAC 7+2 Others 4
Leicester C (£50,000 on 30/1/2001) PL 15

Andy Liddell

LIBURD Richard John
Born: Nottingham, 26 September 1973
Height: 5'9" Weight: 11.1

This hard-working and versatile defender featured regularly for Notts County last season and developed a rather surprising reputation for scoring goals. His effort that provided the 'golden goal' decider in the FA Cup second round replay against Wigan Athletic was undoubtedly the 'Goal of the Season' at Meadow Lane. Picking up a loose ball he flicked it over a defender with his right foot and smashed it home with his left for a truly spectacular winner. New boss Jocky Scott recognised his value to the team by giving him a new two-year contract in the spring.

Middlesbrough (£20,000 from Eastwood T on 25/3/1993) FL 41/1 FLC 4 FAC 2 Others 5
Bradford C (£200,000 on 21/7/1994) FL 75+3/3 FLC 6+2 FAC 2+2 Others 2
Carlisle U (Free on 26/2/1998) FL 9
Notts Co (Free on 4/8/1998) FL 79+18/5 FLC 4+1 FAC 8+4/2

LIDDELL Andrew (Andy) Mark
Born: Leeds, 28 June 1973
Height: 5'7" Weight: 11.6
Club Honours: AMC '99
International Honours: S: U21-12

Andy played an important role for Wigan in their push for promotion in 2000-01. A talented striker who can make as well as score goals, he regularly unlocked defences for his colleagues with his unselfish running. He netted ten goals during the season including a great 30-yard strike against Northampton in September.

Barnsley (From trainee on 6/7/1991) F/PL 142+56/34 FLC 11+2/3 FAC 5+7/1 Others 2+1
Wigan Ath (£350,000 on 15/10/1998) FL 106/27 FLC 6/1 FAC 5/1 Others 13

LIDDLE Craig George
Born: Chester le Street, 21 October 1971
Height: 5'11" Weight: 12.7

Craig once again produced a series of high quality performances in the heart of the Darlington defence in the 2000-01 season. A near ever-present he was an inspiration to those around him with his professional approach and consistency. His reading of the game was of a standard usually only seen at a higher level and he proved effective both in the air and on the ground. If it were not for his presence the Quakers would have suffered many more defeats during the campaign.

Aston Villa (From trainee on 4/7/1990. Free to Blyth Spartans in August 1991)
Middlesbrough (Free on 12/7/1994) P/FL 20+5 FLC 3+2 FAC 2 Others 2
Darlington (Free on 20/2/1998) FL 149/6 FLC 7 FAC 9 Others 9/3

LIGHTBOURNE Kyle Lavince
Born: Bermuda, 29 September 1968
Height: 6'2" Weight: 12.4
Club Honours: AMC '00
International Honours: Bermuda: 22; Yth

Kyle appeared regularly for Stoke City early on last season but found his opportunities limited by the arrival of Andy Cooke and Rikki Dadason. In an attempt to re-launch his career he joined Swindon Town on loan in January but after a lively debut he succumbed to a thigh injury in his second game and returned to the Britannia Stadium. He then spent the following month at Cardiff City as cover for injured strikers Gavin Gordon and Kevin Nugent but received few chances before returning to the Potteries where he played in a handful of games as the season came to a close. He is an experienced striker who works hard and possesses a good shot. Kyle is also a double international having represented Bermuda at both football and cricket. Out of contract in the summer his future was uncertain at the time of writing.

Scarborough (Signed from Pembroke Hamilton, Bermuda on 11/12/1992) FL 11+8/3 FLC 1 Others 0+1
Walsall (Free on 17/9/1993) FL 158+7/65 FLC 8/3 FAC 16+2/12 Others 7/5
Coventry C (£500,000 + on 18/7/1997) PL 1+6 FLC 3
Fulham (Loaned on 13/1/1998) FL 4/2 Others 1/1
Stoke C (£500,000 on 16/2/1998) FL 83+28/21 FLC 7 FAC 3/1 Others 7+2/3
Swindon T (Loaned on 13/1/2001) FL 2
Cardiff C (Loaned on 20/2/2001) FL 2+1

LIGHTFOOT Christopher (Chris) Ian
Born: Warrington, 1 April 1970
Height: 6'2" Weight: 13.6

Chris joined Oldham Athletic on loan last September as Latics' boss Andy Ritchie sought to stem a run of four defeats from five games. He produced a fine performance on his debut in a 0-0 draw against Bristol City but after a handful of games he picked up an injury and returned to Gresty Road. He was subsequently dogged by a succession of injuries and failed to make a single first-team appearance for Crewe during the season. A tall commanding central defender he had a few outings with Kidderminster reserves towards the end of the campaign in a trial period. Out of contract in the summer it was unclear at the time of writing where he would be playing in the 2001-02 season.

Chester C (From trainee on 11/7/1988) FL 263+14/32 FLC 15+2/1 FAC 16+2/1 Others 14+2/5
Wigan Ath (£87,500 on 13/7/1995) FL 11+3/1 FLC 2 FAC 2 Others 3
Crewe Alex (£50,000 on 22/3/1996) FL 63+24/4 FLC 3+2 FAC 1+1/1 Others 3+2
Oldham Ath (Loaned on 15/9/2000) FL 3 FLC 1

LILLEY Derek Symon
Born: Paisley, 9 February 1974
Height: 5'11" Weight: 12.7
Club Honours: S Div 2 '95
International Honours: S: Yth

Derek featured regularly for Oxford United in the first half of last season netting a couple of goals including one in rather bizarre circumstances that led to it being included in the 'What Happened Next' feature of the 'Question of Sport' television programme. The goal came when Reading 'keeper Phil Whitehead slid out of play when trying to prevent a corner and left the ball stranded on the line for Derek to walk it into the net. He subsequently joined Scottish Premier League club Dundee United in December, scoring against Rangers on his debut and finishing with a respectable tally of six goals from 18 appearances. He is an experienced striker who is very quick and has a high work rate.

Greenock Morton (Free from Everton BC on 13/8/1991) SL 157+23/57 SLC 5+1/4 SC 9+4/4 Others 6+4/5
Leeds U (£500,000 + on 27/3/1997) PL 4+17/1 FLC 0+3 FAC 0+1 Others 0+1
Heart of Midlothian (Loaned on 30/12/1998) SL 3+1/1 SC 1
Bury (Loaned on 25/3/1999) FL 5/1
Oxford U (£75,000 on 6/8/1999) FL 51+12/9 FLC 3+4 FAC 6/1 Others 1

LINDLEY James (Jim) Edward
Born: Sutton in Ashfield, 23 July 1981
Height: 6'2" Weight: 13.0

Having developed through Notts County's youth system Jim was loaned to Lincoln City last August as cover for regular 'keeper Alan Marriott. He featured on the subs' bench and in reserve action for the Imps before abruptly returning to Meadow Lane following an injury crisis and replaced Darren Ward for the last ten minutes of the Worthington cup second round second leg tie against Watford. He retained his place for the next two games before losing out to Paul Gibson and spent much of the remainder of the season out on loan, firstly at Mansfield Town and then with Dr Martens League club Gresley Rovers. He was one of several players released by the Magpies in the summer.

Notts Co (From trainee on 1/7/1999) FL 2+1 FLC 0+1

LINIGHAN Andrew (Andy)
Born: Hartlepool, 18 June 1962
Height: 6'3" Weight: 13.10
Club Honours: Div 1 '91; FLC '93; FAC '93; ECWC '94
International Honours: E: B-4

This veteran central defender signed a new one-year contract for Crystal Palace in the summer of 2000 but found himself edged out of the starting line-up by new signing Neil Ruddock. Andy featured just three times for the Eagles but managed to hit the vital last-minute equaliser in the Worthington Cup second round second leg tie against Burnley which earned his team victory on the away goals ruling. His contract was later cancelled by mutual consent and he signed for Second Division Oxford United where he went straight in the first team. He enjoyed a decent unbroken run before dropping out of contention only to return to make a final sentimental appearance from the subs' bench towards the end of the campaign, thus enabling him to enter the record books as the oldest player to appear in Football League action for the U's. Despite his years Andy continued to perform consistently and was still effective in the air, while his vast experience proved invaluable in helping his young team-mates at the Manor Ground. He was released in the summer and was reported to have joined St Albans City.

Hartlepool U (Free from Henry Smiths BC on 19/9/1980) FL 110/4 FLC 7+1/1 FAC 8 Others 1/1
Leeds U (£20,000 on 15/5/1984) FL 66/3 FLC 6/1 FAC 2 Others 2
Oldham Ath (£65,000 on 17/1/1986) FL 87/6 FLC 8/2 FAC 3 Others 4
Norwich C (£350,000 on 4/3/1988) FL 86/8 FLC 6 FAC 10 Others 4
Arsenal (£1,250,000 on 4/7/1990) F/PL 101+17/5 FLC 13+1/1 FAC 12+2/1 Others 9+1/1
Crystal Palace (£150,000 on 27/1/1997) F/PL 108+3/4 FLC 6+3/1 FAC 3+2 Others 4
Queens Park R (Loaned on 25/3/1999) FL 4+3
Oxford U (Free on 16/10/2000) FL 12+1 FAC 2

LISBIE Kevin Anthony
Born: Hackney, 17 October 1978
Height: 5'8' Weight: 10.12
International Honours: E: Yth

Kevin started the 2000-01 campaign in fine form at Charlton and was particularly outstanding against Manchester City and Arsenal. He seemed to do everything but score and although he eventually netted two in the Worthington Cup tie against Stoke City he failed to register a goal in Premiership action. He had a brief spell on loan at First Division strugglers Queens Park Rangers in December but suffered an injury after just two games and returned to The Valley. Kevin is a powerful striker with electric pace who can play either in a central position or wide on the right.

Charlton Ath (From trainee on 24/5/1996) P/FL 10+51/2 FLC 2+5/2 FAC 1+3
Gillingham (Loaned on 5/3/1999) FL 4+3/4
Reading (Loaned on 26/11/1999) FL 1+1
Queens Park R (Loaned on 1/12/2000) FL 1+1

LITMANEN Jari Olaui
Born: Lahti, Finland, 20 February 1971
Height: 5'11" Weight: 12.12
International Honours: Finland: 69

Finland's finest football export, Jari was languishing in Barcelona's second team when Liverpool boss Gerard Houllier signed him up last January. He made his debut as a substitute in the Worthington Cup semi-final first leg match against Crystal Palace and almost immediately made a decisive impact, when with the Reds trailing 2-0, he set up Vladimir Smicer for a goal to reduce the deficit and pave the way for a crushing 5-0 second leg victory in which he also starred. His first goal for Liverpool was a penalty at Sunderland in February to square the match at 1-1 and he scored another spot kick in the FA Cup fifth round victory over Manchester City. Sadly he missed the next four matches with a calf injury, and then after returning to the team in March his season was ended prematurely by a broken wrist incurred ironically while playing for Finland against England at Anfield. Jari was outstanding on that occasion and only a wonderful save by David Seaman kept out his last minute header that might have salvaged a draw for his country. Although he missed the exciting climax to Liverpool's season he did enough to show that he could be a key figure next term. Playing in the 'hole' behind the front two he added a new dimension to the team's attacking play, providing some much needed variety and attacking options.

Liverpool (Free from Barcelona, Spain, ex Reipas, HJK Helsinki, MyPa, Ajax, on 18/1/2001) PL 4+1/1 FLC 1+1 FAC 1+1/1 Others 0+2

LITTLE Colin Campbell
Born: Wythenshawe, 4 November 1972
Height: 5'10" Weight: 11.0

Having been a regular for Crewe Alexandra in 1999-2000, Colin found it difficult to hold down a regular place last term and appeared in little more than half the Railwaymen's First Division games. A quick and lively striker he poses a threat when he runs with the ball at defenders and always tries his hardest for the cause.

Crewe Alex (£50,000 from Hyde U on 7/2/1996) FL 124+46/32 FLC 13+2/7 FAC 5/1 Others 5/3

LITTLE Glen Matthew
Born: Wimbledon, 15 October 1975
Height: 6'3" Weight: 13.0

Burnley's very talented wingman began the 2000-01 campaign in style, coming on as a substitute in the opening game at Bolton and proceeding to torment the home defence, thus providing the key to the Clarets' recovery which gave them a well-earned point. However the season was generally a disappointing one for Glen as hamstring problems severely restricted his appearances. At his best he was still irresistible, the only Burnley player truly capable of turning a game and a constant thorn in the side of opponents who could never fathom his next move. He was mostly used as a right winger, but was also occasionally employed at wing back, despite the fact that defence is certainly not his natural style! Glen's best years lie ahead of him and given better luck with injuries he should be a key player for the club in the coming season.

Crystal Palace (From trainee on 1/7/1994. Free to Glentoran on 11/11/1994)
Burnley (£100,000 on 29/11/1996) FL 119+23/15 FLC 7+2 FAC 6+3 Others 4+1/1

LITTLEJOHN Adrian Sylvester
Born: Wolverhampton, 26 September 1970
Height: 5'9" Weight: 11.0
International Honours: E: Yth

Undoubtedly a naturally gifted player Adrian continued to be something of an enigma for Bury in 2000-01. He showed some impressive early-season form, netting four goals, but then his performances seemed to dip and he spent much of the second half of the campaign on the subs' bench. He is a very quick and direct player with the skill and pace to move past defenders with ease. Out of contract in the summer his future was unclear at the time of writing.

Walsall (From trainee at West Bromwich A juniors on 24/5/1989) FL 26+18/1 FLC 2+1 FAC 1+1 Others 4+1
Sheffield U (Free on 6/8/1991) F/PL 44+25/12 FLC 5+1 FAC 3+2/1 Others 2/1
Plymouth Arg (£100,000 on 22/9/1995) FL 100+10/29 FLC 6 FAC 6+2/3 Others 6
Oldham Ath (Signed on 20/3/1998) FL 16+5/5 FLC 2/1
Bury (£75,000 on 13/11/1998) FL 69+30/14 FLC 4/2 FAC 6/1 Others 2+1

LIVERMORE David
Born: Edmonton, 20 May 1980
Height: 5'11" Weight: 12.1
Club Honours: Div 2 '01

David gave some fine performances in the centre of the park for Millwall last season when he rarely missed a match. An enthusiastic left-sided midfield player he creates pressure for the opposition with his effective runs, is good in the air and very strong in the tackle. He will look forward to the challenge of First Division football in the 2001-02 campaign.

Arsenal (From trainee on 13/7/1998)
Millwall (£30,000 on 30/7/1999) FL 68+3/5 FLC 6/1 FAC 3 Others 3

LIVINGSTONE Stephen (Steve) Carl
Born: Middlesbrough, 8 September 1968
Height: 6'1" Weight: 13.6
Club Honours: AMC '98

After spending almost two seasons as a central defender for Grimsby Town, Steve moved back to his former role as a striker last season following the return to fitness of Peter Handyside. With the Mariners struggling for goals he proved quite effective and finished the campaign as the club's leading scorer. His absence with a calf injury in the vital run-in left the team a little lightweight up front but he returned for the last few matches and notched an important goal in the 3-1 win over fellow strugglers Tranmere. Steve is an old-fashioned striker who works tirelessly and is good in the air.

Coventry C (From trainee on 16/7/1986) FL 17+14/5 FLC 8+2/10 Others 0+1
Blackburn Rov (£450,000 on 17/1/1991) F/PL 25+5/10 FLC 2 FAC 1/1
Chelsea (£350,000 on 23/3/1993) PL 0+1
Port Vale (Loaned on 3/9/1993) FL 4+1
Grimsby T (£140,000 on 29/10/1993) FL 205+51/40 FLC 15+6/4 FAC 11+5/4 Others 4+3

LJUNGBERG Fredrik
Born: Sweden, 16 April 1977
Height: 5'9" Weight: 11.6
Club Honours: CS '99
International Honours: Sweden: 26; U21-12; Yth

Fredrik was again a regular in the Arsenal side last season, playing mainly on the flanks but also occasionally through the middle. A versatile player, he offers pace and skill when attacking, and a high work rate and aggressive ball winning when on the defensive. Freddie scored five goals for the Gunners during the course of the season, including an impressive double against Lazio at Highbury in the Champions' League. A regular for Sweden, he would seem to have a very bright and long future ahead of him at Highbury.

Arsenal (£3,000,000 from BK Halmstad, Sweden on 17/9/1998) PL 57+15/13 FLC 2 FAC 8+2/1 Others 22+6/4

LLEWELLYN Christopher (Chris) Mark
Born: Swansea, 29 August 1979
Height: 5'11" Weight: 11.6
International Honours: W: 2; B-1; U21-14; Yth

Chris continued his education with almost a full season of first-team football at Norwich City in 2000-01. Only a fractured cheekbone, suffered on his 21st birthday, prevented an ever-present season for him, and he also enjoyed a decent time in front of goal, ending the campaign second only to Iwan Roberts in City's goal-scoring charts. An energetic left-sided player, he was at his best when running at defenders in central or wide areas, but because of his incredible appetite for hard work he often played at left wing back or even left back last term. His efforts were rewarded with a new contract that will keep him at Carrow Road until 2005. The regular captain of the Wales U21 side he won four more caps during the season.

Norwich C (From trainee on 21/1/1997) FL 96+28/17 FLC 7+2 FAC 3+1/1

LOCK Anthony (Tony) Charles
Born: Harlow, 3 September 1976
Height: 5'11" Weight: 13.0

Tony featured mainly from the subs' bench for Colchester United and after running into disciplinary problems following two red cards in a spell of three days he was released by the U's. He subsequently joined Conference outfit Dagenham & Redbridge where he featured in a number of games towards the end of the campaign. Tony is a powerful left-sided striker with a high work rate.

Colchester U (From trainee on 18/4/1995) FL 44+58/13 FLC 2+2 FAC 1+5 Others 1+6

LOCKE Adam Spencer
Born: Croydon, 20 August 1970
Height: 5'11" Weight: 12.7

Adam featured regularly for Luton Town for much of last season but was hampered by injuries early in the new year. He is an experienced midfield player who works hard and likes to push forward to support the strikers. He was reported to have signed a one-year extension to his contract during the close season.

Crystal Palace (From trainee on 21/6/1988)
Southend U (Free on 6/8/1990) FL 56+17/4 FLC 5 FAC 2+1 Others 6+1
Colchester U (Loaned on 8/10/1993) FL 4 Others 1
Colchester U (Free on 23/9/1994) FL 64+15/8 FLC 5+1 FAC 5 Others 8+5
Bristol C (Free on 23/7/1997) FL 61+4/4 FLC 6 FAC 3 Others 2/1
Luton T (Free on 24/8/1999) FL 44+15/5 FLC 1+1 FAC 5+2 Others 2

LOCKE Gary
Born: Edinburgh, 16 June 1975
Height: 5'10" Weight: 11.3
International Honours: S: U21-10

Gary began the 2000-01 campaign with Scottish Premier League club Hearts but although he featured fairly regularly he failed to establish himself in the starting line-up and at the end of January he moved south of the border to join Premiership strugglers Bradford City. A versatile player who can feature at wing back on either flank or in his preferred central midfield role, he was mostly employed at right wing back at Valley Parade. He showed some outstanding form, being very pacy and linking up well with the midfield, but nevertheless he was unable to keep the Bantams in the Premiership.

Heart of Midlothian (Free from Whitehill Welfare on 31/7/1992) SL 126+29/5 SLC 14+1 SC 10+1/1 Others 8
Bradford C (Free on 26/1/2001) PL 6+1

LOCKWOOD Matthew (Matt) Dominic
Born: Southend, 17 October 1976
Height: 5'9" Weight: 10.12

An excellent attacking left back Matt enjoyed another fine season for Leyton Orient in 2000-01. A master with free kicks and penalties he finished as the team's third-highest scorer with eight goals, the best and most important of which was undoubtedly a 30-yard screamer in the play-off semi-final win over Hull City. Again watched by several bigger clubs, he was deservedly voted into the PFA's Third Division team for the second successive season.

Queens Park R (From trainee at Southend U on 2/5/1995)
Bristol Rov (Free on 24/7/1996) FL 58+5/1 FLC 2+1 FAC 6 Others 4+2
Leyton Orient (Free on 7/8/1998) FL 108+2/16 FLC 10/2 FAC 10 Others 7/1

Matt Lockwood

LOGAN Richard Anthony
Born: Barnsley, 24 May 1969
Height: 6'1" Weight: 13.3

This experienced central defender was brought in to add height and steel to the Lincoln back line-up. He signed on a three-year contract and for the opening games of last season he appeared in the middle of a five-man defence. However he injured an ankle at Hull at the end of August and his only further first team experience was as a substitute for the final four minutes against Mansfield the following month. Richard developed sciatica and eventually underwent an operation for a prolapsed disc. He was back in light training at the end of the season with the aim of achieving full fitness for the start of the 2001-2002 campaign.

Huddersfield T (Free from Gainsborough Trinity on 15/11/1993) FL 35+10/1 FLC 3 FAC 1 Others 9
Plymouth Arg (£20,000 on 26/10/1995) FL 67+19/12 FLC 4/1 FAC 2+2 Others 8
Scunthorpe U (Free on 2/7/1998) FL 77+3/7 FLC 1 FAC 4 Others 3
Lincoln C (Free on 12/7/2000) FL 4+1 FLC 1

LOGAN Richard James
Born: Bury St Edmunds, 4 January 1982
Height: 6'0" Weight: 12.5
International Honours: E: Yth; Sch

Richard continued his development in Ipswich Town's reserve team last term and his only senior appearance of the campaign came in the FA Cup third round tie at Morecambe when he replaced Marcus Stewart for the final 15 minutes. In January he moved on loan to Cambridge United to gain further experience of first-team football and made an excellent impression in his short spell at the Abbey Stadium. He scored with a header in the 2-0 win at Wycombe before returning to Portman Road and a place in the second string. Richard is a promising right-footed striker who works tirelessly and has a good turn of pace.

Ipswich T (From trainee on 6/1/1999) FL 0+3 FAC 0+1
Cambridge U (Loaned on 25/1/2001) FL 5/1

LOMAS James (Jamie) Duncan
Born: Chesterfield, 18 October 1977
Height: 5'11" Weight: 12.0

Jamie joined Mansfield in the 2000 close season and was initially used from the subs' bench. He quickly broke into the team and just as he seemed to be settling down he sustained medial and cruciate ligament injuries in the away game at Chesterfield in September. He was out of action for several months before returning to the reserves in February although he made no further senior appearances. Jamie can play on the right hand side of either defence or midfield and is an impressive figure bringing the ball forward.

Chesterfield (From trainee on 16/9/1996) FL 17+13 FLC 2+1 FAC 1/1 Others 2+3
Mansfield T (Free on 2/8/2000) FL 4+2 FLC 1

LOMAS Stephen (Steve) Martin
Born: Hanover, Germany, 18 January 1974
Height: 6'0" Weight: 12.8
International Honours: NI: 38; B-1; Yth; Sch

West Ham's club captain was in excellent form in the first half of the 2000-01 campaign but then had the misfortune to suffer a bad knee injury in January and this forced him to miss the remainder of the season. A very effective ball winner on the right-hand side of midfield his searching runs from box to box often caused problems for the opposition. He was a regular for Northern Ireland when fit and captained the side on occasions.

Manchester C (From trainee on 22/1/1991) P/FL 102+9/8 FLC 15/2 FAC 10+1/1
West Ham U (£1,600,000 on 26/3/1997) PL 115/5 FLC 10/2 FAC 8/1 Others 10

LONERGAN Andrew (Andy)
Born: Preston, 19 October 1983
Height: 6'4" Weight: 13.2
International Honours: RoI: Yth; E: Yth

Called up in an injury crisis, Andy made his Preston debut at Coventry in last season's Worthington Cup tie when just 16 years old, making him the club's youngest debutant for nearly 40 years. Despite conceding four goals he gave a virtually faultless display and his confidence did not appear to be harmed. His height helps him command his box, and he also gets down well. Great things are expected of this young goal-keeper, who provided cover on the bench once in December, and again for the last seven games of the season. Previously capped by the Republic of Ireland in an U16 friendly, he made two appearances for England U17s last term.

Preston NE (From trainee on 21/10/2000) FL 1 FLC 1

LOPES Richie
Born: Waterford, 10 August 1981
Height: 5'7" Weight: 10.5

This young right winger joined Northampton Town on transfer deadline day along with Paul Dempsey and went on to make his debut in senior football when he came on from the subs' bench in the 1-0 home defeat by Oldham. Fast and direct, Richie will be hoping to extend his first team experience in the 2001-02 campaign.

Sheffield U (From trainee on 7/7/2000)
Northampton T (Free on 12/3/2001) FL 3+3

LORMOR Anthony (Anth)
Born: Ashington, 29 October 1970
Height: 6'0" Weight: 13.6

This much-travelled forward joined Hartlepool in the 2000 close season as the club sought to resolve what had long been a problem position. Over the years he had been a player who had experienced little trouble in scoring against Pool, but at first he struggled to deliver the goods for his new club. He was relegated to the subs' bench, and it was in this role that he regained his goal-scoring touch with important strikes against Mansfield and Rochdale that kept the club's impressive unbeaten run intact. A bustling striker who leads the line well, Anth is also a qualified Class 1 referee.

Newcastle U (From trainee on 25/2/1988) FL 6+2/3
Lincoln C (£25,000 on 29/1/1990) FL 90+10/30 FLC 1+2/3 FAC 4/2 Others 6
Peterborough U (Free on 4/7/1994) FL 2+3 FAC 1 Others 1+1
Chesterfield (Free on 23/12/1994) FL 97+16/35 FLC 8/4 FAC 5/3 Others 7+1/3
Preston NE (£130,000 + on 5/11/1997) FL 9+3/3 FAC 3 Others 3
Notts Co (Loaned on 20/2/1998) FL 2+5
Mansfield T (£20,000 on 16/7/1998) FL 68+6/20 FLC 2+1 FAC 3/3 Others 4/1
Hartlepool U (£30,000 on 9/8/2000) FL 22+9/8 FLC 1 Others 2+3

LOUIS-JEAN Matthieu
Born: Mont St Aignan, France, 22 February 1976
Height: 5'9" Weight: 10.12
International Honours: France: U21; Yth

Matthieu was a regular in the Nottingham Forest first team in the opening weeks of last season but was then consigned to the subs' bench when manager David Platt changed the tactical formation. He made just one senior appearance after the end of October,

later undergoing a groin operation before disappearing from the first-team picture altogether. He played some very useful games in the reserves and still remains a very good squad player. He is a right back or right wing back who is comfortable on the ball and reads the game well.
Nottingham F (Signed from Le Havre, France on 14/9/1998) P/FL 51+5 FLC 7+2 FAC 2

LOVELL Mark
Born: Beckenham, 16 July 1983
Height: 5'10" Weight: 12.1
This young Gillingham trainee did well enough in the reserve and youth teams to earn his Football League debut in the penultimate home game of the season when he replaced Mark Saunders for the last five minutes against Watford. A promising midfield player he is the son of former Millwall and Gills star Steve Lovell.
Gillingham (From trainee on 10/4/2001) FL 0+1

LOVELL Stephen (Steve) William Henry
Born: Amersham, 6 December 1980
Height: 6'1" Weight: 12.7
Having failed to make much headway at Portsmouth, Steve looked to be on his way from the club when he went to Plymouth for a trial spell early in the new year. However new Pompey boss Graham Rix, saw some potential in the young striker and brought him in for some crucial games towards the end of the season. Steve scored regularly in the reserves and netted for the first time at senior level with a brilliant solo effort that proved to be the winner against Stockport in March. Strong, fast and determined he will be looking to win a regular place in the first-team squad during 2001-02.
Bournemouth (From trainee on 15/7/1999) FL 1+7
Portsmouth (£250,000 on 13/8/1999) FL 5+7/1 FLC 2+1/1
Exeter C (Loaned on 20/3/2000) FL 4+1/1

Steve Lovell

LOVETT Jay
Born: Brighton, 22 January 1978
Height: 6'2" Weight: 12.5
Jay made his debut for Brentford at Port Vale last October but it was not until December that he won a regular place in the first-team squad. He is a right wing back who crosses the ball well and possesses a useful long throw. He scored his first goal for the Bees in the LDV Vans Trophy tie at Oxford.
Brentford (£75,000 from Crawley on 27/7/2000) FL 21+4 Others 3+2/1

LOW Joshua (Josh) David
Born: Bristol, 15 February, 1979
Height: 6'1" Weight: 12.0
International Honours: W: U21-1; Yth
Josh began the 2000-01 campaign on a high by scoring the winner for Cardiff City on the opening day of the season at Exeter. His general play improved as he added composure and an ability to deliver the ball into dangerous areas to his electric pace. He worked hard at the defensive side of his game and made the right-wing-back position his own. He was voted 'Most Improved Player' at Ninian Park and was also selected for the PFA's Third Division team.
Bristol Rov (From trainee on 19/8/1996) FL 11+11 FLC 0+2 FAC 2+2 Others 2
Leyton Orient (Free on 27/5/1999) FL 2+3/1 FLC 1
Cardiff C (Free on 20/11/1999) FL 43+10/6 FLC 1 FAC 2+2 Others 1+1

LOWE Daniel (Danny) James
Born: Barnsley, 12 January 1984
Height: 5'7" Weight: 10.5
Still a trainee at Northampton, Danny made his Football League debut as a substitute in the home game with Colchester in April and went on to make three more appearances from the bench towards the end of the season. A talented right winger he showed a quick turn of speed and some fine ball control.
Northampton T (Trainee) FL 0+4

LOWE Onandi
Born: Kingston, Jamaica, 2 December 1973
Height: 6'3" Weight: 13.12
International Honours: Jamaica
Onandi arrived on loan at Port Vale last January bearing excellent credentials, having been a member of the Rochester Raging Rhinos team that won the US-A League in the 2000 season and also a regular scorer for Jamaica at international level for whom he had netted nine goals in a run of six matches in the previous summer, including a hat-trick in a 4-2 friendly win over Trinidad & Tobago. He made half-a-dozen appearances for Vale scoring twice before departing rather abruptly to return home to join his country's squad for the World Cup qualifiers. He is a powerful striker with good pace and ability on the ball he caused problems for the opposition with his unpredictable style. Onandi subsequently signed for MLS club Kansas City Wizards towards the end of May and got off to a good start, scoring the winner on his debut.
Port Vale (Loaned from Rochester Rhinos, USA, ex Harbour View, Montreal Impact, Waterhouse, Richmond Kickers, on 1/2/2001) FL 4+1/1 Others 1/1

LOWE Ryan Thomas
Born: Liverpool, 18 September 1978
Height: 5'11" Weight: 11.10
Ryan joined Shrewsbury Town in July 2000, arriving from Unibond League club Burscough with a reputation as a prolific goal-scorer. He began the 2000-01 season on the subs' bench and took some time to settle in but once established in the team he began to find the net. He managed a respectable tally of four goals, all towards the end of the season, but is expected to make a much bigger impact in the 2001-02 campaign. He initially featured as an out-and-out striker but looked much more effective when switched to a role just behind the front two.
Shrewsbury T (Free from Burscough on 25/7/2000) FL 13+17/4 FLC 0+2 FAC 0+1 Others 1

LUA LUA Lomano **Tresor**
Born: Zaire, 28 December 1980
Height: 5'8" Weight: 12.2
Tresor began the 2000-01 campaign in excellent form for Colchester and netted a spectacular hat-trick in the 4-1 Worthington Cup demolition of Queens Park Rangers. His performances attracted the attention of Premiership clubs and it was no surprise when he moved on to Newcastle United at the end of September for a fee that was several times in excess of anything previously received by the Layer Road club. Part of manager Bobby Robson's building for the future, he made his debut for the Magpies the following day when he appeared as a substitute in the home game with Charlton. He was an immediate hit with the Toon Army who were impressed by his extravagant ball skills and a willingness to take on opponents inside the box. Well-balanced with two good feet and full of confidence he was unfazed by the step up in class and his dribbling talents were of a standard rarely seen at St James' Park since the days of David Ginola. However he remains relatively inexperienced and he was used predominantly as a substitute striker for the remainder of the season. As he matures and comes to terms with the Premiership he promises to be a talent who will grace the top division for many years to come.
Colchester U (Signed from Leyton College on 25/9/1998) FL 37+24/15 FLC 4/4 FAC 1/1 Others 1
Newcastle U (£2,250,000 on 29/9/2000) PL 3+18 FAC 0+2

LUCAS David Anthony
Born: Preston, 23 November 1977
Height: 6'2" Weight: 13.10
International Honours: E: Yth
Second-choice 'keeper for Preston at the start of last season, David gave a 'Man of the

Match' performance in his first league start for a year at Queens Park Rangers after stepping in for the injured Tepi Moilanen. Retaining his place until a run of defeats in the new year, his 100th senior game came in the home draw with Fulham, and an up and down campaign saw him back as first choice when he came on for the injured Moilanen at Burnley. Still young for a goalkeeper, David has work to do on his decision making and handling of crosses, but is a tremendous shot stopper, as was perfectly demonstrated by two world-class saves at point-blank range in the game at Watford.

Preston NE (From trainee on 12/12/1994) FL 74+1 FLC 5 FAC 6 Others 11
Darlington (Loaned on 14/12/1995) FL 6
Darlington (Loaned on 3/10/1996) FL 7
Scunthorpe U (Loaned on 23/12/1996) FL 6 Others 2

LUCKETTI Christopher (Chris) James
Born: Rochdale, 28 September 1971
Height: 6'0" Weight: 13.6
Club Honours: Div 2 '97

Chris was appointed Huddersfield Town's skipper last term and despite the occasional injury battled on throughout the season rarely missing a match. A commanding central defender with an uncompromising approach, he scored his only goal of the campaign with a 30-yarder in the 2-1 home defeat by Crystal Palace last August. Strong in the air and a good distributor of the ball, he clocked up his 50th appearance for the club against Gillingham. He impressed with his never-say-die attitude but in the end was unable to halt the Terriers slide into Division Two.

Rochdale (Trainee) FL 1
Stockport Co (Free on 23/8/1990)
Halifax T (Free on 12/7/1991) FL 73+5/2 FLC 2/1 FAC 2 Others 4
Bury (£50,000 on 1/10/1993) FL 235/8 FLC 16 FAC 11/1 Others 15/1
Huddersfield T (£750,000 + on 14/6/1999) FL 66/1 FLC 7/1

LUDDEN Dominic James
Born: Basildon, 30 March 1974
Height: 5'8" Weight: 11.0
International Honours: E: Sch

A one-year contract extension followed an ankle operation during the summer, but Dominic again failed to make much impression on the first team at Preston last term when he was once again hampered by persistent injury problems. He made his only appearance of the season (and his first in the league for 15 months) as a substitute against Fulham, which was also his 150th senior game, but despite being a regular on the bench during December this speedy left back was released in the summer.

Leyton Orient (Signed from Billericay T on 6/7/1992) FL 50+8/1 FLC 1 FAC 0+1 Others 6/1
Watford (£100,000 on 7/8/1994) FL 28+5 FLC 3 FAC 2+1 Others 2
Preston NE (Free on 31/7/1998) FL 29+8 FLC 2 FAC 2 Others 3

LUKIC Jovan (John)
Born: Chesterfield, 11 December 1960
Height: 6'4" Weight: 13.12
Club Honours: Div 1 '89, '92; FLC '87; CS '92
International Honours: E: B-1; U21-7; Yth

John made a fairy tale return to the Arsenal first team last autumn after a three-year absence, appearing in Rome against Lazio in the crucial Champions' League match. With first-choice 'keepers David Seaman and Alex Manninger out injured, John put in an accomplished performance as the Gunners earned a vital point. He then went on to play three Premiership matches keeping clean sheets. Now in his 40s, and mainly employed at Highbury as a goalkeeping coach, he provided solid and dependable cover and later spent a large part of the season on the bench. Out of contract in the summer his future as a player remained uncertain at the time of writing.

Leeds U (From apprentice on 16/12/1978) FL 146 FLC 7 FAC 9 Others 3
Arsenal (£50,000 on 25/7/1983) FL 223 FLC 32 FAC 21 Others 4
Leeds U (£1,000,000 on 14/6/1990) F/PL 209 FLC 23 FAC 19 Others 15
Arsenal (Free on 26/7/1996) PL 18 FLC 1 FAC 1 Others 1

LUMSDON Christopher (Chris)
Born: Newcastle, 15 December 1979
Height: 5'7" Weight: 10.6

This young midfielder joined Crewe Alexandra on loan from Sunderland last September and made his debut from the subs' bench in the home defeat by West Bromwich Albion. A skilful hard-working player with great stamina he played regularly in a three-month spell at Gresty Road before returning to the Stadium of Light to continue his football education.

Sunderland (From trainee on 3/7/1997) P/FL 2 FLC 1+1
Blackpool (Loaned on 3/2/2000) FL 6/1
Crewe Alex (Loaned on 11/9/2000) FL 14+2

LUNDEKVAM Claus
Born: Norway, 22 February 1973
Height: 6'3" Weight: 12.10
International Honours: Norway: 10; U21

Claus had another fine season with Southampton in 2000-01 when he was an ever-present for the club in all competitions despite fracturing a cheekbone in October after which he was required to wear a protective mask. Now established as a top-class defender his partnership with Dean Richards continued to flourish as one of the most formidable in the Premiership. An unflappable central defender who loves to surge upfield with the ball, he was recalled for Norway and played in the friendly with Northern Ireland in February.

Southampton (£400,000 from SK Brann, Norway on 3/9/1996) PL 152+6 FLC 18+3 FAC 9

LUNT Kenneth (Kenny) Vincent
Born: Runcorn, 20 November 1979
Height: 5'10" Weight: 10.0
International Honours: E: Yth; Sch

An ever-present for Crewe in first-team games last season, Kenny again showed himself to be an accomplished performer in the centre of the park and contributed a single goal in the 1-0 home win over Sheffield United in March. A right-footed central midfielder with excellent technique, he distributes the ball well and has fine vision. A very competitive player despite his rather slight build, he looks destined for a move to a bigger club in the not too distant future.

Crewe Alex (From trainee on 12/6/1997) FL 120+28/7 FLC 11+3/1 FAC 4+1

LUZHNY Oleg
Born: Ukraine, 5 August 1968
Height: 6'1" Weight: 12.3
Club Honours: CS '99
International Honours: USSR: 8. Ukraine: 40

Despite being unable to dislodge Lee Dixon from the right-back spot for Arsenal, Oleg again proved to be a valuable squad player for the Gunners last term. While filling in mainly at centre back and right back, he can also operate on the right-hand side of midfield. His strength both in the air and in the tackle make him a difficult opponent for opposition strikers. He also likes to get forward and join in the attack whenever possible.

Arsenal (£1,800,000 from Dinamo Kiev, Ukraine on 9/7/1999) PL 32+8 FLC 2 FAC 3 Others 14+1

LYONS Simon Ronald
Born: Watchet, 2 December 1982
Height: 5'9" Weight: 10.10

Simon is equally at home playing as a wing back or wide midfielder on either flank and he proved to be a refreshing addition to the Torquay United squad last season. Mostly used from the subs' bench he gave a particularly precocious performance against Kidderminster in January capped by a fine late equaliser. A confident youngster with the ability to run at defenders, he was offered professional terms by the Gulls at the end of the campaign.

Torquay U (Trainee) FL 0+9/1 FAC 1 Others 1

LYTTLE Desmond (Des)
Born: Wolverhampton, 24 September 1971
Height: 5'9" Weight: 12.13
Club Honours: Div 1 '98

An accomplished right back, Des was a vital figure down the flank for West Bromwich Albion throughout the 2000-01 season. As always he gave 100 per cent every time he took the field and was often to be found in an attacking position deep in the opposition half, occasionally acting as an orthodox winger. He swept some tempting crosses forward and was never found wanting, always quick in recovery, defending with great resilience and clearing his lines with confidence. He scored his first goal for Albion in the 3-1 home defeat by champions-elect Fulham in early December, but came close on a number of occasions to adding to his tally.

Leicester C (From trainee on 1/9/1990)
Swansea C (£12,500 from Worcester C on 9/7/1992) FL 46/1 FLC 2 FAC 5 Others 5
Nottingham F (£375,000 on 27/7/1993) F/PL 177+8/3 FLC 19+1 FAC 16 Others 8
Port Vale (Loaned on 20/11/1998) FL 7
Watford (Free on 28/7/1999) PL 11 FLC 1
West Bromwich A (Free on 21/3/2000) FL 46+3/1 FLC 4 FAC 1 Others 2

Gary McAllister

McALLISTER Gary
Born: Motherwell, 25 December 1964
Height: 6'1" Weight: 11.12
Club Honours: S Div 1 '85; Div 1 '92; CS '92; FLC '01; FAC '01; UEFAC '01
International Honours: S: 57; B-2; U21-1

Gary was a shrewd signing by Liverpool boss Gerard Houllier on a 'Bosman' free transfer from Coventry City in the summer of 2000. Despite his advancing years he had just enjoyed his finest season ever for Coventry and his departure was a severe blow for their manager Gordon Strachan. However neither player nor manager could have foreseen the impact he was to make on the Reds' team at the end of the season as they closed in on their triple targets of the FA Cup, UEFA Cup and Champions League' qualification. His season got off to a disappointing start with a red card at Arsenal and then a niggling injury meant that he did not return to the first team until October. Thereafter he was a regular, although on the bench as often as starting games, as Houllier preferred to use him sparingly. Whether planned or not this was to prove vital in the closing stages of the campaign as he was relatively fresh compared to some of his team-mates. Prior to April his only goal was, almost predictably, against his former team Coventry City in a 4-1 victory at Anfield in November. The second time he found the net proved to be the turning point of the team's season. Liverpool had twice lost the lead in a frenetic 'derby' game with Everton at Goodison on Easter Monday when his late free-kick entered the net from fully 40 yards out to give the Reds a 3-2 victory. Three days later he confidently sent the Barcelona 'keeper the wrong way with his penalty kick to earn the Reds their first European final since 1985. He then converted another penalty in the 3-1 home victory over Tottenham, and scored with two more free kicks late on at both Coventry and Bradford City in 2-0 victories. Five goals in five games and every one of them critical to the club's progress! After playing in seven consecutive games he was surprisingly rested for the FA Cup Final against Arsenal and was sorely missed as the Reds were overrun in midfield for much of the game. However he came on as substitute to play his part in the astonishing recovery as a 1-0 deficit became a 2-1 victory, and was restored to the starting line-up for the UEFA Cup Final against Deportivo Alaves. He went on to give one of his best-ever performances and had a hand in four of his team's five goals in a remarkable 5-4 victory. He set up goals for Markus Babbel and Robbie Fowler, scored a spot kick himself and finally delivered the cunningly-flighted free-kick that a Deportivo defender flicked past his own 'keeper to give the Reds an amazing 5-4 victory. Always the perfect professional, both on and off the field, it is fitting that he should be rewarded with three major honours towards the end of his career, having previously enjoyed little success at club level since moving south of the border some 15 years previously.

Motherwell (Signed from Fir Park BC on 5/9/1981) SL 52+7/6 SLC 3+1 SC 7/2
Leicester C (£125,000 on 15/8/1985) FL 199+2/47 FLC 14+1/3 FAC 5/2 Others 4
Leeds U (£1,000,000 on 2/7/1990) F/PL 230+1/31 FLC 26/5 FAC 24/6 Others 14/4
Coventry C (£3,000,000 on 26/7/1996) PL 119/20 FLC 11/5 FAC 10/1
Liverpool (Free on 6/7/2000) PL 21+9/5 FLC 2+3 FAC 4+1 Others 4+5/2

McANESPIE Kieran
Born: Gosport, 11 September 1979
Height: 5'8" Weight: 10.13
International Honours: S: U21-4

Signed from St Johnstone during the summer, this Scottish U21 left back found it difficult to break into the Fulham first-team squad last term and his only senior appearances came in the two legs of the Worthington Cup tie against Chesterfield. In the new year he had a loan period at Hearts where he featured in half-a-dozen games before returning to fight for a place at Craven Cottage. With Rufus Brevett the regular in his position and internationals Terry Phelan and Paul Trollope ahead in the queue, Kieran is young enough to wait for his opportunity of further first-team action.

St Johnstone (From juniors on 14/9/1995) SL 24+26/5 SC 3+2 Othrs 3+1
Fulham (£80,000 on 11/8/2000) FLC 1+1
Heart of Midlothian (Loaned on 22/1/2001) SL 3+2 SC 0+1

McANESPIE Stephen (Steve)
Born: Kilmarnock, 1 February 1972
Height: 5'9" Weight: 10.7
Club Honours: S Div 1 '95; SLC '95; Div 1 '97
International Honours: S: Yth

Steve joined Cambridge United in the 2000 close season and was a regular in the line-up until the end of November but then lost his place and rarely featured in the second half of the campaign. He appeared mainly for the U's at right back but can also play in midfield. He is a positive player who likes to push forward down the flank and can deliver accurate free kicks.

Aberdeen (From juniors on 12/5/1988. Transferred to Vaesterhaninge, Sweden on 30/6/93)
Raith Rov (Signed on 25/1/1994) SL 37+3 SLC 4 SC 3 Others 5
Bolton W (£900,000 on 30/9/1995) F/PL 19+5 FLC 6
Fulham (£100,000 on 28/11/1997) FL 3+4 FAC 1 Others 2+1
Bradford C (Loaned on 26/3/1998) FL 7
Cambridge U (Free on 9/8/2000) FL 20+3 FLC 2 FAC 1 Others 2

McAREAVEY Paul
Born: Belfast, 3 December 1980
Height: 5'10" Weight: 11.6
International Honours: NI: U21-4; Yth

Paul spent three months on loan with League of Ireland outfit Kilkenny City last season before returning to Swindon in spectacular fashion. Given a place on the subs' bench due to shortage of numbers, he was sent on to assist a side struggling to retain a 1-0 lead over Oldham and he subsequently transformed the match by scoring within two minutes of his arrival. He featured in a handful more games towards the end of the campaign and was reported to have signed a new 12-month contract in the summer.

Swindon T (From trainee on 10/7/1999) FL 2+3/1

McATEER Jason Wynn
Born: Birkenhead, 18 June 1971
Height: 5'10" Weight: 11.12
International Honours: RoI: 40; B-1

Jason had a somewhat mixed season for Blackburn in 2000-01, for after losing out at right back to John Curtis he then took over the wide-right slot for much of the campaign before he was replaced by Keith Gillespie in the second half of the season. However he will still be remembered for scoring the first goal in a Blackburn-Burnley 'derby' for 18 years and was probably 'Man of the Match'; his early defensive excellence saved a certain goal and he produced a dynamic display for the full 90 minutes. Jason is a member of a famous boxing family and the nephew of two former British middleweight champions, Pat and Les McAteer.

Bolton W (Signed from Marine on 22/1/1992) P/FL 109+5/8 FLC 11/2 FAC 11/3 Others 8+1/2
Liverpool (£4,500,000 on 6/9/1995) PL 84+16/3 FLC 12+1 FAC 11+1/3 Others 12+2
Blackburn Rov (£4,000,000 on 28/1/1999) P/FL 57+11/4 FLC 4 FAC 7

McAUGHTRIE Craig James
Born: Burton, 3 March 1981
Height: 6'2" Weight: 14.6

Having been released by Sheffield United at the end of the 1999-2000 campaign Craig joined Third Division Carlisle, but struggled to win a regular place in the squad and was restricted to a handful of outings from the subs' bench and a single appearance in the starting line-up in the LDV Vans Trophy tie at Kidderminster. A promising central defender with undoubted potential he will be looking to gain further senior experience in the coming season.

Sheffield U (From trainee on 5/7/1999)
Carlisle U (Free on 7/8/2000) FL 0+5 Others 1

McAULEY Hugh Francis
Born: Plymouth, 13 May 1976
Height: 5'10" Weight: 11.4

Having previously been known as a striker with Cheltenham Town, Hugh successfully made the switch to midfield last season. Used in either a wide or a central role he produced some impressive performances in the early part of the campaign. His delicate touch and passing ability seem suited to the middle of the park, although he perhaps still needs to develop his strength and stamina to enable him to match some of the more physical opponents in the Third Division.

Cheltenham T (Signed from Leek T on 15/7/1999) FL 52+22/7 FLC 3 FAC 3 Others 2+1/1

Hugh McAuley

McAULEY Sean
Born: Sheffield, 23 June 1972
Height: 5'11" Weight: 11.12
International Honours: S: U21-1; Yth

Sean was Rochdale's left back in the 2000-01 pre-season games, but Lee Todd's arrival relegated him to the reserves. He was appointed captain of the second string and was named as a substitute for the first team on several occasions but his only Third Division game of the season came at Southend in March. Unfortunately he suffered a knee injury just 15 minutes into the game which resulted in him being carried off and missing the remainder of the season.

Manchester U (From trainee on 1/7/1990)
St Johnstone (Signed on 22/4/1992) SL 59+3 SLC 3/1 SC 3 Others 1
Chesterfield (Loaned on 4/11/1994) FL 1/1 FAC 1+1 Others 2
Hartlepool U (Free on 21/7/1995) FL 84/1 FLC 6 FAC 3 Others 3
Scunthorpe U (Signed on 26/3/1997) FL 63+6/1 FLC 5 FAC 5 Others 2
Scarborough (Loaned on 25/3/1999) FL 6+1
Rochdale (Free on 11/2/2000) FL 11+3 Others 1

MACAULEY Stephen (Steve) Roy
Born: Lytham, 4 March 1969
Height: 6'1" Weight: 12.0
Club Honours: FAYC '86

One of the old heads in the Crewe Alexandra squad, Steve was a regular in the line-up until injuries caused him to miss several matches towards the end of the season. A commanding central defender who performs consistently well, he is effective in the air and very useful at set pieces. Steve will have completed ten years service at Gresty Road next March and is looking forward to a well-deserved testimonial.

Manchester C (From trainee on 5/11/1987. Released during 1988 close season)
Crewe Alex (£25,000 from Fleetwood T on 24/3/1992) FL 238+14/26 FLC 19 FAC 16/1 Others 20/3

McAVOY Andrew (Andy) David
Born: Middlesbrough, 28 August 1979
Height: 6'0" Weight: 12.0

Andy was again unable to win a regular place in the Hartlepool first team last season. He was given a handful of opportunities in the first half of the campaign but found himself restricted to reserve team football in the new year. A versatile player who can play either as a right-sided attacking midfielder or as a striker he was released at the end of the campaign.

Blackburn Rov (From trainee on 14/7/1997)
Hartlepool U (Free on 24/11/1999) FL 7+14 Others 1+3

McBRIDE Brian
Born: Arlington Heights, USA, 19 June 1972
Height: 6'1" Weight: 12.7
International Honours: United States: 48

Brian arrived at Preston on a six-month loan deal last September and made his debut two days later, hitting the bar with an early close-range shot. In the first three games he played he impressed the home fans with his intelligent and powerful play, particularly in the air. Unfortunately he picked up a potentially fatal blood clot in his arm that required emergency surgery and he had to rest for three months. Returning to action over the Christmas period, he went on to score his only goal in the 5-0 victory over Queens Park Rangers. A firm favourite with the Deepdale fans he eventually returned home in March. A regular member of the USA national team he continued to represent his country during his stay with North End.

Preston NE (Loaned from Columbus Crew, USA, ex St Louis University, VFL Wolfsburg, on 15/9/2000) FL 8+1/1 FLC 1 FAC 1

McCALL Andrew **Stuart** Murray
Born: Leeds, 10 June 1964
Height: 5'7" Weight: 12.0
Club Honours: Div 3 '85; SPL '92, '93, '94, '95, '96; SLC '92, '93; SC '92, '93, '96
International Honours: S: 40; U21-2

Stuart started the 2000-01 campaign as assistant to new Bradford City manager Chris Hutchings, and when Hutchings was sacked he took over as caretaker-manager for a fortnight until new manager Jim Jeffries arrived, thereafter remaining on the coaching staff. He played as sweeper and right back, as well as in his preferred central midfield role and rarely missed a match all season. Full of energy, he runs around like a teenager, possessing a ferocious tackle and a particularly venomous right foot.

Bradford C (From apprentice on 1/6/1982) FL 235+3/37 FLC 16/3 FAC 12/3 Others 12+1/3
Everton (£850,000 on 1/6/1988) FL 99+4/6 FLC 11/1 FAC 16+2/3 Others 8+1
Glasgow R (£1,200,000 on 15/8/1991) SL 186+8/14 SLC 15/3 SC 25+2 Others 28/2
Bradford C (Free on 4/6/1998) P/FL 112+2/5 FLC 5+1 FAC 4+1 Others 4

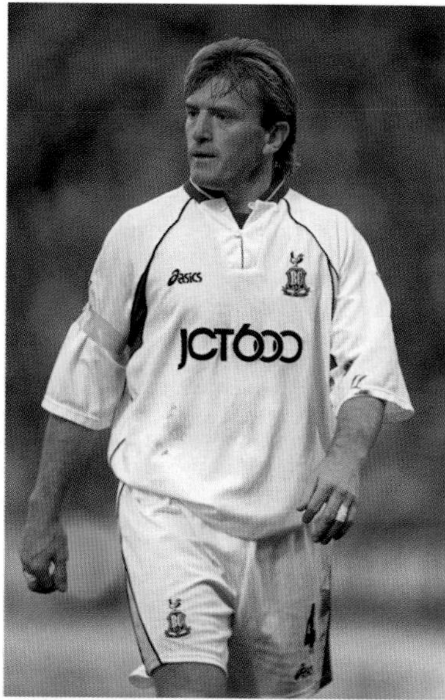

Stuart McCall

McCAMMON Mark Jason
Born: Barnet, 7 August 1978
Height: 6'5" Weight: 14.5

This tall powerful striker made a handful of appearances for Brentford at the start of the 2000-01 campaign but was then injured when scoring his first league goal for his new club at Notts County. It was not until January that he regained a place in the Bees' first-team squad and from then onwards he remained as a regular on the subs' bench as cover for the first-choice pair of Lloyd Owusu and Scott Partridge. He possesses a good work rate but needs to convert more chances to win a regular place in the team. Mark won a runners-up medal in the LDV Vans Trophy coming on as a substitute in the closing minutes of the final against Port Vale when the Bees went down 2-1.

Cambridge U (Free from Cambridge C on 31/12/1996) FL 1+3 FAC 0+1 Others 1
Charlton Ath (Free on 17/3/1999) FL 1+3 FLC 0+1
Swindon T (Loaned on 3/1/2000) FL 4
Brentford (£100,000 + on 18/7/2000) FL 14+10/3 FLC 3/1 Others 2+4/2

McCANN Gavin Peter
Born: Blackpool, 10 January 1978
Height: 5'11" Weight: 11.0
International Honours: E: 1

Gavin finally returned to first-team action at Sunderland last November following a long absence through injury and went on to enjoy a season of significant achievement. The tall central midfielder, renowned for his biting tackles and intelligent distribution, timed his return to perfection, immediately catching the eye of new England boss Sven Goran Eriksson. Selected for the squad for the friendly against Spain in February he received his first full cap as a second half substitute. Other highlights for Gavin included a sensational goal against Arsenal

at Highbury in December when he beat David Seaman from 25 yards, a great strike at Chelsea and a last gasp equaliser against Aston Villa in March. The 2001-02 campaign will be crucial for Gavin with the World Cup just around the corner and a good season with Sunderland could possibly see him on the plane to the Far East.
Everton (From trainee on 1/7/1995) PL 5+6
Sunderland (£500,000 on 27/11/1998) P/FL 48+9/7 FLC 1+3/1 FAC 7+1/2

McCANN Grant Samuel
Born: Belfast, 14 April 1980
Height: 5'10" Weight: 12.0
International Honours: NI: U21-8
This promising West Ham youngster went out on loan to Notts County last August but after looking promising in his first few games he was injured and returned to the Premiership club. In November he joined Third Division Cheltenham Town in a long-term loan deal, staying almost to the end of the season. Performing either at left back or on the left side of midfield he impressed with his attitude, his speed and some fine skills on the ball. He returned to Upton Park at the end of the Nationwide season and went on to make his senior debut as a late substitute in the final game at Middlesbrough before signing a new contract for the Hammers. Grant continued to represent Northern Ireland at U21 level winning a further six caps during the season.
West Ham U (From trainee on 6/7/1998) PL 0+1
Livingston (Loaned on 27/8/1999) SL 0+4
Notts Co (Loaned on 11/8/2000) FL 2 FLC 1
Cheltenham T (Loaned on 17/10/2000) FL 27+3/3 FAC 2 Others 1

McCARTHY Jonathan (Jon) David
Born: Middlesbrough, 18 August 1970
Height: 5'9" Weight: 11.5
International Honours: NI: 18; B-2
Jon returned to fitness for Birmingham City last February after suffering a broken leg towards the end of the 1999-2000 season, and quickly battled through to regain match sharpness. His second start came in the Worthington Cup final against Liverpool and he featured regularly in the squad in the closing weeks of the campaign. Sadly he broke his right leg for the third time within an 18-month period in the unlucky 13th minute of the play-off semi-final second leg at Preston and his future in the game must now be in some doubt. A talented right winger with good pace and tricky ball skills, he had fought his way back into the Northern Ireland squad winning further caps against Norway and Bulgaria before his injury.
Hartlepool U (From juniors on 7/11/1987) FL 0+1 (Free to Shepshed Charterhouse in March 1989)
York C (Free on 22/3/1990) FL 198+1/31 FLC 8/1 FAC 11/3 Others 15/3
Port Vale (£450,000 on 1/8/1995) FL 93+1/12 FLC 10/2 FAC 7/1 Others 8/2
Birmingham C (£1,500,000 on 11/9/1997) FL 104+16/8 FLC 9+1 FAC 4 Others 3+1

Jon McCarthy

McCARTHY Paul Jason
Born: Cork, 4 August 1971
Height: 5'10" Weight: 13.12
International Honours: RoI: U21-10; Yth; Sch
Paul had his best season to date with Wycombe Wanderers in 2000-01, forming an effective partnership with Jamie Bates in the centre of a back four and the pair then joining Jason Cousins in a formidable three-man defence later on. A brave and, strong central defender with great anticipation, he put on a great performance in the FA Cup semi-final against Liverpool. He also proved to be very effective when joining the attack at set pieces and netted a remarkable five goals in FA Cup ties, including a dramatic 119th-minute equaliser in the fifth round replay at Wimbledon. Paul was runner-up to the outstanding Martin Taylor in the club's 'Player of the Season' award.
Brighton & Hove A (From trainee on 26/4/1989) FL 180+1/6 FLC 11/1 FAC 13 Others 12/1
Wycombe W (£100,000 on 5/7/1996) FL 149+11/5 FLC 14+1/3 FAC 17/5 Others 6

Paul McCarthy

McCARTHY Sean Casey
Born: Bridgend, 12 September 1967
Height: 6'1" Weight: 12.12
International Honours: W: B-1
Sean again produced some powerful performances up front for Plymouth last season despite having some disciplinary problems at times. He scored regularly too, finishing with a respectable tally of 11 goals including a brace in the 2-0 win over Devon rivals Exeter City in December. Towards the end of the campaign he switched to a role in the centre of defence where gave some competent performances but it remains to be seen whether this will be a permanent change of position.
Swansea C (Signed from Bridgend T on 22/10/1985) FL 76+15/25 FLC 4+1/3 FAC 5+2/4 Others 9+1/6
Plymouth Arg (£50,000 on 18/8/1988) FL 67+3/19 FLC 7/5 FAC 3/1 Others 0+1/1
Bradford C (£250,000 on 4/7/1990) FL 127+4/60 FLC 10+2/10 FAC 8/2 Others 8+1/7
Oldham Ath (£500,000 on 3/12/1993) P/FL 117+23/42 FLC 10/1 FAC 6+1/1 Others 4/1
Bristol C (Loaned on 26/3/1998) FL 7/1
Plymouth Arg (Signed on 7/8/1998) FL 66+16/19 FLC 3+2/3 FAC 8

McCARTNEY George
Born: Belfast, 29 April 1981
Height: 6'0" Weight: 12.6
International Honours: NI: U21-4; Yth; Sch
This promising young Sunderland defender made his first-team bow last term in the Worthington Cup tie against Luton and went on to appear in a handful more games over

the season. His first Premiership start came against Coventry at Highfield Road in April when he gave an accomplished performance. A left back or central defender whose constructive use of the ball and positional sense belie his tender years, his future at the Stadium of Light looks very promising. He continued to represent Northern Ireland stepping up to make his debut for the U21s against Denmark in October and sitting on the bench for the end of season World Cup qualifiers against Bulgaria and the Czech Republic.
Sunderland (From trainee on 28/5/1998) PL 1+1 FLC 2+1 FAC 0+1

McCLARE Sean Patrick
Born: Rotherham, 12 January 1978
Height: 5'10" Weight: 11.12
International Honours: RoI: U21-3
Sean found himself on the edges of the Barnsley first team last season and enjoyed a short run in the line-up as cover for injuries in the autumn. However soon afterwards he fell out of favour with boss Dave Bassett and went on the transfer list. The change of manager did not improve his prospects and it seems he may need to move on to enable him to get regular first-team football. At his best he is a hard working box-to-box midfield player with an eye for goal.
Barnsley (From trainee on 3/7/1996) FL 29+21/6 FLC 10+3 FAC 5+1/1
Rochdale (Loaned on 22/3/2000) FL 5+4

McCONNELL Barry
Born: Exeter, 1 January 1977
Height: 5'10" Weight: 10.3
Barry suffered a horrific facial injury in a pre-season friendly that required over four hours of surgery and caused him to miss the start of the 2000-01 campaign for Exeter City. He then spent two months on loan at Dr Martens League club Weston-Super-Mare before returning briefly to the Grecians' first-team squad last December. A right wing back or full back he will be hoping for better fortune in the coming season.
Exeter C (From trainee on 4/8/1995) FL 65+44/12 FLC 3+2/1 FAC 2+5 Others 3+1

McCORMICK Luke Martin
Born: Coventry, 15 August 1983
Height: 6'0" Weight: 13.12
Having developed through the club's youth system, Luke made his Football League debut in goal for Plymouth Argyle against Rochdale on the final day of the 2000-01 season. He made several fine saves to deny Argyle's play-off chasing opponents and keep a clean sheet. Luke's promise was further recognised when he appeared for an England Youth XI against a Combined Services team towards the end of the campaign. He will be aiming to extend his experience of first-team football in 2001-02.
Plymouth Arg (Trainee) FL 1

McCULLOCH Lee Henry
Born: Bellshill, 14 May 1978
Height: 6'5" Weight: 13.6
International Honours: S: U21-14
Lee featured regularly for Motherwell in the 2000-01 campaign scoring seven goals in 26 games before joining Second Division Wigan for a club record fee in March. A tall striker whose main strength is his aerial ability, his physical presence makes him a handful for most defences. Lee opened his account for the Latics in the 2-1 win at Wycombe but suffered a number of niggling injuries that ruled him out towards the end of the campaign.
Motherwell (Signed from Cumbernauld U on 17/8/1995) SL 75+47/28 SLC 5+2/2 SC 11+3/4
Wigan Ath (£700,000 on 2/3/2001) FL 10/3 Others 1

McCULLOCH Scott Anderson James
Born: Irvine, 29 November 1975
Height: 6'0" Weight: 13.4
International Honours: S: Sch
This burly defender joined Cardiff City last September and was a regular in the first team squad although he regularly featured on the subs' bench. He was generally used on the left hand side of a back three or in a midfield role but never managed to make any position his own. Scott has considerable ability on the ball and possesses a powerful shot. He was on the open to offers list in the summer.
Glasgow R (From juniors on 1/7/1992)
Hamilton Academical (Signed on 24/3/1995) SL 46+11/4 SLC 1+1 SC 3 Others 4
Dunfermline Ath (Signed on 2/12/1997) SL 37/2 SLC 1 SC 2
Dundee U (Signed on 26/2/1999) SL 19+5 SC 1
Cardiff C (£100,000 on 1/9/2000) FL 9+12/1 FLC 1 FAC 3 Others 1

McDERMOTT Andrew (Andy)
Born: Sydney, Australia, 24 March 1977
Height: 5'9" Weight: 11.3
International Honours: Australia: U23
After joining Notts County shortly before the start of last season Andy produced some exciting displays in the early matches when he was a regular in the line-up. However he struggled with a niggling thigh injury in the second half of the campaign and when he did make the team he appeared in a number of different roles. His contract was cancelled by mutual consent during the summer to allow him to return to Australia and he was reported to have signed for NSL club Northern Spirit at the beginning of June.
Queens Park R (Signed from Australian Institute of Sport on 4/8/1995) FL 6/2
West Bromwich A (£400,000 on 27/3/1997) FL 49+3/1 FLC 4/1 FAC 0+1
Notts Co (Free on 10/8/2000) FL 20+5 FLC 4 FAC 1

McDERMOTT John
Born: Middlesbrough, 3 February 1969
Height: 5'7" Weight: 11.0
Club Honours: AMC '98
John continued to feature for Grimsby Town in 2000-01, his 15th season at Blundell Park, and apart from a mid-season absence through injury he was a regular in the Mariners' defence. In November he achieved the distinction of breaking the club's Football League appearance record, overtaking Keith Jobling's tally of 450 games in the away game against Wolves at Molineux. John is a right-sided defender who provided some of the highlights of a dour season at Grimsby with some exciting forward runs and excellent link up play with Kevin Donovan.
Grimsby T (From trainee on 1/6/1987) FL 455+18/7 FLC 33+2 FAC 29+2/2 Others 21

MacDONALD Charles (Charlie) Lea
Born: Southwark, 13 February 1981
Height: 5'9" Weight: 11.10
Charlie was expected to break into the Charlton Athletic side in 2000-01 but found his chances limited by the abundance of strikers at the club. He is an exciting prospect with a good scoring record in the junior and reserve teams and although he made the starting line up for the home game against Middlesbrough he spent the last couple of months of the season on loan at Cheltenham to gain experience of first-team football. He made a good impression at Whaddon Road and played particularly well in the 2-2 draw at Blackpool when he scored both goals. Although short for a striker Charlie is quick, strong on the ball and has an excellent first touch.
Charlton Ath (From trainee on 10/11/1998) P/FL 1+5 FLC 0+2 FAC 1+1/1
Cheltenham T (Loaned on 16/3/2001) FL 7+1/2

MacDONALD Gary
Born: Germany, 25 October 1979
Height: 6'1" Weight: 12.12
This former Portsmouth trainee had drifted off to Dr Martens League outfit Havant & Waterlooville before Barry Fry snapped him up for Peterborough last January. A promising left-footed central defender he stepped up to make his Football League debut against Rotherham on the final day of the 2000-01 season and put on a fine display.
Portsmouth (From trainee on 3/7/1998. Free to Havant & Waterlooville on 22/7/1999)
Peterborough U (Signed on 16/2/2001) FL 1

McDONALD Thomas (Tom)
Born: Walthamstow, 15 September 1980
Height: 6'2" Weight: 12.4
This young Southend right back was restricted to just one appearance in the first team last season, coming on from the subs' bench for the closing minutes at Scunthorpe in September. Unable to break into the team at Roots Hall he later spent time on loan with Ryman League club Slough Town. Tom is a big strong defender who can also play in the centre of defence if required. He was released by the Blues at the turn of the year and subsequently joined Barking.
Southend U (From trainee on 4/8/1999) FL 1+3

McELHOLM Brendan Anthony
Born: Omagh, 7 July 1982
Height: 5'11" Weight: 12.2
International Honours: NI: Yth
This young Leyton Orient centre half continued to ease gently into senior action last term when he featured fairly regularly in the first-team squad, mostly being used from the subs' bench. Brendan was a member of the O's double-winning youth team and also continued to add to his caps for Northern

Ireland at U18 level. A reliable defender he reads the game well for one so young, and will be looking to make a first team place his own in 2001-02.
Leyton Orient (From trainee on 10/7/2000) FL 6+9 FLC 1+2 Others 1

McEWEN David (Dave)
Born: Westminster, 2 November 1977
Height: 6'0" Weight: 11.0
Dave made good progress in the Tottenham reserve team last season, producing several fine performances. His efforts won a call up to the first-team squad and he made a handful of appearances from the subs' bench early in the new year. A promising youngster he was mostly used in a midfield role last term but was out of contract in the summer and at the time of writing it was unclear what his future would be.
Tottenham H (Free from Dulwich Hamlet on 6/1/2000) PL 0+4

McFLYNN Terence (Terry) Martin
Born: Magherafelt, 27 March 1981
Height: 5'11" Weight: 12.2
International Honours: NI: U21-7; Yth; Sch
This promising Queens Park Rangers youngster stepped up to make his debut from the subs' bench against Stockport last April and then made the starting line-up for the final game of the season at Wolves. A hardworking midfield player he continued to represent Northern Ireland at U21 level winning a further five caps during the season. Terry was one of 15 players released by Rangers in the summer.
Queens Park R (From trainee on 11/5/1998) FL 1+1

McGAVIN Steven (Steve) James
Born: North Walsham, 24 January 1969
Height: 5'9" Weight: 12.8
Club Honours: GMVC '92; FAT '92; Div 2 '95
Having finished the 1999-2000 campaign as Colchester's leading scorer Steve struggled to win a regular place in the starting line-up last season and was regularly used from the subs' bench. An experienced player who can operate either in an attacking midfield role or as a striker he scored just two goals last term, netting a double in the 2-0 win over Cambridge in October. Out of contract in the summer his future was unclear at the time of writing.
Ipswich T (From trainee on 29/1/1987. Free to Thetford T in August 1987)
Colchester U (£10,000 from Sudbury T on 28/7/1992) FL 55+3/17 FLC 2 FAC 6/2 Others 4
Birmingham C (£150,000 on 7/1/1994) FL 16+7/2 FLC 1+1/1 FAC 3+1/2 Others 1+3
Wycombe W (£140,000 on 20/3/1995) FL 103+17/14 FLC 5+2 FAC 6+1/3 Others 4+2
Southend U (Free on 2/2/1999) FL 4+7
Northampton T (Free on 30/7/1999)
Colchester U (Free on 11/10/1999) FL 49+26/18 FLC 3/1 FAC 2 Others 1+1

McGHEE David (Dave) Christopher
Born: Worthing, 19 June 1976
Height: 5'11" Weight: 12.4
A versatile player who can take most positions, Dave was used almost everywhere with the exception of goalkeeper by Leyton Orient last term. He eventually settled down in a central midfield role and by the end of the season he was firmly established in this position. Committed to the cause wherever he plays, he is particularly dangerous from set pieces.
Brentford (From trainee on 15/7/1994) FL 95+22/8 FLC 5+2/1 FAC 9/1 Others 8+1 (Freed on 22/1/1999)
Leyton Orient (Free from Stevenage Borough on 11/11/1999) FL 56+6/4 FLC 4 FAC 4 Others 5

McGIBBON Patrick (Pat) Colm
Born: Lurgan, 6 September 1973
Height: 6'2" Weight: 13.12
Club Honours: AMC '99
International Honours: NI: 7; B-5; U21-1; Sch
This tall and strong defender was a near ever-present for Wigan Athletic during the 2000-01 season. Most effective as a centre back where he formed a solid defensive wall alongside Arjan De Zeeuw, he showed his versatility by also appearing at right back. Pat is quick in the tackle and effective in the air both in defence and when joining the attack at set pieces as was demonstrated by his goal in the 1-1 draw with Luton back in August.
Manchester U (£100,000 from Portadown on 1/8/1992) FLC 1
Swansea C (Loaned on 20/9/1996) FL 1
Wigan Ath (£250,000 on 3/3/1997) FL 145+10/10 FLC 10+1 FAC 8+1 Others 17

McGILL Brendan
Born: Dublin, 22 March 1981
Height: 5'8" Weight: 9.8
International Honours: RoI: Yth (UEFA-U16 '98)
A young right-sided midfielder or right winger, Brendan made his Sunderland debut last season as a second half substitute in the Worthington Cup tie at Luton in September. A regular in the Black Cats' successful reserve team, Brendan was a member of the Republic of Ireland U16 team that defeated Italy to win the UEFA championship in 1998 and is one of a clutch of very promising young players at the Stadium of Light.
Sunderland (Signed from River Valley Rangers on 29/7/1998) FLC 0+1

McGLEISH Scott
Born: Barnet, 10 February 1974
Height: 5'9" Weight: 11.3
Scott started the 2000-01 season in great form for Barnet, netting four times in the first four games, but sadly the goals then dried up and when Tony Cottee took over as manager he found himself playing reserve team football. He played and scored in the LDV Vans Trophy win over Peterborough United but soon afterwards he was transferred to Colchester United, much to the displeasure of the Barnet faithful. He featured regularly in the U's line-up and netted five goals, four of which came in the final month of the season. A tireless forager up front he is also good in the air despite his rather modest height.
Charlton Ath (Free from Edgware T on 24/5/1994) FL 0+6
Leyton Orient (Loaned on 10/3/1995) FL 4+2/1 Others 1/1
Peterborough U (Free on 4/7/1995) FL 3+10 FLC 0+1 FAC 0+1 Others 3+1/2
Colchester U (Loaned on 23/2/1996) FL 10+5/6 Others 2
Cambridge U (Loaned on 2/9/1996) FL 10/7 FLC 1
Leyton Orient (£50,000 on 22/11/1996) FL 36/7 FLC 3/1 FAC 1 Others 1
Barnet (£70,000 on 1/10/1997) FL 106+28/36 FLC 5/4 FAC 3 Others 7+2/1
Colchester U (£15,000 on 11/1/2001) FL 11+10/5

McGLINCHEY Brian Kevin
Born: Londonderry, 26 October 1977
Height: 5'7" Weight: 10.2
International Honours: NI: B-1; U21-14; Yth
Brian struggled to break into the Gillingham first-team squad at the beginning of last season and managed just a single appearance, when he played for 60 minutes of the 1-0 defeat at Grimsby. He subsequently became one of new manager Paul Sturrock's first signings for Plymouth Argyle at the beginning of December, making his debut for the Pilgrims when he came on from the subs' bench in the 2-0 victory at Devon rivals Exeter City. He then continued to hold down a regular first-team position at Home Park, showing excellent close control on the left side of midfield and creating many goal-scoring opportunities from his dangerous crosses into the box.
Manchester C (From trainee on 4/12/1995)
Port Vale (Free on 1/7/1998) FL 10+5/1 FLC 0+1 FAC 1
Gillingham (Free on 3/8/1999) FL 7+7/1 FLC 3+1 FAC 4/1 Others 1
Plymouth Arg (Free on 1/12/2000) FL 17+3 Others 2

McGOVERN Brian
Born: Dublin, 28 April 1980
Height: 6'3" Weight: 12.7
International Honours: RoI: U21-2; Yth
Signed from Arsenal, after an initial loan spell, this versatile defender has yet to win a regular place in the Norwich City starting line-up, despite some assured performances when called upon at senior level. Predominantly a central defender, he likes to play his way out of defence with accurate distribution rather than just clearing it as far from his goal as possible. He has pace, which makes him effective in a right-back role too, and a confidence rare in one so young. Brian has a bright future in the game and will surely figure more regularly in the season ahead.
Arsenal (Signed from Cherry Orchard on 5/9/1997) PL 0+1
Queens Park R (Loaned on 24/12/1999) FL 3+2
Norwich C (£50,000 + on 27/7/2000) FL 3+9/1 FLC 2+1

McGOWAN Gavin Gregory
Born: Blackheath, 16 January 1976
Height: 5'8" Weight: 11.10
Club Honours: FAYC '94
International Honours: E: Yth; Sch
Gavin suffered an ankle injury shortly before the start of the 2000-01 campaign and although he returned to action briefly at the end of September the problem flared up again restricting his first-team opportunities at Luton. A hard-working full back who is strong in the tackle and can operate on either

flank he was one of five players released by new boss Joe Kinnear at the end of April.
Arsenal (From trainee on 1/7/1994) PL 3+3 FAC 1
Luton T (Loaned on 27/3/1997) FL 2
Luton T (Loaned on 11/7/1997) FL 6+2
Luton T (Free on 29/7/1998) FL 42+8 FLC 7 FAC 3

McGOWAN Neil William
Born: Glasgow, 15 April 1977
Height: 5'10" Weight: 10.12
Neil featured regularly for Oxford United at the start of the 2000-01 campaign but then fell out of favour following a change in management and eventually returned to Scotland in March where he played a handful of games for Second Division club Stranraer. He is a pacy tough-tackling defender who has mostly featured at left back for the U's.
Stranraer (Signed from Bonnyton Thistle on 1/8/1995) SL 1+3 SLC 0+1
Albion Rov (Free on 9/8/1996) SL 60+2 SLC 2 SC 4 Others 1
Oxford U (£20,000 on 19/8/1999) FL 26+5 FLC 1+2 FAC 2+1 Others 2

McGRATH John Matthew
Born: Limerick, 27 March 1980
Height: 5'10" Weight: 10.6
International Honours: RoI: U21-5
Having developed with Aston Villa's reserve team over the last couple of seasons, John stepped up to make his Premiership debut when he replaced David Ginola for the second half of the home defeat by Liverpool last January and also featured as a late substitute in the game at Bradford City. A wide left-sided player he can play either as a winger or a wing back. He made his debut for the Republic of Ireland U21s against Holland last September and also featured as a substitute against Estonia the following month.
Aston Villa (Signed from Belvedere YC on 3/9/1999) PL 0+3

McGREAL John
Born: Liverpool, 2 June 1972
Height: 5'11" Weight: 12.8
Having played in the lower divisions all of his career, John was not overawed when he finally reached the top flight and proved that he was capable of holding his own, thus justifying Ipswich boss George Burley's decision to sign him from Tranmere. Very comfortable on the ball he has excellent distribution and the ability to turn defence into attack in an instant. He is a particularly fine crosser of the ball from deep positions. However his best attribute is the last-ditch tackle; on numerous occasions last term he was the last line of defence and managed to win the ball with a clean tackle. He was also very helpful to young Titus Bramble, guiding him through his first full league campaign. Being a Merseyside lad he was particularly satisfied with Town's impressive wins at both Everton and Liverpool. Indeed it was his goal, a superb header from Magilton's floated free kick, which paved the way for the 3-0 win at Goodison.
Tranmere Rov (From trainee on 3/7/1990) FL 193+2/1 FLC 20+1 FAC 8 Others 7+2
Ipswich T (£650,000 on 4/8/1999) P/FL 59+3/1 FLC 9 FAC 2 Others 1

McGREGOR Mark Dale Thomas
Born: Chester, 16 February 1977
Height: 5'11" Weight: 11.5
Mark was in impressive form for Wrexham throughout last season whether he was played as a full back or in a central defensive role. He is a sound defender and particularly useful when pushing up to help out the attack when he uses his height to good effect. He contributed a total of five goals during the campaign including a cracking 35-yard drive which proved to be the winner against Colchester last February. Out of contract in the summer he was reported to have signed for Burnley, much to the displeasure of the Robins' fans.
Wrexham (From trainee on 4/7/1995) FL 237+7/11 FLC 9 FAC 24+1 Others 11

McGREGOR Paul Anthony
Born: Liverpool, 17 December 1974
Height: 5'10" Weight: 11.6
Paul once again showed his goal-scoring potential at Plymouth by netting three goals in three consecutive games last October but unfortunately he could not produce such form consistently throughout the campaign. A skilful player who can play on the right-hand side of midfield or in attack he always gave 100 per cent to the cause but nevertheless he was released by the Pilgrims in April. He was reported to have signed for Northampton in the summer.
Nottingham F (From trainee on 13/12/1991) F/PL 7+23/3 FAC 0+3 Others 0+4/1
Carlisle U (Loaned on 25/9/1998) FL 3/2
Carlisle U (Loaned on 20/11/1998) FL 6+1/1 Others 1
Preston NE (Free on 24/3/1999) FL 1+3
Plymouth Arg (Free on 6/7/1999) FL 75+2/19 FLC 2+1/1 FAC 9/4 Others 0+1

McGUCKIN Thomas **Ian**
Born: Middlesbrough, 24 April 1973
Height: 6'2" Weight: 14.2
Ian joined Oxford United in the 2000 close season and featured regularly for them in the opening games of the campaign before being sidelined by injury at the end of September. He made a brief return in the new year but will be hoping to make a full return to fitness in time for the start of the 2001-02. At his best he is a commanding central defender who is quick for such a big man.
Hartlepool U (From trainee on 20/6/1991) FL 147+5/8 FLC 13+1/1 FAC 6 Others 6
Fulham (£75,000 on 16/6/1997)
Hartlepool U (Loaned on 18/12/1998) FL 8
Oxford U (Free on 7/7/2000) FL 6+1

MACHO Jurgen
Born: Vienna, Austria, 24 August 1977
Height: 6'4" Weight: 13.10
International Honours: Austria: U21
Jurgen arrived at Sunderland from First Vienna in the close season and did not take long to make an impression. When Thomas Sorensen failed appear for the second half of the season's opening game against Arsenal he was pitched straight into action and showed his mettle in impressive fashion, making brilliant stops from Thierry Henry and Robert Pires to preserve the Wearsiders' one-goal lead. With Sorensen sidelined, he remained between the posts for the following four games and although heavy defeats at both Manchester clubs were a rude awakening for him, he made important saves in both matches to save the team from further punishment. Jurgen is an imposing 'keeper who is lightning-quick off his line and he made a second match-winning appearance as a substitute against Manchester United in the Worthington Cup, when an incredible reflex save from a David Healy header in extra time helped the Black Cats to a 2-1 win.
Sunderland (Free from First Vienna, Austria, ex Sportklub, Casino Vienna, on 24/7/2000) PL 4+1 FLC 1+1

McHUGH Frazer
Born: Nottingham, 14 July 1981
Height: 5'9" Weight: 12.5
Frazer found it difficult to break into the Swindon Town line-up last season and managed only a handful of games, all in the second half of the campaign. A hard-working creative midfield player with neat ball control he was released by the Robins in the summer.
Swindon T (From trainee on 5/8/1999) FL 13+6 FLC 0+2 Others 2+1

McINNES Derek John
Born: Paisley, 5 July 1971
Height: 5'8" Weight: 12.0
Club Honours: S Div 2 '95; SPL '97
Having spent a short spell in France with Toulouse, Derek returned across the Channel to sign for West Bromwich Albion, thus linking up again with boss Gary Megson who had previously signed him on loan at Stockport. He was very effective as a midfield anchorman in the early part of the campaign but then suffered a serious cruciate ligament injury to his right knee at Wimbledon towards the end of October. Corrective surgery and a long period of rehabilitation followed and it is hoped he will be fit again for the start of the 2001-02 campaign.
Morton (Signed from Gleniffer Thistle on 13/8/1988) SL 196+25/19 SLC 7+1/1 SC 10+6 Others 10
Glasgow R (£250,000 on 13/11/1995) SL 15+20/1 SLC 4+2/1 SC 0+1 Others 7+2/1 (Transferred to Toulouse, France on 27/12/1999)
Stockport Co (Loaned on 6/11/1998) FL 13 FAC 2
West Bromwich A (£450,000 on 10/8/2000) FL 14/1 FLC 4

McINTYRE James (**Jimmy**)
Born: Dumbarton, 24 May 1972
Height: 5'11" Weight: 12.2
Club Honours: SC '97
International Honours: S: B
Jimmy was a regular in the Reading line-up for much of last season filling the problematic left-midfield berth as well as anyone. A tidy and thoughtful player he crosses the ball accurately and is adept at slipping in at the far post to convert chances.

It was therefore something of a surprise when he was given a free transfer by Royals' boss Alan Pardew at the end of the campaign.

Bristol C (Free from Duntochter BC on 10/10/1991) FL 1 Others 0+1
Exeter C (Loaned on 11/2/1993) FL 12+3/3 Others 4/1
Airdrie (Signed on 23/9/1993) SL 32+22/10 SLC 3+3/1 SC 1+4 Others 2+2/2
Kilmarnock (Signed on 22/3/1996) SL 42+4/9 SLC 2+1 SC 5+1/2 Others 2/1
Reading (£420,000 on 26/3/1998) FL 68+29/14 FLC 2+2 FAC 2+3/1 Others 7+1/1

MACKAY Malcolm (Malky) George
Born: Bellshill, 19 February 1972
Height: 6'1" Weight: 11.7

A traditional stopper-style centre half, Malky won a more regular place in the Norwich City line-up in 2000-2001. His natural competitive spirit earned him many admirers amongst the Canaries' faithful as he combined well in a back three and also in a more orthodox back four. Powerful in the air, he wouldn't claim to be the most graceful player around but he is certainly one of the most effective - his bravery in the challenge preventing many a shot on the City goal.

Queens Park (From juniors on 8/12/1989) SL 68+2/6 SLC 3/2 SC 2 Others 2
Glasgow Celtic (Signed on 6/8/1993) SL 32+5/4 SLC 5+1 SC 4/1 Others 4+1
Norwich C (£350,000 on 18/9/1998) FL 74+12/2 FLC 5+1 FAC 2

McKEEVER Mark Anthony
Born: Londonderry, 16 November 1978
Height: 5'9" Weight: 11.8
International Honours: NI: Yth. RoI: U21-4

Having failed to make a breakthrough at Hillsborough after recovering from injury, Mark joined Bristol Rovers on loan last February and the move became permanent shortly afterwards. A talented young left-winger he impressed with his crossing ability and will be looking to earn a regular place in the Pirates' team in the coming season.

Peterborough U (Trainee) FL 2+1 FLC 1
Sheffield Wed (£500,000 + on 15/4/1997) PL 2+3 FLC 0+1 FAC 0+1
Bristol Rov (Loaned on 10/12/1998) FL 5+2
Reading (Loaned on 8/3/1999) FL 6+1/2
Bristol Rov (Loaned on 8/2/2001) FL 7+5

MACKEN Jonathan Paul
Born: Manchester, 7 September 1977
Height: 5'10" Weight: 12.8
Club Honours: Div 2 '00
International Honours: E: Yth

Jonathan carried on where he had left off the previous season at Preston in 2000-01, finishing as leading scorer again, even though he was now playing at a higher level. He got off to a cracking start at Grimsby in the opening game when a run from the halfway line saw him beat three defenders and finish with a cracking shot, and followed this with his first senior hat-trick in the Worthington Cup tie against Shrewsbury. Groin and hamstring strains meant he missed several games in September, but further highlights included his 50th goal for North End against Barnsley and scoring after only 19 seconds in the return game against Grimsby. Strong on the ball, with a quick turn and a fine footballing brain, Jonathan benefited from playing with the likes of Brian McBride and David Healy, and he can look forward to many more goals in the future.

Manchester U (From trainee on 10/7/1996)
Preston NE (£250,000 on 31/7/1997) FL 127+26/55 FLC 11+2/7 FAC 8+4/1 Others 9+3/1

McKENNA Paul Stephen
Born: Chorley, 20 October 1977
Height: 5'7" Weight: 11.12
Club Honours: Div 2 '00

An increasingly important member of Preston's midfield, where he operated mostly on the left side, Paul made his 100th senior appearance at Huddersfield last October. He went on to be a near ever-present in First Division matches, showing good stamina and deceptive pace. He is a tireless box-to-box player who tackles back and covers well, while he contributed spectacular long-range goals against Crystal Palace, Sheffield Wednesday and Barnsley. His value to the club was shown when he was given an extended contract in mid-season.

Preston NE (From trainee on 2/2/1996) FL 99+15/8 FLC 8 FAC 3+2/2 Others 6+2

McKENZIE Leon Mark
Born: Croydon, 17 May 1978
Height: 5'11" Weight: 11.2

After appearing regularly for Crystal Palace in the second half of 1999-2000 Leon found himself mostly restricted to appearances from the subs' bench at the start of last season and in October he made a permanent move to Peterborough where he had previously enjoyed two successful loan spells. He arrived to a hero's welcome and didn't disappoint the Posh fans, finishing as the club's leading scorer despite some niggling injury problems. He is a talented young striker, lightning-quick and more than a match for most lower division defenders.

Crystal Palace (From trainee on 7/10/1995) F/PL 44+41/7 FLC 5+2/1 FAC 2+4
Fulham (Loaned on 3/10/1997) FL 1+2
Peterborough U (Loaned on 13/8/1998) FL 4/3
Peterborough U (Loaned on 30/11/1998) FL 10/5 Others 1/1
Peterborough U (Free on 13/10/2000) FL 30/13 FAC 3+1

MacKENZIE Neil David
Born: Birmingham, 15 April 1976
Height: 6'2" Weight: 12.12

Neil began the 2000-01 campaign with Cambridge United where he made a number of appearances before being released in November following an off-the-field incident. He subsequently moved on to Third Division new boys Kidderminster where he soon settled in to the team. A talented central midfield player with a great range of passing he is always willing to look for a shot at goal. He netted several spectacular goals for the Harriers, notably with a direct free kick at Halifax in January and with a cracking 35-yarder in the 2-1 win over Barnet the following month.

Stoke C (From trainee at West Bromwich A on 9/11/1995) FL 15+27/1 FLC 1+1 FAC 0+1 Others 0+1
Cambridge U (Loaned on 24/3/1999) FL 3+1/1
Cambridge U (£45,000 on 14/10/1999) FL 20+8 FLC 1+1 FAC 5 Others 0+1
Kidderminster Hrs (Free on 24/11/2000) FL 20+3/3 FAC 0+1 Others 2

MACKIE John
Born: London, 5 July 1976
Height: 6'0" Weight: 12.6

Having spent the 1999-2000 campaign developing in the reserves at Reading, John stepped up to make his senior debut in the Worthington Cup first round first leg tie against Leyton Orient. He enjoyed a short run in the first team when injuries ruled out Barry Hunter and Adrian Williams before losing his place when Adrian Whitbread arrived on loan. A stocky central defender he gave some promising displays and will be hoping to feature more regularly in the coming season.

Reading (Free from Sutton U on 5/11/1999) FL 7+3 FLC 1+1 FAC 3 Others 0+1

McKINLAY William (Billy)
Born: Glasgow, 22 April 1969
Height: 5'9" Weight: 11.6
International Honours: S: 29; B-1; U21-6; Yth; Sch

After recovering from a long-term groin injury, Billy found himself unable to get into the Blackburn Rovers' line-up at the beginning of last term and in October he joined Leicester City on loan. Unfortunately his only appearance for the Foxes was in the nightmare home defeat by First Division Crystal Palace in the Worthington Cup when he had little chance to impress on a generally lacklustre evening. He subsequently moved on to Premiership strugglers Bradford City in another loan deal, becoming new manager Jim Jeffries' first signing. A tough-tackling, no-nonsense midfielder he went straight into the side and enjoyed a decent run of action until his groin problem flared up again in early February and he made just one more first-team appearance for the Bantams. Out of contract in the summer his future was unclear at the time of writing.

Dundee U (Signed from Hamilton Thistle on 24/6/1985) SL 210+10/23 SLC 21/3 SC 23+3/4 Others 17/2
Blackburn Rov (£1,750,000 on 14/10/1995) PL 76+14/3 FLC 4/1 FAC 7+1 Others 1
Leicester C (Loaned on 27/10/2000) FLC 1
Bradford C (Free on 24/11/2000) PL 10+1 FAC 1

McLAREN Paul Andrew
Born: High Wycombe, 17 November 1976
Height: 6'0" Weight: 13.4

Paul was an important figure in the centre of the park for Luton Town last season and was badly missed during a two-month absence after he suffered a knee ligament injury in the match against Reading shortly before Christmas. A hard-working combative mid-field player he was out of contract in the summer and was reported to have signed for Sheffield Wednesday.

Luton T (From trainee on 5/1/1994) FL 137+30/4 FLC 10+4/1 FAC 11/2 Others 9

McLAUGHLIN Brian
Born: Bellshill, 14 May 1974
Height: 5'4" Weight: 8.10
Club Honours: SC '95
International Honours: S: U21-8

Brian was placed on the transfer list by new Wigan Athletic boss Bruce Rioch at the start of the 2000-01 season and struggled to win a regular place in the first team. At his best he is an effective left winger with the ability to accelerate past defenders and deliver accurate crosses into the box. His only goal last season came in the LDV Vans Trophy first round tie at Oldham.

Glasgow Celtic (Free from Giffnock North AFC on 7/7/1992) SL 38+37/5 SLC 1+4 SC 3+4/1 Others 2+3
Dundee U (Free on 27/3/1999) SL 1+2
Wigan Ath (Free on 2/7/1999) FL 13+5 FLC 4+1 FAC 1+1 Others 2/1

McLEAN Aaron
Born: Hammersmith, 25 May 1983
Height: 5'6" Weight: 10.2

Injured at the start of last season, Aaron fought his way back into the Leyton Orient first-team squad in the new year. After making the starting line-up for the first time against Cardiff, he came off the subs' bench to score with a bullet header in the draw at Shrewsbury. However just as he seemed on the verge of winning a regular place in the squad he suffered a broken ankle playing in a Youth Alliance Cup tie against Mansfield and was sidelined until the end of the season. Aaron is a small but pacy forward with bags of enthusiasm.

Leyton Orient (Trainee) FL 1+4/1 Others 0+1

McLEOD Kevin Andrew
Born: Liverpool, 12 September 1980
Height: 5'11" Weight: 11.3

A direct and pacy left winger, Kevin also possesses the streak of ruthlessness necessary to make the grade in the Premiership. He showed this within minutes of his second appearance for Everton, when he came on and was almost immediately booked against Arsenal. If nothing the incident proved that Kevin is certainly no shrinking violet. He went on to make five substitute appearances throughout the campaign and will be looking to add to that experience next season.

Everton (From trainee on 24/9/1998) PL 0+5

McLOUGHLIN Alan Francis
Born: Manchester, 20 April 1967
Height: 5'8" Weight: 10.10
International Honours: RoI: 42; B-3

Alan struggled to find his best form at Wigan last season and his only Second Division outings came from the subs' bench. His only starts came in the LDV Vans Trophy ties when he showed he could still score by netting twice in the 3-2 first round win at Oldham. He is a creative figure in the middle of the park with neat skills and the ability to get forward into good attacking positions.

Manchester U (From apprentice on 25/4/1985)
Swindon T (Free on 15/8/1986) FL 101+5/19 FLC 11+3/5 FAC 4+2 Others 10/1
Torquay U (Loaned on 13/3/1987) FL 21+3/4
Southampton (£1,000,000 on 13/12/1990) FL 22+2/1 FLC 0+1 FAC 4 Others 1
Aston Villa (Loaned on 30/9/1991) Others 1
Portsmouth (£400,000 on 17/2/1992) FL 297+12/54 FLC 27/7 FAC 15+1/7 Others 9/1
Wigan Ath (£250,000 on 9/12/1999) FL 11+8/1 FLC 0+1 Others 3/2

McMAHON David
Born: Dublin, 17 January 1981
Height: 6'1" Weight: 11.5
International Honours: RoI: Yth (UEFA-U16 '98)

This former Republic of Ireland U18 international was loaned by Newcastle to Falkirk in the early part of last season and shortly after his return he had a second loan spell, this time at Third Division Darlington. He scored on his first start against Lincoln City but only found the net once more in ten outings. A tall young striker he impressed with his aerial ability and strong running. Out of contract in the summer his future was uncertain at the time of writing.

Newcastle U (From trainee on 23/2/1998)
Falkirk (Loaned on 5/9/2000) SL 3 SLC 1/1
Darlington (Loaned on 15/12/2000) FL 5+3/1 Others 2+1/1

McMAHON Francis
Born: Fazackerley, 21 December 1981
Height: 6'0" Weight: 13.2

This first-year professional with Wigan Athletic was hampered by a series of minor injuries in 2000-01 and was limited to a single first-team appearance in the LDV Vans Trophy second round tie at Walsall in January. A versatile defender he was released by the Latics in the close season.

Wigan Ath (From trainee on 3/7/2000) Others 1

McMILLAN Stephen Thomas
Born: Edinburgh, 19 January 1976
Height: 5'10" Weight: 11.10
International Honours: S: U21-4

Stephen featured regularly for Scottish Premier League side Motherwell in 2000-01 before moving south to join Wigan Athletic along with his colleague Lee McCulloch. Although essentially a left back he is very versatile and can also play in the centre of defence and in midfield. Strong in the tackle and very confident, he is quick to move up in support of the attack and can deliver a telling cross. He made a sound start for the Latics but after just half-a-dozen games he suffered a hamstring injury that kept him on the sidelines in the closing weeks of the season.

Motherwell (Signed from Troon Juniors on 19/8/1993) SL 144+8/6 SLC 9 SC 13+1
Wigan Ath (£550,000 on 2/3/2001) FL 6

McNEIL Martin James
Born: Rutherglen, 28 September 1980
Height: 6'1" Weight: 12.7

Having been a regular in the Cambridge United line-up in 1999-2000, Martin had to wait until the new year before he got his first chance last season. He enjoyed a brief run in the team before dropping back to continue his development in the reserves. He is a talented young centre half with a commanding presence who is very composed on the ball.

Cambridge U (From trainee on 15/12/1998) FL 38+3 FLC 1 FAC 6 Others 1

McNIVEN David Jonathan
Born: Leeds, 27 May 1978
Height: 5'11" Weight: 12.0

David joined York City in August 2000 and netted a number of crucial goals in the first half of the season, however the goals seemed to dry up in the new year when his formed dipped a little. Nevertheless he finished the 2000-2001 campaign as top scorer for the Minstermen with ten goals. At his best he is a lively forward with good pace and an eye for goal. David is the twin brother of Oldham's Scott McNiven and the son of former Bradford City star David McNiven. He was released in the summer.

Oldham Ath (From trainee on 25/10/1995) FL 8+18/2 FLC 1+2
York C (Free on 9/8/2000) FL 25+16/8 FLC 1+1 FAC 4/2 Others 1

David McNiven

McNIVEN Scott Andrew
Born: Leeds, 27 May 1978
Height: 5'10" Weight: 12.1
International Honours: S: U21-1; Yth

Scott missed the start of the 2000-01 season after suffering a fractured cheekbone during the summer break but quickly returned to the side and rarely missed a game for the remainder of the campaign. A commanding defender with great stamina he is the son of former Bradford City star David McNiven and twin brother of York's David McNiven. He was placed on the open to offers list in the summer.

Oldham Ath (From trainee on 25/10/1995) FL 172+15/3 FLC 11+1 FAC 15+1/1 Others 8

McPHAIL Stephen
Born: Westminster, 9 December 1979
Height: 5'10" Weight: 12.0
Club Honours: FAYC '97
International Honours: RoI: 2; U21-6; Yth; (UEFA-U18 '98)

After establishing himself in the first-team squad in 1999-2000, Leeds United's mercurial Irish midfield player suffered more than most last term in an injury-

ravaged season for the club. He featured in just ten games, appearing in the starting line-up on four occasions, and will be aiming to re-establish himself in the side in 2001-02. A talented midfield player with a sweet left foot, superb vision and the ability to unlock defences, he was sorely missed.
Leeds U (From trainee on 23/12/1996) PL 37+15/2 FLC 2+1 FAC 3 Others 12+2

McSPORRAN Jermaine
Born: Manchester, 1 January 1977
Height: 5'8" Weight: 10.10
Jermaine featured regularly for Wycombe Wanderers last season before suffering cruciate ligament damage in the match against Wigan in December. The injury required corrective surgery and he failed to make a full recovery before the end of the campaign. Featuring as either a right-sided midfielder or striker, he is a talented youngster whose blistering pace enables him to ghost past defenders with ease.
Wycombe W (Signed from Oxford C on 5/11/1998) FL 63+21/15 FLC 8/3 FAC 5+1 Others 2+2/2

McSWEENEY David
Born: Basildon, 28 December 1981
Height: 5'11" Weight: 11.7
David made his Football League debut for Southend last October when he came on as a substitute in the 1-0 home victory over York City. He occasionally deputised at right back for Martin Booty and was given an extended run in the Blues' team in the closing weeks of the season. A strong tackler he showed good positional awareness and was not afraid to push forward when given the opportunity. He will be looking to feature more regularly in the first-team squad in the 2001-02 campaign.
Southend U (From trainee on 30/4/2001) FL 10+1 FAC 0+2 Others 4

McVEIGH Paul
Born: Belfast, 6 December 1977
Height: 5'6" Weight: 10.5
International Honours: NI: 1; U21-11; Yth; Sch
Paul found it difficult to break through into the Norwich side in his first full season at Carrow Road last season, although he did enough to earn himself a year's extension to his contract. A clever ball-playing striker, he has an excellent first touch and a sharpness in front of goal. He also has the ability to create chances for his team-mates with his vision and incisive passing in the final third.
Tottenham H (From trainee on 10/7/1996) PL 2+1/1
Norwich C (Free on 23/3/2000) FL 6+6/1 FLC 0+1

MADDISON Lee Robert
Born: Bristol, 5 October 1972
Height: 5'11" Weight: 12.4
Club Honours: S Div 1 '98
Lee linked up with his old boss Ian Atkins again last October when he joined Carlisle United on loan and impressed sufficiently to earn a permanent move shortly afterwards. He went on to become a near ever-present at left wing back for the Cumbrians in their remaining matches. He provided a solid presence on the left-hand side of the defence and produced some effective forays down the flank to assist the attack.
Bristol Rov (From trainee on 18/7/1991) FL 68+5 FLC 4 FAC 2 Others 6+1
Northampton T (£25,000 on 22/9/1995) FL 55 FLC 3+1 FAC 3 Others 4+1
Dundee (Free on 23/7/1997) SL 59+6/1 SLC 3 SC 3/1
Carlisle U (Free on 13/10/2000) FL 34 FAC 2

MADDISON Neil Stanley
Born: Darlington, 2 October 1969
Height: 5'10" Weight: 12.0
Now very much in the twilight of his career Neil managed just a single appearance for Middlesbrough last term, appearing as a substitute in the Worthington Cup third round tie at Wimbledon. In November he joined Barnsley on a month's loan and was just settling in when he injured his groin in training and returned to the Teesside club. He later joined Bristol City on loan for the final two months of the campaign to provide experienced cover after an injury to Brian Tinnion. He produced a stunning goal in the 2-2 draw with Oldham at the end of March but failed to make the expected impact at Ashton Gate and returned to the Riverside. Out of contract in the summer, he was reported to have signed for Darlington during the summer. A tireless worker in the centre of midfield, he is always willing to take the ball off the defence and start building from the back, while he regularly gets in scoring positions when he moves up to join the attack.
Southampton (From trainee on 14/4/1988) F/PL 149+20/19 FLC 9+5 FAC 8+5 Others 1
Middlesbrough (£250,000 on 31/10/1997) P/FL 32+24/4 FLC 7+1 FAC 4
Barnsley (Loaned on 4/11/2000) FL 3
Bristol C (Loaned on 16/3/2001) FL 4+3/1

MADDIX Daniel (Danny) Shawn
Born: Ashford, 11 October 1967
Height: 5'11" Weight: 12.2
International Honours: Jamaica: 2
Danny spent a large part of last season at Queens Park Rangers recovering from a serious knee injury suffered in November 1999 and it was not until March that he returned to make an appearance from the subs' bench at Watford. He made the starting line-up for the match against Burnley shortly afterwards but was then sidelined through suspension and did not re-appear in the first team before the end of the season. The longest-serving player at Loftus Road he was released in the summer.
Tottenham H (From apprentice on 25/7/1985)
Southend U (Loaned on 1/11/1986) FL 2
Queens Park R (Free on 23/7/1987) F/PL 259+35/13 FLC 25/3 FAC 21+2/2 Others 2+3

MAGILTON James (Jim)
Born: Belfast, 6 May 1969
Height: 6'0" Weight: 14.2
International Honours: NI: 47; U23-2; U21-1; Yth; Sch
One of the main inspirations of Ipswich's successful return to the top flight, Jim used all his experience to set up numerous attacks with a string of delightful, precision passes. His only Premiership goal came early in the season when he converted a second-half penalty at Leicester but when he missed another spot kick in the Worthington Cup tie with Millwall he handed over penalty duties to Marcus Stewart. One of his best performances came in the win at Liverpool, one of his previous clubs, when he provided some inspirational direction from the centre of the park. As soon as the season ended he went into hospital for an operation on his legs but he was expected to be fit for pre-season training for the 2001-02 campaign. Jim continued his international career with Northern Ireland and had the honour of captaining them.
Liverpool (From apprentice on 14/5/1986)
Oxford U (£100,000 on 3/10/1990) FL 150/34 FLC 9/1 FAC 8/4 Others 6/3
Southampton (£600,000 on 11/2/1994) PL 124+6/13 FLC 12+2/2 FAC 12/3
Sheffield Wed (£1,600,000 on 10/9/1997) PL 14+13/1 FLC 2 FAC 1
Ipswich T (£682,500 on 15/1/1999) P/FL 84+6/8 FLC 9/1 FAC 2+1 Others 5/3

MAHER Kevin Andrew
Born: Ilford, 17 October 1976
Height: 6'0" Weight: 12.5
International Honours: RoI: U21-4
Kevin had a fantastic season for Southend United in 2000-01 when he was an inspiration to the side throughout the campaign. Operating in a central midfield role his passing and tackling were of a high quality and he always worked hard for the team. Although he only contributed a couple of goals he set up numerous opportunities for his colleagues. Kevin deservedly won the club's 'Player of the Year' award at the end of the season.
Tottenham H (From trainee on 1/7/1995)
Southend U (Free on 23/1/1998) FL 110+7/7 FLC 7 FAC 5 Others 6+1/1

MAHON Alan Joseph
Born: Dublin, 4 April 1978
Height: 5'10" Weight: 11.5
International Honours: RoI: 1; U21-18; Yth; Sch
Out of contract at Tranmere in the summer, Alan chose to move to Sporting Lisbon where he found it difficult to break into the side, although one of his rare appearances came in a European Champions' League game against Real Madrid. He returned to Blackburn on loan in December and went on to produce some fine performances to assist the club in their bid for promotion. A very skilful and imaginative midfield player he impressed with a fine first touch and some excellent distribution. Alan was reported to have signed permanently for Rovers in the summer.
Tranmere Rov (From trainee on 7/4/1995) FL 84+36/13 FLC 12+6/2 FAC 3+2 (Free to Sporting Lisbon, Portugal on 1/7/2000)
Blackburn Rov (Free on 14/12/2000) FL 14+4 FAC 6

MAHON Gavin Andrew
Born: Birmingham, 2 January 1977
Height: 6'0" Weight: 13.2
Club Honours: Div 3 '99
Gavin began the 2000-01 campaign playing

in a familiar midfield role, but injuries led to him switching to centre back where he produced some excellent performances and attracted the attention of a number of scouts from higher clubs. He is a skilful player, comfortable with either foot and has a useful shot. He scored his only goal of the campaign with a 40-yard drive in the 2-1 win at Bristol City last December and later in the season won a runners-up medal in the LDV Vans Trophy when he appeared for the Bees in the final at Cardiff when they were narrowly defeated by Port Vale.
Wolverhampton W (From trainee on 3/7/1995)
Hereford U (Free on 12/7/1996) FL 10+1/1 FLC 4
Brentford (£50,000 + on 17/11/1998) FL 106/8 FLC 6 FAC 3 Others 12

MAKIN Christopher (Chris) Gregory
Born: Manchester, 8 May 1973
Height: 5'10" Weight: 11.2
Club Honours: Div 1 '99
International Honours: E: U21-5; Yth; Sch
Two-footed and equally adaptable on either flank, Chris's powerful tackling made him something of a cult hero with the Sunderland faithful last term. He was one of the Wearsiders' most consistent performers when he was surprisingly allowed to leave to join Ipswich Town in March. Ironically he made his debut against Aston Villa, the team he had opposed in his last game for the Black Cats, and due to the vagaries of the fixture list it was a month after this that he made his first appearance at Portman Road for Town. He celebrated in style delivering a deep cross from which Alun Armstrong scored the goal that brought a home point against Liverpool. Equally comfortable on either flank or even in the centre of defence, he is a solid tackler who has a good turn of pace and should enhance the quality of the squad at Ipswich.
Oldham Ath (From trainee on 2/11/1991) F/PL 93+1/4 FLC 7 FAC 11 Others 1+1 (Transferred to Marseille, France during 1996 close season)
Wigan Ath (Loaned on 28/8/1992) FL 14+1/2
Sunderland (£500,000 on 5/8/1997) P/FL 115+5/1 FLC 13 FAC 7+1 Others 1+1
Ipswich T (£1,250,000 on 7/3/2001) PL 10

MALESSA Antony George
Born: Ascot, 13 November 1980
Height: 6'0" Weight: 12.12
Antony had few opportunities to demonstrate his ability in goal for Bristol City last season although he proved an effective deputy for Steve Phillips when called upon. He made his senior debut in the Worthington Cup first round first leg tie against Brentford and went on to feature twice more during the season. He was a regular in the reserve team where he showed himself to be a fine shot stopper. Antony was out of contract in the summer when he was released by City.
Bristol C (From trainee at Southampton on 5/2/1999) FL 0+1 FLC 1 Others 1

MALEY Mark
Born: Newcastle, 26 January 1981
Height: 5'9" Weight: 12.3
International Honours: E: Yth; Sch
This young Sunderland full back made one senior appearance last season in the 3-0 Worthington Cup victory against Luton at the Stadium of Light before joining Blackpool on loan a week later. He received a couple of first-team outings for the Seasiders and followed this with another loan spell at Northampton where he played two games at right back before being carried off injured and returning to Wearside.
Sunderland (From trainee on 30/1/1998) FLC 3
Blackpool (Loaned on 6/10/2000) FL 2
Northampton T (Loaned on 24/11/2000) FL 2

MALZ Stefan
Born: Ludwigshafen, Germany, 15 June 1972
Height: 6'0" Weight: 12.3
Stefan again struggled to break into the Arsenal first team last season and remained very much on the fringes of the squad. He had to wait until January before making his first appearance as a substitute in the Premiership game at Charlton and he also featured from the subs' bench in the FA Cup ties at Carlisle and Queens Park Rangers. A left-sided midfield player, he is comfortable on the ball, can pass accurately and tracks back well. He was reported to have signed for Kaiserslautern in the summer.
Arsenal (£610,000 from TSV 1860 Munich, Germany, ex Pfingstweide, Oppau, Ludwigshafen, Darmstadt, VJR Mannheim, on 14/7/1999) PL 2+4/1 FLC 2/1 FAC 2+2 Others 0+2

MAMOUM Blaise Noel Emmanuel
Born: Banmenda, Cameroon, 25 December 1979
Height: 5'9" Weight: 11.5
International Honours: Cameroon: Yth
Blaise had spent the whole of the 1999-2000 campaign on loan at Red Star Paris before being released on his return to St Etienne in the close season. He linked up with Scunthorpe United last August and came on from the subs' bench for the last 20 minutes at Rochdale. He failed to impress and after playing in a reserve game he was released later that week. After a brief trial at Oldham he signed for the German Regionnaliga Nord club Werder Bremen Amateure where he was still playing at the end of the season. A former Cameroon U17 international, he is a right-sided midfielder with a good touch.
Scunthorpe U (Free from St Etienne, France on 25/8/2000) FL 0+1

MANCINI Roberto
Born: Jesi, Italy, 27 November 1964
Height: 5'11" Weight: 11.12
International Honours: Italy: 36
A genuine world-class star, Roberto joined Leicester City from Lazio, where he had been player-coach under Sven Goran Eriksson, He added some much-needed experience to the Foxes' forward line and showed touches of genuine class in an all too brief stay. Indeed he might have been able to mentor Ade Akinbiyi more effectively if he had not been tempted back to his native land to take over as coach of Fiorentina in mid-February.
Leicester C (Loaned from Lazio, Italy, ex Sampdoria, Bologna, on 19/1/2001) PL 3+1 FAC 1

MANN Neil
Born: Nottingham, 19 November 1972
Height: 5'10" Weight: 12.1
After two years of recurring knee problems Neil returned to full fitness last February when he featured in Hull City's win at Cheltenham. He remains a popular figure with the Tigers fans and received a truly emotional ovation after coming on from the subs' bench in the victory over Leyton Orient the following week. Although unable to re-establish a regular place in the play-off bound team his successful recovery was duly rewarded in March when he was offered a new three-year contract. Neil is a skilful left sided midfield player and the son of former Notts County star Arthur Mann.
Grimsby T (From Notts Co juniors on 6/9/1990)
Hull C (Free from Grantham T, ex Spalding, on 30/7/1993) FL 138+37/9 FLC 12+4 FAC 6+2/1 Others 8+2/1

MANNINGER Alexander (Alex)
Born: Salzburg, Austria, 4 June 1977
Height: 6'2" Weight: 13.3
Club Honours: FAC '98; CS '99
International Honours: Austria: 7; U21; Yth
Alex again provided reliable cover for 'keeper David Seaman at Arsenal last term. In November, he deputised for Seaman in nine straight Premiership games, and would have played the previous three had he not been injured himself. With his rival approaching the end of his career, Alex will be hoping to establish himself as the Gunners' first choice in the 2001-02 season. An Austrian international, he is a fine shot stopper, quick off his line and uses his size to command the box at set pieces.
Arsenal (£500,000 from Graz, Austria, ex Vorwaerts, Salzburg, on 17/6/1997) PL 38+1 FLC 7 FAC 9 Others 9

MANSELL Lee Richard Samuel
Born: Gloucester, 28 October 1982
Height: 5'9" Weight: 10.10
Another product of Luton Town's successful youth scheme, Lee burst on the scene when called up for the FA Cup third round replay against Queens Park Rangers, scoring in the first minute of the game. A skilful central or left-sided midfield player he has excellent vision and good distribution. Lee's progress was recognised when he received the 'Young Player of the Season' award at Kenilworth Road and was offered a new three-year contract by new boss Joe Kinnear.
Luton T (From trainee on 16/5/2001) FL 17+1/5 FAC 1/1

MANSLEY Chad Andrew
Born: Newcastle, Australia, 13 November 1980
Height: 6'1" Weight: 10.8
International Honours: Australia: Sch
A promising striker, Chad had a brief trial at Watford before joining Leyton Orient on a non-contract basis. He made his debut as a substitute in the Third Division game against Darlington and also featured from the bench for the whole of the second half of both the FA Cup tie against Northwich and the LDV Vans Trophy game with Wycombe.

A former captain of the Australian schools team, he subsequently returned home and in February rejoined his old club, who had by now reformed under the name Newcastle United.

Leyton Orient (Free from Newcastle Breakers, Australia on 30/11/2000) FL 0+1 FAC 0+1 Others 0+1

[MARCELINO] ELENA SIERRA Marcelino
Born: Santander, Spain, 26 September 1971
Height: 6'2" Weight: 13.0
International Honours: Spain: 5

As in his first season at St James Park, injuries wrecked any chance of Marcelino settling into the Newcastle side on a regular basis in 2000-01. He snapped a tendon in his finger in the opening game of the season at Old Trafford, and on his return he reported a groin strain and was absent again until mid-December when he made three consecutive appearances. However after the turn of the year he only played in another three games, one of them as a substitute, to conclude a very disappointing term. A tall and strong central defender he will be hoping to remain free from injury in 2001-02.

Newcastle U (£5,800,000 from Real Mallorca, Spain, ex Sporting Gijon, on 16/7/1999) PL 15+2 FAC 2+1 Others 2

MARCELLE Clinton (Clint) Sherwin
Born: Trinidad, 9 November 1968
Height: 5'4" Weight: 10.0
International Honours: Trinidad & Tobago

Clint was invited for a trial at Boothferry Park after playing for Goole against Hull in a pre-season friendly, and subsequently stayed with the Tigers on monthly contracts. He shouldered Hull's attacking burden for much of the first half of the 2000-01 campaign until he suffered a foot injury in December. The signing of Kevin Francis and Rodney Rowe brought greater competition and during the club's severe financial problems in the new year he decided to join the mini-exodus from Boothferry Park to Darlington. He struck up a good understanding with big John Williams in a classic 'little and large' strike force but failed to score for the Quakers in the closing games of the season. He is a quick and tricky striker who impressed with his darting runs and nimble footwork.

Barnsley (Free from Felgueiras, Portugal on 8/8/1996) F/PL 37+32/8 FLC 3+5 FAC 6+1/1 (Freed on 29/2/2000)
Scunthorpe U (Loaned on 10/10/1999) FL 8+2 FAC 1
Hull C (Free from Goole T on 1/9/2000) FL 16+7/2 FLC 1 FAC 1
Darlington (Free on 23/2/2001) FL 8+4

[MARCELO] CIPRIANO DOS SANTOS Marcelo
Born: Niteroi, Brazil, 11 October 1969
Height: 6'0" Weight: 13.8

Marcelo began the 2000-01 season as a regular in the Birmingham City team, scoring a fine 25-yarder at Nottingham Forest, but then suffered injury niggles and was in and out of the side. Prior to the defeat by Wimbledon in April, the Blues had won nine and drawn two of the 11 games in which he had started. A striker who is a real trier, he comes alive in the penalty box and many observers felt he deserved an extended run in the team.

Sheffield U (£400,000 from Deportivo Alaves, Spain, ex Benfica, on 6/10/1997) FL 47+19/24 FLC 3+1/2 FAC 10+1/5 Others 1+1/1
Birmingham C (£500,000 on 25/10/1999) FL 30+26/12 FLC 2+3/1 FAC 1+2 Others 3+1/1

MARDON Paul Jonathan
Born: Bristol, 14 September 1969
Height: 6'0" Weight: 12.0
International Honours: W: 1; B-1

This injury-plagued West Bromwich Albion central defender finally returned to match fitness for the start of last season and was then loaned to Third Division Plymouth in September in an attempt to resurrect his career. He made three appearances for the Pilgrims scoring with a header in the 5-2 defeat at Cheltenham. Shortly after his return to The Hawthorns he went out again on loan to Wrexham where he had the misfortune to dislocate a shoulder on his club debut at Reading. After featuring in a handful of league games and an FA Wales Premier Cup tie against Carmarthen he returned to The Hawthorns at the beginning of December. The following month Paul announced his retirement from the game due to recurring knee problems.

Bristol C (From trainee on 29/1/1988) FL 29+13 FLC 3+3/1 Others 1
Doncaster Rov (Loaned on 13/9/1990) FL 3
Birmingham C (£115,000 on 16/8/1991) FL 54+10 FLC 11+1 FAC 1 Others 3
West Bromwich A (£400,000 on 18/11/1993) FL 125+14/3 FLC 10 FAC 3 Others 2
Oldham Ath (Loaned on 8/1/1999) FL 12/3
Plymouth Arg (Loaned on 16/9/2000) FL 3/1
Wrexham (Loaned on 16/10/2000) FL 6+1

MARGAS Javier
Born: Chile, 10 May 1969
Height: 6'1" Weight: 13.8
International Honours: Chile: 62

Javier played well for West Ham in the first three Premiership games of last season but then suffered a knee injury in the Worthington Cup tie against Walsall. He subsequently returned to Chile for treatment and eventually announced in January that he had retired from the game. A classy defender he was good in the air and very effective in the tackle.

West Ham U (£2,000,000 from Catolica University, Chile, ex Colo Colo, FC America, on 3/8/1998) PL 21+3/1 FLC 3 Others 2+1

MARGETSON Martyn Walter
Born: Neath, 8 September 1971
Height: 6'0" Weight: 14.0
International Honours: W: B-1; U21-7; Yth; Sch

Huddersfield Town's reserve goalkeeper eventually got his chance at the MacAlpine Stadium last term some two years after his previous senior appearance. Having set a near record of appearances as an unused substitute he finally stepped off the bench when Nico Vaesen was sent off at Blackburn and then covered for the whole of the following game at Wimbledon when Vaesen was suspended. However Martyn never let the side down, handling the ball well and making some good saves from both close- and long-range efforts.

Manchester C (From trainee on 5/7/1990) F/PL 51 FLC 2+2 FAC 3 Others 1
Bristol Rov (Loaned on 8/12/1993) FL 2+1
Southend U (Free on 3/8/1998) FL 32 FLC 4 FAC 1 Others 1
Huddersfield T (Signed on 6/8/1999) FL 1+1

MARINELLI Carlos Ariel
Born: Buenos Aires, Argentina, 14 March 1982
Height: 5'8" Weight: 11.6
International Honours: Argentina: Yth

This exciting Middlesbrough youngster eased his way into the first team last season when he featured in 13 Premiership games, almost exclusively being used from the substitutes' bench. An attacking midfield player he has skills galore being strong, fast and full of confidence, while he is an explosive dead-ball kicker. Although in the past, like so many others to emerge from South America, he has been burdened with the label 'the next Maradonna', there is certainly no doubt that he has plenty of talent.

Middlesbrough (£1,500,000 from Boca Juniors, Argentina on 27/10/1999) PL 2+13 FLC 0+1

MARRIOTT Alan
Born: Bedford, 3 September 1978
Height: 6'1" Weight: 12.5

Alan was Lincoln City's first choice goalkeeper last season until a knee injury in early December forced him to undergo a cartilage operation. He was out for two months and was then unable to replace loan 'keeper Chris Day, and it was not until Day returned to Watford that he was able to regain his place. He is a fine shot stopper who is improving as he gains greater experience of first-team football.

Tottenham H (From trainee on 3/7/1997)
Lincoln C (Free on 5/8/1999) FL 48 FLC 2 FAC 1 Others 2

MARRIOTT Andrew (Andy)
Born: Sutton in Ashfield, 11 October 1970
Height: 6'1" Weight: 12.6
Club Honours: Div 4 '92; FMC '92; WC '95
International Honours: E: U21-1; Yth; Sch. W: 5

Unable to get in the team at Sunderland, Andy spent two months on loan at Second Division Wigan Athletic as cover for the injured Roy Carroll. Mostly featuring on the subs' bench as deputy to Derek Stillie he made two first-team appearances in the LDV Vans Trophy matches. In March he joined Barnsley on a free transfer as back-up to Kevin Miller after Dave Watson announced his retirement. Although he made a number of appearances as an unused substitute he failed to make it off the bench but nevertheless did enough to impress manager Nigel Spackman and he signed a two-year contract for the Tykes in the summer.

Arsenal (From trainee on 22/10/1988)
Nottingham F (£50,000 on 20/6/1989) F/PL 11 FLC 1 Others 1
West Bromwich A (Loaned on 6/9/1989) FL 3
Blackburn Rov (Loaned on 29/12/1989) FL 2

Colchester U (Loaned on 21/3/1990) FL 10
Burnley (Loaned on 29/8/1991) FL 15 Others 2
Wrexham (£200,000 on 8/10/1993) FL 213 FLC 10 FAC 22 Others 21
Sunderland (£200,000 + on 17/8/1998) P/FL 2 FLC 3
Wigan Ath (Loaned on 1/1/2001) Others 2
Barnsley (Free on 13/3/2001)

MARSDEN Christopher (Chris)
Born: Sheffield, 3 January 1969
Height: 5'11" Weight: 10.12

An enthusiastic and uncompromising player, Chris's no-nonsense and never-say-die attitude in midfield has endeared himself to the Southampton fans. At his best when the chips are down, his motivating qualities bring the best out of players around him. However he struggled at times to make an impact last term and was restricted to just 19 starts in the Premiership campaign.

Sheffield U (From apprentice on 6/1/1987) FL 13+3/1 FLC 1 Others 1
Huddersfield T (Signed on 15/7/1988) FL 113+8/9 FLC 15+1 FAC 6+2 Others 10
Coventry C (Loaned on 2/11/1993) PL 5+2
Wolverhampton W (£250,000 on 11/1/1994) FL 8 FAC 3
Notts Co (£250,000 on 15/11/1994) FL 10 FLC 1 Others 1/1
Stockport Co (£70,000 on 12/1/1996) FL 63+2/3 FLC 13 FAC 4 Others 4/1
Birmingham C (£500,000 on 9/10/1997) FL 51+1/3 FLC 5/3 FAC 2
Southampton (£800,000 on 2/2/1999) PL 52+6/2 FLC 2+2 FAC 3

MARSH Adam
Born: Sheffield, 20 February 1982
Height: 5'10" Weight: 11.7

Adam was signed by Darlington from Unibond League club Worksop Town last November but after making his senior debut as a substitute against Mansfield the following month he made only occasional appearances in the first team and was mainly used as a substitute. A young striker his game is characterised by tenacious harrying to put opposition defenders under constant pressure. He was rewarded with his first goal in the LDV Vans Trophy tie against Shrewsbury Town but managed only one start in a league game.

Darlington (Signed from Worksop T on 30/11/2000) FL 1+6 Others 2/1

MARSH Christopher (Chris) Jonathan
Born: Sedgley, 14 January 1970
Height: 5'11" Weight: 13.2

Chris missed the first couple of months of last season while recovering from an achilles operation and it was not until November that he returned to action with the Walsall first team. He seemed to be settling in when he was allowed to join Wycombe Wanderers for a bargain fee in March after 13 seasons with the Saddlers. He subsequently featured regularly for the Chairboys in the closing weeks of the campaign and showed himself to be as fit as ever. He is a sure-footed right back who is calm under pressure and is famed for his 'step-over' trick.

Walsall (From trainee on 11/7/1988) FL 355+37/23 FLC 23+2/1 FAC 33+3/3 Others 24+1/3
Wycombe W (£30,000 on 23/3/2001) FL 11

MARSH Simon Thomas Peter
Born: Ealing, 29 January 1977
Height: 5'11" Weight: 12.0
International Honours: E: U21-1

Having failed to win his place back in the Birmingham City line-up following a lengthy absence Simon spent last September on loan at Brentford as cover at left back for the injured Paul Gibbs. He soon found his form and showed good distribution skills but elected to return to St Andrews in preference to a second month with the Bees. He continued to play for the Blues reserves until his contract was cancelled by mutual consent at the beginning of April.

Oxford U (From trainee on 22/11/1994) FL 49+7/3 FLC 6+2 FAC 2 Others 2
Birmingham C (£250,000 on 10/12/1998) FL 6+1 FAC 1
Brentford (Loaned on 1/9/2000) FL 3+1 FLC 2

MARSHALL Andrew (Andy) John
Born: Bury St Edmunds, 14 April 1975
Height: 6'2" Weight: 13.7
International Honours: E: U21-4; Yth (UEFA-U18 '93)

In what was likely to be his final season at Norwich City before he takes advantage of the 'Bosman' ruling to move on, Andy produced a string of thrilling displays on a consistent basis to confirm his position as one of the best goalkeepers outside of the top-flight. Tremendously athletic, he possesses fantastic reflexes and agility making him a top-class shot stopper. His handling of crosses improved immensely, as did his kicking, but week-in, week-out, he kept his side in games they might otherwise have lost and also kept the opposition at bay when City were in front. A hugely popular figure with the Canaries' fans he will be sorely missed if, as expected, he moves on from Carrow Road before the 2001-02 season commences.

Norwich C (From trainee on 6/7/1993) P/FL 194+1 FLC 18 FAC 5+1
Bournemouth (Loaned on 9/9/1996) FL 11
Gillingham (Loaned on 21/11/1996) FL 5 FLC 1 Others 1

MARSHALL Ian Paul
Born: Liverpool, 20 March 1966
Height: 6'1" Weight: 13.10
Club Honours: Div 2 '91; FLC '00

Originally signed on a weekly contract at the start of last season by Bolton boss Sam Allardyce, such was the quality of Ian's displays that this soon turned into a season-long agreement. He proved an invaluable member of the first-team squad, although often used from the substitutes' bench, proving that he could still handle the pace of First Division football with his 13 league starts. Providing cover in the centre of defence and as a striker, Ian was as consistent as any Wanderers' player last year. Strong in the tackle and very good at holding the ball when in possession, he added some steel to the side when it was most needed. He also chipped in with a few goals when required, including two in the game at Stockport. A favourite with the fans, he was offered an extended contract by the club in the summer.

Everton (From apprentice on 23/3/1984) FL 9+6/1 FLC 1+1/1 Others 7
Oldham Ath (£100,000 on 24/3/1988) F/PL 165+5/36 FLC 17 FAC 14/3 Others 2+1/1
Ipswich T (£750,000 on 9/8/1993) P/FL 79+5/32 FLC 4/3 FAC 9/3
Leicester C (£875,000 on 31/8/1996) PL 49+34/18 FLC 4+2/4 FAC 6+2/3 Others 2/1
Bolton W (Free on 11/8/2000) FL 13+23/6 FAC 3 Others 0+2

MARSHALL Lee Keith
Born: Islington, 21 January 1979
Height: 6'0" Weight: 11.11
International Honours: E: U21-1

Although still learning the game, Lee made tremendous progress at Norwich last term, attracting many admirers including his former England U21 boss, Peter Taylor. A strong-running midfielder who can also play at full back or in central defence, he loves nothing more than getting forward into goal-scoring positions. With his contract at Carrow Road due to expire in June 2001, his move to Leicester City on transfer deadline day did not come as a surprise to many. Intended as a purchase for the future, the Foxes' spring-time injury crisis meant that he was thrown in at the deep end, making his debut at Charlton. He coped adequately in fairly difficult circumstances and will be looking to establish a regular place in the line-up in 2001-02.

Norwich C (Signed from Enfield on 27/3/1997) FL 95+22/11 FLC 11+1/2 FAC 2
Leicester C (£600,000 on 21/3/2001) PL 7+2

MARSHALL Scott Roderick
Born: Edinburgh, 1 May 1973
Height: 6'1" Weight: 12.5
International Honours: S: U21-5; Yth

Scott was a regular in the centre of the Brentford defence last season until suffering a spine injury in February that put him out of action for a lengthy period. He once again proved to be a solid and effective centre back who reads the game well and is more than useful in set-piece situations. He had been in good form prior to his incapacity despite the club rather surprisingly placing him on the transfer list last November.

Arsenal (From trainee on 18/3/1991) PL 19+5/1 FLC 1+1
Rotherham U (Loaned on 3/12/1993) FL 10/1 Others 1
Sheffield U (Loaned on 25/8/1994) FL 17
Southampton (Free on 3/8/1998) PL 2
Brentford (£250,000 on 15/10/1999) FL 51/2 FLC 4 FAC 3/1 Others 4/2

MARSHALL Shaun Andrew
Born: Fakenham, 3 October 1978
Height: 6'1" Weight: 12.12

This promising young goalkeeper was understudy to Lionel Perez at Cambridge United for most of the 2000-01 campaign but had a brief run in the first team in the new year when Perez was sidelined with an injury. An assured 'keeper who commands his penalty box he had the misfortune to suffer a serious knee injury in the final game of the season at Swansea and is likely to be out of action for several months.

Cambridge U (From trainee on 21/2/1997) FL 55+2 FLC 1 FAC 6 Others 1

MARTIN Andrew (Andy) Peter
Born: Cardiff, 28 February 1980
Height: 6'0" Weight: 10.12
International Honours: W: U21-1; Yth

Andy is a young Crystal Palace striker who scored regularly for the club's reserve side last season. His first-team experience was limited to the final four minutes of extra time in the Worthington Cup Round Four tie against Tranmere. However he had the satisfaction of scoring from his penalty kick as the Eagles won the shoot out on their way to an eventual semi-final tie against Liverpool.

Crystal Palace (From trainee on 28/2/1997) FL 12+10/2 FLC 0+1

MARTIN John (Johnny)
Born: Bethnal Green, 15 July 1981
Height: 5'6" Weight: 9.12

Johnny had his best season to date for Leyton Orient last term. Although of slight build he uses his skill on the ball to beat much bigger and stronger defences. A regular in the O's team until the end of September he lost his place on the left wing soon after Scott Houghton arrived but returned again in the new year to add to his appearances.

Leyton Orient (From trainee on 6/8/1998) FL 24+5 FLC 5 Others 2+3

MARTIN Lee Brendan
Born: Huddersfield, 9 September 1968
Height: 6'0" Weight: 13.0
Club Honours: FC '98
International Honours: E: Sch

Lee was suspended (and at the same time injured) at the start of the 2000-2001 campaign and apart from a short spell in the Macclesfield line-up in November he had to wait until last February to regain his place as first-choice 'keeper for the Moss Rose club. He quickly re-established himself with some commanding performances and produced a wonderful last-minute penalty save at Cheltenham to keep the scores level. Lee is always cool, calm and collected even when under intense pressure and showed strength of character when out of the team, knuckling down in the reserves to win a recall. Outside of football Lee is in the third year of a four-year part-time course at Salford University studying for a BSc (Hons) degree in Physiotherapy.

Huddersfield T (From trainee on 1/7/1987) FL 54 FAC 4 Others 5
Blackpool (Free on 31/7/1992) FL 98 FLC 8 FAC 4 Others 7
Rochdale (Free on 8/11/1996)
Halifax T (Free on 12/8/1997) FL 37 FLC 4 FAC 1 Others 1
Macclesfield T (Free on 19/7/1999) FL 42 FAC 3 Others 1

MARTIN Lilian
Born: Valreas, France, 28 May 1971
Height: 6'0" Weight: 11.10

In need of a specialist right-sided wing back following a succession of heavy defeats, Derby County boss Jim Smith signed Lilian on a short-term contract after a successful trial period. He showed confidence and composure on his debut against West Ham at the beginning of November, displaying both pace and precision in his delivery of the ball. However despite a bright start at Pride Park, a change of tactical formation saw him lose his place to Rory Delap at the end of the year and he had to content himself with a place on the subs' bench for the remainder of the season. He was released by the Rams in the summer.

Derby Co (Free from Olympique Marseille, France, ex Dunkerque, AS Monaco, on 2/11/2000) PL 7+2 FAC 2+1

MARTINEZ Roberto
Born: Balaguer Lerida, Spain, 13 July 1973
Height: 5'10" Weight: 12.2
Club Honours: Div 3 '97

Roberto had a mixed time for Wigan Athletic in 2000-01 being in and out of the side throughout the campaign, however he made the line-up for the play-off encounters with Reading and went on to produce his best performances of the season. He is a skilful right-footed midfield player with the ability to deliver a defence-splitting pass. The last surviving member of the Latics' famed 'Three Amigos' he was released in the close season. Roberto also worked as a summariser on Spanish football for Sky TV.

Wigan Ath (Free from CFS Vipla Balaguer, Spain on 25/7/1995) FL 148+39/17 FLC 11+1/1 FAC 13+2/4 Others 7+5/2

MARTYN Antony **Nigel**
Born: St Austell, 11 August 1966
Height: 6'2" Weight: 14.7
Club Honours: Div 3 '90; FMC '91; Div 1 '94
International Honours: E: 16; B-6; U21-11

Still one of the most consistent goalkeepers in the Premiership, Nigel began last term as he had finished 1999-2000 for Leeds United - producing top quality saves. He kept this up until October when he was carried off towards the end of the home win against Charlton with an injury later diagnosed as a torn groin muscle. It was not until the new year that he returned to action in the FA Cup tie against Liverpool, but he soon shook off the rust and played a prominent part in the club's upturn in form. Among many superb saves one from a Danny Murphy free kick at Anfield, and another in the Champions' League game at Deportivo La Coruna stand out as being particularly memorable. Nigel was again part of the England set-up under Sven Goran Eriksson, and added further caps in the friendlies against Spain and Mexico.

Bristol Rov (Free from St Blazey on 6/8/1987) FL 101 FLC 6 FAC 6 Others 11
Crystal Palace (£1,000,000 on 21/11/1989) F/PL 272 FLC 36 FAC 22 Others 19
Leeds U (£2,250,000 on 26/7/1996) PL 169 FLC 10 FAC 17 Others 28

Nigel Martyn

MATHIE Alexander (Alex)
Born: Bathgate, 20 December 1968
Height: 5'10" Weight: 11.7
Club Honours: Div 2 '00
International Honours: S: Yth

Alex appeared for Dundee United against Celtic on the opening day of the 2000-01 season but after a handful more appearances for the Tannadice Park club he moved south to join York City in September. Although affected by niggling injuries he managed two goals for the Minstermen, scoring on his home debut against Mansfield and netting a real screamer in the FA Cup second round tie against Reading. Providing he returns to full fitness Alex could prove a vital figure for the Bootham Crescent club in 2001-2002.

Glasgow Celtic (From juniors on 15/5/1987) SL 7+4 SC 1 Others 0+1
Morton (£100,000 on 1/8/1991) SL 73+1/31 SLC 2/1 SC 5/3 Others 7/9
Port Vale (Loaned on 30/3/1993) FL 0+3
Newcastle U (£285,000 on 30/7/1993) PL 3+22/4 FLC 2+2
Ipswich T (£500,000 on 24/2/1995) P/FL 90+19/38 FLC 10+3/8 FAC 2+2 Others 6/1
Dundee U (£700,000 on 16/10/1998) SL 13+10/1 SLC 0+1 SC 4+2
Preston NE (Loaned on 17/9/1999) FL 5+7/2 FLC 2/2 FAC 1+2 Others 1
York C (Free on 27/9/2000) FL 13+6/1 FAC 2+2/1 Others 1

MATIAS Pedro Manuel Miguel
Born: Madrid, Spain, 11 October 1973
Height: 6'0" Weight: 12.0
International Honours: Spain: U21

Pedro enjoyed an outstanding season with Walsall in 2000-01 when he snatched some vital goals and netted a great hat-trick in the 5-1 win over Wycombe in March. He made an outstanding contribution to the play-off semi final win against Stoke with a finely angled goal to set up the win and another to settle the issue when his persistence saw a defender's clearance fly off him into the net. A talented left-sided midfield player, his mazy runs down the wing set up many an attack for the Saddlers while he willingly dropped back to help the defence when the going was tough.

Macclesfield T (Free from Logrones, Spain, ex Real Madrid, Almeria, on 3/12/1998) FL 21+1/2 FAC 1
Tranmere Rov (Free on 5/8/1999) FL 1+3
Walsall (Free on 7/10/1999) FL 66+7/15 FLC 3 FAC 4/1 Others 4/2

MATTEO Dominic
Born: Dumfries, 24 April 1974
Height: 6'1" Weight: 11.12
International Honours: E: B-1; U21-4; Yth. S: 3

Having joined Leeds United during the close season, Dominic began last term on the sidelines with a knee injury and it was not until September that he made his debut, featuring in the 1-0 Champions' League victory over AC Milan when he played on the left-hand side of midfield. He scored his first goal for United against Besiktas and remained in the team for the rest of the season. A highlight was undoubtedly his near-post header in the return game against AC Milan in the San Siro Stadium, the 1-1 draw confirming Leeds' qualification for the second stage of the Champions' League. He showed his versatility in the second half of the campaign when he played at left back and in the centre of defence and did equally well in both roles. An intelligent player, with vision, skill and athleticism, he gained his first full cap for Scotland in a friendly against Australia in the autumn and went on to appear twice more during the campaign.

Liverpool (From trainee on 27/5/1992) PL 112+15/1 FLC 9 FAC 6+2/1 Others 10+1
Sunderland (Loaned on 28/3/1995) FL 1
Leeds U (£4,750,000 on 24/8/2000) PL 30 FLC 1 FAC 2 Others 15/2

MATTHEWS Lee Joseph
Born: Middlesbrough, 16 January 1979
Height: 6'3" Weight: 12.6
Club Honours: FAYC '97
International Honours: E: Yth

Having developed through the ranks at Elland Road Lee joined Second Division Bristol City on loan in March and the deal became permanent shortly afterwards. His career at Ashton Gate got off to a great start when he netted a last-minute winner from the penalty spot against Millwall and he scored again in his second game as the Robins won 3-1 at Reading. He is a promising young striker who is tall, quick and has a good first touch.

Leeds U (From trainee on 15/2/1996) PL 0+3 FLC 0+1
Notts Co (Loaned on 24/9/1998) FL 4+1
Gillingham (Loaned on 23/3/2000) FL 2+3
Bristol C (£100,000 on 16/3/2001) FL 4+2/3

Lee Matthews

MATTHEWS Robert (Rob) David
Born: Slough, 14 October 1970
Height: 6'0" Weight: 13.0
Club Honours: Div 2 '97
International Honours: E: Sch

Rob was again hampered by injuries at Stockport in the first half of the 2000-01 campaign but eventually returned to full fitness in the new year. He subsequently joined Third Division Halifax Town on loan where he played a handful of games, scoring twice including a stunning goal in the 3-0 win at Southend in February. However he then made a permanent move to Hull City in March assisting the Boothferry Park club into the play-offs. Like team-mate Rodney Rowe he has achieved the unusual double of being signed by both the Little brothers - Alan having recruited him for York and Brian for Hull. Rob is an experienced right winger capable of some tricky play down the flank.

Notts Co (Free from Loughborough University on 26/3/1992) FL 23+20/11 FLC 0+2 FAC 3+2/2 Others 4+3
Luton T (£80,000 on 17/3/1995) FL 6+5 FLC 0+1
York C (£90,000 on 8/9/1995) FL 14+3/1 FAC 1 Others 3
Bury (£100,000 on 12/1/1996) FL 54+20/11 FLC 4+5/3 FAC 1 Others 3
Stockport Co (£120,000 on 12/11/1998) FL 29+9/4 FAC 2+2
Blackpool (Loaned on 28/12/1999) FL 5+1/2 Others 2/1
Halifax T (Loaned on 9/2/2001) FL 8/2
Hull C (£30,000 on 14/3/2001) FL 8 Others 2

MAUGE Ronald (Ronnie) Carlton
Born: Islington, 10 March 1969
Height: 5'10" Weight: 11.10
International Honours: Trinidad & Tobago: 8

This experienced midfielder returned to action shortly before Christmas following the broken leg he suffered back in February 2000 and immediately re-established himself as a key figure in the centre of the park for Bristol Rovers. He went on to feature regularly in the second half of the season, and also won his place back in the Trinidad & Tobago squad, earning another five caps during the campaign and registering his first goal at international level when he netted in the 3-1 win over Guatemala.

Charlton Ath (From trainee on 22/7/1987)
Fulham (Free on 21/9/1988) FL 47+3/2 FLC 4 FAC 1 Others 2
Bury (£40,000 on 30/7/1990) FL 92+16/10 FLC 8+2/2 FAC 8/2 Others 10+2
Manchester C (Loaned on 26/9/1991) Others 0+1
Plymouth Arg (£40,000 on 22/7/1995) FL 119+16/14 FLC 6 FAC 11/3 Others 5+1/1
Bristol Rov (Free on 5/7/1999) FL 36+2 FLC 4 FAC 1 Others 4

MAWENE Youl
Born: Caen, France, 16 July 1979
Height: 6'2" Weight: 12.6

Signed by Derby County in the close season, Youl spent the first half of the 2000-01 campaign settling in with the reserve team, his progress being hampered by a knee injury. He made his Premiership debut at Southampton at the turn of the year and as injuries and suspensions took hold towards the close of the season, he made several appearances in a right wing-back role. A promising young defender blessed with pace and good vision he is a fine example of the talent being nurtured at Pride Park.

Derby Co (£500,000 from RC Lens, France on 4/8/2000) PL 7+1 FAC 2

MAWSON Craig John
Born: Keighley, 16 May 1979
Height: 6'2" Weight: 13.4
Unable to breakthrough into the first team at Burnley, Craig spent two months on loan at Lincoln last autumn as cover for regular 'keeper Alan Marriott. Although he featured regularly on the subs' bench for the Imps he was never called into action and after returning briefly to Turf Moor he joined Halifax Town last February. He made his Football League debut for the Shaymen at Shrewsbury the following month and had a brief run in the team when Lee Butler was out injured. A promising young goalkeeper the high point of his time at the Shay came when he saved a penalty in the home game against Barnet to pave the way for a vital 3-0 victory. He was released at the end of the season.
Burnley (From trainee on 14/7/1997)
Halifax T (Free on 16/2/2001) FL 9

MAXWELL Leyton Jonathan
Born: Rhyl, 3 October 1979
Height: 5'8" Weight: 11.6
International Honours: W: U21-12; Yth
Having joined Stockport County in a 12-month loan deal during the close season Leyton made an immediate impact with a goal on his debut at Gillingham in the opening game. A regular in the County squad in the first half of the campaign he faded out of the picture somewhat after Christmas and added just one more goal, ironically in the return match against the Gills. A promising young midfield player who is able to play either on the right-hand side or in a central role he also appeared regularly for Wales at U21 level during the season.
Liverpool (From trainee on 17/7/1997) FLC 1/1
Stockport Co (Loaned on 17/7/2000) FL 8+12/2 FLC 1+1 FAC 0+1

MAY David
Born: Oldham, 24 June 1970
Height: 6'0" Weight: 13.5
Club Honours: CS '94, '96; PL '96, '97, '99; FAC '96, '99; EC '99
Having been absent through injury for the best part of 12 months, David made a return to reserve-team action for Manchester United last November but just two minutes into his comeback game he fell victim to hamstring trouble and it was not until much later in the season that he finally returned to full match fitness. He made his long-awaited return to Premiership football as a substitute in the penultimate game at Southampton and made the starting line-up for the final game at Tottenham. A very able central defender with good recovery skills he will be hoping to put all his injury woes behind him in 2001-02.
Blackburn Rov (From trainee on 16/6/1988) F/PL 123/3 FLC 12+1/2 FAC 10/1 Others 5
Manchester U (£1,400,000 on 1/7/1994) PL 66+16/6 FLC 7/1 FAC 6 Others 14+2/1
Huddersfield T (Loaned on 24/12/1999) FL 1

MAYBURY Alan
Born: Dublin, 8 August 1978
Height: 5'11" Weight: 11.12
Club Honours: FAYC '97
International Honours: RoI: 2; B-1; U21-8; Yth
After coming through a torrid period with injuries, this talented youngster appeared regularly in Leeds United's reserve team last term and in October he joined Crewe Alexandra on loan. He played in half-a-dozen First Division games at right back for the Gresty Road club before his four-week loan spell was up and showed some impressive form. On his return to Elland Road he made a single first-team appearance, featuring on the right-hand side of midfield in a much-changed line-up for the 3-3 Champions' League draw with Lazio in March, when the club had already qualified for the quarter-finals. He remains a quality player and will be aiming to win a regular place in the first-team squad in 2001-02.
Leeds U (Free from St Kevin's BC on 17/8/1995) PL 10+3 FLC 1 FAC 2 Others 1
Reading (Loaned on 25/3/1999) FL 8
Crewe Alex (Loaned on 8/10/2000) FL 6

MAYLETT Bradley (Brad)
Born: Manchester, 24 December 1980
Height: 5'8" Weight: 10.10
After missing the whole of the 1999-2000 campaign through injury Brad returned to the first-team picture for Burnley last season and started a league game for the first time when he appeared in the 2-1 defeat at Preston in last December. He was subsequently used as a substitute on a number of occasions when his pace proved troublesome to tired opposition defenders. Mostly used in a right-wing-role he has yet to score for the Clarets but his time will surely come in the future.
Burnley (From trainee on 19/2/1999) FL 2+27 FLC 0+2 Others 1

MAYO Kerry
Born: Haywards Heath, 21 September 1977
Height: 5'10" Weight: 13.4
Club Honours: Div 3 '01
Kerry firmly established himself in the left back position at Brighton last season and apart from a one-match suspension he appeared in every game for the Third Division champions. His tremendous work rate coupled with excellent timing in the tackle contributed greatly to the Seagulls' impressive defensive record. He also possesses a powerful long throw which regularly caused problems for opposition defences.
Brighton & Hove A (From trainee on 3/7/1996) FL 154+15/9 FLC 6 FAC 3+6/2 Others 3+3

MAYO Paul
Born: Lincoln, 13 October 1981
Height: 5'11" Weight: 11.9
This teenaged left back was a regular in the Lincoln City team until new manager Alan Buckley opted for experience as the Imps battled against relegation. In what was his first full season of League football Paul showed plenty of promise both in his defensive qualities and in his ability to push forward.
Lincoln C (From trainee on 6/4/2000) FL 45+1 FLC 2 FAC 2 Others 3

MEAKER Michael John
Born: Greenford, 18 August 1971
Height: 5'11" Weight: 12.0
International Honours: W: B-1; U21-2
Having turned down a move to Exeter City in the 2000-01 close season Michael continued to find it difficult to break into the Bristol Rovers' first team and had to be content with occasional outings in the squad. He subsequently joined Plymouth in February where he featured more regularly although often being used from the subs' bench. He scored his first goal for the Pilgrims when he netted in the 1-1 draw at Leyton Orient in April. Michael is a right-sided attacking midfield player with some tricky skills on the ball. Out of contract in the summer his future was unclear at the time of writing.
Queens Park R (From trainee on 7/2/1990) F/PL 21+13/1 FLC 2/1 FAC 3/1 Others 0+1
Plymouth Arg (Loaned on 20/11/1991) FL 4 Others 1
Reading (£550,000 on 19/7/1995) FL 46+21/2 FLC 3/1 FAC 0+3
Bristol Rov (Free on 7/8/1998) FL 19+8/2 FLC 2+2 FAC 4+1 Others 2
Swindon T (Loaned on 23/3/2000) FL 6
Plymouth Arg (Free on 19/2/2001) FL 5+6/1

MEDOU-OTYE Andre **Parfait**
Born: Ekoundendi, Cameroon, 29 January 1976
Height: 5'10" Weight: 11.12
International Honours: France: Yth
Parfait joined Scottish Division One outfit Morton in the 2000 close season and featured regularly until moving south to join Kidderminster last November. Solidly built, he is a versatile player who can appear in defence or midfield. He initially broke into the Harriers' line-up at left back but he looked far more comfortable when replacing Ian Clarkson at right back for the closing games of the campaign.
Morton (Signed from Le Mans, France, ex Le Havre, on 4/8/2000)
Kidderminster Hrs (Free on 23/11/2000) FL 16+1 Others 2

MEIJER Erik
Born: Meerssem, Holland, 2 August 1969
Height: 6'2" Weight: 13.10
International Honours: Holland: 2; U21
Erik was very much on the fringes of the Liverpool first-team squad last season and made only three brief appearances from the substitutes' bench in the opening weeks of the campaign. In October he was loaned to Preston North End where he set up an injury-time winner against Norwich on his debut. However after nine appearances without a goal for the Deepdale club he opted for a return to the Bundesliga, joining SV Hamburg on a free transfer. A tall striker he has excellent ground skills and is even better in the air.
Liverpool (Free from Bayer Leverkusen, Germany, ex Meerssem, Eindhoven VV, Fortuna Sittard, MVV, on 13/7/1999) PL 7+17 FLC 3/2
Preston NE (Loaned on 17/10/2000) FL 9

MELCHIOT Mario
Born: Amsterdam, Holland, 4 November 1976
Height: 6'1" Weight: 11.8
Club Honours: FAC '00; CS '00
International Honours: Holland: 3; U21-13; Yth

Following his belated entry onto the English football scene, Mario continued to show his value for Chelsea at the beginning of last season, scoring the decisive second goal in the FA Charity Shield game against Manchester United with a ferocious left-footed drive. He went on to claim a regular place in the Blues' line-up and his strength, power in the air and athleticism made him a valued member of the all-star squad at Stamford Bridge. The club recognised his contribution in February with the offer of a two-year extension to his present contract, which he gleefully accepted. To round off an amazing period, his outstanding form was recognised by the Dutch national side and he was rewarded with his first cap against Portugal in October.

Chelsea (Free from Ajax, Holland on 5/7/1999) PL 31+5 FLC 1 FAC 2 Others 2/1

Micky Mellon

MELLON Michael (Micky) Joseph
Born: Paisley, 18 March 1972
Height: 5'10" Weight: 12.11

Always a workman-like player with a liking to go forward from midfield, Micky featured regularly for Burnley last season and it was therefore a surprise when he was transferred back to his previous club Tranmere shortly before the transfer deadline. Although unable to halt Rovers' slide to relegation he showed that he could instigate attacks and is likely to be a key figure for them in their Second Division campaign next term.

Bristol C (From trainee on 6/12/1989) FL 26+9/1 FLC 3 FAC 1+1 Others 5+3
West Bromwich A (£75,000 on 11/2/1993) FL 38+7/6 FLC 3+2 FAC 0+1 Others 6/1
Blackpool (£50,000 on 23/11/1994) FL 123+1/14 FLC 9/1 FAC 4 Others 7/2
Tranmere Rov (£285,000 on 31/10/1997) FL 45+12/3 FLC 4 FAC 3+1
Burnley (£350,000 on 8/1/1999) FL 72+12/5 FLC 3+1 FAC 5
Tranmere Rov (Free on 5/3/2001) FL 11+2/1

MELTON Stephen (Steve)
Born: Lincoln, 3 October 1978
Height: 5'11" Weight: 12.2
Club Honours: Div 3 '01

This versatile player joined Brighton in the 2000 close season, but although he found a regular place in the first-team squad he was generally restricted to appearances from the subs' bench or making the starting line-up as cover for injuries and suspensions. A consistent performer he was mostly used in a central midfield role by the Seagulls and scored the first senior goal of his career in the 3-0 victory over Hull last March.

Nottingham F (From trainee on 9/10/1995) P/FL 2+1 FLC 1
Stoke C (Free on 28/2/2000) FL 0+5 Others 0+2
Brighton & Hove A (Free on 2/8/2000) FL 10+18/1 FLC 0+1 Others 1+1

MELVILLE Andrew (Andy) Roger
Born: Swansea, 29 November 1968
Height: 6'0" Weight: 13.10
Club Honours: WC '89; Div 1 '96, '01
International Honours: W: 46; B-1; U21-2

Andy was one of many in the Fulham side whose passing improved enormously under Jean Tigana. His defensive partnerships with Chris Coleman, and latterly with Kit Symons were the bedrock on which Fulham's title challenge was based. He had one of his best seasons at Craven Cottage and will look forward with confidence to the challenge of Premiership action in the coming season.

Swansea C (From trainee on 25/7/1986) FL 165+10/22 FLC 10 FAC 14+1/5 Others 13/2
Oxford U (£275,000 on 23/7/1990) FL 135/13 FLC 12/1 FAC 6 Others 6/1
Sunderland (£750,000 + on 9/8/1993) P/FL 204/14 FLC 18+1 FAC 11 Others 2
Bradford C (Loaned on 13/2/1998) FL 6/1
Fulham (Free on 1/7/1999) FL 82+1/4 FLC 9 FAC 5

MENDES-RODRIGUEZ Alberto
Born: Nurnberg, Germany, 24 October 1974
Height: 5'11" Weight: 11.9

After spending the previous season on loan in his homeland with Bundesliga side Sp Vgg Unterhaching, Alberto remained very much a fringe player at Arsenal in the 2000-01 season. Although he featured regularly for the reserves, his only senior outing came in the Worthington Cup third round tie against Ipswich when he replaced Jermaine Pennant for the final 30 minutes. An experienced left-sided midfield player he has good pace and excellent close skills.

Arsenal (£250,000 from FC Feucht, Germany on 21/7/1997) PL 1+3 FLC 3+2/1 FAC 1 Others 1/1

MENDY Jules
Born: Pikine, Senegal, 4 September 1973
Height: 5'10" Weight: 12.7

Jules had previously been on trial with Torquay in the summer of 1998, but work permit problems led him to return to France. However he was back at Plainmoor in the 2000 close season and signed a two-year contract for the Gulls. He initially appeared at right back but was used in a variety of roles including centre forward without ever establishing himself in the side. He scored a wonderful goal in the 6-2 defeat at Brighton last September but dropped out of the reckoning in the second half of the campaign.

Torquay U (Free from Racing Paris, France on 9/8/2000) FL 7+14/2 FLC 0+2 FAC 0+2

MENETRIER Mickael
Born: Reims, France, 23 August 1978
Height: 6'3" Weight: 12.10

Mickael joined Bournemouth in August 2000 from Metz where he had been third-choice 'keeper in the 1999-2000 campaign when he was restricted to appearances in the reserve team. He began last season as first-choice 'keeper for the Cherries but lost his place in September and apart from a couple of outings in the LDV Vans Trophy ties his only other senior games came when his rival Gareth Stewart was out injured in the new year. A promising 'keeper he will be aiming to regain his place in the team in 2001-02.

Bournemouth (Free from Metz, France on 11/8/2000) FL 11+1 FLC 2 Others 2

MERSON Paul Charles
Born: Harlesden, 20 March 1968
Height: 6'0" Weight: 13.2
Club Honours: Div 1 '89, '91; FLC '93; FAC '93; ECWC '94
International Honours: E: 21; B-4; U21-4; Yth

Paul picked up where he left off the previous season for Aston Villa in 2000-01, continuing to play some of the best football of his career. One of the most creative players in the Premiership and certainly one of the most influential at Villa, he was mainly used in a 'free' role within the midfield, creating most of the team's moves. Indeed at one point manager John Gregory was reported to have said that the team revolved around him far too much! He netted his 100th league goal against Derby in September and scored a memorable 89th minute winner from all of 35 yards out at Everton. Continuing to captain the side in Gareth Southgate's absence, he was a master with the ball and often out-ran players five years his junior. Regularly in receipt of 'Man of the Match' awards, he was voted 'Player of the Season' by the Villa fans for the second year in a row.

Arsenal (From apprentice on 1/12/1985) F/PL 289+38/78 FLC 38+2/9 FAC 28+3/4 Others 27+2/7
Brentford (Loaned on 22/1/1987) FL 6+1 Others 1+1
Middlesbrough (£4,500,000 + on 15/7/1997) P/FL 48/11 FLC 7/3 FAC 3/1
Aston Villa (£6,750,000 on 10/9/1998) PL 83+13/16 FLC 6+2 FAC 10 Others 3

Paul Merson

MICHOPOULOS Nikalaos (Nik)
Born: Khardsa, Greece, 20 February 1970
Height: 6'3" Weight: 14.5
International Honours: Greece

After arriving relatively unheralded at Turf Moor, this former Greek international goalkeeper saved a penalty on his debut for Burnley in a Worthington Cup tie against Crystal Palace. Four days later he produced a string of brilliant saves at Huddersfield to help the Clarets win three points and became an instant hero of the club's fans. Nik went on to produce a string of outstanding performances throughout last season and a late save at Gillingham earned him the Nationwide 'Save of the Month' award for January. He appears to have it all as a 'keeper: positional sense, good distribution, safe handling and capable of the spectacular when necessary.

Burnley (Free from PAOK Salonika, Greece on 25/8/2000) FL 39 FLC 2 FAC 2

MIDDLETON Craig Dean
Born: Nuneaton, 10 September 1970
Height: 5'10" Weight: 11.12

This experienced midfield player was a near ever-present for Halifax Town last season but really came into his own in the vital closing stages of the campaign. He netted with a cracking volley in the 3-0 win over Macclesfield in mid-April and followed this up with similar strikes to ensure victory over Darlington and a draw at Lincoln, thus almost single-handedly ensuring that the Shaymen retained Football League status. He is a player who likes to push forward and is always willing to shoot on sight.

Coventry C (From trainee on 30/5/1989) F/PL 2+1 FLC 1
Cambridge U (Free on 20/7/1993) FL 55+4/10 FLC 3 FAC 1 Others 1
Cardiff C (Free on 30/8/1996) FL 95+24/8 FLC 3+1 FAC 13+1/3 Others 4+2
Plymouth Arg (Loaned on 27/1/2000) FL 6/2
Halifax T (£25,000 on 16/3/2000) FL 45+2/6 FLC 2 FAC 0+1 Others 2

MIDGLEY Craig Steven
Born: Bradford, 24 May 1976
Height: 5'8" Weight: 11.7

Fully fit after his injury problems of the previous season, Craig began 2000-01 behind Kevin Henderson and Anth Lormor in the pecking order of strikers at Hartlepool. He continued to work hard and was rewarded with a first-team place in November, soon afterwards scoring a hat-trick in the 6-1 victory over Barnet. He subsequently enjoyed a lengthy run in the side and was a member of the squad for all 46 Third Division games, although he often featured from the subs' bench. His career tally of 35 substitute appearances was a new record for the club. Craig was surprisingly released in the summer and was later reported to have joined Halifax.

Bradford C (From trainee on 4/7/1995) FL 0+11/1 FAC 0+4 Others 1
Scarborough (Loaned on 7/12/1995) FL 14+2/1
Scarborough (Loaned on 14/3/1997) FL 6/2
Darlington (Loaned on 1/12/1997) FL 1 Others 0+1/1
Hartlepool U (£10,000 on 13/3/1998) FL 61+35/18 FLC 2+2 FAC 3/2 Others 9+1/1

MIDGLEY Neil Alan
Born: Cambridge, 21 October 1978
Height: 5'11" Weight: 11.10

Neil joined Barnet on the transfer deadline day last season but a combination of lack of match fitness and the Bees relegation problems meant that he received few opportunities. A hard-working young striker he will be aiming to earn regular first-team football in the 2001-02 campaign. He was placed on the open to offers list following the club's relegation to the Conference.

Ipswich T (From trainee on 2/6/1997) FL 1+3/1
Luton T (Loaned on 24/9/1999) FL 8+2/3
Barnet (Free on 22/3/2001) FL 3+1

MIGLIORANZI Stefan
Born: Pocos de Caldas, Brazil, 20 September 1977
Height: 6'0" Weight: 11.12

Stefan was hampered by a recurring knee injury that restricted him to just eight first-team starts for Portsmouth last term. An immensely talented midfield player he impressed with some close ball skills and little shimmies, but is still learning the game and needs to try and develop a greater level of consistency. Having successfully made the transfer from US college soccer to the English professional game he will be looking to establish himself as a regular in the Pompey line-up in 2001-02.

Portsmouth (Free from St John's University, NY, USA on 8/3/1999) FL 24+8/2 FLC 2+3 FAC 1

MIKE Leon Jonathan
Born: Manchester, 4 September 1981
Height: 5'10" Weight: 12.2
International Honours: E: Yth; Sch

Having been capped by England at U16 and U18 levels this promising Manchester City youngster joined Oxford United on loan last September to gain some experience of first-team football. Leon made three appearances for the U's before a change of management at the Manor Ground prevented any extension of the spell and he returned to Maine Road. He subsequently went out on loan again in the new year, this time to Third Division Halifax Town, but although he regularly found space in the box he failed to register a goal for the Shaymen in seven appearances before returning to Maine Road. He is an exciting young striker who will be hoping to make a breakthrough with City in the coming season.

Manchester C (From trainee on 23/9/1998)
Oxford U (Loaned on 21/9/2000) FL 1+2
Halifax T (Loaned on 9/2/2001) FL 2+5

MIKLOSKO Ludek (Ludo)
Born: Ostrava, Czechoslovakia, 9 December 1961
Height: 6'5" Weight: 14.0
International Honours: Czechoslovakia: 44; B-1; U23

Ludo began the 2000-01 season as understudy to the in-form Lee Harper at Queens Park Rangers before being recalled towards the end of November. He retained his place until March before being dropped following a series of heavy defeats. A tall and commanding goalkeeper he was released by Rangers in the summer. He was later reported to have taken up a post as goalkeeping coach at West Ham.

West Ham U (£300,000 from Banik Ostrava, Czechoslovakia on 19/2/1990) F/PL 315 FLC 25 FAC 25 Others 8
Queens Park R (£50,000 on 2/10/1998) FL 57 FLC 2 FAC 4+2

MILDENHALL Stephen (Steve) James
Born: Swindon, 13 May 1978
Height: 6'4" Weight: 14.0

Steve began the 2000-01 campaign as second-choice 'keeper to Bart Griemink at Swindon and it was only after Griemink was suspended early in the new year that he had the chance of a decent run in the side. He seized the opportunity with both hands, keeping ten clean sheets from 24 starts and winning a local newspaper's 'Player of the Year' competition. A tall commanding goalkeeper with a safe pair of hands he is very effective at marshalling his defence. He was reported to have signed for Notts County in the summer.

Swindon T (From trainee on 19/7/1996) FL 29+4 FLC 2 FAC 2 Others 1

MILLEN Keith Derek
Born: Croydon, 26 September 1966
Height: 6'2" Weight: 12.4
Club Honours: Div 3 '92; Div 2 '98

Although now approaching the veteran stage of his career Keith had a fine season in defence for Bristol City, his experience being an important factor in bringing on the young defenders playing alongside him. He provided solid leadership and was a regular in the starting line-up until suffering a knee injury at the beginning of March that sidelined him for the remainder of the campaign. Keith is a consistent central defender with a non-nonsense approach.

Brentford (From apprentice on 7/8/1984) FL 301+4/17 FLC 26/2 FAC 18/1 Others 30+1
Watford (Signed on 22/3/1994) FL 163+2/5 FLC 10+1 FAC 14 Others 1
Bristol C (£35,000 on 12/11/1999) FL 56+1/4 FLC 1 FAC 8 Others 6

MILLER Alan John
Born: Epping, 29 March 1970
Height: 6'3" Weight: 14.6
Club Honours: FAYC '88; ECWC '94; Div 1 '95
International Honours: E: U21-4; Yth; Sch

Alan joined Bristol City on loan to cover for a goalkeeping crisis at the start of the 2000-01 campaign and performed well in the opening games of the season before returning to Ewood Park. However he seemed distinctly out of favour and made just a single appearance in the Worthington Cup second leg game against Portsmouth when Rovers used a number of fringe players. In October he was loaned to Coventry where he was needed as back up to young Chris Kirkland, with both Magnus Hedman and Morten Hyldgaard out injured. In his first appearance on the bench at Stamford Bridge he was called into action early on when Kirkland was sent off but it was to be a miserable afternoon as he let in six goals against a rampant Chelsea attack - even so he won the 'Man of the Match' award. Alan stayed at Coventry for two months, appearing on the bench a number of times without making any further appearances. On his return to Blackburn he found he had slipped further down the pecking order with the arrival of Brad Friedel, although he still featured with the reserves.

Arsenal (From trainee on 5/5/1988) PL 6+2
Plymouth Arg (Loaned on 24/11/1988) FL 13 FAC 2
West Bromwich A (Loaned on 15/8/1991) FL 3
Birmingham C (Loaned on 19/12/1991) FL 15 Others 1
Middlesbrough (£500,000 on 12/8/1994) P/FL 57 FLC 3 FAC 2 Others 2
Grimsby T (Loaned on 28/1/1997) FL 3
West Bromwich A (£400,000 on 28/2/1997) FL 98 FLC 9 FAC 3
Blackburn Rov (£50,000 + on 15/2/2000) FL 1 FLC 1
Bristol C (Loaned on 12/8/2000) FL 4
Coventry C (Loaned on 21/11/2000) PL 0+1

MILLER Charles (Charlie)
Born: Glasgow, 18 March 1976
Height: 5'9" Weight: 10.8
Club Honours: SPD '95, '96, '97; SLC '97
International Honours: S: 1; U21-8; Sch

Charlie made only one first-team appearance for Watford in 2000-01 coming on from the subs' bench in the Worthington Cup first round first leg tie against Cheltenham. He subsequently had a trial with Wigan Athletic before returning north of the border to join Dundee United on a free transfer in November. A scheming midfield player capable of delivering defence-splitting passes he did well with the Scottish Premier League club where he featured regularly, scoring five goals in 24 appearances. He stepped up to make his full international debut in the friendly against Poland in April.

Glasgow R (From juniors on 2/7/1992) SL 54+30/10 SLC 9+2/1 SC 5+1/2 Others 7+9/2
Leicester C (Loaned on 26/3/1999) PL 1+3
Watford (£350,000 + on 1/10/1999) PL 9+5 FLC 1+1 FAC 1

MILLER Kevin
Born: Falmouth, 15 March 1969
Height: 6'1" Weight: 13.0
Club Honours: Div 4 '90

Having firmly established himself as Barnsley's number one 'keeper during the 1999-2000 season, Kevin maintained that position last term and was the club's only ever present. At times he performed heroics in the Reds' goal and when the team suffered a dip in form he kept the ship afloat almost single handedly at times. His shot stopping was second to none and his errors were kept to a minimum. Although booed mercilessly by Palace fans he saved a spot kick at Selhurst Park for the second successive season. Kevin was a deserved winner of the Reds' 'Player of the Year' award.

Exeter C (Free from Newquay on 9/3/1989) FL 163 FLC 7 FAC 12 Others 18
Birmingham C (£250,000 on 14/5/1993) FL 24 FLC 4 Others 2
Watford (£250,000 on 7/8/1994) FL128 FLC 10 FAC 10 Others 3
Crystal Palace (£1,000,000 + on 21/7/1997) P/FL 66 FLC 3 FAC 5 Others 2
Barnsley (£250,000 on 27/8/1999) FL 87 FLC 9 FAC 2 Others 3

MILLER Paul Anthony
Born: Woking, 31 January 1968
Height: 6'0" Weight: 11.7

Paul started the 2000-2001 season on the left side of Lincoln City's midfield where his ability to hold the ball was put to good use. He injured a hamstring at the end of August and was out, on and off, for three months. Shortly after his return to fitness he suffered medial knee ligament damage that kept him out again until March. He only made one start under new manager Alan Buckley and was released in May.

Wimbledon (Signed from Yeovil T on 12/8/1987) F/PL 65+15/10 FLC 3+3 FAC 3 Others 1
Newport Co (Loaned on 20/10/1987) FL 6/2
Bristol C (Loaned on 11/1/1990) FL 0+3 Others 2
Bristol Rov (£100,000 on 16/8/1994) FL 100+5/22 FLC 7/1 FAC 5/4 Others 11/2
Lincoln C (Free on 8/8/1997) FL 93+22/11 FLC 4 FAC 5+1 Others 4+1/1

Tommy Miller

MILLER Thomas (Tommy) William
Born: Easington, 8 January 1979
Height: 6'1" Weight: 11.12

Tommy was an ever-present for Hartlepool in 2000-01 when he had a fine season finishing as the club's top scorer in all competitions and being named in the PFA's Division Three team for the second year in a row. He is a talented attacking midfielder who has the ability to create goals from nothing and is a real match winner. He was again the subject of interest from bigger clubs and it remains to be seen how long Pool can hang on to him.

Hartlepool U (From trainee on 8/7/1997) FL 130+7/35 FLC 6/3 FAC 5/1 Others 12/5

MILLIGAN Jamie
Born: Blackpool, 3 January 1980
Height: 5'6" Weight: 9.12
Club Honours: FAYC '98
International Honours: E: Yth

A former England U18 international, Jamie was unable to break into the Everton first-team squad last season and signed for Third Division Blackpool on the transfer deadline. A slight midfield player who has excellent delivery from dead-ball situations, he made his debut for the Tangerines as a substitute at Macclesfield and was mostly used from the subs' bench in the closing stages of the campaign.

Everton (From trainee on 13/6/1997) PL 0+4
Blackpool (Free on 22/3/2001) FL 1+5 Others 0+3

MILLIGAN Michael (Mike) Joseph
Born: Manchester, 20 February 1967
Height: 5'8" Weight: 11.0
International Honours: RoI: 1; B-2; U23-1; U21-1

This experienced central midfield player joined Blackpool during the 2000 close season and featured regularly in the opening matches. Mike then lost his place and suffered injuries and it was not until January that he returned to first-team action. Strong in the tackle and still a competent ball winner in the centre of the park he netted his first goal for the Tangerines in the 6-0 thrashing of Scunthorpe last February.

Oldham Ath (From apprentice on 2/3/1985) FL 161+1/17 FLC 19+1/1 FAC 12/1 Others 4
Everton (£1,000,000 on 24/8/1990) FL 16+1/1 FLC 0+1 FAC 1 Others 4+1/1
Oldham Ath (£600,000 on 17/7/1991) F/PL 117/6 FLC 11/1 FAC 9 Others 1/1
Norwich C (£800,000 on 27/6/1994) P/FL 113+11/5 FLC 11+1 FAC 6
Blackpool (Free on 24/7/2000) FL 24+2/1 FLC 1 Others 0+1

MILLS Daniel (Danny) John
Born: Norwich, 18 May 1977
Height: 5'11" Weight: 11.9
International Honours: E: 1; U21-14; Yth

Danny more than made his mark in an injury-ravaged season for Leeds United, playing in all four positions in the back four, before making the right-back spot his own at the turn of the year. His bursts of speed and foraging down the flank saw him create a number of goals including one for Robbie Keane at Ipswich, and Mark Viduka's diving header to equalise against Manchester United. He was not only strong going forward, but equally effective in defence where he was particularly sure-footed in the tackle. He was rewarded with his first full cap in the friendly against Mexico in June.

Norwich C (From trainee on 1/11/1994) FL 46+20 FLC 3+2/1 FAC 2
Charlton Ath (£350,000 on 19/3/1998) P/FL 45/3 FLC 3 FAC 1 Others 2
Leeds U (£4,370,000 on 1/7/1999) PL 36+4/1 FLC 1/1 FAC 1+1 Others 17+1

Danny Mills

MILLS Jamie Mark
Born: Swindon, 31 August 1981
Height: 5'10" Weight: 11.6

Jamie stepped up to make his senior debut for Swindon Town in the LDV Vans Trophy tie against Millwall last January and also featured a couple of times from the subs' bench before being released in the summer. A former trainee at the County Ground he is a young midfield player with an excellent attitude.

Swindon T (From trainee on 10/7/1999) FL 0+2 Others 0+1

MILLS Rowan Lee
Born: Mexborough, 10 July 1970
Height: 6'1" Weight: 13.9

Lee did well for Bradford City in the pre-season Inter Toto games, scoring three times in five appearances before Portsmouth paid a club record fee for him shortly before the start of the new campaign. However he had a frustrating time on the south coast, suffering a bad knee injury in the game at Stockport in October that was to keep him out of action until the new year. He eventually made his comeback in Graham Rix's first match in charge, but found it difficult to thrive up front in a team struggling against relegation. A hard-working target man he gave two superb performances in the centre of defence as an emergency replacement for the injured Darren Moore.

Wolverhampton W (Signed from Stocksbridge PS on 9/12/1992) FL 12+13/2 FLC 1 FAC 3+1/1 Others 3/1
Derby Co (£400,000 on 24/2/1995) FL 16/7
Port Vale (£200,000 on 1/8/1995) FL 81+28/35 FLC 7+3/5 FAC 0+3 Others 6/4
Bradford C (£1,000,000 on 7/8/1998) P/FL 63+2/28 FLC 5+1/1 FAC 4/1 Others 5/3
Manchester C (Loaned on 10/3/2000) FL 1+2
Portsmouth (£1,000,000 + on 11/8/2000) FL 22+2/4 FLC 3/1

MILTON Russell Maurice
Born: Folkestone, 12 January 1969
Height: 5'8" Weight: 12.1
Club Honours: FAT '98; NC '99
International Honours: E: SP-2

Russell had the misfortune to suffer a pelvic injury in the 2000 pre-season and as a result he was unable to appear for Cheltenham until the end of November. He continued to be affected by niggling injuries although he featured regularly in the second half of the campaign, contributing a goal in the 4-2 victory over Halifax in April. A set-piece specialist he plays either in the centre or on the left side of midfield.

Arsenal (From apprentice on 26/2/1987. Free to Double Flower, Hong Kong during 1988 close season)
Cheltenham T (Signed from Dover Ath on 12/8/1997) FL 56+1/10 FAC 3+1/2 Others 3/1

MIMMS Robert (Bobby) Andrew
Born: York, 12 October 1963
Height: 6'3" Weight: 14.4
Club Honours: Div 1 '87; CS '87
International Honours: E: U21-3

This veteran 'keeper replaced Ian Bowling as first-choice at Mansfield in the early part of last season and went on to retain his

position right up until the end of the campaign. Bobby performed consistently well plugging what had been a leaking defence and never letting the side down. He also helped the club as a goalkeeping coach and after his release in May he was expected to seek coaching work elsewhere.
Halifax T (From apprentice on 5/8/1981)
Rotherham U (£15,000 on 6/11/1981) FL 83 FLC 7 FAC 3 Others 1
Everton (£150,000 on 30/5/1985) FL 29 FLC 2 FAC 2 Others 4
Notts Co (Loaned on 13/3/1986) FL 2 Others 1
Sunderland (Loaned on 11/12/1986) FL 4
Blackburn Rov (Loaned on 23/1/1987) FL 6
Manchester C (Loaned on 24/9/1987) FL 3
Tottenham H (£325,000 on 25/2/1988) FL 37 FLC 5 FAC 2
Aberdeen (Loaned on 16/2/1990) SL 6 SC 2
Blackburn Rov (£250,000 on 22/12/1990) F/PL 126+2 FLC 15 FAC 9 Others 4
Crystal Palace (Free on 30/8/1996) FL 1
Preston NE (Free on 5/9/1996) FL 27 FLC 2 FAC 2
Rotherham U (Free on 8/8/1997) FL 43 FAC 4
York C (Signed on 14/8/1998) FL 63 FLC 1 FAC 2 Others 2
Mansfield T (Free on 22/3/2000) FL 45 FLC 3 FAC 2

MINTO Scott Christopher
Born: Heswall, 6 August 1971
Height: 5'9" Weight: 12.7
Club Honours: FAC '97
International Honours: E: U21-6; Yth

Scott spent most of last season recuperating from a serious knee injury suffered towards the end of the 1999-2000 campaign, and it was not until the final game at Middlesbrough that he made his long-awaited return to the West Ham line-up. A talented left-sided player who can feature either at full back or wing back he will be hoping that a full pre-season training programme will enable him to win back his place in the Hammers line-up.
Charlton Ath (From trainee on 2/2/1989) FL 171+9/7 FLC 8/2 FAC 8+2 Others 7/1
Chelsea (£775,000 on 28/5/1994) PL 53+1/4 FLC 3/1 FAC 9 Others 5+1 (Free to Benfica, Portugal on 30/6/1997)
West Ham U (£1,000,000 on 15/1/1999) PL 30+4 FLC 1 FAC 1 Others 5

MINTON Jeffrey (Jeff) Simon Thompson
Born: Hackney, 28 December 1973
Height: 5'6" Weight: 11.10
Club Honours: AMC '01

Jeff never really seemed to settle at Port Vale last season, despite scoring a superb goal from 25 yards out in the Worthington Cup first round second leg tie at Chesterfield in September. He had a short spell out due to suspension and was then dropped in the new year before moving on to join Second Division promotion candidates Rotherham United as cover for the suspended Stewart Talbot. He could hardly have made a more dramatic entrance at Millmoor scoring two goals and making the other in a 3-0 win over Bristol Rovers on his debut. Jeff is a talented midfield player with good passing skills who loves to push forward. Having joined the Millers on a short-term contract until the end of the campaign his future was uncertain at the time of writing.
Tottenham H (From trainee on 11/1/1992) FL 2/1 FLC 0+1
Brighton & Hove A (Free on 25/7/1994) FL 167+7/31 FLC 12/1 FAC 7 Others 5
Port Vale (Free on 1/7/1999) FL 34+2/4 FLC 4/2 FAC 3/2 Others 0+2
Rotherham U (Free on 16/3/2001) FL 5+4/2

MISKELLY David Thomas
Born: Newtonards, 3 September 1979
Height: 6'0" Weight: 12.9
International Honours: NI: U21-7; Yth

David was again understudy to first-choice 'keeper Gary Kelly for Oldham in the 2000-01 campaign. He produced some encouraging displays for the reserves but his senior appearances were limited to just two, one as a half-time replacement for the injured Kelly, during a mauling at Reading and the other a start against Swansea in April. Despite this he continue to feature regularly in the Northern Ireland U21 squad and added a further three caps during the season.
Oldham Ath (From trainee on 1/7/1997) FL 4+1 FLC 1

MITCHELL Graham Lee
Born: Shipley, 16 February 1968
Height: 6'1" Weight: 12.13

Graham captained Halifax Town in the early part of the 2000-01 campaign but struggled to find consistent form in the opening games. However, following a spell on the sidelines he put together a string of fine performances and played an important role in helping the Shaymen avoid relegation to the Conference. An experienced central defender who is very comfortable on the ball, his only goal last season came from a header in the 4-3 home defeat by Mansfield Town in February.
Huddersfield T (From trainee on 16/6/1986) FL 235+9/2 FLC 13+2/1 FAC 27/1 Others 24/1
Bournemouth (Loaned on 24/12/1993) FL 4
Bradford C (Signed on 23/12/1994) FL 64+1/1 FLC 8 FAC 2 Others 4
Raith Rov (Signed on 10/10/1996) SL 22+1 SLC 0+1 SC 1 Others 0+1
Cardiff C (Free on 4/8/1998) FL 46 FLC 2 FAC 5 Others 1
Halifax T (£45,000 on 20/7/1999) FL 87/3 FLC 4 FAC 3/1 Others 2

MITCHELL Paul Alexander
Born: Stalybridge, 26 August 1981
Height: 5'11" Weight: 12.3

Paul stepped up to sign a full professional contract for Wigan in July 2000 but found his first-team opportunities at the JJB Stadium very limited. He was eventually allowed to join Third Division Halifax Town on loan in March where he filled in admirably at right back in the closing months of the campaign. Paul is a hard-tackling defender with excellent distribution. He will be aiming to gain further senior experience in the 2001-02 season.
Wigan Ath (From trainee on 3/7/2000) FL 0+1 FLC 2+1 FAC 0+1 Others 1+1
Halifax T (Loaned on 22/3/2001) FL 11

MOHAN Nicholas (Nicky)
Born: Middlesbrough, 6 October 1970
Height: 6'1" Weight: 14.0
Club Honours: AMC '00

Nicky was once again a fixture in the Stoke City back line last term and rarely missed a match. He is an experienced central defender whose strengths lie in his determination, competitiveness and ability to organise his fellow defenders. Although he lost the team captaincy to Tony Dorigo during the season he remained an important figure for City and the defence appeared to lack leadership without his commanding presence.
Middlesbrough (From juniors on 18/11/1987) F/PL 93+6/4 FLC 11 FAC 9+1 Others 11
Hull C (Loaned on 26/9/1992) FL 5/1
Leicester C (£330,000 on 7/7/1994) PL 23 FLC 2 FAC 1
Bradford C (£225,000 on 13/7/1995) FL 83/4 FLC 8 FAC 5 Others 5
Wycombe W (Loaned on 14/8/1997) FL 6
Wycombe W (£75,000 on 10/10/1997) FL 52/2 FLC 3 FAC 4 Others 3
Stoke C (Free on 2/3/1999) FL 92+6 FLC 9 FAC 2 Others 12/1

MOILANEN Teuvo (Tepi) Johannes
Born: Oulu, Finland, 12 December 1973
Height: 6'5" Weight: 13.12
Club Honours: Div 2 '00
International Honours: Finland: 3; U21; Yth

Tepi started the 2000-01 season as first-choice 'keeper at Preston and contributed to the club's tremendous return to First Division football, before missing his first league game in 12 months in September following a back injury. However it was not until a run of defeats early in the new year that he won his place back and he proceeded to demonstrate his value with seven clean sheets in ten games before an injury at Burnley put him on the sidelines again. Tall and commanding, Tepi gets down fast and well for such a tall man, and he was sorely missed during the play-off run-in.
Preston NE (£120,000 from FF Jaro, Finland, ex Ilves, on 12/12/1995) FL 118+1 FLC 11 FAC 8 Others 2
Scarborough (Loaned on 12/12/1996) FL 4
Darlington (Loaned on 17/1/1997) FL 16

MOLENAAR Robert
Born: Zaandam, Holland, 27 February 1969
Height: 6'2" Weight: 14.4

Having finally recovered match fitness after suffering a cruciate knee ligament injury towards the end of 1998, Robert was unable to break into the first team at Leeds and in December he moved on to local rivals Bradford City. He went straight in the first team for the home game against Coventry and retained his place until the end of the season. A commanding central defender with a no-nonsense attitude, he proved to be an outstanding signing for the Bantams but was unable to prevent them dropping down to the First Division.
Leeds U (£1,000,000 from FC Volendam, Holland, ex Zilvermeuwen, on 11/1/1997) PL 47+4/5 FLC 4+1 FAC 5/1 Others 4
Bradford C (£500,000 on 1/12/2000) PL 21/1 FAC 1

MOLLER Peter Nielsen
Born: Gistrup, Denmark, 23 March 1972
Height: 6'3" Weight: 13.5
International Honours: Denmark: 17

Peter joined Fulham on loan in January from Spanish club, Real Oviedo to cover for injuries and suspensions to the strike force.

He only started two games, scoring in the second of these against Queens Park Rangers with rather a soft shot. A very tall target man, he seemed to find it difficult to adapt to the Cottagers' style of play.
Fulham (Loaned from Real Oviedo, Spain, ex Aalborg, FC Copenhagen, Brondby IF, Ajax, on 25/1/2001) FL 2+3/1

MONCUR John Frederick
Born: Stepney, 22 September 1966
Height: 5'7" Weight: 9.10
Although not featuring regularly in the starting line-up for West Ham in 2000-01 John was still a very valuable member of the squad and was often used as a substitute to come on and liven things up. He produced a great display in the vital match with Derby in April, when his all-round enthusiasm helped the Hammers to a 3-1 victory. A hard-working midfield player with good passing skills, he proved his loyalty by signing a contract that will ensure he remains at Upton Park for another season.
Tottenham H (From apprentice on 22/8/1984) FL 10+11/1 FLC 1+2
Doncaster Rov (Loaned on 25/9/1986) FL 4
Cambridge U (Loaned on 27/3/1987) FL 3+1
Portsmouth (Loaned on 22/3/1989) FL 7
Brentford (Loaned on 19/10/1989) FL 5/1 Others 1
Ipswich T (Loaned on 24/10/1991) FL 5+1
Swindon T (£80,000 on 30/3/1992) F/PL 53+5/5 FLC 4 FAC 1 Others 4/1
West Ham U (£900,000 on 24/6/1994) PL 124+25/6 FLC 12+1/2 FAC 6+1/1 Others 5+1

MONINGTON Mark David
Born: Bilsthorpe, 21 October 1970
Height: 6'1" Weight: 14.0
Club Honours: AMC '96
Rochdale's big centre half had to wait for his chance at the start of last season, but when it came he grabbed it in spectacular style. He netted in each of his first three appearances and scored six goals in his first eight starts, an amazing record for a defender. Mark is an uncompromising defender who is a strong tackler and good in the air. He was reported to have signed for Boston United in the summer.
Burnley (From juniors on 23/3/1989) FL 65+19/5 FLC 5 FAC 4+1/1 Others 4+2
Rotherham U (Signed on 28/11/1994) FL 75+4/3 FLC 3 FAC 1 Others 4
Rochdale (Free on 6/7/1998) FL 90+5/12 FAC 8/1 Others 8/3

MONK Garry Alan
Born: Bedford, 6 March 1979
Height: 6'0" Weight: 13.0
This promising Southampton defender joined Oxford United on loan in January to gain further experience of senior football and acquitted himself well in his month at the Manor Ground, despite playing in a struggling team. He subsequently returned to The Dell and was called up to the first-team squad towards the end of the season, appearing in the final two games against Manchester United and Arsenal. A powerfully built central defender who is strong and very quick, he will be hoping to make the breakthrough to a regular place in the Saints' line-up in 2001-02.
Torquay U (Trainee) FL 4+1
Southampton (Signed on 23/5/1997) PL 7+1 FAC 0+1
Torquay U (Loaned on 25/9/1998) FL 6
Stockport Co (Loaned on 9/9/1999) FL 2 FLC 2
Oxford U (Loaned on 12/1/2001) FL 5

MONKHOUSE Andrew (Andy) William
Born: Leeds, 23 October 1980
Height: 6'1" Weight: 11.6
Although one of the most skilful ball players on Rotherham's books, Andy found his first-team appearances limited last season due mainly to the consistent form of the club's other strikers. He scored some absolutely brilliant goals for the reserves but he really needs an extended first-team run to bring out the best in him and fulfil his obvious potential.
Rotherham U (From trainee on 14/11/1998) FL 1+16/1 FAC 0+3 Others 1+1/1

MONKOU Kenneth (Ken) John
Born: Surinam, 29 November 1964
Height: 6'3" Weight: 14.4
Club Honours: FMC '90
International Honours: Holland: U21
This veteran defender only featured briefly for Huddersfield Town during the 2000-01 campaign, appearing in the home games with Bolton Wanderers and Wimbledon last September. Always commanding in defence and a strong leader, Ken unfortunately fell out of favour at the MacAlpine Stadium and found himself on the transfer list. Cardiff City and Reading both showed interest in taking him on loan, but neither move materialised and after being released around the transfer deadline he had a brief trial with Sheffield United.
Chelsea (£100,000 from Feyenoord, Holland on 2/3/1989) FL 92+2/2 FLC 12 FAC 3 Others 10
Southampton (£750,000 on 21/8/1992) PL 190+8/10 FLC 18+1/2 FAC 16/1
Huddersfield T (Free on 23/8/1999) FL 21/1 FLC 4

MONTGOMERY Nicholas (Nick) Anthony
Born: Leeds, 28 October 1981
Height: 5'9" Weight: 11.8
Having joined the professional ranks in the close season Nick made his Football League debut for Sheffield United at Norwich last October and went on to establish himself as a regular in the first-team squad with some most encouraging performances. A hard-working attacking midfielder with the ability to run at defenders his foraging down the flanks often created openings for his colleagues. Voted the supporters' club 'Young Player of the Year' he was also rewarded with a new three-year contract towards the end of the campaign.
Sheffield U (From trainee on 7/7/2000) FL 14+13 FLC 1 FAC 1

MOODY Adrian James Harkin
Born: Birkenhead, 29 September 1982
Height: 6'0" Weight: 12.7
Adrian is a second-year scholar at Wrexham and made his debut in senior football in the FA Wales Premier Cup tie at Carmarthen last October. He then made his bow in the Football League when he came on as a substitute for the Robins at Reading later that month and went on to make the starting line-up on a couple more occasions later in the season. A promising central defender he appeared regularly for the club's reserve team in the Avon Insurance League.
Wrexham (Trainee) FL 2+1

MOODY Paul
Born: Portsmouth, 13 June 1967
Height: 6'3" Weight: 14.9
Club Honours: Div 2 '01
This big, bustling centre forward had a fine season for Second Division champions Millwall in 2000-01 despite having the odd spell out with niggling injuries. Paul is an excellent target man being a constant threat in the air, quick on the turn and able to hold the ball up well. He scored a creditable 14 goals from just 21 starts including a great hat-trick in the 3-1 win over Wigan Athletic in January.
Southampton (£50,000 from Waterlooville on 15/7/1991) F/PL 7+5 FLC 1 FAC 0+1
Reading (Loaned on 9/12/1992) FL 5/1 Others 1
Oxford U (£60,000 on 19/2/1994) FL 98+38/49 FLC 10+4/4 FAC 7+1/5 Others 3/3
Fulham (£200,000 on 4/7/1997) FL 29+11/19 FLC 2+2 FAC 1+1 Others 2/1
Millwall (£150,000 on 5/7/1999) FL 45+14/24 FLC 1+1 FAC 2/1 Others 3+1

MOONEY Thomas (Tommy) John
Born: Billingham, 11 August 1971
Height: 5'10" Weight: 12.6
Club Honours: Div 2 '98
Tommy added a personal landmark to his already illustrious Vicarage Road career by exceeding the 20-goal mark for the first time - the first Watford player to do so for seven seasons. The club's leading scorer and very much a cult hero with the fans he was voted as 'Player of the Year' and served as an inspirational captain in Robert Page's absence. A left-footed striker who is effective either in a central role or wide on the left-hand side he is outstanding in the air. During the summer he was reported to have signed for First Division rivals Birmingham City.
Aston Villa (From trainee on 23/11/1989)
Scarborough (Free on 1/8/1990) FL 96+11/30 FLC 11+2/8 FAC 3 Others 6/2
Southend U (£100,000 on 12/7/1993) FL 9+5/5 FLC 1+1 Others 2+3
Watford (Signed on 17/3/1994) P/FL 221+29/60 FLC 22/3 FAC 11+1/2 Others 4

MOORE Darren Mark
Born: Birmingham, 22 April 1974
Height: 6'2" Weight: 15.6
International Honours: Jamaica: 3
Appointed club captain at Portsmouth for 2000-01, Darren showed some fine form for the first two-thirds of the campaign. Unfortunately he was sidelined with an ankle injury soon after new boss Graham Rix arrived and he failed to recover full fitness before the summer break. A central defender who dominates with his physical presence, he has a tremendous work rate and is a natural leader. Darren is also surprisingly agile in the air and often comes forward for corners to add his tower of strength in the penalty area. His presence was sorely missed in the final run-in, as was

illustrated by the fact that 18 goals were conceded in the last ten games.

Torquay U (From trainee on 18/11/1992) FL 102+1/8 FLC 6 FAC 7/2 Others 8/2
Doncaster Rov (£62,500 on 19/7/1995) FL 76/7 FLC 4 FAC 1 Others 3/1
Bradford C (£310,000 + on 18/6/1997) FL 62/3 FLC 6/1 FAC 2
Portsmouth (£500,000 + on 15/11/1999) FL 56+1/2 FLC 4 FAC 2

MOORE Ian Ronald
Born: Birkenhead, 26 August 1976
Height: 5'11" Weight: 12.0
International Honours: E: U21-7; Yth

Ian hit form early on last season at Stockport, netting two goals in the opening day 3-1 win at Gillingham and he quickly attracted the attention of other clubs. Having turned down Norwich he chose to sign for Second Division rivals Burnley who paid their first-ever £1 million fee to secure his services. Although arriving with a reputation as one of the First Division's top marksmen it soon became clear that his value to the Clarets was his speed, skill and non-stop commitment as much as his goal-scoring exploits. His first goal for the club came at Preston with a beautifully crafted 20-yard shot that curled into the net but the promise of more to come was not really fulfilled until he linked up with loan man Gareth Taylor towards the end of the campaign. Ian's best is yet to come and the Turf Moor fans look forward to more goals in the future.

Tranmere Rov (From trainee on 6/7/1994) FL 41+17/12 FLC 3+2/1 FAC 1+1 Others 0+1
Bradford C (Loaned on 13/9/1996) FL 6
Nottingham F (£1,000,000 on 15/3/1997) F/PL 3+12/1 FLC 0+2 FAC 1
West Ham U (Loaned on 26/9/1997) PL 0+1
Stockport Co (£800,000 on 31/7/1998) FL 83+10/20 FLC 8/2 FAC 3/1
Burnley (£1,000,000 on 20/11/2000) FL 26+1/5 FAC 2/1

MOORE Joe-Max
Born: Tulsa, USA, 23 February 1971
Height: 5'9" Weight: 10.10
International Honours: USA: 91; U21

After bursting onto the Premiership scene with a flurry of goals the previous campaign, Joe-Max couldn't buy a goal in 2000-01. A quick, elusive forward with good finishing skills, he was disappointing throughout his second English season. He was never really helped by a consistent run of matches but showed his versatility by playing in midfield on occasions. After an entire year without a goal he broke his duck in a reserve team match at Manchester City, sadly just a little too late in the season to give him confidence to take into the Premiership campaign. He continued to appear for the USA in international matches and netted a double in the 7-0 World Cup qualifying win over Barbados last August.

Everton (Free from New England Revolution, USA on 7/12/1999) PL 19+17/6 FLC 1+1 FAC 1+4/2

MOREAU Fabrice
Born: Paris, France, 7 October 1967
Height: 5'9" Weight: 11.4

Fabrice was one of several players who arrived at Airdrie from Spanish clubs at the beginning of last season. He did well with the troubled First Division outfit, scoring six goals from 21 starts before moving south of the border to join Notts County on a short-term contract shortly before the transfer deadline. He showed some inspirational form in his early games for the Magpies but faded a little afterwards and was released at the end of the campaign. He is a very skilful midfield play maker who links up well with the strikers to create chances.

Airdrieonians (Signed from CD Numancia, Spain, ex La Roche, Paris St Germain, Le Mans, Meaux, Racing Paris, Olympique Marseille, St Etienne, Toulon, Rayo Vallecano, Talavera, Quan Guoan, on 4/8/2000) SL 21+3/6 SLC 3 SC 1/1 Others 5
Notts Co (Free on 16/3/2001) FL 2+3

MORGAN Alan Meredith
Born: Aberystwyth, 2 November 1973
Height: 5'10" Weight: 11.4
International Honours: W: U21-2; Yth; Sch

Alan suffered from a series of niggling injuries at Tranmere last season and played most of his football in the club's successful reserve team. A versatile player who is equally at home either at full back or in a midfield role he can also make a decent stab at being an emergency attacker if needs be! A gutsy player who never shirks a challenge he will be hoping to stay clear of the treatment room in 2001-02.

Tranmere Rov (From trainee on 8/5/1992) FL 41+22/1 FLC 6+2/1 FAC 3+2

MORGAN David **Bari** Rees
Born: Carmarthen, 13 August 1980
Height: 5'6" Weight: 10.8

After developing through the ranks at Swansea Bari stepped up to make his Football League debut when he came on from the subs' bench for the final minutes of the game at Millwall last September. He made further appearances as a substitute later in the season before being sidelined by a groin injury in April. A promising young midfielder or striker he was one of a number of fringe players at Vetch Field who suffered from the absence of regular reserve-team football last term. Out of contract in the summer his future was unclear at the time of writing.

Swansea C (From trainee on 5/7/1999) FL 0+5 Others 0+1

MORGAN Christopher (Chris) Paul
Born: Barnsley, 9 November 1977
Height: 5'10" Weight: 12.9

Chris was again a first-team regular for Barnsley last term. A big favourite of the Oakwell crowd, not only because he is a local lad but because he never gives less than 100 per cent for the team, he scored his first senior goal when he netted a last-minute winner against Burnley on Boxing Day. He is a tough strong central defender who never shirks a challenge. Chris signed an extension to his contract during the season that will keep him at Oakwell until the summer of 2004.

Barnsley (From trainee on 3/7/1996) P/FL 104+3/1 FLC 11/1 FAC 6 Others 3

MORGAN Dean
Born: Enfield, 3 October 1983
Height: 5'11" Weight: 11.2

This promising Colchester trainee produced some fine performances for the youth team last season and stepped up to make his Football League debut from the subs' bench against Northampton in November. He subsequently made three more appearances as a substitute towards the end of the campaign and will be looking to gain further senior experience in 2001-02. Dean is a pacy striker who linked up well with Scott McGleish in his brief first-team outings.

Colchester U (Trainee) FL 0+4

Lionel Morgan

MORGAN Lionel Anthony
Born: Tottenham, 17 February 1983
Height: 5'11" Weight: 12.7
International Honours: E: Yth

Another product of the successful Wimbledon Academy, Lionel was a surprise starter in the home match with Watford last August. He made an impressive debut and this was followed up by a handful of appearances from the subs' bench but he then had the misfortune to fracture an ankle playing for the U19s against Birmingham in October and it was not until the final two games of the season that he made a return to the Dons' first team. A speedy left winger he concluded a very promising game by netting a hat-trick for the reserves. He was capped by England U17s in the end-of-season game against Italy.

Wimbledon (From trainee on 10/8/2000) FL 1+4 FLC 0+1

MORGAN Mark **Paul** Thomas
Born: Belfast, 23 October 1978
Height: 6'0" Weight: 11.5
International Honours: NI: U21-1

Paul finally made his first-team debut for Preston in the Worthington Cup tie at Shrewsbury last season, when he looked very comfortable on the ball, pushing out of defence with skill and confidence. He was later an unused substitute for the FA Cup game against Stockport and will be looking for further senior experience in 2001-02. A promising young central defender he is effective in the air and times his tackles well. He was reported to have joined Lincoln City on a monthly contract in the summer.

Preston NE (From trainee on 9/5/1997) FLC 1

MORGAN Simon Charles
Born: Birmingham, 5 September 1966
Height: 5'10" Weight: 12.5
Club Honours: Div 2 '99
International Honours: E: U21-2

Injuries plagued Simon's season at Fulham last term to such an extent that he was unable to play in a competitive match until mid-March. In typical fashion however, he appeared in the last seven reserve matches, of which five were won, to clinch the Avon Insurance Combination title in front of a very appreciative audience at Motspur Park. His long-awaited return to the first team came against Wolves on 24 April when he was named on the bench and came on for the final 15 minutes to a rapturous welcome from the spectators present. Out of contract in the summer he was reported to have signed for his former boss Micky Adams at Brighton.

Leicester C (From apprentice on 15/11/1984) FL 147+13/3 FLC 14/1 FAC 4+1 Others 3
Fulham (£100,000 on 12/10/1990) FL 343+10/48 FLC 33/2 FAC 19/3 Others 17/4

MORGAN Stephen (Steve) Alphonso
Born: Oldham, 19 September 1968
Height: 5'11" Weight: 11.8
Club Honours: Div 3 '97
International Honours: E: Yth

This experienced left-sided player joined Halifax Town in the early part of last season and made his debut in the splendid 2-1 away victory against Torquay United. However he fell out of favour following a managerial change and moved on firstly to Altrincham and then to League of Wales club TNS Llansantffraid.

Blackpool (From apprentice on 12/8/1986) FL 135+9/10 FLC 13/2 FAC 16/1 Others 10+1/1
Plymouth Arg (£115,000 on 16/7/1990) FL 120+1/6 FLC 7 FAC 6 Others 5
Coventry C (£110,000 on 14/7/1993) PL 65+3/2 FLC 5/3 FAC 5
Bristol Rov (Loaned on 1/3/1996) FL 5 Others 2
Wigan Ath (Free on 10/7/1996) FL 31+5/2 FLC 2 FAC 1 Others 4
Bury (Loaned on 26/9/1997) FL 5
Burnley (Free on 7/8/1998) FL 17 FLC 2 FAC 1
Hull C (Free on 29/7/1999) FL 17+2/1 FAC 3+1 Others 2/1
Halifax T (Free on 22/9/2000) FL 1

MORINI Emanuele
Born: Rome, Italy, 31 January 1982
Height: 5'8" Weight: 10.7

A free transfer signing from Roma, Emanuele joined Bolton Wanderers on a four-year contract last September. A young striker with quite a reputation, he found his first-team opportunities somewhat limited but he was a consistent scorer at youth and reserve-team level. After an appearance from the subs' bench he made the starting line-up for the FA Cup third round game against Yeovil and also featured in the final game of the regular season against Sheffield United. A promising and very skilful youngster, he will be hoping for more first team opportunities in 2001-02.

Bolton W (Free from Roma, Italy on 4/9/2000) FL 1+1 FAC 1

MORLEY Benjamin (Ben)
Born: Hull, 22 December 1980
Height: 5'9" Weight: 10.1

Ben struggled to win a place in the Hull City first-team squad under new manager Brian Little last season. He was restricted to just three outings from the subs' bench and spent the remainder of the campaign in the Tigers' reserve team. A promising young right wing back he was released at the end of the campaign.

Hull C (From trainee on 10/12/1998) FL 6+17 FLC 1+1 FAC 2/1 Others 1+2

MORLEY David Thomas
Born: St Helens, 25 September 1977
Height: 6'2" Weight: 12.7

David featured regularly for Southend in the early part of last season although he was often used as a substitute. He eventually moved on loan to Carlisle United in January where he created an immediate impact and quickly earned a permanent transfer. He scored his first goal for the Cumbrians with a close-range header in the 2-1 win over Mansfield and went on to produce some fine performances. A tall central defender who is good in the air and quite effective in his occasional forays up the field, he can also play in midfield and up front if required.

Manchester C (From trainee on 3/1/1996) FL 1+2/1
Ayr U (Loaned on 14/3/1998) SL 4
Southend U (Signed on 28/8/1998) FL 63+13 FLC 6 FAC 0+2 Others 2
Carlisle U (Free on 26/1/2001) FL 23/1

MORRELL Andrew (Andy) Jonathan
Born: Doncaster, 28 September 1974
Height: 5'11" Weight: 12.0

Andy began the 2000-01 campaign on the bench at Wrexham before dropping down to the reserve team for whom he scored regularly, but when Lee Trundle joined the Robins the two were paired together up front with some success. He netted excellent goals at home to Northampton and with a diving header at Cambridge, and will be aiming to finally make a breakthrough to regular first-team football in the coming season.

Wrexham (Free from Newcastle Blue Star on 18/12/1998) FL 18+22/4 FLC 1 FAC 0+1 Others 1+1

MORRIS Andrew (Andy)
Born: Prescot, 18 March 1982
Height: 5'10" Weight: 11.1

This former Wigan trainee stepped up to the professional ranks in July 2000 but found senior opportunities few and far between. He was largely restricted to reserve-team football, making just one first team appearance in the LDV Vans Trophy tie against Oldham Athletic. Andy is a right-sided midfield player who is good at keeping possession and passes accurately over both long and short distances. He was one of several players released by the club in the close season.

Wigan Ath (From trainee on 3/7/2000) Others 1+2/1

MORRIS Jody Steven
Born: Hammersmith, 22 December 1978
Height: 5'5" Weight: 10.12
Club Honours: ECWC '98; FAC '00; CS '00
International Honours: E: U21-7; Yth; Sch

This local-born midfielder endured another frustrating season as he strove to claim a regular first-team place at Chelsea last term in the face of intense competition. He spent the campaign shuttling between the starting line-up and a place on the subs' bench. However his prospects looked brighter after Claudio Ranieri's appointment and his publicly stated desire to build a young team with an English backbone. Along with fellow U21 internationals John Terry and Jon Harley he forms a triumvirate of the brightest of home-grown talent at the club. His midfield partnership with overseas youngsters such as Mario Melchiot and Sam Dalla Bona augurs well for the Blues as some of the older players begin to be replaced. Having forced his way into the side, Jody had the misfortune to suffer an ankle ligament injury in the FA Cup fourth round tie at Gillingham and was sidelined for several weeks.

Chelsea (From trainee on 8/1/1996) PL 61+33/5 FLC 6+1/2 FAC 7+3/1 Others 10+9

MORRIS Lee
Born: Blackpool, 30 April 1980
Height: 5'10" Weight: 11.2
International Honours: E: U21-1; Yth

After a disappointing initial season at Derby, Lee must have been hoping for more chances to shine at first-team level last term. However, despite playing in the opening game against Southampton, he found himself having to settle for a series of substitute appearances as the campaign wore on. A left-sided striker, his key strengths are his lightning pace and an ability to ghost past defenders with the ball. Loaned to Huddersfield in March to gain regular first-team football, he made an instant impact at the MacAlpine Stadium by scoring on his debut in an away defeat at local rivals Barnsley. Operating either as a striker or on the wing he worked hard and linked well with his team-mates before returning prematurely to Pride Park due to an injury crisis and he then impressed in a run of games in the successful battle against relegation.

Sheffield U (From trainee on 24/12/1997) FL 14+12/6 FAC 2+5/2 Others 0+1
Derby Co (£1,800,000 + on 7/6/1999) PL 6+17 FLC 0+2 FAC 0+1
Huddersfield T (Loaned on 8/3/2001) FL 5/1

MORRISON Andrew (Andy) Charles
Born: Inverness, 30 July 1970
Height: 6'0" Weight: 14.8

Having missed a large chunk of the previous season due to a bad knee injury, Andy battled back to fitness and in September he returned to his former club Blackpool on loan in a bid to recover match fitness. He appeared regularly for the Tangerines before moving on for another short loan period at Crystal Palace where he did quite well in five appearances for the First Division club. Back at Maine Road he finally returned to the first team for the Worthington Cup fifth round tie against Ipswich in December and played in a handful of games for City over the next few weeks. Although he certainly didn't look out of place in the top flight he faced fierce competition from Steve Howey and Richard Dunne for a place in the line-up and subsequently joined Sheffield United in yet another loan deal on the transfer deadline day. His debut came in the 4-1 defeat at Gillingham but following an excellent performance at Grimsby he was sidelined by an injury and his season came to a premature close. A tall and commanding central defender he will be hoping for a quick return to fitness. Out of contract in the summer his future remained unclear at the time of writing.

Plymouth Arg (From trainee on 6/7/1988) FL 105+8/6 FLC 10+1/1 FAC 6 Others 2+1
Blackburn Rov (£500,000 on 5/8/1993) PL 1+4 FAC 1
Blackpool (£245,000 on 9/12/1994) FL 47/3 FAC 2 Others 4
Huddersfield T (£500,000 on 4/7/1996) FL 43+2/2 FLC 8 FAC 2
Manchester C (£80,000 on 29/10/1998) P/FL 36+1/4 FLC 3 FAC 7/1 Others 1
Blackpool (Loaned on 1/9/2000) FL 6/1
Crystal Palace (Loaned on 12/10/2000) FL 5
Sheffield U (Loaned on 22/3/2001) FL 3+1

Clint Morrison

MORRISON Clinton (Clint) Hubert
Born: Wandsworth, 14 May 1979
Height: 6'1" Weight: 11.2
International Honours: RoI: U21-2

After signing a new four-year contract in the summer of 2000 Clint found himself one of several Crystal Palace players to be placed on the transfer list by new manager Alan Smith. He bounced back in style, hitting a rich goal-scoring vein that saw him take the Nationwide 'Player of the Month' award last December. He continued to impress as a striker with an excellent first touch and a good eye for goal. Clint netted a total of 19 league and cup goals during 2000-01 as he finished leading scorer for the Eagles for the third season in succession. Having opted for an international career with the Republic of Ireland he made his U21 debut against Portugal in the summer and followed this up with a further cap against Estonia when he had a goal disallowed.

Crystal Palace (From trainee on 29/3/1997) P/FL 96+16/40 FLC 13+3/7 FAC 3/1

MORRISON John **Owen**
Born: Londonderry, 8 December 1981
Height: 5'8" Weight: 11.12
International Honours: NI: U21-1; Yth; Sch

Owen had an excellent season for Sheffield Wednesday in 2000-01 when he established himself as a regular in the first-team squad from mid-September playing as a striker or wide on the left of midfield. Quick, skilful and with an eye for goal the Owls have high hopes that he will continue to make good progress in the coming season. His performances won him a call-up for the Northern Ireland U21s and he made his debut as a substitute against Bulgaria last March.

Sheffield Wed (From trainee on 5/1/1999) P/FL 20+11/6 FLC 5/2 FAC 0+2

MORRISON Peter Anthony
Born: Manchester, 29 June 1980
Height: 5'11" Weight: 10.8

Peter made his Football League debut for Scunthorpe on the opening day of last season and was a regular in the squad for the first two months. Effectively used as a substitute, his season was cruelly ended in February when he suffered a double compound fracture of the left leg in a reserve game against Grimsby. The injury was serious enough to cause the match to be abandoned and was expected to keep him out of the game for some time. Peter is a speedy left winger who has great crossing ability.

Bolton W (From trainee on 2/7/1998)
Scunthorpe U (Free on 30/5/2000) FL 8+10 FLC 1+1 FAC 2+1 Others 1

MORROW Andrew (Andy) Gareth
Born: Bangor, NI, 5 October 1980
Height: 5'8" Weight: 9.10
International Honours: NI: U21-1; Yth; Sch

Andy produced some fine displays for Northampton reserves last season and had a couple of outings from the subs' bench before making the starting line-up for the LDV Vans tie at Millwall. He later started a couple of Second Division games and won further caps for Northern Ireland U18s before stepping up to make his debut for the U21s as a substitute against Denmark last October. Out of contract in the summer his future was unclear at the time of writing.

Northampton T (From trainee on 16/12/1998) FL 2+6 Others 3

MORROW Stephen (Steve) Joseph
Born: Bangor, NI, 2 July 1970
Height: 6'0" Weight: 11.6
Club Honours: FAYC '88; FLC '93; ECEC '94
International Honours: NI: 39; B-1; U23-2; Yth; Sch

Having recovered from the shoulder injury that had sidelined him for much of the 1999-2000 campaign, Steve started last season as a first choice in the Queens Park Rangers' defence. He kept his place in the team until the end of October when he was injured, but despite regaining match fitness he only featured occasionally and in March he moved to Second Division Peterborough United on loan as a replacement for Adam Drury. He appeared regularly for Posh in the closing weeks of the campaign firstly at full back, where he looked a little out of position, and later as a central defender where he appeared to be more at home. A versatile player who can also feature in midfield he was released by Rangers in the summer.

Arsenal (From trainee on 5/5/1988) F/PL 39+23/1 FLC 7+4/2 FAC 5+2 Others 1+4
Reading (Loaned on 16/1/1991) FL 10
Watford (Loaned on 14/8/1991) FL 7+1 Others 1
Reading (Loaned on 30/10/1991) FL 3
Barnet (Loaned on 4/3/1992) FL 1
Queens Park R (£1,000,000 on 27/3/1997) FL 84+7/2 FLC 6 FAC 3
Peterborough U (Loaned on 22/3/2001) FL 11

MOSES Adrian (Ade) Paul
Born: Doncaster, 4 May 1975
Height: 5'10" Weight: 12.8
International Honours: E: U21-2

Having missed most of the 1999-2000 campaign through injury, Ade returned to the Barnsley line-up on the opening day of last season. He was employed by Dave Bassett as a central defender and then at right back, however immediately after Bassett was replaced as manager Ade was sold to Huddersfield Town who needed him as extra cover across the back four. A strong and quick player, he had to settle for a place on the substitutes' bench before gaining a regular first-team berth after the turn of the year. A very versatile defender he is solid in the tackle and heads the ball well.

Barnsley (From juniors on 2/7/1993) F/PL 137+14/3 FLC 15 FAC 15
Huddersfield T (£225,000 on 20/12/2000) FL 10+2

MOSS Neil Graham
Born: New Milton, 10 May 1975
Height: 6'2" Weight: 13.10

A more than capable understudy to Paul Jones between the sticks for Southampton, Neil made three early season appearances and was unlucky to lose the first-team spot after performing admirably. Now into his mid-20s he is approaching the stage of his career when he needs regular first-team football and he will be trying to achieve this next term.

Bournemouth (From trainee on 29/1/1993) FL 21+1 FLC 1 FAC 3+1 Others 2
Southampton (£250,000 on 20/12/1995) PL 20+2 FLC 2
Gillingham (Loaned on 8/8/1997) FL 10 FLC 2

MOUNTY Carl Trevor
Born: Caerphilly, 11 December 1981
Height: 5'10" Weight: 12.7
Carl started the 2000-01 season as third-choice goalkeeper at Swansea and in October was sent out on loan to League of Ireland club Waterford where he earned some good reviews. Following another loan spell with League of Wales side Bangor City he was recalled to the Vetch Field and was on the subs' bench for the LDV Vans Trophy tie against Brentford when he made his senior debut after Roger Freestone received a red card. A promising youngster he was out of contract in the summer and his future was unclear at the time of writing.
Swansea C (From trainee on 5/7/2000) Others 0+1

MUDGE James Robert Mark
Born: Exeter, 25 June 1983
Height: 5'11" Weight: 11.9
This young Exeter City striker made his Football League debut in the home game against Macclesfield last February when he came off the subs' bench to replace the injured Paul Read. A prolific marksman at youth-team level, the Grecians' relegation worries ruled out an extended run in the team but James will be looking for more first-team chances in the 2001-02 season.
Exeter C (Trainee) FL 0+3

MUGGLETON Carl David
Born: Leicester, 13 September 1968
Height: 6'2" Weight: 13.4
International Honours: E: U21-1
This experienced 'keeper came into the Stoke City team in October in place of the injured Gavin Ward, and retained his place until the beginning of December shortly after the 8-0 massacre by Liverpool in the Worthington Cup. He was subsequently loaned out to Third Division promotion hopefuls Cardiff City in March where he provided competition for regular 'keeper Mark Walton, but after half-a-dozen games for the Bluebirds he returned to the Britannia Stadium. Carl was released by City in the summer and was reported to have signed for Cheltenham Town.
Leicester C (From apprentice on 17/9/1986) FL 46 FAC 3 Others 5
Chesterfield (Loaned on 10/9/1987) FL 17 Others 2
Blackpool (Loaned on 1/2/1988) FL 2
Hartlepool U (Loaned on 28/10/1988) FL 8 Others 2
Stockport Co (Loaned on 1/3/1990) FL 4
Stoke C (Loaned on 13/8/1993) FL 6 FLC 1 Others 2
Glasgow Celtic (£150,000 on 11/1/1994) SL 12 SC 1
Stoke C (£150,000 on 21/7/1994) FL 148+1 FLC 17 FAC 5 Others 6
Rotherham U (Loaned on 1/11/1995) FL 6 Others 1
Sheffield U (Loaned on 28/3/1996) FL 0+1
Mansfield T (Loaned on 9/9/1999) FL 9
Chesterfield (Loaned on 9/12/1999) FL 5
Cardiff C (Loaned on 15/3/2001) FL 6

MULLER Adam Phillip
Born: Leeds, 17 April 1982
Height: 5'11" Weight: 12.0
Adam is another of the many talented youngsters on Sheffield Wednesday's books and made his debut in senior football when he came on from the subs' bench at Grimsby last August. He featured in a number of early-season games before dropping back into the reserves. He was subsequently loaned to Unibond League club Worksop Town last March to gain further experience. Adam is an intelligent striker with good pace who will be aiming to win a regular place in the Owls' first-team squad in the coming season.
Sheffield Wed (Signed from Ossett T on 18/5/2000) FL 1+4 FLC 0+1

MULLIN John Michael
Born: Bury, 11 August 1975
Height: 6'0" Weight: 11.10
John spent much of the 2000-01 campaign on the subs' bench for Burnley and only made the starting line-up occasionally. He was most often seen in an attacking midfield role from where his foraging runs often troubled opposition defences, but was also occasionally used as a striker and never let the side down when called upon. He scored what proved to be the winner at QPR just four minutes after coming off the bench.
Burnley (From trainee on 18/8/1992) FL 7+11/2 FAC 2
Sunderland (£40,000 + on 12/8/1995) P/FL 23+12/4 FLC 5+1 FAC 2+1
Preston NE (Loaned on 13/2/1998) FL 4+3 Others 1
Burnley (Loaned on 26/3/1998) FL 6
Burnley (Free on 20/7/1999) FL 38+35/8 FLC 1+1 FAC 5+1/1 Others 1

Hayden Mullins

MULLINS Hayden Ian
Born: Reading, 27 March 1979
Height: 6'0" Weight: 11.12
International Honours: E: U21-3
Hayden once again impressed in the 2000-01 season, despite missing a number of games through suspension. An effective ball winner in the centre of the park for Crystal Palace he possesses good passing skills and control. He is a popular player but managed just one goal during the campaign, scoring in the 2-3 home defeat by Blackburn just before Christmas.
Crystal Palace (From trainee on 28/2/1997) FL 123+3/16 FLC 15/1 FAC 4 Others 2

Phil Mulryne

MULRYNE Phillip (Phil) Patrick
Born: Belfast, 1 January 1978
Height: 5'8" Weight: 10.11
Club Honours: FAYC '95
International Honours: NI: 12; B-1; U21-3; Yth
Another injury-interrupted campaign in 2000-01 prevented this talented Norwich City play maker from making the impact his ability suggests he should. On his day Phil has the all-round midfield game to match the best; he is a terrific passer of the ball over both short and long distances and also has the vision to deliver the defence-splitting pass. He loves getting forward and although he is capable of scoring more goals than he does, at the present he would be more than content to play a long sequence of games without injury. A set-piece specialist, he returned to the full Northern Ireland set-up during 2000-2001 winning further caps against Yugoslavia and Denmark.
Manchester U (From trainee on 17/3/1995) PL 1 FLC 3 FAC 0+1
Norwich C (£500,000 on 25/3/1999) FL 40+4/3 FLC 4 FAC 1

MUMFORD Andrew Owen
Born: Neath, 18 June 1981
Height: 6'2" Weight: 13.6
International Honours: W: Yth; Sch
Andrew joined Swansea City from League of Wales outfit Llanelli on a 12-month contract in July 2000 and after enjoying loan spells with Haverfordwest and Port Talbot he stepped up to make his Football League

debut from the subs' bench at Port Vale on Easter Monday when he appeared in an unfamiliar striker's role. He subsequently made a handful more appearances in central midfield where he looked very promising. Out of contract in the summer his future was unclear at the time of writing.
Swansea C (Free from Llanelli T on 14/6/2000) FL 2+4

MUNROE Karl Augustus
Born: Manchester, 23 September 1979
Height: 6'0" Weight: 11.0
Karl provided a real physical presence in the centre of midfield for Macclesfield in the early part of last season but after featuring fairly regularly until December he gave way to the more experienced partnership of Kevin Keen and Chris Priest. The high point of his campaign came in the Worthington Cup first round second leg tie against Bolton when he picked up a loose clearance and chipped the ball into an empty net from 35 yards to score his first goal in senior football.
Swansea C (From trainee on 9/7/1998) FL 0+1
Macclesfield T (Free on 14/10/1999) FL 20+8/1 FLC 4/1 FAC 1 Others 1

MURDOCK Colin James
Born: Ballymena, 2 July 1975
Height: 6'2" Weight: 13.0
Club Honours: Div 2 '00
International Honours: NI: 12; B-3; Yth; Sch
Colin showed his growing skill and confidence at the heart of Preston's defence last term but after receiving a red card in the game at Nottingham Forest he took some time to win his place back. Strong in the air and an increasingly good timer of a tackle, his distribution came on markedly during the campaign and he showed he has matured into a solid and reliable team member. He also established himself as a regular for Northern Ireland, adding several more caps during the season.
Manchester U (From juniors on 21/7/1992)
Preston NE (£100,000 on 23/5/1997) FL 117+13/4 FLC 10 FAC 6+2 Others 10

Danny Murphy

MURPHY Christopher (Chris) Patrick
Born: Leamington Spa, 8 March 1983
Height: 5'6" Weight: 9.8
Chris is one of several fine prospects developing at Shrewsbury and after doing well in the youth and reserve teams he made his Football League debut in the final game of the 2000-01 season at home to Brighton when he came off the subs' bench for the final ten minutes. A diminutive striker with a good scoring record at junior level he will be hoping to gain further senior experience in 2001-02.
Shrewsbury T (Trainee) FL 0+1

MURPHY Daniel (Danny) Benjamin
Born: Chester, 18 March 1977
Height: 5'9" Weight: 10.8
Club Honours: FLC '01; FAC '01; UEFAC '01
International Honours: E: U21-5; Yth; Sch
Having finally broken into the Liverpool first team in the 1999-2000 season Danny continued to make steady progress last term. He had a lengthy run in the side from November through to the end of February as a replacement for the injured Patrik Berger on the left side of midfield. Enjoying some of the best form of his career he celebrated by scoring the winner with a free kick against champions and deadly rivals Manchester United in December to help Liverpool to their first victory at Old Trafford for ten years. He followed this up with double strikes at Aston Villa and in the Worthington Cup semi-final second leg triumph over Crystal Palace. Unfortunately he was then sidelined for several weeks by a calf injury but returned to score more vital goals against Tranmere Rovers in the FA Cup quarter-final and Porto in the UEFA Cup. His form then dipped a little but he made the starting line-up for both the FA and UEFA Cup finals and netted the second goal in the crucial 4-0 victory at Charlton that clinched a coveted Champions' League slot for the Reds. Danny has had to adapt to different roles at Liverpool, sometimes as a hard-tackling destroyer, sometimes as a support striker, but his versatility should ensure that he remains a vital member of the squad at Anfield for the foreseeable future.
Crewe Alex (From trainee on 21/3/1994) FL 110+24/27 FLC 7 FAC 7/4 Others 15+3/3
Liverpool (£1,500,000 + on 17/7/1997) PL 28+39/7 FLC 8+1/7 FAC 6+2/1 Others 6+5/1
Crewe Alex (Loaned on 12/2/1999) FL 16/1

MURPHY John James
Born: Whiston, 18 October 1976
Height: 6'2" Weight: 14.0
This Blackpool striker was again among the goals last season, hitting hat-tricks against Stockport (in the Worthington Cup) and Kidderminster and finishing with his best-ever tally. He forged a very productive

partnership up front with Brett Ormerod, the pair's goals proving vital to the Tangerines' promotion campaign. John's strength in the air, an ability to lead the line and an eye for goal are his main talents and he became a transfer target for bigger clubs during the season.

Chester C (From trainee on 6/7/1995) FL 65+38/20 FLC 6+3/1 FAC 1+2 Others 3+1
Blackpool (Signed on 6/8/1999) FL 78+7/28 FLC 5/5 FAC 5/1 Others 5+1

MURPHY Joseph (Joe)
Born: Dublin, Ireland, 21 August 1981
Height: 6'2" Weight: 13.6
International Honours: RoI: U21-6; Yth; (UEFA-U16 '98)

Joe was understudy to the in-form John Achterberg as Tranmere's 'keeper last term and only played regular first-team football when Achterburg was sidelined with injuries. He enjoyed two short runs in the line-up and continued to show great promise. A lithe and athletic goalkeeper with excellent handling skills and good distribution he commands his area with an authority not usually found in one so young. He continued to be part of the Republic of Ireland U21 set up and won four more caps during the season.

Tranmere Rov (From trainee on 5/7/1999) FL 40+1 FLC 5 FAC 2

MURPHY Matthew (Matt) Simon
Born: Northampton, 20 August 1971
Height: 6'0" Weight: 12.2

After enjoying an excellent season with Oxford United in 1999-2000 Matt found things much tougher last term. Managerial changes and playing in a struggling side did not help him but he seemed to be unable to stamp his authority on games in the manner that he had previously done. Best used in a role just behind the front two or pushing through from midfield he scored seven goals including the winner in the Worthington Cup first round first leg tie at Wolves. Out of contract in the summer his future was unclear at the time of writing.

Oxford U (£20,000 from Corby T on 12/2/1993) FL 168+78/38 FLC 10+9/8 FAC 12+3/6 Others 6+3/3
Scunthorpe U (Loaned on 12/12/1997) FL 1+2 Others 1

Joe Murphy

MURPHY Neil Anthony
Born: Liverpool, 19 May 1980
Height: 5'9" Weight: 11.0
International Honours: E: Yth

This young right back joined Blackpool in the summer of 2000 after being released by Liverpool. He made his Football League debut against Hull on the opening day of last season but after appearing in a run of five consecutive games he was dropped and spent most of the remainder of the season developing in the Tangerines' reserve team.

Liverpool (From trainee on 13/10/1997)
Blackpool (Free on 27/7/2000) FL 3+3 FLC 2

MURPHY Peter
Born: Dublin, 27 October 1980
Height: 5'11" Weight: 12.10
International Honours: RoI: Yth

This Blackburn Rovers defender joined Halifax Town in a long-term loan deal last October and featured regularly for the Third Division club for the remainder of the season. An accomplished left-sided player he looked particularly impressive when pushing forward and scored his first-ever Football League goal with a superb free kick in the 3-2 win over Kidderminster in January. Previously capped by the Republic of Ireland at U18 level he was out of contract in the summer and his future was unclear at the time of writing.

Blackburn Rov (From trainee on 15/7/1998)
Halifax T (Loaned on 26/10/2000) FL 18+3/1 FAC 1 Others 2

MURPHY Shaun Peter
Born: Sydney, Australia, 5 November 1970
Height: 6'1" Weight: 12.0
Club Honours: AIC '95
International Honours: Australia: 15; U23; Yth

Shaun had a superb season for Sheffield United in the centre of defence last season when he became the Blades first ever-present for ten years and signed a further three-year contract midway through the campaign. His understanding with Lee Sandford and then Keith Curle was excellent while he showed perfect timing and his interceptions and aerial ability were of a high standard. A constant danger in the opposition penalty area as his tally of five goals indicates, he was rewarded for his efforts by being voted supporters' club 'Player of the Year'. He added further caps to his international tally for Australia, featuring in the prestigious Confederations Cup tournament when he netted the winner in the third-place play-off tie against Brazil.

Notts Co (Signed from Perth Italia, Australia on

4/9/1992) FL 100+9/5 FLC 5+2 FAC 6/1 Others 12+1/1
West Bromwich A (£500,000 on 31/12/1996) FL 60+11/7 FLC 3 FAC 4
Sheffield U (Free on 22/7/1999) FL 88/8 FLC 9 FAC 3

Shaun Murphy

MURRAY Adam David
Born: Birmingham, 30 September 1981
Height: 5'8" Weight: 10.10
International Honours: E: Yth
Now in his third year as a professional with Derby County, Adam continued to progress towards a more regular first-team spot with the Rams last term. The first half of the season saw him mostly feature from the substitute's bench, but he made the starting line-up for all three of the club's FA Cup ties. After a spell out injured he found himself pitched into the relegation battle at the end of the season and he was especially impressive in the crucial win at Old Trafford. A hard-working right-sided midfield player he is a tenacious tackler and will be hoping to appear more regularly in the coming season.
Derby Co (From trainee on 7/10/1998) PL 5+21 FLC 0+1 FAC 3

MURRAY Daniel (Dan)
Born: Cambridge, 16 May 1982
Height: 6'2" Weight: 12.7
Absent for several weeks in the early part of last season due to torn stomach muscles Dan was only used sparingly by Peterborough boss Barry Fry when fit. One of many talented youngsters to graduate from the club's youth system in recent years he is a tall and skilful central defender.
Peterborough U (From trainee on 7/3/2000) FL 3+2 Others 2

MURRAY Jade (Jay) Alan
Born: Islington, 23 September 1981
Height: 5'9" Weight: 11.5
This promising young Leyton Orient striker was again among the leading scorers for the club's youth and reserve teams last term. He added just a single first-team appearance, coming on from the subs' bench for the final 15 minutes of the Worthington Cup second round second leg tie against Newcastle. In January he had a spell on loan at Dr Martens League club Chelmsford City and in April he was a member of the Orient team that defeated Bradford City to win the Football League Youth Alliance Cup. Having briefly tasted first-team football in each of the last two seasons he will be looking to break into the squad on a more regular basis in 2001-02.
Leyton Orient (From trainee on 10/7/2000) FL 0+2 FLC 0+1

MURRAY Karl Anthony
Born: Islington, 24 June 1982
Height: 5'11" Weight: 12.6
Karl continued to make steady progress at Shrewsbury Town in the 2000-01 campaign, his second season as a full-time professional. He was once again a favourite of the Gay Meadow fans thanks to an impressive work rate and some all-action displays in the centre of the park. He is a hard-tackling midfield player who distributes the ball accurately and will be looking to firmly establish himself in the first team in 2001-02.
Shrewsbury T (From trainee on 7/2/2000) FL 35+12/1 FLC 3 FAC 2

MURRAY Neil
Born: Bellshill, 21 February 1973
Height: 5'9" Weight: 10.10
Club Honours: SC '93
International Honours: S: U21-16; Sch
This experienced Scottish midfielder joined Grimsby Town on a three-month loan from German Second Division club Mainz 05 last November. He made his debut from the subs' bench at Watford but his appearances were restricted by illness and he featured only once more for the Mariners before returning to Germany.
Glasgow R (From juniors on 23/8/1989) SL 47+16/1 SLC 3+1 SC 5/2 Others 4+5 (Transferred to Sion, Switzerland on 12/2/1997)
Dundee U (Signed from Lorient, France on 9/2/1999) SL 2+1 (Freed on 31/5/1999)
Grimsby T (Loaned from FSV Mainz 05, Germany on 3/11/2000) FL 1+1

MURRAY Paul
Born: Carlisle, 31 August 1976
Height: 5'9" Weight: 10.5
International Honours: E: B-1; U21-4; Yth
Paul had a wretched time with injuries at Queens Park Rangers in 2000-01. He missed the start of the campaign after breaking a bone in his ankle in a pre-season match and when he returned to the first team at the end of October he then suffered a recurrence of the same injury. He recovered to make a brief run in the side in the new year but injured his ankle a third time and following surgery he was sidelined until the summer. Paul is a left-footed midfield player who can also turn out as a wing back. Out of contract in the summer his future was uncertain at the time of writing.
Carlisle U (From trainee on 14/6/1994) FL 27+14/1 FLC 2 FAC 1 Others 6+1
Queens Park R (£300,000 on 8/3/1996) P/FL 115+25/7 FLC 8/1 FAC 9

MURRAY Scott George
Born: Aberdeen, 26 May 1974
Height: 5'10" Weight: 11.0
After a slow start to the 2000-01 season, Scott soon hit top form for Bristol City. He scored regularly throughout the campaign, but his performances dipped for a while in the new year before he returned to his best after scoring with a brilliant diving header from Matt Hill's cross in the 1-1 draw with Port Vale in March. A skilful right winger with blistering pace and a powerful shot he was deservedly selected for the PFA's Second Division representative side.
Aston Villa (£35,000 from Fraserburgh on 16/3/1994) PL 4
Bristol C (£150,000 on 12/12/1997) FL 114+28/19 FLC 8+2 FAC 9+1/4 Others 7+1/2

MURRAY Shaun
Born: Newcastle, 7 December 1970
Height: 5'8" Weight: 11.2
International Honours: E: Yth; Sch
Following a change in management at Notts County in the 2000 close season Shaun seemed to fall out of favour and never really got an extended run in the team during the 2000-01 campaign. He eventually joined Kettering Town on loan to try and halt their slide towards relegation from the Conference, but on returning to Meadow Lane he was released in the summer. A predominantly left-footed midfield play maker he has the ability to turn the course of a match with his decisive passing.
Tottenham H (From trainee on 10/12/1987)
Portsmouth (£100,000 on 12/6/1989) FL 21+13/1 FLC 2+1/1 FAC 1+3 Others 2+2
Scarborough (Signed on 1/11/1993) FL 29/5 FAC 2 Others 2
Bradford C (£200,000 on 11/8/1994) FL 105+25/8 FLC 7+2/1 FAC 4+2 Others 4/2
Notts Co (Free on 4/8/1998) FL 43+12/3 FLC 3 FAC 9+1/1 Others 1

MURTY Graeme Stuart
Born: Saltburn, 13 November 1974
Height: 5'10" Weight: 11.10
Although absent from the early-season matches with a knee injury Graeme went on to enjoy a productive and consistent season with Reading last term. He opened his scoring account for the Royals with a long-range effort in the home match with Bristol City but had to miss the play-off games against Wigan after being injured in a training ground clash of heads, the knock being severe enough to warrant him being taken to hospital by air ambulance. A right-sided player who is best in a wing-back role he covers the ground quickly, makes well-

timed last-ditch tackles, and shoots on target.

York C (From trainee on 23/3/1993) FL 106+11/7 FLC 10/2 FAC 5+1 Others 6+2
Reading (£700,000 on 10/7/1998) FL 40+9/1 FAC 4+1 Others 3+2

Graeme Murty

MUSCAT Kevin Vincent
Born: Crawley, 7 August 1973
Height: 5'11" Weight: 12.2
International Honours: Australia: 34; U23; Yth

Thi tough right back was appointed as Wolves' club captain last season but struggled to maintain consistent form although he had some high points, notably when he netted the winner against Sheffield Wednesday at Hillsborough with a lovely right-footed curling free-kick. A rugged defender who enjoys pushing down the flank he held the responsibility for taking penalties at Molineux for a while. Kevin was again a regular for Australia during the campaign netting a remarkable four-goal tally (three were spot-kicks) in the 22-0 victory over Tonga in a World Cup qualifier and also featuring in the end-of-season Confederations Cup tournament.

Crystal Palace (£35,000 from South Melbourne, Australia on 16/8/1996) FL 51+2/2 FLC 4/1 FAC 2 Others 2
Wolverhampton W (£200,000 on 22/10/1997) FL 141+2/14 FLC 10/1 FAC 10

MUSSELWHITE Paul Stephen
Born: Portsmouth, 22 December 1968
Height: 6'2" Weight: 14.2
Club Honours: AMC '93

After trials at Scunthorpe and Darlington during the 2000 summer break Paul had a brief spell with Sheffield Wednesday before joining Hull City last September. He became an instant hit with the Tigers' supporters after saving a penalty on his debut in the 1-1 draw at Barnet and went on to become the first-choice goalkeeper at Boothferry Park, producing a series of outstanding performances. He played a crucial role in helping the club reach the play-offs and this was recognised when he received the 'Young Tigers' Player of the Year' award.

Portsmouth (From apprentice on 1/12/1986)
Scunthorpe U (Free on 21/3/1988) FL 132 FLC 11 FAC 7 Others 13
Port Vale (£20,000 on 30/7/1992) FL 312 FLC 15 FAC 21 Others 19
Sheffield Wed (Free, via trials at Scunthorpe U, Darlington, on 25/8/2000)
Hull C (Free on 19/9/2000) FL 37 FAC 2 Others 3

MUSTOE Neil John
Born: Gloucester, 5 November 1976
Height: 5'9" Weight: 12.10
Club Honours: FAYC '95

Neil featured regularly for Cambridge United for most of last season although he was often used from the subs' bench. He is a tenacious left-sided midfield player who works tirelessly and drives the team forward with his all-action style. He rarely appeared in the first team after a change in management and ended the campaign on the transfer list.

Manchester U (From trainee on 1/7/1995)
Wigan Ath (Signed on 7/1/1998) Others 0+1
Cambridge U (Free on 9/7/1998) FL 71+23/4 FLC 7 FAC 6+1 Others 4

MUSTOE Robin (Robbie)
Born: Witney, 28 August 1968
Height: 5'11" Weight: 11.12
Club Honours: Div 1 '95

This thrusting midfield dynamo suffered his share of absenteeism through injury last term but battled back to match-fitness managing to achieve a respectable appearance total for the season, although he spent a lot of time on the subs' bench. Robbie gave his all for the Middlesborough cause and was sorely missed when absent from the side. His prodding and probing style, is effective and he drives the team forward inspiring his team-mates to greater efforts. He never shirks his own corner and is always prepared to take a snap shot to try and catch the opposition off guard.

Oxford U (From juniors on 2/7/1986) FL 78+13/10 FLC 2 FAC 2 Others 3
Middlesbrough (£375,000 on 5/7/1990) F/PL 296+33/23 FLC 43+2/7 FAC 23+1/2 Others 12+1/1

MUTTON Thomas (Tommy) James
Born: Huddersfield, 17 January 1978
Height: 5'8" Weight: 10.2

Tommy made a handful of early-season appearances for Swansea last term but his only goal came at Barry in an FA Wales Premier Cup tie. In January he went out on loan to Merthyr and shortly afterwards his contract was cancelled and he joined League of Wales club Rhyl on a free transfer. He is a slightly-built striker with electric pace.

Swansea C (£20,000 from Bangor C on 16/9/1999) FL 4+3 FLC 0+3 Others 2/1

MYERS Andrew (Andy) John
Born: Hounslow, 3 November 1973
Height: 5'10" Weight: 13.11
Club Honours: FAC '97; ECWC '98
International Honours: E: U21-4; Yth

Andy had an unfortunate start to the 2000-01 season for Bradford City, suffering a torn hamstring in the home game against Arsenal at the beginning of September. He returned to action at the end of November but found it difficult to re-establish himself in the line-up and it was only when Andy O'Brien was sold to Newcastle that he came back on a regular basis, appearing at centre half. A versatile defender who also played at left back he is quick off the mark and very strong in the tackle.

Chelsea (From trainee on 25/7/1991) F/PL 74+10/2 FLC 2+1 FAC 9+3 Others 4+3
Bradford C (£800,000 on 16/7/1999) PL 25+8/1 FLC 2 FAC 1 Others 3+1
Portsmouth (Loaned on 23/3/2000) FL 4+4

MYERS Peter William
Born: Sheffield, 15 September 1982
Height: 5'11" Weight: 11.3

Having developed in the Halifax Town youth team this wide-right midfield player featured regularly for the club's reserves last season and was called up to the first team squad for the game against Shrewsbury in March. Peter replaced Rob Matthews at half time and did well enough to suggest that he will be threatening to break into the Shaymen's squad on a more regular basis in 2001-02.

Halifax T (Trainee) FL 0+1

MYHRE Thomas
Born: Sarpsborg, Norway, 16 October 1973
Height: 6'4" Weight: 13.12
International Honours: Norway: 19; U21; Yth

Thomas found it impossible to dislodge Paul Gerrard from the goalkeeper's jersey at Everton last term and at the end of November he joined First Division Tranmere on a month's loan, where he not only impressed with some efficient 'keeping but also had a steadying effect on a very young defence. He enjoyed a brief run of first-team appearances at Goodison in the new year when Gerrard was out injured but this included a harrowing 3-0 FA Cup defeat, ironically by Tranmere. However although he dropped back into the reserves things then began to look up. Firstly he was recalled to the Norwegian national team, then in March he moved on loan to FC Copenhagen where he featured regularly in the closing matches of the 2000-01 season, helping them to the Danish League title. An experienced international with a good command of his area and sharp shot-stopping capabilities, it seems that the future for Thomas may well lie away from Merseyside.

Everton (£800,000 from Viking Stavanger, Norway on 28/11/1997) PL 70 FLC 3 FAC 9
Glasgow R (Loaned on 24/11/1999) SL 3 SLC 1 Others 2
Birmingham C (Loaned on 31/3/2000) FL 7 Others 2
Tranmere Rov (Loaned on 28/11/2000) FL 3 FLC 1

Gary Neville

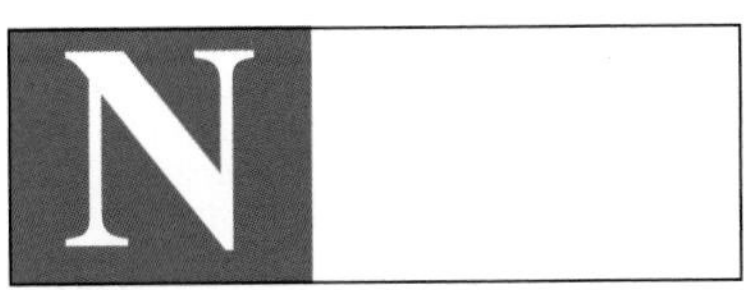

NAISBITT Daniel (Danny) John
Born: Bishop Auckland, 25 November 1978
Height: 6'1" Weight: 11.12

Danny began the 2000-01 campaign as the second choice 'keeper at Barnet, but managed but established himself in the starting line-up for a three-month period after Lee Harrison went down with an injury. He eventually lost his place following the 6-1 defeat at Hartlepool in December and spent much of the remainder of the season on the bench. He was placed on the open to offers list in the summer following the Bees' relegation to the Conference.

Walsall (From trainee at Middlesbrough on 7/7/1997)
Barnet (Free on 3/8/1999) FL 19+4 FLC 1 FAC 2

NANCEKIVELL Kevin William
Born: Barnstable, 22 October 1971
Height: 5'11" Weight: 12.3

Kevin had scored freely with the successful Tiverton Town team in recent seasons and had played in two FA Vase winning sides before signing for Plymouth Argyle after scoring against them in a pre-season friendly last August. He made his Football League debut at the age of 28 and scored his first-ever senior goal in the 1-1 draw at Hartlepool but following a change in management he was loaned back to Tiverton in January. He stayed with the Dr Martens League club until the end of the campaign and helped them win promotion to the Premier Division. Kevin is an enthusiastic striker with a proven goal-scoring record in non-league football.

Plymouth Arg (£5,000 from Tiverton on 25/8/2000) FL 0+6/1 FLC 0+1

NASH Carlo James
Born: Bolton, 13 September 1973
Height: 6'5" Weight: 14.1

Injury and suspension restricted this popular Stockport County 'keeper to just eight league starts last term and in December he moved on loan to Wolves. He failed to make an appearance at Molineux but soon after his return he played his final game for County at Preston when he turned in a magnificent performance to earn the Hatters victory in the FA Cup third round tie. Due to be out of contract in the summer the club then cashed in and accepted Manchester City's bid for him. He initially had to bide his time at Maine Road but eventually made his debut against Arsenal and found himself picking the ball out of the net four times before he even had the chance to make a save! He couldn't be blamed for any of them, and kept his place in the side for the rest of the season, turning in some excellent performances, notably against Manchester United at Old Trafford. He quickly won the crowd over, but alas it was not enough to save City from the drop to the First Division.

Crystal Palace (£35,000 from Clitheroe on 16/7/1996) FL 21 FLC 1 Others 3
Stockport Co (Free on 7/6/1998) FL 89 FLC 5 FAC 4
Manchester C (£100,000 on 12/1/2001) PL 6

NAVARRO Alan Edward
Born: Liverpool, 31 May 1981
Height: 5'11" Weight: 11.7

A regular in Liverpool's reserve team last season, Alan joined Crewe Alexandra on loan last March to gain some valuable experience of first-team football. Initially used as cover for Neil Sorvel and Kenny Lunt he made his debut from the subs' bench against Crystal Palace and scored his first senior goal with a close-range effort in the 2-1 win over Gillingham. He impressed in his spell at Gresty Road and featured regularly in the closing matches before returning to Anfield where he will be hoping for a breakthrough in 2001-02.

Liverpool (From trainee on 27/4/1999)
Crewe Alex (Loaned on 22/3/2001) FL 5+3/1

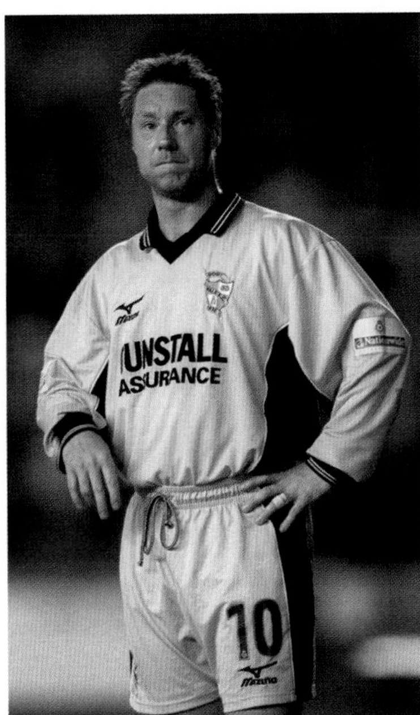

Tony Naylor

NAYLOR Anthony (Tony) Joseph
Born: Manchester, 29 March 1967
Height: 5'7" Weight: 10.8
Club Honours: AMC '01

Tony had an excellent season for Port Vale in 2000-01 rarely missing a match, finishing the campaign as leading scorer and producing a star performance in the LDV Vans Trophy final against Brentford when he had a hand in both goals as Vale ran out 2-1 winners. A small and nippy striker he never seems to give opposing defenders any peace and should once again be an important figure at Vale Park in the 2001-02 campaign.

Crewe Alex (£20,000 from Droylsden on 22/3/1990) FL 104+18/45 FLC 7+2/5 FAC 9/7 Others 12/9
Port Vale (£150,000 on 18/7/1994) FL 207+46/71 FLC 15+1/8 FAC 12+1/2 Others 12+1/8

NAYLOR Glenn
Born: Goole, 11 August 1972
Height: 5'10" Weight: 11.10

One of the longest-serving players at Feethams Glenn started almost every game for Darlington in the 2000-01 season. He had an excellent campaign finishing as the club's leading scorer with 15 goals in all competitions and netting a hat-trick in the 6-1 FA Cup victory over AFC Sudbury in November. He is a pacy striker who works hard and harries opposition defenders into errors.

York C (From trainee on 5/3/1990) FL 78+33/30 FLC 2+4 FAC 4+1/2 Others 3+4
Darlington (Loaned on 13/10/1995) FL 3+1/1 Others 1+1
Darlington (Signed on 26/9/1996) FL 150+40/42 FLC 6+1/2 FAC 12+2/5 Others 6+4

NAYLOR Lee Martyn
Born: Walsall, 19 March 1980
Height: 5'9" Weight: 11.8
International Honours: E: U21-3; Yth

Although he showed somewhat inconsistent form in the early part of the 2000-01 campaign, Lee retained his place in the Wolves' team and eventually came good in the second half of the season. Perhaps his best performance was against Grimsby when he produced an all-action display, excelling in both defence and attack. A very promising young left back he was voted 'Player of the Season' at Molineux. Although he was a regular in the England U21 squad during the campaign it was not until the summer that he won further caps, appearing against Mexico and Greece.

Wolverhampton W (From trainee on 10/10/1997) FL 99+16/4 FLC 12 FAC 9/1

NAYLOR Richard Alan
Born: Leeds, 28 February 1977
Height: 6'1" Weight: 13.7

Richard had a very frustrating time with injuries at Ipswich last term and never managed to get a decent run in the first team. He missed the beginning of the season while recovering from summer operations on both knees and eventually returned to the starting line-up at the end of September when he replaced David Johnson. He scored his first goal in the Middlesbrough game when 'keeper Mark Crossley, under pressure, cleared the ball straight to him and Richard promptly returned it into the net. Shortly afterwards it was discovered that he had been playing with a broken femur! Once he had recovered from that, the old trouble in his knees flared up again and at one point it was thought that he would need further operations on them to resolve the situation. However a second opinion found that he had one leg shorter than the other and suggestions to counteract this problem improved matters greatly. He was soon back in first-team action and scored the equaliser in the last game of the season at Derby when his shot took a wicked deflection and trickled into the net.

Ipswich T (From trainee on 10/7/1995) P/FL 53+58/20 FLC 6+6/1 FAC 1+4 Others 0+4/1

NAYSMITH Gary Andrew
Born: Edinburgh, 16 November 1979
Height: 5'7" Weight: 11.8
Club Honours: SC '98
International Honours: S: 4; U21-22; Sch

Everton won a tug-of-war with Coventry City for the services of the Scottish international full back, and the way the season ended Gary was convinced he chose correctly. Evertonians were also well satisfied with their capture from Hearts, especially after he marked his debut with a dream of a pass at Newcastle to lay on a match-winner for Kevin Campbell. An attack-minded left back or wing back, Gary also weighed in with a couple of invaluable goals, most notably an injury-time winner at Bradford. An appalling gash in his knee which required 37 stitches effectively cut short his first season in English football, but Evertonians saw enough to suggest Gary could become a firm favourite in the seasons ahead.

Heart of Midlothian (From Whitehill Welfare on 17/6/1996) SL 92+5/3 SLC 5/1 SC 10 Others 7/1
Everton (£1,750,000 on 20/10/2000) PL 17+3/2 FAC 1

NDAH George Ehialimolisa
Born: Dulwich, 23 December 1974
Height: 6'1" Weight: 11.4
International Honours: E: Yth

Having missed most of the 1999-2000 campaign with a broken leg, George made a brief return to the Wolves' squad at the beginning of last season but was then sidelined by a groin strain and it was not until November that he came back into the side. He soon celebrated his first goal for Wanderers against Grimsby but it was not until the new year that he really came into his own, netting two in the Black Country 'derby' against West Brom and then racing away from the Birmingham defence to score an early winner at St Andrews. A speedy left-sided forward he has an electrifying turn of pace, a high work rate and a good eye for goal.

Crystal Palace (From trainee on 10/8/1992) F/PL 33+45/8 FLC 7+6/2 FAC 3+1/1 Others 4+1
Bournemouth (Loaned on 13/10/1995) FL 12/2 Others 1
Gillingham (Loaned on 29/8/1997) FL 4
Swindon T (£500,000 on 21/11/1997) FL 66+1/14 FLC 4/1 FAC 3
Wolverhampton W (£1,000,000 on 21/10/1999) FL 29+7/6 FLC 0+1 FAC 0+1

N'DIAYE Seyni
Born: Dakar, Senegal, 6 January 1973
Height: 6'2" Weight: 12.11

Out of favour at French Second Division club Caen, Seyni crossed the Channel to try his luck and after an unsuccessful trial with Gillingham he signed for Tranmere Rovers shortly before the transfer deadline. A bustling striker with an impressive physical presence and a blistering turn of speed he became an instant favourite with the Tranmere fans almost from his debut game that coincidentally came against the Gills. An enthusiastic player who contributed two goals in his short spell at Prenton Park he upset opposition defences with his direct and uncompromising style of play.

Tranmere Rov (Free from Caen, France, ex Vitry-Chatillon, Paris St Germain, Neuchatel Xamax, on 19/3/2001) FL 5+3/2

NDLOVU Peter
Born: Bulawayo, Zimbabwe, 25 February 1973
Height: 5'8" Weight: 10.2
International Honours: Zimbabwe

Transfer-listed in the summer, Peter nevertheless started the 2000-01 season in the Birmingham City team because of injuries and was a most impressive performer. His skilful control and elusive running made him hard to pin down but he then rather unluckily lost his place. In December he joined First Division strugglers Huddersfield Town on loan as Blues' boss Trevor Francis considered a possible exchange for Steve Jenkins. He made a cracking start, scoring two and setting up a third in a 3-0 win over Wolves, and then netting with superb strikes against Nottingham Forest and Tranmere before being recalled to St Andrews. Early in the new year he moved on to Sheffield United in exchange for Curtis Woodhouse and a substantial cash payment, and immediately slotted in on the left flank providing much greater width to the attack. His fast, tricky, sometimes unpredictable play and close control created openings for others, but his first goal did not arrive until the draw at Blackburn in April. He continued to appear for Zimbabwe in African Nations' Cup and World Cup qualifiers and returned to play for the Blades in the final game of the season just 24 hours after scoring against South Africa.

Coventry C (£10,000 from Highlanders, Zimbabwe on 16/8/1991) F/PL 141+36/37 FLC 10/2 FAC 5+4/2 Others 0+1
Birmingham C (£1,600,000 on 15/7/1997) FL 78+29/22 FLC 17+2/4 FAC 3+1/1 Others 2+2
Huddersfield T (Loaned on 8/12/2000) FL 6/4
Sheffield U (Free on 2/2/2001) FL 15/4

NEAL Lewis
Born: Leicester, 14 July 1981
Height: 6'0" Weight: 11.2

Lewis broke into the Stoke City first-team squad in 2000-01 making his senior debut from the subs' bench in the LDV Vans Trophy tie against Scarborough in December. He went on to feature on a handful more occasions during the season and will be hoping to get more opportunities in the future. He is a promising young midfield player who works hard and seems to cover every blade of grass on the pitch in his efforts for the team.

Stoke C (Free from juniors on 17/7/1998) FL 0+1 Others 0+2

NEDERGAARD Steen
Born: Denmark, 25 February 1970
Height: 6'0" Weight: 11.13

Norwich fans have yet to see the best of this Danish midfielder who has not yet fully settled into the demands of the English game. A real enthusiast, he usually plays on the right-hand side of midfield or at right back. He has tremendous stamina and when he gets forward he has the ability to deliver a great variety of telling crosses into the penalty area. He was disrupted by a series of niggling injuries last term, but the high point of his season came with a late winning goal in the home match against high-flying Watford in January. Steen will be hoping for better things in 2001-02.

Norwich C (Free from Odense BK, Denmark on 3/7/2000) FL 10+5/1 FLC 1+2

NEIL Alexander (Alex)
Born: Bellshill, 4 May 1978
Height: 5'8" Weight: 12.10

Having signed for Barnsley during the summer, Alex featured regularly from the substitutes' bench at the beginning of last season but had to wait until November before he made his first start. However once in the side he mostly retained his place, playing either in a central or wide-right midfield role. An effective ball winner he showed that he had the ability to beat opponents but looked unsure in front of goal, although once his first goal goes in there should be many more. He had a successful first season at Oakwell and did well enough to earn a new improved three-year contract.

Airdrieonians (Free from Dunfermline Ath juniors on 8/7/1999) SL 15+1/5 SC 0+1
Barnsley (£25,000 on 11/7/2000) FL 19+13 FLC 0+1 FAC 1

NEIL Gary Derek Campbell
Born: Glasgow, 16 August 1978
Height: 6'0" Weight: 12.10

Gary struggled to break into the first-team squad at Torquay last season and was limited to occasional appearances either as a central defender in the centre of midfield. He is a powerfully built defender who is composed on the ball and has good positional sense. He was released by the Gulls at the end of the season.

Leicester C (From trainee on 3/7/1997)
Torquay U (Free on 25/3/1999) FL 19+8/1 FLC 1 FAC 1 Others 3+1

NEILL Lucas Edward
Born: Sydney, Australia, 9 March 1978
Height: 6'1" Weight: 12.0
Club Honours: Div 2 '01
International Honours: Australia: 2; U23-12; Yth

Lucas made the subs' bench for Millwall in the opening fixture of last season then departed for Australia where he featured in his country's three games in the Sydney Olympics. On his return he appeared regularly for the Lions and proved once again what a great asset he is to the club. He is one of the most technically gifted players at The New Den and has the advantage that he can play in almost any outfield position. Effective in the tackle he works hard, reads the game well and can strike a ball with either foot.

Millwall (Free from Australian Academy of Sport on 13/11/1995) FL 122+26/13 FLC 5+1 FAC 4 Others 11+1

NEILSON Alan Bruce
Born: Wegburg, Germany, 26 September 1972
Height: 5'11" Weight: 12.10
International Honours: W: 5; B-2; U21-7

With just three substitute appearances, it would seem that Alan was very much a fringe member of the Fulham squad last term. However nothing could be further from the truth as he was on the bench for twenty games and two of his appearances helped clinch vital wins for the Cottagers. He came on to replace the injured Sean Davis in midfield at Gillingham when the score was 0-0 with 23 minutes left, played really well and Fulham scored two late goals. In the six-pointer at Blackburn, he took over from the red-carded Rufus Brevett at left back and had an absolute stormer. Fulham were a goal down at the time and went on to win 2-1 and virtually clinch promotion. The versatile defender skippered the reserves to the Avon Insurance Combination title and the regular defenders knew that they needed to be right on top of their game all the time to keep him on the bench. Out of contract in the summer his future was uncertain at the time of writing.

Newcastle U (From trainee on 11/2/1991) F/PL 35+7/1 FLC 4 Others 4
Southampton (£500,000 on 1/6/1995) PL 42+13 FLC 7 FAC 1+1
Fulham (£250,000 on 28/11/1997) FL 24+5/2 FLC 4+2 FAC 4 Others 2

NELSON Michael John
Born: Gateshead, 28 March 1980
Height: 6'2" Weight: 13.12

This former Portsmouth trainee drifted into non-league football with Spennymoor and then Bishop Auckland before joining Second Division Bury on non-contract forms last March. After appearing in just one reserve game and one first-team friendly he was unexpectedly handed his Football League debut by the Shakers when he replaced the suspended Steve Redmond in the home game against Wycombe at the end of April. He scored an excellent goal on his debut and also appeared in the final game of the season at Brentford. A lanky central defender he is commanding in the air and very composed on the ball.

Bury (Free from Bishop Auckland on 22/3/2001) FL 2/1

NETHERCOTT Stuart David
Born: Ilford, 21 March 1973
Height: 6'1" Weight: 13.8
Club Honours: Div 2 '01
International Honours: E: U21-8

Stuart had a brilliant season for Second Division champions Millwall in 2000-01. He initially shared central defensive duties with Joe Dolan and Sean Dyche but he became an automatic choice following an injury to Dolan. A formidable defender he proved an inspirational captain and motivator for the team and was again a strong contender for the club's 'Player of the Season' award. Stuart is one of the best headers of the ball in the lower divisions but also has excellent all-round skills, being strong in the challenge and effective when pushing forward.

Tottenham H (From trainee on 17/8/1991) PL 31+23 FAC 5+3/1
Maidstone U (Loaned on 5/9/1991) FL 13/1 Others 1
Barnet (Loaned on 13/2/1992) FL 3
Millwall (Signed on 22/1/1998) FL 115+4/4 FLC 4 FAC 3 Others 11

NEVILLE Gary Alexander
Born: Bury, 18 February 1975
Height: 5'11" Weight: 12.8
Club Honours: FAYC '92; PL '96, '97, '99, '00, '01; FAC '96, '99; CS '96; EC '99
International Honours: E: 44; Yth (UEFA-U18 '93)

One of Gary's main priorities at the start of the 2000-01 campaign was persuading Manchester United boss Sir Alex Ferguson, that his true role was in the centre of defence. However he went some way to demonstrating this during Jaap Stam's absence in the autumn when he formed a fine partnership with Wes Brown in the Reds' back line. A near ever-present in the first half of the campaign he celebrated his first goal since March 1999 against Aston Villa in January before being sidelined by a knee injury that kept him out of the end-of-season matches for club and country.

Manchester U (From trainee on 29/1/1993) PL 199+4/3 FLC 4+1 FAC 23+2 Others 61+4

NEVILLE Philip (Phil) John
Born: Bury, 21 January 1977
Height: 5'11" Weight: 12.0
Club Honours: FAYC '95; PL '96, '97, '99, '00, '01; FAC '96, '99: CS '96, '97; EC '99
International Honours: E: 33; U21-7; Yth; Sch

Having re-established himself in the Manchester United defence following Jaap Stam's injury at the start of last season Phil went on to keep his place for most of the remainder of the campaign. In December, Sir Alex Ferguson heaped due praise on both him and Nicky Butt as being the two unsung heroes of the team, stating, "They are probably playing their best football they've ever played for the club." Although he has often been in the shadows of his older brother Gary he showed solid form for club and country, finishing up with yet another Premiership winners' medal and as a regular in new boss Sven Goran Eriksson's England side.

Manchester U (From trainee on 1/6/1994) PL 129+31/2 FLC 7+1 FAC 15+4 Others 28+13/1

NEWBY Jonathan (Jon) Philip Robert
Born: Warrington, 28 November 1978
Height: 6'0" Weight: 12.4
Club Honours: FAYC '96

Jon came to Sheffield United on a three-month loan at the beginning of last season to plug a gap in the squad until Patrick Suffo became available. Mostly appearing as a substitute he impressed with his pace although a first-team goal proved elusive. After a brief return to Anfield and Liverpool reserves he was on his way to Bury in another loan deal at the beginning of February. He marked his debut the following day with a goal against Peterborough and his introduction into the Shakers attack completely transformed the team's fortunes over the next few months. His partnership with the more experienced Colin Cramb became the highlight of the club's season as he soon became the fans' new hero. Jon's loan was later extended for a second month, and then on transfer deadline day he signed in a permanent deal. He netted five goals in total for the Shakers, making him the joint-leading scorer and the Gigg Lane faithful will be hoping that he continues to fulfil his promise in 2001-02.

Liverpool (From juniors on 23/5/1997) PL 0+1 FLC 0+1 FAC 0+2
Crewe Alex (Loaned on 3/3/2000) FL 5+1
Sheffield U (Loaned on 4/8/2000) FL 3+10
Bury (£100,000 on 2/2/2001) FL 17/5

NEWELL Michael (Mike) Colin
Born: Liverpool, 27 January 1965
Height: 6'2" Weight: 12.0
Club Honours: AMC '85; PL '95
International Honours: E: B-2; U21-4

This experienced striker provided useful cover at Blackpool for the club's regular front men Brett Ormerod and John Murphy. Although now in the closing stages of his career he still showed that he could hold the ball up well and act as an effective target man. Mike spent two months out following a cartilage operation last autumn and once he had recovered fitness he was restricted to occasional outings from the bench. Out of contract in the summer his future was unclear at the time of writing.

Crewe Alex (From Liverpool juniors on 28/9/1983) FL 3
Wigan Ath (Free on 31/10/1983) FL 64+8/25 FLC 6/1 FAC 8/6 Others 5+1/3
Luton T (£100,000 on 9/1/1986) FL 62+1/18 FAC 5/1
Leicester C (£350,000 on 16/9/1987) FL 81/21 FLC 9/5 FAC 2 Others 4
Everton (£850,000 on 27/7/1989) FL 48+20/15 FLC 7+3/4 FAC 6+4 Others 6/2
Blackburn Rov (£1,100,000 on 15/11/1991) F/PL 113+17/28 FLC 14+2/8 FAC 9+2/6 Others 9+1/6
Birmingham C (£775,000 on 26/7/1996) FL 11+4/1 FLC 4/2 FAC 0+1
West Ham U (Loaned on 21/12/1996) PL 6+1
Bradford C (Loaned on 17/3/1997) FL 7
Aberdeen (£160,000 on 21/7/1997) SL 32+12/6 SLC 4/4 SC 1+1
Crewe Alex (Free on 25/3/1999) FL 1+3 (Free to Doncaster Rov on 3/6/1999)
Blackpool (Free on 10/2/2000) FL 16+2/2 FLC 2 FAC 0+1 Others 0+1

NEWMAN Richard (Ricky) Adrian
Born: Guildford, 5 August 1970
Height: 5'10" Weight: 12.6

Having enjoyed a successful loan spell at Reading towards the end of the 1999-2000 campaign Ricky made a permanent move to the Madejski Stadium in the close season. He went on to feature regularly for the Royals before being sidelined by a knee injury in the run-in to the end of the season. Although generally used at right back he also appeared in a central midfield role and produced some committed displays, showing himself to be very sharp in the tackle.

Crystal Palace (From juniors on 22/1/1988) F/PL 43+5/3 FLC 5 FAC 5+2 Others 2

Maidstone U (Loaned on 28/2/1992) FL 9+1/1
Millwall (£500,000 on 19/7/1995) FL 144+6/5 FLC 11 FAC 5 Others 7
Reading (Free on 17/3/2000) FL 41+5/1 FLC 1 FAC 3/1 Others 1

NEWMAN Robert (Rob) Nigel
Born: Bradford on Avon, 13 December 1963
Height: 6'2" Weight: 13.4
Club Honours: AMC '86

Now reserve coach at Southend United, Rob was only called upon when injury or suspension deprived the Blues of their first-choice centre-halves. Whenever he was selected he showed himself to be as effective as ever and produced a particularly fine performance when partnering debutant Stephen Broad at champions Chesterfield, the pair helping the Blues to earn a 1-1 draw.
Bristol C (From apprentice on 5/10/1981) FL 382+12/52 FLC 29+1/2 FAC 27/2 Others 33/5
Norwich C (£600,000 on 15/7/1991) F/PL 181+24/14 FLC 22+2/2 FAC 13/1 Others 7
Motherwell (Loaned on 12/12/1997) SL 11 SC 3
Wigan Ath (Loaned on 26/3/1998) FL 8
Southend U (Free on 28/7/1998) FL 53+8/9 FLC 4/1 FAC 1 Others 5

NEWTON Adam Lee
Born: Grays, 4 December 1980
Height: 5'10" Weight: 11.6
Club Honours: FAYC '99
International Honours: E: U21-1

After beginning the 2000-01 campaign with West Ham's reserve team Adam joined Notts County on loan in an extended deal that kept him at Meadow Lane until the end of the season. Having previously featured at wing back or full back he was mostly used by the Magpies in a more forward role wide on the right-hand side of midfield where although a little inconsistent he produced some devastating performances. He is a very promising youngster with lightning pace and the ability to turn defenders inside out with his skill on the ball. Earlier in the season he was capped for England U21s when he appeared in the friendly against Georgia.
West Ham U (From trainee on 1/7/1999) PL 0+2 Others 0+1
Portsmouth (Loaned on 2/7/1999) FL 1+2 FLC 2
Notts Co (Loaned on 22/11/2000) FL 13+7/1 FAC 2

NEWTON Edward (Eddie) John Ikem
Born: Hammersmith, 13 December 1971
Height: 5'11" Weight: 12.8
Club Honours: FAC '97; FLC '98; ECWC '98
International Honours: E: U21-2

Eddie joined Barnet last August on a one-month contract but managed just two starts for the Bees without making any real impression on manager John Still and he was then released. He subsequently joined Hayes in December, featuring regularly for the Conference outfit before being released the following month. He then spent time training with Leyton Orient for whom he played an occasional reserve game without being offered a contract. Eddie is an elegant and intelligent central midfield player who provides a steadying influence in the centre of the park.
Chelsea (From trainee on 17/5/1990) F/PL 139+26/8 FLC 15+2/1 FAC 15+3/1 Others 11+2
Cardiff C (Loaned on 23/1/1992) FL 18/4
Birmingham C (Free on 13/7/1999) FL 2+2 FLC 2+2 FAC 0+1
Oxford U (Free on 23/3/2000) FL 7
Barnet (Free on 18/8/2000) FL 2+2 FLC 1+1

NEWTON Shaun O'Neill
Born: Camberwell, 20 August 1975
Height: 5'8" Weight: 11.7
Club Honours: Div 1 '00
International Honours: E: U21-3

2000-01 proved to be a disappointing season for Shaun who only made a handful of appearances in the Charlton Athletic first team. He is extremely quick and loves to go past defenders and deliver the ball into the penalty area, he can also defend well and played at right wing back when coming on in the home game against Aston Villa. A valuable member of the squad Shaun scored the extra-time winner to put Conference side Dagenham & Redbridge out of the FA Cup in January.
Charlton Ath (From trainee on 1/7/1993) P/FL 189+51/20 FLC 19+1/3 FAC 11+6/2 Others 7+1/2

NGONGE Felix **Michel**
Born: Huy, Belgium, 10 January 1967
Height: 6'0" Weight: 12.8
International Honours: DR Congo: 6

Michel struggled to win a place in the Watford line-up at the beginning of the 2000-01 campaign and after making just a handful of appearances from the subs' bench he moved on to Queens Park Rangers. He went straight into the first team but was unable to hold down a regular place and was frequently used as a substitute. A powerfully built striker with a deceptive turn of pace he scored just three goals in his time at Loftus Road, including a penalty against his former colleagues Watford, and failed to make the starting line-up in the last two months of the campaign. Before he left Vicarage Road, a life-sized cardboard replica of Michel in action that had become a popular feature in Watford High Street was successfully auctioned for the Children in Need appeal. Michel was released by Rangers in the summer.
Watford (Free from Samsunspor, Turkey, ex KRC Harelbeks, on 17/7/1998) P/FL 29+18/9 FLC 3+3/1 FAC 1 Others 3/1
Huddersfield T (Loaned on 17/3/2000) FL 0+4
Queens Park R (£50,000 on 13/12/2000) FL 7+6/3 FAC 0+2

NICHOLLS Kevin John Richard
Born: Newham, 2 January 1979
Height: 6'0" Weight: 11.0
International Honours: E: Yth

Kevin received few opportunities at first-team level for Wigan last term until the appointment of Steve Bruce as manager in April. He was then restored to the side and went on to produce some fine performances for the Latics, scoring his first goal for the club in the play-off semi-final second leg against Reading. He is a combative midfielder who is comfortable on the ball and has fine vision.
Charlton Ath (From trainee on 29/1/1996) FL 4+8/1 FLC 2+2
Brighton & Hove A (Loaned on 26/2/1999) FL 4/1
Wigan Ath (£250,000 + on 22/6/1999) FL 19+9 FLC 2 Others 4/1

NICHOLLS Mark
Born: Hillingdon, 30 May 1977
Height: 5'10" Weight: 10.4
Club Honours: FLC '98

Having developed in the Chelsea youth system Mark went on loan to Second Division Colchester United last October but found it hard to make an impression in a struggling team. He returned to Stamford Bridge early and was eventually released at the end of the season. Mark is a talented young striker with a reputation for poaching goals.
Chelsea (From trainee on 1/7/1995) PL 11+25/3 FLC 4+3 FAC 1+3 Others 0+5
Reading (Loaned on 30/12/1999) FL 4+1/1 Others 2/2
Grimsby T (Loaned on 24/2/2000) FL 6
Colchester U (Loaned on 5/10/2000) FL 3+1

NICHOLSON Kevin John
Born: Derby, 2 October 1980
Height: 5'8" Weight: 11.5
International Honours: E: Yth; Sch

Kevin made his debut in senior football for Sheffield Wednesday when he came on from the subs' bench against Blackburn Rovers last August. However he failed to make the first team again and in January he joined Northampton Town on a non-contract basis. He was immediately loaned to Forest Green where it was intended that he should remain until the end of the season, however injuries meant he was recalled to Sixfields after just one appearance for the Conference club. He subsequently featured regularly for the Cobblers before signing a contract for Notts County shortly before the transfer deadline. Kevin opened his scoring account for the Magpies with a fine header in the 3-3 draw against Peterborough and began to establish himself in the team in the closing weeks of the campaign. A left wing back who is capable of making effective runs down the flank he crosses the ball well and can deliver accurate set-piece kicks.
Sheffield Wed (From trainee on 22/10/1997) FL 0+1
Northampton T (Free on 26/1/2001) FL 6+1
Notts Co (Free on 8/3/2001) FL 9+2/2

NICHOLSON Shane Michael
Born: Newark, 3 June 1970
Height: 5'10" Weight: 12.2
Club Honours: GMVC '88

Shane can feel very satisfied after another steady season for Stockport County in 2001-02. Although playing mainly at left back, he occasionally featured in midfield for the Hatters as he chalked up 37 league and cup appearances during the campaign. A calm defender who tackles solidly and can push down the flank to deliver a useful cross he was due to be out of contract in the summer and at the time of writing it was unclear where he would begin the 2001-02 season.
Lincoln C (From trainee on 19/7/1988) FL 122+11/6 FLC 8+3 FAC 6/1 Others 7+1

Derby Co (£100,000 on 22/4/1992) FL 73+1/1 FLC 4 FAC 4/1 Others 5
West Bromwich A (£150,000 on 9/2/1996) FL 50+2 FLC 2 FAC 2 Others 4
Chesterfield (Free on 21/8/1998) FL 23+1 Others 1
Stockport Co (Free on 4/6/1999) FL 73+4/3 FLC 3 FAC 3

NIELSEN Allan
Born: Esbjerg, Denmark, 13 March 1971
Height: 5'8" Weight: 11.2
Club Honours: FLC '99
International Honours: Denmark: 41; U21
Having joined Watford for a club record fee in the 2000 close season Allan was a virtual ever-present last term and exerted a considerable influence on the Hornets' midfield. A player very much in the Graham Taylor mould, his performances tended to mirror those of the team as a whole. At his best, he worked purposefully, passed effectively and scored some useful goals.

Shane Nicholson

His long throw-ins proved a potent weapon when delivered into the opposition penalty area while he also demonstrated leadership qualities as a stand-in captain.

Tottenham H (£1,650,000 from Brondby, Denmark, ex Esbjerg, Bayern Munich, Sion, Odense, FC Copenhagen, on 3/9/1996) PL 78+18/12 FLC 10+1/3 FAC 5+2/3 Others 1
Wolverhampton W (Loaned on 23/3/2000) FL 7/2
Watford (£2,250,000 on 3/8/2000) FL 45/10 FLC 4 FAC 1

NIELSEN David
Born: Denmark, 1 December 1976
Height: 6'0" Weight: 11.13

David joined Grimsby Town on loan last October and quickly impressed the Blundell Park faithful with a well-taken goal on his first appearance in the starting line-up against Queens Park Rangers. He seemed to have solved the Mariners' goal-scoring problem but with the club keen on a permanent transfer no deal could be reached. He left Grimsby in January and shortly afterwards joined Wimbledon where he again made an immediate impact, netting on his home debut against Birmingham. However although he played a number of games for the Dons towards the end of the season he seemed to struggle to find his best form. He is a talented striker who is fast, strong and possesses excellent ball control.

Grimsby T (Loaned from FC Copenhagen, Denmark on 12/10/2000) FL 16+1/5 FAC 1+1/1
Wimbledon (Signed on 27/3/2001) FL 9+2/2

NIGHTINGALE Luke Raymond
Born: Portsmouth, 22 December 1980
Height: 5'10" Weight: 12.5

Luke had to wait until the end of September before he featured in the Portsmouth first-team last term, and then he only appeared as a substitute in the Worthington Cup second leg against Blackburn. However from then on he was a regular member of the squad of 16, although rarely making it into the starting line-up. His only senior goal came in the 2-0 home win over Burnley in March which coincided with Graham Rix's first game in charge at Fratton Park. A fast, agile striker with good distribution skills and an eye for goal he will be hoping to see more regular first-team action in 2001-02.

Portsmouth (From trainee on 23/11/1998) FL 14+31/4 FLC 2+1/3 FAC 2+1/1

NILIS Luc
Born: Hasselt, Holland, 25 May 1967
Height: 6'0" Weight: 11.12
International Honours: Belgium: 56

Signed on a 'Bosman' free from PSV Eindhoven during the summer, Luc scored on his debut for Villa in the Inter Toto Cup game against Dukla Pribram. He also netted on his Premiership debut when he came off the subs' bench against Chelsea in the second game of the season, volleying home a superb goal into the far corner. He featured in the next game at Liverpool but then in the following match at home to Ipswich he was involved in an accidental collision with the visiting 'keeper and suffered a horrific double fracture of his right leg. Despite extensive treatment he failed to recover full match fitness and announced his retirement from the game in January. A talented striker he had great ability with both feet and was always a danger around the penalty area.

Aston Villa (Free from PSV Eindhoven, Holland, ex Winterslag, Anderlecht, on 6/7/2000) PL 3/1 Others 2/1

NIVEN Stuart Thomas
Born: Glasgow, 24 December 1978
Height: 5'11" Weight: 12.8
International Honours: S: Yth

Unable to break into the first-team squad at Ipswich, Stuart joined Third Division Barnet last September and had a memorable entrance to senior football at Underhill, scoring with a vicious drive in the very first minute of the Bees trip to Carlisle to earn his side a 1-0 victory. He went on to establish a superb partnership in midfield with John Doolan, but following Doolan's injury in December his form dipped and his appearances became less frequent. He was placed on the open to offers list following the Bees relegation to the Conference.

Ipswich T (From trainee on 21/9/1996) FL 2
Barnet (Free on 29/9/2000) FL 20+4/2 FAC 2 Others 2+1

NOEL-WILLIAMS Gifton Ruben Elisha
Born: Islington, 21 January 1980
Height: 6'1" Weight: 14.6
Club Honours: Div 2 '98
International Honours: E: Yth

Gifton was again a regular in the Watford line-up last season despite being hampered by a nagging leg injury. He was also absent in the new year following a groin operation but returned to first-team action before the end of the campaign. At his best he is a splendid centre forward in the traditional style, capable of holding the ball up well, getting on the end of crosses and leading the line with aplomb. These qualities, and his popularity with the fans, helped persuaded the Hornets to award him a new contract that will take him through to 2003.

Watford (From trainee on 13/2/1997) P/FL 84+40/27 FLC 5+2/1 FAC 8/4

NOGAN Kurt
Born: Cardiff, 9 September 1970
Height: 5'11" Weight: 12.7
Club Honours: Div 2 '00
International Honours: W: B-1; U21-2

Kurt spent a frustrating time at Cardiff City last season failing to start a match in the club's promotion campaign. Opportunities for regular football were few and far between as the Bluebirds' reserves did not play in a regular competition and he had to be content with irregular outings from the subs' bench for the senior team. His only goal of the campaign came in the 3-2 win over Hartlepool in November when he clinched a remarkable victory with his injury-time effort. Kurt is a lively striker who is a proven goalscorer. He is the younger brother of York's Lee Nogan.

Luton T (From trainee on 11/7/1989) FL 17+16/3 FLC 1+3/1 Others 1+1
Peterborough U (Free on 30/9/1992) Others 1
Brighton & Hove A (Free on 17/10/1992) FL 97/49 FLC 10/7 FAC 5+1 Others 7/4
Burnley (£250,000 on 24/4/1995) FL 87+5/33 FLC 8/5 FAC 3 Others 5/4
Preston NE (£150,000 + on 13/3/1997) FL 74+19/27 FLC 4+3 FAC 6+3/3 Others 4+3/1
Cardiff C (£50,000 + on 23/3/2000) FL 4+14/1 FLC 1 FAC 0+1 Others 1

NOGAN Lee Martin
Born: Cardiff, 21 May 1969
Height: 5'9" Weight: 11.0
Club Honours: AMC '98
International Honours: W: 2; B-1; U21-1

Lee scored for Darlington on the opening day of the 2000-01 season in the 1-1 draw at Rochdale but after contributing four goals in nineteen games for the Quakers he moved on to Luton in November. Just three weeks later he scored one of the goals that helped the Hatters to an FA Cup second round victory over his old colleagues. However he stayed only a short time at Kenilworth Road and was soon back up north joining York City where he became a key figure in the club's campaign to retain their Football League status. He led the attack in fine style with his ability to hold the ball up transforming the Minstermen's attack while his tireless work made him a firm favourite with the club's supporters. Lee also weighed in with six goals notching the winners against Southend and Halifax and an outstanding strike in the 1-1 draw at Leyton Orient. He is the brother of Kurt Nogan who began his career at Kenilworth Road.

Oxford U (From trainee on 25/3/1987) FL 57+7/10 FLC 4+1 FAC 2+1/1 Others 4+1/1
Brentford (Loaned on 25/3/1987) FL 10+1/2
Southend U (Loaned on 17/9/1987) FL 6/1 FLC 2 Others 1/1
Watford (£350,000 on 12/12/1991) FL 97+8/26 FLC 5+2/3 FAC 2/1 Others 1+2
Southend U (Loaned on 17/3/1994) FL 4+1
Reading (£250,000 on 12/1/1995) FL 71+20/26 FLC 5+1/1 FAC 2 Others 3/2
Notts Co (Loaned on 14/2/1997) FL 6
Grimsby T (£170,000 on 24/7/1997) FL 63+11/10 FLC 9+1/2 FAC 4/2 Others 8/2
Darlington (Free on 21/7/1999) FL 37+12/6 FLC 3/2 FAC 3 Others 1+2/1
Luton T (Free on 23/11/2000) FL 7/1 FAC 3/1 Others 0+1
York C (Free on 12/2/2001) FL 16/6

NOLAN Ian Robert
Born: Liverpool, 9 July 1970
Height: 6'0" Weight: 12.1
International Honours: NI: 17

Signed from Sheffield Wednesday during the close season, Ian was a regular for Bradford City in the first half of last season but was then sidelined by a bad knee injury. Although he returned to fitness within a couple of months he had to wait until the closing games to get back in the first team. Out of contract in the summer it was unclear where he would be playing in the 2001-02 campaign at the time of writing. He is a versatile defender who can play in either full-back position and continued to feature for Northern Ireland during the season.

Tranmere Rov (£10,000 from Marine on 2/8/1991) FL 87+1/1 FLC 10/1 FAC 7 Others 9
Sheffield Wed (£1,500,000 on 17/8/1994) PL 164+1/4 FLC 15+1 FAC 15 Others 3
Bradford C (Free on 6/7/2000) PL 17+4 FLC 2/1 Others 4

NOLAN Kevin Anthony Jance
Born: Liverpool, 24 June 1982
Height: 6'1" Weight: 13.5
International Honours: E: Yth

After making a name for himself in the final run-in of the 1999-2000 season, Kevin really came of age at Bolton last term. Although absent from the opening games due to a broken wrist he won a place on the substitutes' bench before forcing his way into the starting line-up and staying there for the remainder of the season. A tireless worker in midfield, he is confident on the ball and is capable of making outstanding runs into the final third of the field. He also has a ferocious shot, although his goal tally of three was a little disappointing. Having firmly established himself as a key member of the Wanderers squad, he was capped twice by England U18s during the season.

Bolton W (From trainee on 22/1/2000) FL 25+10/1 FAC 3+1/2 Others 2

NORRIS David Martin
Born: Stamford, 22 February 1981
Height: 5'7" Weight: 11.6

A promising young midfielder with an eye for goal, David made two appearances for Bolton last season, featuring in both legs of the Worthington Cup first round tie against Macclesfield. A regular in the Wanderers' reserve team, he enjoyed a loan spell back at Boston United at the turn of the year, scoring seven goals in six games, including a 12-minute hat-trick in an FA Trophy game at Tamworth, and will be hoping to break into the first team at the Reebok at some stage during the coming season.

Bolton W (£50,000 from Boston U on 2/2/2000) FLC 2

NORTHMORE Ryan
Born: Plymouth, 5 September 1980
Height: 6'1" Weight: 13.0

Ryan started last season as Torquay's number two 'keeper but soon dislodged Stuart Jones. The two then shared duties for the remainder of the campaign apart from a brief spell when Andy Petterson was brought in on loan from Portsmouth. Ryan is a brilliant shot stopper but like his rival for the position he still needs to find greater consistency when dealing with crosses.

Torquay U (From trainee on 1/7/1999) FL 26+2 Others 3

NOSWORTHY Nyron Paul Henry
Born: Brixton, 11 October 1980
Height: 6'0" Weight: 12.0

Nyron continued his development at Gillingham last term. He made just two first-team appearances, both from the subs' bench, in the first half of the season but broke through for a decent run of games in the new year. A versatile player, he is equally at home at full back, in midfield and even as a makeshift striker. A hard-tackling strong-running player with enormous potential, he came into the side in March when Barry Ashby was suspended and kept his place for the rest of the season in the right-back position.

Gillingham (From trainee on 30/12/1998) FL 23+19/1 FLC 1+2 FAC 2+6 Others 0+3

NOTMAN Alexander (Alex) McKeachie
Born: Edinburgh, 10 December 1979
Height: 5'7" Weight: 10.11
International Honours: S: U21-11; Yth; Sch

Signed from Manchester United in November, this tricky striker showed glimpses of his undoubted talent in his first six months at Norwich City. A clever player with the ability to turn his marker, he is both a goal-maker and a goal-taker. He is always ready to shoot early, but is also quick to see better-placed colleagues and with his clever flicks and lay-offs he often sets up goals for his team-mates. He is adept at receiving the ball with his back to goal and linking up play and has occasionally played in a slightly deeper role behind the main strike force. He continued to represent Scotland at U21 level adding two more caps in the early part of the season.

Manchester U (From trainee on 17/12/1996) FLC 0+1
Aberdeen (Loaned on 11/2/1999) SL 0+2
Sheffield U (Loaned on 20/1/2000) FL 7+3/3
Norwich C (£250,000 on 28/11/2000) FL 10+5/1 FAC 0+1

NOWLAND Adam Christopher
Born: Preston, 6 July 1981
Height: 5'11" Weight: 11.6

Although still in his teens this Blackpool striker completed his fourth season of senior football at Bloomfield Road. Unfortunately Adam was again unable to win a place in the Tangerines' starting line-up due to the success of the partnership between John Murphy and Brett Ormerod and he was restricted to outings from the substitutes' bench. He netted regularly for the reserves but his only senior goal came when he hit the winner at Stockport in a Worthington Cup tie. He was reported to have signed for Wimbledon in the summer.

Blackpool (From trainee on 15/1/1999) FL 18+51/6 FLC 1+5/1 FAC 2+2/1 Others 0+2

NUGENT Kevin Patrick
Born: Edmonton, 10 April 1969
Height: 6'1" Weight: 13.3
International Honours: RoI: Yth

Cardiff City's skipper had the misfortune to suffer a major achilles problem last November that was to keep him out of the remainder of the club's promotion season and he spent the second half of the campaign working in the commentary box for local station Real Radio. Although he is not the quickest of strikers, Kevin is an effective target man who is strong in the air and can also hold the ball up and bring others into the game. He will be aiming to be fully fit and fighting for his first team place at the start of the 2001-02 season.

Leyton Orient (From trainee on 8/7/1987) FL 86+8/20 FLC 9+3/6 FAC 9/3 Others 9+1/1
Plymouth Arg (£200,000 on 23/3/1992) FL 124+7/32 FLC 11/2 FAC 10/3 Others 5+3
Bristol C (Signed on 29/9/1995) FL 48+22/14 FLC 2+2 FAC 3+2/1 Others 2+1
Cardiff C (£65,000 on 4/8/1997) FL 93+5/29 FLC 8+1/1 FAC 9/6

NUNEZ Garcia **Milton** Omar
Born: Honduras, 30 October 1972
Height: 5'5" Weight: 10.8
International Honours: Honduras

This diminutive striker, nicknamed 'Tyson' because of his powerful physique, again failed to establish himself in the Sunderland first team last term and his only senior action came when he appeared as a substitute for the final 30 minutes of the Worthington Cup second leg tie at Luton. For a while he interested Aston Villa, although no transfer materialised and in April his contract was cancelled. A regular for Honduras he featured in their squad for the Central American championships and also in their more promising World Cup qualifying campaign during the season. He subsequently returned to Uruguay and signed once more for Nacional.

Sunderland (£1,600,000 from Nacional Montevideo, Uruguay, via loan at PAOK Salonika, ex Communicaciones, on 23/3/2000) PL 0+1 FLC 0+1

NUTTER John Robert William
Born: Taplow, 13 June 1982
Height: 5'10" Weight: 11.9

A former Blackburn trainee John impressed for Wycombe's youth and reserve team's last season and was rewarded with his Football League debut in the 3-2 defeat at Peterborough in February. A promising young left back he was released at the end of the campaign without making any more senior appearances.

Wycombe W (Trainee) FL 1

NYARKO Alex
Born: Accra, Ghana, 15 October 1973
Height: 6'1" Weight: 11.13
International Honours: Ghana

Signed from leading French club Lens, Alex arrived at Goodison to a fanfare of publicity - likened in many quarters to Arsenal's Patrick Vieira. Physically the pair may have been alike, but there was no real comparison in styles of play. Pre-season Alex looked an elegant and classy midfielder. After scoring with one particularly inventive back-heel against Manchester City the Everton fans sat back in expectation. A solo goal at Tottenham apart, however, he failed to live up to those expectations. He made 13 successive appearances before the first of a number of injury problems began to affect him. His first game back for almost two months saw him harshly red-carded at Ipswich, then came an upsetting incident at Arsenal following which he announced his retirement from professional football. However he later renounced that decision, but stated his firm desire to quit Everton and was transfer listed.

Everton (£4,500,000 from RC Lens, France, ex Asante Kotoko, Dawu Youngsters, Sportul Studentese, FC Basle, Karlruhe SC, on 9/8/2000) PL 19+3/1 FLC 2

Michael Owen

OAKES Andrew (Andy) Mark
Born: Northwich, 11 January 1977
Height: 6'4" Weight: 12.4

Andy was a regular in Derby County's successful reserve side last term before being thrown headlong into the senior team and a battle against relegation after Mart Poom suffered a shoulder injury against Charlton. He made his debut in the home game against Sunderland when he sealed victory with a stunning save in the closing minutes. A series of steady performances in the next half-dozen games impressed all, before his season was cut short when he suffered a medial ligament injury to his right knee in the away game with Coventry.

Hull C (Signed from Winsford U on 8/12/1998) FL 19 Others 1
Derby Co (£460,000 on 7/6/1999) PL 6 FAC 1

OAKES Michael Christian
Born: Northwich, 30 October 1973
Height: 6'2" Weight: 14.6
Club Honours: FLC '96
International Honours: E: U21-6

Michael firmly established himself as Wolves' number one 'keeper last term and went on to become an ever-present in the club's First Division games. Although not completely settled in the early stages of the campaign he grew more confident as the season progressed and his defenders became used to him. A talented young goalkeeper who makes some excellent flying saves he will be looking to show further improvements in his play in 2001-02. He is the son of the former Manchester City player Alan Oakes.

Aston Villa (From juniors on 16/7/1991) PL 49+2 FLC 3 FAC 2 Others 5
Scarborough (Loaned on 26/11/1993) FL 1 Others 1
Wolverhampton W (£400,000 + on 29/10/1999) FL 74 FLC 4 FAC 4

OAKES Scott John
Born: Leicester, 5 August 1972
Height: 5'11" Weight: 11.13
International Honours: E: U21-1

Having recovered from a serious knee injury, Scott was released by Sheffield Wednesday at the end of 1999-2000 and spent some time on trial at Burnley at the start of last season. He then had a brief period training with Crystal Palace before joining Cambridge United on a non-contract basis at the end of August. He featured in a number of games for the U's either on the left or centre of midfield and improved with every match. Despite looking comfortable on the ball and showing great composure in the centre of the park he was released in the summer. Scott is the brother of Stefan Oakes and the son of Showaddywaddy guitarist Trevor Oakes.

Leicester C (From trainee on 9/5/1990) FL 1+2 Others 1
Luton T (Signed on 22/10/1991) FL 136+37/27 FLC 3+3/1 FAC 12+2/5 Others 3+3/1
Sheffield Wed (£425,000 + on 1/8/1996) PL 7+17/1 FLC 0+1 FAC 0+2
Cambridge U (Free on 29/8/2000) FL 7+11 Others 2

OAKES Stefan Trevor
Born: Leicester, 6 September 1978
Height: 5'11" Weight: 12.4
Club Honours: FLC '00

After making great strides at Leicester during 1999-2000, Stefan found it more difficult to establish himself last time around. A handful of appearances, mostly from the bench, gave him little opportunity to settle into any rhythm in the first team, although one glorious 50-yard pass, that completely bamboozled West Ham's Ian Pearce to set up a Robbie Savage goal at Filbert Street will live long in City supporters' memories. He underwent a hernia operation in January, but was soon back in action and enjoyed a brief run in the squad in the closing stages of the campaign. A right-footed midfield player with genuine ability, he will need to take a step forward next season if he is to become a midfield general of the future. Stefan is the younger brother of Scott Oakes and son of Showaddywaddy star Trevor Oakes.

Leicester C (From trainee on 3/7/1997) PL 22+16/1 FLC 7/2 FAC 4+2

OAKLEY Matthew (Matt)
Born: Peterborough, 17 August 1977
Height: 5'10" Weight: 12.1
International Honours: E: U21-4

Matt firmly established himself as a regular in the Southampton line-up last season and rarely missed a match. Having finally begun to fulfil his potential as a member of the Saints' midfield, he was an influential and commanding figure, getting through vast amounts of work and instrumental in many of the team's moves. Having openly acknowledged the role of former boss Glenn Hoddle in his development he showed his loyalty to the club by agreeing an extension to his contract during the campaign.

Southampton (From trainee on 1/7/1995) PL 142+18/10 FLC 16+2/2 FAC 9+2/1

OATWAY Anthony Charlie Philip David Terry Frank Donald Stanley Gerry Gordon Stephen James
Born: Hammersmith, 28 November 1973
Height: 5'7" Weight: 10.10
Club Honours: Div 3 '99, '01

This tough-tackling midfielder had another solid season for Third Division champions Brighton in 2000-01. He was a key figure in the centre of the park for the Seagulls as his uncompromising style enabled his colleagues to play some enterprising football. He missed a short period in the spring when an ongoing knee injury required surgery, but although this was expected to rule him out for the rest of the season he made a quick recovery and was back on the subs' bench just three weeks later. Charlie owes his plethora of names to the fact that he was named after the Queens Park Rangers players of the early 1970s.

Cardiff C (Free from Yeading on 4/8/1994) FL 29+3 FLC 2/1 FAC 1+1 Others 3+1
Torquay U (Free on 28/12/1995) FL 65+2/1 FLC 3 FAC 1
Brentford (£10,000 on 21/8/1997) FL 37+20 FLC 1+2/1 FAC 4 Others 0+1
Lincoln C (Loaned on 21/10/1998) FL 3
Brighton & Hove A (£10,000 on 9/7/1999) FL 78+2/4 FLC 4 FAC 6/1 Others 2

O'BRIEN Andrew (Andy) James
Born: Harrogate, 29 June 1979
Height: 6'3" Weight: 12.4
International Honours: E: U21-1; Yth. RoI: 1; U21-8

Andy had the misfortune to suffer a broken collar bone playing for Bradford City in the early part of last season and it was not until November that he returned to the first team. He then featured regularly for the Bantams, assisting in their struggle to avoid relegation before he was sold to Newcastle shortly before the transfer deadline. Ironically he made his debut against his old club, helping the Magpies fight their way back to earn a draw after going two goals down. He quickly settled into the centre of the defence at St James Park, and was delighted to net his first goal for the club in the derby at Sunderland to earn a useful point. Tall and slim he is a good man-marker who is cool under pressure, and promises to become a fixture in the side in the coming years. Recalled for the Republic of Ireland U21 side, he scored the winning goal against Cyprus in March, and later made his full debut against Estonia in June.

Bradford C (From trainee on 28/10/1996) P/FL 113+20/3 FLC 5 FAC 8 Others 4
Newcastle U (£2,000,000 on 28/3/2001) PL 9/1

O'BRIEN Burton
Born: South Africa, 10 June 1981
Height: 5'10" Weight: 10.12
International Honours: S: Yth

One of many promising youngsters on the books at Ewood Park this attacking midfield player had a somewhat frustrating time for Blackburn last season. Burton made just one first-team appearance when he came on from the substitutes' bench at half-time in a Worthington Cup tie against Portsmouth, an occasion when several fringe players were included, and at times struggled to get a game in the reserves. A regular for Scotland at U18 level in 1999-2000 he finished the campaign on the transfer list.

St Mirren (From juniors on 11/6/1998) SL 17+9/1 SC 2
Blackburn Rov (£300,000 on 19/2/1999) FLC 0+1

O'BRIEN Michael (Mick) George
Born: Liverpool, 25 September 1979
Height: 5'5" Weight: 10.6
Club Honours: FAYC '98
International Honours: E: Sch

Despite the lack of midfield creativity available to Torquay following the injury to Brian Healey Mick received few first team opportunities last season and even when in the squad he was more often than not on the subs' bench. He spent a couple of months on loan to Conference club Southport in the new year and featured occasionally towards

the end of the campaign. A left footed central midfielder his strengths line in the quality of his passing and his ability with free kicks.
Everton (From trainee on 7/10/1997)
Torquay U (Free on 29/7/1999) FL 32+19/5 FLC 3+1 FAC 4+2/2 Others 1+1

O'CALLAGHAN Brian Patrick
Born: Limerick, 24 February 1981
Height: 6'1" Weight: 12.1
International Honours: RoI: Yth
Brian made his debut as a substitute for Barnsley against Norwich on the opening day of last season. Most of his early appearances were at right back as cover for the injured Carl Regan but when Nigel Spackman took over the reins as manager he was generally employed as a central defender where he looked more comfortable. He did well in the games against Fulham and Blackburn, helping the team keep clean sheets on both occasions, before a knee injury brought his season to a premature close. Twice selected for the Republic of Ireland U21 squad he had to withdraw on both occasions due to his injury.
Barnsley (Signed from Pike Rov on 16/7/1998) FL 20+6 FLC 3+2 FAC 1

O'CALLAGHAN George
Born: Cork, 5 September 1979
Height: 6'1" Weight: 10.10
International Honours: RoI: Yth
George struggled to win a place in the Port Vale first team in the 2000-01 campaign and it was not until the Boxing Day visit to Wrexham that he made the starting line-up and then in an accustomed role as striker. Lack of further opportunities led him to make a transfer request but there were no takers and George was confined to the reserves until being recalled at Brentford for the LDV final rehearsal when both teams fielded some fringe players. A slightly built midfield player with a never-say-die approach to the game he was transfer-listed at the end of the season.
Port Vale (From trainee on 10/7/1998) FL 14+9/1 FAC 0+2 Others 0+1

O'CONNOR Garreth
Born: Dublin, 10 November 1978
Height: 5'7" Weight: 11.0
Garreth joined Bournemouth in the 2000 close season and featured regularly from the subs' bench last term, making the starting line-up on only three occasions, two of which were in the LDV Vans Trophy ties. A promising young midfield player he scored a couple of goals including a great last-minute equaliser in the 3-3 draw at Bristol City.
Bournemouth (Free from Bohemians on 5/6/2000) FL 1+21/1 FAC 0+3/1 Others 2/1

O'CONNOR James Kevin
Born: Dublin, 1 September 1979
Height: 5'8" Weight: 11.6
Club Honours: AMC '00
International Honours: RoI: U21-3; Yth
James again showed himself to be a fierce-tackling midfielder at Stoke City last season and his mature and committed performances made him a natural leader on the pitch and a firm favourite of the club's supporters. A key player for City all season the one area of his game where he needs to improve is his disciplinary record as he again accumulated a significant number of yellow cards during the campaign. Having broken into the Republic of Ireland U21 side in 1999-2000 he featured regularly last term alongside his colleague Clive Clark.
Stoke C (From trainee on 5/9/1996) FL 90/14 FLC 8/3 FAC 1+1 Others 13+1/2

O'CONNOR Jonathan (Jon)
Born: Darlington, 29 October 1976
Height: 5'11" Weight: 11.12
International Honours: E: U21-3; Yth
Jon is a young central defender who was released by Sheffield United in the summer of 2000 and later joined Blackpool after trials with a number of clubs including Lincoln. He was a regular in the Tangerines' line-up last autumn, appearing in ten consecutive games before being dropped following the FA Cup defeat at Yeovil. He only featured occasionally in the first team in the second half of the campaign and will be looking to see more regular senior action in 2001-02.
Everton (From trainee on 28/10/1993) PL 3+2
Sheffield U (Signed on 10/2/1998) FL 2+2 FAC 1
Blackpool (Free on 16/10/2000) FL 10+1 FAC 2 Others 1

O'CONNOR Kevin Patrick
Born: Blackburn, 24 February 1982
Height: 5'11" Weight: 12.0
This young striker was hit by a succession of injuries during the 2000-01 campaign and it was not until early December that he appeared in the Brentford first team. When he did play however he showed much greater maturity than in the previous campaign, being much stronger on the ball and displaying improved control. Ray Lewington used him in the 'hole' behind the front two and to date this appears to be his best position. Kevin scored his first goal in senior football when he netted with a stunning right-foot strike against Bristol City last February.
Brentford (From trainee on 4/3/2000) FL 11+6/1 Others 0+2

O'CONNOR Martin John
Born: Walsall, 10 December 1967
Height: 5'9" Weight: 11.8
International Honours: Cayman Isles: 2
Martin was once again a hugely influential figure for Birmingham City last term, and when he wasn't in the team the Blues just weren't the same, as their bad run of results towards the end of the season showed. He won the penalty from which Darren Purse equalised to take the Worthington Cup final against Liverpool into extra time and then hobbled on despite carrying a bad knee injury. That summed up his attitude perfectly. He fought to overcome an achilles tendon injury during the important run-in to the end of the season but still battled away in the play-off semi-final against Preston. Quick in the tackle and with great positional sense, he bound the team together from a central midfield position.

James O'Connor

Crystal Palace (£25,000 from Bromsgrove Rov on 26/6/1992) FL 2 Others 1+1
Walsall (Loaned on 24/3/1993) FL 10/1 Others 2/1
Walsall (£40,000 on 14/2/1994) FL 94/21 FLC 6/2 FAC 10/2 Others 3/1
Peterborough U (£350,000 on 12/7/1996) FL 18/3 FLC 4 FAC 2
Birmingham C (£500,000 + on 29/11/1996) FL 157+6/16 FLC 22/3 FAC 6 Others 6

ODEJAYI Olukayode (Kay)
Born: Nigeria, 21 February 1982
Height: 6'2" Weight: 12.2

One of the exciting crop of youngsters to emerge from Bristol City's flourishing Academy Kay continued to develop at a steady pace in the 2000-01 season. He added a handful of outings from the subs' bench and made his first senior appearance in the starting line-up when he appeared in the LDV Vans Trophy tie at Plymouth. A promising striker who is strong and powerful he will be looking to feature more regularly at first-team level in 2001-02. Kay is a cousin of Leicester striker Ade Akinbiyi.

Bristol C (From trainee on 17/7/2000) FL 0+6 Others 1

O'DONNELL Philip (Phil)
Born: Bellshill, 25 March 1972
Height: 5'10" Weight: 10.10
Club Honours: SC '91, '95; SPD '98
International Honours: S: 1; U21-8

Having missed virtually the whole of 1999-2000 with knee problems Phil was once again dogged by injuries last season. He made several appearances in the early part of the campaign but then went down with groin trouble, and although he returned to the first team in December he then suffered an achilles injury that kept him out of action for some time. When fully fit he is a hard-working left-sided midfield player and he will be hoping to finally put his problems behind him in the coming season.

Motherwell (From juniors on 30/6/1990) SL 123+1/15 SLC 6 SC 11+1/2 Others 3
Glasgow Celtic (£1,750,000 on 9/9/1994) SL 77+13/15 SLC 6+1 SC 12+4/4 Others 7+1/1
Sheffield Wed (Free on 9/7/1999) P/FL 7+5 FLC 0+1

ODUNSI Saheed **Adeleke (Leke)**
Born: Lambeth, 5 December 1980
Height: 5'9" Weight: 11.8

Leke is another excellent product of the Millwall youth set-up. He again featured mainly in the reserves last season but had a couple of short runs in the first-team squad. He is a powerful central midfielder who is comfortable on the ball, gives no quarter in the tackle and has good vision. He will be aiming to gain further senior experience in the 2001-02 campaign.

Millwall (From trainee on 24/2/1999) FL 5+10 FLC 1+2 Others 2+1

O'HALLORAN Keith James
Born: Dublin, 10 November 1975
Height: 5'10" Weight: 12.3
International Honours: RoI: U21-3; Yth; Sch

Having spent several seasons north of the border with St Johnstone Keith joined Swindon Town in the 2000 close season and immediately established himself as a regular in the first team. He went on to become one of the most consistent performers for the Robins, establishing himself as the club's regular penalty taker and also contributing a couple of spectacular strikes in the FA Cup second round tie against Gateshead. He is a right-sided midfield player who is strong and determined in the tackle.

Middlesbrough (Signed from Cherry Orchard on 6/9/1994) F/PL 3+1 FAC 2 Others 1
Scunthorpe U (Loaned on 25/3/1996) FL 6+1
Cardiff C (Loaned on 29/11/1996) FL 8 Others 2
St Johnstone (Free on 27/3/1997) SL 56+19/3 SLC 3+2/1 SC 2+3 Others 2
Swindon T (Free on 27/7/2000) FL 40/5 FLC 4 FAC 2+1/2 Others 2

O'HANLON Kelham Gerard
Born: Saltburn, 16 May 1962
Height: 6'1" Weight: 13.10
Club Honours: Div 4 '89
International Honours: RoI: 1; U21-1

Preston's assistant manager was forced to sit on the bench as emergency cover for six games in September after an injury to first choice Teuvo Moilanen, and this led to him playing his first senior game for three-and-a half years when he came on to replace the injured David Lucas for the final seven minutes of the game against Stockport. He was mightily relieved when his only contribution was to take three goal kicks! Coincidentally, his last game for Preston had also been a home match against the same opponents back in 1997.

Middlesbrough (From apprentice on 21/5/1980) FL 87 FLC 4 FAC 6
Rotherham U (Free on 7/8/1985) FL 248 FLC 22 FAC 18 Others 16
Carlisle U (£25,000 on 5/8/1991) FL 83 FLC 6 FAC 3 Others 5
Preston NE (£25,000 on 20/7/1993) FL 23 FLC 2 FAC 2 Others 1
Dundee U (£30,000 on 16/9/1994) SL 31 SC 4 Others 3
Preston NE (£12,000 on 6/9/1996) FL 13+1 Others 2

O'KANE John Andrew
Born: Nottingham, 15 November 1974
Height: 5'10" Weight: 12.2
Club Honours: FAYC '92; Div 2 '97

A good run of form during the first half of last season saw John enjoy his most successful spell yet in a Bolton shirt. A speedy, attack-minded right back who can supply an excellent ball into the danger area when required, he established himself as an important squad member at the Reebok Stadium. A dip in form shortly after Christmas coupled with some niggling injuries ensured that he did not have as successful an end to the season as he would have liked. Out of contract in the summer he was reported to have joined Blackpool.

Manchester U (From trainee on 29/1/1993) PL 1+1 FLC 2+1 FAC 1 Others 1
Wimbledon (Loaned on 22/6/1995) Others 3
Bury (Loaned on 25/10/1996) FL 2+2/2
Bury (Loaned on 16/1/1997) FL 9/1 Others 1
Bradford C (Loaned on 31/10/1997) FL 7
Everton (£250,000 + on 30/1/1998) PL 14 FAC 1+2
Burnley (Loaned on 31/10/1998) FL 8
Bolton W (Signed on 19/11/1999) FL 32+6/2 FLC 4 FAC 3+1/1

OKON Paul Michael
Born: Sydney, Australia, 5 April 1972
Height: 5'11" Weight: 11.12
International Honours: Australia: 22; U23; Yth

Having joined Middlesbrough during the summer, Paul did well in his first couple of games before suffering a broken foot in the third game of the season. He therefore missed the chance of representing his country in the Olympic Games and indeed it was not until December that he returned to first-team action. A regular in the side thereafter he helped in Boro's revival to escape relegation in the second half of the campaign. An experienced central defender he is likely to be a key figure for the club in 2000-01 now that he has settled in at the Riverside.

Middlesbrough (Free from Fiorentina, Italy, ex Marconi Fairfield, Brugge, Lazio, on 4/8/2000) PL 23+1 FAC 2

Paul Okon

OLAOYE Dolapo (Del)
Born: Lagos, Nigeria, 17 October 1982
Height: 5'10" Weight: 12.4

This young Port Vale trainee was surprisingly called up for first-team duty in the opening home game of last season against Oxford when he came off the subs' bench to replace Tony Naylor for the final five minutes. He subsequently spent the remainder of the campaign continuing his football education in the reserves. Del is a promising striker who will be hoping to gain further senior experience in 2001-02.

Port Vale (Trainee) FL 0+1

OLDFIELD David Charles
Born: Perth, Australia, 30 May 1968
Height: 5'11" Weight: 13.4
International Honours: E: U21-1

Having featured as a striker for Peterborough towards the end of the 1999-2000 season David was mainly confined to a midfield role last term. He worked tirelessly throughout the campaign and was very much a steadying hand in the centre of the park. Rarely absent from the starting line-up, he contributed four goals and his efforts were rewarded when members of the supporters' club voted him 'Player of the Season'.

Luton T (From apprentice on 16/5/1986) FL 21+8/4 FLC 4+2/2 FAC 0+1 Others 2+1/2
Manchester C (£600,000 on 14/3/1989) FL 18+8/6 FLC 2+1/2 Others 0+1/1
Leicester C (£150,000 on 12/1/1990) F/PL 163+25/26 FLC 10+1/1 FAC 6/3 Others 11+3/2
Millwall (Loaned on 24/2/1995) FL 16+1/6
Luton T (£150,000 on 21/7/1995) FL 99+18/18 FLC 11/2 FAC 2 Others 7+2/4
Stoke C (Free on 2/7/1998) FL 50+15/7 FLC 4+1 FAC 2 Others 1+1
Peterborough U (Free on 23/3/2000) FL 41+7/3 FLC 2 FAC 5/1 Others 3

O'LEARY Kristian (Kris) Denis
Born: Port Talbot, 30 August 1977
Height: 6'0" Weight: 13.4
Club Honours: Div 3 '00
International Honours: W: Yth

Kris displayed consistent form for Swansea City during the early part of last season when he was used in a central defensive role and he later featured at right back before being sidelined by a calf injury. He returned for the penultimate game against Brentford when he scored in a 6-0 thrashing and also made the team for the last game at home to Cambridge. A strong tackler with good distribution he can play either in defence or midfield if required.

Swansea C (From trainee on 1/7/1996) FL 83+22/5 FLC 6 FAC 4+1 Others 5+2

OLEKSEWYCZ Stephen (Steve) Michael
Born: Sowerby Bridge, 24 February 1983
Height: 5'7" Weight: 10.7

This Halifax Town youngster was rewarded with a two-and-a-half-year professional contract when Paul Bracewell took over as manager last October and later that month he made his Football League debut when he came on as a substitute in the 2-0 home defeat by Hull City. A promising striker he made a couple more appearances from the subs' bench before continuing his development in the reserves.

Halifax T (Free from juniors on 11/8/2000) FL 0+3

OLIVER Adam
Born: West Bromwich, 25 October 1980
Height: 5'9" Weight: 11.2
International Honours: E: Yth

Adam was challenging strongly for a regular first-team place with West Bromwich Albion at the beginning of last season but was then sidelined by a knee ligament injury in November. He subsequently suffered further problems when he required an emergency operation for a ruptured appendix and it was not until early March that he returned to full fitness. A determined and hard-working midfield player he has signed a new contract that will keep him at The Hawthorns until 2003.

West Bromwich A (From trainee on 15/8/1998) FL 2+21/1 FLC 1+2 FAC 1

OLIVER Michael
Born: Middlesbrough, 2 August 1975
Height: 5'10" Weight: 12.4

Michael had to battle for a place in Rochdale's line-up last season and although he featured regularly in the squad he often had to be content with appearances from the subs' bench. A hard-working midfield player he was originally used out wide but had his best games for Dale later in the season when he was given a more central role.

Middlesbrough (From trainee on 19/8/1992) Others 0+1
Stockport Co (£15,000 on 7/7/1994) FL 17+5/1 FLC 0+2 FAC 2 Others 1
Darlington (Free on 30/7/1996) FL 135+16/14 FLC 7+1/1 FAC 10+1 Others 6+3
Rochdale (Free on 14/7/2000) FL 25+13 FLC 2 FAC 1 Others 1

OLSEN Benjamin (Ben) Robert
Born: Harrisburg, USA, 15 March 1977
Height: 5'8" Weight: 10.4
International Honours: United States: 19

Having appeared in the Sydney Olympics for the USA team that narrowly missed out on a bronze medal, Ben crossed the Atlantic to join Nottingham Forest for an extended loan period last October. He immediately took to English football, proving to be a very pacy and effervescent wide-right midfield player. He featured regularly before suffering a broken ankle in March when he returned to the United States, and at the time of writing had yet to return to action with DC United. He was a regular with both the full and U23 teams for the USA before his injury.

Nottingham F (Loaned from DC United, USA on 12/10/2000) FL 14+4/2

OLSEN James Paul
Born: Bootle, 23 October 1981
Height: 5'10" Weight: 12.0

A former Liverpool trainee James joined Tranmere on the transfer deadline day and immediately impressed with some eye-catching displays in Rovers' reserve team. His performances won a call-up to the first-team squad and he made his Football League debut as a substitute during the last home game of the season against Nottingham Forest. A promising midfield play maker who showed some imaginative distribution and a maturity beyond his years he will be hoping to gain further senior experience in 2001-02.

Tranmere Rov (From trainee at Liverpool on 22/3/2001) FL 0+1

OMOYINMI Emmanuel (Manny)
Born: Nigeria, 28 December 1977
Height: 5'6" Weight: 10.7
International Honours: E: Sch

Manny arrived at Oxford hoping to re-establish his career after a somewhat torrid time at West Ham in the 1999-2000 campaign. He showed plenty of pace and lots of skill in the early months of the season without scoring but fell out of favour under David Kemp who bought in new players. However injuries and unavailability let him back in and the popular striker opened his goal account with two cracking strikes in the 4-3 win over promotion-chasing Rotherham in March.

West Ham U (From trainee on 17/5/1995) PL 1+8/2 FLC 0+2 FAC 1+1
Bournemouth (Loaned on 30/9/1996) FL 5+2
Dundee U (Loaned on 20/2/1998) SL 1+3 SC 0+1
Leyton Orient (Loaned on 19/3/1999) FL 3+1/1
Gillingham (Loaned on 3/9/1999) FL 7+2/3 FLC 2
Scunthorpe U (Loaned on 21/12/1999) FL 6/1 Others 1
Barnet (Loaned on 25/2/2000) FL 1+5
Oxford U (Free on 10/7/2000) FL 16+8/3 FLC 2 FAC 0+1 Others 1

O'NEIL Brian
Born: Paisley, 6 September 1972
Height: 6'1" Weight: 12.4
International Honours: S: 6; U21-7; Yth; Sch

Brian joined Derby County in the exchange deal that saw Stefan Schnoor return to Germany. Unfortunately he suffered a serious knee injury just two minutes into his debut against Manchester United and this led to a long lay-off, although he eventually returned to first-team action before the end of the season. A versatile player who is at home either in defence or a midfield 'holding' role, he is a fine passer of the ball and excellent at breaking up opposition moves.

Glasgow Celtic (Free from Porirua Viard U on 10/7/1991) SL 92+27/8 SLC 6+4/1 SC 10/9 Others 8+3/1
Nottingham F (Loaned on 18/3/1997) PL 4+1
Aberdeen (Free on 3/7/1997) SL 24+4/1 SLC 4 SC 1 (Transferred to Wolfsburg, Germany on 23/7/1998)
Derby Co (Signed on 16/11/2000) PL 3+1 FAC 2

O'NEIL Gary Paul
Born: Bromley, 18 May 1983
Height: 5'10" Weight: 11.0
International Honours: E: Yth

One of the finest prospects to emerge from the Portsmouth youth system in recent seasons, Gary continued to make steady progress last term. He made the starting line-up on eight occasions despite missing a large part of the campaign after undergoing knee surgery and then breaking a bone in his right foot. He is an exciting midfield player with fine vision, composure and an ability to create space for himself. He scored his first senior goals during the campaign, including one in the crucial last-day-of-the-season win over Barnsley and was also capped for England U17s against Italy.

Portsmouth (From trainee on 5/6/2000) FL 7+4/1 FLC 1+2

O'NEILL John Joseph
Born: Glasgow, 2 January 1974
Height: 5'11" Weight: 12.0

After being released by Bournemouth at the end of the 1999-2000 campaign, John had a trial with Carlisle United over the summer before returning to Dean Court on non-contract forms in October. He made three appearances from the subs' bench for the Cherries and then moved on to join Ross County on a short-term contract later that month. He subsequently signed for Queen of the South in January where he had a successful spell, scoring ten goals in 17 games. John is a versatile player who can appear in any of the midfield roles and also as a striker.

Queens Park (From juniors on 25/7/1991) SL 70+21/30 SLC 2+1 SC 2 Others 0+1
Glasgow Celtic (Signed on 16/5/1994) SL 0+2
Bournemouth (Free on 29/3/1996) FL 79+45/10 FLC 4+6 FAC 4+4/2 Others 6+4

O'NEILL Keith Padre Gerard
Born: Dublin, 16 February 1976
Height: 6'1" Weight: 12.7
International Honours: RoI: 13; U21-1; Yth; Sch

Keith continued to feature as a left wing back for Middlesbrough last term. Although his appearances were restricted by niggling injuries. He stamped his authority on games with his fearless tackling and impressed with some fine crossing, a legacy of having previously played as an orthodox left winger. Hopefully if he can stay clear of injury next term he will feature regularly for Boro' throughout the campaign.

Norwich C (From trainee on 1/7/1994) P/FL 54+19/9 FLC 8+3/1 FAC 3
Middlesbrough (£700,000 + on 19/3/1999) PL 32+5 FLC 3+1 FAC 1

O'NEILL Paul Dennis
Born: Farnworth, 17 May 1982
Height: 5'11" Weight: 11.2

This young central defender was outstanding in the Macclesfield youth and reserve teams last season and deputised on several occasions in the senior team. Always calm and confident even under pressure, Paul is a great prospect for the future and signed a new deal that will keep him at Moss Rose until June 2003.

Macclesfield T (From trainee on 5/7/2000) FL 5+8 FAC 1 Others 1

ONUORA Ifem (Iffy)
Born: Glasgow, 28 July 1967
Height: 6'1" Weight: 13.10

Iffy missed the first part of the 2000-01 season after undergoing a knee operation during the summer. His first game back occurred in bizarre circumstances, for when Marlon King and Kevin James were caught up in traffic on the M25 he was named as substitute for the home game against Bolton. Despite not being 100 per cent fit he came on ten minutes from the end to score an injury-time goal against the promotion favourites to earn a point from a 2-2 draw. A regular in the squad of 16 he was fully restored to the starting line-up when Carl Asaba moved to Sheffield United and responded by netting six goals in seven appearances, including a hat-trick in the 4-3 win over Norwich City.

Huddersfield T (Signed from Bradford University on 28/7/1989) FL 115+50/30 FLC 10+6/4 FAC 11+3/3 Others 13+3/3
Mansfield T (£30,000 on 20/7/1994) FL 17+11/8 FAC 0+1 Others 1
Gillingham (£25,000 on 16/8/1996) FL 53+9/23 FLC 6/1 FAC 4/2 Others 1
Swindon T (£120,000 on 13/3/1998) FL 64+9/25 FLC 4 FAC 2+1
Gillingham (£125,000 on 3/1/2000) FL 38+15/15 FAC 1+1/1 Others 3/1

OPARA Kelechi (KK) Chrysantus
Born: Oweri, Nigeria, 21 December 1981
Height: 6'0" Weight: 12.6

KK struggled to make any impression at all with Colchester United in the first half of the 2000-01 campaign and after just a handful of appearances he was released towards the end of the year. He subsequently signed for Third Division Leyton Orient as a third-year trainee and went straight in the team for the game against Darlington. After a few more appearances he went out on loan to Dagenham & Redbridge to gain further experience, before returning to Brisbane Road where he featured again towards the end of the campaign. KK also played for the O's youth team in their victory over Bradford City in the Football League Youth Alliance Cup final, winning the penalty that decided the game. A powerful young striker he will be looking to gain further experience next term.

Colchester U (Trainee) FL 2+17 FLC 1 Others 0+1
Leyton Orient (Free on 4/12/2000) FL 3+3 FAC 1 Others 1

OPINEL Sasha
Born: Bourg-Saint-Maurice, France, 9 April 1977
Height: 5'9" Weight: 11.12

Sasha had an unfortunate start to the 2000-01 campaign for Raith Rovers, receiving red cards in his first two games. He then played a handful of games before falling out of favour. In December he came to Plymouth on trial and made a single appearance in the LDV Vans Trophy second round game at Bristol Rovers playing as a defender. He was released and after impressing in a trial for Bournemouth reserves against Leyton Orient he was signed up by O's boss Tommy Taylor. Quickly nicknamed 'Slasher' at Brisbane Road he featured fairly regularly in the closing weeks of the campaign. However despite scoring with a 25-yard screamer against Cardiff he was released in the summer. He is a right-sided defender or midfield player.

Raith Rov (Signed from Ajaccio, France, via trial at Stockport Co, ex Lille, on 6/12/1999) SL 21+1 SLC 1 SC 1
Plymouth Arg (Free on 22/12/2000) Others 1
Leyton Orient (Free on 15/2/2001) FL 9+2/1

ORD Michael
Born: Huddersfield, 22 May 1981
Height: 6'1" Weight: 11.6

This young Halifax Town striker made the briefest of appearances in senior football when he came on from the subs' bench in the final minutes of the Worthington Cup first round second leg tie last September. He then returned to the club's reserve team but was badly affected by injury and after being released in February he signed for Unibond League outfit Harrogate Town.

Halifax T (Signed from Ripon C on 6/1/2000) FLC 0+1

ORMEROD Brett Ryan
Born: Blackburn, 18 October 1976
Height: 5'11" Weight: 11.4

Brett showed he had made a full recovery from the broken leg he suffered back in October 1999, returning to first-team action for Blackpool at the start of last season and being a near ever-present throughout the campaign. He forged as an excellent striking partnership with John Murphy and finished the campaign on a high by scoring five goals in the play-offs as the Tangerines went on to win promotion. Brett is quick off the mark and this, combined with a high work rate, enabled him to unsettle even the best Third Division defenders.

Blackpool (£50,000 from Accrington Stanley on 21/3/1997) FL 84+23/32 FLC 6/1 FAC 3+1/3 Others 7/6

OSBORN Simon Edward
Born: Croydon, 19 January 1972
Height: 5'9" Weight: 11.4

Simon had a chequered start to the 2000-01 campaign with Wolves and spent a short while out with an injury early on. Returning to the side as skipper he continued to operate in a midfield 'holding' role where he worked hard to harass opponents although this was not always appreciated by the Wanderers' fans. He subsequently damaged a tendon in his big toe in the FA Cup tie at Wycombe and soon after he had regained fitness he was on his way out of Molineux. He joined Tranmere on the transfer deadline day and stayed until the end of the season but was unable to prevent Rovers being relegated from the First Division.

Crystal Palace (From trainee on 3/1/1990) F/PL 47+8/5 FLC 11/1 FAC 2 Others 1+3
Reading (£90,000 on 17/8/1994) FL 31+1/5 FLC 4 Others 3
Queens Park R (£1,100,000 on 7/7/1995) PL 6+3/1 FLC 2
Wolverhampton W (£1,000,000 on 22/12/1995) FL 151+11/11 FLC 7/3 FAC 11+1 Others 2
Tranmere Rov (Free on 22/3/2001) FL 9/1

O'SHEA John Francis
Born: Waterford, 30 April 1981
Height: 6'3" Weight: 11.12
International Honours: RoI: U21-8; Yth; (UEFA-U16 '98)

Another young Manchester United player who emerged from the youth team shadows last term, John featured in the Worthington Cup ties against Watford and Sunderland, before following in the footsteps of Danny Higginbottom and Ronnie Wallwork and joining Royal Antwerp on loan. A promising central defender he was also a regular for the Republic of Ireland U21 team during the season.

Manchester U (Signed from Waterford U on 2/9/1998) FLC 3
Bournemouth (Loaned on 18/1/2000) FL 10/1 Others 1

OSTENSTAD Egil
Born: Haugesun, Norway, 2 January 1972
Height: 6'0" Weight: 13.0
International Honours: Norway: 18; U21; Yth

Egil was a regular in the Blackburn squad in the first half of last season although he was often used as a substitute. He scored in quick succession against Tranmere and Huddersfield towards the end of October but seemed to slip out of the first-team picture and in March he went on loan to Manchester City as Joe Royle sought to give a boost to his strike force. He made his debut against Tottenham from the subs' bench but never played a full 90 minutes during his time at Maine Road. He found it difficult to make an impact in a struggling team that seemed to be constantly changing. At his best he is a powerful striker who is effective in the air and has a good eye for goal.

Southampton (£800,000 from Viking Stavanger, Norway on 3/10/1996) PL 80+16/28 FLC 9/3 FAC 3+1/2
Blackburn Rov (Signed on 18/8/1999) FL 28+13/11 FLC 4+1/1 FAC 2+1
Manchester C (Loaned on 9/2/2001) PL 1+3

OSTER John Morgan
Born: Boston, 8 December 1978
Height: 5'9" Weight: 10.8
International Honours: W: 4; B-1; U21-9; Yth

John had a somewhat frustrating season at Sunderland last term and struggled to win a regular place in the first-team squad. A clever ball-playing winger, he opened his goal-scoring account for the Black Cats in the Worthington Cup tie against Luton, but always struggled to dislodge Kevin Kilbane or Julio Arca from the Wearsiders' line-up.

Grimsby T (From trainee on 11/7/1996) FL 21+3/3 FAC 0+1/1
Everton (£1,500,000 on 21/7/1997) PL 22+18/1 FLC 4+1/1 FAC 2+3/1
Sunderland (£1,000,000 on 6/8/1999) PL 6+12 FLC 6+1/1 FAC 1+1

O'SULLIVAN Wayne St John
Born: Akrotiri, Cyprus, 25 February 1974
Height: 5'9" Weight: 11.2
Club Honours: Div 2 '96
International Honours: RoI: U21-2

Wayne once again performed consistently for Plymouth Argyle last season when he was used either as right wing back or in the centre of midfield. He was a near ever-present although he scored just one goal during the campaign - a header at Home Park in the 1-0 victory over Halifax in January. Wherever he is asked to play Wayne always works hard and shows 100 per cent commitment to the cause. He was voted 'Player of the Year' by the Home Park fans at the end of the season but reportedly turned down a new contract in favour of a move to Australia in the summer.

Swindon T (From trainee on 1/5/1993) FL 65+24/3 FLC 11/1 FAC 1+3 Others 3+2
Cardiff C (£75,000 on 22/8/1997) FL 78+7/4 FLC 1+2 FAC 10/1 Others 2
Plymouth Arg (Free on 30/7/1999) FL 83+2/3 FLC 4 FAC 7 Others 1

OVENDALE Mark John
Born: Leicester, 22 November 1973
Height: 6'2" Weight: 13.2

Mark joined Luton Town in the 2000 close season and although he began last season on the subs' bench he quickly won a place in the first team at Kenilworth Road, subsequently competing with his rival Nathan Abbey for the goalkeeper's jersey throughout the season. An excellent 'keeper he commands his area well, is a fine shot stopper and plucks crosses and corners out of the air with ease.

Northampton T (Free from Wisbech on 15/8/1994) FL 6 Others 2 (Free to Barry T during 1995 close season)
Bournemouth (£30,000 on 14/5/1998) FL 89 FLC 10 FAC 7 Others 5
Luton T (£425,000 on 10/8/2000) FL 26 FLC 4 FAC 2 Others 1

OWEN Gareth
Born: Chester, 21 October 1971
Height: 5'8" Weight: 12.0
Club Honours: WC '95
International Honours: W: B-1; U21-8

Gareth enjoyed a very successful testimonial when Manchester United visited Wrexham's Racecourse Ground and went on to appear regularly in the Robins' line-up until injury struck at the turn of the year. A pulled muscle was quickly followed by a groin problem and the result was a lengthy spell out of action. He was mostly employed in a deep lying central-midfield role where his passing skills and powerful long-range shot were put to good use. Having spent more than a decade at Wrexham he was reported to have signed for Doncaster Rovers in the summer.

Wrexham (From trainee on 6/7/1990) FL 298+52/36 FLC 13+1 FAC 25+7 Others 37+2/1

OWEN Michael James
Born: Chester, 14 December 1979
Height: 5'9" Weight: 11.2
Club Honours: FAYC '96; FLC '01; FAC '01; UEFAC '01
International Honours: E: 29; U21-1; Yth; Sch

Michael started the 2000-01 season in electrifying form with a double at Southampton, a hat-trick against Aston Villa and a tally of seven goals in five games to firmly establish himself as the country's leading marksmen. Unfortunately he suffered a head injury against Derby County in October that sidelined him for five games, and then a back injury and a hamstring problem further disrupted his season. However even when fit he seemed to have lost some of his sharpness in front of goal and with Emile Heskey in outstanding form he found himself frequently on the bench, alternating with Robbie Fowler for the role of second striker. He returned to goal-scoring form with a stunning double in the away leg of the UEFA Cup tie against Roma, but it was not until the season came to its climax that he returned to his early-season brilliance. A goal at Bradford City was followed by a hat-trick against Newcastle and a double against Chelsea. Even this was overshadowed by his performance in the FA Cup final, as much a defining moment in his career as his World Cup goal against Argentina in 1998. After 80 minutes of a one-sided final (in Arsenal's favour) he had scarcely had a sniff of a goal when he reacted quickest to uncertainty in the Arsenal defence to volley home a loose ball in the penalty area. If his first goal was sheer opportunism, his second and winning goal was sheer class. With two minutes remaining on the clock and the match seemingly destined for extra time, he received a through ball out of defence from Patrik Berger, brushed aside Lee Dixon, outpaced Tony Adams and whipped in a cross-shot from the tightest of angles that eluded David Seaman and crept inside the far post. It was a goal worthy of a great occasion and perhaps the mark of a great player that he can go from anonymity to 'Man of the Match' in the space of ten minutes. Four days later he set up two of the Reds' goals in the UEFA Cup final against Deportivo Alaves. He remained a key figure for England under the new management of Sven Goran Eriksson, and scored the vital first goal in the World Cup qualifying games at home to Finland and in Albania to help his country's World Cup qualifying campaign get back on track.

Liverpool (From juniors on 18/12/1996) PL 107+16/64 FLC 9+1/7 FAC 7+1/5 Others 18+3/7

OWERS Gary
Born: Newcastle, 3 October 1968
Height: 5'11" Weight: 12.7
Club Honours: Div 3 '88

Gary was very much an unsung hero once again for Notts County last season. The anchor-man of the Magpies midfield he performed consistently well and his experience proved invaluable to the youngsters in the team around him. Rarely absent he netted four valuable goals to continue his record of having scored in every season of his professional career.

Sunderland (From apprentice on 8/10/1986) FL 259+9/25 FLC 25+1/1 FAC 10+2 Others 11+1/1
Bristol C (£250,000 on 23/12/1994) FL 121+5/9 FLC 9/1 FAC 9 Others 9/2
Notts Co (£15,000 on 30/7/1998) FL 121+3/11 FLC 8+1 FAC 12/1 Others 1

OWUSU Ansah Ossei
Born: Hackney, 22 November 1979
Height: 5'11" Weight: 11.2

Another product of Wimbledon's successful youth policy Ansah made a couple of first-team appearances last term before being sidelined with an injury. After recovering fitness he then spent the last three months of the campaign on loan with Second Division Bristol Rovers where he featured regularly in the attack but failed to score. He is a lively young striker who can also play on the left wing if required and is a handful to any defence.

Wimbledon (From trainee on 22/6/1998) FL 1+3 FLC 1
Raith Rov (Loaned on 23/3/2000) SL 8+2/3
Bristol Rov (Loaned on 9/2/2001) FL 11+6

OWUSU Lloyd Magnus
Born: Slough, 12 December 1976
Height: 6'1" Weight: 14.0
Club Honours: Div 3 '99

Lloyd had the misfortune to suffer a dislocated shoulder playing for Brentford in a Worthington Cup tie at Bristol City at the start of last season that kept him out of action for two months. After recovering fitness he was nursed back into the team appearing primarily as a substitute until he reclaimed his place up front with Scott Partridge in January. It was not until the second half of the campaign that the goals began to flow again and he finished the season by winning a runners-up medal in the LDV Vans Trophy final when the Bees were defeated by Port Vale. Lloyd remains a very effective striker who is strong and fast with an eye for goal.

Brentford (£25,000 from Slough T on 29/7/1998) FL 105+15/44 FLC 2+4/2 FAC 6/2 Others 9+3/3

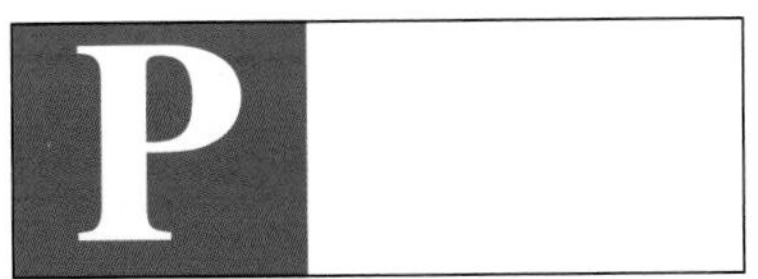

PACKHAM William (Will) Joseph
Born: Brighton, 13 January 1981
Height: 6'2" Weight: 13.0
Will was third-choice 'keeper at Brighton in 2000-01 behind Michels Kuipers and Mark Cartwright and spent much of the season out on loan at local non-league clubs Bognor Regis and Langney Sports. He returned towards the end of the campaign and made his Football League debut in the Seagulls penultimate game at Halifax when he came off the subs' bench for the final half hour and kept a clean sheet.
Brighton & Hove A (From trainee on 29/6/1999) FL 0+1

PACQUETTE Richard Francis
Born: Paddington, 28 January 1983
Height: 6'0" Weight: 12.7
Richard was a member of last season's successful Queens Park Rangers' U19 team that reached the play-off finals of the FA Premier Academy League only to lose in extra time to Nottingham Forest. He stepped up to make his Football League debut from the subs' bench at Huddersfield on the day that Rangers' relegation to the Second Division was confirmed and later made the starting line-up for the home game against Stockport. A promising striker who is fast and strong he will be looking to gain further senior experience in 2001-02.
Queens Park R (From trainee on 1/2/2000) FL 1+1

PADULA Diego **Gino** Mauro
Born: Buenos Aires, Argentina, 11 July 1976
Height: 5'9" Weight: 12.1
Gino was Wigan Athletic manager Bruce Rioch's first signing following his appointment in the 2000 close season but he struggled to win a place in the Latics' line-up in 2000-01, finding his way blocked by the in-form Kevin Sharp. He is a pacy left back who is confident when bringing the ball out of defence and can deliver a quality cross. He scored his only goal of the campaign in the LDV Vans Trophy tie against his former club Walsall. Gino was one of several players released by Wigan in the summer as the club sought to trim its squad.
Bristol Rov (Free from Xerez, Spain on 15/10/1999)
Walsall (Free on 11/11/1999) FL 23+2 FAC 2
Wigan Ath (Free on 21/7/2000) FL 2+2 FLC 0+1 FAC 2 Others 2/1

PAGE Robert John
Born: Llwynpia, 3 September 1974
Height: 6'0" Weight: 12.5
Club Honours: Div 2 '98
International Honours: W: 20; B-1; U21-6; Yth; Sch
Rarely absent from the Watford line-up last season apart from the occasional suspension, Robert again provided inspirational leadership as the club captain. A consistent, hard-tackling central defender he is very commanding in the air and always committed to the cause. He also notched a rare goal when he netted with a header from Peter Kennedy's corner in the defeat at Preston in April. He continued to be selected regularly for Wales although he usually featured at right back rather than in his club role. He was placed on the open to offers list in the summer.
Watford (From trainee on 19/4/1993) P/FL 209+7/2 FLC 17 FAC 12+1 Others 6/1

PAHARS Marians
Born: Latvia, 5 August 1976
Height: 5'9" Weight: 10.9
International Honours: Latvia: 45
Although not as prolific a goal-scorer as in the previous campaign, Marians showed some good form for Southampton last season and his striking partnership with James Beattie was a productive one - even though he scored few goals himself. His ability to trouble defenders and lay off perfect passes more than justified his inclusion in a side that achieved the Saints' best final position in 18 years. He netted six goals in the initial eight games including a fine double against Liverpool when Saints recovered after being three down, but subsequently found the net just three more times. A powerful, pocket-sized striker who is at his best when using his electric pace to cut in from the wings, he remained a regular for Latvia in their World Cup qualifying campaign.
Southampton (£800,000 from Skonto Riga, Latvia on 25/3/1999) PL 61+9/25 FLC 4+1 FAC 6

Marians Pahars

PAINTER Peter **Robert (Robbie)**
Born: Wigan, 26 January 1971
Height: 5'11" Weight: 12.2
Robbie struggled to win a regular place in the Halifax Town line-up last season when he was also affected by one or two niggling injuries. He featured only intermittently during the campaign and was often used from the subs' bench. A right-sided striker with considerable experience in the lower divisions he was released by the Shaymen in May.
Chester C (From trainee on 1/7/1988) FL 58+26/8 FLC 2+2 FAC 7+1/3 Others 3+3
Maidstone U (£30,000 on 16/8/1991) FL 27+3/5 FLC 2 FAC 1+1 Others 0+2
Burnley (£25,000 on 27/3/1992) FL 16+10/2 FLC 2 FAC 1
Darlington (Signed on 16/9/1993) FL 104+11/28 FLC 2+4/1 FAC 5+1/2 Others 9/3
Rochdale (Signed on 10/10/1996) FL 101+11/30 FLC 3/1 FAC 7 Others 4+2
Halifax T (Free on 31/7/1999) FL 46+12/8 FLC 2 FAC 3 Others 1+1

PALLISTER Gary Andrew
Born: Ramsgate, 30 June 1965
Height: 6'4" Weight: 14.13
Club Honours: FAC '90, '94, '96; CS '93, '94, '96, '97; ECWC '91; ESC '91; FLC '92; PL '93, '94, '96, '97
International Honours: E: 22; B-9
Gary had a disappointing season for Middlesbrough in 2000-01 when he was in and out of the side early on before eventually succumbing to a back injury in November. Although he returned to training towards the end of the campaign he did not make any more appearances for the first team. A vastly experienced central defender he is a tower of strength at the back for Boro', skilful in the air and totally dependable. He was reported to have retired from playing in the summer.
Middlesbrough (Free from Billingham T on 7/11/1984) FL 156/5 FLC 10 FAC 10/1 Others 13
Darlington (Loaned on 18/10/1985) FL 7
Manchester U (£2,300,000 on 29/8/1989) F/PL 314+3/12 FLC 36 FAC 38/1 Others 45+1/1
Middlesbrough (£2,500,000 on 24/7/1998) PL 55/1 FLC 4 FAC 2

PALMER Carlton Lloyd
Born: Rowley Regis, 5 December 1965
Height: 6'2" Weight: 13.3
International Honours: E: 18; B-5; U21-4
Carlton made a steady start to the 2000-01 season at Coventry, but following a red card in the home game with Tottenham he seemed to fall out of favour and soon afterwards he was dropped for Lee Carsley. This prompted a loan period at Watford under his former England boss Graham Taylor, but just as he had settled in at Vicarage Road he was recalled by the Sky Blues to cover for injuries and suspensions and made one final appearance as a substitute against Everton. At the end of January he was given a free transfer and he linked up with one of his former clubs, Sheffield Wednesday. His leadership qualities were welcomed at Hillsborough and his arrival coincided with an upturn in the Owls' fortunes. Always a larger-than-life figure and a major influence in the dressing

room, his aggressive midfield play and hard running make him an ideal character for any team needing a boost.

West Bromwich A (From apprentice on 21/12/1984) FL 114+7/4 FLC 7+1/1 FAC 4 Others 6
Sheffield Wed (£750,000 on 23/2/1989) F/PL 204+1/14 FLC 31/1 FAC 18/2 Others 8+1/1
Leeds U (£2,600,000 on 30/6/1994) PL 100+2/5 FLC 12 FAC 12/1 Others 4/1
Southampton (£1,000,000 on 26/9/1997) PL 44+1/3 FLC 5 FAC 2
Nottingham F (£1,100,000 on 21/1/1999) P/FL 14+2/1
Coventry C (£500,000 on 17/9/1999) PL 27+3/1 FLC 2 FAC 3
Watford (Loaned on 15/12/2000) FL 5
Sheffield Wed (Loaned on 13/2/2001) FL 12

PALMER Stephen (Steve) Leonard
Born: Brighton, 31 March 1968
Height: 6'1" Weight: 12.13
Club Honours: Div 2 '92, '98
International Honours: E: Sch

Steve continued to serve Watford well last season although his run of 102 consecutive first-team appearances dating back to October 1998 finally came to an end at the turn of the year when he was relegated to the subs' bench for the game against Bolton. He was also sidelined for a while by a hamstring problem but otherwise he proved to be a model of consistency for the Hornets. A versatile player who can play either as a central defender or just in front of the back four he netted two goals during the campaign.

Ipswich T (Signed from Cambridge University on 1/8/1989) F/PL 87+24/2 FLC 3 FAC 8+3/1 Others 4+2
Watford (£135,000 on 28/9/1995) P/FL 222+13/8 FLC 18+1/1 FAC 9+2 Others 7

PANAYI Sofroni **James (Jimmy)**
Born: Hammersmith, 24 January 1980
Height: 6'1" Weight: 14.0

Jimmy made good progress at Watford in 2000-01 after recovering from a shoulder operation during the close season. He broke into the team for the home match with Fulham in the new year and went on to make a handful of appearances during the remainder of the campaign. A promising defender who can kick with either foot, he can play at left back or in the centre of defence.

Watford (From trainee on 3/7/1998) P/FL 10+1

PANOPOULOS Mikael (Mike)
Born: Melbourne, Australia, 9 October 1976
Height: 6'1" Weight: 11.7

Distinctly out of favour under Portsmouth manager Tony Pulis at the start of the 2000-01 campaign, Mike made a welcome return to the line-up when Steve Claridge took over as caretaker-manager in October. He weighed in with six valuable First Division goals, the best being a super volley in the home game with Norwich in December. A versatile player who can feature at wing back or in midfield, he can kick well with either foot, is strong on the ball and is always willing to track back and help out in defence.

Portsmouth (£500,000 from Aris Salonika, Greece on 8/9/1999) FL 44+8/7 FLC 2 FAC 1

PANUCCI Christian
Born: Savona, Italy, 12 April 1973
Height: 6'1" Weight: 11.12
International Honours: Italy: 17; U21 (UEFA-U21 '94)

The absence through injury of Albert Ferrer and the departure of Dan Petrescu left Chelsea short of cover in the right wing-back position on the eve of the 2000-01 season. The Blues' remedy was to sign Christian Panucci from Inter Milan on a one-year loan deal with the option to make the move permanent. He looked to be yet another valuable Italian acquisition as he settled smoothly into life at Stamford Bridge. He played in the first nine matches of the season during the course of which he scored his only goal for the club - a beautiful chip over the St Gallen 'keeper in the UEFA Cup home leg victory. However Christian subsequently became the most prominent casualty in the post-Luca Vialli fall-out and made his last start of the season at Southampton in November. Subsequently out of contention for a first-team place he eventually opted to spend the remainder of his loan period at Monaco early in the new year.

Chelsea (Loaned from Inter Milan, Italy, ex Genoa, AC Milan, Real Madrid, on 18/8/2000) PL 7+1 Others 2/1

PARKER Kevin James
Born: Plymouth, 20 September 1979
Height: 5'10" Weight: 11.6

Released by Norwich at the end of the 1999-2000 campaign, Kevin impressed sufficiently in pre-season matches for Torquay to earn a contract. A forward or left winger whose key asset is his speed, he was mainly used by the Gulls as an out-and-out striker. An early run in the team was terminated by a knee injury, but after recovering from that he scored a last-minute winner in the Devon 'derby' with Exeter in January. Unfortunately he succumbed to an ankle injury shortly afterwards and failed to recover before the end of the season.

Norwich C (From trainee on 2/6/1999)
Torquay U (Free on 4/8/2000) FL 8+7/2 FLC 2

PARKER Scott Matthew
Born: Lambeth, 13 October 1980
Height: 5'7" Weight: 10.7
Club Honours: Div 1 '00
International Honours: E: U21-4; Yth; Sch

One of the most skilful players on Charlton's books, Scott has an excellent touch, reads the game well and is strong in the tackle. He was unable to break into the Addicks' team on a regular basis at the start of last season and joined Norwich City on loan at the end of October. He impressed all at Carrow Road with some fine performances and netted an opportunist goal in the game at Hillsborough. On returning to The Valley he eventually got his chance when Mark Kinsella was injured and proved to be a revelation when he came into the side, retaining his place until the end of the campaign. He produced some stylish performances in the centre of midfield and was particularly impressive against Manchester United at Old Trafford. Scott made his debut for England U21s in the friendly against Georgia in August and added a further three caps during the season.

Charlton Ath (From trainee on 22/10/1997) P/FL 20+22/2 FLC 3+2 FAC 3+3
Norwich C (Loaned on 31/10/2000) FL 6/1

PARKIN Brian
Born: Birkenhead, 12 October 1965
Height: 6'3" Weight: 14.7
Club Honours: Div 3 '90

This vastly experienced goalkeeper made a couple of outings from the subs' bench for Bristol Rovers last season when standing in for regular 'keeper Nick Culkin. He had the misfortune to suffer a broken rib at Bury in October and eventually announced his retirement after some 17 seasons and almost 400 Football League appearances. Brian is likely to remain in the game in a coaching role.

Oldham Ath (From juniors on 31/3/1983) FL 6 FLC 2
Crewe Alex (Free on 30/11/1984) FL 98 FLC 7 FAC 2 Others 6
Crystal Palace (Free on 1/7/1988) FL 20 FLC 3 Others 2
Bristol Rov (Free on 11/11/1989) FL 241 FLC 15 FAC 12 Others 23
Wycombe W (Free on 24/7/1996) FL 25 FLC 4
Shrewsbury T (Free on 14/9/1998)
Notts Co (Free on 2/10/1998) FL 1
Wimbledon (Free on 26/3/1999. Free to Yeovil during 1999 close season)
Bristol Rov (Free on 22/10/1999) FL 2+3 Others 1

PARKIN Jonathan (Jon)
Born: Barnsley, 30 December 1981
Height: 6'4" Weight: 13.7

Jon missed most of the 2000-01 season at Barnsley through injury but on his return to fitness in April he impressed with his application and determination. Called up as a last-minute replacement for Chris Morgan at Sheffield United, he produced an excellent display and went on to make three more senior appearances before the summer break. He is a versatile player who can feature either as a central defender or a striker, although all his appearances last term were at the back. Big and strong he misses little in the air, but despite his size he still has good control on the floor.

Barnsley (From trainee on 5/1/1999) FL 4+2 FLC 0+1 FAC 0+1

PARKIN Samuel (Sam)
Born: Roehampton, 14 March 1981
Height: 6'2" Weight: 13.0
International Honours: E: Sch

This promising Chelsea youngster spent most of last season out on loan to further his football education. He joined Millwall in September, making a huge impression by scoring twice on what was his Football League debut against Oxford and scoring four goals in five games for the Lions. On his return he was soon off again, this time to Wycombe Wanderers for a three-month spell. He produced some intelligent forward play and went on to play an important role in the Chairboys' FA Cup campaign, netting the winner in the fourth round tie against Wolves and then setting up a vital equaliser in the fifth round replay against Wimbledon. Finally in March he linked up with Oldham

Athletic where he had a great entrance, scoring three goals in three starts. He came off from the bench on his debut against Northampton to help the Latics turn a 1-0 deficit into a 2-1 victory and then netted both goals in the 2-1 win at Swansea. A big and powerful striker who holds the ball up well, he has a good turn of pace and can shoot with either foot.

Chelsea (From juniors on 21/8/1998)
Millwall (Loaned on 12/9/2000) FL 5+2/4
Wycombe W (Loaned on 24/11/2000) FL 5+3/1 FAC 0+3/1 Others 2/1
Oldham Ath (Loaned on 22/3/2001) FL 3+4/3

PARKINSON Andrew (Andy) John
Born: Liverpool, 27 May 1979
Height: 5'8" Weight: 10.12

Having spent five weeks of the close season in plaster, Andy was further dogged by a niggling ankle injury at the start of the 2000-01 campaign and never really got into his stride despite featuring regularly for Tranmere once fit. A slightly built striker who is at his best when played out wide on the right-hand side he has good pace and the ability to create panic in opposition defences with his tricky skills. Playing against Premiership opposition seemed to inspire him for he netted two superb goals in the 3-2 Worthington Cup win over Leeds and was in dazzling form in the FA Cup ties against Everton and Southampton.

Tranmere Rov (From trainee at Liverpool on 12/4/1997) FL 87+36/16 FLC 13+8/5 FAC 11+2/2

PARKINSON Gary Anthony
Born: Thornaby, 10 January 1968
Height: 5'11" Weight: 13.5

Despite signing a new one-year contract in the summer, Gary was never a regular at Preston last season. Having recovered from a serious knee injury, he made his first start for 18 months against Wimbledon at the end of August and then replaced the suspended Graham Alexander for a run of three games in November. Finally he featured in another brief run in the new year before moving on to Lancashire neighbours Blackpool where he appeared regularly at right back for the remainder of the campaign. He is a hard-tackling defender with a powerful shot and capable of delivering an explosive free kick.

Middlesbrough (From Everton juniors on 17/1/1986) FL 194+8/5 FLC 20/1 FAC 17/1 Others 19
Southend U (Loaned on 10/10/1992) FL 6
Bolton W (Free on 2/3/1993) FL 1+2 Others 4
Burnley (Signed on 27/1/1994) FL 134+1/4 FLC 12 FAC 10 Others 6/1
Preston NE (£50,000 on 30/5/1997) FL 82+2/6 FLC 6 FAC 8/1 Others 6/1
Blackpool (£20,000 on 22/3/2001) FL 9 Others 3

PARKINSON Philip (Phil) John
Born: Chorley, 1 December 1967
Height: 6'0" Weight: 12.8
Club Honours: Div 2 '94

Despite approaching the twilight of his career Darren had a fine season with Reading last term and after taking over the captaincy from Darren Caskey he provided some inspirational leadership to his colleagues around him. A tough-tackling midfield player he finished runner-up to Martin Butler as the club's 'Player of the Year' and fully deserved the new two-year contract he received. A perfect ambassador on and off the field he found time to help out with coaching at the Royals' Academy in addition to his studies for a degree in sociology with the Open University.

Southampton (From apprentice on 7/12/1985)
Bury (£12,000 on 8/3/1988) FL 133+12/5 FLC 6+1 FAC 4/1 Others 13/1
Reading (£37,500 on 10/7/1992) FL 300+23/18 FLC 24+1/2 FAC 21/1 Others 11+2

PARKS Anthony (Tony)
Born: Hackney, 28 January 1963
Height: 5'10" Weight: 11.5
Club Honours: UEFAC '84; S Div 1 '94; B&Q '94

Tony made a surprise appearance for Halifax Town on the opening day of last season when he replaced the injured Lee Butler midway through the 2-2 draw at Carlisle. He remained in the team until Butler had recovered fitness and never let the side down. Now in the twilight of his career he is part of the management team at The Shay and following the appointment of new boss Paul Bracewell he was installed as reserve-team manager. Tony is a vastly experienced goalkeeper with over 300 career appearances in senior football.

Tottenham H (From apprentice on 22/9/1980) FL 37 FLC 1 FAC 5 Others 5
Oxford U (Loaned on 1/10/1986) FL 5
Gillingham (Loaned on 1/9/1987) FL 2
Brentford (£60,000 on 24/8/1988) FL 71 FLC 7 FAC 8 Others 5
Fulham (Free on 27/2/1991) FL 2
West Ham U (Free on 15/8/1991) FL 6 FAC 3
Stoke C (Free on 21/8/1992) FL 2 FLC 1
Falkirk (Free on 14/10/1992) SL 112 SLC 8 SC 4 Others 4
Blackpool (Free on 6/9/1996)
Burnley (Free on 13/8/1997) FLC 2 (Free to Barrow on 14/10/1998)
Doncaster Rov (Loaned on 13/2/1998) FL 6
Scarborough (Free on 26/2/1999) FL 15
Halifax T (Free on 5/7/1999) FL 5+1 FLC 3

PARLOUR Raymond (Ray)
Born: Romford, 7 March 1973
Height: 5'10" Weight: 11.12
Club Honours: FLC '93; ECWC '94; PL '98; FAC '93, '98; CS '98, '99
International Honours: E: 10; B-1; U21-12

Ray Parlour

Despite being a regular in the England squad Ray missed out on Euro 2000 through injury. A well-established and at times under-rated midfield player at Arsenal, he spent more time playing through the middle last season as opposed to his usual spot on the right-hand side. He is an industrious player who enjoys attacking the opposition and weighs in with his fair share of goals. He notched a hat-trick at Highbury against Newcastle in December, and scored with a spectacular 30-yard drive against Valencia in the quarter finals of the Champions' League.

Arsenal (From trainee on 6/3/1991) F/PL 227+41/22 FLC 19+3 FAC 30+1/2 Others 34+6/6

PARNABY Stuart
Born: Durham, 19 July 1982
Height: 5'11" Weight: 11.0
International Honours: E: Yth; Sch

A key member of the Middlesbrough team that reached the FA Youth Cup semi-final in 1999-2000 and a regular for England U18s, Stuart made his debut in senior football in last season's Worthington Cup second round first leg tie against Macclesfield. Shortly afterwards he joined Halifax Town on loan where he showed a maturity beyond his years in half-a-dozen outings for the Shaymen. He subsequently returned to the Riverside Stadium to continue his development in the Boro' reserves. Stuart is a versatile player who can turn out either in defence or midfield.

Middlesbrough (From trainee on 21/7/1999) FLC 1
Halifax T (Loaned on 23/10/2000) FL 6

PARRISH Sean
Born: Wrexham, 14 March 1972
Height: 5'10" Weight: 11.8

This infectiously cheerful and whole-hearted player won the Chesterfield fans over from the off last season with some fine goals from midfield. A 45-yard lob against Shrewsbury in August was followed by a hat-trick against Macclesfield, and Sean reached double figures for league goals before a back injury finished his season in March. At his best on the left of a midfield four, Sean's bursting runs, fine skills and determined application set up many chances for others during the campaign.

Shrewsbury T (From trainee on 12/7/1990) FL 1+2 FLC 1 Others 3 (Free to Telford during 1992 close season)
Doncaster Rov (£20,000 on 28/5/1994) FL 64+2/8 FLC 3+1 FAC 2/1 Others 3
Northampton T (£35,000 + on 2/8/1996) FL 103+6/13 FLC 8+1/1 FAC 2 Others 5/2
Chesterfield (Free on 19/7/2000) FL 33+2/10 FLC 4/1 FAC 1 Others 2+1

PARTRIDGE Richard (Richie) Joseph
Born: Dublin, 12 September 1980
Height: 5'8" Weight: 10.10
International Honours: RoI: U21-8; Yth (UEFA-U18 '98)

Richie made his senior debut for Liverpool in the 8-0 Worthington Cup victory at Stoke City last November. After continuing his development in the reserves at Anfield he joined Bristol Rovers on loan in March, where he made a very favourable impression and netted an impressive individual goal in the final match of the season against Wrexham. A speedy ball-playing winger he continued to represent the Republic of Ireland at U21 level winning two more caps.

Liverpool (From trainee on 16/9/1997) FLC 1
Bristol Rov (Loaned on 22/3/2001) FL 4+2/1

PARTRIDGE Scott Malcolm
Born: Leicester, 13 October 1974
Height: 5'9" Weight: 11.2
Club Honours: Div 3 '99

Scott suffered a pre-season injury and although he featured regularly on the subs' bench it was not until November that he reclaimed his place in the Brentford first team. He is a skilful striker who creates plenty of chances for others but is not a prolific goals-corer himself. His confidence reached new heights in the spring when he was paired again with Lloyd Owusu and the two once more proved very effective, their different skills complimenting each other. Scott finished the season by winning a runners-up medal in the LDV Vans Trophy when the Bees went down 2-1 to Port Vale in the final at Cardiff's Millenium Stadium.

Bradford C (From trainee on 10/7/1992) FL 0+5 FLC 1+1
Bristol C (Free on 18/2/1994) FL 24+33/7 FLC 2+3/1 FAC 1+3
Torquay U (Loaned on 13/10/1995) FL 5/2
Plymouth Arg (Loaned on 22/1/1996) FL 6+1/2
Scarborough (Loaned on 8/3/1996) FL 5+2
Cardiff C (£50,000 on 14/2/1997) FL 29+8/2 FLC 2 FAC 2 Others 1
Torquay U (Signed on 26/3/1998) FL 33+1/12 FLC 2 FAC 2/1 Others 2/1
Brentford (£100,000 on 19/2/1999) FL 79+12/21 FLC 3+2 FAC 2+1 Others 7+1/2

PASSI Franck
Born: Bergerac, France, 28 March 1966
Height: 5'9" Weight: 11.9
International Honours: France: U21 (UEFA-U18 '98)

Franck once again proved to be an invaluable member of the Bolton Wanderers squad last season. While it is doubtful that he would make the starting line-up every week, he can be relied upon to produce a whole-hearted and committed display whenever he is called upon. The 'Little General' was a tireless worker in the centre of midfield and often brought a fresh pair of legs into the game when others around him were starting to tire. However following the end-of-season play-off triumph he decided to return to France to conclude his career.

Bolton W (Free from Compostela, Spain on 25/11/1999) FL 21+17 FLC 4 FAC 5+1 Others 0+1

PATTERSON Darren James
Born: Belfast, 15 October 1969
Height: 6'2" Weight: 12.10
International Honours: NI: 17; B-3; U21-1; Yth

Having recovered from a long-standing achilles injury Darren joined York City on a three-month contract last December. He made his debut at Reading in the FA Cup second round replay win and made a handful more senior appearances before moving on to Oxford United in February where he was immediately installed as team captain. He scored on his home debut against Stoke and generally added some much-needed experience to a somewhat besieged defence. He is an experienced centre back who is an excellent motivator and reads the game well.

West Bromwich A (From trainee on 5/7/1988)
Wigan Ath (Free on 17/4/1989) FL 69+28/6 FLC 7+1/3 FAC 5+4/1 Others 7
Crystal Palace (£225,000 on 1/7/1992) PL 22/1 FLC 5 FAC 6
Luton T (£100,000 on 21/8/1995) FL 52+4 FLC 0+1 FAC 2+1 Others 9
Preston NE (Loaned on 4/10/1996) FL 2
Dundee U (Free on 13/7/1998) SL 23+2 SLC 2 SC 4/1
York C (Free on 1/12/2000) FL 4+2 FAC 2 Others 1
Oxford U (Free on 15/2/2001) FL 18/1

PATTERSON Mark
Born: Leeds, 13 September 1968
Height: 5'10" Weight: 12.4

Mark suffered from injuries that prevented him enjoying a lengthy run in the Gillingham first team last term, but after returning to the line-up at the beginning of March he retained his place for the rest of the season. Despite being right-footed he appeared in an uncustomary position of left back, but always gave 100 per cent and never let the side down. Mark signed a new contract in October 2000 that will tie him to the Gills until 2003.

Carlisle U (From trainee on 30/8/1986) FL 19+3 FLC 4 Others 1
Derby Co (£60,000 on 10/11/1987) FL 41+10/3 FLC 5+2 FAC 4 Others 5+1/2
Plymouth Arg (£85,000 on 23/7/1993) FL 131+3/3 FLC 3 FAC 8 Others 9
Gillingham (£45,000 on 30/10/1997) FL 100+2/2 FLC 5+1 FAC 3+2 Others 4

PAYNE Stephen (Steve) John
Born: Pontefract, 1 August 1975
Height: 5'11" Weight: 12.5
Club Honours: GMVC '95, '97; FAT '96
International Honours: E: SP-1

After shouldering the burden of a 'utility' tag in 1999-2000, Steve emerged as a defender of great accomplishment last term. In a back four he was often used a little out of position at right back but seemed to thrive in a back three, helping Chesterfield to nine clean sheets out of ten games between December and February. Comfortable in the air and neat on the ground, Steve's obvious composure enhances his ability.

Huddersfield T (From trainee on 12/7/1993)
Macclesfield T (Free on 23/12/1994) FL 71+6/2 FLC 6 FAC 5 Others 2
Chesterfield (Signed on 8/7/1999) FL 48+5/4 FLC 2+1 Others 3+1/2

PAYNTER William (Billy) Paul
Born: Liverpool, 13 July 1984
Height: 6'1" Weight: 12.0

Billy became Port Vale's youngest player for over 20 years when he made his debut from the subs' bench against Walsall in the penultimate game of the 2000-01 campaign, just 71 days short of his 17th birthday. He earned his call up to the senior squad with some impressive performances for the youth team and did well in his brief first-team

outing. He is a strongly built striker who holds the ball up well and tries to do the simple things correctly. Billy will be aiming to gain further senior experience in the 2001-02 season.
Port Vale (Trainee) FL 0+1

PAYTON Andrew (Andy) Paul
Born: Whalley, 23 October 1967
Height: 5'9" Weight: 11.13
A broken toe kept the Burnley fans' favourite out of action at the start of last season. Once back in the side he was soon into familiar scoring mode, becoming the first Claret to hit a hat-trick as a substitute when he did so in the Worthington Cup victory against Hartlepool. However his well-established striking partnership with Andy Cooke never got into its stride and then when Ian Moore came from Stockport the pair never looked comfortable playing together. Andy was a virtual fixture on the subs' bench for the second half of the season, often coming on too late to make any impact on events, and when Gareth Taylor arrived he was marginalized even more. For all that he remained Burnley's top scorer and he is now approaching the landmark figure of 100 goals for the club he has always supported.
Hull C (From apprentice on 29/7/1985) FL 116+28/55 FLC 9+2/1 FAC 8 Others 3/1
Middlesbrough (£750,000 on 22/11/1991) FL 8+11/3 FAC 1+3
Glasgow Celtic (Signed on 14/8/1992) SL 20+16/15 SLC 3+2/5 SC 1+1 Others 3
Barnsley (Signed on 25/11/1993) FL 100+8/41 FLC 7/3 FAC 6+1/1
Huddersfield T (£350,000 on 4/7/1996) FL 42+1/17 FLC 7/3 FAC 2
Burnley (Signed on 16/1/1998) FL 115+25/64 FLC 4+2/6 FAC 6+1/3 Others 6/3

PEACOCK Darren
Born: Bristol, 3 February 1968
Height: 6'2" Weight: 12.12
Club Honours: WC '90
Unable to get into the team at Blackburn, Darren was loaned to West Ham last September where he served as cover but failed to make a senior appearance. The following month he went on loan again to Wolves where he made a handful of appearances, but just as he was beginning to find his form he injured his neck in the Worthington Cup tie against Fulham. The problem was more serious than first thought and it eventually led to his retirement from the game on medical grounds towards the end of the year. A solid and experienced central defender he fell just short of 500 senior games in a professional career lasting 14 years.
Newport Co (From apprentice on 11/2/1986) FL 24+4 FLC 2 FAC 1 Others 1+1
Hereford U (Free on 23/3/1989) FL 56+3/4 FLC 6 FAC 6/1 Others 6
Queens Park R (£200,000 on 22/12/1990) F/PL 123+3/6 FLC 12/1 FAC 3 Others 2
Newcastle U (£2,700,000 on 24/3/1994) PL 131+2/2 FLC 13+1/2 FAC 11 Others 17+1
Blackburn Rov (Free on 2/7/1998) P/FL 42+5/1 FLC 4 FAC 6 Others 2
Wolverhampton W (Loaned on 14/10/2000) FL 2+2 FLC 1

PEACOCK Gavin Keith
Born: Eltham, 18 November 1967
Height: 5'8" Weight: 11.8
Club Honours: Div 1 '93
International Honours: E: Yth; Sch
Gavin was Queens Park Rangers' captain last season but found his appearances somewhat restricted by a recurring hamstring problem. He eventually returned in the second half of the campaign but was unable to prevent the club from being relegated to the Second Division. He is an experienced central midfield player with the ability to make penetrating runs from the centre of the park. Gavin netted just four goals in 2000-01 including a double in the 2-2 draw with Wolves in November, the second of which was a cracking drive from 25 yards out. Out of contract in the summer his future was uncertain at the time of writing.
Queens Park R (From apprentice on 19/11/1984) FL 7+10/1 FAC 0+1
Gillingham (Loaned on 5/10/1987) FL 6 Others 2
Gillingham (£40,000 on 16/12/1987) FL 63+1/11 FLC 4 FAC 2 Others 3/1
Bournemouth (£250,000 on 16/8/1989) FL 56/8 FLC 6 FAC 2 Others 2
Newcastle U (£275,000 on 30/11/1990) FL 102+3/35 FLC 6/5 FAC 6/2 Others 3/4
Chelsea (£1,250,000 on 12/8/1993) PL 92+11/17 FLC 6/1 FAC 14+4/9 Others 7
Queens Park R (£1,000,000 on 22/11/1996) FL 163+7/33 FLC 9/3 FAC 8+1/3

Gavin Peacock

PEACOCK Lee Anthony
Born: Paisley, 9 October 1976
Height: 6'0" Weight: 12.8
Club Honours: AMC '97
International Honours: S: U21-1; Yth
After signing for Bristol City on the eve of the 2000-01 season Lee went on to have a fine first season at Ashton Gate and looked to have all the attributes to become the club's most revered forward since Bob Taylor. Despite often turning out when not fully fit he scored regularly throughout the campaign and finished with a respectable tally of 15 in all competitions. A big strong striker he is remarkably mobile and athletic, extremely quick on the turn and has a great eye for goal.
Carlisle U (From trainee on 10/3/1995) FL 52+24/11 FLC 2+3 FAC 4+1/1 Others 6+4
Mansfield T (£90,000 on 17/10/1997) FL 79+10/29 FLC 4/1 FAC 4 Others 4/2
Manchester C (£500,000 on 5/11/1999) FL 4+4 FAC 1+1
Bristol C (£600,000 on 10/8/2000) FL 31+4/13 FLC 1/1 FAC 4/1

PEACOCK Richard John
Born: Sheffield, 29 October 1972
Height: 5'10" Weight: 11.5
This versatile midfield man was used in a number of roles by Lincoln City although he became more of a squad player following a change of management at the start of March. Richard mainly appeared in his preferred role wide on the right side of midfield but was also used as a wide-left player and occasionally as a central striker. In spells he showed his potential but his future at Sincil Bank was in doubt after he failed to agree a new contract at the end of the campaign.
Hull C (Signed from Sheffield FC on 14/10/1993) FL 144+30/21 FLC 12+3/2 FAC 7+1/1 Others 5+1
Lincoln C (Free on 21/1/1999) FL 41+27/6 FLC 1+2/1 FAC 2/1 Others 3

PEAKE Jason William
Born: Leicester, 29 September 1971
Height: 5'11" Weight: 12.10
International Honours: E: Yth; Sch
Jason's signing during the 2000 close season was considered a real coup for Plymouth manager Kevin Hodges however he suffered an early-season injury and then fell out of favour following a change of manager at Home Park. He was subsequently loaned to Conference outfit Nuneaton Borough in December and the deal became permanent in March. Jason is an experienced midfield play maker with excellent distribution and a good scoring record.
Leicester C (From trainee on 9/1/1990) FL 4+4/1 Others 1+1
Hartlepool U (Loaned on 13/2/1992) FL 5+1/1
Halifax T (Free on 26/8/1992) FL 32+1/1 FAC 1 Others 2
Rochdale (Signed on 23/3/1994) FL 91+4/6 FLC 3 FAC 5/2 Others 7/1
Brighton & Hove A (Signed on 30/7/1996) FL 27+3/1 FLC 2 FAC 2 Others 1
Bury (Free on 8/10/1997) FL 3+3
Rochdale (Free on 2/7/1998) FL 74+7/11 FLC 4 FAC 7/1 Others 6
Plymouth Arg (Free on 4/7/2000) FL 7+3/2 FLC 1 FAC 1+1/1

PEARCE Dennis Anthony
Born: Wolverhampton, 10 September 1974
Height: 5'10" Weight: 11.0
Club Honours: Div 3 '98
Dennis returned to first-team action with Notts County last September and featured regularly for the Magpies for the remainder of the season apart from a spell out with hamstring trouble early in the new year. A dependable left back who is comfortable on the ball he can produce a devastating overlap when on form. One of several

players released by the Magpies in the summer he was reported to have signed for fellow Second Division club Peterborough United.
Aston Villa (From trainee on 7/6/1993)
Wolverhampton W (Free on 3/7/1995) FL 7+2 FLC 1 FAC 1
Notts Co (Free on 21/7/1997) FL 108+10/3 FLC 7+1 FAC 12+1 Others 3

PEARCE Alexander **Gregory (Greg)**
Born: Bolton, 26 May 1980
Height: 5'10" Weight: 11.7
Greg had few opportunities at Chesterfield in the 2000-01 campaign and spent much of the time out on loan at Unibond League club Worksop Town. He returned to be plunged into the cauldron of a Third Division title decider at Brighton, where he shadowed Bobby Zamora with great dedication and skill. He is an extremely promising centre half and it is hoped that the Spireites will be able to hold on to him despite their financial problems.
Chesterfield (From trainee on 24/3/1998) FL 9+3 Others 0+1

PEARCE Ian Anthony
Born: Bury St Edmunds, 7 May 1974
Height: 6'3" Weight: 14.4
Club Honours: PL '95
International Honours: E: U21-3; Yth
Having suffered a serious knee injury at the start of the 1999-2000 campaign Ian made his long-awaited return for West Ham against Newcastle at the end of October. However he continued to be plagued by niggling injuries that prevented him from fully establishing a place in the line-up. He netted with a header against Manchester City but then suffered a hamstring injury at Leeds and concussion led to his absence from the last few games. A powerful right-sided defender his height and strength in the tackle were badly missed by the Hammers back line when he was absent.
Chelsea (From juniors on 1/8/1991) F/PL 0+4 Others 0+1
Blackburn Rov (£300,000 on 4/10/1993) PL 43+19/2 FLC 4+4/1 FAC 1+2 Others 6+1
West Ham U (£1,600,000 + on 19/9/1997) PL 77+2/4 FLC 6 FAC 7+1/1 Others 1+1

PEARCE Stuart
Born: Hammersmith, 24 April 1962
Height: 5'10" Weight: 13.0
Club Honours: FLC '89, '90; FMC '89, '92
International Honours: E: 78; U21-1
This remarkable veteran returned from two broken legs to take his place in the West Ham side at the start of last season and went on to play in almost every game for the Hammers. Beginning the campaign on monthly contracts he quickly showed that he had lost none of his zest for the game with some fine performances that earned him a contract until the summer. A tough-tackling left-sided defender he certainly let opposition forwards know that he was around and netted with unstoppable strikes against Arsenal and Southampton. However perhaps his finest performance came in the FA Cup quarter-final against Tottenham when he was inspirational throughout the match and netted a cracking goal. He was a deserved winner of the 'Hammer of the Year' award in recognition of his tremendous value to the team. Stuart was reported to have signed for Manchester City in the summer.
Coventry C (£25,000 from Wealdstone on 20/10/1983) FL 52/4 FAC 2
Nottingham F (£200,000 on 3/6/1985) F/PL 401/63 FLC 60/10 FAC 37/9 Others 24/6
Newcastle U (Free on 21/7/1997) PL 37 FLC 2 FAC 7 Others 5+1/1
West Ham U (Free on 5/8/1999) PL 42/2 FLC 4 FAC 4/1

Stuart Pearce

PEER Dean
Born: Stourbridge, 8 August 1969
Height: 6'2" Weight: 12.4
Club Honours: AMC '91
Apart from the occasional game out through injury Dean was a near ever-present for Shrewsbury Town last season. A busy midfielder who was always looking to get in the action he tackled back well and displayed accurate distribution, the only minor disappointment was a lack of goals. Dean was one of several players released in the summer as manager Kevin Ratcliffe put his faith in the youngsters on the club's books.
Birmingham C (From trainee on 9/7/1987) FL 106+14/8 FLC 14+1/3 FAC 2+1 Others 11+1/1
Mansfield T (Loaned on 18/12/1992) FL 10 Others 1
Walsall (Free on 16/11/1993) FL 41+4/8 FLC 2 FAC 4+2 Others 3
Northampton T (Free on 22/8/1995) FL 97+31/6 FLC 6+2/1 FAC 7 Others 9+5
Shrewsbury T (Free on 26/1/2000) FL 53+3 FLC 2 FAC 1 Others 1

PEETERS Thomas (Tom)
Born: Bornem, Belgium, 25 September 1978
Height: 5'10" Weight: 11.4
Having joined Sunderland in the close season, Tom found first-team opportunities hard to come by last term. Indeed, his only sighting in a red and white shirt was during his debut against Luton in the Worthington Cup second round first leg tie in September. On that occasion Tom was one of the top performers on the field, impressing the fans with some simple but effective distribution and solid defensive work. Having now settled in at the Stadium of Light he will be hoping to make more of an impact next term.
Sunderland (£250,000 from KV Mechelen, Belgium on 20/7/2000) FLC 1

PEJIC Shaun Melvyn
Born: Hereford, 16 November 1982
Height: 6'1" Weight: 12.3
This Wrexham scholarship lad appeared regularly for the U19 Academy team and the reserves last season before being given a deserved debut in the senior team as a replacement for Brian Carey at Port Vale last April. Shaun handled the occasion well and will be hoping for more opportunities in the 2001-02 campaign. He is a central defender and the son of former Hereford and Wrexham defender Mel Pejic.
Wrexham (Trainee) FL 1

PEMBERTON Martin Calvin
Born: Bradford, 1 February 1976
Height: 5'11" Weight: 12.6
Martin signed for Mansfield Town in the summer of 2000 after a spell in the Unibond League with Bradford Park Avenue and immediately slotted into the left-back berth at Field Mill. He produced several impressive displays but then suffered a knee injury at the end of August that sidelined him for three months. Returning to the line-up he had just settled in again when the injury flared up once more and he faced another lengthy spell on the sidelines. He is a versatile player who has also appeared as a striker in the past.
Oldham Ath (From trainee on 22/7/1994) FL 0+5 FLC 0+1 Others 0+1
Doncaster Rov (Free on 21/3/1997) FL 33+2/3 FLC 0+1
Scunthorpe U (Free on 26/3/1998) FL 3+3
Hartlepool U (Free on 3/7/1998) FL 0+4 FLC 0+1 (Free to Harrogate T on 30/9/1998)
Mansfield T (£10,000 + from Bradford PA on 3/8/2000) FL 16+2/1 FLC 1 FAC 1 Others 1

PEMBRIDGE Mark Anthony
Born: Merthyr Tydfil, 29 November 1970
Height: 5'8" Weight: 12.0
International Honours: W: 39; B-2; U21-1; Sch
Troubled for long periods of 2000-01 by unrelated calf injuries, it was during his absences that Mark's value to the Everton team was most missed. A dogged and fiercely competitive midfielder, his qualities are enthusiasm, a willingness to work and a refusal to admit defeat. Walter Smith paid him a huge compliment when he said that of all the players the Toffees had missed during an injury-stricken start to the season Mark's loss had been the most significant. Typically he shrugged off the praise, got his head down and carried on doing what he does best . . . working hard.

Luton T (From trainee on 1/7/1989) FL 60/6 FLC 2 FAC 4 Others 4
Derby Co (£1,250,000 on 2/6/1992) FL 108+2/28 FLC 9/1 FAC 6/3 Others 15/5
Sheffield Wed (£900,000 on 19/7/1995) PL 88+5/12 FLC 6/1 FAC 7/1 Others 1 (Free to Benfica, Portugal on 1/7/1998)
Everton (£800,000 on 6/8/1999) PL 49+3/2 FAC 7

PENNANT Jermaine
Born: Nottingham, 15 January 1983
Height: 5'6" Weight: 10.0
Club Honours: FAYC '00, '01
International Honours: E: U21-2; Yth; Sch

Jermaine made his first start for Arsenal, and his only senior appearance of the 2000-01 season, in the Worthington Cup tie against Ipswich Town at Highbury. Although he spent time on the bench as a non-playing substitute to gain experience, he mostly appeared for the Gunners' reserve and U19 teams. A highly thought of right-sided midfield player who likes to attack at every opportunity, he has great dribbling skills and makes clever use of the ball. Honours continued to pour his way with a second successive FA Youth Cup winners' medal for Arsenal, a regular place in the England U18 team and two caps for the U21s in the summer fixtures with Mexico and Greece. Jermaine is an exceptional talent, and considered a player with a great future at Highbury.
Notts Co (Associated Schoolboy) FAC 0+1 Others 0+1
Arsenal (From trainee on 16/3/2000, having been signed for £1,500,000 on 14/1/1999) FLC 1+1

Adrian Pennock

PENNOCK Adrian Barry
Born: Ipswich, 27 March 1971
Height: 6'1" Weight: 13.5

Adrian underwent surgery on an achilles problem just days after Gillingham's victory in the 1999-2000 Second Division play-off final and was ruled out of action until mid-October. On recovering fitness he quickly regained his place at the heart of the defence in the sweepers' role and went on to produce some solid performances, rarely missing a match.
Norwich C (From trainee on 4/7/1989) FL 1
Bournemouth (£30,000 on 14/8/1992) FL 130+1/9 FLC 9 FAC 12/1 Others 8
Gillingham (£30,000 on 4/10/1996) FL 153+2/2 FLC 6 FAC 11/1 Others 11/1

PEPPER Carl
Born: Darlington, 26 July 1980
Height: 5'11" Weight: 11.6

Carl is a local player who came up through the ranks at Darlington but he struggled to break into the first team at the start of last season. He made only two first-team appearances both coming in Worthington Cup ties against Nottingham Forest and Bradford City. However he was surprisingly released in mid-season and linked up with Unibond League club Blyth Spartans. Carl is a composed right-sided defender.
Darlington (From trainee on 8/7/1998) FL 5+1 FLC 4

PEPPER Colin **Nigel**
Born: Rotherham, 25 April 1968
Height: 5'10" Weight: 12.4

Nigel joined Scunthorpe United in the 2000 close season and was immediately named club captain. He led the Iron to victory at Macclesfield on the opening day. But then had the misfortune to suffer a broken leg just 13 minutes into the following game against Kidderminster and the injury ruled him out of action for the remainder of the campaign. He is a hard-tackling midfield player able to break down opposition attacks and always performs with great drive and determination.
Rotherham U (From apprentice on 26/4/1986) FL 35+10/1 FLC 1/1 FAC 1+1 Others 3+3
York C (Free on 18/7/1990) FL 223+12/39 FLC 16+2/3 FAC 12/2 Others 15+1
Bradford C (£100,000 on 28/2/1997) FL 47+5/11 FLC 4/1 FAC 1
Aberdeen (£300,000 on 26/11/1998) SL 11+3 SLC 1
Southend U (Loaned on 24/12/1999) FL 9+3/2
Scunthorpe U (Free on 21/7/2000) FL 2

PEREZ Lionel
Born: Ardeche, France, 24 April 1967
Height: 5'11" Weight: 13.4

This flamboyant goalkeeper joined Cambridge United in the 2000 close season after a successful loan spell during the previous campaign. A firm favourite with the U's fans he made many spectacular saves and his experience proved important in bringing on the young defenders around him. He missed several matches in the new year due to an injury but returned to bolster the back line in the final run-in as the club successfully fought against relegation.
Sunderland (£200,000 from Bordeaux, France, ex Nimes, on 21/8/1996) P/FL 74+1 FLC 2 FAC 4 Others 3
Newcastle U (Free on 2/7/1998)
Scunthorpe U (Loaned on 8/10/1999) FL 13
Cambridge U (Free on 23/3/2000) FL 45+1 FLC 2 FAC 2 Others 1+1

PERKINS Christopher (Chris) Peter
Born: Nottingham, 9 January 1974
Height: 5'11" Weight: 11.0

Chris began last season as Chesterfield's first-choice left back but soon lost his place to Rob Edwards, and made only occasional appearances before moving to Lincoln on a short-term contract in January where he was used as a squad player to fill in for injuries in the second half of the campaign. Chris appeared in both full-back positions and as a wide-left midfield man in his brief time at Sincil Bank. He showed good defensive qualities and the ability to push forward but was released in May.
Mansfield T (From trainee on 19/11/1992) FL 3+5 Others 0+1
Chesterfield (Free on 15/7/1994) FL 136+11/3 FLC 9+1/1 FAC 13 Others 9+3/1
Hartlepool U (Free on 14/7/1999) FL 7+1 FLC 1
Chesterfield (Free on 7/10/1999) FL 37+2 FLC 2+1 Others 3+1
Lincoln C (Free on 5/1/2001) FL 11+1

PERPETUINI David Peter
Born: Hitchin, 26 September 1979
Height: 5'8" Weight: 10.8

After an impressive debut campaign with Watford in the Premiership, David found it difficult to build on his achievements last season and managed only a handful of first-team appearances. A promising youngster with an excellent left foot he featured at left back and in midfield but was placed on the transfer list in the summer by new boss Gianluca Vialli.
Watford (From trainee on 3/7/1997) P/FL 17+2/1 FLC 1+1

PERRETT Russell
Born: Barton on Sea, 18 June 1973
Height: 6'3" Weight: 13.2

Russell had a desperately disappointing season at Cardiff in 2000-01 when he was hit by a series of injuries that kept him out for virtually the whole campaign. He eventually recovered to make two first-team appearances in April but will now need to work hard over the coming pre-season and fight to win his place back in the Bluebirds line-up. He is a centre back who is strong in the air and has considerable ability on the ground.
Portsmouth (Signed from Lymington on 30/9/1995) FL 66+6/2 FLC 5 FAC 4
Cardiff C (£10,000 on 21/7/1999) FL 28+1/1 FAC 5/1 Others 1

PERRY Christopher (Chris) John
Born: Carshalton, 26 April 1973
Height: 5'8" Weight: 11.1

Chris had a very consistent season at Tottenham last term when he was a stable figure in a constantly changing defence. A regular in the line-up apart from the occasional absence through injury he scored his only goal of the campaign in the 4-3 defeat at Leeds in September. An agile central defender who is superb in the air, he will be keen to show that he is capable of filling the gap left by the departing Sol Campbell next term. Chris is also useful when moving forward at set pieces when he draws defenders to him with some intelligent off-the-ball runs.
Wimbledon (From trainee on 2/7/1991) PL 158+9/2 FLC 21 FAC 24/1
Tottenham H (£4,000,000 on 7/7/1999) PL 66+3/2 FLC 5 FAC 6 Others 4/1

PERRY Jason
Born: Caerphilly, 2 April 1970
Height: 6'0" Weight: 11.12
Club Honours: WC '92, '93; Div 3 '93
International Honours: W: 1; B-2; U21-3; Yth; Sch

Jason mainly featured on the subs' bench during the early part of 2000-01, but returned to the Hull City line-up in October as cover for the injured Justin Whittle. He produced a series of fine performances during a brief run in the side but lost his place when Whittle returned to action and soon afterwards he was sidelined for the rest of the term with an ankle injury. Jason was released by the Tigers in May.

Cardiff C (From trainee on 21/8/1987) FL 278+3/5 FLC 22 FAC 14+1 Others 25+1
Bristol Rov (Free on 4/7/1997) FL 24+1 FLC 2 FAC 2+1 Others 2
Lincoln C (Free on 14/7/1998) FL 10+2 FLC 2 FAC 1
Hull C (Free on 18/12/1998) FL 14+1 FAC 2 Others 3+1

PERRY Mark James
Born: Ealing, 19 October 1978
Height: 5'11" Weight: 12.10
International Honours: E: Yth; Sch

Mark began last season in his customary right-wing-back role for Queens Park Rangers but after a spell out injured he returned to the team at the turn of the year on the left side of defence. He went on to make the position his own for the next few months until dropping out when new boss Ian Holloway changed the formation in a vain attempt to reverse the team's fortunes and avoid relegation.

Queens Park R (From trainee on 26/10/1995) FL 41+9/1 FLC 4 FAC 2

PESCHISOLIDO Paolo (Paul) Pasquale
Born: Scarborough, Canada, 25 May 1971
Height: 5'7" Weight: 10.12
Club Honours: Div 2 '99
International Honours: Canada: 44; U23-11

Paul never featured at all in new Fulham coach Jean Tigana's plans last term and his only first-team games came in the Worthington Cup when many fringe players were used. He eventually joined neighbours Queens Park Rangers at the beginning of November where he made an instant impact by scoring after just ten minutes of his debut against Portsmouth. No permanent deal could be reached between the two clubs and he returned to Craven Cottage only to go out on loan again to Sheffield United where he impressed with his striking qualities. Norwich was Paul's final port of call for the season. Signed just 20 minutes ahead of the transfer deadline, he was brought in to add experience to the front line for the important run-in to the end of the season. He linked well with Iwan Roberts, displaying the skills and techniques that have made him such a success throughout his career. Quick to see openings, he has the ability to take on defenders in very tight situations and to anticipate where the ball might go inside the penalty area. He continued to appear regularly for Canada winning nine more caps and featuring in the Confederations Cup matches during the summer.

Birmingham C (£25,000 from Toronto Blizzards, Canada on 11/11/1992) FL 37+6/16 FLC 2/1 FAC 0+1 Others 1+1
Stoke C (£400,000 on 1/8/1994) FL 59+7/19 FLC 6/3 FAC 3 Others 5+1/2
Birmingham C (£400,000 on 29/3/1996) FL 7+2/1
West Bromwich A (£600,000 on 24/7/1996) FL 36+9/18 FLC 4+1/3 FAC 1
Fulham (£1,100,000 on 24/10/1997) FL 69+26/24 FLC 7+1/4 FAC 9+1/2 Others 2
Queens Park R (Loaned on 3/11/2000) FL 5/1
Sheffield U (Loaned on 19/1/2001) FL 4+1/2
Norwich C (Loaned on 22/3/2001) FL 3+2

PETHICK Robert (Robbie) John
Born: Tavistock, 8 September 1970
Height: 5'10" Weight: 11.12

Robbie began the 2000-01 season for Bristol Rovers playing in the unfamiliar role of centre back. He endured something of a roller-coaster time, being put on the transfer list in October and struggling to win a place during the middle part of the campaign, before returning briefly towards the end of the season in his more accustomed position at right back. He is a tough-tackling defender with a powerful right foot.

Portsmouth (£30,000 from Weymouth on 1/10/1993) FL 157+32/3 FLC 13+3 FAC 9 Others 3+1
Bristol Rov (£15,000 on 19/2/1999) FL 60+3/2 FLC 5 FAC 1 Others 2+1

PETRESCU Daniel (Dan) Vasile
Born: Bucharest, Romania, 22 December 1967
Height: 5'9" Weight: 11.9
Club Honours: FAC '97; FLC '98; ECWC '98
International Honours: Romania: 95; U21

Signed by Bradford City in the summer of 2000, Dan featured both at right back and on the right-hand side of midfield for the Bantams last term, but wherever he played he always tried his best. A quality signing for the Valley Parade club he produced some intelligent play, but was sold to Southampton at the beginning of the new year as new boss Jim Jeffries began to cut the wage bill for City. Quickly settling in at The Dell under his former manager Glenn Hoddle, he used his experience to great effect. His attacking flair gave an extra edge to the Saints' attack and he netted winners against Leicester and Manchester City in quick succession.

Sheffield Wed (£1,250,000 from Genoa, Italy, ex Steava and Foggia, on 6/8/1994) PL 28+9/3 FLC 2 FAC 0+2 Others 1/1
Chelsea (£2,300,000 on 18/11/1995) PL 134+16/18 FLC 8/2 FAC 20+1/1 Others 24+5/3
Bradford C (£1,000,000 on 2/8/2000) PL 16+1/1 FLC 2 FAC 0+1
Southampton (£100,000 on 12/1/2001) PL 8+1/2

PETTEFER Carl James
Born: Burnham, 22 March 1981
Height: 5'7" Weight: 10.5

Having come up through the ranks at Portsmouth Carl stepped up to make his Football League debut when he replaced Lee Mills for the final ten minutes of the 2-0 home defeat by Nottingham Forest last season. A promising young midfield player he will be hoping for more senior action in 2001-02.

Portsmouth (From trainee on 23/11/1998) FL 0+1

Dan Petrescu

PETTERSON Andrew (Andy) Keith
Born: Freemantle, Australia, 29 September 1969
Height: 6'2" Weight: 14.7

Andy found himself to be third-choice 'keeper behind Russell Hoult and Aaron Flahavan for Portsmouth last term, and then slipped even further down the pecking order with the emergence of Chris Tardif. In March he joined Third Division Torquay on loan, making an outstanding debut in the 1-0 defeat at Carlisle when he produced a number of stunning saves to prevent a much heavier defeat. His assured performances gave Torquay's back four renewed confidence as Colin Lee strove to rebuild the side's fortunes and it was a blow when an injury to Flahavan forced Pompey to exercise the recall clause in his loan deal. He returned to feature against Fulham and Blackburn, doing well on both occasions before giving way again when the first-choice 'keeper returned to fitness.

Luton T (Signed from East Freemantle, Australia on 30/12/1988) FL 16+3 FLC 2 Others 2
Ipswich T (Loaned on 26/3/1993) PL 1
Charlton Ath (£85,000 on 15/7/1994) P/FL 68+4 FLC 6 FAC 1 Others 4
Bradford C (Loaned on 8/12/1994) FL 3
Ipswich T (Loaned on 26/9/1995) FL 1
Plymouth Arg (Loaned on 19/1/1996) FL 6
Colchester U (Loaned on 8/3/1996) FL 5
Portsmouth (Loaned on 13/11/1998) FL 13
Portsmouth (Free on 5/7/1999) FL 19 FLC 1+1
Torquay U (Loaned on 15/3/2001) FL 6

PETTINGER Paul Alan
Born: Sheffield, 1 October 1975
Height: 6'1" Weight: 13.7
Club Honours: FAYC '93
International Honours: E: Yth; Sch

Paul spent much of the 2000-01 campaign on the substitutes' bench for Rotherham as cover for regular 'keeper Ian Gray but forced his way into the first team in the run-in to the end of the season. An excellent shot stopper, he made a brilliant save to keep out a penalty and earn the Millers a point at Swansea City. His run of six successive appearances in February and March was his best since he moved to Millmoor. Out of contract in the summer he was reported to have joined Lincoln City.

Leeds U (From trainee on 16/10/1992)
Torquay U (Loaned on 23/12/1994) FL 3
Rotherham U (Loaned on 11/8/1995) FL 0+1
Gillingham (Free on 28/3/1996)
Carlisle U (Free on 2/8/1996)
Rotherham U (Free on 1/8/1997) FL 16 FLC 2 Others 1

PETTY Benjamin (Ben) James
Born: Solihull, 22 March 1977
Height: 6'0" Weight: 12.5
Club Honours: AMC '00

Ben failed to establish himself in any one position for Stoke City last term and played a number of bit parts for the team filling in commendably in defence, at wing back and in the midfield 'holding' role. A committed and competitive player he has signed a new one-year contract for City.

Aston Villa (From trainee on 10/5/1995)
Stoke C (Free on 27/11/1998) FL 26+20 FLC 4+1 FAC 3 Others 7+4/1

PEYTON Warren
Born: Manchester, 13 December 1979
Height: 5'10" Weight: 10.9

Warren impressed sufficiently in pre-season trials at Bury to be taken on by Shakers' boss Andy Preece but he spent much of the campaign developing in the club's reserve team. He received a few glimpses of first-team action, appearing on two occasions as a substitute and also making the starting line-up for the friendly game against the Pakistan national team. A promising young midfield player he will be aiming to gain further senior experience in the coming season.

Rochdale (Signed from Morecambe on 25/10/1999) FL 1
Bury (Free on 18/9/2000) FL 0+1 Others 0+1

PHELAN Leeyon
Born: Hammersmith, 6 October 1982
Height: 5'11" Weight: 12.6

Leeyon scored prolifically for the Wycombe reserve and youth teams last season and was rewarded with his Football League debut when he came on from the subs' bench in the home game against Stoke City in March. A powerful striker with plenty speed and a high work rate he will be hoping to feature more often in the coming season.

Wycombe W (Trainee) FL 0+2

PHELAN Terence (Terry) Michael
Born: Manchester, 16 March 1967
Height: 5'8" Weight: 10.6
Club Honours: FAC '88
International Honours: RoI: 41: B-1; U23-1; U21-1; Yth

Terry had a season he will want to forget at Fulham in 2000-01. An injury during the pre-season meant that Rufus Brevett was able to reclaim the left back berth in the defence and he subsequently played so well that he couldn't be left out. Apart from an outing in the Worthington Cup against Northampton, Terry had to wait until January for his first appearance from the subs' bench and despite several fine performances in the reserves his only other first-team action came when he replaced the suspended Brevett for the final game at Grimsby. Out of contract in the summer his future was unclear at the time of writing.

Leeds U (From apprentice on 3/8/1984) FL 12+2 FLC 3 Others 2
Swansea C (Free on 30/7/1986) FL 45 FLC 4 FAC 5 Others 3
Wimbledon (£100,000 on 29/7/1987) FL 155+4/1 FLC 13+2 FAC 16/2 Others 8
Manchester C (£2,500,000 on 25/8/1992) PL 102+1/2 FLC 11 FAC 8/1
Chelsea (£900,000 on 15/11/1995) PL 13+2 FLC 0+1 FAC 8
Everton (£850,000 on 1/1/1997) PL 23+2 FLC 1+1 FAC 1
Crystal Palace (Loaned on 23/10/1999) FL 14
Fulham (Free on 3/2/2000) FL 18+1/2 FLC 1

PHILLIPS Gareth Russell
Born: Pontypridd, 19 August 1979
Height: 5'8" Weight: 9.8
International Honours: W: U21-1; Yth; Sch

After featuring from the subs' bench in a couple of early-season games for Swansea Gareth enjoyed a successful loan spell with Merthyr before breaking through to earn an extended run in the team in the final third of the campaign. A tireless worker in the midfield engine-room he made his debut for Wales at U21 level when he came on as a second half substitute against Ukraine at the Vetch Field.

Swansea C (From trainee on 9/7/1998) FL 11+15 FLC 0+1 Others 1

PHILLIPS Kevin Mark
Born: Hitchin, 25 July 1973
Height: 5'7" Weight: 11.0
Club Honours: Div 1 '99
International Honours: E: 6; B-1

Last season was always going to be a testing one for Kevin following his 30-goal haul of the previous term, but the prolific striker was still one of Sunderland's top performers over the campaign. His final tally of 16 goals was one of the best in the Premiership and his overall contribution to the side was impressive. With tremendous pace and a great competitiveness Kevin still proved to be a handful for any defence. The highlights of his season were a hat-trick at Bradford on Boxing Day, helping him to break Gary Rowell's post-war goal-scoring record for the club, and the award of his sixth England cap against Italy. Although Kevin was subsequently omitted from further international squads, it is surely only a matter of time before he is back and searching for his first goal at that level.

Watford (£10,000 from Baldock on 19/12/1994) FL 54+5/23 FLC 2/1 FAC 2 Others 0+2
Sunderland (£325,000 + on 17/7/1997) P/FL 138+1/96 FLC 8+1/4 FAC 9/6 Others 3/2

Kevin Phillips

PHILLIPS Lee Paul
Born: Penzance, 16 September 1980
Height: 5'11" Weight: 12.0

Lee continued to make steady progress at Plymouth in the early part of last season but had few senior opportunities. Following a change in management he moved on loan to Weymouth in January and the move was made permanent in March. Lee is a young striker with good pace.

Plymouth Arg (From trainee on 9/7/1998) FL 18+32/1 FLC 0+1 FAC 3+3 Others 2+2

PHILLIPS Martin John
Born: Exeter, 13 March 1976
Height: 5'10" Weight: 11.10

Martin joined Plymouth during the close season after impressing against the Pilgrims in a pre-season friendly. Always willing to take on opposing defenders his skill and trickery created many goal-scoring opportunities for his team-mates and his excellent form was one of the highlights of a generally disappointing campaign for the Pilgrims. A skilful winger who can play on either flank he scored his first goal for Plymouth in home game against Chesterfield in March.

Exeter C (From trainee on 4/7/1994) FL 36+16/5 FLC 1+2 FAC 2+2 Others 1+5
Manchester C (£500,000 on 25/11/1995) P/FL 3+12 FLC 0+1
Scunthorpe U (Loaned on 5/1/1998) FL 2+1 Others 1
Exeter C (Loaned on 19/3/1998) FL 7+1
Portsmouth (£50,000 + on 27/8/1998) FL 4+20/1 FLC 2+2 FAC 0+1
Bristol Rov (Loaned on 24/2/1999) FL 2
Plymouth Arg (£25,000 on 11/8/2000) FL 36+6/1 FLC 2 FAC 2 Others 2

PHILLIPS Michael Edward
Born: Dulwich, 22 January 1983
Height: 5'10" Weight: 10.10

A slightly built young Gillingham midfield player, Michael made his senior debut when he came off the subs' bench in the last minute of the final game of the 2000-01 season against Blackburn. Despite only being on the pitch for a short time he had a major impact on the course of the game, delivering the cross from which the Gills snatched a late equaliser. A promising youngster he will be looking to gain more senior experience in 2001-02.

Gillingham (From trainee on 10/4/2001) FL 0+1

PHILLIPS Steven (Steve) John
Born: Bath, 6 May 1978
Height: 6'1" Weight: 11.10

With Billy Mercer out injured for the whole of the 2000-01 campaign Steve seized his chance to become Bristol City's regular first-choice 'keeper again. He showed greater maturity and comfortably held off the challenge of Antony Malessa to retain his place all season. The high point of his campaign came in the Bristol 'derby' match at the Memorial Ground in early April when his last-minute penalty save earned City a point and himself a place in local footballing folklore. Steve was voted 'Most Improved Player of the Season' by the club's Junior Strikers.

Bristol C (Signed from Paulton Rov on 21/11/1996) FL 78 FLC 5 FAC 8 Others 1

PHILLIPS Wayne
Born: Bangor, 15 December 1970
Height: 5'10" Weight: 11.2
International Honours: W: B-1

Having spent the best part of 16 months out injured Wayne returned to the Wrexham squad last December and was on the verge of establishing himself in the team when he suffered a damaged cartilage at Bristol City towards the end of January. Fortunately his return to fitness was much quicker this time and he was back playing in the Robins' Avon Insurance League side by the end of the season. When free from injury he is a hard-working central midfield player or full back.

Wrexham (From trainee on 23/8/1989) FL 184+23/16 FLC 17+1 FAC 12+2/1 Others 18+6/1
Stockport Co (£200,000 on 13/2/1998) FL 14+8 FLC 1 FAC 1
Wrexham (£50,000 on 23/7/1999) FL 7+3/1 FLC 1

PHILPOTT Lee
Born: Barnet, 21 February 1970
Height: 5'10" Weight: 12.9
Club Honours: Div 3 '91

Lee linked up again with new Hull boss Brian Little during the 2000 close season, having previously played for him when he was manager at Leicester. He produced some outstanding displays from the turn of the year and contributed to the Tigers rise up the table. His first goal for the Boothferry Park club was the winner against Halifax in March and coincided with the 450th appearance of his career. Lee is a skilful wide left midfield player with the ability to beat defenders and deliver an accurate cross.

Peterborough U (From trainee on 17/7/1986) FL 1+3 FAC 0+1 Others 0+2
Cambridge U (Free on 31/5/1989) FL 118+16/17 FLC 10/1 FAC 19/3 Others 15/2
Leicester C (£350,000 on 24/11/1992) F/PL 57+18/3 FLC 2+1 FAC 6+2 Others 4+1
Blackpool (£75,000 on 22/3/1996) FL 51+20/5 FLC 5/1 FAC 4 Others 0+2
Lincoln C (Free on 21/7/1998) FL 33+14/3 FLC 1+2 FAC 1+2 Others 1+3
Hull C (Free on 10/8/2000) FL 36+6/1 FLC 1 FAC 2 Others 0+2

Lee Philpott

PIERCY John William
Born: Forest Gate, 18 September 1979
Height: 5'11" Weight: 12.4
International Honours: E: Yth
Having made his senior debut for Tottenham in the 1999-2000 season, John continued to make steady progress last term and added a further five appearances from the substitutes' bench in the closing stages of the campaign. A versatile midfield player, he is still something of a raw talent but is very quick and strong and has plenty of confidence.
Tottenham H (From trainee on 2/7/1998) PL 1+7 FLC 1

PILKINGTON Kevin William
Born: Hitchin, 8 March 1974
Height: 6'1" Weight: 13.0
Club Honours: FAYC '92
International Honours: E: Sch
Kevin did the rounds in the summer of 2000 after his release by Port Vale, and after trials and brief spells with a number of clubs including Macclesfield, Mansfield (where he played in a pre-season friendly), Aberystwyth Town and Wigan Athletic (one outing as an unused substitute) he returned to Field Mill in September signing as cover for Bobby Mimms. Although mostly a reserve for the Stags he played in the LDV Vans tie against Bury and also featured in two games right at the end of the campaign. An excellent shot stopper he may yet get his chance of regular first-team football with the Stags in 2001-02 following the club's decision to release Mimms in the summer.
Manchester U (From trainee on 6/7/1992) PL 4+2 FLC 1 FAC 1
Rochdale (Loaned on 2/2/1996) FL 6
Rotherham U (Loaned on 22/1/1997) FL 17
Port Vale (Free on 1/7/1998) FL 23 FLC 1 FAC 1 (Freed during 2000 close season)
Wigan Ath (Free, via a trial at Macclesfield, on 31/8/2000. Freed on 4/9/2000)
Mansfield T (Free from Aberystwyth T on 8/9/2000) FL 2 Others 1

PILVI Tero
Born: Vihti, Finland, 21 February 1976
Height: 5'8" Weight: 10.11
Tero joined Scottish First Division club Airdrie at the end of the Scandinavian 2000 season and got off to a great start, netting a fine goal to clinch a 2-0 win at Falkirk just minutes after coming off the subs' bench. He moved south of the border to join Cambridge United on the transfer deadline day and after scoring on his debut for the reserves he went on to feature in a number of games in the closing stages of the campaign. He is a quick and strong striker who added width to the U's attack.
Airdrieonians (Signed from Enkopings SK, Sweden, ex HJK Helsinki, FC Jokerit, Atlantis Helsinki, on 14/12/2000) SL 4+5/2 SC 1/1
Cambridge U (Free on 22/3/2001) FL 3+2

PINAMONTE Lorenzo
Born: Foggia, Italy, 9 May 1978
Height: 6'3" Weight: 13.4
Lorenzo began the 2000-01 campaign on the subs' bench at Brentford making the starting line-up for the game against Bournemouth in September when he produced a particularly good performance scoring once himself and setting up two goals for Andy Scott. He subsequently dropped out of the squad and in February he went on loan to Third Division Leyton Orient. He scored on his debut in a 3-0 win over Halifax and added another in the victory at Lincoln but with the return of injured players to fitness he lost his place and returned to Griffin Park. He was on the open to offers list in the summer.
Bristol C (Free from Foggia, Italy on 18/9/1998) FL 3+4/1 FLC 1+2
Brighton & Hove A (Loaned on 17/12/1999) FL 8+1/2
Brentford (£75,000 on 4/2/2000) FL 8+15/2 FLC 1 FAC 0+1/1 Others 0+1
Leyton Orient (Loaned on 3/2/2001) FL 5+6/2

PINAULT Thomas
Born: Grasse, France, 4 December 1981
Height: 5'10" Weight: 11.1
Although Thomas netted a great 25-yarder when coming on from the subs' bench for Colchester against Luton in December, U's boss Steve Whitton seemed reluctant to play him on a regular basis and it was only when the club were safe from relegation that he was introduced to the starting line-up. He is a very promising central midfield player who has shown great composure in his first-team outings.
Colchester U (Free from AS Cannes, France on 5/7/1999) FL 4+5/1 FLC 0+1

PINKNEY Grant Edward
Born: Evesham, 31 January 1983
Height: 5'6" Weight: 11.7
Grant is a scholarship boy who was a regular in Lincoln's reserves last season before making his senior debut when he came on as a substitute for the final few minutes of the FA Cup first round tie with Bracknell Town. He was also an unused sub on several occasions. He is a central midfield player who showed plenty of promise in his first season at Sincil Bank.
Lincoln C (Trainee, having earlier been a trainee at Birmingham C) FAC 0+1

PIRES Robert
Born: Reims, France, 29 October 1973
Height: 6'1" Weight: 12.4
International Honours: France: 47 (UEFA '00)
Robert joined Arsenal after triumphing at Euro 2000 with France when he set up David Trezeguet's 'golden goal' in the final against Italy. After taking a couple of months to settle in at Highbury, he began to show the sort of form that earned him a regular spot in his national side. He is a quick, skilful ball-player, equally comfortable on either left or right flank, and is exciting to watch when attacking opposition defences. Robert scored regularly throughout the season, including a spectacular equaliser in Rome against Lazio in the Champions' League as well as the winner against Tottenham in the FA Cup semi-final. He also performed well for his country and was a member of the team that defeated Japan to win the FIFA Confederations Cup during the summer.
Arsenal (£6,000,000 from Olympique Marseille, France, ex Metz, on 24/7/2000) PL 29+4/4 FAC 6/3 Others 11+1/1

PISTONE Alessandro
Born: Milan, Italy, 27 July 1975
Height: 5'11" Weight: 12.1
International Honours: Italy: U21 (UEFA-U21 '96)
The Italian defender's season was symptomatic of Everton's injury-troubled campaign. After a solid debut at Leeds on the opening day of the season, he lasted just 38 minutes of his first home game against Charlton before bowing out with a hamstring injury. After shaking off that problem, Alessandro lasted just six minutes of his next appearance before pulling up with cruciate knee ligament damage - and then spent six months on the sidelines. In his few first-team forays he showed the pace and willingness to get forward that Everton lacked all season. But a campaign to forget was compounded when he received a red card in his comeback game against Manchester City. A left back, equally at home in central defence and also capable of playing down the right, he will be hoping Evertonians see more of his talents next season.
Newcastle U (£4,300,000 from Inter Milan, Italy, ex Vicenza, Solbiatese, Crevalcore, on 31/7/1997) PL 45+1/1 FLC 1+1 FAC 8 Others 7
Everton (£3,000,000 on 12/7/2000) PL 5+2 FLC 1

PITTS Matthew
Born: Middlesbrough, 25 December 1979
Height: 5'11" Weight: 12.8
Matthew started the 2000-01 campaign on a short-term contract at Carlisle but found first-team opportunities few and far between. He was released at the end of October and later signed for Unibond League club Workington. He is a promising youngster who can play either at right back or on the right-hand side of midfield.
Sunderland (From trainee on 25/6/1998)
Carlisle U (Free on 1/7/1999) FL 21+13/1 FLC 2+2 Others 2/1

PLATT Clive Linton
Born: Wolverhampton, 27 October 1977
Height: 6'4" Weight: 13.0
Clive started the 2000-01 season in brilliant form for Rochdale, scoring six times in the space of eight games early on. Later on a goal drought affected his confidence for a while, but after a short spell out injured he returned and although the goals continued to elude him, he struck up a devastating partnership with new signing Paul Connor. Clive is a big tall striker who is an excellent leader of the line.
Walsall (From trainee on 25/7/1996) FL 18+14/4 FLC 1+2/1 FAC 0+1 Others 1+6
Rochdale (£70,000 + on 5/8/1999) FL 70+14/17 FLC 2/1 FAC 4/2 Others 5

PLATT David Andrew
Born: Chadderton, 10 June 1966
Height: 5'10" Weight: 11.12
Club Honours: PL '98; FAC '98
International Honours: E: 62; B-3; U21-3
Nottingham Forest's player-manager again

made a handful of early-season appearances last term, scoring in the 3-2 win at Crystal Palace. A talented midfield player who showed he still had something to offer, he subsequently hung up his boots once more to concentrate on his managerial role at the City Ground.

Manchester U (Signed from Chadderton on 24/7/1984)
Crewe Alex (Free on 25/1/1985) FL 134/55 FLC 8/4 FAC 3/1 Others 7
Aston Villa (£200,000 on 2/2/1988) FL 121/50 FLC 14/10 FAC 4/2 Others 6/6 (£5,500,000 to Bari, Italy on 20/7/1991)
Arsenal (£4,750,000 from Sampdoria, Italy on 14/7/1995) PL 65+23/13 FLC 7+3/2 FAC 3+3 Others 2+2 (Retired on 23/7/1998)
Nottingham F (Free on 3/8/1999) FL 3+2/1 FLC 1+1

PLATTS Mark Anthony
Born: Sheffield, 23 May 1979
Height: 5'8" Weight: 11.13
International Honours: E: Yth; Sch

Mark showed that he had the ability to succeed in the professional game in a handful of outings for Torquay at the beginning of last season but he never appeared to be settled at Plainmoor. His contract with the Gulls was cancelled in October and he subsequently returned north to join the former England star Chris Waddle at Worksop Town. He is a skilful left-sided player who can play at left wing back and in midfield.

Sheffield Wed (From trainee on 16/10/1996) PL 0+2
Torquay U (Free on 9/3/1999) FL 16+18/1 FLC 1+2 FAC 0+2 Others 2

PLUCK Lee Kenneth
Born: Enfield, 27 February 1982
Height: 6'0" Weight: 11.11

A product of the Barnet youth system, Lee spent much of his first season as a professional developing in the reserve team before spending a month on loan at Ryman League club Grays Athletic early in the new year. He made his Football League debut last February when he made a late appearance from the subs' bench in the Bees 3-0 victory over Darlington. Lee is a promising central defender and has been rewarded with a two-year contract at Underhill. He was placed on the open to offers list following the Bees' relegation to the Conference.

Barnet (From trainee on 2/7/2000) FL 0+1

PLUMMER Christopher (Chris) Scott
Born: Isleworth, 12 October 1976
Height: 6'3" Weight: 12.9
International Honours: E: U21-5; Yth

Chris was not a first choice for Queens Park Rangers at the start of last season and only made the line-up in December when injuries robbed the team of more experienced defenders. He did well enough to retain his place until the end of the season and broke his goal-scoring duck when he netted in the 2-0 win over West Bromwich Albion in January. He is a tall central defender who uses his height to good effective and is comfortable on the ball.

Queens Park R (From trainee on 1/7/1994) F/PL 53+6/2 FLC 2 FAC 6

PLUMMER Dwayne Jermaine
Born: Bristol, 12 May 1978
Height: 5'9" Weight: 11.8

After spells in non-league with Stevenage and Chesham United Dwayne returned to the full-time game when he joined Bristol Rovers last September. Soon after signing he kept his nerve to net the winning penalty in the Worthington Cup second round shoot-out against Premiership Everton but it was not until the appointment of caretaker-manager Garry Thompson that he established himself as a regular in the first team. A promising midfielder he netted his first league goal in the 2-0 win over Bury and impressed with his ball-winning skills and some superb passing.

Bristol C (From trainee on 5/9/1995) FL 1+13 FLC 1+2 Others 0+1 (Free to Stevenage Borough on 18/11/1998)
Bristol Rov (£15,000 + from Chesham U on 7/9/2000) FL 17+3/1 FLC 0+2

POLLET Ludovic (Ludo)
Born: Valenciennes, France, 18 June 1970
Height: 6'1" Weight: 12.11

Having begun the 2000-01 campaign brightly for Wolves Ludo was sidelined by injury early on and missed several weeks following a hernia operation. He was sorely missed in his absence and although he returned to action he suffered further injuries including a broken nose. He is an experienced central defender who is particularly effective in the air and is a key figure in the Wanderers' back line when fit, so the club were relieved that he signed a new long-term contract during the campaign.

Wolverhampton W (Free from Le Havre, France on 10/9/1999) FL 67+1/7 FAC 4

POLLITT Michael (Mike) Francis
Born: Farnworth, 29 February 1972
Height: 6'4" Weight: 14.0

This experienced goalkeeper joined Chesterfield in the 2000 close season and went on to become an ever-present for the Spireites while enjoying being a member of a Third Division promotion team for the second year in succession. The big man looked unruffled throughout the season, offering a consistency and reliability that turned a defence that had leaked in the 1999-2000 campaign into one that let in only 42 last time round. Anticipation, good positioning and confident handling allow him to make it all look rather more comfortable than it actually is, and should one day earn him the chance to play at a higher level. A member of the PFA's Third Division team he was reported to have joined Rotherham United again in the summer.

Manchester U (From trainee on 1/7/1990)
Bury (Free on 10/7/1991)
Lincoln C (Free on 1/12/1992) FL 57 FLC 5 FAC 2 Others 4
Darlington (Free on 11/8/1994) FL 55 FLC 4 FAC 3 Others 5
Notts Co (£75,000 on 14/11/1995) FL 10 Others 2
Oldham Ath (Loaned on 29/8/1997) FL 16
Gillingham (Loaned on 12/12/1997) FL 6
Brentford (Loaned on 22/1/1998) FL 5
Sunderland (£75,000 on 23/2/1998)
Rotherham U (Free on 14/7/1998) FL 92 FLC 4 FAC 7 Others 5
Chesterfield (Free on 15/6/2000) FL 46 FLC 3 FAC 1 Others 4

POLLOCK Jamie
Born: Stockton, 16 February 1974
Height: 5'11" Weight: 14.0
Club Honours: Div 1 '95, '97
International Honours: E: U21-3; Yth

Jamie joined Crystal Palace in the 2000 close season adding bite and experience for the Eagles' in the centre of the park. He proved a useful acquisition and contributed four goals before a sending off led to a period of suspension and shortly after his return he was placed on the transfer list. A loan move to Birmingham followed as Blues' manager Trevor Francis sought cover for injuries to Danny Sonner and Martin O'Connor, but despite playing for the club at a difficult time he tried his best and always worked to make things happen. He is a combative midfield player who is sharp in the tackle and always gives 100 per cent.

Middlesbrough (From trainee on 18/12/1991) F/PL 144+11/17 FLC 17+2/1 FAC 13+1/1 Others 4+1 (Free to Osasuna, Spain on 6/9/96)
Bolton W (£1,500,000 on 22/11/1996) F/PL 43+3/5 FLC 4+1/1 FAC 4/2
Manchester C (£1,000,000 on 19/3/1998) FL 49+9/5 FLC 5 FAC 4+1 Others 1+1
Crystal Palace (£750,000 on 11/8/2000) FL 29+2/4 FLC 5+1
Birmingham C (Loaned on 16/3/2001) FL 4+1

POOLE Kevin
Born: Bromsgrove, 21 July 1963
Height: 5'10" Weight: 12.11
Club Honours: FLC '97

Kevin was second choice in goal to Ian Bennett for Birmingham City during the whole of last season and although he regularly featured on the substitutes' bench his only first-team action came when he stepped in for the 3-2 home defeat by Barnsley in January. An excellent shot stopper who performs consistently well when called upon, he was out of contract in the summer and at the time of writing it was unclear what the future held for him.

Aston Villa (From apprentice on 26/6/1981) FL 28 FLC 2 FAC 1 Others 1
Northampton T (Loaned on 8/11/1984) FL 3
Middlesbrough (Signed on 27/8/1987) FL 34 FLC 4 FAC 2 Others 2
Hartlepool U (Loaned on 27/3/1991) FL 12
Leicester C (£40,000 on 30/7/1991) F/PL 163 FLC 10 FAC 8 Others 12
Birmingham C (Free on 4/8/1997) FL 56 FLC 6 FAC 2 Others 2

POOM Mart
Born: Tallin, Estonia, 3 February 1972
Height: 6'4" Weight: 13.6
International Honours: Estonia: 75

Now recognised as one of the top goalkeepers in the Premiership, Mart produced some stunning performances in the first half of last season, and his injury against Charlton was a big blow to the club at the time. His commanding presence in the area and ability to intercept crosses was especially important in a season when, due to a run of injuries, he was playing behind a constantly changing defence. He returned from injury towards the end of the campaign and made some vital saves at Old Trafford in the win that guaranteed Premiership survival for the Rams. The first-choice 'keeper for Estonia, he added to his already considerable collection of caps during the season.

Portsmouth (£200,000 from FC Wil, Switzerland, ex Flora, on 4/8/1994) FL 4 FLC 3 (Signed by Tallin SC, Estonia on 9/5/1996)
Derby Co (£500,000 on 26/3/1997) PL 115+3 FLC 10 FAC 7

POPE Craig
Born: Islington, 17 September 1982
Height: 5'10" Weight: 11.7

This young Barnet midfield player made the briefest of entrances in senior football when he came on as a substitute in the last minute of the Bees' LDV Vans Trophy tie against Rushden & Diamonds last November. Craig is still a trainee at Underhill and will be looking to gain more experience in the first team in the 2001-02 campaign. He was placed on the open to offers list following the Bees' relegation to the Conference in the summer.

Barnet (Trainee) Others 0+1

POTTER Graham Stephen
Born: Solihull, 20 May 1975
Height: 6'1" Weight: 11.12
International Honours: E: U21-1; Yth

Graham joined York City in July 2000 and featured regularly for the Minstermen last season. He looked particularly strong when playing in the left-wing-back role where his pace was effective and he also showed he could deliver useful crosses from free kicks and corners. He took time to get used to the hurly burly of the Third Division but after a spell out through injury he returned to find his best form in the closing weeks of the campaign. He scored three goals during the campaign, netting a dramatic last-minute equaliser direct from a corner at Torquay in April which ensured that York retained their Football League status.

Birmingham C (From trainee on 1/7/1992) FL 23+2/2 FAC 1 Others 6
Wycombe W (Loaned on 17/9/1993) FL 2+1 FLC 1 Others 1
Stoke C (£75,000 on 20/12/1993) FL 41+4/1 FLC 3+1 FAC 4 Others 5
Southampton (£250,000 + on 23/7/1996) FL 2+6 FLC 1+1
West Bromwich A (£300,000 + on 14/2/1997) FL 31+12 FLC 0+3 FAC 1
Northampton T (Loaned on 24/10/1997) FL 4 Others 1
Reading (Loaned on 2/12/1999) FL 4 Others 1
York C (Free on 7/7/2000) FL 34+4/2 FLC 2 FAC 4/1

POTTER Lee
Born: Salford, 3 September 1978
Height: 5'11" Weight: 12.10

Mart Poom

Lee had a very frustrating time at Halifax Town in the 2000-01 season for he featured from the subs' bench in only a handful of senior games last October despite finishing as leading scorer for the club's reserve team. A promising young striker he was out of contract in the summer and at the time of writing his future was unclear.
Bolton W (From trainee on 3/7/1997) FLC 0+1
Halifax T (£30,000 on 17/12/1999) FL 13+9/2

POTTS Steven (Steve) John
Born: Hartford, USA, 7 May 1967
Height: 5'8" Weight: 10.11
International Honours: E: Yth
Still a valued member of the West Ham squad, Steve provided excellent cover whenever he was called upon in 2000-01. Loyal, honest and reliable he played in his 500th first-team game during the campaign. He is a dependable defender who is quick in the tackle and reads the game well.
West Ham U (From apprentice on 11/5/1984) F/PL 362+37/1 FLC 39+3 FAC 41+1 Others 21+2

POUTON Alan
Born: Newcastle, 1 February 1977
Height: 6'0" Weight: 12.8
Alan had a frustrating time with injuries at Grimsby Town last season. He began the campaign as a regular in the line-up, but suffered concussion in the home match with Nottingham Forest in September and then shortly afterwards sustained a knee injury that kept him on the sidelines for three months. However he returned to the Mariners' team towards the end of the campaign, scoring an important goal from the penalty spot to earn a point in the 1-1 draw with Birmingham City. He is a hard-running midfield player capable of making effective runs into the opposition penalty box.
Oxford U (From trainee at Newcastle U on 7/11/1995)
York C (Free on 8/12/1995) FL 79+11/7 FLC 5+1 FAC 5/1 Others 2
Grimsby T (£150,000 on 5/8/1999) FL 35+21/2 FLC 7+2 FAC 1+1

POWELL Christopher (Chris) George Robin
Born: Lambeth, 8 September 1969
Height: 5'10" Weight: 11.7
Club Honours: Div 1 '00
International Honours: E: 3
2000-01 was a memorable season for Chris. One of Charlton Athletic's most consistent performers in recent years he was actually dropped following the Boxing Day defeat at West Ham but was quickly recalled at the start of January. This set off a remarkable chain of events that saw him become only the third Addicks' player since 1946 to play for the full England side when he won caps against Spain, Finland and Mexico. A skilful and unflappable left-sided defender Chris can play as an orthodox left back or as a left wing back and loves to push forward down the flank and cross the ball from the by-line. A very popular figure at The Valley he rarely has a bad game and scored his long-awaited first goal for the club in the FA Cup tie against Tottenham Hotspur.
Crystal Palace (From trainee on 24/12/1987) FL 2+1 FLC 0+1 Others 0+1
Aldershot (Loaned on 11/1/1990) FL 11
Southend U (Free on 30/8/1990) FL 246+2/3 FLC 13 FAC 8 Others 21
Derby Co (£750,000 on 31/1/1996) F/PL 89+2/1 FLC 5 FAC 5/1
Charlton Ath (£825,000 on 1/7/1998) P/FL 109+2 FLC 4+1 FAC 6/1

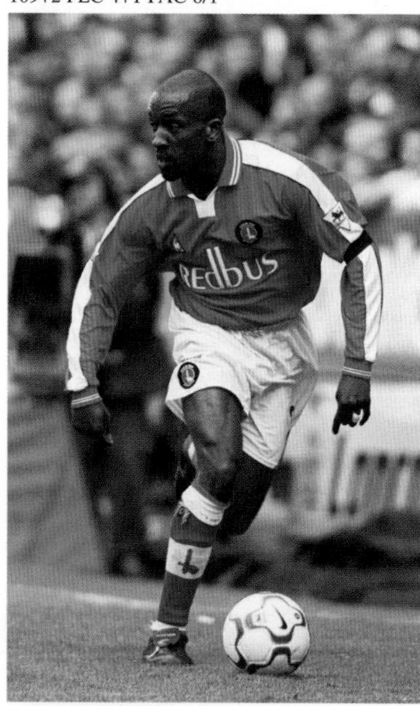

Chris Powell

POWELL Darren David
Born: Hammersmith, 10 March 1976
Height: 6'3" Weight: 13.2
Club Honours: Div 3 '99
Brentford's huge central defender missed the first half of last season due to hamstring and pelvic problems and it was not until the new year that he returned to the first-team squad. Darren soon settled down to become a valuable figure in the Bees' back line, once again proving a difficult player for opposing strikers to beat. He won a runners-up medal in the LDV Vans Trophy after appearing against Port Vale in the final last April.
Brentford (£15,000 from Hampton on 27/7/1998) FL 87/5 FLC 5 FAC 2 Others 7+1/1

POWELL Darryl Anthony
Born: Lambeth, 15 November 1971
Height: 6'0" Weight: 12.10
International Honours: Jamaica: 16
Darryl had another consistent campaign for Derby County in 2000-01 when he was again team captain. A regular in the centre of midfield, his enthusiasm and capacity for hard work were key factors in the successful fight against relegation. Although the first to admit that he is not blessed with the skills of some of his contemporaries, he was badly missed when absent on international duty. He missed the closing weeks of the season due to a knee injury but is expected to be fit in time for the start of the 2001-02 campaign. He continued to represent Jamaica, winning a further ten caps during the season.
Portsmouth (From trainee on 22/12/1988) FL 83+49/16 FLC 11+3/3 FAC 10 Others 9+5/4
Derby Co (£750,000 on 27/7/1995) F/PL 164+20/9 FLC 10+1/1 FAC 7+1

POWELL Paul
Born: Wallingford, 30 June 1978
Height: 5'8" Weight: 11.6
Paul had a frustrating time with injuries for much of last term after damaging his knee ligaments in an early-season game at Walsall. It was only really towards the end of the campaign that he recovered full fitness and enjoyed a decent run in the line-up, although it was too late to halt the U's slide towards relegation. A quality left-sided player who can play either as a wing back or in a wide-midfield role, he will be hoping to re-establish himself in the line-up in 2001-02.
Oxford U (From trainee on 2/7/1996) FL 106+22/11 FLC 6+2 FAC 7+1/3 Others 2+2/3

POWER Graeme Richard
Born: Harrow, 7 March 1977
Height: 5'10" Weight: 10.10
International Honours: E: Yth; Sch
Despite breaking a wrist during the pre-season Graeme appeared in the Exeter City line-up on the opening day of the 2000-01 campaign and featured regularly for the Grecians. A versatile defender who can play at centre half or left back he is calm on the ball and can deliver an accurate pass. He scored his first senior goal with a low free kick from the edge of the box against Leyton Orient last January and has now made over 100 appearances for the St James Park club.
Queens Park R (From trainee on 11/4/1995)
Bristol Rov (Free on 15/7/1996) FL 25+1 FAC 1 Others 1+2
Exeter C (Free on 6/8/1998) FL 102+2/1 FLC 3 FAC 7 Others 5

POYET Gustavo (Gus) Augusto
Born: Montevideo, Uruguay, 15 November 1967
Height: 6'2" Weight: 13.0
Club Honours: ECWC '98; ESC '98; FAC '00; CS '00
International Honours: Uruguay: 31; Yth
This ebullient midfielder suffered another injury-marred season at Chelsea last term. A damaged ankle sustained against Arsenal in September led to a seven-match absence and his loss was keenly felt in the shock UEFA Cup exit at the hands of St Gallen. Fortunately for the Blues, Gus quickly returned to demonstrate his knack of snatching vital goals with efforts against Southampton, Leeds United, Derby County and Bradford City before Christmas and on New Year's Day he skippered the team in the absence of Dennis Wise and Marcel Desailly. He maintained his reputation as the most prolific midfielder in the Premiership with a final tally of 11 goals a vital contribution that helped the club to a place in the 2001-02 UEFA Cup - and made all the

more remarkable by the fact that he was consigned to the substitutes' bench for much of the second half of the campaign. He notched another two goals in the 4-0 win at Derby in April but rather surprisingly handed in a transfer request at the beginning of the summer break. He was reported to have signed for Tottenham in the summer.
Chelsea (Free from Real Zaragoza, Spain, ex River Plate, Grenoble, Bella Vista, on 15/7/1997) PL 79+26/36 FLC 3+1/2 FAC 8+1/7 Others 20+7/4

PREECE Andrew (Andy) Paul
Born: Evesham, 27 March 1967
Height: 6'1" Weight: 12.0
Bury's player-manager used himself mainly as a substitute during the 2000-2001 season, although he still made the starting line-up on a handful of occasions. Despite being a great success off the field in his role as the Shakers' boss he made little impact as a player and netted just two goals during the campaign. His appearances were restricted in the new year when a long-standing back injury flared up and it remains to be seen how long he will continue in his dual role. Andy is a tall striker who uses his height to good effect and holds the ball up well.
Northampton T (Free from Evesham on 31/8/1988) FL 0+1 FLC 0+1 Others 0+1 (Free to Worcester C during 1989 close season)
Wrexham (Free on 22/3/1990) FL 44+7/7 FLC 5+1/1 FAC 1/2 Others 5/1
Stockport Co (£10,000 on 18/12/1991) FL 89+8/42 FLC 2+1 FAC 7/3 Others 12+2/9
Crystal Palace (£350,000 on 23/6/1994) PL 17+3/4 FLC 4+2/1 FAC 2+3
Blackpool (£200,000 on 5/7/1995) FL 114+12/35 FLC 8+2/1 FAC 2+3/2 Others 12/2
Bury (Free on 6/7/1998) FL 62+50/17 FLC 6+3 FAC 2+2 Others 2

PREECE David William
Born: Bridgnorth, 28 May, 1963
Height: 5'6" Weight: 11.6
Club Honours: FLC '88
International Honours: E: B-3
Now in the twilight of his career David spent most of his time on his coaching duties with Cambridge United last season and only stepped up to make occasional appearances from the subs' bench as cover. Even in a few brief outings he showed some of the touches that made him such a stylish midfield player in his younger days.
Walsall (From apprentice on 22/7/1980) FL 107+4/5 FLC 18/5 FAC 6/1 Others 1
Luton T (£150,000 on 6/12/1984) FL 328+8/21 FLC 23/3 FAC 27/2 Others 8+1/1
Derby Co (Free on 11/8/1995) FL 10+3/1 FLC 2
Birmingham C (Loaned on 24/11/1995) FL 6 Others 1
Swindon T (Loaned on 21/3/1996) FL 7/1
Cambridge U (Free on 6/9/1996) FL 40+35/2 FLC 3+2 Others 2+2

PRENDERVILLE Barry
Born: Dublin, 16 October 1976
Height: 6'0" Weight: 12.8
Having been released by Ayr United at the end of the 1999-2000 campaign, Barry began last season with League of Ireland outfit St Patricks before joining Oldham Athletic at the beginning of September. He netted with a 30-yard screamer in a reserve friendly against Glossop but after a brief run in the squad shortly after signing he was beset with injuries, and was restricted to occasional first-team outings later in the season. A commanding full back he produced some strong displays and was rewarded by the Latics with a new contract.
Coventry C (Signed from Cherry Orchard on 5/8/1994)
Hibernian (Loaned on 11/9/1998) SL 13/2
Ayr U (Free on 7/6/1999) SL 3+2 SLC 1 (Freed on 20/10/1999)
Oldham Ath (Free from St Patricks on 7/9/2000) FL 6+3 FLC 1+1 FAC 1

PRESSMAN Kevin Paul
Born: Fareham, 6 November 1967
Height: 6'1" Weight: 15.5
International Honours: E: B-3; U21-1; Yth; Sch
Kevin began 2000-01 in dramatic style when he created a new record by being sent off for handling the ball outside the penalty area just 13 seconds into the opening game of the season at Wolves. He was once again first-choice 'keeper for Sheffield Wednesday and produced some fine displays, notably in the Worthington Cup tie against West Ham. He is an excellent shot stopper and went on to make his 350th senior appearance for the Owls against Tranmere last February.
Sheffield Wed (From apprentice on 7/11/1985) F/PL 302+3 FLC 38 FAC 17 Others 4
Stoke C (Loaned on 10/3/1992) FL 4 Others 2

PRICE Jason Jeffrey
Born: Pontypridd, 12 April 1977
Height: 6'2" Weight: 11.5
Club Honours: Div 3 '00
International Honours: W: U21-7
Jason was a near ever-present for Swansea last season when he was mostly employed at right back covering for the injured Steve Jones rather than in the right-sided midfield position he has previously occupied. His ability to create openings for his colleagues from the centre of the park was badly missed by the Swans but he still found time to score four goals including two crackers against Brentford in the LDV Vans Trophy and Wycombe. Out of contract in the summer, his future was unclear at the time of writing.
Swansea C (Free from Aberaman on 17/7/1995) FL 133+11/17 FLC 10/1 FAC 4/1 Others 4+1/1

PRIEST Christopher (Chris)
Born: Leigh, 18 October 1973
Height: 5'9" Weight: 10.10
Chris underwent a double hernia operation last September and it was not until the end of November that he returned to action for Macclesfield. A quality box-to-box midfield player he quickly regained his best form, working hard throughout every match and contributing a number of crucial goals for the Moss Rose club. It was therefore disappointing when he suffered an ankle injury in February that eventually ruled him out for the remainder of the season.
Everton (From trainee on 1/6/1992)
Chester C (Loaned on 9/9/1994) FL 11/1 Others 2
Chester C (Free on 11/1/1995) FL 151+5/25 FLC 6 FAC 6/1 Others 6
Macclesfield T (Free on 5/7/1999) FL 48+3/8 FLC 2/1 FAC 2 Others 1

PRIMUS Linvoy Stephen
Born: Forest Gate, 14 September 1973
Height: 6'0" Weight: 14.0
A powerful and consistent centre back and accomplished defender in the lower divisions, Linvoy settled into First Division football very quickly at Portsmouth last term after signing under the 'Bosman' ruling. A clean tackler, with good pace, he is strong on the ball, dominant in the air and not afraid to go forward when the opportunity arises. His confidence and experience helped strengthen the Pompey defence before he was sidelined by a thigh problem at the end of November, then by a groin injury, and it was not until the last few games that he returned to the side.
Charlton Ath (From trainee on 14/8/1992) FL 4 FLC 0+1 Others 0+1
Barnet (Free on 18/7/1994) FL 127/7 FLC 9+1 FAC 8/1 Others 4
Reading (£400,000 on 29/7/1997) FL 94+1/1 FLC 9 FAC 6 Others 4
Portsmouth (Free on 4/8/2000) FL 23 FLC 3

PRINGLE Ulf **Martin**
Born: Sweden, 18 November 1970
Height: 6'2" Weight: 12.3
Club Honours: Div 1 '00
International Honours: Sweden: 2; B-1
Martin is a tall, quick striker who had the misfortune to suffer a frustrating time in the 2000-01 season when he was plagued with persistent injury problems. Effective in the air and with sufficient pace to enable him to beat defenders to through balls he also has fine vision and an excellent work rate. He started only one Premiership game, against Liverpool at Anfield, but made several appearances from the subs' bench and came on to score the winning goal against Chelsea at The Valley. Martin is a useful squad member and if he can stay free of injury he will be hoping to win a place in the Addicks' starting line-up in the coming season.
Charlton Ath (Signed from Benfica, Portugal on 8/1/1999) P/FL 28+30/8 FLC 2 FAC 3

PRIOR Spencer Justin
Born: Southend, 22 April 1971
Height: 6'3" Weight: 13.4
Club Honours: FLC '97
Having played a major part in Manchester City's promotion in 1999-2000, Spencer was in the starting line up at the beginning of last season and retained his place until early December. However he was dropped after a run of six consecutive defeats and although never completely out of the running for the first team after this, he often found himself on the substitutes' bench towards the end of the campaign. His only goal came at West Ham in November when he gave City a half-time lead, only for the Hammers to come back with a vengeance to win 4-1. With a surplus of central defenders at Maine Road, it was always going to be tough to get into the first team once the partnership of Steve Howey and Richard Dunne had become established.

Southend U (From trainee on 22/5/1989) FL 135/3 FLC 9 FAC 5 Others 7/1
Norwich C (£200,000 on 24/6/1993) P/FL 67+7/1 FLC 10+1/1 FAC 0+2 Others 2
Leicester C (£600,000 on 17/8/1996) PL 61+3 FLC 7 FAC 5 Others 2
Derby Co (£700,000 on 22/8/1998) PL 48+6/1 FLC 5 FAC 4
Manchester C (£500,000 + on 23/3/2000) P/FL 27+3/4 FLC 4 FAC 2+1

PROCTOR Michael Anthony
Born: Sunderland, 3 October 1980
Height: 5'11" Weight: 12.7

This young striker spent the first half of the 2000-01 campaign on loan with Danish club Hvidovre and shortly after his return he was loaned out again to Third Division Halifax Town. His high work rate and skilful play made him a popular figure with the club's supporters and netted four crucial goals in his time at The Shay. He returned to the Stadium of Light at the end of the season and will be aiming to break into the first team during 2001-02.

Sunderland (From trainee on 29/10/1997) FLC 0+1
Halifax T (Loaned on 14/3/2001) FL 11+1/4

PROKAS Richard
Born: Penrith, 22 January 1976
Height: 5'9" Weight: 11.4
Club Honours: Div 3 '95; AMC '97

Richard again provided a combative presence in the centre of midfield for Carlisle United last season. He featured regularly throughout the campaign, producing a particularly effective performance in the FA Cup tie against Premiership Arsenal before a rather surprising move to Cambridge United just before the transfer deadline. He made his debut for the U's in the 1-0 win against Oxford United but featured in only a handful of games in the closing weeks of the campaign.

Carlisle U (From trainee on 18/7/1994) FL 184+20/3 FLC 11+1 FAC 10 Others 19+5/1
Cambridge U (Signed on 22/3/2001) FL 1+2

Richard Prokas

Steve Purches

PROUDLOCK Adam David
Born: Telford, 9 May 1981
Height: 6'0" Weight: 13.0
International Honours: E: Yth

Loaned out to Scottish First Division club Clyde at the beginning of last season Adam responded in style with a hat-trick on his debut against Falkirk and a tally of five goals in six appearances. On his return to Wolves he scored in his first game to clinch the Worthington Cup tie against Oxford and although he was to some extent in and out of the side he finished the campaign as the club's leading scorer with nine goals in all competitions. Two of these were especially memorable - a cracking winner in the FA Cup tie at Nottingham Forest and a 25-yard beauty at Grimsby. A tall hard-working striker who is still learning the game his control and strength on the ball improved during the season.

Wolverhampton W (From trainee on 15/7/1999) FL 28+7/8 FLC 3+1/2 FAC 2/1
Clyde (Loaned on 1/8/2000) SL 4/4 SLC 2/1

PRUTTON David Thomas
Born: Hull, 12 September 1981
Height: 6'1" Weight: 11.10
International Honours: E: U21-6; Yth

Although still a teenager David was a near ever-present for Nottingham Forest last term and continued to make good progress. Although sometimes played away from his favoured central midfield role he showed great stamina, playing in a similar style to former City Ground legend Roy Keane. David continued to be a part of the England set-up, making his debut for the U21s against Georgia and winning a further five caps during the season.

Nottingham F (From trainee on 1/10/1998) FL 74+2/3 FLC 4 FAC 3

PURCHES Stephen (Steve) Robert
Born: Ilford, 14 January 1980
Height: 5'11" Weight: 12.0

Having been released by West Ham at the end of the 1999-2000 campaign Steve joined Bournemouth in the close season and immediately established himself as a regular in the Cherries' line-up. He was sidelined for six weeks after suffering a hamstring injury in the New Years' Day fixture with Luton Town but returned to regain his place in the squad. A talented young full back who is equally at home on either flank he is effective when pushing forward and delivers some fine crosses.

West Ham U (From trainee on 6/7/1998)
Bournemouth (Free on 4/7/2000) FL 25+9 FLC 2 FAC 2

PURSE Darren John
Born: Stepney, 14 February 1977
Height: 6'2" Weight: 12.8
International Honours: E: U21-2

Darren grew in stature to become an inspirational figure at the heart of the Birmingham City defence last season. Entrusted with the vital injury-time penalty in the Worthington Cup final against Liverpool he kept his nerve to fire the ball home and then followed up with another penalty in the shoot-out. A talented central defender he attacks the ball in the air with power and determination and is very strong in the tackle. Despite the disappointment of the play-off defeat by Preston, Darren finished the campaign on a personal high when he was voted as the Blues' 'Player of the Year'.

Leyton Orient (From trainee on 22/2/1994) FL 48+7/3 FLC 2 FAC 1 Others 7+1/2
Oxford U (£100,000 on 23/7/1996) FL 52+7/5 FLC 10+1/2 FAC 2
Birmingham C (£800,000 on 17/2/1998) FL 80+23/5 FLC 15+2/2 FAC 2 Others 4+1

PURSER Wayne Montague
Born: Basildon, 13 April 1980
Height: 5'9" Weight: 11.13

Wayne began last season in fine style for Barnet, scoring with a header in the 3-0 victory over Shrewsbury in the opening match which was also his debut in senior football. However although he regularly featured from the subs' bench it was not until the end of the campaign that he got much of an opportunity in the first team. A promising young striker he scored an outstanding individual goal for the Bees in their 3-2 defeat at Barnet in April. He was placed on the open to offers list in the summer following the Bees' relegation to the Conference.

Queens Park R (From trainee on 21/4/1997)
Barnet (Free on 18/8/2000) FL 4+14/3 FLC 1+1 FAC 0+2 Others 1+1/1

QUAILEY Brian Sullivan
Born: Leicester, 21 March 1978
Height: 6'1" Weight: 13.11
International Honours: St Kitts & Nevis: U23

Brian seemed to find it difficult to rediscover his best form for Scunthorpe United at the start of last season and it was not until the closing months of the campaign that he featured regularly in first-team action. Although still not at his best he netted a few goals, including two in the 4-1 victory over Plymouth in March. Brian is a pacy forward with great strength and an eye for goal.

West Bromwich A (Signed from Nuneaton Borough on 22/9/1997) FL 1+6 FLC 0+1
Exeter C (Loaned on 23/12/1998) FL 8+4/2 Others 2/1
Blackpool (Loaned on 3/12/1999) FL 1 Others 1
Scunthorpe U (Free on 3/2/2000) FL 24+17/8 FLC 0+1 Others 0+1/1

QUASHIE Nigel Francis
Born: Peckham, 20 July 1978
Height: 6'0" Weight: 12.4
International Honours: E: B-1; U21-7; Yth

A very talented midfield player, Nigel impressed in his first season at Portsmouth with some powerful shooting. He netted three spectacular goals, the best of which came against Norwich when he ran with the ball from the halfway line before unleashing a tremendous 40-yard shot into the top corner of the net. A player with a fine first touch, useful turn of pace and a good pass, he still needs to find greater consistency to his game. He was unfortunately hampered by a knee injury that restricted his appearances in the closing stages of the campaign but he is likely to be a key figure for Pompey once more when he returns to match fitness.

Queens Park R (From trainee on 1/8/1995) P/FL 50+7/3 FLC 0+1 FAC 4/2
Nottingham F (£2,500,000 on 24/8/1998) P/FL 37+7/2 FLC 7/1 FAC 1+1
Portsmouth (£200,000 + on 7/8/2000) FL 29+2/5 FLC 4 FAC 1

QUINN Alan
Born: Dublin, 13 June 1979
Height: 5'9" Weight: 11.7
International Honours: RoI: U21-7; Yth (UEFA-U18 '98)

This hard-working teenager made rapid strides with Sheffield Wednesday in 2000-01, establishing himself as a regular in the first team before his season ended prematurely when he suffered a broken leg in the local 'derby' against Sheffield United in April. Although primarily right-footed, he was mostly used in a wide-left midfield role where his fiery challenges and all-out commitment were put to good use. Alan added to his Republic of Ireland U21 caps with further appearances against Netherlands, Portugal and Cyprus.

Sheffield Wed (Signed from Cherry Orchard on 6/12/1997) P/FL 56+2/5 FLC 5/1 FAC 4+1

QUINN Barry Scott
Born: Dublin, 9 May 1979
Height: 6'0" Weight: 12.2
International Honours: RoI: 3; U21-16; Yth (UEFA-U18 '98)

Having made just a handful of appearances in the previous two seasons, Barry became a first-team regular for Coventry City during the 2000-01 campaign. He made a couple of early-season appearances in midfield but was then handed the troublesome left-back role at the beginning of December and performed with great aplomb. Despite being right-footed he adapted well to the role and on Marcus Hall's return he switched to right back displacing the incumbent, Marc Edworthy. While not the fastest full back in the Premiership he makes up for a certain lack of speed with good positional sense and strong passing skills, not to mention his crossing which created Lee Carsley's headed goal at Leicester. He gained three caps for the Republic of Ireland during the summer of 2000 and his regular place in the Coventry side won him a recall to the squad in April.

Coventry C (From trainee on 28/11/1996) PL 36+7 FLC 3 FAC 2

Niall Quinn

QUINN Stephen **James**
Born: Coventry, 15 December 1974
Height: 6'1" Weight: 12.10
International Honours: NI: 21; B-2; U21-1; Yth

James hardly figured in West Bromwich Albion manager Gary Megson's plans until last February and then bounced back with the opening goal in an important 3-0 home win over fellow play-off hopefuls Watford. He had struggled early on with his form but still managed to add to his collection of Northern Ireland caps while battling away in the reserves. A good ball player, he likes to occupy a position wide on the right and if required can play through the centre as well. Although willing to fight for a place in the first team he finished the campaign on the transfer list.

Birmingham C (Trainee) FL 1+3
Blackpool (£25,000 on 5/7/1993) FL 128+23/37 FLC 10+4/5 FAC 5+1/4 Others 7+4/2
Stockport Co (Loaned on 4/3/1994) FL 0+1
West Bromwich A (£500,000 on 20/2/1998) FL 84+23/9 FLC 3+2/1 FAC 2

QUINN Niall John
Born: Dublin, 6 October 1966
Height: 6'4" Weight: 15.10
Club Honours: FLC '87; Div 1 '99
International Honours: RoI: 84; B-1; U23-1; U21-6; Yth; Sch

The big Irishman could not have started last season better, with goals in the first two matches against his former clubs Arsenal and Manchester City - both trademark headers - and he continued to be the focal point for Sunderland's attacking play. His power in the air and awareness of his team-mates' positions were again crucial for the Wearsiders, although the wear and tear caused by his physical contributions began to show last term and he was plagued by a persistent back injury throughout the campaign. Niall continued to be a regular for the Republic of Ireland, but is still searching for the elusive goal that will give him his country's outright goal-scoring record. A hugely popular figure on Wearside he did no harm to his reputation by netting the winning goal against Newcastle at St James Park in November.

Arsenal (From juniors on 30/11/1983) FL 59+8/14 FLC 14+2/4 FAC 8+2/2 Others 0+1
Manchester C (£800,000 on 21/3/1990) F/PL 183+20/66 FLC 20+2/7 FAC 13+3/4 Others 3/1
Sunderland (£1,300,000 on 17/8/1996) F/PL 144+13/55 FLC 5+1/4 FAC 7+1/2 Others 2/2

QUINN Robert (Rob) John
Born: Sidcup, 8 November 1976
Height: 5'11" Weight: 11.2
Club Honours: Div 3 '99
International Honours: RoI: U21-5; B-1

This tough-tackling and versatile player began last season playing at right back for Brentford. He later moved to centre back before settling in a central midfield role alongside Paul Evans. Having been a near-ever present for the Bees it was something of a surprise when he was sold to Second Division strugglers Oxford United along with Andy Scott last January. He mostly featured in a midfield anchor role for the U's and although affected by suspension and injury he contributed one of the goals in the surprise 4-3 win over promotion-chasing Rotherham.

Crystal Palace (From trainee on 11/3/1995) F/PL 18+5/1 FLC 2+1/1 Others 2+1
Brentford (£40,000 on 9/7/1998) FL 98+11/2 FLC 9+1 FAC 6/2 Others 7/1
Oxford U (£75,000 on 12/1/2001) FL 12+1/2

QUINN Wayne Richard
Born: Truro, 19 November 1976
Height: 5'10" Weight: 11.12
International Honours: E: B-1; U21-2; Yth

After starting the 2000-01 season on the left side of midfield for Sheffield United, Wayne soon reverted to his role as a left wing back. He continued to show an improved positional sense and was a regular in the Blades' line-up until moving to Premiership Newcastle United early in the new year. He initially arrived on a month's loan, but his form persuaded manager Bobby Robson to make the move permanent as he sought to fill the gap left by Didier Domi's departure. Calm under pressure, he provided a balance that the Magpies had previously lacked. He quickly settled into the team and seemed comfortable at the higher level, which augers well for the 2001-02 season by which time he should be fully established on Tyneside.

Sheffield U (From trainee on 6/12/1994) FL 131+8/5 FLC 14+1 FAC 12+1 Others 2
Newcastle U (£750,000 + on 1/1/2001) PL 14+1

Rob Quinn

RACHUBKA Paul Stephen
Born: California, USA, 21 May 1981
Height: 6'1" Weight: 13.5
International Honours: E: Yth

Paul made his domestic debut for Manchester United when he came on as a late substitute in the Worthington Cup third round tie at Watford after Rai Van Der Gouw had received a red card. A goal-keeping crisis in March then gave him a rare opportunity to shine in the 2-0 defeat of Leicester at Old Trafford. The Reds' rookie 'keeper said he had sleepless nights thinking about being called up for the first-team, but performance-wise he was excellent. The signing of Andy Goram from Motherwell in April then put paid to a more regular slot, although judging by his limited appearances to date his future in the game looks well assured.

Manchester U (From trainee on 7/7/1999) PL 1 FLC 0+1 Others 0+1

RADEBE Lucas
Born: Johannesburg, South Africa, 12 April 1969
Height: 6'1" Weight: 11.8
International Honours: South Africa (ANC '96)

With Leeds ravaged by injuries at the start of the 2000-01 campaign, 'the Chief' found himself playing in midfield as well as in his customary central defensive role. However he suffered a serious injury in the closing minutes of the Champions' League defeat at Barcelona when he collided with Michael Duberry and was stretchered from the field in a neck brace. Although soon back in action he was carried off again after a clash of heads with Les Ferdinand and the injury kept him out for a run of seven matches. On his return he shackled Chelsea's Jimmy Hasselbaink, producing a 'Man of the Match' performance in the 1-1 draw at Stamford Bridge. As skipper he remained a key figure in the side, and enjoyed some marvellous nights in Europe. Unfortunately just as he began to form a formidable partnership with Rio Ferdinand, he suffered a bad knee injury at Sunderland in March, which required an operation and kept him out for the rest of the season. A very skilful defender, Lucas makes many last-ditch tackles and interceptions and is also a first class man-marker.

Leeds U (£250,000 from Kaizer Chiefs, South Africa on 5/9/1994) PL 152+12 FLC 9+4 FAC 15+2/1 Others 24/2

RAE Alexander (Alex) Scott
Born: Glasgow, 30 September 1969
Height: 5'9" Weight: 11.12
Club Honours: Div 1 '99
International Honours: S: B-4; U21-8

Alex featured regularly in the Sunderland first-team from the end of September, scoring the winner at Charlton in November. However he was sidelined by a bout of tendonitis that caused him to miss the last few months of the season and eventually required corrective surgery. A combative midfield player who is always willing to get stuck in, he also shows undoubted ability on the ball.

Falkirk (Free from Bishopbriggs on 15/6/1987) SL 71+12/20 SLC 5/1 SC 2+1
Millwall (£100,000 on 20/8/1990) FL 205+13/63 FLC 13+2/1 FAC 13/6 Others 10/1
Sunderland (£750,000 on 14/6/1996) F/PL 89+22/12 FLC 12+1/3 FAC 7 Others 0+2

RAMAGE Craig Darren
Born: Derby, 30 March 1970
Height: 5'9" Weight: 11.8
International Honours: E: U21-3

Craig featured fairly regularly for Notts County in the early part of last season, scoring a fine brace of goals in the 4-3 home defeat by Millwall at the end of August but was then sidelined by a knee injury in November and failed to return to the first team before the end of the campaign. A creative midfield playmaker who loves to link up with the attack he was one of several players released by the Magpies in the summer.

Derby Co (From trainee on 20/7/1988) FL 33+9/4 FLC 6+1/2 FAC 3+1/1 Others 0+3
Wigan Ath (Loaned on 16/2/1989) FL 10/2 Others 0+1
Watford (£90,000 on 21/2/1994) FL 99+5/27 FLC 8+1/2 FAC 7
Peterborough U (Loaned on 10/2/1997) FL 7 Others 1
Bradford C (Free on 24/6/1997) FL 24+11/1 FLC 0+2
Notts Co (Free on 5/8/1999) FL 50+5/7 FLC 7/2 FAC 2

RAMMELL Andrew (Andy) Victor
Born: Nuneaton, 10 February 1967
Height: 6'1" Weight: 13.12

Unable to break into the Walsall line-up Andy moved on to Second Division rivals Wycombe Wanderers who were faced with an injury crisis with their strike force. He was an immediate success at Adams Park, scoring regularly including a brace against his old club in October. Although he struggled with hamstring trouble in the new year he will be hoping to have recovered full fitness in time for the start of the new season. An excellent leader of the line he is strong on the ball and very effective in the air.

Manchester U (£40,000 from Atherstone U on 26/9/1989)
Barnsley (£100,000 on 14/9/1990) FL 149+36/44 FLC 11+3/1 FAC 12+1/4 Others 8/1
Southend U (Signed on 22/2/1996) FL 50+19/13 FLC 3+3/1 FAC 2+1 Others 1
Walsall (Free on 15/7/1998) FL 60+9/23 FLC 3/1 FAC 3+1 Others 5/1
Wycombe W (£75,000 on 7/9/2000) FL 25+1/10 FLC 2/1 FAC 9/2 Others 3

RAMSAY Scott Alan
Born: Hastings, 16 October 1980
Height: 6'0" Weight: 13.0

The 2000-2001 campaign proved to be a disappointing one for this young Brighton striker. Opportunities were few and far between and he only made the starting line-up for two league games. Strong on the ball and hard working, Scott will be hoping to feature more regularly for the Seagulls in the coming season.

Brighton & Hove A (From trainee on 29/6/1999) FL 10+25/2 FAC 0+2 Others 2

RANKIN Isaiah
Born: Edmonton, 22 May 1978
Height: 5'10" Weight: 11.6

Isaiah scored a pre-season goal for Bradford City in their Inter Toto Cup tie against Lithuanian outfit FK Atlantas before joining Bolton on loan at the start of the 2000-01 campaign as manager Sam Allardyce sought some extra attacking options. He made an explosive entrance, scoring two goals in his first four games, his cracker against Preston being particularly memorable, but this fine start fizzled out, however, and he returned to Bradford upon completion of his three-month loan period. He made his only Premiership appearance when coming on as a late substitute at Leicester on New Year's Day and soon afterwards he was sold to neighbours Barnsley, becoming new manager Nigel Spackman's first signing for the club. Although initially asked to play in an unaccustomed wide role, his pace proved a real asset as he helped pull the Tykes away from the relegation zone. He scored in the 3-2 win against Tranmere but niggling injuries brought his campaign to a premature halt and he later underwent a hernia operation.

Arsenal (From trainee on 12/9/1995) PL 0+1
Colchester U (Loaned on 25/9/1997) FL 10+1/5 Others 1
Bradford C (£1,300,000 on 14/8/1998) P/FL 15+22/4 FLC 2/1 FAC 0+2 Others 1+1/1
Birmingham C (Loaned on 19/1/2000) FL 11+2/4
Bolton W (Loaned on 11/8/2000) FL 9+7/2 FLC 2
Barnsley (£350,000 on 19/1/2001) FL 6+3/1

RANKINE Simon **Mark**
Born: Doncaster, 30 September 1969
Height: 5'9" Weight: 12.11
Club Honours: Div 2 '00

Having waited almost two years since his last league goal for Preston, Mark went goal crazy, scoring twice in September and then in successive matches in November, and adding a fifth in December, to double his previous tally for the club which had been achieved over a five-year period. Always giving 100 per cent, he remained a first choice in central midfield throughout the season - indeed no other player has played as often under manager David Moyes. Other milestones included marking his 550th senior appearance with a win at Fulham in October and playing his 200th game for North End on New Year's Day.

Doncaster Rov (From trainee on 4/7/1988) FL 160+4/20 FLC 8+1/1 FAC 8/2 Others 14/2
Wolverhampton W (£70,000 on 31/1/1992) FL 112+20/1 FLC 9+1 FAC 14+2 Others 7+2
Preston NE (£100,000 on 17/9/1996) FL 182+6/8 FLC 14+1/1 FAC 13/1 Others 6/1

RAPLEY Kevin John
Born: Reading, 21 September 1977
Height: 5'9" Weight: 10.8
Club Honours: Div 3 '99

Kevin found himself out of favour at Notts

County at the beginning of last season and after being restricted to outings from the subs' bench he spent much of the remainder of the campaign away from Meadow Lane. He spent two months on loan at Exeter in the autumn as manager Noel Blake sought to boost his fire power, but failed to score in nine outings for the Devon club and subsequently joined Scunthorpe, again on loan, in March. He came off the substitutes' bench to make his debut for the Iron at half-time in the 4-1 win over Plymouth, showing an excellent touch, pace and movement up front. However he then suffered a shin injury in training that put him on the sidelines for a few weeks. A quick right-footed striker he makes effective darting runs and is capable of scoring spectacular goals.

Brentford (From trainee on 8/7/1996) FL 27+24/12 FLC 3+5/3 FAC 0+2 Others 1
Southend U (Loaned on 20/11/1998) FL 9/4
Notts Co (£50,000 on 23/2/1999) FL 21+31/5 FLC 0+3 FAC 1+1/1 Others 1
Exeter C (Loaned on 1/11/2000) FL 6+1 FAC 1 Others 1
Scunthorpe U (Loaned on 17/3/2001) FL 1+4

RAVEN Paul Duncan
Born: Salisbury, 28 July 1970
Height: 6'1" Weight: 12.12
International Honours: E: Sch

Paul linked up with his old boss Alan Buckley at Grimsby in July 2000 and featured regularly for Grimsby Town in the opening matches of last season. His first team opportunities were subsequently limited by the return to fitness of Peter Handyside, the on-loan signing of Zhang Enhua and some niggling injuries. Paul is a reliable central defender who is effective both in the air and on the ground.

Doncaster Rov (From juniors on 6/6/1988) FL 52/4 FLC 2 FAC 5 Others 2
West Bromwich A (£100,000 on 23/3/1989) FL 249+10/15 FLC 20/2 FAC 10/3 Others 15/1
Doncaster Rov (Loaned on 27/11/1991) FL 7
Rotherham U (Loaned on 29/10/1998) FL 11/2
Grimsby T (Free on 13/7/2000) FL 11+4 FLC 2

RAWLE Mark Anthony
Born: Leicester, 27 April 1979
Height: 5'11" Weight: 12.0

This young striker joined Southend United last February from Conference club Boston United for whom he had scored an impressive 38 goals in 84 appearances in the previous two campaigns. Although only slightly built, Mark has good body strength and neat skills on the ball. He produced an excellent performance on his home debut against Rochdale but it was not until the penultimate game of the season against Cheltenham that he netted his first goal for the Blues.

Southend U (£60,000 + from Boston U on 23/2/2001) FL 11+3/1

RAWLINSON Mark David
Born: Bolton, 9 June 1975
Height: 5'10" Weight: 11.4

Mark occupied a regular place in the centre of midfield for Exeter City in 2000-01 until he suffered an ankle injury against Barnet last February which kept him out for five weeks. Accurate passing and non-stop running were both prominent features of his game and his experience of a higher level of football was evident. He was released by the Grecians in May.

Manchester U (From trainee on 5/7/1993)
Bournemouth (Free on 1/7/1995) FL 48+31/2 FLC 3+1 FAC 2+1 Others 4
Exeter C (Free on 18/7/2000) FL 18+7/2 FLC 1/1 FAC 1 Others 0+1

REA Simon
Born: Kenilworth, 20 September 1976
Height: 6'1" Weight: 13.2

Having broken into the Peterborough United team towards the end of the 1999-2000 campaign Simon went on to firmly establish himself as a regular in the line-up last term. A left-sided central defender who is very effective in the air and a fine reader of the game he also found time to score a couple of goals for Posh.

Birmingham C (From trainee on 27/1/1995) FL 0+1 Others 1+1
Peterborough U (Free on 24/8/1999) FL 46+4/3 FLC 2+1 FAC 3 Others 3/1

READ Paul Colin
Born: Harlow, 25 September 1973
Height: 5'10" Weight: 12.11
International Honours: E: Sch

Having spent the summer months with Swedish club OFK Ostersund, Paul returned to join Exeter City last November and went straight into the first team. He was one of the first-choice strikers for the Grecians until he fractured his pelvis in an innocuous looking collision during the game with Macclesfield in February. He returned to first-team action by the end of the season but managed just one goal for the Devon club.

Arsenal (From trainee on 11/10/1991)
Leyton Orient (Loaned on 10/3/1995) FL 11 Others 1
Southend U (Loaned on 6/10/1995) FL 3+1/1 Others 1
Wycombe W (£130,000 on 17/1/1997) FL 32+25/9 FLC 4/2 FAC 1+2/1 Others 1 (Freed during 1999 close season)
Luton T (Free from OFK Ostersund, Sweden on 6/12/1999) Others 0+1 (Free to OFK Ostersund in January 2000)
Exeter C (Free on 10/11/2000) FL 10+1/1

READY Karl
Born: Neath, 14 August 1972
Height: 6'1" Weight: 13.3
International Honours: W: 5; B-2; U21-5; Sch

Karl was one of several Queens Park Rangers' players to have a frustrating time with injuries in the 2000-01 campaign. He suffered a broken leg in the third game of the season against Crewe and then went down with an ankle injury in December soon after returning to the team. When he finally recovered fitness he began to form an effective defensive partnership with Chris Plummer and the flood of goals conceded was reduced. Karl is an experienced central defender who is comfortable both in the air and on the ground. He was one of 15 players to be released by the Loftus Road club in the summer.

Queens Park R (From trainee on 13/8/1990) F/PL 206+20/10 FLC 10+2/1 FAC 8

REBROV Sergei
Born: Donetsk, Ukraine, 3 June 1974
Height: 5'7" Weight: 11.1
International Honours: Ukraine: 43

Having chosen to join Tottenham in preference to playing in Italy, Sergei took some time to settle in at White Hart Lane and there was considerable media speculation of an early departure at the beginning of last season. He netted a double in the 3-2 win over Everton at the start of September and another against Leeds shortly afterwards, but it was not until the turn of the year that he began to establish himself and demonstrate his powers as a lethal striker. He went on to finish as the club's leading scorer with 12 goals in all competitions and by the end of the season he had become a firm favourite of the Tottenham faithful.

Tottenham H (£11,000,000 from Dynamo Kiev, Ukraine on 6/6/2000) PL 28+1/9 FLC 2 FAC 5/3

REDDINGTON Stuart
Born: Lincoln, 21 February 1978
Height: 6'2" Weight: 13.6

Once a junior with Lincoln City, Stuart opted to complete his education and it was from the Unibond League club Lincoln United that he joined Premiership Chelsea. Although he is yet to make his senior debut at Stamford Bridge he spent the summer of 2000 gaining experience in Sweden with Kalmar FF and after spending the first half of last season with the Blues' reserves he went out on loan to Third Division Mansfield to cover for injuries. A central or right-sided defender he made his Football League debut for the Stags at Blackpool and impressed with his skill in the air and distribution.

Chelsea (Signed from Lincoln U on 24/8/1999)
Mansfield T (Loaned on 16/3/2001) FL 9

REDDY Michael
Born: Kilkenny City, Ireland, 24 March 1980
Height: 6'1" Weight: 11.7
International Honours: RoI: U21-8; Yth

This exciting young striker featured in a handful of games for Sunderland in the early part of last season, and scored in the Worthington Cup second leg win at Luton. In January he joined Second Division Swindon Town for an extended loan period in a move that proved beneficial to both player and club. He announced his arrival in spectacular fashion, scoring within three minutes of his debut against Bury, and then winning a penalty when he was brought down in the box following a mazy run. He is a very lively forward with great pace, who can take on and beat defenders with his direct style of play. He continued to be a regular for the Republic of Ireland U21 team winning five more caps during the season.

Sunderland (£50,000 from Kilkenny C on 30/8/1999) PL 0+10/1 FLC 2+1/1 FAC 0+1
Swindon T (Loaned on 27/1/2001) FL 17+1/4 Others 1+1/1

REDFEARN Neil David
Born: Dewsbury, 20 June 1965
Height: 5'9" Weight: 13.0
Club Honours: Div 2 '91

This vastly experienced midfield player was placed on the transfer list by new Wigan boss Bruce Rioch at the start of the 2000-01 season and was restricted to infrequent appearances in the first team. He moved on to join Halifax Town as player-coach shortly before the transfer deadline and featured regularly for the Shaymen proving a steadying influence in the closing stages of the campaign as they successfully fought to retain their Football League status. A hard-tackling figure in the centre of midfield Neil is expected to become more involved with coaching at The Shay in 2001-02.

Bolton W (From Nottingham F juniors on 23/6/1982) FL 35/1 FLC 2 FAC 4
Lincoln C (£8,250 on 23/3/1984) FL 96+4/13 FLC 4 FAC 3/1 Others 7
Doncaster Rov (£17,500 on 22/8/1986) FL 46/14 FLC 2 FAC 3/1 Others 2
Crystal Palace (£100,000 on 31/7/1987) FL 57/10 FLC 6 FAC 1 Others 1
Watford (£150,000 on 21/11/1988) FL 22+2/3 FLC 1 FAC 6/3 Others 5/1
Oldham Ath (£150,000 on 12/1/1990) FL 56+6/16 FLC 3/1 FAC 7+1/3 Others 1
Barnsley (£150,000 on 5/9/1991) F/PL 289+3/71 FLC 21/6 FAC 20/6 Others 5
Charlton Ath (£1,000,000 on 1/7/1998) PL 29+1/3 FLC 2/1 FAC 1
Bradford C (£250,000 on 3/8/1999) PL 14+3/1 FLC 1+1 FAC 2
Wigan Ath (£112,500 on 17/3/2000) FL 18+4/7 FAC 1 Others 5
Halifax T (Free on 16/3/2001) FL 12

REDMILE Matthew (Matt) Ian
Born: Nottingham, 12 November 1976
Height: 6'3" Weight: 14.10
Club Honours: Div 3 '98

Matt started last season as a regular in the Notts County defence but lost his place following a heavy defeat at Walsall and in November he moved on loan to Shrewsbury Town. He quickly settled in at Gay Meadow and the deal became permanent as he went on to establish an effective partnership in the heart of the defence with Andrew Tretton. He is a commanding central defender who likes to get forward at set-pieces where his height is a great advantage.

Notts Co (From trainee on 4/7/1995) FL 140+7/7 FLC 11 FAC 13/1 Others 4
Shrewsbury T (£30,000 on 3/11/2000) FL 24/3 FAC 1

REDMOND Stephen (Steve)
Born: Liverpool, 2 November 1967
Height: 5'11" Weight: 11.7
Club Honours: FAYC '86
International Honours: E: U21-14; Yth

Steve's incredible appetite for the game was still in evidence during 2000-01 as he competed in his 17th consecutive season of senior football. He performed his twin roles as player and assistant-manager for Bury with great success and his vast experience was particularly important in steadying the young defenders around him. A solid and reliable central defender he is cool under pressure and reads the game well. Out of contract in the summer it was unclear at the time of writing whether he would continue as a player.

Manchester C (From apprentice on 3/12/1984) FL 231+4/7 FLC 24 FAC 17 Others 11
Oldham Ath (£300,000 on 10/7/1992) P/FL 195+10/4 FLC 20 FAC 10+2 Others 1+1
Bury (Free on 3/7/1998) FL 93+5/3 FLC 6 FAC 5 Others 3

REED Adam Maurice
Born: Bishop Auckland, 18 February 1975
Height: 6'1" Weight: 12.0

Adam was regularly paired alongside the experienced Neil Aspin in the centre of defence for Darlington in the first half of last season, but when Aspin left just after Christmas he found himself relegated to the subs' bench. He is now a fairly experienced defender himself having made over 100 league appearances for the Quakers and can always be relied upon to stand in very capably wherever he is asked to play. Adam is strong in the air and reads the game well.

Darlington (From trainee on 16/7/1993) FL 45+7/1 FLC 1+1 FAC 1 Others 3
Blackburn Rov (£200,000 on 9/8/1995)
Darlington (Loaned on 21/2/1997) FL 14
Rochdale (Loaned on 5/12/1997) FL 10 Others 2/1
Darlington (Free on 17/7/1998) FL 73+13/2 FLC 6 FAC 5+1 Others 2+3

REED Martin John
Born: Scarborough, 10 January 1978
Height: 6'0" Weight: 11.6

Martin struggled to break into the York City squad last season and managed just one start, appearing in the home game against Leyton Orient in October. He featured from the subs' bench at Kidderminster the following month but was released in March and later joined Scarborough. He is a strong-tackling no-nonsense central defender.

York C (From trainee on 4/7/1996) FL 39+7 FLC 2 FAC 3+1 Others 1

REES Jason Mark
Born: Aberdare, 22 December 1969
Height: 5'5" Weight: 10.6
International Honours: W: 1; B-1; U21-3; B-1; Yth; Sch

After surprisingly being released by Exeter Jason started last season with Tiverton Town before joining injury-hit Torquay United on non-contract terms in December. He immediately established himself in the Gulls' line-up and endeared himself to the club's supporters with his whole-hearted attitude and a tough-tackling, no-nonsense style. Originally played in a central midfield role he later moved to a position wide on the right. Jason confirmed his value to the club when he scored the opening goal in the crucial last day victory at Barnet that secured another season of Third Division football at Plainmoor. Out of contract in the summer his future was unclear at the time of writing.

Luton T (From trainee on 1/7/1988) FL 59+23 FLC 3+2 FAC 2+1 Others 5+1/2
Mansfield T (Loaned on 23/12/1993) FL 15/1 Others 1
Portsmouth (Free on 18/7/1994) FL 30+13/3 FLC 2+1 FAC 0+1
Exeter C (Loaned on 31/1/1997) FL 7
Cambridge U (Free on 8/8/1997) FL 17+3 FLC 2 Others 1
Exeter C (Free on 29/7/1998) FL 86+1/5 FLC 4 FAC 8 Others 6 (Freed during 2000 close season)
Torquay U (Free from Tiverton on 13/12/2000) FL 25/2

REEVES Alan
Born: Birkenhead, 19 November 1967
Height: 6'0" Weight: 12.0

Alan was a fixture in the heart of the Swindon Town defence last term, leading the team by example with a series of gritty determined displays. He weighed in with a few useful goals during the early part of the season, netting the winner at Ashton Gate and a last-minute effort at home to Wycombe to earn a point after the Robins had been reduced to ten men. He is a tall central defender who is particularly effective in the air.

Norwich C (Free from Heswall on 20/9/1988)
Gillingham (Loaned on 9/2/1989) FL 18
Chester C (£10,000 on 18/8/1989) FL 31+9/2 FLC 1+1 FAC 3 Others 3
Rochdale (Free on 2/7/1991) FL 119+2/9 FLC 12/1 FAC 6 Others 5
Wimbledon (£300,000 on 6/9/1994) PL 52+5/4 FLC 2+2 FAC 8
Swindon T (Free on 23/6/1998) FL 108+3/6 FLC 7/2 FAC 3 Others 1

REEVES David Edward
Born: Birkenhead, 19 November 1967
Height: 6'0" Weight: 12.6
Club Honours: Div 3 '95

David took a while to get going for Chesterfield last season but following a spell out injured he returned fresh to the team and became the irrepressible imaginative forward of old. He linked well with Luke Beckett and scored regularly, at one point briefly overtaking his strike partner as leading scorer. Dave passed the milestone of 500 Football League appearances at Macclesfield in March.

Sheffield Wed (Free from Heswall on 6/8/1986) FL 8+9/2 FLC 1+1/1 FAC 1+1 Others 0+1
Scunthorpe U (Loaned on 17/12/1986) FL 3+1/2
Scunthorpe U (Loaned on 1/10/1987) FL 6/4
Burnley (Loaned on 20/11/1987) FL 16/8 Others 2/1
Bolton W (£80,000 on 17/8/1989) FL 111+23/29 FLC 14+1/1 FAC 8+5/5 Others 9+2/7
Notts Co (£80,000 on 25/3/1993) FL 9+4/2 FLC 1+1
Carlisle U (£121,000 on 1/10/1993) FL 127/48 FLC 9/5 FAC 9/4 Others 23/7
Preston NE (Signed on 9/10/1996) FL 45+2/12 FLC 3+1/3 FAC 2/3 Others 1
Chesterfield (Signed on 6/11/1997) FL 140+6/42 FLC 9+1/4 FAC 3+1/1 Others 7/4

REGAN Carl Anthony
Born: Liverpool, 9 September 1980
Height: 6'0" Weight: 11.5
Club Honours: FAYC '98
International Honours: E: Yth

Signed from Everton during the close season, Carl went straight in the Barnsley first team at the beginning of last term but had the misfortune to be sent off just 20 minutes into his debut against Norwich. He returned from this, and was beginning to show considerable potential when he was sidelined by a knee ligament injury at the beginning of November and it was not until February that he regained match fitness. However once back in the team he was a regular through to the end of the season. A pacy right back with good control he will have learnt considerably from his introduction to senior football last term.

Everton (From trainee on 19/1/1998)
Barnsley (£20,000 on 15/6/2000) FL 25+2 FLC 3

REID Andrew Matthew
Born: Dublin, 29 July 1982
Height: 5'7" Weight: 11.12
International Honours: RoI: Yth (UEFA-U16 '98)

Andy made a superb Football League debut for Nottingham Forest against Sheffield United last November and scored the second goal to clinch a 2-0 victory for his side. He subsequently enjoyed a brief run in the squad and also netted against Huddersfield the following month. Initially used as a central striker he was later switched to a wide-left midfield role where he showed vision, pace and the ability to get the ball into the box. Andy was a member of the Republic of Ireland team that won the UEFA U16 title in 1998, when he set up the winning goal in the final, and was a regular with the U18s last term.

Nottingham F (From trainee on 16/8/1999) FL 9+5/2 FAC 1

REID Brian Robertson
Born: Paisley, 15 June 1970
Height: 6'2" Weight: 11.12
International Honours: S: U21-4

This experienced left-sided central defender began last season in the Scottish Premier League with Dunfermline. Brian featured twice for the Pars in early season fixtures before moving south to join Blackpool, initially for a three-month loan period. He produced some outstanding performances for the Tangerines, his strength in the air proving a real asset. Rarely absent apart from the occasional injury and suspension, he deputised as club captain when Ian Hughes was absent.

Morton (Free from Renfrew Waverley on 27/7/1988) SL 57/1 SLC 2 SC 7 Others 2/1
Glasgow R (Signed on 25/3/1991) SL 5
Morton (Signed on 11/3/1996) SL 68/3 SLC 4 SC 3 Others 5
Burnley (Signed on 4/9/1998) FL 30+1/3 FAC 1 Others 1
Dunfermline Ath (Free on 7/7/1999) SL 23+4/3 SLC 2 SC 1 Others 1
Blackpool (Free on 6/10/2000) FL 29/2 FAC 2 Others 3/1

REID Paul Robert
Born: Oldbury, 19 January 1968
Height: 5'9" Weight: 11.8

A totally committed, tough-tackling midfield battler, Paul was once again an automatic choice in Bury's line-up in 2000-01 when he enjoyed another consistent season. A player who can always be relied on when the going gets tough, his experience proved invaluable in helping bring on the youngsters in the Shakers' team. He netted four goals during the campaign including two from the penalty spot. Out of contract in the summer his future was unclear at the time of writing.

Leicester C (From apprentice on 9/1/1986) FL 140+22/21 FLC 13/4 FAC 5+1 Others 6+2
Bradford C (Loaned on 19/3/1992) FL 7
Bradford C (£25,000 on 27/7/1992) FL 80+2/15 FLC 3/2 FAC 3 Others 5/1
Huddersfield T (£70,000 on 20/5/1994) FL 70+7/6 FLC 9/1 FAC 5+1 Others 1
Oldham Ath (£100,000 on 27/3/1997) FL 93/6 FLC 4/1 FAC 8 Others 1
Bury (Free on 2/7/1999) FL 79+3/6 FLC 4 FAC 4 Others 3

REID Steven John
Born: Kingston, 10 March 1981
Height: 6'1" Weight: 12.4
Club Honours: Div 2 '01
International Honours: E: Yth; RoI: U2-3

Steven was a regular in the Millwall first-team squad last season and produced some excellent performances for the Second Division champions. He provided numerous chances for his colleagues and scored a respectable tally of six goals himself. His two major achievements during the campaign were to pass a career total of 100 senior appearances for the Lions and to win his first cap for the Republic of Ireland at U21 level when he appeared against Cyprus in February. Steven is a tall winger who is strong in the challenge and can also play at full back if required.

Millwall (From trainee on 18/5/1998) FL 63+21/7 FLC 4+2 FAC 4 Others 8+1

REILLY Alan
Born: Dublin, 22 August 1980
Height: 5'11" Weight: 12.6

Alan spent the early part of last season struggling for form but kept battling away and was rewarded with a regular place in the Halifax Town squad from December until the end of the campaign. A first choice in the starting line-up from March he netted two goals including a great 25-yarder in the 4-3 home defeat by Scunthorpe United. He is a talented left winger with great crossing ability.

Manchester C (From trainee on 23/9/1998)
Halifax T (Free on 3/12/1999) FL 30+13/2 FLC 1 Others 1+2

REUSER Martijn Franciscus
Born: Amsterdam, Holland, 1 February 1975
Height: 5'9" Weight: 11.7
International Honours: Holland: 1; U21-12

Having created a great impact at Ipswich in the closing stages of the 1999-2000 campaign, Martijn found it difficult to repeat this last term and in the first half of the season he was mainly used as a substitute. It was not until the final third of the campaign that he established himself in the side and he proved his worth by scoring six goals in those 11 games. Capable of playing anywhere in midfield or as an outright striker, he is an expert striker of a dead ball, whether a corner or a free-kick. He scored twice in the 3-1 win against Bradford, one an individual run in which he beat three defenders before curling the ball into the net, the second direct from a free-kick, and he then struck the only goal of the game at West Ham with a curling free-kick. However, perhaps his most significant goal was the header from Alun Armstrong's cross in the closing stages of the game against Manchester City that sealed his opponents' relegation to Division One.

Ipswich T (£1,000,000 + from Vitesse Arnhem, Holland, ex Ajax, on 23/3/2000) P/FL 15+19/8 FLC 3+4 FAC 1 Others 0+3/2

REVELL Alexander (Alex) David
Born: Cambridge, 7 July 1983
Height: 6'3" Weight: 12.0

Alex was one of several promising youngsters to be introduced to first-team football by new Cambridge United boss John Beck in the closing weeks of last season when he came off the subs' bench for the last 15 minutes of the game at Northampton in April. A tall and pacy forward with good technique he can play either as an out-and-out striker or wide on the right. Alex was rewarded with a professional contract by the U's towards the end of the campaign.

Cambridge U (From trainee on 21/4/2001) FL 2+2

REZAI Carl Sarbaz
Born: Manchester, 16 October 1982
Height: 5'10" Weight: 11.8

Carl is another youngster who has developed through the ranks with Halifax Town. He signed a two-and-a-half-year contract last October shortly after Paul Bracewell took over as manager and marked his senior debut with a stunning goal against Cheltenham. He then went on to enjoy a short run in the first team and will be looking to build on that experience in the 2001-02 campaign. He can play either at right back or in a central midfield role.

Halifax T (From trainee on 28/10/2000) FL 8+3 FAC 1 Others 1

RIBEIRO Bruno
Born: Setubal, Portugal, 22 October 1975
Height: 5'8" Weight: 12.2

Bruno again failed to establish himself in the Sheffield United first team last season and after a handful of early-season appearances he returned to Portugal in November, signing a long-term loan deal with Uniao Leiria. A skilful and determined midfield player who is a favourite of the Bramall Lane crowd it was unclear at the time of writing whether he would be back with the Blades in 2001-02.

Leeds U (£500,000 from Vittoria Setubal, Portugal on 18/7/1997) PL 35+7/4 FLC 3+1/1 FAC 4/1 Others 1+1
Sheffield U (£500,000 on 25/10/1999) FL 12+13/1 FLC 3 FAC 1+1

RICARD Cuesta **Hamilton**
Born: Colombia, 12 January 1974
Height: 6'2" Weight: 14.5
International Honours: Colombia: 29; U21

'Ham the Man' struggled to score goals for Middlesbrough in the first half of the 2000-01 campaign, although ironically on the one occasion that he did find the net, in the Worthington Cup game against Macclesfield, he actually scored a hat-trick. However he turned things round after Christmas to net six goals and thus finish second-top scorer for the season. Despite a rather languid style this striker is quite lethal around the box and has scored some remarkable goals, ably assisted by his acceleration from a standing start and an ability to flight the ball with deceptive speed. His penalty kicks too are almost casual, yet invariably successful. He almost strolls up to the spot before launching the ball which is soon wrapped up in the net about to be retrieved by some unfortunate 'keeper.

Middlesbrough (£2,000,000 + from Deportivo Cali, Colombia on 13/3/1998) P/FL 86+20/33 FLC 11+1/8 FAC 5/2

RICHARDS Dean Ivor
Born: Bradford, 9 June 1974
Height: 6'2" Weight: 13.5
International Honours: E: U21-4

Dean proved his worth for Southampton last season with a series of commanding performances that must have brought him close to international recognition. Without doubt his central defensive partnership with Claus Lundekvam was the cornerstone on which the Saints' best league performance for 18 years was built, and they were particularly effective in the early part of 2001 when just one Premiership goal was conceded in the first three months of the year. Although there was media talk of a transfer to a bigger club he remained loyal to the Saints, signing a two-year extension to his contract in March.

Bradford C (From trainee on 10/7/1992) FL 82+4/4 FLC 7/1 FAC 4/1 Others 3+2
Wolverhampton W (£1,850,000 on 25/3/1995) FL 118+4/7 FLC 11 FAC 10/1 Others 2
Southampton (Free on 28/7/1999) PL 63/3 FLC 6/2 FAC 4+1/2

RICHARDS Ian
Born: Barnsley, 5 October 1979
Height: 5'8" Weight: 11.5

Ian appeared in the starting line-up for Halifax at Carlisle on the opening day of last season but then struggled with niggling injuries and never really established himself in the side. When called upon he never let the side down although he failed to add to his goal tally for the Shaymen. He is a young midfield player with good distribution who is an effective ball winner. Out of contract in the summer his future was uncertain at the time of writing.

Blackburn Rov (From trainee on 11/7/1997)
Halifax T (Free on 5/7/1999) FL 13+11 FLC 1 FAC 1

RICHARDS Justin
Born: West Bromwich, 16 October 1980
Height: 5'10" Weight: 11.0

Unable to break into the first team at The Hawthorns Justin moved on to Second Division Bristol Rovers last January. However he found it difficult to establish himself in a team struggling against relegation and made only occasional appearances for the Pirates in the closing weeks of the season. A lightning-quick striker, he impressed the Rovers faithful with his hard work and an eagerness to learn.

West Bromwich A (From trainee on 8/1/1999) FL 0+1 FAC 0+1
Bristol Rov (£75,000 on 19/1/2001) FL 3+4 Others 0+1

RICHARDS Marc John
Born: Wolverhampton, 8 July 1982
Height: 6'0" Weight: 12.7
International Honours: E: Yth

Marc is a bustling old-fashioned-style centre forward with a proven record as a goal-scorer at junior level. Previously capped by England U17s he was a regular in the U18s last term and gave an encouraging performance on his first-team debut for Blackburn in the Worthington Cup third round tie against West Ham. One of many promising youngsters on the books at Ewood Park he will be aiming for more senior outings in 2001-02.

Blackburn Rov (From trainee on 12/7/1999) FLC 1

RICHARDS Tony Spencer
Born: Newham, 17 September 1973
Height: 5'11" Weight: 13.1

Tony joined Barnet from Leyton Orient just days before the start of the 2000-01 campaign but injuries limited his appearances until October. He then produced some fine displays, finding the net regularly until the supply of goals dried up in the new year. An effective striker who is adept at holding the ball up he will be hoping to break his lean spell early in the 2001-02 season. He was placed on the open to offers list following the Bees' relegation to the Conference.

West Ham U (From trainee on 14/8/1992. Free to Hong Kong R during 1993 close season)
Cambridge U (Signed from Sudbury T on 10/8/1995) FL 29+13/5 FLC 1 Others 3
Leyton Orient (£10,000 on 21/7/1997) FL 47+16/11 FLC 3+3/1 FAC 2/3 Others 5
Barnet (Free on 11/8/2000) FL 27+6/8 FLC 1/1 FAC 1/1 Others 1

RICHARDSON Ian George
Born: Barking, 22 October 1970
Height: 5'10" Weight: 11.1
Club Honours: Div 3 '98
International Honours: E: SP-1

Ian switched from a midfield role to a position on the left-side of central defence for Notts County last season but continued to perform with his usual effectiveness. Although absent with a knee injury for a lengthy spell in the new year he returned to the line-up for the closing matches. A player who has great pace and is very strong in the air, he is popular with the Meadow Lane faithful.

Birmingham C (£60,000 from Dagenham & Redbridge on 23/8/1995) FL 3+4 FLC 3+1 FAC 2 Others 1+2
Notts Co (£200,000 on 19/1/1996) FL 136+9/15 FLC 12 FAC 14/1 Others 6

RICHARDSON Jonathan (Jon) Derek
Born: Nottingham, 29 August 1975
Height: 6'0" Weight: 12.6

Jon joined Oxford United shortly before the start of the 2000-01 campaign and despite playing in a struggling side that at times seemed to leak goals he performed consistently in the back line, rarely missing a match. An experienced right-sided central defender he occasionally captained the U's and never let the team down.

Exeter C (From trainee on 7/7/1994) FL 242+5/8 FLC 11/3 FAC 15/1 Others 13
Oxford U (Free on 8/8/2000) FL 41/2 FLC 2 FAC 2 Others 1

RICHARDSON Leam Nathan
Born: Leeds, 19 November 1979
Height: 5'7" Weight: 11.4

Yet another inspired recruit by Bolton manager Sam Allardyce, Leam was signed in the close season after being released by Blackburn. He made his debut for Wanderers in the opening game against Preston and followed this up with occasional substitute appearances before figuring prominently in the side during the final six weeks of the season. His tenacious battling qualities were exactly what was needed at this crucial stage of the campaign, and if he continues to display similar form in 2001-02 he should start to feature prominently in the first-team line-up.

Blackburn Rov (From trainee on 31/12/1997) FLC 1
Bolton W (£50,000 on 13/7/2000) FL 5+7 FLC 1+1 FAC 1

RICHARDSON Lee James
Born: Halifax, 12 March 1969
Height: 5'11" Weight: 11.0

Lee was very much the unsung hero of Chesterfield's promotion campaign last season. Having fought a lengthy battle to overcome injuries he joined the Spireites in August 2000 and settled down well in the midfield, providing a firm platform for other less experienced players. Lee used his vision to great effect and also did much of the ball winning for Marcus Ebdon. As the campaign progressed his stamina improved and he developed into a great asset for the club.

Halifax T (From trainee on 6/7/1987) FL 43+13/2 FLC 4 FAC 4+2 Others 6
Watford (£175,000 on 9/2/1989) FL 40+1/1 FLC 1+1 FAC 1
Blackburn Rov (£250,000 on 15/8/1990) FL 50+12/3 FLC 1 Others 2+2
Aberdeen (£152,000 on 16/9/1992) SL 59+5/6 SLC 2/1 SC 8/2 Others 3/1
Oldham Ath (£300,000 on 12/8/1994) FL 82+6/21 FLC 6/2 FAC 3 Others 4
Stockport Co (Loaned on 15/8/1997) FL 4+2
Huddersfield T (£65,000 on 24/10/1997) FL 29+7/3 FAC 0+2
Bury (Loaned on 27/8/1999) FL 5/1
Livingston (Free on 3/2/2000) SL 6 SC 1
Chesterfield (Free on 11/8/2000) FL 30 FLC 2 Others 2

RICHARDSON Marcus Glenroy
Born: Reading, 31 August 1977
Height: 6'2" Weight: 13.2

Having spent the 1999-2000 campaign with Slough Town Marcus had trials with a number of Football League clubs in the early part of last season including Cambridge, Reading and Wycombe before joining Ryman League club Harrow Borough in January. He finally signed for Cambridge United in March and made a sensational start to his senior career, coming off the bench at Stoke to score a last-minute winner when he beat the offside trap, ran 30 yards and slotted the ball home. He subsequently featured regularly from the subs' bench as he took time to adjust to the standards of Second Division football. Marcus is a promising young striker who is quick off the mark and very strong on the ball.

Cambridge U (Free from Harrow Borough on 16/3/2001) FL 3+7/2

RICHARDSON Nicholas (Nick) John
Born: Halifax, 11 April 1967
Height: 6'1" Weight: 12.6
Club Honours: Div 3 '93; WC '93

Nick went on the transfer list at Conference club Chester in July 2000 and rarely featured last season. He was released in February and returned to Third Division football signing for York City. He appeared in the starting line-up for the first time in the vital win at Rochdale that ended a long lean run for the Minstermen, and went on to play an impressive role as the club finished the 2000-2001 campaign strongly. A creative and efficient worker in midfield he scored just one goal, netting in the 2-0 home win over Darlington.

Halifax T (Free from Emley on 15/11/1988) FL 89+12/17 FLC 6+4/2 FAC 2+1/1 Others 6/1
Cardiff C (£35,000 on 13/8/1992) FL 106+5/13 FLC 4 FAC 6 Others 12+2/2
Wrexham (Loaned on 21/10/1994) FL 4/2
Chester C (Loaned on 16/12/1994) FL 6/1
Bury (£22,500 on 8/8/1995) FL 3+2 FLC 1
Chester C (£40,000 on 7/9/1995) FL 158+11/11 FLC 11/1 FAC 8/2 Others 5/1
York C (Free on 16/2/2001) FL 16+1/1

RICKERS Paul Steven
Born: Pontefract, 9 May 1975
Height: 5'10" Weight: 11.0

Paul was once again a regular in the Oldham Athletic line-up last season. Solid but unspectacular, he worked tirelessly in midfield and has now made over 200 Football League appearances for the club. The high point of his campaign was surely the 2-0 win at Huddersfield in the Worthington Cup first round second leg when he gave a fine performance and scored the two goals that knocked the First Division club out of the competition.

Oldham Ath (From trainee on 16/7/1993) FL 229+8/18 FLC 11/2 FAC 16+1 Others 4+1

RICKETTS Michael Barrington
Born: Birmingham, 4 December 1978
Height: 6'2" Weight: 11.12

What a phenomenal first season with Bolton for this young Birmingham-born striker! Signed for a bargain fee, he scored in his first game against Preston and continued to find the net with some regularity for the remainder of the campaign. His early chances were mostly limited to substitute appearances but this didn't stop him from scoring consistently, and he went on to finish the season as the Wanderers' leading scorer by a comfortable margin. If Michael works on improving his all round game, the results, when coupled with his natural goal-scoring ability, are likely to be devastating for opposing defenders.

Walsall (From trainee on 13/9/1996) FL 31+45/14 FLC 2+4 FAC 2+2 Others 3+1/1
Bolton W (£500,000 on 17/7/2000) FL 24+15/19 FLC 0+1/1 FAC 2+2/2 Others 1+2/2

RICKETTS Samuel (Sam) Derek
Born: Aylesbury, 11 October 1981
Height: 6'0" Weight: 11.12

Having graduated through the ranks at Oxford Sam made his Football League debut at Swindon last October and went on to enjoy a brief run in the side under caretaker-manager Mike Ford. He broke into the side again in the new year and will be looking to establish himself in the U's squad in the coming season. He is a promising right-sided player who featured both at full back and in midfield. Sam is the son of the show jumper Derek Ricketts and a nephew of the former jockey John Francombe.

Oxford U (From trainee on 20/4/2000) FL 13+1 Others 1

RIDEOUT Paul David
Born: Bournemouth, 14 August 1964
Height: 5'11" Weight: 12.10
Club Honours: FAC '95; CS '95
International Honours: E: U21-5; Yth; Sch

Paul returned to English football last summer after several years abroad and put his plans to move into coaching on hold as he elected to join Tranmere Rovers shortly before the start of the 2000-01 campaign. He showed his versatility by appearing both as a striker and in a midfield role and despite his advancing years produced several 'Man of the Match' performances. Undoubtedly the high point of his campaign came in the FA Cup fifth round replay against Southampton when he netted a stunning hat-trick as Rovers fought back from a three-goal deficit to win 4-3. Paul has since signed a further contract that should keep him at Prenton Park for another season.

Swindon T (From apprentice on 15/8/1981) FL 90+5/38 FLC 3/2 FAC 7/1
Aston Villa (£200,000 on 1/6/1983) FL 50+4/19 FLC 4+2/3 FAC 1+1 Others 1 (£400,000 to Bari, Italy on 1/7/1985)
Southampton (£430,000 on 5/7/1988) FL 68+7/19 FLC 13/2 FAC 5+2 Others 1
Swindon T (Loaned on 28/3/1991) FL 9/1
Notts Co (£250,000 on 16/9/1991) FL 9+2/3 FLC 2 FAC 1 Others 2
Glasgow R (£500,000 on 10/1/1992) SL 7+5/1 SLC 0+1 SC 1
Everton (£500,000 on 14/8/1992) PL 86+26/29 FLC 11+2/3 FAC 9+1/3 Others 5/1 (£250,000 to Huang Dong Vanguards, China on 16/4/1997)
Tranmere Rov (Free from Shengzhen, China on 14/7/2000) FL 28+3/2 FLC 5/2 FAC 5/3

RIDLER David (Dave) George
Born: Liverpool, 12 March 1976
Height: 6'1" Weight: 12.2

This reliable and unhurried defender performed well both at full back and as a partner to Brian Carey in the centre of the Wrexham defence last season. Unfortunately he missed some games through suspension and this is an area where he needs to show some improvement. Dave has been an important member of the Robins' back line in recent seasons but was out of contract in the summer at the time of writing his future was unclear.

Wrexham (Free from Rockys on 3/7/1996) FL 104+12/1 FLC 5 FAC 10+2 Others 8+2/1

RIDLEY Lee
Born: Scunthorpe, 5 December 1981
Height: 5'9" Weight: 11.2

Scunthorpe's youth-team captain made his Football League debut in March at Darlington when he gave a solid performance at left back in place of the suspended Andy Dawson. Lee is a strong and versatile left-sided player who can also play in midfield or at centre half. He was reported to have been offered professional terms for the 2001-02 season.

Scunthorpe U (Trainee) FL 1+1

RIEDLE Karl-Heinz
Born: Weiler, Germany, 16 September 1965
Height: 5'10" Weight: 11.6
Club Honours: Div 1 '01
International Honours: Germany: 42; U21; Yth

Injuries blighted Karl-Heinz's first full season at Fulham, while the goal-scoring exploits of Messrs Saha, Boa Morte and Hayles restricted him mostly to substitute appearances when he was fit. Even so he played a very important part as Jean Tigana rotated his strikers later in the season and headed a vital clinching goal in the 2-0 win at Queens Park Rangers. Out of contract in the summer it was unclear where he would be playing in 2001-01 at the time of writing.

Liverpool (£1,600,000 from Borussia Dortmund, Germany, ex Augsburg, Blau-Weiss 90, Werder Bremen, Lazio, on 4/8/1997) PL 34+26/11 FLC 3+4/2 FAC 2 Others 3+4/2
Fulham (£250,000 on 28/9/1999) FL 16+19/6 FAC 1

RIGGOTT Christopher (Chris)
Born: Derby, 1 September 1980
Height: 6'3" Weight: 12.2
International Honours: E: U21-4; Yth

Having begun the 2000-01 season as one of a number of promising young players at Pride Park, Chris made such progress during the campaign that he was soon regarded as a regular in the first team. A right-sided centre back who tackles cleanly and can dominate in the penalty area, he fitted in well in a three-man defensive formation and clearly benefited from the coaching provided by Colin Todd. He was outstanding on many occasions, none more so than in the drawn game at Anfield. His sterling performances earned him a place in the England U21 squad and after making his debut in the friendly against Spain he won three more caps. A lifelong Rams supporter himself, he signed an extended contract with the club that will run until June 2005.

Derby Co (From trainee on 5/10/1998) PL 29+3/3 FLC 3/1 FAC 2/1

RIIHILAHTI Aki
Born: Helsinki, Finland, 9 September 1976
Height: 6'1" Weight: 12.6
International Honours: Finland: 20

Aki joined Crystal Palace shortly before the transfer deadline and made his debut in the 1-0 win at home to Crewe. A talented midfield player he is an established figure in the Finland national side who scored the winner against Albania last September and also netted in the 2-1 defeat by England at Anfield.

Crystal Palace (£200,000 from Valerenga, Norway, ex HJK Helsinki, on 22/3/2001) FL 9/1

RIOCH Gregor (Greg) James
Born: Sutton Coldfield, 24 June 1975
Height: 5'11" Weight: 12.10

This Macclesfield utility player missed the start of the 2000-2001 season with a hamstring injury and played his first match at the end of September, coming on from the bench to take the right-back position. He featured just a handful of times until the beginning of January when he was introduced on the left side of midfield where his speed and agility were put to good use. He then moved to Shrewsbury Town on transfer deadline day making his debut in the 2-2 draw at Lincoln. He featured at left back for the Gay Meadow club performing with commitment and enthusiasm. Greg holds both UEFA 'A' and 'B' coaching certificates and is the son of the former Wigan manager Bruce Rioch.

Luton T (From trainee on 19/7/1993)
Barnet (Loaned on 17/9/1993) FL 3 FLC 2 Others 1
Peterborough U (Free on 11/8/1995) FL 13+5 FLC 2 FAC 2+1 Others 2+1
Hull C (Free on 10/7/1996) FL 86+5/6 FLC 7/3 FAC 5/1 Others 3
Macclesfield T (Free on 5/7/1999) FL 58+1/6 FLC 2 FAC 2 Others 2
Shrewsbury T (Free on 22/3/2001) FL 8

RIPLEY Stuart Edward
Born: Middlesbrough, 20 November 1967
Height: 5'11" Weight: 13.0
Club Honours: PL '95
International Honours: E: 2; U21-8; Yth

Stuart found it difficult to win a place in the Southampton team at the beginning of the 2000-01 season and started just one Premiership match. In November he moved on loan to Barnsley and was an instant hit, scoring a spectacular goal on his debut against Blackburn. He did well in two months at Oakwell but a change of manager did not help his cause for a permanent transfer and he returned to The Dell. He subsequently joined Sheffield Wednesday for another loan period in March and had a successful time at Hillsborough. The Owls' caretaker-manager Peter Shreeves used him in a wide-left midfield role and his know-how and professionalism proved an asset to the team as they finally turned their season around to finish well clear of any relegation worries. An old-fashioned winger with the ability to beat defenders and deliver a telling cross, he is always willing to track back and help out in defence.

Middlesbrough (From apprentice on 23/12/1985) FL 210+39/26 FLC 21+2/3 FAC 17+1/1 Others 20+1/1
Bolton W (Loaned on 18/2/1986) FL 5/1 Others 0+1
Blackburn Rov (£1,300,000 on 20/7/1992) PL 172+15/13 FLC 18 FAC 14/3 Others 8+1
Southampton (£1,500,000 on 10/7/1998) PL 35+13/1 FLC 4 FAC 2+1
Barnsley (Loaned on 7/11/2000) FL 8+2/1
Sheffield Wed (Loaned on 22/3/2001) FL 5+1/1

RISOM Henrik
Born: Denmark, 24 July 1968
Height: 5'11" Weight: 11.13
International Honours: Denmark: 9

This experienced Dane joined Stoke City last August following an impressive pre-season trial but never really established himself in the first team in 2000-01. Principally used as cover in a midfield 'holding' role his main strengths are his thoughtful distribution and his ability to deliver set pieces. Henrik was released by City in the summer.

Stoke C (£20,000 from Vejle BK, Denmark, ex Lyngby, Dynamo Dresden, Odense BK, Silkeborg, on 1/8/2000) FL 9+16 FLC 2+2 FAC 1 Others 4

RITCHIE Andrew (Andy) Timothy
Born: Manchester, 28 November 1960
Height: 5'10" Weight: 12.13
Club Honours: Div 2 '91
International Honours: E: U21-1; Yth; Sch

The 2000-01 campaign was Andy's third as manager of Oldham and it was generally a case of aiming high on a low budget with the end result being a respectable mid-table finish. On the field, he hung up his boots with a swansong against rivals Wigan Athletic in the LDV Vans Trophy. With a flu' bug affecting the Latics, Andy called himself into action aged 40 yrs 42 days and he played for the final 11 minutes before Wigan scored an extra-time golden goal to win the tie 3-2.

Manchester U (From apprentice on 5/12/1977) FL 26+7/13 FLC 3+2 FAC 3+1
Brighton & Hove A (£500,000 on 17/10/1980) FL 82+7/23 FLC 3+1/1 FAC 9/2
Leeds U (£150,000 on 25/3/1983) FL 127+9/40 FLC 11/3 FAC 9/1 Others 2+1
Oldham Ath (£50,000 on 14/8/1987) F/PL 187+30/82 FLC 18+2/18 FAC 8+2/4 Others 3
Scarborough (Free on 3/8/1995) FL 59+9/17 FLC 4+1/2 FAC 4/1 Others 1
Oldham Ath (Free on 21/2/1997) FL 14+12/2 FLC 1/1 FAC 1+2 Others 0+1

RITCHIE Paul Simon
Born: Kirkcaldy, 21 August 1975
Height: 5'11" Weight: 12.0
Club Honours: SC '98
International Honours: S: 6; B; U21-7; Sch

After failing to secure a first-team place with Rangers, Paul became available for transfer and moved south of the border to join Manchester City shortly before the 2000-01 season started. He made his debut in the away game at Leeds when City won 2-1 and retained his place for a decent run in the side until injury struck. A groin problem kept him out of action for two months and although he returned briefly in the new year the injury flared up again and he was out of action for the remainder of the campaign.

Heart of Midlothian (From Links U on 31/7/1992) SL 132+1/5 SLC 10+1 SC 11/3 Others 6
Bolton W (Free on 22/12/1999) FL 13+1 FLC 1 FAC 3+1 Others 2
Glasgow R (Free on 26/2/2000)
Manchester C (£500,000 on 22/8/2000) PL 11+1 FLC 3 FAC 1

RIVERS Mark Alan
Born: Crewe, 26 November 1975
Height: 5'11" Weight: 11.2

A regular member of the Crewe Alexandra first team since graduating through the club's youth programme in the mid-1990's, Mark had another fine season at Gresty Road last term. A versatile forward with good pace, he is particularly effective when cutting in from wide positions, but can also play as an out-and-out striker if required. He continued to score regularly and his tally of ten goals made him the Railwaymen's second-top scorer for the season. He was reported to have joined Norwich City for a substantial fee in the summer.

Crewe Alex (From trainee on 6/5/1994) FL 177+26/43 FLC 14+1/8 FAC 12/4 Others 6+3/3

RIZA Omer Kerime
Born: Enfield, 8 November 1979
Height: 5'9" Weight: 11.2

After beginning last season with West Ham's reserves Omer joined Barnet on loan in October and made a huge impact with the Third Division club. The Bees were keen to make the transfer a permanent one but no deal could be agreed and he returned to Upton Park. He was loaned out again to Cambridge United in March and after scoring on his debut against Oldham he became an instant hit with the U's fans. Omer is an exciting right-sided striker with blistering pace and a great eye for goal.

Arsenal (From trainee on 1/7/1998) FLC 0+1
West Ham U (£20,000 on 7/12/1999)
Barnet (Loaned on 20/10/2000) FL 7+3/4 FAC 1 Others 2/1
Cambridge U (Loaned on 2/3/2001) FL 10+2/3

ROACH Neville
Born: Reading, 29 September 1978
Height: 5'10" Weight: 11.1

After being released by Southend United at the end of the 1999-200 campaign Neville had pre-season trials with Kingstonian before jetting off to Australia to sign for NSL club Eastern Pride. He returned home at the end of January and after a very brief liaison with St Albans City he linked up with Oldham Athletic. Fitness blighted his short spell at Boundary Park and he managed just one substitute appearance, coming on for the final 30 minutes of the 5-0 defeat at champions Millwall on the last day of the season. However although he looked the pick of the Latics' side he was not offered a contract. Neville is a promising young striker who is very quick and has good skills on the ball.

Reading (From trainee on 10/5/1997) FL 5+11/1 FLC 1+4/1 FAC 0+1 Others 0+1
Southend U (£30,000 on 26/2/1999) FL 13+3/2 FLC 1+1 Others 0+1 (Freed during 2000 close season)
Oldham Ath (Free from Eastern Pride, Australia, via St Albans C, on 20/3/2001) FL 0+1

ROBERTS Andrew (Andy) James
Born: Dartford, 20 March 1974
Height: 5'10" Weight: 13.0
Club Honours: FAYC '91
International Honours: E: U21-5

An ongoing injury prevented Andy from playing in the opening games of the 2000-01 season for Wimbledon but once he had returned to fitness he took his place in the team, forming an effective unit with Trond Andersen and Damien Francis in the centre of the park. Very much an unsung hero for the Dons he is a defensive central midfield player who brings a hardened edge to the middle line.

Millwall (From trainee on 29/10/1991) FL 132+6/5 FLC 12/2 FAC 7 Others 4/1
Crystal Palace (£2,520,000 on 29/7/1995) F/PL 106+2/2 FLC 7+1 FAC 8 Others 6/1
Wimbledon (£1,200,000 + on 10/3/1998) P/FL 74+9/5 FLC 11+1/1 FAC 3+2

ROBERTS Christian (Chris) John
Born: Cardiff, 22 October 1979
Height: 5'10" Weight: 12.8
International Honours: W: U21-1; Yth

Chris was in superb form for Exeter City throughout 2000-01 and appeared in almost every game although his partners up front were chopped and changed. Lightning fast and with a powerful shot he was willing to take on defenders at every opportunity and finished as the club's second-top scorer. He missed a number of games around the turn of the year due to a knee operation but was back in the starting line-up in a matter of weeks. One of the highlights of his season was a superb double bagged against York in the 3-1 win last September. Chris was moved from a centre-forward role to playing behind the front players in the final matches of the campaign.

Cardiff C (From trainee on 8/10/1997) FL 6+17/3 FLC 2 FAC 2+3 Others 0+2
Exeter C (Free on 24/7/2000) FL 33+9/7 FLC 1+1 FAC 0+1 Others 1

ROBERTS Darren Anthony
Born: Birmingham, 12 October 1969
Height: 6'0" Weight: 12.4

This experienced striker began the 2000-01 campaign as a regular for Exeter City and netted a glorious equaliser in the 1-1 draw at Barnet in September. However he then fell out of favour and in November he moved on loan to Unibond League club Barrow. Darren appeared for the Cumbrian club in their FA Cup tie against Leyton Orient and after returning to Devon briefly in January he spent the remainder of the season at Barrow.

Wolverhampton W (£20,000 from Burton A on 23/4/1992) FL 12+9/5 FLC 0+1 Others 1+1
Hereford U (Loaned on 18/3/1994) FL 5+1/5
Chesterfield (Free on 18/7/1994) FL 10+15/1 FLC 3/1 FAC 1+1 Others 2+5/3
Darlington (Free on 30/7/1996) FL 76+20/33 FLC 6+2/4 FAC 5/1 Others 3
Peterborough U (Loaned on 20/2/1998) FL 2+1
Scarborough (Free on 5/2/1999) FL 18/3
Exeter C (Free on 18/7/2000) FL 3+5/1 FLC 0+1

Darren Roberts

ROBERTS Gareth Wyn
Born: Wrexham, 6 February 1978
Height: 5'7" Weight: 12.6
Club Honours: FAYC '96
International Honours: W: 4; B-1; U21-10

Gareth had another solid and steady campaign for Tranmere last season and was rarely absent in a campaign that ended with the disappointment of relegation. A tenacious defender who is equally at home at either left back or left wing back he tackles hard and is always fully committed to the cause. Something of an unsung hero at Prenton Park he was a regular in the Welsh international squad in the first half of the season winning a further cap against Belarus.

Liverpool (From trainee on 22/5/1996. £50,000 to Panionios, Greece on 15/1/1999)
Tranmere Rov (Free on 5/8/1999) FL 69+2/1 FLC 12 FAC 5+1

ROBERTS Iwan Wyn
Born: Bangor, 26 June 1968
Height: 6'3" Weight: 14.2
International Honours: W: 13; B-1; Yth; Sch

Iwan once again provided the bulk of Norwich's goals in their disappointing 2000-01 campaign, finishing as top scorer for the third season in succession. His style is not spectacular, but it is certainly effective - he is a big, awkward centre forward who is very difficult to play against. He receives the ball from all angles and at all heights, and then uses it efficiently to keep possession - but it is when he is in the penalty area that he comes into his own. He has a natural goal-scoring instinct to arrive in the right place at the right time and registered the 200th goal of his career while netting a hat-trick against Stockport at Carrow Road in February. He was a regular for Wales last term where he often teamed up with his former Canary colleague, Craig Bellamy.

Watford (From trainee on 4/7/1988) FL 40+23/9 FLC 6+2/3 FAC 1+6 Others 5
Huddersfield T (£275,000 on 2/8/1990) FL 141+1/50 FLC 13+1/6 FAC 12/4 Others 14/8
Leicester C (£100,000 on 25/11/1993) P/FL 92+8/41 FLC 5/1 FAC 5/2 Others 1
Wolverhampton W (£1,300,000 + on 15/7/1996) FL 24+9/12 FLC 2 FAC 0+1 Others 2
Norwich C (£900,000 on 9/7/1997) FL 157+7/56 FLC 14+2/10 FAC 3/2

ROBERTS Jason Andre Davis
Born: Park Royal, 25 January 1978
Height: 5'11" Weight: 12.7
International Honours: Grenada: 6

Signed by West Bromwich Albion for a club record fee during the close season, Jason quickly established a fine understanding up front with Lee Hughes. His direct approach, aggressive style and goal-awareness, allied to hard work, good ball control and spirited endeavour made him a handful for any defender. Despite suffering an occasional dip in form he always gave 100 per cent effort and scored some fine goals, his best coming against Nottingham Forest just prior to Christmas - smart control, a quick turn and a thumping right-foot drive high into the net from 25 yards. He also netted twice at Hillsborough in October when Albion recorded their first victory on Wednesday soil for 35 years. Jason is a cousin of former Baggies' favourite Cyrille Regis.

Wolverhampton W (£250,000 from Hayes on 12/9/1997)
Torquay U (Loaned on 19/12/1997) FL 13+1/6 Others 1
Bristol C (Loaned on 26/3/1998) FL 1+2/1
Bristol Rov (£250,000 on 7/8/1998) FL 73+5/38 FLC 6/3 FAC 6/7 Others 3
West Bromwich A (£2,000,000 on 27/7/2000) FL 32+11/14 FLC 3+1/2 FAC 1 Others 2/1

ROBERTS Neil Wyn
Born: Wrexham, 7 April 1978
Height: 5'10" Weight: 11.0
International Honours: W: 1; B-1; U21-2; Yth

Neil was at his best for Wigan last season when coming off the subs' bench to score important goals. Although not a prolific goal-scorer, he led the line well, holding the ball up to bring his colleagues into play and also showed an excellent work rate. Having settled in well at the JJB Stadium he will be looking to win a regular place in the starting line-up in the 2001-02 campaign. Neil is the older brother of Wrexham defender Steve Roberts.

Wrexham (From trainee on 3/7/1996) FL 58+17/17 FLC 1/1 FAC 11+1/4 Others 2+2/2
Wigan Ath (£450,000 on 18/2/2000) FL 25+18/7 FLC 0+1/1 FAC 2/1 Others 1+1

ROBERTS Stephen (Steve) Wyn
Born: Wrexham, 24 February 1980
Height: 6'0" Weight: 12.7
International Honours: W: U21-4; Yth

Steve was just beginning to establish himself in the Wrexham team when he had the misfortune to suffer a broken leg in the Robins' 4-3 win at Oxford last October. It was not until February that he was able to resume training and he eventually returned to action with the reserves towards the end of the season. He is an assured central defender capable of playing his way out of trouble and will be looking to fulfil the promise he has already shown next season at the Racecourse Ground. He won two further caps for Wales at U21 level appearing against Belarus and Norway last August. Steve is the younger brother of the Wigan striker Neil Roberts.

Wrexham (From trainee on 16/1/1998) FL 22+4 FLC 1 FAC 3/1 Others 0+1

ROBERTS Stuart Ian
Born: Carmarthen, 22 July 1980
Height: 5'7" Weight: 9.8
International Honours: W: U21-8

Stuart had his best season to date with Swansea City in 2000-01 and was regularly in the squad although often featuring from the subs' bench. He showed his versatility by appearing in a wide role, as a partner for Giovanni Savarese and as a third striker but wherever he was employed his pace and ability to beat his opponent were always evident. He continued to be part of the Wales U21 set up, winning a further five caps during the campaign. Out of contract in the summer it was unclear at the time of writing where he would be playing in 2001-02.

Swansea C (From trainee on 9/7/1998) FL 45+34/9 FLC 4+3 FAC 4 Others 7+2

ROBERTSON John Alexander
Born: Irvine, 28 March 1976
Height: 6'0" Weight: 11.4
Club Honours: SCC '97

John moved south of the border to join Oxford United in the summer of 2000 and although he faced the difficult task of replacing the long-serving Les Robinson in the U's defence he established himself in the side and rarely missed a game all season. He is a reliable right back who is sound defensively and likes to push forward down the wing. He was reported to have rejoined Ayr during the summer.

Stranraer (Signed from Bonnyton on 19/9/1994) SL 55+13/1 SLC 1 SC 1 Others 2+2
Ayr U (Free on 24/7/1997) SL 74+9/1 SLC 5+2 SC 11+1 Others 3
Oxford U (Free on 11/7/2000) FL 37+3 FLC 2 FAC 1 Others 1

ROBERTSON Mark William
Born: Sydney, Australia, 6 April 1977
Height: 5'9" Weight: 11.4
International Honours: Australia: U23-5; Yth

Mark enjoyed a successful loan spell in Australia during the summer of 2000, coming off the bench to help his club Wollongong Wolves overturn a 3-0 deficit to win the NSL Grand Final in a dramatic penalty shoot-out. On his return to England he linked up with Second Division club Swindon Town where he mostly featured from the bench, scoring his only goal from the penalty spot in the home defeat by Bristol Rovers before he returned to Burnley. He subsequently moved on to Dundee in March where he featured in a handful of games towards the end of the season. Mostly used as a right-sided attacking midfielder, he also occasionally played up front for the Robins.

Burnley (Free from Marconi Stallions, Australia on 3/10/1997) FL 27+9/1 FLC 1+1 Others 3+2
Swindon T (Loaned on 22/8/2000) FL 4+6/1 FLC 2+1

ROBINS Mark Gordon
Born: Ashton under Lyne, 22 December 1969
Height: 5'8" Weight: 11.11
Club Honours: FAC '90; ECWC '91; ESC '91; FLC '97
International Honours: E: U21-6

Mark chose to move to Rotherham in the 2000 close season when he could have stayed at Walsall and had a superb season for the Millers, registering his best-ever scoring return as he topped 20 goals for the first time in a lengthy career. His tally included several cracking efforts as he showed all his experience in the opposing penalty area. The highlight of a magnificent campaign was his classical hat-trick against Swindon Town at the end of March: a header, a left-foot shot and a right-foot shot.

Manchester U (From apprentice on 23/12/1986) FL 19+29/11 FLC 0+7/2 FAC 4+4/3 Others 4+3/1
Norwich C (£800,000 on 14/8/1992) PL 57+10/20 FLC 6+3/1 Others 1+1
Leicester C (£1,000,000 on 16/1/1995) P/FL 40+16/12 FLC 5+4/5 FAC 4+2 Others 1+1
Reading (Loaned on 29/8/1997) FL 5 (Signed by Deportivo Orense, Spain on 15/1/1998)
Manchester C (Free from Panionios, Greece on 25/3/1999) FL 0+2
Walsall (Free on 5/8/1999) FL 30+10/6 FLC 4/1 FAC 2/1
Rotherham U (Free on 5/7/2000) FL 42/24 FLC 2/1 FAC 3 Others 1/1

ROBINSON Carl Phillip
Born: Llandrindod Wells, 13 October 1976
Height: 5'10" Weight: 12.10
International Honours: W: 4; B-2; U21-6; Yth

Carl was in and out of the Wolves team in the first half of last season and although he netted several goals with some well-timed runs into the box, it was only in the new year that he really began to blossom. He was particularly effective in the Black Country 'derby' against West Brom and retained his place in the starting line-up until just before the end of the campaign. A right-sided midfield player he is a good ball winner and has the capacity to deliver a defence-splitting pass. He continued to represent Wales last term winning two more caps.

Wolverhampton W (From trainee on 3/7/1995) FL 114+27/17 FLC 11+1/1 FAC 14/3
Shrewsbury T (Loaned on 28/3/1996) FL 2+2 Others 1

ROBINSON John Robert Campbell
Born: Bulawayo, Rhodesia, 29 August 1971
Height: 5'10" Weight: 11.7
Club Honours: Div 1 '00
International Honours: W: 26; U21-5

John holds the record for international appearances by a Charlton Athletic player and was once again a regular in the Wales team, adding a further four caps during the 2000-01 season. However he was not a regular in the Addicks' line-up and after losing his place in mid-November he only started a handful of games during the remainder of the campaign. John is a tricky right-footed winger who can play on either flank or as a right wing back. He loves to take on players and delivers an accurate cross with either foot. He netted two goals last season, scoring in the opening day victory against Manchester City and contributing a late equaliser when coming on as a substitute in the home game against Manchester United.

Brighton & Hove A (From trainee on 21/4/1989) FL 57+5/6 FLC 5/1 FAC 2+1 Others 1+2/2
Charlton Ath (£75,000 on 15/9/1992) P/FL 270+21/34 FLC 17+3/4 FAC 15+3/3 Others 5+1

ROBINSON Leslie (Les)
Born: Shirebrook, 1 March 1967
Height: 5'9" Weight: 12.4

Les returned to Field Mill in the summer of 2000 after an absence of 14 years and had an excellent season with Mansfield in 2000-01. A versatile player who can appear in midfield or defence he took a while to settle in but was soon producing some sterling performances. He occasionally played in the centre of the defence when covering for

John Robinson

injuries but was much more impressive in a midfield role. Les finished the season just short of a landmark 700 appearances in senior football and capped a fine campaign when he received the club's 'Player of the Year' award.

Mansfield T (From Nottingham F juniors on 6/10/1984) FL 11+4 Others 1
Stockport Co (£10,000 on 27/11/1986) FL 67/3 FLC 2 FAC 4 Others 4
Doncaster Rov (£20,000 on 24/3/1988) FL 82/12 FLC 4 FAC 5 Others 5/1
Oxford U (£150,000 on 19/3/1990) FL 379+5/3 FLC 38/3 FAC 22+1 Others 13
Mansfield T (Free on 13/7/2000) FL 44 FLC 4 FAC 2 Others 1

ROBINSON Mark
Born: Guisborough, 24 July 1981
Height: 5'9" Weight: 11.0

Mark impressed for Hartlepool in the 2000-01 pre-season matches and went on to make his Football League debut at Lincoln on the opening day of the campaign. He was given a short run in the first team before being replaced by the more experienced Sam Shilton and then found his opportunities somewhat limited. A promising young left back he will be looking to gain further senior experience in 2001-02.

Hartlepool U (From trainee on 2/7/1999) FL 5+1 FLC 1

ROBINSON Mark James
Born: Rochdale, 21 November 1968
Height: 5'9" Weight: 12.4
Club Honours: Div 2 '96

Swindon Town's longest-serving player struggled to find his form at times last season but eventually came good again towards the end of the campaign and put in an outstanding display in the home defeat by Reading. He usually played at right back although he has the ability to play in the centre of defence if needed. Mark is a reliable defender who brings the ball confidently out of defence.

West Bromwich A (From apprentice on 10/1/1987) FL 2 FLC 0+1
Barnsley (Free on 23/6/1987) FL 117+20/6 FLC 7+2 FAC 7+1 Others 3+2/1
Newcastle U (£450,000 on 9/3/1993) F/PL 14+11 FAC 1
Swindon T (£600,000 on 22/7/1994) FL 249+12/4 FLC 21+1 FAC 13 Others 9+1

ROBINSON Marvin Leon St
Born: Crewe, 11 April 1980
Height: 6'0" Weight: 12.9
International Honours: E: Sch

This Derby County youngster joined Stoke City on loan last September to gain more experience of first-team football. He endeared himself to the club's supporters by scoring on his debut against Oxford but then suffered a badly broken leg in his third game for City and this brought his season to a premature close. A powerfully built striker it is hoped he will have made a full recovery by the start of the 2001-02 season.

Derby Co (From trainee on 8/7/1998) PL 3+6
Stoke C (Loaned on 13/9/2000) FL 3/1

ROBINSON Matthew Richard
Born: Exeter, 23 December 1974
Height: 5'11" Weight: 11.8

Matthew was first choice at left back for Reading last season, only missing games through injury of suspension. Although he suffered a fractured rib in the home defeat by Millwall he soon returned to the line-up within a few weeks. A solid but unspectacular defender he is comfortable on the ball and makes effective surges down the left flank in support of the attack.

Southampton (From trainee on 1/7/1993) PL 3+11 FAC 1+2
Portsmouth (£50,000 on 20/2/1998) FL 65+4/1 FLC 3+2 FAC 3
Reading (£150,000 on 28/1/2000) FL 48+3 FLC 2 FAC 2 Others 4

ROBINSON Paul Derrick
Born: Sunderland, 20 November 1978
Height: 5'11" Weight: 11.12

This young Wimbledon striker began last season on the subs' bench at Selhurst Park and found it difficult to settle at his new club. In October he moved on loan to First Division rivals Burnley but he was again restricted to a role as substitute and he returned south after the Clarets signed Ian Moore. Still unable to break into the Dons team he spent time on loan with Dundee United in the new year where he made a handful of appearances. Used predominantly as a right-sided striker Paul can be a handful for any defender on his day.

Darlington (From trainee on 14/7/1997) FL 7+19/3 FLC 0+1 FAC 2+4/1 Others 0+1
Newcastle U (£250,000 + on 27/3/1998) PL 2+9 FLC 0+1 Others 0+4/1
Wimbledon (£1,500,000 on 9/8/2000) FL 0+3 FLC 1+1
Burnley (Loaned on 10/10/2000) FL 0+4
Dundee (Loaned on 21/2/2001) SL 2+4

ROBINSON Paul Peter
Born: Watford, 14 December 1978
Height: 5'9" Weight: 11.12
Club Honours: Div 2 '98
International Honours: E: U21-3

Paul was once again a regular in the Watford line-up last season and is now an established member of the first team at Vicarage Road. A left back who is very strong in the tackle he was an asset at set pieces and worked hard to improve his passing. However he tended to accumulate bookings during the campaign and this is an area of his game where he needs to show improvement. Paul's value to the Hornets was recognised when he was awarded an extended contract during the season that will keep him at the club until 2005.

Watford (From trainee on 13/2/1997) P/FL 116+18/2 FLC 8+1 FAC 6+2 Others 5

ROBINSON Paul William
Born: Beverley, 15 October 1979
Height: 6'2" Weight: 13.4
Club Honours: FAYC '97
International Honours: E: U21-5

Paul took over in goal for Leeds United when Nigel Martyn went off injured against Charlton in October and went on to retain his pace until the end of January, his longest run to date of first-team football. He produced many inspirational performances, none more so than in the home Champions' League encounter with Barcelona when at times it seemed like 'Robbo' versus Rivaldo. A regular for England U21s he was called up to the full squad for the friendly against Italy but still awaits his debut.

Leeds U (From trainee on 13/5/1997) PL 19+2 FLC 2 FAC 1 Others 6

ROBINSON Stephen (Steve)
Born: Lisburn, 10 December 1974
Height: 5'9" Weight: 11.3
International Honours: NI: 5; B-4; U21-1; Yth; Sch

Signed by Preston during the summer of 2000, Steve made his debut for North End as a substitute in the opening game at Grimsby. Although better known as a high-scoring attacking midfielder, his first league start came as a makeshift striker against Tranmere, and he continued in this role for three matches. After spells as a regular substitute and again as an emergency forward, he netted his first goal for the club direct from a free-kick at Wimbledon. He would have been hoping for a regular place in the starting line-up following the transfer of Michael Appleton, but knee and ankle injuries effectively ended his season early and he will be looking for the chance to impress the North End fans next season after a rather frustrating start to his Deepdale career.

Tottenham H (From trainee on 27/1/1993) PL 1+1
Bournemouth (Free on 20/10/1994) FL 227+13/51 FLC 14/1 FAC 15+1/5 Others 16/3
Preston NE (£375,000 on 26/5/2000) FL 6+16/1 FLC 3

Steve Robinson (Preston North End)

ROBINSON Steven (Steve) Eli
Born: Nottingham, 17 January 1975
Height: 5'9" Weight: 11.3

Steve had little chance of shining for Birmingham City last term and although he featured in a handful of first-team games he was put up for sale. In February he signed for Swindon Town where he went straight in

the side and kept his place for the remainder of the campaign, endearing himself to the club's fans with two expertly struck volleys to secure a 2-0 win at local rivals Oxford United. An energetic dynamic midfielder who fully justified his nickname of 'turbo', he also has excellent distribution.
Birmingham C (From trainee on 9/6/1993) FL 53+28 FLC 6+2/1 FAC 2+2/1 Others 2
Peterborough U (Loaned on 15/3/1996) FL 5
Swindon T (£50,000 on 12/2/2001) FL 18/2 Others 1

ROCHE Barry Christopher
Born: Dublin, 6 April 1982
Height: 6'4" Weight: 12.6
International Honours: RoI: Yth
A promising young goalkeeper, Barry made an immediate impression on his debut for Nottingham Forest. Coming on from the subs' bench after Dave Beasant had received a red card, he saved a penalty in the dying minutes of the game. His only other senior action came when he stepped in for the suspended Beasant for the home game against Sheffield Wednesday when he kept a clean sheet. Tall and commanding in the box, he featured for the Republic of Ireland at U18 level during the season.
Nottingham F (From trainee on 29/6/1999) FL 1+1

Lee Roche

ROCHE Lee Paul
Born: Bolton, 28 October 1980
Height: 5'10" Weight: 10.12
International Honours: E: U21-1; Yth
Lee joined Wrexham on a full season's loan from Manchester United last August and was a near-ever-present in the Robins' line-up during 2000-01. He impressed with a series of consistent displays at right back and also proved to be more than useful when attacking down the flank. Previously capped by England at U18 level he stepped up to make his debut for the U21s in their 2-2 draw in Finland last October.
Manchester U (From trainee on 11/2/1999)
Wrexham (Loaned on 24/7/2000) FL 41 FLC 2 FAC 1 Others 1

RODGER Simon Lee
Born: Shoreham, 3 October 1971
Height: 5'9" Weight: 11.9
Club Honours: Div 1 '94
Simon is an effective left-sided Crystal Palace midfield player who works hard and is strong in the tackle. 2000-01 was a relatively injury-free period for him and he missed few games although he failed to add to his goals tally. He is the longest-serving player at Selhurst Park and will be due a testimonial game in the 2001-02 season.
Crystal Palace (£1,000 from Bognor Regis T on 2/7/1990) F/PL 213+27/10 FLC 27+1/1 FAC 9+3 Others 5+3
Manchester C (Loaned on 28/10/1996) FL 8/1
Stoke C (Loaned on 14/2/1997) FL 5

RODGERS Luke John
Born: Birmingham, 1 January 1982
Height: 5'7" Weight: 11.2
Luke spent much of last season on the subs' bench for Shrewsbury Town and it was not until February that he appeared in the starting line-up. Having waited so long he scored at Plymouth on his second start and then netted a hat-trick before being sent off (for two yellow cards) in the sensational 7-1 victory at Rochdale. Luke is an extremely promising striker who is quick, direct and always willing to run at opposition defenders. He benefited greatly from playing alongside the experienced Nigel Jemson and if he continues to make progress in the coming season he will become a key figure for the Gay Meadow club.
Shrewsbury T (From trainee on 10/7/2000) FL 13+19/8 FAC 0+1 Others 0+2

RODRIGUEZ Daniel (Dani) Ferreira
Born: Madeira, Portugal, 3 March 1980
Height: 6'0" Weight: 11.8
International Honours: Portugal: U21
The skill and electric pace of this early-season loan signing from Southampton made him an instant hit with the Bristol City fans, but unfortunately he suffered a fractured ankle just before half time in the 4-0 home win over Reading at the end of October and this brought his stay at Ashton Gate to a premature conclusion. He recovered sufficiently to begin training with Southampton later in the season but then sustained another break that ended all hope of any return to action in the 2000-01 campaign.
Bournemouth (Loaned from CS Farense, Portugal on 1/10/1998) FL 0+5 Others 0+2
Southampton (£170,000 on 3/3/1999) PL 0+2
Bristol C (Loaned on 3/10/2000) FL 3+1

ROGERS Alan
Born: Liverpool, 3 January 1977
Height: 5'9" Weight: 12.6
Club Honours: Div 1 '98
International Honours: E: U21-3
Alan was in fine form down the left flank for Nottingham Forest at the beginning of last season, terrorising opposition defenders with his trademark bursting runs. Unfortunately he suffered a serious knee injury at Gillingham, tearing the anterior cruciate ligament, and he was subsequently sidelined for most of the remainder of the season. He made a brief come back in April, ironically for the return encounter against the Gills, and will be looking forward to a full return to fitness in 2001-02. A pacy left winger he can deliver a terrific cross and also has a great eye for goal.
Tranmere Rov (From trainee on 1/7/1995) FL 53+4/2 FLC 1 FAC 1
Nottingham F (£2,000,000 on 10/7/1997) P/FL 132+2/17 FLC 14/2 FAC 2+1/1

ROGERS David (Dave) Raymond
Born: Liverpool, 25 August 1975
Height: 6'1" Weight: 12.4
Unable to get a game at Ayr, Dave moved south to join Peterborough for a three-month loan period last October but he struggled to break into the team and was replaced early on in his only league start. He subsequently returned to Scotland before joining Scunthorpe United on a short-term contract in March. He looked strong and assured on his debut for the Iron at Torquay, helping his new team to a 2-0 win but unfortunately he sustained a dislocated shoulder and ankle injury during that game which ruled him out of action for the rest of the campaign. Dave is an effective defender who is equally at home at left-back or in the centre of defence. Out of contract in the summer his future was uncertain at the time of writing.
Tranmere Rov (From trainee on 6/7/1994)
Chester C (Free on 7/8/1995) FL 18+7/1 FLC 2+2 FAC 0+1 Others 1 (Free to Southport on 25/11/1996)
Dundee (Free on 6/8/1997) SL 38+5/1 SLC 2 SC 4+1 Others 1
Ayr U (Free on 23/6/1999) SL 13+3/1 SLC 2 SC 1 Others 1
Partick Thistle (Loaned on 31/3/2000) SL 6
Peterborough U (Loaned on 6/10/2000) FL 1+2 Others 1
Scunthorpe U (Free on 2/3/2001) FL 1

ROGERS Kristian Raleigh John
Born: Chester, 2 October 1980
Height: 6'3" Weight: 12.6
International Honours: E: Sch
Kristian began the 2000-01 campaign as first-choice 'keeper for Wrexham but he was replaced by the more experienced Kevin Dearden in mid-September and was unable to win back his position in the team. He played a couple of times for Conference club Rushden & Diamonds during a loan period last December before returning to the Racecourse Ground to compete with Dearden, David Walsh and Paul Whitfield for a place in the Robins' line-up. He is a promising young goalkeeper who needs to gain more first-team experience to develop further.
Wrexham (From Chester C juniors on 14/8/1998) FL 6 FLC 1

ROGERS Mark Alvin
Born: Guelph, Ontario, Canada, 3 November 1975
Height: 6'1" Weight: 12.12
International Honours: Canada: 1

Mark firmly established himself as a regular in the Wycombe line-up last season and created a piece of history by becoming the first Wanderers' player to win a full international cap while on the club's books when he appeared for Canada in a World Cup qualifier against Panama in October. He retained his place until suffering ankle ligament damage in the FA Cup fifth round tie against Wimbledon and the injury brought his campaign to a premature close. A right back who is strong in the tackle and comfortable on the ball, he is expected to be fit in time for the start of the coming season.
Wycombe W (Free from Burnaby Canadians, Canada on 23/12/1998) FL 38+9/1 FLC 4/1 FAC 8+1/1 Others 3

ROGERS Paul Anthony
Born: Portsmouth, 21 March 1965
Height: 6'0" Weight: 12.0
Club Honours: Div 3 '97, '01; AMC '99
International Honours: E: SP-6
This experienced central midfield player once again captained Brighton in 2000-01 and had the distinction of leading the Seagulls to the Third Division title. A near ever-present alongside Richard Carpenter and Charlie Oatway he was able to get forward more last season and contributed some spectacular goals, notably in the away victories at Blackpool and Hull. A steady influence on the team as a whole, Paul gains respect from his team-mates by use of a quiet word rather than shouting.
Sheffield U (£35,000 from Sutton U on 29/1/1992) F/PL 120+5/10 FLC 8+1/1 FAC 4 Others 1
Notts Co (Signed on 29/12/1995) FL 21+1/2 FAC 1 Others 6/1
Wigan Ath (Loaned on 13/12/1996) FL 7+2/3
Wigan Ath (£50,000 on 7/3/1997) FL 85+6/2 FLC 6 FAC 3 Others 8/1
Brighton & Hove A (Free on 8/7/1999) FL 85+5/14 FLC 3+1 FAC 6/1 Others 3

Paul Rogers

ROGET Leo Thomas Earl
Born: Ilford, 1 August 1977
Height: 6'1" Weight: 12.2
Leo established a strong central defensive partnership with Phil Whelan at Southend at the beginning of last season, although he again ran into disciplinary problems. He subsequently moved on loan to First Division Stockport County in March and the deal became permanent shortly before the end of the campaign. He played the odd game in midfield for the Hatters but looked much more impressive when employed on the left-hand side of a three-man defensive formation where his pace, mobility and strength in the air were used to good effect.
Southend U (From trainee on 5/7/1995) FL 105+15/7 FLC 8 FAC 6/1 Others 3/1
Stockport Co (Loaned on 1/3/2001) FL 8+1

ROMO David
Born: Nimes, France, 7 August 1978
Height: 6'0" Weight: 12.6
International Honours: France: Yth
David joined Swansea last September following a successful trial period and although he took time to settle into his new surroundings he went on to become a regular in the first-team squad. A talented midfield player who is a specialist with dead-ball kicks one of the high points of his campaign was his performance in the 6-0 thrashing of Brentford when he set up four of the Swans' goals with his corners.
Swansea C (Free from Guingamp, France on 13/10/2000) FL 28+5 FAC 1 Others 3

ROPER Ian Robert
Born: Nuneaton, 20 June 1977
Height: 6'3" Weight: 13.4
Although Ian began the 2000-01 campaign as Andy Tillson's partner in the heart of the Walsall defence he was soon replaced by Tony Barras and was subsequently in and out of the side. However he was still a vital member of the Saddlers' promotion squad and always gave 100 per cent when called upon. A central defender who is effective in the air and firm in the tackle he was placed on the transfer list during the summer.
Walsall (From trainee on 15/5/1995) FL 107+21/2 FLC 3+5 FAC 5+1/1 Others 11+3

ROSCOE Andrew (Andy) Ronald
Born: Liverpool, 4 June 1973
Height: 5'11" Weight: 12.0
Club Honours: AMC '96
This experienced left wing back featured in virtually every game for Exeter City last season. Andy loves to get forward and attack down the left-hand side at every opportunity and his enthusiasm and desire to win made him a great crowd favourite at St James Park. His only goal of the campaign came from a free kick in the 1-1 draw at Darlington last August.
Bolton W (From trainee at Liverpool on 17/7/1991) FL 2+1 Others 1+1
Rotherham U (£70,000 on 27/10/1994) FL 184+18/18 FLC 10 FAC 10/2 Others 11/2
Mansfield T (Free on 5/8/1999) FL 29+10/2 FLC 2 FAC 1 Others 0+1/1
Exeter C (Free on 18/7/2000) FL 33+10/1 FLC 2 FAC 1 Others 1

ROSE Matthew David
Born: Dartford, 24 September 1975
Height: 5'11" Weight: 11.1
Club Honours: FAYC '94
International Honours: E: U21-2
This influential Queens Park Rangers player was sorely missed during an early season absence through injury but returned to become a mainstay of the defence. He was one of the few players who managed to retain his place at a disruptive time when the formation was altered and there was a change in management. He regularly featured in the centre of defence, although he can also play as a sweeper and in a 'holding' midfield role. He was released in the summer.
Arsenal (From trainee on 19/7/1994) PL 2+3
Queens Park R (£500,000 on 20/5/1997) FL 94+7/1 FLC 6 FAC 3

ROSE Richard Alan
Born: Pembury, 8 September 1982
Height: 6'0" Weight: 11.9
A highly talented left back or central defender, Richard made his Football League debut for Gillingham when he came on as an early substitute for Mark Patterson in the Easter Monday game at Crewe and gave a composed and cultured performance. He went on to appear twice more from the bench before making the starting line-up in the penultimate home game against Watford. His progress was rewarded by the club when he was given a three-year professional contract in February.
Gillingham (From trainee on 10/4/2001) FL 1+3

Uwe Rosler

ROSLER Uwe
Born: Magdeburg, Germany, 15 November 1968
Height: 6'0" Weight: 12.4
International Honours: East Germany: 5

Uwe joined Southampton after becoming a free agent when his former club Borussia Tennis Berlin folded, but he had an unfortunate time at The Dell last term and struggled to make an impact. Hampered by a nagging groin problem that required two operations and sidelined him for long periods, he found his way blocked by a rejuvenated James Beattie and when fit he spent much of his time on the substitutes' bench. He managed just a single goal all season - and that was in the Worthington Cup victory at Third Division Mansfield - but as a true professional he will no doubt put these troubles behind him when the 2001-02 campaign begins.

Manchester C (£375,000 from FC Nurnberg, Germany on 2/3/1994) P/FL 141+11/50 FLC 10+1/5 FAC 14/9 (Free to Kaiserslautern, Germany during 1998 close season)
Southampton (Free from Tennis Borussia, Germany on 24/7/2000) PL 6+14 FLC 1+1/1 FAC 0+2

ROUGIER Anthony (Tony) Leo
Born: Tobago, 17 July 1971
Height: 6'0" Weight: 14.1
International Honours: Trinidad & Tobago

Tony joined Reading for a substantial fee shortly before the start of the 2000-01 season and although he took a little while to settle in he soon endeared himself to the club's supporters when he scored twice in the 4-3 win over Oxford. Thereafter he was generally used on the left-hand side of midfield where he was able to open up defences with his pace and trickery. A committed Christian, he continued to assist Trinidad & Tobago in their World Cup qualifying campaign, winning a further nine caps in the process.

Raith Rov (Free from Trinity Prospect, Trinidad on 9/3/1995) SL 47+10/2 SLC 3/3 SC 4+1/1 Others 4+1/1
Hibernian (Signed on 10/7/1997) SL 34+11/4 SLC 4
Port Vale (£175,000 on 4/1/1999) FL 41+10/8 FLC 2/1 FAC 1
Reading (£325,000 on 11/8/2000) FL 14+17/2 FLC 1 FAC 1+1 Others 2+2

ROUSSEL Cedric
Born: Mons, Belgium, 6 January 1978
Height: 6'2" Weight: 12.5
International Honours: Belgium: U21

Cedric found it difficult to recreate the excellent form he had displayed in 2000-01 at Coventry last term and clearly missed playing alongside Robbie Keane. He headed the winner at The Dell in August, but this was the only goal he scored in the first six matches of the season as he struggled to form a partnership with new signing Craig Bellamy. He injured shoulder ligaments at Highbury and when fit found he could only make the substitutes' bench. Although he scored a consolation goal at Chelsea he was affected by back and then hamstring injuries that further restricted his appearances. He was eventually sold to Wolves in the new year, but struggled to find full match fitness and although he showed some neat touches he failed to score for the First Division club. A big solid striker he will be hoping to steer clear of the treatment room in 2001-02.

Coventry C (£1,200,000 from KAA Ghent, Belgium on 19/10/1999) PL 28+11/8 FLC 1 FAC 2+1/3
Wolverhampton W (£1,530,000 + on 15/2/2001) FL 3+6

ROWAN Jonathan (Jonny) Robert
Born: Grimsby, 29 November 1981
Height: 5'10" Weight: 11.4

This youngster signed his first professional contract with Grimsby Town in July 2000 and made a sensational entry to senior football when he came off the subs' bench in the Worthington Cup second round first leg tie against Wolves to score with almost his first touch of the ball. He was then sidelined by a groin strain but returned for a brief run in the Mariners' first team in the new year. Jonny is a promising young striker with a good eye for goal. He was voted as the club's 'Young Player of the Year'.

Grimsby T (From trainee on 12/7/2000) FL 2+3 FLC 0+2/1

ROWBOTHAM Jason
Born: Cardiff, 3 January 1969
Height: 5'9" Weight: 11.12
Club Honours: S Div 1 '95; SLC '95

Having been released by Plymouth at the end of the 1999-2000 campaign this experienced defender began last season at Dorchester Town before joining Torquay United on a non-contract basis in October to cover for an injury crisis. He made a handful of appearances for the Gulls before leaving in January when he linked up with his brother Darren at Weymouth.

Plymouth Arg (From trainee on 20/7/1987) FL 8+1 FLC 0+1
Shrewsbury T (Free on 26/3/1992)
Hereford U (Free on 17/10/1992) FL 3+2/1 FAC 1
Raith Rov (Free on 31/7/1993) SL 47+9/1 SLC 3+2 SC 2+1 Others 1
Wycombe W (£40,000 on 14/9/1995) FL 27 FLC 2 FAC 2 Others 2
Plymouth Arg (Free on 11/10/1996) FL 42+9/1 FLC 3 FAC 1+1 Others 2+1 (Freed during 2000 close season)
Torquay U (Free from Dorchester T on 26/10/2000) FL 4+1

ROWE Rodney Carl
Born: Huddersfield, 30 July 1975
Height: 5'8" Weight: 12.8

Rodney found himself out of favour at Gillingham at the start of last season and he made his only senior appearance as a late substitute in the Worthington Cup tie at Torquay. In January he moved on to join Third Division Hull City on an 18-month contract. He quickly established an effective partnership with another new signing, target man Kevin Francis, and together they helped fire City into the play-offs. Rodney scored his first goal for the Tigers in the memorable 1-0 victory over Leyton Orient - the first game after the club was plunged into administration - and with four penalties he took his tally to six to clinch the title of the Tigers' leading scorer in league matches. He is a lively striker with good pace who is always a danger in the penalty box.

Huddersfield T (From trainee on 12/7/1993) FL 14+20/2 FLC 0+2 FAC 6+1/2 Others 3/1
Scarborough (Loaned on 11/8/1994) FL 10+4/1 FLC 4/1
Bury (Loaned on 20/3/1995) FL 1+2
York C (£80,000 on 19/2/1997) FL 74+23/20 FLC 5+1/2 FAC 2+3/3 Others 2/2
Halifax T (Loaned on 24/9/1999) FL 7+2/2 FAC 1
Gillingham (£45,000 on 25/11/1999) FL 8+14/4 FLC 0+1 Others 1
Hull C (Free on 2/1/2001) FL 14+7/6 Others 1+1

ROWETT Gary
Born: Bromsgrove, 6 March 1974
Height: 6'0" Weight: 12.10

A right back or central defender Gary became Peter Taylor's first, and arguably most effective, signing after he took over as manager last summer. Arriving for a fee that equalled the then club record, he slotted neatly into a back three alongside Matt Elliott and Gerry Taggart, and quickly adapted to life in the Premiership once more. He even found time to pop up with some crucial goals: a left-foot volley to break the deadlock in the FA Cup tie with York, a close range effort to claim the winner at home to Chelsea and a low drive from a half-cleared corner against Tottenham. Having settled in nicely at Filbert Street he will be looking forward to another season of regular first-team football in 2001-02.

Cambridge U (From trainee on 10/9/1991) FL 51+12/9 FLC 7/1 FAC 5+2 Others 5/3
Everton (£200,000 on 21/5/1994) PL 2+2
Blackpool (Loaned on 23/1/1995) FL 17
Derby Co (£300,000 on 20/7/1995) P/FL 101+4/2 FLC 8/2 FAC 5+2
Birmingham C (£1,000,000 on 17/8/1998) FL 87/6 FLC 9/3 FAC 3/1 Others 4/1
Leicester C (£3,000,000 + on 7/7/2000) PL 38/2 FLC 1 FAC 4/1 Others 2

ROWLAND Keith
Born: Portadown, 1 September 1971
Height: 5'10" Weight: 10.0
International Honours: NI: 18; B-3; Yth

Keith struggled to break into the Queens Park Rangers first team last season and was restricted to a handful of early season outings as cover for the non-availability of other players. In January he moved on loan to Second Division Luton Town where he settled in straight away, featuring regularly during his stay. He is a left-sided player who operates either as a wing back or in a more attacking midfield role. He returned to Loftus Road and was released in the summer.

Bournemouth (From trainee on 2/10/1989) FL 65+7/2 FLC 5 FAC 8 Others 3
Coventry C (Loaned on 8/1/1993) PL 0+2
West Ham U (£110,000 on 6/8/1993) PL 63+17/1 FLC 3+2 FAC 5+1
Queens Park R (Signed on 30/1/1998) FL 32+24/3 FLC 1+1 FAC 1+1
Luton T (Loaned on 27/1/2001) FL 12/2

ROWLANDS Martin Charles
Born: Hammersmith, 8 February 1979
Height: 5'9" Weight: 10.10
Club Honours: Div 3 '99
International Honours: RoI: U21-8

Martin began the 2000-01 campaign playing on the right-hand side of midfield for Brentford however he switched to a position in the 'hole' behind the front two strikers under Ray Lewington and finished the season appearing alongside Paul Evans in a central midfield role. Although he missed a

number of games through suspension he added a creative dimension to the centre of the park with his excellent dribbling and passing skills. He won a runners-up medal in the LDV Vans Trophy after appearing for the Bees in their 2-1 defeat by Port vale in the final of the competition.
Brentford (£45,000 from Farnborough T on 6/8/1998) FL 102+6/12 FLC 8+2/1 FAC 5+1 Others 12/2

ROY Eric
Born: Nice, France, 26 September 1967
Height: 5'9" Weight: 10.10
This stylish midfield player featured in only a handful of early season games for the Sunderland last term before dropping out of the first-team picture. He subsequently returned to France, signing for Troyes in January, but the move was not particularly successful and in the summer he was reported to have moved on again to Rayo Vallecano.
Sunderland (£200,000 from Olympique Marseille, France, ex Nice, Toulon, Lyon, on 25/8/1999) PL 20+7 FLC 5/1 FAC 2

ROYCE Simon Ernest
Born: Forest Gate, 9 September 1971
Height: 6'2" Weight: 12.8
Having previously played for Peter Taylor at Southend, Simon linked up once more with his old boss when he joined Leicester City in July 2000. Initially second-choice in goal to Tim Flowers he stepped up to make his debut in the surprise Worthington Cup defeat by Crystal Palace when he was beaten by two immaculate long-range strikes. However he bounced back to make the most of the opportunities presented by Flowers' injuries and featured regularly for the Foxes over the next few months. Simon earned a reputation as a genuine shot stopper with a series of high class saves against an array of opponents and will be challenging for the number one jersey on merit in 2001-02. Before he can lay claim to first-choice status, however, he perhaps needs to work on his all-round dominance of his penalty box.
Southend U (£35,000 from Heybridge Swifts on 15/10/1991) FL 147+2 FLC 9 FAC 5 Others 6
Charlton Ath (Free on 2/7/1998) PL 8
Leicester C (Free on 17/7/2000) PL 16+3 FLC 1 FAC 4

RUBINS Andrejs
Born: Latvia, 26 November 1978
Height: 5'9" Weight: 10.5
International Honours: Latvia: 23
Andrejs began the 2000-01 season with Latvian club Skonto Riga for whom he made two appearances in the UEFA Champions' League qualifying competition. He signed for Crystal Palace soon after his club colleague Alex Kolinko and featured regularly for the Eagles for the remainder of the campaign. Andrejs is a pacy winger who possesses a fierce shot and he scored brilliant goals in the Worthington Cup ties at Leicester and in the home leg of the semi-final against Liverpool. An experienced international he won six further caps after joining Palace.
Crystal Palace (£2,000,000 from Skonto Riga, Latvia on 17/10/2000) FL 17+5 FLC 3/2 FAC 2

RUDDOCK Neil
Born: Wandsworth, 9 May 1968
Height: 6'2" Weight: 12.12
Club Honours: FLC '95
International Honours: E: 1; B-1; U21-4; Yth
Neil began the 2000-01 season as the Crystal Palace club captain a role he only briefly held. His campaign was interrupted by a series of injuries and suspensions and he was eventually released by mutual consent in the final weeks of the season. At his best Neil is a powerful and effective defender, strong in the air and with a good left foot.
Millwall (From apprentice on 3/3/1986) Others 3+1/1
Tottenham H (£50,000 on 14/4/1986) FL 7+2 FAC 1+1/1
Millwall (£300,000 on 29/6/1988) FL 0+2/1 FLC 2/3 Others 1+1
Southampton (£250,000 on 13/2/1989) FL 100+7/9 FLC 14+1/1 FAC 10/3 Others 6
Tottenham H (£750,000 on 29/7/1992) PL 38/3 FLC 4 FAC 5
Liverpool (£2,500,000 on 22/7/1993) PL 111+4/11 FLC 19+1/1 FAC 11 Others 5+1
Queens Park R (Loaned on 26/3/1998) FL 7
West Ham U (£100,000 + on 31/7/1998) PL 39+3/2 FLC 4+1 FAC 3 Others 5+1/1
Crystal Palace (Signed on 28/7/2000) FL 19+1/2 FLC 5/1 FAC 0+1

RUDI Petter
Born: Kristiansund, Norway, 17 September 1973
Height: 6'2" Weight: 12.0
International Honours: Norway: 27; U21; Yth
This tall left-sided attacking midfield player made a single appearance for Sheffield Wednesday last season, coming on from the subs' bench as a replacement for Gilles De Bilde at half-time against Huddersfield Town last August. He was then transferred back to Norwegian club Molde FK where he was still playing when the Scandinavian season resumed in the spring.
Sheffield Wed (£800,000 from Molde, Norway on 17/10/1997) P/FL 70+7/8 FLC 5/1 FAC 6+1/1

RUDONJA Mladen
Born: Koper, Yugoslavia, 26 July 1971
Height: 5'9" Weight: 11.6
International Honours: Slovenia: 47
A natural left-sided midfield player, despite being predominantly right-footed, Mladen took some time to settle in after signing for Portsmouth following his appearances for Slovenia in the Euro 2000 finals. His cause was certainly not helped by the constant

Eric Roy

managerial changes at Fratton Park last term, but with Graham Rix now firmly established as the new boss he will be hoping for a regular place in the first team in 2001-02. An experienced international for his country he continued to add to his caps during the season.

Portsmouth (£200,000 from St Truiden, Belgium, ex Belvedur Izola, NK Zagreb, Koper, Olympija, Marsonia, HIT Gorica, Lugano, Primorje, on 11/8/2000) FL 2+9 FLC 1+2 FAC 1

RUFUS Richard Raymond
Born: Lewisham, 12 January 1975
Height: 6'1" Weight: 11.10
Club Honours: Div 1 '00
International Honours: E: U21-6

Richard had a superb season in the heart of the Charlton defence in 2000-01 and is now looking very much the finished article. Strong and determined in the tackle he is extremely quick, calm under pressure and provides a commanding presence in the air. He reads the game well and his distribution has improved beyond recognition. He likes to move forward at set pieces and corners and scored an opportunist goal at Coventry to help Charlton earn a share of the points. If Richard is able to maintain such excellent form it only seems a matter of time before he is called up to the full England squad. He was deservedly voted as the Addicks' 'Player of the Season' for the second year in a row.

Charlton Ath (From trainee on 1/7/1993) P/FL 245+3/9 FLC 13 FAC 14 Others 5/1

RUSHBURY Andrew (Andy) James
Born: Carlisle, 7 March 1983
Height: 5'10" Weight: 11.7

This Chesterfield trainee earned his promotion to the first-team squad at the end of last season after a fine goal-scoring run with the reserves and juniors. He made his debut from the subs' bench in the closing stages of the penultimate game at Brighton and also featured briefly in the home game with Halifax. Andy is a compact left-footed striker who is very lively and has a great eye for goal. He is the son of Dave Rushbury the former Sheffield Wednesday and Carlisle defender who is currently the physio at Saltergate.

Chesterfield (Trainee) FL 0+2

RUSSELL Alexander (Alex) John
Born: Crosby, 17 March 1973
Height: 5'9" Weight: 11.7

Having made a full recovery from the injuries that had plagued him in the 1999-2000 season, Alex made a full return to fitness last term but had a somewhat disappointing campaign with Cambridge United. He struggled to find his best form, then lost his place following a change in management and after being put on the transfer list he was released in the summer. He is an influential midfield player and an expert with dead-ball kicks. He is the son of Alex Russell who played for Southport in the 1960s and early 1970s.

Rochdale (£4,000 from Burscough on 11/7/1994) FL 83+19/14 FLC 5/1 FAC 1+1 Others 2+3
Cambridge U (Free on 4/8/1998) FL 72+9/8 FLC 7+1 FAC 7 Others 3

RUSSELL Darel Francis Roy
Born: Stepney, 22 October 1980
Height: 5'11" Weight: 11.9
International Honours: E: Yth

Darel was a near ever-present for Norwich City in the 2000-01 campaign. A powerful midfielder, he has the ability to take a game by the scruff of the neck and drive his team forward by virtue of his work-rate and ball-winning qualities. A naturally attacking player he loves to set his sights from long range and shoot at goal, although his tally last term was not as he would have liked. Although only just out of his teens he has already played nearly 100 senior games for the Canaries, advancing his career at an early stage which can only benefit him as he continues to improve year upon year.

Norwich C (From trainee on 29/11/1997) FL 70+18/7 FLC 7/2 FAC 2

Darel Russell

RUSSELL Kevin John
Born: Portsmouth, 6 December 1966
Height: 5'9" Weight: 10.12
Club Honours: Div 2 '93
International Honours: E: Yth

This veteran player returned to the Wrexham team last November and featured regularly for the remainder of the season, mostly appearing in a left-sided midfield role although he also had a spell partnering Craig Faulconbridge up front for the Robins. His high work rate, enthusiasm and eye for goal make him a useful member of the squad and more than compensate for his advancing years. Out of contract in the summer it was unclear at the time of writing where he would be playing in 2001-02.

Portsmouth (From apprentice at Brighton & Hove A on 9/10/1984) FL 3+1/1 FLC 0+1 FAC 0+1 Others 1+1
Wrexham (£10,000 on 17/7/1987) FL 84/43 FLC 4/1 FAC 4 Others 8/3
Leicester C (£175,000 on 20/6/1989) FL 24+19/10 FLC 0+1 FAC 1 Others 5/2
Peterborough U (Loaned on 6/9/1990) FL 7/3
Cardiff C (Loaned on 17/1/1991) FL 3
Hereford U (Loaned on 7/11/1991) FL 3/1 Others 1/1
Stoke C (Loaned on 2/1/1992) FL 5/1
Stoke C (£95,000 on 16/7/1992) FL 30+10/5 FLC 3 FAC 2 Others 4+1/1
Burnley (£150,000 on 28/6/1993) FL 26+2/6 FLC 4/1 FAC 4 Others 1/1
Bournemouth (£125,000 on 3/3/1994) FL 30/1 FLC 3/1 FAC 2/1
Notts Co (£60,000 on 24/2/1995) FL 9+2
Wrexham (£60,000 on 21/7/1995) FL 163+24/17 FLC 6+1/1 FAC 18+5/4 Others 9+1

RUSSELL Lee Edward
Born: Southampton, 3 September 1969
Height: 5'11" Weight: 12.0

This solid and reliable defender was badly affected by injuries in the first half of last season and could only watch as Torquay plunged towards the relegation zone. Returning to action in January he worked in a professional, no-nonsense way to shore up the Gulls' defence. Lee established an effective partnership with Jimmy Aggrey in the centre of defence and when Mark Ford left for Darlington he took over as club captain.

Portsmouth (From trainee on 12/7/1988) FL 103+20/3 FLC 8+2 FAC 4+2 Others 5+2
Bournemouth (Loaned on 9/9/1994) FL 3
Torquay U (Free on 25/3/1999) FL 71 FLC 2 FAC 4 Others 1

RYAN Keith James
Born: Northampton, 25 June 1970
Height: 5'11" Weight: 12.8
Club Honours: FAT '91, '93; GMVC '93

Keith enjoyed a pre-season testimonial against Leicester City last term but injuries meant that it was not until November that he was able to resume his place in the Wycombe Wanderers' line-up. A loyal and committed servant of the club for more than a decade, it was rather fitting that he should score in the FA Cup semi-final against Liverpool, skilfully chipping the 'keeper to give the Chairboys a glimmer of hope in the closing minutes of the tie. A hard-working player who is particularly strong in the air, he mostly featured in his customary central midfield role but towards the end of the campaign he played as an emergency striker to cover for an injury crisis.

Wycombe W (Signed from Berkhamstead T during 1990 close season) FL 209+16/23 FLC 13/3 FAC 18+4/5 Others 13+1/1

RYAN Robert (Robbie) Paul
Born: Dublin, 16 May 1977
Height: 5'10" Weight: 12.0
Club Honours: Div 2 '01
International Honours: RoI: U21-12; Yth; Sch

This hard-tackling left back has become a firm favourite with the Millwall fans with his no-nonsense style of defending. He was a regular in the starting line-up throughout the 2000-01 campaign and apart from the occasional absence due to suspension he rarely missed a match. Robbie has now made over 130 senior appearances for the Lions and although he loves to get forward he has yet to score a goal for the club.

Huddersfield T (Free from Belvedere YC on 26/7/1994) FL 12+3 FLC 2
Millwall (£10,000 on 30/1/1998) FL 113+5 FLC 6 FAC 4 Others 5

Paul Scholes

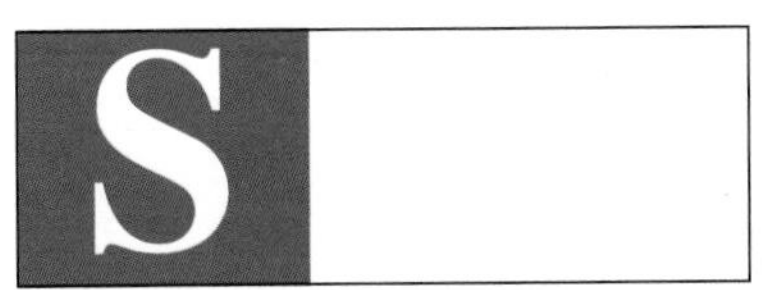

SADLIER Richard Thomas
Born: Dublin, 14 January 1979
Height: 6'2" Weight: 12.10
Club Honours: Div 2 '01
International Honours: RoI: U21-1; Yth

Richard had a wretched time with injuries at Millwall last season, missing the opening matches with a broken arm and then suffering a knee injury towards the end of the campaign. In between he gave some fine performances showing a greater maturity to his play. He is a talented young striker who holds the ball up well, can turn a defender and sets up chances for his team-mates with some deft flicks. He will be hoping to avoid injuries and win a regular place in the Lions team in the 2001-02 campaign.

Millwall (Signed from Belvedere YC on 14/8/1996) FL 65+36/19 FLC 4/1 FAC 3+1 Others 7+2/3

SAHA Louis
Born: Paris, France, 8 August 1978
Height: 5'11" Weight: 11.10
Club Honours: Div 1 '01
International Honours: France: U21; Yth (UEFA-U18 '97)

Louis had a sensational first season at Fulham and proved to be an inspirational signing by coach Jean Tigana. His searing pace, the ability to turn both ways on the proverbial sixpence and a powerful shot with either foot make him close to being the perfect striker. He scored 22 goals during the season from open play, to which he added a further ten penalties (from ten attempts) to finish the campaign as the leading scorer in Division One. One of six Fulham players in the PFA First Division team, he will surely prove a handful for many Premiership defences in the coming season.

Newcastle U (Loaned from Metz, France on 8/1/1999) PL 5+6/1 FAC 1/1
Fulham (£2,100,000 on 29/6/2000) FL 39+4/27 FLC 3+1/5 FAC 1

SAHNOUN Nicolas Omar Mickael
Born: Bordeaux, France, 3 September 1980
Height: 6'2" Weight: 12.10

A midfield player with a talent for long-range passing, Nicolas spent the 2000-01 season at Fulham in a long-term loan deal. He made a handful of senior appearances, mostly from the subs' bench and his best performances for the Cottagers came in the Worthington Cup tie with Derby County and the FA Cup game against Manchester United when he deputised for Sean Davis as the 'holding' midfield player. He is the son of Omar Sahnoun a former Nantes player who won six caps for France before tragically dying on the pitch just months before Nicolas was born.

Fulham (Loaned from Bordeaux, France on 13/10/2000) FL 2+5 FLC 1 FAC 1/1

SALAKO John Akin
Born: Nigeria, 11 February 1969
Height: 5'10" Weight: 12.8
Club Honours: FMC '91; Div 1 '94, '00
International Honours: E: 5

John was used mainly as a substitute by Charlton Athletic last season and started just six first-team games. His only goal proved of vital importance as it was the late equaliser that earned the Addicks an FA Cup replay against Conference outfit Dagenham & Redbridge, thus preventing a major upset. A vastly experienced player, John showed glimpses of the form that earned him five England caps in the early '90's but although he often looked impressive when coming off the bench he seemed unable to sustain his performance for a full 90 minutes. Not as quick as he once was, John is still an excellent crosser of the ball and is especially effective with free kicks and corners.

Crystal Palace (From apprentice on 3/11/1986) F/PL 172+43/22 FLC 19+5/5 FAC 20/4 Others 11+3/2
Swansea C (Loaned on 14/8/1989) FL 13/3 Others 2/1
Coventry C (£1,500,000 on 7/8/1995) PL 68+4/4 FLC 9/3 FAC 4/1
Bolton W (Free on 26/3/1998) PL 0+7
Fulham (Free on 22/7/1998) FL 7+3/1 FLC 2/1 FAC 2+2 Others 1
Charlton Ath (£150,000 + on 20/8/1999) P/FL 8+36/2 FLC 1+1 FAC 3+4/1

Louis Saha (left) and Phil Gilchrist

SALLI Janne
Born: Finland, 14 December 1977
Height: 6'2" Weight: 11.13
International Honours: Finland: 8
Signed by Barnsley at the end of the Scandinavian domestic season, Janne delayed his arrival at Oakwell so that he could complete his university studies. He quickly settled in showing himself to be a very able defender. Unfortunately he suffered a serious knee injury after just eight games for his new club and he was expected to be out of action for around 12 months. A right back or central defender he is very effective in the air with a strong tackle and good distribution.
Barnsley (£200,000 from FC Haka, Finland, ex TP Sjoki, on 7/11/2000) FL 6+1 FAC 1

SALT Phillip (Phil) Thomas
Born: Oldham, 2 March 1979
Height: 5'11" Weight: 11.9
The only local-born player in the Oldham Athletic squad, Phil is a young midfield player with plenty of reserve team experience. He was very much a fringe member of the first team last season, going down with an injury after initially breaking into the side and making a handful of appearances towards the end of the campaign. He scored one goal during 2000-01, netting in the LDV Vans Trophy tie against Wigan Athletic.
Oldham Ath (From trainee on 1/7/1997) FL 12+10 FLC 1+3 FAC 1+1/1 Others 3/1

SAM Hector McLeod
Born: Mount Hope, Trinidad, 25 February 1978
Height: 5'9" Weight: 11.5
International Honours: Trinidad & Tobago: 10
Hector joined Wrexham along with Carlos Edwards in the summer of 2000 and was an instant success at the Racecourse Ground, scoring six goals in his first six games. Loss of form and then a hernia operation subsequently hampered his progress but by the end of the season he had returned to a place on the subs' bench. An exciting young striker he was previously studying to become a doctor before becoming a professional footballer. Hector made his international debut for Trinidad & Tobago back in 1999 and won a further two more caps after signing for the Robins.
Wrexham (£125,000 from CL Financial San Juan Jabloteh, Trinidad on 8/8/2000) FL 11+9/6 FLC 1 FAC 1 Others 1

SAMPSON Ian
Born: Wakefield, 14 November 1968
Height: 6'2" Weight: 13.3
This reliable central defender was again an important figure for Northampton Town last season and deservedly finished the campaign as the club's 'Player of the Year'. Ian is excellent in the air, cool on the ground and a constant danger when he moves up to help out in attack. He was a near ever-present in 2000-01 and is now one of the Cobblers' top ten all-time appearance makers.
Sunderland (Signed from Goole T on 13/11/1990) FL 13+4/1 FLC 1 FAC 0+2 Others 0+1
Northampton T (Loaned on 8/12/1993) FL 8
Northampton T (Free on 5/8/1994) FL 282+3/23 FLC 16/1 FAC 9/1 Others 17/2
Tottenham H (Loaned on 22/6/1995) Others 3/1

SAMUEL JLloyd
Born: Trinidad, 29 March 1981
Height: 5'11" Weight: 11.4
International Honours: E: Yth
JLloyd gained some valuable European experience for Aston Villa in the pre-season Inter Toto Cup games before dropping back to the reserve team. He later returned to the first-team squad at the turn of the year to make a handful more senior appearances and will be hoping to make a further breakthrough at Villa Park in 2001-02. A former England youth international, he is a powerful young central defender.
Aston Villa (From trainee on 2/2/1999) PL 6+6 FLC 0+1 FAC 1 Others 3

SANDFORD Lee Robert
Born: Basingstoke, 22 April 1968
Height: 6'1" Weight: 13.4
Club Honours: AMC '92; Div 2 '93
International Honours: E: Yth
Lee's place in the Sheffield United line-up seemed to be under threat following the summer signing of Keith Curle and for a while he found himself on the transfer list. However, injuries to Curle meant that Lee started the season in central defence and he continued where he had left off at the end of the 1999-2000 campaign. Playing within his limitations his anticipation and excellent understanding with Shaun Murphy more than compensated for a certain lack of pace. Although he lost his place in the team in October injuries allowed him to return, before he was sidelined by a neck problem in February that required surgery. However having signed a new two-year contract for the Blades during the campaign he will be looking forward to regaining a first-team place in 2001-02.
Portsmouth (From apprentice on 4/12/1985) FL 66+6/1 FLC 11 FAC 4 Others 2+1
Stoke C (£140,000 on 22/12/1989) FL 255+3/8 FLC 19 FAC 16/2 Others 31/4
Sheffield U (£500,000 on 22/7/1996) FL 137+8/4 FLC 12+1 FAC 15/1 Others 3+1
Reading (Loaned on 5/9/1997) FL 5

SANTOS Georges
Born: Marseille, France, 15 August 1970
Height: 6'3" Weight: 14.0
A close-season signing for Sheffield United boss Neil Warnock, Georges took time to establish himself at Bramall Lane last term. He initially played both in the centre of the park and in defence but was used mainly as a substitute until mid-November when he settled into a midfield role. Always appearing to have time when in possession, he created openings with his decisive passing and impressed with his ball-winning abilities and all round commitment. Unfortunately a serious injury brought his season to an end in March when he sustained a broken nose and shattered eye socket in the game against Nottingham Forest.
Tranmere Rov (Free from Toulon, France on 29/7/1998) FL 46+1/2 FLC 6 FAC 1
West Bromwich A (£25,000 on 23/3/2000) FL 8
Sheffield U (Free on 5/7/2000) FL 23+8/4 FLC 1+2 FAC 1

SAUNDERS Dean Nicholas
Born: Swansea, 21 June 1964
Height: 5'8" Weight: 10.6
Club Honours: FAC '92; FLC '94
International Honours: W: 75
Dean made three appearances for Bradford City in the pre-season Inter Toto Cup matches but was then out of action for two months with a series of injuries including hamstring trouble and a knee cartilage problem. On his return to fitness he made a handful of Premiership appearances but it became clear that he was not a part of new boss Jim Jeffries' plans. On the international front he established a new record of caps for an outfield player for Wales when he made his 74th appearance in the World Cup qualifier against Armenia. Dean was out of contract at Valley Parade in the summer and at the time of writing his future was uncertain.
Swansea C (From apprentice on 24/6/1982) FL 42+7/12 FLC 2+1 FAC 1 Others 1+1
Cardiff C (Loaned on 29/3/1985) FL 3+1
Brighton & Hove A (Free on 7/8/1985) FL 66+6/21 FLC 4 FAC 7/5 Others 3
Oxford U (£60,000 on 12/3/1987) FL 57+2/22 FLC 9+1/8 FAC 2/2 Others 2/1
Derby Co (£1,000,000 on 28/10/1988) FL 106/42 FLC 12/10 FAC 6 Others 7/5
Liverpool (£2,900,000 on 19/7/1991) F/PL 42/11 FLC 5/2 FAC 8/2 Others 6/10
Aston Villa (£2,300,000 on 10/9/1992) F/PL 111+1/37 FLC 15/7 FAC 9/4 Others 8/1 (£2,350,000 to Galatasaray, Turkey on 1/7/1995)
Nottingham F (£1,500,000 on 16/7/1996) F/PL 39+4/5 FLC 5+1/2 FAC 2/2
Sheffield U (Free on 5/12/1997) FL 42+1/17 FLC 4/3 FAC 6/2 Others 2 (£500,000 to Benfica, Portugal on 10/12/1998)
Bradford C (Free on 6/8/1999) PL 32+12/3 FLC 1+2/1 FAC 2+1/2 Others 3

SAUNDERS Mark Philip
Born: Reading, 23 July 1971
Height: 5'11" Weight: 11.12
Mark was troubled by a knee injury for most of last season, and although he featured regularly in the Gillingham squad of 16 he only made the starting line-up for around half their First Division fixtures. He is a versatile performer and appeared during the season at full back, central defender and his normal position of midfield, from where he managed to score four goals in seven games with away doubles against Crystal Palace and Huddersfield. A box-to-box midfielder who never gives up, he is a strong tackler and excellent in the air.
Plymouth Arg (Signed from Tiverton T on 22/8/1995) FL 60+12/11 FLC 1+1 FAC 2+3 Others 2
Gillingham (Free on 1/6/1998) FL 72+23/10 FLC 3+2 FAC 7+1/1 Others 3+3

SAVAGE David (Dave) Thomas Patrick
Born: Dublin, 30 July 1973
Height: 6'1" Weight: 12.7
International Honours: RoI: 5; U21-5
This versatile Northampton midfield player prefers a role in the centre of the park, although he can also play wide on either

flank if required. A regular in the Cobblers' line-up throughout 2000-01 he finished the campaign as the club's second-top scorer with eight league goals. Comfortable on the ball, Dave likes to run at opposition defender and also has a powerful shot. Out of contract in the summer his future was unclear at the time of writing.
Brighton & Hove A (Signed from Kilkenny on 5/3/1991. Free to Longford T in May 1992)
Millwall (£15,000 on 27/5/1994) FL 104+28/6 FLC 11/2 FAC 6+2/2 Others 2/1
Northampton T (£100,000 on 7/10/1998) FL 98+15/18 FLC 3 FAC 5 Others 2+1

SAVAGE Robert (Robbie) William
Born: Wrexham, 18 October 1974
Height: 6'1" Weight: 11.11
Club Honours: FAYC '92; FLC '00
International Honours: W: 20; U21-5; Yth; Sch
Once again a truly inspirational figure for Leicester City last term, Robbie appeared to revel in the extra responsibility handed to him when Neil Lennon departed. Very much a cult figure at Filbert Street, he seemed to have a never-ending supply of energy. He also found himself in the opposition box more often than in the past and duly took advantage with some cool finishes, notably a memorable strike at home to West Ham. Unfortunately he was injured in the Wycombe FA Cup tie and subsequently had to undergo a cartilage operation. His influence was clearly missed in the next few games although, remarkably, he was back playing just 17 days after submitting himself to the surgeon's knife. A right-footed midfielder or wing back, he has a level of skill that is easily overlooked. Robbie also represented Wales during the campaign winning four more caps.
Manchester U (From trainee on 5/7/1993)
Crewe Alex (Free on 22/7/1994) FL 74+3/10 FLC 5 FAC 5 Others 8/1
Leicester C (£400,000 on 23/7/1997) PL 125+12/8 FLC 13+2 FAC 11/1 Others 2+1

Robbie Savage

SAVARESE Giovanni
Born: Caracas, Venezuela, 14 July 1971
Height: 6'0" Weight: 13.2
International Honours: Venezuela: 20
Giovanni joined Swansea last October after several seasons playing in the MLS where his career tally of 41 goals made him one of the leading scorers in the brief history of that competition. He got off to a great start netting seven goals in his first nine games and although he seemed to lose his scoring touch later on he hit a hat-trick in the 5-3 defeat at Luton, before finishing up as the club's leading scorer with a respectable total of 13 goals. A striker with a high work rate who is always capable of finding space in the box, he is also a Venezuelan international and added a further cap during his stay at the Vetch Field when he appeared in the World Cup qualifying tie against Colombia in April. Out of contract in the summer his future was uncertain at the time of writing.
Swansea C (Free from San Jose Earthquakes, USA, ex New England Revolution, on 13/10/2000) FL 28+3/12 FAC 0+1 Others 3/2

SAWYERS Robert (Rob)
Born: Dudley, 20 November 1978
Height: 5'10" Weight: 11.7
2000-01 was probably Rob's best campaign for Barnet since his arrival at Underhill some three seasons previously. He began as the Bees regular left back but despite some consistent performances he lost his place in the new year when Lee Flynn was signed from Hayes. However he returned to the team in March playing in midfield, a role that he adapted to well. The highlight of his season was without doubt his performance at Saltergate in the 2-1 win over Chesterfield in September. He defended outstandingly throughout the 90 minutes and contributed a rare goal when he drilled home a left-foot shot to put the Bees on their way to victory. He was placed on the open to offers list following the Bees' relegation to the Conference.
Barnet (From trainee at Wolverhampton W on 22/10/1997) FL 78+6/3 FLC 5 FAC 2 Others 6/1

SCALES John Robert
Born: Harrogate, 4 July 1966
Height: 6'2" Weight: 13.5
Club Honours: FAC '88; FLC '95, '99
International Honours: E: 3; B-2
Having been released by Tottenham at the end of the 1999-2000 season John joined Ipswich Town during the summer. He began brightly, making his debut at Leicester at the beginning of September but he was constantly dogged by injuries and made only three more first-team appearances at Portman Road. He finally left the club by mutual consent in April announcing that he intended to gain coaching qualifications and also concentrate on his business interests. A strong and versatile defender he played in over 400 Football League and Premiership games.
Bristol Rov (From Leeds U juniors on 11/7/1985) FL 68+4/2 FLC 3 FAC 6 Others 3+1
Wimbledon (£70,000 on 16/7/1987) F/PL 235+5/11 FLC 18+1 FAC 20+1 Others 7+1/4

Liverpool (£3,500,000 on 2/9/1994) PL 65/2 FLC 10/2 FAC 14 Others 4+1
Tottenham H (£2,600,000 on 11/12/1996) PL 29+4 FLC 4/1
Ipswich T (Free on 5/7/2000) PL 2 FLC 2

SCARLETT Andre Pierre
Born: Wembley, 11 January 1980
Height: 5'4" Weight: 9.6
A right-sided midfielder with boundless energy Andre was again on the fringe of the first-team squad at Luton last season, his cause not being helped by the fact that he played under three different managers during the campaign. He is a skilful player who always gives 100 per cent for the cause but was one of five players released by the Hatters at the end of April.
Luton T (From trainee on 8/7/1998) FL 9+9/1 FLC 2/1 FAC 0+2 Others 0+2

SCHEMMEL Sebastien
Born: Nancy, France, 2 June 1975
Height: 5'10" Weight: 11.12
International Honours: France: U21
After joining West Ham on loan from Metz last January Sebastien went on to produce a string of impressive performances for the Hammers. He did well on his debut at Charlton and played brilliantly in the FA Cup fourth round tie at Old Trafford when he successfully curbed the threat of Ryan Giggs. However despite this no permanent deal was pursued and he returned to France in the summer.
West Ham U (Loaned from Metz, France, ex Nancy, on 19/1/2001) PL 10+2 FAC 3

SCHNOOR Stefan
Born: Neumunster, Germany, 24 April 1971
Height: 5'10" Weight: 11.10
After undergoing close-season surgery for a groin injury, Stefan featured in most of Derby County's games during the opening months of the 2000-01 season, but with his contract due to expire in the summer he moved back to the Bundesliga, joining Wolfsburg in exchange for Brian O'Neil. A left-sided wing back able to strike a dead ball with great power, he showed that he could play equally well in a more central position.
Derby Co (Free from SV Hamburg, Germany, ex Neumunster FC, on 13/7/1998) PL 48+12/2 FLC 4+2 FAC 3

SCHOFIELD Daniel (Danny) James
Born: Doncaster, 10 April 1980
Height: 5'10" Weight: 11.3
Danny was a regular in Huddersfield's reserve team last term but managed just a single first-team outing when he came off the subs' bench for the final 25 minutes of the 3-0 defeat at Fulham. He is a promising young striker with a good touch who is always willing to chase every cause.
Huddersfield T (£2,000 from Brodsworth on 8/2/1999) FL 1+3 FLC 0+2 FAC 0+1

SCHOFIELD John David
Born: Barnsley, 16 May 1965
Height: 5'11" Weight: 11.8
This hard-tackling midfield man returned to Lincoln City in the summer of 2000 as youth development officer but was pressed into first team action as a result of an early-season injury crisis. John battled hard in the centre of the park being used on occasions as a man-marker. He remained part of the first-team squad until the end of February when he went back to full-time coaching.
Lincoln C (Free from Gainsborough Trinity on 10/11/1988) FL 221+10/11 FLC 15/2 FAC 5+2 Others 13+1
Doncaster Rov (Free on 18/11/1994) FL 107+3/12 FLC 4 FAC 2 Others 3
Mansfield T (£10,000 on 8/8/1997) FL 81+5 FLC 4 FAC 4 Others 4
Hull C (Free on 28/7/1999) FL 13+12 FLC 4 FAC 2+2 Others 1+1
Lincoln C (Free on 8/8/2000) FL 13+6 FAC 1 Others 3+1/1

SCHOLES Paul
Born: Salford, 16 November 1974
Height: 5'7" Weight: 11.10
Club Honours: PL '96, '97, '99, '00, '01; FAC '96, '99; CS '96, '97
International Honours: E: 35; Yth (UEFA-U18 '93)
One of England's few successes during Euro 2000, Paul had a fine start to the 2000-01 season. However after impressing both at club level and in a friendly for England against France in September he was strangely subdued in the World Cup qualifier against Germany at Wembley in October. Despite a lack of goals in the Premiership, he scored regularly in the Champions' League including a strike against PSV in October and a double against Panathinaikos in November. He continued to remain a key figure for both United and England as the season reached its climax and finished on a high with goals in the end-of-season internationals against Mexico and Greece.
Manchester U (From trainee on 29/1/1993) PL 145+47/47 FLC 6+2/5 FAC 8+6/4 Others 47+10/16

SCHWARZ Stefan Hans
Born: Malmo, Sweden, 18 April 1969
Height: 5'10" Weight: 12.6
International Honours: Sweden: 69; U21
Stefan was still recovering from an achilles injury suffered in the 1999-2000 season at the beginning of last term, and it was not until shortly before Christmas that he finally returned to first-team action for Sunderland.

Stefan Schwarz

A tremendous competitor on the left side of midfield, he scored his only goal of the campaign in the 4-1 win over Ipswich on New Year's Day and went on to secure a regular place in the line-up for the remainder of the season. An experienced figure in the centre of the park, his calm approach brought much greater stability to the Wearsiders' midfield.

Arsenal (£1,750,000 from Benfica, Portugal, ex Malmo, on 31/5/1994) PL 34/2 FLC 4 FAC 1 Others 10/2 (£2,500,000 to Fiorentina, Italy on 27/7/1995)
Sunderland (£3,500,000 from Valencia, Spain on 9/8/1999) PL 44+3/2 FLC 1 FAC 6

SCHWARZER Mark
Born: Sydney, Australia, 6 October 1972
Height: 6'5" Weight: 13.6
International Honours: Australia: 16; Yth

Having begun the 2000-01 campaign as Middlesbrough's first-choice 'keeper, Mark was sidelined by an injury early on and it was not until November that he returned to first-team action for the Riverside club. Although not always able to find his best form in a struggling side, he improved steadily as the season progressed with Boro' eventually pulling clear of relegation problems. He remained a first-choice for Australia too, and was a key member of the side that defeated Brazil to take third place in the FIFA Confederations Cup tournament in the summer.

Bradford C (£350,000 from Kaiserslautern, Germany, ex Blacktown, Marconi, Dynamo Dresden, on 22/11/1996) FL 13 FAC 3
Middlesbrough (£1,500,000 on 26/2/1997) F/PL 144 FLC 15 FAC 8

SCIMECA Ricardo
Born: Leamington Spa, 13 June 1975
Height: 6'1" Weight: 12.9
Club Honours: FLC '96
International Honours: E: B-1; U21-9

Having lost the Nottingham Forest captain's armband to Chris Bart-Williams at the start of last season, Ricardo went on to retain his first-team place for most of the campaign. However manager David Platt never seemed sure of his best position and he was tried at full back, in the centre of the defence, and in central midfield before eventually settling on the right-hand side of midfield. A versatile player with good skills on the ball, the constant changing of roles seemed to affect his confidence somewhat.

Aston Villa (From trainee on 7/7/1993) PL 50+23/2 FLC 4+3 FAC 9+1 Others 5+2
Nottingham F (£3,000,000 on 23/7/1999) FL 72+2/4 FLC 4 FAC 3

Mark Schwarzer

SCOTT Andrew (Andy)
Born: Epsom, 2 August 1972
Height: 6'1" Weight: 11.5
Club Honours: Div 3 '99

This left-sided player began the 2000-01 season playing in a wide-midfield role, but when Brentford hit an injury crisis he was switched to striker with devastating effect. He hit a total of 15 goals in 27 league and cup games for the Bees before he was surprisingly sold to Oxford United along with Rob Quinn last January. However, although he took some time to settle in a struggling U's side he finished the campaign with a flourish, netting five goals in 12 games to provide a hint of what may be to come in 2001-02. A hard-working striker he established a useful partnership up front with Phil Gray at the Manor Ground.

Sheffield U (£50,000 from Sutton U on 1/12/1992) P/FL 39+36/6 FLC 5/2 FAC 2+1 Others 3+1/3
Chesterfield (Loaned on 18/10/1996) FL 4+1/3
Bury (Loaned on 21/3/1997) FL 2+6
Brentford (£75,000 on 21/11/1997) FL 109+9/28 FLC 8+1/4 FAC 3 Others 6/3
Oxford U (£75,000 on 12/1/2001) FL 21/5

SCOTT Dion Elijah
Born: Birmingham, 24 December 1980
Height: 5'11" Weight: 11.3

This promising youngster stepped up to make his senior debut for Walsall in the LDV Vans Trophy tie against Wigan and also featured in the next round against Stoke before making his bow in the Second Division when he came off the subs' bench in the last match of the season against Northampton. A confident and extremely mobile defender he is still remembered for an outstanding display for the Saddlers' youths against Spurs a couple of seasons ago.

Walsall (From trainee on 18/5/1999) FL 0+1 Others 2

SCOTT Keith James
Born: Westminster, 9 June 1967
Height: 6'3" Weight: 14.3
Club Honours: GMVC '93; FAT '93

Keith featured in the opening game of the 2000-01 campaign for Reading but thereafter he was very much a forgotten figure at the Madejski Stadium. In October he joined Colchester United and impressed during his spell at Layer Road, scoring on his debut at Port Vale. He subsequently returned to the Royals with a knee injury but failed to win a return to the first team and was allowed to join the U's once again in March, this time on a short-term contract. However his second spell at Layer Road proved to be somewhat less successful and he was released before the end of the season. Keith is a big bustling target man with a wealth of experience.

Lincoln C (Free from Leicester U on 22/3/1990) FL 7+9/2 FLC 0+1 Others 1+1
Wycombe W (£30,000 in March 1991 on 1/3/1991) FL 15/10 FLC 4/2 FAC 6/1 Others 2/2
Swindon T (£375,000 on 18/11/1993) P/FL 43+8/12 FLC 5/3 Others 3/1
Stoke C (£300,000 on 30/12/1994) FL 22+3/3 FAC 2/1 Others 0+1
Norwich C (Signed on 11/11/1995) FL 10+15/5 FLC 0+2 FAC 0+2

Bournemouth (Loaned on 16/2/1996) FL 8/1
Watford (Loaned on 7/2/1997) FL 6/2 Others 2
Wycombe W (£55,000 on 27/3/1997) FL 60+3/20 FLC 1+1/1 FAC 5/1 Others 1+1
Reading (£250,000 on 24/3/1999) FL 20+15/5 FLC 2+1/2 FAC 2+1 Others 1+2/1
Colchester U (Loaned on 12/10/2000) FL 5/1
Colchester U (Free on 19/3/2001) FL 3+1

SCOTT Richard Paul
Born: Dudley, 29 September 1974
Height: 5'9" Weight: 12.8

Richard started the 2000-01 season as first choice at right back for Peterborough United but although he performed well he lost his place and only came back in the side towards the end of the season due to injuries. A hard-working player with accurate distribution he can also play on the right-hand side of midfield. Although he was offered a new contract, at the time of writing it appeared that he would be leaving London Road in the summer under the 'Bosman' ruling.

Birmingham C (From trainee on 17/5/1993) FL 11+1 FLC 3+1 Others 3
Shrewsbury T (Signed on 22/3/1995) FL 91+14/18 FLC 6 FAC 8+1/3 Others 8+1/1
Peterborough U (Signed on 20/7/1998) FL 65+16/7 FLC 1+3 FAC 1 Others 6+1

SCOTT Robert (Rob)
Born: Epsom, 15 August 1973
Height: 6'1" Weight: 11.10

Converted from a striker, Rob settled into his role at the centre of the Rotherham back three with ease last season. He played a key role in the team's successful campaign and his long throws deep into the opposing penalty area set up several goals for his colleagues. Blessed with great pace and the ability to read a game superbly, he suffered somewhat from disciplinary problems and this is an area of his game where he needs to improve.

Sheffield U (£20,000 from Sutton U on 1/8/1993) FL 2+4/1 FLC 0+1 Others 2+1
Scarborough (Loaned on 22/3/1995) FL 8/3
Northampton T (Loaned on 24/11/1995) FL 5 Others 1
Fulham (£30,000 on 10/1/1996) FL 65+19/17 FLC 3+5 FAC 3/1 Others 2+2/1
Carlisle U (Loaned on 18/8/1998) FL 7/3
Rotherham U (£50,000 on 17/11/1998) FL 77+2/4 FLC 3+1 FAC 6/1 Others 6

SCOWCROFT James (Jamie) Benjamin
Born: Bury St Edmunds, 15 November 1975
Height: 6'1" Weight: 12.2
International Honours: E: U21-5

Jamie found it hard to match his achievements of the 1999-2000 campaign last season at Ipswich. He started in the opening game but found himself on the bench for the home game with Manchester United. He then had to wait until the end of the year before he got back into the side on a regular basis and formed a useful partnership up front with Marcus Stewart. Once Alun Armstrong had joined the club Jamie was used as a striker for the first half with Armstrong taking over some time in the second period, allowing him to attack from a deeper midfield berth. His lack of opportunities as an out-and-out striker reduced his chances of scoring regularly, however it gave him the opportunity to arrive in the penalty area late and get on the end of crosses unchallenged. His aerial power is still his biggest asset but his passing skills have improved in his midfield role and he is always willing to drop back and help out defensively.

Ipswich T (From trainee on 1/7/1994) P/FL 163+39/47 FLC 21+4/7 FAC 9+1 Others 7+4/1

SCULLY Anthony (Tony) Derek Thomas
Born: Dublin, 12 June 1976
Height: 5'7" Weight: 11.12
International Honours: RoI: B-1; U21-10; Yth; Sch

Tony found first-team opportunities very limited at Queens Park Rangers in 2000-01. He featured briefly in the new year, making one appearance from the subs' bench and starting in the home match against Watford at the beginning of March, but was otherwise restricted to reserve-team football. A skilful ball winner he suffered somewhat due to the fact that the team generally employed more defensive players on the right side of midfield while Tony is essentially more suited to an attacking role. He was released by Rangers in the summer.

Crystal Palace (From trainee on 2/12/1993) FL 0+3
Bournemouth (Loaned on 14/10/1994) FL 6+4 Others 2
Cardiff C (Loaned on 5/1/1996) FL 13+1
Manchester C (£80,000 on 12/8/1997) FL 1+8
Stoke C (Loaned on 27/1/1998) FL 7
Queens Park R (£155,000 on 17/3/1998) FL 20+20/2 FLC 4+1 FAC 0+1

SEABURY Kevin
Born: Shrewsbury, 24 November 1973
Height: 5'10" Weight: 11.11

Kevin made the starting line-up for Shrewsbury Town in the opening game of the 2000-01 campaign but then went down with a hernia problem. The injury required an operation and once he had returned to fitness he found it difficult to win a regular place in the line-up. He was restricted to just a handful of appearances in the second half of the season and will be hoping to re-establish himself in the side in 2001-02. He is a right wing back who is strong in the tackle and shows good pace when bringing the ball out of defence. He was placed on the open to offers list in the summer.

Shrewsbury T (From trainee on 6/7/1992) FL 206+23/7 FLC 10+2/1 FAC 12 Others 10+2

SEAMAN David Andrew
Born: Rotherham, 19 September 1963
Height: 6'4" Weight: 14.10
Club Honours: Div 1 '91; PL '98; FAC '93, '98; FLC '93; ECWC '94; CS '98
International Honours: E: 65; B-6; U21-10

2000-2001 was quite a season for David. He had an excellent Euro 2000, but despite missing England's final game against Romania through injury he began last term with the media scrutinising his displays for both club and country. Then after missing several weeks in the middle of the season with shoulder and ankle injuries he returned to the Arsenal side to provide a boost for the defence. A string of fine performances and clean sheets during this period persuaded new national coach Sven Goran Eriksson that he was still the country's best 'keeper, and David repaid this faith by producing a great save in the dying minutes of the World Cup qualifier against Finland at Anfield to secure three valuable points. David holds the Gunners' club record of appearances for a goalkeeper, and remains quite simply one of the best around. His size, presence and composure instil confidence in all those around him. Having spent more than a decade at Highbury he received a well-deserved testimonial in May when Barcelona provided the opposition.

Leeds U (From apprentice on 22/9/1981)
Peterborough U (£4,000 on 13/8/1982) FL 91 FLC 10 FAC 5
Birmingham C (£100,000 on 5/10/1984) FL 75 FLC 4 FAC 5
Queens Park R (£225,000 on 7/8/1986) FL 141 FLC 13 FAC 17 Others 4
Arsenal (£1,300,000 on 18/5/1990) F/PL 360 FLC 32 FAC 48 Others 56+1

SEARLE Damon Peter
Born: Cardiff, 26 October 1971
Height: 5'11" Weight: 10.4
Club Honours: WC '92, '93; Div 3 '93
International Honours: W: B-1; U21-6; Yth; Sch

This whole-hearted left back was an ever-present for Southend United in 2000-01, filling the gap left by departing 'Player of the Year' Nathan Jones more than adequately. Equally strong with both feet and possessing great stamina, Damon provided a string of decent crosses to set up chances for his colleagues throughout the season. He scored just one goal for the Blues - netting with a memorable 30-yard free kick in injury time of the final game of the season against Mansfield Town.

Cardiff C (From trainee on 20/8/1990) FL 232+2/3 FLC 9/1 FAC 13 Others 29
Stockport Co (Free on 28/5/1996) FL 34+7 FLC 2+1 FAC 2 Others 1
Carlisle U (Free on 6/7/1998) FL 57+9/3 FLC 4 FAC 1 Others 4+1/1
Rochdale (Loaned on 17/9/1999) FL 13+1
Southend U (Free on 10/7/2000) FL 46/1 FLC 2 FAC 4 Others 6/1

SEDGEMORE Benjamin (Ben) Redwood
Born: Wolverhampton, 5 August 1975
Height: 5'11" Weight: 12.10
International Honours: E: Sch

This tall midfielder performed impressively for Macclesfield during the 2000-2001 season and was ever present apart from a brief spell out with an ankle injury last February. Heeding his manager's advice to push forward he scored a number of important goals, notably in the Worthington Cup ties against Bolton and Middlesbrough. Although mostly operating in a central role he occasionally appeared wide on the right and even took over in goal at Southend after Tony Bullock was sent off. He made a surprise move to Lincoln in the spring where he appeared mostly in a right-sided central role but found it difficult to establish himself as anything more than a squad player following a change in management. He was

David Seaman

placed on the open to offers list in May. Away from football Ben is mid-way through a part time degree course in Psychology and Law at Warwick University.
Birmingham C (From trainee on 17/5/1993)
Northampton T (Loaned on 22/12/1994) FL 1
Mansfield T (Loaned on 25/8/1995) FL 4+5 Others 1
Peterborough U (Free on 10/1/1996) FL 13+4 FAC 1
Mansfield T (Free on 6/9/1996) FL 58+9/6 FLC 1 FAC 2+1 Others 2
Macclesfield T (£25,000 on 19/3/1998) FL 84+18/6 FLC 8/2 FAC 7/1 Others 2
Lincoln C (Signed on 16/2/2001) FL 3+7/1 Others 0+1

SEDGLEY Stephen (Steve) Philip
Born: Enfield, 26 May 1968
Height: 6'1" Weight: 13.13
Club Honours: FAC '87, '91
International Honours: E: U21-11

Having eventually signed a further contract for Wolves last summer, Steve was back in the first-team squad for the early matches and scrambled a decisive goal against Burnley. However shortly afterwards he was sidelined by a knee injury, and when this failed to clear up following an operation his contract was cancelled by mutual consent and he returned to London to recuperate. An experienced central defender and midfield player he was something of a dead-ball specialist.
Coventry C (From apprentice on 2/6/1986) FL 81+3/3 FLC 9/2 FAC 2+2 Others 5+1
Tottenham H (£750,000 on 28/7/1989) F/PL 147+17/9 FLC 24+3/1 FAC 22+1/1 Others 5+3
Ipswich T (£1,000,000 on 15/6/1994) P/FL 105/15 FLC 10/2 FAC 5 Others 5/1
Wolverhampton W (£700,000 on 29/7/1997) FL 96+10/9 FLC 8+1 FAC 8+1/1

SEDGWICK Christopher (Chris) Edward
Born: Sheffield, 28 April 1980
Height: 5'11" Weight: 10.10

After breaking down in pre-season training Chris had to undergo a knee operation that kept him out of the Rotherham first-team squad until Christmas. He then mainly featured from the subs' bench coming on with great effect on a number of occasions to demonstrate his speed in a wide-right midfield role. Perhaps the best illustration of this was in the televised game at Walsall when he came on to score a wonderful equaliser.
Rotherham U (From trainee on 16/8/1997) FL 55+41/11 FLC 1+2 FAC 3+5 Others 2+2/1

SELLARS Scott
Born: Sheffield, 27 November 1965
Height: 5'8" Weight: 10.0
Club Honours: FMC '87; Div 1 '93, '97
International Honours: E: U21-3

This skilful midfielder started the early part of the 2000-01 season on the substitutes' bench for Huddersfield, often called upon late in the game to add extra fuel to the midfield fires. With his bright and inventive style of play he was able to conjure up that vital tackle or pass to unlock opposition defences. Scott became a regular in the side in late October, before a sending off and then injury put him on the sidelines. Still considered for first-team duties when fully fit, the experienced midfielder turned down a loan deal to Hartlepool before deadline day and in mid-April moved to Denmark to join Aarhus on a free transfer.
Leeds U (From apprentice on 25/7/1983) FL 72+4/12 FLC 4/1 FAC 4 Others 2/1
Blackburn Rov (£20,000 on 28/7/1986) FL 194+8/35 FLC 12/3 FAC 11/1 Others 20/2
Leeds U (£800,000 on 1/7/1992) PL 6+1 FLC 1+1 Others 1
Newcastle U (£700,000 on 9/3/1993) F/PL 56+5/5 FLC 6+1/2 FAC 3 Others 4/1
Bolton W (£750,000 on 7/12/1995) P/FL 106+5/15 FLC 8+1 FAC 5/1 Others 0+1
Huddersfield T (Free on 30/7/1999) FL 29+19/1 FLC 1+2/1 FAC 1+1

SELLEY Ian
Born: Chertsey, 14 June 1974
Height: 5'10" Weight: 11.0
Club Honours: FLC '93; FAC '93; ECWC '94
International Honours: E: U21-3; Yth

Ian joined Wimbledon on a free transfer during the 2000 close season from Fulham where he had not played for the first team since suffering a badly broken leg some three years previously. He made a handful of appearances for the Dons in the opening games but then dropped out of the scene as he found it impossible to win his place back. An experienced hard-working midfield player, at his best he is an effective ball winner and man marker.
Arsenal (From trainee on 6/5/1992) PL 35+6 FLC 5+1 FAC 3 Others 8+2/2
Southend U (Loaned on 3/12/1996) FL 3+1
Fulham (£500,000 on 17/10/1997) FL 3
Wimbledon (Free on 8/8/2000) FL 1+3

SENDA Daniel (Danny) Luke
Born: Harrow, 17 April 1981
Height: 5'10" Weight: 10.0
International Honours: E: Yth

Danny continued to develop slowly with Wycombe last term and he was a near ever-present in the first-team squad, although most of his appearances came from the subs' bench. He enjoyed a fine end to the season capped by two goals, the first at Bristol City when he cut inside and superbly chipped in

from the edge of the area. He is an attacking midfield player whose pacy runs down the right cause many problems for opposition defenders.
Wycombe W (From Southampton juniors on 26/1/1999) FL 17+47/3 FLC 0+3 FAC 1+3 Others 0+4

SENIOR Michael Graham
Born: Huddersfield, 3 March 1981
Height: 5'9" Weight: 11.6
This promising local-born youngster made his debut for Huddersfield Town when he replaced Kevin Gray for the closing minutes against Crewe in the autumn. He subsequently made a further three appearances as a substitute before dropping back to continue his footballing education in the Terriers' reserves. Michael is a determined character, never afraid to get stuck in to the midfield action and with a keen eye for goal.
Huddersfield T (From trainee on 8/7/1999) FL 0+4 FLC 0+1

SERTORI Mark Anthony
Born: Manchester, 1 September 1967
Height: 6'2" Weight: 14.2
Club Honours: GMVC '88
Mark was a regular in the centre of the defence for York City last season losing his place after the home defeat by Exeter in February. Shortly afterwards his contract was cancelled by mutual consent and he joined Shrewsbury on a monthly contract. He made just a single appearance from the subs' bench for the Gay Meadow club before signing a three-month contract for Cheltenham. He was used as cover for injured central defenders Mark freeman and Neil Howarth although he made one appearance as a makeshift striker, a position he had played in regularly in the early days of his career. Carl is a strong tackling central defender who uses his height to good effect and always gives 100 per cent effort for the cause. Out of contract in the summer his future was unclear at the time of writing.
Stockport Co (Signed from East Manchester on 7/2/1987) FL 3+1 FLC 1
Lincoln C (Free on 1/7/1988) FL 43+7/9 FLC 6 FAC 4/1 Others 5/2
Wrexham (£30,000 on 9/2/1990) FL 106+4/3 FLC 8+1 FAC 6 Others 9+1
Bury (Free on 22/7/1994) FL 4+9/1 FLC 1 FAC 2+1 Others 1+2/1
Scunthorpe U (Free on 22/7/1996) FL 82+1/2 FLC 6 FAC 7 Others 4+1
Halifax T (Free on 7/7/1998) FL 44+1 FLC 6 FAC 1 Others 2
York C (£25,000 on 3/9/1999) FL 63+3/2 FLC 1+1 FAC 4 Others 2
Shrewsbury T (Free on 9/3/2001) FL 0+1
Cheltenham T (Free on 16/3/2001) FL 10

SHAIL Mark Edward David
Born: Sandviken, Sweden, 15 October 1966
Height: 6'1" Weight: 13.3
International Honours: E: SP-1
Mark finally arrived at Kidderminster almost ten years after the club first showed an interest in him and he featured regularly for most of last season, only losing his place for the last few games. A typical old-fashioned central defender he is effective in the air, strong in the tackle and always gives 100 per cent. He scored just one goal, heading home a corner in the Harriers' 1-1 draw at Southend in September.
Bristol C (£45,000 from Yeovil on 25/3/1993) FL 117+11/4 FLC 5+1 FAC 11/1 Others 4
Kidderminster Hrs (Free on 14/7/2000) FL 36/1 FLC 2 FAC 3 Others 2

SHANDRAN Anthony Mark
Born: Newcastle, 17 September 1981
Height: 5'11" Weight: 12.0
Anthony was a regular scorer for Burnley's reserve team last season and his performances won a call up to the Clarets' first-team squad. He made his Football League debut last February when he came on from the subs' bench for the last nine minutes at Crewe. He is a promising striker who will be looking to feature more regular for the Turf Moor club in the coming season.
Burnley (From trainee on 13/11/2000) FL 0+1

SHANNON Gregg Zachary
Born: Magherafelt, 15 February 1981
Height: 6'0" Weight: 11.8
International Honours: NI: Yth; Sch
Gregg joined Halifax Town on a month-to-month contract last August and provided useful cover for 'keeper Lee Butler. His only senior appearance came in the Worthington Cup first round second leg tie against Tranmere Rovers when he gave an excellent performance. Gregg was released by the Shaymen in mid-February.
Sunderland (Free from Maghera Colts on 19/2/1998)
Halifax T (Free on 17/8/2000) FLC 1

SHARP James
Born: Reading, 2 January 1976
Height: 6'1" Weight: 14.6
This former Reading trainee joined Hartlepool from Wessex League club Andover last August and made his Football League debut in the opening game at Lincoln. He settled in quickly and by the second half of the campaign he had established himself as a regular in the first team. James is a powerful left-sided defender with an effective long throw. His willingness to give 100 per cent to the cause made him a popular figure with the club's supporters and he scooped the 'Player of the Year' awards at the end of the season.
Hartlepool U (Free from Andover on 10/8/2000) FL 31+3/2 FLC 2 Others 4+1

SHARP Kevin Phillip
Born: Ontario, Canada, 19 September 1974
Height: 5'9" Weight: 11.11
Club Honours: FAYC '93; Div 3 '97; AMC '99
International Honours: E: Yth (UEFA-U18 '93); Sch
This reliable and solid left back had a fine season at Wigan in 2000-01, seeing off the challenge of newcomer Gino Padula to keep his place in the team. Having made a big contribution to the Latics campaign into the play-offs he suffered the agony of conceding a last-minute penalty that led to defeat in the final against Reading. Nevertheless as a committed professional he will no doubt put this disappointment behind him when the 2001-02 season commences.
Leeds U (£60,000 from Auxerre, France on 20/10/1992) PL 11+6 Others 0+1
Wigan Ath (£100,000 on 30/11/1995) FL 155+21/10 FLC 6+2/1 FAC 7+3 Others 17+1/1

SHARPE Lee Stuart
Born: Halesowen, 27 May 1971
Height: 6'0" Weight: 12.12
Club Honours: ECWC '91; FLC '92; PL '93, '94, '96; CS '94
International Honours: E: 8; B-1; U21-8
Lee had a frustrating time at Bradford City in the first half of the 2000-01 season. He was tried in several different left-sided roles (full back, wing back and midfield) but as soon as he began to establish himself in the team he was hit by injury - first his foot, then a hamstring. In February he joined Portsmouth on loan and featured regularly in a central midfield role during the remainder of the season, helping the club to avoid relegation down to the Second Division. His experience proved invaluable for Pompey as he showed a high work rate, some fine close control and the ability to shake off defenders.
Torquay U (From trainee on 31/5/1988) FL 9+5/3 Others 2+3
Manchester U (£185,000 on 10/6/1988) F/PL 160+33/21 FLC 15+8/9 FAC 22+7/3 Others 18+2/3
Leeds U (£4,500,000 on 14/8/1996) PL 28+2/5 FLC 3/1 FAC 0+1 Others 1+2
Bradford C (£200,000 on 25/3/1999) P/FL 25+13/2 FLC 2+1 FAC 1+1 Others 3
Portsmouth (Loaned on 2/2/2001) FL 17

Lee Sharpe

SHAW Paul
Born: Burnham, 4 September 1973
Height: 5'11" Weight: 12.4
International Honours: E: Yth
Having joined First Division new boys Gillingham for a substantial fee in the summer Paul had the misfortune to suffer an ankle injury on the opening day of the

season against Stockport. He returned to the line-up at the end of September and was rarely absent thereafter. An experienced striker, he was at his best playing just behind the front two where his subtle touches and alertness made him a dangerous player.

Arsenal (From trainee on 18/9/1991) PL 1+11/2 FAC 0+1
Burnley (Loaned on 23/3/1995) FL 8+1/4
Cardiff C (Loaned on 11/8/1995) FL 6
Peterborough U (Loaned on 20/10/1995) FL 12/5 Others 2
Millwall (£250,000 on 15/9/1997) FL 88+21/26 FLC 6/2 FAC 2 Others 5+6
Gillingham (£450,000 on 11/7/2000) FL 27+6/1 FAC 2/2

SHAW Richard Edward
Born: Brentford, 11 September 1968
Height: 5'9" Weight: 12.8
Club Honours: FMC '91; Div 1 '94

Richard looked as if he would face a major challenge to win a place in Coventry's back four at the start of the 2000-01 season. However after one game out he was back in the side and enjoyed a decent run in the line-up before being dropped in November, firstly in favour of Mo Konjic and later Gary Breen. He returned to the side in February and put in several polished performances during the run-in, although he was unable to prevent the Sky Blues from being relegated to the First Division. A player who never gives less than 100 per cent, he remains the best man-to-man marker at Highfield Road and has now played over 200 games for the club without scoring a goal.

Crystal Palace (From apprentice on 4/9/1986) F/PL 193+14/3 FLC 28+2 FAC 18 Others 12+1
Hull C (Loaned on 14/12/1989) FL 4
Coventry C (£1,000,000 on 17/11/1995) PL 175+4 FLC 15 FAC 14+1

SHEARER Alan
Born: Newcastle, 13 August 1970
Height: 6'0" Weight: 12.6
Club Honours: PL '95
International Honours: E: 63; B-1; U21-11; Yth

Having become Newcastle's most capped England player, club captain Alan retired from international football after Euro 2000 so that he could spend more time with his family and concentrate his attention on assisting his club. However he got off to a slow start last term and it was not until the fourth game of the season that he opened his account with a penalty at Coventry to give him his 200th league goal. However a promising striking partnership with Carl Cort was interrupted when Cort was sidelined by injury in September and Alan was largely left to carry the weight of the Magpies' attack on his own. Tendonitis in the left knee continued to be a problem, although he attempted to play on with the help of steroid injections. He eventually succumbed to the surgeon's knife at the end of the year, and his remarkable powers of recovery enabled him to return to action earlier than expected at the end of February. However after two games he broke down in training and after consulting a specialist he conceded that his season was over. He subsequently underwent further surgery at the beginning of May and is expected to be fit in time for the 2001-02 campaign. Despite his advancing years he remains a dangerous striker. His great body strength makes it difficult for defenders to knock him off the ball; his tremendous shooting power makes him a threat anywhere within striking range, while his poaching instincts enable him to snap up half chances with ease. Alan was made an Honorary Freeman of Newcastle in March - only the second footballer after the legendary Jackie Milburn to receive that honour - and his heart clearly remains in the city, a popular view being that he will eventually take over as manager of the club. He was further honoured when he received an OBE for services to Association Football in the Queen's Birthday Honours List.

Southampton (From trainee on 14/4/1988) FL 105+13/23 FLC 16+2/11 FAC 11+3/4 Others 8/5
Blackburn Rov (£3,600,000 on 24/7/1992) PL 132+6/112 FLC 16/14 FAC 8/2 Others 9/2
Newcastle U (£15,000,000 on 30/7/1996) PL 130+4/69 FLC 8/4 FAC 21/16 Others 13/4

SHEFFIELD Jonathan (Jon)
Born: Bedworth, 1 February 1969
Height: 5'11" Weight: 12.10

Jon began last season as first-choice 'keeper for Plymouth Argyle and produced some sound performances until dropping out with an injury in November. He returned to the team once fit again, but then lost his place in the new year to new signing Romain Larrieu. Jon is a fine shot stopper who is quick off his line to thwart opposing forwards.

Norwich C (From apprentice on 16/2/1987) FL 1
Aldershot (Loaned on 22/9/1989) FL 11 Others 1
Aldershot (Loaned on 21/8/1990) FL 15 Others 1
Cambridge U (Free on 18/3/1991) FL 56 FLC 3 FAC 4 Others 6
Colchester U (Loaned on 23/12/1993) FL 6
Swindon T (Loaned on 28/1/1994) PL 2
Hereford U (Loaned on 15/9/1994) FL 8 FLC 2
Peterborough U (£150,000 on 20/7/1995) FL 62 FLC 8 FAC 6 Others 5
Plymouth Arg (£100,000 on 28/7/1997) FL 155 FLC 7 FAC 11 Others 2

SHELDON Gareth Richard
Born: Birmingham, 31 January 1980
Height: 5'11" Weight: 12.0

Gareth made excellent progress last season and established himself as a regular in the Scunthorpe United line-up for the first time. He is a very fast and direct striker who started the campaign at centre forward before switching to a role wide on the right. Although his goals return was disappointing he netted with a brilliant 75-yard individual effort in the LDV Vans Trophy tie against Hartlepool. Collecting a loose ball from the edge of his own area he dribbled straight up the field before netting with a great 20-yard drive into the bottom of the net. He missed the last few games after suffering a leg injury at Shrewsbury.

Scunthorpe U (From trainee on 4/2/1999) FL 46+27/4 FLC 3 FAC 4+1/1 Others 3+3/4

SHEPHEARD Jonathan (Jon) Thomas
Born: Oxford, 31 March 1981
Height: 6'3" Weight: 12.4

This promising Oxford United youngster followed up his breakthrough in 1999-2000 to make seven more starts at the beginning of last season. Before being sidelined by injury, he netted his first senior goal in a Worthington Cup tie against Wolves. A tall lanky central defender he will be hoping to return to first-team action in the coming season.

Oxford U (From trainee on 28/6/1999) FL 6+1 FLC 2/1 Others 2

SHEPHERD Paul David
Born: Leeds, 17 November 1977
Height: 5'11" Weight: 12.0
International Honours: E: Yth

Paul returned from a spell in Iceland at the start of the 2000-01 campaign and after a trial with Crewe he joined Scunthorpe United last September. He came on from the subs' bench in the home win against Torquay and looked comfortable at right wing-back but he was released after three weeks and then spent time training with Wimbledon before joining Luton Town on a short-term contract. He featured regularly for the Hatters in the closing weeks of the campaign but was unable to prevent them dropping into the Third Division. Out of contract in the summer his future was unclear at the time of writing.

Leeds U (From trainee on 15/9/1995) PL 1
Ayr U (Loaned on 31/3/1997) SL 6/1
Tranmere Rov (Loaned on 23/2/1999) FL 0+1
Ayr U (Free on 13/9/1999) SL 20+2/1 SLC 1 SC 4+1 (Free to Keflavic, Iceland on 13/6/2000)
Scunthorpe U (Free on 29/9/2000) FL 0+1
Luton T (Free, via trials at Crewe Alex and Wimbledon, on 22/3/2001) FL 7

SHERIDAN Darren Stephen
Born: Manchester, 8 December 1967
Height: 5'5" Weight: 11.5

Darren began the 2000-01 campaign in the Wigan first-team line-up but suffered a broken rib early on that kept him out for several weeks. He came back into the team in November and featured regularly for the remainder of the season, either in midfield or at full back. Darren is a hard working left-footed player who tackles enthusiastically and distributes the ball with care. Out of contract in the summer, he was surprisingly released by the Latics. Darren is the younger brother of Oldham's John Sheridan.

Barnsley (£10,000 from Winsford U on 12/8/1993) F/PL 149+22/5 FLC 9+4/1 FAC 9+2/1 Others 1+1
Wigan Ath (Free on 2/7/1999) FL 50+8/3 FLC 5 FAC 1+2 Others 5/1

SHERIDAN John Joseph
Born: Stretford, 1 October 1964
Height: 5'10" Weight: 12.0
Club Honours: FLC '91; Div 1 '97
International Honours: RoI: 34; B-1; U23-2; U21-2; Yth

Although now in the twilight of his playing career John continued to be an influential figure in the centre of the park for Oldham Athletic last season. Despite being struck down by injury early on, he fought his way back into the Latics' team and featured in more than half their Second Division games during the campaign. He is still a quality

play maker and one of the best passers of the ball in the division. He will be sorely missed by all at Boundary Park when he finally decides to hang his boots up. John is the older brother of Darren Sheridan.
Leeds U (From Manchester C juniors on 2/3/1982) FL 225+5/47 FLC 14/3 FAC 11+1/1 Others 11/1
Nottingham F (£650,000 on 3/8/1989) FLC 1
Sheffield Wed (£500,000 on 3/11/1989) F/PL 187+10/25 FLC 24/3 FAC 17+1/3 Others 5/2
Birmingham C (Loaned on 9/2/1996) FL 1+1 FLC 2
Bolton W (£180,000 on 13/11/1996) F/PL 24+8/2 FLC 2 FAC 2 (Free to Doncaster Rov in 1998 close season)
Oldham Ath (Free on 20/10/1998) FL 86+5/7 FLC 1+1 FAC 8+1/1 Others 1

SHERINGHAM Edward (Teddy) Paul
Born: Highams Park, 2 April 1966
Height: 5'11" Weight: 12.5
Club Honours: Div 2 '88; FMC '92; CS '97; PL '99, '00, '01; FAC '99; EC '99
International Honours: E: 41; U21-1; Yth
Like vintage wine, Teddy just seemed to get better and better with each passing game during the 2000-01 campaign. Instead of dwelling over the proposed summer signing of Ruud Van Nistelrooy from PSV, he started the season so well that he not only froze out his regular partner on the bench, Ole Gunner Solskjaer, but also Dwight Yorke. The other pleasing aspect of his game was his sensational strike rate. While he has never been what you might call a prolific scorer during his four years with United, he took a leaf out of Solskjaer's book, and hit an amazing 13 goals before the turn of the year. Memorable highlights included four in successive games against Bradford, Sunderland and Anderlecht in September, then a brace against Leicester in the top of the table clash at Filbert Street in October, and a hat-trick against Southampton at the end of that month. Also during October, he earned a recall into the England side for the vital World Cup qualifier against Finland, proving once again, that he can still hack it on the international stage. He continued to impress, winning plaudits from all quarters and finished the season with an array of awards: 'Footballer of the Year', PFA 'Player of the Year' and the Manchester Evening News-GMR Sports Personality of the Year in January. He was also honoured by his fellow professionals with a place in the PFA's Premiership team. A superb goal from a free-kick in the 4-0 win over Mexico in the summer added a fitting touch to an exceptional season.
Millwall (From apprentice on 19/1/1984) FL 205+15/93 FLC 16+1/8 FAC 12/5 Others 11+2/5
Aldershot (Loaned on 1/2/1985) FL 4+1 Others 1
Nottingham F (£2,000,000 on 23/7/1991) FL 42/14 FLC 10/5 FAC 4/2 Others 6/2
Tottenham H (£2,100,000 on 28/8/1992) PL 163+3/75 FLC 14/10 FAC 17/13
Manchester U (£3,500,000 on 1/7/1997) PL 73+31/31 FLC 1/1 FAC 4+5/5 Others 23+16/9

SHERON Michael (Mike) Nigel
Born: St Helens, 11 January 1972
Height: 5'10" Weight: 11.13
International Honours: E: U21-16
Mike failed to reach the heights of form he had shown at Barnsley in 1999-2000 last term and struggled to find the net in First Division games. However he seemed to have no trouble in the Worthington Cup matches, scoring five goals in five games including doubles against Rotherham and Crewe. He spent much of the season in an unfamiliar wide-right role and following a change of manager his confidence seemed to drop, leading to fewer senior opportunities. A skilful striker who links up well with his colleagues, he will be hoping for better fortune in 2001-02.
Manchester C (From trainee on 5/7/1990) F/PL 82+18/24 FLC 9+1/1 FAC 5+3/3 Others 1
Bury (Loaned on 28/3/1991) FL 1+4/1 Others 2
Norwich C (£1,000,000 on 26/8/1994) P/FL 19+9/2 FLC 6/3 FAC 4/2
Stoke C (£450,000 on 13/11/1995) FL 64+5/34 FLC 4/5 FAC 1 Others 2
Queens Park R (£2,750,000 on 2/7/1997) FL 57+6/19 FLC 2+2/1 FAC 2
Barnsley (£1,000,000 on 27/1/1999) FL 63+22/12 FLC 9/7 FAC 2+2

SHERWOOD Timothy (Tim) Alan
Born: St Albans, 6 February 1969
Height: 6'0" Weight: 12.9
Club Honours: PL '95
International Honours: E: 3; B-1; U21-4
Tim was again a highly influential figure for Tottenham last term, often taking over the captain's armband in the absence of Sol Campbell. He performed consistently all season, perhaps his only weakness being a lack of goals - he netted just twice in the wins over Sunderland and Liverpool. A talented midfield play maker, he is a stabilising figure in the centre of the park and his pace is very effective when joining the attack. His superb organisational skills are a great benefit to the team although it remains to be seen whether he has a long-term future at White Hart Lane under new boss Glenn Hoddle.
Watford (From trainee on 7/2/1987) FL 23+9/2 FLC 4+1 FAC 9 Others 4+1
Norwich C (£175,000 on 18/7/1989) FL 66+5/10 FLC 7/1 FAC 4 Others 5+1/2
Blackburn Rov (£500,000 on 12/2/1992) F/PL 239+7/25 FLC 24+1/2 FAC 15+2/4 Others 12
Tottenham H (£3,800,000 on 5/2/1999) PL 66+8/12 FLC 4/1 FAC 9/1 Others 3/1

SHIELDS Anthony (Tony) Gerald
Born: Londonderry, 4 June 1980
Height: 5'7" Weight: 10.10
Tony continued to develop at a steady rate with Peterborough last term and now finally appears to have made a breakthrough to a regular place in the first team. A tenacious midfield dynamo who is very strong in the tackle, he produced some effective performances and is a fine prospect. His talents were recognised by members of the Posh supporters' club who voted him 'Young Player of the Year'.
Peterborough U (From trainee on 6/7/1998) FL 49+18/2 FLC 3+1/1 FAC 2+3/1 Others 0+1

SHIELDS Greg
Born: Falkirk, 21 August 1976
Height: 5'9" Weight: 11.2
Club Honours: Div 1 '00
International Honours: S: U21-2; Yth; Sch
Greg was beset by injury problems in 2000-01 and as a result he only started four first-team games for Charlton Athletic. Even when fit he found it difficult to displace new signing Radostin Kishishev in his favoured right-back position and he appeared in a central defensive role for the Worthington Cup tie against Stoke City. Greg is a very capable defender who is strong in the tackle and has the ability to push down the flank and deliver an accurate cross. Once tipped as a future Scottish international he will be aiming to re-establish himself in the Addicks' line-up in the coming season.
Glasgow R (From juniors on 1/7/1993) SL 7 SLC 1+1 Others 2
Dunfermline Ath (Signed on 30/6/1997) SL 75 SLC 6 SC 4 Others 1
Charlton Ath (£580,000 on 26/8/1999) P/FL 23+2/2 FLC 4 FAC 3

SHILTON Samuel (Sam) Roger
Born: Nottingham, 21 July 1978
Height: 5'10" Weight: 11.6
Sam was a regular choice at left back for Hartlepool for most of 2000-01, only losing his place to Ian Clark in the closing weeks of the campaign. A left-sided player who is also comfortable in midfield, he scored five valuable goals for Pool during the season. He was surprisingly released by boss Chris Turner in the summer. Sam is the son of the former England 'keeper Peter Shilton.
Plymouth Arg (Trainee) FL 1+2 FAC 0+1
Coventry C (£12,500 on 31/10/1995) PL 3+4 FLC 1+1 FAC 0+1
Hartlepool U (Free on 9/7/1999) FL 45+9/7 FLC 1+1 FAC 3 Others 3+1

SHIPPERLEY Neil Jason
Born: Chatham, 30 October 1974
Height: 6'1" Weight: 13.12
International Honours: E: U21-7
Having started the 2000-01 season in good form for Barnsley, Neil was sidelined by a knee injury at the end of October and he did not return to first-team action until shortly before Christmas. Once back he took time to settle in but eventually regained his scoring touch, proving to be the Reds' most consistent outfield player. His final tally of 16 goals was a true reflection of the hard work and no little skill that he showed. Always willing to battle for the cause, he is particularly effective with his back to goal from where he can bring his colleagues into play. Strong in the air, he also packs a punch with his right foot and his winning goal in the 'derby' match at Bramall Lane was a perfect example of this.
Chelsea (From trainee on 24/9/1992) PL 26+11/7 FLC 4+2/1 FAC 3/1 Others 2
Watford (Loaned on 7/12/1994) FL 5+1/1
Southampton (£1,250,000 on 6/1/1995) PL 65+1/12 FLC 5+1/2 FAC 10/5
Crystal Palace (£1,000,000 on 25/10/1996) F/PL 49+12/20 FLC 3 FAC 2 Others 5/1
Nottingham F (£1,500,000 on 22/9/1998) PL 12+8/1 FAC 1
Barnsley (£700,000 on 7/7/1999) FL 70+8/27 FLC 4+1/3 FAC 2 Others 3/1

SHITTU Daniel (Danny) Olusola
Born: Lagos, Nigeria, 2 September 1980
Height: 6'3" Weight: 16.0
Danny is a powerfully built Charlton central defender who was loaned to Blackpool for the final months of last season to provide

him with first-team action. He scored with a header on his Football League debut against Lincoln and produced some impressive displays for the Bloomfield Road club. He was called up by Nigeria for their friendly game against Libya in April but turned down the opportunity, preferring to help the Tangerines in their promotion campaign, and went on to play a vital role right up to the play-off semi-finals. Unfortunately his loan period expired before the final and he had to watch from the sidelines as his team-mates defeated Leyton Orient to win promotion to the Second Division.

Charlton Ath (Free from Carshalton Ath on 15/9/1999)
Blackpool (Loaned on 16/2/2001) FL 15+2/2 Others 2

SHOREY Nicholas (Nicky)
Born: Romford, 19 February 1981
Height: 5'9" Weight: 10.10

One of a number of very promising youngsters on Leyton Orient's books, Nicky made several appearances at both left back and left midfield during the first half of last season. His exploits soon attracted the attention of bigger clubs and in February he was sold to Reading. He continued his development in the Royals' reserves and will be hoping to make his senior debut in 2001-02.

Leyton Orient (From trainee on 5/7/1999) FL 12+3 FAC 1
Reading (£25,000 on 9/2/2001)

SHORT Craig Jonathan
Born: Bridlington, 25 June 1968
Height: 6'1" Weight: 13.8

Having finally put all his injury problems behind him, Craig stepped forward to win a regular place in the Blackburn Rovers line-up last term. He came under pressure from Martin Taylor for a time but eventually fought off the challenge and went on to score his first goal in five years. Netting the opener for Rovers in what was to be a 5-0 thrashing of local rivals Burnley he brought the house down, and then had a major contribution to the second goal although it was credited to an opponent. Ironically his career at Ewood Park might have almost ended if transfer target Lucien Mettomo had not failed a medical. Instead Short and Taylor combined to prove that in-house solutions could be found to the club's defensive problems. Indeed in the vital closing stages of the campaign Craig was in commanding form and will be hoping to retain his place on returning to the Premiership in 2001-02.

Scarborough (Free from Pickering T on 15/10/1987) FL 61+2/7 FLC 6 FAC 2 Others 7/1
Notts Co (£100,000 on 27/7/1989) FL 128/6 FLC 6/1 FAC 8/1 Others 16/2
Derby Co (£2,500,000 on 18/9/1992) FL 118/9 FLC 11 FAC 7/4 Others 7
Everton (£2,700,000 on 18/7/1995) PL 90+9/4 FLC 7 FAC 4 Others 3
Blackburn Rov (£1,700,000 + on 3/8/1999) FL 52/1 FLC 1 FAC 3

SHUKER Christopher (Chris) Alan
Born: Liverpool, 9 May 1982
Height: 5'5" Weight: 10.1

Highly rated by Joe Royle, Chris spent the majority of the season playing for Manchester City reserves where he produced some impressive appearances. He was loaned to Third Division Macclesfield on the transfer deadline day to gain experience of first-team football and made his senior debut from the subs' bench in the home win against Blackpool. A tricky and pacy left winger who is not afraid to tackle, Chris scored his first senior goal with a fine header to give Macc a 1-0 victory over Kidderminster at the beginning of April.

Manchester C (From trainee on 21/9/1999)
Macclesfield T (Loaned on 27/3/2001) FL 6+3/1

SIBON Gerald
Born: Dalen, Holland, 19 April 1974
Height: 6'5" Weight: 13.5

Gerald had an excellent season with Sheffield Wednesday in 2000-01, putting the disappointment of relegation from the Premiership behind him to produce some fine displays and win over the Hillsborough fans. He finished top scorer with 15 league and cup goals and his hat-trick against Queens Park Rangers in December was one of the highlights of the campaign. Tall and skilful he often played in a midfield role rather than as a striker and Owls' fans are hoping that he will become the play maker that the team has lacked for several years.

Sheffield Wed (£2,000,000 from Ajax, Holland, ex Twente, VVV Groningen, Roda JC, on 16/7/1999) P/FL 44+25/18 FLC 5+2/1 FAC 5+1/2

SIGURDSSON Larus Orri
Born: Akureyri, Iceland, 4 June 1973
Height: 6'0" Weight: 13.11
International Honours: Iceland: 33; U21-16; Yth

Larus was still fighting his way back from a serious injury to his right knee at the start of last season and once fit he found it difficult to win his place back in the West Bromwich Albion team. Biding his time, he eventually returned from the subs' bench in the 1-0 win at Bolton in December but it was not until the end of February that he made the first-team squad on a regular basis. A rugged defender who can appear on the right-hand side or in a more central role he also won a recall to the Iceland national team before the end of the campaign.

Stoke C (£150,000 from Thor, Iceland on 21/10/1994) FL 199+1/7 FLC 15 FAC 6+1 Others 6
West Bromwich A (£325,000 on 17/9/1999) FL 34+5 FAC 1 Others 0+1

SILVESTRE Mikael Samy
Born: Tours, France, 9 August 1977
Height: 6'0" Weight: 13.1
Club Honours: PL '00, '01
International Honours: France: 6; U21; Yth (UEFA-U18 '96)

What a huge asset Mikael was in the Manchester United back four following the long-term absence of Jaap Stam during the first half of last season. His value and versatility kept United firing on all cylinders in both the Premiership and Europe up to Stam's return in January. Switching to left back on a more full-time basis, he had an almost unbroken run in the side up until March. His consistency at club level was rewarded on the international stage when he made his debut for France as a substitute for Marcel Desailly in the friendly against Germany in February. He celebrated his first goal for the Reds in their 2-0 Premiership victory over Leicester at Old Trafford in March.

Manchester U (£4,000,000 from Inter Milan, Italy on 10/9/1999) PL 55+6/1 FAC 2 Others 19+3

[SILVINHO] SILVIO DE CAMPOS Junior
Born: Sao Paulo, Brazil, 30 June 1974
Height: 5'9" Weight: 10.9
Club Honours: CS '99
International Honours: Brazil: 2

Silvinho is an exciting, attacking left back who gets forward at every opportunity and is often on the score sheet. He netted a vital goal in Arsenal's opening Champions' League game against Sparta Prague last September, jinking past several defenders before firing past the 'keeper. His fantastic skill, strong tackles and pinpoint distribution have enabled him to break into the Brazil national squad. However he had a somewhat frustrating time at Highbury in the middle of the season when he was sidelined with a hamstring injury and then lost his place to impressive youngster Ashley Cole. Nevertheless he won a place in the PFA's Premiership team selected by his fellow professionals.

Arsenal (£4,000,000 from Corinthians, Brazil on 20/7/1999) PL 46+9/3 FLC 2 FAC 4+2 Others 14+3/2

SIMONSEN Steven (Steve) Preben
Born: South Shields, 3 April 1979
Height: 6'3" Weight: 13.2
International Honours: E: U21-4; Yth

Steve had a frustrating time at Everton last term when he failed to make a single first-team start for the Toffees. His only glimpse of the Premiership came as a 90th minute substitute for the injured Paul Gerrard against West Ham in December. Winning an FA Premier Reserve League championship medal was scant consolation, as he sought to build on his limited Premiership experience. An England U21 international, Steve was once one of the brightest goalkeeping talents in the country, but he may now have to move away from Goodison to realise that potential.

Tranmere Rov (From trainee on 9/10/1996) FL 35 FLC 4 FAC 3
Everton (£3,300,000 on 23/9/1998) PL 0+2 FLC 2

SIMPKINS Michael (Mike) James
Born: Sheffield, 28 November 1978
Height: 6'1" Weight: 12.0

Mike's versatility helped Chesterfield Manager Nicky Law operate two defensive systems with equal success in the 2000-01 season. Although able to play as a left back in a back four, he is more comfortable as one of three centre halves, where his positional sense and ability to read a game comes more to the fore. He proved to be a valuable squad member for the Spireites in their successful promotion campaign. He was reported to have signed for Cardiff in the summer.

Sheffield Wed (From trainee on 4/7/1997)
Chesterfield (Free on 26/3/1998) FL 22+4 FLC 2+1 FAC 1 Others 2

SIMPSON Fitzroy
Born: Trowbridge, 26 February 1970
Height: 5'8" Weight: 12.0
International Honours: Jamaica: 33

Fitzroy featured in a number of early season games for Hearts in the 2000-01 campaign, including a UEFA Cup tie against Stuttgart, but then fell out of favour and in March he moved south of the border to join Second Division Walsall in a loan deal. He scored in the first half of his debut for the Saddlers and made a big impression in the handful of games that he played before being injured in the play-off semi final at Stoke. A combative midfield player with good pace and stamina he can deliver accurate corners and free kicks.

Swindon T (From trainee on 6/7/1988) FL 78+27/9 FLC 15+2/1 FAC 2+1 Others 3+2
Manchester C (£500,000 on 6/3/1992) P/FL 58+13/4 FLC 5+1 FAC 4+1
Bristol C (Loaned on 16/9/1994) FL 4
Portsmouth (£200,000 on 17/8/1995) FL 139+9/10 FLC 12+1 FAC 8
Heart of Midlothian (£100,000 on 8/12/1999) SL 7+4 SLC 0+1 SC 2
Walsall (Loaned on 2/3/2001) FL 8+2/1 Others 1

SIMPSON Michael
Born: Nottingham, 28 February 1974
Height: 5'9" Weight: 10.8
Club Honours: AIC '95

Michael enjoyed his best season to date in the Wycombe engine room last term. He has become something of an institution in the side and in many ways embodies the style of the current team. A hard-working midfield player with good close control, great stamina and a fierce determination he often seems to deliver an astonishing number of passes in a game. The provider of many chances for his colleagues he netted several vital goals himself during the campaign including strikes in the FA Cup ties against Grimsby and Wimbledon.

Notts Co (From trainee on 1/7/1992) FL 39+10/3 FLC 4+1 FAC 2+1 Others 7+3
Plymouth Arg (Loaned on 4/10/1996) FL 10+2
Wycombe W (£50,000 on 5/12/1996) FL 144+18/8 FLC 9+1 FAC 16+2/4 Others 8

SIMPSON Paul David
Born: Carlisle, 26 July 1966
Height: 5'6" Weight: 11.10
International Honours: E: U21-5; Yth

This experienced left-sided midfielder proved to be an inspirational signing for Blackpool manager Steve McMahon. A creative player with a good eye for goal he became the Bloomfield Road club's dead-ball specialist, delivering accurate corners and creating numerous chances with his free kicks. Paul was a pivotal figure for the Tangerines and was rewarded for some excellent performances when he was voted the club's 'Player of the Year' and also selected for the PFA Third Division team.

Manchester C (From apprentice on 4/8/1983) FL 99+22/18 FLC 10+1/2 FAC 10+2/4 Others 8+3
Oxford U (£200,000 on 31/10/1988) FL 138+6/43 FLC 10/3 FAC 9/2 Others 5/2
Derby Co (£500,000 on 20/2/1992) P/FL 134+52/48 FLC 12+3/6 FAC 4+4/1 Others 14+2/2
Sheffield U (Loaned on 6/12/1996) FL 2+4
Wolverhampton W (£75,000 on 10/10/1997) FL 32+20/6 FLC 2+1 FAC 2+5
Walsall (Loaned on 17/9/1998) FL 4/1
Walsall (Loaned on 11/12/1998) FL 6
Blackpool (Free on 11/8/2000) FL 44/12 FLC 4 FAC 2 Others 3/1

SINCLAIR Frank Mohammed
Born: Lambeth, 3 December 1971
Height: 5'9" Weight: 12.9
Club Honours: FAC '97; FLC '98, '00
International Honours: Jamaica: 19

A right-footed wing back or central defender, Frank missed the start of the 2000-01 campaign after undergoing a groin operation in the summer. It was not until October that he returned to Premiership action for Leicester, stepping in at right wing back for the injured Andrew Impey. He slotted in very effectively and hit his best form almost immediately, but sadly he was dogged by injuries throughout the campaign, in particular a nasty calf strain. In total he made few senior appearances and the team looked decidedly less effective when he was absent. He continued to represent Jamaica when fit, assisting in their campaign to qualify for the 2002 World Cup finals.

Chelsea (From trainee on 17/5/1990) F/PL 163+6/7 FLC 17+1/1 FAC 18/1 Others 13/3
West Bromwich A (Loaned on 12/12/1991) FL 6/1
Leicester C (£2,000,000 on 14/8/1998) PL 78+4/1 FLC 14 FAC 6/1

SINCLAIR Trevor Lloyd
Born: Dulwich, 2 March 1973
Height: 5'10" Weight: 12.10
International Honours: E: B-1; U21-14; Yth

Trevor missed the start of the 2000-01 season for West Ham with a niggling groin strain, but once settled in the side he was a key figure for the Hammers and particularly impressive in the away victories at Leeds and Southampton. He scored with a cracking 30-yard volley into the roof of the net in the 5-0 win over Charlton on Boxing Day and the strike was later selected as 'Goal of the Month'. Unfortunately he then suffered a knee cartilage injury in mid-January and this forced him out of action for the remainder of the season. Trevor was mainly used on the right wing last term where his speed and tricky skills were put to good use, although he occasionally featured at right wing back.

Blackpool (From trainee on 21/8/1990) FL 84+28/15 FLC 8 FAC 6+1 Others 8+5/1
Queens Park R (£750,000 on 12/8/1993) P/FL 162+5/16 FLC 13/3 FAC 10/2
West Ham U (£2,300,000 + on 30/1/1998) PL 105/24 FLC 8+1 FAC 4 Others 10/1

SINTON Andrew (Andy)
Born: Cramlington, 19 March 1966
Height: 5'8" Weight: 11.5
Club Honours: FLC '99
International Honours: E: 12; B-3; Sch

Andy was hampered by niggling injuries that restricted his appearances for Wolves in the first half of last season. He came more into the picture in the new year after netting his first goal at Portsmouth in January. He added a second with a delightful lob at Crystal Palace, but still failed to make the same sort of impact as he had in his first campaign at Molineux. An experienced left-sided midfield player he is still capable of beating defenders down the flank and going on to deliver a pinpoint centre. Out of contract in the summer his future was unclear at the time of writing.

Cambridge U (From apprentice on 13/4/1983) FL 90+3/13 FLC 6/1 FAC 3 Others 2/1
Brentford (£25,000 on 13/12/1985) FL 149/28 FLC 8/3 FAC 11/1 Others 14/2
Queens Park R (£350,000 on 23/3/1989) F/PL 160/22 FLC 14 FAC 13/2 Others 3/1
Sheffield Wed (£2,750,000 on 19/8/1993) PL 54+6/3 FLC 13 FAC 5 Others 2+1
Tottenham H (£1,500,000 on 23/1/1996) PL 66+17/6 FLC 6+3 FAC 4+4/1
Wolverhampton W (Free on 13/7/1999) FL 59+6/2 FLC 3+1 FAC 5

SISSOKHO Habib
Born: Paris, France, 24 May 1971
Height: 6'3" Weight: 14.6

Having spent the 1999-2000 campaign engaged in a battle against relegation from the Belgian Second Division, Habib joined Torquay in the close season and became embroiled in their struggle to avoid the drop down to the Conference. He scored a close-range goal for the Gulls in his third outing for the club against Blackpool but then missed some time through injury and shortly after returning to the side he fell out of favour. New manager Colin Lee offered him a second chance but he departed in controversial circumstances following the defeat at Plymouth in April. Habib is a big target man who is strong in the air and lays the ball off well.

Preston NE (Free from Louhans Cuiseaux, France, ex Creteil, Noisy-le-Sec, on 19/2/1998) FL 4+3
Airdrieonians (Free on 20/8/1998) SL 0+1 (Free to Uniao de Madera, Portugal on 2/10/1998)
Torquay U (Free from R Capellen FC, Belgium, ex Uniao Leiria, on 11/8/2000) FL 7+7/2 FAC 2

SISSON Michael Anthony
Born: Sutton in Ashfield, 24 November 1978
Height: 5'9" Weight: 10.10

Michael started the 2000-01 season in excellent form in central midfield for Mansfield Town, but had the misfortune to suffer a serious knee injury at Exeter early in September that put him out of action for the remainder of the campaign. A hard-working player who is strong in the tackle and closes opponents down quickly, it is hoped that he will make a full recovery in time for the start of the 2001-02 campaign.

Mansfield T (From trainee on 27/1/1998) FL 26+5/2 FLC 3 Others 2

SKELTON Aaron Matthew
Born: Welwyn Garden City, 22 November 1974
Height: 5'11" Weight: 12.6

Aaron had his most productive campaign to date for Colchester United in the 2000-01 season. He stayed clear of the injuries that had previously plagued his career and was a near ever-present in the first team. A versatile player who can appear at centre back or in midfield he is very composed on the ball and has a tremendous long-range shot. He was the club's regular penalty taker last term and weighed in with a total of six goals.

Luton T (From trainee on 16/12/1992) FL 5+3 FLC 0+1 FAC 2 Others 2
Colchester U (Free on 3/7/1997) FL 114+11/17 FLC 4 FAC 5+1 Others 5+1

SKELTON Craig Eric
Born: Middlesbrough, 14 September 1980
Height: 5'9" Weight: 11.11

This young defender came through the ranks at Darlington and made his Football League debut when he came on as a late substitute in the 2-0 defeat at Cardiff last October. However he was released shortly afterwards and joined Unibond League side Whitby Town.

Darlington (From trainee on 17/7/1999) FL 0+1

SKOVBJERG Thomas
Born: Denmark, 25 October 1974
Height: 5'7" Weight: 11.8
Club Honours: NC '00

Thomas was sorely missed by Kidderminster for most of last season while he recovered from a knee ligament injury. He eventually made his Football League debut against Lincoln in March and quickly became a regular in the Harriers' line-up. A tricky right winger capable of terrorising opposition defenders and delivering lethal crosses, he was surprisingly released at the end of the campaign.

Kidderminster Hrs (Free from Esbjerg, Denmark on 24/8/1999) FL 7+5/1

SLADE Steven (Steve) Anthony
Born: Hackney, 6 October 1975
Height: 6'0" Weight: 11.2
International Honours: E: U21-4

Having been released by Queens Park Rangers at the end of the 1999-2000 campaign, Steve joined Cambridge United on a weekly contract at the start of last season. He gave some promising early-season performances but then seemed to suffer a dip in form and he was released at the beginning of November. He subsequently re-emerged at Luton Town where he had a trial with the reserves in April. He is a right-sided striker with good off-the-ball movement.

Tottenham H (From trainee on 1/7/1994) PL 1+4 FLC 0+1 FAC 0+2 Others 4
Queens Park R (£350,000 on 12/7/1996) FL 27+41/6 FLC 3+4/1 FAC 1+2
Brentford (Loaned on 13/2/1997) FL 4
Cambridge U (Free on 17/8/2000) FL 4+5/1 FLC 0+1

SMALL Bryan
Born: Birmingham, 15 November 1971
Height: 5'9" Weight: 11.9
International Honours: E: U21-12; Yth

Having been hampered by injury in the 1999-2000 season, Bryan found it difficult to get fixed up with a club last term despite having trials at several clubs including Carlisle and Brentford. He eventually joined Walsall on a short-term contract at the end of January to provide strength to a squad looking to win promotion. However his only first-team opportunities came in the LDV Vans Trophy games against Wigan and Stoke and he was released in the summer. At his best he is a tenacious left wing back who can overlap down the wing and cross the ball accurately.

Aston Villa (From trainee on 9/7/1990) F/PL 31+5 FLC 2 FAC 2+1 Others 4
Birmingham C (Loaned on 9/9/1994) FL 3
Bolton W (Free on 20/3/1996) F/PL 11+1 FLC 1 FAC 3
Luton T (Loaned on 8/9/1997) FL 15
Bradford C (Loaned on 19/12/1997) FL 5
Bury (Free on 30/1/1998) FL 18/1
Stoke C (Free on 14/7/1998) FL 40+5 FLC 3 FAC 2 Others 2
Walsall (Free, via trials at Carlisle, Brentford, on 29/1/2001) Others 2

SMART Allan Andrew Colin
Born: Perth, 8 July 1974
Height: 6'2" Weight: 12.10
Club Honours: AMC '97

Allan had another frustrating season with injuries at Watford last term and spent lengthy periods in the treatment room. He missed the early matches while recovering from a knee operation carried out during the summer, but after undergoing rehabilitation at Lilleshall he returned to fitness and netted four goals in a reserve game against Chelsea in November. However he failed to win his place back in the side and mostly featured from the subs' bench, before suffering another set back when he broke a toe in February. An honest and hard-working striker he is overdue a change of fortune.

St Johnstone (From juniors on 24/1/1991)
Brechin C (Free on 30/12/1991)
Inverness Caledonian Thistle (Free on 28/7/1993) SL 2+2 SLC 1+1
Preston NE (£15,000 on 22/11/1994) FL 17+4/6 FAC 2/1 Others 1+1
Carlisle U (Loaned on 24/11/1995) FL 3+1
Northampton T (Loaned on 13/9/1996) FL 1
Carlisle U (Signed on 9/10/1996) FL 41+3/16 FLC 1/1 FAC 4 Others 4+1
Watford (£75,000 + on 2/7/1998) P/FL 48+9/12 FLC 1+2 FAC 1 Others 0+3/1

SMICER Vladimir (Vlad)
Born: Czechoslovakia, 24 May 1973
Height: 5'11" Weight: 11.3
Club Honours: FLC '01; FAC '01; UEFAC '01
International Honours: Czech Republic: 48; U21-7. Czechoslovakia: 1

After starting the 2000-01 season as a first choice on the right flank for Liverpool, Vlad suffered a hamstring injury that sidelined him until October. Thereafter although always in the squad he rarely enjoyed a prolonged run in the team, and was evenly occasionally employed as a makeshift striker to cover for injuries. The most important of his seven goals during the season was that at Crystal Palace in the first leg of the Worthington Cup semi-final when he snatched a vital goal to set the Reds up for their second leg victory. He went on to make the starting line-up in both the FA and Worthington Cup finals, but was only used from the subs' bench in the UEFA Cup final against Deportivo Alaves. However he made a telling contribution as it was his run late in extra time that forced a foul, resulting in the free kick from which Gary McAllister produced the 'golden goal' winner.

Liverpool (£3,750,000 from RC Lens, France, ex SK Slavia Praha, on 14/7/1999) PL 29+19/3 FLC 7+1/4 FAC 6+1/1 Others 6+5

SMITH Adrian (Adie) Jonathan
Born: Birmingham, 11 August 1973
Height: 5'10" Weight: 12.0
Club Honours: NC '00
International Honours: E: SP-3

Adie became one of Kidderminster's most consistent performers last season. Apart from a short absence through injury in March that coincided with the club's worst run of the season he was a near ever-present. Essentially a central defender he can also play in a midfield role and it was from that position that he scored most of his six goals last term.

Kidderminster Hrs (£19,000 from Bromsgrove Rov on 17/6/1997) FL 32+2/5 FLC 1+1 FAC 3 Others 1/1

SMITH Alan
Born: Rothwell, 28 October 1980
Height: 5'9" Weight: 11.10
International Honours: E: 2; U21-5; Yth

After a relatively quiet 1999-2000, Alan had a season to remember last term. He began like a house on fire, scoring in both legs of the Champions' League qualifying round with Munich 1860, adding a double in the 2-0 win over Everton and a single in the 2-1 victory at Middlesbrough. He began to forge a formidable partnership with Mark Viduka and further goals came at regular intervals throughout the campaign. A striker who is a real team player, he is full of unselfish running and works hard to close down defenders. He netted several valuable goals in Europe, including the winner against Lazio in the Olympic Stadium after being set up by Viduka's back heel, and an audacious chip in the 4-1 win in Anderlecht. While his combative style and never-say-die attitude are really appreciated by the Elland Road faithful they also seem to attract the attention of referees and his game would improve if he could cut down the number of yellow cards he receives. Alan was rewarded for a fine season with his first England cap in the friendly against Mexico and retained his place in the squad for the World Cup qualifier in Greece.

Leeds U (From trainee on 26/3/1998) PL 61+20/22 FLC 1+1 FAC 5+4/3 Others 18+6/8

SMITH Alexander (Alex) Philip
Born: Liverpool, 15 February 1976
Height: 5'7" Weight: 11.10
Club Honours: AMC '01

Alex featured regularly for Port Vale last season and was an ever-present in the LDV Vans Trophy run. He scored the club's first goal in their opening round tie against Notts County and went on to gain a winners' medal when he appeared in the final against Brentford, a match that was undoubtedly one of the highlights of his career. He is a skilful left winger who causes havoc among opposition defenders with his pace and jinking runs.

Everton (From trainee on 1/7/1994)
Swindon T (Free on 12/1/1996) FL 17+14/1
Huddersfield T (Free on 6/2/1998) FL 4+2
Chester C (Free on 8/7/1998) FL 32/2 FLC 4/1 Others 1
Port Vale (£75,000 on 25/3/1999) FL 52+6/2 FLC 2+1 FAC 2 Others 7/1

Alan Smith

SMITH Andrew (Andy) William
Born: Lisburn, 25 September 1980
Height: 5'11" Weight: 11.10

Andy made his senior debut for Sheffield United as a substitute in the Worthington Cup tie at Lincoln and went on to feature from the bench on several occasions last term. Having signed a three-year deal in October he moved on loan to Bury to gain more first-team experience, making his debut in the 4-1 defeat at Bristol City. He created a favourable impression in his brief spell with the Shakers before returning to Bramall Lane where he contributed to the United reserve team's double success, featuring in the Avon Insurance League Cup final victory over Stoke City when he came on to net the closing goal in a 3-1 victory for the Blades. Andy is a promising young striker who is strong, very quick and has a high work rate.

Sheffield U (Signed from Ballyclare Comrades on 11/9/1999) FL 0+6 FLC 0+4
Bury (Loaned on 30/11/2000) FL 2 Others 1

SMITH Daniel (Danny) Lee
Born: Southampton, 17 August 1982
Height: 5'11" Weight: 11.4

Danny made several first-team appearances for Bournemouth during the club's injury crisis at the beginning of last season but then dropped back to the reserves and only received occasional opportunities in the remainder of the campaign. A promising young central defender he will be looking to extend his first-team experience in 2001-02.

Bournemouth (From trainee on 12/4/2000) FL 7+8 FLC 2 FAC 0+1 Others 2

SMITH David
Born: Stonehouse, 29 March 1968
Height: 5'8" Weight: 10.7
Club Honours: AMC '98
International Honours: E: U21-10

David found his opportunities with Grimsby Town rather limited last season due to the consistency of regular left back Tony Gallimore and most of his appearances came during two spells when Gallimore was out injured. David himself was then sidelined after being injured in the match at Nottingham Forest in February, but returned before the end of the campaign to make a couple of appearances from the subs' bench. A pacy left-sided player he had previously appeared as a left winger for the Mariners.

Coventry C (From apprentice on 7/7/1986) P/FL 144+10/19 FLC 17 FAC 6 Others 4+1
Bournemouth (Loaned on 8/1/1993) FL 1
Birmingham C (Signed on 12/3/1993) FL 35+3/3 FLC 4 FAC 0+1 Others 1
West Bromwich A (£90,000 on 31/1/1994) FL 82+20/2 FLC 4+2 FAC 1+3 Others 4+1
Grimsby T (£200,000 on 16/1/1998) FL 97+11/8 FLC 9+3/1 FAC 2 Others 7/1

SMITH David (Dave) Christopher
Born: Liverpool, 26 December 1970
Height: 5'9" Weight: 12.9

Dave had another efficient season in the centre of the park for Stockport County for whom he was a regular in the line-up. He scored just a single goal, netting with a 25-yard drive in the 3-1 defeat by his former club Norwich City back in September. A hard-working left-sided midfield player he still has the ability to find time and space in today's crowded midfield areas and once on the ball he rarely gives it away.

Norwich C (From trainee on 4/7/1989) F/PL 13+5 FAC 2+1 Others 1+1
Oxford U (£100,000 on 5/7/1994) FL 193+5/2 FLC 23+1/1 FAC 9+1 Others 7
Stockport Co (Free on 4/2/1999) FL 55+5/3 FLC 2+1 FAC 2

SMITH Dean
Born: West Bromwich, 19 March 1971
Height: 6'1" Weight: 12.10

Dean once again captained Leyton Orient last term, providing inspirational leadership to guide the team into the play-off finals before they eventually fell to Blackpool. A powerful central defender he showed some excellent form when marking Alan Shearer and Sergei Rebrov in the cup ties against Tottenham and Newcastle respectively. Strong both on the ground and in the air he is a difficult player to pass and will undoubtedly be a key figure for the O's as they try put last season's disappointment behind them in 2001-02.

Walsall (From trainee on 1/7/1989) FL 137+5/2 FLC 10 FAC 4 Others 10
Hereford U (£75,000 on 17/6/1994) FL 116+1/19 FLC 10/3 FAC 7 Others 11+1/4
Leyton Orient (£42,500 on 16/6/1997) FL 167/27 FLC 15 FAC 13/3 Others 9

SMITH James (Jamie) Jade Anthony
Born: Birmingham, 17 September 1974
Height: 5'7" Weight: 11.4

Jamie made the starting line-up for Crystal Palace's opening game of the 2000-01 season, but was then dropped and for a while found himself on the transfer list. He was soon back in the team however, and held down a regular place until affected by injuries in the last few weeks of the campaign. He is a right back or wing back who works hard and brings the ball out of defence well.

Wolverhampton W (From trainee on 7/6/1993) FL 81+6 FLC 10+1 FAC 2 Others 4/1
Crystal Palace (Signed on 22/10/1997) P/FL 93+7 FLC 13/2 FAC 6+1 Others 1+1
Fulham (Loaned on 25/3/1999) FL 9/1

SMITH Jason Leslie
Born: Bromsgrove, 6 September 1974
Height: 6'3" Weight: 13.7
Club Honours: Div 3 '00
International Honours: E: Sch

Jason was again an inspirational leader in the Swansea defence during the first half of last season but then suffered a twisted ankle in the LDV Vans Trophy tie against Brentford. Although he returned shortly afterwards he suffered another ankle injury in his comeback game and was sidelined for the remainder of the campaign. A powerful central defender who is very effective in the air, he was sorely missed by the Swans as they fought an unsuccessful battle against relegation. Jason signed a new three-year contract extension last September.

Coventry C (Signed from Tiverton T on 5/7/1993. Free to Tiverton T on 15/7/1995)
Swansea C (£10,000 on 1/7/1998) FL 107/5 FLC 7 FAC 7/1 Others 8/1

SMITH Jay Mark
Born: Hammersmith, 29 December 1981
Height: 5'11" Weight: 11.7

Captain of the Brentford U19s last term, Jay made his Football League debut as a substitute against Walsall in April and subsequently returned to make the starting line-up for the final two home games against Luton and Bury. A promising young midfield player he will be looking to gain further senior experience next term.

Brentford (From trainee on 5/7/2000) FL 2+1

SMITH Jeffrey (Jeff)
Born: Middlesbrough, 28 June 1980
Height: 5'10" Weight: 11.8

Jeff's story last season would not have been out of place in a fairy-tale book! Having started the campaign with Unibond League outfit Bishop Auckland and working as a postman, he took up the offer of trials with Bolton Wanderers. Promptly giving up his day job to pursue his dream of a full-time career in football, he made some impressive appearances for the reserves before receiving his Football League debut in the final game of the regular season against Sheffield United. Starting out on the left wing, he made some confident runs with the ball and acquitted himself very well, supplying several pinpoint crosses to boot. At the time of writing it was unclear whether he would be given a longer-term contract by Wanderers to keep him at the Reebok.

Hartlepool U (From trainee on 3/7/1998) FL 2+1 Others 1 (Free to Barrow in October 1999)
Bolton W (Free from Bishop Auckland on 21/3/2001) FL 1

SMITH Martin Geoffrey
Born: Sunderland, 13 November 1974
Height: 5'11" Weight: 12.6
Club Honours: Div 1 '96
International Honours: E: U21-1; Yth; Sch

Martin got off to a good start to the 2000-01 campaign at Huddersfield netting two goals in an early season win at Sheffield Wednesday. He continued to get among the goals and also netted against his old club Sheffield United. Unfortunately he also suffered a knee injury in the same match and he was sidelined for the remainder of the campaign. A very skilful player he can play either as a left-sided striker or in an attacking midfield role.

Sunderland (From trainee on 9/9/1992) P/FL 90+29/25 FLC 10+6/2 FAC 7+3/1
Sheffield U (Free on 6/8/1999) FL 24+2/10 FLC 3+1/4 FAC 3/1
Huddersfield T (£300,000 on 3/2/2000) FL 37+5/12 FLC 1

SMITH Neil James
Born: Lambeth, 30 September 1971
Height: 5'9" Weight: 12.12
Club Honours: FAYC '90; Div 2 '99

Neil had a short run in the Reading first team in the middle part of last season and headed an equaliser against Bristol Rovers on Boxing Day, but once Jamie Harper was signed it was clear his chances would be limited. Otherwise he appeared regularly for the Royals' successful reserve team and featured in the side that was narrowly defeated by Norwich in the Avon Insurance Combination Cup final. An experienced defensive midfield player who is strong in the tackle and works hard, he was placed on the open to offers list in the summer.

Tottenham H (From trainee on 24/7/1990)
Gillingham (£40,000 on 17/10/1991) FL 204+9/10 FLC 14+1/1 FAC 18/2 Others 7+1/2
Fulham (Signed on 4/7/1997) FL 62+11/1 FLC 3+1 FAC 6+3/1 Others 1+1
Reading (£100,000 on 20/8/1999) FL 30+21/2 FLC 3+1 FAC 1+1 Others 2+1

SMITH Ian **Paul**
Born: Easington, 22 January 1976
Height: 6'0" Weight: 13.3

Unable to break into the Burnley team at the start of last season, Paul spent two months on loan at Oldham Athletic where he made a handful of appearances before being struck down by a freak injury when he fell into an uncovered manhole. This put him out of action for several weeks and on returning to fitness he finally broke through to the Clarets' first team shortly before Christmas, later enjoying another brief run in the starting line-up towards the end of the campaign when injuries gave him an opportunity in the left-wing-back-role. Paul poses a threat going forward with his speed and accurate crosses and when he scored against QPR in March he ended a four-year spell without a goal. He was released on a free transfer in the summer.

Burnley (From trainee on 10/7/1994) FL 79+33/5 FLC 3+1 FAC 6+1 Others 5
Oldham Ath (Loaned on 22/9/2000) FL 3+1 FLC 1

SMITH Paul Antony
Born: Hastings, 25 January 1976
Height: 5'11" Weight: 11.7

This right-sided midfield man was used in different roles by Lincoln City as the Imps underwent a number of changes in style during the 2000-01 season. He began the campaign at right back but was moved forward to right wing back before finishing up on the right of midfield in a 4-4-2 system. Paul was most effective pushing forward but also showed good defensive qualities as well as providing eight league and cup goals.

Nottingham F (£50,000 from Hastings T on 13/1/1995)
Lincoln C (£30,000 on 17/10/1997) FL 95+17/17 FLC 5+1/1 FAC 8/1 Others 7

SMITH Paul Daniel
Born: Epsom, 17 December 1979
Height: 6'4" Weight: 14.0

Paul was understudy to Olafur Gottskalksson as Brentford goalkeeper last season. He made two brief appearances in the first team from the subs' bench, coming on for the final five minutes of the league game at Bury in January, and playing the final half hour of the LDV Vans Trophy Southern Area final when he achieved instant hero status with the Bees' fans by making a miraculous save to deny Southend an equaliser.

Charlton Ath (Free from Walton & Hersham on 2/7/1998. Free to Walton & Hersham during 1999 close season)
Brentford (Free from Carshalton Ath on 27/7/2000) FL 1+1 Others 0+1

SMITH Paul William
Born: East Ham, 18 September 1971
Height: 5'11" Weight: 13.0

Paul again served Gillingham as club captain last term and his midfield performances went from strength to strength during the course of the season. Although not the fastest of players, his value is in his quickness in both feet and thought, and his excellent close control. He missed several games early on in the campaign, but returned in mid-September and was an ever present until the end, during which time he made his 200th appearance for the Gills. He was deservedly named as the club's 'Player of the Year'.

Southend U (From trainee on 16/3/1990) FL 18+2/1 Others 0+1
Brentford (Free on 6/8/1993) FL 159/11 FLC 12/1 FAC 12/3 Others 15/2
Gillingham (Signed on 25/7/1997) FL 176+1/13 FLC 9/1 FAC 12 Others 9+2/2

Paul Smith (Gillingham)

SMITH Peter Lee
Born: Rhyl, 15 September 1978
Height: 5'10" Weight: 10.8
International Honours: E: Yth; Sch

Peter had a disappointing season at Crewe last term and only made the first team on a handful of occasions. In February he was loaned out to Conference club Doncaster Rovers and although he featured as a substitute at Stockport on his return he was released in the summer. A skilful young striker he was reported to have signed for Telford United.

Crewe Alex (From trainee on 12/7/1996) FL 3+19 FLC 4+1 FAC 0+1
Macclesfield T (Loaned on 25/9/1998) FL 12/3 Others 1

SMITH Richard Geoffrey
Born: Lutterworth, 3 October 1970
Height: 6'0" Weight: 13.12

After missing most of 1999-2000 with a back injury Richard finally returned to action in mid-November but after a brief run in the Grimsby Town first team at the turn of the year he was once again sidelined with a knee ligament problem. When fully fit he is a classy centre back who possesses a powerful long throw. Out of contract in the summer his future was unclear at the time of writing.

Leicester C (From trainee on 15/12/1988) F/PL 82+16/1 FLC 4 FAC 6/1 Others 12
Cambridge U (Loaned on 6/9/1989) FL 4 FLC 1
Grimsby T (Loaned on 8/9/1995) FL 8
Grimsby T (£50,000 on 11/3/1996) FL 72+7/1 FLC 10 FAC 4

SMITH Gareth **Shaun**
Born: Leeds, 9 April 1971
Height: 5'10" Weight: 11.0

Shaun had another excellent season in the Crewe Alexandra defence last term when he was a near ever-present at left back. A hard-tackling defender with a no-nonsense attitude he is an expert at delivering dead-ball kicks. Also the Railwaymen's penalty taker, his tally of four goals included two spot kicks in the 4-2 win over Burnley in February. His consistency throughout the campaign was recognised when he walked away with all the various supporters' 'Player of the Year' awards.

Shaun Smith

Halifax T (From trainee on 1/7/1989) FL 6+1 Others 1 (Free to Emley in May 1991)
Crewe Alex (Free on 31/12/1991) FL 339+21/40 FLC 21+1/3 FAC 16+2/4 Others 19+2/3

SMITH Thomas (Tommy) William
Born: Hemel Hempstead, 22 May 1980
Height: 5'8" Weight: 11.4
International Honours: E: U21-1; Yth

The 2000-01 campaign proved an excellent one for Watford's exciting young striker who established himself as a first-team regular at Vicarage Road and also featured for the England U21 squad, scoring on his debut in the 6-1 win over Georgia back in August. Playing either wide on the right-hand side or down the middle he combines blistering pace with good control and is now much stronger on the ball. He produced a particularly memorable performance against Portsmouth when he scored two fine goals and went on to reach a double-figure tally for the first time in his career. His younger brother Jack, who is a central defender, is also on Watford's books.
Watford (From trainee on 21/10/1997) P/FL 54+20/15 FLC 4+1/1 FAC 1+1

Tommy Smith

SNEEKES Richard
Born: Amsterdam, Holland, 30 October 1968
Height: 5'11" Weight: 12.2

Richard was in and out of the West Bromwich Albion team in the early part of last season but took on a much greater responsibility after Derek McInnes was sidelined by injury and was rarely absent after that. Although not a great tackler he enjoyed battling it out in the centre of the park even though it meant that his scoring opportunities were severely restricted. A clean striker of the ball from distance, he was always involved in the Baggies' build-up play but generously allowed others to play a more attacking role. He was released in the summer.
Bolton W (£200,000 from Fortuna Sittard, Holland, ex Ajax, Volendam, on 12/8/1994) P/FL 51+4/7 FLC 11+1/3 FAC 2/1
West Bromwich A (£385,000 on 11/3/1996) FL 208+19/30 FLC 14+3/2 FAC 7/2 Others 2

SODJE Efetobore (Efe)
Born: Greenwich, 5 October 1972
Height: 6'1" Weight: 12.0
Club Honours: GMVC '96
International Honours: Nigeria: 2

Having joined Crewe Alexandra in the close season Efe had an excellent campaign in 2000-01. He made his debut at Fulham in the opening game and rarely missed a match before dropping back to the sidelines in the new year. A classy defender easily recognised by his trademark bandanna, he has a great turn of pace and is very strong in the tackle. Efe is the brother of the Sheffield Eagles' Rugby League player Bright Sodje.
Macclesfield T (£30,000 from Stevenage Borough on 11/7/1997) FL 83/6 FLC 6 FAC 6/1 Others 1
Luton T (Free on 12/8/1999) FL 5+4 FLC 2 FAC 2+1 Others 1
Colchester U (Free on 23/3/2000) FL 3
Crewe Alex (Free on 21/7/2000) FL 29+3 FLC 2+1 FAC 2

SOLANO Nolberto (Nobby) Albino
Born: Lima, Peru, 12 December 1974
Height: 5'8" Weight: 10.8
International Honours: Peru: 52; Yth

Nobby's performances on the right side of midfield were a key feature of Newcastle United's play last season. His ability to run at opponents at pace with the ball under close control, and his subsequent accurate centres provided a major source of scoring opportunities for the strikers. He also proved

Richard Sneekes

a potent threat from dead-ball situations, enabling him to finish up as equal-top scorer for the Magpies in Premiership games. Very highly regarded back in Peru where he is reportedly among the country's top paid sportsmen, he was surprisingly dropped for the World Cup clash with Paraguay in November but was soon reinstated to the side.

Newcastle U (£2,763,958 from Boca Juniors, Argentina, ex Cristal Alianza Lima, Sporting, Deportivo Municipal, on 17/8/1998) PL 84+8/15 FLC 5+1 FAC 11/1 Others 7+1/1

SOLEY Stephen (Steve)
Born: Widnes, 22 April 1971
Height: 5'11" Weight: 12.8
International Honours: E: SP-1

Steve had a good start to the 2000-01 campaign for Carlisle, netting both goals in the 2-2 draw with Halifax on the opening day of the season and following this up with a last-minute equaliser in the home game with York City. He went on to produce some determined performances although his season was hampered by a series of injuries. He bravely returned for the penultimate match at Lincoln to help secure a vital draw that ensured safety from relegation. Steve is an attacking midfield player who works hard and has a good record for goal-scoring.

Portsmouth (£30,000 from Leek T on 22/7/1998) FL 1+7 FLC 0+4
Macclesfield T (Loaned on 19/3/1999) FL 5+5
Carlisle U (Signed on 6/8/1999) FL 56+6/12 FLC 2 FAC 2 Others 3+1/2

Steve Soley

SOLLITT Adam James
Born: Sheffield, 22 June 1977
Height: 6'0" Weight: 11.4
International Honours: E: SP-3

This tall and agile 'keeper was second choice to Keith Welch for Northampton Town last season. Adam made his debut in senior football in the LDV Vans Trophy defeat at Millwall in December, the first of a three-match run in the team and he also enjoyed a short run in the starting line-up in April. A former England Semi-Professional cap, Adam never let the team down when he was called upon.

Barnsley (From trainee on 4/7/1995. Free to Gainsborough Trinity during 1997 close season)
Northampton T (£30,000 from Kettering T on 25/7/2000) FL 6 FAC 1 Others 1

SOLSKJAER Ole Gunnar
Born: Kristiansund, Norway, 26 February 1973
Height: 5'10" Weight: 11.10
Club Honours: PL '97, '99, '00, '01; FAC '99; EC '99
International Honours: Norway: 41; U21

Ole was once again content to play his usual waiting game last term, while holding firm to his own 'title' as Manchester United's most-used substitute. One area that he continued to shine, irrespective of appearances, was in the goal-scoring stakes. A super strike against Everton in only his second full start in September was followed by a brace against Watford in the Worthington Cup, and a second Premiership goal in the top-of-the-table clash with Leicester City at Filbert Street. Moving into December, and his strike rate intensified, with two in successive games against Spurs and Charlton, a brace against Ipswich, followed by the solitary winner against Aston Villa. As the old year ended, Ole was already planning for the new with his fourth goal of the Premiership campaign against West Ham at Old Trafford on New Year's Day. He netted one of the six goals against Arsenal in February and shortly afterwards he signed a new contract for United.

Manchester U (£1,500,000 from Molde, Norway on 29/7/1996) PL 83+50/57 FLC 6/5 FAC 6+9/4 Others 24+28/7

SOLTVEDT Trond Egil
Born: Voss, Norway, 15 February 1967
Height: 6'1" Weight: 12.8
International Honours: Norway: 4

A player with a true professional attitude to the game, quiet man Trond was plagued with injuries at Southampton last season, and a persistent groin problem sidelined him for over six weeks. Although not a regular in the side he remained an important cog in the wheel and always performed to the maximum of his abilities. Given a free transfer in January, he was loaned to Sheffield Wednesday where he performed well enough to gain a permanent deal in March. He settled in straight away at Hillsborough and with his former colleague Carlton Palmer became the driving force behind the Owls' revival towards the end of the campaign. He netted just one goal for Wednesday but made a great impact at the club and will be in line for a leading role in the coming season. He is a hard-working midfield player who is strong in the tackle and has good ball-control skills.

Coventry C (£500,000 from Rosenborg, Norway, ex Ny-Khronborg, Viking Stavanger, Brann, on 24/7/1997) PL 47+10/3 FLC 1+4/1 FAC 5+2
Southampton (£300,000 on 13/8/1999) PL 20+10/2 FLC 6/3 FAC 2+1
Sheffield Wed (Free on 13/2/2001) FL 15/1

SOMA Ragnvald
Born: Norway, 10 November 1979
Height: 6'2" Weight: 12.2

This stylish defender had been tracked by West Ham boss Harry Redknapp for some time before he eventually signed for the Hammers in January. He was introduced sparingly towards the end of the season, making his debut from the substitutes' bench in the closing minutes of the epic 1-0 FA Cup fourth round win at Old Trafford. He went on to give two fine performances in the Premiership games against Arsenal and Tottenham and will be aiming to establish himself in the team next term.

West Ham U (£800,000 from Bryne, Norway on 19/1/2001) PL 2+2 FAC 0+1

SOMMER Juergen Petersen
Born: New York, USA, 27 February 1969
Height: 6'5" Weight: 15.12
International Honours: USA

A free agent at the beginning of 2001 after failing to sign a new deal with Columbus Crew, Juergen crossed the Atlantic and signed non-contract forms for Bolton Wanderers to help solve a goalkeeping crisis for manager Sam Allardyce. He played in the FA Cup tie against Blackburn, but after a confident start he sustained a leg injury and subsequently spent much of the game limping around his area, unable to kick out with his right foot. He then returned to the United States, signing for New England Revolution in April, but ruptured his left achilles tendon in June and was expected to be out of action for some time.

Luton T (Signed from USSF, USA on 5/9/1991) FL 82 FLC 6 FAC 11 Others 2
Brighton & Hove A (Loaned on 13/11/1991) FL 1
Torquay U (Loaned on 31/10/1992) FL 10 Others 1
Queens Park R (£600,000 on 28/8/1995) P/FL 66 FLC 3 FAC 3 (Free to Columbus Crew, USA on 19/2/1998)
Bolton W (Free from New England Revolution, USA on 8/2/2001) FAC 1

SOMNER Matthew James
Born: Isleworth, 8 December 1982
Height: 5'11" Weight: 12.4

After doing well with Brentford's reserve and youth teams last term, Matthew stepped up to make his debut at senior level when he came on as a substitute in the shock 6-0 defeat at Swansea towards the end of last season. A promising young midfield player he subsequently made the starting line-up for the last two games and will be hoping for more senior action next term.

Brentford (Trainee) FL 2+1

SONG Bahanag **Rigobert**
Born: Nkanglicock, Cameroon, 1 July 1976
Height: 5'9" Weight: 11.10

International Honours: Cameroon (ANC '00)

Having lost his place in the Liverpool side at the end of 1999-2000 Rigobert again found himself on the fringes of the squad last term. He played four games at right back in September, when Sami Hyypia was injured and Markus Babbel was moved to central defence, and gave some competent performances. However he saw no further senior action at Anfield and in November he moved on to West Ham where he quickly settled in on the right-hand side of defence. A regular for the remainder of the season apart from a brief spell in the new year when his form dipped, he finished the campaign strongly. A string of saving tackles won him 'Man of the Match' awards against Aston Villa and Leicester and he was mostly in impressive form for the Hammers. A tough-tackling right-sided defender he also continued to represent Cameroon, leading them to early qualification for the 2002 World Cup finals.

Liverpool (£2,720,000 from Salernitana, Italy, ex Tonnerre Yaoundi, Metz, on 29/1/1999) PL 27+7 FLC 2 FAC 0+1 Others 1

West Ham U (£2,500,000 on 29/11/2000) PL 18+1 FLC 1 FAC 1

SONNER Daniel (Danny) James

Born: Wigan, 9 January 1972

Height: 5'11" Weight: 12.8

International Honours: NI: 7; B-4

Danny formed a very strong and influential pairing with Martin O'Connor in the heart of the Birmingham City midfield last term. A busy player who constantly wanted to be part of the action, his runs all over the field made him hard to counter. He netted the Blues' first goal of the season in the home defeat by Fulham and also contributed a powerful header in the 2-0 Worthington Cup quarter-final win over his former club Sheffield Wednesday. However, although he appeared in the heart-breaking final against Liverpool an achilles tendon injury then restricted his appearances.

Burnley (From trainee at Wigan Ath on 6/8/1990) FL 1+5 FLC 0+1/1 Others 0+2 (Free to Preussen Koln, Germany during 1993 close season)

Bury (Loaned on 21/11/1992) FL 5/3 FAC 3 Others 1/1

Ipswich T (Free from FC Erzgebirge Aue, Germany on 12/6/1996) FL 28+28/3 FLC 6+4/1 FAC 1+1 Others 0+1

Sheffield Wed (£75,000 on 15/10/1998) PL 42+11/3 FLC 3+1/1 FAC 4+2

Birmingham C (Free on 4/8/2000) FL 22+4/1 FLC 9/1 FAC 1 Others 2

SORENSEN Thomas

Born: Denmark, 12 June 1976

Height: 6'4" Weight: 13.10

Club Honours: Div 1 '99

International Honours: Denmark: 1; B-1; U21

Now firmly established as one of the Premiership's top goalkeepers, Thomas once again proved himself to be invaluable to Sunderland last term, keeping them in games when they might often have lost. A powerful imposing figure, his shot stopping and handling skills make him almost the complete 'keeper, while his immense popularity at the Stadium of Light was assured when he saved Alan Shearer's penalty at St James Park in November to ensure the Wearsiders' 2-1 victory over Newcastle. At times, the Danish keeper's bravery worked against him and he twice left the field injured during the season in the matches against Arsenal and Manchester United. Thomas made the starting line-up for his country for the first time against Germany last September and with Peter Schmeichel announcing his retirement from international football, he was elevated to Denmark's number one goalkeeper.

Sunderland (£500,000 + from Odense BK, Denmark on 6/8/1998) P/FL 116 FLC 13 FAC 8

SORVEL Neil Simon

Born: Whiston, 2 March 1973

Height: 6'0" Weight: 12.9

Club Honours: GMVC '95, '97; FAT '96

Neil had another fine campaign at Crewe in 2000-01 when he featured in every match for the second season in a row. He netted just one goal, scoring with a low drive in the 4-1 defeat at Bolton. A hard-working midfielder with great stamina, he uses the ball with care and possesses a powerful shot.

Crewe Alex (From trainee on 31/7/1991) FL 5+4 FAC 1+1 Others 4

Macclesfield T (Free on 21/8/1992) FL 79+7/7 FLC 4+1 FAC 5 Others 0+1

Crewe Alex (Free on 9/6/1999) FL 88+4/7 FLC 9 FAC 4

SOUTHALL Leslie **Nicholas (Nicky)**

Born: Stockton, 28 January 1972

Height: 5'10" Weight: 12.12

Nicky had another excellent season for Gillingham in 2000-01. Although he did not score as many as in the previous campaign he created numerous chances for his colleagues with some telling crosses and deadly free kicks and corners. Having played at wing back in 1999-2000 he returned to his more favoured position in an attacking midfield role last term, thus giving him more opportunities to push forward. He was reported to have signed for Bolton in the summer.

Hartlepool U (From Darlington juniors on 21/2/1991) FL118+20/24 FLC 6+1/3 FAC 4+4 Others 6+2

Grimsby T (£40,000 on 12/7/1995) FL 55+17/5 FLC 3+3/1 FAC 4+3/2

Gillingham (Free on 9/12/1997) FL 141+13/17 FLC 6+1/1 FAC 10/3 Others 12

SOUTHGATE Gareth

Born: Watford, 3 September 1970

Height: 6'0" Weight: 12.8

Club Honours: Div 1 '94; FLC '96

International Honours: E: 42

Gareth continued to wear the captain's armband for Aston Villa last season, despite a summer transfer request. A steadying influence in the heart of the defence, he suffered a rare injury in the FA Cup replay against Newcastle United, damaging a medial ligament in his knee that caused him to miss seven weeks of first-team action. He forged an excellent understanding with new signing Alpay, proving once again to be an intelligent, articulate centre back and a model of consistency. Solid in defence and extremely comfortable on the ball he was very much a class act. He continued to represent England when fit, winning a further five caps during the campaign.

Crystal Palace (From trainee on 17/1/1989) F/PL 148+4/15 FLC 23+1/7 FAC 9 Others 6

Aston Villa (£2,500,000 on 1/7/1995) PL 191/7 FLC 17/1 FAC 20/1 Others 15

SPARROW Matthew (Matt)

Born: Wembley, 3 October 1981

Height: 5'11" Weight: 10.6

This talented youngster made a couple of early-season appearances at right-back for Scunthorpe United in 2000-01 but failed to make much impression and he did not re-appear in the first team until last March. A switch into centre midfield seemed to offer him the chance to show off his skills, determination and eye for goal as he cracked in three in two games to re-launch Scunthorpe's season. Sadly though he picked up an ankle injury after netting the winner against Brighton which ruled him out for a few weeks but he returned to the squad for the final matches. Matt signed a professional contract with the Iron in the spring and will be looking to establish himself as a regular in the first-team squad at Glanford Park in the coming season.

Scunthorpe U (Trainee) FL 11+11/4 FLC 0+3 Others 0+1

SPEAKMAN Robert (Rob)

Born: Swansea, 5 December 1980

Height: 5'11" Weight: 11.6

This young striker made just two appearances from the sub's bench for Exeter City last season and in between he spent time on loan at non-league outfits Bashley and Tiverton Town. Alert in the box and a natural finisher Rob was released by the Grecians in the summer.

Exeter C (From trainee on 2/7/1999) FL 4+15/3 FLC 0+3 FAC 0+1 Others 1+3/2

SPEDDING Duncan

Born: Camberley, 7 September 1977

Height: 6'1" Weight: 11.1

This left-sided Northampton player can play as a wing back or in a wide-midfield role. When fit he appeared regularly for the Sixfields club last season but he had some injury problems which necessitated a cartilage operation last February. Duncan delivers a useful cross from the wing and links well with John Frain down the left flank for the Cobblers.

Southampton (From trainee on 24/5/1996) PL 4+3 FLC 0+1

Northampton T (£60,000 on 14/7/1998) FL 76+13/2 FLC 5+2 FAC 2 Others 4

SPEED Gary Andrew

Born: Deeside, 8 September 1969

Height: 5'10" Weight: 12.10

Club Honours: Div 2 '90, Div 1 '92; CS '92

International Honours: W: 65; U21-3; Yth

Once again Gary proved highly influential in midfield for Newcastle last season. Always comfortable on the ball he was often employed as a play maker in Rob Lee's absence, although when Lee was in the side he tended to play in a more attacking role, making bursting runs though into advanced positions. His aerial ability made him a constant threat at set pieces, and he again claimed his share of goals. He also worked hard for the team, and could always be relied upon to track back and help out his defence when they were under pressure. Gary was a regular in the Wales team, proudly serving his country as captain, and scored in the World Cup qualifying game in Belarus last September.

Leeds U (From trainee on 13/6/1988) F/PL 231+17/39 FLC 25+1/11 FAC 21/5 Others 14+3/2
Everton (£3,500,000 on 1/7/1996) PL 58/16 FLC 5/1 FAC 2/1
Newcastle U (£5,500,000 on 6/2/1998) PL 118+4/19 FLC 6+1/1 FAC 18/5 Others 8/1

SPENCER Damian Michael
Born: Ascot, 19 September 1981
Height: 6'1" Weight: 14.5

After bursting on the scene with Bristol City in the 1999-2000 campaign Damian struggled to make an impact last season and only featured in the first team on a handful of occasions before being loaned out to Exeter City in March to gain more experience of senior football. He featured mostly from the subs' bench for the Grecians but failed to score in six outings and returned to Ashton Gate. Damian is a strong and hard-working young striker with good pace and an eye for goal.

Bristol C (From trainee on 14/6/2000) FL 8+5/1 FLC 0+1 Others 1+3/1
Exeter C (Loaned on 22/3/2001) FL 2+4

SPERREVIK Tim
Born: Norway, 1 January 1976
Height: 6'3" Weight: 14.12

This tall striker caused the Hartlepool defence major problems with his unorthodox style when playing against them for Norwegian Second Division club Fana in a pre-season friendly. After a short period on trial he signed a two-year contract but found it difficult to meet the demands of full-time football. He was given a number of run-outs in the first team, mostly from the subs' bench, but failed to establish himself and was released towards the end of the campaign when he returned to Norway to rejoin his old club.

Hartlepool U (Free from Fana, Norway on 11/8/2000) FL 4+11/1 FLC 1 Others 0+1

Gary Speed

SPRING Matthew John
Born: Harlow, 17 November 1979
Height: 5'11" Weight: 11.5

Matthew again retained a regular first-team place for Luton Town in 2000-01, when he was a driving force in the centre of the park in what was a very disappointing season for the Hatters. A tenacious midfield player with a biting tackle and impressive vision he scored four goals but was unable to prevent the club from being relegated down to the Third Division.

Luton T (From trainee on 2/7/1997) FL 136+7/13 FLC 12 FAC 12+1/2 Others 2

SQUIRES James (Jamie) Alexander
Born: Preston, 15 November 1975
Height: 6'2" Weight: 13.11

Jamie returned to Nationwide League football after two seasons in Scotland and was expected to be a cornerstone of the Carlisle United defence in 2000-01. However after featuring in just a handful of early season games he was stretchered off at Plymouth after tearing the ligaments in his left knee and the injury brought his campaign to a very early conclusion. A big strong central defender he is effective in the air and cool under pressure. Out of contract in the summer his future was uncertain at the time of writing.

Preston NE (From trainee on 26/4/1994) FL 24+7 FLC 1 FAC 0+1 Others 5+1
Mansfield T (Loaned on 22/8/1997) FL 1
Dunfermline Ath (Free on 30/3/1998) SL 21+5/2
Carlisle U (Free on 4/8/2000) FL 2+3 FLC 1

STALLARD Mark
Born: Derby, 24 October 1974
Height: 6'0" Weight: 13.6

Mark got off to a great start at Notts County last season netting the winner at Luton in the opening game and going on to score regularly throughout the campaign. He established a fine rapport with Danny Allsopp up front for the Magpies the pair hitting nearly 40 goals between them in all competitions. A skilful striker who can turn his marker and shoot with either foot he signed a new long-term contract towards the end of the season.

Derby Co (From trainee on 6/11/1991) FL 19+8/2 FLC 2+1/2 FAC 2+1 Others 3/2
Fulham (Loaned on 23/9/1994) FL 4/3
Bradford C (£110,000 on 12/1/1996) FL 33+10/10 FLC 2/1 FAC 0+1 Others 3/2
Preston NE (Loaned on 14/2/1997) FL 4/1
Wycombe W (£100,000 on 7/3/1997) FL 67+3/23 FLC 5+1/1 Others 2/1
Notts Co (£10,000 on 3/3/1999) FL 86+6/34 FLC 8/4 FAC 6/3 Others 1

STAM Jakob (Jaap)
Born: Kampen, Holland, 17 July 1972
Height: 6'3" Weight: 14.0
Club Honours: EC '99; FAC '99; PL '99, '00, '01
International Honours: Holland: 39

After performing solidly for Holland during Euro 2000, Jaap had a wretched start to his second Premiership campaign for Manchester United, suffering a troublesome achilles injury that forced him out of the side after only four games. During the next three months his name was conspicuous by its absence from the United team-sheet, as he underwent surgery, and battled back to fitness. While United coped well without him, his return in January was a much-needed boost in the run-in to domestic and European honours. His presence inspired the team to go on a five-game run without conceding a goal in the Premiership and when contracts were being discussed in February he pledged his future to United, hoping to end his career at Old Trafford before moving to the United States. That, of course, remains much in the future. His main concern at present is to keep United at the top of the footballing tree over the next 12 months. He was honoured by his fellow professionals with a place in the PFA's Premiership team for the season.

Manchester U (£10,750,000 from PSV Eindhoven, Holland, ex Zwolle, Cambuur, Willem II, on 17/7/1998) PL 78/1 FAC 7+1 Others 38+1

STAMP Darryn Michael
Born: Beverley, 21 September 1978
Height: 6'2" Weight: 12.0

A tall striker with good ball skills, Darryn scored regularly for Scunthorpe reserves last season but found first-team opportunities limited. He only started four games and managed just one goal, a last-minute equaliser at home to Macclesfield Town on New Year's Day. Available for transfer all season, he turned down a loan move to Yeovil and permanent switches to Exeter and Carlisle fell through before he moved to Conference club Scarborough on loan in March. Unfortunately he then fractured his cheekbone on his debut against Kingstonian and this brought an end to his season. Released in the summer he was reported to have signed for Scarborough.

Scunthorpe U (Signed from Hessle on 7/7/1997) FL 18+39/6 FLC 1+3 FAC 2+2 Others 3+1/1
Halifax T (Loaned on 18/2/2000) FL 5

STAMP Neville
Born: Reading, 7 July 1981
Height: 5'11" Weight: 12.7

Neville joined York City last October following a successful trial period and although troubled at times by a calf injury he was a regular in the first-team squad for much of the season. A strong-tackling and solid left back he gave a number of impressive displays for the Minstermen and will be looking to gain a regular place in the starting line-up in 2001-02.

Reading (From trainee on 22/6/1999) FL 0+1
York C (Free on 10/10/2000) FL 12+1 FAC 0+2 Others 1

STAMP Philip (Phil) Lawrence
Born: Middlesbrough, 12 December 1975
Height: 5'10" Weight: 13.5
International Honours: E: Yth

Now firmly established in a wing-back role at Middlesbrough, Phil provided useful service last term although his appearances were restricted by a series of injuries. A local lad his robust all-action style leaves him prone to injury as was the case with his former boss Bryan Robson. Hard-working and tenacious, Boro' would have no relegation worries if they could field a team of players with as much fire in their bellies as Phil. His only goal came in the 2-1 home defeat by Leeds last August.

Middlesbrough (From trainee on 4/2/1993) P/FL 72+38/6 FLC 13+4/1 FAC 8+4/1 Others 5+1

STAMPS Scott
Born: Birmingham, 20 March 1975
Height: 5'10" Weight: 11.10
Club Honours: NC '00

This tough-tackling left back featured regularly for Kidderminster Harriers in their inaugural season in the Football League. Scott was handed the penalty taker's duty at Aggborough but he had to wait until the penultimate game of the season before the club were awarded a spot kick, and then found that by the time he had arrived to take the kick Drewe Broughton had already stepped in! He is a versatile left-sided player who can also take a more attacking role if required.

Torquay U (From trainee on 6/7/1993) FL 80+6/5 FLC 5 FAC 2 Others 2+1/1
Colchester U (£10,000 on 26/3/1997) FL 52+4/1 FLC 4 FAC 3+1 Others 1+1
Kidderminster Hrs (Free on 17/9/1999) FL 34 FLC 1 FAC 3 Others 1

STANIC Mario
Born: Sarajevo, Yugoslavia, 10 April 1972
Height: 6'2" Weight: 12.12
Club Honours: CS '00
International Honours: Croatia: 38

Mario followed an established trend in that he impressed in a European match against Chelsea and subsequently joined the club - a precedent set by the likes of Gustavo Poyet, Bjarne Goldbaek and Gabriele Ambrosetti - although in this case there was a five-year delay in him playing for FC Brugge and signing for the Blues. 'Super Mario' is an extremely versatile player, able to play wing back, defensive or attacking midfield and even as a striker. An influential member of Croatia's team that reached the semi-final of the 1998 World Cup, he made an impressive debut in Chelsea's FA Charity Shield victory at Wembley occupying the wide-right position in midfield. However his first match in the Premiership against West Ham six days later was nothing short of sensational. He controlled an awkward bouncing ball with his chest, juggled it onto his left knee and smashed home a beautiful volley from 30 yards to score one of the goals of the season - and for good measure headed home a last-minute free-kick to put the seal on a 4-2 victory. In his next game however he suffered a serious knee ligament injury that required keyhole surgery and a lengthy period of rehabilitation. When Mario hobbled away from first-team football in August, Chelsea's prospects seemed boundless with Vialli at the helm and the team credible contenders in four competitions but the loss of this outstanding talent was symptomatic of a disappointing season when autumn optimism turned to a winter of discontent. He eventually returned towards the end of the season but it was too late to help the Blues to a place in the Champions' League for 2001-02 and they had to be content with a slot in the UEFA Cup.

Chelsea (£5,600,000 from Parma, Italy, ex Zeljeznicar Sarajevo, Croatio Zagreb, Sporting Gijon, Benfica, Brugge, on 12/7/2000) PL 8+4/2 FAC 0+2 Others 1

STANSFIELD James Edward
Born: Dewsbury, 18 September 1978
Height: 6'2" Weight: 13.0

This young centre back started last season on a three-month contract at Halifax Town and featured in the opening two games of the campaign, but was released in October and joined Unibond League outfit Ossett Town. He subsequently moved on to Liversidge and later had unsuccessful trials with Conference clubs Leigh RMI (where he played in the Nationwide Trophy defeat at Morecambe) and Kettering Town.

Huddersfield T (From trainee on 21/7/1997)
Halifax T (Free on 7/7/1998) FL 24+2/1 FAC 1 Others 3

STANT Phillip (Phil) Richard
Born: Bolton, 13 October 1962
Height: 6'0" Weight: 13.4
Club Honours: Div 3 '93; WC '93

This veteran striker had more or less hung up his boots after taking over as manager at Lincoln in the summer of 2000, but after his dismissal by the new Imps' board in March he joined Brighton as a player on non-contract terms. Although no longer possessing the pace that he had earlier in his career, he showed that he could still perform a useful role as a target man for a short period in matches and his experience proved valuable to the Seagulls in the run-in to the Third Division title. His appearances were restricted to outings from the subs' bench but he increased his tally of goals when he netted with a close-range header in the 3-0 win over Hull City. Phil was released at the end of the season.

Reading (Free from Camberley on 19/8/1982) FL 3+1/2
Hereford U (Free from Army on 25/11/1986) FL 83+6/38 FLC 3/2 FAC 3/2 Others 11/7
Notts Co (£175,000 on 18/7/1989) FL 14+8/6 FLC 2/1 FAC 0+1 Others 3+2
Blackpool (Loaned on 5/9/1990) FL 12/5
Lincoln C (Loaned on 22/11/1990) FL 4
Huddersfield T (Loaned on 3/1/1991) FL 5/1
Fulham (£60,000 on 8/2/1991) FL 19/5 Others 1
Mansfield T (£50,000 on 1/8/1991) FL 56+1/32 FLC 4/1 FAC 2 Others 2
Cardiff C (£100,000 on 4/12/1992) FL 77+2/34 FLC 2/2 FAC 6+1/4 Others 10/3
Mansfield T (Loaned on 12/8/1993) FL 4/1 FLC 1/1
Bury (£90,000 on 27/1/1995) FL 49+13/23 FLC 5+1/4 FAC 1 Others 5

Northampton T (Loaned on 22/11/1996) FL 4+1/2
Lincoln C (£30,000 on 26/12/1996) FL 42+22/20 FLC 2+1/1 FAC 2+6 Others 1+1
Brighton & Hove A (Free on 2/3/2001) FL 0+7/1

STANTON Nathan
Born: Nottingham, 6 May 1981
Height: 5'9" Weight: 11.3
International Honours: E: Yth

Nathan continued to shine for Scunthorpe United last season whether at centre back or full back and his pace and strength made him one of the Third Division's best defenders. Highly-rated he was always a first choice at Glanford Park and captained the side in Steve Torpey's absence even though he is still a teenager. Nathan picked up a knee ligament injury in February, which sidelined him for four weeks, but he quickly recovered and was back in the team by the end of the campaign.

Scunthorpe U (From trainee on 19/3/1999) FL 64+13 FLC 3 FAC 5+1 Others 3

STAUNTON Stephen (Steve)
Born: Drogheda, Ireland, 19 January 1969
Height: 6'1" Weight: 12.12
Club Honours: FAC '89; Div 1 '90; FLC '94, '96
International Honours: RoI: 89; U21-4; Yth

Steve was very much on the fringes of the Liverpool first-team squad at the beginning of last season and apart from two brief appearances from the substitutes' bench he failed to feature in the senior team. In October he moved on loan to Crystal Palace where he is best remembered for his spectacular goal in the 3-2 home victory over Tranmere. He collected a clearance wide on the left-hand side some 50 yards from goal and his amazing shot sailed over the Rovers 'keeper and into the net. Steve later returned to Aston Villa where he started 12 games in a row, covering in the centre of defence for the injured Gareth Southgate before switching to a more familiar left-wing-back role. He continued to add to his total of appearances for the Republic of Ireland and now holds the all-time record for the number of caps received.

Liverpool (£20,000 from Dundalk on 2/9/1986) FL 55+10 FLC 6+2/4 FAC 14+2/1 Others 1/1
Bradford C (Loaned on 13/11/1987) FL 7+1 FLC 2 Others 1
Aston Villa (£1,100,000 on 7/8/1991) F/PL 205+3/16 FLC 17+2/1 FAC 19+1/1 Others 15+1
Liverpool (Free on 3/7/1998) PL 38+6 FLC 5/1 FAC 2 Others 5+2
Crystal Palace (Loaned on 20/10/2000) FL 6/1
Aston Villa (Free on 7/12/2000) PL 13+1 FAC 3

STEELE Lee Anthony James
Born: Liverpool, 7 December 1973
Height: 5'8" Weight: 12.7
Club Honours: Div 3 '01

Out of contract at Shrewsbury, Lee joined Brighton in the summer of 2000 but rather appropriately for a player wearing the number 13 shirt he enjoyed very little luck last season. He suffered a hand injury that kept him out for a few weeks in the early part of the campaign and injured his knee in a car accident towards the end of the year. Then when Bobby Zamora was injured in late March, Lee missed his opportunity due to suspension. He is a tough centre forward with a low centre of gravity that enables him to turn defenders, and he will surely hope for better fortune in the coming season. He was placed on the open to offers list in the summer.

Shrewsbury T (£30,000 + from Northwich Vic on 23/7/1997) FL 104+9/37 FLC 5/3 FAC 4+1 Others 3
Brighton & Hove A (Free on 19/7/2000) FL 4+19/2 FAC 0+2 Others 1

STEIN Earl **Mark** Sean
Born: Capetown, South Africa, 29 January 1966
Height: 5'6" Weight: 11.10
Club Honours: FLC '88; AMC '92; Div 2 '93
International Honours: E: Yth

Mark answered Ricky Hill's call to arms in the 2000 close season and rejoined his old club Luton Town to help them through a transitional period. Although troubled by niggling injuries he featured regularly throughout the campaign, but despite adding some much-needed experience he only scored four times. A hard-working striker he is still quick off the mark and sharp in the box. Mark was appointed reserve-team coach at Kenilworth Road in the summer.

Luton T (From juniors on 31/1/1984) FL 41+13/19 FLC 4+1 FAC 9/3 Others 3/1
Aldershot (Loaned on 29/1/1986) FL 2/1
Queens Park R (£300,000 on 26/8/1988) FL 20+13/4 FLC 4/2 FAC 2+1/1 Others 4
Oxford U (Signed on 15/9/1989) FL 72+10/18 FLC 4 FAC 2+1 Others 3
Stoke C (£100,000 on 15/9/1991) FL 94/50 FLC 8/8 FAC 4 Others 17/10
Chelsea (£1,400,000 on 28/10/1993) PL 46+4/21 FLC 0+1 FAC 9/2 Others 2+1/2
Stoke C (Loaned on 22/11/1996) FL 11/4
Ipswich T (Loaned on 22/8/1997) FL 6+1/2 FLC 3+1/1
Bournemouth (Signed on 4/3/1998) FL 90/30 FLC 10/7 FAC 7/2 Others 8/5
Luton T (Free on 14/7/2000) FL 19+11/3 FLC 3/1 FAC 1+1 Others 0+1

STEPANOVS Igors
Born: Ogre, Latvia, 21 January 1976
Height: 6'4" Weight: 13.7
International Honours: Latvia: 42

Igors joined Arsenal in September 2000 from Skonto Riga after a successful trial and scored with a well-taken header on his first-team debut in the Worthington Cup defeat by Ipswich Town. A big, strong, imposing centre half he provided coach Arsene Wenger with new options in the middle of defence. He made a string of starts in the second half of the season, due mainly to injuries to first choices Tony Adams and Martin Keown. Despite questions being raised over his performance as part of an inexperienced defence in the heavy defeat at Old Trafford, Igors bounced back six weeks later in the 4-0 drubbing of Manchester City. He is solid, resolute and will continue to develop to the mental and physical demands of the English game the more matches he plays.

Arsenal (£1,000,000 from Skonto Riga, Latvia, ex FK Ventspils, on 5/9/2000) PL 9 FLC 1/1 FAC 3

STEPHENSON Paul
Born: Wallsend, 2 January 1968
Height: 5'10" Weight: 12.12
International Honours: E: Yth

Paul had another excellent season for Hartlepool in 2000-01 when he was a near ever-present. His career seems to have undergone a rejuvenation since he switched from playing as a winger to a central midfield role two seasons ago. He once again linked up well with his colleagues and showed he has the ability to control the speed of the game. Paul was rewarded for his fine performances when manager Chris Turner gave him a new contract.

Newcastle U (From apprentice on 2/1/1986) FL 58+3/1 FLC 3+1 FAC 2 Others 2
Millwall (£300,000 on 10/11/1988) FL 81+17/6 FLC 3/1 FAC 9/2 Others 8/1
Gillingham (Loaned on 21/11/1992) FL 12/2 Others 2
Brentford (£30,000 on 4/3/1993) FL 70/2 FLC 6/1 FAC 1+1 Others 5
York C (£35,000 on 7/8/1995) FL 91+6/8 FLC 9+2 FAC 5 Others 2+2/1
Hartlepool U (Free on 20/3/1998) FL 113+3/9 FLC 4+1/2 FAC 4+1 Others 12

STERGIOPOULOS Marcus
Born: Melbourne, Australia, 12 June 1973
Height: 5'10" Weight: 12.2

This left-sided midfield player signed a three-month contract for Lincoln City last August following a successful pre-season trial. He showed tremendous skill on the ball and was quick to get forward, scoring his only goal with a long-range shot that proved the winner in the home leg of the Worthington Cup first round clash with Sheffield United. Despite his considerable promise he was released in November and returned to Australia where he signed for National Soccer League outfit Eastern Pride. In March he had a pre-season trial with MSL club Columbus Crew, but failed to make the final roster for the 2001 campaign.

Lincoln C (Free from Auckland Kingz, New Zealand, ex Gippsland Falcons, Carlton, on 18/8/2000) FL 2+5 FLC 1+1/1

STEVENS Ian David
Born: Malta, 21 October 1966
Height: 5'10" Weight: 12.6
Club Honours: AMC '89

Ian enjoyed something of an Indian summer in his career last season after joining Carlisle in August 2000. He scored in five consecutive appearances early in the campaign, and netted four goals in the 5-1 FA Cup first round victory over Woking, the best haul by any United player for almost twenty years. Arguably his most important strike, however, was the goal he scored at Barnet to clinch victory in a game that was ultimately decisive in keeping the Cumbrians in Division Three. A hard-working striker with the ability to be in the right place at the right time he has scored consistently throughout his career.

Preston NE (From apprentice on 22/11/1984) FL 9+2/2 Others 1
Stockport Co (Free on 27/10/1986) FL 1+1 FAC 0+1 Others 0+1 (Free to Lancaster C on 27/11/1986)
Bolton W (Free on 25/3/1987) FL 26+21/7 FLC 1+2 FAC 4/2 Others 3+1

Bury (Free on 3/7/1991) FL 100+10/38 FLC 3+1 FAC 2+2 Others 7+1/2
Shrewsbury T (£20,000 on 11/8/1994) FL 94+17/37 FLC 2+1 FAC 4+2/2 Others 10+2/12
Carlisle U (£100,000 on 13/5/1997) FL 64+14/26 FLC 2 FAC 2/1 Others 3/2
Wrexham (Free on 5/7/1999) FL 14+2/4 FLC 2 FAC 1+1
Cheltenham T (Loaned on 21/3/2000) FL 1
Carlisle U (Free on 7/8/2000) FL 41/12 FLC 2/1 FAC 3/4

STEWART Gareth John
Born: Preston, 3 February 1980
Height: 6'0" Weight: 12.8
International Honours: E: Yth; Sch

Having spent the 1999-2000 campaign as understudy to regular 'keeper Mark Ovendale, Gareth began last season as second choice to new signing Mickael Menetrier at Bournemouth. However he finally made his breakthrough at the beginning of October and went on to establish himself as first choice in the line-up. A fine prospect he produced several outstanding performances and matured as the season progressed.

Blackburn Rov (From trainee on 11/2/1997)
Bournemouth (Free on 2/7/1999) FL 38 FAC 3

STEWART William Paul **Marcus**
Born: Bristol, 7 November 1972
Height: 5'10" Weight: 11.0
International Honours: E: Sch

Marcus enjoyed an incredible season at Ipswich last term. After a shaky start that saw him relegated to the subs' bench against Aston Villa he promptly came on to score and never looked back. The rest of the football world really started to take him seriously when he scored in seven successive games between 26 December and 20 January, which took him to the top of the Premiership scoring charts. One of his highlights was his hat-trick at the Dell against Southampton in a 3-0 win. The three goals displayed his full repertoire - a tap in, a header and a cheekily chipped in penalty. He was in contention for the Golden Boot for being the Premiership's leading scorer right up to the last game of the season, made the short-list of six for the PFA's 'Player of the Season' and was voted 'Player of the Year' by the Ipswich supporters. However there is more to his game than scoring goals and he was always involved in the thick of the action, as often as not creating chances for his colleagues. At Middlesbrough it was his cross that enabled Alun Armstrong to notch the winning goal. He also established himself as the club's penalty taker during the course of the season.

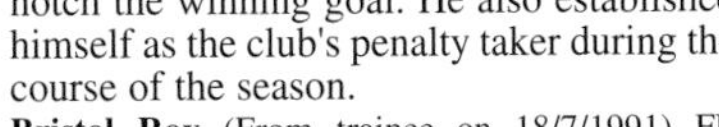

Bristol Rov (From trainee on 18/7/1991) FL 137+34/57 FLC 11/5 FAC 7+1/3 Others 16+1/14
Huddersfield T (£1,200,000 + on 2/7/1996) FL 129+4/58 FLC 18/7 FAC 9/3
Ipswich T (£2,500,000 on 1/2/2000) P/FL 42+2/21 FLC 3+2/1 FAC 2/1 Others 3/3

Marcus Stewart

STEWART Michael James
Born: Edinburgh, 26 February 1981
Height: 5'11" Weight: 11.11
International Honours: S: U21-6; Sch

Michael was another young Manchester United player to make his mark in the first team last season. He made two substitute appearances in the Worthington Cup before making his bow in the Premiership at Middlesbrough towards the end of the campaign. A promising young central midfield player he was a regular for Scotland at U21 level winning four more caps during the campaign.

Manchester U (From trainee on 19/3/1998) PL 3 FLC 0+2

STILLIE Derek Daniel
Born: Irvine, 3 December 1973
Height: 6'0" Weight: 12.0
International Honours: S: U21-14

Wigan's second-choice 'keeper once again proved to be a capable deputy for Roy Carroll last season. He had a three-month run in the team at the turn of the year when Carroll broke a toe and produced some impressive performances. A fine shot stopper with a long kick, Derek will be waiting in the wings should his rival move on to a bigger club in the near future.

Aberdeen (From juniors on 3/5/1991) SL 22+1 SLC 2 SC 3
Wigan Ath (Free on 5/8/1999) FL 29+2 FLC 2+1 FAC 4 Others 3

STIMAC Igor
Born: Metkovic, Croatia, 6 September 1967
Height: 6'2" Weight: 13.0
International Honours: Croatia: 47

West Ham's tough-tackling central defender had a frustrating time with injuries in the 2000-01 campaign. He suffered a bad knee injury at Ipswich in October that kept him out of action for five weeks and soon after his return he was sidelined again with a calf injury and did not play again until March. An established international he continued to represent Croatia when fit.

Derby Co (£1,570,000 from Hadjuk Split, Croatia, ex Cibalia Vinkovic, on 31/10/1995) F/PL 84/3 FLC 2 FAC 7
West Ham U (£600,000 on 10/9/1999) PL 43/1 FLC 5 FAC 2 Others 2

STIRLING Jude Barrington
Born: Enfield, 29 June 1982
Height: 6'2" Weight: 11.12

Having progressed through the ranks at Luton, Jude stepped up to make his Football League debut at Swansea last September only to have the misfortune to receive a red card for a handball offence. He continued to impress in reserve matches but it was not until new boss Joe Kinnear arrived that he was selected more often for the first team. A young defender with a powerful long throw, he is strong in the tackle and his surging runs down the wing put opposing defences under pressure.

Luton T (From trainee on 9/7/1999) FL 5+4 FAC 0+2

STOCCO Thomas (Tom) Luca
Born: London, 4 January 1983
Height: 6'2" Weight: 12.5

This second-year trainee made steady but unspectacular progress at Torquay last season. He made three appearances from the subs' bench in the early part of the campaign when he was used as a striker, but after returning to the Gulls' youth team he switched to playing in the centre of defence. Tom holds the ball up well and is strong in the air although it still remains to be seen in which position he will be used in the future. At the time of writing he was considering the offer of a professional contract at Plainmooor for the 2001-02 season.

Torquay U (Trainee) FL 2+8/2 FLC 0+1

STOCK Brian Benjamin
Born: Winchester, 24 December 1981
Height: 5'11" Weight: 11.2

One of the many youngsters to graduate through Bournemouth's successful youth system in recent seasons, Brian struggled to make an impact at first-team level in 2000-01 making a single brief appearance from the subs' bench at Northampton and also featuring in the two LDV Vans Trophy ties. A quick midfield player who is not afraid to run at defenders he will be hoping to receive more opportunities in the coming season.

Bournemouth (From trainee on 25/1/2000) FL 4+2 Others 1+1

STOCKDALE Robert (Robbie) Keith
Born: Redcar, 30 November 1979
Height: 5'11" Weight: 11.3
International Honours: E: U21-1

Robbie was unable to break into the Middlesbrough team last season and moved to Sheffield Wednesday on loan in mid-September where he covered for injuries at full back. He performed competently enough but returned to the North-East when the four-week period was over and continued his development in the club's reserve team. Robbie won his first England U21 cap last August when he came on from the subs' bench for the final 20 minutes of the 6-1 friendly win over Georgia.

Middlesbrough (From trainee on 2/7/1998) P/FL 24+7/1 FLC 5 FAC 1
Sheffield Wed (Loaned on 13/9/2000) FL 6

STOCKLEY Samuel (Sam) Joshua
Born: Tiverton, 5 September 1977
Height: 6'0" Weight: 12.0

Sam had an absolutely outstanding campaign for Barnet in 2000-01 when he was a near ever-present. Playing at right back or in midfield he showed a good work rate and linked up well with Darren Currie down the flank. Although not noted for his goalscoring ability he netted with a great swirling header in the home game against Mansfield last August. A popular figure with the Underhill fans he was deservedly voted 'Player of the Year' at the end of the season.

Southampton (From trainee on 1/7/1996)
Barnet (Free on 31/12/1996) FL 177+5/2 FLC 10 FAC 4 Others 11

Micky Stockwell

STOCKWELL Michael (Micky) Thomas
Born: Chelmsford, 14 February 1965
Height: 5'9" Weight: 11.4
Club Honours: Div 2 '92

Micky defied his years to enjoy an outstanding season for his new club Colchester United last term. The only U's player to start every league and cup game, he finished up as the leading scorer with 11 goals and was also voted 'Player of the Season' by the Layer Road faithful. A model professional in every sense of the word, he performed in an attacking midfield role and was a key figure in ensuring that the club retained their Division Two status. He was reported to have signed an extension to his contract at the end of the campaign.

Ipswich T (From apprentice on 17/12/1982) F/PL 464+42/35 FLC 43+5/5 FAC 28+3/2 Others 22+4/2
Colchester U (Free on 27/7/2000) FL 46/11 FLC 4 FAC 1 Others 1

STOLCERS Andrejs
Born: Latvia, 8 July 1974
Height: 5'10" Weight: 11.4
Club Honours: Div 1 '01
International Honours: Latvia: 51

Andrejs began last season on loan at Spartak Moscow and appeared for them in the early rounds of the Champions' League before joining Fulham at the beginning of December. He scored on his debut at West Bromwich Albion, but was in and out of the side for the remainder of the campaign. Often used as a second-half substitute for Bjarne Goldbaek, he can play on either wing or up front. Andrejs is a regular for Latvia at international level and will be going all out to cement a regular place in Fulham's Premiership campaign in 2001-02.

Fulham (£2,000,000 + from Shakhtjor Donetsk, Ukraine, ex Olympija Riga, Skonto Riga, on 7/12/2000) FL 8+7/2 FLC 0+1 FAC 0+1

STONE Steven (Steve) Brian
Born: Gateshead, 20 August 1971
Height: 5'8" Weight: 12.7
Club Honours: Div 1 '98
International Honours: E: 9

Restored as a regular in the Aston Villa line-up last term, Steve had a fine season and was rarely absent from first-team duties. He adapted well to the right-wing-back role and linked nicely with Paul Merson down the flank. Deceptively fast, he loves to run at defenders with the ball and possesses an accurate cross. Later in the campaign boss John Gregory changed the formation around and he appeared in a more familiar position on the right-hand side of midfield where his talents were again put to good use. He netted three goals during the season, the most memorable being a spectacular volley in the FA Cup third round tie against Newcastle.

Nottingham F (From trainee on 20/5/1989) F/PL 189+4/23 FLC 14+1/2 FAC 9 Others 12/2
Aston Villa (£5,500,000 on 12/3/1999) PL 52+16/3 FLC 4+3/1 FAC 5+4/2 Others 4

STONEBRIDGE Ian Robert
Born: Lewisham, 30 August 1981
Height: 6'0" Weight: 11.4
International Honours: E: Yth

Having recovered from the groin injury that affected him in the closing months of the 1999-2000 campaign Ian returned to the Plymouth Argyle starting line-up on the opening day of last season, but it was not until the new year that he finally put his injuries behind him. He went on to produce some consistent performances, finding the net regularly and ending the season as the club's leading scorer with 12 goals in all competitions. Ian is a big strong striker with an excellent eye for goal.

Plymouth Arg (From trainee at Tottenham H on 13/7/1999) FL 44+18/20 FLC 2/1 FAC 7+2/1 Others 2+1/1

STONEMAN Paul
Born: Tynemouth, 26 February 1973
Height: 6'1" Weight: 13.6
Club Honours: FC '98

Paul's versatility shone through once again for Halifax Town last season. Essentially a central defender he had to cover in midfield on a number of occasions but his commitment to the club was exemplary. He scored with a penalty against York in October and with an 18-yard shot in the excellent 2-0 win over Plymouth in December. Paul is currently the longest-serving player at The Shay.

Blackpool (From trainee on 26/7/1991) FL 38+5 FLC 5 FAC 3 Others 3
Colchester U (Loaned on 23/12/1994) FL 3/1
Halifax T (Free on 12/7/1995) FL 105+2/10 FLC 7 FAC 4 Others 4

STOWELL Michael (Mike)
Born: Portsmouth, 19 April 1965
Height: 6'2" Weight: 14.2

After enjoying a testimonial match against Aston Villa during the close season Mike spent virtually the whole of the 2001-02 campaign in the Wolves' reserve team. Unable to displace Michael Oakes in goal he was restricted to a couple of outings in the cup competitions before coming off the subs' bench on the final day of the season for an emotional farewell. A vastly experienced 'keeper he was released by the club at the end of the season.

Preston NE (Free from Leyland Motors on 14/2/1985)
Everton (Free on 12/12/1985) Others 1
Chester C (Loaned on 3/9/1987) FL 14 Others 2
York C (Loaned on 24/12/1987) FL 6
Manchester C (Loaned on 2/2/1988) FL 14 FAC 1
Port Vale (Loaned on 21/10/1988) FL 7 Others 1
Wolverhampton W (Loaned on 17/3/1989) FL 7
Preston NE (Loaned on 8/2/1990) FL 2
Wolverhampton W (£250,000 on 28/6/1990) FL 377+1 FLC 30 FAC 22 Others 11

STRACHAN Gavin David
Born: Aberdeen, 23 December 1978
Height: 5'11" Weight: 11.7
International Honours: S: U21-8; Yth

Gavin made just two Premiership appearances for Coventry last term as he continued to be gently eased into first-team football. His first game unfortunately came at Liverpool when the Sky Blues were overrun and he then had to wait until the final game of the season against Bradford City for his second outing. He also featured twice in the Worthington Cup as a substitute, scoring from the penalty spot in the away tie at Preston. Although a regular in midfield for the reserves, he seems to have slipped behind John Eustace and Barry Quinn in the pecking order for first-team places. Gavin's brother Craig is also on the books at Highfield Road and both are the sons of Sky Blues' boss Gordon Strachan.

Coventry C (From trainee on 28/11/1996) PL 5+9 FLC 1+3/1 FAC 2+2
Dundee (Loaned on 27/1/1999) SL 4+2

STREET Kevin
Born: Crewe, 25 November 1977
Height: 5'10" Weight: 10.8

Although affected by injuries that kept him out of the line-up for several weeks in the middle of the campaign, Kevin still gave useful service to Crewe Alexandra last term. However despite playing in an attacking role he scored just once during the season with a snap shot in the 4-2 home win over Burnley. He is a hard-working midfield player who can play in a number of positions, but often featured in a wide-right role.

Crewe Alex (From trainee on 4/7/1996) FL 55+51/8 FLC 4+3 FAC 1+1

STREVENS Benjamin (Ben) John
Born: Edgware, 24 May 1980
Height: 6'1" Weight: 11.0

This promising young striker appeared regularly in the first team squad for Barnet last season although he often featured on the subs' bench rather than in the starting line-up. One of several players to fall out of favour during Tony Cottee's brief spell as manager he spent two months on loan at Ryman League club St Albans City early in the new year. He returned to Underhill a stronger and more determined player and fought his way back in to the squad towards the end of the campaign. He was placed on the open to offers list following the Bees' relegation to the Conference.

Barnet (Free from Wingate & Finchley on 13/1/1999) FL 13+21/4 FLC 1+2 Others 0+2

STRINGER Christopher (Chris)
Born: Sheffield, 19 September 1983
Height: 6'6" Weight: 12.0

This young goalkeeper graduated to the Sheffield Wednesday first-team squad from the U19s last season and was immediately pushed into action when Kevin Pressman was sent off in the first minute of the opening game against Wolves. He performed competently on that occasion and never let the team down whenever he was called up for action. He is considered a great prospect at Hillsborough and he will be aiming to gain more first-team experience in the coming season.

Sheffield Wed (From trainee on 20/6/2000) FL 4+1 FLC 0+1 FAC 1

STRODDER Gary John
Born: Cleckheaton, 1 April 1965
Height: 6'1" Weight: 13.3
Club Honours: Div 3 '98

Hartlepool's most experienced player had a frustrating time in the 2000-01 season due to missing long spells through injury. Having been absent at the start of the campaign due to a suspension, he had a run in the team at centre half before an achilles injury flared up. He was then out of the first-team picture for the remainder of the season apart from the briefest of re-appearances. A tough-tackling no-nonsense defender he was released by Pool at the end of the season.

Lincoln C (From apprentice on 8/4/1983) FL 122+10/6 FLC 7+1 FAC 2+1 Others 5+1
West Ham U (£150,000 on 20/3/1987) FL 59+6/2 FLC 8 FAC 4+2 Others 2
West Bromwich A (£190,000 on 22/8/1990) FL 123+17/8 FLC 8+1 FAC 7/1 Others 10
Notts Co (£145,000 on 14/7/1995) FL 116+5/10 FLC 9 FAC 10+1 Others 7
Rotherham U (Loaned on 29/1/1999) FL 3
Hartlepool U (£25,000 on 25/2/1999) FL 58+3 FLC 2 FAC 1 Others 3

STRUPAR Branko
Born: Croatia, 9 February 1970
Height: 6'3" Weight: 13.7
International Honours: Belgium: 12

Great things were expected of Branko at Pride Park last season but the campaign turned out to be one of extreme frustration all round due to long-term injury problems that were eventually diagnosed as a pelvic muscle injury. Not blessed with great pace but very much the old-fashioned type of centre forward, he started off in great style, scoring in each of the Rams' first four games before his injury problems struck. He then made only one appearance between mid-September and mid-February but a brief return to the side in March included two goals in the vital home win over Tottenham. It is hoped that he will be fully fit next term and able to resume his partnership up front with Malcolm Christie.

Derby Co (£3,000,000 from KRC Genk, Belgium, ex Spansko, on 17/12/1999) PL 20+4/11 FLC 1

STUART Graham Charles
Born: Tooting, 24 October 1970
Height: 5'9" Weight: 11.10
Club Honours: FAC '95; Div 1 '00
International Honours: E: U21-5; Yth

Graham had a great season in the heart of Charlton Athletic's midfield in 2000-01 and was one of the Addicks' star performers throughout the season. He is a hard-working attacking midfield player who is strong in the tackle and an excellent distributor of the ball. He has developed a fine relationship with Charlton skipper Mark Kinsella and most of the side's attacking moves stem from one of these two. Usually playing just behind the front two, he also took over the captaincy when Kinsella was absent through injury. Graham scored five times, his most important strike being the goal at Newcastle which gave the Addicks their first away win of the season.

Chelsea (From trainee on 15/6/1989) F/PL 70+17/14 FLC 11/2 FAC 5+2/1 Others 3+2/1
Everton (£850,000 on 19/8/1993) PL 116+20/22 FLC 9/3 FAC 10+3/5 Others 2+1/1
Sheffield U (£850,000 on 28/11/1997) FL 52+1/11 FLC 4 FAC 10+1/1 Others 0+1
Charlton Ath (£1,100,000 on 25/3/1999) P/FL 75+6/16 FLC 2 FAC 5

STUART Jamie Christopher
Born: Southwark, 15 October 1976
Height: 5'10" Weight: 11.0
International Honours: E: U21-4; Yth

Jamie was mainly restricted to reserve-team football for Millwall last season and made only one brief first-team appearance, coming off the subs' bench for the final ten minutes of the match against Bristol City in October. He is a versatile defender who can play at left back or as a sweeper. He was released in the summer.

Charlton Ath (From trainee on 18/1/1995) FL 49+1/3 FLC 8+1 FAC 3 Others 0+1
Millwall (Free on 25/9/1998) FL 42+3 FLC 2 FAC 1 Others 6

STURRIDGE Dean Constantine
Born: Birmingham, 27 July 1973
Height: 5'8" Weight: 12.1

Dean struggled to win a regular place in the Derby County line-up last term and featured almost exclusively as a substitute. He managed just a single goal - a header in the

2-2 draw at Everton in August - and eventually moved on to Leicester City as boss Peter Taylor sought to boost his strike force. His experience proved of particular value in bringing along Ade Akinbiyi, while he showed that he had lost none of his predatory skills by scoring on three successive Saturdays in February, twice from close range and once with a neat looping header against Sunderland. He also came close to scoring in the FA Cup tie against Wycombe, but on this occasion his effort was disallowed. With the benefit of hindsight, it is possible to earmark that moment as potentially the one that dramatically altered the course of the Foxes' entire season. Unusually, a chest injury put him out of first-team action in April. Dean is a speedy and nimble striker with the ability to take on opposition defenders with his mazy runs.

Derby Co (From trainee on 1/7/1991) P/FL 142+48/53 FLC 9+4/4 FAC 8/2 Others 2+1
Torquay U (Loaned on 16/12/1994) FL 10/5
Leicester C (£350,000 on 19/1/2001) PL 12+1/3 FAC 2/1

SUFFO Kengne Herve **Patrick**
Born: Ebolowa, Cameroon, 17 January 1978
Height: 5'9" Weight: 12.12
International Honours: Cameroon
Having missed much of the 1999-2000 campaign while under suspension at Nantes, Patrick began last season in brighter fashion appearing for the Cameroon team in the Sydney Olympic Games. He featured several times as a substitute and won a gold medal even though he did not make it off the bench in the dramatic final against Spain that was decided by a penalty shoot-out. He subsequently joined Sheffield United where he again spent much of his time on the bench although he often made an impact when coming on, and netted a fine winner against Crystal Palace in February. A pacy striker who is strong on the ball he also occasionally appeared for his country in their World Cup qualifying campaign.
Sheffield U (£150,000 from Nantes, France, ex Tonerre Yaounde, Barcelona, on 20/11/2000) FL 6+10/1 FAC 0+1

Patrick Suffo

SUGDEN Ryan Stephen
Born: Bradford, 26 December 1980
Height: 6'1" Weight: 11.10
Having concluded the 1999-2000 season on a high with his first-ever senior goal, Ryan found himself further down in the pecking order of strikers at Oldham last season following the arrival of Carlo Corrazin and the improvement in form of Matthew Tipton and Craig Dudley. He found first-team opportunities very much at a premium and after making just two starts he joined Nigel Clough's Burton Albion on loan at the end of March where he scored eight goals in 10 games for the championship-chasing Dr Martens League outfit. A tall striker with a good eye for goal he will be hoping to gain more senior experience with the Latics in the coming season.
Oldham Ath (From trainee on 25/11/1998) FL 4+17/1 FLC 1+2 Others 1

SUKER Davor
Born: Osijek, Croatia, 1 January 1968
Height: 6'1" Weight: 12.5
International Honours: Croatia: 63. Yugoslavia: 2; Yth (World Yth-U20 '87)
Davor showed some excellent early-season form for West Ham and netted late equalisers against Manchester United and Sunderland. However niggling injuries, the form of Frederic Kanoute and then the arrival of Svetoslav Todorov all saw him edged out to the fringes of the squad and he had few opportunities in the second half of the campaign. At his best he is a powerful striker with a great left-foot shot. Out of contract in the summer he appeared likely to be on his way from Upton Park. He continued to play for Croatia during the season.
Arsenal (Free from Real Madrid, Spain, ex Osijek, Dinamo Zagreb, Seville, on 20/8/1999) PL 8+14/8 FLC 1/1 FAC 3 Others 3+10/2
West Ham U (Free on 5/7/2000) PL 7+4/2 FLC 1+1/1

SULLIVAN Neil
Born: Sutton, 24 February 1970
Height: 6'0" Weight: 12.1
International Honours: S: 22
Having joined Tottenham in the close season, Neil quickly established himself as the number one 'keeper at White Hart Lane and missed only three Premiership matches all season. He was in outstanding form and while it is difficult to single out any one performance, perhaps his finest display was in the 1-1 draw at home to Arsenal in December. With amazing ability at close range, Neil stands big and seems to dwarf the goal, yet has superb agility in the air. His anticipation and quick mind have ensured his place for Scotland at international level and he seems destined to remain first choice

at Spurs for some time. A total of 13 clean sheets proved his quality and his ability to settle into his new team was evident from day one. He was rewarded for an outstanding season when the club's supporters voted him as the 'Player of the Season'.

Wimbledon (From trainee on 26/7/1988) F/PL 180+1 FLC 18 FAC 25
Crystal Palace (Loaned on 1/5/1992) FL 1
Tottenham H (Free on 5/6/2000) PL 35 FLC 3 FAC 5

SUMMERBEE Nicholas (Nicky) John
Born: Altrincham, 26 August 1971
Height: 5'11" Weight: 12.8
Club Honours: Div 1 '99
International Honours: E: B-1; U21-3

Unable to get a game at Sunderland, Nicky eventually joined Bolton last January and although it was apparent that he was lacking match fitness he was soon pitched into first-team action. Not surprisingly he took some time to settle down, but he gradually won over the Wanderers' fans with a string of quality displays. While never the toughest of competitors, his qualities lie in his skill on the ball, and an ability to supply some breathtaking crosses into the penalty area. An important player for Wanderers in the final months of the season as he helped the team to a place in the Premiership via the play-offs, he was out of contract in the summer and his future at the time of writing was unclear.

Swindon T (From trainee on 20/7/1989) F/PL 89+23/6 FLC 9+1/3 FAC 2+4 Others 7/1
Manchester C (£1,500,000 on 24/6/1994) P/FL 119+12/6 FLC 11+2/2 FAC 12/2
Sunderland (£1,000,000 on 14/11/1997) P/FL 87+6/7 FLC 6+1 FAC 4+1 Others 3/1
Bolton W (Signed on 4/1/2001) FL 9+3/1 FAC 3

SUMMERBELL Mark
Born: Durham, 30 October 1976
Height: 5'9" Weight: 11.9

Mark enjoyed a short run of first-team football at Middlesbrough in 2000-01, scoring with a header in his first game of the season against Tottenham. However he dropped out of the squad in mid-November and although he occasionally featured as an unused substitute after that he made no further senior appearances. A versatile and industrious young midfielder he still looks to have a good future at the Riverside.

Middlesbrough (From trainee on 1/7/1995) F/PL 35+16/1 FLC 4+3/3

SUTCH Daryl
Born: Beccles, 11 September 1971
Height: 6'0" Weight: 12.0
International Honours: E: U21-4; Yth

Daryl had another tremendously consistent season for Norwich City last season when he once again proved his versatility by playing in defence in both full-back and wing-back roles, and also in midfield in both wide and central positions. Despite this constant changing of position he featured in almost every match, showing a selfless attitude throughout. Most suited to the right-back position, he covers his central defenders very well, he is also a good timer of challenges and when the opportunity arises comfortable in possession when going forward.

Norwich C (From trainee on 6/7/1990) F/PL 249+37/9 FLC 24+3 FAC 9+3 Others 2+3

SVENSSON Mathias (Matt)
Born: Boras, Sweden, 24 September 1974
Height: 6'0" Weight: 12.4
Club Honours: Div 1 '00
International Honours: Sweden: 3

Matt missed the first few games of the 2000-01 campaign after sustaining a broken wrist in a pre-season friendly but went on to feature regularly for Charlton. He scored almost immediately after coming on from the subs' bench against Middlesbrough in his first game of the season and then had a run in the starting line-up playing alongside Jonatan Johansson before making way for loan signing Shaun Bartlett. Matt is a strong aggressive striker who is unselfish, useful in the air and a hard worker. He was watched by the Swedish selectors during the season and if he continues to maintain this form he could soon add to his total of international caps.

Portsmouth (£200,000 from Elfsborg, Sweden on 6/12/1996) FL 34+11/10 FLC 1/1 FAC 3+2/1 (£100,000 to Tirol Innsbruck, Austria on 15/7/1998)
Crystal Palace (£100,000 on 29/9/1998) FL 26+6/10 FLC 2 FAC 1
Charlton Ath (£600,000 on 28/1/2000) P/FL 31+9/7 FAC 2+1/1

SWAILES Christopher (Chris) William
Born: Gateshead, 19 October 1970
Height: 6'2" Weight: 12.11

Chris enjoyed a superb season for Bury in 2000-01 when he was once again a rock in the defence throughout the campaign. A central defender who is commanding in the air and determined in the tackle, he also proved useful when joining the attack and contributed five valuable goals. Chris was runner-up in the supporters' poll for 'Player of the Season'. He was reported to have signed for Rotherham United in the summer.

Ipswich T (From trainee on 23/5/1989)
Peterborough U (£10,000 on 28/3/1991. Free to Boston U in August 1991)
Doncaster Rov (Free from Bridlington T on 27/10/1993) FL 49 FLC 2/1 FAC 1 Others 2
Ipswich T (£225,000 on 23/3/1995) P/FL 34+3/1 FLC 3 Others 2
Bury (£200,000 on 14/11/1997) FL 125+1/10 FLC 9 FAC 8 Others 3/1

SWAILES Daniel (Danny)
Born: Bolton, 1 April 1979
Height: 6'3" Weight: 13.0

This promising Bury youngster was largely overshadowed by the likes of Sam Collins, Steve Redmond and his namesake Chris Swailes in the running for a place in the first team last season. His appearances were mostly restricted to cover for injuries and suspensions but when drafted in he performed creditably. A central defender who is excellent in the air, Danny will be hoping to make a breakthrough to regular first-team action in 2001-02.

Bury (From trainee on 9/7/1997) FL 28+7/3 FLC 0+3 FAC 4+1 Others 2

SWALES Stephen (Steve) Colin
Born: Whitby, 26 December 1973
Height: 5'8" Weight: 10.6

New Hull manager Brian Little gave Steve the chance to display his skills in midfield during the early months of 2000-01. His progress was soon checked by a knee problem, and although he returned to the team he suffered another setback in February when he picked up a foot injury against Barnet. A tough-tackling player he has previously appeared in a wing-back role on either flank. Out of contract in the summer his future was unclear at the time of writing.

Scarborough (From trainee on 3/8/1992) FL 51+3/1 FAC 5 Others 3
Reading (£70,000 on 13/7/1995) FL 33+10/1 FLC 6+1 FAC 6
Hull C (Free on 7/12/1998) FL 57+11 FLC 4+1 FAC 1 Others 3

SWAN Peter Harold
Born: Leeds, 28 September 1966
Height: 6'2" Weight: 15.9
Club Honours: AMC '93

Peter was appointed captain of York City for the 2000-01 season but sadly after just two matches he suffered a serious cartilage injury and following surgery he was forced to retire from the game on specialist's advice. An imposing central defender who occasionally appeared as a striker he made more than 400 appearances in senior football.

Leeds U (From trainee on 6/8/1984) FL 43+6/11 FLC 3/2 FAC 3 Others 1+2
Hull C (£200,000 on 23/3/1989) FL 76+4/24 FLC 2+3/1 FAC 2 Others 1
Port Vale (£300,000 on 16/8/1991) FL 105+6/5 FLC 6 FAC 9/1 Others 12/1
Plymouth Arg (£300,000 on 22/7/1994) FL 24+3/2 FLC 2/1 FAC 2
Burnley (£200,000 on 4/8/1995) FL 47+2/7 FLC 2 FAC 3 Others 6
Bury (£50,000 on 8/8/1997) FL 26+11/6 FLC 1+1 FAC 1
Burnley (Free on 28/8/1998) FL 11+8
York C (Free on 14/3/2000) FL 11

SYMONS Christopher (Kit) Jeremiah
Born: Basingstoke, 8 March 1971
Height: 6'2" Weight: 13.7
Club Honours: Div 2 '99; Div 1 '01
International Honours: W: 33; B-1; U21-2; Yth

Kit was the unlucky central defender to miss out when Fulham's new manager Jean Tigana opted to switch to a back four instead of a formation of three central defenders and two wing backs. Nevertheless, he helped a very young side through four rounds of the Worthington Cup and when Chris Coleman was badly injured in a car crash, he stepped into the breach to do a superb job for the rest of the season. A regular member of the Wales international squad, Kit won back his place in the team for the World Cup qualifiers late in the season.

Portsmouth (From trainee on 30/12/1988) FL 161/10 FLC 19 FAC 10 Others 13+1/1
Manchester C (£1,600,000 on 17/8/1995) P/FL 124/4 FLC 6 FAC 9
Fulham (Free on 30/7/1998) FL 94+4/13 FLC 14+1/1 FAC 12

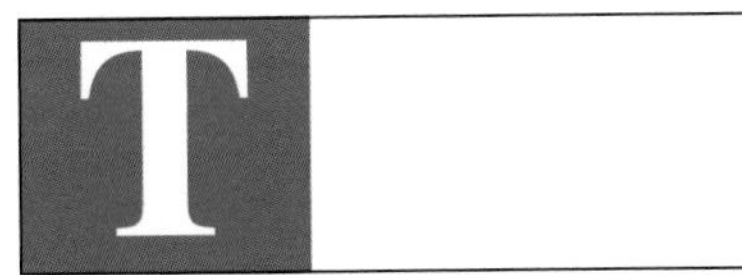

TABB Jay Anthony
Born: London, 21 February 1984
Height: 5'5" Weight: 9.7

A product of Brentford's youth team, Jay was one of several youngsters drafted in to the senior squad following the 6-0 defeat at Swansea in the final week of last season and he made his debut in the penultimate game against Luton. He gave an accomplished performance and also featured as a substitute for the whole of the second half in the final game against Bury. A promising young midfield player he will be hoping to gain more first-team experience in 2001-02.

Brentford (Trainee) FL 1+1

TAGGART Gerald (Gerry) Paul
Born: Belfast, 18 October 1970
Height: 6'1" Weight: 13.12
Club Honours: Div 1 '97; FLC '00
International Honours: NI: 50; U23-2; Yth; Sch

Massively popular with the Leicester City faithful, Gerry did not have quite the same impact last term as he had managed in 1999-2000. He was troubled by a knee injury in the early weeks of the campaign but nevertheless managed to net the winner against Southampton and also scored to put City back into the UEFA tie against Red Star Belgrade. However after that his season became more patchy as further injuries intervened, including groin, buttock and hip strains. He did, however, gain his 50th full cap for Northern Ireland during the campaign and was made captain for the night to mark the occasion, although Norway rather spoiled the party by winning the World Cup qualifier 4-0 in Belfast. He subsequently took over the Foxes' captaincy after Matt Elliott was injured. A solid left-footed central defender he is always willing to get stuck in when the chips are down.

Manchester C (From trainee on 1/7/1989) FL 10+2/1 Others 1
Barnsley (£75,000 on 10/1/1990) FL 209+3/16 FLC 15/1 FAC 14/2 Others 6/1
Bolton W (£1,500,000 on 1/8/1995) F/PL 68+1/4 FLC 8/1 FAC 4
Leicester C (Free on 23/7/1998) PL 63+7/8 FLC 12+2/2 FAC 8+1 Others 2/1

TAIT Jordan Alexander
Born: Berwick, 27 September 1979
Height: 5'10" Weight: 11.5

This young left back joined Darlington from Oldham Athletic last October and made his first team debut as a substitute at Cardiff City later that month. He then started the next two games but despite a number of appearances on the bench he failed to get any further opportunities of senior experience with the Third Division club. Out of contract in the summer his future was unclear at the time of writing.

Newcastle U (From trainee on 2/7/1998)
Oldham Ath (Free on 19/8/1999) FL 0+1 FLC 0+1
Darlington (Signed on 12/10/2000) FL 2+1

TAIT Paul
Born: Newcastle, 24 October 1974
Height: 6'1" Weight: 11.10

After an excellent first season with Crewe, Paul struggled to win a regular place in the first-team squad last term. He made the starting line-up on just nine occasions and towards the end of the campaign found that Rob Hulse and Dean Ashton had a firm hold on the strikers' positions at Gresty Road. A tall target man with good control, he flicks the ball on very effectively and can always be relied upon to give his best.

Everton (From trainee on 8/7/1993)
Wigan Ath (Free on 22/7/1994) FL 1+4 (Free to Runcorn on 16/2/1996)
Crewe Alex (Signed from Northwich Vic on 9/6/1999) FL 28+23/6 FLC 0+1 FAC 1+1

TAIT Paul Ronald
Born: Sutton Coldfield, 31 July 1971
Height: 6'1" Weight: 10.10
Club Honours: Div 2 '95; AMC '95

Paul's form in the centre of the park was one of the few bright features of a very dismal 2000-01 season at Oxford United. Unfortunately he missed a lengthy period in mid-season with an ankle problem and was again sidelined by injury in the closing weeks of the campaign. In between he proved to be a key influence in midfield, creating chances and tidying up the loose ends, while he also found time to net three goals including the winner at Northampton.

Birmingham C (From trainee on 2/8/1988) FL 135+35/14 FLC 13+2 FAC 6+2 Others 13+5/4
Northampton T (Loaned on 24/12/1997) FL 2+1
Oxford U (Free on 15/1/1999) FL 73+4/3 FLC 7 FAC 4 Others 2

Gerry Taggart

TAL Idan
Born: Petach Tikva, Israel, 13 September 1975
Height: 5'10" Weight: 11.8
International Honours: Israel: 24

Everton were forced to wait until a work permit wrangle was finalised before completing Idan's transfer from Maccabi Petach Tikva. It proved well worth the wait. A slightly built left-winger, he is a tricky, skilful player with a voracious appetite for hard work. He is also unfazed by the physical aspect of the English game. His performances seemed to improve as the season progressed, and his last two displays - against Chelsea and Sunderland - suggested, a bright future ahead for the player. In those games he was employed as a right winger, where his ability to cut inside on to his left foot proved particularly dangerous. After settling well during 2000-01, the new season could be a big one for him.

Everton (£700,000 from Maccabi Petach Tikva, Israel, ex Hapoel Tel Aviv, on 20/10/2000) PL 12+10/2 FAC 0+2

Idan Tal

TALBOT Stewart Dean
Born: Birmingham, 14 June 1973
Height: 5'11" Weight: 13.7

Signed from Port Vale during the summer, Stewart quickly settled into his role as a midfield dynamo for Rotherham United last season. He impressed with his ability to win the ball and a willingness to push forward while he netted a crucial goal for the Millers to earn victory at Northampton when the team produced a tremendous performance after playing for most of the game with ten men. His influence on the team was such that he was sorely missed whenever absent.

Port Vale (Signed from Moor Green on 10/8/1994) FL 112+25/10 FLC 4+3 FAC 4+1 Others 2+3/1
Rotherham U (Free on 13/7/2000) FL 37+1/5 FLC 2 FAC 3

TALIA Francesco (Frank)
Born: Melbourne, Australia, 20 July 1972
Height: 6'1" Weight: 13.6
Club Honours: Div 2 '96
International Honours: Australia: Sch

Having joined Wolves in the close season, Frank moved on to Sheffield United last September without registering a senior appearance at Molineux. He joined as cover for regular 'keeper Simon Tracey but his opportunities were limited to reserve games and a seat on the subs' bench until an injury to Tracey gave him his chance towards the end of the season. He had little to do on his debut in the home draw against Norwich and went on to record two clean sheets from six appearances before he lost his place again.

Blackburn Rov (Free from Sunshine George Cross, Australia on 28/8/1992)
Hartlepool U (Loaned on 29/12/1992) FL 14 Others 1
Swindon T (£150,000 on 8/9/1995) FL 107 FLC 9 FAC 2
Wolverhampton W (Free on 11/8/2000)
Sheffield U (Free on 26/9/2000) FL 6

TANKARD Allen John
Born: Fleet, 21 May 1969
Height: 5'10" Weight: 12.10
Club Honours: AMC '01
International Honours: E: Yth

Allen featured regularly for Port Vale in the first half of last season but was mostly confined to the subs' bench in the second half of the campaign. Generally used on the left-hand side of a three-man defence he still managed to find time to net five goals including one in the LDV Vans Trophy victory over Darlington. He is approaching his 600th senior appearance but was out of contract in the summer and it was unclear what the future held at the time of writing.

Southampton (From apprentice on 27/5/1987) FL 5 Others 2
Wigan Ath (Free on 4/7/1988) FL 205+4/4 FLC 15/1 FAC 13 Others 20
Port Vale (£87,500 on 26/7/1993) FL 261+14/11 FLC 21 FAC 16/1 Others 11+1/1

TANN Adam John
Born: Kings Lynn, 12 May 1982
Height: 6'0" Weight: 11.5
International Honours: E: Yth

Having been capped several times by England at U18 level in 1999-2000 Adam continued his development in Cambridge United's reserves last term. A promising defender who can play at right back or centre half he was loaned to Cambridge City in March to gain some senior experience and on his return made his Football League debut at Swansea in the final game of the season.

Cambridge U (From trainee on 7/9/1999) FL 1 Others 1

TANNER Adam David
Born: Maldon, 25 October 1973
Height: 6'0" Weight: 12.1
Club Honours: FAT '01

Adam found it difficult to win a place in the Colchester United line-up last season due to the abundance of central defenders on the club's books and was restricted to just a handful of first-team appearances. He moved on to Ryman League club Canvey Island in January and appeared as a substitute in their FA Trophy Final victory over Forest Green in May.

Ipswich T (From trainee on 13/7/1992) P/FL 49+24/7 FLC 2+2 FAC 5+2 Others 3+1/1
Peterborough U (Free on 23/3/2000)
Colchester U (Free on 7/8/2000) FL 1+3 FLC 1+1

TARDIF Christopher (Chris) Luke
Born: Guernsey, 19 September 1979
Height: 5'11" Weight: 12.7

This young Portsmouth goalkeeper was well down the pecking order at Portsmouth at the start of the 2000-01 campaign, but following the departure of Russell Hoult in the new year he found himself raised to second choice to Aaron Flahavan. He was unexpectedly given his senior debut in the FA Cup tie against Tranmere when Pompey were decimated by illness and injuries and did his best under difficult circumstances, before going on to make two more senior appearances later in the season. A promising 'keeper who shows good command of his area, he earned a three-year contract from new boss Graham Rix in the summer.

Portsmouth (From trainee on 3/7/1998) FL 2+2 FAC 1

TARICCO Mauricio Ricardo
Born: Buenos Aires, Argentine, 10 March 1973
Height: 5'9" Weight: 11.7

Mauricio had a frustrating time at Tottenham last term and after featuring in a handful of games early on he was sidelined by an injury in September and later required a hernia operation. He remained out of action until May when he returned for the reserves in a 4-0 defeat at the hands of Arsenal. An agile wing back who has great pace and the ability to deliver well-timed passes into the heart of the action, he will be looking forward to renewing his career under new boss Glenn Hoddle in 2001-02.

Ipswich T (£175,000 from Argentinos Juniors, Argentina on 9/9/1994) FL 134+3/4 FLC 18/3 FAC 8 Others 7
Tottenham H (£1,800,000 on 4/12/1998) PL 43+4 FLC 2 FAC 3+1 Others 3

TARRANT Neil Kenneth
Born: Darlington, 24 June 1979
Height: 6'1" Weight: 12.0
International Honours: S: U21-5

This Scottish U21 international joined York City on loan from Aston Villa last October and scored on what was his Football League debut in the 1-1 draw against Leyton Orient. The tall striker impressed at times but on occasions found it difficult to come to terms with Third Division football. He returned to Villa Park in December to continue his development in the club's reserve team.

Darlington (From trainee on 15/7/1997. Free to Shamrock Rov on 9/10/1997)
Ross Co (Signed on 12/12/1997) SL 34+10/20 SLC 4/2 SC 3+3/5
Aston Villa (£250,000 on 28/4/1999)
Ayr U (Loaned on 10/12/1999) SL 15/4 SC 5/3
York C (Loaned on 19/10/2000) FL 6+1/1 FAC 1

TATE Christopher (Chris) Douglas
Born: York, 27 December 1977
Height: 6'0" Weight: 11.10

Having begun last season with Conference outfit Scarborough, Chris was snapped up by Leyton Orient boss Tommy Taylor in the autumn. Although appearing mainly as a substitute he netted some vital goals including a double in the 2-1 win at Barnet - a smart volley and a brilliant overhead kick. He went on to score one of the fastest goals in a domestic final when he netted after just 30 seconds in the play-off final against Blackpool, although eventually the O's fell to defeat. A big and strong striker he will be looking to win a regular place in the line-up in 2001-02.

Sunderland (From trainee at York C on 17/7/1996)
Scarborough (Free on 5/8/1997) FL 21+28/13 FLC 0+1 FAC 0+1 Others 2+1
Halifax T (£150,000 on 5/7/1999) FL 18/4 FLC 2 FAC 2/1 (£80,000 to Scarborough on 16/12/1999)
Leyton Orient (£25,000 on 3/11/2000) FL 9+13/3 FAC 1+2/1 Others 1+2/1

TAYLOR Craig
Born: Plymouth, 24 January 1974
Height: 6'1" Weight: 13.2

Craig was an extremely influential figure for Plymouth Argyle in 2000-01 and this was recognised when he was appointed captain in the absence of the injured Mick Heathcote. A commanding centre back he takes a powerful free kick and is a constant danger when coming up to join the attack for set pieces. He had the misfortune to suffer a broken ankle against Southend in April that put him out of action for the last few weeks of the campaign but it is hoped he will be fit in time for the start of the 2001-02 season.

Exeter C (From trainee on 13/6/1992) FL 2+3 FLC 1 Others 2+2 (Free to Bath C on 18/3/1994)
Swindon T (£25,000 from Dorchester T on 15/4/1997) FL 47+8/2 FLC 0+1 FAC 3
Plymouth Arg (Loaned on 16/10/1998) FL 6/1
Plymouth Arg (£30,000 on 20/8/1999) FL 79+1/6 FLC 2 FAC 7 Others 1/1

TAYLOR Gareth Keith
Born: Weston super Mare, 25 February 1973
Height: 6'2" Weight: 13.8
International Honours: W: 8; U21-7

Unable to get a game in the first team at Manchester City, Gareth eventually moved on loan to Burnley in the new year and his arrival proved something of a masterstroke for Clarets' manager Stan Ternent. On his debut for the club he set up a goal for Ian Moore as league leaders Fulham were despatched 2-1 and a fortnight later he scored the winner in a 1-0 win at Watford. His striking partnership with Moore was a key factor in Burnley's revival towards the end of the season with Gareth playing as a target man and bringing the best out of his more deep-lying partner. Gareth was a constant threat to opposition defences always giving 100 per cent and a permanent signing would be much welcomed by the Burnley faithful.

Bristol Rov (From trainee at Southampton on 29/7/1991) FL 31+16/16 FLC 3+1 FAC 1+1 Others 5
Crystal Palace (£750,000 on 27/9/1995) FL 18+2/1 FAC 2/1
Sheffield U (Signed on 8/3/1996) FL 56+28/25 FLC 8+3/2 FAC 5+2 Others 1+2
Manchester C (£400,000 on 26/11/1998) FL 28+15/9 FLC 2+1/1 FAC 3 Others 1+3
Port Vale (Loaned on 21/1/2000) FL 4
Queens Park R (Loaned on 14/3/2000) FL 2+4/1
Burnley (Loaned on 20/2/2001) FL 15/4

TAYLOR Ian Kenneth
Born: Birmingham, 4 June 1968
Height: 6'1" Weight: 12.4
Club Honours: AMC '93; FLC '96

Ian had another consistent season in the Aston Villa midfield last term and apart from a spell on the sidelines with a hamstring injury he was a near ever-present. A Villa man through-and-through having supported the club from the terraces in his youth, his dedication, industry and work rate are second to none. He netted four valuable goals and was once again a key member of John Gregory's first-team squad.

Port Vale (£15,000 from Moor Green on 13/7/1992) FL 83/28 FLC 4/2 FAC 6/1 Others 13/4
Sheffield Wed (£1,000,000 on 12/7/1994) PL 9+5/1 FLC 2+2/1
Aston Villa (£1,000,000 on 21/12/1994) PL 186+18/25 FLC 17+2/7 FAC 13+2/1 Others 15+1/4

TAYLOR John Patrick
Born: Norwich, 24 October 1964
Height: 6'2" Weight: 13.12
Club Honours: Div 3 '91

Although he is now player-coach of the reserve team at Cambridge United John continued to feature regularly for the first team last season. 'The King of the Abbey', as he is known, extended his own club record goal tally by three including important last-minute strikes against Stoke and Notts County to earn some vital points. His experience up front proved invaluable in the development of the promising Tom Youngs and he still showed he had an eye for goal when it mattered.

Colchester U (From juniors on 17/12/1982)
Cambridge U (Signed from Sudbury T on 24/8/1988) FL 139+21/46 FLC 9+2/2 FAC 21/10 Others 12+2/2
Bristol Rov (Signed on 28/3/1992) FL 91+4/44 FLC 4/1 FAC 3 Others 5
Bradford C (£300,000 on 5/7/1994) FL 35+1/11 FLC 4/2 FAC 2 Others 3
Luton T (£200,000 on 23/3/1995) FL 27+10/3 FLC 2 Others 1/1
Lincoln C (Loaned on 27/9/1996) FL 5/2
Colchester U (Loaned on 8/11/1996) FL 8/5 Others 1
Cambridge U (Free on 10/1/1997) FL 97+68/40 FLC 3+6/2 FAC 6+6/1 Others 1+2/1

Gareth Taylor

TAYLOR Maik Stefan
Born: Hildeshein, Germany, 4 September 1971
Height: 6'4" Weight: 14.2
Club Honours: Div 2 '99; Div 1 '01
International Honours: NI: 15; B-1; U21-1
Maik missed only a handful of first-team games in goal for Fulham last term and proved himself to be the best 'keeper in the First Division, recording a total of 19 clean sheets during the season. His command of the penalty area was second to none and if he came for crosses or corners he got them. He made numerous crucial saves and enjoyed playing as a 'sweeper' using his excellent distribution to start numerous attacks. Having lost out to Roy Carroll for part of the season he eventually came back to regain his place for Northern Ireland in the friendly against Norway. He was rewarded by his fellow professionals with a place in the PFA's First Division team.
Barnet (Free from Farnborough on 7/6/1995) FL 70 FLC 6 FAC 6 Others 2
Southampton (£500,000 on 1/1/1997) PL 18
Fulham (£800,000 + on 17/11/1997) FL 164 FLC 17 FAC 14 Others 3

TAYLOR Martin
Born: Ashington, 9 November 1979
Height: 6'4" Weight: 15.0
International Honours: E: U21-1; Yth
Having previously been only on the fringes of the Blackburn Rovers' first-team squad Martin emerged last season as deputy to Craig Short in the centre of the defence and even kept him out of the team for a while. Tall and powerfully built he added a degree of steel to his play, while he remained very comfortable on the ball. He also developed something of a reputation as a goal-scorer netting three times in the First Division and also adding one in the FA Cup win over Chester when he was in particularly impressive form. Martin made his debut for England U21s in the end-of-season game against Mexico.
Blackburn Rov (From trainee on 13/8/1997) P/FL 17+8/3 FLC 7 FAC 7/1 Others 0+1
Darlington (Loaned on 18/1/2000) FL 4
Stockport Co (Loaned on 23/3/2000) FL 7

TAYLOR Martin James
Born: Tamworth, 9 December 1966
Height: 6'0" Weight: 14.6
Martin had another magnificent season in goal for Wycombe Wanderers in the 2000-01 campaign when he regularly produced match-winning performances. Perhaps his best display came in the FA Cup fifth round replay against Wimbledon at Selhurst Park when he blocked an 89th minute penalty to take the game into extra time, saved two spot kicks in the penalty shoot-out and even scored one himself to help the Chairboys to victory. A strong all-round 'keeper he is good in the air and has the ability to kick out with either foot. He was comfortably voted 'Player of the Season' by the club's supporters for the second time in a row.
Derby Co (Signed from Mile Oak Rov on 2/7/1986) F/PL 97 FLC 7 FAC 5 Others 11
Carlisle U (Loaned on 23/9/1987) FL 10 FLC 1 FAC 1 Others 2
Scunthorpe U (Loaned on 17/12/1987) FL 8
Crewe Alex (Loaned on 20/9/1996) FL 6
Wycombe W (Free on 27/3/1997) FL 181 FLC 12 FAC 19 Others 7

TAYLOR Matthew Simon
Born: Oxford, 27 November 1981
Height: 5'10" Weight: 11.10
Matthew continued to impress in a struggling Luton Town side last season and was a near ever-present during the campaign. A fast-raiding midfielder or wing back, he created panic in opposition defences with his surging runs and showed that he can shoot equally well with either foot. He scored an amazing goal against Cambridge when he fired home a shot from 40 yards over the retreating 'keeper and into the net to clinch a 1-0 victory for the Hatters. His efforts during the campaign were rewarded when he received the supporters' club 'Player of the Season' and players' 'Player of the Season' awards.
Luton T (From trainee on 9/2/1999) FL 84+2/5 FLC 5 FAC 9/1 Others 1

TAYLOR Robert (Bob)
Born: Horden, 3 February 1967
Height: 5'10" Weight: 12.12
West Bromwich Albion boss Gary Megson preferred a twin strike-force of Jason Roberts and Lee Hughes for much of the 2000-01 season but 'Super Bob' was always there in the wings, waiting to enter the fray, ready for the challenge and eager to score goals ... which he did at crucial times and indeed, in crucial matches. He hit a vital brace in a 2-1 win over Tranmere Rovers after Albion had suffered two successive defeats that had seriously dented their play-off chances, while a late equaliser at Burnley also proved important. Powerful in the air he acted as the perfect supporting foil to either Roberts or Hughes when called into action and he was still as keen and eager as ever to play when called up.
Leeds U (Free from Horden Colliery on 27/3/1986) FL 33+9/9 FLC 5+1/3 FAC 1 Others 4+1/1
Bristol C (£175,000 on 23/3/1989) FL 96+10/50 FLC 6+1/2 FAC 9+1/5 Others 3/1
West Bromwich A (£300,000 on 31/1/1992) FL 211+27/96 FLC 16/6 FAC 6+2/3 Others 16+3/8
Bolton W (Free on 8/1/1998) P/FL 57+20/21 FLC 6+5/2 FAC 4+1/2 Others 3/2
West Bromwich A (£90,000 on 23/3/2000) FL 25+23/10 FLC 2+1 FAC 0+1/1 Others 0+2

TAYLOR Robert Anthony
Born: Norwich, 30 April 1971
Height: 6'1" Weight: 13.8
Having joined Wolves for a substantial fee during the close season Robert struggled to make an impact in the early games last term, despite applying plenty of effort. He scored in the Worthington Cup tie at Oxford and another two against Grimsby in the same competition but was hampered by a mystery injury that was later diagnosed as a rare muscle problem that was causing him to suffer cramp-like symptoms. He returned briefly to the squad in December but did not feature at all for the first team after Christmas. A big striker who shields the ball well he will be hoping for better fortune in 2001-02.
Norwich C (From trainee on 26/3/1990)
Leyton Orient (Loaned on 28/3/1991) FL 0+3/1
Birmingham C (Signed on 31/8/1991)
Leyton Orient (Free on 21/10/1991) FL 54+19/20 FLC 1+1 FAC 2+1 Others 2+1
Brentford (£100,000 on 24/3/1994) FL 172+1/56 FLC 16/6 FAC 10/8 Others 14/4
Gillingham (£500,000 on 6/8/1998) FL 56+2/31 FLC 2+1/1 FAC 3/2 Others 7/5
Manchester C (£1,500,000 on 30/11/1999) FL 14+2/5
Wolverhampton W (£1,550,000 on 15/8/2000) FL 5+4 FLC 3/3

TAYLOR Scott Dean
Born: Portsmouth, 28 November 1970
Height: 5'9" Weight: 11.8
Club Honours: Div 2 '94; FLC '97
Having signed a further 12-month contract for Wolves in the close season Scott featured regularly in the early games last term. However he then had the misfortune to suffer a ruptured knee cap playing against Tranmere in September and the injury kept him out of action for the remainder of the campaign. A lively midfield player he was released in the summer.
Reading (From trainee on 22/6/1989) FL 164+43/24 FLC 7+5/1 FAC 11+2/3 Others 12+4/1
Leicester C (£250,000 on 12/7/1995) P/FL 59+5/6 FLC 7+3 FAC 2+1 Others 3
Wolverhampton W (Free on 23/9/1999) FL 21+11/3 FLC 2

TAYLOR Scott James
Born: Chertsey, 5 May 1976
Height: 5'10" Weight: 11.4
A great crowd favourite at Tranmere Scott again featured regularly last season although he often found himself on the subs' bench. A hard-working striker his build-up play was impressive and showed himself to be a master of holding up the action to allow his colleagues to regroup. Committed and tenacious as ever he chipped in with six valuable goals, thus making him Rovers' joint-second-top scorer for the season.
Millwall (£15,000 from Staines on 8/2/1995) FL 13+15 FLC 0+2/2 FAC 1+1
Bolton W (£150,000 on 29/3/1996) P/FL 2+10/1 FLC 0+4/1 FAC 1/1
Rotherham U (Loaned on 12/12/1997) FL 10/3 Others 1
Blackpool (Loaned on 26/3/1998) FL 3+2/1
Tranmere Rov (£50,000 on 9/10/1998) FL 78+30/17 FLC 16/5 FAC 2+5

TAYLOR Stuart James
Born: Romford, 28 November 1980
Height: 6'4" Weight: 13.4
International Honours: E: Yth
Finding himself third in line at Highbury behind full internationals David Seaman and Alex Manninger, Stuart began last season on loan at Crystal Palace. He played in the opening ten matches for the Eagles performing competently but only keeping two clean sheets before returning to the Gunners. On his return he made his debut for Arsenal in the Worthington Cup third round defeat by Ipswich Town before gaining some valuable European experience in the Champions' League game Shakhtjor Donetsk. Later in the season he had a spell on loan at Peterborough as cover for the injured Mark Tyler and again acquitted

himself well. A big, solid 'keeper with a fine all-round game, hopes are high that Stuart will become an Arsenal regular in the future.
Arsenal (From trainee on 8/7/1998) FLC 1 Others 1
Bristol Rov (Loaned on 24/9/1999) FL 4
Crystal Palace (Loaned on 9/8/2000) FL 10
Peterborough U (Loaned on 15/2/2001) FL 6

TELFER Paul Norman
Born: Edinburgh, 21 October 1971
Height: 5'9" Weight: 11.6
International Honours: S: 1; B-2; U21-3
Coventry City's 'Mr Dependable' had a good solid season in 2000-01, playing in several positions including central midfield and right back. Although his place in the team seemed under threat following the arrival of David Thompson, injuries, suspensions, international call-ups and loss of form all meant that Paul was generally in the team or on the bench and when called upon he rarely let the side down. His doggedness, strong tackling and excellent crossing ability were all characteristics that endeared him to the Sky Blues' fans. He failed to score during the season but was responsible for setting up many chances with his corners, and delivered two stunning crosses at Old Trafford from which John Hartson scored. Paul had the misfortune to suffer a broken leg in the vital end-of-season game at Villa Park but will be looking to return to action early in the 2001-02 campaign.
Luton T (From trainee on 7/11/1988) FL 136+8/19 FLC 5 FAC 14/2 Others 2/1
Coventry C (£1,500,000 on 11/7/1995) PL 178+13/6 FLC 15/2 FAC 15+4/4

TENNEBO Thomas
Born: Bergen, Norway, 19 March 1975
Height: 6'2" Weight: 12.2
Having spent the 1999-2000 campaign coming to terms with the demands of Third Division football Thomas was looking to gain regular first-team football last season. He featured in a handful of early season games before unfortunately suffering a broken leg playing for the reserves in September and the injury kept him out of action until the summer. He is an attacking midfielder with some good touches who makes effective use of his height and pace.
Hartlepool U (Free from Fana, Norway on 13/8/1999) FL 6+7 FLC 1+2 Others 1

Paul Telfer

TERESKINAS Andrejus
Born: Telsiai, Lithuania, 10 July 1970
Height: 6'3" Weight: 13.10
International Honours: Lithuania: 55
This experienced left back appeared for Skonto Riga in the Champions' League qualifying rounds at the start of last season before joining Macclesfield Town on a non-contract basis for a taste of English football. Injury and administrative problems over his work permit meant that Andrejus was ineligible for selection for competitive games until the middle of February and he made his debut in the Football League when he came on from the subs' bench against Hartlepool in March, featuring on the left side of midfield. Tall and powerfully built, Andrejus has represented Lithuania for over a decade and currently holds the record number of caps for his country.
Macclesfield T (Free from Skonto Riga, Latvia, ex Zalgiris Vilnius, Stomil Olsztyn, on 27/11/2000) FL 0+1

TERRY John George
Born: Barking, 7 December 1980
Height: 6'0" Weight: 12.4
Club Honours: FAC '00
International Honours: E: U21-6
This highly rated central defender made his long-awaited breakthrough at Chelsea during the 2000-01 season. In October he won his first England U21 cap against Finland and he claimed a regular first-team place at Stamford Bridge alongside Marcel Desailly and Frank Leboeuf as new manager Claudio Ranieri tried a three-man central defensive system. Tough in the tackle and commanding in the air, John has the confidence to constructively play his way out of trouble and is capable of hitting long passes to attacking players on either flank. When Ranieri switched to a flat back four at the turn of the year, John retained his place, easing Leboeuf out of the side. He claimed his first Premiership goal at Arsenal in January to clinch a draw and was made captain of England's U21 side for the return fixture with Finland, when he scored with a towering header. The enforced retirement of Jes Hogh, the sale of Emerson Thome and the unsettled future of Frank Leboeuf all combined to give John a great opportunity of becoming a regular for the Blues, a fact further recognised when he agreed a new four-and-a-half-year deal with the club in February.
Chelsea (From trainee on 18/3/1998) PL 21+7/1 FLC 2+1 FAC 7+3/1 Others 1
Nottingham F (Loaned on 23/3/2000) FL 5+1

TESSEM Jo
Born: Orlandet, Norway, 28 February 1972
Height: 6'3" Weight: 12.10
International Honours: Norway: 3

2000-01 was a memorable season for this attack-minded midfielder, the highlight possibly being his long-awaited international debut for Norway against Northern Ireland in March. A late developer at the highest level, his move to the English game has paid dividends both for himself and the Southampton team. Considered the fittest player on the club's books, he combines his speed with good ball control to supply perfect crosses and is also known to have a fierce shot. He netted one of the most memorable goals in recent years at The Dell when he pushed and ran around the Everton defence to score from just outside the area.

Southampton (£600,000 from Molde, Norway, ex Lyn, on 19/11/1999) PL 50+8/8 FLC 3/1 FAC 5+1/1

THATCHER Benjamin (Ben) David
Born: Swindon, 30 November 1975
Height: 5'10" Weight: 12.7
International Honours: E: U21-4; Yth

An old-fashioned no-nonsense left back, Ben struggled to make an impact in his first season at Tottenham last term and after succumbing to a combination of groin and hip injuries in November he failed to regain match fitness before the end of the season. Tenacious and hard working he will be aiming to establish himself in the Spurs line-up in 2001-02.

Millwall (From trainee on 8/6/1992) FL 87+3/1 FLC 6 FAC 7 Others 1
Wimbledon (£1,840,00 on 5/7/1996) PL 82+4 FLC 12 FAC 5
Tottenham H (£5,000,000 on 12/7/2000) PL 10+2 FLC 3

THELWELL Alton Anthony
Born: Islington, 5 September 1980
Height: 6'0" Weight: 12.7
International Honours: E: U21-1

After spending the summer of 2000 on loan with Swedish Third Division club IFK Hassleholm, Alton returned to Tottenham and made fine progress last term. He made his Premiership debut in the 2-1 win over Liverpool in November and went on to feature in the first-team squad on a regular basis in the second half of the season. A versatile player who can play at left back, in the centre of defence or in midfield he capped a fine season with his debut for England U21s against Spain in February.

Tottenham H (From trainee on 27/1/1999) PL 13+3 FAC 0+2

THEOBALD David John
Born: Cambridge, 15 December 1978
Height: 6'3" Weight: 12.0

David began the 2000-01 campaign on the fringes of the Brentford first-team squad and it was not until last February that he finally got a decent run in the side, replacing the injured Scott Marshall. A tall and capable central defender he impressed with some solid work at the back for the Bees and finished the season with a runners-up medal for the LDV Vans Trophy after appearing in the final against Port Vale.

Ipswich T (From trainee on 2/6/1997)
Brentford (Free on 8/7/1999) FL 21+4 Others 5

THETIS Jean-Manuel (Manu)
Born: Dijon, France, 5 November 1971
Height: 6'3" Weight: 14.12

The big central defender joined Wolverhampton Wanderers on loan from Ipswich at the beginning of last season and made a solid debut against Burnley when he helped support young Joleon Lescott in the back line. However after two more first-team appearances he headed back to East Anglia. Manu subsequently joined Sheffield United on the transfer deadline day, signing on a match-by-match basis. His single appearance for the Blades came when he appeared as a half-time substitute at Gillingham and was employed out of position as a striker, but nevertheless he gave a competent display and came close to scoring. An experienced centre half he is very effective when bringing the ball out of defence.

Ipswich T (£50,000 from Seville, Spain on 11/9/1998) FL 44+3/2 FLC 5/1 FAC 2 Others 2+1
Wolverhampton W (Loaned on 25/8/2000) FL 3
Sheffield U (Free on 22/3/2001) FL 0+1

THIRLWELL Paul
Born: Washington, 13 February 1979
Height: 5'11" Weight: 11.4
International Honours: E: U21-1

The busy Sunderland midfielder found senior opportunities somewhat limited last term, but still enjoyed two notable 'firsts'. He gained his first England U21 cap in the friendly against Georgia in August and followed this up with his first-ever senior goal in the home leg of the Worthington Cup tie against Luton in September. Although central midfield is Paul's best position, he can also operate wide on the right-hand side and will be hoping to win himself a regular first-team slot in 2001-02.

Sunderland (From trainee on 14/4/1997) P/FL 11+4 FLC 4+1/1 FAC 0+1
Swindon T (Loaned on 8/9/1999) FL 12

THOGERSEN Thomas
Born: Copenhagen, Denmark, 2 April 1968
Height: 6'2" Weight: 12.10

Thomas was a regular in the Portsmouth line-up for most of the 2000-01 campaign before being sidelined by a knee ligament injury soon after Graham Rix took over as manager in March. A versatile player who can switch from his midfield role to the right-wing-back position with ease, he did particularly well in October when he scored in three consecutive matches. Experienced and hard working, he possesses a tremendous right foot and has excellent distribution.

Portsmouth (£100,000 from Brondby, Denmark, ex Frem, on 5/8/1998) FL 93+10/8 FLC 9 FAC 1+1

THOM Stuart Paul
Born: Dewsbury, 27 December 1976
Height: 6'2" Weight: 11.12

This tall central defender is strong both in the air and on the ground and Scunthorpe were delighted to sign him on a permanent basis last September after an impressive month on loan. However a series of niggling

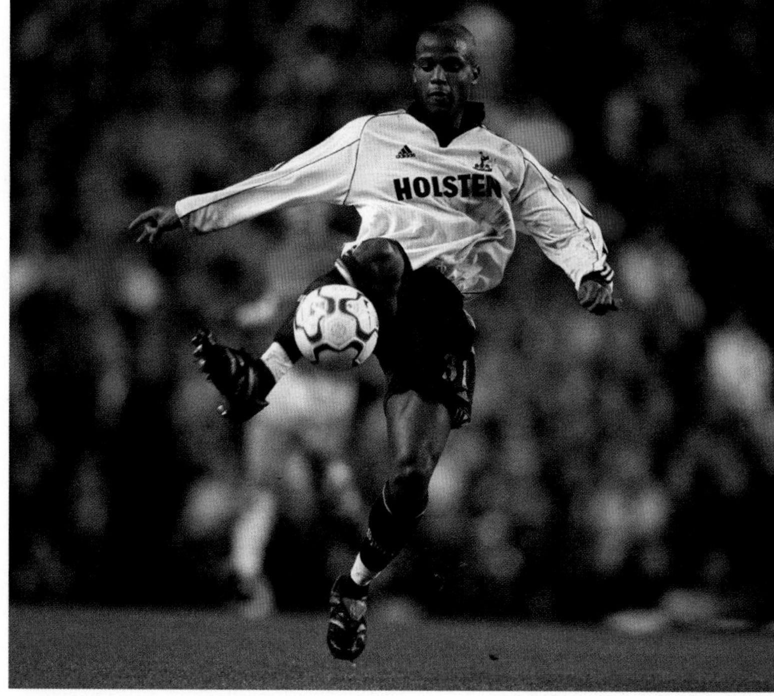

Alton Thelwell

injuries then restricted him to just one start in three months and on his return he had the misfortune to concede a late own goal to give Chesterfield a victory. Stuart then suffered further injury woes when he tore a calf muscle at Cardiff in February and this kept him out of action for a further six weeks.

Nottingham F (From trainee on 11/1/1994)
Mansfield T (Loaned on 24/12/1997) FL 5 Others 2
Oldham Ath (£45,000 on 21/10/1998) FL 28+6/3 FLC 1 FAC 1 Others 1
Scunthorpe U (Signed on 10/8/2000) FL 17+4 FAC 0+1 Others 1

THOMAS David (Dai) John
Born: Caerphilly, 26 September 1975
Height: 5'10" Weight: 12.7
Club Honours: Div 2 '98
International Honours: W: U21-2

Dai's career went sharply downhill following much publicised off the field events in the summer of 2000. He made just one senior appearance for Cardiff coming on from the subs' bench for the last few minutes of the Worthington Cup first round second leg tie against Crystal Palace. He then had a spell at Dr Martens League club Merthyr Tydfil before finishing the season playing in the South Wales Amateur League for Bryntirion. A burly striker he was later reported to be considering offers to play in Cyprus.

Swansea C (From trainee on 25/7/1994) FL 36+20/10 FLC 2 FAC 0+1 Others 5+3/3
Watford (£100,000 on 17/7/1997) FL 8+8/3 FAC 1+3
Cardiff C (£50,000 on 20/8/1998) FL 21+10/5 FLC 0+1 FAC 0+3 Others 1

THOMAS Geoffrey (Geoff) Robert
Born: Manchester, 5 August 1964
Height: 6'1" Weight: 13.2
Club Honours: FMC '91; Div 1 '98
International Honours: E: 9; B-3

Although still involved on the playing side at Barnsley last term, Geoff was given the job of coaching the reserve team from the start of the season. Despite being used almost exclusively as a substitute he continued to do a decent job for the senior squad, coming on to provide extra backbone to the midfield. However he reverted to his former role as a player under new boss Nigel Spackman, receiving limited opportunities before moving on to Notts County on a short-term contract at the beginning of March. Required to help resolve an injury crisis at Meadow Lane, he approached the task in his usual whole-hearted fashion but nevertheless he was released by the Magpies at the end of the campaign.

Rochdale (Free from Littleborough on 13/8/1982) FL 10+1/1 Others 0+1
Crewe Alex (Free on 22/3/1984) FL 120+5/20 FLC 8 FAC 2 Others 2+1
Crystal Palace (£50,000 on 8/6/1987) F/PL 192+3/26 FLC 24/3 FAC 13+1/2 Others 15+1/4
Wolverhampton W (£800,000 on 18/6/1993) FL 36+10/8 FLC 1 FAC 1 Others 6
Nottingham F (Free on 18/7/1997) P/FL 18+7/4 FLC 2/1
Barnsley (Free on 1/7/1999) FL 14+24/4 FLC 2+2 FAC 1 Others 0+2
Notts Co (Free on 1/3/2001) FL 8/1

THOMAS James Alan
Born: Swansea, 16 January 1979
Height: 6'0" Weight: 13.0
International Honours: W: U21-18

This young Welshman made his long-awaited senior debut for Blackburn when he came off the subs' bench at Sheffield United and went on to score a double in the 4-1 Worthington Cup win over Portsmouth and another goal against Bolton. When Marcus Bent arrived from Sheffield United he journeyed in the opposite direction in a loan deal that allowed him to stay at Bramall Lane until the end of the season. He was mostly used as a substitute by the Blades, and after being sidelined by an injury at the beginning of the new year he came back to score the winner in the 3-2 home win over Preston. A pacy striker he showed skill in holding the ball and patience in his build up. James again appeared regularly for Wales U21s winning seven more caps during the season.

Blackburn Rov (From trainee on 2/7/1996) FL 1+3/1 FLC 1/2
West Bromwich A (Loaned on 29/8/1997) FL 1+2
Blackpool (Loaned on 21/3/2000) FL 9/2
Sheffield U (Loaned on 24/11/2000) FL 3+7/1 FAC 0+1

THOMAS Martin Russell
Born: Lymington, 12 September 1973
Height: 5'8" Weight: 12.6
Club Honours: Div 3 '00

Martin began the 2000-01 campaign in the first team at Swansea but was placed on the transfer list before Christmas following a breakdown in contract talks. He then suffered an ankle injury at Wycombe sand he struggled to recapture his place. On transfer deadline day he moved to Brighton where he was mostly restricted to outings from the subs' bench as the Seagulls went on to clinch the Third Division title. Initially recruited on a short-term contract he was unable to impress enough to earn a longer deal at the Withdean Stadium. A tireless worker in midfield he is always looking to score goals and he possesses a powerful long-range shot.

Southampton (From trainee on 19/6/1992)
Leyton Orient (Free on 24/3/1994) FL 5/2
Fulham (Free on 21/7/1994) FL 59+31/8 FLC 6+1 FAC 4/1 Others 7+1/2
Swansea C (Free on 30/7/1998) FL 70+21/8 FLC 8 FAC 5/2 Others 4/1
Brighton & Hove A (Free on 22/3/2001) FL 1+7

THOMAS Michael Lauristen
Born: Lambeth, 24 August 1967
Height: 5'10" Weight: 12.4
Club Honours: FLC '87, '95; Div 1 '89, '91; FAC '92
International Honours: E: 2; B-5; U21-12; Yth; Sch

This vastly experienced player returned from Portugal to join Wimbledon during the 2000 close season but after featuring on a number of occasions in the early part of the campaign he fell out of contention and dropped back into the reserves. A hard-tackling and strong-running midfield player he will be hoping for regular first-team football in 2001-02.

Arsenal (From apprentice on 31/12/1984) FL 149+14/24 FLC 21 FAC 8 Others 14+1
Portsmouth (Loaned on 30/12/1986) FL 3
Liverpool (£1,500,000 on 16/12/1991) F/PL 96+28/9 FLC 7+3/1 FAC 15+2/2 Others 10+2 (Free to Benfica, Portugal on 17/7/1998)
Middlesbrough (Loaned on 3/2/1998) FL 10
Wimbledon (Free on 11/8/2000) FL 5+3 FLC 1

THOMAS Mitchell Anthony
Born: Luton, 2 October 1964
Height: 6'2" Weight: 13.0
International Honours: E: B-1; U21-3; Yth

Although now in the twilight of his career Mitchell remained a commanding presence in a Burnley defence that was the key to the side's First Division success in 2000-01. Usually employed on the right of a back three playing alongside Steve Davis and Ian Cox he presented a formidable barrier to opposing attackers, his defensive soundness more than compensating for any lack of pace. Mitchell enjoys going forward but has yet to score his first goal for the Clarets. He was an automatic choice until a rib injury put him briefly out of action towards the end of the season.

Luton T (From apprentice on 27/8/1982) FL 106+1/1 FLC 5 FAC 18
Tottenham H (£233,000 on 7/7/1986) FL 136+21/6 FLC 28+1/1 FAC 12/1
West Ham U (£525,000 on 7/8/1991) FL 37+1/3 FLC 5 FAC 4 Others 2
Luton T (Free on 12/11/1993) FL 170+15/5 FLC 12+1 FAC 6 Others 5+1
Burnley (Free on 2/7/1999) FL 85+2 FLC 6 FAC 6 Others 1

THOMAS Roderick (Rod) Clive
Born: Harlesden, 10 October 1970
Height: 5'5" Weight: 11.0
Club Honours: FAYC '89; Div 3 '95; AMC '97
International Honours: E: U21-1; Yth; Sch

Rod had a frustrating time at Brighton last season. Made available on a free transfer in the summer of 2000 he only featured from the subs' bench in a handful of early games and spent the remainder of the campaign languishing in the reserves. His contract with the Seagulls expired in May and he was released by the club. Rod is a lively winger with good ball control and the ability to beat opposition defenders.

Watford (From trainee on 3/5/1988) FL 63+21/9 FLC 3+2 FAC 0+1 Others 3+1
Gillingham (Loaned on 27/3/1992) FL 8/1 Others 1
Carlisle U (Free on 12/7/1993) FL 124+22/16 FLC 11+1/3 FAC 9+4 Others 22+4/9
Chester C (Free on 4/7/1997) FL 28+16/7 FLC 3+2 FAC 2
Brighton & Hove A (£25,000 on 8/10/1998) FL 25+23/4 FLC 2+1 FAC 2+1

THOMAS Stephen (Steve)
Born: Hartlepool, 23 June 1979
Height: 5'10" Weight: 12.0
International Honours: W: U21-2; Yth

This young Wrexham midfield player was yet again affected by injuries in the 2000-01 season for he missed the early part of the campaign with a foot injury and then underwent an operation for a double hernia in January. It was not until last April that he finally returned to first team action at the Racecourse Ground when coming on from the subs' bench against Notts County. Steve is a combative figure in the centre of the park who is adept at breaking up opposition attacks. He will be hoping to avoid major injury problems in the coming season and to make the breakthrough to a regular place in the Robins' first-team squad. He made his debut for Wales U21s against Poland in June.

Wrexham (From trainee on 4/7/1997) FL 5+8 FLC 0+1

THOMAS Wayne
Born: Walsall, 28 August 1978
Height: 5'9" Weight: 12.10

Wayne featured in a handful of early-season games for Shrewsbury Town in the 2000-01 campaign but was then sidelined with an injury and once he had recovered fitness he was unable to win his place back. A skilful midfielder who is confident going forward and comfortable on the ball he was released by manager Kevin Ratcliffe in the summer.

Walsall (From trainee on 25/7/1996) FL 18+20 FLC 0+1 FAC 2 Others 1+4/1
Mansfield T (Loaned on 6/8/1999) FL 4+1
Shrewsbury T (Free on 20/1/2000) FL 15+2/1 FLC 1

THOMAS Wayne Junior Robert
Born: Gloucester, 17 May 1979
Height: 5'11" Weight: 11.12

A summer signing of some potential, Wayne quickly established himself in the Stoke City side last term and showed a growing level of confidence throughout the season. A promising central defender he is good in the air, firm in the tackle and is physically fit and strong. Having made such a good start to his career at the Britannia Stadium he will be looking to continue to develop at a similar rate in the coming campaign.

Torquay U (From trainee on 4/7/1997) FL 89+34/5 FLC 2+1/1 FAC 7/1 Others 6+4
Stoke C (£200,000 + on 5/6/2000) FL 33+1 FLC 3+1 FAC 1 Others 6

THOME Emerson August
Born: Porto Alegre, Brazil, 30 March 1972
Height: 6'1" Weight: 13.4

Having appeared for Chelsea in the surprise 2-0 defeat at Bradford City last August, Emerson was quickly on his way to Sunderland, signing for a new record fee for the Wearsiders. Nicknamed 'The Wall' due to his imposing physical stature, the Brazilian centre back made his debut against West Ham and then scored his first goal for his new club in the home game against Coventry when he powered home a header that proved to be the only goal of the game. A strong tackler, his defensive qualities particularly impressed the Sunderland fans while his partnership with Jody Craddock at the centre of the defence was very effective.

Sheffield Wed (Free from Benfica, Portugal on 23/3/1998) PL 60+1/1 FLC 5+1 FAC 4/1
Chelsea (£2,700,000 on 23/12/1999) PL 19+2 Others 1
Sunderland (£4,500,000 on 1/9/2000) PL 30+1/1 FLC 2 FAC 3

THOMPSON Alan
Born: Newcastle, 22 December 1973
Height: 6'0" Weight: 12.8
Club Honours: Div 1 '97
International Honours: E: U21-2; Yth

Alan appeared for Aston Villa in both legs of the Inter Toto Cup semi-final against Celta Vigo, receiving a red card in the home game, but that was the extent of his first-team experience for John Gregory's side last term and at the beginning of September he was sold to Celtic. He went on to become a regular member of Martin O'Neill's successful side, winning Scottish Cup and League championship medals during the season. A dead-ball expert of some repute he is mainly employed on the left-hand side of midfield.

Newcastle U (From trainee on 11/3/1991) FL 13+3 FAC 1 Others 3
Bolton W (£250,000 on 22/7/1993) P/FL 143+14/33 FLC 24+1/5 FAC 6+2/2 Others 7+1/1
Aston Villa (£4,500,000 on 12/6/1998) PL 36+10/4 FLC 3+3/1 FAC 1 Others 4+1

THOMPSON Andrew (Andy) Richard
Born: Cannock, 9 November 1967
Height: 5'5" Weight: 10.1
Club Honours: Div 4 '88, Div 3 '89; AMC '88

Andy was one of several Cardiff City players to have their season disrupted by injury in 2000-2001. He suffered torn stomach muscles in the first home game of the campaign and after surgery he made a brief return in December but it was not until towards the end of April that he featured regularly for the Bluebirds. He is an experienced full back who is more effective as an organiser than a creative force. He was placed on the open to offers list in the summer.

West Bromwich A (From apprentice on 16/11/1985) FL 18+6/1 FLC 0+1 FAC 2 Others 1+1
Wolverhampton W (£35,000 on 21/11/1986) FL 356+20/43 FLC 22 FAC 20/1 Others 33/1
Tranmere Rov (Free on 21/7/1997) FL 91+5/4 FLC 13+1 FAC 5+1
Cardiff C (Free on 11/8/2000) FL 5+2 FAC 0+1 Others 1

THOMPSON David Anthony
Born: Birkenhead, 12 September 1977
Height: 5'7" Weight: 10.0
Club Honours: FAYC '96
International Honours: E: U21-7; Yth

David was seen as a major capture for Coventry when he signed in the summer of 2000 but last term proved to be a rather frustrating season for him. Injury and suspension meant that he didn't become a regular in the team until early November, but his performances were then excellent, with his all-action style and skills on the ball winning favour with the fans. On his return to Anfield he got a warm reception and scored a stunning goal from all of 25 yards. He was also on the score-sheet against Southampton with a curling free-kick that deceived everyone. However after Christmas his performances stuttered a little and he was dropped after the Spurs away game, but returned at Old Trafford with a more disciplined display.

Liverpool (From trainee on 8/11/1994) PL 24+24/5 FLC 5 FAC 0+1 Others 2
Swindon T (Loaned on 21/11/1997) FL 10
Coventry C (£3,000,000 on 8/8/2000) PL 22+3/3 FLC 1+1 FAC 1

THOMPSON Marc
Born: York, 15 January 1982
Height: 5'10" Weight: 12.3

After making several appearances as a trainee in 1999-2000 Marc was hit by a series of injuries that limited his senior appearances for York City last season. He is a very combative performer on the right side of defence or midfield who is strong in the tackle and gives 100 per cent commitment to the cause. He will be hoping to break into the first-team squad more regularly in the 2001-02 campaign.

York C (From trainee on 1/6/2000) FL 18+4 FLC 1 FAC 2 Others 1

THOMPSON Niall Joseph
Born: Birmingham, 16 April 1974
Height: 6'0" Weight: 12.2
International Honours: Canada: 9

Having spent the 2000 season with San Francisco club Bay Area Seals, Niall joined Wycombe Wanderers for a trial period last October. Although he suffered from a number of niggling injuries he played in a handful of games and scored the winning goal in the LDV Vans Trophy tie at Exeter. He was eventually released at the end of February and after returning to Canada he signed for US-A League outfit Montreal Impact. He is a big striker with good close control and a useful scoring record in US football.

Crystal Palace (From juniors on 16/7/1992. Freed on 24/3/1994)
Colchester U (Free from Hong Kong on 4/11/1994) FL 5+8/5 FAC 0+1 (Freed during 1995 close season)
Brentford (Free from Zultse VV, Belgium, ex Montreal Impact, Osters, on 27/2/1998) FL 6+2 (Freed during 1998 close season)
Airdrieonians (Signed from Vancouver 86ers, Canada on 27/9/1999) SL 19+6/5 SC 1 (Freed on 22/6/2000)
Wycombe W (Free from Bay Area Seals, USA on 27/10/2000) FL 6+2 FAC 2 Others 0+2/1

THOMPSON Peter David
Born: Bury, 30 July 1977
Height: 6'3" Weight: 12.6

Once at Bury, Peter had a spell in Holland with NAC Breda before returning across the Channel at the beginning of September. Seen by manager Ricky Hill as an answer to some of his problems up front he found it difficult to settle back in the English game, although the rapid turnover of managers at Kenilworth Road did not help the situation. A striker who never really fulfilled the promise he sometimes showed he scored twice in the 3-1 win at Stoke in December but was made available on a free transfer at the end of the season.

Bury (Signed from Stand Ath on 3/11/1995. Free to Chorley during 1997 close season)
Luton T (£100,000 from NAC Breda, Holland on 8/9/2000) FL 4+7/2 FLC 1+1 FAC 1+1 Others 1

THOMPSON Philip (Phil) Paul
Born: Blackpool, 1 April 1981
Height: 5'11" Weight: 12.0

Phil spent most of last season in Blackpool's reserve team, his first-team opportunities being limited to cover for injuries and suspension. He is a promising young central

defender who never let the team down when called upon and he will be aiming to feature more regularly for the Tangerines in 2001-02.
Blackpool (From trainee on 4/9/1998) FL 27+7/2+5/2 FLC 3 FAC 0+1 Others 1+1

THOMPSON Ryan James Daley
Born: Lambeth, 24 June 1982
Height: 5'11" Weight: 11.11
Ryan again scored regularly for Northampton's reserve team last season and forced his way into the first-team squad in the new year when he appeared as a substitute in the home games against Wigan and Swansea. A young striker with good pace who is adept at holding the ball up, he was out of contract in the summer and his future was unclear at the time of writing.
Northampton T (From trainee on 13/7/2000) FL 0+2 Others 0+1

THOMPSON Steven (Steve) James
Born: Oldham, 2 November 1964
Height: 5'10" Weight: 13.5
Club Honours: AMC '89
Steve joined Halifax Town from Rotherham in July 2000 and had a good season in the heart of midfield for the Shaymen. He scored twice, including the opener in the 3-2 victory over Kidderminster last January which was the 100th senior goal of his career. Steve has excellent distribution and a well-earned reputation for scoring with free kicks from the edge of the box. He was released in the summer.
Bolton W (From apprentice on 4/11/1982) FL 329+6/49 FLC 27/2 FAC 21/4 Others 39/2
Luton T (£180,000 on 13/8/1991) FL 5 FLC 2
Leicester C (Signed on 22/10/1991) P/FL 121+6/18 FLC 6/2 FAC 8/1 Others 11+3/4
Burnley (£200,000 on 24/2/1995) FL 44+5/1 FLC 2 Others 1+1
Rotherham U (Free on 24/7/1997) FL 87+16/14 FLC 3 FAC 6+2/1 Others 4+1
Halifax T (Free on 19/7/2000) FL 35+1/2 FLC 1 FAC 1 Others 2

THOMPSON Tyrone
Born: Sheffield, 8 May 1982
Height: 5'9" Weight: 11.2
A first-year professional at Sheffield United, Tyrone made a lively senior debut in the Worthington Cup tie against Lincoln City and went on to make one more first-team appearance in the early part of last season. Despite signing a three-year contract he subsequently dropped back into the Blades reserves, contributing to their successful double-winning campaign. A promising young striker he will be aiming for more first-team experience next term.
Sheffield U (From trainee on 10/7/2000) FLC 1+1

THOMSON Andrew (Andy)
Born: Motherwell, 1 April 1971
Height: 5'10" Weight: 10.13
Andy had an excellent goal-scoring record for Gillingham last term with eight goals from 14 starts, however this was not enough to win a guaranteed place in the team and he was often restricted to a place on the subs' bench. In March he moved on to First Division strugglers Queens Park Rangers and although unable to prevent their relegation at the end of the season he established an excellent understanding up front with Peter Crouch. Andy is a hardworking striker who is constantly looking for goal-scoring chances.
Queen of the South (Free from Jerviston BC on 28/7/1989) SL 163+12/93 SLC 8/3 SC 7+2/5 Others 9/8
Southend U (£250,000 on 4/7/1994) FL 87+35/28 FLC 4+1 FAC 3+2 Others 1+2
Oxford U (Free on 21/7/1998) FL 25+13/7 FLC 1 FAC 0+1
Gillingham (Signed on 5/8/1999) FL 32+20/14 FLC 5+1/3 FAC 5+1/4 Others 0+1/1
Queens Park R (Signed on 22/3/2001) FL 7+1/4

THOMSON Andrew (Andy) John
Born: Swindon, 28 March 1974
Height: 6'3" Weight: 14.12
Andy was appointed captain of Bristol Rovers following the departure of Andy Tillson shortly before the start of last season. A key figure in the early games he then had the misfortune to suffer a stress fracture of his foot in September and this kept him out of action for several weeks. He netted his only goal of the campaign in the 2-2 draw with Reading on Boxing Day and went on to form a useful defensive partnership with Steve Foster and Scott Jones in the second half of the campaign. A strong and determined central defender he is always a threat to opposition defences when joining the attack at set-pieces and corners.
Swindon T (From trainee on 1/5/1993) P/FL 21+1 FLC 5/1 Others 3
Portsmouth (£75,000 on 29/12/1995) FL 85+8/3 FLC 4 FAC 6+1
Bristol Rov (£60,000 on 15/1/1999) FL 95+1/5 FLC 6 FAC 2 Others 3

THOMSON Steven (Steve)
Born: Glasgow, 23 January 1978
Height: 5'8" Weight: 10.4
International Honours: S: Yth
This talented young midfield player returned to the Crystal Palace first-team squad last October but struggled to win a place in the starting line-up. Strong in the tackle and an excellent ball winner the highlight of his season was undoubtedly his goal in the 3-0 Worthington Cup victory at Leicester - a brilliant strike from 30 yards out.
Crystal Palace (From trainee on 9/12/1995) FL 40+15 FLC 6+2/2 FAC 2/1 Others 1+1

THORDARSON Stefan
Born: Reykjavik, Iceland, 27 March 1975
Height: 6'1" Weight: 12.1
International Honours: Iceland: 5; U21-8; Yth
Stefan made an immediate impact on his pre-season home debut for Stoke City, scoring with a thunderous free kick against Liverpool. His eye for a spectacular goal was confirmed with a brilliant effort against Charlton in the Worthington Cup at the Valley that was later selected as City's 'Goal of the Season'. However despite this he failed to win a regular place in the starting line-up and often featured from the subs' bench. He is an exciting left winger who is skilful on the ball and has a very languid style.
Stoke C (Free from Bayer Uerdingen, Germany, ex IA Akranes, Osters IF, BK Brann Bergen, on 26/6/2000) FL 15+15/4 FLC 4+2/2 FAC 2 Others 3+2/1

THORNE Peter Lee
Born: Manchester, 21 June 1973
Height: 6'0" Weight: 13.6
Club Honours: Div 2 '96; AMC '00
Peter missed the opening weeks of the 2000-01 campaign while recovering from a knee injury picked up in the previous season's play-off semi-final and it was not until mid-September that he returned to first-team duties for Stoke City. He soon re-established himself as a key member of the side scoring a healthy quota of goals including a hat-trick in the 3-0 win at Bristol Rovers, his second in successive seasons at The Memorial Ground. He went on to finish the season as leading scorer with 19 goals in all competitions and signed a further 12-month extension to his contract with City. He is a striker who is good with his back to goal and is a constant threat in the air.
Blackburn Rov (From trainee on 20/6/1991) Others 0+1
Wigan Ath (Loaned on 11/3/1994) FL 10+1
Swindon T (£225,000 on 18/1/1995) FL 66+11/27 FLC 5+1/4 FAC 4+2 Others 1+1/1
Stoke C (£350,000 + on 25/7/1997) FL 142+11/61 FLC 12+1/6 FAC 5+1 Others 9+3/9

THORNLEY Benjamin (Ben) Lindsay
Born: Bury, 21 April 1975
Height: 5'9" Weight: 11.12
Club Honours: FAYC '92
International Honours: E: U21-3; Sch
Although he featured regularly for Huddersfield Town last term Ben struggled to find a consistent level of form. He often seemed to start games well, but couldn't always match this for the full 90 minutes. A very skilful left winger, at his best he is effective at foraging down the flank, can deliver a fine cross and willingly tracks back to help out in defence. The campaign ended with the Terriers relegated to Division Two and Ben was released in the summer.
Manchester U (From trainee on 29/1/1993) PL 1+8 FLC 3 FAC 2
Stockport Co (Loaned on 6/11/1995) FL 8+2/1 Others 1
Huddersfield T (Loaned on 22/2/1996) FL 12/2
Huddersfield T (£175,000 + on 3/7/1998) FL 77+22/5 FLC 10 FAC 5/1

THORPE Anthony (Tony) Lee
Born: Leicester, 10 April 1974
Height: 5'9" Weight: 12.6
Although he failed to match the form he had shown for Bristol City at the end of the 1999-2000 campaign Tony still scored consistently throughout last season and became the first player at Ashton Gate to top 20 league and cup goals for over a decade. He netted hat-tricks against Bournemouth and Cambridge but his late header from Aaron Brown's cross to clinch a 3-2 win over local rivals Bristol Rovers was perhaps his most acclaimed strike of the season. Tony is a nippy striker with quick reflexes who always seems to find himself in the right place at the right time in the opposition penalty box.

Luton T (From trainee at Leicester C on 18/8/1992) FL 93+27/50 FLC 5+4/5 FAC 4+3/2 Others 4+3/3
Fulham (£800,000 on 26/2/1998) FL 5+8/3 Others 1+1
Bristol C (£1,000,000 on 23/6/1998) FL 66+20/34 FLC 3+2/3 FAC 5+1/3 Others 5/3
Reading (Loaned on 5/2/1999) FL 6/1
Luton T (Loaned on 25/3/1999) FL 7+1/4
Luton T (Loaned on 26/11/1999) FL 3+1/1

THORPE Lee Anthony
Born: Wolverhampton, 14 December 1975
Height: 6'1" Weight: 12.4

Lee missed the first two months of Lincoln City's 2000-01 season as he recovered from a groin injury sustained in the final month of the previous campaign. On his return the hard-working striker found league goals hard to come by, although he netted six in the LDV Vans Trophy games including his first ever senior hat-trick in the 3-2 win over Morecambe. He began to form a useful strike partnership with Tony Battersby towards the end of the season and he finished with 13 league and cup goals, a respectable tally in a struggling team.

Blackpool (From trainee on 18/7/1994) FL 2+10 FLC 0+1 FAC 1 Others 1
Lincoln C (Free on 4/8/1997) FL 146+9/45 FLC 4+1/1 FAC 12/1 Others 8+1/7

THURGOOD Stuart Anthony
Born: Enfield, 4 November 1981
Height: 5'7" Weight: 11.8

Stuart returned to England after spending two seasons with Steve Perryman's Shimizu S-Pulse in the Japanese J-League and after impressing in a trial match signed a contract with Third Division Southend United. A tigerish midfield player, his tough tackling and ability to play the simple ball should earn him a place in the Blues' team in the 2001-02 campaign.

Southend U (Free from Shimuzu-S-Pulse, Japan on 30/1/2001) FL 8+5/1 Others 0+1

THURSTAN Mark Richard
Born: Cockermouth, 10 February 1980
Height: 6'2" Weight: 11.8

Mark stepped up to make his Football League debut for Carlisle United at Torquay last October when he replaced John Inglis for the final 45 minutes. He went on to feature on a handful more occasions, earning a 'Man of the Match' rating in the defeat at Brighton, and will be looking to gain further senior experience in 2001-02. He is a promising youngster who can play either in defence or midfield.

Carlisle U (From juniors on 6/7/1998) FL 3+2 FAC 1+1 Others 1

THWAITES Adam
Born: Kendal, 8 December 1981
Height: 5'10" Weight: 11.0

Another product of Carlisle United's youth scheme, Adam joined the professional ranks in June 2000 and made his senior debut from the subs' bench in the Worthington Cup first round second leg tie against Grimsby Town. A promising player who can feature anywhere on the left flank he went on to make two more first-team appearances and will be aiming to feature more regularly in the squad in 2001-02.

Carlisle U (From trainee on 6/6/2000) FLC 0+1 FAC 0+1 Others 1

TIATTO Daniele (Danny) Amadio
Born: Melbourne, Australia, 22 May 1973
Height: 5'7" Weight: 12.0
International Honours: Australia: 19; U23

Danny was in fine form for Manchester City in 2000-01 despite the club's relegation from the Premiership. He scored twice for the Blues, but more memorable was the 'goal' that was disallowed at Middlesbrough when he picked the ball up inside his own half and went on a long run, finally putting the ball in the net, only for the superb strike to be disallowed as Darren Huckerby was deemed to have been in an offside position. Comfortable either at left back or on the left-hand side of midfield, his speed down the flank caused plenty of problems for defenders. Voted as the supporters' 'Player of the Year' he appeared for Australia in a World Cup qualifier against New Zealand in the summer.

Stoke C (Loaned from FC Baden, Switzerland on 25/11/1997) FL 11+4/1
Manchester C (£300,000 on 15/7/1998) P/FL 65+20/2 FLC 8/1 FAC 2+1 Others 1

TIERNEY Francis (Fran)
Born: Liverpool, 10 September 1975
Height: 5'10" Weight: 11.0
International Honours: E: Yth

After being released by Notts County in May 2000 Fran had trials with Altrincham and Chesterfield before joining Unibond League club Witton Albion. He subsequently returned to the Football League later in the autumn when he signed non-contract forms for Exeter City. His career at St James Park got off to a great start when he scored just seven minutes into his debut against Scunthorpe but shortly after appearing in the 6-1 New Year's Day mauling by Cardiff he returned to Witton. He finished the season playing in the Conference with Doncaster Rovers.

Crewe Alex (From trainee on 22/3/1993) FL 57+30/10 FLC 6 FAC 1+4 Others 5+6/3
Notts Co (Free on 2/7/1998) FL 19+14/4 FLC 0+1 FAC 1+4/1 Others 2 (Freed during 2000 close season)
Exeter C (Free from Witton A on 10/11/2000) FL 4+3/1 FAC 0+1

TIHINEN Hannu
Born: Keminmaa, Finland, 1 July 1976
Height: 6'2" Weight: 13.6

This young Finnish defender came to West

Danny Tiatto

Ham on loan during the Scandinavian close season and produced a series of excellent performances culminating with a superb display in the FA Cup fourth round tie at Old Trafford when he helped the Hammers secure a surprise victory. However, although boss Harry Redknapp was keen on a permanent deal, no agreement could be reached on a fee and he returned to Viking.

West Ham U (Loaned from Viking, Norway, ex KePS, HJK Helsinki, on 8/12/2000) PL 5+3 FAC 2

TILER Carl
Born: Sheffield, 11 February 1970
Height: 6'3" Weight: 13.10
International Honours: E: U21-13

Carl is a tall, strong and dominant centre half who started last season as first choice alongside Richard Rufus in the Charlton Athletic defence but lost his place after being sent off at Everton. He returned for just a single game before being replaced by Steve Brown and after the arrival of Mark Fish in November he became surplus to requirements at The Valley. He spent a brief loan spell at Birmingham last February where he made a single appearance in the 3-1 defeat at Sheffield United and was then sold to Portsmouth in March. Required as a replacement for the injured Darren Moore he added his considerable physical presence to the back line, but took some time to settle and was unable to plug a leaky defence in the closing weeks of the season. Carl is the son of the former Chesterfield and Brighton defender Ken Tiler.

Barnsley (From trainee on 2/8/1988) FL 67+4/3 FLC 4 FAC 4+1 Others 3+1
Nottingham F (£1,400,000 on 30/5/1991) F/PL 67+2/1 FLC 10+1 FAC 6 Others 1
Swindon T (Loaned on 18/11/1994) FL 2
Aston Villa (£750,000 on 28/10/1995) PL 10+2/1 FLC 1 FAC 2
Sheffield U (£650,000 on 26/3/1997) FL 23/2 FLC 5 Others 3
Everton (£500,000 on 28/11/1997) PL 21/1 FLC 1 FAC 1
Charlton Ath (£700,000 on 30/9/1998) P/FL 38+7/2 FAC 1+1
Birmingham C (Loaned on 9/2/2001) FL 1
Portsmouth (£250,000 on 13/3/2001) FL 9/1

TILLSON Andrew (Andy)
Born: Huntingdon, 30 June 1966
Height: 6'2" Weight: 12.10

Walsall manager Ray Graydon had been pursuing this strong central defender for two years before finally landing him in the 2000 close season. His rock-like presence at the heart of the defence meant that the Saddlers hardly missed the departed Adrian Viveash and Andy went on to play in all but four Second Division games during the campaign. The major contribution he made to the club's promotion campaign was recognised when he was selected for the PFA's Division Two team.

Grimsby T (Free from Kettering T on 14/7/1988) FL 104+1/5 FLC 8 FAC 10 Others 5
Queens Park R (£400,000 on 21/12/1990) FL 27+2/2 FLC 2 Others 1
Grimsby T (Loaned on 15/9/1992) FL 4 Others 1
Bristol Rov (£370,000 on 7/11/1992) FL 250+3/11 FLC 16/1 FAC 11 Others 19+1/2
Walsall (£10,000 on 9/8/2000) FL 42/1 FLC 4 FAC 3/2 Others 3

TINDALL Jason
Born: Mile End, 15 November 1977
Height: 6'1" Weight: 11.10

Jason switched from a midfield role to playing in the centre of the defence during Bournemouth's injury crisis at the start of last season and adapted so well to his new position that he stayed there. He forged an excellent partnership with Eddie Howe in the back line for the Cherries and missed just two matches throughout the campaign. A versatile player he can also play in the centre of midfield and at left back.

Charlton Ath (From trainee on 18/7/1996)
Bournemouth (Free on 3/7/1998) FL 54+16/2 FLC 3+2 FAC 3 Others 2

TINKLER Mark Roland
Born: Bishop Auckland, 24 October 1974
Height: 5'11" Weight: 13.3
Club Honours: FAYC '93
International Honours: E: Yth (UEFA-U18 '93); Sch

A classy midfielder who can also play as sweeper, Mark featured regularly in the Southend United squad at the beginning of last season before being sold to Third Division rivals Hartlepool United soon after David Webb became manager at Roots Hall. He added some much needed bite to the Pool midfield, and shortly after his arrival the team started a 21-match unbeaten run in Third Division games. Mark went on to become part of an outstanding trio in the centre of the park along with Tommy Miller and Paul Stephenson, although he accumulated a number of yellow cards and this is an area of his game where he needs to improve. He is a player who always appears to have time on the ball, and can find a colleague with a pass regardless of the number of opponents in close proximity.

Leeds U (From trainee on 29/11/1991) PL 14+11 FLC 1 Others 0+1
York C (£85,000 on 25/3/1997) FL 88+2/8 FLC 6 FAC 5 Others 2
Southend U (£40,000 on 13/8/1999) FL 55+1/1 FLC 2+1 FAC 1 Others 1
Hartlepool U (Free on 2/11/2000) FL 28/3 Others 5/1

TINNION Brian
Born: Stanley, 23 February 1968
Height: 6'0" Weight: 13.0

After a slow start to the 2000-01 season Brian switched to a central midfield role for Bristol City and went on to impress with some of the most exhilarating form of his long career at Ashton Gate. He combined a talented left foot with exceptional passing ability over both long and short distances and fully merited his selection in the PFA's Second Division side. He also topped the PFA internet poll for the best player in the division and made a near clean-sweep of City's end-of-season awards winning both the supporter's club and the Junior Strikers 'Player of the Season' titles.

Newcastle U (From apprentice on 26/2/1986) FL 30+2/2 FLC 5 Others 1+1
Bradford C (£150,000 on 9/3/1989) FL 137+8/22 FLC 12/1 FAC 9/4 Others 7+1/2
Bristol C (£180,000 on 23/3/1993) FL 299+14/21 FLC 22 FAC 22+2/5 Others 10+2

TINSON Darren Lee
Born: Birmingham, 15 November 1969
Height: 6'0" Weight: 13.12
Club Honours: GMVC '97

The powerfully built Macclesfield skipper mostly played in his favoured centre-back position last season. A commanding figure with a good turn of speed he is also one of the best defensive headers of the ball in the Third Division. Darren has committed himself to the Moss Rose club for the foreseeable future and outside football he is in the first year of a four-year part-time course at Salford University leading to a BSc (Hons) degree in Physiotherapy.

Macclesfield T (£10,000 from Northwich Vic on 14/2/1996) FL 172/4 FLC 12 FAC 7 Others 3

TIPTON Matthew John
Born: Conway, 29 June 1980
Height: 5'10" Weight: 11.7
International Honours: W: U21-6; Yth

Matthew finally made his long-awaited first-team breakthrough at Oldham during the 2000-01 campaign. Taking advantage of injuries and loss of form by Carlo Corazzin and Mark Allott, he enjoyed a brief spell as the Latics' main striker and netted a total of seven goals in all competitions. A promising youngster who has good pace and excellent skills on the ground he will be looking to firmly establish himself as a regular in the starting line-up in the coming season.

Oldham Ath (From trainee on 1/7/1997) FL 40+50/10 FLC 2+3 FAC 2+5/1 Others 1+3/1

TISTIMITANU Ivan
Born: Moldova, 27 April 1974
Height: 5'10" Weight: 11.2
International Honours: Moldova: 34

After being such a big hit in his early days with Bristol City Ivan struggled to make an impact in the 2000-01 campaign and after a few early season appearances he was relegated to the subs' bench. With 18 months of his contract still to run he was eventually allowed to join his former club Zimbru on loan at the beginning of January. A hard-tackling defender or midfield ball-winner he continued to be a regular for the Moldova national team.

Bristol C (£225,000 from FC Zimbru Chisinau, Moldova on 24/12/1998) FL 23+12/2 FLC 1 FAC 3+1 Others 4

TOD Andrew (Andy)
Born: Dunfermline, 4 November 1971
Height: 6'3" Weight: 12.0
Club Honours: S Div 1 '96

Out of favour with Scottish Premier League club Dunfermline, Andy made just a single brief appearance from the subs' bench in the early part of last season before joining Stockport County on loan. The move was a huge success and he went on to score three times in 11 first-team appearances for the Hatters before returning north of the border where he moved closer to a regular first-team slot. A big central defender he is very powerful in the air and solid in the tackle.

Dunfermline Ath (Signed from Kelty Hearts on 4/11/1993) SL 206+12/35 SLC 14 SC 11+2/2 Others 8+1/2
Stockport Co (Loaned on 6/10/2000) FL 11/3

TODD Andrew (Andy) John James
Born: Derby, 21 September 1974
Height: 5'10" Weight: 11.10
Club Honours: Div 1 '97, '00

Andy is a versatile player equally comfortable at right back, as a central defender or in midfield. He found it difficult to break into the Charlton Athletic team at the beginning of last season and was restricted to a couple of appearances at right back in October. However when Radostin Kishishev was moved from right back to midfield Mark Fish took over at full back and Andy was able to seize his chance as a central defender. He slotted into the side brilliantly, holding off Steve Brown, Carl Tiler and Greg Shield to make the position his own. He is a strong competitive player, sharp in the tackle, confident on the ball and calm under pressure. Andy scored his first goal for the Addicks with a firm header against Leicester City at The Valley.

Middlesbrough (From trainee on 6/3/1992) FL 7+1 FLC 1+1 Others 5
Swindon T (Loaned on 27/2/1995) FL 13
Bolton W (£250,000 on 1/8/1995) P/FL 66+18/2 FLC 14+5/1 FAC 1 Others 3
Charlton Ath (£750,000 on 18/11/1999) P/FL 24+11/1 FLC 2 FAC 6+1

TODD Christopher (Chris)
Born: Swansea, 22 August 1981
Height: 6'0" Weight: 11.4

Chris graduated to the professional ranks with Swansea City in July 2000 and after stepping up to make his Football League debut against Northampton in March he retained his place in the line-up, providing the club with a rare bright spot in what was otherwise a very gloomy season. A promising central defender who is quick and very composed he won a number of 'Man of the Match' awards and netted his first senior goal in the 6-0 thrashing of Brentford. Having made such a fine start to his career he will be looking to firmly establish himself in the squad in the 2001-02 campaign.

Swansea C (Trainee) FL 11/1

TODD Lee
Born: Hartlepool, 7 March 1972
Height: 5'6" Weight: 11.2

Having appeared twice for Bradford City in the pre-season Inter Toto Cup matches, Lee moved on to Rochdale shortly before the start of the 2000-01 campaign and soon showed his class, proving to be a terrific signing by Steve Parkin. Superb throughout the campaign his full-back partnership with Wayne Evans helped Dale maintain one of the one of the best defensive records in the Football League. Lee's three goals all came from free kicks on the edge of the box and his last gasp equaliser against Brighton was a strong contender for Dale's goal of the season.

Stockport Co (From trainee at Hartlepool U on 23/7/1990) FL 214+11/2 FLC 24+2 FAC 17/2 Others 33+1
Southampton (£500,000 on 28/7/1997) PL 9+1 FLC 1
Bradford C (£250,000 + on 6/8/1998) FL 14+1 FLC 2 Others 2
Walsall (Loaned on 17/9/1999) FL 1 FLC 1
Rochdale (Free on 9/8/2000) FL 40/3 FLC 2 FAC 1

TODOROV Svetoslav
Born: Bulgaria, 30 August 1978
Height: 6'0" Weight: 11.11
International Honours: Bulgaria: 23; Yth

After joining West Ham in January Svetoslav was slowly eased into the Premiership by boss Harry Redknapp and was mostly used as a substitute. He scored his first goal in the FA Cup quarter-final against Tottenham and also netted in the final game at Middlesbrough. He was extremely unlucky against Manchester City when he had a volley, close-range shot and header all brilliantly saved, while he superbly set up goals for Paolo Di Canio and Joe Cole against Southampton. Svetoslav is a speedy young striker with a direct style and an excellent first touch. Already established as an international he continued to represent Bulgaria.

West Ham U (£500,000 + from Liteks Lovech, Bulgaria on 30/1/2001) PL 2+6/1 FAC 0+1/1

TOLLEY Jamie Christopher
Born: Ludlow, 12 May 1983
Height: 6'0" Weight: 11.3
International Honours: W: U21-2

Jamie is yet another of the talented youngsters on Shrewsbury's books and having won a place in the starting line-up shortly before Christmas he went on to feature regularly in the second half of last season. A busy midfield player he has a positive approach to the game and some of his link play with the strikers showed a level of maturity beyond his years. He will be aiming to gain further experience of Third Division football in the coming campaign. Jamie made his debut for Wales U21s against Poland at the start of June.

Shrewsbury T (From trainee on 9/1/2001) FL 22+4/2 FLC 0+1 FAC 0+2 Others 1

TOLSON Neil
Born: Stourbridge, 25 October 1973
Height: 6'2" Weight: 12.4

After making just a handful of appearances for Southend United at the start of last season Neil was struck down with pelvic trouble. The problem required surgery to insert a pin into his stomach to prevent the pelvic bone moving and it was not until March that he returned to serious training. He will be hoping for a full return to fitness in time for the start of the 2001-02 campaign. Neil is a tall striker who is quick off the mark and effective in the air. He was out of contract in the summer and his future was unclear at the time of writing.

Walsall (From trainee on 17/12/1991) FL 3+6/1 FAC 0+1/1 Others 1+2
Oldham Ath (£150,000 on 24/3/1992) PL 0+3
Bradford C (£50,000 on 2/12/1993) FL 32+31/12 FLC 1+4/1 FAC 3+1/1 Others 2+2/3
Chester C (Loaned on 6/1/1995) FL 3+1
York C (£50,000 on 15/7/1996) FL 66+18/18 FLC 7+2/3 FAC 6+1/2 Others 0+2/1
Southend U (Free on 2/7/1999) FL 34+2/11 FLC 4 FAC 1

TOMLINSON Graeme Murdoch
Born: Watford, 10 December 1975
Height: 5'10" Weight: 12.7

Graeme started the 2000-01 campaign as a first-choice striker for Exeter City but indifferent form and the consistency of Steve Flack kept him out of the side for long periods and he was used mainly from the bench. He scored just one goal, netting with a great 25-yard drive on his debut for the Grecians against Cardiff on the opening day of the season. He is a useful front man who holds the ball up well and shows good awareness in the penalty box although he needs to try and improve his goals-per-game ratio.

Bradford C (Trainee) FL 12+5/6 FAC 0+1
Manchester U (£100,000 on 12/7/1994) FLC 0+2
Wimbledon (Loaned on 22/6/1995) Others 4
Luton T (Loaned on 22/3/1996) FL 1+6
Bournemouth (Loaned on 8/8/1997) FL 6+1/1
Millwall (Loaned on 26/3/1998) FL 2+1/1
Macclesfield T (Free on 9/7/1998) FL 22+24/6 FLC 2+2 FAC 4+2/4 Others 1
Exeter C (Free on 21/7/2000) FL 13+11/1 FLC 2 Others 0+1

TOMS Frazer Peter
Born: Ealing, 13 September 1979
Height: 6'1" Weight: 11.0

This talented youngster started the 2000-01 season at Barnet in promising fashion, but like several others he fell out of favour under Tony Cottee's reign before eventually returning to the side in February. Frazer is a skilful wide-left midfield player with good pace and capable of producing mazy runs down the flank. He was placed on the open to offers list following the club's relegation to the Conference.

Charlton Ath (From trainee on 2/7/1998)
Barnet (Free on 2/7/1999) FL 46+19/1 FLC 4 FAC 2+1 Others 1+3/1

TONGE Michael William
Born: Manchester, 7 April 1983
Height: 6'0" Weight: 11.10

Captain of Sheffield United's youth team, Michael had a fine season at Bramall Lane in 2000-01, appearing for the reserves in their Avon Insurance League Cup final victory over Stoke and stepping up to make his Football League debut from the subs' bench against Wimbledon in April. He subsequently made the starting line-up for the last game of the campaign at Bolton and will be hoping to gain more senior experience in 2001-02. A very promising midfield player he performed creditably in both his first-team appearances.

Sheffield U (From trainee on 16/3/2001) FL 1+1

TORPEY Stephen (Steve) David James
Born: Islington, 8 December 1970
Height: 6'3" Weight: 14.6
Club Honours: AMC '94

Scunthorpe's record signing had a good season at Glanford Park in 2000-01, his aerial strength making him a handful for most Division Three defences. He was appointed club captain when Nigel Pepper was ruled out early on through injury and he netted nine times before Christmas, but then struggled for goals during the second half of the campaign. He unfortunately suffered

disciplinary problems which saw him miss several matches through suspension and this is an area of his game which he needs to improve on in the coming season.
Millwall (From trainee on 14/2/1989) FL 3+4 FLC 0+1
Bradford C (£70,000 on 21/11/1990) FL 86+10/22 FLC 6 FAC 2+1 Others 8/6
Swansea C (£80,000 on 3/8/1993) FL 151+11/44 FLC 9+2/2 FAC 10/5 Others 18+3/6
Bristol C (£400,000 on 8/8/1997) FL 53+17/13 FLC 4+1/1 FAC 3 Others 3+1
Notts Co (Loaned on 7/8/1998) FL 4+2/1 FLC 1+1/1
Scunthorpe U (£175,000 on 3/2/2000) FL 55/11 FLC 2/1 FAC 4/1

TOWNSEND Benjamin (Ben)
Born: Reading, 8 October 1981
Height: 5'10" Weight: 11.3
Ben made excellent progress at Wycombe last season although he was used sparingly by manager Lawrie Sanchez. Mostly employed in the second half of the campaign he gave a mature display in the FA Cup sixth round tie at Leicester and won more praise for his semi-final performance against Liverpool. A gutsy young right back he will be looking to establish himself as a regular member of the first-team squad in the coming season.
Wycombe W (From trainee on 13/1/2001) FL 10+1 FAC 5+1 Others 1

TOWNSON Kevin
Born: Liverpool, 19 April 1983
Height: 5'8" Weight: 10.3
International Honours: E: Yth
Kevin joined Rochdale in July 2000 and spent much of last season learning his trade in the club's youth and reserve sides. Dale manager Steve Parkin resisted the temptation to pitch him into the first team until an injury crisis in March when he made his debut from the subs' bench at Southend. He made the starting line-up for the following game at Hartlepool when he produced a superb performance, harassing much bigger and more experienced defenders. A small and sharp striker, he was easily the top scorer for Dale's reserves. He made his debut for England U17s in the end-of-season game against Italy.
Rochdale (Free from Everton juniors on 6/7/2000) FL 1+2

TRACEY Richard Shaun
Born: Dewsbury, 9 July 1979
Height: 5'11" Weight: 11.0
Richard began the 2000-01 campaign on a short-term contract with Carlisle United but struggled to win a regular place in the line-up. He was released in November and joined Macclesfield Town at the end of January following a successful trial period. He made his debut from the subs' bench in the home defeat by Cardiff when he scored with his first touch but then picked up injuries in his next two appearances and consequently was out of action until the middle of March when he returned to put in some steady performances. Away from football Richard is in his second year of a four-year part-time course studying for a Bsc (Hons) degree in Sports Science.
Sheffield U (From trainee on 4/6/1997)
Rotherham U (Free on 24/2/1998) FL 0+3 FAC 1+1
Carlisle U (Free on 12/3/1999) FL 39+14/11 FLC 3+1 FAC 1 Others 1+1
Macclesfield T (Free on 25/1/2001) FL 11+2/3

TRACEY Simon Peter
Born: Woolwich, 9 December 1967
Height: 6'0" Weight: 13.12
Simon began his 13th season at Bramall Lane with no serious challenger for the number one spot between the posts and he had probably his best campaign to date for Sheffield United. He looked sure with crosses into the box, his shot stopping was as good as ever and there were very few unforced errors. After signing a new two-year deal he passed his 300th league and cup appearance for the Blades and looked like being an ever-present before a groin injury brought his run of 91 consecutive first-team games to an end.
Wimbledon (From apprentice on 3/2/1986) FL 1 Others 1
Sheffield U (£7,500 on 19/10/1988) F/PL 288+3 FLC 20 FAC 18 Others 10
Manchester C (Loaned on 27/10/1994) PL 3
Norwich C (Loaned on 31/12/1994) PL 1 FAC 2
Wimbledon (Loaned on 2/11/1995) PL 1

TRAORE Demba
Born: Stockholm, Sweden, 22 April 1982
Height: 6'1" Weight: 11.10
Demba spent most of last season developing in the Cambridge United youth and reserve teams but stepped up to make his Football League debut from the subs' bench at Bristol City in January. He also featured in the LDV Vans Trophy tie at Southend before going out on loan to Wisbech Town in the closing weeks of the campaign to gain more experience of senior football. A quick hard-working striker he was rewarded with a contract towards the end of the season.
Cambridge U (Free from Vasalunds IF, Sweden on 28/12/2000) FL 0+1 Others 0+1

TRAORE Djimi
Born: Paris, France, 1 March 1980
Height: 6'3" Weight: 13.10
International Honours: France: U21; Yth
Having made just two Worthington Cup appearances for Liverpool in 1999-2000 it was a big surprise when Djimi started last season as first-choice left back and held his place for eight games before being displaced by new signing Christian Ziege. He then returned for another brief spell in November but the UEFA Cup tie against Olympiakos in Athens was his last appearance in the first team for the season. He subsequently had some problems with hamstring and knee injuries but otherwise appeared in the club's reserve team. He remains a promising youngster but now faces strong competition from Gregory Vignal as he tries to displace Jamie Carragher from the left-back slot.
Liverpool (£550,000 from Laval, France on 18/2/1999) PL 8 FLC 3 Others 2+1

TRETTON Andrew (Andy) David
Born: Derby, 9 October 1976
Height: 6'0" Weight: 12.9
Andy was once again affected by injuries last season but he returned to the Shrewsbury Town line-up in the new year and established a useful partnership with Matt Redmile in the centre of defence. A popular defender who is strong in the air and assured on the ball he would benefit greatly from an extended run of first-team football.
Derby Co (From trainee on 18/10/1993)
Shrewsbury T (Free on 12/12/1997) FL 90+2/6 FLC 2 FAC 3 Others 2

TROLLOPE Paul Jonathan
Born: Swindon, 3 June 1972
Height: 6'0" Weight: 12.6
Club Honours: Div 2 '99
International Honours: W: 5; B-1
Paul had another season on the fringe of the Fulham squad in 2000-01, playing occasional games at left back or left midfield as cover for injuries and suspensions. He was a regular in the reserve side that won the Avon Insurance Combination for the first time in the club's history and when he did appear for the first team he set up many goals with his overlapping runs.
Swindon T (From trainee on 23/12/1989)
Torquay U (Free on 26/3/1992) FL 103+3/16 FLC 9+1/1 FAC 7 Others 8+1
Derby Co (£100,000 on 16/12/1994) F/PL 47+18/5 FLC 3+2/1 FAC 3+1
Grimsby T (Loaned on 30/8/1996) FL 6+1/1
Crystal Palace (Loaned on 11/10/1996) FL 0+9
Fulham (£600,000 on 28/11/1997) FL 54+22/5 FLC 9+2 FAC 3+5 Others 4/1

TRUDGIAN Ryan
Born: Truro, 15 September 1983
Height: 6'0" Weight: 12.1
Ryan spent most of last season developing with Plymouth Argyle's youth team but was called up to the first-team squad for the last game of the campaign against Rochdale. He went on to make his Football League debut, coming off the subs' bench to replace Martin Gritton for the final ten minutes of the match. He is a young centre forward who should receive more senior opportunities in the future providing he continues to work at his game.
Plymouth Arg (Trainee) FL 0+1

TRUNDLE Lee Christopher
Born: Liverpool, 10 October 1976
Height: 6'0" Weight: 13.3
Lee began the 2000-01 campaign with League of Wales outfit Rhyl Town but after notching a hat-trick in a friendly game against Wrexham in the new year he was signed up by Robins' manager Brian Flynn. He became an overnight sensation at the Racecourse Ground, netting with a spectacular overhead kick at Walsall and then hitting a hat-trick in the 5-3 win over Oxford. Having scored eight goals in his first 11 games he then suffered an achilles injury at the beginning of April but he recovered in time to play in the last few games of the season. Lee is an extremely promising striker who has the ability to hold up the ball, turn his opponent and shoot at goal in one quick movement.
Wrexham (£60,000 from Rhyl, ex Burscough, Chorley, Stalybridge Celtic, Southport, on 16/2/2001) FL 12+2/8

TUDOR Shane Anthony
Born: Wolverhampton, 10 February 1982
Height: 5'8" Weight: 11.2

Caretaker-manager John Ward gave this Wolves youngster his Football League debut when he came on from the subs' bench for the final eight minutes of the game at Sheffield Wednesday shortly before Christmas. An exciting right winger he will be aiming for further senior experience in 2001-02.

Wolverhampton W (From trainee on 9/8/1999) FL 0+1

TULLY Stephen (Steve) Richard
Born: Paignton, 10 February 1980
Height: 5'9" Weight: 11.0

This promising Torquay youngster dislodged the more experienced Paul Holmes from the right-back position last season and retained his place in the Gulls' line-up until suffering an injury in February that caused him to miss the remainder of the campaign. Steve is a determined defender with great stamina who is always willing to push forward down the flank.

Torquay U (From trainee on 18/5/1998) FL 73+15/3 FLC 3+1 FAC 4+1 Others 7

TUOMELA Marko
Born: Finland, 3 March 1972
Height: 6'4" Weight: 14.6
International Honours: Finland: 21

Marko joined Swindon Town on loan from Norwegian club Tromso last September as boss Colin Todd sought to shore up a leaking defence but he failed to establish himself in the team and returned to Scandinavia in November. A tall, strong central defender he was recalled to the Finland national team in the new year and started the new 2001 season at Swedish club Sundsvall.

Swindon T (Loaned from Tromso, Norway, ex FC Kuusysi, TPV Tampere, FF Jaro, on 11/9/2000) FL 1+1 FLC 2

TURLEY James
Born: Manchester, 24 June 1981
Height: 5'6" Weight: 10.6

This diminutive striker made a number of senior appearances for York City last season, chiefly operating on the right side of the attack. He failed to find the net for the first team but once again headed the scoring charts for the club's reserves. A lively and enthusiastic player James was released at the end of the campaign.

York C (From trainee on 29/6/1999) FL 14+7/2 Others 0+1

TURNER Andrew (Andy) Peter
Born: Woolwich, 23 March 1975
Height: 5'10" Weight: 11.12
International Honours: RoI: U21-7. E: Yth; Sch

Apart from a brief spell in the first team last September Andy struggled to find his form for Rotherham at the start of the 2000-01 campaign. He had a loan spell at Conference club Boston United in November and in March was loaned out again, this time to Third Division Rochdale. Intended to give Dale an authentic left-sided attacker, Andy was unfortunately injured in only his third game but made a quick return for one final appearance before going back to Millmoor. He is a wide left-sided player with excellent ball skills and the ability to deliver crosses from apparently impossible positions. Out of contract in the summer he was reported to have signed for Yeovil.

Tottenham H (From trainee on 8/4/1992) PL 8+12/3 FLC 0+2/1 FAC 0+1 Others 1
Wycombe W (Loaned on 26/8/1994) FL 3+1
Doncaster Rov (Loaned on 10/10/1994) FL 4/1 Others 1/1
Huddersfield T (Loaned on 28/11/1995) FL 2+3/1
Southend U (Loaned on 28/3/1996) FL 4+2
Portsmouth (£250,000 on 4/9/1996) FL 34+6/3 FLC 2+2 FAC 1
Crystal Palace (Free on 27/10/1998) FL 0+2
Wolverhampton W (Free on 25/3/1999)
Rotherham U (Free on 1/7/1999) FL 29+7/1 FLC 2 Others 1
Rochdale (Loaned on 22/3/2001) FL 2+2

TUTILL Stephen (Steve) Alan
Born: York, 1 October 1969
Height: 5'10" Weight: 12.6
International Honours: E: Sch

Steve formed an effective partnership with Steve Blatherwick at the centre of Chesterfield's defence last season. He featured regularly until suffering an achilles injury in December that failed to clear up and eventually required corrective surgery. Steve is powerful in the air and shows more composure on the deck than might be expected of a Third Division defender.

York C (From trainee on 27/1/1988) FL 293+8/6 FLC 21 FAC 18+1 Others 22+3/1
Darlington (Free on 20/2/1998) FL 65+5 FLC 1 FAC 6/1 Others 5
Chesterfield (Free on 19/7/2000) FL 17+2/1 FLC 3 FAC 1 Others 1

TUTTLE David (Dave) Philip
Born: Reading, 6 February 1972
Height: 6'1" Weight: 12.10
Club Honours: FAYC '90
International Honours: E: Yth

This experienced defender played only a handful of games for Millwall last season as he found himself unable to win a regular place in a very strong squad. He played a valuable role helping the club's youngsters in the reserves and was always outstanding when called upon by the first team. A strong-tackling centre back he is an excellent squad member for the Lions.

Tottenham H (From trainee on 8/2/1990) F/PL 10+3 FLC 3+1 Others 1/1
Peterborough U (Loaned on 21/1/1993) FL 7
Sheffield U (£350,000 on 1/8/1993) P/FL 63/1 FLC 2 FAC 3
Crystal Palace (Signed on 8/3/1996) F/PL 73+8/5 FLC 7 FAC 2 Others 6
Barnsley (£150,000 on 18/8/1999) FL 11+1 FAC 1
Millwall (£200,000 on 2/3/2000) FL 13+4 FLC 2 Others 3

TWISS Michael John
Born: Salford, 18 December 1977
Height: 5'11" Weight: 12.8
Club Honours: AMC '01

Michael joined Port Vale in July 2000 and after an impressive pre-season he scored on the opening day of the campaign at Oldham. He lost his place in October following a poor run of results for Vale and although generally in the squad of 16 he did not return to the starting line-up until the new year. Initially used in a left-sided midfield role he later featured as a striker before being released in the summer.

Manchester U (From trainee on 5/7/1996) FLC 1 FAC 0+1
Sheffield U (Loaned on 6/8/1998) FL 2+10/1 FAC 2+3
Port Vale (Free on 27/7/2000) FL 15+3/2 FLC 2 FAC 0+2 Others 1+1

TWYNHAM Gary Steven
Born: Manchester, 8 February 1976
Height: 6'0" Weight: 12.1

Gary impressed in trials for Macclesfield in the summer of 2000 and was rewarded with a one-year contract, but only managed a handful of first team appearances mostly in a midfield role. He offered glimpses of his talents, often beating several opposing players with powerful runs into the area and he showed clean tackling and accurate distribution. Unfortunately illness and injury kept him out of contention and his registration was cancelled by mutual consent in February. He subsequently moved back in to the non-league game signing for Dr Martens League club Halesowen Town in March.

Manchester U (From trainee on 1/7/1994)
Darlington (Free on 28/3/1996) FL 23+8/3 FLC 4 Others 1 (Free to Gateshead on 27/8/1997)
Macclesfield T (Free from Hednesford T on 7/8/2000) FL 5+4 FLC 2

TYLER Mark Richard
Born: Norwich, 2 April 1977
Height: 6'0" Weight: 12.9
International Honours: E: Yth

Mark was again first-choice 'keeper for Peterborough United last season and apart from a brief spell out injured he played in almost every senior match. An agile goalkeeper who is a fine shot stopper he produced several magnificent saves, performing with an ever-increasing level of maturity. Capable of playing at a higher level it remains to be seen how long he will stay at London Road.

Peterborough U (From trainee on 7/12/1994) FL 152+1 FLC 9 FAC 11 Others 13

TYNE Thomas (Tommy) Richard
Born: Lambeth, 2 March 1981
Height: 6'1" Weight: 12.5

Having signed from Kent League club Slade Green towards the end of the 1999-2000 campaign, Tommy made his senior debut for Millwall in the Worthington Cup first round first leg tie against Brighton and featured in a number of games in the early part of last season. He continued his development with some excellent performances in the reserves and in February he went on an extended loan to Dr Martens League club Fisher Athletic to gain more first-team experience. He is an old-fashioned centre forward who is strong on the ball and packs a powerful shot. He was released by the Lions in the summer.

Millwall (Signed from Slade Green on 24/2/1999) FL 0+3 FLC 0+3

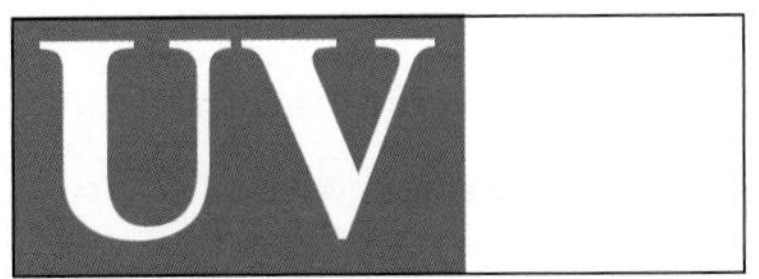

UHLENBEEK Gustav (Gus) Reinier
Born: Paramaribo, Surinam, 20 August 1970
Height: 5'10" Weight: 12.6
Club Honours: Div 2 '99

Gus joined Sheffield United on a two-year deal in the 2000 close season and immediately slotted into the right-wing-back spot becoming a fixture in the side until December when he lost his place to Rob Kozluk. Thereafter he was in and out of the team playing at times in the centre of defence or on the left but always giving of his best. A versatile defender with tremendous pace, he linked well with Paul Devlin down the right-hand side and created chances for his colleagues with some accurate crosses.

Ipswich T (£100,000 from Tops SV, Holland, ex Ajax, Cambuur, on 11/8/1995) FL 77+12/4 FLC 5+3 FAC 4+3 Others 7+1
Fulham (Free on 22/7/1998) FL 22+17/1 FLC 4+1 FAC 3+2 Others 1
Sheffield U (Free on 10/8/2000) FL 28+3 FLC 4 FAC 1

ULLATHORNE Robert (Rob)
Born: Wakefield, 11 October 1971
Height: 5'8" Weight: 11.3
International Honours: E: Yth

Having finally recovered full fitness after suffering a badly broken leg back in March 1999, Rob joined Newcastle on a non-contract basis last September following unsuccessful trials in Spain and after featuring regularly in their reserve team he signed for Sheffield United towards the end of the year. Although sidelined by a hamstring injury after just two games he enjoyed a good run in the side after Wayne Quinn's departure before sustaining ankle and knee ligament damage in the Sheffield derby at Hillsborough. An experienced left-sided defender he made good use of his pace and anticipation, linking well with Peter Ndlovu down the wing. Out of contract in the summer his future was unclear at the time of writing.

Norwich C (From trainee on 6/7/1990) F/PL 86+8/7 FLC 10+2/1 FAC 7+1 Others 1 (Free to Osasuna, Spain during 1996 close season)
Leicester C (£600,000 on 18/2/1997) PL 28+3/1 FLC 8+1 FAC 2/1
Sheffield U (Free, following an injury and trials at Huddersfield T, Real Zaragoza, Tenerife, Newcastle, on 1/12/2000) FL 13+1

UNSWORTH David Gerald
Born: Chorley, 16 October 1973
Height: 6'1" Weight: 14.2
Club Honours: FAC '95; CS '95
International Honours: E: 1; U21-6; Yth

David came through a dip in form at Everton in the early part of the 2000-01 season to re-establish himself as one of the most popular players at the club. Having shown strength of character and resolve to come through the period he ended the season with a flourish, scoring four goals in a decisive six-match spell. His usual dead-eye accuracy from the penalty spot was marred by a last day miss against Sunderland, but typically he refused to let that affect his concentration and picked up a 'Man of the Match' award at the end of the game. Happiest on the left of a three-man defensive formation, he was largely employed at left wing back throughout the season where he acquitted himself diligently and enthusiastically.

Everton (From trainee on 25/6/1992) F/PL 108+8/11 FLC 5+2 FAC 7 Others 4/1
West Ham U (£1,000,000 + on 18/8/1997) PL 32/2 FLC 5 FAC 4
Aston Villa (£3,000,000 on 28/7/1998)
Everton (£3,000,000 on 22/8/1998) PL 82+4/12 FLC 6 FAC 9/4

UNSWORTH Lee Peter
Born: Eccles, 25 February 1973
Height: 5'11" Weight: 11.8

Lee had a wretched time with injuries at Bury in the 2000-01 season. Although he started the campaign as first-choice right back he was sidelined early on after suffering an ankle ligament injury against Northampton. He returned to the first team in October but in January he was out again with a serious knee injury. However he came back again in mid-April only to break a toe at Reading and he failed to recover full fitness by the summer. Lee will be hoping to steer clear of the treatment table in the coming season! Out of contract in the summer his future was unclear at the time of writing.

Crewe Alex (Signed from Ashton U on 20/2/1995) FL 93+33 FLC 10+1/1 FAC 5+1/1 Others 8+2
Bury (Free on 4/8/2000) FL 12+3 FLC 1 FAC 2 Others 2

UPSON Matthew James
Born: Stowmarket, 18 April 1979
Height: 6'1" Weight: 11.4
International Honours: E: U21-10; Yth

Matthew spent the first part of the 2000-01 season battling back to full fitness after rupturing a cruciate ligament in December 1999. He made a handful of appearances for Arsenal in the autumn, featuring in the defeats against Ipswich Town and Shakhtar Donetsk in the Worthington Cup and Champions' League competitions, but made only one substitute appearance in the Premiership away at Everton. He subsequently joined Nottingham Forest on loan where he made a single appearance against Portsmouth in an unfamiliar midfield role before returning early to North London with a back injury. He later moved to Crystal Palace for another loan period and featured regularly for the Eagles in the run-in to the end of the season, contributing to their struggle to avoid relegation. Back at Highbury he added a further appearance from the subs' bench when he replaced Robert Pires in the final stages of the last game of the season at Southampton. Matthew is a strong, intelligent central defender who is comfortable on the ball and has good distribution skills. He continued to feature in the England U21 squad winning a further three caps.

Luton T (From trainee on 24/4/1996) FL 0+1 Others 1
Arsenal (£1,000,000 on 14/5/1997) PL 10+10 FLC 7 FAC 2 Others 3+1
Nottingham F (Loaned on 8/12/2000) FL 1
Crystal Palace (Loaned on 2/3/2001) FL 7

VAESEN Nico Jos-Theodor
Born: Ghent, Belgium, 28 September 1969
Height: 6'3" Weight: 12.8

Regarded as one of the best goalkeepers outside the Premier League, Nico has firmly established himself in English football and has won the hearts of the Huddersfield Town fans. He celebrated his 100th league appearance for the Terriers in the away defeat at Grimsby Town, and only suspension following a red card at Blackburn prevented him from being an ever-present for the second consecutive season. A superb all-round 'keeper he handles the ball well, is quick to turn defence into attack and generally makes at least one outstanding save every match. Nico was reported to have signed for Birmingham City during the summer.

Huddersfield T (£80,000 from SC Eendracht Aalst, Belgium on 10/7/1998) FL 134 FLC 12 FAC 7

VALAKARI Simo
Born: Helsinki, Finland, 28 April 1973
Height: 5'10" Weight: 11.10
International Honours: Finland: 18

A close-season 'Bosman' signing for Derby County, Simo joined the Rams on a four-year contract. A combative midfield player he is suited to a central position where his ability to dictate the pace of the game is best employed. Goal-scoring has never been his forte and the early-season strike against Charlton was his first for three years, however he dropped out of the squad through injury in November and was subsequently restricted to reserve-team action on his return to fitness.

Motherwell (Signed from MyPa, Finland on 6/2/1997) SL 98+6 SLC 3+1 SC 7+2
Derby Co (Free on 6/7/2000) PL 9+2/1 FLC 3

VAN BLERK Jason
Born: Sydney, Australia, 16 March 1968
Height: 6'1" Weight: 13.0
International Honours: Australia: 27; Yth

This tough-tackling Australian international featured at left back, centre half and in midfield for Albion during the 2000-01 season. His performances were both vigorous and competitive and with Neil Clement behind him he found more time to venture forward in an attempt to create goal-scoring opportunities for his colleagues. Sidelined for a while with a hamstring problem, his competitive approach was admired by all and he was key member of the Baggies' squad. He was released in the summer.

Millwall (£300,000 from Go Ahead Eagles, Holland on 8/9/1994) FL 68+5/2 FLC 5 FAC 6+1 Others 1+1
Manchester C (Free on 9/8/1997) FL 10+9 FLC 0+1 FAC 0+1
West Bromwich A (£250,000 on 13/3/1998) FL 106+3/3 FLC 8+1 FAC 1 Others 2

VAN DER GEEST Franciscus (Frank) Wilhelmus
Born: Beverwijk, Holland, 30 April 1973
Height: 6'2" Weight: 13.0

Frank joined Darlington in the 2000 close season, signing from Dutch club Heracles with Tom Kaak. He made his debut in the home leg of the Worthington Cup tie with Nottingham Forest and also appeared in the second leg at the City Ground. He subsequently played in the next two league matches but after that his only other first-team outings came in the LDV Vans Trophy ties. When an opportunity arose due to the injury to Andy Collett in the new year Frank was also injured and unable to take advantage. He is a tall and commanding goalkeeper who will be looking to gain regular first-team football in the 2001-02 campaign.

Darlington (Free from Heracles, Holland, ex AZ Alkmaar, Sparta Rotterdam, on 21/8/2000) FL 2 FLC 2 Others 3

VAN DER GOUW Raimond (Rai)
Born: Oldenzaal, Holland, 24 March 1963
Height: 6'3" Weight: 13.10
Club Honours: EC '99; FAC '99; PL '00, '01

With Fabien Barthez claiming the goal-keeper's jersey at Old Trafford from Mark Bosnich in the summer, Rai appeared to be the most likely candidate to be frozen out at Old Trafford. However after Bosnich fell out of favour, Rai started his fourth Premiership campaign as the surprise understudy to the flamboyant Frenchman. Not that he was expecting to be called upon quite so early, when Barthez pulled up with a hamstring problem in the Premiership match against Everton in mid-September. Having kept a clean sheet in the vital Champions' League tie against Dynamo Kiev, Rai was then beaten on six occasions in his next two games, against Chelsea at Old Trafford and PSV Eindhoven in Holland. In December, when contracts were in the offing, Rai suggested that a possible move to Florida in the summer would satisfy a longing to play in the USA. However, with Bosnich moving on to Chelsea, and only the inexperienced Paul Rachubka left as cover, his 'American Dream' might just have to be put on hold for another season.

Manchester U (Signed from Vitesse Arnhem, Holland, ex Go Ahead Eagles, on 12/7/1996) PL 26+10 FLC 8 FAC 1 Others 13

VAN DER LAAN Robertus (Robin) Petrus
Born: Schiedam, Holland, 5 September 1968
Height: 6'0" Weight: 13.8
Club Honours: AMC '93

Robin signed a new two-year contract for Barnsley at the start of last season and featured regularly for the Reds in a midfield role in the opening matches. Always a handful at set pieces or when manager Dave Bassett decided to play him in attack, he scored in consecutive games against Queens Park Rangers and in the Worthington Cup against Crewe. However after injuring a knee he underwent surgery early in the new year and he later had a second operation before announcing his retirement from the game in March. A sad end to a very popular player's career.

Port Vale (£80,000 from Wageningen, Holland on 21/2/1991) FL 154+22/24 FLC 11+1/1 FAC 9+1/1 Others 11+1/1
Derby Co (£675,000 on 2/8/1995) F/PL 61+4/8 FLC 6+2 FAC 3+1/3
Wolverhampton W (Loaned on 11/10/1996) FL 7
Barnsley (£325,000 + on 17/7/1998) FL 52+15/5 FLC 10+1/4 FAC 0+1 Others 1

VAN DER LINDEN Antoine
Born: Rotterdam, Holland, 17 March 1976
Height: 6'3" Weight: 13.4

Having been released by Sparta Rotterdam at the end of the 1999-2000 campaign Antoine joined Swindon Town in August following a successful trial. However it was not until October that he won a regular place in the first-team squad and even then he was regularly used from the subs' bench. A confident and composed left-footed player he was mostly used in the centre of defence but he also featured at left back and as a striker when the need arose. He was reported to have returned to Holland and signed for Emmen during the summer.

Swindon T (Free from Sparta Rotterdam, Holland, ex Alexandria, Zwervers, Sparta Rotterdam, on 10/8/2000) FL 17+16/1 FLC 1 FAC 2 Others 3

VAN HEUSDEN Arjan
Born: Alphen, Holland, 11 December 1972
Height: 6'3" Weight: 14.7

Arjan was first choice 'keeper at Exeter last season and endeared himself to the club's fans with a string of superb performances. Perhaps the highlight of his campaign was his display at Mansfield in February when he pulled off a pair of one-handed wonder saves to earn the Grecians a draw. A popular member of the squad he will be aiming for the same level of consistency in the 2001-02 campaign.

Port Vale (£4,500 from VV Noordwijk, Holland on 15/8/1994) FL 27 FLC 4 Others 2
Oxford U (Loaned on 26/9/1997) FL 11 FLC 2
Cambridge U (Free on 4/8/1998) FL 41+1 FLC 6 FAC 1 Others 4
Exeter C (Free on 31/7/2000) FL 41 FLC 1 FAC 1

VARGA Stanislav (Stan)
Born: Czechoslovakia, 8 October 1972
Height: 6'2" Weight: 14.8
International Honours: Slovakia: 32

A giant central defender who joined Sunderland from Slovan Bratislava in the close season, Stan made his debut in the opening game against Arsenal and his first contribution was a 40-yard pass in the opening minutes to set up an attack. Not surprisingly dominant in the air, his distribution from the back was excellent, but his season was turned on its head in the very next game at Maine Road when he was stretchered off with a torn leg muscle; the injury developed complications due to internal bleeding and led ultimately to Stan requiring four operations. He returned to first-team action by the end of October and scored his first goal for the Black Cats at West Ham in January. Although he missed some more games towards the end of the campaign, Stan can be reasonably satisfied with his first season in the Premiership.

Sunderland (£650,000 + from SK Slovan Bratislave, Slovakia, ex Tetran Presov, on 14/8/2000) PL 9+3/1 FLC 2+1 FAC 4

VARTY John William (Will)
Born: Workington,, 1 October 1976
Height: 6'0" Weight: 12.4
Club Honours: AMC '97

Will had to be content with a fringe role at Rotherham last season where his appearances were restricted to cover for injuries and suspensions although he featured regularly in the reserves. A defender who is equally at home on the right side of the defence or being used as a sweeper he occasionally turned out in a midfield role for the second string. He was released by the Millers in the summer.

Carlisle U (From trainee on 10/7/1995) FL 79+3/1 FLC 8+1 FAC 3 Others 9+1
Rotherham U (Free on 12/3/1999) FL 45+2 FLC 2+2 FAC 2 Others 2+1

VASSELL Darius
Born: Birmingham, 13 June 1980
Height: 5'7" Weight: 12.0
International Honours: E: U21-7; Yth

A powerful young striker with superb close control and electric pace, Darius is still learning the game at Aston Villa but he continued to show considerable promise last season. Mostly featuring from the substitutes' bench he scored some valuable goals including the winner in the FA Cup third round replay against Newcastle and a double in the 3-0 win at Bradford City. A regular for England U21s for whom he won five more caps, he will be aiming to win a regular place up front for Villa in 2001-02.

Aston Villa (From trainee on 14/4/1998) PL 6+34/4 FLC 1+6 FAC 2+3/1 Others 0+6/2

VASSEUR Emmanuel
Born: Calais, France, 3 September 1976
Height: 5'7" Weight: 10.2

One of the heroes of French CFA (Fourth Division) club Calais's incredible run to the 1999-2000 cup final (they were only defeated by a last-minute penalty in front of 78,000 fans), Emmanuel opted to cross the Channel for a career with Leyton Orient last February. He made his debut from the subs' bench against Halifax and also featured against Torquay but struggled to adjust to the pace of the full-time game at times. A left-footed midfield player with plenty of vision he was reported to have returned to Calais during the summer.

Leyton Orient (Free from Calais, France on 31/1/2001) FL 0+2

VAUGHAN Anthony (Tony) John
Born: Manchester, 11 October 1975
Height: 6'1" Weight: 11.2
International Honours: E: Yth; Sch

Very much a favourite of the Nottingham Forest fans because of his hard-tackling, combative approach to the game, Tony was a regular in the team for most of last term. However after being shown a red card at Crewe, boss David Platt put him on the transfer list and he made just one more first-team appearance. He is a powerful defender

who can play either at left back or as a centre half.
Ipswich T (From trainee on 1/7/1994) P/FL 56+11/3 FLC 4+2 FAC 2 Others 4
Manchester C (£1,350,000 on 9/7/1997) FL 54+4/2 FLC 6+1 FAC 3 Others 3+1
Cardiff C (Loaned on 15/9/1999) FL 14 Others 1
Nottingham F (£350,000 on 8/2/2000) FL 33+2/1 FLC 2

VAUGHAN David Owen
Born: Rhuddlan, 18 February 1983
Height: 5'7" Weight: 10.10
One of the latest players to develop through Crewe Alexandra's successful youth scheme, David stepped in to make his Football League debut in the home game against Blackburn last August when he played for the whole of the first half before being replaced by Kevin Street at the break. A left-sided midfield player he showed some neat touches and will be looking for more senior experience in 2001-02.
Crewe Alex (From trainee on 6/2/2001) FL 1

VEGA Ramon
Born: Zurich, Switzerland, 14 June 1971
Height: 6'3" Weight: 13.0
Club Honours: FLC '99
International Honours: Switzerland: 24; B-1
Ramon again struggled to win a place in George Graham's Tottenham side in the first half of last season and made the starting line-up for just eight Premiership games. Transferred to Celtic in December he received the regular first-team place he craved, and after scoring twice on his debut against Aberdeen he went on to gain winners' medals in the Scottish League Cup and Scottish Cup and become a key member of Martin O'Neill's championship-winning side. An effective defender who is strong in the air and quick on the ball, he was reported to have signed for Watford in the summer.
Tottenham H (£3,750,000 from Cagliari, Italy, ex Trimbach, Grasshoppers, on 11/1/1997) PL 53+11/7 FLC 9+2/1 FAC 8+1

VENUS Mark
Born: Hartlepool, 6 April 1967
Height: 6'0" Weight: 13.11
Club Honours: Div 3 '89
Mark's performances at the centre of Ipswich's defence last season proved that he is still capable of playing at the highest level and surprised a few people into the bargain. He scored Town's first Premiership goal of the campaign when he drilled home a free-kick in the ninth minute at Tottenham in the opening game. Although sometimes seen as lacking a degree of pace, he more than compensated for this with some great anticipation that enabled him to cut out danger at an early stage. He remained an expert from dead-ball situations and scored goals against Middlesbrough and Leeds with powerful left-footed free kicks.
Hartlepool U (From juniors on 22/3/1985) FL 4 Others 0+1
Leicester C (Free on 6/9/1985) FL 58+3/1 FLC 3 FAC 2 Others 2+1
Wolverhampton W (£40,000 on 23/3/1988) FL 271+16/7 FLC 17+1/1 FAC 15+1 Others 17/2
Ipswich T (£150,000 on 29/7/1997) P/FL 107+4/15 FLC 15/3 FAC 4 Others 7

VERHOENE Kenny
Born: Belgium, 15 April 1973
Height: 6'3" Weight: 12.12
This experienced defender joined Crystal Palace on loan shortly before the transfer deadline and made his debut as a late substitute in the 1-1 draw at home to Crewe. Earlier in the season he had made three appearances for Belgian First Division club Harelbeke.
Crystal Palace (Loaned from KRC Harelbeke, Belgium, ex St Truiden VV, KAA Gent, KVC Westerlo, on 22/3/2001) FL 0+1

VERNAZZA Paolo Andrea Pietro
Born: Islington, 1 November 1979
Height: 6'0" Weight: 11.10
International Honours: E: U21-2; Yth
Beginning the 2000-01 campaign with Arsenal, Paolo scored a late winner in his first appearance of the season as a substitute at Coventry. However after a couple more outings from the bench and a place in the starting line-up in the Worthington Cup tie against Ipswich, he moved on to Watford in December where he received regular first-team football for the remainder of the campaign. A busy purposeful midfield player he has good awareness, passes the ball accurately and looks an excellent investment for the Hornets. Having previously been capped by England at youth level Paolo stepped up to make his U21 debut against Germany last October and also featured in the friendly game against Mexico in the summer.
Arsenal (From trainee on 18/11/1997) PL 2+3/1 FLC 4 Others 1+2
Ipswich T (Loaned on 2/10/1998) FL 2
Portsmouth (Loaned on 14/1/2000) FL 7
Watford (£350,000 + on 15/12/2000) FL 20+3/2 FAC 1

VERSCHAVE Matthias
Born: Lille, France, 24 December 1977
Height: 5'9" Weight: 11.5
Matthias joined Swansea City from top French club Paris St Germain last February in a loan deal that kept him at Vetch Field until the end of the season. An extremely quick striker with an excellent first touch he took some time to settle in but finished the season with a flourish, netting a goal in the 6-0 thrashing of Brentford and another against Cambridge in the final game. Matthias was selected to play for the French Universities team against Libya during his stay with the Swans.
Swansea C (Loaned from Paris St Germain, France on 6/2/2001) FL 12/3 Others 1

VICKERS Stephen (Steve)
Born: Bishop Auckland, 13 October 1967
Height: 6'1" Weight: 12.12
Club Honours: AMC '90; Div 1 '95
Steve was in excellent form for Middlesbrough last term and was one of the few players at the Riverside to enjoy a decent run of form even when the team were struggling. A very dependable 'stopper' centre half he gave his best at all times and produced some quality performances. His strong tackles and hefty clearances were just what the situation required and although he enjoys going forward for set pieces to try and nick a goal, he failed to find the net during the season.
Tranmere Rov (Signed from Spennymoor U on 11/9/1985) FL 310+1/11 FLC 20+1/5 FAC 19/3 Others 36/1
Middlesbrough (£700,000 on 3/12/1993) P/FL 246+11/8 FLC 27+2/3 FAC 17+1 Others 2

VICTORY Jamie Charles
Born: Hackney, 14 November 1975
Height: 5'10" Weight: 12.0
Club Honours: FAT '98; NC '99
International Honours: E: SP-1
Jamie had a frustrating time for Cheltenham Town in the 2000-01 campaign, suffering cruciate knee ligament damage in the 2-0 victory over Torquay in August. His rehabilitation took most of the season and it was only in the closing weeks that he began full training again. He is a left-sided defender with good pace who is very comfortable on the ball. He was sorely missed by the Robins last season and his long-awaited return will be akin to signing a new player.
West Ham U (From trainee on 1/7/1994)
Bournemouth (Free on 1/7/1995) FL 5+11/1 FLC 1+1 Others 1+1
Cheltenham T (Free on 1/7/1996) FL 49/5 FLC 3/1 FAC 2 Others 2

VIDUKA Mark Anthony
Born: Australia, 9 October 1975
Height: 6'2" Weight: 13.9
Club Honours: SLC '00
International Honours: Australia: 16; U23; Yth
Having missed the final six weeks of the 1999-2000 season with an ankle injury and then sorted out a new work permit, Mark eventually signed for Leeds United in the summer in time for the pre-season tour of Sweden, when he duly netted a hat-trick in his first game. However he remained without a goal in the first four competitive games of the campaign before departing to join the Australian squad for the Sydney Olympics tournament. Despite the Olyroos poor showing he returned a different player, and promptly scored on his first game back in the 6-0 thrashing of Besiktas, following this up with doubles in the next two games against Tottenham and Charlton. His most telling game was against Liverpool when he became the first Leeds striker to score four goals in a league game since Allan Clarke against Burnley in 1971. In a topsy-turvy game, he had four different types of chances and took them all to give Leeds a 4-3 victory. Superbly skilful for a big man and full of unselfish running, he complemented those around him brilliantly, particularly Alan Smith. Mark had an excellent season, notably in the Champions' League where his combative style gave him the edge over opponents and all at Elland Road look forward to a repeat performance next term.
Glasgow Celtic (Signed from NK Croatia Zagreb, Croatia, ex Melbourne Knights, on 2/12/1998) SL 36+1/30 SLC 4/1 SC 3/3 Others 4/1
Leeds U (£6,000,000 on 25/7/2000) PL 34/17 FLC 1 FAC 2/1 Others 16/4

Jamie Victory

VIEIRA Patrick
Born: Dakar, Senegal, 23 June 1976
Height: 6'4" Weight: 13.0
Club Honours: PL '98; FAC '98; CS '98, '99
International Honours: France: 44 (WC '98, UEFA '00)

After experiencing the sweet success of winning Euro 2000 with France, the start of Patrick's season was soured by two red cards in the opening two games. He quickly put his disciplinary problems behind him and went on to produce some excellent performances for the Gunners. A world-class figure in the centre of midfield he is a fantastic ball winner who uses quick, short passes and one-twos as a platform to spring forward into attack. He has the ability to take the game to the opposition and produce driving runs through the middle of the park. Patrick is also capable of scoring spectacular goals. His total of six for the 2000-2001 season included a brace at Chelsea in a two-goal comeback, and the all-important equaliser in the FA Cup semi-final at Old Trafford against Tottenham. He was honoured by his fellow professionals with a place in the PFA's Premiership team.

Arsenal (£3,500,000 from AC Milan, Italy, ex Cannes, on 14/8/1996) PL 152+6/14 FLC 5 FAC 23+2/2 Others 34

VIGNAL Gregory
Born: Montpellier, France, 19 July 1981
Height: 6'0" Weight: 12.4
Club Honours: FAC '01; UEFAC '01
International Honours: France: Yth (UEFA-U18 '00)

Having done well for the France U18 team that won the UEFA championship in the summer, Gregory joined Liverpool soon afterwards but was not expected to see much senior action in his first season at Anfield. However he made rapid progress and after making his debut as a substitute in the FA Cup third round tie against Rotherham in January he was called up for his first full game at home to West Ham United the following month as a replacement for Jamie Carragher. He held his place for the subsequent game at Sunderland when he performed admirably, and several further appearances followed, enabling him to rise above his compatriot Djimi Traore in the pecking order for the left-back slot at Anfield.

Liverpool (£500,000 from Montpellier, France on 29/9/2000) PL 4+2 FAC 0+1

VILJANEN Ville
Born: Finland, 2 February 1971
Height: 6'2" Weight: 13.5
International Honours: Finland: 1

Although Ville was a regular in the Port Vale line-up in the first half of last season he failed to live up to the promise he had shown in the 1999-2000 campaign and struggled to score goals. He then lost his place in the team to newcomer Stephen Brooker and rarely featured after that. A tall and solid striker he was released by Vale in May.

Port Vale (Free from Vastra Frolunda, Sweden, ex Sandarna, BK Hacken, on 25/2/1999) FL 26+8/6 FLC 2 FAC 1 Others 0+1

VINCENT Jamie Roy
Born: Wimbledon, 18 June 1975
Height: 5'10" Weight: 11.8

Jamie had a somewhat frustrating time at Huddersfield last term. He began the season wearing a cast on a wrist that had been broken in a freak domestic accident and then missed some time with an ankle injury. A return against Barnsley at the McAlpine, marked his 50th appearance for the club, before another injury put him on the sidelines yet again. He returned for the 1-1 draw against Nottingham Forest but in February he was sold on to Portsmouth for a substantial fee. Steve Claridge's only signing during his time as caretaker-manager at Pompey he more than adequately filled the gap left by the injured Justin Edinburgh on the left-hand side of the defence. Jamie is a solid left back who defends strongly and is always willing to support the attack with his accurate crossing and passes.

Crystal Palace (From trainee on 13/7/1993) FL 19+6 FLC 2+1/1 FAC 1
Bournemouth (Loaned on 18/11/1994) FL 8
Bournemouth (£25,000 + on 30/8/1996) FL 102+3/5 FLC 7+1 FAC 8 Others 9/1
Huddersfield T (£440,000 + on 25/3/1999) FL 54+5/2 FLC 3+2 FAC 2
Portsmouth (£800,000 on 23/2/2001) FL 14

VINE Rowan Lewis
Born: Basingstoke, 21 September 1982
Height: 6'1" Weight: 12.2

A product of Portsmouth's youth system, Rowan did well enough in the club's reserve and youth teams to earn a call-up for the

first-team squad, He made his Football League debut when he came on as a substitute for the home game with Sheffield United shortly before Christmas. A promising striker who is a good header of the ball, he also featured from the bench against Fulham later in the season. A former trainee he was reported to have signed a new long-term contract for boss Graham Rix.
Portsmouth (From trainee on 27/4/2001) FL 0+2

VINNICOMBE Christopher (Chris)
Born: Exeter, 20 October 1970
Height: 5'9" Weight: 10.12
Club Honours: SPD '91
International Honours: E: U21-12

Chris had his best season to date for Wycombe in 2000-01 when he was a fixture in the left-back position. A tireless worker the hallmarks of his game are a dogged shadowing of opposition strikers and some surging runs down the wing. He netted his first senior goal for the Chairboys with a spectacular 30-yard free kick against Wrexham in April.
Exeter C (From trainee on 1/7/1989) FL 35+4/1 FLC 5/1 Others 2
Glasgow R (£150,000 on 3/11/1989) SL 14+9/1 SLC 1+2 Others 1
Burnley (£200,000 on 30/6/1994) FL 90+5/3 FLC 9 FAC 2 Others 7+1/1
Wycombe W (Free on 6/8/1998) FL 114+4/1 FLC 9 FAC 12 Others 4

Jamie Vincent

VIRGO Adam John
Born: Brighton, 25 January 1983
Height: 6'2" Weight: 13.7
This young Brighton central defender made his debut in senior football when coming on as a substitute in the LDV Vans tie against Brentford. Although still in his teens he showed maturity and composure in his subsequent appearances and never let the team down. Strong in the air and calm under pressure he looks to have a promising future in the game.
Brighton & Hove A (From juniors on 4/7/2000) FL 2+4 Others 0+1

VIVAS Nelson David
Born: Buenos Aires, Argentina, 18 October 1969
Height: 5'6" Weight: 10.6
International Honours: Argentina: 34
A valuable member of the Arsenal squad, Nelson is a very versatile player who is equally comfortable in either a defensive or midfield berth. He was very much on the fringe of the first team for much of last season, filling in when needed and making a total of eight starts. A stocky, competitive player who never gives less than a 100 per cent, Nelson still occasionally featured for Argentina.
Arsenal (£1,600,000 from Lugano, Switzerland, ex Quilmes, Boca Juniors, on 5/8/1998) PL 14+26 FLC 4/1 FAC 5+4 Others 6+10

VIVEASH Adrian Lee
Born: Swindon, 30 September 1969
Height: 6'2" Weight: 12.13
Signed by Reading on a 'Bosman' free transfer during the 2000 close season Adrian settled down quickly and showed that he had matured considerably since his previous loan spells at the club. A near ever-present he proved himself to be a tough competitor in the heart of the defence playing with great composure. Strong in the air and with a great determination to win, he saved many dangerous situations for the Royals with his expert sliding tackles.
Swindon T (From trainee on 14/7/1988) FL 51+3/2 FLC 6+1 FAC 0+1 Others 2
Reading (Loaned on 4/1/1993) FL 5 Others 1/1
Reading (Loaned on 20/1/1995) FL 6
Barnsley (Loaned on 10/8/1995) FL 2/1
Walsall (Free on 16/10/1995) FL 200+2/13 FLC 12 FAC 15/2 Others 13/1
Reading (Free on 6/7/2000) FL 40/2 FLC 2 FAC 3 Others 5

VOLZ Moritz
Born: Siegen, Germany, 21 January 1983
Height: 5'11" Weight: 12.7
Club Honours: FAYC '00, '01
International Honours: Germany: Yth
A former captain of Germany U15s, Moritz has been a key figure for the Arsenal youth team in recent seasons, appearing in their FA Youth Cup winning teams in both 1999-2000 and last term when he scored in the first leg of the final against Blackburn. A powerful, pacy right back who is highly rated at Highbury he made his first-team debut in the Worthington Cup defeat against Ipswich Town in November.
Arsenal (Free from Schalke 04, Germany on 25/1/2000) FLC 1

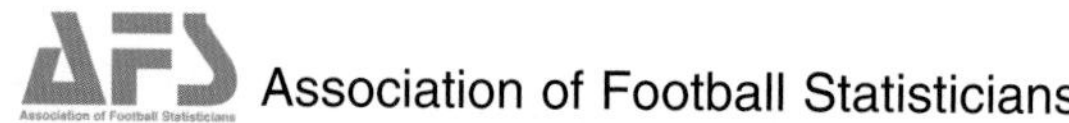

Association of Football Statisticians

The AFS is the world's largest organisation for football statisticians with 1200 members throughout the world.

We have the most comprehensive web-based databases of football and player statistics, which are updated daily. On the AFS website you'll find all manner of statistics, historical archives and latest news, together with our live Matchtracker where you can follow games live on the net. As a member you can also enjoy the members only area of the website, where you can read and help build the AFS Reports online and take part in the Members Bulletin Board, a forum for football discussion on the net.

As a subscriber to the AFS you will receive quarterly AFS Reports packed full of football articles, statistical analyses, members feedback, obituaries and classified advertisements.

If you would like to subscribe to the AFS, please photocopy, complete and send the form below to our office.

Please return this form to our office along with cheques made payable to "The AFS".

Subscription Rates 2001-2002

UK & Europe £21.00 .... ☐

Overseas £30.00 .... ☐

Corporate £100.00* .... ☐

I am a New Member .... ☐

Individual Life Membership .... ☐

Age Band (see right) .... ☐

Reduced to £25.00 for Charitable & Educational Institutions.

AFS Individual Life Membership

Age Band	Current Age	£
A	Under 25	525
B	25 to 29	511
C	30 to 34	483
D	35 to 39	462
E	40 to 44	420
F	45 to 49	385
G	50 to 54	329
H	55 to 59	315
I	60 to 64	273
J	65 to 69	168
K	70 and over	105

Name ______________________

Address ______________________

____

______________________ Postcode ______________________

Telephone ______________________ Team/Club ______________________

E-mail address: ______________________

*Credit Card Number: ______________________ Exp: ______________________

SUMMER 2001
REPORT 112
THE ASSOCIATION OF FOOTBALL STATISTICIANS

***If you wish The AFS to automatically renew your subscription each period until otherwise advised using the above credit card details, please tick this box**......... ☐

AFS, 18 St Philip Square, London SW8 3RS, UK
Tel. 020 7498 8906 Fax. 020 7720 7525
http://www.the-afs.com

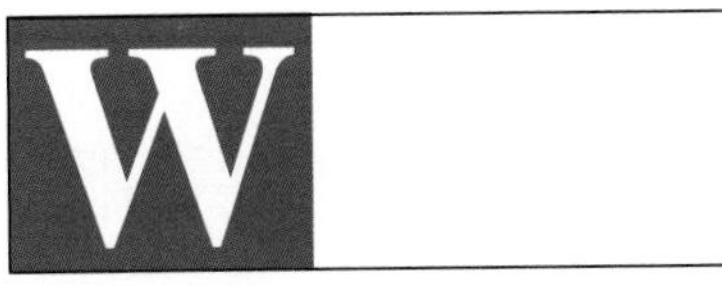

WAINWRIGHT Neil
Born: Warrington, 4 November 1977
Height: 6'0" Weight: 11.5

This tall Sunderland winger made his only appearance of the 2000-01 season for the Black Cats against Luton in a 3-0 Worthington Cup victory in September before joining Halifax on loan the following month. He made his debut for the Shaymen against Hull City and impressed in a three-month spell with the Third Division club, creating numerous opportunities with his tricky wing play. He returned to the Stadium of Light in January to continue his development in the reserves.

Wrexham (From trainee on 3/7/1996) FL 7+4/3 FAC 1 Others 1
Sunderland (£100,000 + on 9/7/1998) FL 0+2 FLC 5+1
Darlington (Loaned on 4/2/2000) FL 16+1/4
Halifax T (Loaned on 13/10/2000) FL 13 FAC 1 Others 2

WALKER Desmond (Des) Sinclair
Born: Hackney, 26 November 1965
Height: 5'11" Weight: 11.13
Club Honours: FLC '89, '90; FMC '89, '92
International Honours: E: 59; U21-7

Des was once again a rock-like figure in the centre of the Sheffield Wednesday defence last season. He produced some outstanding displays, captaining the team and offering a great role model to the club's younger professionals. He is still quick, although perhaps a little slower than in his prime, but his ability to read the game is what makes him such a quality defender. Des played his 350th senior game for the Owls against Tranmere last February but he was out of contract in the summer and at the time of writing it was unclear whether he would remain at Hillsborough.

Nottingham F (From apprentice on 2/12/1983) FL 259+5/1 FLC 40 FAC 27 Others 14 (£1,500,000 to Sampodoria on 1/8/92)
Sheffield Wed (£2,700,000 on 22/7/1993) P/FL 307 FLC 28 FAC 24 Others 3

WALKER Ian Michael
Born: Watford, 31 October 1971
Height: 6'2" Weight: 13.1
Club Honours: FAYC '90; FLC '99
International Honours: E: 3; B-1; U21-9; Yth

Ian had a disappointing time at Tottenham last season when he lost his place as the club's number one 'keeper to new signing Neil Sullivan. He received very few first-team chances and even when he kept two consecutive clean sheets against Southampton and West Ham he could not persuade boss George Graham to restore him to the line-up. Still a very talented and agile goalkeeper it would seem that he might have to move on if he is to gain regular first-team football in the near future.

Tottenham H (From trainee on 4/12/1989) F/PL 257+2 FLC 22+1 FAC 25 Others 6
Oxford U (Loaned on 31/8/1990) FL 2 FLC 1

WALKER James Barry
Born: Sutton in Ashfield, 9 July 1973
Height: 5'11" Weight: 13.5

This brave and agile goalkeeper enjoyed a highly successful eighth season with Walsall in 2000-01. He gave one of his finest-ever displays in the Worthington Cup tie against West Ham and made a vital penalty save in the late-season game at Stoke when a play-off place hung in the balance. His safe handling was an inspiration to the whole side and he was selected for the PFA Division Two team. James has now overtaken his mentor Mick Kearns as the goalkeeper with most appearances in the history of the club.

Notts Co (From trainee on 9/7/1991)
Walsall (Free on 4/8/1993) FL 274+2 FLC 19 FAC 22 Others 19

WALKER Justin Matthew
Born: Nottingham, 6 September 1975
Height: 5'11" Weight: 12.12
International Honours: E: Yth; Sch

This skilful central midfield man had an excellent first campaign at Lincoln City culminating in him being voted 'Player of the Season' by the club's supporters. His partnership with his former Nottingham Forest team-mate John Finnigan in the middle of the park was one of Lincoln's successes of what was generally a disappointing season for the Imps. Justin created many chances for his colleagues but scored just twice himself - both against Chesterfield.

Nottingham F (From juniors on 10/9/1992)
Scunthorpe U (Signed on 26/3/1997) FL 126+6/2 FLC 8 FAC 6 Others 7/1
Lincoln C (Free on 12/7/2000) FL 44+1/1 FLC 1+1 FAC 1 Others 5/1

WALKER Richard Martin
Born: Birmingham, 8 November 1977
Height: 6'0" Weight: 12.0

A regular player within Aston Villa's reserve team last term, Richard appeared in the Inter Toto Cup semi-final second leg against Celta Vigo and also featured as a substitute in the FA Cup replay against Newcastle. In February he joined Blackpool for an extended loan period where he was required as cover for regular strikers John Murphy and Brett Ormerod. He proved most effective when coming on from the subs' bench and netted a total of three goals to help the Seasiders win a place in the play-offs. He is a quick striker who holds the ball up well and is good in the air.

Aston Villa (From trainee on 13/12/1995) PL 2+4/2 FLC 1+1 FAC 0+1 Others 1
Cambridge U (Loaned on 31/12/1998) FL 7+14/3 Others 1+2/1
Blackpool (Loaned on 9/2/2001) FL 6+12/3

WALKER Richard Neil
Born: Derby, 9 November 1971
Height: 6'0" Weight: 12.0
Club Honours: NC '99

Richard enjoyed a consistent season with Cheltenham Town last term. Operating at either left back in the absence of Jamie Victory, or in the centre of defence he produced some consistent performances for the Robins. A good all-round defender with fine positional sense and heading ability he is also a useful man-marker.

Notts Co (From trainee on 3/7/1990) FL 63+4/4 FLC 10 FAC 1+2 Others 8+1 (Free to Hereford U on 24/7/1997)
Mansfield T (Loaned on 23/3/1995) FL 4
Cheltenham T (Signed on 23/10/1998) FL 41+2 FLC 2

WALKER Richard Stuart
Born: Stafford, 17 September 1980
Height: 6'2" Weight: 13.0

One of the latest youngsters to graduate through Crewe's successful academy set-up, Richard stepped in to make his Football League debut at Preston last November. He also featured in the home game with Sheffield Wednesday soon afterwards, before being loaned to Dr Martens League outfit Halesowen Town in March. He was subsequently recalled to Gresty Road and played in the 3-3 draw at Wimbledon the following month. A very confident central defender he looks to be a great prospect.

Crewe Alex (From trainee on 6/7/1999) FL 2+1

WALKLATE Steven
Born: Durham, 27 September 1979
Height: 5'11" Weight: 12.0

This young midfielder gave some steady performances for Darlington at the start of last season and impressed with his calm approach and direct passing. He made his debut from the subs' bench against York City in early September and started four days later in the Worthington Cup tie at Nottingham Forest. However he then made only a handful of senior appearances for the Quakers before being released early in the new year and after a brief spell with Blyth Spartans he signed for Queen of the South where he featured regularly in the closing weeks of the campaign.

Middlesbrough (From trainee on 2/7/1998)
Darlington (Free on 14/2/2000) FL 2+4 FLC 2 FAC 0+1

WALLWORK Ronald (Ronnie)
Born: Manchester, 10 September 1977
Height: 5'10" Weight: 12.9
Club Honours: FAYC '95; PL '01
International Honours: E: Yth

Although Ronnie's contribution to Manchester United's continuing quest for honours was a little short in supply last season, he was determined to show Sir Alex Ferguson that he was ready for a place in the senior squad. After making a good start in a central defensive role at Ipswich at in August, he did a similar job against Bradford at Old Trafford in early September and featured mostly in the first half of the campaign. Ronnie will be hoping to make further progress at Old Trafford.

Manchester U (From trainee on 17/3/1995) PL 4+14 FLC 2+2 FAC 0+1 Others 1+1
Carlisle U (Loaned on 22/12/1997) FL 10/1 Others 2
Stockport Co (Loaned on 18/3/1998) FL 7

WALSCHAERTS Wim
Born: Antwerp, Belgium, 5 November 1972
Height: 5'10" Weight: 12.4

Wim was again a vital member of the

Leyton Orient team last term and only missed one Second Division game all season. He also netted some vital goals, but although he made the team for the play-off final against Blackpool he was unable to inspire the O's to victory. A consistent box-to-box player on the right-hand side of midfield he was out of contract at the end of the season and left the club on a free transfer.

Leyton Orient (Free from KFC Tielen, Belgium on 30/7/1998) FL 120+5/9 FLC 9+1 FAC 10/2 Others 5

WALSH David (Dave)
Born: Wrexham, 29 April 1979
Height: 6'1" Weight: 12.8
International Honours: W: U21-5

Dave had to be content with being second choice to Wrexham 'keeper Kevin Dearden for most of the 2000-01 campaign and spent a short spell on loan at League of Wales club Rhyl Town last February. He was eventually given his Football League debut against Luton in April and featured regularly for the Robins in the closing stages of the season. He is developing into a fine and alert shot stopper although he still needs to work to improve his distribution. He won further caps for Wales at U21 level against Belarus, Armenia and Ukraine.

Wrexham (From trainee on 4/7/1997) FL 5 Others 2

WALSH David Andrew
Born: Rochdale, 12 July 1983
Height: 6'1" Weight: 12.8

Having been at Spotland since U13 level this young Rochdale striker had worked his way up to the club's reserve team at the start of last season. He netted early on for the second string and with other strikers injured, suspended or ineligible he was a surprise choice on the subs' bench for the Worthington Cup tie at Blackburn. He came on for the last 25 minutes for his debut in senior football and looked extremely promising.

Rochdale (Trainee) FLC 0+1

WALSH Gary
Born: Wigan, 21 March 1968
Height: 6'3" Weight: 15.10
Club Honours: ECWC '91; ESC '91; FAC '94
International Honours: E: U21-2

Having been out injured for over six months, Gary returned to the Bradford City line-up for the Inter Toto Cup third round tie against Waalwijk but otherwise had to be content with being second choice to Matt Clarke in the early part of the 2000-01 campaign. In September he moved on loan to Middlesbrough to cover for the injured Mark Schwarzer but after three games he returned to Valley Parade with a muscle tear in his thigh. Sidelined for two months he regained his place in mid-December and held on to it for the remainder of the season. He produced a few 'Man of the Match' performances and showed great command of his area, but was unable to prevent the Bantams from dropping down to the First Division. Gary was voted as City's 'Players Player of the Year'.

Manchester U (From juniors on 25/4/1985) F/PL 49+1 FLC 7 Others 6
Airdrie (Loaned on 11/8/1988) SL 3 SLC 1
Oldham Ath (Loaned on 19/11/1993) PL 6
Middlesbrough (£500,000 on 11/8/1995) PL 44 FLC 9 FAC 4
Bradford C (£500,000 + on 26/9/1997) P/FL 111 FLC 7 FAC 4 Others 1
Middlesbrough (Loaned on 15/9/2000) PL 3

WALSH Michael Shane
Born: Rotherham, 5 August 1977
Height: 6'0" Weight: 13.2
Club Honours: AMC '01

Michael was in excellent form for Port Vale in 2000-01, coming in to the line-up for the local 'derby' against Stoke City in September and retaining his place for the remainder of the campaign. He seemed to play better as the season progressed and was a key figure in both the club's 16-match unbeaten run and their victory in the LDV Vans Trophy final against Brentford. Michael is a tall, solid defender who is strong in the tackle and possesses a powerful long throw.

Scunthorpe U (From trainee on 3/7/1995) FL 94+9/1 FLC 4 FAC 9 Others 5
Port Vale (£100,000 on 30/7/1998) FL 66+4/3 FLC 3+1 FAC 2 Others 7

WALSH Steven (Steve)
Born: Preston, 3 November 1964
Height: 6'3" Weight: 14.9
Club Honours: AMC '85; FLC '97, '00

This left-footed central defender had become 'Mr Leicester City' after spending over a decade at Filbert Street, but finally severed his connections with the Foxes last September when he stood in fifth place in all-time appearances for the club. He joined Norwich City on a free transfer, linking up with his former boss Bryan Hamilton, however injuries and other circumstances kept him out of the side and his contract was cancelled by mutual consent in December. After leaving Carrow Road he briefly figured for Tamworth, before setting up a coaching school for local youngsters back in Leicester in the spring.

Wigan Ath (From juniors on 11/9/1982) FL 123+3/4 FLC 7 FAC 6 Others 10+2
Leicester C (£100,000 on 24/6/1986) P/FL 352+17/53 FLC 39+1/4 FAC 16+1/1 Others 23/4
Norwich C (Free on 18/9/2000) FL 1+3 FLC 1

WALSHE Benjamin (Ben) Matthew
Born: Hammersmith, 24 May 1983
Height: 6'1" Weight: 12.12

Ben was yet another of the very promising youngsters at Queens Park Rangers who was blooded in the senior team in the closing weeks of the 2000-01 campaign. He made his Football League debut when he came off the subs' bench in the final home game of the season against Stockport County. A fast and direct winger he was a member of the U19s team that reached the FA Premier Academy final only to lose to Nottingham Forest in extra time.

Queens Park R (From trainee on 4/7/2000) FL 0+1

WALTERS Mark Everton
Born: Birmingham, 2 June 1964
Height: 5'10" Weight: 12.8
Club Honours: FAYC '80; ESC '82; SPD '89, '90, '91; SLC '89, '91; FAC '92; FLC '95
International Honours: E: 1; B-1; U21-9; Yth; Sch

Mark experienced a somewhat frustrating season with Bristol Rovers in 2000-01 when he made many of his appearances from the subs' bench. One of several players transfer listed by the Pirates in January he was then appointed temporary boss of the reserve team after Garry Thompson became caretaker-manager. Despite the disappointment of Rovers' relegation he finished the campaign on a personal high, netting two goals in the final day victory over Wrexham. Although now entering the twilight of his career Mark is still one of the most talented wide attacking players in the lower divisions and providing he remains fit he looks to have plenty more football left in him.

Aston Villa (From apprentice on 18/5/1982) FL 168+13/39 FLC 20+1/6 FAC 11+1/1 Others 7+3/2
Glasgow R (£500,000 on 31/12/1987) SL 101+5/32 SLC 13/11 SC 14/6 Others 10/2
Liverpool (£1,250,000 on 13/8/1991) F/PL 58+36/14 FLC 10+2/4 FAC 6+3 Others 8+1/1
Stoke C (Loaned on 24/3/1994) FL 9/2
Wolverhampton W (Loaned on 9/9/1994) FL 11/3
Southampton (Free on 18/1/1996) PL 4+1 FAC 4
Swindon T (Free on 31/7/1996) FL 91+21/25 FLC 9+1/2 FAC 3+1/2
Bristol Rov (Free on 17/11/1999) FL 39+17/13 FLC 0+5 FAC 0+1 Others 0+3

WALTON David (Dave) Lee
Born: Bedlington, 10 April 1973
Height: 6'2" Weight: 14.8
Club Honours: Div 3 '94

Dave was again troubled by injuries at Crewe for much of last season and only featured on a regular basis in the early part of the campaign. He returned for a brief spell in February, but was then sidelined again in the following month with hamstring trouble and failed to return to the line-up before the summer break. A commanding central defender he is particularly effective in the air.

Sheffield U (Free from Ashington on 13/3/1992)
Shrewsbury T (Signed on 5/11/1993) FL 127+1/10 FLC 7 FAC 10/1 Others 11/1
Crewe Alex (£500,000 + on 20/10/1997) FL 90+6/1 FLC 6 FAC 1

WALTON Mark Andrew
Born: Merthyr Tydfil, 1 June 1969
Height: 6'4" Weight: 15.8
International Honours: W: U21-1

Mark was ever-present in goal for Cardiff City last season until Carl Muggleton arrived to provide him with some competition. He returned for the last few games to help the Bluebirds clinch promotion to the Second Division and will be aiming to be first choice once again at Ninian Park in the 2001-02 campaign.

Luton T (From juniors on 21/2/1987)
Colchester U (£15,000 on 5/11/1987) FL 40 FLC 3 FAC 8 Others 5
Norwich C (£75,000 on 15/8/1989) FL 22 FLC 1 FAC 5

Wrexham (Loaned on 27/8/1993) FL 6
Dundee (Free on 27/1/1994)
Bolton W (Free on 2/3/1994) FL 3 (Free to Wroxham on 9/9/1994)
Fulham (Free from Fakenham T on 12/8/1996) FL 40 FLC 5 Others 3
Gillingham (Loaned on 6/2/1998) FL 1
Brighton & Hove A (£20,000 on 15/7/1998) FL 58 FLC 2 FAC 4 Others 2
Cardiff C (Free on 11/8/2000) FL 40 FLC 2 FAC 4 Others 1

WANCHOPE Pablo (Paulo) Cesar
Born: Costa Rica, 31 July 1976
Height: 6'4" Weight: 12.6
International Honours: Costa Rica

Signed from West Ham for a new club record fee, Paulo got off to a cracking start with a hat-trick for Manchester City on his home debut against Sunderland. However despite finishing the season as leading scorer he found himself on the transfer list and he didn't appear in the first-team line-up from the end of January until early April. He also appeared regularly for Costa Rica as the Central American nation mounted an effective campaign to qualify for the 2002 World Cup finals.

Derby Co (£600,000 from CS Heridiano, Costa Rica on 27/3/1997) PL 65+7/23 FLC 6+1/5 FAC 4
West Ham U (£3,250,000 on 28/7/1999) PL 33+2/12 FLC 3 FAC 0+1 Others 7+1/3
Manchester C (£3,650,000 on 16/8/2000) PL 25+2/9 FLC 3/1 FAC 1

Paulo Wanchope

WANLESS Paul Steven
Born: Banbury, 14 December 1973
Height: 6'1" Weight: 13.12

Paul had another fine campaign for Cambridge United in 2000-01 when he was voted 'Player of the Season' by the club's fans for the third successive year. A brave and tough-tackling midfield player he led the team from the front, always giving 100 per cent and also developed something of a goal-scoring touch netting ten goals during the season. Once again a near ever-present for the U's he has now made more than 200 Football League appearances for the club.

Oxford U (From trainee on 3/12/1991) FL 12+20 FLC 0+3/1 Others 2+2
Lincoln C (Free on 7/7/1995) FL 7+1 Others 2
Cambridge U (Free on 8/3/1996) FL 209+7/33 FLC 11 FAC 12+2/1 Others 5/1

WARD Ashley Stuart
Born: Manchester, 24 November 1970
Height: 6'2" Weight: 13.10

Having joined Bradford City during the close season, Ashley started the first four matches of the 2000-01 campaign on the substitutes' bench before breaking into the starting line-up. He was a regular choice for the next three months until a thigh strain forced him to miss five matches. Although he showed tremendous work rate he found goals hard to come by, and it was not until November that he found the net, hitting a double in the Worthington Cup game against Newcastle. His first Premiership goal was even longer in coming - not until March in fact - but even so the Bantams' fans were won over by his non-stop running and enthusiasm.

Manchester C (From trainee on 5/8/1989) FL 0+1 FAC 0+2
Wrexham (Loaned on 10/1/1991) FL 4/2 Others 1
Leicester C (£80,000 on 30/7/1991) FL 2+8 FLC 2+1 FAC 0+1 Others 0+1
Blackpool (Loaned on 21/11/1992) FL 2/1
Crewe Alex (£80,000 on 1/12/1992) FL 58+3/25 FLC 4/2 FAC 2/4 Others 7/5
Norwich C (£500,000 on 8/12/1994) P/FL 53/18 FLC 6/3 FAC 1
Derby Co (£1,000,000 on 19/3/1996) F/PL 32+8/9 FLC 1+1 FAC 2/1
Barnsley (£1,300,000 + on 5/9/1997) P/FL 45+1/20 FLC 9/4 FAC 6/1
Blackburn Rov (£4,250,000 + on 31/12/1998) P/FL 52+2/13 FLC 2 FAC 4+1
Bradford C (£1,500,000 on 18/8/2000) PL 24+9/4 FLC 2+1/2

WARD Darren
Born: Worksop, 11 May 1974
Height: 6'2" Weight: 14.2
Club Honours: Div 3 '98
International Honours: W: 1; B-1; U21-2

Darren was once again in fine form for Notts County last season and despite having a spell out through injury he produced his usual quota of superb displays, saving the Magpies time and time again. An accomplished shot stopper he was out of contract in the summer and was reported to have signed for local rivals Nottingham Forest.

Mansfield T (From trainee on 27/7/1992) FL 81 FLC 5 FAC 5 Others 6
Notts Co (£160,000 on 11/7/1995) FL 251 FLC 18 FAC 23 Others 10

WARD Darren Philip
Born: Harrow, 13 September 1978
Height: 6'0" Weight: 12.6

One of Watford's success stories of the 2000-01 season, Darren finally put his injury problems behind him and established himself as a first choice in the centre of defence partnering Robert Page. Tall and strong, Darren is commanding in the air, reads the game well and poses a considerable threat when he joins the attack at set pieces. He suffered a setback in November when he sustained what seemed to be a serious thigh injury, but was quickly back in the line-up. Darren's progress was recognised when he signed a new four-year contract for the Hornets during the campaign.

Watford (From trainee on 13/2/1997) P/FL 56+2/2 FLC 5/1 FAC 2 Others 0+1
Queens Park R (Loaned on 17/12/1999) FL 14 FAC 1

WARD Gavin John
Born: Sutton Coldfield, 30 June 1970
Height: 6'3" Weight: 14.12
Club Honours: Div 3 '93; WC '93; AMC '00

Stoke City's popular 'keeper held his place in the starting line-up for most of the early part of last season before succumbing to a back injury that kept him out of action for almost six months. He eventually returned towards the end of March and re-established himself in the side in the closing weeks of the campaign. A goalkeeper who is an excellent shot stopper and has firm control over his box he was sorely missed by City during his absence.

Shrewsbury T (From trainee at Aston Villa on 26/9/1988)
West Bromwich A (Free on 18/9/1989)
Cardiff C (Free on 5/10/1989) FL 58+1 FAC 1 Others 7
Leicester C (£175,000 on 16/7/1993) F/PL 38 FLC 3 FAC 0+1 Others 4
Bradford C (£175,000 on 13/7/1995) FL 36 FLC 6 FAC 3 Others 2
Bolton W (£300,000 on 29/3/1996) F/PL 19+3 FLC 2 FAC 4
Burnley (Loaned on 14/8/1998) FL 17
Stoke C (Free on 25/2/1999) FL 69 FLC 7 FAC 1 Others 11

WARD Mark Steven
Born: Sheffield, 27 January 1982
Height: 6'0" Weight: 11.2
International Honours: E: Sch

A regular for the England Schools' U18 team in 1999-2000 Mark signed forms for Sheffield United in the close season and did well for the club's double-winning reserve team. His performances earned him a call up to the first-team squad and he made his Football League debut at Bolton in the final game of the season when he came off the subs' bench for the last ten minutes. A promising striker who is a natural goal-scorer he will hope to add to his senior appearances in the coming season.

Sheffield U (Signed from Sheffield Colleges on 7/7/2000) FL 0+1

WARD Mitchum (Mitch) David
Born: Sheffield, 19 June 1971
Height: 5'8" Weight: 11.7

Having signed from Everton during the close season, Mitch took some time to win over the Barnsley fans, mostly due to a previous association with local rivals Sheffield United. However he featured regularly in the side throughout the campaign, despite suffering from a recurring ankle problem which kept him out from time to time. He received a boost when new boss Nigel Spackman took over early in the new year and along with the rest of the team his performances showed much improvement. Used mostly as a midfield ball winner at Oakwell he can also play equally well on either flank or at full back.

Mitch Ward

Sheffield U (From trainee on 1/7/1989) F/PL 135+19/11 FLC 8+3/2 FAC 7+2/2 Others 5+1/1
Crewe Alex (Loaned on 1/11/1990) FL 4/1 FAC 1/1 Others 2
Everton (£850,000 on 25/11/1997) PL 18+6 FLC 2+1 FAC 2
Barnsley (£20,000 on 14/7/2000) FL 34+2 FLC 3+1 FAC 1

WARD Scott
Born: Harrow, 5 October 1981
Height: 6'2" Weight: 13.0
Scott is yet another product of Luton Town's successful youth policy. A promising young goalkeeper he made his Football League debut in dramatic circumstances, coming on from the subs' bench after Mark Ovendale had received a red card at Brentford. His first task was to face the resulting penalty and he did so in style, turning Lloyd Owusu's spot kick round the left-hand post for a corner. With the departure of Nathan Abbey he will step up the pecking order of 'keepers at Kenilworth Road and will be looking to gain more senior experience in 2001-02.
Luton T (From trainee on 7/10/1998) FL 0+1

WARDLEY Shane David
Born: Ipswich, 26 February 1980
Height: 5'7" Weight: 9.10
Signed from Dr Martens League club Cambridge City, left-back Shane became the 34th player to make a first-team appearance for Southend United when he came on as a substitute at Darlington last March, thus establishing a new club record for the number of players used in a season. Small and nimble he will be aiming to win a regular place in Dave Webb's first team squad during the 2001-02 campaign.
Southend U (£5,000 from Cambridge C on 18/12/2000) FL 0+2

WARDLEY Stuart James
Born: Cambridge, 10 September 1975
Height: 5'11" Weight: 12.7
Although Stuart failed to repeat his fine form of the previous campaign in 2000-01 he still managed to retain his place in the Queens Park Rangers line-up for most of the season. A busy midfield player he seemed to lose his touch in front of goal and he eventually lost his place following a change in management and the arrival of Leon Knight on loan.
Queens Park R (£15,000 from Saffron Walden T on 22/7/1999) FL 67+10/4 FLC 1 FAC 3+2/3

WARE Paul David
Born: Congleton, 7 November 1970
Height: 5'9" Weight: 11.8
Paul started the 2000-01 campaign as a regular in the Rochdale squad however he suffered a couple of injuries and was absent for a large chunk in the middle of the season before regaining his place towards the end of February. A hard-working midfield player he will be aiming to feature more regularly in the starting line-up next term.
Stoke C (From trainee on 15/11/1988) FL 92+23/10 FLC 7+1 FAC 4+1 Others 12+2/4
Stockport Co (Signed on 8/9/1994) FL 42+12/4 FLC 6+1/1 FAC 2 Others 3/1 (Free to Hednesford T on 15/7/1997)
Cardiff C (Loaned on 29/1/1997) FL 5
Macclesfield T (Free on 14/7/1999) FL 9+9/2 FLC 1
Rochdale (Free on 10/7/2000) FL 17+13/2 FLC 2 FAC 1 Others 1

WARHURST Paul
Born: Stockport,, 26 September 1969
Height: 6'1" Weight: 13.6
Club Honours: PL '95
International Honours: E: U21-8
Paul's injury problems of old returned to haunt him last season and prevented him from getting a consistent run in the Bolton first team. Out for two months with hamstring trouble early on he still made a significant contribution to the club's successful promotion campaign. One of the most gifted and committed members of the Wanderers' squad, he was a vital member of the team when fit. Employed either in the centre of defence or midfield, he showed he was a highly gifted technical player, an excellent distributor of the ball and ferocious in the tackle. If he can remain injury free next term, he is likely to continue to feature regularly for the Reebok club as they fight to establish themselves in the Premiership.
Manchester C (From trainee on 1/7/1988)
Oldham Ath (£10,000 on 27/10/1988) FL 60+7/2 FLC 8 FAC 5+4 Others 2
Sheffield Wed (£750,000 on 17/7/1991) F/PL 60+6/6 FLC 9/4 FAC 7+1/5 Others 5/3
Blackburn Rov (£2,700,000 on 17/8/1993) PL 30+27/4 FLC 6+2 FAC 2+1 Others 4+2
Crystal Palace (£1,250,000 on 31/7/1997) P/FL 27/4 FLC 2 FAC 1
Bolton W (£800,000 on 25/11/1998) FL 51+8 FLC 2+3 FAC 3+1 Others 2+2

WARNE Paul
Born: Norwich, 8 May 1973
Height: 5'9" Weight: 11.2
Paul was the workhorse of the Rotherham team last season, when he seemed to cover every blade of grass on the pitch during each game. He set up many chances for his colleagues although his own goal tally was perhaps less than he would have liked. An all-action striker with a phenomenal work rate he will be looking forward to the experience of First Division football in the 2001-02 campaign. He was deservedly voted as the Millers 'Player of the Year'.

Wigan Ath (£25,000 from Wroxham on 30/7/1997) FL 11+25/3 FLC 0+1 FAC 1 Others 1+2/1
Rotherham U (Free on 15/1/1999) FL 102+4/25 FLC 3+1 FAC 5 Others 5

WARNER Anthony (Tony) Randolph
Born: Liverpool, 11 May 1974
Height: 6'4" Weight: 13.9
Club Honours: Div 2 '01

Tony had a great season in goal for Second Division champions Millwall in 2000-01. His substantial frame makes him a formidable opponent for opposing strikers while he is very agile for such a big man. He made many crucial saves and was able to see off the challenge of his able understudy Willy Gueret who provided him with some stiff competition for the first-team slot. A firm favourite of the club's fans he will no doubt approach the challenge of First Division football with his customary confidence.

Liverpool (From juniors on 1/1/1994)
Swindon T (Loaned on 5/11/1997) FL 2
Glasgow Celtic (Loaned on 13/11/1998) SL 3
Aberdeen (Loaned on 31/3/1999) SL 6
Millwall (Free on 16/7/1999) FL 80 FLC 6 FAC 4 Others 3

Tony Warner

WARREN Christer Simon
Born: Weymouth, 10 October 1974
Height: 5'10" Weight: 11.10

Christer joined Queens Park Rangers on a 'Bosman' free in June 2000 but had to wait until Ian Baraclough was sidelined with injury at the end of August to claim a regular first-team place. He later suffered an ankle injury himself although he recovered to feature a couple of times towards the end of the campaign. He is a pacy left wing back who is capable of delivering a fine cross from the flank.

Southampton (£40,000 from Cheltenham T on 31/3/1995) PL 1+7 FLC 1
Brighton & Hove A (Loaned on 11/10/1996) FL 3
Fulham (Loaned on 6/3/1997) FL 8+3/1
Bournemouth (£50,000 on 8/10/1997) FL 94+9/13 FLC 4+3 FAC 10/1 Others 7
Queens Park R (Free on 15/6/2000) FL 16+6

WARREN Mark Wayne
Born: Clapton, 12 November 1974
Height: 6'0" Weight: 12.2
International Honours: E: Yth

Mark began the 2000-01 season as an automatic choice in the Notts County line-up but was sidelined with a hamstring injury in October and although he made a brief return to the side in the new year he failed to shake off the problem before the end of the campaign. A pacy no-nonsense central defender who is strong in the tackle he will be hoping for a return to full fitness in the summer.

Leyton Orient (From trainee on 6/7/1992) FL 134+18/5 FLC 8+1/2 FAC 5+1 Others 10+4/1
Oxford U (Loaned on 24/12/1998) FL 4
Notts Co (Signed on 28/1/1999) FL 64+3/1 FLC 7 FAC 1 Others 2

WATERMAN David (Dave) Graham
Born: Guernsey, 16 May 1977
Height: 5'10" Weight: 13.2
International Honours: NI: U21-14

Dave made the Portsmouth squad under boss Tony Pulis at the beginning of last season, but was then affected by the managerial changes at Fratton Park and it was only towards the end of the campaign that he featured on a regular basis again. His preferred role is in the centre of defence where he excels as a man-marker, but he is also a tireless worker who is very effective in the challenge. Now approaching his mid-20s he will be hoping to finally establish himself in the team under new boss Graham Rix in 2001-02.

Portsmouth (From trainee on 4/7/1995) FL 52+19 FLC 4+1 FAC 3

WATKIN Stephen (Steve)
Born: Wrexham, 16 June 1971
Height: 5'10" Weight: 11.10
Club Honours: WC '95; Div 3 '00
International Honours: W: B-2; Sch

Steve featured regularly in attack for Swansea City last season until he was sidelined in the final weeks firstly with an ankle injury and then with a wrist problem. He is a hard-working striker with good control who is able to hold the ball up to bring his colleagues into play. Although never a prolific goal-scorer he still managed a respectable tally of seven goals in what was a very disappointing campaign for the Swans.

Wrexham (From juniors on 24/7/1989) FL 167+33/55 FLC 11+3/4 FAC 16+6/12 Others 17+5/4
Swansea C (£108,000 on 26/9/1997) FL 127+22/34 FLC 7/1 FAC 6+2/1 Others 2+2/1

WATSON Alexander (Alex) Francis
Born: Liverpool, 5 April 1968
Height: 6'1" Weight: 13.0
Club Honours: CS '88
International Honours: E: Yth

Perhaps distracted by his role as assistant-manager of a struggling team Alex never quite seemed to hit the high standards he had previously shown for Torquay during the 2000-01 campaign. He eventually lost his place following the defeat at Halifax towards the end of February and his only subsequent appearance was when he came off the subs' bench for the final minutes of the vital last-day encounter at Barnet. A commanding central defender who is good in the air he compensates for a certain lack of pace with an ability to read the game well.

Liverpool (From apprentice on 18/5/1985) FL 3+1 FLC 1+1 FAC 1+1 Others 1
Derby Co (Loaned on 30/8/1990) FL 5
Bournemouth (£150,000 on 18/1/1991) FL 145+6/5 FLC 14/1 FAC 12/1 Others 5
Gillingham (Loaned on 11/9/1995) FL 10/1
Torquay U (£50,000 on 23/11/1995) FL 201+1/8 FLC 11 FAC 10 Others 7/1

WATSON Kevin Edward
Born: Hackney, 3 January 1974
Height: 6'0" Weight: 12.6

Kevin captained Rotherham United to promotion from the Second Division last season when he was the only ever-present player in the squad. A midfield play maker who spreads passes around to great effect, he took the majority of free kicks and corners and enjoyed a purple patch of goal-scoring in October when he netted in four successive games. His efforts were rewarded with the offer of an extended contract before his current one had expired.

Tottenham H (From trainee on 15/5/1992) PL 4+1 FLC 1+1/1 FAC 0+1 Others 4
Brentford (Loaned on 24/3/1994) FL 2+1
Bristol C (Loaned on 2/12/1994) FL 1+1
Barnet (Loaned on 16/2/1995) FL 13
Swindon T (Free on 15/7/1996) FL 39+24/1 FLC 2+2 FAC 1+2
Rotherham U (Free on 31/7/1999) FL 90/6 FLC 4/1 FAC 5 Others 3

WATSON Mark Stewart
Born: Vancouver, Canada, 8 September 1970
Height: 6'0" Weight: 12.6
International Honours: Canada: 58 (Gold Cup 2000); U23-13

Having been released by Oxford United at the end of the 1999-2000 season Mark had trials with Wolves and DC United before linking up with his international colleague Carlo Corazzin at Oldham as boss Andy Ritchie sought to halt what appeared to be a slide towards relegation. Although he impressed in a reserve outing he made just two senior appearances before being released. He subsequently had a further trial with St Johnstone before returned to the United States and signing a contract with DC United in mid-January. Mark is an effective centre back who is solid in the air and able to anticipate danger quickly. He continued to represent Canada being a regular in the side and featuring in the Confederations Cup tournament during the summer.

Watford (Signed from Vancouver 86ers, Canada on 19/11/1993) FL 18 FAC 1+2 (Freed during 1995 close season)
Oxford U (Free from Osters IFV, Sweden on 17/12/1998) FL 57+1 FLC 2 FAC 8 Others 1
Oldham Ath (Free on 29/9/2000) FL 1+1 FLC 1

WATSON Paul Douglas
Born: Hastings, 4 January 1975
Height: 5'8" Weight: 10.10
Club Honours: Div 3 '99, '01

Paul was an ever-present for Third Division champions Brighton last season for whom he mostly featured at right back. He performed consistently throughout the campaign, creating many chances when moving up to join the attack and showing excellent distribution. Paul's dead-ball skills proved useful when taking free kicks and corners and he was also the club's penalty-taker for part of the campaign.

Gillingham (From trainee on 8/12/1992) FL 57+5/2 FLC 4 FAC 6 Others 5+3
Fulham (£13,000 on 30/7/1996) FL 48+2/4 FLC 3/1 FAC 2 Others 2
Brentford (£50,000 on 12/12/1997) FL 37 FLC 2 FAC 2 Others 0+1
Brighton & Hove A (£20,000 on 9/7/1999) FL 86+2/9 FLC 3/1 FAC 6/3 Others 4

WATSON Stephen (Steve) Craig
Born: North Shields, 1 April 1974
Height: 6'0" Weight: 12.7
International Honours: E: B-1; U21-12; Yth

Steve joined Everton in the summer of 2000, and immediately established himself as one of the club's most consistent players, both in terms of form and fitness. Whether used as an adventurous wing back, more restrained full back or out-and-out centre half, Steve's versatility was matched by his performances throughout a difficult Everton campaign. His high point was undoubtedly a dramatic injury-time FA Cup winner at Watford, but throughout the season Steve lent his support to Everton attacks and was responsible for directly creating a large proportion of the side's goals. Defensively he also proved solid, and an early season aberration apart at home to Ipswich, he enjoyed a sound first season at Goodison.

Newcastle U (From trainee on 6/4/1991) F/PL 179+29/12 FLC 10+6/1 FAC 13+4 Others 18+4/1
Aston Villa (£4,000,000 on 15/10/1998) PL 39+2 FLC 8+1/1 FAC 4
Everton (£2,500,000 on 12/7/2000) PL 34 FLC 2 FAC 2/1

WATTS Julian
Born: Sheffield, 17 March 1971
Height: 6'3" Weight: 13.7
Club Honours: FLC '97

Julian is an accomplished central defender who is strong in the air and tenacious in the tackle. He produced some confident displays at the back for Luton Town last season, his experience steadying the young defenders around him but he missed two months of the campaign with a hamstring problem and was unable to prevent the Hatters from being relegated to the Third Division. He was reported to have signed for Australian club Northern Spirit in the summer.

Rotherham U (Signed from Frecheville CA on 10/7/1990) FL 17+3/1 FLC 1 FAC 4 Others 2
Sheffield Wed (£80,000 on 13/3/1992) PL 12+4/1 FLC 1 Others 3
Shrewsbury T (Loaned on 18/12/1992) FL 9 Others 1
Leicester C (£210,000 on 29/3/1996) P/FL 31+7/1 FLC 6+1 FAC 2+1 Others 4
Crewe Alex (Loaned on 29/8/1997) FL 5
Huddersfield T (Loaned on 5/2/1998) FL 8
Bristol C (Free on 6/7/1998) FL 16+1/1 FLC 3+1
Lincoln C (Loaned on 18/12/1998) FL 2 Others 1
Blackpool (Loaned on 25/3/1999) FL 9
Luton T (Free on 6/8/1999) FL 71+2/8 FLC 6 FAC 8

WATTS Steven (Steve)
Born: Lambeth, 11 July 1976
Height: 6'1" Weight: 13.7

Steve was again a vital member of the Leyton Orient forward line last term, scoring a total of 11 valuable goals including one in the Worthington Cup tie against Newcastle and the first goal in the play-off semi-final against Hull. However he was later sent off in the latter game and missed the final through suspension. Steve originally entered the professional game as the winner of the Sun newspaper's 'Search for a Striker' competition in 1998 and is a big powerful front man.

Leyton Orient (Signed from Fisher on 14/10/1998) FL 45+51/20 FLC 4+2/2 FAC 4+2/1 Others 6/1

WEAH George
Born: Monrovia, Liberia, 1 October 1966
Height: 6'1" Weight: 12.10
Club Honours: FAC '00
International Honours: Liberia

A surprise signing by Manchester City boss Joe Royle during the summer, George formed a classy strike force with Paulo Wanchope at the start of last season. He played a major role in the 3-1 win over Sunderland when Wanchope notched a hat-trick and bagged a double himself in the Worthington Cup win over Gillingham. He also found the net on the Blues visit to Anfield, but shortly afterwards he was left out of the side and in October he moved on to join Marseilles. An extremely talented player, despite his advancing years, he showed tremendous skill on the ball but never really settled at Maine Road.

Chelsea (Loaned from AC Milan, Italy, ex Young Survivors, Bongrange, Mighty Barolle, Invincible Eleven, Tonerre Yaounde, AS Monaco, Paris St Germain, on 12/1/2000) PL 9+2/3 FAC 4/2
Manchester C (Free on 4/8/2000) PL 5+2/1 FLC 2/3

WEATHERSTONE Ross
Born: Reading, 16 May 1981
Height: 5'11" Weight: 11.10

Having recovered from the knee injury he suffered during the 1999-2000 and put his well-publicised off the field problems behind him Ross struggled to break into the Oxford United first-team squad last season. He made just one senior appearance featuring at right back against Bournemouth on Boxing Day before moving on to Conference club Boston United early in the new year. A versatile young defender who can also play at centre back he is the younger brother of Simon Weatherstone.

Oxford U (From trainee on 29/10/1999) FL 4 FAC 1 Others 2

WEATHERSTONE Simon
Born: Reading, 26 January 1980
Height: 5'10" Weight: 11.12

Simon found it difficult to win a place in the Oxford United team last season although he made a handful of appearances when Mike Ford was caretaker-manager following the departure of Dennis Smith. Mostly used as a striker by the U's he eventually moved on to Conference club Boston United with his brother Ross early in the new year. He did well with the York Street club netting five goals from 13 appearances and such form may well win another chance in the Football League in due course. He is a versatile player who is at home in a number of different positions.

Oxford U (From trainee on 27/3/1997) FL 25+27/3 FLC 1+3/1 Others 1

WEAVER Luke Dennis Spencer
Born: Woolwich, 26 June 1979
Height: 6'2" Weight: 13.2
International Honours: E: Yth; Sch

Luke had a disappointing season for Carlisle United in 2000-01. He began the campaign as first-choice 'keeper but lost his place after the defeat at Torquay and failed to regain it after Matty Glennon arrived on loan from Bolton. He remains a good shot stopper and he will be hoping to a return to first-team football in the coming season.

Leyton Orient (From trainee on 26/6/1996) FL 9 FAC 1 Others 1
Sunderland (£250,000 on 9/1/1998)
Scarborough (Loaned on 10/12/1998) FL 6
Carlisle U (Free on 6/8/1999) FL 43 FLC 4 Others 1

WEAVER Nicholas (Nicky) James
Born: Sheffield, 2 March 1979
Height: 6'3" Weight: 13.6
International Honours: E: U21-8

Having come up two divisions in two seasons with Manchester City, this highly rated 'keeper was keen to prove himself at the highest level. However the 2000-01 campaign proved to be a somewhat torrid time for Nicky, although playing in a struggling team did not help his cause. In the end he lost his place to newcomer Carlo Nash in April and failed to return before the summer break. His season was summed up by an incident playing for the reserves in the Manchester Senior Cup final, when with City cruising to a 4-1 victory he advanced to challenge for the ball, came in rather late and picked up both a yellow card and a bad knee injury. On a brighter note he added two more caps for the U21s and also appeared in the game in Italy that was abandoned after just 11 minutes. Nicky will be hoping for better fortune and a return to first-team football in 2001-02.

Mansfield T (Trainee) FL 1
Manchester C (£200,000 on 2/5/1997) P/FL 121 FLC 12 FAC 9 Others 3

WEBB Daniel (Danny) John
Born: Poole, 2 July 1983
Height: 6'1" Weight: 11.8
International Honours: E:

Danny was signed by Southend from Premiership club Southampton last December and showed considerable promise when thrown into the first team at Roots Hall. Although still a teenager he showed no signs of nerves and displayed

good vision, an excellent first touch and the ability to hold the ball up. He scored his first goal in senior football in the 3-3 draw at Plymouth last April and will be aiming to win a regular place in the starting line-up in the coming season. Danny is the son of Blues' manager Dave Webb.
Southend U (From trainee at Southampton on 4/12/2000) FL 6+9/1 FAC 1+1 Others 3

WEBB Paul Andrew
Born: Wolverhampton, 30 November 1967
Height: 5'9" Weight: 13.7
Club Honours: NC '00
International Honours: E: SP-11
At the age of 33 Paul took the big step of giving up his full-time job as a warehouse manager for a career as a professional footballer. A former trainee at Shrewsbury he went on to make his Football League debut for Kidderminster against Torquay on the opening day of the 2000-01 campaign and featured regularly for the Harriers in the first half of the season. He was then one of several players put on the transfer list by manager Jan Molby last January but forced his way back into the team and scored his only goal of the season with a 20-yard drive in the 3-1 win over local rivals Cheltenham in April.
Shrewsbury T (From apprentice on 30/11/1985. Free to Bromsgrove Rov during 1986 close season)
Kidderminster Hrs (£17,500 on 20/7/1994) FL 23+9/1 FAC 0+1 Others 1

Paul Webb

WEBBER Daniel (Danny) Vaughn
Born: Manchester, 28 December 1981
Height: 5'9" Weight: 10.8
International Honours: E: Yth
One of the many fine prospects at Old Trafford, Danny has scored regularly for the youth teams in recent seasons and was called up to the first team for the Worthington Cup fourth road tie against Sunderland, coming on as a substitute for Ronnie Wallwork during extra time. He is a lively young striker who is a constant threat inside the penalty box.
Manchester U (From trainee on 7/1/1999) FLC 0+1

WEBER Nicolas
Born: Metz, France, 28 October 1970
Height: 6'0" Weight: 12.10
A regular for French First Division side Le Havre in 1999-2000 Nicolas moved to Sheffield United on a three-month loan deal in the close season following his club's relegation. He began the new campaign in the Blades' first team but then lost his place to the in-form Wayne Quinn and was subsequently sidelined by injury until shortly before his loan period was due to end. He duly returned to Le Havre only to find some difficulty in regaining his first team place there. He is a left-sided wing back who is quick and has excellent control. He was reported to have joined Grenoble in the summer.
Sheffield U (Loaned from Le Havre, France, ex INF Vichy, Sochaux, Chateauroux, on 9/8/2000) FL 3+1 FLC 2

Davie Weir

WEIR David (Davie) Gillespie
Born: Falkirk, 10 May 1970
Height: 6'2" Weight: 13.7
Club Honours: S Div 1 '94; B&Q '94
International Honours: S: 20
One of the most commanding and consistent members of the Everton squad last term, Davie's status at Goodison was confirmed when he was made captain in the continued absence through injury of Richard Gough. A sharp, thoughtful centre half his reading of the game is impeccable and he has the ability to bring the ball intelligently out of defence, providing an excellent counter-attacking weapon. While a quiet and reserved demeanour means he rarely receives the praise his play deserves, Everton's fans are in no doubt as to his value to the team.
Falkirk (From Celtic BC on 1/8/1992) SL 133/8 SLC 5 SC 6 Others 5
Heart of Midlothian (Signed on 29/7/1996) SL 92/8 SLC 10/2 SC 9/2 Others 6
Everton (£250,000 on 17/2/1999) PL 83+3/3 FLC 3 FAC 7

WELCH Keith James
Born: Bolton, 3 October 1968
Height: 6'2" Weight: 13.7
Keith once again performed consistently in goal for Northampton Town last season. A vastly experienced 'keeper he is confident, calm under pressure and excellent at handling crosses. He also showed his versatility with a willingness to dribble the ball out of tricky situations when outside of his penalty area. He rarely missed a match throughout the campaign and he will be aiming to continue as first-choice at Sixfields in the coming season.
Rochdale (From Bolton W juniors on 3/3/1987) FL 205 FLC 12 FAC 10 Others 12
Bristol C (£200,000 on 25/7/1991) FL 271 FLC 20 FAC 13 Others 14
Northampton T (Free on 7/7/1999) FL 79 FLC 3 FAC 2 Others 1

WELLENS Richard Paul
Born: Manchester, 26 March 1980
Height: 5'9" Weight: 11.6
International Honours: E: Yth
Richard missed the opening matches of the 2000-01 season due to suspension but then went on to establish himself as a regular in the centre of the Blackpool midfield for the remainder of the campaign. Tigerish in the tackle he also displays some neat creative touches and has a good scoring record. He netted the winner against York last January with a brilliant free kick curled in from the edge of the penalty box.
Manchester U (From trainee on 19/5/1997) FLC 0+1
Blackpool (Signed on 23/3/2000) FL 39+5/8 FLC 2+1 FAC 1 Others 3+1

WELLER Paul Anthony
Born: Brighton, 6 March 1975
Height: 5'8" Weight: 11.2
One of the most satisfying aspects of Burnley's 2000-01 campaign was the re-emergence of Paul Weller after being sidelined for much of the previous two years with a stomach complaint. He began brightly, scoring the winning goal against Wimbledon in the first home league match of the season and he went on to enjoy his best season to date for the Clarets. Playing on the right, either as a wing back or in a more attacking role, Paul was a tigerish figure whose sheer effort was enough to win

Richard Wellens

a place in the side. Despite being one of the longest-serving players at Turf Moor he is also one of the youngest in the first-team squad and he can look forward to the future now that he has recovered full fitness. He was rewarded for his efforts when he won seven separate 'Player of the Year' awards from the various Clarets' supporters' clubs.
Burnley (From trainee on 30/11/1993) FL 119+28/9 FLC 7+2 FAC 6+2/1 Others 7

WELSH Stephen (Steve) George
Born: Glasgow, 19 April 1968
Height: 6'1" Weight: 12.6
This left-sided central defender had a frustrating season that saw him out of senior action until late February for although he overcame a pre-season ankle injury he was then kept out by a groin strain. When he finally returned to fitness he gave some excellent performances at the heart of Lincoln City's defence. However, at the end of the campaign Steve chose to retire from playing full-time to take up the post of Football in the Community officer at Sincil Bank.
Cambridge U (Free from Wimborne T on 22/6/1990) FL 0+1 Others 2
Peterborough U (Free on 8/8/1991) FL 146/2 FLC 20 FAC 8 Others 13
Partick Thistle (£40,000 on 23/12/1994) SL 55 SLC 3 SC 1
Peterborough U (Loaned on 9/7/1996) FL 6 FLC 3
Dunfermline Ath (£65,000 on 8/11/1996) SL 24+2 SC 2
Ayr U (Signed on 4/7/1998) SL 24+1 SLC 4/1
Lincoln C (Free on 5/8/1999) FL 42+1 FLC 1 Others 4+1

WEST Dean
Born: Morley, 5 December 1972
Height: 5'10" Weight: 12.2
Club Honours: Div 2 '97
Dean was Burnley's 'forgotten man' for much of 2000-01 but he finally broke into the first team eight matches from the end of the season. His performance was a key feature of the Clarets' biggest win of the campaign against Preston - solid in defence, dangerous going forward and playing a major part in the opening goal. A stocky and competitive right back he at least provided a timely reminder that he was still in contention for a first-team place.
Lincoln C (From trainee on 17/8/1991) FL 93+26/20 FLC 11/1 FAC 6/1 Others 5+2/1
Bury (Signed on 29/9/1995) FL 100+10/7 FLC 6 FAC 3 Others 2+1
Burnley (Free on 26/7/1999) FL 36+5 FLC 1+1 FAC 4 Others 1

WEST Taribo
Born: Port Harcourt, Nigeria, 26 March 1974
Height: 6'1" Weight: 12.7
International Honours: Nigeria: (OLYM '96)
This vastly experienced Nigerian international initially joined Derby County in a three-month loan deal and the agreement was later extended until the end of the season. He quickly settled into a position on the left side of a three-man defensive formation, adding invaluable experience to a struggling team. He lived up to his reputation as a highly skilled defender, proving to be quick in the tackle and in possession of superb distribution. His arrival quickly tightened up a defence which had been leaking far too many goals, and he was sorely missed when absent on international duty. An inspiration both to the younger players around him and to the Pride Park faithful for whom he soon became a cult figure, he was a key figure in ensuring the Rams preserved their Premiership status for another season.
Derby Co (Loaned from AC Milan, Italy, ex Sharks Port Harcourt, Enugu Rangers, Julius Berger, Auxerre, Inter Milan, on 16/11/2000) PL 18 FLC 1 FAC 1

WESTERVELD Sander
Born: Enschede, Holland, 23 October 1974
Height: 6'3" Weight: 13.12
Club Honours: FLC '01; FAC '01; UEFAC '01
International Honours: Holland: 5; U21; Yth
Having enjoyed an excellent first season at Liverpool Sander remained first choice throughout last term, appearing in every senior game with the exception of two Worthington Cup ties. He looked a little shaky during the first half of the campaign although the Reds' defence as a whole lacked a certain amount of cohesion but his form improved after Christmas. He was particularly impressive in the titanic battles with Roma and Barcelona in the UEFA Cup ties and finished with three winners' medals for the Worthington, FA and UEFA Cups. A superb shot stopper he spreads his huge frame to deny opposition strikers a clear sight of their target but still needs to improve on his handling of crosses and corners.
Liverpool (£4,000,000 from Vitesse Arnhem, Holland, ex Twente, on 18/6/1999) PL 74 FLC 5 FAC 8 Others 13

WESTON Rhys David
Born: Kingston, 27 October 1980
Height: 6'1" Weight: 12.3
International Honours: E: Yth; Sch. W: 1; U21-4
After developing with Arsenal reserves, Rhys made the starting line-up for the Worthington Cup third round tie against Ipswich Town before Sam Hammam came in to sign him for Cardiff City. Rhys had something of a mixed season at Ninian Park showing moments of real quality at times but seeming to lose concentration on other occasions. A versatile player who appeared for the Bluebirds in defence, at wing back

and in midfield he can generally feel satisfied with his first campaign of regular senior football which ended with the club winning promotion from the Third Division. He also appeared regularly for the Wales U21 team during the season winning four more caps.

Arsenal (From trainee on 8/7/1999) PL 1 FLC 1+1
Cardiff C (£300,000 on 21/11/2000) FL 25+3 FAC 3 Others 1

WESTWOOD Ashley Michael
Born: Bridgnorth, 31 August 1976
Height: 6'0" Weight: 12.8
Club Honours: FAYC '95
International Honours: E: Yth

Ashley appeared in a couple of Inter Toto fixtures for Bradford City in the 2000 close season before moving on loan to Sheffield Wednesday last August. He did well enough to earn a permanent transfer and he went on to become a regular figure in the centre of the Owls' defence. He linked up again with his old manager Paul Jewell and looked a useful acquisition, helping to provide a more solid look to the back line at Hillsborough. Ashley has great drive and enthusiasm and his height and mobility make him very useful when joining the attack for set pieces.

Manchester U (From trainee on 1/7/1994)
Crewe Alex (£40,000 on 26/7/1995) FL 93+5/9 FLC 8 FAC 9/2 Others 10
Bradford C (£150,000 on 20/7/1998) P/FL 18+6/2 FLC 1 FAC 2+1 Others 1+1
Sheffield Wed (£150,000 + on 10/8/2000) FL 32+1/2 FLC 5/3

WESTWOOD Christopher (Chris) John
Born: Dudley, 13 February 1977
Height: 6'0" Weight: 12.2

Chris gave some solid performances at the heart of the Hartlepool defence in the 2000-01 campaign when he was one of the club's most consistent players. An ever-present in what was usually a three-man central defence, he was a key figure for Pool providing stability at a time when other senior defenders were sidelined for long spells through injury. He is a hard-working and stylish defender who has great composure on the ball.

Wolverhampton W (From trainee on 3/7/1995) FL 3+1/1 FLC 1+1 (Released during 1998 close season)
Hartlepool U (Signed from Telford U on 24/3/1999) FL 82+5/1 FLC 2 FAC 3 Others 10

Sander Westerveld

WETHERALL David
Born: Sheffield, 14 March 1971
Height: 6'3" Weight: 13.12
International Honours: E: Sch

David began last season as a regular in the heart of the Bradford City defence but had the misfortune to suffer a groin injury in November that required corrective surgery and it was not until the end of February that he returned to the Bantams' line-up. However he then suffered a further groin problem that kept him out of the last eight games of the campaign. One of the club's most consistent players over the previous two seasons he was sorely missed when he was out injured. A dominant centre half his distribution was outstanding and his height proved useful when joining the attack at set pieces.

Sheffield Wed (From trainee on 1/7/1989)
Leeds U (£125,000 on 15/7/1991) F/PL 188+14/12 FLC 19+1/2 FAC 21+3/4 Others 4
Bradford C (£1,400,000 on 7/7/1999) PL 56/3 FLC 4/2 FAC 1 Others 3

David Wetherall

WHALLEY Gareth
Born: Manchester, 19 December 1973
Height: 5'10" Weight: 11.12

Gareth started the 2000-01 campaign as a regular in midfield for Bradford City but then had to miss three months in the middle of the season after having a hernia operation. Best used in a 'holding' role in the centre of the park, his passing and distribution are excellent, and he has a thoughtful approach to his play, showing fine vision. He returned for the Bantams in the middle of March and was soon back to top form.

Crewe Alex (From trainee on 29/7/1992) FL 174+6/9 FLC 10+1/1 FAC 15+1/4 Others 24/3
Bradford C (£600,000 on 24/7/1998) P/FL 78+2/3 FLC 10/2 FAC 2 Others 5+1

WHEATCROFT Paul Michael
Born: Bolton, 22 November 1980
Height: 5'9" Weight: 9.11
International Honours: E: Yth; Sch

Capped by England at both U16 and U18 levels, Paul had spent part of the 1999-2000 season in South Africa with Manchester United's satellite club FC Fortune before being released and joining Bolton Wanderers. A pacy striker who impressed at reserve level, he made his senior debut in the Worthington Cup first round second leg tie at Macclesfield and also featured in the FA Cup games against Scunthorpe and Blackburn. Having received a taste of first-team football he will be hoping to gain further experience in 2001-02.

Manchester U (From trainee on 8/7/1998)
Bolton W (Free on 6/7/2000) FLC 0+1 FAC 0+2

WHELAN Noel David
Born: Leeds, 30 December 1974
Height: 6'2" Weight: 12.3
Club Honours: FAYC '93
International Honours: E: U21-2; Yth (UEFA-U18 '93)

Having joined Middlesbrough in the close season, Noel slotted in well at the Riverside and helped invigorate the Boro' side with his enthusiasm and gusto. He featured regularly in the squad, although more often than not from the subs' bench, but managed just a single Premiership goal. A lively front runner with good ball skills he will be hoping to get back on the goal trail in the 2001-02 campaign.

Leeds U (From trainee on 5/3/1993) PL 28+20/7 FLC 3+2/1 FAC 2 Others 3
Coventry C (£2,000,000 on 16/12/1995) PL 127+7/31 FLC 6/1 FAC 15+1/7
Middlesbrough (£2,200,000 on 4/8/2000) PL 13+14/1 FLC 3/1 FAC 0+2

WHELAN Philip (Phil) James
Born: Stockport, 7 March 1972
Height: 6'4" Weight: 14.7
International Honours: E: U21-3

Phil joined Southend United in the 2000 summer break and was immediately appointed club captain. Commanding in the air and with an excellent sense of timing on the ground, he helped to shore up a defence that had conceded far too many goals in recent seasons. He firstly formed an effective partnership with Leo Roget and later with Carl Hutchings in the centre of the Blues' defence. Phil opened his goals account at Roots Hall when he netted in the 3-0 win over Rochdale last March.

Ipswich T (From juniors on 2/7/1990) F/PL 76+6/2 FLC 6+1 FAC 3+1 Others 1
Middlesbrough (£300,000 on 3/4/1995) PL 18+4/1 FLC 5 FAC 3
Oxford U (£150,000 on 15/7/1997) FL 51+3/2 FLC 3/1 FAC 5 Others 3
Rotherham U (Loaned on 12/3/1999) FL 13/4
Southend U (Free on 4/7/2000) FL 40+2/1 FLC 1+1 FAC 4 Others 5/1

WHITBREAD Adrian Richard
Born: Epping, 22 October 1971
Height: 6'1" Weight: 12.12

Having been captain at Portsmouth in the 1999-2000 campaign, Adrian found himself surplus to requirements last term and in November new Luton boss Lil Fuccillo snapped him up to try and plug a leaking defence. The move was a success but attempts to make the deal permanent fell through and he subsequently returned to Fratton Park before joining Reading on loan. He established a very effective central defensive partnership with Adrian Viveash and was a key figure in the Royals' line-up to the extent that they lost just two of the 19 games in which he appeared. Unfortunately, his loan period could not be extended to cover the play-off matches, but he has since reportedly joined the club on a two-year contract. He is a solid and dependable central defender who is an excellent man-marker and a good motivator of his colleagues in the back line.

Leyton Orient (From trainee on 13/11/1989) FL 125/2 FLC 10+1 FAC 11/1 Others 8
Swindon T (£500,000 on 29/7/1993) P/FL 35+1/1 FAC 2
West Ham U (£650,000 on 17/8/1994) PL 3+7 FLC 2+1 FAC 1
Portsmouth (Loaned on 9/11/1995) FL 13
Portsmouth (£250,000 on 24/10/1996) FL 133+1/2 FLC 8/1 FAC 3
Luton T (Loaned on 23/11/2000) FL 9 FAC 4
Reading (Loaned on 8/2/2001) FL 19

WHITE Alan
Born: Darlington, 22 March 1976
Height: 6'1" Weight: 13.2

Alan began the 2000-01 campaign as a regular in the Colchester United defence but lost his place in the team following the disastrous Boxing Day defeat at Millwall. He returned to the starting line-up in March and played an important role for the U's as they successfully avoided the drop to the Third Division. A commanding centre half in either a back four or three he can dominate opposing strikers with his supremacy in the air.

Middlesbrough (From trainee on 8/7/1994) Others 1
Luton T (£40,000 on 22/9/1997) FL 60+20/3 FLC 3+3 FAC 2 Others 4
Colchester U (Loaned on 12/11/1999) FL 4 Others 1
Colchester U (Free on 19/7/2000) FL 29+3 FLC 4 FAC 1

WHITE Andrew (Andy)
Born: Swanwick, 6 November 1981
Height: 6'4" Weight: 13.4

Andy is one of several talented youngsters on Mansfield Town's books and made his Football League debut when he came on from the subs' bench in the 2-1 win over Cardiff last April. A big strong target man he made a few more appearances as a substitute towards the end of last season and will be aiming to feature more regularly in the first-team squad in 2001-02.

Mansfield T (Signed from Hucknall T on 13/7/2000) FL 0+4

WHITE Jason Gregory
Born: Meriden, 19 October 1971
Height: 6'0" Weight: 12.10

Jason joined Cheltenham Town in July 2000 but although he made regularly appearances in the early part of last season, he never really seemed to find his best form and failed to score a single goal. As the campaign progressed he was increasingly limited to late appearances from the subs' bench and he was eventually placed on the transfer list by manager Steve Cotterill, despite having another year of his contract to run. He is a brave and strong striker with a good goals-per-game record throughout his career and given the right opportunities he will no doubt start scoring again.

Derby Co (From trainee on 4/7/1990)
Scunthorpe U (Free on 6/9/1991) FL 44+24/16 FLC 2 FAC 3+3/1 Others 4+4/1
Darlington (Loaned on 20/8/1993) FL 4/1
Scarborough (Free on 10/12/1993) FL 60+3/20 FLC 2+1 FAC 5/1 Others 1
Northampton T (£35,000 on 15/6/1995) FL 55+22/18 FLC 1+4 FAC 3 Others 5+2
Rotherham U (£25,000 on 9/9/1997) FL 52+21/22 FLC 2 FAC 3+1/1 Others 3/1
Cheltenham T (Free on 10/7/2000) FL 8+19 FLC 1 FAC 0+1 Others 1

WHITEHALL Steven (Steve) Christopher
Born: Bromborough, 8 December 1966
Height: 5'10" Weight: 11.5

Steve managed just three brief appearances from the subs' bench for Oldham Athletic last season before joining Conference outfit Chester City on loan in September. He got off to a great start, netting two goals on his debut at Kingstonian and the transfer was made permanent a couple of weeks later. He went on to find the net regularly for the remainder of the season finishing with a respectable tally of 12 goals in 32 games. He is a strong-running striker with a good goal-scoring record throughout his career.

Rochdale (£20,000 from Southport on 23/7/1991) FL 212+26/75 FLC 10+3/4 FAC 13+2/3 Others 15+1/10
Mansfield T (£20,000 on 8/8/1997) FL 42+1/24 FLC 2 FAC 2/1 Others 2/1
Oldham Ath (£50,000 on 10/7/1998) FL 55+21/13 FLC 0+3 FAC 6+1/2 Others 2

WHITEHEAD Damien Stephen
Born: Whiston, 24 April 1979
Height: 5'10" Weight: 11.7

This young Macclesfield striker remained a favourite with the club's supporters last season for his goal-scoring ability and unpredictability although he mostly featured from the subs' bench. His pace within the 18-yard box upsets defenders and he certainly has an eye for goal, scoring regularly with a mixture of headers and close-range efforts. However, Damien is still on a learning curve, but with additional work on some aspects of his overall play he could develop into a quality player.

Macclesfield T (Signed from Warrington T on 6/8/1999) FL 19+37/14 FLC 0+2 FAC 0+1 Others 1+1

WHITEHEAD Dean
Born: Oxford, 12 January 1982
Height: 5'11" Weight: 12.1

Having received a brief introduction to senior football in the 1999-2000 campaign Dean began to fulfil some of his promise last season. He featured in several games early on but then took some time to win over new boss David Kemp before he was given another run in the side. He is a busy midfield player who always wants to be in on the action and uses the ball very effectively. He was rewarded for his efforts when he received the club's 'Young Player of the Year' award.

Oxford U (From trainee on 20/4/2000) FL 16+4 FLC 2 FAC 0+1 Others 0+1

WHITEHEAD Philip (Phil) Matthew
Born: Halifax, 17 December 1969
Height: 6'3" Weight: 15.10

An ever-present for Reading in their Second Division campaign last season, Phil provided a launch pad for many of the team's successes with some fine performances. A tall and commanding 'keeper he dominates his penalty box and is an excellent shot stopper. Having now firmly established himself as first choice at the Madejski Stadium he will be aiming to continue in a similar vein in the 2001-02 campaign.

Halifax T (From trainee on 1/7/1988) FL 42 FLC 2 FAC 4 Others 4
Barnsley (£60,000 on 9/3/1990) FL 16
Halifax T (Loaned on 7/3/1991) FL 9
Scunthorpe U (Loaned on 29/11/1991) FL 8 Others 2
Scunthorpe U (Loaned on 4/9/1992) FL 8 FLC 2
Bradford C (Loaned on 19/11/1992) FL 6 Others 4
Oxford U (£75,000 on 1/11/1993) FL 207 FLC 15 FAC 13 Others 3
West Bromwich A (£250,000 on 1/12/1998) FL 26 FLC 1/1 FAC 1
Reading (Signed on 7/10/1999) FL 57 FLC 2 FAC 5 Others 3

WHITEHEAD Stuart David
Born: Bromsgrove, 17 July 1976
Height: 5'11" Weight: 12.4

Stuart produced another season of consistent performances for Carlisle United in 2000-01. He was team captain and a virtual ever-present, playing a significant role in the closing weeks of the campaign when he marshalled the defence as they went on to record several clean sheets in key fixtures. He featured in the centre of defence and occasionally in a midfield role, scoring his first goal for the Cumbrians in the 2-1 victory over Mansfield in January.

Bolton W (Signed from Bromsgrove Rov on 18/9/1995)
Carlisle U (Free on 31/7/1998) FL 110+1/1 FLC 5 FAC 4 Others 2

WHITLEY James (Jim)
Born: Zambia, 14 April 1975
Height: 5'9" Weight: 11.0
International Honours: NI: 3; B-1

Jim was not in the first-team picture at all for Manchester City last term and spent virtually the whole of the season out on loan. He began at Norwich where he did a great job, even when asked to play out of position in a wide-left role, and scored an excellent goal in the 3-1 win at Stockport. He then enjoyed a spell at Swindon Town at the turn of the year where he looked promising in the centre of the park but returned to Maine Road after injuring a shoulder. Finally he joined Second Division Northampton Town in February remaining until the end of the season, he was again effective, mostly playing at right back. Essentially a neat and tidy midfielder he is best employed in a central role from where his busy style ensures that the opposition seldom get time to settle on the ball, although clearly he is a very versatile player. Out of contract in the summer he was released by City. Jim is the older brother of Jeff Whitley.

Manchester C (From juniors on 1/8/1994) FL 27+11 FLC 3+1/1 FAC 2+1 Others 0+1
Blackpool (Loaned on 20/8/1999) FL 7+1 FLC 1
Norwich C (Loaned on 24/8/2000) FL 7+1/1
Swindon T (Loaned on 15/12/2000) FL 2 FAC 1
Northampton T (Loaned on 27/2/2001) FL 13

WHITLEY Jeffrey (Jeff)
Born: Zambia, 28 January 1979
Height: 5'8" Weight: 11.2
International Honours: NI: 6; B-2; U21-17

At the start of the 2000-01 season Jeff found himself replaced in the Manchester City line-up by new signing Alfie Haaland, but he was soon back in the side for the game at Leeds and went on to enjoy an extended run in the line-up. He then suffered a knee injury that kept him out of action over the Christmas period, and although he returned in the new year he was in and out of the side for the remainder of the campaign. A hard-tackling midfield player who always gives 100 per cent effort he continued to feature for Northern Ireland, captaining the U21s and adding two appearances for the senior team.

Manchester C (From trainee on 19/2/1996) P/FL 96+25/8 FLC 9+1 FAC 2+2 Others 4
Wrexham (Loaned on 14/1/1999) FL 9/2

WHITLOW Michael (Mike) William
Born: Northwich, 13 January 1968
Height: 6'0" Weight: 12.12
Club Honours: Div 2 '90, Div 1 '92; FLC '97

Mike had a frustrating time last term at Bolton when his season was blighted by injuries. The worst of these was a groin problem that kept him out for over half the campaign, although other minor injuries meant that he only featured in a handful of first-team games. A vastly experienced competitor, Mike is an important part of the back four when fully fit and will be hoping for an injury-free season next time around.

Leeds U (£10,000 from Witton A on 11/11/1988) FL 62+15/4 FLC 4+1 FAC 1+4 Others 9
Leicester C (£250,000 on 27/3/1992) F/PL 141+6/8 FLC 12/1 FAC 6 Others 14
Bolton W (£500,000 + on 19/9/1997) P/FL 82+4/2 FLC 13+1 FAC 8 Others 2+3

WHITMORE Theodore (Theo)
Born: Jamaica, 5 August 1972
Height: 6'2" Weight: 11.2
International Honours: Jamaica

This very gifted Hull City midfield player displayed some excellent skills during the first half of the 2000-01 campaign attracting the attention of many higher grade clubs. However he suffered a tragic set back while back home on international duty last January when he was involved in a horrific car accident that saw the death of his fellow Jamaican international and close friend Steve Malcolm. Although Theo was only slightly injured he took some time to recover match fitness and his return to the team coincided with the Tigers' remarkable change of fortunes. He was allowed to miss the play-off games to play in the Copa Caribe tournament in Trinidad where he captained Jamaica for the first time. Theo remained a regular for his country winning a further 19 caps last season. He was placed on the open to offers list in the summer.

Hull C (Free from Seba U, Jamaica on 22/10/1999) FL 40+3/7 FLC 1 FAC 5+1 Others 2

WHITNEY Jonathan (Jon) David
Born: Nantwich, 23 December 1970
Height: 5'10" Weight: 13.8

Jon often had to be content with time on the bench in the 2000-01 campaign due to the fine form of other Hull City defenders. However with Steve Harper's departure to Darlington in February he stepped in at left back, only losing his place when Andy Holt arrived from Oldham. When Holt was moved further forward, Jon returned to the team and responded with the opening goal in the local 'derby' with Scunthorpe which set the Tigers on their way to victory. He followed with a series of typically solid performances to help guide Hull through to the play-offs. Out of contract in the summer his future was unclear at the time of writing.

Huddersfield T (£10,000 from Winsford, ex Wigan Ath YTS, Skelmersdale, on 21/10/1993) FL 17+1 FLC 0+1 Others 4/1
Wigan Ath (Loaned on 17/3/1995) FL 12
Lincoln C (£20,000 on 31/10/1995) FL 98+3/8 FLC 9/1 FAC 6+1/2 Others 4
Hull C (Signed on 18/12/1998) FL 54+3/3 FLC 2 FAC 2 Others 6

WHITTINGHAM Guy
Born: Evesham, 10 November 1964
Height: 5'9" Weight: 12.2

Not part of the first-team plans at Portsmouth under manager Tony Pulis, Guy was loaned to Peterborough United at the beginning of last season where he scored on his debut for the club at Oldham but was mostly used from the subs' bench during his month's stay. In October he was off on loan again, this time to Oxford United, becoming one of the few players to have played for both Oxford City and United, and scoring a goal on his debut at Swindon. However a change of management at Fratton Park saw him return early and he served as assistant to caretaker-manager Steve Claridge until Graham Rix took over at the end of February. Guy was released shortly afterwards and moved on to

Wycombe Wanderers on a short-term contract. He brought some much-needed experience to a forward line decimated by injury and featured on a number of occasions, including a brief appearance from the subs' bench in the FA Cup semi-final against Liverpool. A mobile striker who is still adept at holding the ball to bring his colleagues in to play, he was released in the summer.

Portsmouth (Free from Yeovil on 9/6/1989) FL 149+11/88 FLC 7+2/3 FAC 7+3/10 Others 9/3
Aston Villa (£1,200,000 on 1/8/1993) PL 17+8/5 FLC 4+1/1 Others 2+1
Wolverhampton W (Loaned on 28/2/1994) FL 13/8 FAC 1
Sheffield Wed (£700,000 on 21/12/1994) PL 90+23/22 FLC 7+2/2 FAC 7+1/1 Others 1+2
Wolverhampton W (Loaned on 2/11/1998) FL 9+1/1
Portsmouth (Loaned on 28/1/1999) FL 9/7
Watford (Loaned on 18/3/1999) FL 4+1
Portsmouth (Free on 13/7/1999) FL 15+11/4 FLC 2 FAC 1
Peterborough U (Loaned on 25/8/2000) FL 1+4/1 FLC 1
Oxford U (Loaned on 6/10/2000) FL 1/1
Wycombe W (Free on 22/3/2001) FL 9+3/1 FAC 0+1

Guy Whittingham

WHITTLE Justin Phillip

Born: Derby, 18 March 1971
Height: 6'1" Weight: 12.12

The Hull City skipper once again proved his worth last season with a string of excellent performances. Justin was an ever-present until he picked up a knee injury in the win at Exeter in October sidelined him for nine games, but once fit again he rarely missed a match. His central defensive partnership with Ian Goodison was the foundation of the Tigers' remarkable rise to the play-offs. A big and powerful defender he made the 200th appearance of his senior career in the Easter match against York.

Glasgow Celtic ((Free from Army during 1994 close season))
Stoke C (Free on 20/10/1994) FL 66+13/1 FLC 3+4 FAC 2 Others 2
Hull C (£65,000 on 27/11/1998) FL 100/1 FLC 6 FAC 4+2 Others 4

WHITWORTH Neil Anthony

Born: Wigan, 12 April 1972
Height: 6'2" Weight: 12.6
International Honours: E: Yth

Neil was a virtual ever-present in the Exeter City defence until picking up an ankle injury against Cheltenham last March. This put him out of action for some time and it was not until the penultimate game of the season that he returned to the first team. A big strong central defender he is composed on the ball and reads the game well.

Wigan Ath (Trainee) FL 1+1
Manchester U (£45,000 on 1/7/1990) FL 1
Preston NE (Loaned on 16/1/1992) FL 6
Barnsley (Loaned on 20/2/1992) FL 11
Rotherham U (Loaned on 8/10/1993) FL 8/1 Others 2
Blackpool (Loaned on 10/12/1993) FL 3
Kilmarnock (£265,000 on 2/9/1994) SL 74+1/3 SLC 3 SC 4 Others 1
Wigan Ath (Loaned on 11/3/1998) FL 1+3
Hull C (Free on 16/7/1998) FL 18+1/2 FLC 4 FAC 1
Exeter C (Free on 4/8/2000) FL 34/1 FLC 2 FAC 1 Others 1

WICKS Matthew Jonathan

Born: Reading, 8 September 1978
Height: 6'2" Weight: 13.5
Club Honours: Div 3 '01
International Honours: E: Yth

Matthew initially joined Brighton on loan last September before moving permanently to the South Coast. A hard-working and committed central defender he also proved more than useful when joining the attack and scored a number of crucial goals for the Seagulls. Matthew is the son of former Chelsea and QPR defender Steve Wicks.

Arsenal (From trainee at Manchester U on 23/1/1996)
Crewe Alex (£100,000 on 15/6/1998) FL 4+2
Peterborough U (Free on 3/3/1999) FL 28+3 FLC 2 FAC 1 Others 1
Brighton & Hove A (£25,000 on 1/9/2000) FL 23+1/3 FLC 1 FAC 2/1 Others 1

WIDDRINGTON Thomas (Tommy)

Born: Newcastle, 1 October 1971
Height: 5'9" Weight: 11.12
Club Honours: AMC '01

Tommy was a regular in the Port Vale line-up last season until dropping out through suspension in the new year. Although he was the club captain he then found it difficult to win his place back and he was forced to sit on the subs' bench for the LDV Vans Trophy final win over Brentford at Cardiff's Millenium Stadium. He netted one of Vale's goals of the season with a cracking 30-yard volley at Swindon in January but was eventually released at the end of the campaign. He is a hard-tackling midfield player who is adept at breaking up opposition attacks.

Southampton (From trainee on 10/5/1990) F/PL 67+8/3 FLC 3+1 FAC 11
Wigan Ath (Loaned on 12/9/1991) FL 5+1 FLC 2
Grimsby T (£300,000 on 11/7/1996) FL 72+17/8 FLC 10+3 FAC 3+1 Others 1
Port Vale (Free on 24/3/1999) FL 77+5/8 FLC 2 FAC 2 Others 3

WIEKENS Gerard

Born: Tolhuiswyk, Holland, 25 February 1973
Height: 6'0" Weight: 13.4

Having come up through the divisions with Manchester City Gerard certainly did not look out of place in the Premiership last term. He was a near ever-present for the Blues and netted goals in the 2-1 win at Leeds and in the draw at Valley Parade. A stylish player who always seemed to have time on the ball he mostly featured in the midfield anchor role. Although not the quickest of players, he was able to link up play between the back four and midfield and he formed a useful partnership with Jeff Whitley in the centre of the park.

Manchester C (£500,000 from SC Veendam, Holland on 28/7/1997) P/FL 138+9/10 FLC 11+1 FAC 9+1 Others 3

WIJNHARD Clyde

Born: Surinam, 9 November 1973
Height: 5'11" Weight: 12.4

Clyde will want to put memories of the 2000-01 season firmly behind him. Having appeared five times for Huddersfield in the early weeks of the campaign he was involved in a road accident from which he considered himself lucky to be alive at all. He suffered a broken arm but his injuries kept him out of action for the whole of the season. Sorely missed by the Terriers who were relegated in his absence, he is a big bustling striker with a proven scoring record. It is hoped he will be able to return to action for the start of the 2001-02 campaign.

Leeds U (£1,500,000 from Willem II, Holland, ex Ajax, Groningen, RKC Waelwijk, on 22/7/1998) PL 11+7/3 FLC 1 FAC 1+1/1 Others 1+3
Huddersfield T (£750,000 on 22/7/1999) FL 49/15 FLC 7/1 FAC 1

WILBRAHAM Aaron Thomas

Born: Knutsford, 21 October 1979
Height: 6'3" Weight: 12.4

After spending the close season on loan in Norway with Moss FK, Aaron returned to Stockport and went on to enjoy his best season to date for the Hatters. He netted regularly throughout the campaign finishing as the club's leading scorer and carring off a number of awards including the 'Players' Player of the Year'. A product of the Edgeley Park youth policy, the big striker not only looked strong in the air and skilful on the ball but he added a much greater degree of consistency to his game.

Stockport Co (From trainee on 29/8/1997) FL 59+36/17 FLC 3+2/1 FAC 3

WILCOX Jason Malcolm

Born: Farnworth, 15 July 1971
Height: 5'11" Weight: 11.10
Club Honours: PL '95
International Honours: E: 3; B-2

After being ruled out of England's Euro 2000 campaign through injury, Jason missed the start of last season while still recuperating. He eventually made the Leeds United first-team squad for the game at Coventry in September but when on the verge of a run in the team he broke his leg in training in Barcelona. However he made a quick return to fitness two months later and was part of the squad for much of the remainder of the campaign. He netted just one goal - a blistering volley in the 3-3 draw with Lazio. An experienced winger he gave the side an extra dimension with his play down the flank.

Blackburn Rov (From trainee on 13/6/1989) F/PL 242+27/31 FLC 16+1/1 FAC 18+2/2 Others 7
Leeds U (£3,000,000 on 17/12/1999) PL 22+15/3 FAC 2+1 Others 5+4/2

WILCOX Russell (Russ)
Born: Hemsworth, 25 March 1964
Height: 6'0" Weight: 12.12
Club Honours: Div 4 '87; Div 3 '96
International Honours: E: SP-3

Scunthorpe's assistant manager was expected to wind down his lengthy career in 2000-01 but ended up playing a huge role in the club's promotion challenge. Injuries led to him being given a chance at right back in the second match of the season and he kept his place on merit, switching to his usual central defensive position where his experience and organisation helped a young team. He missed a short spell after suffering a knee injury at the end of February, but returned for the run-in and was a strong contender for the Iron's 'Player of the Season' award.

Doncaster Rov (Apprentice) FL 1
Northampton T (£15,000 from Frickley Ath on 30/6/1986) FL 137+1/9 FLC 6 FAC 10 Others 8/1
Hull C (£120,000 on 6/8/1990) FL 92+8/7 FLC 5 FAC 5/1 Others 5+1
Doncaster Rov (£60,000 on 30/7/1993) FL 81/6 FLC 5/2 FAC 3 Others 3
Preston NE (£60,000 on 22/9/1995) FL 62/1 FLC 4 FAC 3/1 Others 2
Scunthorpe U (£15,000 on 8/7/1997) FL 100+9/4 FLC 7+1 FAC 11/2 Others 8

WILDER Christopher (Chris) John
Born: Stocksbridge, 23 September 1967
Height: 5'11" Weight: 12.8

Chris was a model of consistency at right back for Halifax Town last season until suffering a back injury in the away game at Blackpool on Boxing Day. He struggled to shake off the problem but despite receiving extensive physiotherapy he failed to make a return before the end of the campaign. Chris is a cultured defender who creates chances with his accurate crosses. He eventually announced his retirement in the summer.

Southampton (From apprentice on 26/9/1985)
Sheffield U (Free on 20/8/1986) FL 89+4/1 FLC 8+1 FAC 7 Others 3
Walsall (Loaned on 2/11/1989) FL 4 FAC 1 Others 2
Charlton Ath (Loaned on 12/10/1990) FL 1
Charlton Ath (Loaned on 28/11/1991) FL 2
Leyton Orient (Loaned on 27/2/1992) FL 16/1 Others 1
Rotherham U (£50,000 on 30/7/1992) FL 129+3/11 FLC 11 FAC 6+2/1 Others 6+1
Notts Co (£150,000 on 2/1/1996) FL 46 FLC 2 FAC 4 Others 1
Bradford C (£150,000 on 27/3/1997) FL 35+7 FLC 2 FAC 1
Sheffield U (£150,000 on 25/3/1998) FL 11+1 FLC 0+1 Others 1
Northampton T (Loaned on 6/11/1998) FL 1
Lincoln C (Loaned on 25/3/1999) FL 2+1
Brighton & Hove A (Free on 30/7/1999) FL 11 FLC 2
Halifax T (Free on 22/10/1999) FL 51/1 FLC 1 FAC 4 Others 2

WILDING Peter John
Born: Shrewsbury, 28 November 1968
Height: 6'1" Weight: 12.12

Peter never managed to establish himself in the Shrewsbury Town first team last season although his versatility made him a useful squad player. A strong and determined player who always showed a positive attitude he was in and out of the side. He scored a rare goal when he hit a real cracker in the closing stages of the 2-0 victory over Exeter in October.

Shrewsbury T (£10,000 from Telford on 10/6/1997) FL 130+8/4 FLC 7 FAC 6+1/1 Others 3/1

WILKIE Lee
Born: Dundee, 20 April 1980
Height: 6'4" Weight: 13.4
International Honours: S:

Lee made several early-season appearances for Scottish Premier League side Dundee in 2000-01 before dropping out of the reckoning and in January and he joined Third Division Plymouth Argyle on loan. He played in two away games for the Pilgrims before returning north of the border but his only subsequent appearance in the starting line-up came in the last game of the season against Hearts. Lee is a highly rated central defender who has been tracked by several top English clubs.

Dundee (Signed from Downfield Juniors on 8/9/1998) SL 25+6 SLC 3/1 SC 2
Plymouth Arg (Loaned on 12/1/2001) FL 2

WILKINSON John Colbridge
Born: Exeter, 24 August 1979
Height: 5'9" Weight: 11.0

John had a frustrating time in the 2000-01 season. Having spent some time battling back against a serious cruciate knee ligament injury his only first-team football came when he appeared as a substitute for the final 12 minutes of Exeter's game at Macclesfield last February. A left winger who has good skill on the ball and excellent vision, he was released by the Grecians in the summer.

Exeter C (From trainee on 9/7/1998) FL 6+14/2 FLC 0+1 FAC 1+1 Others 0+2

WILKINSON Shaun Frederick
Born: Portsmouth, 12 September 1981
Height: 5'8" Weight: 10.13

The young Brighton midfield player spent most of last season developing with the club's successful youth team and was restricted to a single first-team outing when he came off the subs' bench for the final 20 minutes of the 4-1 win over Barnet in March. He is a tenacious player with excellent distribution and will be aiming to feature more regularly for the Seagulls in the 2001-02 campaign.

Brighton & Hove A (Trainee) FL 0+3

WILLEMS Menno
Born: Amsterdam, Holland, 10 March 1977
Height: 6'0" Weight: 14.6

Having spent the 1999-2000 campaign on an extended loan with Den Bosch, Menno again failed to win a place in the Vitesse Arnhem line-up last season and opted to join Grimsby Town on loan in November. After impressing with his high work rate and strong tackling he joined the Mariners permanently in the new year. A left-sided midfield player who is also a dead-ball specialist he featured regularly for the Blundell Park club scoring just once when he netted with a classic free kick in the 2-1 win at Preston shortly before Christmas.

Grimsby T (Signed from Vitesse Arnhem, Holland, ex Den Bosch, Ajax, on 24/11/2000) FL 17+7/1 FAC 2

WILLIAMS Adrian
Born: Reading, 16 August 1971
Height: 6'2" Weight: 13.2
Club Honours: Div 2 '94
International Honours: W: 12

Adrian missed the start of the 2000-01 campaign at Reading after suffering a knee injury during the pre-season and soon after resuming his place in the first team he was carried off with an injury to his other knee during the game at Bristol City in October. He bravely fought back to appear in the play-offs only to endure the heartbreak of defeat in the final by Walsall at the Millenium Stadium. A reliable and committed central defender he is particularly effective in the air.

Reading (From trainee on 4/3/1989) FL 191+5/14 FLC 16/1 FAC 16/2 Others 14/2
Wolverhampton W (£750,000 on 3/7/1996) FL 26+1 FLC 3 FAC 2+2 Others 2/1
Reading (Loaned on 15/2/2000) FL 5/1 Others 1
Reading (Free on 26/3/2000) FL 15 Others 2

WILLIAMS Andrew (Andy) Phillip
Born: Bristol, 8 October 1977
Height: 5'10" Weight: 10.10
International Honours: W: 2; U21-9

Andy made a number of appearances for Swindon Town in the early part of the 2000-01 campaign but was then sidelined by a hernia problem that required surgery. Although he returned to the squad in April he struggled to find his best form and was released at the end of the season. A natural left winger he creates problems for opposition defences with some surging runs and dangerous crosses.

Southampton (From trainee on 24/5/1996) PL 3+18 FLC 1+2 FAC 0+1
Swindon T (£65,000 on 8/9/1999) FL 38+6/1 FLC 1+3 FAC 1

WILLIAMS Anthony (Tony) Simon
Born: Bridgend, 20 September 1977
Height: 6'1" Weight: 13.5
International Honours: W: U21-16; Yth

Tony joined Hartlepool in July 2000 and began last season as second-choice 'keeper to Martin Hollund, but within a month he had won a place in the starting line-up where he remained for the rest of the campaign. He is a very capable goalkeeper who commands his area well, gives confidence to his defenders and has a reputation for saving penalties. Tony holds the record for the number of Wales U21 caps.

Blackburn Rov (From trainee on 4/7/1996)
Macclesfield T (Loaned on 16/10/1998) FL 4
Bristol Rov (Loaned on 24/3/1999) FL 9
Gillingham (Loaned on 5/8/1999) FL 2 FLC 2
Macclesfield T (Loaned on 28/1/2000) FL 11
Hartlepool U (Free on 7/7/2000) FL 41 FLC 1 FAC 1 Others 5

WILLIAMS Daniel (Danny) Ivor Llewellyn
Born: Wrexham, 12 July 1979
Height: 6'1" Weight: 13.0
International Honours: W: U21-9

Danny began the 2000-01 campaign in the Wrexham first-team squad and scored in the 4-1 triumph at Bury last August but then dropped out the side and spent time on loan with Conference club Doncaster Rovers in the new year. He was involved with the Robins' senior team once again on his return and he will be looking to establish a regular presence in the squad in the 2001-02 season. He is a forceful and combative midfield player, strong in the tackle and able to play in defence if called upon. He added a further cap for Wales at U21 level when he appeared against Belarus last September. He was reported to have joined Kidderminster in the summer.

Liverpool (From trainee on 14/5/1997)
Wrexham (Free on 22/3/1999) FL 38+1/3 FLC 4 FAC 4/1 Others 1

WILLIAMS Daniel (Danny) Josef
Born: Sheffield, 2 March 1981
Height: 5'9" Weight: 9.13

Danny was very much on the fringes of the Chesterfield first-team squad last season and his only start came against Rochdale in March when the club was under a transfer embargo. The simplicity of his play suited Chesterfield's midfield and he showed he could read the game well and also handle the pressures of senior football. He will be aiming to gain further experience with the Spireites in the 2001-02 campaign.

Chesterfield (From trainee on 2/7/1999) FL 4+3 FLC 0+1 Others 0+3

WILLIAMS Darren
Born: Middlesbrough, 28 April 1977
Height: 5'10" Weight: 11.12
Club Honours: Div 1 '99
International Honours: E: B-1; U21-2

Often referred to by Peter Reid as his best value-for-money signing, this dependable Sunderland utility man signed a five-year extension to his contract at the Stadium of Light last September. Darren can operate in the centre of defence, at full back, or in midfield and although he has stressed that he would like to establish himself in one position, he remains an extremely useful squad player who can do a job almost anywhere on the field. A good tackler and competitor Darren will be challenging for a regular place in the Wearsiders defence in 2001-02.

York C (From trainee on 21/6/1995) FL 16+4 FLC 4+1 FAC 1 Others 3/1
Sunderland (£50,000 on 18/10/1996) F/PL 95+30/4 FLC 14+1/2 FAC 7+1 Others 3

WILLIAMS Eifion Wyn
Born: Anglesey, 15 November 1975
Height: 5'11" Weight: 11.12
International Honours: W: B-1

Eifion had a difficult time in a somewhat unsettled Torquay team for much of last season, but to his credit he knuckled down to some hard work and showed great improvement in his play outside the box. His haul of nine goals included several crucial match-winners: of particular note was an injury-time brace against Blackpool back in August that turned defeat into an unlikely victory. His goal supply seemed to dry up in the new year but no doubt this able striker will find the net regularly again in the 2001-02 campaign.

Torquay U (£70,000 from Barry T on 25/3/1999) FL 76+10/23 FLC 3 FAC 3 Others 2

WILLIAMS Gareth John
Born: Glasgow, 16 December 1981
Height: 5'11" Weight: 11.10
International Honours: S: Yth

Having broken into the Nottingham Forest first team in 1999-2000 Gareth spent most of last term continuing his development in the club's reserves, although he enjoyed a decent run of senior action from November to the turn of the year. A promising young midfield player he is composed on the ball, passes accurately and has a high work rate. He will be hoping to win a regular place in the squad of 16 in 2001-02.

Nottingham F (From trainee on 23/12/1998) FL 11+8 FAC 2

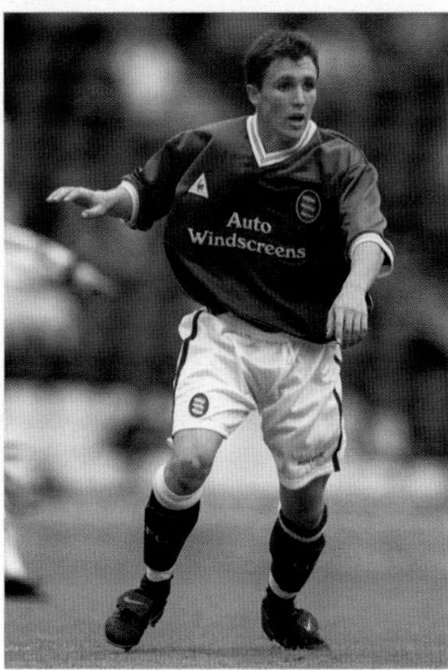

Jacques Williams

WILLIAMS Jacques
Born: Wallasey, 25 April 1981
Height: 5'9" Weight: 11.0

This promising Birmingham City youngster got into the team on a couple of occasions early on last season and certainly did not look out of place in a midfield role. Although slightly built, Jacques gave as good as he got in the physical battles and passed the ball very well. He was encouraged to take more risks and express himself a little more, which he did, but his development was hampered by a hernia operation before Christmas and groin problems thereafter.

Birmingham C (Free from Bordeaux, France on 31/7/1999) FL 1+2 FLC 0+1

WILLIAMS James
Born: Liverpool, 15 July 1982
Height: 5'7" Weight: 10.8

Although not used to the same extent as in the previous campaign, James continued to develop at a steady rate with Swindon last term and enjoyed a brief run in the starting line-up early in the new year. Highly regarded by Robins' boss Andy King he can play in a number of different roles in defence or midfield and will be looking to breakthrough to win a regular place in the first-team squad in the coming season.

Swindon T (From trainee on 9/12/1999) FL 21+15/1 FAC 0+1 Others 3

WILLIAMS John Nelson
Born: Birmingham, 11 May 1968
Height: 6'1" Weight: 13.12

John made the starting line-up just once for York City last season and featured in a handful of games from the subs' bench before being released in December and joining Darlington shortly afterwards. He made his debut for the Quakers in the home game against Lincoln shortly before Christmas and opened his account with a goal at Plymouth. He missed only three games in the second half of the campaign and added another four goals. A tall rangy striker his ability to win the ball in the air immediately added an extra dimension to the Darlington attack and his speed down the right flank provided a number of opportunities his team-mates. He was reported to have signed for Swansea in the summer.

Swansea C (£5,000 from Cradley T on 19/8/1991) FL 36+3/11 FLC 2+1 FAC 3 Others 1
Coventry C (£250,000 on 1/7/1992) PL 66+14/11 FLC 4 FAC 2
Notts Co (Loaned on 7/10/1994) FL 3+2/2
Stoke C (Loaned on 23/12/1994) FL 1+3
Swansea C (Loaned on 3/2/1995) FL 6+1/2
Wycombe W (£150,000 on 15/9/1995) FL 34+14/8 FLC 4+1/2 FAC 5/4 Others 2
Hereford U (Free on 14/2/1997) FL 8+3/3
Walsall (Free on 21/7/1997) FL 0+1
Exeter C (Free on 29/8/1997) FL 16+20/4
Cardiff C (Free on 3/8/1998) FL 25+18/12 FLC 2/1 FAC 5/3 Others 1
York C (£20,000 on 12/8/1999) FL 29+13/3 FLC 2 FAC 0+1 Others 1
Darlington (Free on 21/12/2000) FL 23+1/5 Others 1

WILLIAMS Lee
Born: Birmingham, 3 February 1973
Height: 5'7" Weight: 11.13
International Honours: E: Yth

Lee appeared regularly for Mansfield Town in a right-sided midfield role last season but never quite managed to reach the high standards he had set in 1999-2000. At his best he is very effective when linking up

with the attack and can deliver a fine cross from the flank. Lee was placed on the open to offers list in the summer.
Aston Villa (From trainee on 26/1/1991)
Shrewsbury T (Loaned on 8/11/1992) FL 2+1 FAC 1+1/1 Others 2
Peterborough U (Signed on 23/3/1994) FL 83+8/1 FLC 4+1 FAC 5+1/1 Others 7 (Free to Shamrock Rov during 1996 close season)
Mansfield T (Free on 27/3/1997) FL 149+26/9 FLC 8 FAC 4+2 Others 4+1

WILLIAMS Mark Ross
Born: Chatham, 19 October 1981
Height: 5'9" Weight: 11.0
Mark is an exciting Brentford right winger who has the ability to take on and beat opposition defenders and deliver an accurate cross for his team-mates. He made his senior debut for the Bees against Millwall last September and was a regular in the squad for the remainder of the season, although he was mostly used from the subs' bench. He scored his first goal for the club with a cracking shot against Stoke in March and went on to win a runners-up medal in the LDV Vans Trophy coming on as a substitute for the closing minutes.
Brentford (From trainee on 2/11/2000) FL 6+24/2 FLC 0+1 FAC 0+1 Others 0+2

WILLIAMS Mark Stuart
Born: Stalybridge, 28 September 1970
Height: 6'0" Weight: 13.0
Club Honours: Div 3 '94
International Honours: NI: 17; B-1
Mark had an outstanding season for Wimbledon in 2000-01 when he was a model of consistency. An effective central defender he stops, blocks and clears and is always a handful when moving forward to join the attack for set pieces. He continued to notch the occasional goal and was very unlucky not to score a hat-trick in the 5-0 home win over Queens Park Rangers when he netted twice and had another cleared off the line. He showed great character and spirit to lift himself after the disappointing FA Cup defeat by Wycombe and finished the campaign by being deservedly voted the fans' 'Player of the Year'. He continued to appear regularly for Northern Ireland and managed to score his first-ever international goal against Bulgaria in March.
Shrewsbury T (Free from Newtown on 27/3/1992) FL 96+6/3 FLC 7+1 FAC 6 Others 6/1
Chesterfield (£50,000 on 7/8/1995) FL 168/12 FLC 10 FAC 13/1 Others 7/1
Watford (Free on 13/7/1999) P/FL 20+2/1 FLC 2
Wimbledon (Signed on 26/7/2000) FL 42/6 FLC 4 FAC 6/1

WILLIAMS Martin Keith
Born: Luton, 12 July 1973
Height: 5'9" Weight: 11.12
Martin came close to joining Swindon during the 2000 close season but a recurrence of a knee injury put the move on hold and it was not until September that he eventually signed a three month-contract. However despite a high work rate he found goals hard to come by and he was released in January, moving on to Peterborough United on another short-term contract. He featured regularly up front for Posh and scored a couple of goals but was released at the end of the season. He is an experienced striker who is quick, brave and shows skill on the ball.
Luton T (From trainee at Leicester C on 13/9/1991) FL 12+28/2 FLC 1 FAC 0+1 Others 2+1
Colchester U (Loaned on 9/3/1995) FL 3
Reading (Free on 13/7/1995) FL 99+29/26 FLC 10+6/2 FAC 8+2/1 Others 3
Swindon T (Free on 30/8/2000) FL 17+2/2 FLC 3 FAC 2/1
Peterborough U (Free on 19/1/2001) FL 13+2/1

WILLIAMS Paul Darren
Born: Burton, 26 March 1971
Height: 6'0" Weight: 13.0
International Honours: E: U21-6
Combative in the air and strong in the tackle Paul is one of the most under-rated central defenders in the Premiership and his re-signing in the summer of 2000 was good news for Coventry City. Despite the potentially stiff competition from Colin Hendry and Mo Konjic, Paul started the campaign as first choice centre-half playing alongside firstly Hendry (for one game), then Richard Shaw and later Konjic. Suspensions then cost him his place in the squad and he eventually lost out to the outstanding Gary Breen.
Derby Co (From trainee on 13/7/1989) FL 153+7/26 FLC 10+2/2 FAC 8/3 Others 14+1/2
Lincoln C (Loaned on 9/11/1989) FL 3 FAC 2 Others 1
Coventry C (£975,000 on 6/8/1995) PL 149+15/5 FLC 16+1/1 FAC 13

WILLIAMS Ryan Neil
Born: Sutton in Ashfield, 31 August 1978
Height: 5'5" Weight: 11.4
International Honours: E: Yth
Although nominally a midfielder, Ryan operated down the wings for Chesterfield last season, usually favouring the right but able to pop up anywhere to torment opponents. Difficult to dispossess, he weighed in with many important goals and set up countless more with fine crosses. Irrepressible, persistent and cheerful, Ryan's obvious enjoyment of his role has endeared him greatly to the Spireites' supporters. He was reported to have signed for Hull City in the summer.
Mansfield T (Trainee) FL 9+17/3 FLC 2 FAC 0+1
Tranmere Rov (£70,000 + on 8/8/1997) FL 2+3
Chesterfield (£80,000 on 10/11/1999) FL 69+6/13 FLC 3 FAC 1 Others 5+1/1

WILLIAMS Thomas (Tommy) Andrew
Born: Carshalton, 8 July 1980
Height: 6'0" Weight: 11.8
This young West Ham United full back was loaned to Peterborough United on the transfer deadline day to get some experience of first-team football and featured on two occasions for Posh towards the end of the season. An excellent prospect who reads the game well he always seems to have time on the ball and possesses a powerful long throw. He was reported to have joined Peterborough permanently during the summer.
West Ham U (£60,000 from Walton & Hersham on 3/4/2000)
Peterborough U (Loaned on 22/3/2001) FL 1+1

WILLIAMSON Garry
Born: Darlington, 24 January 1982
Height: 6'0" Weight: 12.7
This Darlington trainee burst through onto the first-team scene at the beginning of last season after scoring freely for the club's reserves in 1999-2000. He made his Football League debut from the subs' bench in the opening game of the campaign and made the starting line-up for the two Worthington Cup ties against Nottingham Forest. He went on to make a handful more appearances as a substitute and also had a spell on loan at Spennymoor United in the new year. Garry is a strong-running young forward with great enthusiasm for the game and will be looking to gain further senior experience in the coming season.
Darlington (Trainee) FL 1+5 FLC 2 Others 0+2

WILLIAMSON Lee Trevor
Born: Derby, 7 June 1982
Height: 5'10" Weight: 10.4
This promising youngster progressed from being captain of the Mansfield Town youth team to a regular in the reserves last season. He was used sparingly in the first team although he will be pushing for a more regular place in the senior squad in the 2001-02 campaign. Lee is a right-sided midfielder and despite his slight build is extremely strong in the tackle.
Mansfield T (From trainee on 3/7/2000) FL 10+9 FLC 0+3 FAC 1+1 Others 1

WILLIAMSON Russell Ian
Born: Epping, 17 March 1980
Height: 5'4" Weight: 8.10
This tiny midfield dynamo had a trial period at Clyde at the beginning of last season before Dave Webb signed him for Third Division Southend last November. One of the smallest players in the Football League, he endeared himself to the Blues' fans with a series of all-action displays. Quick and light on his feet, Russell tackled ferociously and supported his forwards with some deep runs that brought him goals in the two FA Cup matches against Torquay United. Out of contract in the summer his future was unclear at the time of writing.
Wimbledon (From trainee on 22/6/1998)
Southend U (Free, via trial at Clyde, on 3/11/2000) FL 9+3 FAC 3+1/2 Others 3+3/1

WILLIS Adam Peter
Born: Nuneaton, 21 September 1976
Height: 6'1" Weight: 12.2
Adam was a first choice in the heart of the Swindon defence at the beginning of last season, but was then sidelined with a heel injury and it was not until April that he eventually returned to the side. He is a tall and steady central defender who is good in the air and not easily ruffled by opposing strikers.
Coventry C (From trainee on 1/7/1995)
Swindon T (Free on 21/4/1998) FL 48+7 FLC 1+1 FAC 2/1 Others 1
Mansfield T (Loaned on 25/3/1999) FL 10

WILLIS Roger Christopher
Born: Sheffield, 17 June 1967
Height: 6'1" Weight: 12.0
Club Honours: GMVC '91

International Honours: E: SP-1

'Harry' was used as a regular substitute by Chesterfield last season, coming on 21 times to inject pace and keep pressure on tiring opponents. Usually the first to come in up front if David Reeves or Luke Beckett were absent, he adapted his game intelligently to form effective partnerships with both players and netted five times. A brave and experienced striker his season was ended in April by a cut above an eye that required nine stitches.

Grimsby T (Signed from Dunkirk on 20/7/1989) FL 1+8 FLC 0+1
Barnet (£10,000 on 1/8/1990) FL 39+5/13 FLC 2 FAC 5+1/3 Others 1+4/1
Watford (£175,000 on 6/10/1992) FL 30+6/2 FAC 1
Birmingham C (£150,000 on 31/12/1993) FL 12+7/5 FAC 0+1
Southend U (Signed on 16/9/1994) FL 30+1/7 FAC 1 Others 1
Peterborough U (Free on 13/8/1996) FL 34+6/6 FLC 3 FAC 5+1 Others 5
Chesterfield (£100,000 on 11/7/1997) FL 57+54/17 FLC 11+4/2 FAC 2+2/1 Others 1+4

WILLMOTT Christopher (Chris) Alan
Born: Bedford, 30 September 1977
Height: 6'2" Weight: 11.12

Chris enjoyed a short run in the Wimbledon line-up at the start of last season as cover for injuries before dropping back to the reserves where he continued to produce some fine performances. He made the odd first-team appearance after this and netted his first goal in senior football with a powerful header in the 3-3 draw against Crewe in April. A dependable central defender who continues to learn his trade he is strong in the tackle and always tries to use the ball constructively.

Luton T (From trainee on 1/5/1996) FL 13+1
Wimbledon (£350,000 on 14/7/1999) P/FL 20+1/1 FLC 2+1 FAC 2

WILLOCK Calum Daniel
Born: London, 29 October 1981
Height: 5'11" Weight: 12.7
International Honours: E: Sch

A regular for the England Schools U18 team in 1999-2000, Calum was leading scorer for Fulham's U19 team last term and also netted seven goals for the reserves including a hat-trick against Bristol Rovers. He was rewarded with his Football League debut in the game at Huddersfield when he came on for Louis Saha in the closing minutes of the Cottagers' 3-0 victory. He is a pacy young striker who is strong on the ball and has a great eye for goal.

Fulham (From ADT College, Putney on 18/7/2000) FL 0+1

WILLS Kevin Michael
Born: Torquay, 15 October 1980
Height: 5'8" Weight: 10.7

Kevin was on the fringe of Plymouth's first-team squad for the first half of the 2000-01 season but it was not until the LDV Vans Trophy tie against Bristol City in December that he made the starting line-up. He later had a short run in the team and scored his first goal in senior football when he netted with a right-foot shot in the 3-1 victory over local rivals Torquay in April. He is a central midfield player who is strong in the tackle and likes to get forward into goal-scoring positions.

Plymouth Arg (From trainee on 16/7/1999) FL 4+10/1 FAC 0+2 Others 2

WILNIS Fabian
Born: Surinam, 23 August 1970
Height: 5'8" Weight: 12.6

After being left out of the Ipswich line-up for the opening game of last season, Fabian made his Premiership debut in the home game with Manchester United. He got off to a fine start and it was his goal, a superb low drive after he exchanged passes with David Johnson, which gave him and the team the confidence that they could do well in this division. He maintained his position as the right back or wing back for most of the season, scoring once more - an injury-time header from Martijn Reuser's cross to secure the points in the 1-0 win at Coventry. He gave the team extra attacking options with his ability to push down the right flank and deliver an excellent cross, while defensively not many opponents got the better of him.

Ipswich T (£200,000 from De Graafschap, Holland, ex NAC Breda, on 6/1/1999) P/FL 74+8/3 FLC 6+2 FAC 4 Others 3+1

WILSON Che Christian Aaron Clay
Born: Ely, 17 January 1979
Height: 5'9" Weight: 11.3

Che joined Bristol Rovers in the 2000 close season and immediately slotted in well in a left-back role. However he was then injured in the FA Cup defeat at Cardiff and on his return he showed his versatility by appearing at right back and also in the centre of midfield. A fine all-round defender he is solid in the tackle, capable of passing the ball accurately and has a very calm approach to the game.

Norwich C (From trainee on 3/7/1997) FL 16+6 FLC 3
Bristol Rov (Free on 13/7/2000) FL 36+1 FLC 5 FAC 1 Others 2

WILSON Kevin James
Born: Banbury, 18 April 1961
Height: 5'8" Weight: 11.4
Club Honours: Div 2 '89; FMC '90
International Honours: NI: 42

Northampton's player-manager named himself as a substitute on several occasions last season when the squad was affected by injury problems. He made a total of six appearances from the bench, the final one coming against Oxford at the end of March just days before his 40th birthday, thus making him the oldest outfield player to appear in the Football League for the Cobblers. He played in midfield or up front but remains one goal short of the landmark total of 200 in senior football.

Derby Co (£20,000 from Banbury U on 21/12/1979) FL 106+16/30 FLC 8+3/8 FAC 8/3
Ipswich T (£100,000 on 5/1/1985) FL 94+4/34 FLC 8/8 FAC 10/3 Others 7/4
Chelsea (£335,000 on 25/6/1987) FL 124+28/42 FLC 10+2/4 FAC 7+1/1 Others 14+5/8
Notts Co (£225,000 on 27/3/1992) FL 58+11/3 FLC 3+1 FAC 2 Others 5+1
Bradford C (Loaned on 13/1/1994) FL 5
Walsall (Free on 4/8/1994) FL 124+1/38 FLC 8/3 FAC 13/7 Others 6/1
Northampton T (Free on 28/7/1997) FL 13+18/2 FLC 1+1 FAC 0+2

WILSON Philip (Phil) John
Born: Oxford, 17 October 1982
Height: 6'3" Weight: 14.12

Another of the promising youngsters to graduate at Oxford United last season, Phil made his Football League debut when he came on from the subs' bench at Bristol Rovers after regular 'keeper Richard Knight had received a red card. He went on to receive his first start when he played in the final game at Notts County when Knight was suspended. A talented young 'keeper he will be looking to gain more first-team experience in the 2001-02 campaign.

Oxford U (Trainee) FL 1+1

WILSON Stephen (Steve) Lee
Born: Hull, 24 April 1974
Height: 5'10" Weight: 10.12

Unable to get in the first team at Hull, Steve moved on loan to Macclesfield last March to provide goalkeeping cover for Lee Martin after Tony Bullock was transferred to Lincoln. He made a single appearance for Macc in the home match against Southend when he was in good form and kept a clean sheet. Out of contract in the summer he was released on a free transfer.

Hull C (From trainee on 13/7/1992) FL 180+1 FLC 13 FAC 13 Others 11+1
Macclesfield T (Loaned on 22/3/2001) FL 1

WILSON Stuart Kevin
Born: Leicester, 16 September 1977
Height: 5'8" Weight: 9.12
Club Honours: FLC '00

Unable to break into Leicester's Premiership side Stuart joined Cambridge United last December and made his debut from the subs' bench at Walsall shortly afterwards. He gave a fine performance on Boxing Day against Wycombe Wanderers when he showed some fine skills and was named 'Man of the Match'. A right back or right-sided or midfield player he featured in a handful more games but fell out of favour following a change in management and was released in the summer.

Leicester C (From trainee on 4/7/1996) PL 1+21/3 FLC 1+7/1 FAC 0+4
Sheffield U (Loaned on 23/3/2000) FL 4+2
Cambridge U (Free on 22/12/2000) FL 3+3 Others 1

WILSTERMAN Brian Hank
Born: Surinam, 19 November 1966
Height: 6'1" Weight: 13.8

Brian battled back well after losing his place in the Rotherham United line-up last September but from then onwards he was mainly used as a squad player. He was brought back into the team for the game at Walsall in January specifically to cope with the Saddlers' big forwards and performed the task admirably. A strong defender who can always be relied upon to give his all, he netted a vital goal in the victory over Wrexham. Out of contract in the summer his future was uncertain at the time of writing.

Oxford U (£200,000 from Beerschot, Belgium on 28/2/1997) FL 28+14/2 FLC 2 FAC 1
Rotherham U (Free on 1/7/1999) FL 47+5/4 FLC 3 FAC 2 Others 2

WILTORD Sylvain
Born: Paris, France, 10 May 1974
Height: 5'9" Weight: 12.2
International Honours: France: 29 (UEFA '00)

Having helped his country to victory in Euro 2000 when he netted the equaliser in the final against Italy, Sylvain joined Arsenal for a new club record fee at the end of August. A livewire striker, full of flair and pace, Sylvain is an exciting signing for the Gunners. After taking the customary period of time to settle into the English game, he weighed in with 15 goals, including a fantastic hat-trick against West Ham at Highbury in March, and six in Arsenal's run to the FA Cup final. He showed his willingness to work hard and make life difficult for defenders in the FA Cup semi-final victory over Spurs, putting in an excellent all-round performance.
Arsenal (£13,000,000 from Bordeaux, France, ex Rennes, Girondins, on 31/8/2000) PL 20+7/8 FLC 1 FAC 5+1/6 Others 2+11/1

WINDASS Dean
Born: Hull, 1 April 1969
Height: 5'10" Weight: 12.6

An ever-present at Bradford City last season apart from suspensions, Dean featured both as a striker and in midfield showing great enthusiasm and a will to win whatever the circumstances. In March he was rather surprisingly allowed to move on to Middlesbrough where he made an immediate impact by scoring on his debut at Chelsea. Readily joining in Boro's fight against relegation he gave his all as ever and was a real asset in their ultimately successful struggle. Dean is the original 'rough diamond' in the best Alf Tupper 'Tough of the Track' traditions [a fictional working-class hero in the Victor comic of the 1960s for the uninitiated]. A man who would run through the proverbial brick wall for his team, he knows no fear in goalmouth melees, aware only that he is there to score goals.
Hull C (Free from North Ferriby on 24/10/1991) FL 173+3/57 FLC 11/4 FAC 7 Others 12/3
Aberdeen (£700,000 on 1/12/1995) SL 60+13/21 SLC 5+2/6 SC 7/3 Others 6/1
Oxford U (£475,000 on 6/8/1998) FL 33/15 FLC 2 FAC 3/3
Bradford C (£950,000 + on 5/3/1999) P/FL 64+10/16 FLC 6/2 FAC 2 Others 6/3
Middlesbrough (£600,000 + on 15/3/2001) PL 8/2

WINSTANLEY Mark Andrew
Born: St Helens, 22 January 1968
Height: 6'1" Weight: 12.7
Club Honours: AMC '89

Released by Shrewsbury Town at the end of the 1999-2000 campaign, Mark joined Carlisle United in the close season and went on to produce some fine performances for the Cumbrian club. He played particularly well in the crucial victory at Barnet and in the game at Southend when a vital point was secured. One of the more experienced players in the squad he is a central defender who is strong in the air and very effective on the left-hand side.
Bolton W (From trainee on 22/7/1986) FL 215+5/3 FLC 19+1 FAC 19 Others 26/3
Burnley (Signed on 5/8/1994) FL 151+1/5 FLC 13 FAC 8 Others 8+1
Shrewsbury T (Loaned on 17/9/1998) FL 8
Preston NE (Free on 22/3/1999)
Shrewsbury T (Free on 22/7/1999) FL 32+1/1 FLC 2 FAC 1
Carlisle U (Free on 7/8/2000) FL 34+2 FLC 2 FAC 3

WINTERBURN Nigel
Born: Nuneaton, 11 December 1963
Height: 5'9" Weight: 11.4
Club Honours: Div 1 '89, '91; PL '98; FAC '93, '98; FLC '93; ECWC '94; CS '98 '99
International Honours: E: 2; B-3; U21-1; Yth

Having signed for West Ham in the summer Nigel had a fine season in the Hammers' defence in 2000-01. Rarely absent he was a model of consistency, hardly putting a foot wrong and becoming a firm favourite of the Upton Park fans. Whether used as a left wing back or on the left-hand side of midfield he linked well with Paolo Di Canio and his only goal came with a diving header to secure a 1-0 victory at Leeds.
Birmingham C (From apprentice on 14/8/1981)
Wimbledon (Free on 22/9/1983) FL 164+1/8 FLC 13 FAC 12 Others 2
Arsenal (£407,000 on 26/5/1987) F/PL 429+11/8 FLC 49/3 FAC 47 Others 50+1/1
West Ham U (£250,000 on 5/7/2000) PL 33/1 FLC 3 FAC 4

Nigel Winterburn

WISE Dennis Frank
Born: Kensington, 15 December 1966
Height: 5'6" Weight: 10.10
Club Honours: FAC '88, '97, '00; FLC '98; ECWC '98; ESC '98; CS '00
International Honours: E: 21; B-3; U21-1

The 2000-01 season was a topsy-turvy affair for Dennis at Chelsea. Shortly after lifting his sixth major trophy - the FA Charity Shield - he was voted the 'Player of the Year' for 2000, his second such award in three years, and as a measure of his importance to the club he signed a one-year extension to his contract with the offer of a coaching role on his retirement as a player. His next landmark was to break the 400 first-team appearance barrier and so put himself in fourth place in the club's all-time list of appearance makers before his fortunes plummeted with the departure of Luca Vialli. New boss Claudio Ranieri played him on the left of midfield and sometimes as a left wing back rather than in his customary central role. Nevertheless he remained a regular in the line-up and scored his third goal of the season in the final match at Maine Road to help clinch a UEFA Cup place for 2001-02. However his future at Stamford Bridge remained uncertain and he was reported to have signed for Leicester City in the summer.
Wimbledon (From trainee at Southampton on 28/3/1985) FL 127+8/27 FLC 14 FAC 11/3 Others 5
Chelsea (£1,600,000 on 3/7/1990) F/PL 322+10/53 FLC 30/6 FAC 38/9 Others 44+1/8

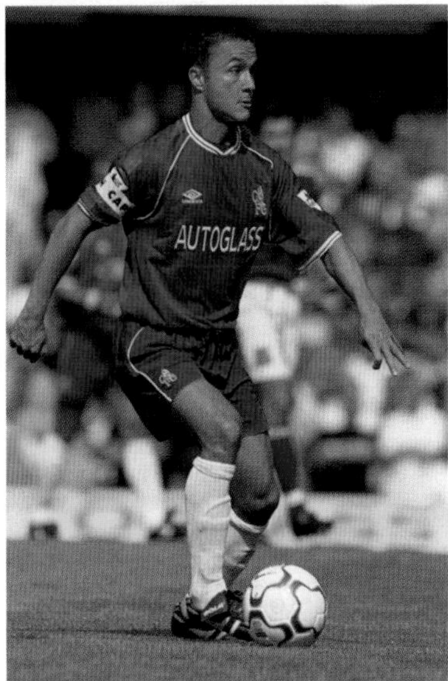

Dennis Wise

WISS Jarkko
Born: Finland, 17 April 1972
Height: 6'0" Weight: 12.8
International Honours: Finland: 32

Having joined Stockport County shortly before the start of last season Jarkko's career at Edgeley Park got off to the worst possible start when he suffered badly damaged ankle ligaments on his debut in a Worthington Cup tie against Blackpool. However once fully fit again he showed just why County boss Andy Kilner had been prepared to shell out a substantial fee for him. Tenacious in the tackle, with a phenomenal work rate and an eye for goal he soon became a firm favourite of the Edgeley Park faithful. Unfortunately a knee injury, the legacy of playing 18 months continuous football, brought his campaign to a premature close. A regular member of the Finland squad when fit he won a further four caps during the season, featuring in both World Cup qualifiers against England.

Stockport Co (£350,000 from Moss FK, Norway, ex TPV Tampere, FF Jaro, HJK Helsinki, Molde, Lillestrom, on 10/8/2000) FL 27+3/6 FLC 1 FAC 3/1

WOAN Ian Simon
Born: Heswall, 14 December 1967
Height: 5'10" Weight: 12.4
Club Honours: Div 1 '98

Ian joined Barnsley on a two-month contract last August but although he showed that he clearly had a cultured left foot he failed to win a longer deal at Oakwell. In October he moved on to Swindon Town, arriving soon after Andy King was appointed manager and went on to be a key figure in the centre of the park for the Robins. An expert with dead-ball kicks he set up numerous goals for his colleagues and netted a few himself, including a great strike with a 45-yard free kick at Rotherham and another direct from a corner against Northampton. Very much a favourite with the County Ground faithful he was runner up for the 'Player of the Season' award before moving to the United States to play for Columbus Crew in the summer.

Nottingham F (£80,000 from Runcorn on 14/3/1990) F/PL 189+32/31 FLC 15+3/1 FAC 20+1/6 Others 13/2
Barnsley (Free on 25/8/2000) FL 2+1 FLC 3
Swindon T (Free on 27/10/2000) FL 21+1/3 FAC 3

WOLLEASTON Robert Ainsley
Born: Perivale, 21 December 1979
Height: 5'11" Weight: 12.2

This promising Chelsea youngster was loaned to Portsmouth just before transfer deadline day as new boss Graham Rix used his knowledge of the Stamford Bridge set-up to strengthen his squad for the closing stages of the season. A tall, powerfully built attacking midfield player he showed some neat controlled football and occasional touches of brilliance in six appearances for Pompey. A natural two-footed player with outstanding potential, he likes to roam forward and tease opposition defences.

Chelsea (From trainee on 3/6/1998) PL 0+1 FLC 0+1
Bristol Rov (Loaned on 23/3/2000) FL 0+4
Portsmouth (Loaned on 8/3/2001) FL 5+1

WOOD Jamie
Born: Salford, 21 September 1978
Height: 5'10" Weight: 13.0
International Honours: Cayman Islands: 2

Jamie started the first three games of the 2000-01 season and it appeared that new Hull manager Brian Little had decided that he was the man to lead his Tigers' attack. However, an untimely ankle injury wrecked his hopes and the only other occasion when he made the starting line-up was for the LDV Vans Trophy defeat at Chester in December. Jamie continued to provide enthusiastic backup from the bench but with City signing Kevin Francis and Rodney Rowe his opportunities became increasingly limited. Jamie is a promising striker who works hard. He was released by Hull in May.

Manchester U (From trainee on 10/7/1997)
Hull C (Free on 21/7/1999) FL 15+32/6 FLC 2+3 FAC 3+2/1 Others 2+1

WOOD Leigh James
Born: York, 21 May 1983
Height: 6'1" Weight: 11.2

A youth-team trainee with York City, Leigh was thrust into senior action in January, making his Football League debut at Blackpool. He greatly impressed in his five appearances and will be aiming to extend his experience of first-team football in 2001-02. He is a composed midfield player with good ball skills and an ability to read the game. Leigh was voted the Minstermen's 'Young Player of the Year' last season.

York C (Trainee) FL 4+1

WOOD Steven (Steve) Ronald
Born: Oldham, 23 June 1963
Height: 5'9" Weight: 10.10
Club Honours: FAT '96; GMVC '95, '97

Steve is Macclesfield's longest-serving player and is extremely popular with the fans, not only for his playing ability but also for his sense of humour. He appeared regularly in midfield in the early part of last season until the partnership of Chris Priest and Kevin Keen was formed, after which he rarely featured in the senior side although he often captained the reserves. Now approaching the veteran stage of his career he is currently studying for the UEFA 'B' coaching certificate.

Macclesfield T (Free from Ashton U on 22/7/1993) FL 129+22/19 FLC 11+1/1 FAC 5+1/2 Others 3

WOODGATE Jonathan Simon
Born: Middlesbrough, 22 January 1980
Height: 6'2" Weight: 13.0
Club Honours: FAYC '97
International Honours: E: 1; U21-1; Yth

Jonathan began the 2000-01 season as a first choice in the centre of defence for Leeds and looked in fine form. However he picked up an injury in only the second game at Middlesbrough putting him on the sidelines for a short while. He returned with some high quality performances, notably in the Champions' League draws with Besiktas and Barcelona when the side was up against extreme pressure. He again limped off in November in the Premiership encounter with Liverpool, but returned against Real Madrid to hit a post after five minutes with the scores at 0-0, and saved probably his best performance of the season for the 1-0 victory at Lazio when he was simply world-class. He appeared in the FA Cup fourth round defeat by Liverpool at the end of January before stepping back to focus on an off the field matter that at the time of writing remained unresolved.

Leeds U (From trainee on 13/5/1997) PL 71+2/4 FLC 5 FAC 9 Others 16

WOODHOUSE Curtis
Born: Beverley, 17 April 1980
Height: 5'8" Weight: 11.0
International Honours: E: U21-4; Yth

Although he featured regularly for Sheffield United in the first half of last season and always gave his best for the cause, Curtis never quite seemed to reach the high standards of play that he had shown in the 1999-2000 campaign. In the new year his name was circulated to other clubs as available for transfer and he was sold to Birmingham City in February in a deal which saw the Blades receive Peter Ndlovu and a substantial cash payment. He went on to feature regularly for the Blues in the closing stages of the campaign scoring both goals in the 2-1 win at Huddersfield in the final game of the regular season. A hard-working midfield player who harries the opposition for 90 minutes, he uses the ball simply but effectively.

Sheffield U (From trainee on 31/12/1997) FL 92+12/7 FLC 5+3 FAC 10
Birmingham C (£1,000,000 on 2/2/2001) FL 17/2 Others 2

WOODMAN Andrew (Andy) John
Born: Camberwell, 11 August 1971
Height: 6'3" Weight: 13.7
Club Honours: Div 3 '99

Andy joined Southend United on loan from Brentford shortly before the start of the 2000-01 season, and made 19 appearances before new manager Dave Webb brought in Darryl Flahavan. He moved on for another loan spell, this time at Colchester and the transfer was made permanent early in the new year. He proved to be a great success at Layer Road, turning in a string of outstanding performances that earned him runner-up to Micky Stockwell in the club's 'Player of the Season' award. A goalkeeper who commands his area, his shot stopping and general handling are excellent.

Crystal Palace (From trainee on 1/7/1989)
Exeter C (Free on 4/7/1994) FL 6 FLC 1 FAC 1 Others 2
Northampton T (Free on 10/3/1995) FL 163 FLC 13 FAC 8 Others 13
Brentford (Signed on 22/1/1999) FL 61 FLC 1 FAC 2 Others 3
Southend U (Loaned on 8/8/2000) FL 17 FLC 2
Colchester U (Free on 10/11/2000) FL 28 Others 1

WOODMAN Craig Alan
Born: Tiverton, 22 December 1982
Height: 5'9" Weight: 9.11

A product of the FA School of Excellence at Lilleshall, Craig stepped up to make his senior debut for Bristol City in the LDV Vans Trophy tie at Plymouth and also featured in a couple of Second Division games last season. A promising left wing back he will be looking to extend his first-team experience in the 2001-02 campaign.

Bristol C (From trainee on 17/2/2000) FL 1+1 Others 1

WOODTHORPE Colin John
Born: Ellesmere Port, 13 January 1969
Height: 5'11" Weight: 11.8

Colin began last season on the subs' bench for Stockport and featured regularly in the squad in the first half of the campaign. Essentially a left back he was also used in midfield and towards the end of the season even appeared as a central defender, but wherever he was asked to play he always

gave a competent performance. A model professional, and an excellent example to the club's many younger players, Colin's mature approach to the game earned him the offer of another two-year contract at Edgeley Park.
Chester C (From trainee on 23/8/1986) FL 154+1/6 FLC 10 FAC 8+1 Others 18/1
Norwich C (£175,000 on 17/7/1990) P/FL 36+7/1 FLC 0+2 FAC 6 Others 1+1
Aberdeen (£400,000 on 20/7/1994) SL 43+5/1 SLC 5+1/1 SC 4 Others 5+2
Stockport Co (£200,000 on 29/7/1997) FL 92+27/4 FLC 10+1/2 FAC 3+1/1

WOODWARD Andrew (Andy) Stephen
Born: Stockport, 23 September 1973
Height: 5'11" Weight: 13.6
Club Honours: Div 2 '97

Andy made a single appearance for Sheffield United in the Worthington Cup tie against Lincoln City last August before joining Scunthorpe on loan. He made his debut for the Iron at Southend on his 27th birthday and immediately became a favourite with the club's fans. He enjoyed a three-month period at Glanford Park interrupted for five weeks by a knee operation, however with no permanent deal being agreed he returned to Bramall Lane at the end of January. He is a versatile defender who can play right back, left back or in a central defensive role but whatever position he is asked to play in he performs with composure and commitment. He was reported to have signed for Halifax Town in the summer.
Crewe Alex (From trainee on 29/7/1992) FL 9+11 FLC 2 Others 0+3
Bury (Signed on 13/3/1995) FL 95+20/1 FLC 6+2 FAC 6+1 Others 5
Sheffield U (£35,000 on 23/3/2000) FL 2+1 FLC 1
Scunthorpe U (Loaned on 22/9/2000) FL 9
Scunthorpe U (Loaned on 22/12/2000) FL 3

WOOLLEY Matthew (Matt) David
Born: Manchester, 22 February 1982
Height: 5'10" Weight: 11.2

A local lad who made his mark in the Macclesfield youth and reserve teams as a speedy attacking midfield player with the ability to score sensational goals, Matt made his Football League debut from the subs' bench very late in the match at Barnet at the beginning of last October. Soon afterwards he signed a new contract for Macc that will keep him at Moss Rose for the next couple of seasons.
Macclesfield T (From trainee at Stockport Co on 19/7/1999) FL 1+1 Others 1

WOOTER Nordin
Born: Surinam, 24 August 1976
Height: 5'8" Weight: 11.1
International Honours: Holland: U21-15

Nordin made a fitful start to the 2000-01 season at Watford, injury problems limiting his opportunities, but his form and fitness improved as the campaign progressed and his attitude was never in doubt. A diminutive, ball-playing winger whose dribbling skills make him a firm favourite with the Watford fans he netted a fine individual goal in the 4-1 win against Norwich in March.
Watford (£975,000 from Real Zaragoza, Spain, ex Ajax, on 14/9/1999) P/FL 30+16/2 FLC 2+1 FAC 1

WOOZLEY David (Dave) James
Born: Ascot, 6 December 1979
Height: 6'0" Weight: 12.10

Dave joined Bournemouth on a month's loan last September to gain regular first-team football and did well in half-a-dozen outings for the Cherries. However he failed to gain a place in the Crystal Palace squad on his return and then had the misfortune to suffer a double fracture of his leg when playing for the reserves against Leyton Orient. The injury put him out of action for the remainder of the campaign and he will be hoping to have made a full recovery in time for the start of the 2001-02 season. He is a tall left-sided defender who is good in the air and solid on the ground.
Crystal Palace (From trainee on 17/11/1997) FL 21+9 FLC 3+1 FAC 0+1
Bournemouth (Loaned on 15/9/2000) FL 6

WORRELL David
Born: Dublin, 12 January 1978
Height: 5'11" Weight: 12.4
International Honours: RoI: U21-17

David was new Plymouth manager Paul Sturrock's first signing, arriving from Dundee United last November initially on loan. His consistent performances at right back ensured a permanent deal but his season was then cruelly cut short when he suffered a broken ankle playing against Barnet in March. A former Republic of Ireland U21 international he looked comfortable on the ball and produced some good link-up play with the midfield.
Blackburn Rov (Signed from Shelbourne on 12/1/1995)
Dundee U (Free on 30/3/1999) SL 13+4 SLC 2
Plymouth Arg (Signed on 23/11/2000) FL 14 Others 2

WOTTON Paul Anthony
Born: Plymouth, 17 August 1977
Height: 5'11" Weight: 12.0

Paul linked up well with Craig Taylor in the heart of the Plymouth Argyle defence last season and their partnership was an important factor in ensuring the Pilgrims maintained an excellent defensive record at Home Park, conceding just 17 goals in 23 league games. He was also the club's penalty taker and netted two goals from the spot. Paul is a strong and powerful central defender who is very comfortable on the ball.
Plymouth Arg (From trainee on 10/7/1995) FL 132+20/7 FLC 5 FAC 12/1 Others 6+1/2

WRACK Darren
Born: Cleethorpes, 5 May 1976
Height: 5'9" Weight: 12.10

Darren was hampered by an attack of tendonitis during the 2000-01 campaign but always gave his best for Walsall when selected. He made several useful contributions towards the Saddlers' promotion campaign, heading the equaliser and setting up the winner in the opening home game against Oldham and laying on a late winner against Swindon. A purposeful midfield player known for his darting runs he was made available on the transfer list in the summer.
Derby Co (From trainee on 12/7/1994) FL 4+22/1 FLC 0+3 FAC 0+2
Grimsby T (£100,000 + on 19/7/1996) FL 5+8/1 Others 0+1
Shrewsbury T (Loaned on 17/2/1997) FL 3+1 Others 1
Walsall (Free on 6/8/1998) FL 91+27/21 FLC 7 FAC 5+1/1 Others 7+1/1

WREH Christopher (Chris)
Born: Liberia, 14 May 1975
Height: 5'8" Weight: 11.13
Club Honours: PL '98; FAC '98; CS '98
International Honours: Liberia

After spending a long period of the 1999-2000 season away from Highbury, Chris featured only briefly for Arsenal last term. His only first-team outing came as a substitute in the Worthington Cup third round defeat by Ipswich Town in November before he was sold to top Saudi Arabian club Al-Hilal shortly before Christmas. He is a quick and confident striker with the ability to run at defences.
Arsenal (£300,000 from Guingamp, France, ex AS Monaco, on 14/8/1997) PL 10+18/3 FLC 3+4 FAC 2+4/1 Others 3+2/1
Birmingham C (Loaned on 22/10/1999) FL 6+1/1

WRIGHT Alan Geoffrey
Born: Ashton under Lyne, 28 September 1971
Height: 5'4" Weight: 9.9
Club Honours: FLC '96
International Honours: E: U21-2; Yth; Sch

Alan had another consistent season in the Aston Villa defence in 2000-01 when he was a near ever-present in the first team. Although he tended to play as a left wing back in the early stages of the campaign, he later switched to a conventional left-back role as manager John Gregory changed the formation from 3-5-2 to 4-4-2. A small and pacy defender who loves to push forward, he is one of the most reliable members of the Villa squad.
Blackpool (From trainee on 13/4/1989) FL 91+7 FLC 10+2 FAC 8 Others 11+2
Blackburn Rov (£400,000 on 25/10/1991) F/PL 67+7/1 FLC 8 FAC 5+1 Others 3
Aston Villa (£1,000,000 on 10/3/1995) PL 223+4/5 FLC 18 FAC 23 Others 18

WRIGHT David
Born: Warrington, 1 May 1980
Height: 5'11" Weight: 10.8
International Honours: E: Yth

David was once again a near ever-present in the Crewe Alexandra back line last term when he was in excellent form. Mostly featuring at right back he was very solid in defence and also enjoyed pushing forward to help out with the attack. He is yet another fine prospect to develop through the very productive Gresty Road youth scheme.
Crewe Alex (From trainee on 18/6/1997) FL 106+4/1 FLC 7+1 FAC 3

WRIGHT Jermaine Malaki
Born: Greenwich, 21 October 1975
Height: 5'9" Weight: 11.9
International Honours: E: Yth

After being excluded from the Ipswich Town starting line-up for the opening game of last season Jermaine was brought into the side for the next game and kept his place for the remainder of the campaign, missing only one game. He mostly played on the right-hand side of midfield, linking well with Fabian Wilnis down the flank, but his best performances came when he replaced Jim Magilton in central midfield and really controlled the game, spraying passes all around the pitch. He showed his potential with two fine goals - a one-two with Marcus Stewart on the edge of the box followed by a low drive at Leeds and a rocket of a shot against Coventry after picking up a loose ball some 25 yards out from goal. Jermaine was voted the 'Most Improved Player' in the squad this season by the club's coaching staff.

Millwall (From trainee on 27/11/1992)
Wolverhampton W (£60,000 on 29/12/1994) FL 4+16 FLC 1+3/1 Others 0+1
Doncaster Rov (Loaned on 1/3/1996) FL 13
Crewe Alex (£25,000 on 19/2/1998) FL 47+2/5 FLC 5 FAC 1
Ipswich T (£500,000 on 23/7/1999) P/FL 56+15/3 FLC 8+2 FAC 2+1/1 Others 1

WRIGHT Mark Anthony
Born: Wolverhampton, 24 February 1982
Height: 5'11" Weight: 11.4

Mark almost made a dream debut in senior football after coming off the subs' bench for Walsall in the Worthington Cup second round tie at West Ham when with his first touch he had a potential equaliser cleared off the line. He received a handful of opportunities later in the season and his crossing ability was highlighted when he provided the centre from which Brett Angell scored the second goal of his hat-trick in the final Second Division game at Northampton. A promising youngster who can play in central midfield or on the right wing he won the club's 'Young Player of the Season' trophy. Mark is the son of former Walsall striker Evran Wright who is currently winding down his career with local club Rushall Olympic.

Walsall (From trainee on 26/1/2001) FL 0+4 FLC 0+1 Others 2

WRIGHT Nicholas (Nick) John
Born: Ilkeston, 15 October 1975
Height: 5'10" Weight: 11.7

Nick had another very frustrating time at Watford in 2000-01 and managed only one senior appearance, featuring in the Worthington Cup second round second leg tie against Notts County. He underwent a groin operation during the 2000 close season and then picked up a knee injury that proved troublesome as the joint kept swelling up as he fought to regain match fitness. A hard-working right-sided midfielder with a good eye for goal he has hardly played at all in the last two seasons and is long overdue a change in fortune.

Derby Co (From trainee on 12/7/1994)
Carlisle U (£35,000 on 28/11/1997) FL 25/5 Others 2/2
Watford (£100,000 on 6/7/1998) P/FL 32+5/6 FLC 3 FAC 1+1 Others 3/1

WRIGHT Richard Ian
Born: Ipswich, 5 November 1977
Height: 6'2" Weight: 13.0
International Honours: E: 1; U21-15; Yth; Sch

Richard was a near ever-present for Premiership new boys Ipswich Town last term and enhanced his credentials as a top-class 'keeper with a string of outstanding performances. His best display was probably in the game at Highbury when he was called upon to make a series of great saves, with one from a Dennis Bergkamp shot that was destined for the top corner of world-class standard. His 12 clean sheets in the Premiership are a measure of the quality of his performance. He also gave confidence to his defenders who could rest assured that the final line of defence was a particularly effective one. On the international front he was named in the first three England squads picked by new boss Sven Goran Ericsson but failed to add to his single cap. He played the last few games of the season with a slight injury and at the start of the summer break he entered hospital for a hernia operation, although he is expected to be fully fit for the start of the 2001-02 campaign. He was reported to have joined Arsenal in the summer.

Ipswich T (From trainee on 2/1/1995) P/FL 240 FLC 27 FAC 13 Others 11

Richard Wright

WRIGHT Stephen (Steve) John
Born: Liverpool, 8 February 1980
Height: 6'2" Weight: 12.0
Club Honours: UEFAC '01
International Honours: E: U21-3; Yth

Another outstanding prospect from Liverpool's youth scheme Steve, had already appeared for England U21s before he made his debut for the Reds as a substitute in the Worthington Cup tie at Stoke in November. Further appearances off the bench followed in February against West Ham and Sunderland before he made the starting line-up for the FA Cup quarter-final tie at Tranmere, but although he performed admirably this was his last first-team action of the season. With three U21 caps to his name already this young right back is likely to feature more regularly in the squad in 2001-02.

Liverpool (From trainee on 13/10/1997) PL 0+2 FLC 0+1 FAC 1
Crewe Alex (Loaned on 6/8/1999) FL 17+6 FLC 1

WRIGHT Thomas (Tommy) James
Born: Belfast, 29 August 1963
Height: 6'1" Weight: 14.5
Club Honours: Div 1 '93
International Honours: NI: 31; U23-1

Tommy continued to show great patience as back-up 'keeper for Manchester City last season and managed just one appearance against Newcastle at Maine Road, when he gave a superb performance yet still failed to keep his place in the team. In January he joined Bolton on a three-month loan deal as Wanderers' boss Sam Allardyce sought to ease his goalkeeping crisis. This deal was subsequently made permanent until the end of the season to free-up a further loan spot so that Wanderers could sign Matt Clarke from Bradford. Tommy made his debut when he came on against Queens Park Rangers in February to replace red-card victim Steve Banks and went on to make three more appearances before serving as a reliable deputy to Clarke in the closing matches. Out of contract in the summer his future remained uncertain at the time of writing.

Newcastle U (£30,000 from Linfield on 27/1/1988) F/PL 72+1 FLC 6 FAC 4 Others 1
Hull C (Loaned on 14/2/1991) FL 6
Nottingham F (£450,000 on 24/9/1993) P/FL 11 FLC 2
Reading (Loaned on 4/10/1996) FL 17
Manchester C (Loaned on 17/1/1997) FL 5
Manchester C (£450,000 on 3/3/1997) P/FL 29 FLC 1 FAC 2 Others 1
Wrexham (Loaned on 26/2/1999) FL 16
Newcastle U (Loaned on 25/8/1999) PL 3
Bolton W (Loaned on 18/1/2001) FL 3+1

WRIGHT-PHILLIPS Shaun Cameron
Born: Greenwich, 25 October 1981
Height: 5'6" Weight: 10.1

Shaun made a fine start to his career in the Premiership with Manchester City last term, featuring in a total of 15 games and showing some fine form that had the crowd on the edge of their seats at times. A talented young midfield player, his light frame enabled him to turn on the proverbial sixpence making it difficult for defenders to stop him, while he also made several exciting runs with the ball taking on defenders. Although he later dropped back to the reserves and then faced relegation at the end of the season he will have learnt a lot from his introduction to Premiership football. Shaun is the son of the former England striker Ian Wright.

Manchester C (From trainee on 28/10/1998) P/FL 11+8 FLC 3+2

XAVIER Abel
Born: Mozambique, 30 November 1972
Height: 6'2" Weight: 13.6
International Honours: Portugal: 17; U21; Yth (UEFA-U16 '89; U18 '90)

After a bright and purposeful first full season in the English Premiership, the Portuguese international with the distinctive appearance was sidelined by a series of unfortunate injuries. During the early part of the campaign, Abel boasted a happy record for the Blues as his first five appearances of the season saw three Everton victories from testing trips to Newcastle, Middlesbrough and Bradford. But a succession of injury problems limited his appearances after that. There is no doubt Everton missed his commanding presence. Equally at home at right back, centre half or in midfield, Abel is a strong, crisp tackler with fine distribution.

Everton (£1,500,000 from PSV Eindhoven, Holland on 8/9/1999) PL 28+3 FLC 1 FAC 3

YATES Mark Jason
Born: Birmingham, 24 January 1970
Height: 5'11" Weight: 13.2
Club Honours: NC '99
International Honours: E: SP-2

Mark enjoyed an excellent campaign for Cheltenham Town in the centre of midfield last season winning much praise for his hard work and consistent displays. Partnering Lee Howells in the centre of the park his ball-winning skills were to the fore and he also contributed six valuable goals. He was deservedly awarded the title of 'Player of the Season' at Whaddon Road at the end of the campaign.

Birmingham C (From trainee on 8/7/1988) FL 38+16/6 FLC 5/1 FAC 0+2 Others 5
Burnley (£40,000 on 30/8/1991) FL 9+9/1 FLC 1 FAC 0+2 Others 2+1
Lincoln C (Loaned on 19/2/1993) FL 10+4
Doncaster Rov (Signed on 30/7/1993) FL 33+1/4 FLC 2 FAC 1 Others 1 (Transferred to Kidderminster Hrs on 13/8/1994)
Cheltenham T (Signed on 28/1/1999) FL 91/8 FLC 4 FAC 4 Others 2+1

YATES Stephen (Steve)
Born: Bristol, 29 January 1970
Height: 5'11" Weight: 12.2
Club Honours: Div 3 '90

A near ever-present for Tranmere in 2000-01 Steve again proved to be a calm and reliable figure in defence. Very solid and with a no-nonsense approach he is particularly effective in the air, both at the back and when coming up to help out in attack. His high point of the season was undoubtedly the FA Cup victory over Everton when he contributed two stunning headers to Rovers' 3-0 victory. Despite the campaign ending in relegation he received some consolation when he was voted as the 'Young Supporters' Player of the Year'.

Abel Xavier

Bristol Rov (From trainee on 1/7/1988) FL 196+1 FLC 9 FAC 11 Others 21
Queens Park R (£650,000 on 16/8/1993) P/FL 122+12/2 FLC 8 FAC 7
Tranmere Rov (Free on 5/8/1999) FL 73+3/4 FLC 10+1/2 FAC 6/4

YORKE Dwight
Born: Canaan, Tobago, 3 November 1971
Height: 5'10" Weight: 12.4
Club Honours: FLC '96; FAC '99; PL '99, '00, '01; EC '99
International Honours: Trinidad & Tobago

That enigmatic smile, as much a trademark of Dwight's game as his penchant for scoring spectacular goals, was in real danger of being wiped away by the early season exploits of Teddy Sheringham for Manchester United. It looked at one stage as though a big money move might be the only way of solving his problem, but happily things soon improved, and it wasn't long before Dwight was showing his worth in front of goal again. A fine strike against Leeds at Old Trafford in October was followed by another superb effort at Derby in November. Despite falling behind on the appearances stakes, Dwight had better luck on the Champions' League stage, where his only missing link was the match against Valencia in February. At the turn of the year, he showed his predatory instincts with a hat-trick against Arsenal at Old Trafford, and a goal against Leicester. He continued to feature regularly for Trinidad & Tobago, scoring six goals in 12 appearances, although his country's campaign to qualify for the 2002 World Cup finals fizzled out in the summer.

Aston Villa (£120,000 from Signal Hill, Tobago on 19/12/1989) F/PL 195+36/73 FLC 20+2/8 FAC 22+2/13 Others 10/3
Manchester U (£12,600,000 on 22/8/1998) PL 76+10/47 FLC 2/2 FAC 6+4/3 Others 30+8/12

YOUNG Alan James
Born: Swindon, 12 August 1983
Height: 5'6" Weight: 10.2
International Honours: E: Yth

A regular scorer for Swindon Town's reserve and youth teams Alan stepped up to make his Football League debut from the subs' bench at Luton in September and went on to make a handful of first-team appearances last term, registering his first senior goal in the FA Cup victory over Ilkeston Town. A promising young striker he was voted the club's 'Young Player of the Year'.

Swindon T (Trainee) FL 0+4 FAC 0+3/1 Others 1

YOUNG Luke Paul
Born: Harlow, 19 July 1979
Height: 6'0" Weight: 12.4
Club Honours: FLC '99
International Honours: E: U21-9; Yth

A promising Tottenham wing back, Luke had just begun to establish himself in the first team when he was struck down by injuries. An ankle problem kept him out for several weeks in September and he had only been back for a short while before he broke a bone in his foot, putting him on the sidelines for a further six weeks. Extremely confident on the ball and strong in the challenge he will be hoping to benefit from Sol Campbell's summer departure. He continued to represent England U21s when fit and won a further four caps during the season. Luke is the younger brother of Neil Young.

Tottenham H (From trainee on 3/7/1997) PL 44+14 FLC 1+3 FAC 9+2 Others 2+1

YOUNG Neil Anthony
Born: Harlow, 31 August 1973
Height: 5'9" Weight: 12.0

Neil featured regularly for Bournemouth at the beginning of the 2000-01 campaign but then suffered a serious knee injury at the end of September that required surgery and a long period of rehabilitation. A dependable right back who likes to get forward and put crosses in he will be hoping to recover full fitness in time to resume his career at the start of the coming season. He is the older brother of Tottenham's Luke Young.

Tottenham H (From trainee on 17/8/1991)
Bournemouth (Free on 11/10/1994) FL 247+2/3 FLC 19 FAC 16 Others 15

YOUNG Scott
Born: Pontypridd, 14 January 1976
Height: 6'2" Weight: 12.6
International Honours: W: B-1; U21-5

This solid central defender bounced back from a disappointing 1999-2000 campaign with a series of powerful performances for Cardiff City last season. He missed just one league game and revealed his hidden talents as a goalscorer, scoring ten times thus more than doubling his previous career total. He was a major contender for the club's 'Player of the Year' award and was only just edged out by Andy Legg.

Cardiff C (From trainee on 4/7/1994) FL 216+16/17 FLC 13+1/1 FAC 17/1 Others 13+3/1

YOUNGS Thomas (Tom) Anthony John
Born: Bury St Edmunds, 31 August 1979
Height: 5'9" Weight: 10.4

Tom continued to make excellent progress at Cambridge United last season and established himself as the club's main striker for the first time. A tireless and unselfish worker up front he scored regularly throughout the campaign and finished up as the U's leading scorer. His form attracted the attention of several bigger clubs and if he continues to develop at such a rate it remains to be seen how long United will be able to keep him at the Abbey Stadium.

Cambridge U (From juniors on 3/7/1997) FL 51+22/22 FLC 1+2 FAC 2/1 Others 2+2/1

ZABEK Lee Kevin
Born: Bristol, 13 October 1978
Height: 6'0" Weight: 12.0

A strong and powerful ball-winner, Lee made an instant impact in the centre of the midfield for Exeter City last season. Although affected by illness and injury he appeared regularly in the first team and if he continues to show such promise it seems only a matter of time before he is transferred to a higher-level club. He has a good disciplinary record, despite a combative approach to the game, and he is more than useful in the air.

Bristol Rov (From trainee on 28/7/1997) FL 21+8/1 FLC 2 FAC 2+1/1 Others 4
Exeter C (Free on 10/8/2000) FL 26+5 FLC 2 FAC 1

ZAMORA Robert (Bobby) Lester
Born: Barking, 16 January 1981
Height: 6'0" Weight: 11.0
Club Honours: Div 3 '01

Bobby joined Brighton permanently in the summer of 2000 after enjoying a successful loan spell in 1999-2000 and continued where he had left off, scoring goals regularly throughout the campaign. His tally of 31 in all competitions included hat-tricks against Torquay and Macclesfield and he became the first Seagulls' player since Garry Nelson back in 1987-88 to score more than 30 goals in a season. A powerful and stylish striker he is effective both in the air and on the ground and attracted attention from a number of scouts from higher-level clubs. His goals were a key factor in Brighton winning the Third Division title last season and he will be aiming to continue scoring in the Second Division in the 2001-02 campaign. Bobby was honoured by his fellow professionals with a place in the PFA's Third Division team.

Bristol Rov (From trainee on 1/7/1999) FL 0+4 FLC 0+1 FAC 0+1
Brighton & Hove A (Loaned on 11/2/2000) FL 6/6
Brighton & Hove A (£100,000 on 10/8/2000) FL 42+1/28 FLC 2 FAC 2/2 Others 1/1

ZEGHDANE Lehit
Born: Revin, France, 3 October 1977
Height: 6'1" Weight: 12.7

Having been released by French club Sedan at the end of the 1999-2000 campaign Lehit had trials with a number of clubs before joining Darlington last September. He made his debut at the City Ground against Nottingham Forest in the Worthington Cup first round second leg tie, but managed only a handful more appearances before returning to France in October. He is a pacy hard-working striker.

Darlington (Free from Sedan, France on 1/9/2000) FL 1+2 FLC 0+2

ZHIYI Fan
Born: Shanghai, China, 6 November 1969
Height: 6'2" Weight: 12.1
International Honours: China

Fan had another brilliant season playing for Crystal Palace in 2000-01. An excellent all-round central defender he possesses excellent passing skills, good pace and a phenomenal work rate. He missed several games in the new year with hamstring trouble and was absent from the final weeks of the season on World Cup duty. An ever-present for China in the six first round qualifying games, he scored twice in a 10-1 win over the Maldives. Fan was deservedly voted as the Eagles' 'Player of the Year'.

Crystal Palace (£500,000 from Shanghai, China on 10/9/1998) FL 85+1/4 FLC 11/2 FAC 3

Bobby Zamora

ZIEGE Christian
Born: Germany, 1 February 1972
Height: 6'1" Weight: 12.12
Club Honours: FLC '01
International Honours: Germany: 58 (UEFA '96)

Having enjoyed a fine season at Middlesbrough in 1999-2000, Christian took advantage of an 'escape clause' in his contract to sign for Liverpool at the end of August. However the controversy surrounding the deal seemed to affect his form at club level and he took some time to settle in at Anfield. He scored his first goal for the Reds in the 4-3 defeat at Leeds in November but was then briefly replaced by the youngster Djimi Traore. Soon after his return he was sidelined by a hamstring problem and then a back injury. On his return to fitness he found that Jamie Carragher had claimed the left-back position and manager Gerard Houllier redeployed him on the left side of midfield where he was in competition with Danny Murphy and Patrik Berger. He made a decisive contribution to the unexpected UEFA Cup victory away to Roma, when chasing a loose ball to the bye line he was able to successfully cut the ball back to set up Michael Owen's second and decisive goal. However he then only made fleeting appearances for the Reds' first team in the climax to their treble-winning season. He continued to be a key figure for Germany in their quest for World Cup qualification.

Middlesbrough (£4,000,000 from AC Milan, Italy, ex Bayern Munich, on 6/8/1999) PL 29/6 FLC 3+1/1 FAC 1
Liverpool (£5,500,000 on 29/8/2000) PL 11+5/1 FLC 1+3/1 FAC 2+1 Others 6+3

ZOLA Gianfranco (Franco)
Born: Sardinia Italy, 5 July 1966
Height: 5'6" Weight: 10.10
Club Honours: FAC '97, '00; FLC '98; ECWC '98; ESC '98; CS '00
International Honours: Italy: 35

Although nearing the veteran stage of his career at Chelsea, Franco tormented the Manchester United defence in the FA Charity Shield at Wembley and deservedly won the 'Man of the Match' award. Preferred to Tore Andre Flo he struck up an immediate rapport with Jimmy-Floyd Hasselbaink who fully appreciated his quicksilver skills. No season would be complete without one of his trademark free-kicks, and he duly obliged in the opening match, curling a sublime effort up and over the West Ham wall. Following Luca Vialli's shock departure Franco was reunited with Claudio Ranieri, his former mentor from his Napoli days, and was regularly switched to a position in the 'hole' behind front runners Hasselbaink and Eidur Gudjohnsen to devastating effect. He went on to produce some excellent form and was a key factor in the Blues' progression to a UEFA Cup spot. A perfect illustration of this came with his virtuoso performance at Pride Park, when he inspired Chelsea to a 4-0 victory. In May he finally settled any doubts about his future by signing a new two-year deal that is likely to see him end his playing career at Stamford Bridge.

Chelsea (£4,500,000 from Parma, Italy, ex Napoli, Torres, Nuorese, on 15/11/1996) PL 136+20/42 FLC 5/1 FAC 21+1/8 Others 32+1/8

ZUNIGA Yanez Herlin **Ysrael**
Born: Lima, Peru, 27 August 1976
Height: 5'10" Weight: 11.5
International Honours: Peru: 15

Ysrael had few opportunities to display his talents for Coventry in the Premiership last term, starting only nine games and completing only one. His best performances were when he came off the bench at Highbury and in the home game with Manchester United, when he scored his only league goal of the campaign. He generally looked a little lightweight alongside Moustafa Hadji in attack and looked as if he would benefit from being paired with a bigger partner. He featured for Peru in the early part of the campaign before losing his place and will really need regular first-team football to get back in the squad.

Coventry C (£750,000 from FCB Melgar, Peru on 3/3/2000) PL 10+12/3 FLC 2/1

Where Did They Go?

Below is a list of all players who were recorded in the 2000-2001 *Factfile* as making a first-team appearance in 1999-2000, but failed to make the current book, which covers last season. They are listed alphabetically, and show their leaving dates as well as their first port of call if known. Of course, they may well have moved on by now, but space does not allow further reference.

* Shows that the player in question is still with his named club but failed to make an appearance in 2000-2001, the most common reason being injury.

\+ Players retained by Chester C, who were relegated to the Conference.

Player	Club	Date	Destination
ABIODUN Yemi	Southend U	01.01	Kingstonian
ABLETT Gary	Blackpool	06.00	*Retired*
ABOU Samassi	West Ham U	06.00	
AGOGO Junior	Sheffield Wed	02.00	Chicago Fire (USA)
ALDRIDGE Martin	Blackpool	01.00	*Deceased*
ALJOFREE Hasney	Bolton W	06.00	Dundee U
ALLARDYCE Craig	Mansfield T	03.00	Boston U
ALLEN Chris	Stockport Co	06.00	Slough T
ALLEN Rory	Portsmouth	*	
ALLOU Bernard	Nottingham F	05.01	
ALMEIDA Marco	Southampton	12.99	Sporting Lisbon (Portugal)
AMBROSETTI Gabriele	Chelsea	*	
ANDRESEN Martin	Wimbledon	06.00	Stabaek (Norway)
ANSELIN Cedric	Norwich C	*	
ANSELL Gary	Barnet	06.00	St Albans C
ANTHONY Graham	Carlisle U	06.00	Barrow
ARENDSE Andre	Fulham	07.00	Sparta Rotterdam (Holland)
ARMSTRONG Paul	Brighton & Hove A	06.00	Airdrieonians
ATKINSON Graeme	Rochdale	06.01	
AVDIU Kemajl	Bury	05.00	Vasalund (Sweden)
BABB Phil	Liverpool	06.00	Sporting Lisbon (Portugal)
BADIR Walid	Wimbledon	07.00	Maccabi Haifa (Israel)
BAIANO Francesco	Derby Co	11.99	Ternana (Italy)
BAILEY John	Bournemouth	10.00	*Retired*
BAKER Matt	Hull C	06.00	Hereford U
BAKER Paul	Carlisle U	05.00	*Retired*
BARDSLEY David	Blackpool	06.00	*Retired*
BARKER Simon	Port Vale	12.99	*Retired*
BARNES Steve	Barnet	06.00	Hayes
BARNETT Dave	Lincoln C	09.00	*Retired*
BARR Billy	Carlisle U	06.00	Workington
BARWICK Terry	Scunthorpe U	*	
BASSINDER Gavin	Mansfield T	06.00	Gainsborough Trinity
BASTOW Darren	Plymouth Arg	*	
BEARD Mark	Southend U	06.00	Kingstonian
BECK Mikkel	Derby Co	07.00	OSC Lille (France)
BEESLEY Mark	Preston NE	06.00	Chester C
BEESLEY Paul	Blackpool	07.00	Chester C
BEHARALL David	Newcastle U	*	
BELGRAVE Barrington	Plymouth Arg	06.00	Yeovil T
BENGTSSON Robert	Barnsley	12.99	
BENNETT Frankie	Exeter C	03.00	Forest Green Rov
BENNETT Gary	Darlington	06.00	*Retired*
BENT Junior	Blackpool	06.01	
BERESFORD John	Southampton	10.00	*Retired*
BERNAL Andy	Reading	06.00	*Retired*
BERNTSEN Tommy	Portsmouth	11.99	Lillestrom (Norway)
BERRY Paul	Chester C	+	
BEWERS Jonathan	Aston Villa	*	

Player	Club	Date	Destination
{BICA} DI GIUSEPPE Marcos	Walsall	12.99	
BLACKBURN Chris	Chester C	+	
BLACKMORE Clayton	Notts Co	06.00	Leigh RMI
BONALAIR Thierry	Nottingham F	04.00	*Retired*
BONNOT Alex	Watford	06.01	
BORBOKIS Vass	Derby Co	12.99	PAOK Salonika (Greece)
BOSNICH Mark	Manchester U	01.01	Chelsea*
BOSSU Bert	Barnet	*	
BOWEN Mark	Reading	01.00	*Retired*
BOWMAN Rob	Carlisle U	06.00	Bohemians
BOXALL Danny	Brentford	*	
BOYLAN Lee	Exeter C	01.00	Kingstonian
BRACE Deryn	Wrexham	06.00	Llanelli
BROWN Greg	Macclesfield T	01.00	Morecambe
BROWN Wayne	Chester C	+	
BRYAN Del	Brentford	*	
BRYANT Matt	Gillingham	06.01	
BUCKLEY Adam	Grimsby T	*	
BULL Garry	Wolverhampton W	06.00	Grantham T
BULLOCK Matthew	Stoke C	*	
BURNS John	Bristol C	*	
BUTLER Peter	Halifax T	04.01	*Retired*
BUTLER Steve	Gillingham	06.00	*Retired*
BYRNE Shaun	West Ham U	*	
CADETE Jorge	Bradford C	05.00	Estrela Amadora (Portugal)
CAMILIERI-GIOIA Carlo	Mansfield T	11.99	
CAMPAGNA Sam	Swindon T	06.01	
CAMPBELL Neil	Southend U	03.00	Doncaster Rov
CANHAM Scott	Leyton Orient	06.00	Chesham U
CARDEN Paul	Chester C	+	
CAREY Shaun	Norwich C	04.00	Rushden & Diamonds
CARSON Danny	Chester C	03.00	Winsford U
CARTER Rob	Leyton Orient	11.00	Billericay T
CARVER Joe	Chester C	10.99	
CASPER Chris	Reading	*	
CASSIDY Jamie	Cambridge U	07.00	Northwich Victoria
CHALLINOR Paul	Bury	06.00	Ilkeston T
CHAPPLE Phil	Peterborough U	*	
CHENERY Ben	Cambridge U	06.00	Canvey Island
CLARKE Adrian	Southend U	06.00	Stevenage Borough
CLARKE Richard	Scunthorpe U	04.00	
COLLETER Patrick	Southampton	11.00	AS Cannes (France)
COOPER Steve	Wrexham	06.00	Rhyl
CORICA Steve	Wolverhampton W	03.00	Sanfrecce Hiroshima (Japan)
COUZENS Andy	Blackpool	06.00	Harrogate T
COWLING Lee	Mansfield T	06.00	Kettering T
CRAWFORD Jimmy	Reading	07.00	Shelbourne
CRITCHLEY Neil	Crewe Alex	06.00	Leigh RMI
CROSS David	Notts Co	*	
CROSS Jon	Chester C	06.00	Colwyn Bay

Player	Club	Date	Destination
CROUDSON Steve	Grimsby T	*	
CRUYFF Jordi	Manchester U	06.00	Deportivo Alaves (Spain)
CUERVO Philippe	Swindon T	06.00	
CULVERHOUSE Ian	Brighton & Hove A	05.00	*Retired*
CUNDY Jason	Portsmouth	12.00	*Retired*
CURRAN Danny	Leyton Orient	03.00	Purfleet

Player	Club	Date	Destination
DALEY Tony	Walsall	09.99	Forest Green Rov
DALTON Paul	Huddersfield T	03.00	Gateshead
DANIELSSON Einer Thor	Stoke C	01.00	KR Rejkjavik (Iceland)
DARBY Duane	Notts Co	06.00	Rushden & Diamonds
DAVIES Gareth	Swindon T	*	
DAVIS Steve	Oxford U	06.00	Northwich Victoria
DE FREITAS Fabian	West Bromwich A	09.00	Cambuur (Holland)
DEGN Peter	Everton	*	
DELORGE Laurent	Coventry C	*	
DE ORNELAS Fernando	Crystal Palace	12.99	Real Zaragoza (Spain)
DESCHAMPS Didier	Chelsea	07.00	Valencia (Spain)
DEVINE Sean	Wycombe W	*	
DIAF Farid	Preston NE	06.00	
DICKSON Mark	Northampton T	06.00	Newry T
DIGBY Fraser	Crystal Palace	10.00	Barry T
DI LELLA Gustavo	Hartlepool U	01.00	Durham C
DILLON Paul	Rotherham U	04.01	
DIOP Pape	Norwich C	12.99	RC Lens (France)
DIXON Kevin	Leeds U	*	
DOBSON Tony	Northampton T	06.00	Forest Green Rov
DONALDSON O'Neill	Torquay U	06.00	
DONIS George	Huddersfield T	07.00	
DOUGHTY Matt	Chester C	+	
DOWE Julian	Rochdale	06.00	Morecambe
DUMAS Franck	Newcastle U	01.00	Marseille (France)
DYSON James	Birmingham C	06.01	

Player	Club	Date	Destination
EARLE Robbie	Wimbledon	10.00	*Retired*
EDWARDS Jake	Wrexham	11.99	Telford U
EINARSSON Gunnar	Brentford	04.00	Roda JC (Holland)
ELLINGTON Lee	Exeter C	04.00	Walton & Hersham
EMBLEN Paul	Wycombe W	06.01	
ENCKELMAN Peter	Aston Villa	*	
ETHERINGTON Craig	West Ham U	*	
EVANS Andy	Barnsley	*	
EVANS Rhys	Chelsea	*	
EVE Angus	Chester C	+	

Player	Club	Date	Destination
FAERBER Winston	Cardiff C	05.00	FC Den Bosch (Holland)
FAIRCLOUGH Chris	York C	02.01	
FARLEY Craig	Colchester U	09.00	Chesham U
FENTON Tony	Portsmouth	06.00	Colwyn Bay
FEUER Ian	West Ham U	06.00	Wimbledon*
FINCH Keith	Darlington	*	
FINNEY Steve	Chester C	+	
FISHER Neil	Chester C	+	
FLANAGAN Alan	Swindon T	06.00	
FLO Havard	Wolverhampton W	06.01	
FOE Marc-Vivien	West Ham U	05.00	Lyonnaise (France)
FORBES Steve	Colchester U	03.00	Stevenage Borough
FORBES Terrell	West Ham U	*	
FORRESTER Mark	Torquay U	03.00	
FOSTER Craig	Crystal Palace	11.00	
FOYLE Martin	Port Vale	06.00	*Retired*
FRAIL Steve	Tranmere Rov	02.00	St Johnstone
FRENCH Jon	Hull C	06.00	Barry T
FRIARS Sean	Ipswich T	*	
FROGGATT Steve	Coventry C	*	
FUERTES Esteban	Derby Co	06.00	FC Lens (France)
FUGLESTAD Erik	Norwich C	04.00	
[FUMACA] ANTUNES Jose	Newcastle U	05.00	

Player	Club	Date	Destination
GALE Shaun	Exeter C	06.00	Havant & Waterlooville
GARVEY Steve	Blackpool	06.01	
GAYLE Mark	Chesterfield	06.00	Hednesford T
GERMAIN Steve	Colchester U	12.99	
GHRAYIB Naj	Aston Villa	02.01	Hapoel Haifa (Israel)
GIJSBRECHTS Davy	Sheffield U	*	
GISLASON Siggi	Stoke C	02.00	KR Rejkjavik (Iceland)
GITTENS Jon	Exeter C	06.00	Nuneaton Borough
GOODING Mick	Southend U	06.00	*Retired*
GOODMAN Jon	Wimbledon	01.00	*Retired*
GOODWIN Tommy	Leicester C	*	
GOUGH Neil	Leyton Orient	*	
GOULD Ronnie	Leyton Orient	*	
GRAHAM Mark	Cambridge U	09.99	Glenavon
GRAHAM Richard	Oldham Ath	06.00	*Retired*
GRANT Stephen	Burnley	09.99	
GRAVELAINE Xavier	Watford	01.00	Le Havre (France)
GREGORY Andy	Barnsley	06.00	Emley
GRIFFITHS Michael	Torquay U	06.00	Halesowen T
GUSTAFSSON Tomas	Coventry C	*	

Player	Club	Date	Destination
HAARHOFF Jimmy	Birmingham C	01.01	Chester C
HACKETT Warren	Barnet	06.01	
HAILS Julian	Southend U	04.00	*Retired*
HALEY Grant	Peterborough U	12.00	Bedford T
HALLWORTH Jon	Cardiff C	06.00	
HANKIN Sean	Crystal Palace	*	
HANNON Kevin	Wrexham	06.01	
HARRIES Paul	Carlisle U	10.00	
HEALY Brian	Torquay U	*	
HEANEY Neil	Darlington	07.00	Dundee U
[HELDER] CHRISTOVAO Rodriguez	Newcastle U	05.00	Deportivo la Coruna (Spain)
HELMER Thomas	Sunderland	11.00	Hertha Berlin (Germany)
HERBERT Craig	Shrewsbury T	06.00	
HEWITT Jamie	Chesterfield	*	
HIBBURT James	Crystal Palace	06.01	
HICKEY Ben	Darlington	09.99	
HICKS Graham	Rochdale	*	
HIDEN Martin	Leeds U	06.00	SV Salzburg (Austria)
HOCKTON Danny	Millwall	01.00	Stevenage Borough
HODOUTO Kwami	Huddersfield T	04.00	
HOGH Jes	Chelsea	02.01	*Retired*
HOLSGROVE Lee	Wycombe W	06.00	Aldershot T
HOLSGROVE Paul	Darlington	05.00	Barry T
HOLT Michael	Rochdale	06.00	St Patricks Ath
HOUSHAM Steve	Scunthorpe U	06.00	Barrow
HRISTOV Georgi	Barnsley	06.00	NEC Nijmegen (Holland)
HUGHES Jamie	Cardiff C	06.00	Bangor C
HUNT Steve	Crystal Palace	06.01	
HYLDGAARD Morten	Coventry C	*	

Player	Club	Date	Destination
INGHAM Michael	Sunderland	*	
INGRAM Denny	Hartlepool U	06.00	Scarborough
INMAN Niall	Peterborough U	01.01	Kettering T

Player	Club	Date	Destination
JACKSON Justin	Halifax T	08.99	Morecambe
JAMES Clement	Brentford	05.00	Slough T
JEANNE Leon	Queens Park R	02.01	
JENKINS Steve	Brentford	05.00	
JOBLING Kevin	Shrewsbury T	06.00	Telford U
JOHANSEN Michael	Bolton W	05.00	FC Copenhagen (Denmark)
JOHNSON Tommy	Everton	10.99	Glasgow Celtic
JOHNSTON Allan	Bolton W	06.00	Glasgow Rangers
JONES Graeme	Wigan Ath	11.99	St Johnstone
JONES Jon	Chester C	06.00	TNS Llansantffraid
JOSEPH Roger	Leyton Orient	06.00	*Retired*

JOYCE Warren	Hull C	04.00	*Retired*
[JUNINHO] JUNIOR Oswaldo	Middlesbrough	05.00	Atletico Madrid (Spain)

KAPRELIAN Mickael	Bolton W	06.01	
KARELSE John	Newcastle U	*	
KATCHOURO Petr	Sheffield U	03.00	Chengdu (China)
KAVANAGH Jason	Cambridge U	07.00	Burton A
KEEGAN John	York C	10.00	
KELLY Seamus	Cardiff C	07.00	St Patricks Ath
KERR David	Mansfield T	06.00	Chester C
KERRIGAN Danny	Southend U	*	
KILGANNON Sean	Middlesbrough	*	
KING Stuart	Preston NE	*	
KNIGHT Alan	Portsmouth	06.00	*Retired*
KOOGI Anders	Peterborough U	05.00	
KRIZAN Ales	Barnsley	03.00	
KYD Michael	Cambridge U	06.00	*Retired*

LAIRD Kamu	Chester C	01.00	
LAMBERT Jamie	Oxford U	01.00	Barry T
LANCASTER Martyn	Chester C	+	
LAUNDERS Brian	Sheffield U	12.99	
LAURSEN Jacob	Derby Co	08.00	
LEANING Andy	Chesterfield	06.00	*Retired*
LEE David	Exeter C	03.00	*Retired*
LEITCH Scott	Swindon T	06.00	Motherwell
LEONI Stephane	Bristol Rov	06.00	Dundee U
LEWIS Mickey	Oxford U	05.00	*Retired*
LING Martin	Brighton & Hove A	05.00	*Retired*
LINIGHAN Brian	Bury	06.00	Gainsborough Trinity
LINIGHAN David	Mansfield T	06.00	Southport
LOWE David	Wrexham	06.00	*Retired*
LUCAS Richard	Halifax T	06.00	Boston U
LUND Andreas	Wimbledon	*	
LUNDIN Pal	Oxford U	05.00	Umea (Sweden)

McCALL Steve	Plymouth Arg	05.00	*Retired*
McCLEN Jamie	Newcastle U	*	
McINDOE Michael	Luton T	07.00	Hereford U
McINTOSH Martin	Stockport Co	02.00	Hibernian
McKINNON Ray	Luton T	09.99	Livingston
McKINNON Rob	Carlisle U	05.00	Clydebank
McLAREN Andy	Reading	01.00	
McLEAN Ian	Oldham Ath	06.00	Gainsborough Trinity
McPHEE Chris	Brighton & Hove A	*	
McPHERSON Keith	Brighton & Hove A	06.00	Slough T
McSHEFFREY Gary	Coventry C	04.01	
MALONE Steve	Chester C	03.00	Glencairn
MANNINI Marino	Nottingham F	01.00	*Retired*
MARESCA Enzo	West Bromwich A	01.00	Juventus
MARIC Silvio	Newcastle U	07.00	Porto (Portugal)
MARSHALL Lee	Scunthorpe U	06.00	Grantham T
MARTIN Jae	Peterborough U	06.00	Woking
MARTINDALE Gary	Rotherham U	06.00	Telford U
MASON Gary	Manchester C	12.00	Dunfermline Ath
MATRECANO Salvatore	Nottingham F	03.01	*Retired*
MATTHEW Damian	Northampton T	11.99	*Retired*
MATTHEWS Jason	Exeter C	06.00	Aberystwyth T
MAUTONE Steve	Gillingham	06.00	Slough T
MAVRAK Darko	Walsall	05.00	
MEAN Scott	Bournemouth	06.00	Crawley T
MEECHAN Alex	Bristol C	12.00	Forest Green Rov
MENDONCA Clive	Charlton Ath	*	
MERCER Billy	Bristol C	*	
MERINO Carlos	Nottingham F	07.00	Atletico Bilbao (Spain)
MILLER Barry	Gillingham	10.00	Doncaster Rov
MILLER Rob	Cambridge U	12.99	Stevenage Borough
MILOSAVLJEVIC Goran	Chester C	06.00	
MITTEN Charlie	Gillingham	05.01	

MOORE Neil	Macclesfield T	03.00	Telford U
MORALEE Jamie	Colchester U	06.00	Barry T
MORRIS Andy	Rochdale	06.00	Hucknall T
MORRISON Dave	Leyton Orient	06.00	Bohemians
MORRISON-HILL Jamie	Plymouth Arg	11.00	Weymouth
MORTIMER Paul	Bristol C	06.01	
MOSS Darren	Chester C	+	
MOWBRAY Tony	Ipswich T	*	
MURPHY Stephen	Halifax T	06.00	

NASH Martin	Chester C	01.00	St Johnstone (trial)
NAYLOR Stuart	Exeter C	06.00	Rushden & Diamonds
NEWHOUSE Aidan	Brighton & Hove A	11.99	Sutton U
NEWSOME Jon	Sheffield Wed	06.00	*Retired*
NEWTON Chris	Halifax T	06.00	Gainsborough Trinity
NICHOLS Jon	Torquay U	06.00	Dorchester T
NIESTROJ Robert	Wolverhampton W	07.00	OF Iraklion (Greece)
NIMNI Avi	Derby Co	02.00	Maccabi Tel Aviv (Israel)
NIXON Eric	Tranmere Rov	06.00	*Retired*
NORMANN Runar	Coventry C	*	
NUZZO Raffaele	Coventry C	02.00	
NYAMAH Kofi	Exeter C	06.00	Stevenage Borough

OGRIZOVIC Steve	Coventry C	05.00	*Retired*
O'NEILL Michael	Wigan Ath	06.00	St Johnstone
O'REILLY Alex	West Ham U	03.01	Bristol Rov (trial)
ORMEROD Anthony	Middlesbrough	*	
ORMEROD Mark	Brighton & Hove A	06.00	Woking
OSBORN Mark	Wycombe W	*	
OVERMARS Marc	Arsenal	08.00	Barcelona (Spain)

PALMER Ryan	Brighton & Hove A	06.00	Sutton U
PAMAROT Noe	Portsmouth	06.00	
PARSONS David	Leyton Orient	*	
PATERSON Jamie	Halifax T	07.00	Doncaster Rov
PATERSON Scott	Plymouth Arg	05.00	Peterhead
PATTERSON Jamie	Torquay U	02.00	Weymouth
PEARCEY Jason	Brentford	10.00	*Retired*
PEDERSEN Tore	Wimbledon	01.01	
PENRICE Gary	Bristol Rov	06.00	*Retired*
PERCASSI Luca	Chelsea	10.00	Monza (Italy)
PERON Jean	Wigan Ath	06.00	
PETIT Manu	Arsenal	08.00	Barcelona (Spain)
PETRACHI Gianluca	Nottingham F	08.00	Perugia (Italy)
PHILLIPS David	Lincoln C	06.00	Stevenage Borough
PHILLIPS Jimmy	Bolton W	06.01	
PHILLIPS Lee	Cardiff C	06.00	Barry T
PICKERING Ally	Chester C	03.00	Hyde U
PIERRE Nigel	Bristol Rov	04.00	Joe Public (Trinidad)
PINNOCK James	Gillingham	06.01	Kingstonian
POINTON Neil	Chesterfield	06.00	Hednesford T
POLSTON John	Reading	04.01	
POPPLETON David	Lincoln C	12.99	Bradford PA
PORTER Andy	Wigan Ath	10.00	Chester C
POTTER Danny	Exeter C	06.00	Weymouth
POUNEWATCHY Stephane	Scunthorpe U	03.00	
POWER Lee	Halifax T	11.99	Boston U
PREECE Roger	Shrewsbury T	03.00	Telford U
PRICE Ryan	Macclesfield T	12.99	Telford U
PRIESTLEY Phil	Rochdale	06.01	
PRITCHARD Dave	Bristol Rov	06.01	
PRUDHOE Mark	Southend U	10.00	Carlisle U (trial)

QUIGLEY Michael	Hull C	06.00	
QUINN Jimmy	Swindon T	04.00	Weymouth

RACHEL Adam	Blackpool	06.01	
REDKNAPP Jamie	Liverpool	*	

Player	Club	Date	Destination
REID Paul	Carlisle U	07.00	Glasgow Rangers
REID Shaun	Chester C	06.00	*Retired*
RICHARD Fabrice	Colchester U	03.00	
RICHARDSON Barry	Lincoln C	06.00	Doncaster Rov
RICHARDSON Kevin	Barnsley	05.00	*Retired*
RICHARDSON Neil	Mansfield T	06.00	
RIGBY Tony	Shrewsbury T	01.00	Burscough
RIMMER Steve	Port Vale	06.00	Marine
RIZZO Nicky	Crystal Palace	07.00	Ternana (Italy)
ROBERTS Ben	Middlesbrough	07.00	Charlton Ath*
ROBINSON Jamie	Chester C	06.00	
ROBINSON Phil	Blackpool	06.00	Bamber Bridge
ROBINSON Phil	Stoke C	06.00	Hereford U
ROBSON Mark	Notts Co	09.00	Boreham Wood
ROCHA Carlos	Bury	11.99	Lincoln C (trial)
RODDIE Andy	Carlisle U	08.99	Clydebank
RODRIGUEZ Bruno	Bradford C	11.99	Paris St Germain (France)
ROSS Neil	Stockport Co	06.01	
ROWBOTHAM Darren	Exeter C	06.00	Weymouth
RUSSELL Craig	Manchester C	03.00	St Johnstone
RUSSELL Matthew	Halifax T	10.99	Scarborough
RYAN Michael	Wrexham	06.00	Woodley Sports
SAMWAYS Mark	Darlington	06.00	Matlock T
SAROYA Nevin	Brentford	10.00	Grays Ath
SARR Mass	Reading	05.00	
SCHWINKENDORF Jorn	Cardiff C	09.00	Vfl Osnabruck (Germany)
SCOTT Phil	Sheffield Wed	*	
SEARLE Stevie	Barnet	*	
SEBOK Vilmos	Bristol C	01.00	Waldhof Mannheim (Germany)
SERRANT Carl	Newcastle U	*	
SHARPLING Chris	Crystal Palace	*	
SHEERIN Joe	Bournemouth	10.00	
SHELTON Andy	Chester C	+	
SHORT Chris	Stoke C	08.00	*Retired*
SHUTTLEWORTH Barry	Blackpool	06.00	Scarborough
SIMB Jean-Pierre	Torquay U	02.00	
SIMBA Amara	Leyton Orient	03.00	Kingstonian
SKELTON Gavin	Carlisle U	10.00	Workington
SKINNER Craig	York C	*	
SKINNER Steve	Carlisle U	10.00	Queen of South
SMEETS Axel	Sheffield U	06.00	
SMITH Bryan	Swindon T	*	
SMITH Pete	Exeter C	12.00	Cambridge C
SNIJDERS Mark	Port Vale	06.00	
SOUTAR Ryan	Bury	10.00	Newport Co
SOUTHALL Neville	Bradford C	05.00	*Retired*
SPINK Dean	Wrexham	06.00	Chester C
SPINK Nigel	Millwall	06.00	Forest Green Rov
SPOONER Nicky	Chester C	03.00	Charleston (USA)
SRNICEK Pavel	Sheffield Wed	06.00	Brescia (Italy)
STATON Luke	Bolton W	06.00	Barry T
STEINER Rob	Queens Park R	05.01	*Retired*
STEWART Jordan	Leicester C	*	
STOKES Dean	Rochdale	06.00	Leek T
STONES Craig	Lincoln C	06.00	Spalding U
STRONG Greg	Bolton W	07.00	Motherwell
STURRIDGE Simon	Northampton T	06.00	
SUTTON Chris	Chelsea	07.00	Glasgow Celtic
SWAN Iain	Oldham Ath	03.00	Leigh RMI
TAAFE Steve	Stoke C	*	
TAIBI Massimo	Manchester U	07.00	Reggina (Italy)
TALBOT Paul	York C	06.00	Gateshead
TALLON Gary	Mansfield T	08.00	*Retired*
TAYLOR Danny	Rochdale	*	
TAYLOR Shaun	Bristol C	06.01	
TEALE Shaun	Carlisle U	05.00	Southport
THOMAS Danny	Leicester C	*	
THOMPSON Barry	Carlisle U	01.00	Ross Co
THOMPSON Glyn	Fulham	*	
THOMPSON Neil	York C	02.00	Scarborough
THOMPSON Richard	Wycombe W	06.00	Sutton U
THORPE Jeff	Carlisle U	06.00	
TINKLER Eric	Barnsley	*	
TOWNSEND Andy	West Bromwich A	07.00	*Retired*
TREES Rob	Bristol Rov	11.00	Leigh RMI
TROUGHT Mike	Bristol Rov	*	
TURNER Ross	Scunthorpe U	05.00	
TYSON Nathan	Reading	*	
VAN DER KWAAK Peter	Reading	05.00	GAE Deventer (Holland)
VANINEN Jukka	Exeter C	12.00	
VAUGHAN John	Lincoln C	06.00	*Retired*
VEYSEY Ken	Plymouth Arg	06.00	
VINDHEIM Rune	Hartlepool U	12.99	
VLACHOS Michail	Walsall	05.00	Ionikos (Greece)
WALKER Andy	Carlisle U	09.99	Partick Thistle
WALKER Andy	Colchester U	*	
WALSH Danny	Oldham Ath	06.01	
WARNER Phil	Southampton	*	
WARNER Vance	Rotherham U	06.00	
WARREN David	Wrexham	*	
WASSALL Darren	Birmingham C	05.00	Burton A
WATKINS Dale	Cheltenham T	12.99	Kettering T
WATSON Dave	Everton	05.01	*Retired*
WATSON Gordon	Bournemouth	05.00	*Retired*
WAUGH Warren	Exeter C	06.00	Cambridge C
WEARE Ross	Queens Park R	06.01	
WEBB Simon	Leyton Orient	06.00	Bohemians
WEBSTER Adam	Notts Co	03.00	Bedworth U
WEST Colin	Hartlepool U	05.00	*Retired*
WESTHEAD Mark	Wycombe W	06.01	
WHELAN Spencer	Shrewsbury T	12.00	
WHITE Tom	Bristol Rov	06.00	Yeovil T
WHITTAKER Stuart	Macclesfield T	06.00	Southport
WIGNALL Jack	Colchester U	03.01	Dagenham & Redbridge
WILKINS Ian	Lincoln C	06.00	Spalding U
WILKINS Richard	Colchester U	06.00	*Retired*
WILKINSON Steve	Chesterfield	06.00	Kettering T
WILLIAMS Gareth	Hull C	12.99	Scarborough
WILLIAMS Marc	York C	12.00	Bangor C
WILLIAMS Mike	Halifax T	02.00	
WILLIAMS Paul	Bury	06.00	Ilkeston T
WILSON Clive	Cambridge U	05.00	*Retired*
WILSON Mark	Manchester U	*	
WILSON Paul	Barnet	10.00	Boston U
WILSON Scott	Rochdale	06.00	Radcliffe Borough
WOODS Mattie	Chester C	+	
WOODS Steve	Chesterfield	06.01	
WOOLLISCROFT Ashley	Stoke C	06.01	
WORRALL Ben	Exeter C	01.00	
WORTHINGTON Martin	Torquay U	02.00	
WRIGHT Ben	Bristol C	12.00	
WRIGHT Darren	Chester C	+	
WRIGHT Ian	Burnley	05.00	*Retired*
WRIGHT Mark	Preston NE	*	
WRIGHT Steve	Bradford C	05.00	Dundee U
YOUDS Eddie	Charlton Ath	*	
ZAGORAKIS Theo	Leicester C	06.00	AEK Athens (Greece)
ZAHANA-ONI Landry	Luton T	06.00	

The Official PFA Transfer Directory

The Official PFA Transfer Directory is the definitive source of information on players available for transfer. The Directory is produced by the Association of Football Statisticians and aims to provide the most accurate, comprehensive and up-to-date information in the most accessible and user-friendly fashion for the benefit of managers, fans and players. The Directory can be accessed at http://www.profootballers.co.uk

The foundations for the Transfer Directory have been laid by the Association of Football Statisticians and their on-line database which includes over 15,000 current players, including all players playing in the Premiership and Division 1, 2 and 3 (England and Scotland) and all players in the Premier Leagues of France, Italy, Spain, Germany, Holland, Portugal, Belgium and Turkey. This database displays a player's positions, details, photo, career history and performance history.

The Transfer Directory lists of players available are built using information from a variety of sources, including the PFA, the players themselves, clubs, managers and the AFS network of statisticians. The Directory is endorsed by the League Managers' Association.

Although accessing the information in the Directory is free, a login with a password is required so we can keep track of the site's usage (which areas are popular, which need to be improved) and to let you know when there are any updates/improvements to the service.

The Login page has a number of input boxes. If you have logged in before and already have a password you can put your surname (not case sensitive) in the top box and your password (case sensitive) in the password box underneath. If you tick the box 'Remember Password' the page will remember your password to make logging in easier. We would recommend ticking this box.

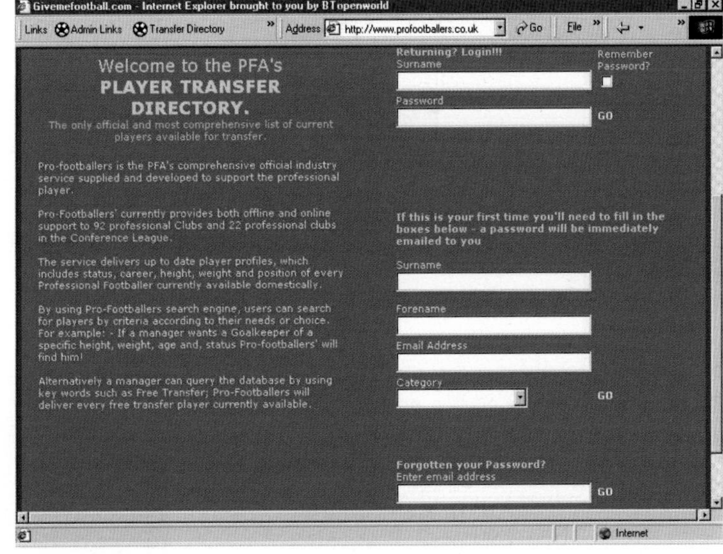

If this is your first visit you will need to enter your surname, first name, email address and category in the next four boxes. Once you have done this you will immediately be taken into the site and your password will be emailed to you. You can use your surname and password to log in.

If you can't remember your password, enter your email address into the bottom box and (if it exists) your password will immediately be emailed to you. This is an automatic process - it usually takes a couple of seconds for the email to turn up.

If you have any problems, please email enquiries@exxus.co.uk

The Transfers Page

The first page you come to is the Main Transfers page. This page has a list of all the players who are available for transfer. Clicking on the player name will take you through to the Player Card for that player with their basic details (height, weight, age etc) as well as their career history and performance history.

At the top of the transfers page are a series of drop-down lists which you can use to filter the list. For example, if you want to see all the players currently Open To Offer you can choose this option from the first drop down list and the page will refresh with only Open To Offer players displayed. As well as Status, you can also filter the players by position, age group, weight and height. Initially, only the first 30 players are displayed (it's quite a big list). The last box can be used to display 10, 30, 50 or all the players - or alternatively you can click on one of the letters at the top of the list to display the players whose surname starts with that letter.

Clicking the headings of each column (e.g.: last club, weight or position) will sort by that category.

To display the player's photos, click the Show Photos tick box.

You can switch between European or Imperial units by clicking the Imperial Units tick box.

Printable version

At the top of each page is a printer logo which, if clicked, displays a black on white, low graphic version of the site for easy printing. Clicking the blue one will return you to PFA colours.

The Player Card

Clicking on a player name will take you through to a Player Card page.

This page will display the player's details where available. Unless the player is new to the scene, this will include a career history and performance history. The menu on the left will take you back to the Player Directory, or on to the Player Match list.

FA Carling Premiership and Nationwide League Clubs

Summary of Appearances and Goals for 2000-2001.

KEY TO TABLES: P/FL = Premier Football League. FLC = Football League Cup. FAC = FA Cup. Others = Other first team appearances. Left hand figures in each column list number of full appearances + appearances as substitute. Right hand figures list number of goals scored.

	P/FL		FLC		FAC		Others	
	App	Goals	App	Goals	App	Goals	App	Goals
ARSENAL (PREM: 2nd)								
ADAMS Tony	26	1			4	1	8	
BARRETT Graham			1					
BERGKAMP Dennis	19 + 6	3			4 + 1	1	3 + 2	1
CANOVILLE Lee			0 + 1					
COLE Ashley	15 + 2	3	1		5 + 1		8 + 1	
DANILEVICIUS Tomas	0 + 2				0 + 1			
DIXON Lee	26 + 3	1			6		11	1
EDU	2 + 3							
GRIMANDI Gilles	28 + 2	1			2 + 1		8	
HENRY Thierry	27 + 8	17			3 + 1	1	14	4
KANU Nwankwo	13 +14	3			0 + 1		11 + 3	2
KEOWN Martin	28				2		9	2
LAUREN	15 + 3	2			4		6 + 5	1
LJUNGBERG Fredrik	25 + 5	6			4 + 1	1	10 + 3	2
LUKIC John	3						1	
LUZHNY Oleg	16 + 3				2		8	
MALZ Stefan	0 + 1				0 + 2			
MANNINGER Alex	11				1		2	
MENDEZ-RODRIGUEZ Alberto			0 + 1					
PARLOUR Ray	28 + 5	4			3 + 1		9 + 1	2
PENNANT Jermaine			1					
PIRES Robert	29 + 4	4			6	3	11 + 1	1
SEAMAN David	24				5		10	
SILVINHO	23 + 1	2			1 + 2		6 + 1	2
STEPANOVS Igors	9		1	1	3			
TAYLOR Stuart			1				1	
UPSON Matthew	0 + 2		1				1	
VERNAZZA Paolo	0 + 2	1	1				0 + 1	
VIEIRA Patrick	28 + 2	5			5 + 1	1	12	
VIVAS Nelson	3 + 9		1		1 + 2		3 + 4	
VOLZ Moritz			1					
WESTON Rhys			1					
WILTORD Sylvain	20 + 7	8	1		5 + 1	6	2 +11	1
WREH Chris			0 + 1					
ASTON VILLA (PREM: 8th)								
ALPAY	33		1		2			
ANGEL Juan Pablo	7 + 2	1			1			
BARRY Gareth	29 + 1		1		2 + 1		4	1
BOATENG George	29 + 4	1	1		3		4	
COOKE Stephen							0 + 1	
De BILDE Gilles	4							
DELANEY Mark	12 + 7		0 + 1				1	
DUBLIN Dion	29 + 4	8	1		2 + 1		3	1
EHIOGU Ugo	1 + 1						2	
GINOLA David	14 +13	3			1			
HENDRIE Lee	27 + 5	6	0 + 1		1		1 + 2	
HITZLSPERGER Thomas	0 + 1							
JAMES David	38		1		3		4	
JOACHIM Julian	11 + 9	7	1		0 + 1	1	1 + 2	
McGRATH John	0 + 3							
MERSON Paul	38	6	1		3		3	
NILIS Luc	3	1					2	1
SAMUEL Jlloyd	1 + 2				1		3	
SOUTHGATE Gareth	31	2	1		2		2	
STAUNTON Steve	13 + 1				3			
STONE Steve	33 + 1	2	1		3	1	4	
TAYLOR Ian	25 + 4	4	1		1		4	1
THOMPSON Alan							1 + 1	
VASSELL Darius	5 +18	4	0 + 1		2 + 1	1	0 + 3	
WALKER Richard					0 + 1		1	
WRIGHT Alan	35 + 1	1	1		3		4	

	P/FL		FLC		FAC		Others	
	App	Goals	App	Goals	App	Goals	App	Goals
BARNET (DIV 3: 24th)								
ARBER Mark	45	7	2		2		3	
BASHAM Mike	8		1				1	
BELL Leon	7 + 4		0 + 1				3	
BERKLEY Austin							1 + 1	
BROWN Danny	22 + 7				0 + 1		2	
CHARLERY Kenny	6 + 1	3						
COLLIS Dave	1 + 1							
COTTEE Tony	16	9			2	1		
CURRIE Darren	43 + 2	10	2		2	1	1	
D'ARCY Ross	0 + 3							
DAWSON Kevin	5							
DOOLAN John	31	3	2	1	2			
FLYNN Lee	17						1	
GLEDHILL Lee	1 + 4				0 + 1		2	
GOODHIND Warren	30 + 1	1			1		1	
GOWER Mark	10 + 4	1					1	1
HARRISON Lee	30		2				3	
HEALD Gregg	39	3	2		2		2	
McGLEISH Scott	14 + 5	5	1	1			1	1
MIDGLEY Neil	3 + 1							
NAISBETT Danny	16 + 3				2			
NEWTON Eddie	2 + 2		1 + 1					
NIVEN Stuart	20 + 4	2			2		2 + 1	
PLUCK Lee	0 + 1							
POPE Craig							0 + 1	
PURSER Wayne	4 +14	3	1 + 1		0 + 2		1 + 1	1
RICHARDS Tony	27 + 6	8	1	1	1	1	1	
RIZA Omer	7 + 3	4			1		2	1
SAWYERS Rob	25 + 4	1	2		2		2	1
STOCKLEY Sam	45	1	2		2		3	
STREVENS Ben	13 +15	4	1 + 1				0 + 1	
TOMS Frazer	19 + 7		2		1 + 1		0 + 1	
BARNSLEY (DIV 2: 16th)								
APPLEBY Matty	17 + 2	2	1 + 1		1			
AUSTIN Kevin			0 + 1					
BARKER Chris	39 + 1		4 + 1		1			
BARNARD Darren	26 + 4	2	1 + 1	2				
BARROWCLOUGH Carl	2 + 5							
BERTOS Leo	0 + 2							
BROWN Keith	1							
BULLOCK Martin	15 + 3	1						
CHETTLE Steve	35		3		1			
CORBO Mateo	10 + 7		2	1	0 + 1			
DYER Bruce	27 +11	15	4	1	0 + 1			
FALLON Rory	1							
HAYWARD Steve	10	1						
JONES Lee	15 +12	5	2 + 3	1				
KAY Antony	3 + 4							
McCLARE Sean	5 + 5	1	3		0 + 1			
MADDISON Neil	3							
MILLER Kevin	46		5		1			
MORGAN Chris	40	1	4		1			
MOSES Ade	11 + 3		2					
NEIL Alex	19 +13		0 + 1		1			
O'CALLAGHAN Brian	20 + 6		3 + 2		1			
PARKIN Jon	4							
RANKIN Isaiah	6 + 3	1						
REGAN Carl	25 + 2		3					
RIPLEY Stuart	8 + 2	1						
SALLI Janne	6 + 1				1			
SHERON Mike	21 +13	1	5	5	1			
SHIPPERLEY Neil	38 + 1	14	2	2	1			

	P/FL		FLC		FAC		Others	
	App	Goals	App	Goals	App	Goals	App	Goals
THOMAS Geoff	1 +10		0 + 2					
VAN DER LAAN Robin	16 + 2	1	5	1				
WARD Mitch	34 + 2		3 + 1		1			
WOAN Ian	2 + 1		3					
BIRMINGHAM CITY (DIV 2: 5th)								
ADEBOLA Dele	16 +15	6	6 + 2	5	1	1		
ATHERTON Peter	10						2	
BASS Jon	0 + 1							
BENNETT Ian	45		10		1		2	
BURCHILL Mark	4 + 9	4	3 + 1	1				
BURROWS David	8 + 5		0 + 2					
CHARLES Gary	3							
EADEN Nicky	44 + 1	2	10	1	1		1 + 1	1
EDGHILL Richard	3							
FURLONG Paul	0 + 4							
GILL Jerry	21 + 8		7		1			
GRAINGER Martin	35	6	10	1	1	1	1	
HOLDSWORTH David	24 + 5	1	4				0 + 1	
HORSFIELD Geoff	25 + 9	7	5 + 1	3	0 + 1		2	1
HUGHES Bryan	38 + 7	4	6 + 3	1	0 + 1		0 + 2	
HYDE Graham	1 + 2		0 + 1					
JENKINS Steve	3		1					
JOHNSON Andy	20 +14	4	1 + 6	3				
JOHNSON Michael	39	2	8	2	1		2	
LAZARIDIS Stan	26 + 5	2	5 + 2		1		1 + 1	
McCARTHY Jon	7 + 8		1				1 + 1	
MARCELO	16 +15	7	2 + 3	1	0 + 1		2	
NDLOVU Peter	10 + 2	2	5 + 1	1	1			
O'CONNOR Martin	28 + 2	5	9		1		2	
POLLOCK Jamie	4 + 1							
POOLE Kevin	1							
PURSE Darren	34 + 3	3	8 + 1	1	1		2	
ROBINSON Steve	0 + 4		0 + 2					
SONNER Danny	22 + 4	1	9	1	1		2	
TILER Carl	1							
WILLIAMS Jacques	1 + 2		0 + 1					
WOODHOUSE Curtis	17	2					2	
BLACKBURN ROVERS (DIV 2: 2nd)								
BENT Marcus	21 + 7	8			5 + 1	3		
BERG Henning	41	1	1		3			
BERKOVIC Eyal	4 + 7	2			3			
BJORNEBYE Stig Inge	30 + 3	1	2		2 + 1			
BLAKE Nathan	11 + 1	6	1	1	0 + 1			
BROOMES Marlon	1		2					
BURGESS Ben			1					
CARSLEY Lee	3 + 5		4	1				
CURTIS John	46		4		5			
DAILLY Christian	3 + 7		2 + 1					
DIAWARA Kaba	1 + 4		1	1				
DOUGLAS Jonathan			0 + 1		0 + 1			
DUFF Damien	31 + 1	1	2	2	3 + 2			
DUNN David	41 + 1	12	3 + 2	4	5	2		
DUNNING Darren	1		1		1			
FILAN John	12 + 1		2					
FLITCROFT Garry	41	3	2 + 1		5	2		
FRIEDEL Brad	27				6			
GILLESPIE Keith	12 + 6		1					
GRAYSON Simon			1					
HAMILTON Gary			0 + 1					
HARKNESS Steve			1					
HIGNETT Craig	15 +15	3			2 + 3	2		
HUGHES Mark	21 + 8	5			3 + 2			
JANSEN Matt	31 + 9	23	2		3 + 3	1		
JOHNSON Damien	12 + 4		3 + 2		0 + 1			
KELLER Marc	0 + 2				0 + 3			
KELLY Alan	7		2					
KENNA Jeff	5 + 1		2 + 2					
McATEER Jason	20 + 7	1	4		4			
MAHON Alan	14 + 4				6			

	P/FL		FLC		FAC		Others	
	App	Goals	App	Goals	App	Goals	App	Goals
MILLER Alan			1					
O'BRIEN Burton			0 + 1					
OSTENSTAD Egil	7 + 6	3	3 + 1	1	1			
RICHARDS Marc			1					
SHORT Craig	35	1			3			
TAYLOR Martin	12 + 4	3	5		6	1		
THOMAS James	1 + 3	1	1	2				
BLACKPOOL (DIV 3: 7th)								
BARNES Phil	34		3		1		4	
BUSHELL Steve	16 + 8	1	4		1 + 1		0 + 1	
CAIG Tony	6		1					
CLARKSON Phil	16 +12	5	1 + 1		0 + 2		4	
COID Danny	45 + 1	1	4		2		4	
COLLINS Lee	23 + 5		2		2		1	
HAWE Steve	2							
HILLS John	18	2			2		2 + 1	1
HUGHES Ian	31 + 3	1	4		2		2 + 1	1
JASZCZUN Tommy	32 + 3		4				3	
JONES Eifion	4 + 3		4					
KENNEDY Jon	6				1			
MALEY Mark	2							
MILLIGAN Jamie	1 + 5						0 + 3	
MILLIGAN Mike	24 + 2	1	1				0 + 1	
MORRISON Andy	6	1						
MURPHY John	44 + 2	18	4	5	2	1	4	
MURPHY Neil	3 + 3		2					
NEWELL Mike	4 + 1		2		0 + 1		0 + 1	
NOWLAND Adam	0 +10		0 + 3	1	0 + 1			
O'CONNOR Jon	10 + 1				2		1	
ORMEROD Brett	36 + 5	17	2	1	2	2	4	6
PARKINSON Gary	9						3	
REID Brian	29	2			2		3	1
SHITTU Danny	15 + 2	2					2	
SIMPSON Paul	44	12	4		2		3	1
THOMPSON Phil	6 + 2				0 + 1		1 + 1	
WALKER Richard	6 +12	3						
WELLENS Richard	34 + 2	8	2 + 1		1		3 + 1	
BOLTON WANDERERS (DIV 2: 3rd)								
BANKS Steve	8 + 1		2		3			
BARNESS Anthony	17 + 3		2		2		3	
BERGSSON Gudni	44	8	1 + 1		2		3	2
CAMPBELL Andy	3 + 3							
CHARLTON Simon	18 + 4				3 + 1		3	
CLARKE Matt	8						3	
DOWNEY Chris	0 + 1							
ELLIOTT Robbie	31 + 2	2			2		1 + 1	
FARRELLY Gareth	36 + 5	3	1		2 + 1		3	1
FISH Mark	13 + 1		2					
FRANDSEN Per	35 + 4	7	1 + 1		2 + 2		2 + 1	1
FREDGAARD Carsten	1 + 4							
GARDNER Ricardo	27 + 5	3			2		3	2
GOPE-FENEPEJ John	0 + 2							
HANSEN Bo	38 + 3	5	1 + 1		1 + 2		3	
HENDRY Colin	22	3			1		3	
HOLDEN Dean	1	1						
HOLDSWORTH Dean	22 + 9	11	2	1	2 + 1	3	3	
HUNT Nicky	0 + 1							
JAASKELAINEN Jussi	27							
MARSHALL Ian	13 +23	6			3		0 + 2	
MORINI Emanuele	1 + 1				1			
NOLAN Kevin	25 + 6	1			3 + 1	2	2	
NORRIS David			2					
O'KANE John	25 + 2	1	2		2	1		
PASSI Franck	14 + 9		2		3			
RANKIN Isaiah	9 + 7	2	2					
RICHARDSON Leam	5 + 7		1 + 1		1			
RICKETTS Michael	24 +15	19	0 + 1	1	2 + 2	2	1 + 2	2
SMITH Jeff	1							
SOMMER Jurgen					1			

	P/FL App	P/FL Goals	FLC App	FLC Goals	FAC App	FAC Goals	Others App	Others Goals
SUMMERBEE Nicky	9 + 3	1			3			
WARHURST Paul	19 + 1		1		2			
WHEATCROFT Paul			0 + 1		0 + 2			
WHITLOW Mike	7 + 1	1			1		0 + 3	
WRIGHT Tommy	3 + 1							
BOURNEMOUTH (DIV 2: 7th)								
ANGUS Stevland	7 + 2							
BERNARD Narada	6 + 8				1		2	
BROADHURST Karl	25 + 5				2		1	
CUMMINGS Warren	10	1					1	
DAY Jamie	6 + 1				2 + 1		1	
DEFOE Jermaine	27 + 2	18			1	1	1	
ELLIOTT Wade	27 + 9	9	0 + 1		3	2	0 + 1	
ERIBENNE Chukki	6 +11	1	2		0 + 3		2	
FEENEY Warren	3 + 7	4						
FENTON Nicky	4 + 1							
FLETCHER Carl	43	6	2		2	1	0 + 1	
FLETCHER Steve	45	9	2		3		1	
FORD James	0 + 3							
GRANT Peter	14 + 1		2				1	
HAYTER Jamie	29 +11	11	0 + 1		3	1	0 + 1	
HOWE Eddie	30 + 1	2			3		1	
HUCK William	1 + 7		0 + 2				2	
HUGHES Richard	44	8	2		2	1	1	
JORGENSEN Claus	43	8	2	1	3			
KEELER Justin	0 + 1						0 + 2	
MENETRIER Mickael	11 + 1		2				2	
O'CONNOR Garreth	1 +21	1			0 + 3	1	2	1
O'NEILL John	0 + 3							
PURCHES Steve	25 + 9		2		2			
SMITH Danny	7 + 7		2		0 + 1		2	
STEWART Gareth	35				3			
STOCK Brian	0 + 1						1 + 1	
TINDALL Jason	44 + 1	1	2		3		1	
WOOZLEY Dave	6							
YOUNG Neil	7		2					
BRADFORD CITY (PREM: 20th)								
ATHERTON Peter	25		3		1		4	
BEAGRIE Peter	9 +10	1			0 + 1		0 + 1	
BLAKE Robbie	14 + 7	4			1		3 + 1	2
BOWER Mark			1				1	
CARBONE Beni	29 + 2	5	2	2	0 + 1			
CLARKE Matt	17		1				3	
COLLYMORE Stan	5 + 2	2	1					
DAVISON Aidan	2		2				2 + 1	
GRANT Gareth	0 + 5		1 + 2	1			0 + 2	1
HALLE Gunnar	10 + 3		2	1			2	
HARDY Adam			0 + 1					
HOPKIN David	8 + 3		1				3 + 1	
JACOBS Wayne	19 + 2	2	1 + 1		1		2	
JESS Eoin	17	3			1			
KERR Scott	0 + 1		0 + 1				1	
LAWRENCE Jamie	15 + 2	1	2				0 + 2	
LOCKE Gary	6 + 1							
McCALL Stuart	36 + 1	1	0 + 1		1		4	
McKINLAY Billy	10 + 1				1			
MILLS Lee							5	3
MOLENAAR Robert	21	1			1			
MYERS Andy	15 + 5	1					3 + 1	
NOLAN Ian	17 + 4		2	1			4	
O'BRIEN Andy	17 + 1				1		4	
PETRESCU Dan	16 + 1	1	2		0 + 1			
RANKIN Isaiah	0 + 1						1 + 1	1
SAUNDERS Dean	4 + 6		0 + 1		1		3	
SHARPE Lee	6 + 5		2				3	
TODD Lee							2	
WALSH Gary	19				1		1	
WARD Ashley	24 + 9	4	2 + 1	2				
WESTWOOD Ashley							1 + 1	

	P/FL App	P/FL Goals	FLC App	FLC Goals	FAC App	FAC Goals	Others App	Others Goals
WETHERALL David	18	1	2				3	
WHALLEY Gareth	17 + 2		3	2			5 + 1	
WINDASS Dean	22 + 2	3	3	2	1		6	3
BRENTFORD (DIV 2: 14th)								
ANDERSON Ijah	1							
AUSTIN Kevin	3							
CHARLES Julian	4 + 6							
CROWE Jason	9		2					
DOBSON Michael	23 + 3		0 + 1				7	3
EVANS Paul	43	7	4		1		7	2
FOLAN Tony	11 +10	2	1 + 1					
GIBBS Paul	26 + 1	1	1		1		6	
GOTTSKALKSSON Olafur	45		4		1		7	
GRAHAM Gareth	0 + 1							
HUTCHINSON Eddie	5 + 2							
INGIMARSSON Ivar	42	3	4		1		6	1
JAVARY Jean-Phillipe	4 + 2		2				1	
KENNEDY Richard	1						0 + 1	
LOVETT Jay	21 + 4						3 + 2	1
McCAMMON Mark	14 +10	3	3	1			2 + 4	2
MAHON Gavin	40	1	4		1		6	
MARSH Simon	3 + 1		2					
MARSHALL Scott	29		4		1		4	2
O'CONNOR Kevin	5 + 6	1					0 + 1	
OWUSU Lloyd	24 + 9	10	1		1		6 + 1	2
PARTRIDGE Scott	29 + 7	8	1 + 2		1		6	2
PINAMONTE Lorenzo	3 + 5	1	1		0 + 1	1		
POWELL Darren	18	1					4	
QUINN Rob	22		4		1		1	
ROWLANDS Martin	32	2	3 + 1	1	1		6	1
SCOTT Andy	22	13	3	2	1		1	
SMITH Jay	2 + 1							
SMITH Paul	1 + 1						0 + 1	
SOMNER Matthew	2 + 1							
TABB Jay	1 + 1							
THEOBALD David	15						4	
WILLIAMS Mark	6 +24	2	0 + 1		0 + 1		0 + 2	
BRIGHTON & HOVE ALBION (DIV 3: 1st)								
ASPINALL Warren	0 + 1							
BROOKER Paul	25 +16	3	1 + 1		0 + 2		2	1
CARPENTER Richard	42	6	2		2	1	1	
CARR Darren	2							
CARTWRIGHT Mark	12 + 1		2					
CROSBY Andy	28 + 6	2	1		0 + 1		2	
CULLIP Danny	38	2	2		2		2	1
FREEMAN Darren	5 +11		1				0 + 1	
HAMMOND Dean							0 + 1	
HART Gary	43 + 2	7	2		2		1 + 1	
JOHNSON Lee							1	1
JONES Nathan	27 +13	4	1 + 1	1	2		1	
KUIPERS Michel	34				2		2	
MAYO Kerry	43 + 2	1	2		2		2	
MELTON Steve	10 +18	1	0 + 1				1 + 1	
OATWAY Charlie	36 + 2		2		2	1		
PACKHAM Will	0 + 1							
RAMSAY Scott	2 + 9						1	
ROGERS Paul	41 + 4	6	1 + 1		2		1	
STANT Phil	0 + 7	1						
STEELE Lee	4 +19	2			0 + 2		1	
THOMAS Martin	1 + 7							
THOMAS Rod	0 + 2		0 + 1					
VIRGO Adam	2 + 4						0 + 1	
WATSON Paul	46	5	2	1	2	2	2	
WICKS Matthew	23 + 1	3	1		2	1	1	
WILKINSON Shaun	0 + 1							
ZAMORA Bobby	42 + 1	28	2		2	2	1	1
BRISTOL CITY (DIV 2: 9th)								
AMANKWAAH Kevin	8 + 6				0 + 1		1	

	P/FL App	P/FL Goals	FLC App	FLC Goals	FAC App	FAC Goals	Others App	Others Goals
BEADLE Peter	18+15	4	1		3+ 2	1	1	
BELL Mickey	41	4	2		6			
BROWN Aaron	27+ 8	2			6		1	
BROWN Marvin	0+ 5				0+ 1			
BURNELL Joe	19+ 4				0+ 3		1	
CAREY Louis	46	3	2		6			
CLIST Simon	36+ 2	4			6	2	0+ 1	
COLES Danny	1+ 1						1	
DOHERTY Tommy							1	
DUNNING Darren	9							
GOODRIDGE Greg	1+ 6		1				1	
HILL Matt	32+ 2		1		6			
HOLLAND Paul	5	1	2	1				
HULBERT Robin	14+ 5		0+ 2					
JONES Darren							0+ 1	
JORDAN Andy	1+ 1		0+ 1					
LAVIN Gerard	3		2					
LEVER Mark	2		1					
LOURENCO	1+ 2	1						
MADDISON Neil	4+ 3	1						
MALESSA Antony	0+ 1		1				1	
MATTHEWS Lee	4+ 2	3						
MILLEN Keith	28+ 1	2	1		6			
MILLER Alan	4							
MURRAY Scott	46	10	2		6	1		
ODEJAYI Kay	0+ 3						1	
PEACOCK Lee	31+ 4	13	1	1	4	1		
PHILLIPS Steve	42		1		6			
RODRIGUEZ Dani	3+ 1							
SPENCER Damian	2+ 2		0+ 1				0+ 1	
THORPE Tony	33+ 6	19	1	1	5+ 1	3		
TINNION Brian	40+ 2	1	2		6			
TISTIMETANU Ivan	4+ 7		1				1	
WOODMAN Craig	1+ 1						1	
BRISTOL ROVERS (DIV 2: 21st)								
ALLSOP Danny	4+ 2							
ANDREASSON Marcus	4	1	2					
ASTAFJEVS Vitalijs	34+ 7	5	5		1		3	2
BARRETT Graham	0+ 1							
BIGNOT Marcus	26	1	5	2	1		3	
BRYANT Simon	27+ 3	1	5		1		3	
CAMERON Martin	6+ 8	2	1	1				
CHALLIS Trevor	19+ 3		1				1	
CULKIN Nick	45		5		1		3	
CURETON Jamie	1	1						
DAGNOGO Moussa	0+ 2							
ELLINGTON Nathan	36+ 6	15	5	2	1		3	1
ELLIS Clint	2+13	1	2+ 2		0+ 1		0+ 1	
EVANS Micky	19+ 2	4	2				3	2
FORAN Mark	9+ 3		1+ 1				1	
FOSTER Steve	44	4	5		1		3	
GALL Kevin	3+ 7	2						
GLENNON Matty	1							
HILLIER David	3+ 1						0+ 1	
HOGG Lewis	31+ 3	3	5	1	1		1	
JOHANSEN Rune	0+ 2				1			
JONES Scott	37+ 2	3	3		1		1+ 1	
LEE Christian	8+ 1	2						
McKEEVER Mark	7+ 5							
MAUGE Ronnie	14+ 2						2	
MEAKER Michael	2+ 3		0+ 1				2	
OWUSU Ansah	11+ 6							
PARKIN Brian	0+ 2							
PARTRIDGE Richie	4+ 2	1						
PETHICK Robbie	11+ 2		1				0+ 1	
PLUMMER Dwayne	17+ 3	1	0+ 2					
RICHARDS Justin	3+ 4						0+ 1	
THOMSON Andy	31+ 1	1	2		1		2	
WALTERS Mark	11+15	4	0+ 5		0+ 1		0+ 1	
WILSON Che	36+ 1		5		1		2	

	P/FL App	P/FL Goals	FLC App	FLC Goals	FAC App	FAC Goals	Others App	Others Goals
BURNLEY (DIV 1: 7th)								
ARMSTRONG Gordon	14+ 5		1		0+ 1			
BALL Kevin	40	2	4		1			
BRANCH Graham	26+ 9	5	2+ 2		2			
BRISCOE Lee	25+ 4		3					
COOK Paul	38+ 2	3	3+ 1		2			
COOKE Andy	10+ 1	2	4	3				
COX Ian	35+ 3	1	4		2			
CRICHTON Paul	7+ 1		2					
DAVIS Steve	44	5	4	1	2			
GRAY Phil	5	1	2+ 1					
JEPSON Ronnie	0+13		0+ 2					
JOHNROSE Lenny	9+10	1			1+ 1	1		
LITTLE Glen	27+ 7	3	3		0+ 2			
MAYLETT Brad	2+10		0+ 2					
MELLON Micky	19+ 3		1+ 1		1			
MICHOPOULOS Nik	39		2		2			
MOORE Ian	26+ 1	5			2	1		
MULLIN John	11+25	3	1+ 1		1+ 1			
PAYTON Andy	18+22	9	2+ 2	5	1+ 1	1		
ROBINSON Paul	0+ 4							
SHANDRAN Anthony	0+ 1							
SMITH Paul	10+ 4	1			1			
TAYLOR Gareth	15	4						
THOMAS Mitchell	41+ 2		4		2			
WELLER Paul	39+ 5	3	2		2			
WEST Dean	6+ 1							
BURY (DIV 2: 16th)								
ARMSTRONG Chris	22	1					3	
BARNES Paul	12+ 4	4			2		1	
BARRASS Matt	4+ 1		1					
BARRICK Dean	9+ 1				1			
BHUTIA Bhaichung	11+ 9	1	2		1		2	
BILLY Chris	46		2		2		0+ 1	
BUGGIE Lee							0+ 1	
BULLOCK Darren	9+ 1	2	2	2	1			
COLLINS Sam	33+ 1	2	2		0+ 1			
CONNELL Lee	0+ 1	1					1	
CRAMB Colin	15	5						
CROWE Dean	1+ 6	1						
DAWS Nick	44	3	2		2	1	1+ 2	2
FORREST Martyn	20+ 7		0+ 2				1	
HALFORD Steve	2+ 1							
HILL Nicky	8+ 2						2+ 1	
JAMES Lutel	7+21		0+ 1				2+ 1	
JARRETT Jason	13+12	2			0+ 2		2	1
KENNY Paddy	46		2		2		3	
LITTLEJOHN Adrian	24+13	4	2	1	2		1+ 1	
NELSON Michael	2	1						
NEWBY Jon	17	5						
PEYTON Warren	0+ 1						0+ 1	
PREECE Andy	13+17	2	0+ 2		0+ 1		2	
REDMOND Steve	39	2	2		1		2	
REID Paul	42+ 1	4	2		2		3	
SMITH Andy	2						1	
SWAILES Chris	43	4	2		2		2	1
SWAILES Danny	10+ 1		0+ 1		2		2	
UNSWORTH Lee	12+ 3		1		2		2	
CAMBRIDGE UNITED (DIV 2: 19th)								
ABBEY Zema	14	5	1+ 1		1		1	
ASHBEE Ian	43+ 1	3	2		2		1	
AXELDAL Jonas	12+ 6	2	2		1	1	2	1
BUTTERWORTH Adam	0+ 1							
CHILLINGWORTH Daniel	0+ 1							
CONNOR Paul	12+ 1	5			1			
COWAN Tom	41	2	1		1			
DREYER John	40		2		1		1	1
DUNCAN Andy	39	1	2		2		2	

	P/FL App	P/FL Goals	FLC App	FLC Goals	FAC App	FAC Goals	Others App	Others Goals
FLEMING Terry	9+ 1	1						
GREENE David	1							
GUDMUNDSSON Johann	3							
GUTTRIDGE Luke	1	1					0+ 2	
HANSEN John	7+ 5		1		0+ 2	1	1	
HANSON Christian	8							
HUMPHREYS Richie	7	3						
JOSEPH Marc	29+ 1				2		2	
KITSON Dave	6+ 2	1						
LAMEY Nathan	0+ 3							
LOGAN Richard	5	1						
McANESPIE Steve	20+ 3		2		1		2	
MacKENZIE Neil	1+ 5		1+ 1					
McNEIL Martin	5+ 1						1	
MARSHALL Shaun	10+ 1						1	
MUSTOE Neil	15+12	1	2		2		2	
OAKES Scott	7+11						2	
PEREZ Lionel	36+ 1		2		2		1+ 1	
PILVI Tero	3+ 2							
PREECE David	0+ 2						0+ 1	
PROKAS Richard	1+ 2							
REVELL Alex	2+ 2							
RICHARDSON Marcus	3+ 7	2						
RIZA Omer	10+ 2	3						
RUSSELL Alex	22+ 7	2	1+ 1		2		1	
SLADE Steve	4+ 5	1	0+ 1					
TANN Adam	1							
TAYLOR John	12+18	3	0+ 1		1+ 1		0+ 1	
TRAORE Demba	0+ 1						0+ 1	
WANLESS Paul	42+ 1	10	2		1+ 1		1	1
WILSON Stuart	3+ 3						1	
YOUNGS Tom	32+ 6	14	1+ 1		2	1		
CARDIFF CITY (DIV 3: 2nd)								
BOLAND Willie	25	1	1		1+ 2			
BONNER Mark	17+ 7	1	2		2		1	
BOWEN Jason	35+ 5	12			4			
BRAYSON Paul	25+15	15	1		0+ 3		1	
BRAZIER Matt	23+ 3	2	1		2+ 1			
COLLINS James	0+ 3				0+ 2		1	
EARNSHAW Robert	21+15	19	0+ 1		4	6		
ECKHARDT Jeff	6+ 2							
EVANS Kevin	24+ 6	3	1		3	2	0+ 1	
FORTUNE-WEST Leo	28+ 9	12			4	1		
FOWLER Jason	3+ 2							
GABBIDON Danny	42+ 1	3	2		4			
GILES Martyn	1+ 4							
GORDON Gavin	4+ 6	1						
GREENE David	10		2				1	
HARPER Jamie	3							
HILL Danny	7+ 2	1	1				1	
HUGHES David	11+ 1							
JONES Gethin	0+ 2		1					
JORDAN Andy	3+ 2				1			
LEGG Andy	39	3	2		4			
LIGHTBOURNE Kyle	2+ 1							
LOW Josh	31+ 5	4	1		1+ 2		1	
McCULLOCH Scott	9+12	1	1		3		1	
MUGGLETON Carl	6							
NOGAN Kurt	0+12	1	1		0+ 1		1	
NUGENT Kevin	14	4	2					
PERRETT Russell	2							
THOMAS Dai			0+ 1					
THOMPSON Andy	5+ 2				0+ 1		1	
WALTON Mark	40		2		4		1	
WESTON Rhys	25+ 3				3		1	
YOUNG Scott	45	10	1	1	4	1		
CARLISLE UNITED (DIV 3: 22nd)								
ALLAN Jon							0+ 1	
ANTHONY Paul							1	

	P/FL App	P/FL Goals	FLC App	FLC Goals	FAC App	FAC Goals	Others App	Others Goals
BIRCH Mark	44		2		3		1	
CARR Darren	10							
CARSS Tony	6+ 1		2					
CONNELLY Gordon	21+ 7	1			3	1		
CULLEN Jon	10+ 1							
DARBY Julian	15+ 3	1	2		1		1	
DAWSON Andy							0+ 1	
DOBIE Scott	41+ 3	10	1+ 1		3	2		
GALLOWAY Mick	26	1			2			
GLENNON Matty	29				3		1	
HALLIDAY Steve	3+21	1			0+ 2		1	
HEGGS Carl	16+14	5	1		0+ 3		1	
HEMMINGS Tony	16+ 6		1		2			
HOPPER Tony	4+ 5							
HORE John	1						1	
INGLIS John	8							
KEEN Peter	3	1						
LEE David	1+12		1+ 1					
LEMARCHAND Stephane	4+ 1	1						
McAUGHTRIE Craig	0+ 5						1	
MADDISON Lee	34				2			
MORLEY David	23	1						
PITTS Matthew	1+ 4		0+ 2					
PROKAS Richard	26+ 3		1		3		1	
SOLEY Steve	21+ 4	4	2		1		0+ 1	1
SQUIRES Jamie	2+ 3		1					
STEVENS Ian	41	12	2	1	3	4		
THURSTAN Mark	3+ 2				1+ 1		1	
THWAITES Adam			0+ 1		0+ 1		1	
TRACEY Richard	4+ 2	1	1+ 1					
WEAVER Luke	14		2					
WHITEHEAD Stuart	45	1	1		3			
WINSTANLEY Mark	34+ 2		2		3			
CHARLTON ATHLETIC (PREM: 9th)								
BAGHERI Karim	0+ 1							
BARTLETT Shaun	16+ 2	7			2			
BROWN Steve	15+10		1		1			
CAIG Tony	0+ 1							
FISH Mark	24	1			3			
HUNT Andy	8	4						
ILIC Sasa	13		1		1			
JENSEN Claus	37+ 1	5	2		2			
JOHANSSON JJ	27+ 4	11	2	3				
KIELY Dean	25		1		2			
KINSELLA Mark	27+ 5	2						
KISHISHEV Radostin	25+ 2		1		2			
KONCHESKY Paul	11+12		1+ 1		2			
LISBIE Kevin	5+13		2	2	1+ 1			
MacDONALD Charlie	1+ 2		0+ 2		0+ 1			
NEWTON Shaun	1+ 9		2		1+ 2	1		
PARKER Scott	15+ 5	1	2		2+ 1			
POWELL Chris	31+ 2		1+ 1		1	1		
PRINGLE Martin	1+ 7	1			1			
ROBINSON John	21+ 8	2	1+ 1		1+ 1			
RUFUS Richard	32	2			3			
SALAKO John	4+13		1+ 1		1+ 2	1		
SHIELDS Greg	2+ 2		2					
STUART Graham	33+ 2	5			2			
SVENSSON Matt	18+ 4	5			2+ 1	1		
TILER Carl	7							
TODD Andy	19+ 4	1	2		3			
CHELSEA (PREM: 6th)								
ALEKSIDZE Rati	0+ 2						0+ 1	
BABAYARO Celestine	19+ 5		1		2		1	
BOGARDE Winston	2+ 7		1				1	
CUDICINI Carlo	23+ 1				3		2	
DALLA BONA Sam	26+ 3	2			1		1+ 1	
DE GOEY Ed	15		1				1	
DESAILLY Marcel	34	2	1		2		2	

	P/FL App	P/FL Goals	FLC App	FLC Goals	FAC App	FAC Goals	Others App	Others Goals
DI MATTEO Robbie	7						3	
FERRER Albert	12 + 2				3			
FLO Tore Andre	5 + 9	3	1				2	
GRØNKJAER Jesper	6 + 8	1			1 + 1	2		
GUDJOHNSEN Eidur	17 +13	10	0 + 1		1 + 2	3	0 + 3	
HARLEY Jon	6 + 4				2			
HASSELBAINK Jimmy Floyd	35	23	1		2	2	3	1
JOKANOVIC Slavisa	7 +12		1		2			
LAMBOURDE Bernard	0 + 1							
LEBOEUF Frank	23 + 2				1 + 1		3	
LE SAUX Graeme	18 + 2				0 + 2		2 + 1	
MELCHIOT Mario	27 + 4		1		1		2	1
MORRIS Jody	13 + 8		0 + 1		1		1 + 2	
PANUCCI Christian	7 + 1						2	1
POYET Gus	22 + 8	11	0 + 1		2 + 1	1	1	
STANIC Mario	8 + 4	2			0 + 2		1	
TERRY John	19 + 3	1	1		3			
THOME Emerson	1							
WISE Dennis	35 + 1	3	1		3		2	
ZOLA Franco	31 + 5	9	1	1	3	2	3	
CHELTENHAM TOWN (DIV 3: 9th)								
ALSOP Julian	29 +10	5	2		1 + 1	1		
BANKS Chris	40	1	2		2		1	
BLOOMER Bob	5 + 7	1	2				1	
BOOK Steve	46		2		2			
BROUGH John	4 + 6		1					
CLARE Daryl	4							
DEVANEY Martin	23 +11	10	1		1 + 1		1	
DUFF Michael	39	5	2		2		1	
FREEMAN Mark	25 + 2		1		2			
GOODRIDGE Greg	10 + 1	1						
GRAYSON Neil	23 + 8	13			1	2		
GRIFFIN Antony	14 + 8	1			1		0 + 1	
HIGGS Shane	0 + 1						1	
HOPKINS Gareth	1 + 3		0 + 1				1	
HOWARTH Neil	19 + 4	3	2		1 + 1			
HOWELLS Lee	36	1			2	1		
IWELUMO Chris	2 + 2	1						
JACKSON Michael	2 + 4		0 + 1		0 + 1		1	
JONES Marcus	1 + 1						1	
McAULEY Hugh	30 + 5	3	1		2		0 + 1	
McCANN Grant	27 + 3	3			2		1	
MacDONALD Charlie	7 + 1	2						
MILTON Russell	18 + 1	1			1 + 1	1	1	
SERTORI Mark	10							
VICTORY Jamie	3	1	1					
WALKER Richard	35 + 1		2					
WHITE Jason	8 +19		1		0 + 1		1	
YATES Mark	45	6	2		2		0 + 1	
CHESTERFIELD (DIV 3: 3rd)								
ARMSTRONG Joel	0 + 1		1					
BARRETT Danny	0 + 1							
BEAUMONT Chris	4 +10						0 + 4	
BECKETT Luke	38 + 3	16	4	2	1		3	
BLATHERWICK Steve	38	1	4		1		2	
BRECKIN Ian	45	3	4	1	1		4	1
D'AURIA David	4 + 2				0 + 1		1	
DUDFIELD Lawrie	4 +10	3					3 + 1	1
EBDON Marcus	41	3	4		1		3	3
EDWARDS Rob	34	4	2		1		4	
GALLOWAY Mick	4 + 1		2 + 1					
HOWARD Jon	13 +18	5	1 + 2				1	
INGLEDOW Jamie	14 +10	3	0 + 1				3	
JONES Mark	0 + 3				0 + 1		1	1
PARRISH Sean	33 + 2	10	4	1	1		2 + 1	
PAYNE Steve	33 + 2	1	1 + 1				3	2
PEARCE Greg	1							
PERKINS Chris	8		2 + 1				1	
POLLITT Mike	46		3		1		4	
REEVES David	34 + 3	13	2 + 1	1			2	2
RICHARDSON Lee	30		2				2	
RUSHBURY Andy	0 + 2							
SIMPKINS Mike	14 + 2				1		2	
TUTILL Steve	17 + 2	1	3		1		1	
WILLIAMS Danny	1 + 1						0 + 2	
WILLIAMS Ryan	39 + 6	8	3		1		2 + 1	1
WILLIS Roger	11 +21	5	2 + 2		1		0 + 2	
COLCHESTER UNITED (DIV 2: 17th)								
ARNOTT Andy	1 + 2		0 + 1				1	
BROWN Simon	18		4		1			
CLARK Simon	33 + 1		4		0 + 1			
CONLON Barry	23 + 3	8			1		1	
DOZZELL Jason	22		4		1		1	
DUGUID Karl	34 + 7	5	3		1	1	1	
DUNNE Joe	31 + 3	1	3		0 + 1		1	
FITZGERALD Scott	30				1		1	
GREGORY David	27 + 1	3	1		1		1	
IZZET Kem	5 + 1	1						
JOHNSON Gavin	33 + 4	2	3 + 1		1			
JOHNSON Ross	17 + 1							
KEEBLE Chris	10 + 6	1	1 + 1				1	
KEITH Joe	21 + 6	3	1 + 2					
LOCK Tony	3 +11	2	2		0 + 1			
LUA-LUA Tresor	7	2	2	3				
McGAVIN Steve	19 +22	2	3	1	1		0 + 1	
McGLEISH Scott	11 +10	5						
MORGAN Dean	0 + 4							
NICHOLLS Mark	3 + 1							
OPARA KK	0 + 2		1					
PINAULT Thomas	3 + 2	1						
SCOTT Keith	8 + 1	1						
SKELTON Aaron	43 + 1	6	3		1		1	
STOCKWELL Micky	46	11	4		1		1	
TANNER Adam	1 + 3		1 + 1					
WHITE Alan	29 + 3		4		1			
WOODMAN Andy	28						1	
COVENTRY CITY (PREM: 19th)								
ALOISI John	8 +11	3	2 + 1	3				
BELLAMY Craig	33 + 1	6	3	1	2	1		
BETTS Robert	0 + 1							
BOTHROYD Jay	3 + 5		0 + 1		1			
BREEN Gary	29 + 2	1	2 + 2		2			
CARSLEY Lee	21	2			2			
CHIPPO Youssef	18 +14		4		1			
DAVENPORT Calum	0 + 1							
EDWORTHY Marc	18 + 6	1	2		2			
EUSTACE John	22 +10	2	4	2	1			
GUERRERO Ivan	3		1					
HADJI Moustapha	28 + 1	6	3 + 1		1	1		
HALL Marcus	21		2	1	1			
HARTSON John	12	6						
HEDMAN Magnus	15		2		1			
HENDRY Colin	1 + 1							
KIRKLAND Chris	23		2 + 1		1			
KONJIC Mo	8		1					
MILLER Alan	0 + 1							
PALMER Carlton	12 + 3		1					
QUINN Barry	25		2		2			
ROUSSEL Cedric	10 + 7	2	1					
SHAW Richard	23 + 1		3		1			
STRACHAN Gavin	2		0 + 2	1				
TELFER Paul	27 + 4		2		1 + 1			
THOMPSON David	22 + 3	3	1 + 1		1			
WILLIAMS Paul	27 + 3		4		2			
ZUNIGA Ysrael	7 + 8	1	2	1				
CREWE ALEXANDRA (DIV 2: 14th)								
ASHTON Dean	12 + 9	8			1 + 1			

	P/FL App	P/FL Goals	FLC App	FLC Goals	FAC App	FAC Goals	Others App	Others Goals
BANKOLE Ade	21		0 + 1		3			
CHARNOCK Phil	4 + 5		0 + 1					
COLLINS James	2 + 2		0 + 1					
CRAMB Colin	10 + 3	4	0 + 1		1			
FOSTER Steve	21 + 9		2	1	3			
GANNON Jim	5 + 2				3			
GRANT John	0 + 2		1 + 1					
HOWELL Dean	0 + 1							
HULSE Rob	22 +11	11	2 + 1		1 + 1			
INCE Clayton	0 + 1							
JACK Rodney	23 + 7	4	3		3			
KEARTON Jason	25 + 1		4					
LITTLE Colin	24 + 3	4	3	1				
LUMSDON Chris	14 + 2							
LUNT Kenny	46	1	4		3			
MACAULEY Steve	30	1	3		3			
MAYBURY Alan	6							
NAVARRO Alan	5 + 3	1						
RIVERS Mark	32 + 1	7	2	2	3	1		
SMITH Peter	2 + 3		1 + 1					
SMITH Shaun	44 + 1	4	4		2	1		
SODJE Efe	29 + 3		2 + 1		2			
SORVEL Neil	42 + 4	1	4		3			
STREET Kevin	16 + 7	1	3					
TAIT Paul	9 + 9		0 + 1		0 + 1			
VAUGHAN David	1							
WALKER Richard	2 + 1							
WALTON Dave	17 + 3		2					
WRIGHT David	42		4		2			
CRYSTAL PALACE (DIV 1: 21st)								
AUSTIN Dean	38 + 1	3	7 + 1		2			
BERHALTER Gregg	4 + 1							
BLACK Tommy	30 +10	4	8	1	0 + 1			
CARLISLE Wayne	4 +10		3 + 2		1			
EVANS Steve	0 + 1							
FORSSELL Mikael	31 + 8	13	8	2	1 + 1			
FRAMPTON Andy	8 + 2				1			
FREEDMAN Dougie	16 +10	11			1 + 1			
FULLARTON Jamie	1 + 1		0 + 1					
FULLER Ricardo	2 + 6							
GRAY Julian	12 +11	1	1 + 4					
GREGG Matt	1		2 + 1					
HARRIS Richard	1 + 1		1 + 1					
HARRISON Craig	30 + 2		8		2			
HOPKIN David	8 + 1	1						
KABBA Steve	0 + 1		0 + 1					
KARIC Amir	3							
KITSON Paul	4							
KOLINKO Alex	35		7		2			
LINIGHAN Andy	0 + 1		1 + 1	1				
McKENZIE Leon	2 + 6		1 + 2					
MARTIN Andy			0 + 1					
MORRISON Andy	5							
MORRISON Clint	41 + 4	14	8 + 1	4	2	1		
MULLINS Hayden	40 + 1	1	8		2			
POLLOCK Jamie	29 + 2	4	5 + 1					
RIIHILAHTI Aki	9	1						
RODGER Simon	28 + 5		6		2			
RUBINS Andrejs	17 + 5		3	2	2			
RUDDOCK Neil	19 + 1	2	5	1	0 + 1			
SMITH Jamie	25 + 4		6		1			
STAUNTON Steve	6	1						
TAYLOR Stuart	10							
THOMSON Steve	12 + 6		4 + 1	1	2	1		
UPSON Matthew	7							
VERHOENE Kenny	0 + 1							
ZHIYI Fan	28	1	7		1			
DARLINGTON (DIV 3: 20th)								
ANGEL Mark	1 + 4		2 + 1	1				

	P/FL App	P/FL Goals	FLC App	FLC Goals	FAC App	FAC Goals	Others App	Others Goals
ASPIN Neil	21		2		3			
ATKINSON Brian	17 + 6	4			3			
BEAVERS Paul	3 + 4	1	1					
BERNARD Olivier	9 + 1	2						
BRIGHTWELL David	12 + 2							
BRUMWELL Phil	19 + 2				0 + 2		3	
BUTLER Thomas	8				2			
CAMPBELL Paul	11 + 5	1	1 + 2	1			2	
CAU Jean-Michel	0 + 1							
COLLETT Andy	37		2		3			
CONVERY Mark	5 + 6						1	
ELLIOTT Stuart	20 + 4		3 + 1	3	1 + 1		3	1
FORD Mark	11	2						
GRAY Martin	25		3 + 1		3		2	
HARPER Steve	17							
HECKINGBOTTOM Paul	17 + 1	1	2		1		2	
HIMSWORTH Gary	14 + 1		2 + 1		3			
HJORTH Jesper	8 +15	1	4		0 + 2		2 + 1	
HODGSON Richard	20 +15	2	2 + 1		2 + 1	2	2 + 1	1
JACKSON Kirk	5 + 5	1						
JEANNIN Alex	11							
KAAK Tom	7 + 1	2	0 + 2					
KEEN Peter	7							
KILTY Mark	18	1	1		0 + 1		3	
KYLE Kevin	5	1			3	1		
LIDDLE Craig	45	2	3		3		3	2
McMAHON David	5 + 3	1					2 + 1	1
MARCELLE Clint	8 + 4							
MARSH Adam	1 + 6						2	1
NAYLOR Glenn	42 + 2	11	3	1	3	3	1 + 1	
NOGAN Lee	18	4	1					
PEPPER Carl			2					
REED Adam	28 + 6		4		3		1	
SKELTON Craig	0 + 1							
TAIT Jordan	2 + 1							
VAN DER GEEST Frank	2		2				3	
WALKLATE Steven	2 + 4		2		0 + 1			
WILLIAMS John	23 + 1	5					1	
WILLIAMSON Garry	1 + 5		2				0 + 2	
ZEGHDANE Lehit	1 + 2		0 + 2					
DERBY COUNTY (PREM: 17th)								
BLATSIS Con	2							
BOERTIEN Paul	7 + 1	1			1 + 2			
BOHINEN Lars	1 + 1							
BOLDER Adam	0 + 2							
BRAGSTAD Bjorn Otto	10 + 2		3	2	1			
BURLEY Craig	24	2	3	2	1			
BURTON Deon	25 + 7	5	2 + 1	1	2			
CARBONARI Horacio	27	1	1		3			
CHRISTIE Malcolm	29 + 5	8	4	2	3	2		
DELAP Rory	32 + 1	3	2	1	1			
ELLIOTT Steve	5 + 1		1					
ERANIO Stefano	25 + 3	2	1		3	2		
EVATT Ian	0 + 1							
GUDJONSSON Thordur	2 + 8	1						
HIGGINBOTHAM Danny	23 + 3		3 + 1		2 + 1			
JACKSON Richard	1 + 1		1					
JOHNSON Seth	30	1	4					
KINKLADZE Georgi	13 +11	1	2		1			
MARTIN Lilian	7 + 2				2 + 1			
MAWENE Youl	7 + 1				2			
MORRIS Lee	4 +16		0 + 2		0 + 1			
MURRAY Adam	4 +10		0 + 1		3			
OAKES Andy	6				1			
O'NEIL Brian	3 + 1				2			
POOM Mart	32 + 1		4		2			
POWELL Darryl	27	1	3	1				
RIGGOTT Chris	29 + 2	3	3	1	2	1		
SCHNOOR Stefan	6 + 2		2 + 1					
STRUPAR Branko	7 + 2	6	1					

	P/FL App	P/FL Goals	FLC App	FLC Goals	FAC App	FAC Goals	Others App	Others Goals
STURRIDGE Dean	3+11	1	0+2					
VALAKARI Simo	9+2	1	3					
WEST Taribo	18		1		1			
EVERTON (PREM: 16th)								
ALEXANDERSSON Niclas	17+3	2	2		1			
BALL Michael	29	3	1+1		2			
CADAMARTERI Danny	7+9	4			2			
CAMPBELL Kevin	27+2	9	1+1	1	1			
CLARKE Peter	0+1							
CLELAND Alex	2+3		1+1					
DUNNE Richard	3		1					
FERGUSON Duncan	9+3	6			1			
GASCOIGNE Paul	10+4		0+1					
GEMMILL Scot	25+3	2			1+1			
GERRARD Paul	32		2					
GOUGH Richard	9				0+1			
GRAVESEN Thomas	30+2	2	1		2			
HIBBERT Tony	1+2							
HUGHES Mark	6+3		1					
HUGHES Stephen	16+2		1+1		2	1		
JEFFERS Francis	10+2	6	2	1				
JEVONS Phil	0+4							
McLEOD Kevin	0+5							
MOORE Joe-Max	8+13		1+1		0+2			
MYHRE Thomas	6				2			
NAYSMITH Gary	17+3	2			1			
NYARKO Alex	19+3	1	2					
PEMBRIDGE Mark	20+1				2			
PISTONE Alessandro	5+2		1					
SIMONSEN Steve	0+1							
TAL Idan	12+10	2			0+2			
UNSWORTH David	17+12	5	2		1			
WATSON Steve	34		2		2	1		
WEIR Davie	37	1	1		1			
XAVIER Abel	10+1				1			
EXETER CITY (DIV 3: 19th)								
AMPADU Kwame	29+7		1	1	0+1			
ASHTON Jon	7+6		0+2				1	
BIRCH Gary	6+3	2						
BLAKE Noel	3+2							
BRESLAN Geoff	0+2							
BUCKLE Paul	39+2	3			1		1	
BURROWS Mark	21+8		2		1			
CAMPBELL Jamie	42	2	1		1		1	
CORNFORTH John	11+1							
CURRAN Chris	26		2		1			
EPESSE-TITI Steeve	5+1							
FLACK Steve	33+7	13	2					
FRANCIS Kevin	3+4	1			1		1	
FRASER Stuart	5+1		1				1	
HOLLIGAN Gavin	3							
HOLLOWAY Chris	0+4							
HUTCHINGS Carl	2						1	
INGLETHORPE Alex	11+7	2	2					
McCONNELL Barry	3+1							
MUDGE James	0+3							
POWER Graeme	34+1	1					1	
RAPLEY Kevin	6+1				1		1	
RAWLINSON Mark	18+7	2	1	1	1		0+1	
READ Paul	10+1	1						
ROBERTS Chris	33+9	7	1+1		0+1		1	
ROBERTS Darren	3+5	1	0+1					
ROSCOE Andy	33+10	1	2		1		1	
SPEAKMAN Rob	0+1		0+1					
SPENCER Damian	2+4							
TIERNEY Fran	4+3	1			0+1			
TOMLINSON Graeme	13+11	1	2				0+1	
VAN HEUSDEN Arjan	41		1		1			
WHITWORTH Neil	34	1	2		1		1	
WILKINSON John	0+1							
ZABEK Lee	26+5		2		1			
FULHAM (DIV 1: 1st)								
BETSY Kevin	2+3		2					
BOA MORTE Luis	21+18	18	5+1	3	1			
BREVETT Rufus	39		2		1			
CLARK Lee	45	7	4		1			
COLEMAN Chris	25		1					
COLLINS John	25+2	3						
COLLINS Wayne	3+2		4					
CORNWALL Luke			1+1					
DAVIS Sean	37+3	6	3+1	1				
FERNANDES Fabrice	23+6	2	4+2	1	1			
FINNAN Steve	45	2	1+1		1			
GOLDBAEK Bjarne	41+3	2	3		1			
GOMA Alain	3							
HAHNEMANN Marcus	2		2					
HAMMOND Elvis			0+1					
HAYLES Barry	28+7	18	3+1	1				
HAYWARD Steve	0+1		3+1	1				
HUDSON Mark			2					
KNIGHT Zat			3					
LEWIS Eddie	1+6		6	1				
McANESPIE Kieran			1+1					
MELVILLE Andy	42+1	1	3		1			
MOLLER Peter	2+3	1						
MORGAN Simon	0+1							
NEILSON Alan	0+3		4					
PESCHISOLIDO Paul			2					
PHELAN Terry	1+1		1					

Kwame Ampadu (Exeter City)

	P/FL App	P/FL Goals	FLC App	FLC Goals	FAC App	FAC Goals	Others App	Others Goals
RIEDLE Karl-Heinz	1 +13	1						
SAHA Louis	39 + 4	27	3 + 1	5	1			
SAHNOUN Nicolas	2 + 5		1		1	1		
STOLCERS Andrejs	8 + 7	2	0 + 1		0 + 1			
SYMONS Kit	22 + 2		5	1	1			
TAYLOR Maik	44		5		1			
TROLLOPE Paul	5 + 5		3					
WILLOCK Calum	0 + 1							
GILLINGHAM (DIV 1: 13th)								
ASABA Carl	18 + 7	10	3	2				
ASHBY Barry	38 + 2	1	3		1			
BARTRAM Vince	46		4		2			
BROWNING Marcus	22 + 9		4		0 + 1			
BUTTERS Guy	12	3	4		1			
CROFTS Andrew	0 + 1							
EDGE Roland	19 + 1		3		2			
GOODEN Ty	17 + 1		2					
HESSENTHALER Andy	19 + 4	2	3		1	1		
HOPE Chris	46	2	4		2	1		
IPOUA Guy	0 + 9							
JAMES Kevin	1 + 6		0 + 1					
KING Marlon	26 +12	15	3		1 + 1			
LEWIS Junior	10 + 7	2	2 + 2		2			
LOVELL Mark	0 + 1							
McGLINCHEY Brian	1							
NOSWORTHY Nyron	8 + 2							
ONUORA Iffy	17 +14	9			1 + 1	1		
PATTERSON Mark	26 + 2		2 + 1		0 + 2			
PENNOCK Adrian	34 + 1				2			
PHILLIPS Michael	0 + 1							
ROSE Richard	1 + 3							
ROWE Rodney			0 + 1					
SAUNDERS Mark	24 +11	5	0 + 2		1			
SHAW Paul	27 + 6	1			2	2		
SMITH Paul	42	3	2	1	2			
SOUTHALL Nicky	40 + 4	2	3		2			
THOMSON Andy	12 +12	5	2 + 1	3	0 + 1			
GRIMSBY TOWN (DIV 1: 18th)								
ALLEN Bradley	15 + 6	3	4	3				
BLACK Kingsley	4 + 1		0 + 2					
BLOOMER Matt	3 + 3		0 + 2					
BURNETT Wayne	20 + 3	1			0 + 2			
BUTTERFIELD Danny	23 + 7	1	3		2			
CAMPBELL Stuart	38	2			2			
CHAPMAN Ben	0 + 2							
CLARE Daryl	6 +11		1 + 3					
COLDICOTT Stacy	34 + 3	1	4	1	1 + 1			
CORNWALL Luke	9 + 1	4						
COYNE Danny	46		4		2			
DONOVAN Kevin	36 + 5	5	2		2			
ENHUA Zhang	16 + 1	3						
FOSTERVOLD Knut Anders	9 + 1							
GALLIMORE Tony	26 + 2		2	1	2			
GROVES Paul	45	4	4		1			
HANDYSIDE Peter	17 + 2	1	3		1 + 1			
JEFFREY Mike	15 +14	1	3 + 1		1	1		
LIVINGSTONE Steve	27 + 5	7	2		2			
McDERMOTT John	36		3		1			
MURRAY Neil	1 + 1							
NIELSEN David	16 + 1	5			1 + 1	1		
POUTON Alan	16 + 5	1	4					
RAVEN Paul	11 + 4		2					
ROWAN Jonny	2 + 3		0 + 2	1				
SMITH David	16 + 8	1	3					
SMITH Richard	2 + 4	1			2			
WILLEMS Menno	17 + 7	1			2			
HALIFAX TOWN (DIV 3: 23rd)								
BRADSHAW Mark	15 + 2	2	2					

	P/FL App	P/FL Goals	FLC App	FLC Goals	FAC App	FAC Goals	Others App	Others Goals
BRASS Chris	6							
BUTLER Lee	33				1		2	
CLARKE Chris	26	1	1				1	
CLARKE Matthew	12 + 7	1					0 + 2	
FITZPATRICK Ian	9 + 3	2	1 + 1					
GAUGHAN Steve	6 + 3	1	0 + 1					
HARRISON Gerry	7 + 2	1	2					
HAWE Steve	6 + 2				1		1	
HERBERT Robert	3 + 6	1	0 + 1		0 + 1			
HOLT Grant	0 + 2		1	1				
JONES Gary	30 + 3	5	2		1		2	2
JULES Mark	16 + 4	1	1					
KERRIGAN Steve	40 + 1	19	1 + 1		1		2	1
MATTHEWS Rob	8	2						
MAWSON Craig	9							
MIDDLETON Craig	35 + 2	5	2		0 + 1		2	
MIKE Leon	2 + 5							
MITCHELL Graham	42	1	2				2	
MITCHELL Paul	11							
MORGAN Steve	1							
MURPHY Peter	18 + 3	1			1		2	
MYERS Peter	0 + 1							
OLEKSEWYCZ Steve	0 + 3							
ORD Michael			0 + 1					
PAINTER Robbie	8 + 8						0 + 1	
PARKS Tony	4 + 1		1					
PARNABY Stuart	6							
POTTER Lee	0 + 3							
PROCTOR Michael	11 + 1	4						
REDFEARN Neil	12							
REILLY Alan	15 + 8	2	1				0 + 2	
REZAI Carl	8 + 3				1		1	
RICHARDS Ian	8 +10		1		1			
SHANNON Gregg			1					
STANSFIELD James	2							
STONEMAN Paul	29 + 1	2	1		1		2	
THOMPSON Steve	35 + 1	2	1		1		2	
WAINWRIGHT Neil	13				1		2	
WILDER Chris	20		1		1		1	
HARTLEPOOL UNITED (DIV 3: 4th)								
ARNISON Paul	26 + 1	1	1		1		3	1
ASPIN Neil	5 + 5						0 + 1	
BAKER Steve	9							
BARRON Michael	27 + 1				1		5	
BOYD Adam	3 + 2				0 + 1			
CLARK Ian	15 + 9				1		4	1
EASTER Jermaine	0 + 4						0 + 2	
FERGUSON Barry	4		1					
FITZPATRICK Lee	12 +11	4	2	1			0 + 3	
HENDERSON Kevin	40	17	2		1		4 + 1	2
HOLLUND Martin	5		1					
KNOWLES Darren	22 + 3	1	1 + 1				2	
LEE Graeme	3 + 3						1 + 1	
LORMOR Anth	22 + 9	8	1				2 + 3	
McAVOY Andy	2 + 3							
MIDGLEY Craig	24 +17	8	0 + 1		1	1	4	
MILLER Tommy	46	16	2	2	1		5	2
ROBINSON Mark	5 + 1		1					
SHARP James	31 + 3	2	2				4 + 1	
SHILTON Sam	29 + 4	4	1 + 1		1		1 + 1	
SPERREVIK Tim	4 +11	1	1				0 + 1	
STEPHENSON Paul	40	2	2	1	1		5	
STRODDER Gary	17 + 2		1		1			
TENNEBO Thomas	0 + 2		0 + 2					
TINKLER Mark	28	3					5	1
WESTWOOD Chris	46	1	2		1		5	
WILLIAMS Tony	41		1		1		5	
HUDDERSFIELD TOWN (DIV 1: 22nd)								
ARMSTRONG Craig	44	3	1		1			

	P/FL		FLC		FAC		Others	
	App	Goals	App	Goals	App	Goals	App	Goals
BALDRY Simon	26 + 9	2	0 + 2		1			
BEECH Chris	10		1					
BERESFORD David	0 + 2		1					
BOOTH Andy	8	3						
BRENNAN Jim	0 + 2							
DYSON Jon	25 + 5	3	1		1			
FACEY Delroy	22 +12	10	1 + 1		1			
GALLEN Kevin	30 + 8	10			1			
GORRE Dean	23 +11	2	1		0 + 1			
GRAY Kevin	13 + 4				1			
HAY Chris	0 + 4		2					
HEARY Thomas	25 + 3		2		1			
HOLLAND Chris	29		1		1			
IRONS Kenny	18 +15		1					
JENKINS Steve	30							
KOZLUK Rob	14							
KYLE Kevin	0 + 4							
LUCKETTI Chris	40	1	2					
MARGETSON Martyn	1 + 1							
MONKOU Ken	2							
MORRIS Lee	5	1						
MOSES Ade	10 + 2							
NDLOVU Peter	6	4						
SCHOFIELD Danny	0 + 1							
SELLARS Scott	6 + 8		0 + 1		0 + 1			
SENIOR Michael	0 + 4							
SMITH Martin	27 + 3	8	1					
THORNLEY Ben	29 + 7		2		1			
VAESEN Nico	45		2		1			
VINCENT Jamie	14 + 2		2		1			
WIJNHARD Clyde	4		1					
HULL CITY (DIV 3: 6th)								
ATKINS Mark	8						1 + 1	
BRABIN Gary	31 + 6	2	1 + 1		2		2	
BRACEY Lee	9 + 1		2					
BRADSHAW Gary	0 + 2							
BRIGHTWELL David	24 + 3	2	2		2		1	
BROWN David	24 +13	4	1 + 1		2		1 + 1	
BRUMWELL Phil	1 + 3		1 + 1					
EDWARDS Michael	40 + 2	4	1		1		3	
EYRE John	19 + 9	5	1	1	2		1 + 2	1
FLETCHER Gary	1 + 4							
FRANCIS Kevin	22	5					2	
GOODISON Ian	36	1	1		1		2	
GREAVES Mark	28 + 2	2	1		2		3	
HARPER Steve	27		1		2		1	
HARRIS Jason	1 + 8						0 + 1	
HOLT Andy	10	2					2	
MANN Neil	11 + 2							
MARCELLE Clint	16 + 7	2	1		1			
MATTHEWS Rob	8						2	
MORLEY Ben	0 + 2						0 + 1	
MUSSELWHITE Paul	37				2		3	
PERRY Jason	6				2			
PHILPOTT Lee	36 + 6	1	1		2		0 + 2	
ROWE Rodney	14 + 7	6					1 + 1	
SWALES Steve	20 + 6		2		1		1	
WHITMORE Theo	23 + 3	5	1		0 + 1		1	
WHITNEY Jon	14 + 1	1	2				3	
WHITTLE Justin	38		2				2	
WOOD Jamie	2 +13		1 + 1		0 + 1		1	
IPSWICH TOWN (PREM: 5th)								
ABIDALLAH Nabil	0 + 2							
ARMSTRONG Alun	15 + 6	7			2	1		
BRAMBLE Titus	23 + 3	1	4 + 1	2	2			
BRANAGAN Keith	2		1					
BROWN Wayne	0 + 4							
BURCHILL Mark	2 + 5	1						
CLAPHAM Jamie	28 + 7	2	7	1	0 + 2			
CROFT Gary	6 + 2		3 + 1		1			
HOLLAND Matt	38	3	6 + 1	2	2			
HREIDARSSON Hermann	35 + 1	1	7		2			
JOHNSON David	6 + 8		5	3				
KARIC Amir			0 + 3					
LOGAN Richard					0 + 1			
McGREAL John	25 + 3	1	5		1			
MAGILTON Jim	32 + 1	1	6	1	1 + 1			
MAKIN Chris	10							
NAYLOR Richard	5 + 8	1	1 + 1		0 + 1			
REUSER Martijn	13 +13	6	3 + 4		1			
SCALES John	2		2					
SCOWCROFT Jamie	22 +12	4	5 + 2	2	1 + 1			
STEWART Marcus	33 + 1	19	3 + 2	1	2	1		
VENUS Mark	23 + 2	3	3	1	1			
WILNIS Fabian	27 + 2	2	5 + 1		2			
WRIGHT Jermaine	35 + 2	2	5 + 2		2	1		
WRIGHT Richard	36		6		2			
KIDDERMINSTER HARRIERS (DIV 3: 16th)								
BARNETT Gary	2							
BENNETT Dean	35 + 7	4	2		1 + 2		1	
BIRD Tony	16 + 9	1	2		1 + 1	1	1 + 1	1
BOGIE Ian	14 + 7	1	2		2 + 1	1	1 + 1	
BROCK Stuart	21		1		3			
BROUGHTON Drewe	19	7						
CLARKE Tim	25		1				2	
CLARKSON Ian	37 + 1		2		3		1	
CORBETT Andy	3 + 3							
DAVIES Ben	2 + 1						1	
DOYLE Daire	13 + 2							
DUCROS Andy	29 + 5	2	1		3			
DURNIN John	28 + 3	9			1			
FOSTER Ian	9 + 1	2	1		2		1	
HADLEY Stewart	18 +15	6	2	1	2 + 1	2	1	
HINTON Craig	46	2	2		3		2	
HORNE Barry	21 + 6	1	2		3		2	
KERR Dylan	0 + 1							
MacKENZIE Neil	20 + 3	3			0 + 1		2	
MEDOU-OTYE Parfait	16 + 1						2	
SHAIL Mark	36	1	2		3		2	
SKOVBJERG Thomas	7 + 5	1						
SMITH Adie	32 + 2	5	1 + 1		3		1	1
STAMPS Scott	34		1		3		1	
WEBB Paul	23 + 9	1			0 + 1		1	
LEEDS UNITED (PREM: 4th)								
BAKKE Eirik	24 + 5	2	1		2		10 + 2	1
BATTY David	13 + 3				2		7 + 1	
BOWYER Lee	38	9			1		15	6
BRIDGES Michael	6 + 1						4	
BURNS Jacob	3 + 1		1				3 + 1	
DACOURT Olivier	33	3			1		14	
DUBERRY Michael	5						4	
EVANS Gareth	0 + 1						0 + 1	
FERDINAND Rio	23	2			2		7	1
HACKWORTH Tony			0 + 1				0 + 2	
HARTE Ian	29	7	1		1		17	4
HAY Danny	2 + 2		1				0 + 1	
HUCKERBY Darren	2 + 5		1	2			0 + 3	1
JONES Matthew	3 + 1		1				1	
KEANE Robbie	12 + 6	9			2			
KELLY Garry	22 + 2		1		1		11 + 1	
KEWELL Harry	12 + 5	2					6 + 3	
McPHAIL Stephen	3 + 4						1 + 2	
MARTYN Nigel	23				1		12	
MATTEO Dominic	30		1		2		15	2
MAYBURY Alan							1	
MILLS Danny	20 + 3				1		15 + 1	
RADEBE Lucas	19 + 1		0 + 1		1		10	
ROBINSON Paul	15 + 1		1		1		6	

	P/FL		FLC		FAC		Others	
	App	Goals	App	Goals	App	Goals	App	Goals
SMITH Alan	26 + 7	11	0 + 1		1 + 1		16	7
VIDUKA Mark	34	17	1		2	1	16	4
WILCOX Jason	7 +10				0 + 1		2 + 3	1
WOODGATE Jonathan	14	1	1		1		5	
LEICESTER CITY (PREM: 13th)								
AKINBIYI Ade	33 + 4	9			4	1	2	
BENJAMIN Trevor	7 +14	1	0 + 1		1 + 2			
COLLYMORE Stan	1 + 4	1					0 + 1	
COTTEE Tony	0 + 2							
CRESSWELL Richard	3 + 5		1		0 + 2	1	0 + 2	
DAVIDSON Callum	25 + 3	1	1		2		0 + 1	
DELANEY Damien	3 + 2				1 + 1			
EADIE Darren	16 + 8	2	1		0 + 1		2	
ELLIOTT Matt	34	2	0 + 1		4		2	
ELLISON Kevin	0 + 1							
FLOWERS Tim	22						2	
GILCHRIST Phil	6 + 6		1		1 + 1			
GUNNLAUGSSON Arnie	3 +14	3	1		0 + 3	1	0 + 1	
GUPPY Steve	17 +11	1	1		3		2	
IMPEY Andy	29 + 4				3		2	
IZZET Muzzy	27	7	0 + 1		3	3	2	1
JONES Matthew	10 + 1				3			
LENNON Neil	15		1				2	
LEWIS Junior	15							
McKINLAY Billy			1					
MANCINI Roberto	3 + 1				1			
MARSHALL Lee	7 + 2							
OAKES Stefan	5 + 8				1 + 2			
ROWETT Gary	38	2	1		4	1	2	
ROYCE Simon	16 + 3		1		4			
SAVAGE Robbie	33	4			4		2	
SINCLAIR Frank	14 + 3		1		1			
STURRIDGE Dean	12 + 1	3			2	1		
TAGGART Gerry	24	2			2		2	1
WALSH Steve	0 + 1							
LEYTON ORIENT (DIV 3: 5th)								
BARRETT Scott	7							
BAYES Ashley	39		4		4		4	
BEALL Matthew	12 + 5				0 + 2		1	
BRISSETT Jason	2 + 2		1 + 1					
BRKOVIC Ahmet	34 + 6	3	3	2	2 + 2		1 + 2	
CADIOU Frederic	0 + 3							
CASTLE Steve	2 + 7				0 + 1		2 + 1	
CHRISTIE Iyseden	1 + 6	2	2 + 1	1				
DORRIAN Chris	2		1					
DOWNER Simon	20 +11		1 + 1		2 + 1		3	
FORGE Nicolas	1							
GARCIA Richard	18	4	3					
GRIFFITHS Carl	35 + 2	14	2 + 1		3	4		
HARRIS Andy	44		4		4		1 + 1	
HATCHER Danny	0 + 2						0 + 1	
HOUGHTON Scott	17 + 4	1			3	1	4	1
IBEHRE Jabo	1 + 4	2	0 + 1				3	
JONES Billy	1							
JOSEPH Matt	44		3		4		4	
LEE Christian	2 + 1							
LOCKWOOD Matt	31 + 1	7	4		4		4	1
McELHOLM Brendan	3 + 9		1 + 2				1	
McGHEE Dave	39	3	4		4		4	
McLEAN Aaron	1 + 1	1						
MANSLEY Chad	0 + 1				0 + 1		0 + 1	
MARTIN John	15 + 4		3				0 + 3	
MURRAY Jay			0 + 1					
OPARA KK	3 + 3				1		1	
OPINEL Sasha	9 + 2	1						
PINAMONTE Lorenzo	5 + 6	2						
SHOREY Nicky	8				1			
SMITH Dean	43	5	3		4		4	
TATE Chris	9 +13	3			1 + 2	1	1 + 2	1

	P/FL		FLC		FAC		Others	
	App	Goals	App	Goals	App	Goals	App	Goals
VASSEUR Emmanuel	0 + 2							
WALSCHAERTS Wim	44 + 1	3	3		4		4	
WATTS Steve	14 +22	8	2 + 1	1	3 + 1	1	2	1
LINCOLN CITY (DIV 3: 18th)								
BARNETT Jason	27 + 6	1	1		1 + 1		5	
BATTERSBY Tony	24 +11	6	2		0 + 2		5 + 1	1
BIMSON Stuart	17 + 3						3	
BLACK Kingsley	5							
BROWN Grant	20	2	2		2		2	
BULLOCK Tony	2							
CAMERON David	10 + 6	2	2		0 + 1		0 + 5	
CAMM Mark	3						0 + 2	
CARR Darren	3							
DAY Chris	14						4	
DUDFIELD Lawrie	2 + 1							
DUDGEON James	20 + 2	3					3	
EUSTACE Scott	0 + 1							
FINNIGAN John	40		2		2		5	
GAIN Peter	19 + 5	5	1 + 1		2	1	3 + 1	
GARRATT Martin	2						1	
GHENT Matthew	0 + 1				1			
GORDON Gavin	18	9			2	1		
GRANT Gareth	3						1	1
HENRY Anthony	1							
HOLMES Steve	37 + 1	11	2		1		4	
LEWIS Graham	0 + 2		0 + 1					
LOGAN Richard	4 + 1		1					
MARRIOTT Alan	30		2		1		2	
MAYO Paul	26 + 1		2		2		3	
MILLER Paul	10 + 9		1		0 + 1		1 + 1	
PEACOCK Richard	22 +12	3	0 + 1		2	1	3	
PERKINS Chris	11 + 1							
PINKNEY Grant					0 + 1			
SCHOFIELD John	13 + 6				1		3 + 1	1
SEDGEMORE Ben	3 + 7	1					0 + 1	
SMITH Paul	35 + 5	7	2	1	2		4	
STERGIOPOULOS Marcus	2 + 5		1 + 1	1				
THORPE Lee	29 + 2	7			2		6	6
WALKER Justin	44 + 1	1	1 + 1		1		5	1
WELSH Steve	10 + 1						3 + 1	
LIVERPOOL (PREM: 3rd)								
ARPHEXAD Pegguy			2					
BABBEL Markus	38	3	4	1	5	1	13	1
BARMBY Nick	21 + 5	2	2 + 4	1	2 + 3	1	6 + 3	4
BERGER Patrik	11 + 3	2	1		0 + 1		3 + 2	
BISCAN Igor	8 + 5		4	1	3 + 1			
CARRAGHER Jamie	30 + 4		6		6		12	
DIOMEDE Bernard	1 + 1						2	
FOWLER Robbie	15 +12	8	5	6	3 + 2	2	6 + 5	1
GERRARD Steven	29 + 4	7	4		2 + 2	1	9	2
HAMANN Dietmar	26 + 4	2	2 + 3		5	1	13	
HEGGEM Vegard	1 + 2						1	
HENCHOZ Stephane	32		6		5		10	
HESKEY Emile	33 + 3	14	3 + 1		3 + 2	5	9 + 2	3
HYYPIA Sami	35	3	6	1	6		11	
LITMANEN Jari	4 + 1	1	1 + 1		1 + 1	1	0 + 2	
McALLISTER Gary	21 + 9	5	2 + 3		4 + 1		4 + 5	2
MEIJER Erik	0 + 3							
MURPHY Danny	13 +14	4	5	4	4 + 1	1	6 + 4	1
OWEN Michael	20 + 8	16	1 + 1	1	4 + 1	3	10 + 1	4
PARTRIDGE Richie			1					
SMICER Vlad	16 +11	2	5 + 1	4	4 + 1	1	6 + 5	
SONG Rigobert	3						1	
STAUNTON Steve	0 + 1						0 + 1	
TRAORE Djimi	8		1				2 + 1	
VIGNAL Gregory	4 + 2				0 + 1			
WESTERVELD Sander	38		4		6		13	
WRIGHT Steve	0 + 2		0 + 1		1			
ZIEGE Christian	11 + 5	1	1 + 3	1	2 + 1		6 + 3	

	P/FL		FLC		FAC		Others	
	App	Goals	App	Goals	App	Goals	App	Goals
LUTON TOWN (DIV 2: 22nd)								
ABBEY Nathan	20				3			
AYRES James							1	
BAPTISTE Rocky	0+ 3							
BOYCE Emmerson	42	3	4		2+ 1			
BREITENFELDER Friedrich	2+ 3							
BRENNAN Dean	2+ 7		1+ 2					
DOUGLAS Stuart	15+ 6	4			1+ 1	1		
DRYDEN Richard	20							
FOTIADIS Andrew	12+10	3	1		3	1	1	
FRASER Stuart	10+ 5		4		4		1	
GEORGE Liam	37+ 6	7	3+ 1		4	2		
HELIN Petri	23	1			3		1	
HOLMES Peter	12+ 6	1	2+ 1		1			
HOWARD Steve	12	3						
JOHNSON Marvin	9				2			
KANDOL Tresor	6+ 7	3	2+ 1	1				
KARLSEN Kent	4+ 2				2		1	
LOCKE Adam	17+ 8	2	1+ 1		2+ 1		1	
McGOWAN Gavin	5+ 1				1			
McLAREN Paul	35	2	4		3	1	1	
MANSELL Lee	17+ 1	5			1	1		
NOGAN Lee	7	1			3	1	0+ 1	
OVENDALE Mark	26		4		2		1	
ROWLAND Keith	12	2						
SCARLETT Andre	5+ 4		2	1	0+ 1			
SHEPHERD Paul	7							
SPRING Matthew	41	4	4		5		1	
STEIN Mark	19+11	3	3	1	1+ 1		0+ 1	
STIRLING Jude	5+ 4				0+ 2			
TAYLOR Matthew	45	1	4		4		1	
THOMPSON Peter	4+ 7	2	1+ 1		1+ 1		1	
WARD Scott	0+ 1							
WATTS Julian	26+ 2	4	4		3			
WHITBREAD Adrian	9				4			
MACCLESFIELD TOWN (DIV 3: 14th)								
ABBEY George	13+ 5		3+ 1		1			
ADAMS Danny	36+ 1		1+ 1		1		1	
ASKEY John	29+ 8	3	2+ 2		1		0+ 1	
BAMBER Mike	2+ 3		0+ 1				0+ 1	
BARKER Richie	23	7	4	2	1			
BETTNEY Chris	0+ 2							
BULLOCK Tony	24		4				1	
CAME Shaun	3+ 4						0+ 1	
COLLINS Simon	15+ 2		2					
CONNELL Darren	0+ 1							
DURKAN Keiron	26+ 5	4	3		0+ 1			
GLOVER Lee	29+ 8	8	0+ 1		1		1	2
HITCHEN Steve	37		3		1		1	
INGRAM Rae	32+ 1	1	3					
KEEN Kevin	30+ 2	2	1+ 1		0+ 1			
LAMBERT Rickie	4+ 5							
MARTIN Lee	21				1			
MUNROE Karl	19+ 4	1	4	1	1		1	
O'NEILL Paul	5+ 7				1		1	
PRIEST Chris	14+ 1	4					1	
RIOCH Greg	16+ 1	1					1	
SEDGEMORE Ben	23+ 4	3	4	2	1			
SHUKER Chris	6+ 3	1						
TERESKINAS Andrejus	0+ 1							
TINSON Darren	45	3	4		1		1	
TRACEY Richard	11+ 2	3						
TWYNHAM Gary	5+ 4		2					
WHITEHEAD Damien	9+24	8	0+ 2		0+ 1		1	
WILSON Steve	1							
WOOD Steve	27+ 3	1	4					
WOOLLEY Matt	1+ 1						1	

	P/FL		FLC		FAC		Others	
	App	Goals	App	Goals	App	Goals	App	Goals
MANCHESTER CITY (PREM: 18th)								
ALLSOP Danny	0+ 1							
BISHOP Ian	3+ 7		2+ 3		0+ 1			
CHARVET Laurent	16+ 4				0+ 1			
CROOKS Lee	0+ 2		2					
DICKOV Paul	15+ 6	4	2+ 1	1	0+ 1			
DUNFIELD Terry	0+ 1							
DUNNE Richard	24+ 1				3			
EDGHILL Richard	6				1			
GOATER Shaun	20+ 6	6	3	2	2+ 1	3		
GRANT Tony	5+ 5				1+ 1			
GRANVILLE Danny	16+ 3		0+ 3		3			
HAALAND Alfie	35	3	5		3			
HORLOCK Kevin	14	2	4	1				
HOWEY Steve	36	6	2		1			
HUCKERBY Darren	8+ 5	1			3	1		
JOBSON Richard			1+ 1					
KANCHELSKIS Andrei	7+ 3				1	1		
KENNEDY Mark	15+10		1+ 4	1				
MORRISON Andy	3		1		3	1		
NASH Carlo	6							
OSTENSTAD Egil	1+ 3							
PRIOR Spencer	18+ 3	1	4		2+ 1			
RITCHIE Paul	11+ 1		3		1			
TIATTO Danny	31+ 2	2	4		2			
WANCHOPE Paulo	25+ 2	9	3	1	1			
WEAH George	5+ 2	1	2	3				
WEAVER Nicky	31		5		3			
WHITLEY Jeff	28+ 3	1	5		1			
WIEKENS Gerard	29+ 5	2	3+ 1		2+ 1			
WRIGHT Tommy	1							
WRIGHT-PHILLIPS Shaun	9+ 6		3+ 1					
MANCHESTER UNITED (PREM: 1st)								
BARTHEZ Fabien	30				1		13	
BECKHAM David	29+ 2	9			2		12+ 1	
BERG Henning	0+ 1							
BROWN Wes	25+ 3		1		1		9+ 2	
BUTT Nicky	24+ 4	3			2		8+ 3	1
CHADWICK Luke	6+10	2	2		0+ 1		1+ 2	
CLEGG Michael			2					
COLE Andy	15+ 4	9			1		10+ 1	4
DJORDJIC Bojand	0+ 1							
FORTUNE Quinton	6+ 1	2	2				0+ 2	
GIGGS Ryan	24+ 7	5			2		10+ 2	2
GORAM Andy	2							
GREENING Jonathan	3+ 4		2				1+ 1	
HEALY David	0+ 1		0+ 1					
IRWIN Denis	20+ 1				1		8	2
JOHNSEN Ronny	11	1	1				5	
KEANE Roy	28	2			2		14	1
MAY David	1+ 1							
NEVILLE Gary	32	1			2		15	
NEVILLE Phil	24+ 5	1	2		1		4+ 2	
O'SHEA John			2					
RACHUBKA Paul	1		0+ 1					
SCHOLES Paul	28+ 4	6					13	6
SHERINGHAM Teddy	23+ 6	15			1+ 1	1	9+ 3	5
SILVESTRE Mickael	25+ 5	1			2		14+ 1	
SOLSKJAER Ole Gunnar	19+12	10	2	2	1+ 1	1	4+ 8	
STAM Jaap	15				1		6+ 1	
STEWART Michael	3		0+ 2					
VAN DER GOUW Rai	5+ 5		2		1		2	
WALLWORK Ronnie	4+ 8		2		0+ 1		0+ 1	
WEBBER Danny			0+ 1					
YORKE Dwight	15+ 7	9	2	2	1+ 1		7+ 5	1
MANSFIELD TOWN (DIV 3: 13th)								
ANDREWS John	5+ 3		4		2			
ASHER Alistair	23+ 5		2+ 2		1		1	

	P/FL App	P/FL Goals	FLC App	FLC Goals	FAC App	FAC Goals	Others App	Others Goals
BACON Danny	7+15	1	1+2		0+1		1	1
BARRETT Adam	8	1					1	
BLAKE Mark	38+3	8	3		2		1	
BOULDING Michael	12+21	6	1+1		2		0+1	
BOWLING Ian	4		1					
BRADLEY Shayne	21+5	7	0+1		0+2		1	
CLARKE Darrell	30+2	6	4	1				
CORDEN Wayne	31+3	3	4	2	1		1	
DISLEY Craig	16+8				1		1	
FORTUNE Jon	14							
GREENACRE Chris	46	19	4	1	2	1	0+1	
HASSELL Bobby	39+1	1	2+1		1			
HICKS Stuart	25		4		1			
JERVIS David	17+5				2			
LAWRENCE Liam	7+11	4						
LOMAS Jamie	4+2		1					
MIMMS Bobby	40		3		2			
PEMBERTON Martin	16+2	1	1		1		1	
PILKINGTON Kevin	2						1	
REDDINGTON Stuart	9							
ROBINSON Les	44		4		2		1	
SISSON Michael	2+2		1					
WHITE Andy	0+4							
WILLIAMS Lee	36+5	4	4		1+1			
WILLIAMSON Lee	10+5		0+3		1+1		1	

MIDDLESBROUGH (PREM: 14th)

	P/FL App	P/FL Goals	FLC App	FLC Goals	FAC App	FAC Goals	Others App	Others Goals
ARMSTRONG Alun			1					
BENNION Chris			1					
BERESFORD Marlon	0+1							
BOKSIC Alen	26+2	12	0+1		2+1			
CAMPBELL Andy	5+2		1		0+2			
COOPER Colin	26+1	2	2		2			
CROSSLEY Mark	4+1		2					
DEANE Brian	13+12	2	1		1			
EHIOGU Ugo	21	3			3			
FESTA Gianluca	21+4	2	3		3			
FLEMING Curtis	29+1		2		3			
GAVIN Jason	10+4		1					
GORDON Dean	12+8	1	3		2			
HUDSON Mark	0+3				0+1			
INCE Paul	30	2	2		3			
JOB Josephe-Desire	8+4	3	1+1					
KAREMBEU Christian	31+2	4	1		1+1			
MADDISON Neil			0+1					
MARINELLI Carlos	2+11		0+1					
MUSTOE Robbie	13+12				1+1			
OKON Paul	23+1				2			
O'NEILL Keith	14+1		0+1		1			
PALLISTER Gary	8		1					
PARNABY Stuart			1					
RICARD Hamilton	22+5	4	3	3	3	2		
SCHWARZER Mark	31				3			
STAMP Phil	11+8	1	0+1		2			
SUMMERBELL Mark	5+2	1	3	1				
VICKERS Steve	29+1		1		1			
WALSH Gary	3							
WHELAN Noel	13+14	1	3	1	0+2			
WINDASS Dean	8	2						

MILLWALL (DIV 2: 1st)

	P/FL App	P/FL Goals	FLC App	FLC Goals	FAC App	FAC Goals	Others App	Others Goals
BIRCHAM Marc	13+7	2	1		3	1	2	
BOWRY Bobby	0+1		0+1					
BRANIFF Kevin	2+3		3+1	1	0+1			
BUBB Byron	2+1							
BULL Ronnie	2						1	
CAHILL Tim	40+1	9	4	1	0+2		0+1	
CLARIDGE Steve	6	3						
CONSTANTINE Leon	0+1						1	
COTTEE Tony	0+2							
DOLAN Joe	20	1	4		3	1	2	
DYCHE Sean	33		0+1		2			
FITZGERALD Scott	0+1							
GILKES Michael	2+1		0+1					
GUERET Willy	11						2	
HARRIS Neil	39+3	27	3		3	1	1+1	
IFILL Paul	28+7	6	2	1	3		1	
KINET Christophe	18+9	2	3	1	1+2		2	3
LAWRENCE Matty	45		4		3		2	
LIVERMORE David	39	3	4	1	3			
MOODY Paul	21+6	13			2	1	0+1	
NEILL Lucas	19+5	2					1	
NETHERCOTT Stuart	33+2	2	2		1		1	
ODUNSI Leke	2+6		1+2				2	
PARKIN Sam	5+2	4						
REID Steven	27+10	7	3+1		3		1+1	
RYAN Robbie	42		4		2			
SADLIER Richard	16+13	6			1+1		2	1
STUART Jamie	0+1							
TUTTLE Dave	6+3		2				1	
TYNE Tommy	0+3		0+3					
WARNER Tony	35		4		3			

NEWCASTLE UNITED (PREM: 11th)

	P/FL App	P/FL Goals	FLC App	FLC Goals	FAC App	FAC Goals	Others App	Others Goals
ACUNA Clarence	23+3	3	1		2			
AMEOBI Shola	12+8	2			2			
BARTON Warren	27+2		1		1+1			
BASSEDAS Christian	17+5	1	1+1		2			
CALDWELL Steve	5+4		1	1				
CHARVET Laurent	6+1		2					
COPPINGER James	0+1							
CORDONE Daniel	12+9	2	1+3	1	0+2			
CORT Carl	13	6	2	1				
DABIZAS Nicos	9							
DOMI Didier	11+3		1+1					
DYER Kieron	25+1	5	4	1	1			
GALLACHER Kevin	12+7	2	2	1	1			
GAVILAN Diego	0+1		0+1					
GIVEN Shay	34		1					
GLASS Stephen	5+9	3			1+1			
GOMA Alain	18+1	1	3		2			
GRIFFIN Andy	14+5		4		2			
HARPER Steve	4+1		3		2			
HUGHES Aaron	34+1		3		2			
KERR Brian	0+1							
LEE Rob	21+1		3+1					
LUA-LUA Tresor	3+18				0+2			
MARCELINO	5+1				1			
O'BRIEN Andy	9	1						
QUINN Wayne	14+1							
SHEARER Alan	19	5	4	2				
SOLANO Nobby	31+2	6	3+1		1	1		
SPEED Gary	35	5	4	1	2			

NORTHAMPTON TOWN (DIV 2: 18th)

	P/FL App	P/FL Goals	FLC App	FLC Goals	FAC App	FAC Goals	Others App	Others Goals
CANOVILLE Lee	2							
CARRUTHERS Chris	1+2							
CHILVERS Liam	7							
CLARE Daryl	3+1						0+1	
CROOKS Lee	3							
DEMPSEY Paul	5+1							
DRYDEN Richard	9+1							
FERGUSON Barry	1+2							
FORRESTER Jamie	42+1	17	2		2	2		
FRAIN John	27	1	1		1	1		
GABBIADINI Marco	34+10	6	2	1	1+1		1	
GOULD James	0+1						1	1
GREEN Richard	34+4		2		2		1	
HARGREAVES Chris	29+2		1		2		1	
HENDON Ian	9	1	2					
HODGE John	24+9	1	0+2		0+1			
HOPE Richard	30+3		1		2		1	

	P/FL		FLC		FAC		Others	
	App	Goals	App	Goals	App	Goals	App	Goals
HOWARD Steve	23+10	8	2		2		1	
HOWEY Lee	2+1							
HUGHES Garry	12+4	1	2		1+1		1	
HUNT James	41	1	2		2	1		
HUNTER Roy	1+3							
LOPES Richie	3+3							
LOWE Danny	0+4							
MALEY Mark	2							
MORROW Andy	2+2						1	
NICHOLSON Kevin	6+1							
SAMPSON Ian	41	2	1	1	2		1	
SAVAGE Dave	37+6	8	1		2		0+1	
SOLLITT Adam	6				1		1	
SPEDDING Duncan	17+4		1		1		1	
THOMPSON Ryan	0+2							
WELCH Keith	40		2		1			
WHITLEY Jim	13							
WILSON Kevin	0+6							
NORWICH CITY (DIV 1: 15th)								
ABBEY Zema	11+9	1						
BELLAMY Craig	1							
BRADY Garry	2		2					
COOTE Adrian	3+11		0+3		0+1			
COTTEE Tony	5+2	1	1+1	1				
DALGLISH Paul	0+7		1					
DE BLASIIS Jean Yves	2+5							
DERVELD Fernando	15+2	1	3					
DE WAARD Raymond	0+6		1+2					
DRURY Adam	6							
FLEMING Craig	39		5		1			
FORBES Adrian	13+16	3	1+2		1			
GIALLANZA Gaetano	5+6	2	3+1	3				
GRANVILLE Danny	6							
GREEN Robert	5							
HOLT Gary	3+1							
JACKSON Matt	26		1		1			
KENTON Darren	24+5	2	3		0+1			
LLEWELLYN Chris	41+1	8	3		1			
McGOVERN Brian	3+9	1	2+1					
MACKAY Malky	34+4	1	1		1			
McVEIGH Paul	6+5	1	0+1					
MARSHALL Andy	41		5		1			
MARSHALL Lee	34+2	3	4	1	1			
MULRYNE Phil	27+1	1	2		1			
NEDERGAARD Steen	10+5	1	1+2					
NOTMAN Alex	10+5	1			0+1			
PARKER Scott	6	1						
PESCHISOLIDO Paul	3+2							
ROBERTS Iwan	44	15	5	3	1	1		
RUSSELL Darel	34+7	2	5	2	1			
SUTCH Daryl	39+1		5		1			
WALSH Steve	1+3		1					
WHITLEY Jim	7+1	1						
NOTTINGHAM FOREST (DIV 1: 11th)								
BART-WILLIAMS Chris	46	14	2	1	1			
BEASANT Dave	45		2		1			
BENALI Francis	15							
BLAKE Robbie	9+2	1	1					
BRENNAN Jim	9+3		2		1			
CALDERWOOD Colin	1+1							
COOPER Richard	0+2							
DAWSON Kevin	1							
DOIG Chris	14+1		2					
EDDS Gareth	9+4	1			1			
EDWARDS Chris	35+1	3			1			
FOY Keith	17+3	1						
FREEDMAN Dougie	2+3		0+1					
FREEMAN David	2+3				0+1			
GRAY Andy	11+7				1			

	P/FL		FLC		FAC		Others	
	App	Goals	App	Goals	App	Goals	App	Goals
HAREWOOD Marlon	13+20	3	1		1			
HJELDE Jon Olav	10+1	2						
JENAS Jermaine	1				1			
JOHN Stern	16+13	2	2	1	0+1			
JOHNSON Andy	29+2	3	1					
JOHNSON David	19	2						
JONES Gary	22+9	1	1+1		1			
LESTER Jack	18+1	7						
LOUIS-JEAN Matthieu	10+3		2					
OLSEN Ben	14+4	2						
PLATT David	2	1	1+1					
PRUTTON David	41+1	1	2					
REID Andrew	9+5	2			1			
ROCHE Barry	1+1							
ROGERS Alan	16+1	3	1	1				
SCIMECA Ricardo	34+2	4						
UPSON Matthew	1							
VAUGHAN Tony	23+2	1	2					
WILLIAMS Gareth	11+6				1			
NOTTS COUNTY (DIV 2: 8th)								
ALLSOP Danny	26+3	13			4			
BOLLAND Paul	7		1		0+1		1	
BROUGH Michael	11+5	1			1+2			
CALDERWOOD Colin	5							
CRAMB Colin	2+1							
DUNN Mark							1	
DYER Alex	8+1		3					
FARRELL Sean	9+10	3	0+1		0+1			
FENTON Nicky	30	2	1		5			
FORD Ryan							1	
GELLERT Brian							1	
GIBSON Paul	9		1				1	
HAMILTON Ian	23+2		3+1		3+1		1	
HEFFERNAN Paul	0+1						0+1	
HOLMES Richard	3+2				0+1		1	
HUGHES Andy	20+10	5	1+1	1	5	2		
IRELAND Craig	16							
JACOBSON Anders	27+2	2			5			
JORGENSEN Henrik	3+2						1	
JOSEPH David	13+14	4	3+1		0+1		1	
LIBURD Richard	28+3	3	3		4+1	2		
LINDLEY Jim	2		0+1					
McCANN Grant	2		1					
McDERMOTT Andy	20+5		4		1			
MOREAU Fabrice	2+3							
MURRAY Shaun	7+4				2+1		1	
NEWTON Adam	13+7	1			2			
NICHOLSON Kevin	9+2	2						
OWERS Gary	40	4	3		5			
PEARCE Dennis	26+1		2		3			
RAMAGE Craig	14+1	3	3					
RAPLEY Kevin	0+7		0+3					
REDMILE Matt	7+1		1					
RICHARDSON Ian	24+1	1	4		5			
STALLARD Mark	42	17	4	4	5	3		
THOMAS Geoff	8	1						
WARD Darren	35		3		5			
WARREN Mark	15+1		3				1	
OLDHAM ATHLETIC (DIV 2: 15th)								
ADAMS Neil	18	2	2					
ALLOTT Mark	26+13	7	3+1		1+2			
BOSHELL Danny	11+7	1	3	1	2		1	
CARSS Tony	35	2			3			
CORAZZIN Carlo	37+1	7	3	1	3	1		
DUDLEY Craig	10+16	4	2		3	2		
DUXBURY Lee	40	8	4	1	1	1		
EYRES David	30	3			3		1	
FUTCHER Ben	1+4							
GARNETT Shaun	39	1	2		3		1	

	P/FL		FLC		FAC		Others	
	App	Goals	App	Goals	App	Goals	App	Goals
HOLT Andy	12 + 8	1	4		0 + 3		1	
HOTTE Mark	25 + 3		2		0 + 1		1	
INNES Mark	27 + 3		2 + 2		3		0 + 1	
JONES Paul	10 + 2	2	3					
KELLY Gary	45		4		3		1	
LIGHTFOOT Chris	3		1					
McNIVEN Scott	43 + 2		3		3		1	
MISKELLY David	1 + 1							
PARKIN Sam	3 + 4	3						
PRENDERVILLE Barry	6 + 3		1 + 1		1			
RICKERS Paul	38	2	2	2	3		1	
RITCHIE Andy							0 + 1	
ROACH Neville	0 + 1							
SALT Phil	4 + 2		0 + 2		0 + 1		1	1
SHERIDAN John	22 + 3	4			1 + 1			
SMITH Paul	3 + 1		1					
SUGDEN Ryan	1 + 1		0 + 1				1	
TIPTON Matthew	15 +15	5	1 + 3		0 + 1	1	1	1
WATSON Mark	1 + 1		1					
WHITEHALL Steve	0 + 2		0 + 1					
OXFORD UNITED (DIV 2: 24th)								
ANDREWS Keith	4	1					1	
ANTHROBUS Steve	13 + 7	1	2		1		0 + 1	1
BEAUCHAMP Joey	32 +11	7	1 + 1		2		1	
BROOKS Jamie	3 + 1	1						
BROWN Keith	3				2		1	
BUSBY Hubert	0 + 1							
COOK Jamie	4 + 5	1						
CUTLER Neil	11							
FEAR Peter	14 + 5	2			2			
FOLLAND Rob	1 + 4	1	0 + 2					
FORD Mike	1							
GLASS Jimmy	1						1	
GRAY Phil	21 + 2	7			2	2	1	
HACKETT Chris	10 + 6	2			1		0 + 1	
HATSWELL Wayne	26 + 1						1	
HOLDER Jordan	0 + 2							
JARMAN Lee	15 + 6	1	2		2			
KING Simon	2							
KNIGHT Richard	33		2		2			
LILLEY Derek	15 + 4	2	0 + 2		1			
LINIGHAN Andy	12 + 1				2			
McGOWAN Neil	11		1					
McGUCKIN Ian	6 + 1							
MIKE Leon	1 + 2							
MONK Garry	5							
MURPHY Matt	37 + 3	6	1 + 1	1	2	1	1	
OMOYIMNI Manny	16 + 8	3	2		0 + 1		1	
PATTERSON Darren	18	1						
POWELL Paul	15 + 5	1	1					
QUINN Rob	12 + 1	2						
RICHARDSON Jon	41	2	2		2		1	
RICKETTS Sam	13 + 1						1	
ROBERTSON John	37 + 3		2		1		1	
SCOTT Andy	21	5						
SHEPHEARD Jon	5		2	1				
TAIT Paul	22 + 4	3	2					
WEATHERSTONE Ross	1							
WEATHERSTONE Simon	6 + 1							
WHITEHEAD Dean	16 + 4		2		0 + 1			
WHITTINGHAM Guy	1	1						
WILSON Phil	1 + 1							
PETERBOROUGH UNITED (DIV 2: 12th)								
CLARKE Andy	36 + 6	9	1	1	4	1	1	
CONNOR Dan							2	
CULLEN Jon	12 + 6	1	0 + 1		1		2	1
DANIELSSON Helgi	3 + 3							
DRURY Adam	29		2		5		0 + 1	
EDWARDS Andy	43	1	2		5	1		

	P/FL		FLC		FAC		Others	
	App	Goals	App	Goals	App	Goals	App	Goals
FARRELL Dave	39 + 5	7	1 + 1	1	5	1		
FORINTON Howard	2 + 6	1	1		0 + 2		2	
FORSYTH Richard	25 + 5	2	2		5	1	0 + 1	
FRENCH Daniel	1 + 1						1 + 1	
GILL Matthew	11 + 6	1			3		1	
GREEN Francis	18 +14	6	2		2		2	1
HANLON Richie	21 + 5	1	1 + 1		0 + 1		2	
HOOPER Dean	28 + 5		2		3 + 1		2	
JELLEYMAN Gareth	6 + 2				1 + 1		2	
LEE Jason	14 +16	8			4	1	0 + 1	
MacDONALD Gary	1							
McKENZIE Leon	30	13			3 + 1			
MORROW Steve	11							
MURRAY Dan	1 + 2						2	
OLDFIELD David	32 + 7	3	2		5	1		
REA Simon	35 + 1	2	2		3		1	
ROGERS Dave	1 + 2						1	
SCOTT Richard	18 + 2		0 + 2				1	
SHIELDS Tony	28 + 5	1	1 + 1		1 + 3	1		
TAYLOR Stuart	6							
TYLER Mark	40		2		5			
WHITTINGHAM Guy	1 + 4	1	1					
WILLIAMS Martin	13 + 2	1						
WILLIAMS Tommy	1 + 1							
PLYMOUTH ARGYLE (DIV 3: 12th)								
ADAMS Steve	12 + 5				1		1	
BANCE Danny	1							
BARLOW Martin	17 + 3		2		2			
BARRETT Adam	9		2					
BESWETHERWICK Jon	44 + 1		2		2		1	
BETTS Robert	3 + 1							
CONNOLLY Paul	0 + 1							
ELLIOTT Stuart	11 + 1							
EVANS Micky	10	4						
EVERS Sean	2 + 5							
FLEMING Terry	15 + 2		2		2		0 + 2	
FRIIO David	26	5					1	
GRITTON Martin	1 + 9	1	1 + 1		0 + 1		2	1
GUINAN Steve	7 +15	1	2		2		0 + 1	
HEATHCOTE Mick	4 + 1						1	
HODGES John	2				2			
JAVARY Jean-Phillipe	4							
LARRIEU Romain	14 + 1						2	
LEADBITTER Chris	9				2		1	
McCARTHY Sean	31 + 6	10	1 + 1	1				
McCORMICK Luke	1							
McGLINCHEY Brian	17 + 3						2	
McGREGOR Paul	31 + 2	6	0 + 1	1	2	1	0 + 1	
MARDON Paul	3	1						
MEAKER Michael	5 + 6	1						
NANCEKIVELL Kevin	0 + 6	1	0 + 1					
OPINEL Sasha							1	
O'SULLIVAN Wayne	38 + 2	1	2					
PEAKE Jason	7 + 3	2	1		1 + 1	1		
PHILLIPS Lee	4 + 2		0 + 1				0 + 1	
PHILLIPS Martin	36 + 6	1	2		2		2	
SHEFFIELD Jon	29		2					
STONEBRIDGE Ian	17 +14	11			0 + 2		2	1
TAYLOR Craig	38 + 1	3	2		2		1	1
TRUDGIAN Ryan	0 + 1							
WILKIE Lee	2							
WILLS Kevin	4 + 6	1			0 + 2		2	
WORRELL David	14						2	
WOTTON Paul	38 + 4	4	1		2		1	
PORTSMOUTH (DIV 1: 20th)								
AWFORD Andy	2							
BIRMINGHAM David			0 + 1					
BRADBURY Lee	35 + 4	10	3 + 1		1	1		
BRADY Garry	8							

	P/FL		FLC		FAC		Others	
	App	Goals	App	Goals	App	Goals	App	Goals
CLARIDGE Steve	24 + 7	11	2		0 + 1			
CROWE Jason	21 + 2				1			
CURTIS Tom	4		1 + 1					
DERRY Shaun	27 + 1		4		1			
EDINBURGH Justin	16 + 1		3					
FLAHAVAN Aaron	20							
HARPER Kevin	15 + 9	2			1			
HILEY Scott	34		1		1			
HOULT Russell	22		4					
HUGHES Ceri	16 + 3		3		0 + 1			
KELLER Marc	3							
LAMBOURDE Bernard	6							
LOVELL Steve	5 + 4	1						
MIGLIORANZI Stefan	8 + 4		0 + 2					
MILLS Lee	22 + 2	4	3	1				
MOORE Darren	31 + 1	1	4		1			
NIGHTINGALE Luke	7 +12	1	0 + 1	1	1			
O'NEIL Gary	7 + 3	1	1 + 2					
PANOPOULOS Mike	26 + 4	6						
PETTEFER Carl	0 + 1							
PETTERSON Andy	2							
PRIMUS Linvoy	23		3					
QUASHIE Nigel	29 + 2	5	4		1			
RUDONJA Mladen	2 + 9		1 + 2		1			
SHARPE Lee	17							
TARDIF Chris	2 + 2				1			
THOGERSEN Thomas	32 + 2	3	4		1			
TILER Carl	9	1						
VINCENT Jamie	14							
VINE Rowan	0 + 2							
WATERMAN David	12 +10		3 + 1					
WHITTINGHAM Guy	0 + 1							
WOLLEASTON Robert	5 + 1							
PORT VALE (DIV 2: 11th)								
BERESFORD David	4							
BRAMMER Dave	33 + 2	3			2	1	7	
BRIDGE-WILKINSON Marc	40 + 2	9	1	1	2	1	7	3
BRISCO Neil	16 + 1	1					4 + 1	
BROOKER Stephen	20 + 3	8					5	2
BURGESS Richard	0 + 1							
BURNS Liam	5 + 8				1		0 + 1	
BURTON-GODWIN Sagi	24 + 5		2	1	1		4 + 1	
BYRNE Paul	1							
CARRAGHER Matt	45		2		2		7	
CUMMINS Michael	43 + 2	2	2		2		7	1
DELANEY Dean	7 + 1						1	
DODD Ashley	3							
DONNELLY Paul	0 + 1							
EYRE Richard	1 + 5		1				0 + 1	
FREEMAN David	2 + 1							
GOODLAD Mark	39 + 1		2		2		6	
GRAY Wayne	2 + 1							
LOWE Onandi	4 + 1	1					1	1
MINTON Jeff	11 + 2	1	2	1	2	2	0 + 2	
NAYLOR Tony	41 + 1	14	2		2	1	7	5
O'CALLAGHAN George	2 + 6	1			0 + 1		0 + 1	
OLAOYE Del	0 + 1							
PAYNTER Billy	0 + 1							
SMITH Alex	36 + 1	2	0 + 1		2		7	1
TANKARD Allen	28 + 5	4	2		1		3	1
TWISS Michael	15 + 3	3	2		0 + 2		1 + 1	
VILJANEN Ville	15 + 4	2	2		1		0 + 1	
WALSH Michael	38 + 1	1			1		7	
WIDDRINGTON Tommy	31 + 4	2	2		1		3	
PRESTON NORTH END (DIV 1: 4th)								
ALEXANDER Graham	34	5	4	2			3	
ANDERSON Iain	19 +12	6	2				1 + 2	
APPLETON Michael	25 + 1	5	1		1			
BARRY-MURPHY Brian	2 +12		1 + 2		1			
BASHAM Steve	11	2	4					
CARTWRIGHT Lee	29 + 9		4		0 + 1		3	
CRESSWELL Richard	5 + 6	2					1 + 2	
EATON Adam	1				1			
EDWARDS Rob	41 + 1		4				3	
EYRES David	0 + 5		0 + 2					
GREGAN Sean	39 + 2	2	3				3	
GUNNLAUGSSON Bjarki	5 +14	1						
HEALY David	19 + 3	9			1		3	1
JACKSON Michael	27 + 3	1	2		1			
KEANE Michael	0 + 2							
KIDD Ryan	13 + 2		0 + 1		1		3	
LONERGAN Andy	1		1					
LUCAS David	28 + 1		3		1		3	
LUDDEN Dominic	0 + 2							
McBRIDE Brian	8 + 1	1	1		1			
MACKEN Jonathan	37 + 1	19	2	3	0 + 1		3	
McKENNA Paul	43 + 1	5	2		1		2 + 1	
MEIJER Erik	9							
MOILANEN Tepi	17							
MORGAN Paul			1					
MURDOCK Colin	33 + 4		4				3	
O'HANLON Kelham	0 + 1							
PARKINSON Gary	11				1			
RANKINE Mark	43 + 1	4	2 + 1	1	1		2	1
ROBINSON Steve	6 +16	1	3					
QUEENS PARK RANGERS (DIV 1: 23rd)								
BARACLOUGH Ian	26 + 3		1		3			
BIGNOT Marcus	8 + 1	1						
BREACKER Tim	8 + 2		1					
BROOMES Marlon	5							
BROWN Wayne	2							
BRUCE Paul	5 + 2	1	0 + 1					
BUBB Alvin	0 + 1							
BURGESS Oliver	0 + 1							
CARLISLE Clarke	27	3	2		3			
COCHRANE Justin	0 + 1							
CONNOLLY Karl	17 + 6	4	1		2 + 1			
CROUCH Peter	38 + 4	10	1 + 1		3	2		
DARLINGTON Jermaine	32 + 1		1		3			
DOWIE Iain	0 + 1							
FURLONG Paul	3	1						
HARPER Lee	29		2					
HEINOLA Antti	0 + 1		0 + 1					
HIGGINS Alex	0 + 1							
KIWOMYA Chris	20 + 6	6	2	2	1 + 1	2		
KNIGHT Leon	10 + 1							
KOEJOE Sammy	8 +13	2	1 + 1		2 + 1			
KULSCAR George	9 + 5				1			
LANGLEY Richard	26	1	2		3			
LISBIE Kevin	1 + 1							
McFLYNN Terry	1 + 1							
MADDIX Danny	1 + 1							
MIKLOSKO Ludo	17				3			
MORROW Steve	18 + 6		2		1			
MURRAY Paul	4 + 2							
NGONGE Michel	7 + 6	3			0 + 2			
PACQUETTE Richard	1 + 1							
PEACOCK Gavin	31 + 1	3	1		1 + 1	1		
PERRY Mark	23 + 6		2		2			
PESCHISOLIDO Paul	5	1						
PLUMMER Chris	24 + 1	2			3			
READY Karl	19 + 4		1					
ROSE Matthew	27		1		2			
ROWLAND Keith	4							
SCULLY Tony	1 + 1							
THOMSON Andy	7 + 1	4						
WALSHE Ben	0 + 1							
WARDLEY Stewart	26 + 8	3	1		0 + 2			
WARREN Christer	16 + 6							

	P/FL		FLC		FAC		Others	
	App	Goals	App	Goals	App	Goals	App	Goals
READING (DIV 2: 3rd)								
ASHDOWN Jamie	0+1							
BUTLER Martin	42+3	24	1+1		3	2	3+1	2
CASKEY Darren	35+8	9	1		1	1	3+1	
CURETON Jamie	37+6	26	2	1	2+1	1	5	2
EVERS Sean			1					
FORSTER Nicky	0+9	1					0+3	1
GAMBLE Joe	0+1		0+1		0+1			
GRAY Stuart	2+1				1		1	
GURNEY Andy	15+6	1	2		0+1		2+1	
HADDOW Alex	0+1							
HARPER Jamie	9+3	1					1+1	
HENDERSON Darius	0+4		1				0+1	
HODGES Lee	23+6	2	1		3	1	0+1	
HOWIE Scott							2	
HUNTER Barry	21+2	1	1		0+1		3+1	
IGOE Sammy	15+16	6	2		2		5	
JONES Keith	18+5				3	1	2	
McINTYRE Jim	25+8	4	0+1		0+1		5	1
MACKIE John	7+3		1+1		3		0+1	
MURTY Graeme	18+5	1					3	
NEWMAN Ricky	37+2		1		3	1	1	
PARKINSON Phil	44	4	1		3		4	
ROBINSON Matthew	29+3		2		2		3	
ROUGIER Tony	14+17	2	1		1+1		2+2	
SCOTT Keith	1							
SMITH Neil	4+11	1	0+1		0+1			
VIVEASH Adrian	40	2	2		3		5	
WHITBREAD Adrian	19							
WHITEHEAD Phil	46		2		3		3	
WILLIAMS Adrian	5						2	
ROCHDALE (DIV 3: 8th)								
BAYLISS Dave	41	3	2				1	
BUGGIE Lee	0+2							
COLEMAN Simon	5							
CONNOR Paul	14	10						
DAVIES Simon	7+5	1	1+1		0+1		0+1	
EDWARDS Neil	44		2		1		1	
ELLIS Tony	25+3	6	1	1	0+1		1	
EVANS Wayne	45	2	2		1		1	
FLITCROFT Dave	40+1		1+1				0+1	
FORD Tony	36+2	2	2		1			
GILKS Matty	2+1							
HADLAND Phil	12+20	2	0+1		1		1	
HAMILTON Gary	0+3							
HILL Keith	22+3		2		1			
HOWELL Dean	2+1							
JONES Gary	44	8	1+1		1		1	1
KYLE Kevin	3+3							
LANCASHIRE Graham	6+10	3			0+1		0+1	
LEE Christian	2+3	1						
McAULEY Sean	1						1	
MONINGTON Mark	31+3	7			1		1	
OLIVER Michael	25+13		2		1		1	
PLATT Clive	39+4	8	2	1	1	1	1	
TODD Lee	40	3	2		1			
TOWNSON Kevin	1+2							
TURNER Andy	2+2							
WALSH David			0+1					
WARE Paul	17+13	2	2		1		1	
ROTHERHAM UNITED (DIV 2: 2nd)								
ARTELL David	35+1	4			3		1	
BARKER Richie	7+12	1						
BEECH Chris	8+7		1		0+1			
BERRY Trevor	5+6		0+1		0+1		0+1	
BOLIMA Cedric	0+1							
BRANSTON Guy	41	6	2		3			
BRYAN Marvin	23+5		2		1		1	

	P/FL		FLC		FAC		Others	
	App	Goals	App	Goals	App	Goals	App	Goals
CARR Darren	1						1	
FORTUNE-WEST Leo	5	1	2					
GARNER Darren	30+1	1	1+1		3		1	
GRAY Ian	33		2		3		1	
HUDSON Danny	1+4							
HURST Paul	42+2	3	1+1		3		1	
LEE Alan	29+2	13			3	1	1	1
LEMARCHAND Stephane					0+1			
MINTON Jeff	5+4	2						
MONKHOUSE Andy	1+11				0+2		0+1	1
PETTINGER Paul	13							
ROBINS Mark	42	24	2	1	3		1	1
SCOTT Rob	39	2	2		2		1	
SEDGWICK Chris	2+19	2			0+1			
TALBOT Stuart	37+1	5	2		3			
TURNER Andy	3+1							
VARTY Will	5+1		0+2					
WARNE Paul	44	7	2		3		1	
WATSON Kevin	46	5	2	1	3		1	
WILSTERMAN Brian	9+1	1	1					
SCUNTHORPE UNITED (DIV 3: 10th)								
BANGER Nicky	0+1							
BERRY Trevor	6	1						
BROUGH Scott	0+4				0+1		0+1	
CALVO-GARCIA Alex	30+4	4	1		5	1		
CARRUTHERS Martin	8	1						
COTTERILL James	4							
DAWSON Andy	41	4	2		5	1	1	
DEWHURST Rob			1					
EVANS Tommy	46		2		5		1	
FICKLING Ashley	3+6		1		0+1			
GRAVES Wayne	25+9	2	2		0+4		1	
HARSLEY Paul	22+11	1	2		1+1		0+1	

Rob Scott (Rotherham United)

	P/FL App	P/FL Goals	FLC App	FLC Goals	FAC App	FAC Goals	Others App	Others Goals
HODGES Lee	32 + 6	8	2		5	1		
IPOUA Guy	22 + 3	14			4	4	1	
JACKSON Mark	28 + 4	1			5		1	
LARUSSON Bjarni	33	4			5		1	
MAMOUM Blaise	0 + 1							
MORRISON Peter	8 +10		1 + 1		2 + 1		1	
PEPPER Nigel	2							
QUAILEY Brian	11 +16	3	0 + 1				0 + 1	1
RAPLEY Kevin	1 + 4							
RIDLEY Lee	1 + 1							
ROGERS Dave	1							
SHELDON Gareth	33 + 6	1	2		4	1	1	1
SHEPHERD Paul	0 + 1							
SPARROW Matt	9 + 2	4	0 + 2					
STAMP Darryn	4 + 8	1			0 + 2		1	
STANTON Nathan	34 + 4		2		5		1	
THOM Stuart	17 + 4				0 + 1		1	
TORPEY Steve	40	10	2	1	4	1		
WILCOX Russ	33 + 3	1	2		5			
WOODWARD Andy	12							

SHEFFIELD UNITED (DIV 1: 10th)

	P/FL App	P/FL Goals	FLC App	FLC Goals	FAC App	FAC Goals	Others App	Others Goals
ASABA Carl	10	5						
BENT Marcus	16	5	5	3				
BROWN Michael	36	1	4	1				
BULLOCK Darren	6							
BURLEY Adam	0 + 1		0 + 1					
CRYAN Colin	0 + 1		0 + 2					
CURLE Keith	23 + 2		2					
DEVLIN Paul	41	5	4	3	1			
D'JAFFO Laurent	16 + 6	5			0 + 1			
DOANE Ben	3							
FORD Bobby	33 + 2	3	2 + 2		1			
JAGIELKA Phil	3 +12		3					
KELLY David	21 +14	6	4	2	1			
KOZLUK Rob	23 + 4				1			
MONTGOMERY Nick	14 +13		1		1			
MORRISON Andy	3 + 1							
MURPHY Shaun	46	5	5		1			
NDLOVU Peter	15	4						
NEWBY Jon	3 +10							
PESCHISOLIDO Paul	4 + 1	2						
QUINN Wayne	21 + 3	2	3					
RIBEIRO Bruno	3 + 2		3					
SANDFORD Lee	20 + 2	1	3		1			
SANTOS Georges	23 + 8	4	1 + 2		1			
SMITH Andy	0 + 6		0 + 4					
SUFFO Patrick	6 +10	1			0 + 1			
TALIA Frank	6							
THETIS Manu	0 + 1							
THOMAS James	3 + 7	1			0 + 1			
THOMPSON Tyrone			1 + 1					
TONGE Michael	1 + 1							
TRACEY Simon	40		5		1			
UHLENBEEK Gus	28 + 3		4		1			
ULLATHORNE Rob	13 + 1							
WARD Mark	0 + 1							
WEBER Nicolas	3 + 1		2					
WOODHOUSE Curtis	23 + 2		2 + 1		1			
WOODWARD Andy			1					

SHEFFIELD WEDNESDAY (DIV 1: 17th)

	P/FL App	P/FL Goals	FLC App	FLC Goals	FAC App	FAC Goals	Others App	Others Goals
BERESFORD Marlon	4							
BLATSIS Con	6				2			
BOOTH Andy	17 + 1	3	2 + 1		1	1		
BROMBY Leigh	17 + 1				1 + 1			
COOKE Terry	16 + 1	1						
CRANE Tony	7 + 8	2	3 + 2		0 + 2			
CRESSWELL Richard	4							
DE BILDE Gilles	13 + 8	3	2	1				
DI PIEDI Michele	6 +19	4	0 + 3	1				

	P/FL App	P/FL Goals	FLC App	FLC Goals	FAC App	FAC Goals	Others App	Others Goals
DONNELLY Simon	0 + 3	1						
EKOKU Efan	31 + 1	7	3	2	1 + 1			
GEARY Derek	1 + 4		4 + 1					
GRAYSON Simon	5							
HAMSHAW Matthew	9 + 9		3	1	1	1		
HARKNESS Steve	28 + 2	1			2			
HASLAM Steven	24 + 3	1	3		2			
HENDON Ian	31	2			2			
HINCHCLIFFE Andy	9	2						
HUMPHREYS Richie	7		3					
JONK Wim	2							
LESCOTT Aaron	17 +13		3		2			
MORRISON Owen	20 +10	6	5	2	0 + 2			
MULLER Adam	1 + 4		0 + 1					
NICHOLSON Kevin	0 + 1							
O'DONNELL Phil	7 + 4		0 + 1					
PALMER Carlton	12							
PRESSMAN Kevin	38 + 1		5		1			
QUINN Alan	37	2	5	1	2			
RIPLEY Stuart	5 + 1	1						
RUDI Petter	0 + 1							
SIBON Gerald	32 + 9	13	4 + 1	1	2	1		
SOLTVEDT Trond Egil	15	1						
STOCKDALE Robbie	6							
STRINGER Chris	4 + 1		0 + 1		1			
WALKER Des	43		5		2			
WESTWOOD Ashley	32 + 1	2	5	3				

SHREWSBURY TOWN (DIV 3: 15th)

	P/FL App	P/FL Goals	FLC App	FLC Goals	FAC App	FAC Goals	Others App	Others Goals
AISTON Sam	40 + 2	2	2		1			
BROWN Mickey	20 +14	4	0 + 1		0 + 1		1	
COLLINS Simon	12							
DAVIDSON Ross	31 + 2		2	1	1		1	
DRYSDALE Leon	16 + 2		0 + 1					
DUNBAVIN Ian	20 + 2		2		1			
EDWARDS Paul	26						1	
FRESTONE Chris	16 + 4		2	1	1	1	0 + 1	
GAYLE John	0 + 1							
HANMER Gareth	18 + 4		2				1	
HARRIS Jason	1 + 3							
HUGHES David	24	2	1		1		1	
JAGIELKA Steve	21 +10	6	1		1			
JEMSON Nigel	41	15	2		1		1	
JENKINS Iain	16		2		1		1	
JONES Matthew	5 + 1							
KEISTER John	8				1			
LOWE Ryan	13 +17	4	0 + 2		0 + 1		1	
MURPHY Chris	0 + 1							
MURRAY Karl	29 + 6		1					
PEER Dean	34 + 3		2		1		1	
REDMILE Matthew	24	3			1			
RIOCH Greg	8							
RODGERS Luke	13 +13	7					0 + 1	
SEABURY Kevin	9 + 2						1	
SERTORI Mark	0 + 1							
THOMAS Wayne	4		1					
TOLLEY Jamie	22 + 2	2	0 + 1				1	
TRETTON Andy	21 + 1	2	1					
WILDING Peter	14 + 7	1	1		0 + 1			

SOUTHAMPTON (PREM: 10th)

	P/FL App	P/FL Goals	FLC App	FLC Goals	FAC App	FAC Goals	Others App	Others Goals
ASHFORD Ryan			1					
BEATTIE James	29 + 8	11	2		4	1		
BENALI Francis	0 + 4							
BLEIDELIS Imants	0 + 1		1 + 1		0 + 1			
BRIDGE Wayne	38		2 + 1		4			
DAVIES Kevin	21 + 6	1	1		2	1		
DODD Jason	29 + 2	1	3		3	2		
DRAPER Mark	16 + 6	1	1		3 + 1			
EL KHALEJ Tahar	25 + 7	1	1 + 2		1 + 1			
GIBBENS Kevin	1 + 2				1			

	P/FL App	P/FL Goals	FLC App	FLC Goals	FAC App	FAC Goals	Others App	Others Goals
JONES Paul	35		3		4			
KACHLOUL Hassan	26+ 6	4	1		2+ 1	1		
LE TISSIER Matt	2+ 6	1	2	1				
LUNDEKVAM Claus	38		2+ 1		4			
MARSDEN Chris	19+ 4		2		2			
MONK Garry	2							
MOSS Neil	3							
OAKLEY Matt	35	1	2+ 1		3			
PAHARS Marians	26+ 5	9	1+ 1		4			
PETRESCU Dan	8+ 1	2						
RICHARDS Dean	28	1	2		3+ 1	1		
RIPLEY Stuart	1+ 2		1					
ROSLER Uwe	6+14		1+ 1	1	0+ 2			
SOLTVEDT Trond Egil	3+ 3	1	2	2	1			
TESSEM Jo	27+ 6	4	2	1	3+ 1	1		

SOUTHEND UNITED (DIV 3: 11th)

	P/FL App	P/FL Goals	FLC App	FLC Goals	FAC App	FAC Goals	Others App	Others Goals
ABBEY Ben	15+ 9	8			4	1	3+ 1	1
BLACK Michael	10+ 5	1					1	
BOOTY Martyn	32		2		4		2	
BRAMBLE Tes	12+ 4	6					2+ 1	
BROAD Stephen	10							
CAPLETON Mel	0+ 1							
CARRUTHERS Martin	31+ 1	7	2		4		4+ 1	3
CONNELLY Gordon	8+ 1		1					
CROSS Garry	4+ 4		0+ 1					
EDWARDS Craig	0+ 1						1	
FITZPATRICK Trevor	8+ 3	3			0+ 1		0+ 1	
FLAHAVAN Darryl	29				4		6	
FORBES Scott	27+ 7	3	0+ 1		4	1	4	
HOUGHTON Scott	7+ 2	2	1+ 1					
HUNTER Leon			0+ 1					
HUTCHINGS Carl	14				1			
JOHNSON Leon	19+ 1	1			0+ 1		5	
LEE David	37+ 5	8	2		3		5	2
McDONALD Tom	0+ 1							
McSWEENEY David	10+ 1				0+ 2		4	
MAHER Kevin	40+ 1	2	2		4		5+ 1	
MORLEY David	8+ 9		2				1	
NEWMAN Rob	3+ 3	2					4	
RAWLE Mark	11+ 3	1						
ROGET Leo	26	4	2		4	1	2	1
SEARLE Damon	46	1	2		4		6	1
THURGOOD Stuart	8+ 5	1					0+ 1	
TINKLER Mark	14+ 1	1	1+ 1					
TOLSON Neil	5	1	2					
WARDLEY Shane	0+ 2							
WEBB Danny	6+ 9	1			1+ 1		3	
WHELAN Phil	40+ 2	1	1+ 1		4		5	1
WILLIAMSON Russell	9+ 3				3+ 1	2	3+ 3	1
WOODMAN Andy	17		2					

STOCKPORT COUNTY (DIV 1: 19th)

	P/FL App	P/FL Goals	FLC App	FLC Goals	FAC App	FAC Goals	Others App	Others Goals
BAILEY Alan	1+ 3		0+ 1					
BERGERSEN Kent	8+ 1	1						
BREBNER Grant	3+ 3							
BRIGGS Keith					0+ 1			
BRYNGELSSON Fredrik	4+ 1		2					
BYRNE Chris	0+ 1							
CARRATT Phil	0+ 2							
CARRIGAN Brian	3+10	1	1		1+ 1			
CLARE Robert	19+ 3				2			
CLARK Peter	33+ 4	2	2		3			
CONNELLY Sean	11+ 2		1		0+ 1			
COOPER Kevin	34	5	2		3			
DALY Jon			1					
DIBBLE Andy	9+ 1							
DINNING Tony	6		1	1				
FLYNN Mike	44		2		3			
FRADIN Karim	27+ 4	6			2+ 1	1		
GIBB Ally	38+ 1		2		2			
GRAY Kevin	1							
GRAYSON Simon	13				1			
HANCOCK Glynn	1+ 1							
HURST Glynn	10+ 1							
JONES Lee	27		2		2			
KELLY Alan	2							
KUQI Shefki	17	6			1			
LAWSON Ian	1+ 9							
MATTHEWS Rob	7+ 4	1			1+ 1			
MAXWELL Leyton	8+12	2	1+ 1		0+ 1			
MOORE Ian	17	7	2	1				
NASH Carlo	8				1			
NICHOLSON Shane	31+ 4	2			2			
ROGET Leo	8+ 1							
SMITH Dave	31+ 3	1	1+ 1		2			
TOD Andy	11	3						
WILBRAHAM Aaron	32+ 4	12			3			
WISS Jarko	27+ 3	6	1		3	1		
WOODTHORPE Colin	14+10	1	1+ 1		1			

STOKE CITY (DIV 2: 5th)

	P/FL App	P/FL Goals	FLC App	FLC Goals	FAC App	FAC Goals	Others App	Others Goals
CLARKE Clive	12+ 9		5+ 1		1+ 1		5	1
COLLINS Lee					0+ 1			
CONNOR Paul	1+ 6		1+ 1	2				
COOKE Andy	21+ 1	6					3+ 2	1
DADASON Rikki	13+15	6	0+ 1	1	0+ 1		3+ 2	1
DORIGO Tony	34+ 2		3		1		1	
FENTON Graham	2+ 3	1	2					
GOODFELLOW Marc	0+ 7		0+ 2	1	0+ 1		2	1
GUDJONSSON Bjarni	41+ 1	6	5	2	2		4+ 1	2
GUNNARSSON Brynjar	46	5	6	1	1		3+ 1	
HANSSON Mikael	36+ 2	2	4		2		2+ 1	
HEATH Robert			1	1				
HENRY Karl							0+ 1	
IWELUMO Chris	0+ 2	1	0+ 2	1				
KAVANAGH Graham	42+ 1	8	4+ 1		2		4	1
KIPPE Frode	15+ 4						5	
KRISTINSSON Birkir	18						4	
LIGHTBOURNE Kyle	11+11	5	3		1			
MOHAN Nicky	37	1	6		2		4	1
MUGGLETON Carl	11+ 1		3		2			
NEAL Lewis	0+ 1						0+ 2	
O'CONNOR James	44	8	5	2	0+ 1		4	
PETTY Ben	10+12		3+ 1		2		4+ 1	1
RISOM Henrik	9+16		2+ 2		1		4	
ROBINSON Marvin	3	1						
THOMAS Wayne	33+ 1		3+ 1		1		6	
THORDARSON Stefan	15+15	4	4+ 2	2	2		3+ 2	1
THORNE Peter	35+ 3	16	3+ 1		2		3+ 2	3
WARD Gavin	17		3				2	

SUNDERLAND (PREM: 7th)

	P/FL App	P/FL Goals	FLC App	FLC Goals	FAC App	FAC Goals	Others App	Others Goals
ARCA Julio	26+ 1	2	2	1	1			
BOULD Steve	0+ 1							
BUTLER Paul	3		3	1				
BUTLER Thomas	0+ 4		0+ 1					
CARTERON Patrice	8	1						
CLARK Ben			1					
CRADDOCK Jody	33+ 1		1		1			
DICHIO Danny	2+13	1	4		2+ 2	1		
FREDGAARD Carsten			0+ 1					
GRAY Michael	36	1	3		2			
HOLLOWAY Darren	5		1					
HUTCHISON Don	30+ 2	8	2	2	3			
KILBANE Kevin	26+ 4	4	1		0+ 3	1		
KYLE Kevin	0+ 3							
McCANN Gavin	22	3	0+ 2		4			
McCARTNEY George	1+ 1		2+ 1		0+ 1			
McGILL Brendan			0+ 1					
MACHO Jurgen	4+ 1		1+ 1					
MAKIN Chris	21+ 2		2		2+ 1			

	P/FL		FLC		FAC		Others	
	App	Goals	App	Goals	App	Goals	App	Goals
MALEY Mark			1					
NUNEZ Milton			0 + 1					
OSTER John	2 + 6		3 + 1	1	1 + 1			
PEETERS Tom			1					
PHILLIPS Kevin	34	14	3 + 1	2	4	2		
QUINN Niall	32 + 2	7			2 + 1	1		
RAE Alex	18	2	4	1	3			
REDDY Michael	0 + 2		2	1				
ROY Eric	1 + 2		2					
SCHWARZ Stefan	17 + 3	1	1		4			
SORENSEN Thomas	34		4		4			
THIRWELL Paul	3 + 2		2	1				
THOME Emerson	30 + 1	1	2		3			
VARGA Stan	9 + 3	1	2 + 1		4			
WAINWRIGHT Neil			1					
WILLIAMS Darren	21 + 7		4 + 1		4			
SWANSEA CITY (DIV 2: 23rd)								
APPLEBY Richie	0 + 5							
BOUND Matthew	39 + 1	3	2	1	1		0 + 1	
BOYD Walter	14 + 3	3	2				1	
CASEY Ryan	3 + 6	1			0 + 1		0 + 1	
COATES Jonathan	16 + 3	1	1					
CUSACK Nicky	30 +10	2	1		1		0 + 1	
DAVIES Alex	0 + 1							
DE-VULGT Leigh	6 + 1						2	
FABIANO Nicholas	12 + 4	1						
FREESTONE Roger	43		2		1		3	
HOWARD Mike	39 + 2		2		1		2	
JENKINS Lee	29 +10		1		1		2	
JONES Jason	3							
JONES Steve	13	1			1			
KEEGAN Michael	4		1 + 1		0 + 1		2	
LACEY Damian	17 + 1						3	1
MORGAN Bari	0 + 5							
MOUNTY Carl							0 + 1	
MUMFORD Andrew	2 + 4							
MUTTON Tommy	3 + 2		0 + 2					
O'LEARY Kris	22 + 2	2	2				3	
PHILLIPS Gareth	9 + 6							
PRICE Jason	41	4	2				2	1
ROBERTS Stuart	21 +15	5	1 + 1		1		3	
ROMO David	28 + 5				1		3	
SAVARESE Giovanni	28 + 3	12			0 + 1		3	2
SMITH Jason	22		1		1		3	
THOMAS Martin	12 + 9	1	2		1			
TODD Chris	11	1						
VERSCHAVE Matthias	12	3					1	
WATKIN Steve	27 + 8	7	2		1		0 + 1	
SWINDON TOWN (DIV 2: 20th)								
ALEXANDER Gary	30 + 7	7	3		2 + 1		2 + 1	2
BAKALLI Adrian	1							
COBIAN Juan	3		2		1		0 + 2	
COWE Steve	5 + 4	1	0 + 1		1 + 1	2		
DAVIS Sol	35 + 1		3		3		1	
DRYDEN Richard	7				1			
DUKE David	24 + 8	1	4		1 + 2		3	
GRAZIOLI Guiliano	10 +18	2	1 + 2					
GRIEMINK Bart	24 + 1		4		2		2	
GRIFFIN Charlie	1 + 1							
HALL Gareth	3 + 4				1		1 + 1	
HALLIDAY Kevin							0 + 1	
HEISELBERG Kim	1		1					
HEWLETT Matt	25 + 1		4				1	
HEYWOOD Matty	21	2					2	
HOWE Bobby	17 + 2	1	2	1	2	2		
INVINCIBLE Danny	32 +10	9	1 + 1	1	3		2	
LIGHTBOURNE Kyle	2							
McAREAVEY Paul	2 + 1	1						
McHUGH Frazer	3 + 1						2 + 1	

	P/FL		FLC		FAC		Others	
	App	Goals	App	Goals	App	Goals	App	Goals
MILDENHALL Steve	22 + 1				1		1	
MILLS Jamie	0 + 2						0 + 1	
O'HALLORAN Keith	40	5	4		2 + 1	2	2	
REDDY Michael	17 + 1	4					1 + 1	1
REEVES Alan	42 + 2	3	4	1	3		1	
ROBERTSON Mark	4 + 6	1	2 + 1					
ROBINSON Mark	29 + 5	1	2 + 1		1		3	
ROBINSON Steve	18	2					1	
TUOMELA Marko	1 + 1		2					
VAN DER LINDEN Antoine	17 +16	1	1		2		3	
WHITLEY Jim	2				1			
WILLIAMS Andy	3 + 5		0 + 2					
WILLIAMS James	6 + 1				0 + 1		3	
WILLIAMS Martin	17 + 2	2	3		2	1		
WILLIS Adam	21		1 + 1		1	1	1	
WOAN Ian	21 + 1	3			3			
YOUNG Alan	0 + 4				0 + 3	1	1	
TORQUAY UNITED (DIV 3: 21st)								
AGGREY Jimmy	41	2	2		1		1	
ASHINGTON Ryan	9 + 5		1 + 1		0 + 1			
BEDEAU Tony	33 + 1	5	1	2	2		1	
BENEFIELD Jimmy	0 + 1							
BRANDON Chris	1 + 1							
CHALQI Khalid	20 + 1	1			2	1	1	
DOUGLIN Troy	3		2					
FORD Mark	28	3	2		2	1	1	
GAYLE John	5 + 8	1						
GRAHAM David	5	2						
GREEN Ryan	10							
HERRERA Robbie	29	1	1		1		1	
HILL Kevin	43 + 1	9	2	1	2			
HOCKLEY Matt	4 + 2	1			2		1	
HOLMES Paul	28 + 4	2	2					
JONES Stuart	16		2		2		1	
KELL Richard	15	3						
LAW Gareth	2 + 8	1					0 + 1	
LYONS Simon	0 + 9	1			1		1	
MENDY Jules	7 +14	2	0 + 2		0 + 2			
NEIL Gary	9 + 4	1	1		1		0 + 1	
NORTHMORE Ryan	24 + 1							
O'BRIEN Mick	7 +14	1	1 + 1		0 + 2		0 + 1	
PARKER Kevin	8 + 7	2	2					
PETTERSON Andy	6							
PLATTS Mark	2 + 2		0 + 1					
REES Jason	25	2						
ROWBOTHAM Jason	4 + 1							
RUSSELL Lee	27							
SISSOKHO Habib	7 + 7	2			2			
STOCCO Tom	0 + 2		0 + 1					
TULLY Steve	28 + 1	1	1		2		1	
WATSON Alex	29 + 1		1		2		1	
WILLIAMS Eifion	31 + 6	9	1				1	
TOTTENHAM HOTSPUR (PREM: 12th)								
ANDERTON Darren	22 + 1	2	1	1	2	1		
ARMSTRONG Chris	3 + 6	2						
BOOTH Andy	3 + 1							
CAMPBELL Sol	21	2	1		5			
CARR Stephen	27 + 1	3	3		1 + 1			
CLEMENCE Stephen	27 + 2	1	2		4			
DAVIES Simon	9 + 4	2	0 + 1		0 + 1	2		
DOHERTY Gary	18 + 4	3			5	3		
DOMINGUEZ Jose	0 + 2		0 + 2					
ETHERINGTON Matthew	1 + 5		1					
FERDINAND Les	25 + 3	10	2 + 1		4			
FREUND Steffen	19 + 2		3		3			
GARDNER Anthony	5 + 3							
IVERSEN Steffen	10 + 4	2	2	1	2			
KING Ledley	18	1			4 + 1	1		
KORSTEN Willem	8 + 6	3	1		0 + 3			

	P/FL App	P/FL Goals	FLC App	FLC Goals	FAC App	FAC Goals	Others App	Others Goals
LEONHARDSEN Oyvind	23 + 2	3	2	1	3 + 1	1		
McEWEN Dave	0 + 3							
PERRY Chris	30 + 2	1	3		4			
PIERCY John	0 + 5							
REBROV Sergei	28 + 1	9	2		5	3		
SHERWOOD Tim	31 + 2	2	2		4			
SULLIVAN Neil	35		3		5			
TARICCO Mauricio	2 + 3							
THATCHER Ben	10 + 2		3					
THELWELL Alton	13 + 3				0 + 2			
VEGA Ramon	8 + 2		2 + 1					
WALKER Ian	3 + 1		0 + 1					
YOUNG Luke	19 + 4		0 + 1		4			
TRANMERE ROVERS (DIV 1: 24th)								
ACHTERBERG John	24 + 1		4		5			
ALDRIDGE Paul	0 + 2							
ALLEN Graham	21 + 1		2		5			
ALLISON Wayne	32 + 4	6	4 + 2	1	0 + 1	1		
BARLOW Stuart	12 +15	2	1 + 3	1	2 + 2	1		
CHALLINOR Dave	18 + 4		5		1 + 2			
FLYNN Sean	35	1	5		4			
GILL Wayne	7 + 9	2	3 + 2	1	0 + 1			
HAMILTON Des	5 + 1		1		3			
HAZELL Reuben	11 + 2		2					
HENRY Nick	17 + 3		3 + 1		1 + 3			
HILL Clint	34	5	6	1	3			
HINDS Richard	24 + 5		3 + 3		5			
HUME Iain	0 +10				0 + 1			
JOBSON Richard	16				5			
KENNA Jeff	11							
KOUMAS Jason	34 + 5	10	3 + 1		4	1		
MELLON Micky	11 + 2	1						
MORGAN Alan	3 + 4							
MURPHY Joe	19 + 1		1					
MYHRE Thomas	3		1					
N'DIAYE Seyni	5 + 3	2						
OLSEN James	0 + 1							
OSBORN Simon	9	1						
PARKINSON Andy	29 +10	6	2 + 4	2	5	1		
RIDEOUT Paul	28 + 3	2	5	2	5	3		
ROBERTS Gareth	33 + 1		5		2 + 1			
TAYLOR Scott	24 +13	5	6	1	0 + 2			
YATES Steve	41 + 2	2	4	1	5	4		
WALSALL (DIV 2: 4th)								
ANGELL Brett	23 +18	13	2 + 1		1 + 2	1	0 + 1	
ARANALDE Zigor	45		4		3		3	
BARRAS Tony	33 + 3	1	3		3	1	4	
BENNETT Tom	34 + 4	5	1 + 1		2		3	
BIRCH Gary							2	1
BRIGHTWELL Ian	43 + 1		4		3		3	
BUKRAN Gabor	30 + 6	2	4		3		1 + 1	
BYFIELD Darren	21 +19	9	2 + 2	1	2 + 1		2 + 2	1
CARTER Alfie	0 + 1							
EKELUND Ronnie	2 + 7	1			0 + 1		1 + 1	
EMBERSON Carl	3						2	
EYJOLFSSON Sigi			0 + 1					
GADSBY Matthew	2 + 3						2 + 3	
GAUNT Ian							2	1
GOODMAN Don	8	2					3	1
HALL Paul	36 + 6	6	4		3	1	3	
HAWLEY Karl							0 + 2	
HORNE Barry	1 + 2							
KEATES Dean	21 +12	4	3		1 + 2		3 + 1	1
LEITAO Jorge	40 + 4	18	4	2	3	1	3	
MARSH Chris	4 + 3				0 + 2			
MATIAS Pedro	36 + 4	9	3		2	1	4	2
ROPER Ian	20 + 5		1 + 1				0 + 2	
SCOTT Dion	0 + 1						2	
SIMPSON Fitzroy	8 + 2	1					1	

	P/FL App	P/FL Goals	FLC App	FLC Goals	FAC App	FAC Goals	Others App	Others Goals
SMALL Bryan							2	
TILLSON Andy	42	1	4		3	2	3	
WALKER James	43 + 1		4		3		3	
WRACK Darren	11 +17	4	1		1 + 1	1	1 + 1	
WRIGHT Mark	0 + 4		0 + 1				2	
WATFORD (DIV 1: 9th)								
ARMSTRONG Stephen	0 + 3							
BAARDSEN Espen	27		2					
CHAMBERLAIN Alec	19 + 2		3 + 1		1			
COOK Lee	2 + 2							
COX Neil	43 + 1	5	5		1			
EASTON Clint	5 + 6		1 + 2					
FOLEY Dominic	0 + 5	1	2 + 2					
FORDE Fabian	0 + 1							
GIBBS Nigel	3 + 3		1					
GUDMUNDSSON Johann			1 + 1					
HEIGUSON Heidar	23 +10	8	2 + 2	1	0 + 1			
HYDE Micah	17 + 9	6	1					
JOBSON Richard	2							
JOHNSON Richard	1 + 2							
KENNEDY Peter	11 + 6				1			
MILLER Charlie			0 + 1					
MOONEY Tommy	38 + 1	19	5	2	1	1		
NGONGE Michel	0 + 2		0 + 2					
NIELSEN Allan	45	10	4		1			
NOEL-WILLIAMS Gifton	28 + 4	8	2 + 1		1			
PAGE Robert	36	1	5		1			
PALMER Carlton	5							
PALMER Steve	37 + 2	1	5	1	0 + 1			

Gifton Noel-Williams (Watford)

	P/FL App	P/FL Goals	FLC App	FLC Goals	FAC App	FAC Goals	Others App	Others Goals
PANAYI Jimmy	8 + 1							
PERPETUINI David	4 + 1		1 + 1					
ROBINSON Paul	39		4		1			
SMART Allan	1 + 7							
SMITH Tommy	38 + 5	11	4	1	1			
VERNAZZA Paolo	20 + 3	2			1			
WARD Darren	40	1	5	1	1			
WOOTER Nordin	14 +12	1	1 + 1					
WRIGHT Nick			1					
WEST BROMWICH ALBION (DIV 1: 6th)								
ADAMSON Chris					1			
APPLETON Michael	15						2	
BALIS Igor	1 + 6				0 + 1			
BURGESS Daryl	1 + 2							
BUTLER Tony	44	1	4		1		2	
CARBON Matt	19 + 5		1 + 1		1			
CHAMBERS Adam	4 + 7	1	1 + 1				0 + 1	
CHAMBERS James	27 + 4		4		1			
CLEMENT Neil	45	5	4	2	1		2	
CUMMINGS Warren	1 + 2							
DERVELD Fernando	1 + 1							
FOX Ruel	36 + 2	1	3		1		2	
GILCHRIST Phil	8						2	
GRANT Tony	3 + 2							
HOULT Russell	13						2	
HUGHES Lee	41	21	3 + 1		1	1	2	1
JENSEN Brian	33		4					
JORDAO	28 + 7	1	3	1	1		0 + 2	
LYTTLE Des	38 + 2	1	4		1		2	
McINNES Derek	14	1	4					
OLIVER Adam	1 + 6		1 + 1					
QUINN James	3 +11	1						
ROBERTS Jason	32 +11	14	3 + 1	2	1		2	1
SIGURDSSON Larus	7 + 5						0 + 1	
SNEEKES Richard	39 + 6	2	0 + 3	1	1		2	
TAYLOR Bob	17 +23	5	2 + 1		0 + 1	1	0 + 2	
VAN BLERK Jason	35 + 1	2	3				2	
WEST HAM UNITED (PREM: 15th)								
BASSILA Christian	0 + 3				0 + 1			
BYWATER Steve	1							
CAMARA Titi	5 + 1				1			
CARRICK Michael	32 + 1	1	4		4			
CHARLES Gary	0 + 1							
COLE Joe	24 + 6	5	2		4			
DAILLY Christian	11 + 1				3			
DEFOE Jermaine	0 + 1		0 + 1	1				
DIAWARA Kaba	6 + 5							
DI CANIO Paolo	31	9	3	1	3	1		
FERDINAND Rio	12		2					
FORREST Craig	3 + 1							
FOXE Hayden	3 + 2							
HISLOP Shaka	34		4		4			
KANOUTE Frederic	32	11	3		4	3		
KELLER Marc			1					
KITSON Paul	0 + 2							
LAMPARD Frank	30	7	3	1	4	1		
LOMAS Steve	20	1	3	1				
McCANN Grant	0 + 1							
MARGAS Javier	3		1					
MINTO Scott	1							
MONCUR John	6 +10		0 + 1					
PEARCE Ian	13 + 2	1	1		0 + 1			
PEARCE Stuart	34	2	4		4	1		
POTTS Steve	2 + 6		2 + 1					
SCHEMMEL Sebastien	10 + 2				3			
SINCLAIR Trevor	19	3	3		1			
SOMA Ragnvald	2 + 2				0 + 1			
SONG Rigobert	18 + 1		1		1			
STIMAC Igor	19		3		2			
SUKER Davor	7 + 4	2	1 + 1	1				
TIHINEN Hannu	5 + 3				2			
TODOROV Svetoslav	2 + 6	1			0 + 1	1		
WINTERBURN Nigel	33	1	3		4			
WIGAN ATHLETIC (DIV 2: 6th)								
ASHCROFT Lee	23 + 7	5	1		2 + 1	1	0 + 2	
BALMER Stuart	22 + 2	1	2		1		1	
BEAGRIE Peter	7 + 3	1					2	
BIDSTRUP Stefan	10 + 5	2			2	1		
BRADSHAW Carl	22 + 5	3	1				2	
BRANNAN Ged	12 + 1							
CARROLL Roy	29		3		1		2	
CUNNINGHAM Craig							0 + 1	
DALGLISH Paul	5 + 1							
DE ZEEUW Arjan	45	1	4		2		2	
DICKSON Hugh	0 + 1				0 + 1		2	
GILLESPIE Keith	4 + 1				2			
GREEN Scott	27 + 8	2	4		3		2	
GRIFFITHS Gareth	14 + 3	1			3		2	
HAWORTH Simon	25 + 5	11	3	2			1 + 1	
HERNANDEZ Dino					1			
JOHNSON Ian							0 + 2	
JOHNSON Joel							1	
KAY Ben							1	
KILFORD Ian	23 + 1	2	3 + 1	1	2	1		
LIDDELL Andy	37	9	3	1	2		2	
McCULLOCH Lee	10	3					1	
McGIBBON Pat	38 + 2	2	4		0 + 1		2	
McLAUGHLIN Brian	13 + 5		4		1 + 1		1	1
McLOUGHLIN Alan	0 + 4		0 + 1				2	2
McMAHON Francis							1	
McMILLAN Stephen	6							
MARRIOTT Andy							2	
MARTINEZ Roberto	25 + 9		3 + 1		3		2	
MITCHELL Paul	0 + 1		2		0 + 1		1	
MORRIS Andy							1	
NICHOLLS Kevin	13 + 7		2				4	1
PADULA Gino	2 + 2		0 + 1		2		2	1
REDFEARN Neil	6 + 4	1			1		2	
ROBERTS Neil	17 +17	6	0 + 1	1	2	1	1 + 1	
SHARP Kevin	29 + 2		3	1	1		2	
SHERIDAN Darren	25 + 2		1		0 + 1			
STILLIE Derek	17 + 1		1 + 1		2			
WIMBLEDON (DIV 1: 8th)								
AGYEMANG Patrick	16 +13	4	1 + 1		6	1		
AINSWORTH Gareth	8 + 4	2			5 + 1	1		
ANDERSEN Trond	40 + 2	5	4		6	1		
ARDLEY Neal	36 + 1	3	2		4 + 1	2		
BLACKWELL Dean	5 + 1		1		1			
COOPER Kevin	11	3						
CUNNINGHAM Kenny	15				4 + 1			
DAVIS Kelvin	45		4		6			
EUELL Jason	33 + 3	19	1		6	1		
FRANCIS Damien	29	8	3		4			
GAYLE Marcus	24 + 8	3	3	1	0 + 4			
GIER Rob	13 + 1		1 + 1					
GRAY Wayne	1 +10				0 + 3	1		
HARLEY Jon	6	2						
HARTSON John	19	8	4	2				
HAWKINS Peter	29 + 1		3		5			
HEALD Paul	1 + 2							
HOLLOWAY Darren	30 + 1				4			
HREIDARSSON Hermann	1							
HUGHES Michael	5 + 5	1						
HUNT Jon	8 + 4		1 + 1		0 + 2	1		
JUPP Duncan	4		2					
KARLSSON Par	7 + 9		1		5	1		
KIMBLE Alan	21 + 4		1		3			
LEABURN Carl	2 + 1							

	P/FL		FLC		FAC		Others	
	App	Goals	App	Goals	App	Goals	App	Goals
MORGAN Lionel	1 + 4		0 + 1					
NIELSEN David	9 + 2	2						
OWUSU Ansah	1 + 3		1					
ROBERTS Andy	25 + 2	2	3	1	0 + 1			
ROBINSON Paul	0 + 3		1 + 1					
SELLEY Ian	1 + 3							
THOMAS Michael	5 + 3		1					
WILLIAMS Mark	42	6	4		6	1		
WILLMOTT Chris	13 + 1	1	2		1			
WOLVERHAMPTON WANDERERS (DIV 1: 12th)								
AL JABER Sami	0 + 4		1					
ANDREWS Keith	20 + 2				2			
BAZELEY Darren	23 + 1	1	5					
BRANCH Michael	31 + 7	4	2 + 1		2			
BUTLER Paul	12							
CAMARA Mohamed	4 +14		1 + 1		0 + 1			
CONNELLY Sean	6							
DINNING Tony	31	6			1			
EMBLEN Neil	21 + 7		4		1 + 1			
GREEN Ryan	5 + 2		2		0 + 2			
KETSBAIA Temuri	14 + 8	3	3 + 1	1				
LARKIN Colin	0 + 2							
LESCOTT Joleon	31 + 6	2	5		2			
MUSCAT Kevin	37	3	4	1	1			
NAYLOR Lee	44 + 2	1	5		2			
NDAH George	23 + 6	6	0 + 1		0 + 1			
OAKES Michael	46		4		1			
OSBORN Simon	16 + 4		2	1	2			
PEACOCK Darren	2 + 2		1					
POLLET Ludo	29	2			1			
PROUDLOCK Adam	28 + 7	8	3 + 1	2	2	1		
ROBINSON Carl	36 + 4	3	4 + 1	1	2	1		
ROUSSEL Cedric	3 + 6							
SEDGLEY Steve	5	1	1 + 1					
SINTON Andy	28 + 2	2	2 + 1		2			
STOWELL Mike	0 + 1		1		1			
TAYLOR Robert	5 + 4		3	3				
TAYLOR Scott	3 + 1		2					
THETIS Manu	3							
TUDOR Shane	0 + 1							
WREXHAM (DIV 2: 10th)								
BARRETT Paul	22 + 2		0 + 1		1			
BLACKWOOD Michael	3 +12				0 + 1			
BOUANANE Emad	13 + 4				1		1	
CAREY Brian	33	3	1				1	
CHALK Martyn	22 + 2	4	0 + 2		1		1	
DEARDEN Kevin	36		1		1			
EDWARDS Carlos	31 + 5	4	1 + 1		1			
FAULCONBRIDGE Craig	33 + 6	10	2		1		1	
FERGUSON Darren	43	9	2	1	1		1	
GIBSON Robin	17 +11	1	1 + 1				0 + 1	
HARDY Phil	13						1	
KILLEN Chris	11 + 1	3						
LAWRENCE Denis	1 + 2							
McGREGOR Mark	43	5	2		1		1	
MARDON Paul	6 + 1							
MOODY Adrian	2 + 1							
MORRELL Andy	10 +10	3	1					
OWEN Gareth	18 + 4	2	2				1	
PEJIC Shaun	1							
PHILLIPS Wayne	4 + 3	1						
RIDLER Dave	22 + 2		2		1		0 + 1	
ROBERTS Steve	6 + 1		1					
ROCHE Lee	41		2		1		1	
ROGERS Kristian	5		1					
RUSSELL Kevin	24 + 2	4			0 + 1		0 + 1	
SAM Hector	11 + 9	6	1		1		1	
THOMAS Steve	4 + 2							
TRUNDLE Lee	12 + 2	8						
WALSH Dave	5						1	
WILLIAMS Danny	14 + 1	2	2					

	P/FL		FLC		FAC		Others	
	App	Goals	App	Goals	App	Goals	App	Goals
WYCOMBE WANDERERS (DIV 2: 13th)								
BAIRD Andy	9 + 4	3	1 + 3	1	3 + 2		1 + 1	
BATES Jamie	37 + 2	3	4	1	5 + 2	2	1	
BEETON Alan	3				1			
BRADY Matt	2 + 3				2 + 1		2	1
BROWN Steve	30 + 2	4	4		7 + 3	1	2	1
BULMAN Dannie	36	4	4		8 + 1		3	
CARROLL Dave	8 + 4	2			2 + 2	1		
CASTLEDINE Stewart	6 +11		0 + 3	1	0 + 2		0 + 1	
CLEGG George	2 + 8				1			
COUSINS Jason	26 + 6		0 + 1		9		3	
ESSANDOH Roy	8 + 5				0 + 2	1		
HARKIN Mo	10 + 5		4		3		1	
JOHNSON Roger	0 + 1							
JONES Steve	5		1					
LAVIN Gerard	2						1	
LEE Martyn	13 + 8	3			4 + 1		1 + 1	
McCARTHY Paul	38	2	4	1	9	5	2	
McSPORRAN Jermaine	20	2	4	1	1 + 1		0 + 1	
MARSH Chris	11							
NUTTER John	1							
PARKIN Sam	5 + 3	1			0 + 3	1	2	1
PHELAN Leeyon	0 + 2							
RAMMELL Andy	25 + 1	10	2	1	9	2	3	
ROGERS Mark	19 + 3	1	4	1	5 + 1	1	2	
RYAN Keith	21 + 9	4			6 + 1	1		
SENDA Danny	12 +19	2	0 + 3		1 + 3		0 + 3	
SIMPSON Michael	45	3	4		9	3	3	
TAYLOR Martin	46		4		10		3	
THOMPSON Niall	6 + 2				2		0 + 2	1
TOWNSEND Ben	9 + 1				5 + 1		1	
VINNICOMBE Chris	42	1	4		8		2	
WHITTINGHAM Guy	9 + 3	1			0 + 1			
YORK CITY (DIV 3: 17th)								
AGNEW Steve	37 + 2	2	1		3	1	1	
ALCIDE Colin	24 +14	5	1		2 + 1	1	1	
BASHAM Mike	6 + 1	1						
BOWER Mark	21	1			3		0 + 1	
BRASS Chris	8 + 2	1						
BULLOCK Lee	29 + 4	3	1 + 1		1 + 1	1		
CONLON Barry	2 + 6		0 + 2					
COOPER Richard	14							
DARLOW Kieran	0 + 1							
DUFFIELD Peter	6	3	1					
DURKAN Keiron	7							
EDMONDSON Darren	22 + 1		2		2			
EMMERSON Scott	3 + 5	1						
FETTIS Alan	46		1		4			
FOX Christian	3 + 5				1		1	
HALL Wayne	16 + 3		2		1 + 1		0 + 1	
HOBSON Gary	8 + 3		1					
HOCKING Matt	24 + 2		1		1 + 1			
HOWARTH Russell			1				1	
HULME Kevin	11 + 4	3	2		3		1	
IWELUMO Chris	11 + 1	2			4	1		
JONES Barry	28 + 1		2	1				
JORDAN Scott	6 + 6				1 + 1	1		
McNIVEN David	25 +16	8	1 + 1		4	2	1	
MATHIE Alex	13 + 6	1			2 + 2	1	1	
NOGAN Lee	16	6						
PATTERSON Darren	4 + 2				2		1	
POTTER Graham	34 + 4	2	2		4	1		
REED Martin	1 + 1							
RICHARDSON Nick	16 + 1	1						
SERTORI Mark	26	1	1 + 1		3		1	
STAMP Neville	12 + 1				0 + 2		1	
SWAN Peter	2							
TARRANT Neil	6 + 1	1			1			
THOMPSON Marc	9 + 3		1		2		1	
TURLEY James	5 + 5						0 + 1	
WILLIAMS John	1 + 5		1					
WOOD Leigh	4 + 1							

PFA AWARDS 2001

Player of the Year
TEDDY SHERINGHAM

Young Player of the Year
STEVEN GERRARD

Special Merit Award
JIMMY HILL

DIVISIONAL AWARDS

FA Carling Premiership

Fabien Barthez	Manchester United
Stephen Carr	Tottenham Hotspur
Silvinho	Arsenal
Jaap Stam	Manchester United
Wes Brown	Manchester United
Roy Keane	Manchester United
Ryan Giggs	Manchester United
Steven Gerrard	Liverpool
Patrick Vieira	Arsenal
Teddy Sheringham	Manchester United
Thierry Henry	Arsenal

Nationwide League Division One

Maik Taylor	Fulham
Steve Finnan	Fulham
Martin Grainger	Birmingham City
Chris Coleman	Fulham
Henning Berg	Blackburn Rovers
Lee Clark	Fulham
David Dunn	Blackburn Rovers
Damien Duff	Blackburn Rovers
Sean Davis	Fulham
Louis Saha	Fulham
Matt Jansen	Blackburn Rovers

Nationwide League Division Two

James Walker	Walsall
Matty Lawrence	Millwall
Mickey Bell	Bristol City
Arjan De Zeeuw	Wigan Athletic
Andy Tillson	Walsall
Scott Murray	Bristol City
Graham Kavanagh	Stoke City
Brian Tinnion	Bristol City
Tim Cahill	Millwall
Neil Harris	Millwall
Martin Butler	Reading

Nationwide League Division Three

Mike Pollitt	Chesterfield
Josh Low	Cardiff City
Matthew Lockwood	Leyton Orient
Steve Blatherwick	Chesterfield
Danny Cullip	Brighton & Hove Albion
Lee Hodges	Scunthorpe United
Darren Currie	Barnet
Paul Simpson	Blackpool
Tommy Miller	Hartlepool United
Bobby Zamora	Brighton & Hove Albion
Robert Earnshaw	Cardiff City